LECTIONARY
FOR MASS

THE ROMAN MISSAL

REVISED BY DECREE OF THE
SECOND VATICAN COUNCIL AND
PUBLISHED BY AUTHORITY OF POPE PAUL VI

LECTIONARY
FOR MASS

ENGLISH TRANSLATION APPROVED BY
THE NATIONAL CONFERENCE OF
CATHOLIC BISHOPS AND CONFIRMED
BY THE APOSTOLIC SEE

With the
NEW AMERICAN VERSION
of sacred scripture from the original languages
made by members of the
CATHOLIC BIBLICAL ASSOCIATION
and sponsored by the Bishop's Committee
of the Division of Religious Education
(Confraternity of Christian Doctrine)

CATHOLIC BOOK PUBLISHING CO.
New York
1970

NIHIL OBSTAT:

Stephen J. Hartdegen, O.F.M., S.S.L,
Censor Deputatus

IMPRIMATUR:

✠ Patrick Cardinal O'Boyle, D.D.
Archbishop of Washington, D.C.

February 11, 1970

Published by authority of the Bishops' Conference on the Liturgy,
National Conference of Catholic Bishops.

The poetic English translations of the sequences of the Roman Missal are taken from *The Roman Missal* approved by the National Conference of Bishops of the United States, © 1964 by the National Catholic Welfare Conference, Inc.

The prose English translations of the sequences of the Roman Missal are taken from Joseph Connolly, *Hymns of the Roman Liturgy* (London: Longmans, Green, 1954).

Published by Catholic Book Publishing Co., New York
Printed and bound in the U.S.A.

SACRED CONGREGATION FOR DIVINE WORSHIP

DECREE

Prot. n. 106/69

The Constitution on the Sacred Liturgy directed that the treasures of the bible be opened up more lavishly so that richer fare might be provided for the faithful at the table of God's word and a more representative portion of sacred scripture be read to the people over a set cycle of years (article 51). In response to these directives, the Consilium for the Implementation of the Constitution on the Sacred Liturgy prepared this lectionary for Mass, and Pope Paul VI approved it in his apostolic constitution, Missale Romanum, April 3, 1969.

Therefore this Sacred Congregation, acting on the directive of the pope, publishes this order of readings for Mass to be used beginning November 30, 1969, the first Sunday of Advent. Since this date is the beginning of the 1970 liturgical year, the readings used will be from Series B of the Sunday readings and from Series II of the first readings for the weekdays of the year.

Since the typical edition of the new order of readings provides only text references, it is the responsibility of the conferences of bishops to prepare the complete vernacular texts, following the guidelines in the Instruction on the Translation of Liturgical Texts (Consilium for the Implementation of the Constitution on the Sacred Liturgy, January 25, 1969). Vernacular texts may be taken from bible translations already canonically approved for individual regions, with the confirmation of the Apostolic See. If newly translated, they should be submitted for confirmation by this congregation.

Anything to the contrary notwithstanding.

From the Sacred Congregation for Divine Worship, May 25, 1969, Pentecost Sunday.

Benno Card. Gut
prefect
A. Bugnini
secretary

CONTENTS

4 Contents

FOREWORD

This lectionary contains the complete texts of the biblical readings and chants for the liturgy of the word in the celebration of Mass. The selection of texts and the arrangement follow the Roman *Ordo Lectionum Missae*, authorized in the apostolic constitution *Missale Romanum* (April 3, 1969) and published by decree of the Congregation for Divine Worship (May 29, 1969). It is authorized for use in the dioceses of the United States by the National Conference of Catholic Bishops beginning Palm Sunday, March 22, 1970; it is mandatory beginning the first Sunday of Advent, November 28, 1971.

In addition to the texts, indices, and tables (indicating the use of the years in the cycles of readings), the first two chapters of *Praenotanda* are included. These explain in some detail the rationale for the arrangement of readings in the pattern of this lectionary. Since the biblical passages have been chosen with great care, their effectiveness in the eucharistic celebration will be increased if they are explained to the faithful and if they are further unfolded and applied in the homily. The brief title which precedes each reading is intended to indicate in summary fashion why the passage was selected (that is, what particular aspect or value of the reading prompted the selection) and also to identify the text. While this brief title is not to be read aloud by the reader, it may suggest the kind of introduction which may be helpful.

In the celebration of Mass with a congregation the readers are to conclude the first and second readings: "This is the Word of the Lord," so that the people may respond: "Thanks be to God."

The deacon (or, in the absence of a deacon, the priest) adds: "This is the gospel of the Lord" at the end of the gospel in order to introduce the acclamation, the people sing or say: "Praise to you, Lord Jesus Christ."

The complete details of the rite for the readings and chants of the liturgy of the word are given in the *Order of Mass* and the *General Instruction* of the Roman Missal, both published by decree of the Congregation of Rites, April 6, 1969. For convenience, pertinent excerpts are reprinted below.

FROM THE ORDER OF MASS
Liturgy of the Word

7. *The reader goes to the lectern for the first reading. All sit and listen.*
To indicate the end, the reader adds:
This is the Word of the Lord.
All respond:
Thanks be to God.

8. *The cantor of the psalm sings or recites the psalm, and the people make the response.*

9. *If there is a second reading, it is read at the lectern as before.*
To indicate the end, the reader adds:
This is the Word of the Lord.
All respond:
Thanks be to God.

10. *The alleluia or other chant follows.*

11. *Meanwhile, if incense is used, the priest puts some*

in the censer. Then the deacon who is to proclaim the gospel bows before the priest and in a low voice asks the blessing:
Father, give me your blessing.
The priest says in a low voice:
The Lord be in your heart and on your lips
that you may worthily proclaim his gospel.
In the name of the Father, and of the Son, ✠ and of the Holy Spirit.
The deacon answers:
Amen.

If there is no deacon, the priest bows before the altar and says quietly:
Almighty God, cleanse my heart and my lips
that I may worthily proclaim your gospel.

12. *Then the deacon (or the priest) goes to the lectern. He may be accompanied by ministers with incense and candles. He sings or says:*
The Lord be with you.
The people answer:
And also with you.
The deacon (or priest) sings or says:
A reading from the holy gospel according to N.
He makes the sign of the cross on the book, and then on his forehead, lips, and breast.
The people respond:
Glory to you, Lord.
Then, if incense is used, the deacon (or priest) incenses the book and proclaims the gospel.

13. *At the end of the gospel, the deacon (or priest) adds:*
This is the gospel of the Lord.
All respond:
Praise to you, Lord Jesus Christ.
Then he kisses the book, saying quietly:
May the words of the gospel wipe away our sins.

14. *A homily shall be given on all Sundays and holydays of obligation; it is recommended for other days.*

15. *After the homily, the profession of faith is made if prescribed.*
We believe in one God,
  the Father, the Almighty,
  maker of heaven and earth,
  of all that is seen and unseen.
We believe in one Lord, Jesus Christ,
  the only Son of God,
  eternally begotten of the Father,
  God from God, Light from Light,
  true God from true God,
  begotten, not made, one in Being with the Father.
  Through him all things were made.
  For us men and for our salvation
    he came down from heaven:
  by the power of the Holy Spirit
    he was born of the Virgin Mary, and became man.
  For our sake he was crucified under Pontius Pilate;
    he suffered, died, and was buried.

on the third day he rose again
   in fulfillment of the Scriptures;
he ascended into heaven
   and is seated at the right hand of the Father.
He will come again in glory to judge the living and
the dead,
   and his kingdom will have no end.
We believe in the Holy Spirit, the Lord, the giver of life,
   who proceeds from the Father and the Son.
With the Father and the Son he is worshiped and
glorified.
He has spoken through the Prophets.
We believe in one holy catholic and apostolic Church.
We acknowledge one baptism for the forgiveness of
sins.
We look for the resurrection of the dead,
   and the life of the world to come. Amen.

*16. Then follow the general intercessions (prayer of
the faithful).*

FROM THE GENERAL INSTRUCTION

B) Liturgy of the Word

33. Readings from scripture and the chants between the
readings form the main part of the liturgy of the word.
The homily, profession of faith, and general intercessions
or prayer of the faithful develop and complete it. In the
readings, God speaks to his people of the mystery of
salvation and nourishes their spirit; Christ is present
through his word. The homily then explains the readings, and the chants and profession of faith comprise the
people's acceptance of God's word. Finally, moved by
this word, they pray in the general intercessions for the
needs of the Church and the world.

Liturgy of the Word

34. In the readings the treasures of the bible are opened
to the people; this is the table of God's word. Reading
the scriptures is traditionally considered a ministerial,
not a presidential, function. It is desirable that the gospel
be read by the deacon or, in his absence, by a priest other
than the celebrant; the other readings are read by the
subdeacon or reader. In the absence of a deacon or another priest, the celebrant reads the gospel.

35. The liturgy indicates that the reading of the gospel
should be done with reverence; it is distinguished from
the other readings by special marks of honor. A special
minister proclaims it, preparing himself by a blessing or
prayer. By standing to hear the reading and by their acclamations, the people recognize and acknowledge that
Christ is present and speaking to them. Marks of honor
are also given to the gospel book itself.

Chants Between the Readings

36. The responsorial psalm or gradual comes after the
first reading. The psalm is an integral part of the liturgy
of the word and is usually taken from the lectionary,
since these texts are directly related to and depend upon
the respective readings. To make the people's response
easier, however, some texts of psalms and responses
have also been selected for the several seasons of the
year or for the different kinds of saints. These may be
used instead of the text corresponding to the reading
whenever the psalm is sung.

The cantor of the psalm sings the verse at the lectern or
other suitable place, while the people remain seated and
listen. Unless the psalm is sung straight through without
response, the congregation takes part by singing the response.

If sung, the following texts may be chosen: the psalm in
the lectionary, the gradual in the Roman Gradual, or the
responsorial or alleluia psalm in the Simple Gradual, as
these books indicate.

37. According to the season, the second reading is followed by the alleluia or other chant.

   (a) The alleluia is sung outside Lent. It is begun by all
present or by the choir or cantor; it way then be repeated.
The verses are taken from the lectionary or the Gradual.

   (b) The other chant consists of the verse before the gospel or another psalm or tract, as found in the lectionary
or the Gradual.

38. When there is only one reading before the gospel:

   (a) during the time when the alleluia is said, either the
alleluia psalm, or the psalm and alleluia with its verse, or
only the psalm or alleluia may be used;

   (b) during the time when the alleluia is not said, either
the psalm or the verse before the gospel may be used.

39. If the psalm after the reading is not sung, it is re-
cited. The alleluia or the verse before the gospel may be
omitted if not sung.

40. Except on Easter Sunday and Pentecost the sequences
are optional.

Liturgy of the Word

89. After the opening prayer, the reader goes to the lectern for the first reading. All sit and listen and make the
acclamation at the end.

90. After the reading, the cantor of the psalm, or the
reader, sings or recites the psalm, and the people make
the response (see no. 36).

91. If there is a second reading before the gospel, it is
read at the lectern, as before. All sit and listen and make
the acclamation at the end.

92. The alleluia or other chant, depending on the season,
follows (see nos. 37-39).

93. During the singing of the alleluia or other chant, if
incense is being used, the priest puts some in the censer.
Then he bows before the altar, with his hands joined,
and says quietly: Almighty God, cleanse my heart.

94. If the gospel book is on the altar, he takes it and goes
to the lectern. The ministers, who may carry the censer
and candles, walk ahead of him.

95. At the lectern the priest opens the book and says:
The Lord be with you. Then he says: A reading from . . . ,
and makes the sign of the cross with his thumb on the
book and on his forehead, mouth, and breast. If incense
is used, he incenses the book. After the acclamation of
the people, he proclaims the gospel. At the end he kisses

the book, saying quietly: May the words of the gospel wipe away our sins. After the reading the people make the customary acclamation.

96. If no reader is present, the priest proclaims all the readings at the lectern and, if necessary, also the chants between the readings. If incense is used, he puts some in the censer and then, bowing, says: Almighty God, cleanse my heart.

Liturgy of the Word

131. If incense is used, the deacon assists the priest when he puts incense in the censer during the singing of the alleluia or other chant. Then he bows before the priest and asks for the blessing, saying in a low voice: Father, give me your blessing. The priest blesses him: The Lord be in your heart . . . The deacon answers: Amen. If the gospel book is on the altar, he takes it and goes to the lectern, preceded by the ministers, if present, who may carry the candles and censer. There he greets the people, incenses the book, and proclaims the gospel. After the reading, he kisses the book, saying quietly: May the words of the gospel wipe away our sins, and returns to the celebrant. If there is no homily or profession of faith, he may remain at the lectern for the general intercessions, but the ministers leave.

132. After the priest introduces the general intercessions, the deacon announces the intentions at the lectern or other suitable place.

Liturgy of the Word

145. The subdeacon reads the epistle or other reading before the gospel at the lectern and afterwards returns to the priest.

146. He assists the priest when he puts incense in the censer and accompanies the deacon for the proclamation of the gospel. He assists the deacon at the lectern; after the gospel, both return to the priest.

CHOICE OF READINGS

The *General Instruction* of the Roman Missal gives the norms for the use or choice of Mass formularies according to the calendar and in special cases (nos. 314-316; 326-341). The general rules are as follows:

313. The pastoral effectiveness of a celebration depends in great measure on choosing readings, prayers, and songs which correspond to the needs, spiritual preparation, and attitude of the participants. This will be achieved by an intelligent use of the options which are described below. In planning the celebration, the priest should consider the spiritual good of the assembly rather than his own desires. The choice of texts is to be made in consultation with the ministers and others who have a function in the celebration, including the faithful.

Since a variety of options is provided, it is necessary for the deacon, readers, cantors, commentator, and choir to know beforehand the texts for which they are responsible, so that nothing will upset the celebration. This careful planning will help dispose the people to take their part in the eucharist.

In addition, there are particular norms for the choice of individual texts, including the readings:

318. Sundays and feasts have three readings, i.e., from the Old Testament, the writings of the apostles, and the gospel. These readings teach the Christian people God's plan for salvation.

It is strongly recommended that the three readings be used, but for pastoral reasons and by decree of the conference of bishops the use of two readings is allowed in some places. In such a case, the choice between the first two readings should be based on the norms in the lectionary and the desire to lead the people to a deeper knowledge of scripture and never simply on the brevity or simplicity of the reading.

319. In the weekday lectionary readings are provided for each day of the year. Unless a solemnity or feast occurs, these readings are to be used regularly on the days to which they are assigned.

The continuous reading during the week, however, is sometimes interrupted by the occurrence of a feast or particular celebration. In this case the priest should consider in advance the entire week's readings and, if the weekday readings which will be suppressed are important, he may combine the weekday readings to include them, or he may omit the less important ones.

In Masses for special groups, the priest may choose from the readings of that week those most suitable for the group.

320. The lectionary has a special selection of readings for Masses in which certain sacraments or sacramentals are celebrated and also for particular circumstances.

These selections provide the people with more suitable readings of God's word and lead them to a fuller understanding of the mystery in which they take part. In this way they are formed in a deeper love of his word.

Pastoral considerations and the permission to choose readings should determine which texts are proclaimed to the assembly.

For the dioceses of the United States, the National Conference of Catholic Bishops decided on November 13, 1969, concerning no. 318 (above), that the pattern of three readings for Sundays and feast days, in accord with the *Ordo Lectionum*, be completely implemented.

At the same time the National Conference of Catholic Bishops employed the faculty of no. 325 (concerning further adaptations of readings) to authorize that the priest, when he is otherwise free to choose the readings of Mass in accord with no. 319 of the *Institutio Generalis*, may choose readings not found in the current week, provided they are within the approved lectionary, and appropriate to the particular celebration, and are not chosen to the disadvantage of the ordinary use of the weekday lectionary.

CHANTS BETWEEN THE READINGS

The norms for the singing or saying of the psalm verses between the readings are given in the *General Instruction* above.

Responsorial Psalm

In the lectionary the responsorial psalm is printed to indicate the way in which the response is employed. The sign ℟. prefixed to the response indicates that the text is first sung (or said) by the cantor or other leader or by the reader, and that it is then *repeated* by the congregation of the faithful. Then the several verses of the psalm are sung (or said). The response by the people is indicated after each verse.

The full form of the responsorial psalm may thus be indicated in the following example:

Cantor: ℟. To you, O Lord, I lift my soul.

People: ℟. To you, O Lord, I lift my soul.

Cantor: Your ways, O Lord, make known to me;
                teach me your paths,
            Guide me in your truth and teach me,
                for you are God my savior,
                and for you I wait all the day.

People: ℟. To you, O Lord, I lift my soul.

Cantor: Good and upright is the Lord;
                thus he shows sinners the way.
            He guides the humble to justice,
                he teaches the humble his way.

People: ℟. To you, O Lord, I lift my soul.

Cantor: All the paths of the Lord are kindness
                and constancy
            toward those who keep his covenant
                and his desires.
            The friendship of the Lord is with those
                who fear him,
            and his covenant, for their instruction.

People: ℟. To you, O Lord, I lift my soul.

Unless the psalm is sung straight through without response, the people take part by singing the response (no. 36, above).

Alleluia

A similar pattern is followed for the alleluias which introduce the gospel and for which the people stand. The cantor sings the alleluia, marked ℟., and it may then be repeated by the people; the cantor sings the verse, and the people sing the alleluia.

Depending on the musical setting, a double or triple alleluia may be sung and then repeated; the double or triple alleluia will then be sung again by the people after the verse. The *General Instruction* (nos. 37-40, above) gives fuller information, including the case when not even the alleluia itself is sung.

The form of the alleluia and verse may be spelled out in the following example:

Cantor: ℟. Alleluia.

People: ℟. Alleluia.

Cantor: [Verse] Lord, let us see your kindness,
                and grant us your salvation.

People: ℟. Alleluia.

Verse before the Gospel

During Lent, when the alleluia is not sung, a verse before the gospel is given in the lectionary for use with a response which is employed as a substitute for the alleluia. Because four recommended responses are provided for this purpose, it is not possible to print them repeatedly (see chapter I, no. 9 of the *Praenotanda* of this lectionary). The response —either one of the four given or a similar response—is sung by the cantor, repeated by the people; the cantor then sings the verse given in the lectionary, and the people sing the response. For example:

Cantor: ℟. Glory and praise to you, Lord Jesus Christ!

People: ℟. Glory and praise to you, Lord Jesus Christ!

Cantor: [Verse] Now is the acceptable time,
                now is the day of salvation.

People: ℟. Glory and praise to you, Lord Jesus Christ!

The four sample responses for this use during Lent are:

A Praise to you, Lord Jesus Christ, king of endless glory!

B Praise and honor to you, Lord Jesus Christ!

C Glory and praise to you, Lord Jesus Christ!

D Glory to you, Word of God, Lord Jesus Christ!

MASS WITHOUT A CONGREGATION

FROM THE ORDER OF MASS

Liturgy of the Word

8. *Then the minister (or the priest himself) reads the first reading, the psalm and, if there is one, the second reading, with the second chant.*

9. *Then the priest bows and says quietly:*
Almighty God, cleanse my heart and my lips
that I may worthily proclaim your gospel.

10. *With hands joined, he says:*
The Lord be with you.

    The minister answers:
And also with you.

    The priest:
A reading from the holy gospel according to N.

    He makes the sign of the cross on the book, and then on his forehead, lips, and breast.

    The minister responds:
Glory to you, Lord.

    Then the priest reads the gospel. At the end of the gospel he kisses the book, saying quietly:
May the words of the gospel wipe away our sins.

    The minister answers:
Praise to you, Lord Jesus Christ.

11. *If prescribed, the priest and minister make the profession of faith together.*

12. *The general intercessions (prayer of the faithful) may follow. The priest gives the intentions and the minister answers.*

FROM THE GENERAL INSTRUCTION
Liturgy of the Word
217. After the opening prayer, the minister or the priest himself reads the first reading and psalm, and, when it is to be said, the second reading and the alleluia verse or other chant.

218. The priest remains in the same place, bows, and says: Almighty God, cleanse my heart. He then reads the gospel, kissing the book at the end and saying quietly: May the words of the gospel . . . The minister makes the acclamation.

219. If the profession of faith is to be added, the priest says it with the minister.

220. The general intercessions may be said in this form of Mass. The priest gives the intentions, and the minister answers.

INTRODUCTION

Chapter I

GENERAL ARRANGEMENT OF THE LECTIONARY FOR MASS

I. General Principles

1

The Church loves sacred scripture and is anxious to deepen its understanding of the truth and to nourish its own life by studying these sacred writings. The Second Vatican Council likened the bible to a fountain of renewal within the community of God's people and directed that in the revision of liturgical celebrations there should be "more abundant, varied, and appropriate reading from sacred scripture." [1] The council further directed that at Mass "the treasures of the bible should be opened up more lavishly so that richer fare might be provided for the faithful at the table of God's word. In this way a more representative portion of sacred scripture will be read to the people over a set cycle of years." [2]

It is clear why the council expressed such principles. By means of sacred scripture, read during the liturgy of the word and explained during the homily, "God speaks to his people, revealing the mystery of their redemption and salvation and offering them spiritual nourishment. Through his word, Christ himself is present in the assembly of his people." [3] Thus the Church at Mass "receives the bread of life from the table of Christ's body and God's word and unceasingly offers it to the faithful." [4]

2

In response to the directives of the council, the Consilium for the Implementation of the Constitution on the Sacred Liturgy has prepared this order of readings, which lists texts for Sundays and feasts, for weekdays throughout the year, for Masses of the saints and for other special occasions.

In arranging these texts the purpose was to assign those of greatest importance to Sundays and feasts when the Christian people are bound to celebrate the eucharist together. In this way the faithful will be able to hear the principal portions of God's revealed word over a suitable period of time. Other biblical readings which to some degree complement these texts are arranged in a separate series for weekdays. Neither part of the lectionary is dependent on the other: the readings for Sundays and feasts proceed independently of the weekday readings and vice versa.

The selection of texts for Masses of the saints, ritual Masses, votive Masses, and other special Masses has been determined by their own rules.

II. Lectionary for Sundays and Feasts

3

The following norms apply to the readings for Sundays and feasts:

a) Three readings are provided for each Mass: the first from the Old Testament, the second from the writings of the apostles (from an epistle or from the Book of Revelation, depending on the time of the year), and the third from the gospel. This arrangement best illustrates the basic unity of both Testaments and of the history of salvation: a unity which has Christ in the memorial of his paschal mystery as its center; a unity which should be one of the main subjects of instruction. Furthermore this arrangement is traditional and has long been followed in the Eastern Churches.

b) This lectionary provides a more and varied reading of sacred scripture on Sundays and feasts by arranging the texts in a three-year cycle. Thus the same text is read only once every fourth year.

Each year is designated A, B, or C. Year C is a year whose number is equally divisible by three, as if the cycle began with the first year of the Christian era. Thus 1968 is year C, 1969 is year A, 1970 is year B, 1971 is year C, etc.

c) Readings for Sundays and feasts have been arranged according to two principles which are called "semi-continuous" or "thematic." The different seasons of the year and the themes of each liturgical season determine which principle applies in specific cases.

The Old and New Testament readings best harmonize when their relationship is self-evident, that is, when the events and teachings of the New Testament are more or less explicitly related to those of the Old. The Old Testament readings in this lectionary have been chosen primarily because of their relationship to the New Testament selections, especially the gospel reading.

Common themes provide another kind of harmonization among the readings for each Mass. Seasons which best illustrate this principle are Advent, Lent, and Easter, each of which has its own spirit and message.

The Sundays of the year, on the other hand, have no particular theme. The epistle and gospel readings for these days are arranged semi-continuously, while the Old Testament readings have been chosen because of their relationship to the gospel passages.

III. Weekday Lectionary

4

The following norms apply to the weekday readings:

a) The Lenten cycle is based on the principal themes of this season, baptism and penance.

b) The gospel readings for other weekdays are arranged in a single series. During the thirty-four weeks of the year the first reading is arranged in a two-year cycle with separate readings for alternate years. Series I is for the odd years (1969, 1971, etc.), and series II is for the even years (1970, 1972, etc.).

c) The reading in the weekday lectionary, as in the Sunday lectionary, are arranged either semi-continuously or thematically depending on the presence of a theme for a particular season.

IV. Lectionary for the Celebrations of the Saints

5

Two series of readings are provided for Masses of the saints:

a) The Proper of the Saints provides the first series of readings for solemnities, feasts, and memorials, especially if a reading is especially appropriate for an individual feast. Sometimes, however, a more appropriate text is indicated as preferable and will be found in the Common of the Saints.

b) The Common of the Saints provides a more complete series of readings especially appropriate for various kinds of celebrations of saints (martyrs, pastors, virgins), as well as an extensive selection of texts speaking of holiness in general, for optional use whenever one is referred to the Common to choose a reading.

Texts in this Common are arranged in the order in which they are read at Mass: Old Testament selections, texts from the writings of the apostles, psalms and verses between the readings, and finally gospel selections. Unless expressly stated otherwise, the celebrant may choose the readings at will, considering the pastoral needs of the participating group.

V. Lectionary for Ritual Masses, Masses for Special Occasions, and Votive Masses

6

Texts for use at ritual Masses, votive Masses, and other special Masses are arranged in the same way. An extensive list of optional texts is provided, as in the Common of the Saints, to enable the celebrant to consider the particular occasion and the pastoral needs of the participating group when he chooses from a variety of readings.

VI. Criteria for the Choice and Arrangement of Readings

7

In addition to the principles governing the arrangement of readings in specific parts of the lectionary, these general norms also apply:

a) *Liturgical seasons*

The importance of scriptural reading at Mass, as well as liturgical tradition, demands that in this new lectionary certain scriptural books should be reserved for specific liturgical seasons. The tradition of reading the Acts of the Apostles during the Easter season is preserved, as common to East and West (in the Ambrosian and Spanish rites). These readings beautifully illustrate how the total life of the Church springs from the paschal mystery. The Eastern and Western traditions of reading John's Gospel during the last weeks of Lent and throughout the Easter season is likewise preserved, since it is the "spiritual" gospel which brings out the mystery of Christ more deeply.

The reading of Isaiah, especially the first part of the book, is traditionally assigned to Advent. Parts of this prophet's writings are also read during the Christmas season, along with the First Letter of John.

b) *Length of texts.* The new lectionary has tried to establish a balance in determining the length of texts. A distinction has been made between narratives which demand a longer reading but are likely to hold the listeners' attention and other texts which should not be too lengthy because of their doctrinal depth.

Certain lengthy passages have been carefully abbreviated and appear in both long and short forms. The celebrant may decide which to use. Optional verses should be indicated by appropriate typographical signs.

c) *Difficult texts.* Biblical texts which contain serious literary, critical, or exegetical problems or which the faithful may find difficult to understand have been omitted from the readings for Sundays and solemnities. It would be wrong, of course, to keep from the faithful the wealth of spiritual meaning contained in these texts on the premise that they are too difficult to understand, if this difficulty can be overcome, since every faithful member of the Church should have a basic Christian education and every pastor should have a basic biblical formation. Frequently a passage will become easier to grasp when associated with another reading from the same Mass.

d) *Omission of verses.* Many liturgies, including the Roman liturgy, traditionally omit certain verses from biblical readings. One should not be too quick to do this because the style, purpose, or meaning of the scriptural text may easily be damaged. But, for pastoral reasons, it seemed best to continue this tradition, taking care that the essential meaning of the text remain unchanged. Otherwise some texts would be too lengthy or readings of greater spiritual value to the people would have to be entirely omitted because of the one or two verses of little pastoral worth or involving truly difficult questions.

VII. Celebrant's Choice of Texts

8

This lectionary sometimes provides the celebrant with a choice of two texts or a choice among several optional texts for one reading. This seldom occurs on Sundays, solemnities, and feasts because such a choice might easily obscure the spirit of the liturgical season or unduly interrupt the semi-continuous reading of a book of the bible. However, such a choice is frequently possible in Masses of the saints, ritual Masses, votive Masses, and other special Masses.

To keep a sound order in the choice of readings, these guidelines should be noted:

a) When three readings are assigned for a Mass, it is most desirable that all three be read. If, however, for pastoral reasons, the conference of bishops decides to permit only two readings, one of the first two should be chosen which is of greater value in presenting the mystery of salvation to the faithful. Unless expressly stated otherwise in another part of the lectionary, it is preferable to choose the reading which is more closely related to the day's gospel, more helpful in presenting an organized and unified instruction over a period of time, or which permits a semi-continuous reading of a book of the bible.

For instance, the Old Testament readings throughout Lent present the development of salvation history. Semi-continuous selections from the writings of the apostles are provided for Sundays of the year. The priest should choose the readings systematically for a number of Sundays so that his teaching will be logically and coherently presented. It would hardly be consistent to choose a reading from the Old Testament one week and from the writings of the apostles the next week, with no order or harmony at all.

b) Pastoral reasons should also determine the choice between the long and the short forms of the same text. These reasons are the capacity of the hearers to listen to a longer or shorter reading with profit, their ability to understand difficult texts correctly, and their appreciation of a more complete text which is to be explained in the homily.

Whenever this choice is given it should be indicated by the way the text is printed.

c) When a choice between appointed texts is permitted, the needs of the people should be considered by choosing a text which is easier or more suited to the congregation, by repeating or postponing a text appointed for a particular celebration and using it optionally on another occasion when it is helpful pastorally.

These provisions are especially useful in circumstances where a text may present difficulties for a certain group, or when the same text might be repeated within a few days, on Sunday and again during the week.

d) When the weekday lectionary is used, it is important to determine in advance whether any feasts will occur in a given week to interrupt the course of weekday readings. Then the priest, considering the entire week's readings, may omit less important selections from the weekday lectionary or combine them with other readings when this will give a unified presentation of a specific theme.

e) For Masses of the saints *special readings* are sometimes provided which are appropriate to the saint's life or the mystery remembered at the Mass (feast of the conversion of Paul, memorial of Mary Magdalene). Even in the case of a memorial, these readings should replace those prescribed by the weekday lectionary for that day.

Sometimes *appropriate readings* are provided to focus on a certain aspect of the spiritual life or the saint's accomplishments. It is not necessary to use these readings every time they are provided, unless pastoral reasons so demand. Generally it would be preferable to use the semi-continuous readings from the book assigned in the weekday lectionary to that liturgical season.

In addition, the Common of the Saints provides *general readings* which are appropriate for various kinds of saints (martyrs, pastors, virgins) or for the saints in general. When several texts are given for the same reading, the celebrant may choose the one most suitable for the congregation. However:

1) On solemnities, when three readings are assigned the first choice should be from the Old Testament, the second from the writings of the apostles, and the third from the gospel, unless the conference of bishops decides to permit only two readings.

2) On feasts and memorials, when only two readings are assigned the first choice is from the Old Testament or from the writings of the apostles, and the second from the gospel. During Easter time, however, it is customary to use the writings of the apostles for the first reading and John's Gospel for the second.

f) The guidelines above, governing the choice of readings from the Common of the Saints, also apply to ritual Masses, votive Masses, and other special Masses when several texts are provided for the same reading.

VIII. Chants between the Readings

9

According to the norms of the General Instruction of the Roman Missal (nos. 36-40), there is to be a song after each reading.

The more important song is the psalm following the first reading. Ordinarily the psalm should be the one assigned to the reading, except for readings from the Common of the Saints, ritual Masses, votive Masses, and other special Masses for which the celebrant may choose the psalm most pastorally useful.

To make it easier for the people to join in the psalm, some selected texts and responses have been chosen for different times of the year and for different kinds of saints, and these may be used in place of the assigned response if the psalm is sung.

The other song, between the second reading and the gospel, is either specified for the Mass and related to the day's gospel, or it may be chosen from the series of texts given for the particular season or in the Common.

During Lent the following acclamations (or similar ones) may be used before and after the verse which precedes the gospel:

Praise to you, Lord Jesus Christ, king of endless glory!
Praise and honor to you, Lord Jesus Christ!
Glory and praise to you, Lord Jesus Christ!
Glory to you, Word of God, Lord Jesus Christ!

IX. Purpose of the Lectionary
10

The purpose of this lectionary is primarily a pastoral one, in the spirit of the Second Vatican Council. The general principles governing it and the wealth of texts within it are all pastorally oriented. It is the result of cooperation and effort among a large number of people from all parts of the world: experts in scripture, pastoral work, catechetics, and liturgy.

This extended reading and explanation of sacred scripture to Christians during the celebration of the eucharist will, it is hoped, help to reach the goal which the Second Vatican Council so often spoke of and which Pope Paul VI expressed in these words: "The revision of the lectionary was indeed a wise directive, aimed at developing among the faithful an ever-increasing hunger for God's word, the word which leads the people of the new covenant to the perfect unity of the Church under the guidance of the Holy Spirit. We are fully confident that priests and faithful alike will prepare their hearts together more earnestly for the Lord's Supper, meditating more thoughtfully on sacred scripture, nourishing themselves daily with the words of the Lord. The fulfillment of the wishes of the Second Vatican Council will be the inevitable consequence of this experience of God's word: sacred scripture will become a perpetual source of spiritual life, an important instrument for transmitting Christian teachings, and the center of all theological formation." [5]

Chapter II

DESCRIPTION OF THE ORDER
OF READINGS

This arrangement of the order of readings according to the different seasons of the year is to help clarify the structure of the entire lectionary and its relationship to the liturgical year.

I. Season of Advent
11

1. *Sundays.* Each gospel reading has a specific theme: the Lord's coming in glory at the end of time (first Sunday), John the Baptist (second and third Sundays), and the events which immediately prepared for the Lord's birth (fourth Sunday).

The Old Testament readings are prophecies about the Messiah and messianic times, especially those taken from the Book of Isaiah.

The selections from the writings of the apostles present exhortations and instructions on different themes of this season.

2. *Weekdays.* Two series of readings are given: one from the beginning of Advent to December 16, the other from December 17 to December 24.

The first part of Advent is devoted to a semi-continuous reading of the Book of Isaiah, including those important passages which are also read on Sundays. Gospel passages for these days have been chosen because of their relationship to the first reading.

Beginning on Thursday of the second week the gospel passages are about John the Baptist, while the first readings either continue the Book of Isaiah or come from a text related to the day's gospel.

The gospels of the last week before Christmas are from Matthew (Chapter 1) and Luke (Chapter 1), the events which immediately prepared for the Lord's birth. Selections for the first reading are from different books of the Old Testament which have important messianic prophecies and a relationship to the gospel texts.

II. Christmas Season
12

1. *Solemnities, Feasts, and Sundays.* For the Vigil and the three Masses of Christmas, the first reading is from Isaiah. These passages are traditional in the Roman liturgy and have been retained in various local rites. With two exceptions, the other readings follow the Roman Missal.

The gospel of the Sunday within the octave of Christmas (the feast of the Holy Family) tells of Jesus' childhood. The other readings concern family life.

The readings for the octave of Christmas and solemnity of Mary the Mother of God are about the virgin-mother of God (the gospel and second reading) and about the naming of the child Jesus (the gospel and first reading, since this feast is no longer in the calendar).

The readings for the second Sunday after Christmas refer to the mystery of the incarnation.

On Epiphany the second reading speaks of the call of all people to salvation.

The readings for the Sunday after Epiphany (the feast of the Lord's Baptism) speak of that mystery.

2. *Weekdays.* The reading of the First Letter of John begins on his feast, December 27. It is continued on the feast of the Holy Innocents (December 28) and the following days.

The gospels present the Lord's manifestations: the events of Jesus' childhood from Luke's Gospel (December 29-30), the first chapter of John's Gospel (December 31-January 5), and the significant manifestations recorded in the three synoptic gospels (January 7-12).

III. Lenten Season
13

1. *Sundays.* The gospel selections for the first two Sundays recount the Lord's temptations and transfiguration as recorded in the synoptic gospels.

For year A the gospel accounts concerning the Samaritan woman, the man born blind, and Lazarus are assigned to the following three Sundays. Since these passages are very important in relation to Christian initiation they may also be used for years B and C, especially when candidates for baptism are present. However, for pastoral reasons, many wished another choice of texts for years B and C and alternative selections have been provided: year B, John's text about Christ's future glorification through his cross and resurrection; year C, Luke's texts on conversion.

The Old Testament readings are about the history of salvation, one of the main topics of Lenten instruction. A series of texts has been prepared for each year to present the principal elements of this history from the beginning to the promise of the new covenant; especially readings about Abraham (second Sunday) and about the deliverance of God's people from slavery (third Sunday).

The selections from the writings of the apostles have been chosen because of their relationship to the gospel and Old Testament readings, and as far as possible should harmonize with them.

2. *Weekdays.* The gospel and Old Testament readings were chosen for their mutual relationship and for their treatment of various themes for Lenten instruction. Whenever possible, most of the readings from the Roman Missal were preserved. It seemed best, however, to arrange the readings from John's Gospel in a better sequence since most of it used to be read without any special order. Therefore a semi-continuous reading of John's Gospel, with a better relation to Lenten themes, begins on Monday of the fourth week.

Since the readings about the Samaritan woman, the man born blind, and Lazarus are assigned for Sundays only in year A (and are optional in years B and C), additional Masses with these texts have been inserted at the beginning of the third, fourth, and fifth weeks. During years B and C they may be used on any day of these weeks in place of the assigned weekday readings.

IV. Easter Season

14

1. *Sundays.* Until the third Sunday of Easter the gospel selections recount the appearances of the risen Christ. To avoid interrupting the narrative, the reading about the Good Shepherd, previously assigned to the second Sunday after Easter, is now assigned to the fourth Sunday of Easter (that is, the third Sunday after Easter). The gospels of the fifth, sixth, and seventh Sundays of Easter are excerpts from the teaching and prayer of Christ after the last supper.

The first reading is from the Acts of the Apostles, arranged in a three-year cycle of parallel and progressive selections. Thus the life, growth, and witness of the early Church are presented every year.

The selections from the writings of the apostles are year A, First Letter of Peter; year B, First Letter of John; year C, the Book of Revelation. These texts seem most appropriate to the spirit of the Easter season, a spirit of joyful faith and confident hope.

2. *Weekdays.* As on Sunday, the first reading is from the Acts of the Apostles, arranged semi-continuously.

The gospel readings during Easter week tell of the Lord's appearances with the conclusions of the synoptic gospels reserved for the Ascension. A semi-continuous

reading of John's Gospel follows, appropriate for the Easter theme and complementary to the Lenten readings. These readings are largely devoted to the teaching and prayer of the Lord after the last supper.

V. Season "of the Year"

I. Arrangement and Choice of Texts

15

The remainder of the liturgical year consists of thirty-three or thirty-four weeks of the year. It begins on Monday after the Sunday following January 6 and goes to the Tuesday before Ash Wednesday inclusive, and from Monday after Pentecost Sunday until first Vespers of the first Sunday of Advent.

This lectionary provides readings for all thirty-four weeks. Sometimes, however, there are only thirty-three weeks since certain seasonal feasts, e.g., the Lord's Baptism and Pentecost as well as other solemnities, e.g., Holy Trinity, Christ the King, replace some of these Sundays.

The following guidelines should be followed for the correct use of the readings during the weeks of the year.

1. The Sunday celebrated as the feast of the Lord's Baptism takes the place of the first Sunday of the year. Therefore the readings for the first week begin on Monday after the first Sunday following January 6.

2. The Sunday following the feast of the Lord's Baptism is the second Sunday of the year, and the following Sundays are numbered consecutively until the beginning of Lent. The readings for the week in which Lent begins continue until Tuesday inclusive. On Ash Wednesday the Lenten readings begin.

3. The weeks of the year begin again after Pentecost Sunday in the following order:

a) When there are thirty-four Sundays of the year, the readings are resumed at the week immediately following the last one used before Lent. For instance, if Lent begins during the sixth week of the year, then the Monday after Pentecost Sunday begins the seventh week of the year. The Solemnity of the Trinity takes the place of a Sunday of the year.

b) When there are only thirty-three Sundays of the year, the week of the year which would ordinarily follow Pentecost is omitted. Thus the eschatological readings with which the liturgical year concludes will still be read during the last two weeks of the year. For instance, if Lent begins during the fifth week of the year, the sixth week is omitted and the seventh week begins on Monday after Pentecost.

2. Sunday Readings

16

1. *Gospel readings:* The gospel for the second Sunday of the year refers to the manifestation of the Lord, already celebrated on Epiphany, with the traditional passage about the wedding at Cana and two other passages from John's Gospel.

The third Sunday of the year begins the semi-continuous reading of the three synoptic gospels. This arrangement provides a presentation of each gospel's distinctive doctrine as well as a development of the Lord's life and preaching.

The above arrangement and distribution of texts also allows a certain harmony between the meaning of each gospel and the development of the liturgical year. The readings after Epiphany are concerned with the beginning of the Lord's preaching and are related to His Baptism and first manifestation, which are celebrated on Epiphany and the following Sundays. At the end of the liturgical year the eschatological themes of these last Sundays occur in sequence because the chapters of the synoptic gospels which precede the passion narratives treat these themes more or less extensively.

In year B after the sixteenth Sunday of the year, there are five readings from the sixth chapter of John's Gospel (the teaching on the bread of life). This insertion is only natural since the multiplication of the bread in John's Gospel parallels the same narrative in Mark. In year C the first text in the semi-continuous reading of Luke (third Sunday of the year) is the preface to his gospel in which he outlines his purpose for writing the gospel; there did not seem to be another appropriate place for this reading.

2. *Old Testament readings* were chosen for their relationship to each gospel passage. This serves a twofold purpose: any great contrast between the readings in the same Mass is avoided, and at the same time the unity of Old and New Testaments is clearly shown. This relationship between the readings for each Mass is indicated by the careful selection of titles for the readings.

As far as possible the selection of readings has been made so that the texts are short and easy to grasp, but another purpose is to read the most important parts of the Old Testament on Sundays. Although these readings are ordinarily related to the gospel passage and thus lack their own set order, nevertheless the treasures of the word of God are opened up so that all who participate in Sunday Mass will hear most of the Old Testament's principal sections.

3. *Writings of the Apostles:* A semi-continuous reading of the letters of Paul and James is presented. (The letters of Peter and John are read during the Easter and Christmas seasons.)

Paul's First Letter to the Corinthians, since it is lengthy and discusses so many different questions, is arranged in a three-year cycle at the beginning of this season of the year. It seemed best to divide the Letter to the Hebrews into one part for year B and another for year C.

All selections are short and should be quite easy for the faithful to understand.

Table II (below, page 15) indicates the distribution of passages from the epistles in the three-year cycle of the Sundays of the year.

4. The theme of the readings chosen for the thirty-fourth and last Sunday of the liturgical year is Christ the King, prefigured by David and proclaimed in the humiliations he suffered by dying for us on the cross, who governs and guides his Church until his return at the end of time.

3. Weekday Readings

17

1. *The gospel selections* are arranged so that Mark is read first (weeks 1-9), then Matthew (weeks 10-21), and finally Luke (weeks 22-34). The first twelve chapters of Mark are read in their entirety, omitting only those two passages from the sixth chapter which are read on weekdays at other times of the year. Everything omitted in Mark is read from Matthew and Luke. Thus all the elements which give the different gospels their distinctive style and which are necessary for an intelligent understanding of each gospel are read two or three times. The complete eschatological teaching of Luke's Gospel completes the readings of the liturgical year.

2. *The first reading* consists of selections from either Testament, depending on the length of books to be read.

a) Extensive selections from the books of the *New Testament* are read so that the listener is given something of each letter's substance. However, passages having little pastoral relevance today have been omitted, such as those concerning the gift of tongues or the discipline of the early Church.

b) The limited readings from the *Old Testament* are an attempt to give something of the individual character of each book. The historical texts have been chosen for their presentation of an overall view of the history of salvation before the incarnation. Lengthy narratives could not be included; sometimes a few verses have been selected to make up a short reading. In addition the religious significance of some historical events is brought out by selections from the wisdom books which serve as introductions or conclusions to a series of historical events.

Almost all the Old Testament books will be found in the weekday lectionary in the proper of the season. The only books omitted are the very short prophetic books (Abdiah, Zephaniah) and a poetic book not suited to reading (Song of Songs). Some texts written for edification require a lengthy reading to be understood. Of these the books of Tobit and Ruth are read and the rest omitted (Esther and Judith). Texts from these are also assigned to Sundays and weekdays at other times of the year.

Table III (below, page 15) indicates the distribution of the books of each Testament in a two-year cycle among the weekdays of the year.

c) The Books of Daniel and Revelation are assigned to the end of the liturgical year since they have appropriate eschatological themes.

NOTES

1. Second Vatican Council, *Constitution on the Sacred Liturgy*, n. 35: *A.A.S.* 56 (1964), p. 109.
2. *Ibid.*, n. 51, p. 114.
3. General Instruction on the Roman Missal, n. 33.
4. Second Vatican Council, *Dogmatic Constitution on Divine Revelation*, n. 21: *A.A.S.* 58 (1966), p. 827.
5. Pope Paul VI, Apostolic Constitution on the Roman Missal, April 3, 1969: *A.A.S.* 61 (1969), pp. 220-221.

TABLE I Seasonal Table of feasts and Sundays for determining the readings

Year	Lectionary Cycle Sunday Cycle	Week Cycle	Ash Wednesday	Easter	Ascension	Pentecost	Corpus Christi	Weeks in Ordinary Time before Lent Number of weeks	Ending	after Easter Season Beginning	Number of weeks	First Sunday of Advent
1986	C	II	12 February	30 March	8 May	18 May	1 June	5	11 February	19 May	7	30 November
1987	A	I	4 March	19 April	28 May	7 June	21 June	8	3 March	8 June	10	29 November
1988	B	II	17 February	3 April	12 May	22 May	5 June	6	16 February	23 May	8	27 November
1989	C	I	8 February	26 March	4 May	14 May	28 May	5	7 February	15 May	6	3 December
1990	A	II	28 February	15 April	24 May	3 June	17 June	8	27 February	4 June	9	2 December
1991	B	I	13 February	31 March	9 May	19 May	2 June	5	12 February	20 May	7	1 December
1992	C	II	4 March	19 April	28 May	7 June	21 June	8	3 March	8 June	10	29 November
1993	A	I	24 February	11 April	20 May	30 May	13 June	7	23 February	31 May	9	28 November
1994	B	II	16 February	3 April	12 May	22 May	5 June	6	15 February	23 May	8	27 November
1995	C	I	1 March	16 April	25 May	4 June	18 June	8	28 February	5 June	9	3 December
1996	A	II	21 February	7 April	16 May	26 May	9 June	7	20 February	27 May	8	1 December
1997	B	I	12 February	30 March	8 May	18 May	1 June	5	11 February	19 May	7	30 November
1998	C	II	25 February	12 April	21 May	31 May	14 June	7	24 February	1 June	9	29 November
1999	A	I	17 February	4 April	13 May	23 May	6 June	6	16 February	24 May	8	28 November
2000	B	II	8 March	23 April	1 June	11 June	25 June	9	7 March	12 June	10	3 December

TABLE II Order of the second reading on Sundays "of the year"

Sunday	Year A	Year B	Year C
2	1 Cor, 1—4	1 Cor, 6—11	1 Cor, 12—15
3	"	"	"
4	"	"	"
5	"	"	"
6	"	"	"
7	"	2 Cor	"
8	"	"	"
9	Rom	"	Gal
10	"	"	"
11	"	"	"
12	"	"	"
13	"	"	"
14	"	"	"
15	"	Eph	Col
16	"	"	"
17	"	"	"
18	"	"	"
19	"	"	Heb, 11—12
20	"	"	"
21	"	"	"
22	"	James	"
23	"	"	Philm
24	"	"	1 Tm
25	Phil	"	"
26	"	"	"
27	"	Heb, 2—10	2 Tm
28	"	"	"
29	1 Thes	"	"
30	"	"	"
31	"	"	2 Thes
32	"	"	"
33	"	"	"

TABLE III Order of the first reading on weekdays "of the year"

Week	Year I	Year II
1	Heb	1 Samuel
2	"	"
3	"	"
4	"	2 Sm; 1 Kings, 1—16
5	Gen 1—11	1 Kings, 1—16
6	"	James
7	Sir	"
8	"	1 Peter; Jude
9	Tobit	2 Peter; 2 Tm
10	2 Cor	1 Kings, 17—22
11	"	1 Kgs, 17—22; 2 Kgs
12	Gen 12—50	2 Kings; Lm
13	"	Amos
14	"	Hos; Is
15	Ex;	Is; Mi
16	"	Micah; Jer
17	Ex Lv	Jeremiah
18	Nm; Dt	Jer; Nah; Hb
19	Dt; Jos	Ezekiel
20	Jgs; Ruth	"
21	1 Thes	2 Thes; 1 Cor
22	1 Thes; Col	1 Corinthians
23	Col; 1 Tm	"
24	1 Tm	"
25	Ezra; Haggai; Zec	Prv; Eccl
26	Zec; Neh; Bar	Job
27	Jonah; Mal; Joel	Galatians
28	Romans	Gal; Eph
29	"	Ephesians
30	"	"
31	"	Eph; Phil
32	Wisdom	Ti; Philm; 2 and 3 John
33	1 and 2 Mc	Revelation
34	Daniel	"

ABBREVIATIONS OF BOOKS OF THE BIBLE

Acts — Acts of the Apostles	Jb — Job	Neh — Nehemiah
Am — Amos	Jdt — Judith	Nm — Numbers
Bar — Baruch	Jer — Jeremiah	Ob — Obadiah
1 Chr — 1 Chronicles	Jl — Joel	1 Pt — 1 Peter
2 Chr — 2 Chronicles	Jgs — Judges	2 Pt — 2 Peter
Col — Colossians	Jn — John	Phil — Philippians
1 Cor — 1 Corinthians	1 Jn — 1 John	Phlm — Philemon
2 Cor — 2 Corinthians	2 Jn — 2 John	Prv — Proverbs
Dn — Daniel	3 Jn — 3 John	Ps(s) — Psalms
Dt — Deuteronomy	Jon — Jonah	Rom — Romans
Eccl — Ecclesiastes	Jos — Joshua	Ru — Ruth
Eph — Ephesians	Jude — Jude	Rv — Revelation
Est — Esther	1 Kgs — 1 Kings	Sg — Song of Songs
Ex — Exodus	2 Kgs — 2 Kings	Sir — Sirach
Ez — Ezekiel	Lam — Lamentations	1 Sm — 1 Samuel
Ezr — Ezra	Lk — Luke	2 Sm — 2 Samuel
Gal — Galatians	Lv — Leviticus	Tb — Tobit
Gn — Genesis	Mal — Malachi	1 Thes — 1 Thessalonians
Hb — Habakkuk	1 Mc — 1 Maccabees	2 Thes — 2 Thessalonians
Heb — Hebrews	2 Mc — 2 Maccabees	Ti — Titus
Hg — Haggai	Mi — Micah	1 Tm — 1 Timothy
Hos — Hosea	Mk — Mark	2 Tm — 2 Timothy
Is — Isaiah	Mt — Matthew	Wis — Wisdom
Jas — James	Na — Nahum	Zec — Zechariah
		Zep — Zephaniah

NOTE: Text references (to chapter and verse) follow the English translation of the Bible used in this lectionary and thus are not always the same as in the "Ordo Lectionum Missae" (which employs the Vulgate numbering). Some of the references to books of the Bible also differ:

1 Samuel	=	1 Kings
2 Samuel	=	2 Kings
1 Kings	=	3 Kings
2 Kings	=	4 Kings
1 Chronicles	=	1 Paralipomenon
2 Chronicles	=	2 Paralipomenon
Ezra	=	1 Ezra
Nehemiah	=	2 Ezra

PROPER OF SEASONS

ADVENT SEASON

1   FIRST SUNDAY OF ADVENT   A

READING I
Is 2, 1-5

A reading from the book of the prophet Isaiah
The Lord will gather all nations in eternal peace to form the kingdom of God

This is what Isaiah, son of Amoz, saw concerning Judah and Jerusalem.

In days to come,
The mountain of the Lord's house
  shall be established as the highest mountain
  and raised above the hills.
All nations shall stream toward it;
  many peoples shall come and say:
"Come, let us climb the Lord's mountain,
  to the house of the God of Jacob,
That he may instruct us in his ways,
  and we may walk in his paths."
For from Zion shall go forth instruction,
  and the word of the Lord from Jerusalem.
He shall judge between the nations,
  and impose terms on many peoples.
They shall beat their swords into plowshares
  and their spears into pruning hooks;
One nation shall not raise the sword against another,
  nor shall they train for war again.
O house of Jacob, come,
  let us walk in the light of the Lord!

    This is the Word of the Lord.

Responsorial Psalm
Ps 122, 1-2. 3-4. 4-5. 6-7. 8-9

℞. (1) I rejoiced when I heard them say:
  let us go to the house of the Lord.

I rejoiced because they said to me,
  "We will go up to the house of the Lord."
And now we have set foot
  within your gates, O Jerusalem.

℞. I rejoiced when I heard them say:
  let us go to the house of the Lord.

Jerusalem, built as a city
  with compact unity.
To it the tribes go up,
  the tribes of the Lord.

℞. I rejoiced when I heard them say:
  let us go to the house of the Lord.

According to the decree for Israel,
  to give thanks to the name of the Lord.
In it are set up judgment seats,
  seats for the house of David.

℞. I rejoiced when I heard them say:
  let us go to the house of the Lord.

Pray for the peace of Jerusalem!
  May those who love you prosper!
May peace be within your walls,
  prosperity in your buildings.

℞. I rejoiced when I heard them say:
  let us go to the house of the Lord.

Because of my relatives and friends
  I will say, "Peace be within you!"
Because of the house of the Lord, our God,
  I will pray for your good.

℞. I rejoiced when I heard them say:
  let us go to the house of the Lord.

READING II
Rom 13, 11-14

A reading from the letter of Paul to the Romans
The time has come, our salvation is near.

You know the time in which we are living. It is now the hour for you to wake from sleep, for our salvation is closer than when we first accepted the faith. The night is far spent; the day draws near. Let us cast off deeds of darkness and put on the armor of light. Let us live honorably as in daylight; not in carousing and drunkenness, not in sexual excess and lust, not in quarreling and jealousy. Rather, put on the Lord Jesus Christ and make no provision for the desires of the flesh.

    This is the Word of the Lord.

GOSPEL
Mt 24, 37-44

Alleluia
Ps 85, 8

℞. Alleluia. Lord, let us see your kindness, and grant us your salvation. ℞. Alleluia

✠ **A reading from the holy gospel according to Matthew**
Stay awake, you must be ready.

Jesus said to his disciples: "The coming of the Son of Man will repeat what happened in Noah's time. In the days before the flood people were eating and drinking, marrying and being married, right up to the day Noah entered the ark. They were totally unconcerned until the flood came and destroyed them. So will it be at the coming of the Son of Man. Two men will be out in the field; one will be taken and one will be left. Two women will be grinding meal; one will be taken and one will be left. Stay awake, therefore! You cannot know the day your Lord is coming.

"Be sure of this: if the owner of the house knew when the thief was coming he would keep a watchful eye and not allow his house to be broken into. You must be prepared in the same way. The Son of Man is coming at the time you least expect."

This is the gospel of the Lord.

---

2   FIRST SUNDAY OF ADVENT   B

READING I   Is 63, 16-17. 19; 64, 2-7

A reading from the book of the prophet Isaiah

Oh, that you would tear the heavens apart and come down.

You, Lord, are our father,
  our redeemer you are named forever.
Why do you let us wander, O Lord, from your ways,
  and harden our hearts so that we fear you not?
Return for the sake of your servants,
  the tribes of your heritage.
Oh, that you would rend the heavens and come down,
  with the mountains quaking before you,
While you wrought awesome deeds we could not hope for,
  such as they had not heard of from of old.
No ear has ever heard, no eye ever seen,
  any God but you
  doing such deeds for those who wait for him.
Would that you might meet us doing right,
  that we were mindful of you in our ways!
Behold, you are angry, and we are sinful;
  all of us have become like unclean men,
  all our good deeds are like polluted rags;
We have all withered like leaves,
  and our guilt carries us away like the wind.

There is none who calls upon your name,
  who rouses himself to cling to you;
For you have hidden your face from us
  and have delivered us up to our guilt.
Yet, O Lord, you are our father;
  we are the clay and you are the potter:
  we are all the work of your hands.
      This is the Word of the Lord.

Responsorial Psalm   Ps 80, 2-3. 15-16. 18-19

℟. (4) Lord, make us turn to you,
  let us see your face and we shall be saved.
O shepherd of Israel, hearken,
  from your throne upon the cherubim, shine forth.
Rouse your power,
  and come to save us.
℟. Lord, make us turn to you,
  let us see your face and we shall be saved.
Once again, O Lord of hosts,
  look down from heaven, and see;
Take care of this vine,
  and protect what your right hand has planted
  [the son of man whom you yourself made strong].
℟. Lord, make us turn to you,
  let us see your face and we shall be saved.
May your help be with the man of your right hand,
  with the son of man whom you yourself made strong.
Then we will no more withdraw from you;
  give us new life, and we will call upon your name.
℟. Lord, make us turn to you,
  let us see your face and we shall be saved.

READING II   1 Cor 1, 3-9

A reading from the first letter of Paul to the Corinthians

The revelation we looked for, Christ Jesus our Lord.

Grace and peace from God our Father and the Lord Jesus Christ.

I continually thank my God for you because of the favor he has bestowed on you in Christ Jesus, in whom you have been richly endowed with every gift of speech and knowledge. Like-

wise, the witness I bore to Christ has been so confirmed among you that you lack no spiritual gift as you wait for the revelation of our Lord Jesus [Christ.] He will strengthen you to the end, so that you will be blameless on the day of our Lord Jesus Christ. God is faithful, and it was he who called you to fellowship with his Son, Jesus Christ our Lord.
This is the Word of the Lord.

GOSPEL   Mk 13, 33-37
Alleluia   Ps 85, 8

℞. Alleluia. **Lord, let us see your kindness, and grant us your salvation.** ℞. Alleluia.

✠   **A reading from the holy gospel according to Mark**

Stay awake! You never know when the Lord will come

Jesus said to his disciples: "Be constantly on the watch! Stay awake! You do not know when the appointed time will come. It is like a man traveling abroad. He leaves home and places his servants in charge, each with his own task; and he orders the man at the gate to watch with a sharp eye. Look around you! You do not know when the master of the house is coming, whether at dusk, at midnight, when the cock crows, or at early dawn. Do not let him come suddenly and catch you asleep. What I say to you, I say to all: Be on guard!"
This is the gospel of the Lord.

---

3   FIRST SUNDAY OF ADVENT   🄲

READING I   Jer 33, 14-16
A reading from the book of the prophet Jeremiah

I will cause a good seed to spring forth from David.

The days are coming, says the Lord, when I will fulfill the promise I made to the house of Israel and Judah. In those days, in that time, I will raise up for David a just shoot; he shall do what is right and just in the land. In those days Judah shall be safe and Jerusalem shall dwell secure; this is what they shall call her: "The Lord our justice."
This is the Word of the Lord.

Responsorial Psalm   Ps 25, 4-5. 8-9. 10. 14

℞. (1) To you, O Lord, I lift my soul.
**Your ways, O Lord, make known to me;
teach me your paths,
Guide me in your truth and teach me,
for you are God my savior,
and for you I wait all the day.**
℞. To you, O Lord, I lift my soul.
**Good and upright is the Lord;
thus he shows sinners the way.
He guides the humble to justice,
he teaches the humble his way.**
℞. To you, O Lord, I lift my soul.
**All the paths of the Lord are kindness and constancy
toward those who keep his covenant and his decrees.
The friendship of the Lord is with those who fear him,
and his covenant, for their instruction.**
℞. To you, O Lord, I lift my soul.

READING II   1 Thes 3, 12-4, 2
A reading from the first letter of Paul to the Thessalonians

When Christ comes may he strengthen your hearts in holiness.

May the Lord increase you and make you overflow with love for one another and for all, even as our love does for you. May he strengthen your hearts, making them blameless and holy before our God and Father at the coming of our Lord Jesus with all his holy ones.

Now, my brothers, we beg and exhort you in the Lord Jesus that, even as you learned from us how to conduct yourselves in a way pleasing to God—which you are indeed doing—so you must learn to make still greater progress. You know the instructions we gave you in the Lord Jesus.
This is the Word of the Lord.

GOSPEL   Lk 21, 25-28. 34-36
Alleluia   Ps 85, 8

℟. Alleluia. **Lord, let us see your kindness,
and grant us your salvation.** ℟.Alleluia.

✠ **A reading from the holy gospel according
to Luke**
Your redemption is near at hand.

Jesus said to his disciples: "There will be signs
in the sun, the moon and the stars. On the
earth, nations will be in anguish, distraught
at the roaring of the sea and the waves. Men
will die of fright in anticipation of what is
coming upon the earth. The powers in the
heavens will be shaken. After that, men will
see the Son of Man coming on a cloud with
great power and glory. When these things begin to happen, stand up straight and raise your
heads, for your ransom is near at hand.

"Be on guard lest your spirits become
bloated with indulgence and drunkenness and
worldly cares. The great day will suddenly
close in on you like a trap. The day I speak
of will come upon all who dwell on the face
of the earth, so be on the watch. Pray constantly for the strength to escape whatever is
in prospect, and to stand secure before the
Son of Man."
        This is the gospel of the Lord.

---

4   SECOND SUNDAY OF ADVENT   A

READING I   Is 11, 1-10
A reading from the book of the prophet Isaiah
He judges the poor with justice.
On that day
A shoot shall sprout from the stump of Jesse,
    and from his roots a bud shall blossom.
The spirit of the Lord shall rest upon him:
    a spirit of wisdom and of understanding,
A spirit of counsel and of strength,
    a spirit of knowledge and of fear of the Lord,
    and his delight shall be the fear of the Lord.
Not by appearance shall he judge,
    nor by hearsay shall he decide,
But he shall judge the poor with justice,
    and decide aright for the land's afflicted.
He shall strike the ruthless with the rod of

his mouth,
    and with the breath of his lips he shall slay
    the wicked.
Justice shall be the band around his waist,
    and faithfulness a belt upon his hips.

Then the wolf shall be a guest of the lamb,
    and the leopard shall lie down with the kid;
The calf and the young lion shall browse to-
    gether,
    with a little child to guide them.
The cow and the bear shall be neighbors,
    together their young shall rest;
    the lion shall eat hay like the ox.
The baby shall play by the cobra's den,
    and the child lay his hand on the adder's
    lair.
There shall be no harm or ruin on all my holy
    mountain;
    for the earth shall be filled with knowledge
    of the Lord,
    as water covers the sea.

On that day,
The root of Jesse,
    set up as a signal for the nations,
The Gentiles shall seek out,
    for his dwelling shall be glorious.
        This is the Word of the Lord.

Responsorial Psalm   Ps 72, 1-2. 7-8. 12-13. 17

℟. (7)Justice shall flourish in his time,
    and fullness of peace for ever.
O God, with your judgment endow the king,
    and with your justice, the king's son;
He shall govern your people with justice
    and your afflicted ones with judgment.
℟.Justice shall flourish in his time,
    and fullness of peace for ever.
Justice shall flower in his days,
    and profound peace, till the moon be no
    more.
May he rule from sea to sea,
    and from the River to the ends of the earth.
℟.Justice shall flourish in his time,
    and fullness of peace for ever.
For he shall rescue the poor man when he
    cries out,
    and the afflicted when he has no one to
    help him.

He shall have pity for the lowly and the poor;
 the lives of the poor he shall save.
℟. Justice shall flourish in his time,
 and fullness of peace for ever.
May his name be blessed forever;
 as long as the sun his name shall remain.
In him shall all the tribes of the earth be
 blessed;
 all the nations shall proclaim his happiness.
℟. Justice shall flourish in his time,
 and fullness of peace for ever.

READING II   Rom 15, 4-9
A reading from the letter of Paul to the Romans
Christ, the hope of all men.

Everything written before our time was
written for our instruction, that we might derive hope from the lessons of patience and the
words of encouragement in the Scriptures.
May God, the source of all patience and encouragement, enable you to live in perfect
harmony with one another according to the
spirit of Christ Jesus, so that with one heart
and voice you may glorify God, the Father of
our Lord Jesus Christ.

Accept one another, then, as Christ accepted
you, for the glory of God. Yes, I affirm that
Christ became the servant of the Jews because of God's faithfulness in fulfilling the
promises to the patriarchs whereas the Gentiles glorify God because of his mercy. As
Scripture has it, "Therefore I will praise you
among the Gentiles and I will sing to your
name."
            This is the Word of the Lord.

GOSPEL   Mt 3, 1-12
Alleluia Lk 3, 4. 6

℟. Alleluia. **Prepare the way for the Lord,
make straight his paths:**
all mankind shall see the salvation of God.
℟. Alleluia.

✠ A reading from the holy gospel according
            to Matthew
Repent, for the kingdom of heaven is close at hand.

When John the Baptizer made his appearance
as a preacher in the desert of Judea, this was

his theme: "Reform your lives! The reign of
God is at hand." It was of him that the prophet
Isaiah had spoken when he said,
     "A herald's voice in the desert:
      'Prepare the way of the Lord,
       make straight his paths.' "
John was clothed in a garment of camel's
hair and wore a leather belt around his waist.
Grasshoppers and wild honey were his food.
At that time Jerusalem, all Judea, and the
whole region around the Jordan were going out
to him. They were being baptized by him in
the Jordan River as they confessed their sins.

When he saw that many of the Pharisees
and Sadducees were stepping forward for this
bath, he said to them: "You brood of vipers!
Who told you to flee from the wrath to come?
Give some evidence that you mean to reform.
Do not pride yourselves on the claim, 'Abraham is our father.' I tell you, God can raise
up children to Abraham from these very
stones. Even now the ax is laid to the root of
the tree. Every tree that is not fruitful will be
cut down and thrown into the fire. I baptize
you in water for the sake of reform, but the
one who will follow me is more powerful than
I. I am not even fit to carry his sandals. He it is
who will baptize you in the Holy Spirit and fire.
His winnowing-fan is in his hand. He will
clear his threshing floor, and gather his grain
into the barn, but the chaff he will burn in unquenchable fire."
     This is the gospel of the Lord.

---

5   SECOND SUNDAY OF ADVENT **B**

READING I   Is 40, 1-5. 9-11
A reading from the book of the prophet Isaiah
Make straight in the desert the way of the Lord.

Comfort, give comfort to my people,
 says your God.
Speak tenderly to Jerusalem, and proclaim to
 her
 that her service is at an end,
 her guilt is expiated;
Indeed, she has received from the hand of the
 Lord
 double for all her sins.

A voice cries out:
In the desert prepare the way of the Lord!
Make straight in the wasteland a highway
for our God!
Every valley shall be filled in,
every mountain and hill shall be made low;
The rugged land shall be made a plain,
the rough country, a broad valley.
Then the glory of the Lord shall be revealed,
and all mankind shall see it together;
for the mouth of the Lord has spoken.

Go up onto a high mountain,
Zion, herald of glad tidings;
Cry out at the top of your voice,
Jerusalem, herald of good news!
Fear not to cry out
and say to the cities of Judah:
Here is your God!
Here comes with power
the Lord God,
who rules by his strong arm;
Here is his reward with him,
his recompense before him.
Like a shepherd he feeds his flock;
in his arms he gathers the lambs,
Carrying them in his bosom,
and leading the ewes with care.
This is the Word of the Lord.

Responsorial Psalm   Ps 85, 9-10. 11-12. 13-14

℞. (8) Lord, let us see your kindness,
and grant us your salvation.
I will hear what God proclaims;
the Lord—for he proclaims peace to his people.
Near indeed is his salvation to those who fear
him,
glory dwelling in our land.
℞. Lord, let us see your kindness,
and grant us your salvation.
Kindness and truth shall meet;
justice and peace shall kiss.
Truth shall spring out of the earth,
and justice shall look down from heaven.
℞. Lord, let us see your kindness,
and grant us your salvation.
The Lord himself will give his benefits;

our land shall yield its increase.
Justice shall walk before him,
and salvation, along the way of his steps.
℞. Lord, let us see your kindness,
and grant us your salvation.

READING II   2 Pt 3, 8-14

A reading from the second letter of Peter
We wait for new heavens and a new earth.

This point must not be overlooked, dear
friends. In the Lord's eyes, one day is as a
thousand years and a thousand years are as
a day. The Lord does not delay in keeping his
promise—though some consider it "delay."
Rather, he shows you generous patience, since
he wants none to perish but all to come to repentance. The day of the Lord will come like a
thief, and on that day the heavens will vanish
with a roar; the elements will be destroyed by
fire, and the earth and all its deeds will be made
manifest.

Since everything is to be destroyed in this
way, what sort of men must you not be! How
holy in your conduct and devotion, looking for
the coming of the day of God and trying to
hasten it! Because of it, the heavens will be
destroyed in flames and the elements will melt
away in a blaze. What we await are new
heavens and a new earth where, according to
his promise, the justice of God will reside. So,
beloved, while waiting for this, make every effort to be found without stain or defilement,
and at peace in his sight.
This is the Word of the Lord.

GOSPEL   Mk 1, 1-8
Alleluia   Lk 3, 4. 6

℞. Alleluia. **Prepare the way for the Lord,
make straight his paths:**
all mankind shall see the salvation of God.
℞. Alleluia.

✠ **The beginning of the holy gospel according
to Mark**
Prepare a way for the Lord.

Here begins the gospel of Jesus Christ, the Son
of God. In Isaiah the prophet, it is written:

"I send my messenger before you
   to prepare your way:
   a herald's voice in the desert, crying,
   'Make ready the way of the Lord,
      clear him a straight path.' "

Thus it was that John the Baptizer appeared in the desert proclaiming a baptism of repentance which led to the forgiveness of sins. All the Judean countryside and the people of Jerusalem went out to him in great numbers. They were being baptized by him in the Jordan River as they confessed their sins. John was clothed in camel's hair, and wore a leather belt around his waist. His food was grasshoppers and wild honey. The theme of his preaching was: "One more powerful than I is to come after me. I am not fit to stoop and untie his sandal straps. I have baptized you in water; he will baptize you in the Holy Spirit."

This is the gospel of the Lord.

---

6   SECOND SUNDAY OF ADVENT   C

READING I   Bar 5, 1-9

A reading from the book of the prophet Baruch
Jerusalem—God will show your splendor.

Jerusalem, take off your robe of mourning and
   misery;
   put on the splendor of glory from God forever:
Wrapped in the cloak of justice from God,
   bear on your head the mitre
   that displays the glory of the eternal name.
For God will show all the earth your splendor:
   you will be named by God forever
   the peace of justice, the glory of God's worship.

Up, Jerusalem! stand upon the heights;
   look to the east and see your children
Gathered from the east and the west
   at the word of the Holy One,
   rejoicing that they are remembered by God.
Led away on foot by their enemies they left
   you:
   but God will bring them back to you
   borne aloft in glory as on royal thrones.
For God has commanded

that every lofty mountain be made low,
And that the age-old depths and gorges
   be filled to level ground,
   that Israel may advance secure in the glory
      of God.
The forests and every fragrant kind of tree
   have overshadowed Israel at God's command;
For God is leading Israel in joy
   by the light of his glory,
   with his mercy and justice for company.
      This is the Word of the Lord.

Responsorial Psalm   Ps 126, 1-2. 2-3. 4-5. 6

℟. (3) The Lord has done great things for us;
   we are filled with joy.
When the Lord brought back the captives of
      Zion,
   we were like men dreaming.
Then our mouth was filled with laughter,
   and our tongue with rejoicing.

℟. The Lord has done great things for us;
   we are filled with joy.
Then they said among the nations,
   "The Lord has done great things for them."
The Lord has done great things for us;
   we are glad indeed.

℟. The Lord has done great things for us;
   we are filled with joy.
Restore our fortunes, O Lord,
   like the torrents in the southern desert.
Those that sow in tears
   shall reap rejoicing.

℟. The Lord has done great things for us;
   we are filled with joy.
Although they go forth weeping,
   carrying the seed to be sown,
They shall come back rejoicing,
   carrying their sheaves.

℟. The Lord has done great things for us;
   we are filled with joy.

READING II   Phil 1, 4-6. 8-11

**A reading from the letter of Paul
to the Philippians**
Show yourselves sinless and without blame in the day
of Christ.

In every prayer I utter, I rejoice as I plead on your behalf, at the way you have all continually helped promote the gospel from the very first day.

I am sure of this much: that he who has begun the good work in you will carry it through to completion, right up to the day of Christ Jesus. God himself can testify how much I long for each of you with the affection of Christ Jesus! My prayer is that your love may more and more abound, both in understanding and wealth of experience, so that with a clear conscience and blameless conduct you may learn to value the things that really matter, up to the very day of Christ. It is my wish that you may be found rich in the harvest of justice which Jesus Christ has ripened in you, to the glory and praise of God.

This is the Word of the Lord.

GOSPEL Lk 3, 1-6
Alleluia Lk 3, 4. 6

R̶. Alleluia. **Prepare the way for the Lord, make straight his paths:**
all mankind shall see the salvation of God.
R̶. Alleluia.

✠ A reading from the holy gospel according to Luke
All mankind shall see the salvation of God.

In the fifteenth year of the rule of Tiberius Caesar, when Pontius Pilate was procurator of Judea, Herod tetrarch of Galilee, Philip his brother tetrarch of the region of Ituraea and Trachonitis, and Lysanias tetrarch of Abilene, during the high-priesthood of Annas and Caiaphas, the word of God was spoken to John son of Zechariah in the desert. He went about the entire region of the Jordan proclaiming a baptism of repentance which led to the forgiveness of sins, as is written in the book of the words of Isaiah the prophet:

"A herald's voice in the desert, crying,
'Make ready the way of the Lord,
  clear him a straight path.
Every valley shall be filled
  and every mountain and hill shall be
  leveled.
The windings shall be made straight

and the rough ways smooth,
and all mankind shall see the salvation of
  God.' "
This is the gospel of the Lord.

_____

7 **THIRD SUNDAY OF ADVENT** **A**

READING I Is 35, 1-6. 10
A reading from the book of the prophet Isaiah
God himself will come and save us.

The desert and the parched land will exult;
  the steppe will rejoice and bloom.
They will bloom with abundant flowers,
  and rejoice with joyful song.
The glory of Lebanon will be given to them,
  the splendor of Carmel and Sharon;
They will see the glory of the Lord,
  the splendor of our God.

Strengthen the hands that are feeble,
  make firm the knees that are weak,
Say to those whose hearts are frightened:
  Be strong, fear not!
Here is your God,
  he comes with vindication;
With divine recompense
  he comes to save you.
Then will the eyes of the blind be opened,
  the ears of the deaf be cleared;
Then will the lame leap like a stag,
  then the tongue of the dumb will sing.

Those whom the Lord has ransomed will return
  and enter Zion singing,
  crowned with everlasting joy;
They will meet with joy and gladness,
  sorrow and mourning will flee.
This is the Word of the Lord.

Responsorial Psalm Ps 146, 6-7. 8-9. 9-10
R̶. (See Is 35, 4) Lord, come and save us.
The Lord God keeps faith forever,
  secures justice for the oppressed,
  gives food to the hungry.
The Lord sets captives free.
R̶. Lord, come and save us.
The Lord gives sight to the blind;

the Lord raises up those that were bowed down.
The Lord loves the just;
  the Lord protects strangers.
R̷. Lord, come and save us.
The fatherless and the widow he sustains,
  but the way of the wicked he thwarts.
The Lord shall reign forever;
  your God, O Zion, through all generations.
R̷. Lord, come and save us.
R̷. Or: Alleluia.

READING II   Jas 5, 7-10

A reading from the letter of James
You also must be patient; do not lose heart,
the Lord's coming will be soon.

Be patient, my brothers, until the coming of the Lord. See how the farmer awaits the precious yield of the soil. He looks forward to it patiently while the soil receives the winter and the spring rains. You too, must be patient. Steady your hearts, because the coming of the Lord is at hand. Do not grumble against one another, my brothers, lest you be condemned. See! The judge stands at the gate. As your models in suffering hardships and in patience, brothers, take the prophets who spoke in the name of the Lord.
    This is the Word of the Lord.

GOSPEL   Mt 11, 2-11
Alleluia   Is 61, 1

R̷. Alleluia. The Spirit of the Lord is upon me; he sent me to bring Good News to the poor.
    R̷. Alleluia.

✠ A reading from the holy gospel according to Matthew
Are you the one who is to come, or must we wait for someone else?

John in prison heard about the works Christ performed, and sent a message through his disciples to ask him, "Are you 'He who is to come' or do we look for another?" In reply, Jesus said to them: "Go back and report to John what you hear and see: the blind recover their sight, cripples walk, lepers are cured, the deaf hear, dead men are raised to life, and the poor have the

good news preached to them. Blest is the man who finds no stumbling block in me."
    As the messengers set off, Jesus began to speak to the crowds about John: "What did you go out to the wasteland to see—a reed swaying in the wind? Tell me, what did you go out to see—someone luxuriously dressed? Remember, those who dress luxuriously are to be found in royal palaces. Why then did you go out—to see a prophet? A prophet indeed, and something more! It is about this man that Scripture says,
    'I send my messenger ahead of you
    to prepare your way before you.'
"I solemnly assure you, history has not known a man born of woman greater than John the Baptizer. Yet the least born into the kingdom of God is greater than he."
    This is the gospel of the Lord.

8   **THIRD SUNDAY OF ADVENT**   B

READING I   Is 61, 1-2. 10-11
A reading from the book of the prophet Isaiah
I exult for joy in the Lord.
The spirit of the Lord God is upon me,
  because the Lord has anointed me;
He has sent me to bring glad tidings to the
    lowly,
  to heal the brokenhearted,
To proclaim liberty to the captives
  and release to the prisoners,
To announce a year of favor from the Lord
  and a day of vindication by our God.

I rejoice heartily in the Lord,
  in my God is the joy of my soul;
For he has clothed me with a robe of salvation,
  and wrapped me in a mantle of justice,
Like a bridegroom adorned with a diadem,
  like a bride bedecked with her jewels.
As the earth brings forth its plants,
  and a garden makes its growth spring up,
So will the Lord God make justice and praise
  spring up before all the nations.
    This is the Word of the Lord.

Responsorial Psalm   Lk 1, 46-48. 49-50. 53-54

R̸. (Is 61, 10) My soul rejoices in my God.
My being proclaims the greatness of the Lord,
    my spirit finds joy in God my savior,
For he has looked upon his servant in her
        lowliness;
    all ages to come shall call me blessed.
R̸. My soul rejoices in my God.
God who is mighty has done great things for
        me,
    holy is his name;
His mercy is from age to age
    on those who fear him.
R̸. My soul rejoices in my God.
The hungry he has given every good thing,
    while the rich he has sent empty away.
He has upheld Israel his servant,
    ever mindful of his mercy.
R̸. My soul rejoices in my God.

READING II   1 Thes 5, 16-24

A reading from the first letter of Paul to the
        Thessalonians
May you all be kept blameless, spirit, soul and body,
    for the coming of our Lord Jesus Christ.
Rejoice always, never cease praying, render
constant thanks; such is God's will for you in
Christ Jesus.
    Do not stifle the spirit. Do not despise proph-
ecies. Test everything; retain what is good.
Avoid any semblance of evil.
    May the God of peace make you perfect in
holiness. May you be preserved whole and entire, spirit, soul, and body, irreproachable at
the coming of our Lord Jesus Christ. He who
calls us is trustworthy, therefore he will do it.
    This is the Word of the Lord.

GOSPEL   Jn 1, 6-8. 19-28

Alleluia   Is 61. 1

R̸. Alleluia. The Spirit of the Lord is upon me;
he sent me to bring Good News to the poor.
    R̸. Alleluia.

✠ A reading from the holy gospel according
            to John

There stands among you, unknown to you, the one who is
    coming after me.
There was a man named John sent by God,
who came as a witness to testify to the light,
so that through him all men might believe—
but only to testify to the light, for he himself
was not the light.
    The testimony John gave when the Jews
sent priests and Levites from Jerusalem to ask
"Who are you?" was the absolute statement,
"I am not the Messiah." They questioned him
further, "Who, then? Elijah?" "I am not Elijah,"
he answered. "Are you the prophet?" "No,"
he replied.
    Finally they said to him: "Tell us who you
are, so that we can give some answer to those
who sent us. What do you have to say for your
self?" He said, quoting the prophet Isaiah, "I
am
        'a voice in the desert, crying out:
        Make straight the way of the Lord!' "
    Those whom the Pharisees had sent pro-
ceeded to question him further: "If you are not
the Messiah, nor Elijah, nor the prophet, why
do you baptize?" John answered them: "I baptize with water. There is one among you whom
you do not recognize—the one who is to come
after me—the strap of whose sandal I am not
worthy to unfasten." This happened in Bethany, across the Jordan, where John was baptizing.
    This is the gospel of the Lord.

---

9   THIRD SUNDAY OF ADVENT   Ⓒ

READING I   Zep 3, 14-18

A reading from the book of the prophet
            Zephaniah
The Lord will exult you, over you, he will renew you
    by his love.
Shout for joy, O daughter Zion!
    sing joyfully, O Israel!
Be glad and exult with all your heart,
    O daughter Jerusalem!
The Lord has removed the judgment against
        you,
    he has turned away your enemies;
The King of Israel, the Lord, is in your midst,

you have no further misfortune to fear.
On that day, it shall be said to Jeru-
  salem:
Fear not, O Zion, be not discouraged!
The Lord, your God, is in your midst,
  a mighty savior;
He will rejoice over you with gladness,
  and renew you in his love.
He will sing joyfully because of you,
  as one sings at festivals.
    This is the Word of the Lord.

Responsorial Psalm   Is 12, 2-3. 4. 5-6

R̴. (6) Cry out with joy and gladness:
  for among you is the great and Holy One of
  Israel.
God indeed is my savior;
  I am confident and unafraid.
My strength and my courage is the Lord,
  and he has been my savior.
With joy you will draw water
  at the fountain of salvation.
R̴. Cry out with joy and gladness:
  for among you is the great and Holy One of
  Israel.
Give thanks to the Lord, acclaim his name;
  among the nations make known his deeds,
  proclaim how exalted is his name.
R̴. Cry out with joy and gladness:
  for among you is the great and Holy One of
  Israel.
Sing praise to the Lord for his glorious achievement;
  let this be known throughout all the earth.
Shout with exultation, O city of Zion,
  for great in your midst
  is the Holy One of Israel!
R̴. Cry out with joy and gladness:
  for among you is the great and Holy One of
  Israel.

READING II   Phil 4, 4-7

A reading from the letter of Paul to the
Philippians
The Lord is near

Rejoice in the Lord always! I say it again.
Rejoice! Everyone should see how unselfish

you are. The Lord himself is near. Dismiss all
anxiety from your minds. Present your needs
to God in every form of prayer and in petitions
full of gratitude. Then God's own peace, which
is beyond all understanding, will stand guard
over your hearts and minds, in Christ Jesus.
    This is the Word of the Lord.

GOSPEL   Lk 3, 10-18

Alleluia   Is 61, 1 (cited in Lk 4, 18)

R̴. Alleluia. The Spirit of the Lord is upon me;
he sent me to bring Good News to the poor.
  R̴. Alleluia.

✠ A reading from the holy gospel according
                to Luke
What, then, must we do?

The crowds asked John, "What ought we to
do?" In reply he said, "Let the man with two
coats give to him who has none. The man who
has food should do the same."

Tax collectors also came to be baptized, and
they said to him, "Teacher, what are we to do?"
He answered them, "Exact nothing over and
above your fixed amount."

Soldiers likewise asked him, "What about
us?" He told them, "Do not bully anyone. Denounce no one falsely. Be content with your
pay."

The people were full of anticipation, wondering in their hearts whether John might be
the Messiah. John answered them all by saying: "I am baptizing you in water, but there
is one to come who is mightier than I. I am
not fit to loosen his sandal strap. He will
baptize you in the Holy Spirit and in fire.
His winnowing-fan is in his hand to clear his
threshing floor and gather the wheat into his
granary, but the chaff he will burn in unquenchable fire." Using exhortations of this
sort, he preached the good news to the people.
    This is the gospel of the Lord.

10   FOURTH SUNDAY OF ADVENT   A

READING I   Is 7, 10-14

A reading from the book of the prophet Isaiah

The virgin shall conceive.

The Lord spoke to Ahaz: Ask for a sign from the Lord, your God; let it be deep as the nether world, or high as the sky! But Ahaz answered, "I will not ask! I will not tempt the Lord!" Then he said: Listen, O house of David! Is it not enough for you to weary men, must you also weary my God? Therefore the Lord himself will give you this sign: the virgin shall be with child, and bear a son, and shall name him Immanuel.

This is the Word of the Lord.

Responsorial Psalm   Ps 24, 1-2. 3-4. 5-6

℟. (7. 10) Let the Lord enter; he is king of
    glory.
**The Lord's are the earth and its fullness;
    the world and those who dwell in it.
For he founded it upon the seas
    and established it upon the rivers.**
℟. Let the Lord enter; he is king of glory.
**Who can ascend the mountain of the Lord?
    or who may stand in his holy place?
He whose hands are sinless, whose heart is
    clean,
    who desires not what is vain.**
℟. Let the Lord enter; he is king of glory.
**He shall receive a blessing from the Lord,
    a reward from God his savior.
Such is the race that seeks for him,
    that seeks the face of the God of Jacob.**
℟. Let the Lord enter; he is king of glory.

READING II   Rom 1, 1-7

**The beginning of the letter of Paul to the
    Romans**

Jesus Christ, a descendant of David, is the Son of God.

Greetings from Paul, a servant of Christ Jesus, called to be an apostle and set apart to proclaim the gospel of God which he promised long ago through his prophets, as the holy Scriptures record—the gospel concerning his Son, who was descended from David according to the

flesh but was made Son of God in power, according to the spirit of holiness, by his resurrection from the dead: Jesus Christ our Lord. Through him we have been favored with apostleship, that we may spread his name and bring to obedient faith all the Gentiles, among whom are you who have been called to belong to Jesus Christ.

To all in Rome, beloved of God and called to holiness, grace and peace from God our Father and the Lord Jesus Christ.

This is the Word of the Lord.

GOSPEL   Mt 1, 18-24

Alleluia   Mt 1, 23

℟. Alleluia. **A virgin will give birth to a son; his name will be Emmanuel: God is with us.**
℟. Alleluia.

✠ **A reading from the holy gospel according
    to Matthew**

Jesus was born of Mary who was betrothed to Joseph, a relative of David.

**This is how the birth of Jesus Christ came about. When his mother Mary was engaged to Joseph, but before they lived together, she was found with child through the power of the Holy Spirit. Joseph her husband, an upright man unwilling to expose her to the law, decided to divorce her quietly. Such was his intention when suddenly the angel of the Lord appeared in a dream and said to him: "Joseph, son of David, have no fear about taking Mary as your wife. It is by the Holy Spirit that she has conceived this child. She is to have a son and you are to name him Jesus because he will save his people from their sins." All this happened to fulfill what the Lord had said through the prophet:
    "The virgin shall be with child
    and give birth to a son,
    and they shall call him Emmanuel,"
a name which means "God is with us." When Joseph awoke he did as the angel of the Lord had directed him and received her into his home as his wife.**

This is the gospel of the Lord.

11   FOURTH SUNDAY OF ADVENT   **B**

READING I   2 Sm 7, 1-5. 8-11. 16

A reading from the second book of Samuel

The Lord will make the house of David secure for ever.

When King David was settled in his palace, and the Lord had given him rest from his enemies on every side, he said to Nathan the prophet, "Here I am living in a house of cedar, while the ark of God dwells in a tent!" Nathan answered the king, "Go, do whatever you have in mind, for the Lord is with you." But that night the Lord spoke to Nathan and said: "Go, tell my servant David, 'Thus says the Lord: Should you build me a house to dwell in?'

"'It was I who took you from the pasture and from the care of the flock to be commander of my people Israel. I have been with you wherever you went, and I have destroyed all your enemies before you. And I will make you famous like the great ones of the earth. I will fix a place for my people Israel; I will plant them so that they may dwell in their place without further disturbance. Neither shall the wicked continue to afflict them as they did of old, since the time I first appointed judges over my people Israel. I will give you rest from all your enemies. The Lord also reveals to you that he will establish a house for you. Your house and your kingdom shall endure forever before me; your throne shall stand firm forever.'"

This is the Word of the Lord.

Responsorial Psalm   Ps 89, 2-3. 4-5. 27. 29

℞. (2) For ever I will sing the goodness of the Lord.

The favors of the Lord I will sing forever; through all generations my mouth shall proclaim your faithfulness.

For you have said, "My kindness is established forever"; in heaven you have confirmed your faithfulness.

℞. For ever I will sing the goodness of the Lord.

"I have made a covenant with my chosen one,

I have sworn to David my servant: Forever will I confirm your posterity and establish your throne for all generations."

℞. For ever I will sing the goodness of the Lord.

"He shall say of me, 'You are my father, my God, the Rock, my savior.'

Forever I will maintain my kindness toward him, and my covenant with him stands firm."

℞. For ever I will sing the goodness of the Lord.

READING II   Rom 16, 25-27

A reading from the letter of Paul to the Romans

The mystery kept secret for endless ages is now made clear.

To him who is able to strengthen you in the gospel which I proclaim when I preach Jesus Christ, the gospel which reveals the mystery hidden for many ages but now manifested through the writings of the prophets, and, at the command of the eternal God, made known to all the Gentiles that they may believe and obey—to him, the God who alone is wise, may glory be given through Jesus Christ unto endless ages. Amen.

This is the Word of the Lord.

GOSPEL   Lk 1, 26-38

Alleluia Lk 1, 38

℞. Alleluia. I am the servant of the Lord: may his will for me be done. ℞. Alleluia.

✠ **A reading from the holy gospel according to Luke**

You shall conceive and bear a son.

The angel Gabriel was sent from God to a town of Galilee named Nazareth, to a virgin betrothed to a man named Joseph, of the house of David. The virgin's name was Mary. Upon arriving, the angel said to her: "Rejoice, O highly favored daughter! The Lord is with you Blessed are you among women." She wa deeply troubled by his words, and wonder what his greeting meant. The angel went or

say to her: "Do not fear, Mary. You have found favor with God. You shall conceive and bear a son and give him the name Jesus. Great will be his dignity and he will be called Son of the Most High. The Lord God will give him the throne of David his father. He will rule over the house of Jacob forever and his reign will be without end."

Mary said to the angel, "How can this be since I do not know man?" The angel answered her: "The Holy Spirit will come upon you and the power of the Most High will overshadow you; hence, the holy offspring to be born will be called Son of God. Know that Elizabeth your kinswoman has conceived a son in her old age; she who was thought to be sterile is now in her sixth month, for nothing is impossible with God."

Mary said: "I am the maidservant of the Lord. Let it be done to me as you say." With that the angel left her.

This is the gospel of the Lord.

12　FOURTH SUNDAY OF ADVENT　C

READING I　　　　　　　　　　Mi 5, 1-4

A reading from the book of the prophet Micah

Out of you will be born the one who is to rule over Israel.

Thus says the Lord:
You, Bethlehem-Ephrathah
　too small to be among the clans of Judah,
From you shall come forth for me
　one who is to be ruler in Israel;
Whose origin is from of old,
　from ancient times.
(Therefore the Lord will give them up, until the time
　when she who is to give birth has borne,
And the rest of his brethren shall return
　to the children of Israel.)
He shall stand firm and shepherd his flock
　by the strength of the Lord,
　in the majestic name of the Lord, his God;
And they shall remain, for now his greatness
　shall reach to the ends of the earth;
　he shall be peace.
This is the Word of the Lord.

Responsorial Psalm　　　Ps 80, 2-3. 15-16. 18-19

℟. (4) Lord, make us turn to you,
　let us see your face and we shall be saved.
O shepherd of Israel, hearken,
　from your throne upon the cherubim, shine
　　forth.
Rouse your power,
　and come to save us.
℟. Lord, make us turn to you,
　let us see your face and we shall be saved.
Once again, O Lord of hosts,
　look down from heaven, and see;
Take care of this vine,
　and protect what your right hand has planted
　[the son of man whom you yourself made
　　strong].
℟. Lord, make us turn to you,
　let us see your face and we shall be saved.
May your help be with the man of your right
　hand,
　with the son of man whom you yourself
　　made strong.
Then we will no more withdraw from you;
　give us new life, and we will call upon your
　　name.
℟. Lord, make us turn to you,
　let us see your face and we shall be saved.

READING II　　　　　　　　　　Heb 10, 5-10

**A reading from the letter of Paul
to the Hebrews**

I am coming to do your will.

On coming into the world Jesus said:
"Sacrifice and offering you did not desire,
　but a body you have prepared for me;
Holocausts and sin offerings you took no
　delight in.
Then I said, 'As is written of me in the book,
　I have come to do your will, O God.'"
First he says,
"Sacrifices and offerings, holocausts and sin
　offerings
you neither desired nor delighted in."
(These are offered according to the prescriptions of the law.) Then he says,
"I have come to do your will."
In other words, he takes away the first covenant to establish the second.

By this "will," we have been sanctified through the offering of the body of Jesus Christ once for all.

This is the Word of the Lord.

GOSPEL   Lk 1, 39-45
Alleluia   Lk 1, 38

℟. Alleluia. I am the servant of the Lord: may his will for me be done. ℟. Alleluia.

✠ A reading from the holy gospel according to Luke

Why should it happen that I am honored with a visit from the mother of my Lord?

Mary set out, proceeding in haste into the hill country to a town of Judah, where she entered Zechariah's house and greeted Elizabeth. When Elizabeth heard Mary's greeting, the baby stirred in her womb. Elizabeth was filled with the Holy Spirit, and cried out in a loud voice: "Blessed are you among women and blessed is the fruit of your womb. But who am I that the mother of my Lord should come to me? The moment your greeting sounded in my ears, the baby stirred in my womb for joy. Blessed is she who trusted that the Lord's words to her would be fulfilled."

This is the gospel of the Lord.

---

13   **CHRISTMAS SEASON**

December 25   CHRISTMAS
Vigil   **A** **B** **C**

These readings are for use at Masses on the afternoon of December 24, either before or after first Vespers of Christmas.

READING I   Is 62, 1-5
A reading from the book of the prophet Isaiah

The Lord takes delight in you.

For Zion's sake I will not be silent,
    for Jerusalem's sake I will not be quiet,
Until her vindication shines forth like the dawn
    and her victory like a burning torch.

Nations shall behold your vindication,
    and all kings your glory;
You shall be called by a new name
    pronounced by the mouth of the Lord.

You shall be a glorious crown in the hand of the Lord,
    a royal diadem held by your God.
No more shall men call you "Forsaken,"
    or your land "Desolate,"
But you shall be called "My Delight,"
    and your land "Espoused."
For the Lord delights in you,
    and makes your land his spouse.
As a young man marries a virgin,
    your Builder shall marry you;
And as a bridegroom rejoices in his bride
    so shall your God rejoice in you.

This is the Word of the Lord.

Responsorial Psalm   Ps 89, 4-5. 16-17. 27. 29

℟. (2a) For ever I will sing the goodness of the Lord.

I have made a covenant with my chosen one,
    I have sworn to David my servant:
Forever will I confirm your posterity
    and establish your throne for all generations.

℟. For ever I will sing the goodness of the Lord.

Happy the people who know the joyful shout;
    in the light of your countenance, O Lord,
    they walk.
At your name they rejoice all the day,
    and through your justice they are exalted.

℟. For ever I will sing the goodness of the Lord.

He shall say of me, "You are my father,
    my God, the Rock, my savior."
Forever I will maintain my kindness toward him,
    and my covenant with him stands firm.

℟. For ever I will sing the goodness of the Lord.

READING II   Acts 13, 16-17. 22-25

A reading from the Acts of the Apostles

Paul spoke of Christ, the son of David.

[When Paul came to Antioch Pisidia, he entered the synagogue there] and motioning to them for silence, he began: "Fellow Israelites and you others who reverence our God, listen to what I have to say! The God of the people

Israel once chose our fathers. He made this people great during their sojourn in the land of Egypt, and 'with an outstretched arm' he led them out of it. God raised up David as their king; on his behalf he testified, 'I have found David son of Jesse to be a man after my own heart who will fulfill my every wish.'

"According to his promise, God has brought forth from this man's descendants Jesus, a savior for Israel. John heralded the coming of Jesus by proclaiming a baptism of repentance to all the people of Israel. As John's career was coming to an end, he would say, 'What you suppose me to be I am not. Rather, look for the one who comes after me. I am not worthy to unfasten the sandals on his feet.' "

This is the Word of the Lord.

GOSPEL   Mt 1, 1-25 or 1, 18-25
Alleluia

℞. Alleluia. **Tomorrow the wickedness of the earth will be destroyed:**
the Savior of the world will be our king.
℞. Alleluia.

✠ The beginning of the holy gospel according to Matthew
A genealogy of Jesus Christ, son of David.

(Long Form)

A family record of Jesus Christ, son of David, son of Abraham. Abraham was the father of Isaac, Isaac the father of Jacob, Jacob the father of Judah and his brothers.
Judah was the father of Perez and Zerah, whose mother was Tamar.
Perez was the father of Hezron,
Hezron the father of Ram.
Ram was the father of Amminadab,
Amminadab the father of Nahshon,
Nahshon the father of Salmon.
Salmon was the father of Boaz, whose mother was Rahab,
Boaz was the father of Obed, whose mother was Ruth.
Obed was the father of Jesse,
Jesse the father of King David.
David was the father of Solomon, whose

mother had been the wife of Uriah.
Solomon was the father of Rehoboam,
Rehoboam the father of Abijah,
Abijah the father of Asa.
Asa was the father of Jehoshaphat,
Jehoshaphat the father of Joram,
Joram the father of Uzziah.
Uzziah was the father of Jotham,
Jotham the father of Ahaz,
Ahaz the father of Hezekiah.
Hezekiah was the father of Manasseh,
Manasseh the father of Amos,
Amos the father of Josiah.
Josiah became the father of Jechoniah and his brothers at the time of the Babylonian exile.
After the Babylonian exile
Jechoniah was the father of Shealtiel,
Shealtiel the father of Zerubbabel.
Zerubbabel was the father of Abiud,
Abiud the father of Eliakim,
Eliakim the father of Azor.
Azor was the father of Zadok,
Zadok the father of Achim,
Achim the father of Eliud.
Eliud was the father of Eleazar,
Eleazar the father of Matthan,
Matthan the father of Jacob.
Jacob was the father of Joseph the husband of Mary.
It was of her that Jesus who is called the Messiah was born.
Thus the total number of generations is:
from Abraham to David, fourteen generations;
from David to the Babylonian captivity, fourteen generations;
from the Babylonian captivity to the Messiah,
fourteen generations.

Now this is how the birth of Jesus Christ came about. When his mother Mary was engaged to Joseph, but before they lived together, she was found with child through the power of the Holy Spirit. Joseph her husband, an upright man unwilling to expose her to the law, decided to divorce her quietly. Such was his intention when suddenly the angel of the Lord appeared in a dream and said to him: "Joseph, son of David, have no fear about taking Mary as your wife. It is by the Holy Spirit that she has conceived this child. She is to have a son and you are to name him Jesus because he will save his people from their sins." All this happened to fulfill what the Lord had said through the prophet:

> "The virgin shall be with child
> and give birth to a son,
> and they shall call him Emmanuel,"

a name which means "God is with us." When Joseph awoke he did as the angel of the Lord had directed him and received her into his home as his wife. He had no relations with her at any time before she bore a son, whom he named Jesus.

> This is the gospel of the Lord.

OR
(Short Form)

This is how Jesus came to be born.

Now this is how the birth of Jesus Christ came about. When his mother Mary was engaged to Joseph, but before they lived together, she was found with child through the power of the Holy Spirit. Joseph her husband, an upright man unwilling to expose her to the law, decided to divorce her quietly. Such was his intention when suddenly the angel of the Lord appeared in a dream and said to him: "Joseph, son of David, have no fear about taking Mary as your wife. It is by the Holy Spirit that she has conceived this child. She is to have a son and you are to name him Jesus because he will save his people from their sins." All this happened to fulfill what the Lord had said through the prophet:

> "The virgin shall be with child
> and give birth to a son,
> and they shall call him Emmanuel,"

a name which means "God is with us." When Joseph awoke he did as the angel of the Lord had directed him and received her into his home as his wife. He had no relations with her at any time before she bore a son, whom he named Jesus.

> This is the gospel of the Lord.

These texts may also be used for Masses on Christmas day, with a choice of readings from one of the three Christmas Masses, as the pastoral needs of each congregation suggest.

14   MASS AT MIDNIGHT A B C

READING I   Is 9, 1-6
A reading from the book of the prophet Isaiah
A son is given to us.

The people who walked in darkness
   have seen a great light;
Upon those who dwelt in the land of gloom
   a light has shone.
You have brought them abundant joy
   and great rejoicing,
As they rejoice before you as at the harvest,
   as men make merry when dividing spoils.
For the yoke that burdened them,
   the pole on their shoulder,
And the rod of their taskmaster
   you have smashed, as on the day of Midian.
For every boot that tramped in battle,
   every cloak rolled in blood,
      will be burned as fuel for flames.

For a child is born to us, a son is given us;
   upon his shoulder dominion rests.
They name him Wonder-Counselor, God-Hero,
   Father-Forever, Prince of Peace.
His dominion is vast
   and forever peaceful,
From David's throne, and over his kingdom,
   which he confirms and sustains
By judgment and justice,
   both now and forever.
The zeal of the Lord of hosts will do this!
      This is the Word of the Lord.

Responsorial Psalm   Ps 96, 1-2. 2-3. 11-12. 13

℟. (Luke 2:11) Today is born our Savior,
   Christ the Lord.
Sing to the Lord a new song;
   sing to the Lord, all you lands.
Sing to the Lord; bless his name.
℟. Today is born our Savior, Christ the Lord.
Announce his salvation, day after day.
   Tell his glory among the nations;

Among all peoples, his wondrous deeds.

℟. Today is born our Savior, Christ the Lord.

Let the heavens be glad and the earth rejoice;
   let the sea and what fills it resound;
   let the plains be joyful and all that is in them!
Then shall all the trees of the forest exult.

℟. Today is born our Savior, Christ the Lord.

They shall exult before the Lord, for he comes;
   for he comes to rule the earth.
He shall rule the world with justice
   and the peoples with his constancy.

℟. Today is born our Savior, Christ the Lord.

READING II   Ti 2, 11-14

A reading from the letter of Paul to Titus
God's grace has been revealed to all men.

The grace of God has appeared, offering salvation to all men. It trains us to reject godless ways and worldly desires, and live temperately, justly, and devoutly in this age as we await our blessed hope, the appearing of the glory of the great God and of our Savior Christ Jesus. It was he who sacrificed himself for us, to redeem us from all unrighteousness and to cleanse for himself a people of his own, eager to do what is right.

   This is the Word of the Lord.

GOSPEL   Lk 2, 1-14

Alleluia Lk 2, 10-11

℟. Alleluia. **Good News and great joy to all the world:**
today is born our Savior, Christ the Lord.
   ℟. Alleluia.

✠ **A reading from the holy gospel according to Luke**
Today a savior has been born for you.

In those days Caesar Augustus published a decree ordering a census of the whole world. This first census took place while Quirinius was governor of Syria. Everyone went to register, each to his own town. And so Joseph went from the town of Nazàreth in Galilee to Judea, to David's town of Bethlehem—because he was of the house and lineage of David —to register with Mary, his espoused wife, who was with child.

While they were there the days of her confinement were completed. She gave birth to her first-born son and wrapped him in swaddling clothes and laid him in a manger, because there was no room for them in the place where travelers lodged.

There were shepherds in the locality, living in the fields and keeping night watch by turns over their flock. The angel of the Lord appeared to them, as the glory of the Lord shone around them, and they were very much afraid. The angel said to them: "You have nothing to fear! I come to proclaim good news to you— tidings of great joy to be shared by the whole people. This day in David's city a savior has been born to you, the Messiah and Lord. Let this be a sign to you: in a manger you will find an infant wrapped in swaddling clothes." Suddenly, there was with the angel a multitude of the heavenly host, praising God and saying,

   "Glory to God in high heaven,
      peace on earth to those on whom his
         favor rests."
   This is the gospel of the Lord.

---

15   MASS AT DAWN   🅐🅑🅒

READING I   Is 62, 11-12

A reading from the book of the prophet Isaiah
Your savior is born

See, the Lord proclaims
   to the ends of the earth:
Say to daughter Zion,
   your savior comes!
Here is his reward with him,
   his recompense before him.
They shall be called the holy people,
   the redeemed of the Lord,
and you shall be called "Frequented,"
   a city that is not forsaken.
      This is the Word of the Lord.

Responsorial Psalm   Ps 97, 1. 6. 11-12

℟. A light will shine on us this day:
   the Lord is born for us.

The Lord is king; let the earth rejoice;
  let the many isles be glad.
The heavens proclaim his justice,
  and all peoples see his glory.
℟. A light will shine on us this day:
  the Lord is born for us.
Light dawns for the just;
  and gladness, for the upright of heart.
Be glad in the Lord, you just,
  and give thanks to his holy name.
℟. A light will shine on us this day:
  the Lord is born for us.

READING II   Ti 3, 4-7

A reading from the letter of Paul to Titus
                His own compassion saved us

When the kindness and love of God our Savior
appeared, he saved us, not because of any
righteous deeds we had done, but because of
his mercy. He saved us through the baptism
of new birth and renewal by the Holy Spirit.
This Spirit he lavished on us through Jesus
Christ our Savior, that we might be justified by
his grace and become heirs, in hope, of eternal
life.
              This is the Word of the Lord.

GOSPEL   Lk 2, 15-20

Alleluia   Lk 2, 14

℟. Alleluia. **Glory to God in heaven,**
peace and grace to his people on earth. ℟. Alleluia.

✠ A reading from the holy gospel according
              to Luke
  The shepherds found Mary and Joseph, and the baby,
              lying in the manger

When the angels had returned to heaven, the
shepherds said to one another: "Let us go over
to Bethlehem and see this event which the Lord
has made known to us." They went in haste
and found Mary and Joseph, and the baby lying
in the manger; once they saw, they understood
what had been told them concerning this child.
All who heard of it were astonished at the
report given them by the shepherds.
  Mary treasured all these things and reflected
on them in her heart. The shepherds returned,

glorifying and praising God for all they had
heard and seen, in accord with what had been
told them.
          This is the gospel of the Lord.

---

16   **MASS DURING THE DAY** 🅰🅱🅲

READING I   Is 52, 7-10
A reading from the book of the prophet Isaiah
All the ends of the earth shall see the salvation of our God

How beautiful upon the mountains
  are the feet of him who brings glad tidings,
Announcing peace, bearing good news,
  announcing salvation, and saying to Zion,
  "Your God is King!"

Hark! Your watchmen raise a cry,
  together they shout for joy,
For they see directly, before their eyes,
  the Lord restoring Zion.
Break out together in song,
  O ruins of Jerusalem!
For the Lord comforts his people,
  he redeems Jerusalem.
The Lord has bared his holy arm
  in the sight of all the nations;
All the ends of the earth will behold
  the salvation of our God.
          This is the word of the Lord.

Responsorial Psalm   Ps 98, 1. 2-3. 3-4. 5-6
℟. (3) All the ends of the earth have seen the
  saving power of God.
Sing to the Lord a new song,
  for he has done wondrous deeds;
His right hand has won victory for him,
  his holy arm.
℟. All the ends of the earth have seen the
  saving power of God.
The Lord has made his salvation known:
  in the sight of the nations he has revealed his
  justice.
He has remembered his kindness and his faith-
  fulness
  toward the house of Israel.
℟. All the ends of the earth have seen the
  saving power of God.

All the ends of the earth have seen
  the salvation by our God.

Sing joyfully to the Lord, all you lands;
  break into song; sing praise.

℟ All the ends of the earth have seen the
  saving power of God.

Sing praise to the Lord with the harp,
  with the harp and melodious song.

With trumpets and the sound of the horn
  sing joyfully before the King, the Lord.

℟. All the ends of the earth have seen the
  saving power of God.

READING II   Heb 1, 1-6

A reading from the letter of Paul
to the Hebrews
In our own times, God speaks to us through his Son

In times past, God spoke in fragmentary and
varied ways to our fathers through the
prophets; in this, the final age, he has spoken
to us through his Son, whom he has made
heir of all things and through whom he first
created the universe. This Son is the reflection
of the Father's glory, the exact representation
of the Father's being, and he sustains all things
by his powerful word. When the Son had
cleansed us from our sins, he took his seat
at the right hand of the Majesty in heaven, as
far superior to the angels as the name he has
inherited is superior to theirs.

  To which of the angels did God ever say,
"You are my son; today I have begotten you"?
Or again,
"I will be his father, and he shall be my son"?
And again when he leads his first-born into the
world, he says,
"Let all the angels of God worship him."
  This is the Word of the Lord.

GOSPEL   Jn 1, 1-18 or 1-5. 9-14

Alleluia

℟. Alleluia. A holy day has dawned upon us.
Come, you nations, and adore the Lord.
Today a great light has come upon the earth.
℟. Alleluia.

✠ The beginning of the holy gospel according
    to John

(Long Form)
The Word was made flesh, he lived among us,
      and we saw his glory

In the beginning was the Word;
  the Word was in God's presence,
  and the Word was God.
He was present to God in the beginning.
Through him all things came into being,
  and apart from him nothing came to be.
Whatever came to be in him, found life,
  life for the light of men.
The light shines on in darkness,
  a darkness that did not overcome it.
There was a man named John sent by God,
who came as a witness to testify to the light,
so that through him all men might believe—
but only to testify to the light, for he himself
was not the light. The real light which gives
light to every man was coming into the world.
  He was in the world,
  and through him the world was made,
  yet the world did not know who he was.
  To his own he came,
  yet his own did not accept him.
  Any who did accept him
  he empowered to become children of God.
These are they who believe in his name—who
were begotten not by blood, nor by carnal desire, nor by man's willing it, but by God.
  The Word became flesh
  and made his dwelling among us,
  and we have seen his glory:
  the glory of an only Son coming from the
      Father,
  filled with enduring love.
John testified to him by proclaiming, "This is
he of whom I said, 'The one who comes after
me ranks ahead of me, for he was before me.' "
  Of his fullness
  we have all had a share—
  love following upon love.
For while the law was a gift through Moses,
this enduring love came through Jesus Christ.
No one has ever seen God. It is God the only
Son, ever at the Father's side, who has revealed him.
  This is the gospel of the Lord.

OR

(Short Form)

In the beginning was the Word;
the Word was in God's presence,
and the Word was God.
He was present to God in the beginning.
Through him all things came into being,
and apart from him nothing came to be.
Whatever came to be in him, found life,
life for the light of men.
The light shines on in darkness,
a darkness that did not overcome it.
The real light which gives light to every man
was coming into the world.

He was in the world
and through him the world was made,
yet the world did not know who he was.
To his own he came,
yet his own did not accept him.
Any who did accept him
he empowered to become children of God.
These are they who believe in his name—who
were begotten not by blood, nor by carnal
desire, nor by man's willing it, but by God.

The Word became flesh
and made his dwelling among us,
and we have seen his glory:
the glory of an only Son coming from the
Father,
filled with enduring love.
This is the gospel of the Lord.

SUNDAY IN THE OCTAVE OF CHRISTMAS

17   HOLY FAMILY   A B C

READING I   Sir 3, 2-6. 12-14

A reading from the book of Sirach
He who fears the Lord honors his parents.

The Lord sets a father in honor over his chil-
dren;
a mother's authority he confirms over her
sons.
He who honors his father atones for sins;
he stores up riches who reveres his mother.
He who honors his father is gladdened by
children,
and when he prays he is heard.
He who reveres his father will live a long life;

he obeys the Lord who brings comfort to his
mother.
My son, take care of your father when he is
old;
grieve him not as long as he lives.
Even if his mind fail, be considerate with him;
revile him not in the fullness of your
strength.
For kindness to a father will not be forgotten,
it will serve as a sin offering—it will take
lasting root.
This is the Word of the Lord.

Responsorial Psalm   Ps 128, 1-2. 3. 4-5

℟. (1) Happy are those who fear the Lord
     and walk in his ways.

Happy are you who fear the Lord,
who walk in his ways!
For you shall eat the fruit of your handiwork;
happy shall you be, and favored.

℟. Happy are those who fear the Lord and
     walk in his ways.

Your wife shall be like a fruitful vine
in the recesses of your home;
Your children like olive plants
around your table.

℟. Happy are those who fear the Lord and
     walk in his ways.

Behold, thus is the man blessed
who fears the Lord.
The Lord bless you from Zion:
may you see the prosperity of Jerusalem
all the days of your life.

℟. Happy are those who fear the Lord and
     walk in his ways.

READING II   Col 3, 12-21

A reading from the letter of Paul
to the Colossians
Concerning the Christian life in the world

Because you are God's chosen ones, holy and
beloved, clothe yourselves with heartfelt
mercy, with kindness, humility, meekness, and
patience. Bear with one another; forgive what-
ever grievances you have against one another.
Forgive as the Lord has forgiven you. Over all
these virtues put on love, which binds the rest
together and makes them perfect. Christ's

peace must reign in your hearts, since as members of the one body you have been called to that peace. Dedicate yourselves to thankfulness. Let the word of Christ, rich as it is, dwell in you. In wisdom made perfect, instruct and admonish one another. Sing gratefully to God from your hearts in psalms, hymns, and inspired songs. Whatever you do, whether in speech or in action, do it in the name of the Lord Jesus. Give thanks to God the Father through him.

You who are wives, be submissive to your husbands. This is your duty in the Lord. Husbands, love your wives. Avoid any bitterness toward them. You children, obey your parents in everything as the acceptable way in the Lord. And fathers, do not nag your children lest they lose heart.

This is the Word of the Lord.

A

GOSPEL   Mt 2, 13-15. 19-23

Alleluia   Col 3, 15. 16

℟. Alleluia. May the peace of Christ rule in your hearts;
and the fullness of his message live within you.
℟. Alleluia.

✠ **A reading from the holy gospel according to Matthew**

Take the child and his mother, and flee to Egypt

After the astrologers had left, the angel of the Lord suddenly appeared in a dream to Joseph with the command: "Get up, take the child and his mother, and flee to Egypt. Stay there until I tell you otherwise. Herod is searching for the child to destroy him." Joseph got up and took the child and his mother and left that night for Egypt. He stayed there until the death of Herod, to fulfill what the Lord had said through the prophet:

"Out of Egypt I have called my son."

But after Herod's death, the angel of the Lord appeared in a dream to Joseph in Egypt with the command: "Get up, take the child and his mother, and set out for the land of Israel. Those who had designs on the life of the child

are dead." He got up, took the child and his mother, and returned to the land of Israel. He heard, however, that Archelaus had succeeded his father Herod as king of Judea, and he was afraid to go back there. Instead, because of a warning received in a dream, Joseph went to the region of Galilee. There he settled in a town called Nazareth. In this way what was said through the prophets was fulfilled:

"He shall be called a Nazorean."

This is the gospel of the Lord.

B

GOSPEL   Lk 2, 22-40 or 2, 22. 39-40

Alleluia   Col 3, 15. 16

℟. Alleluia. May the peace of Christ rule in your hearts;
and the fullness of his message live within you.
℟. Alleluia.

✠ **A reading from the holy gospel according to Luke**

The child grew to maturity, and he was filled with wisdom.

(Long Form)

When the day came to purify them according to the law of Moses, Mary and Joseph brought Jesus up to Jerusalem so that he could be presented to the Lord, for it is written in the law of the Lord, "Every first-born male shall be consecrated to the Lord." They came to offer in sacrifice "a pair of turtledoves or two young pigeons," in accord with the dictate in the law of the Lord.

There lived in Jerusalem at the time a certain man named Simeon. He was just and pious, and awaited the consolation of Israel, and the Holy Spirit was upon him. It was revealed to him by the Holy Spirit that he would not experience death until he had seen the Anointed of the Lord. He came to the temple now, inspired by the Spirit; and when the parents brought in the child Jesus to perform for him the customary ritual of the law, he took him in his arms and blessed God in these words:

"Now, Master, you can dismiss your servant in peace;

you have fulfilled your word.
For my eyes have witnessed your saving
    deed
  displayed for all the peoples to see:
  A revealing light to the Gentiles,
    the glory of your people Israel."
The child's father and mother were marveling at what was being said about him. Simeon
blessed them and said to Mary his mother:
"This child is destined to be the downfall and
the rise of many in Israel, a sign that will be
opposed—and you yourself shall be pierced
with a sword—so that the thoughts of many
hearts may be laid bare."
  There was also a certain prophetess, Anna
by name, daughter of Phanuel of the tribe of
Asher. She had seen many days, having lived
seven years with her husband after her marriage and then as a widow until she was eighty-
four. She was constantly in the temple, worshiping day and night in fasting and prayer.
Coming on the scene at this moment, she gave
thanks to God and talked about the child to
all who looked forward to the deliverance of
Jerusalem.
  When the pair had fulfilled all the prescriptions of the law of the Lord, they returned
to Galilee and their own town of Nazareth. The
child grew in size and strength, filled with
wisdom, and the grace of God was upon him.
        This is the gospel of the Lord.

OR
(Short Form)

When the day came to purify them according
to the law of Moses, Mary and Joseph brought
Jesus up to Jerusalem so that he could be
presented to the Lord. When they had fulfilled
all the prescriptions of the law of the Lord,
they returned to Galilee and their own town of
Nazareth. The child grew in size and strength,
filled with wisdom, and the grace of God was
upon him.
    This is the gospel of the Lord.

C

GOSPEL   Lk 2, 41-52
Alleluia   Col 3, 15. 16

℟. Alleluia. **May the peace of Christ rule in
  your hearts;**
and the fullness of his message live within you.
  ℟. Alleluia.

✠ A reading from the holy gospel according
            to Luke
His parents found him in the temple, sitting among the
          doctors, listening to them.

**The parents of Jesus used to go every year to
Jerusalem for the feast of the Passover, and
when he was twelve they went up for the
celebration as was their custom. As they were
returning at the end of the feast, the child
Jesus remained behind unknown to his parents. Thinking he was in the party, they continued their journey for a day, looking for him
among their relatives and acquaintances.**
  **Not finding him, they returned to Jerusalem
in search of him. On the third day they came
upon him in the temple sitting in the midst of
the teachers, listening to them and asking them
questions. All who heard him were amazed at
his intelligence and his answers.**
  **When his parents saw him they were aston-
ished, and his mother said to him: "Son, why
have you done this to us? You see that your
father and I have been searching for you in
sorrow." He said to them: "Why did you
search for me? Did you not know I had to be
in my Father's house?" But they did not grasp
what he said to them.**
  **He went down with them then, and came to
Nazareth, and was obedient to them. His
mother meanwhile kept all these things in
memory. Jesus, for his part, progressed steadily in wisdom and age and grace before God
and men.**

    This is the gospel of the Lord.

January 1—OCTAVE OF CHRISTMAS
SOLEMNITY OF MARY,
MOTHER OF GOD **A** **B** **C**

READING I
Nm 6, 22-27

A reading from the book of Numbers

They will call down my name on the sons of Israel and I will bless them.

The Lord said to Moses: "Speak to Aaron and his sons and tell them: This is how you shall bless the Israelites. Say to them:
The Lord bless you and keep you!
The Lord let his face shine upon you, and be gracious to you!
The Lord look upon you kindly and give you peace!
So shall they invoke my name upon the Israelites, and I will bless them."
This is the Word of the Lord.

Responsorial Psalm
Ps 67, 2-3. 5. 6. 8

R̸. (2) May God bless us in his mercy.
May God have pity on us and bless us;
  may he let his face shine upon us.
So may your way be known upon earth;
  among all nations, your salvation.
R̸. May God bless us in his mercy.
May the nations be glad and exult
  because you rule the peoples in equity;
  the nations on the earth you guide.
R̸. May God bless us in his mercy.
May the peoples praise you, O God;
  may all the peoples praise you!
May God bless us,
  and may all the ends of the earth fear him!
R̸. May God bless us in his mercy.

READING II
Gal 4, 4-7

A reading from the letter of Paul to the Galatians

When his appointed time came. God sent his Son, born of a woman.

When the designated time had come, God sent forth his Son born of a woman, born under the law, to deliver from the law those who were subjected to it, so that we might receive our status as adopted sons. The proof that you are sons is the fact that God has sent forth into our hearts the spirit of his Son which cries out "Abba!" ("Father!"). You are no longer a slave but a son! And the fact that you are a son makes you an heir, by God's design.
This is the Word of the Lord.

GOSPEL
Lk 2, 16-21

Alleluia Heb 1, 1-2

R̸. Alleluia. In the past God spoke to our fathers through the prophets;
now he speaks to us through his Son. R̸. Alleluia.

✠ **A reading from the holy gospel according to Luke**

The shepherds found Mary and Joseph, and the infant lying in the crib . . . When the eighth day came they gave him the name of Jesus.

The shepherds went in haste to Bethlehem and found Mary and Joseph, and the baby lying in the manger; once they saw, they understood what had been told them concerning this child. All who heard of it were astonished at the report given them by the shepherds.

Mary treasured all these things and reflected on them in her heart. The shepherds returned, glorifying and praising God for all they had heard and seen, in accord with what had been told them.

When the eighth day arrived for his circumcision, the name Jesus was given the child, the name the angel had given him before he was conceived.
This is the gospel of the Lord.

---

19 **SECOND SUNDAY** **A** **B** **C**
AFTER CHRISTMAS

READING I
Sir 24, 1-4. 8-12

A reading from the book of Sirach

The wisdom of God lives in his people.

Wisdom sings her own praises,
  before her own people she proclaims her glory;
In the assembly of the Most High she opens her mouth,

in the presence of his hosts she declares her
worth:
"From the mouth of the Most High I came
forth,
and mistlike covered the earth.
In the highest heavens did I dwell,
my throne on a pillar of cloud.

"Then the Creator of all gave me his command,
and he who formed me chose the spot for my
tent,
Saying, 'In Jacob make your dwelling,
in Israel your inheritance.'
Before all ages, in the beginning, he created me,
and through all ages I shall not cease to be.
In the holy tent I ministered before him,
and in Zion I fixed my abode.
Thus in the chosen city he has given me rest,
in Jerusalem is my domain.
I have struck root among the glorious people,
in the portion of the Lord, his heritage.
This is the Word of the Lord.

Responsorial Psalm   Ps 147, 12-13. 14-15. 19-20

℞. (Jn 1, 14) The Word of God became man,
and lived among us.
Glorify the Lord, O Jerusalem;
praise your God, O Zion.
For he has strengthened the bars of your gates;
he has blessed your children within you.
℞. The Word of God became man,
and lived among us.

He has granted peace in your borders;
with the best of wheat he fills you.
He sends forth his command to the earth;
swiftly runs his word!
℞. The Word of God became man,
and lived among us.

He has proclaimed his word to Jacob,
his statutes and his ordinances to Israel.
He has not done thus for any other nation;
his ordinances he has not made known to
them. Alleluia
℞. The Word of God became man,
and lived among us.

℞. Or: Alleluia.

READING II   Eph 1, 3-6. 15-18
**A reading from the letter of Paul to the
Ephesians**
He has blessed us with all the spiritual blessings of heaven
in Jesus.

Praised be the God and Father of our Lord
Jesus Christ, who has bestowed on us in Christ
every spiritual blessing in the heavens! God
chose us in him before the world began to be
holy and blameless in his sight, to be full of
love; he likewise predestined us through Christ
Jesus to be his adopted sons—such was his
will and pleasure—that all might praise the
divine favor he has bestowed on us in his beloved.
For my part, from the time I first heard of
your faith in the Lord Jesus and your love for
all the members of the church, I have never
stopped thanking God for you and recommending you in my prayers. May the God of our
Lord Jesus Christ, the Father of glory, grant
you a spirit of wisdom and insight to know
him clearly. May he enlighten your innermost
vision that you may know the great hope to
which he has called you, the wealth of his
glorious heritage to be distributed among the
members of the church.
This is the Word of the Lord.

GOSPEL   Jn 1, 1-18 or 1, 1-5. 9-14
Alleluia   See 1 Tm 3, 16

℞. Alleluia. Glory to Christ who is proclaimed
to the world;
glory from all who believe in him! ℞. Alleluia.

✠ The beginning of the holy gospel according
to John
The Word was made flesh, he lived among us, and we saw
his glory.

(Long Form)

In the beginning was the Word;
the Word was in God's presence,
and the Word was God.
He was present to God in the beginning.
Through him all things came into being,
and apart from him nothing came to be.
Whatever came to be in him, found life,

life for the light of men.
The light shines on in darkness,
a darkness that did not overcome it.
There was a man named John sent by God,
who came as a witness to testify to the light,
so that through him all men might believe—but
only to testify to the light, for he himself was
not the light. The real light which gives light
to every man was coming into the world.
He was in the world,
and through him the world was made,
yet the world did not know who he was.
To his own he came,
yet his own did not accept him.
Any who did accept him
he empowered to become children of God.
These are they who believe in his name—who
were begotten not by blood, nor by carnal desire, nor by man's willing it, but by God.
The Word became flesh
and made his dwelling among us,
and we have seen his glory:
the glory of an only Son coming from the
Father,
filled with enduring love.
John testified to him by proclaiming: "This is
he of whom I said, 'The one who comes after
me ranks ahead of me, for he was before me.'"
Of his fullness
we have all had a share—
love following upon love.
For while the law was a gift through Moses,
this enduring love came through Jesus Christ.
No one has ever seen God. It is God the only
Son, ever at the Father's side, who has revealed
him.

This is the gospel of the Lord.

OR

(Short Form)

In the beginning was the Word;
the Word was in God's presence,
and the Word was God.
He was present to God in the beginning.
Through him all things came into being,
and apart from him nothing came to be.
Whatever came to be in him, found life,
life for the light of men.

The light shines on in darkness,
a darkness that did not overcome it.
The real light which gives light to every man
was coming into the world.
He was in the world,
and through him the world was made,
yet the world did not know who he was.
To his own he came,
yet his own did not accept him.
Any who did accept him
he empowered to become children of God.
These are they who believe in his name—who
were begotten not by blood, nor by carnal desire, nor by man's willing it, but by God.
The Word became flesh
and made his dwelling among us,
and we have seen his glory:
the glory of an only Son coming from the
Father,
filled with enduring love.

This is the gospel of the Lord.

---

20   January 6—EPIPHANY   A B C

READING I   Is 60, 1-6

A reading from the book of the prophet Isaiah

The glory of the Lord shines upon you.

Rise up in splendor, Jerusalem! Your light has
come,
the glory of the Lord shines upon you.
See, darkness covers the earth,
and thick clouds cover the peoples;
But upon you the Lord shines,
and over you appears his glory.
Nations shall walk by your light,
and kings by your shining radiance.
Raise your eyes and look about;
they all gather and come to you:
Your sons come from afar,
and your daughters in the arms of their
nurses.

Then you shall be radiant at what you see,
your heart shall throb and overflow,
For the riches of the sea shall be emptied out
before you,
the wealth of nations shall be brought to
you.

Caravans of camels shall fill you,
   dromedaries from Midian and Ephah;
All from Sheba shall come
   bearing gold and frankincense,
   and proclaiming the praises of the Lord.
      This is the Word of the Lord.

Responsorial Psalm   Ps 72, 1-2. 7-8. 10-11. 12-13

℟. (11) Lord, every nation on earth will adore
you.

O God, with your judgment endow the king,
   and with your justice, the king's son;
He shall govern your people with justice
   and your afflicted ones with judgment.
℟. Lord, every nation on earth will adore you.
Justice shall flower in his days,
   and profound peace, till the moon be no
      more.
May he rule from sea to sea,
   and from the River to the ends of the earth.
℟. Lord, every nation on earth will adore you.
The kings of Tarshish and the Isles shall offer
      gifts;
   the kings of Arabia and Seba shall bring
      tribute.
All kings shall pay him homage,
   all nations shall serve him.
℟. Lord, every nation on earth will adore you.
For he shall rescue the poor man when he cries
      out,
   and the afflicted when he has no one to help
      him.
He shall have pity for the lowly and the poor;
   the lives of the poor he shall save.
℟. Lord, every nation on earth will adore you.

READING II   Eph 3, 2-3. 5-6

A reading from the letter of Paul
to the Ephesians
The revelation means that pagans now share the same
inheritance, that they are parts of the same body.

I am sure you have heard of the ministry which
God in his goodness gave me in your regard.
God's secret plan, as I have briefly described
it, was revealed to me, unknown to men in
former ages but now revealed by the Spirit to
the holy apostles and prophets. It is no less

than this: in Christ Jesus the Gentiles are now
co-heirs with the Jews, members of the same
body and sharers of the promise through the
preaching of the gospel.
   This is the Word of the Lord.

GOSPEL   Mt 2, 1-12
Alleluia Mt 2, 2

℟. Alleluia. We have seen his star in the east,
and have come to adore the Lord. ℟. Alleluia.

✠ **A reading from the holy gospel according
to Matthew**
We have come from the East to worship the king.

After Jesus' birth in Bethlehem of Judea during
the reign of King Herod, astrologers from the
east arrived one day in Jerusalem inquiring,
"Where is the newborn king of the Jews? We
observed his star at its rising and have come to
pay him homage." At this news King Herod became greatly disturbed, and with him all Jerusalem. Summoning all of the chief priests and
scribes of the people, he inquired of them
where the Messiah was to be born. "In Bethlehem of Judea," they informed him. "Here is
what the prophet has written:
   'And you, Bethlehem, land of Judah,
      are by no means least among the princes
         of Judah,
   since from you shall come a ruler
   who is to shepherd my people Israel.' "
Herod called the astrologers aside and found
out from them the exact time of the star's appearance. Then he sent them to Bethlehem, after having instructed them: "Go and get de-
tailed information about the child. When you
have discovered something, report your find-
ings to me so that I may go and offer him
homage too."
   After their audience with the king, they set
out. The star which they had observed at its
rising went ahead of them until it came to a
standstill over the place where the child was.
They were overjoyed at seeing the star, and on
entering the house, found the child with Mary
his mother. They prostrated themselves and
did him homage. Then they opened their

coffers and presented him with gifts of gold, frankincense, and myrrh.

They received a message in a dream not to return to Herod, so they went back to their own country by another route.

This is the gospel of the Lord.

---

21   **Sunday after January 6**
        BAPTISM OF THE LORD **A** **B** **C**

READING I   Is 42, 1-4. 6-7

A reading from the book of the prophet Isaiah

Here is my servant, my chosen one in whom
my soul delights.

Here is my servant whom I uphold,
    my chosen one with whom I am pleased,
Upon whom I have put my spirit;
    he shall bring forth justice to the nations,
Not crying out, not shouting,
    not making his voice heard in the street.
A bruised reed he shall not break,
    and a smoldering wick he shall not quench,
Until he establishes justice on the earth;
    the coastlands will wait for his teaching.

I, the Lord, have called you for the victory of
        justice,
    I have grasped you by the hand;
I formed you, and set you
        as a covenant of the people,
        a light for the nations,
To open the eyes of the blind,
        to bring out prisoners from confinement,
        and from the dungeon, those who live in
    darkness.
        This is the Word of the Lord.

Responsorial Psalm   Ps 29, 1-2. 3-4. 3. 9-10

℟. (11) The Lord will bless his people with
    peace.
Give to the Lord, you sons of God,
    give to the Lord glory and praise,
Give to the Lord the glory due his name;
    adore the Lord in holy attire.
℟. The Lord will bless his people with peace.
The voice of the Lord is over the waters,
    the Lord, over vast waters.

The voice of the Lord is mighty;
    the voice of the Lord is majestic.
℟. The Lord will bless his people with peace.
The God of glory thunders,
    and in his temple all say, "Glory!"
The Lord is enthroned above the flood;
    the Lord is enthroned as king forever.
℟. The Lord will bless his people with peace.

READING II   Acts 10, 34-38

A reading from the Acts of the Apostles

God anointed him with the Holy Spirit and with power.

Peter addressed Cornelius and the people assembled at his house in these words: "I begin to see how true it is that God shows no partiality. Rather, the man of any nation who fears God and acts uprightly is acceptable to him. This is the message he has sent to the sons of Israel, 'the good news of peace' proclaimed through Jesus Christ who is Lord of all. I take it you know what has been reported all over Judea about Jesus of Nazareth, beginning in Galilee with the baptism John preached; of the way God anointed him with the Holy Spirit and power. He went about doing good works and healing all who were in the grip of the devil, and God was with him.

This is the Word of the Lord.

A

GOSPEL   Mt 3, 13-17

Alleluia   See Mk 9, 6

℟. Alleluia. **The heavens were opened and the
    Father's voice was heard:**
this is my beloved Son, hear him. ℟. Alleluia.

✠ **A reading from the holy gospel according
            to Matthew**

When Jesus was baptized the heavens were opened and
the Spirit of God came upon him.

Jesus, coming from Galilee, appeared before John at the Jordan to be baptized by him. John tried to refuse him with the protest, "I should be baptized by you, yet you come to me!" Jesus answered, "Give in for now. We must do this if we would fulfill all of God's demands." So John gave in. After Jesus was baptized, he came directly out of the water. Suddenly the sky opened and he saw the Spirit of God descend like a dove and hover over him. With that, a voice from the heavens said, "This is my beloved Son. My favor rests on him."

This is the gospel of the Lord.

B

GOSPEL Mk 1, 7-11

Alleluia See Mk 9, 6

℟. Alleluia. The heavens were opened and the Father's voice was heard:
this is my beloved Son; hear him. ℟. Alleluia.

✠ A reading from the holy gospel according to Mark

You are my Son, the beloved; my favor rests on you.

The theme of John's preaching was: "One more powerful than I is to come after me. I am not fit to stoop and untie his sandal straps. I have baptized you in water; he will baptize you in the Holy Spirit."

During that time, Jesus came from Nazareth in Galilee and was baptized in the Jordan by John. Immediately on coming up out of the water he saw the sky rent in two and the Spirit descending on him like a dove. Then a voice came from the heavens: "You are my beloved Son. On you my favor rests."

This is the gospel of the Lord.

C

GOSPEL Lk 3, 15-16. 21-22

Alleluia See Mk 9, 6

℟. Alleluia. The heavens were opened and the Father's voice was heard:
this is my beloved Son; hear him. ℟. Alleluia.

✠ A reading from the holy gospel according to Luke

Someone is coming who is more powerful than I am, he will baptize you with the Holy Spirit and with fire.

The people were full of anticipation, wondering in their hearts whether John might be the Messiah. John answered them all by saying: "I am baptizing you in water, but there is one to come who is mightier than I. I am not fit to loosen his sandal strap. He will baptize you in the Holy Spirit and in fire.

When all the people were baptized, and Jesus was at prayer after likewise being baptized, the skies opened and the Holy Spirit descended on him in visible form like a dove. A voice from heaven was heard to say, "You are my beloved Son. On you my favor rests."

This is the gospel of the Lord.

The readings for the Sundays of the Year (see no. 65) begin on the Sunday following the feast of the Baptism of the Lord.

---

22 **LENTEN SEASON**

A

FIRST SUNDAY OF LENT

READING I Gn 2, 7-9; 3, 1-7

A reading from the book of Genesis

Creation of our first parents, and Sin.

The Lord God formed man out of the clay of the ground and blew into his nostrils the breath of life, and so man became a living being.

Then the Lord God planted a garden in Eden, in the east, and he placed there the man whom he had formed. Out of the ground the Lord God made various trees grow that were delightful to look at and good for food, with the tree of life in the middle of the garden and the tree of the knowledge of good and bad.

Now the serpent was the most cunning of all the animals that the Lord God had made. The serpent asked the woman, "Did God really tell you not to eat from any of the trees in the garden?" The woman answered the serpent: "We may eat of the fruit of the trees in the garden; it is only about the fruit of the tree in the middle of the garden that God said, 'You shall not eat it or even touch it, lest you die.' " But the serpent said to the woman: "You certainly will not die! No, God knows well that the moment you eat of it you will be like gods who know what is good and what is bad." The woman saw that the tree was good for food, pleasing to the eyes, and desirable for gaining wisdom. So she took some of its fruit and ate it; and she also gave some to her husband, who

was with her, and he ate it. Then the eyes of both of them were opened, and they realized that they were naked; so they sewed fig leaves together and made loincloths for themselves.
This is the Word of the Lord.

Responsorial Psalm   Ps 51, 3-4. 5-6. 12-13. 14. 17

℟. (3) Be merciful, O Lord, for we have sinned.
Have mercy on me, O God, in your goodness;
  in the greatness of your compassion wipe
    out my offense.
Thoroughly wash me from my guilt
  and of my sin cleanse me.
℟. Be merciful, O Lord, for we have sinned.
For I acknowledge my offense,
  and my sin is before me always:
"Against you only have I sinned,
  and done what is evil in your sight."
℟. Be merciful, O Lord, for we have sinned.
A clean heart create for me, O God,
  and a steadfast spirit renew within me.
Cast me not out from your presence,
  and your holy spirit take not from me.
℟. Be merciful, O Lord, for we have sinned.
Give me back the joy of your salvation,
  and a willing spirit sustain in me.
O Lord, open my lips,
  and my mouth shall proclaim your praise.
℟. Be merciful, O Lord, for we have sinned.

READING II   Rom 5, 12-19 or 5, 12. 17-19
A reading from the letter of Paul to the Romans
The results of the gift, Jesus Christ, outweigh
one man's sin.
(Long Form)

Through one man sin entered the world and with sin death, death thus coming to all men inasmuch as all sinned—before the law there was sin in the world, even though sin is not imputed when there is no law—I say, from Adam to Moses death reigned, even over those who had not sinned by breaking a precept as did Adam, that type of the Man to come.
But the gift is not like the offense. For if by the offense of the one man all died, much more did the grace of God and the gracious gift of the one man, Jesus Christ, abound for all. The

gift is entirely different from the sin committed by the one man. In the first case, sentence followed upon one offense and brought condemnation, but in the second, the gift came after many offenses and brought acquittal. If death began its reign through one man because of his offense, much more shall those who receive the overflowing grace and gift of justice live and reign through the one man, Jesus Christ. To sum up, then: just as a single offense brought condemnation to all men, a single righteous act brought all men acquittal and life. Just as through one man's disobedience all became sinners, so through one man's obedience all shall become just.
This is the Word of the Lord.

OR
(Short Form)

Through one man sin entered the world and with sin death, death thus coming to all men inasmuch as all sinned. If death began its reign through one man because of his offense, much more shall those who receive the overflowing grace and gift of justice live and reign through the one man, Jesus Christ.
To sum up, then: just as a single offense brought condemnation to all men, a single righteous act brought all men acquittal and life. Just as through one man's disobedience all became sinners, so through one man's obedience all shall become just.
This is the Word of the Lord.

GOSPEL   Mt 4, 1-11
Verse before the Gospel   Mt 4, 4

Man does not live on bread alone,
but on every word that comes from the mouth
  of God.

✠ **A reading from the holy gospel according to Matthew**
Jesus fasted for forty days and nights.

Jesus was led into the desert by the Spirit to be tempted by the devil. He fasted forty days and forty nights, and afterward was hungry. The tempter approached and said to him, "If you are the Son of God, command these stones

to turn into bread." Jesus replied, "Scripture
has it:

> 'Not on bread alone is man to live
> but on every utterance that comes from
> the mouth of God.' "

Next the devil took him to the holy city, set
him on the parapet of the temple, and said,
"If you are the Son of God, throw yourself
down. Scripture has it:

> 'He will bid his angels take care of you;
> with their hands they will support you
> that you may never stumble on a stone.' "

Jesus answered him, "Scripture also has it:

> 'You shall not put the Lord your God to
> the test.' "

The devil then took him to a lofty mountain
peak and displayed before him all the kingdoms of the world in their magnificence, promising, "All these will I bestow on you if you
prostrate yourself in homage before me." At
this, Jesus said to him, "Away with you, Satan!
Scripture says:

> 'You shall do homage to the Lord your
> God;
> him alone shall you adore.' "

At that the devil left him, and angels came and
waited on him.

This is the gospel of the Lord.

---

23   FIRST SUNDAY OF LENT   B

READING I   Gn 9, 8-15

A reading from the book of Genesis

I will recall the covenant between myself and you . . . the
waters shall never again become a flood to destory all flesh

**God said to Noah and to his sons with him:
"See, I am now establishing my covenant with
you and your descendants after you and with
every living creature that was with you: all the
birds, and the various tame and wild animals
that were with you and came out of the ark.
I will establish my covenant with you, that
never again shall all bodily creatures be destroyed by the waters of a flood; there shall not
be another flood to devastate the earth." God
added: "This is the sign that I am giving for
all ages to come, of the covenant between me**

and you and every living creature with you: I
set my bow in the clouds to serve as a sign
of the covenant between me and the earth.
When I bring clouds over the earth, and the
bow appears in the clouds, I will recall the
covenant I have made between me and you and
all living beings, so that the waters shall never
again become a flood to destroy all mortal beings."

This is the Word of the Lord.

Responsorial Psalm   Ps 25, 4-5 6-7. 8-9

℟. (10) Your ways, O Lord, are love and truth,
    to those who keep your covenant.

**Your ways, O Lord, make known to me;
    teach me your paths,
Guide me in your truth and teach me.
    for you are God my savior.**

℟. Your ways, O Lord, are love and truth,
    to those who keep your covenant.

**Remember that your compassion, O Lord,
    and your kindness are from of old.
In your kindness remember me,
    because of your goodness, O Lord.**

℟. Your ways, O Lord, are love and truth,
    to those who keep your covenant.

**Good and upright is the Lord;
    thus he shows sinners the way.
He guides the humble to justice,
    he teaches the humble his way.**

℟. Your ways, O Lord, are love and truth,
    to those who keep your covenant.

READING II   1 Pt 3, 18-22

A reading from the first letter of Peter

The water of the flood is a type of the baptism which saves
you now

**This is why Christ died for sins once for all, a
just man for the sake of the unjust: so that he
could lead you to God. He was put to death insofar as fleshly existence goes, but was given
life in the realm of the spirit. It was in the
spirit also that he went to preach to the spirits in prison. They had disobeyed as long ago
as Noah's day, while God patiently waited until the ark was built. At that time, a few persons, eight in all, escaped in the ark through**

the water. You are now saved by a baptismal bath which corresponds to this exactly. This baptism is no removal of physical stain, but the pledge to God of an irreproachable conscience through the resurrection of Jesus Christ. He went to heaven and is at God's right hand, with angelic rulers and powers subjected to him.

This is the Word of the Lord.

GOSPEL   Mk 1, 12-15
Verse before the Gospel   Mt 4, 4

Man does not live on bread alone,
but on every word that comes from the mouth
  of God.

✠ A reading from the holy gospel according to Mark

He was tempted by Satan, and the angels looked after him.

The Spirit sent Jesus out toward the desert. He stayed in the wasteland forty days, put to the test there by Satan. He was with the wild beasts, and angels waited on him.

After John's arrest, Jesus appeared in Galilee proclaiming God's good news: "This is the time of fulfillment. The reign of God is at hand! Reform your lives and believe in the goods news!"

This is the gospel of the Lord.

---

24   FIRST SUNDAY OF LENT   C

READING I   Dt 26, 4-10

A reading from the book of Deuteronomy

The confession of faith of the elect.

Moses told the people: "The priest shall then receive the basket from you and shall set it in front of the altar of the Lord, your God. Then you shall declare before the Lord, your God, 'My father was a wandering Aramean who went down to Egypt with a small household and lived there as an alien. But there he became a nation great, strong, and numerous. When the Egyptians maltreated and op-

pressed us, imposing hard labor upon us, we cried to the Lord, the God of our fathers, and he heard our cry and saw our affliction, our toil and our oppression. He brought us out of Egypt with his strong hand and outstretched arm, with terrifying power, with signs and wonders; and bringing us into this country, he gave us this land flowing with milk and honey. Therefore, I have now brought you the first fruits of the products of the soil which you, O Lord, have given me.' And having set them before the Lord, your God, you shall bow down in his presence. Then you and your family, together with the Levite and the aliens who live among you, shall make merry over all these good things which the Lord, your God, has given you.

This is the Word of the Lord.

Responsorial Psalm   Ps 91, 1-2. 10-11. 12-13. 14-15

℟. (15) Be with me, Lord, when I am in
  trouble.
You who dwell in the shelter of the Most High,
  who abide in the shadow of the Almighty,
Say to the Lord, "My refuge and my fortress,
  my God, in whom I trust."
℟. Be with me, Lord, when I am in trouble.
No evil shall befall you,
  nor shall affliction come near your tent,
For to his angels he has given command about
  you,
  that they guard you in all your ways.
℟. Be with me, Lord, when I am in trouble.
Upon their hands they shall bear you up,
  lest you dash your foot against a stone.
You shall tread upon the asp and the viper;
  you shall trample down the lion and the
  dragon.
℟. Be with me, Lord, when I am in trouble.
Because he clings to me, I will deliver him;
  I will set him on high because he acknowl-
  edges my name.
He shall call upon me, and I will answer him;
  I will be with him in distress;
I will deliver him and glorify him.
℟. Be with me, Lord, when I am in trouble

READING II   Rom 10, 8-13

A reading from the letter of Paul to the Romans

The confession of faith of the believers in Christ.

What does Scripture say? "The word is near you, on your lips and in your heart (that is, the word of faith which we preach)." For if you confess with your lips that Jesus is Lord, and believe in your heart that God raised him from the dead, you will be saved. Faith in the heart leads to justification, confession on the lips to salvation. Scripture says, "No one who believes in him will be put to shame." Here there is no difference between Jew and Greek; all have the same Lord, rich in mercy toward all who call upon him. "Everyone who calls on the name of the Lord will be saved."

This is the Word of the Lord.

GOSPEL   Lk 4, 1-13

Verse before the Gospel   Mt 4, 4

Man does not live on bread alone
   but on every word that comes from the mouth of God.

✠ A reading from the holy gospel according to Luke

Filled with the Holy Spirit, Jesus was led by the Spirit through the wilderness where he was tempted.

Jesus, full of the Holy Spirit, returned from the Jordan and was led by the Spirit into the desert for forty days, where he was tempted by the devil. During that time he ate nothing, and at the end of it he was hungry. The devil said to him, "If you are the Son of God, command this stone to turn into bread." Jesus answered him, "Scripture has it, 'Not on bread alone shall man live.'"

Then the devil took him up higher and showed him all the kingdoms of the world in a single instant. He said to him, "I will give you all this power and the glory of these kingdoms; the power has been given to me and I give it to whomever I wish. Prostrate yourself in homage before me, and it shall all be yours." In reply, Jesus said to him, "Scripture has it, 'You shall do homage to the Lord your God; him alone shall you adore.'"

Then the devil led him to Jerusalem, set him on the parapet of the temple, and said to him, "If you are the Son of God, throw yourself down from here, for Scripture has it,

'He will bid his angels watch over you';

and again,

'With their hands they will support you,
   that you may never stumble on a stone.'"

Jesus said to him in reply, "It also says, 'You shall not put the Lord your God to the test.'"

When the devil had finished all this tempting he left him, to await another opportunity.

This is the gospel of the Lord.

---

25   SECOND SUNDAY OF LENT   A

READING I   Gn 12, 1-4

A reading from the book of Genesis

The call of Abraham, the father of God's people.

The Lord said to Abram: "Go forth from the land of your kinsfolk and from your father's house to a land that I will show you.

"I will make of you a great nation,
   and I will bless you;
I will make your name great,
   so that you will be a blessing.
I will bless those who bless you
   and curse those who curse you.
All the communities of the earth
   shall find blessing in you."

Abram went as the Lord directed him, and Lot went with him. Abram was seventy-five years old when he left Haran.

This is the Word of the Lord.

Responsorial Psalm   Ps 33, 4-5. 18-19. 20. 22

℟. (22) Lord, let your mercy be on us,
   as we place our trust in you.

Upright is the word of the Lord,
   and all his works are trustworthy.

He loves justice and right;
   of the kindness of the Lord the earth is full.

℟. Lord, let your mercy be on us,
   as we place our trust in you.

See, the eyes of the Lord are upon those who
   fear him,
   upon those who hope for his kindness,
To deliver them from death
   and preserve them in spite of famine.
℟. Lord, let your mercy be on us,
   as we place our trust in you.
Our soul waits for the Lord,
   who is our help and our shield.
May your kindness, O Lord, be upon us
   who have put our hope in you.
℟. Lord, let your mercy be on us,
   as we place our trust in you.

READING II   2 Tm 1, 8-10

A reading from the second letter of Paul
to Timothy

God has saved us and called us to be holy.

Bear your share of the hardship which the gospel entails.

   God has saved us and has called us to a holy life, not because of any merit of ours but according to his own design—the grace held out to us in Christ Jesus before the world began but now made manifest through the appearance of our Savior. He has robbed death of its power and has brought life and immortality into clear light through the gospel.
   This is the Word of the Lord.

GOSPEL   Mt 17, 1-9

Verse before the Gospel

From the shining cloud the Father's voice is
   heard:
this is my beloved Son; hear him.

✠ A reading from the holy gospel according
   to Matthew

His face shone like the sun.

Jesus took Peter, James, and his brother John and led them up on a high mountain by themselves. He was transfigured before their eyes. His face became as dazzling as the sun, his clothes as radiant as light. Suddenly Moses and Elijah appeared to them conversing with him. Upon this, Peter said to Jesus, "Lord, how good it is for us to be here! With your per-

mission I will erect three booths here, one for you, one for Moses, and one for Elijah." He was still speaking when suddenly a bright cloud overshadowed them. Out of the cloud came a voice which said, "This is my beloved Son on whom my favor rests. Listen to him." When they heard this the disciples fell forward on the ground, overcome with fear. Jesus came toward them and laying his hand on them, said, "Get up! Do not be afraid." When they looked up they did not see anyone but Jesus.

   As they were coming down the mountainside Jesus commanded them, "Do not tell anyone of the vision until the Son of Man rises from the dead."
   This is the gospel of the Lord.

---

26   SECOND SUNDAY OF LENT   **B**

READING I   Gn 22, 1-2. 9. 10-13. 15-18

A reading from the book of Genesis

The sacrifice of Abraham, our father in faith.

God put Abraham to the test. He called to him, "Abraham!" "Ready!" he replied. Then God said: "Take your son Isaac, your only one, whom you love, and go to the land of Moriah. There you shall offer him up as a holocaust on a height that I will point out to you."

   When they came to the place of which God had told him, Abraham built an altar there and arranged the wood on it. Then he reached out and took the knife to slaughter his son. But the Lord's messenger called to him from heaven, "Abraham, Abraham!" "Yes, Lord," he answered. "Do not lay your hand on the boy," said the messenger. "Do not do the least thing to him. I know now how devoted you are to God, since you did not withhold from me your own beloved son." As Abraham looked about, he spied a ram caught by its horns in the thicket. So he went and took the ram and offered it up as a holocaust in place of his son.

   Again the Lord's messenger called to Abraham from heaven and said: "I swear by myself, declares the Lord, that because you acted as you did,in not withholding from me your be-

loved son, I will bless you abundantly and make your descendants as countless as the stars of the sky and the sands of the seashore; your descendants shall take possession of the gates of their enemies, and in your descendants all the nations of the earth shall find blessing— all this because you obeyed my command."
This is the Word of the Lord.

Responsorial Psalm   Ps 116, 10. 15. 16-17. 18-19

℟. (Ps 116, 9) I will walk in the presence of the Lord,
  in the land of the living.
I believed, even when I said,
  "I am greatly afflicted."
Precious in the eyes of the Lord
  is the death of his faithful ones.

℟. I will walk in the presence of the Lord,
  in the land of the living.

O Lord, I am your servant;
  I am your servant, the son of your hand-
  maid;
  you have loosed my bonds.
To you will I offer sacrifice of thanksgiving,
  and I will call upon the name of the Lord.

℟. I will walk in the presence of the Lord,
  in the land of the living.

My vows to the Lord I will pay
  in the presence of all his people,
In the courts of the house of the Lord,
  in your midst, O Jerusalem.

℟. I will walk in the presence of the Lord,
  in the land of the living.

READING II   Rom 8, 31-34

A reading from the letter of Paul to the Romans
God did not spare his own Son.

If God is for us, who can be against us? Is it possible that he who did not spare his own Son but handed him over for the sake of us all will not grant us all things besides? Who shall bring a charge against God's chosen ones? God, who justifies? Who shall condemn them? Christ Jesus, who died or rather was raised up, who is at the right hand of God and who intercedes for us?
This is the Word of the Lord.

GOSPEL   Mk 9, 2-10
Verse before the Gospel

From the shining cloud the Father's voice is heard:
this is my beloved Son; hear him.

✠ **A reading from the holy gospel according to Mark**
This is my Son, the beloved; listen to him.

Jesus took Peter, James and John off by themselves with him and led them up a high mountain. He was transfigured before their eyes and his clothes became dazzlingly white—whiter than the work of any bleacher could make them. Elijah appeared to them along with Moses; the two were in conversation with Jesus. Then Peter spoke to Jesus: "Rabbi, how good it is for us to be here. Let us erect three booths on this site, one for you, one for Moses, and one for Elijah." He hardly knew what to say, for they were all overcome with awe. A cloud came, overshadowing them, and out of the cloud a voice: "This is my Son, my beloved. Listen to him." Suddenly looking around they no longer saw anyone with them—only Jesus.

As they were coming down the mountain, he strictly enjoined them not to tell anyone what they had seen before the Son of Man had risen from the dead. They kept this word of his to themselves, though they continued to discuss what "to rise from the dead" meant.
This is the gospel of the Lord.

---

27   SECOND SUNDAY OF LENT   C

READING I   Gn 15, 5-12. 17-18

A reading from the book of Genesis
Abraham put his faith in the Lord.

God took Abram outside and said: "Look up at the sky and count the stars, if you can. Just so," he added, "shall your descendants be." Abram put his faith in the Lord, who credited it to him as an act of righteousness.

He then said to him, "I am the Lord who brought you from Ur of the Chaldeans to give you this land as a possession." "O Lord God," he asked, "how am I to know that I shall possess it?" He answered him, "Bring me a three-year-old heifer, a three-year-old she-goat, a three-year-old ram, a turtledove, and a young pigeon." He brought him all these, split them in two, and placed each half opposite the other; but the birds he did not cut up. Birds of prey swooped down on the carcasses, but Abram stayed with them. As the sun was about to set, a trance fell upon Abram, and a deep, terrifying darkness enveloped him.

When the sun had set and it was dark, there appeared a smoking brazier and a flaming torch, which passed between those pieces. It was on that occasion that the Lord made a covenant with Abram, saying: "To your descendants I give this land from the Wadi of Egypt to the Great River [the Euphrates].

This is the Word of the Lord.

Responsorial Psalm   Ps 27, 1 7-8. 8-9. 13-14

℟. (1) The Lord is my light and my salvation.
The Lord is my light and my salvation;
   whom should I fear?
The Lord is my life's refuge;
   of whom should I be afraid?
℟. The Lord is my light and my salvation.
Hear, O Lord, the sound of my call;
   have pity on me, and answer me.
Of you my heart speaks; you my glance seeks.
℟. The Lord is my light and my salvation.
Your presence, O Lord, I seek.
   Hide not your face from me;
Do not in anger repel your servant.
   You are my helper: cast me not off.
℟. The Lord is my light and my salvation.
I believe that I shall see the bounty of the Lord
   in the land of the living.
Wait for the Lord with courage;
   be stouthearted, and wait for the Lord.
℟. The Lord is my light and my salvation.

READING II   Phil 3, 17—4, 1 or 3, 20—4, 1

A reading from the letter of Paul to the Philippians

Christ will transfigure these wretched bodies of ours into copies of his glorious body.

(Long Form)

Be imitators of me, my brothers. Take as your guide those who follow the example that we set. Unfortunately, many go about in a way which shows them to be enemies of the cross of Christ. I have often said this to you before; this time I say it with tears. Such as these will end in disaster! Their god is their belly and their glory is in their shame. I am talking about those who are set upon the things of this world. As you well know, we have our citizenship in heaven; it is from there that we eagerly await the coming of our savior, the Lord Jesus Christ. He will give a new form to this lowly body of ours and remake it according to the pattern of his glorified body, by his power to subject everything to himself.

For these reasons, my brothers, you whom I so love and long for, you who are my joy and my crown, continue, my dear ones, to stand firm in the Lord.

This is the Word of the Lord.

OR
(Short Form)

As you well know, we have our citizenship in heaven; it is from there that we eagerly await the coming of our savior, the Lord Jesus Christ. He will give a new form to this lowly body of ours and remake it according to the pattern of his glorified body, by his power to subject everything to himself.

This is the Word of the Lord.

GOSPEL   Lk 9, 28-36

Verse before the Gospel

From the shining cloud the Father's voice is heard:
   this is my beloved Son; hear him.

✠ A reading from the holy gospel according
to Luke

*As Jesus prayed, the aspect of his face was changed and
his clothing became brilliant as lightning.*

Jesus took Peter, John and James, and went
up onto a mountain to pray. While he was
praying, his face changed in appearance and
his clothes became dazzlingly white. Suddenly
two men were talking with him—Moses and
Elijah. They appeared in glory and spoke of
his passage which he was about to fulfil in
Jerusalem. Peter and those with him had fallen
into a deep sleep; but awakening, they saw his
glory and likewise saw the two men who were
standing with him. When these were leaving,
Peter said to Jesus, "Master, how good it is for
us to be here. Let us set up three booths, one for
you, one for Moses, and one for Elijah." (He
did not really know what he was saying.)
While he was speaking, a cloud came and overshadowed them, and the disciples grew fearful as the others entered it. Then from the
cloud came a voice which said, "This is my
Son, my Chosen One. Listen to him." When
the voice fell silent, Jesus was there alone. The
disciples kept quiet, telling nothing of what
they had seen at that time to anyone.

This is the gospel of the Lord.

---

28   THIRD SUNDAY OF LENT   A

READING I   Ex 17, 3-7

A reading from the book of Exodus

Give us water to drink.

In their thirst for water, the people grumbled
against Moses, saying, "Why did you ever
make us leave Egypt? Was it just to have us die
here of thirst with our children and our livestock?" So Moses cried out to the Lord, "What
shall I do with this people? A little more and
they will stone me!" The Lord answered
Moses, "Go over there in front of the people,
along with some of the elders of Israel,
holding in your hand, as you go, the staff with
which you struck the river. I will be standing
there in front of you on the rock in Horeb.
Strike the rock, and the water will flow from

it for the people to drink." This Moses did,
n the presence of the elders of Israel. The
place was called Massah and Meribah, because the Israelites quarreled there and tested
the Lord, saying, "Is the Lord in our midst or
not?"

This is the Word of the Lord.

Responsorial Psalm   Ps 95, 1-2. 6-7. 8-9

℟. (8) If today you hear his voice,
   harden not your hearts.
Come, let us sing joyfully to the Lord;
   let us acclaim the Rock of our salvation.
Let us greet him with thanksgiving;
   let us joyfully sing psalms to him.
℟. If today you hear his voice,
   harden not your hearts.
Come, let us bow down in worship;
   let us kneel before the Lord who made us.
For he is our God,
   and we are the people he shepherds, the
      flock he guides.
℟. If today you hear his voice,
   harden not your hearts.
Oh, that today you would hear his voice:
   "Harden not your hearts as at Meribah,
   as in the day of Massah in the desert,
Where your fathers tempted me;
   they tested me though they had seen my
      works.
℟. If today you hear his voice,
   harden not your hearts.

READING II   Rom 5, 1-2. 5-8

A reading from the letter of Paul to the Romans

*The love of God has been poured into our hearts by the
Holy Spirit which has been given to us.*

Now that we have been justified by faith, we
are at peace with God through our Lord Jesus
Christ. Through him we have gained access by
faith to the grace in which we now stand,
and we boast of our hope for the glory of God.
And this hope will not leave us disappointed,
because the love of God has been poured out in
our hearts through the Holy Spirit who has
been given to us. At the appointed time, when
we were still powerless, Christ died for us godless men. It is rare that anyone should lay

down his life for a just man, though it is barely possible that for a good man someone may have the courage to die. It is precisely in this that God proves his love for us: that while we were still sinners, Christ died for us.

This is the Word of the Lord.

GOSPEL   Jn 4, 5-42 or 4, 5-15. 19-26. 39. 40-42
Verse before the Gospel   Jn 4, 42. 15

Lord, you are truly the Savior of the world; give me living water, that I may never thirst again.

✠ A reading from the holy gospel according to John

The water that I shall give will turn into a spring of eternal life.

(Long Form)

Jesus had to pass through Samaria, and his journey brought him to a Samaritan town named Shechem near the plot of land which Jacob had given to his son Joseph. This was the site of Jacob's well. Jesus, tired from his journey, sat down at the well.

The hour was about noon. When a Samaritan woman came to draw water, Jesus said to her, "Give me a drink." (His disciples had gone off to the town to buy provisions.) The Samaritan woman said to him, "You are a Jew. How can you ask me, a Samaritan and a woman, for a drink?" (Recall that Jews have nothing to do with Samaritans.) Jesus replied:

"If only you recognized God's gift,
and who it is that is asking you for a drink,
you would have asked him instead,
and he would have given you living water."

"Sir," she challenged him, "you don't have a bucket and this well is deep. Where do you expect to get this flowing water? Surely you don't pretend to be greater than our ancestor Jacob, who gave us this well and drank from it with his sons and his flocks?" Jesus replied:

"Everyone who drinks this water
will be thirsty again.
But whoever drinks the water I give him
will never be thirsty;

no, the water I give
shall become a fountain within him,
leaping up to provide eternal life."

The woman said to him, "Give me this water, sir, so that I won't grow thirsty and have to keep coming here to draw water."

He told her, "Go, call your husband, and then come back here." "I have no husband," replied the woman. "You are right in saying you have no husband!" Jesus exclaimed. "The fact is, you have had five, and the man you are living with now is not your husband. What you said is true enough."

"Sir," answered the woman, "I can see you are a prophet. Our ancestors worshiped on this mountain, but you people claim that Jerusalem is the place where men ought to worship God." Jesus told her:

"Believe me, woman,
an hour is coming
when you will worship the Father
neither on this mountain
nor in Jerusalem.
You people worship what you do not understand,
while we understand what we worship;
after all, salvation is from the Jews.
Yet an hour is coming, and is already here,
when authentic worshipers
will worship the Father in Spirit and truth.
Indeed, it is just such worshipers
the Father seeks.
God is Spirit,
and those who worship him
must worship in Spirit and truth."

The woman said to him: "I know there is a Messiah coming. (This term means Anointed.) When he comes, he will tell us everything." Jesus replied, "I who speak to you am he."

His disciples, returning at this point, were surprised that Jesus was speaking with a woman. No one put a question, however, such as "What do you want of him?" or "Why are you talking with her?" The woman then left her water jar and went off into the town. She said to the people: "Come and see someone who told me everything I ever did! Could this not be the Messiah?" With that they set out from the town to meet him.

Meanwhile the disciples were urging him, "Rabbi, eat something." But he told them:

"I have food to eat
of which you do not know."

At this the disciples said to one another, "You do not suppose anyone has brought him something to eat?" Jesus explained to them:

"Doing the will of him who sent me
and bringing his work to completion
is my food.
Do you not have a saying:
'Four months more
and it will be harvest!'?
Listen to what I say:
Open your eyes and see!
The fields are shining for harvest!
The reaper already collects his wages
and gathers a yield for eternal life,
that sower and reaper may rejoice to-
gether.
Here we have the saying verified:
'One man sows; another reaps.'
I sent you to reap
what you had not worked for.
Others have done the labor,
and you have come into their gain."

Many Samaritans from that town believed in him on the strength of the woman's word of testimony: "He told me everything I ever did." The result was that, when these Samaritans came to him, they begged him to stay with them awhile. So he stayed there two days, and through his own spoken word many more came to faith. As they told the woman: "No longer does our faith depend on your story. We have heard for ourselves, and we know that this really is the Savior of the world."

This is the gospel of the Lord.

OR
(Short Form)

Jesus had to pass through Samaria, and his journey brought him to a Samaritan town named Shechem near the plot of land which Jacob had given to his son Joseph. This was the site of Jacob's well. Jesus, tired from his journey, sat down at the well.

The hour was about noon. When a Samaritan woman came to draw water, Jesus said to her, "Give me a drink." (His disciples had gone off of the town to buy provisions.) The Samaritan woman said to him, "You are a Jew. How can you ask me, a Samaritan and a woman, for a drink?" (Recall that Jews have nothing to do with Samaritans.) Jesus replied:

"If only you recognized God's gift,
and who it is that is asking you for a drink,
you would have asked him instead,
and he would have given you living
water."

"Sir," she challenged him, "you don't have a bucket and this well is deep. Where do you expect to get this flowing water? Surely you don't pretend to be greater than our ancestor Jacob, who gave us this well and drank from it with his sons and his flocks?" Jesus replied:

"Everyone who drinks this water
will be thirsty again.
But whoever drinks the water I give him
will never be thirsty;
no, the water I give
shall become a fountain within him,
leaping up to provide eternal life."

The woman said to him, "Give me this water, sir, so that I won't grow thirsty and have to keep coming here to draw water. I can see you are a prophet. Our ancestors worshiped on this mountain, but you people claim that Jerusalem is the place where men ought to worship God." Jesus told her:

"Believe me, woman,
an hour is coming
when you will worship the Father
neither on this mountain
nor in Jerusalem.
You people worship what you do not understand,
while we understand what we worship;
after all, salvation is from the Jews.
Yet an hour is coming, and is already here,
when authentic worshipers
will worship the Father in Spirit and truth.
Indeed, it is just such worshipers

the Father seeks.
God is Spirit,
and those who worship him
must worship in Spirit and truth."
The woman said to him: "I know there is a
Messiah coming. (This term means Anointed.)
When he comes, he will tell us everything."
Jesus replied, "I who speak to you am he."
   Many Samaritans from that town believed in
him on the strength of the woman's word of
testimony. The result was that, when these
Samaritans came to him, they begged him to
stay with them awhile. So he stayed there two
days, and through his own spoken word many
more came to faith. As they told the woman:
"No longer does our faith depend on your
story. We have heard for ourselves, and we
know that this really is the Savior of the
world."
   This is the gospel of the Lord.

---

29   THIRD SUNDAY OF LENT   B

READING I   Ex 20, 1-17 or 20, 1-3. 7-8. 12-17

A reading from the Book of Exodus
The law was given through Moses.

(Long Form)

God delivered all these commandments:
"I, the Lord, am your God, who brought you
out of the land of Egypt, that place of slavery.
You shall not have other gods besides me. You
shall not carve idols for yourselves in the shape
of anything in the sky above or on the earth
below or in the waters beneath the earth; you
shall not bow down before them or worship
them. For I, the Lord, your God, am a jealous
God, inflicting punishment for their fathers'
wickedness on the children of those who hate
me, down to the third and fourth generation;
but bestowing mercy down to the thousandth
generation, on the children of those who love
me and keep my commandments.
   "You shall not take the name of the Lord,
your God, in vain. For the Lord will not leave
unpunished him who takes his name in vain.
   "Remember to keep holy the sabbath day.
Six days you may labor and do all your work,

but the seventh day is the sabbath of the Lord,
your God. No work may be done then either by
you, or your son or daughter, or your male or
female slave, or your beast, or by the alien who
lives with you. In six days the Lord made the
heavens and the earth, the sea and all that is in
them; but on the seventh day he rested. That is
why the Lord has blessed the sabbath day and
made it holy.
   "Honor your father and your mother, that
you may have a long life in the land which the
Lord, your God, is giving you.
   "You shall not kill.
   "You shall not commit adultery.
   "You shall not steal.
   "You shall not bear false witness against
your neighbor.
   "You shall not covet your neighbor's house.
You shall not covet your neighbor's wife, nor
his male or female slave, nor his ox or ass, nor
anything else that belongs to him."
   This is the Word of the Lord.

OR
(Short Form)

God delivered all these commandments:
   "I, the Lord, am your God, who brought you
out of the land of Egypt, that place of slavery.
You shall not have other gods besides me.
   "You shall not take the name of the Lord,
your God, in vain. For the Lord will not leave
unpunished him who takes his name in vain.
   "Remember to keep holy the sabbath day.
   "Honor your father and your mother, that
you may have a long life in the land which the
Lord, your God, is giving you.
   "You shall not kill.
   "You shall not commit adultery.
   "You shall not steal.
   "You shall not bear false witness against
your neighbor.
   "You shall not covet your neighbor's house.
You shall not covet your neighbor's wife, nor
his male or female slave, nor his ox or ass, nor
anything else that belongs to him."
   This is the Word of the Lord.

Responsorial Psalm   Ps 19, 8. 9. 10. 11

℟. (Jn 6, 69) Lord, you have the words of everlasting life.

The law of the Lord is perfect,
   refreshing the soul;
The decree of the Lord is trustworthy,
   giving wisdom to the simple.

℟. Lord, you have the words of everlasting
   life.

The precepts of the Lord are right,
   rejoicing the heart;
The command of the Lord is clear,
   enlightening the eye.

℟. Lord, you have the words of everlasting
   life.

The fear of the Lord is pure,
   enduring forever;
The ordinances of the Lord are true,
   all of them just.

℟. Lord, you have the words of everlasting
   life.

They are more precious than gold,
   than a heap of purest gold;
Sweeter also than syrup
   or honey from the comb.

℟. Lord, you have the words of everlasting
   life.

READING II   1 Cor 1, 22-25
**A reading from the first letter of Paul to the
                  Corinthians**

We are preaching a crucified Christ, a scandal to men,
but to those who have been called, the wisdom of God.

Jews demand "signs" and Greeks look for
"wisdom," but we preach Christ crucified, a
stumbling block to Jews, and an absurdity to
Gentiles; but to those who are called, Jews and
Greeks alike, Christ is the power of God and
the wisdom of God. For God's folly is wiser
than men, and his weakness more powerful
than men.
             This is the Word of the Lord.

GOSPEL   Jn 2, 13-25
Verse before the Gospel

See no. 224.

✠ **A reading from the holy gospel according
              to John**

Destroy this sanctuary and in three days I will raise it up.

As the Jewish Passover was near, Jesus went
up to Jerusalem. In the temple precincts he
came upon people engaged in selling oxen,
sheep and doves, and others seated changing
coins. He made a [kind of] whip of cords and
drove them all out of the temple area, sheep
and oxen alike, and knocked over the money-
changers' tables, spilling their coins. He told
those who were selling doves: "Get them out of
here! Stop turning my Father's house into a
marketplace!" His disciples recalled the words
of Scripture: "Zeal for your house consumes
me."

    At this the Jews responded, "What sign can
you show us authorizing you to do these
things?" "Destroy this temple," was Jesus' answer, "and in three days I will raise it up."
They retorted, "This temple took forty-six
years to build, and you are going to 'raise it up
in three days'!" Actually he was talking about
the temple of his body. Only after Jesus had
been raised from the dead did his disciples recall that he had said this, and come to believe
the Scripture and the word he had spoken.

    While he was in Jerusalem during the Pass-
over festival, many believed in his name, for
they could see the signs he was performing.
For his part, Jesus would not trust himself to
them because he knew them all. He needed no
one to give him testimony about human nature.
He was well aware of what was in man's heart.
             This is the Word of the Lord.

OR

The readings given for Year A, no. 28, may be used in place
of these.

_____

30   THIRD SUNDAY OF LENT   C

READING I   Ex 3, 1-8. 13-15
A reading from the book of Exodus

This is what you must say to the sons of Israel: "I am
           has sent me to you."

Moses was tending the flock of his father-in-
law Jethro, the priest of Midian. Leading the

flock across the desert, he came to Horeb, the mountain of God. There an angel of the Lord appeared to him in fire flaming out of a bush. As he looked on, he was surprised to see that the bush, though on fire, was not consumed. So Moses decided, "I must go over to look at this remarkable sight, and see why the bush is not burned."

When the Lord saw him coming over to look at it more closely, God called out to him from the bush, "Moses! Moses!" He answered, "Here I am." God said, "Come no nearer! Remove the sandals from your feet, for the place where you stand is holy ground. I am the God of your father," he continued, "the God of Abraham, the God of Isaac, the God of Jacob." Moses hid his face, for he was afraid to look at God. But the Lord said, "I have witnessed the affliction of my people in Egypt and have heard their cry of complaint against their slave drivers, so I know well what they are suffering. Therefore I have come down to rescue them from the hands of the Egyptians and lead them out of that land into a good and spacious land, a land flowing with milk and honey."

"But," said Moses to God, "when I go to the Israelites and say to them, 'The God of your fathers has sent me to you,' if they ask me, 'What is his name?' what am I to tell them?" God replied, "I am who am." Then he added, "This is what you shall tell the Israelites: I AM sent me to you."

God spoke further to Moses, "Thus shall you say to the Israelites: The Lord, the God of your fathers, the God of Abraham, the God of Isaac, the God of Jacob, has sent me to you.

"This is my name forever;
 this is my title for all generations."

This is the Word of the Lord.

Responsorial Psalm   Ps 103. 1-2. 3-4. 6-7. 8. 11

℟. (8) The Lord is kind and merciful.
Bless the Lord, O my soul;
 and all my being, bless his holy name.
Bless the Lord, O my soul,
 and forget not all his benefits.
℟. The Lord is kind and merciful.

He pardons all your iniquities,
 he heals all your ills.
He redeems your life from destruction,
 he crowns you with kindness and compassion.
℟. The Lord is kind and merciful.
The Lord secures justice
 and the rights of all the oppressed.
He has made known his ways to Moses,
 and his deeds to the children of Israel.
℟. The Lord is kind and merciful.
Merciful and gracious is the Lord,
 slow to anger and abounding in kindness.
For as the heavens are high above the earth,
 so surpassing is his kindness toward those
 who fear him.
℟. The Lord is kind and merciful.

READING II   1 Cor 10, 1-6. 10-12

A reading from the first letter of Paul to the Corinthians

All this that happened to the people of Moses in the desert was written for our benefit.

I want you to remember this: our fathers were all under the cloud and all passed through the sea; by the cloud and the sea all of them were baptized into Moses. All ate the same spiritual food. All drank the same spiritual drink (they drank from the spiritual rock that was following them, and the rock was Christ), yet we know that God was not pleased with most of them, for "they were struck down in the desert."

These things happened as an example to keep us from wicked desires such as theirs. Nor are you to grumble as some of them did, to be killed by the destroying angel. The things that happened to them serve as an example. They have been written as a warning to us, upon whom the end of the ages has come. For all these reasons, let anyone who thinks he is standing upright watch out lest he fall!

This is the Word of the Lord.

GOSPEL   Lk 13, 1-9
Verse before the Gospel
See no. 224, e.g., 9.

✠ A reading from the holy gospel according
to Luke
Unless you repent you will all perish as they did.

At that time some were present who told Jesus
about the Galileans whose blood Pilate had
mixed with their sacrifices. He said in reply:
"Do you think that these Galileans were the
greatest sinners in Galilee just because they suffered this? By no means! But I tell you, you will
all come to the same end unless you reform. Or
take those eighteen who were killed by a falling
tower in Siloam. Do you think they were more
guilty than anyone else who lived in Jerusalem?
Certainly not! But I tell you, you will all come
to the same end unless you begin to reform."

Jesus spoke this parable: "A man had a fig
tree growing in his vineyard, and he came out
looking for fruit on it but did not find any. He
said to the vinedresser, 'Look here! For three
years now I have come in search of fruit on this
fig tree and found none. Cut it down. Why
should it clutter up the ground?' In answer, the
man said, 'Sir, leave it another year while I hoe
around it and manure it; then perhaps it will
bear fruit. If not, it shall be cut down.'"
This is the gospel of the Lord.

OR

The readings given for Year A, no. 28, may be used in place
of these.

31   **FOURTH SUNDAY OF LENT**   **A**

READING I   1 Sm 16, 1. 6-7. 10-13

A reading from the first book of Samuel
In the presence of the Lord God, they anointed David king
of Israel.

The Lord said to Samuel: "I am sending you to
Jesse of Bethlehem, for I have chosen my king
from among his sons.

As Jesse and his sons came to the sacrifice,
Samuel looked at Eliab and thought, "Surely
the Lord's anointed is here before him." But
the Lord said to Samuel: "Do not judge from

his appearance or from his lofty stature, because I have rejected him. Not as man sees
does God see, because man sees the appearance
but the Lord looks into the heart." In the same
way Jesse presented seven sons before Samuel,
but Samuel said to Jesse, "The Lord has not
chosen any one of these." Then Samuel asked
Jesse, "Are these all the sons you have?" Jesse
replied, "There is still the youngest, who is
tending the sheep." Samuel said to Jesse,
"Send for him; we will not begin the sacrificial
banquet until he arrives here." Jesse sent and
had the young man brought to them. He was
ruddy, a youth handsome to behold and making a splendid appearance. The Lord said,
"There—anoint him, for this is he!" Then Samuel, with the horn of oil in hand, anointed him
in the midst of his brothers; and from that day
on, the spirit of the Lord rushed upon David.
This is the Word of the Lord.

Responsorial Psalm   Ps 23, 1-3. 3-4. 5. 6

℟. (1) The Lord is my shepherd, there is noth-
ing I shall want.
The Lord is my shepherd; I shall not want.
In verdant pastures he gives me repose;
Beside restful waters he leads me;
he refreshes my soul.
℟. The Lord is my shepherd, there is nothing
I shall want.
He guides me in right paths
for his name's sake.
Even though I walk in the dark valley
I fear no evil; for you are at my side
With your rod and your staff
that give me courage.
℟. The Lord is my shepherd, there is nothing
I shall want.
You spread the table before me
in the sight of my foes;
You anoint my head with oil;
my cup overflows.
℟. The Lord is my shepherd, there is nothing
I shall want.
Only goodness and kindness follow me
all the days of my life;
And I shall dwell in the house of the Lord
for years to come.

℟. The Lord is my shepherd, there is nothing I shall want.

READING II   Eph 5, 8-14

A reading from the letter of Paul to the Ephesians

Rise from the dead, and Christ will shine on you.

There was a time when you were darkness, but now you are light in the Lord. Well, then, live as children of light. Light produces every kind of goodness and justice and truth. Be correct in your judgment of what pleases the Lord. Take no part in vain deeds done in darkness; rather, condemn them. It is shameful even to mention the things these people do in secret; but when such deeds are condemned, they are seen in the light of day, and all that then appears is light. That is why we read:

"Awake, O sleeper,
    arise from the dead,
    and Christ will give you light."
        This is the Word of the Lord.

GOSPEL   Jn 9, 1-41 or 9, 1. 6-9. 13-17. 34-38

Verse before the Gospel   Jn 8, 12

I am the light of the world, says the Lord: the man who follows me will have the light of life.

✠ **A reading from the holy gospel according to John**

The blind man went off and washed himself and came away with his sight restored.

(Long Form)

As Jesus walked along, he saw a man who had been blind from birth. His disciples asked him, "Rabbi, was it his sin or his parents' that caused him to be born blind?" "Neither," answered Jesus:

"It was no sin, either of this man or of his parents.
    Rather, it was to let God's works show forth in him.
    We must do the deeds of him who sent me while it is day.
    The night comes on

when no one can work.
    While I am in the world
    I am the light of the world."

With that Jesus spat on the ground, made mud with his saliva, and smeared the man's eyes with the mud. Then he told him, "Go, wash in the pool of Siloam." (This name means "One who has been sent.") So the man went off and washed, and came back able to see.

His neighbors and the people who had been accustomed to see him begging began to ask, "Isn't this the fellow who used to sit and beg?" Some were claiming it was he; others maintained it was not but someone who looked like him. The man himself said, "I'm the one, all right." They said to him then, "How were your eyes opened?" He answered: "That man they call Jesus made mud and smeared it on my eyes, telling me to go to Siloam and wash. When I did go and wash, I was able to see." "Where is he?" they asked. He replied, "I have no idea."

Next, they took the man who had been born blind, to the Pharisees. (Note that it was on a sabbath that Jesus had made the mud paste and opened his eyes.) The Pharisees, in turn, began to inquire how he had recovered his sight. He told them, "He put mud on my eyes. I washed it off, and now I can see." This prompted some of the Pharisees to assert, "This man cannot be from God because he does not keep the sabbath." Others objected, "If a man is a sinner, how can he perform signs like these?" They were sharply divided over him. Then they addressed the blind man again: "Since it was your eyes he opened, what do you have to say about him?" "He is a prophet," he replied.

The Jews refused to believe that he had really been born blind and had begun to see, until they summoned the parents of this man who now could see. "Is this your son?" they asked, "and if so, do you attest that he was blind at birth? How do you account for the fact that he now can see?" His parents answered, "We know this is our son, and we know he was blind at birth. But how he can see now, or who opened his eyes, we have no idea. Ask him. He is old enough to speak for himself." (His parents answered in this fashion because they were afraid of the Jews, who had already agreed among themselves that anyone who acknowledged Jesus as the Messiah would be put out of the synagogue. That was why his parents said, "He is of age—ask him.")

A second time they summoned the man who had been born blind and said to him, "Give glory to God! First of all, we know this man is a sinner." "I would not know whether he is a sinner or not," he answered. "I know this much: I was blind before; now I can see." They persisted: "Just what did he do to you? How did he open your eyes?" "I have told you once, but you would not listen to me," he answered them. "Why do you want to hear it all over again? Do not tell me you want to become his disciples too?" They retorted scornfully, "You are the one who is that man's disciple. We are disciples of Moses. We know that God spoke to Moses, but we have no idea where this man comes from." He came back at them: "Well, this is news! You do not know where he comes from, yet he opened my eyes. We know that God does not hear sinners, but that if someone is devout and obeys his will he listens to him. It is unheard of that anyone ever gave sight to a person blind from birth. If this man were not from God, he could never have done such a thing." "What!" they exclaimed, "You are steeped in sin from your birth, and you are giving us lectures?" With that they threw him out bodily.

When Jesus heard of his expulsion, he sought him out and asked him, "Do you believe in the Son of Man?" He answered, "Who is he, sir, that I may believe in him?" "You have seen him," Jesus replied. "He is speaking to you now." ["I do believe, Lord," he said, and bowed down to worship him. Then Jesus said:]

"I came into this world to divide it,
    to make the sightless see
    and the seeing blind."

Some of the Pharisees around him picked this up, saying, "You are not counting us in with the blind, are you?" To which Jesus replied: "If you were blind

there would be no sin in that.
'But we see,' you say,
and your sin remains.
    This is the gospel of the Lord.

OR
(Short Form)

As Jesus walked along, he saw a man who had been blind from birth. Jesus spat on the ground, made mud with his saliva, and smeared the man's eyes with the mud. Then he told him, "Go, wash in the pool of Siloam." (This name means "One who has been sent.") So the man went off and washed, and came back able to see.

His neighbors and the people who had been accustomed to see him begging began to ask, "Isn't this the fellow who used to sit and beg?" Some were claiming it was he; others maintained it was not but someone who looked like him. The man himself said, "I'm the one, all right."

Next, they took the man who had been born blind, to the Pharisees. (Note that it was on a sabbath that Jesus had made the mud paste and opened his eyes.) The Pharisees, in turn, began to inquire how he had recovered his sight. He told them, "He put mud on my eyes. I washed it off, and now I can see." This prompted some of the Pharisees to assert, "This man cannot be from God because he does not keep the sabbath." Others objected, "If a man is a sinner, how can he perform signs like these?" They were sharply divided over him. Then they addressed the blind man again: "Since it was your eyes he opened, what do you have to say about him?" "He is a prophet," he replied.

"What!" they exclaimed, "You are steeped in sin from your birth, and you are giving us lectures?" With that they threw him out bodily.

When Jesus heard of his expulsion, he sought him out and asked him, "Do you believe in the Son of Man?" He answered, "Who is he, sir, that I may believe in him?" "You have seen him," Jesus replied. "He is speaking to you

now." ["I do believe, Lord," he said, and bowed
down to worship him.]

    This is the gospel of the Lord.

---

32   FOURTH SUNDAY OF LENT   B

READING I   2 Chr 36, 14-17. 19-23

A reading from the second book of Chronicles

They ridiculed the prophets of God until at last his wrath
rose so high, there was no remedy.

All the princes of Judah, the priests and the
people added infidelity to infidelity, practicing
all the abominations of the nations and pollut-
ing the Lord's temple which he had consecrated in Jerusalem.

    Early and often did the Lord, the God of
their fathers, send his messengers to them, for
he had compassion on his people and his dwelling place. But they mocked the messengers of
God, despised his warnings, and scoffed at his
prophets, until the anger of the Lord against
his people was so inflamed that there was no
remedy. Then he brought up against them the
king of the Chaldeans, who slew their young
men in their own sanctuary building, sparing
neither young man nor maiden, neither the
aged nor the decrepit; he delivered all of them
over into his grip. Finally, their enemies burnt
the house of God, tore down the walls of
Jerusalem, set all its palaces afire, and destroyed all its precious objects. Those who
escaped the sword he carried captive to Babylon, where they became his and his sons' servants until the kingdom of the Persians came
to power. All this was to fulfill the word of the
Lord spoken by Jeremiah: "Until the land has
retrieved its lost sabbaths, during all the time
it lies waste it shall have rest while seventy
years are fulfilled."

    In the first year of Cyrus, king of Persia, in
order to fulfill the word of the Lord spoken by
Jeremiah, the Lord inspired King Cyrus of
Persia to issue this proclamation throughout
his kingdom, both by word of mouth and in
writing: "Thus says Cyrus, king of Persia: 'All
the kingdoms of the earth the Lord, the God of
heaven, has given to me, and he has also

charged me to build him a house in Jerusalem,
which is in Judah. Whoever, therefore, among
you belongs to any part of his people, let him
go up, and may his God be with him!' "

    This is the Word of the Lord.

Responsorial Psalm   Ps 137, 1-2. 3 4-5. 6

℟. (6) Let my tongue be silenced, if I ever
    forget you!

By the streams of Babylon
    we sat and wept
    when we remembered Zion.
On the aspens of that land
    we hung up our harps.

℟. Let my tongue be silenced, if I ever forget
    you!

Though there our captors asked of us
    the lyrics of our songs,
And our despoilers urged us to be joyous:
    "Sing for us the songs of Zion!"

℟. Let my tongue be silenced, if I ever forget
    you!

How could we sing a song of the Lord
    in a foreign land?
If I forget you, Jerusalem,
    may my right hand be forgotten!

℟. Let my tongue be silenced, if I ever forget
    you!

May my tongue cleave to my palate
    if I remember you not,
If I place not Jerusalem
    ahead of my joy.

℟. Let my tongue be silenced, if I ever forget
    you!

READING II   Eph 2, 4-10

**A reading from the letter of Paul to the
Ephesians**

When we were dead through sins, he brought us to life.

God is rich in mercy; because of his great love
for us he brought us to life with Christ when
we were dead in sin. By this favor you were
saved. Both with and in Christ Jesus he raised
us up and gave us a place in the heavens, that
in the ages to come he might display the
great wealth of his favor, manifested by his

kindness to us in Christ Jesus. I repeat, it is owing to his favor that salvation is yours through faith. This is not your own doing, it is God's gift; neither is it a reward for anything you have accomplished, so let no one pride himself on it. We are truly his handiwork, created in Christ Jesus to lead the life of good deeds which God prepared for us in advance.

This is the Word of the Lord.

GOSPEL   Jn 3, 14-21
Verse before the Gospel   Jn 3, 16

God loved the world so much, he gave us his
only Son,
that all who believe in him might have eternal
life.

✠ A reading from the holy gospel according
to John

God loved the world so much that he gave his only Son.

Jesus said to Nicodemus:
"Just as Moses lifted up the serpent in
the desert,
so must the Son of Man be lifted up,
that all who believe
may have eternal life in him.
Yes, God so loved the world
that he gave his only Son,
that whoever believes in him may not die
but may have eternal life.
God did not send the Son into the world
to condemn the world,
but that the world might be saved through
him.
Whoever believes in him avoids condemnation,
but whoever does not believe is already
condemned
for not believing in the name of God's
only Son.
The judgment in question is this:
the light came into the world,
but men loved darkness rather than light
because their deeds were wicked.
Everyone who practices evil
hates the light;
he does not come near it

for fear his deeds will be exposed.
But he who acts in truth
comes into the light,
to make clear
that his deeds are done in God."
This is the gospel of the Lord.

OR

The readings given for Year A, no. 31, may be used in place
of these.

---

33   FOURTH SUNDAY OF LENT   C

READING I   Jos 5, 9. 10-12
A reading from the book of Joshua

The people of God went to the promised land and
there kept the passover

The Lord said to Joshua, "Today I have removed the reproach of Egypt from you."
While the Israelites were encamped at Gilgal
on the plains of Jericho, they celebrated the
Passover on the evening of the fourteenth of
the month. On the day after the Passover they
ate of the produce of the land in the form of
unleavened cakes and parched grain. On that
same day after the Passover on which they ate
of the produce of the land, the manna ceased.
No longer was there manna for the Israelites, who that year ate of the yield of the land
of Canaan.
This is the Word of the Lord.

Responsorial Psalm   Ps 34, 2-3. 4-5. 6-7

℟. (9) Taste and see the goodness of the
Lord.
I will bless the Lord at all times;
  his praise shall be ever in my mouth.
Let my soul glory in the Lord;
  the lowly will hear me and be glad.
℟. Taste and see the goodness of the Lord.
Glorify the Lord with me,
  let us together extol his name.
I sought the Lord, and he answered me
  and delivered me from all my fears.
℟. Taste and see the goodness of the Lord.
Look to him that you may be radiant with
  joy,
  and your faces may not blush with shame.

When the afflicted man called out, the Lord
   heard,
   and from all his distress he saved him.
℟. Taste and see the goodness of the Lord.

READING II   2 Cor 5, 17-21
A reading from the second letter of Paul to the
                        Corinthians
God reconciled us to himself through Christ.

If anyone is in Christ, he is a new creation.
The old order has passed away; now all is
new! All this has been done by God, who has
reconciled us to himself through Christ and
has given us the ministry of reconciliation.
I mean that God, in Christ, was reconciling
the world to himself, not counting men's transgressions against them, and that he has entrusted the message of reconciliation to us.
This makes us ambassadors for Christ, God
as it were appealing through us. We implore
you, in Christ's name: be reconciled to God!
For our sakes God made him who did not know
sin to be sin, so that in him we might become the very holiness of God.
          This is the Word of the Lord.

GOSPEL   Lk 15, 1-3. 11-32
Verse before the Gospel

I will rise and go to my father and tell him:
Father, I have sinned against heaven and
   against you.

✠ A reading from the holy gospel according
                     to Luke
Your brother here was dead and has come to life.

The tax collectors and the sinners were all
gathering around Jesus to hear him, at which
the Pharisees and the scribes murmured, "This
man welcomes sinners and eats with them."
Then he addressed this parable to them: "A
man had two sons. The younger of them said
to his father, 'Father, give me the share of the
estate that is coming to me.' So the father divided up the property. Some days later this
younger son collected all his belongings and
went off to a distant land, where he squan-

dered his money on dissolute living. After he
had spent everything, a great famine broke
out in that country and he was in dire need.
So he attached himself to one of the propertied
class of the place, who sent him to his farm
to take care of the pigs. He longed to fill his
belly with the husks that were fodder for the
pigs, but no one made a move to give him
anything. Coming to his senses at last, he
said: 'How many hired hands at my father's
place have more than enough to eat, while
here I am starving! I will break away and
return to my father, and say to him, "Father,
I have sinned against God and against you;
I no longer deserve to be called your son.
Treat me like one of your hired hands."' With
that he set off for his father's house. While
he was still a long way off, his father caught
sight of him and was deeply moved. He ran
out to meet him, threw his arms around his
neck, and kissed him. The son said to him,
'Father, I have sinned against God and against
you; I no longer deserve to be called your
son.' The father said to his servants: 'Quick!
bring out the finest robe and put it on him;
put a ring on his finger and shoes on his
feet. Take the fatted calf and kill it. Let us
eat and celebrate because this son of mine was
dead and has come back to life. He was lost and
is found.' Then the celebration began.

"Meanwhile the elder son was out on the
land. As he neared the house on his way home,
he heard the sound of music and dancing.
He called one of the servants and asked him
the reason for the dancing and the music. The
servant answered, 'Your brother is home, and
your father has killed the fatted calf because
he has him back in good health.' The son
grew angry at this and would not go in; but
his father came out and began to plead with
him.

"He said in reply to his father: 'For years
now I have slaved for you. I never disobeyed
one of your orders, yet you never gave me so
much as a kid goat to celebrate with my
friends. Then, when this son of yours returns
after having gone through your property with
loose women, you kill the fatted calf for him.'

" 'My son,' replied the father, 'you are with me always, and everything I have is yours. But we had to celebrate and rejoice! This brother of yours was dead, and has come back to life. He was lost, and is found.' "

This is the gospel of the Lord.

OR

The readings given for Year A, no. 31, may be used in place of these.

---

34   FIFTH SUNDAY OF LENT   🅐
READING I   Ez 37, 12-14
A reading from the book of the prophet Ezekiel
I shall put my spirit in you, and you will live.
Thus says the Lord God: O my people, I will open your graves and have you rise from them, and bring you back to the land of Israel. Then you shall know that I am the Lord, when I open your graves and have you rise from them, O my people! I will put my spirit in you that you may live, and I will settle you upon your land; thus you shall know that I am the Lord. I have promised, and I will do it, says the Lord.

This is the Word of the Lord.

Responsorial Psalm   Ps 130, 1-2. 3-4. 5-6. 7-8
℟. (7) **With the Lord there is mercy,**
   and fullness of redemption.
Out of the depths I cry to you, O Lord;
   Lord, hear my voice!
Let your ears be attentive
   to my voice in supplication.
℟. With the Lord there is mercy,
   and fullness of redemption.
If you, O Lord, mark iniquities,
   Lord, who can stand?
But with you is forgiveness,
   that you may be revered.
℟. With the Lord there is mercy,
   and fullness of redemption.
I trust in the Lord;
   my soul trusts in his word.
More than sentinels wait for the dawn,
   let Israel wait for the Lord.

℟. **With the Lord there is mercy,**
   and fullness of redemption.
For with the Lord is kindness
   and with him is plenteous redemption;
And he will redeem Israel
   from all their iniquities.
℟. With the Lord there is mercy,
   and fullness of redemption.

READING II   Rom 8, 8-11
A reading from the letter of Paul to the Romans
If the Spirit of him who raised Jesus from the dead is living in you then he will give life to your own mortal bodies.
Those who are in the flesh cannot please God. But you are not in the flesh; you are in the spirit, since the Spirit of God dwells in you. If anyone does not have the Spirit of Christ, he does not belong to Christ. If Christ is in you, the body is indeed dead because of sin, while the spirit lives because of justice. If the Spirit of him who raised Jesus from the dead dwells in you, then he who raised Christ from the dead will bring your mortal bodies to life also through his Spirit dwelling in you.

This is the Word of the Lord.

GOSPEL   Jn 11, 1-45 or 11, 3-7. 17. 20-27. 33-45
Verse before the Gospel   Jn 11, 25. 26

I am the resurrection and the life, said the Lord:
he who believes in me will not die for ever.

✠ **A reading from the holy gospel according to John**
I am the resurrection and the life.
(Long Form)
There was a certain man named Lazarus who was sick. He was from Bethany, the village of Mary and her sister Martha. (This Mary whose brother Lazarus was sick was the one who anointed the Lord with perfume and dried his feet with her hair.) The sisters sent word to Jesus to inform him, "Lord, the one you love is sick." Upon hearing this, Jesus said:
   "This sickness is not to end in death;
   rather it is for God's glory,
      that through it the Son of God may be glorified."

Jesus loved Martha and her sister and Lazarus very much. Yet, after hearing that Lazarus was sick, he stayed on where he was for two days more. Finally he said to his disciples, "Let us go back to Judea." "Rabbi," protested the disciples, "with the Jews only recently trying to stone you, you are going back up there again?" Jesus answered:

"Are there not twelve hours of daylight?
If a man goes walking by day he does
    not stumble,
because he sees the world bathed in light.
But if he goes walking at night he will
    stumble,
since there is no light in him."

After uttering these words, he added, "Our beloved Lazarus has fallen asleep, but I am going there to wake him." At this the disciples objected, "Lord, if he is asleep his life will be saved." Jesus had been speaking about his death, but they thought he meant sleep in the sense of slumber. Finally Jesus said plainly, "Lazarus is dead. For your sakes I am glad I was not there, that you may come to believe. In any event, let us go to him." Then Thomas (the name means "Twin") said to his fellow disciples, "Let us go along, to die with him."

When Jesus arrived at Bethany, he found that Lazarus had already been in the tomb four days. The village was not far from Jerusalem—just under two miles—and many Jewish people had come out to console Martha and Mary over their brother. When Martha heard that Jesus was coming she went to meet him, while Mary sat at home. Martha said to Jesus, "Lord, if you had been here, my brother would never have died. Even now, I am sure that God will give you whatever you ask of him." "Your brother will rise again," Jesus assured her. "I know he will rise again," Martha replied, "in the resurrection on the last day." Jesus told her:

"I am the resurrection and the life:
whoever believes in me,
    though he should die, will come to life;
and whoever is alive and believes in me
    will never die.

Do you believe this?" "Yes, Lord," she replied. "I have come to believe that you are the Messiah, the Son of God: he who is to come into the world."

When she had said this she went back and called her sister Mary. "The Teacher is here, asking for you," she whispered. As soon as Mary heard this, she got up and started out in his direction. (Actually Jesus had not yet come into the village but was still at the spot where Martha had met him.) The Jews who were in the house with Mary consoling her saw her get up quickly and go out, so they followed her, thinking she was going to the tomb to weep there. When Mary came to the place where Jesus was, seeing him, she fell at his feet and said to him, "Lord, if you had been here my brother would never have died." When Jesus saw her weeping, and the Jewish folk who had accompanied her also weeping, he was troubled in spirit, moved by the deepest emotions. "Where have you laid him?" he asked. "Lord, come and see," they said. Jesus began to weep, which caused the Jews to remark, "See how much he loved him!" But some said, "He opened the eyes of that blind man. Why could he not have done something to stop this man from dying?" Once again troubled in spirit, Jesus approached the tomb.

It was a cave with a stone laid across it. "Take away the stone," Jesus directed. Martha, the dead man's sister, said to him, "Lord, it has been four days now; surely there will be a stench!" Jesus replied, "Did I not assure you that if you believed you would see the glory of God?" They then took away the stone and Jesus looked upward and said:

"Father, I thank you for having heard me.
I know that you always hear me
but I have said this for the sake of the
    crowd,
that they may believe that you sent me."

Having said this, he called loudly, "Lazarus, come out!" The dead man came out, bound hand and foot with linen strips, his face wrapped in a cloth. "Untie him," Jesus told them, "and let him go free."

This caused many of the Jews who had

come to visit Mary, and had seen what Jesus did, to put their faith in him.

This is the gospel of the Lord.

OR
(Short Form)

The sisters of Lazarus sent word to Jesus to inform him, "Lord, the one you love is sick." Upon hearing this, Jesus said:

"This sickness is not to end in death;
rather it is for God's glory,
that through it the Son of God may be glorified."

Jesus loved Martha and her sister and Lazarus very much. Yet, after hearing that Lazarus was sick, he stayed on where he was for two days more. Finally he said to his disciples, "Let us go back to Judea."

When Jesus arrived at Bethany, he found that Lazarus had already been in the tomb four days. When Martha heard that Jesus was coming she went to meet him, while Mary sat at home. Martha said to Jesus, "Lord, if you had been here, my brother would never have died. Even now, I am sure that God will give you whatever you ask of him." "Your brother will rise again," Jesus assured her. "I know he will rise again," Martha replied, "in the resurrection on the last day." Jesus told her:

"I am the resurrection and the life:
whoever believes in me,
though he should die, will come to life;
and whoever is alive and believes in me
will never die.

Do you believe this?" "Yes, Lord," she replied. "I have come to believe that you are the Messiah, the Son of God: he who is to come into the world."

Jesus was troubled in spirit, moved by the deepest emotions. "Where have you laid him?" he asked. "Lord, come and see," they said. Jesus began to weep, which caused the Jews to remark, "See how much he loved him!" But some said, "He opened the eyes of that blind man. Why could he not have done something to stop this man from dying?" Once again troubled in spirit, Jesus approached the tomb. It was a cave with a stone laid across it.

"Take away the stone," Jesus directed. Martha, the dead man's sister, said to him, "Lord, it has been four days now; surely there will be a stench!" Jesus replied, "Did I not assure you that if you believed you would see the glory of God?" They then took away the stone and Jesus looked upward and said:

"Father, I thank you for having heard me.
I know that you always hear me
but I have said this for the sake of the crowd,
that they may believe that you sent me."

Having said this, he called loudly, "Lazarus, come out!" The dead man came out, bound hand and foot with linen strips, his face wrapped in a cloth. "Untie him," Jesus told them, "and let him go free."

This caused many of the Jews who had come to visit Mary, and had seen what Jesus did, to put their faith in him.

This is the gospel of the Lord.

---

35   FIFTH SUNDAY OF LENT   B

READING I   Jer 31, 31-34

A reading from the book of the prophet Jeremiah

The days are coming when I will make a new covenant with Israel and I will forgive their iniquity.

The days are coming, says the Lord, when I will make a new covenant with the house of Israel and the house of Judah. It will not be like the covenant I made with their fathers the day I took them by the hand to lead them forth from the land of Egypt; for they broke my covenant, and I had to show myself their master, says the Lord. But this is the covenant which I will make with the house of Israel after those days, says the Lord. I will place my law within them, and write it upon their hearts; I will be their God, and they shall be my people. No longer will they have need to teach their friends and kinsmen how to know the Lord. All, from least to greatest, shall know me, says the Lord, for I will forgive their evildoing and remember their sin no more.

This is the Word of the Lord.

Responsorial Psalm   Ps 51, 3-4. 12-13. 14-15

℞. (12) Create a clean heart in me, O God.

Have mercy on me, O God, in your goodness;
  in the greatness of your compassion wipe
  out my offense.
Thoroughly wash me from my guilt
  and of my sin cleanse me.

℞. Create a clean heart in me, O God.

A clean heart create for me, O God,
  and a steadfast spirit renew within me.
Cast me not out from your presence,
  and your holy spirit take not from me.

℞. Create a clean heart in me, O God.

Give me back the joy of your salvation,
  and a willing spirit sustain in me.
I will teach transgressors your ways,
  and sinners shall return to you.

℞. Create a clean heart in me, O God.

READING II   Heb 5, 7-9

**A reading from the letter of Paul to the
Hebrews**

He learned to obey and became for all the source of eternal
salvation.

In the days when Christ was in the flesh, he
offered prayers and supplications with loud
cries and tears to God, who was able to save
him from death, and he was heard because of
his reverence. Son though he was, he learned
obedience from what he suffered; and when
perfected, he became the source of eternal salvation for all who obey him.

This is the Word of the Lord.

GOSPEL   Jn 12, 20-33
Verse before the Gospel   Jn 12, 26

If you serve me, follow me, says the Lord;
and where I am, my servant will also be.

✠ **A reading from the holy gospel according
to John**

If a grain of wheat falls on the ground and dies, it yields
a rich harvest.

Among those who had come up to worship at
the feast of Passover were some Greeks. They
approached Philip, who was from Bethsaida in
Galilee, and put this request to him: "Sir, we

should like to see Jesus." Philip went to tell
Andrew; Philip and Andrew in turn came to
inform Jesus. Jesus answered them:
  "The hour has come
  for the Son of Man to be glorified.
  I solemnly assure you,
  unless the grain of wheat falls to the earth
    and dies,
  it remains just a grain of wheat.
  But if it dies,
  it produces much fruit.
  The man who loves his life
  loses it,
  while the man who hates his life in this
    world
  preserves it to life eternal.
  If anyone would serve me,
  let him follow me;
  where I am,
  there will my servant be.
  Anyone who serves me,
  the Father will honor.
  My soul is troubled now,
  yet what should I say—
  Father, save me from this hour?
  But it was for this that I came to this hour.
  Father, glorify your name!"
Then a voice came from the sky:
  "I have glorified it,
  and will glorify it again."
When the crowd of bystanders heard the voice,
they said it was thunder. Others maintained,
"An angel was speaking to him." Jesus answered, "That voice did not come for my sake,
but for yours.
  "Now has judgment come upon this
    world,
  now will this world's prince be driven out,
  and I—once I am lifted up from earth—
  will draw all men to myself."
(This statement of his indicated the sort of
death he was going to die.)
  This is the gospel of the Lord.

OR

The readings given for Year A, no. 34, may be used in place
of these.

36   FIFTH SUNDAY OF LENT   **C**

READING I   Is 43, 16-21

A reading from the book of the prophet Isaiah

I am doing a new thing and I will give drink to my people.

Thus says the Lord,
  who opens a way in the sea
  and a path in the mighty waters,
Who leads out chariots and horsemen,
  a powerful army,
Till they lie prostrate together, never to rise,
  snuffed out and quenched like a wick.
Remember not the events of the past,
  the things of long ago consider not;
See, I am doing something new!
  Now it springs forth, do you not perceive it?
In the desert I make a way,
  in the wasteland, rivers.
Wild beasts honor me,
  jackals and ostriches,
For I put water in the desert
  and rivers in the wasteland
  for my chosen people to drink,
The people whom I formed for myself,
  that they might announce my praise.
                This is the Word of the Lord.

Responsorial Psalm   Ps 126, 1-2. 2-3. 4-5. 6

℟. (3) The Lord has done great things for us;
  we are filled with joy.

When the Lord brought back the captives of
    Zion,
  we were like men dreaming.
Then our mouth was filled with laughter,
  and our tongue with rejoicing.

℟. The Lord has done great things for us;
  we are filled with joy.

Then they said among the nations,
  "The Lord has done great things for them."
The Lord has done great things for us;
  we are glad indeed.

℟. The Lord has done great things for us;
  we are filled with joy.

Restore our fortunes, O Lord,
  like the torrents in the southern desert.

Those that sow in tears
  shall reap rejoicing.

℟. The Lord has done great things for us;
  we are filled with joy.

Although they go forth weeping,
  carrying the seed to be sown,
They shall come back rejoicing,
  carrying their sheaves.

℟. The Lord has done great things for us;
  we are filled with joy.

READING II   Phil 3, 8-14

**A reading from the letter of Paul to the
Philippians**

Because of Christ I look upon everything else as useless
in order to gain him.

I have come to rate all as loss in the light of
the surpassing knowledge of my Lord Jesus
Christ. For his sake I have forfeited everything;
I have accounted all else rubbish so that Christ
may be my wealth and I may be in him, not
having any justice of my own based on observance of the law. The justice I possess is that
which comes through faith in Christ. It has its
origin in God and is based on faith. I wish to
know Christ and the power flowing from his
resurrection; likewise to know how to share in
his sufferings by being formed into the pattern
of his death. Thus do I hope that I may arrive
at resurrection from the dead.

It is not that I have reached it yet, or have
already finished my course; but I am racing to
grasp the prize if possible, since I have been
grasped by Christ [Jesus]. Brothers, I do not
think of myself as having reached the finish
line. I give no thought to what lies behind but
push on to what is ahead. My entire attention
is on the finish line as I run toward the prize to
which God calls me—life on high in Christ
Jesus.

                This is the Word of the Lord.

GOSPEL Jn 8, 1-11

Verse before the Gospel

See no. 224, e.g., nos. 4-7.

✠ A reading from the holy gospel according
to John

Let the man without sin be the first to throw a stone.

Jesus went out to the Mount of Olives. At daybreak he reappeared in the temple area; and when the people started coming to him, he sat down and began to teach them. The scribes and the Pharisees led a woman forward who had been caught in adultery. They made her stand there in front of everyone. "Teacher," they said to him, "this woman has been caught in the act of adultery. In the law, Moses ordered such women to be stoned. What do you have to say about the case?" (They were posing this question to trap him, so that they could have something to accuse him of.) Jesus simply bent down and started tracing on the ground with his finger. When they persisted in their questioning, he straightened up and said to them, "Let the man among you who has no sin be the first to cast a stone at her." A second time he bent down and wrote on the ground. Then the audience drifted away one by one, beginning with the elders. This left him alone with the woman, who continued to stand there before him. Jesus finally straightened up again and said to her, "Woman, where did they all disappear to? Has no one condemned you?" "No one, sir," she answered. Jesus said, "Nor do I condemn you. You may go. But from now on, avoid this sin."
This is the gospel of the Lord.

OR

The readings given for Year A, no. 34, may be used in place of these.

---

37 **PASSION SUNDAY** **A**
[PALM SUNDAY]
The Procession with Palms

GOSPEL Mt 21, 1-11

✠ A reading from the holy gospel according
to Matthew

Blessed is he who comes in the name of the Lord.

As the crowd drew near Jerusalem, entering Bethphage on the Mount of Olives, Jesus sent off two disciples with the instruction: "Go into the village straight ahead of you and you will immediately find an ass tethered and her colt with her. Untie them and lead them back to me. If anyone says a word to you, say, 'The Master needs them.' Then he will let them go at once." This came about to fulfill what was said through the prophet:
"Tell the daughter of Zion,
Your king comes to you without display
astride an ass, astride a colt,
the foal of a beast of burden."
So the disciples went off and did what Jesus had ordered; they brought the ass and the colt and laid their cloaks on them, and he mounted. The huge crowd spread their cloaks on the road, while some began to cut branches from the trees and laid them along his path. The groups preceding him as well as those following kept crying out:
"God save the Son of David!
Blessed be he who comes in the name of
the Lord!
God save him from on high!"
As he entered Jerusalem the whole city was stirred to its depths, demanding, "Who is this?" And the crowd kept answering, "This is the prophet Jesus from Nazareth in Galilee."
This is the gospel of the Lord.

B

GOSPEL Mk 11, 1-10

✠ A reading from the holy gospel according
to Mark

Blessed is he who comes in the name of the Lord.

As the crowd drew near Bethphage and Bethany on the Mount of Olives, close to Jerusalem,

Jesus sent off two of his disciples with the instruction: "Go to the village straight ahead of you, and as soon as you enter it you will find tethered there a colt on which no one has ridden. Untie it and bring it back. If anyone says to you, 'Why are you doing that?' say, 'The Master needs it but he will send it back here at once.' " So they went off, and finding a colt tethered out on the street near a gate, they untied it. Some of the bystanders said to them, "What do you mean by untying that colt?" They answered as Jesus had told them to, and the men let them take it. They brought the colt to Jesus and threw their cloaks across its back, and he sat on it. Many people spread their cloaks on the road, while others spread reeds which they had cut in the fields. Those preceding him as well as those who followed cried out:

"Hosannah!
Blessed be he who comes in the name of
   the Lord!
Blessed be the reign of our father David
   to come!
God save him from on high!"
This is the gospel of the Lord.

OR

GOSPEL   Jn 12, 12-16

✠ A reading from the holy gospel according
               to John
Blessed is he who comes in the name of the Lord.

The great crowd that had come for the feast heard that Jesus was to enter Jerusalem, so they got palm branches and came out to meet him. They kept shouting:

"Hosanna!
Blessed is he who comes in the name of
   the Lord!
Blessed is the King of Israel!"
Jesus found a donkey and mounted it, in accord with Scripture:

"Fear not, O daughter of Zion!
Your king approaches you
   on a donkey's colt."
(At first, the disciples did not understand all

this, but after Jesus was glorified they recalled that the people had done to him precisely what had been written about him.)
This is the gospel of the Lord.

C

GOSPEL   Lk 19, 28-40

✠ A reading from the holy gospel according
               to Luke
Blessed is he who comes in the name of the Lord.

Jesus went ahead with his ascent to Jerusalem. As he approached Bethphage and Bethany on the mount called Olivet, he sent two of the disciples with these instructions: "Go into the village straight ahead of you. Upon entering it you will find an ass tied there which no one has yet ridden. Untie it and lead it back. If anyone should ask you, 'Why are you untying the beast?' say, 'The Master has need of it.' "

They departed on their errand and found things just as he had said. As they untied the ass, its owners said to them, "Why are you doing that?" They explained that the Master needed it. Then they led the animal to Jesus, and laying their cloaks on it, helped him mount. They spread their cloaks on the roadway as he moved along; and on his approach to the descent from Mount Olivet, the entire crowd of disciples began to rejoice and praise God loudly for the display of power they had seen, saying:

"Blessed be he who comes as king
   in the name of the Lord!
Peace in heaven
   and glory in the highest!"
Some of the Pharisees in the crowd said to him, "Teacher, rebuke your disciples." He replied, "If they were to keep silence, I tell you the very stones would cry out."
This is the gospel of the Lord.

38   **PASSION SUNDAY** A B C
            [PALM SUNDAY]

Mass

READING I   Is 50, 4-7

A reading from the book of the prophet Isaiah
I did not cover my face against insult and I know I will
not be ashamed (Third song of the Servant of Yahweh).

The Lord God has given me
   a well-trained tongue,
That I might know how to speak to the weary
   a word that will rouse them.
Morning after morning
   he opens my ear that I may hear;
And I have not rebelled,
   have not turned back.
I gave my back to those who beat me,
   my cheeks to those who plucked my beard;
My face I did not shield
   from buffets and spitting.

The Lord God is my help,
   therefore I am not disgraced;
I have set my face like flint,
   knowing that I shall not be put to shame.
       This is the Word of the Lord.

Responsorial Psalm   Ps 22, 8-9. 17-18. 19-20. 23-24

℟. (2) My God, my God, why have you aban-
   doned me?
All who see me scoff at me;
   they mock me with parted lips, they wag
   their heads:
"He relied on the Lord; let him deliver him,
   let him rescue him, if he loves him."
℟. My God, my God, why have you abandoned
   me?
Indeed, many dogs surround me,
   a pack of evildoers closes in upon me;
They have pierced my hands and my feet;
   I can count all my bones.
℟. My God, my God, why have you abandoned
   me?
They divide my garments among them,
   and for my vesture they cast lots.
But you, O Lord, be not far from me;
   O my help, hasten to aid me.

℟. My God, my God, why have you abandoned
   me?
I will proclaim your name to my brethren;
   in the midst of the assembly I will praise
   you:
"You who fear the Lord, praise him;
   all you descendants of Jacob, give glory to
   him."
℟. My God, my God, why have you abandoned
   me?

READING II   Phil 2, 6-11

**A reading from the letter of Paul to the
Philippians**
He humbled himself to become like us and God raised
him on high.

Your attitude must be Christ's:
   though he was in the form of God
   he did not deem equality with God
   something to be grasped at.
Rather, he emptied himself
   and took the form of a slave,
   being born in the likeness of men.
He was known to be of human estate,
   and it was thus that he humbled himself,
   obediently accepting even death,
   death on a cross!
Because of this,
   God highly exalted him
   and bestowed on him the name
   above every other name,
So that at Jesus' name
   every knee must bend
   in the heavens, on the earth,
   and under the earth,
   and every tongue proclaim
   to the glory of God the Father:
   JESUS CHRIST IS LORD!
       This is the Word of the Lord.

A

GOSPEL   Mt 26, 14-27, 66 or 27, 11-54
Verse before the Gospel   Phil 2, 8-9

Christ became obedient for us even to death
dying on the cross.
Therefore God raised him on high
and gave him a name above all other names.

The Passion of our Lord Jesus Christ according to Matthew

(Long Form)

One of the Twelve whose name was Judas Iscariot went off to the chief priests and said, "What are you willing to give me if I hand Jesus over to you?" They paid him thirty pieces of silver, and from that time on he kept looking for an opportunity to hand him over.

On the first day of the feast of Unleavened Bread, the disciples came up to Jesus and said, "Where do you wish us to prepare the Passover supper for you?" He said, "Go to this man in the city and tell him, 'The Teacher says, My appointed time draws near. I am to celebrate the Passover with my disciples in your house.' "

The disciples then did as Jesus had ordered, and prepared the Passover supper.

When it grew dark he reclined at table with the Twelve. In the course of the meal he said, "I give you my word, one of you is about to betray me." Distressed at this, they began to say to him one after another, "Surely it is not I, Lord?" He replied: "The man who has dipped his hand into the dish with me is the one who will hand me over. The Son of Man is departing, as Scripture says of him, but woe to that man by whom the Son of Man is betrayed. Better for him if he had never been born."

Then Judas, his betrayer, spoke: "Surely it is not I, Rabbi?" Jesus answered, "It is you who have said it."

During the meal Jesus took bread, blessed it, broke it, and gave it to his disciples. "Take this and eat it," he said, "this is my body." Then he took a cup, gave thanks, and gave it to them. "All of you must drink from it," he said, "for this is my blood, the blood of the covenant, to be poured out in behalf of many for the forgiveness of sins. I tell you, I will not drink this fruit of the vine from now until the day I drink new wine with you in my Father's reign." Then, after singing songs of praise, they walked out to the Mount of Olives. Jesus then said to them, "Tonight your faith in me will be shaken, for Scripture has it:

'I will strike the shepherd
 and the sheep of the flock will be dispersed.'

But after I am raised up, I will go to Galilee ahead of you." Peter responded, "Though all may have their faith in you shaken, mine will never be shaken!" Jesus said to him, "I give you my word before the cock crows tonight you will deny me three times." Peter replied, "Even though I have to die with you, I will never disown you." And all the other disciples said the same.

Then Jesus went with them to a place called Gethsemani. He said to his disciples, "Stay here while I go over there and pray." He took along Peter and Zebedee's two sons, and began to experience sorrow and distress. Then he said to them, "My heart is nearly broken with sorrow. Remain here and stay awake with me." He advanced a little and fell prostrate in prayer. "My Father, if it is possible, let this cup pass me by. Still, let it be as you would have it, not as I." When he returned to his disciples, he found them asleep. He said to Peter, "So you could not stay awake with me for even an hour? Be on guard, and pray that you may not undergo trial. The spirit is willing but nature is weak." Withdrawing a second time, he began to pray: "My Father, if this cannot pass me by without my drinking it, your will be done!" Once more, on his return, he found them asleep; they could not keep their eyes open. He left them again, withdrew somewhat, and began to pray a third time, saying the same words as before. Finally he returned to his disciples and said to them, "Sleep on now. Enjoy your rest! The hour is on us when the Son of Man is to be handed over to the power of evil men. Get up! Let us be on our way! See, my betrayer is here."

While he was still speaking, Judas, one of the Twelve, arrived accompanied by a great crowd with swords and clubs. They had been sent by the chief priests and elders of the people. His betrayer had arranged to give them a signal, saying, "The man I shall embrace is the one; take hold of him." He immediately went over to Jesus, said to him, "Peace, Rabbi," and embraced him. Jesus answered, "Do what you are here for, friend!" At that moment they stepped forward to lay hands on Jesus, and arrested him. Suddenly one of those who accompanied Jesus put his hand to his sword, drew it, and slashed at the high priest's servant, cutting off his ear. Jesus said to him: "Put back your sword where it belongs. Those who use the sword are sooner or later destroyed by it. Do you not suppose I can call on my Father to provide at a moment's notice more than twelve legions of angels? But then how would the Scriptures be fulfilled which say it must happen this way?"

At that very time Jesus said to the crowd: "Am I a brigand, that you have come armed with swords and clubs to arrest me? From day to day I sat teaching in the temple precincts, yet you never arrested me. Nonetheless, all this has happened in fulfillment of the writings of the prophets." Then all the disciples deserted him and fled.

Those who had apprehended Jesus led him off to Caiaphas the high priest, where the scribes and elders were convened. Peter kept following him at a distance as far as the high priest's residence. Going inside, he sat down with the guards to see the outcome. The chief priests, with the whole Sanhedrin, were busy trying to obtain false testimony against Jesus so that they might put him to death. They discovered none, despite the many false witnesses who took the stand. Finally two came forward who stated: "This man has declared, 'I can destroy God's sanctuary and rebuild it in three days.'" The high priest rose to his feet and addressed him: "Have you no answer to the testimony leveled against you?" But Jesus remained silent. The high priest then said to him: "I order you to tell us under oath before the living God whether you are the Messiah, the Son of God." Jesus answered: "It is you who say it. But I tell you this: Soon you will see the Son of Man seated at the right hand of the Power and coming on the clouds of heaven." At this the high priest tore his robes: "He has blasphemed! What further need have we

of witnesses? Remember, you heard the blasphemy. What is your verdict?" They answered, "He deserves death!" Then they began to spit in his face and hit him. Others slapped him, saying: "Play the prophet for us, Messiah! Who struck you?"

Peter was sitting in the courtyard when one of the serving girls came over to him and said, "You too were with Jesus the Galilean." He denied it in front of everyone: "I don't know what you are talking about!" When he went out to the gate another girl saw him and said to those nearby, "This man was with Jesus the Nazorean." Again he denied it with an oath: "I don't know the man!" A little while later some bystanders came over to Peter and said, "You are certainly one of them! Even your accent gives you away!" At that he began cursing and swore, "I don't even know the man!" Just then a rooster began to crow and Peter remembered the prediction Jesus had made: "Before the rooster crows you will three times disown me." He went out and began to weep bitterly.

At daybreak all the chief priests and the elders of the people took formal action against Jesus to put him to death. They bound him and led him away to be handed over to the procurator Pilate.

Then Judas, who had handed him over, seeing that Jesus had been condemned, began to regret his action deeply. He took the thirty pieces of silver back to the chief priests and elders and said, "I did wrong to deliver up an innocent man!" They retorted, "What is that to us? It is your affair!" So Judas flung the money into the temple and left. He went off and hanged himself. The chief priests picked up the silver, observing, "It is not right to deposit this in the temple treasury since it is blood money." After consultation, they used it to buy the potter's field as a cemetery for foreigners. That is why that field, even today, is called Blood Field. On that occasion, what was said through Jeremiah the prophet was fulfilled:

"They took the thirty pieces of silver, the value of a man with a price on his head, a price set by the Israelites, and they paid it out for the potter's field just as the Lord had commanded me."

Jesus was arraigned before the procurator, who questioned him: "Are you the king of the Jews?" Jesus responded, "As you say." Yet when he was accused by the chief priests and elders, he had made no reply. Then Pilate said to him, "Surely you hear how many charges they bring against you?" He did not answer him on a single count, much to the procurator's surprise.

Now on the occasion of a festival the procurator was accustomed to release one prisoner, whom the crowd would designate. They had at the time a notorious prisoner named Barabbas. Since they were already assembled, Pilate said to them, "Which one do you wish me to release for you, Barabbas or Jesus the so-called Messiah?" He knew, of course, that it was out of jealousy that they had handed him over.

While he was still presiding on the bench, his wife sent him a message: "Do not interfere in the case of that holy man. I had a dream about him today which has greatly upset me."

Meanwhile, the chief priests and elders convinced the crowds that they should ask for Barabbas and have Jesus put to death. So when the procurator asked them, "Which one do you wish me to release for you?" they said, "Barabbas." Pilate said to them, "Then what am I to do with Jesus, the so-called Messiah?" "Crucify him!" they all cried. He said, "Why, what crime has he committed?" But they only shouted the louder, "Crucify him!" Pilate finally realized that he was making no impression and that a riot was breaking out instead. He called for water and washed his hands in front of the crowd, declaring as he did so, "I am innocent of the blood of this just man. The responsibility is yours." The whole people said in reply, "Let his blood be on us and on our children." At that, he released Barabbas to them. Jesus, however, he first had scourged; then he handed him over to be crucified.

The procurator's soldiers took Jesus inside the praetorium and collected the whole cohort around him. They stripped off his clothes and wrapped him in a scarlet military cloak. Weaving a crown out of thorns they fixed it on his head, and stuck a reed in his right hand. Then they began to mock him by dropping to their knees before him, saying, "All hail, king of the Jews!" They also spat at him. Afterward they took hold of the reed and kept striking him on the head. Finally, when they had finished making a fool of him, they stripped him of the cloak, dressed him in his own clothes, and led him off to crucifixion.

On their way out they met a Cyrenian named Simon. This man they pressed into service to carry the cross. Upon arriving at a site called Golgotha (a name which means Skull Place), they gave him a drink of wine flavored with gall, which he tasted but refused to drink.

When they had crucified him, they divided his clothes among them by casting lots; then they sat down there and kept watch over him. Above his head they had put the charge against him in writing: "This is Jesus, King of the Jews." Two insurgents were crucified along with him, one at his right and one at his left. People going by kept insulting him, tossing their heads and saying: "So you are the one who was going to destroy the temple and rebuild it in three days! Save yourself, why don't you? Come down off that cross if you are God's Son!" The chief priests, the scribes and the elders also joined in the jeering: "He saved others but he cannot save himself! So he is the king of Israel! Let's see him come down from that cross, then we will believe in him. He relied on God; let God rescue him now if he wants to. After all, he claimed, 'I am God's Son.'" The insurgents who had been crucified with him kept taunting him in the same way.

From noon onward, there was darkness over the whole land until midafternoon. Then toward midafternoon Jesus cried out in a loud tone, "Eli, Eli, lema sabachthani?", that is, "My God, my God, why have you forsaken me?" This made some of the bystanders who heard it remark, "He is invoking Elijah!" Immediately one of them ran off and got a sponge. He soaked it in cheap wine, and sticking it on a reed, tried to make him drink. Meanwhile the rest said, "Leave him alone. Let's see whether Elijah comes to his rescue." Once again Jesus cried out in a loud voice, and then gave up his spirit.

Suddenly the curtain of the sanctuary was torn in two from top to bottom. The earth quaked, boulders split, tombs opened. Many bodies of saints who had fallen asleep were raised. After Jesus' resurrection they came forth from their tombs and entered the holy city and appeared to many. The centurion and and his men who were keeping watch over Jesus were terror-stricken at seeing the earthquake and all that was happening, and said, "Clearly this was the Son of God!"

Many women were present looking on from a distance. They had followed Jesus from Galilee to attend to his needs. Among them were Mary Magdalene, and Mary the mother of James and Joseph, and the mother of Zebedee's sons.

When evening fell, a wealthy man from Arimathea arrived, Joseph by name. He was another of Jesus' disciples, and had gone to request the body of Jesus. Thereupon Pilate issued an order for its release. Taking the body, Joseph wrapped it in fresh linen and laid it in his own new tomb which had been hewn from a formation of rock. Then he rolled a huge stone across the entrance of the tomb and went away. But Mary Magdalene and the other Mary remained sitting there, facing the tomb.

The next day, the one following the Day of Preparation, the chief priests and the Pharisees called at Pilate's residence. "Sir," they said, "we have recalled that that impostor while he was still alive made the claim, 'After three days I will rise.' You should issue an order having the tomb kept under surveillance until the third day. Otherwise his disciples may go and steal him and tell the people, 'He has been raised from the dead!' This final imposture would be worse than the first." Pilate told them, "You have a guard. Go and secure the tomb as best you can." So they went and kept it under surveillance of the guard, after fixing a seal to the stone.

OR
(Short Form)

✠ A reading from the holy gospel according to Matthew

The passion of our Lord Jesus Christ

Jesus was arraigned before the procurator, Pontius Pilate, who questioned him: "Are you the king of the Jews?" Jesus responded, "As you say." Yet when he was accused by the chief priests and elders he had made no reply. Then Pilate said to him, "Surely you hear how many charges they bring against you?" He did not answer him on a single count, much to the procurator's surprise.

Now on the occasion of a festival the procurator was accustomed to release one prisoner, whom the crowd would designate. They had at the time a notorious prisoner named Barabbas. Since they were already assembled, Pilate said to them, "Which one do you wish me to release for you, Barabbas or Jesus the so-called Messiah?" He knew, of course, that it was out of jealousy that they had handed him over.

While he was still presiding on the bench, his wife sent him a message: "Do not interfere in the case of that holy man. I had a dream about him today which has greatly upset me."

Meanwhile, the chief priests and elders convinced the crowds that they should ask for Barabbas and have Jesus put to death. So when the procurator asked them, "Which one do you wish me to release for you?" they said, "Barabbas." Pilate said to them, "Then what am I to do with Jesus, the so-called Messiah?" "Crucify him!" they all cried. He said, "Why, what crime has he committed?" But they only shouted the louder, "Crucify him!" Pilate finally realized that he was making no impression and that a riot was breaking out instead. He called for water and washed his hands in front of the crowd, declaring as he did so, "I am innocent of the blood of this just man. The responsibility is yours." The whole people said in reply, "Let his blood be on us and on our children." At that, he released Barabbas to them. Jesus, however, he first had scourged; then he handed him over to be crucified.

The procurator's soldiers took Jesus inside the praetorium and collected the whole cohort around him. They stripped off his clothes and wrapped him in a scarlet military cloak. Weaving a crown out of thorns they fixed it on his head, and stuck a reed in his right hand. Then they began to mock him by dropping to their knees before him, saying, "All hail, king of the Jews!" They also spat at him. Afterward they took hold of the reed and kept striking him on the head. Finally, when they had finished making a fool of him, they stripped him of the cloak, dressed him in his own clothes, and led him off to crucifixion.

On their way out they met a Cyrenian named Simon. This man they pressed into service to carry the cross. Upon arriving at a site called Golgotha (a name which means Skull Place), they gave him a drink of wine flavored with gall, which he tasted but refused to drink.

When they had crucified him, they divided his clothes among them by casting lots; then they sat down there and kept watch over him. Above his head they had put the charge against him in writing: "This is Jesus, King of the Jews." Two insurgents were crucified along with him, one at his right and one at his left. People going by kept insulting him, tossing their heads and saying: "So you are the one who was going to destroy the temple and rebuild it in three days! Save yourself, why don't you? Come down off that cross if you are God's Son!" The chief priests, the scribes and the elders also joined in the jeering: "He saved others but he cannot save himself! So he's the king of Israel! Let's see him come down from that cross, and then we will believe. He relied on God; let God rescue him now if he wants to. After all, he claimed, 'I am God's Son.'" The insurgents who had been crucified with him kept taunting him in the same way.

From noon onward, there was darkness over the whole land until midafternoon. Then toward midafternoon Jesus cried out in a loud tone, "Eli, Eli, lema sabachthani?", that is, "My God, my God, why have you forsaken me?"

This made some of the bystanders who heard it remark, "He is invoking Elijah!" Immediately one of them ran off and got a sponge. He soaked it in cheap wine, and sticking it on a reed, tried to make him drink. Meanwhile the rest said, "Leave him alone. Let's see whether Elijah comes to his rescue." Once again Jesus cried out in a loud voice, and then gave up his spirit.

Suddenly the curtain of the sanctuary was torn in two from top to bottom. The earth quaked, boulders split, tombs opened. Many bodies of saints who had fallen asleep were raised. After Jesus' resurrection they came forth from their tombs and entered the holy city and appeared to many. The centurion and his men who were keeping watch over Jesus were terror-stricken at seeing the earthquake and all that was happening, and said, "Clearly this was the Son of God!"

This is the gospel of the Lord.

B

GOSPEL Mk 14, 1—15, 47 or 15, 1-39
Verse before the Gospel Phil 2, 8-9

Christ became obedient for us even to death dying on the cross.
Therefore God raised him on high
and gave him a name above all other names.

The Passion of our Lord Jesus Christ according to Mark

(Long Form)

The feasts of Passover and Unleavened Bread were to be observed in two days' time, and therefore the chief priests and scribes began to look for a way to arrest Jesus by some trick and kill him. Yet they pointed out, "Not during the festival, or the people may riot."

When Jesus was in Bethany reclining at table in the house of Simon the leper, a woman entered carrying an alabaster jar of perfume made from expensive aromatic nard. Breaking the jar, she began to pour the perfume on his head. Some were saying to themselves indignantly: "What is the point of this extravagant waste of perfume? It could have been sold for over three hundred silver pieces and the money given to the poor." They were infuriated at her. But Jesus said: "Let her alone. Why do you criticize her? She has done me a kindness. The poor you will always have with you and you can be generous to them whenever you wish, but you will not always have me. She has done what she could. By perfuming my body she is anticipating its preparation for burial. I assure you, wherever the good news is proclaimed throughout the world, what she has done will be told in her memory."

Then Judas Iscariot, one of the Twelve, went off to the chief priests to hand Jesus over to them. Hearing what he had to say, they were jubilant and promised to give him money. He for his part kept looking for an opportune way to hand him over.

On the first day of Unleavened Bread, when it was customary to sacrifice the paschal lamb, his disciples said to him, "Where do you wish us to go to prepare the Passover supper for you?" He sent two of his disciples with these instructions: "Go into the city and you will come upon a man carrying a water jar. Follow him. Whatever house he enters, say to the owner, 'The Teacher asks, Where is my guest-room where I may eat the Passover with my disciples?' Then he will show you an upstairs room, spacious, furnished, and all in order. That is the place you are to get ready for us." The disciples went off. When they reached the city they found it just as he had told them, and they prepared the Passover supper.

As it grew dark he arrived with the Twelve. They reclined at table, and in the course of the meal Jesus said, "I give you my word, one of you is about to betray me, yes, one who is eating with me." They began to say to him sorrowfully, one by one, "Surely not I!" He said, "It is one of the Twelve—a man who dips into the dish with me. The Son of Man is going the way the Scripture tells of him. Still, accursed be that man by whom the Son of Man is betrayed. It were better for him had he never been born."

During the meal he took bread, blessed and broke it, and gave it to them. "Take this," he said, "this is my body." He likewise took a cup, gave thanks and passed it to them, and they all drank from it. He said to them: "This is my blood, the blood of the covenant, to be poured out on behalf of many. I solemnly assure you, I will never again drink of the fruit of the vine until the day when I drink it in the reign of God."

After singing songs of praise, they walked out to the Mount of Olives.

Jesus then said to them: "Your faith in me shall be shaken, for Scripture has it,

'I will strike the shepherd
and the sheep will be dispersed.'

But after I am raised up, I will go to Galilee ahead of you." Peter said to him, "Even though all are shaken in faith, it will not be that way with me." Jesus answered, "I give you my assurance, this very night before the cock crows twice, you will deny me three times." But Peter kept reasserting vehemently, "Even if I have to die with you, I will not disown you." They all said the same.

They went then to a place named Gethsemani. "Sit down here while I pray," he said to his disciples; at the same time he took along with him Peter, James, and John. Then he began to be filled with fear and distress. He said to them, "My heart is filled with sorrow to the point of death. Remain here and stay awake." He advanced a little and fell to the ground, praying that if it were possible this hour might pass him by. He kept saying, "Abba **(O Father)**, you have the power to do all things. Take this cup away from me. But let it be as you would have it, not as I." When he returned he found them asleep. He said to Peter, "Asleep, Simon? You could not stay awake for even an hour? Be on guard and pray that you may not be put to the test. The spirit is willing but nature is weak." Going back again he began to pray in the same words. Once again he found them asleep on his return. They could not keep their eyes open, nor did they know what to say to him. He returned a third time and said to them, "Still sleeping? Still taking your ease? It will have to do. The hour is on us. You will see that the Son of Man is to be handed over into the clutches of evil men. Rouse yourselves and come along. See! My betrayer is near."

Even while he was still speaking, Judas, one of the Twelve, made his appearance accompanied by a crowd with swords and clubs; these people had been sent by the chief priests, the scribes, and the elders. The betrayer had arranged a signal for them, saying, "The man I shall embrace is the one; arrest him and lead him away, taking every precaution." He then went directly over to him and said, "Rabbi!" and embraced him. At this, they laid hands on him and arrested him. One of the bystanders drew his sword and struck the high priest's slave, cutting off his ear. Addressing himself to them, Jesus said, "You have come out to arrest me armed with swords and clubs as if against a brigand. I was within your reach daily, teaching in the temple precincts, yet you never arrested me. But now, so that the Scriptures may be fulfilled. . . ." With that, all deserted him and fled. There was a young man following him who was covered by nothing but a linen cloth. As they seized him he left the cloth behind and ran off naked.

Then they led Jesus off to the high priest, and all the chief priests, the elders and the scribes came together. Peter followed him at a distance right into the high priest's courtyard, where he found a seat with the temple guard and began to warm himself at the fire. The chief priests with the whole Sanhedrin were busy soliciting testimony against Jesus that would lead to his death, but they could not find any. Many spoke against him falsely under oath but their testimony did not agree. Some, for instance, on taking the stand, testified falsely by alleging, "We heard him declare, 'I will destroy this temple made by human hands,' and 'In three days I will construct another not made by human hands.'" Even so, their testimony did not agree.

The high priest rose to his feet before the court and began to interrogate Jesus: "Have you no answer to what these men testify against you?" But Jesus remained silent; he made no reply. Once again the high priest

interrogated him: "Are you the Messiah, the Son of the Blessed One?" Then Jesus answered: "I am; and you will see the Son of Man seated at the right hand of the Power and coming with the clouds of heaven." At that the high priest tore his robes and said: "What further need do we have of witnesses? You have heard the blasphemy. What is your verdict?" They all concurred in the verdict "guilty," with its sentence of death. Some of them then began to spit on him. They blindfolded him and hit him, saying, "Play the prophet!" while the officers manhandled him.

While Peter was down in the courtyard, one of the servant girls of the high priest came along. When she noticed Peter warming himself, she looked more closely at him and said, "You too were with Jesus of Nazareth." But he denied it: "I don't know what you are talking about! What are you getting at?" Then he went out into the gateway. At that moment a rooster crowed. The servant girl, keeping an eye on him, started again to tell the bystanders, "This man is one of them." Once again he denied it. A little later the bystanders said to Peter once more, "You are certainly one of them! You're a Galilean, are you not?" He began to curse, and to swear, "I don't even know the man you are talking about!" Just then a second cockcrow was heard and Peter recalled the prediction Jesus had made to him, "Before the cock crows twice you will disown me three times." He broke down and began to cry.

As soon as it was daybreak the chief priests, with the elders and scribes (that is, the whole Sanhedrin), reached a decision. They bound Jesus, led him away, and handed him over to Pilate. Pilate interrogated him: "Are you the king of the Jews?" "You are the one who is saying it," Jesus replied. The chief priests, meanwhile, brought many accusations against him. Pilate interrogated him again: "Surely you have some answer? See how many accusations they are leveling against you." But greatly to Pilate's surprise, Jesus made no further response.

Now on the occasion of a festival he would release for them one prisoner—any man they asked for. There was a prisoner named Barabbas jailed along with the rebels who had committed murder in the uprising. When the crowd came up to press their demand that he honor the custom, Pilate rejoined, "Do you want me to release the king of the Jews for you?" He was aware, of course, that it was out of jealousy that the chief priests had handed him over. Meanwhile, the chief priests incited the crowd to have him release Barabbas instead. Pilate again asked them, "What am I to do with the man you call the king of the Jews?" They shouted back, "Crucify him!" Pilate protested, "Why? What crime has he committed?" They only shouted the louder, "Crucify him!" So Pilate, who wished to satisfy the crowd, released Barabbas to them, and after he had had Jesus scourged, he handed him over to be crucified.

The soldiers now led Jesus away into the hall known as the praetorium; at the same time they assembled the whole cohort. They dressed him in royal purple, then wove a crown of thorns and put it on him, and began to salute him, "All hail! King of the Jews!" Continually striking Jesus on the head with a reed and spitting at him, they genuflected before him and pretended to pay him homage. When they had finished mocking him, they stripped him of the purple, dressed him in his own clothes, and led him out to crucify him.

A man named Simon of Cyrene, the father of Alexander and Rufus, was coming in from the fields and they pressed him into service to carry the cross. When they brought Jesus to the site of Golgotha (which means "Skull Place"), they tried to give him wine drugged with myrrh, but he would not take it. Then they crucified him and divided up his garments by rolling dice for them to see what each should take. It was about nine in the morning when they crucified him. The inscription proclaiming his offense read, "The King of the Jews."

With him they crucified two insurgents, one at his right and one at his left. People going by kept insulting him, tossing their heads and saying, "Ha, ha! So you were going to destroy the temple and rebuild it in three days! Save yourself now by coming down from that cross!" The chief priests and the scribes also joined in and jeered: "He saved others but he cannot save himself! Let the 'Messiah,' the 'king of Israel,' come down from that cross here and now so that we can see it and believe in him!" The men who had been crucified with him likewise kept taunting him.

When noon came, darkness fell on the whole countryside and lasted until midafternoon. At that time Jesus cried in a loud voice, "Eloi, Eloi, lama sabachthani?" which means, "My God, my God, why have you forsaken me?" A few of the bystanders who heard it remarked, "Listen! He is calling on Elijah!" Someone ran off, and soaking a sponge in sour wine, stuck it on a reed to try to make him drink. The man said, "Now let's see whether Elijah comes to take him down."

Then Jesus, uttering a loud cry, breathed his last. At that moment the curtain in the sanctuary was torn in two from top to bottom. The centurion who stood guard over him, on seeing the manner of his death, declared, "Clearly this man was the Son of God!" There were also women present looking on from a distance. Among them were Mary Magdalene, Mary the mother of James the younger and Joses, and Salome. These women had followed Jesus when he was in Galilee and attended to his needs. There were also many others who had come up with him to Jerusalem.

As it grew dark (it was Preparation Day, that is, the eve of the sabbath), Joseph from Arimathea arrived—a distinguished member of the Sanhedrin. He was another who looked forward to the reign of God. He was bold enough to seek an audience with Pilate, and urgently requested the body of Jesus. Pilate was surprised that Jesus should have died so soon. He summoned the centurion and inquired whether Jesus was already dead. Learning from him that he was dead, Pilate released the corpse to Joseph. Then, having bought a linen shroud, Joseph took him down, wrapped him in the linen, and laid him in a tomb which had been cut out of rock. Finally he rolled a stone across the entrance of the tomb. Meanwhile, Mary Magdalene and Mary the mother of Joses observed where he had been laid.

OR
(Short Form)

✠ A reading from the holy gospel according to Mark

The passion of our Lord Jesus Christ

As soon as it was daybreak the chief priests, with the elders and scribes (that is, the whole Sanhedrin), reached a decision. They bound Jesus, led him away, and handed him over to Pilate. Pilate interrogated him: "Are you the king of the Jews?" "You are the one who is saying it," Jesus replied. The chief priests, meanwhile, brought many accusations against him. Pilate interrogated him again: "Surely you have some answer? See how many accusations they are leveling against you." But greatly to Pilate's surprise, Jesus made no further response.

Now on the occasion of a festival he would release for them one prisoner—any man they asked for. There was a prisoner named Barabbas jailed along with the rebels who had committed murder in the uprising. When the crowd came up to press their demand that he honor the custom, Pilate rejoined, "Do you want me to release the king of the Jews for you?" He was aware, of course, that it was out of jealousy that the chief priests had handed him over. Meanwhile, the chief priests incited the crowd to have him release Barabbas instead. Pilate again asked them, "What am I to do with the man you call the king of the Jews?" They shouted back, "Crucify him!" Pilate protested, "Why? What crime has he committed?" They only shouted the louder, "Crucify him!" So Pilate, who wished to satisfy the crowd, released Barabbas to them; and after he had had Jesus scourged, he handed him over to be crucified.

The soldiers now led Jesus away into the hall known as the praetorium; at the same time they assembled the whole cohort. They dressed him in royal purple, then wove a crown of thorns and put it on him, and began to salute him, "All hail! King of the Jews!" Continually striking Jesus on the head with a reed and spitting at him, they genuflected before him and pretended to pay him homage. When they had finished mocking him, they stripped him of the purple, dressed him in his own clothes, and led him out to crucify him.

A man named Simon of Cyrene, the father of Alexander and Rufus, was coming in from the fields and they pressed him into service to carry the cross. When they brought Jesus to the site of Golgotha (which means "Skull Place"), they tried to give him wine drugged with myrrh, but he would not take it. Then they crucified him and divided up his garments by rolling dice for them to see what each should take. It was about nine in the morning when they crucified him. The inscription proclaiming his offense read, "The King of the Jews."

With him they crucified two insurgents, one at his right and one at his left. People going by kept insulting him, tossing their heads and saying, "Ha, ha! So you were going to destroy the temple and rebuild it in three days! Save yourself now by coming down from that cross!" The chief priests and the scribes also joined in and jeered: "He saved others, but he cannot save himself! Let the 'Messiah,' the 'king of Israel,' come down from that cross here and now so that we can see it and believe in him!" The men who had been crucified with him likewise kept taunting him.

When noon came, darkness fell on the whole countryside and lasted until midafternoon. At that time Jesus cried in a loud voice, "Eloi, Eloi, lama sabachthani?" which means, "My God, my God, why have you forsaken me?" A few of the bystanders who heard it remarked, "Listen! He is calling on Elijah!" Someone ran off, and soaking a sponge in sour wine, stuck it on a reed to try to make him drink. The man said, "Now let's see whether Elijah comes to take him down."

Then Jesus, uttering a loud cry, breathed his last. At that moment the curtain in the sanctuary was torn in two from top to bottom. The centurion who stood guard over him, on seeing the manner of his death, declared, "Clearly this man was the Son of God!"

This is the gospel of the Lord.

C

Lk 22, 14—23, 56 or 23, 1-49

Verse before the Gospel   Phil 2, 8-9

Christ became obedient for us even to death dying on the cross.
Therefore God raised him on high
and gave him a name above all other names.

The Passion of our Lord Jesus Christ according to Luke
(Long Form)

When the hour arrived, Jesus took his place at table, and the apostles with him. He said to them: "I have greatly desired to eat this Passover with you before I suffer. I tell you, I will not eat again until it is fulfilled in the kingdom of God."

Then taking a cup he offered a blessing in thanks and said: "Take this and divide it among you; I tell you, from now on I will not drink of the fruit of the vine until the coming of the reign of God."

Then taking bread and giving thanks, he broke it and gave it to them, saying: "This is my body to be given for you. Do this as a remembrance of me." He did the same with the cup after eating, saying as he did so: "This cup is the new covenant in my blood, which will be shed for you.

"And yet the hand of my betrayer is with me at this table. The Son of Man is following out his appointed course, but woe to that man by whom he is betrayed." Then they began to dispute among themselves as to which of them would do such a deed.

A dispute arose among them about who would be regarded as the greatest. He said:

"Earthly kings lord it over their people. Those who exercise authority over them are called their benefactors. Yet it cannot be that way with you. Let the greater among you be as the junior, the leader as the servant. Who, in fact, is the greater—he who reclines at table or he who serves the meal? Is it not the one who reclines at table? Yet I am in your midst as the one who serves you. You are the ones who have stood loyally by me in my temptations. I for my part assign to you the dominion my Father has assigned to me. In my kingdom, you will eat and drink at my table, and you will sit on thrones judging the twelve tribes of Israel.

"Simon, Simon! Remember that Satan has asked for you to sift you all like wheat. But I have prayed for you that your faith may never fail. You in turn must strengthen your brothers." "Lord," he said to him, "at your side I am prepared to face imprisonment and death itself." Jesus replied, "I tell you, Peter, the rooster will not crow today until you have three times denied that you know me."

He asked them, "When I sent you on mission without purse or traveling bag or sandals, were you in need of anything?" "Not a thing," they replied. He said to them: "Now, however, the man who has a purse must carry it; the same with the traveling bag. And the man without a sword must sell his coat and buy one. It is written in Scripture,

'He was counted among the wicked,'
and this, I tell you, must come to be fulfilled in me. All that has to do with me approaches its climax." They said, "Lord, here are two swords!" He answered, "Enough."

Then he went out and made his way, as was his custom, to the Mount of Olives; his disciples accompanied him. On reaching the place he said to them, "Pray that you may not be put to the test." He withdrew from them about a stone's throw, then went down on his knees and prayed in these words: "Father, if it is your will, take this cup from me; yet not my will but yours be done." An angel then appeared to him from heaven to strengthen him. In his anguish he prayed with all the greater intensity, and his sweat became like drops of blood falling to the ground. Then he rose from prayer and came to his disciples, only to find them asleep, exhausted with grief. He said to them, "Why are you sleeping? Wake up, and pray that you may not be subjected to the trial."

While he was still speaking a crowd came, led by the man named Judas, one of the Twelve. He approached Jesus to embrace him. Jesus said to him, "Judas, would you betray the Son of Man with a kiss?" When the companions of Jesus saw what was going to happen, they said, "Lord, shall we use the sword?" One of them went so far as to strike the high priest's servant and cut off his right ear. Jesus said in answer to their question, "Enough!" Then he touched the ear and healed the man. But to those who had come out against him—the chief priests, the chiefs of the temple guard, and the ancients—Jesus said, "Am I a criminal that you come out after me armed with swords and clubs? When I was with you day after day in the temple you never raised a hand against me. But this is your hour—the triumph of darkness!"

They led him away under arrest and brought him to the house of the high priest, while Peter followed at a distance. Later they lighted a fire in the middle of the courtyard and were sitting beside it, and Peter sat among them. A servant girl saw him sitting in the light of the fire. She gazed at him intently, then said, "This man was with him." He denied the fact, saying, "Woman, I do not know him." A little while later someone else saw him and said, "You are one of them too." But Peter said, "No, sir, not I!" About an hour after that another spoke more insistently: "This man was certainly with him, for he is a Galilean." Peter responded, "My friend, I do not know what you are talking about." At the very moment he was saying this, a rooster crowed. The Lord turned around and looked at Peter, and Peter remembered the word that the Lord had spoken to him, "Before the rooster crows today you will deny me three times." He went out and wept bitterly.

Meanwhile the men guarding Jesus amused themselves at his expense. They blindfolded

him first, slapped him, and then taunted him: "Play the prophet; which one struck you?" And they directed many other insulting words at him.

At daybreak the council, which was made up of the elders of the people, the chief priests, and the scribes, assembled again. Once they had brought him before their council, they said, "Tell us, are you the Messiah?" He replied, "If I tell you, you will not believe me, and if I question you, you will not answer. This much only will I say: 'From now on, the Son of Man will have his seat at the right hand of the Power of God.'" "So you are the Son of God?" they asked in chorus. He answered, "It is you who say I am." They said, "What need have we of witnesses? We have heard it from his own mouth."

Then the entire assembly rose up and led him before Pilate. They started his prosecution by saying, "We found this man subverting our nation, opposing the payment of taxes to Caesar, and calling himself the Messiah, a king." Pilate asked him, "Are you the king of the Jews?" He answered, "That is your term." Pilate reported to the chief priests and the crowds, "I do not find a case against this man." But they insisted, "He stirs up the people by his teaching throughout the whole of Judea, from Galilee, where he began, to this very place." On hearing this Pilate asked if the man was a Galilean; and when he learned that he was under Herod's jurisdiction, he sent him to Herod, who also happened to be in Jerusalem at the time.

Herod was extremely pleased to see Jesus. From the reports about him he had wanted for a long time to see him, and he was hoping to see him work some miracle. He questioned Jesus at considerable length, but Jesus made no answer. The chief priests and scribes were at hand to accuse him vehemently. Herod and his guards then treated him with contempt and insult, after which they put a magnificent robe on him and sent him back to Pilate. Herod and Pilate, who had previously been set against each other, became friends from that day.

Pilate then called together the chief priests, the ruling class, and the people, and said to them: "You have brought this man before me as one who subverts the people. I have examined him in your presence and have no charge against him arising from your allegations. Neither has Herod, who therefore has sent him back to us; obviously this man has done nothing to deserve death. Therefore I mean to release him, once I have taught him a lesson." The whole crowd cried out, "Away with this man; release Barabbas for us!" This Barabbas had been thrown in prison for causing an uprising in the city, and for murder. Pilate addressed them again, for he wanted Jesus to be the one he released.

But they shouted back, "Crucify him, crucify him!" He said to them for the third time, "What wrong is this man guilty of? I have not discovered anything about him deserving the death penalty. I will therefore chastise him and release him." But they demanded with loud cries that he be crucified, and their shouts increased in violence. Pilate then decreed that what they demanded should be done. He released the one they asked for, who had been thrown in prison for insurrection and murder, and delivered Jesus up to their wishes.

As they led him away, they laid hold of one Simon the Cyrenean who was coming in from the fields. They put a crossbeam on Simon's shoulder for him to carry along behind Jesus. A great crowd of people followed him, including women who beat their breasts and lamented over him. Jesus turned to them and said: "Daughters of Jerusalem, do not weep for me. Weep for yourselves and for your children. The days are coming when they will say, 'Happy are the sterile, the wombs that never bore and the breasts that never nursed.' Then they will begin saying to the mountains, 'Fall on us,' and to the hills, 'Cover us.' If they do these things in the green wood, what will happen in the dry?"

Two others who were criminals were led along with him to be crucified. When they came to Skull Place, as it was called, they crucified him there and the criminals as well, one on his right and the other on his left. [Jesus said, "Father, forgive them; they do not know what they are doing."] They divided his garments, rolling dice for them.

The people stood there watching, and the leaders kept jeering at him, saying, "He saved others; let him save himself if he is the Messiah of God, the chosen one." The soldiers also made fun of him, coming forward to offer him their sour wine and saying, "If you are the king of the Jews, save yourself." There was an inscription over his head:

"THIS IS THE KING OF THE JEWS."

One of the criminals hanging in crucifixion blasphemed him, "Aren't you the Messiah? Then save yourself and us." But the other one rebuked him: "Have you no fear of God, seeing you are under the same sentence? We deserve it, after all. We are only paying the price for what we've done, but this man has done nothing wrong." He then said, "Jesus, remember me when you enter upon your reign." And Jesus replied, "I assure you: this day you will be with me in paradise."

It was now around midday, and darkness came over the whole land until midafternoon with an eclipse of the sun. The curtain in the sanctuary was torn in two. Jesus uttered a loud cry and said,

"Father, into your hands I commend my spirit."

After he said this, he expired. The centurion, upon seeing what had happened, gave glory to God by saying, "Surely this was an innocent man." After the crowd assembled for this spectacle witnessed what had happened, they returned beating their breasts. All his friends and the women who had accompanied him from Galilee were standing at a distance watching everything.

There was a man named Joseph, an upright and holy member of the Sanhedrin, who had not been associated with their plan or their action. He was from Arimathea, a Jewish town, and he looked expectantly for the reign of God. This man approached Pilate with a request for Jesus' body. He took it down, wrapped it in fine linen, and laid it in a tomb hewn out of the rock, in which no one had yet been buried.

That was the day of Preparation, and the sabbath was about to begin. The women who had come with him from Galilee followed along behind. They saw the tomb and how his body was buried. Then they went back home to prepare spices and perfumes. They observed the sabbath as a day of rest, in accordance with the law.

OR
(Short Form)

✠ A reading from the holy gospel according to Luke

The passion of our Lord Jesus Christ

The elders of the people and chief priests and scribes rose up and led Jesus before Pilate. They started his prosecution by saying, "We found this man subverting our nation, opposing the payment of taxes to Caesar, and calling himself the Messiah, a king." Pilate asked him, "Are you the king of the Jews?" He answered, "That is your term." Pilate reported to the chief priests and the crowds, "I do not find a case against this man." But they insisted, "He stirs up the people by his teaching throughout the whole of Judea, from Galilee, where he began, to this very place." On hearing this Pilate asked if the man was a Galilean; and when he learned that he was under Herod's jurisdiction, he sent him to Herod, who also happened to be in Jerusalem at the time.

Herod was extremely pleased to see Jesus. From the reports about him he had wanted for a long time to see him, and he was hoping to see him work some miracle. He questioned Jesus at considerable length, but Jesus made no answer. The chief priests and scribes were at hand to accuse him vehemently. Herod and his guards then treated him with contempt and insult, after which they put a magnificent robe on him and sent him back to Pilate. Herod and Pilate, who had previously been set against each other, became friends from that day.

Pilate then called together the chief priests, the ruling class, and the people, and said to them: "You have brought this man before me as one who subverts the people. I have examined him in your presence and have no charge against him arising from your allegations. Neither has Herod, who therefore has sent him back to us; obviously this man has done nothing to deserve death. Therefore I mean to release him, once I have taught him a lesson." The whole crowd cried out, "Away with this man; release Barabbas for us!" This Barabbas had been thrown in prison for causing an uprising in the city, and for murder. Pilate addressed them again, for he wanted Jesus to be the one he released.

But they shouted back, "Crucify him, crucify him!" He said to them for the third time, "What wrong is this man guilty of? I have not discovered anything about him deserving the death penalty. I will therefore chastise him and release him." But they demanded with loud cries that he be crucified, and their shouts increased in violence. Pilate then decreed that what they demanded should be done. He released the one they asked for, who had been thrown in prison for insurrection and murder, and delivered Jesus up to their wishes.

As they led him away, they laid hold of one Simon the Cyrenean who was coming in from the fields. They put a crossbeam on Simon's shoulder for him to carry along behind Jesus. A great crowd of people followed him, including women who beat their breasts and lamented over him. Jesus turned to them and said: "Daughters of Jerusalem, do not weep for me. Weep for yourselves and for your children. The days are coming when they will say, 'Happy are the sterile, the wombs that never bore and the breasts that never nursed.' Then they will begin saying to the mountains, 'Fall on us,' and to the hills, 'Cover us.' If they do these things in the green wood, what will happen in the dry?"

Two others who were criminals were led along with him to be crucified. When they came to Skull Place, as it was called, they crucified him there and the criminals as well, one on his right and the other on his left. [Jesus said, "Father, forgive them; they do not know what they are doing."] They divided his garments, rolling dice for them.

The people stood there watching, and the leaders kept jeering at him, saying, "He saved others; let him save himself if he is the Messiah of God, the chosen one." The soldiers also made fun of him, coming forward to offer him their sour wine and saying, "If you are the king of the Jews, save yourself." There was an inscription over his head:

"THIS IS THE KING OF THE JEWS."

One of the criminals hanging in crucifixion blasphemed him, "Aren't you the Messiah? Then save yourself and us." But the other one rebuked him: "Have you no fear of God, seeing you are under the same sentence? We deserve it, after all. We are only paying the price for what we've done, but this man has done nothing wrong." He then said, "Jesus, remember me when you enter upon your reign." And Jesus replied, "I assure you: this day you will be with me in paradise."

It was now around midday, and darkness came over the whole land until midafternoon with an eclipse of the sun. The curtain in the sanctuary was torn in two. Jesus uttered a loud cry and said,

"Father, into your hands I commend my spirit."

After he said this, he expired. The centurion, upon seeing what had happened, gave glory to God by saying, "Surely this was an innocent man." After the crowd assembled for this spectacle witnessed what had happened, they returned beating their breasts. All his friends and the women who had accompanied him from Galilee were standing at a distance watching everything.

This is the gospel of the Lord.

It is strongly recommended that all three readings prescribed for the Passion Sunday Mass be used, unless pastoral reasons demand otherwise.

However, since the most important reading is the account of the Lord's Passion, the priest, considering the needs of the individual congregation, may use only one of the two readings prescribed before the gospel. If necessary, he may read only the Passion, even in the shorter form. This permission applies only to Masses celebrated with a congregation.

EASTER TRIDUUM AND EASTER SEASON

39　　**HOLY THURSDAY** Ⓐ Ⓑ Ⓒ

Chrism Mass

READING I　　　　　　Is 61, 1-3. 6. 8-9

A reading from the book of the prophet Isaiah

The Lord has anointed me, he has sent me to bring Good News to the poor, to give them the oil of gladness

The spirit of the Lord God is upon me,
　because the Lord has anointed me;
He has sent me to bring glad tidings to the
　　lowly,
　to heal the brokenhearted,
To proclaim liberty to the captives
　and release to the prisoners,
To announce a year of favor from the Lord
　and a day of vindication by our God,
　to comfort all who mourn;
To place on those who mourn in Zion
　a diadem instead of ashes,
To give them oil of gladness in place of
　　mourning,
　a glorious mantle instead of a listless spirit.

You yourselves shall be named priests of the
　　Lord,
　ministers of our God you shall be called.
I will give them their recompense faithfully,
　a lasting covenant I will make with them.
Their descendants shall be renowned among
　　the nations,
　and their offspring among the peoples;
All who see them shall acknowledge them
　as a race the Lord has blessed.
　　　This is the Word of the Lord.

Responsorial Psalm　　Ps 89, 21-22. 25. 27

℟. (2) For ever I will sing the goodness of the
　　Lord.
I have found David, my servant;
　with my holy oil I have anointed him,
That my hand may be always with him,
　and that my arm may make him strong.
℟. For ever I will sing the goodness of the
　　Lord.
My faithfulness and my kindness shall be with
　　him,

and through my name shall his horn be
exalted.
"He shall say of me, 'You are my father,
my God, the rock, my savior.'
℟. For ever I will sing the goodness of the
Lord.

READING II Rv 1, 5-8
A reading from the book of Revelation
Christ has made us a line of kings, priests to serve his
God and Father

[Grace and peace to you] from Jesus Christ the
faithful witness, the first-born from the dead
and ruler of the kings of earth. To him who
loves us and freed us from our sins by his own
blood, who has made us a royal nation of
priests in the service of his God and Father—
to him be glory and power forever and ever!
Amen.
See, he comes amid the clouds!
Every eye shall see him,
even of those who pierced him.
All the peoples of the earth
shall lament him bitterly.
So it is to be! Amen!
The Lord God says, "I am the Alpha and the
Omega, the One who is and who was and who
is to come, the Almighty!"
This is the Word of the Lord.

GOSPEL Lk 4, 16-21
Verse before the Gospel Is 61, 1: cited in Lk 4, 18

The spirit of the Lord is upon me;
he sent me to bring Good News to the poor.

✠ A reading from the holy gospel according
to Luke
The spirit of the Lord has been given to me, for he has
anointed me.

Jesus came to Nazareth where he had been
reared, and entering the synagogue on the
sabbath as he was in the habit of doing, he
stood up to do the reading. When the book of
the prophet Isaiah was handed him, he unrolled
the scroll and found the passage where it was
written:
"The spirit of the Lord is upon me;
therefore he has anointed me.

He has sent me to bring glad tidings to the
poor,
to proclaim liberty to captives,
Recovery of sight to the blind
and release to prisoners,
To announce a year of favor from the
Lord."
Rolling up the scroll, he gave it back to the
assistant and sat down. All in the synagogue
had their eyes fixed on him. Then he began by
saying to them, "Today this Scripture passage
is fulfilled in your hearing."
This is the gospel of the Lord.

---

40 **HOLY THURSDAY** Ⓐ Ⓑ Ⓒ
Mass of the Lord's Supper

READING I Ex 12, 1-8. 11-14
A reading from the book of Exodus
The law for the passover meal.

The Lord said to Moses and Aaron in the land
of Egypt, "This month shall stand at the head
of your calendar; you shall reckon it the first
month of the year. Tell the whole community
of Israel: On the tenth of this month every one
of your families must procure for itself a lamb,
one apiece for each household. If a family is
too small for a whole lamb, it shall join the
nearest household in procuring one and shall
share in the lamb in proportion to the number
of persons who partake of it. The lamb must be
a year-old male and without blemish. You may
take it from either the sheep or the goats. You
shall keep it until the fourteenth day of this
month, and then, with the whole assembly of
Israel present, it shall be slaughtered during
the evening twilight. They shall take some of
its blood and apply it to the two doorposts and
the lintel of every house in which they partake
of the lamb. That same night they shall eat its
roasted flesh with unleavened bread and bitter
herbs.
"This is how you are to eat it: with your
loins girt, sandals on your feet and your staff
in hand, you shall eat like those who are in
flight. It is the Passover of the Lord. For on this
same night I will go through Egypt, striking
down every first-born of the land, both man

and beast, and executing judgment on all the gods of Egypt—I, the Lord! But the blood will mark the houses where you are. Seeing the blood, I will pass over you; thus, when I strike the land of Egypt, no destructive blow will come upon you.

"This day shall be a memorial feast for you, which all your generations shall celebrate with pilgrimage to the Lord, as a perpetual institution."

This is the Word of the Lord.

Responsorial Psalm   Ps 116, 12-13. 15-16. 17-18

℟. (See 1 Cor 10, 16) Our blessing-cup is a communion with the blood of Christ.

How shall I make a return to the Lord
    for all the good he has done for me?
The cup of salvation I will take up,
    and I will call upon the name of the Lord.

℟. Our blessing-cup is a communion with the blood of Christ.

Precious in the eyes of the Lord
    is the death of his faithful ones.
I am your servant, the son of your handmaid;
    you have loosed my bonds.

℟. Our blessing-cup is a communion with the blood of Christ.

To you will I offer sacrifice of thanksgiving,
    and I will call upon the name of the Lord.
My vows to the Lord I will pay
    in the presence of all his people.

℟. Our blessing-cup is a communion with the blood of Christ.

READING II   1 Cor 11, 23-26

A reading from the first letter of Paul to the Corinthians

Until the Lord comes, every time you eat this bread and drink this cup, you proclaim his death.

I received from the Lord what I handed on to you, namely, that the Lord Jesus on the night in which he was betrayed took bread, and after he had given thanks, broke it and said, "This is my body, which is for you. Do this in remembrance of me." In the same way, after the supper, he took the cup, saying, "This cup is the new covenant in my blood. Do this, whenever you drink it, in remembrance of me."

Every time, then, you eat this bread and drink this cup, you proclaim the death of the Lord until he comes!

This is the Word of the Lord.

GOSPEL   Jn 13, 1-15

Verse before the Gospel   Jn 13, 34

I give you a new commandment:
love one another as I have loved you.

✠ A reading from the holy gospel according to John

Now he showed how perfect was his love

Before the feast of Passover, Jesus realized that the hour had come for him to pass from this world to the Father. He had loved his own in this world, and would show his love for them to the end. The devil had already induced Judas, son of Simon Iscariot, to hand Jesus over; and so, during the supper, Jesus—fully aware that he had come from God and was going to God, the Father who had handed everything over to him—rose from the meal and took off his cloak. He picked up a towel and tied it around himself. Then he poured water into a basin and began to wash his disciples' feet and dry them with the towel he had around him. Thus he came to Simon Peter, who said to him, "Lord, are you going to wash my feet?" Jesus answered, "You may not realize now what I am doing, but later you will understand." Peter replied, "You shall never wash my feet!" "If I do not wash you," Jesus answered, "you will have no share in my heritage." "Lord," Simon Peter said to him, "then not only my feet, but my hands and head as well." Jesus told him, "The man who has bathed has no need to wash [except for his feet]; he is entirely cleansed, just as you are; though not all." (The reason he said, "Not all are washed clean," was that he knew his betrayer.)

After he had washed their feet, he put his cloak back on and reclined at table once more. He said to them:

"Do you understand what I just did for you?
You address me as 'Teacher' and 'Lord,'

and fittingly enough,
for that is what I am.
But if I washed your feet—
I who am Teacher and Lord—
then you must wash each other's feet.
What I just did was to give you an
    example:
as I have done, so you must do.
    This is the gospel of the Lord.

---

41   **GOOD FRIDAY** A B C
          The Passion of the Lord

READING I   Is 52, 13-53, 12
A reading from the book of the prophet Isaiah

He surrendered himself to death, while bearing the faults
of many (Fourth song of the Servant of Yahweh).

See, my servant shall prosper,
    he shall be raised high and greatly exalted.
Even as many were amazed at him—
    so marred was his look beyond that of man,
    and his appearance beyond that of mortals—
So shall he startle many nations,
    because of him kings shall stand speechless;
For those who have not been told shall see,
    those who have not heard shall ponder it.

Who would believe what we have heard?
    To whom has the arm of the Lord been
        revealed?
He grew up like a sapling before him,
    like a shoot from the parched earth;
There was in him no stately bearing to make us
    look at him,
    nor appearance that would attract us to him.
He was spurned and avoided by men,
    a man of suffering, accustomed to infirmity,
One of those from whom men hide their faces,
    spurned, and we held him in no esteem.

Yet it was our infirmities that he bore,
    our sufferings that he endured,
While we thought of him as stricken,
    as one smitten by God and afflicted.
But he was pierced for our offenses,
    crushed for our sins;
Upon him was the chastisement that makes us
    whole,

by his stripes we were healed.
We had all gone astray like sheep,
    each following his own way;
But the Lord laid upon him
    the guilt of us all.

Though he was harshly treated, he submitted
    and opened not his mouth;
Like a lamb led to the slaughter
    or a sheep before the shearers,
    he was silent and opened not his mouth.
Oppressed and condemned, he was taken
    away,
    and who would have thought any more of his
        destiny?
When he was cut off from the land of the
    living,
    and smitten for the sin of his people,
A grave was assigned him among the wicked
    and a burial place with evildoers,
Though he had done no wrong
    nor spoken any falsehood.
[But the Lord was pleased
    to crush him in infirmity.]

If he gives his life as an offering for sin,
    he shall see his descendants in a long life,
    and the will of the Lord shall be accom-
        plished through him.

Because of his affliction
    he shall see the light in fullness of days;
Through his suffering, my servant shall justify
    many,
    and their guilt he shall bear.
Therefore I will give him his portion among
    the great,
    and he shall divide the spoils with the
        mighty,
Because he surrendered himself to death
    and was counted among the wicked;
And he shall take away the sins of many,
    and win pardon for their offenses.
    This is the Word of the Lord.

Responsorial Psalm   Ps 31, 2. 6. 12-13. 15-16. 17. 25
℟. (Lk 23, 46) Father, I put my life in your
    hands.

In you, O Lord, I take refuge;
    let me never be put to shame.
    In your justice rescue me.
Into your hands I commend my spirit;
    you will redeem me, O Lord, O faithful God.
R̸. Father, I put my life in your hands.
For all my foes I am an object of reproach,
    a laughingstock to my neighbors, and a
        dread to my friends;
    they who see me abroad flee from me.
I am forgotten like the unremembered dead;
    I am like a dish that is broken.
R̸. Father, I put my life in your hands.
But my trust is in you, O Lord;
    I say, "You are my God."
In your hands is my destiny; rescue me
    from the clutches of my enemies and my
        persecutors.
R̸. Father, I put my life in your hands.
Let your face shine upon your servant;
    save me in your kindness.
Take courage and be stouthearted,
    all you who hope in the Lord.
R̸. Father, I put my life in your hands.

READING II   Heb 4, 14-16; 5, 7-9
A reading from the letter of Paul to the Hebrews

He submitted humbly and became for all the source of
eternal salvation.

We have a great high priest who has passed
through the heavens, Jesus, the Son of God; let
us hold fast to our profession of faith. For we
do not have a high priest who is unable to
sympathize with our weakness, but one who
was tempted in every way that we are, yet
never sinned. So let us confidently approach
the throne of grace to receive mercy and favor
and to find help in time of need.

In the days when he was in the flesh, Christ
offered prayers and supplications with loud
cries and tears to God, who was able to save
him from death, and he was heard because of
his reverence. Son though he was, he learned
obedience from what he suffered; and when
perfected, he became the source of eternal
salvation for all who obey him.

This is the Word of the Lord.

GOSPEL   Jn 18, 1-19, 42
Verse before the Gospel   Phil 2, 8-9

Christ became obedient for us even to death,
dying on the cross.
Therefore God raised him on high
and gave him the name above all other names.

The Passion of our Lord Jesus Christ according to John

Jesus went out with his disciples across the
Kidron valley. There was a garden there, and
he and his disciples entered it. The place was
familiar to Judas as well (the one who was to
hand him over) because Jesus had often met
there with his disciples. Judas took the cohort
as well as police supplied by the chief priests
and the Pharisees, and came there with lan-
terns, torches and weapons. Jesus, aware of all
that would happen to him, stepped forward
and said to them, "Who is it you want?" "Jesus
the Nazorean," they replied. "I am he," he
answered. (Now Judas, the one who was to
hand him over, was right there with them.) As
Jesus said to them, "I am he," they retreated
slightly and fell to the ground. Jesus put the
question to them again, "Who is it you want?"
"Jesus the Nazorean," they repeated. "I have
told you, I am he," Jesus said. "If I am the one
you want, let these men go." (This was to
fulfill what he had said, "I have not lost one
of those you gave me.")

Then Simon Peter, who had a sword, drew it
and struck the slave of the high priest, sever-
ing his right ear. (The slave's name was
Malchus.) At that Jesus said to Peter, "Put
your sword back in its sheath. Am I not to
drink the cup the Father has given me?"

Then the soldiers of the cohort, their tribune,
and the Jewish police arrested Jesus and bound
him. They led him first to Annas, the father-
in-law of Caiaphas who was high priest that
year. (It was Caiaphas who had proposed to
the Jews the advantage of having one man die
for the people.)

Simon Peter, in company with another disciple, kept following Jesus closely. This disciple, who was known to the high priest,

stayed with Jesus as far as the high priest's courtyard, while Peter was left standing at the gate. The disciple known to the high priest came out and spoke to the woman at the gate, and then brought Peter in. This servant girl who kept the gate said to Peter, "Aren't you one of this man's followers?" "Not I," he replied.

Now the night was cold, and the servants and the guards who were standing around had made a charcoal fire to warm themselves by. Peter joined them and stood there warming himself.

The high priest questioned Jesus, first about his disciples, then about his teaching. Jesus answered by saying:

"I have spoken publicly to any who would
  listen.
I always taught in a synagogue or in the
  temple area
where all the Jews come together.
There was nothing secret about anything
  I said.

Why do you question me? Question those who heard me when I spoke. It should be obvious they will know what I said." At this reply, one of the guards who was standing nearby gave Jesus a sharp blow on the face. "Is that any way to answer the high priest?" he said. Jesus replied, "If I said anything wrong produce the evidence, but if I spoke the truth why hit me?" Annas next sent him, bound, to the high priest Caiaphas.

All through this, Simon Peter had been standing there warming himself. They said to him, "Are you not a disciple of his?" He denied: "I am not!" "But did I not see you with him in the garden?" insisted one of the high priest's slaves—as it happened, a relative of the man whose ear Peter had severed. Peter denied it again. At that moment a cock began to crow.

At daybreak they brought Jesus from Caiaphas to the praetorium. They did not enter the praetorium themselves, for they had to avoid ritual impurity if they were to eat the Passover supper. Pilate came out to them. "What accusation do you bring against this man?" he

demanded. "If he were not a criminal," they retorted, "we would certainly not have handed him over to you." At this Pilate said, "Why do you not take him and pass judgment on him according to your law?" "We may not put anyone to death," the Jews answered. (This was to fulfill what Jesus had said, indicating the sort of death he would die.)

Pilate went back into the praetorium and summoned Jesus. "Are you the King of the Jews?" he asked him. Jesus answered, "Are you saying this on your own, or have others been telling you about me?" "I am no Jew!" Pilate retorted. "It is your own people and the chief priests who have handed you over to me. What have you done?" Jesus answered:

"My kingdom does not belong to this
  world.
If my kingdom were of this world,
my subjects would be fighting
to save me from being handed over to the
  Jews.
As it is, my kingdom is not here."

At this Pilate said to him, "So, then, you are a king?" Jesus replied:

"It is you who say I am a king.
The reason I was born,
the reason why I came into the world,
is to testify to the truth.
Anyone committed to the truth hears my
  voice."

"Truth!" said Pilate, "What does that mean?"

After this remark, Pilate went out again to the Jews and told them: "Speaking for myself, I find no case against this man. Recall your custom whereby I release to you someone at Passover time. Do you want me to release to you the king of the Jews?" They shouted back, "We want Barabbas, not this one!" (Barabbas was an insurrectionist.)

Pilate's next move was to take Jesus and have him scourged. The soldiers then wove a crown of thorns and fixed it on his head, throwing around his shoulders a cloak of royal purple. Repeatedly they came up to him and said, "All hail, King of the Jews!", slapping his face as they did so.

Pilate went out a second time and said to the

crowd: "Observe what I do. I am going to bring him out to you to make you realize that I find no case against him." When Jesus came out wearing the crown of thorns and the purple cloak, Pilate said to them, "Look at the man!" As soon as the chief priests and the temple police saw him they shouted, "Crucify him! Crucify him!" Pilate said, "Take him and crucify him yourselves; I find no case against him." "We have our law," the Jews responded, "and according to that law he must die because he made himself God's Son." When Pilate heard this kind of talk, he was more afraid than ever.

Going back into the praetorium, he said to Jesus, "Where do you come from?" Jesus would not give him any answer. "Do you refuse to speak to me?" Pilate asked him. "Do you not know that I have the power to release you and the power to crucify you?" Jesus answered:

"You would have no power over me whatever

unless it were given you from above.

That is why he who handed me over to you

is guilty of the greater sin."

After this, Pilate was eager to release him, but the Jews shouted, "If you free this man you are no 'Friend of Caesar.' Anyone who makes himself a king becomes Caesar's rival." Pilate heard what they were saying, then brought Jesus outside and took a seat on a judge's bench at the place called the Stone Pavement—Gabbatha in Hebrew. (It was the Preparation Day for Passover, and the hour was about noon.) He said to the Jews, "Look at your king!" At this they shouted, "Away with him! Away with him! Crucify him!" "What!" Pilate exclaimed. "Shall I crucify your king?" The chief priests replied, "We have no king but Caesar." In the end, Pilate handed Jesus over to be crucified.

Jesus was led away, and carrying the cross by himself, went out to what is called the Place of the Skull (in Hebrew, Golgotha). There they crucified him, and two others with him: one on either side, Jesus in the middle. Pilate had an inscription placed on the cross which read,

JESUS THE NAZOREAN
THE KING OF THE JEWS

This inscription, in Hebrew, Latin and Greek, was read by many of the Jews, since the place where Jesus was crucified was near the city. The chief priests of the Jews tried to tell Pilate, "You should not have written, 'The King of the Jews.' Write instead, 'This man claimed to be king of the Jews.'" Pilate answered, "What I have written, I have written."

After the soldiers had crucified Jesus they took his garments and divided them four ways, one for each soldier. There was also his tunic, but this tunic was woven in one piece from top to bottom and had no seam. They said to each other, "We shouldn't tear it. Let's throw dice to see who gets it." (The purpose of this was to have the Scripture fulfilled:

"They divided my garments among them;
for my clothing they cast lots.")

And this was what the soldiers did.

Near the cross of Jesus there stood his mother, his mother's sister, Mary the wife of Clopas, and Mary Magdalene. Seeing his mother there with the disciple whom he loved, Jesus said to his mother, "Woman, there is your son." In turn he said to the disciple, "There is your mother." From that hour onward, the disciple took her into his care.

After that, Jesus, realizing that everything was now finished, to bring the Scripture to fulfillment said, "I am thirsty." There was a jar there, full of common wine. They stuck a sponge soaked in this wine on some hyssop and raised it to his lips. When Jesus took the wine, he said, "Now it is finished." Then he bowed his head, and delivered over his spirit.

Since it was the Preparation Day the Jews did not want to have the bodies left on the cross during the sabbath, for that sabbath was a solemn feast day. They asked Pilate that the legs be broken and the bodies be taken away. Accordingly, the soldiers came and broke the legs of the men crucified with Jesus, first of one, then of the other. When they came to Jesus and saw that he was already dead, they did not break his legs. One of the soldiers ran a lance into his side, and immediately blood and water flowed out. (This testimony has been given by an eyewitness, and his testimony is true. He tells what he knows is true, so that you may believe.) These events took place for the fulfillment of Scripture:

"Break none of his bones."

There is still another Scripture passage which says:

They shall look on him whom they have pierced."

Afterward, Joseph of Arimathea, a disciple of Jesus (although a secret one for fear of the Jews), asked Pilate's permission to remove Jesus' body. Pilate granted it, so they came and took the body away. Nicodemus (the man who had first come to Jesus at night) likewise came, bringing a mixture of myrrh and aloes which weighed about a hundred pounds. They took Jesus' body, and in accordance with Jewish burial custom bound it up in wrappings of cloth with perfumed oils. In the place where he had been crucified there was a garden, and in the garden a new tomb in which no one had ever been laid. Because of the Jewish Preparation Day they laid Jesus there, for the tomb was close at hand.

This is the gospel of the Lord.

---

42   EASTER
THE RESURRECTION OF THE LORD
Easter Vigil   A B C

Nine readings are assigned to the Easter Vigil: seven from the Old Testament and two from the New. If circumstances demand in individual cases, the number of prescribed readings may be reduced. However, three selections from the Old Testament should be read before the Epistle and Gospel, although when necessary, two may be read. In any case, the reading from Exodus about the escape through the Red Sea (reading 3) should always be used.

READING I   Gn 1, 1-2, 2 or 1, 1. 26-31

A reading from the book of Genesis

God saw all he had made, and indeed it was good.

(Long Form)

In the beginning, when God created the heavens and the earth, the earth was a formless

25-4

wasteland, and darkness covered the abyss, while a mighty wind swept over the waters.

Then God said, "Let there be light," and there was light. God saw how good the light was. God then separated the light from the darkness. God called the light "day," and the darkness he called "night." Thus evening came, and morning followed—the first day.

Then God said, "Let there be a dome in the middle of the waters, to separate one body of water from the other." And so it happened: God made the dome, and it separated the water above the dome from the water below it. God called the dome "the sky." Evening came, and morning followed—the second day.

Then God said, "Let the water under the sky be gathered into a single basin, so that the dry land may appear." And so it happened: the water under the sky was gathered into its basin, and the dry land appeared. God called the dry land "the earth," and the basin of the water he called "the sea." God saw how good it was. Then God said, "Let the earth bring forth vegetation: every kind of plant that bears seed and every kind of fruit tree on earth that bears fruit with its seed in it." And so it happened: the earth brought forth every kind of plant that bears seed and every kind of fruit tree on earth that bears fruit with its seed in it. God saw how good it was. Evening came, and morning followed—the third day.

Then God said: "Let there be lights in the dome of the sky, to separate day from night. Let them mark the fixed times, the days and the years, and serve as luminaries in the dome of the sky, to shed light upon the earth." And so it happened: God made the two great lights, the greater one to govern the day, and the lesser one to govern the night; and he made the stars. God set them in the dome of the sky, to shed light upon the earth, to govern the day and the night, and to separate the light from the darkness. God saw how good it was. Evening came, and morning followed—the fourth day.

Then God said, "Let the water teem with an abundance of living creatures, and on the earth let birds fly beneath the dome of the sky." And so it happened: God created the great sea monsters and all kinds of swimming creatures with which the water teems, and all kinds of winged birds. God saw how good it was, and God blessed them, saying, "Be fertile, multiply, and fill the water of the seas; and let the birds multiply on the earth." Evening came, and morning followed—the fifth day.

Then God said, "Let the earth bring forth all kinds of living creatures: cattle, creeping things, and wild animals of all kinds." And so it happened: God made all kinds of wild animals, all kinds of cattle, and all kinds of creeping things of the earth. God saw how good it was. Then God said: "Let us make man in our image, after our likeness. Let them have dominion over the fish of the sea, the birds of the air, and the cattle, and over all the wild animals and all the creatures that crawl on the ground."

> God created man in his image;
> in the divine image he created him;
> male and female he created them.

God blessed them, saying: "Be fertile and multiply; fill the earth and subdue it. Have dominion over the fish of the sea, the birds of the air, and all the living things that move on the earth." God also said: "See, I give you every seed-bearing plant all over the earth and every tree that has seed-bearing fruit on it to be your food; and to all the animals of the land, all the birds of the air, and all the living creatures that crawl on the ground, I give all the green plants for food." And so it happened. God looked at everything he had made, and he found it very good. Evening came, and morning followed—the sixth day.

Thus the heavens and the earth and all their array were completed. Since on the seventh day God was finished with the work he had been doing, he rested on the seventh day from all the work he had undertaken.

> This is the Word of the Lord.

OR
(Short Form)

In the beginning, when God created the heavens and the earth, God said: "Let us make man in our image, after our likeness. Let them have dominion over the fish of the sea, the birds of the air, and the cattle, and over all the wild animals and all the creatures that crawl on the ground."

> God created man in his image;
> in the divine image he created him;
> male and female he created them.

God blessed them, saying: "Be fertile and multiply; fill the earth and subdue it. Have dominion over the fish of the sea, the birds of the air, and all the living things that move on the earth." God also said: "See, I give you every seed-bearing plant all over the earth and every tree that has seed-bearing fruit on it to be your food; and to all the animals of the land, all the birds of the air, and all the living creatures that crawl on the ground, I give all the green plants for food." And so it happened. God looked at everything he had made, and he found it very good.

> This is the Word of the Lord.

Responsorial Psalm Ps 104, 1-2. 5-6. 10. 12. 13-14. 24. 35

℟. (30) Lord, send out your Spirit,
  and renew the face of the earth.

Bless the Lord, O my soul!
  O Lord, my God, you are great indeed!
You are clothed with majesty and glory,
  robed in light as with a cloak.

℟. Lord, send out your Spirit,
  and renew the face of the earth.

You fixed the earth upon its foundation,
  not to be moved forever;
With the ocean, as with a garment, you covered it;
  above the mountains the waters stood.

℟. Lord, send out your Spirit,
  and renew the face of the earth.

You send forth springs into the watercourses
  that wind among the mountains.
Beside them the birds of heaven dwell;
  from among the branches they send forth their song.

℟. Lord, send out your Spirit,
  and renew the face of the earth.

You water the mountains from your palace;

the earth is replete with the fruit of your works.
You raise grass for the cattle,
 and vegetation for men's use,
Producing bread from the earth.
℟. Lord, send out your Spirit,
 and renew the face of the earth.
How manifold are your works, O Lord!
 In wisdom you have wrought them all—
 the earth is full of your creatures.
Bless the Lord, O my soul! Alleluia.
℟. Lord, send out your Spirit,
 and renew the face of the earth.

OR

Responsorial Psalm   Ps 33, 4-5. 6-7. 12-13. 20-22

℟. (5) The earth is full of the goodness of the Lord.
Upright is the word of the Lord,
 and all his works are trustworthy.
He loves justice and right;
 of the kindness of the Lord the earth is full.
℟. The earth is full of the goodness of the Lord.
By the word of the Lord the heavens were made;
 by the breath of his mouth all their host.
He gathers the waters of the sea as in a flask;
 in cellars he confines the deep.
℟. The earth is full of the goodness of the Lord.
Happy the nation whose God is the Lord,
 the people he has chosen for his own inheritance.
From heaven the Lord looks down;
 he sees all mankind.
℟. The earth is full of the goodness of the Lord
Our soul waits for the Lord,
 who is our help and our shield.
May your kindness, O Lord, be upon us
 who have put our hope in you.
℟. The earth is full of the goodness of the Lord.

READING II   Gn 22, 1-18 or 22, 1-2. 9. 10-13. 15-18

A reading from the book of Genesis
Abraham's Sacrifice of Isaac.

(Long Form)

God put Abraham to the test. He called to him, "Abraham!" "Ready!" he replied. Then God said: "Take your son Isaac, your only one, whom you love, and go to the land of Moriah. There you shall offer him up as a holocaust on a height that I will point out to you." Early the next morning Abraham saddled his donkey, took with him his son Isaac, and two of his servants as well, and with the wood that he had cut for the holocaust, set out for the place of which God had told him.

On the third day Abraham got sight of the place from afar. Then he said to his servants: "Both of you stay here with the donkey, while the boy and I go on over yonder. We will worship and then come back to you." Thereupon Abraham took the wood for the holocaust and laid it on his son Isaac's shoulders, while he himself carried the fire and the knife. As the two walked on together, Isaac spoke to his father Abraham. "Father!" he said. "Yes, son," he replied. Isaac continued, "Here are the fire and the wood, but where is the sheep for the holocaust?" "Son," Abraham answered, "God himself will provide the sheep for the holocaust." Then the two continued going forward.

When they came to the place of which God had told him, Abraham built an altar there and arranged the wood on it. Next he tied up his son Isaac, and put him on top of the wood on the altar. Then he reached out and took the knife to slaughter his son. But the Lord's messenger called to him from heaven, "Abraham, Abraham!" "Yes, Lord," he answered. "Do not lay your hand on the boy," said the messenger. "Do not do the least thing to him. I know now how devoted you are to God, since you did not withhold from me your own beloved son." As Abraham looked about, he spied a ram caught by its horns in the thicket. So he went and took the ram and offered it up as a holocaust in place of his son. Abraham named the site Yahweh-yireh; hence people now say, "On the mountain the Lord will see."

Again the Lord's messenger called to Abraham from heaven and said: "I swear by myself, declares the Lord, that because you acted as you did in not withholding from me your beloved son, I will bless you abundantly and make your descendants as countless as the

stars of the sky and the sands of the seashore; your descendants shall take possession of the gates of their enemies, and in your descendants all the nations of the earth shall find blessing— all this because you obeyed my command."
This is the Word of the Lord.

OR (Short Form)

God put Abraham to the test. He called to him, "Abraham!" "Ready!" he replied. Then God said: "Take your son Isaac, your only one, whom you love, and go to the land of Moriah. There you shall offer him up as a holocaust on a height that I will point out to you."

When they came to the place of which God had told him, Abraham built an altar there and arranged the wood on it. Then he reached out and took the knife to slaughter his son. But the Lord's messenger called to him from heaven, "Abraham, Abraham!" "Yes, Lord," he answered. "Do not lay your hand on the boy," said the messenger. "Do not do the least thing to him. I know now how devoted you are to God, since you did not withhold from me your own beloved son." As Abraham looked about, he spied a ram caught by its horns in the thicket. So he went and took the ram and offered it up as a holocaust in place of his son.

Again the Lord's messenger called to Abraham from heaven and said: "I swear by myself, declares the Lord, that because you acted as you did in not withholding from me your beloved son, I will bless you abundantly and make your descendants as countless as the stars of the sky and the sands of the seashore; your descendants shall take possession of the gates of their enemies, and in your descendants all the nations of the earth shall find blessing —all this because you obeyed my command."
This is the Word of the Lord.

Responsorial Psalm   Ps 16, 5. 8. 9-10. 11

℟. (1) Keep me safe, O God;
    you are my hope.

O Lord, my allotted portion and my cup,
    you it is who hold fast my lot.
I set the Lord ever before me;
    with him at my right hand I shall not be disturbed.

℟. Keep me safe, O God;
    you are my hope.

Therefore my heart is glad and my soul rejoices,
    my body, too, abides in confidence;
Because you will not abandon my soul to the nether world,
    nor will you suffer your faithful one to undergo corruption.

℟. Keep me safe, O God;
    you are my hope.

You will show me the path to life,
    fullness of joys in your presence,
    the delights at your right hand forever.

℟. Keep me safe, O God;
    you are my hope.

READING III   Ex 14, 15—15, 1

A reading from the book of Exodus

Tell the sons of Israel to march on, to walk through the sea on dry ground.

The Lord said to Moses, "Why are you crying out to me? Tell the Israelites to go forward. And you, lift up your staff and, with hand outstretched over the sea, split the sea in two, that the Israelites may pass through it on dry land. But I will make the Egyptians so obstinate that they will go in after them. Then I will receive glory through Pharaoh and all his army, his chariots and charioteers. The Egyptians shall know that I am the Lord, when I receive glory through Pharaoh and his chariots and charioteers."

The angel of God, who had been leading Israel's camp, now moved and went around behind them. The column of cloud also, leaving the front, took up its place behind them, so that it came between the camp of the Egyptians and that of Israel. But the cloud now became dark, and thus the night passed without the rival camps coming any closer together all night long. Then Moses stretched out his hand over the sea, and the Lord swept the sea with a strong east wind throughout the night and so turned it into dry land. When the water was thus divided, the Israelites marched into the midst of the sea on dry land, with the water like a wall to their right and to their left.

The Egyptians followed in pursuit; all Pharaoh's horses and chariots and charioteers went after them right into the midst of the sea. In the night watch just before dawn the Lord cast through the column of the fiery cloud upon the Egyptian force a glance that threw it into a panic; and he so clogged their chariot wheels that they could hardly drive. With that the Egyptians sounded the retreat before Israel, because the Lord was fighting for them against the Egyptians.

Then the Lord told Moses, "Stretch out your hand over the sea, that the water may flow back upon the Egyptians, upon their chariots and their charioteers." So Moses stretched out his hand over the sea, and at dawn the sea flowed back to its normal depth. The Egyptians were fleeing head on toward the sea, when the Lord hurled them into its midst. As the water flowed back, it covered the chariots and the charioteers of Pharaoh's whole army which had followed the Israelites into the sea. Not a single one of them escaped. But the Israelites had marched on dry land through the midst of the sea, with the water like a wall to their right and to their left. Thus the Lord saved Israel on that day from the power of the Egyptians. When Israel saw the Egyptians lying dead on the seashore and beheld the great power that the Lord had shown against the Egyptians, they feared the Lord and believed in him and in his servant Moses.

Then Moses and the Israelites sang this song to the Lord:
I will sing to the Lord, for he is gloriously triumphant;
    horse and chariot he has cast into the sea.
This is the Word of the Lord.

Responsorial Psalm   Ex 15, 1-2. 3-4. 5-6. 17-18

℟. (1) Let us sing to the Lord;
    he has covered himself in glory.
I will sing to the Lord, for he is gloriously triumphant;
    horse and chariot he has cast into the sea.

My strength and my courage is the Lord,
    and he has been my savior.
He is my God, I praise him;
    the God of my father, I extol him.
℟. Let us sing to the Lord;
    he has covered himself in glory.
The Lord is a warrior,
    Lord is his name!
Pharaoh's chariots and army he hurled into the sea;
    the elite of his officers were submerged in the Red Sea.
℟. Let us sing to the Lord;
    he has covered himself in glory.
The flood waters covered them,
    they sank into the depths like a stone.
Your right hand, O Lord, magnificent in power,
    your right hand, O Lord, has shattered the enemy.
℟. Let us sing to the Lord;
    he has covered himself in glory.
You brought in the people you redeemed
    and planted them on the mountain of your inheritance.
The place where you made your seat, O Lord,
    the sanctuary, O Lord, which your hands established.
The Lord shall reign forever and ever.
℟. Let us sing to the Lord;
    he has covered himself in glory.

READING IV   Is 54, 5-14

A reading from the book of the prophet Isaiah
But with everlasting love I have taken pity on you, says the Lord, your redeemer.

He who has become your husband is your Maker;
    his name is the Lord of hosts;
Your redeemer is the Holy One of Israel,
    called God of all the earth.
The Lord calls you back,
    like a wife forsaken and grieved in spirit,
A wife married in youth and then cast off,
    says your God.
For a brief moment I abandoned you,
    but with great tenderness I will take you back.
In an outburst of wrath, for a moment

I hid my face from you;
But with enduring love I take pity on you,
　　says the Lord, your redeemer.
This is for me like the days of Noah,
　　when I swore that the waters of Noah
　　should never again deluge the earth;
So I have sworn not to be angry with you,
　　or to rebuke you.
Though the mountains leave their place
　　and the hills be shaken,
My love shall never leave you
　　nor my covenant of peace be shaken,
　　says the Lord, who has mercy on you.
O afflicted one, storm-battered and uncon-
　　soled,
　　I lay your pavements in carnelians,
　　and your foundations in sapphires;
I will make your battlements of rubies,
　　your gates of carbuncles,
　　and all your walls of precious stones.
All your sons shall be taught by the Lord,
　　and great shall be the peace of your children.
In justice shall you be established,
　　far from the fear of oppression,
　　where destruction cannot come near you.
　　　　This is the Word of the Lord.

Responsorial Psalm   Ps 30, 2. 4. 5-6. 11-12. 13

R⁄. (2) I will praise you, Lord,
　　for you have rescued me.
I will extol you, O Lord, for you drew me clear
　　and did not let my enemies rejoice over me.
O Lord, you brought me up from the nether
　　world;
　　you preserved me from among those going
　　down into the pit.
R⁄. I will praise you, Lord,
　　for you have rescued me.
Sing praise to the Lord, you his faithful ones,
　　and give thanks to his holy name.
For his anger lasts but a moment;
　　a lifetime, his good will.
At nightfall, weeping enters in,
　　but with the dawn, rejoicing.
R⁄. I will praise you, Lord,
　　for you have rescued me.

Hear, O Lord, and have pity on me;
　　O Lord, be my helper.
You changed my mourning into dancing;
　　O Lord, my God, forever will I give you
　　thanks.
R⁄. I will praise you, Lord,
　　for you have rescued me.

READING V   Is 55, 1-11
A reading from the book of the prophet Isaiah
Come to me and your soul will live. With you I will make
an everlasting covenant.

Thus says the Lord:
All you who are thirsty,
　　come to the water!
You who have no money,
　　come, receive grain and eat;
Come, without paying and without cost,
　　drink wine and milk!
Why spend your money for what is not bread;
　　your wages for what fails to satisfy?
Heed me, and you shall eat well,
　　you shall delight in rich fare.
Come to me heedfully,
　　listen, that you may have life.
I will renew with you the everlasting covenant,
　　the benefits assured to David.
As I made him a witness to the peoples,
　　a leader and commander of nations,
So shall you summon a nation you knew not,
　　and nations that knew you not shall run to
　　you,
Because of the Lord, your God,
　　the Holy One of Israel, who has glorified
　　you.
Seek the Lord while he may be found,
　　call him while he is near.
Let the scoundrel forsake his way,
　　and the wicked man his thoughts;
Let him turn to the Lord for mercy;
　　to our God, who is generous in forgiving.
For my thoughts are not your thoughts,
　　nor are your ways my ways, says the Lord.
As high as the heavens are above the earth,
　　so high are my ways above your ways
　　and my thoughts above your thoughts.
For just as from the heavens
　　the rain and snow come down

And do not return there
   till they have watered the earth,
   making it fertile and fruitful,
Giving seed to him who sows
   and bread to him who eats,
So shall my word be
   that goes forth from my mouth;
It shall not return to me void,
   but shall do my will,
   achieving the end for which I sent it.
      This is the Word of the Lord.

Responsorial Psalm   Is 12, 2-3. 4. 5-6

℞. (3) You will draw water joyfully from the
   springs of salvation.
God indeed is my savior;
   I am confident and unafraid.
My strength and my courage is the Lord,
   and he has been my savior.
With joy you will draw water
   at the fountain of salvation.
℞. You will draw water joyfully from the
   springs of salvation.
Give thanks to the Lord, acclaim his name;
   among the nations make known his deeds,
   proclaim how exalted is his name.
℞. You will draw water joyfully from the
   springs of salvation.
Sing praise to the Lord for his glorious achievement;
   let this be known throughout all the earth.
Shout with exultation, O city of Zion,
   for great in your midst
   is the Holy One of Israel!
℞. You will draw water joyfully from the
   springs of salvation.

READING VI   Bar 3, 9-15. 32—4, 4

A reading from the book of the prophet Baruch
Walk in the way of God and you will live in peace for ever.
Hear, O Israel, the commandments of life:
   listen, and know prudence!
How is it, Israel,
   that you are in the land of your foes,
   grown old in a foreign land,
Defiled with the dead,

accounted with those destined for the nether
   world?
You have forsaken the fountain of wisdom!
   Had you walked in the way of God,
   you would have dwelt in enduring peace.
Learn where prudence is,
   where strength, where understanding;
That you may know also
   where are length of days, and life,
   where light of the eyes, and peace.

Who has found the place of wisdom,
   who has entered into her treasuries?
He who knows all things knows her;
   he has probed her by his knowledge—
He who established the earth for all time,
   and filled it with four-footed beasts;
He who dismisses the light, and it departs,
   calls it, and it obeys him trembling;
Before whom the stars at their posts
   shine and rejoice;
When he calls them, they answer, "Here we
   are!"
   shining with joy for their Maker.
Such is our God;
   no other is to be compared to him:
He has traced out all the way of understanding,
   and has given her to Jacob, his servant,
   to Israel, his beloved son.

Since then she has appeared on earth,
   and moved among men.
She is the book of the precepts of God,
   the law that endures forever;
All who cling to her will live,
   but those will die who forsake her.
Turn, O Jacob, and receive her:
   walk by her light toward splendor.
Give not your glory to another,
   your privileges to an alien race.
Blessed are we, O Israel;
   for what pleases God is known to us!
      This is the Word of the Lord.

Responsorial Psalm   Ps 19, 8. 9. 10. 11

℞. (Jn 6, 69) Lord, you have the words of
   everlasting life.
The law of the Lord is perfect,
   refreshing the soul;

The decree of the Lord is trustworthy,
    giving wisdom to the simple.
℟. Lord, you have the words of everlasting
    life.
The precepts of the Lord are right,
    rejoicing the heart;
The command of the Lord is clear,
    enlightening the eye.
℟. Lord, you have the words of everlasting
    life.
The fear of the Lord is pure,
    enduring forever;
The ordinances of the Lord are true,
    all of them just.
℟. Lord, you have the words of everlasting
    life.
They are more precious than gold,
    than a heap of purest gold;
Sweeter also than syrup
    or honey from the comb.
℟. Lord, you have the words of everlasting
    life.

READING VII   Ez 36, 16-28

**A reading from the book of the prophet
Ezekiel**

I shall pour clean water over you and I shall give you a
new heart.

Thus the word of the Lord came to me: Son of
man, when the house of Israel lived in their
land, they defiled it by their conduct and deeds.
In my sight their conduct was like the defilement of a menstruous woman. Therefore I
poured out my fury upon them [because of
the blood which they poured out on the ground,
and because they defiled it with idols]. I scattered them among the nations, dispersing them
over foreign lands; according to their conduct
and deeds I judged them. But when they came
among the nations [wherever they came], they
served to profane my holy name, because it
was said of them: "These are the people of the
Lord, yet they had to leave their land." So I
have relented because of my holy name which
the house of Israel profaned among the nations
where they came. Therefore say to the house
of Israel: Thus says the Lord God: Not for
your sakes do I act, house of Israel, but for

the sake of my holy name, which you profaned among the nations to which you came. I
will prove the holiness of my great name, profaned among the nations, in whose midst you
have profaned it. Thus the nations shall know
that I am the Lord, says the Lord God, when
in their sight I prove my holiness through you.
For I will take you away from among the nations, gather you from all the foreign lands, and
bring you back to your own land. I will sprinkle clean water upon you to cleanse you from
all your impurities, and from all your idols I
will cleanse you. I will give you a new heart
and place a new spirit within you, taking from
your bodies your stony hearts and giving you
natural hearts. I will put my spirit within you
and make you live by my statutes, careful to
observe my decrees. You shall live in the land
I gave your fathers; you shall be my people,
and I will be your God.

   This is the Word of the Lord.

Responsorial Psalm   Ps 42, 3. 5; 43, 3. 4

℟. (Ps 42, 2) Like a deer that longs for running
    streams,
    my soul longs for you, my God.
Athirst is my soul for God, the living God.
    When shall I go and behold the face of God?
℟. Like a deer that longs for running streams,
    my soul longs for you, my God.
I went with the throng
    and led them in procession to the house of
        God,
Amid loud cries of joy and thanksgiving,
    with the multitude keeping festival.
℟. Like a deer that longs for running streams,
    my soul longs for you, my God.
Send forth your light and your fidelity;
    they shall lead me on
And bring me to your holy mountain,
    to your dwelling-place.
℟. Like a deer that longs for running streams,
    my soul longs for you, my God.
Then will I go in to the altar of God,
    the God of my gladness and joy;
Then will I give you thanks upon the harp,
    O God, my God!

℟. Like a deer that longs for running streams,
   my soul longs for you, my God.

OR

When baptism is celebrated, the Responsorial Psalm after
Reading V (Is 12, 2-3. 4. 5-6) as above may be used; or the
following:

OR

Responsorial Psalm   Ps 51, 12-13. 14-15. 18-19

℟. (12) Create a clean heart in me, O God.
A clean heart create for me, O God,
   and a steadfast spirit renew within me.
Cast me not out from your presence,
   and your holy spirit take not from me.
℟. Create a clean heart in me, O God.
Give me back the joy of your salvation,
   and a willing spirit sustain in me.
I will teach transgressors your ways,
   and sinners shall return to you.
℟. Create a clean heart in me, O God.
For you are not pleased with sacrifices;
   should I offer a holocaust, you would not
      accept it.
My sacrifice, O God, is a contrite spirit;
   a heart contrite and humbled, O God, you
      will not spurn.
℟. Create a clean heart in me, O God.

EPISTLE   Rom 6, 3-11

A reading from the letter of Paul to the Romans
Christ, having been raised from the dead, will never die
again.

Are you not aware that we who were baptized
into Christ Jesus were baptized into his death?
Through baptism into his death we were buried
with him, so that, just as Christ was raised
from the dead by the glory of the Father, we
too might live a new life. If we have been
united with him through likeness to his death,
so shall we be through a like resurrection.
This we know: our old self was crucified with
him so that the sinful body might be destroyed
and we might be slaves to sin no longer. A man
who is dead has been freed from sin. If we have
died with Christ, we believe that we are also to
live with him. We know that Christ, once
raised from the dead, will never die again;
death has no more power over him. His death
was death to sin, once for all; his life is life for
God. In the same way, you must consider yourselves dead to sin but alive for God in Christ
Jesus.
                This is the Word of the Lord.

Responsorial Psalm   Ps 118, 1-2. 16. 17. 22-23

℟. Alleluia. Alleluia. Alleluia.
Give thanks to the Lord, for he is good,
   for his mercy endures forever.
Let the house of Israel say,
   "His mercy endures forever."
℟. Alleluia. Alleluia. Alleluia.
The right hand of the Lord has struck with
      power;
   the right hand of the Lord is exalted.
I shall not die, but live,
   and declare the works of the Lord.
℟. Alleluia. Alleluia. Alleluia.
The stone which the builders rejected
   has become the cornerstone.
By the Lord has this been done;
   It is wonderful in our eyes.
℟. Alleluia. Alleluia. Alleluia.

A

GOSPEL   Mt 28, 1-10

✠ **A reading from the holy gospel according**
            to Matthew
He has risen from the dead and now he is going before
you to Galilee.

After the sabbath, as the first day of the week
was dawning, Mary Magdalene came with the
other Mary to inspect the tomb. Suddenly there
was a mighty earthquake, as the angel of the
Lord descended from heaven. He came to the
stone, rolled it back, and sat on it. In appearance he resembled a flash of lightning while
his garments were as dazzling as snow. The
guards grew paralyzed with fear of him and
fell down like dead men. Then the angel spoke,
addressing the women: "Do not be frightened.
I know you are looking for Jesus the crucified,
but he is not here. He has been raised, exactly
as he promised. Come and see the spot where
he was laid. Then go quickly and tell his disciples: 'He has been raised from the dead and

now goes ahead of you to Galilee, where you will see him.' That is the message I have for you."

They hurried away from the tomb half-overjoyed, half-fearful, and ran to carry the good news to his disciples. Suddenly, without warning, Jesus stood before them and said, "Peace!" The women came up and embraced his feet and did him homage. At this Jesus said to them, "Do not be afraid! Go and carry the news to my brothers that they are to go to Galilee, where they will see me."

This is the gospel of the Lord.

B

GOSPEL   Mk 16, 1-8

✠ A reading from the holy gospel according to Mark

Jesus of Nazareth, who was crucified, has risen

When the sabbath was over, Mary Magdalene, Mary the mother of James, and Salome bought perfumed oils with which they intended to go and anoint Jesus. Very early, just after sunrise, on the first day of the week they came to the tomb. They were saying to one another, "Who will roll back the stone for us from the entrance to the tomb?" When they looked, they found that the stone had been rolled back. (It was a huge one.) On entering the tomb they saw a young man sitting at the right, dressed in a white robe. This frightened them thoroughly, but he reassured them: "You need not be amazed! You are looking for Jesus of Nazareth, the one who was crucified. He has been raised up; he is not here. See the place where they laid him. Go now and tell his disciples and Peter, 'He is going ahead of you to Galilee, where you will see him just as he told you.' " They made their way out and fled from the tomb bewildered and trembling; and because of their great fear, they said nothing to anyone.

This is the gospel of the Lord.

C

GOSPEL   Lk 24, 1-12

✠ A reading from the holy gospel according to Luke

Why look among the dead for someone who is alive?

On the first day of the week, at dawn, the women came to the tomb bringing the spices they had prepared. They found the stone rolled back from the tomb; but when they entered the tomb, they did not find the body of the Lord Jesus. While they were still at a loss what to think of this, two men in dazzling garments appeared beside them. Terrified, the women bowed to the ground. The men said to them: "Why do you search for the living One among the dead? He is not here; he has been raised up. Remember what he said to you while he was still in Galilee—that the Son of Man must be delivered into the hands of sinful men, and be crucified, and on the third day rise again." With this reminder, his words came back to them.

On their return from the tomb, they told all these things to the Eleven and the others. The women were Mary of Magdala, Joanna, and Mary the mother of James. The other women with them also told the apostles, but the story seemed like nonsense and they refused to believe them. Peter, however, got up and ran to the tomb. He stooped down but could see nothing but the wrappings. So he went away full of amazement at what had occurred.

This is the gospel of the Lord.

43　　　　　**EASTER SUNDAY**　**A B C**

READING I　　　　　　　　　　Acts 10, 34. 37-43

A reading from the Acts of the Apostles

We have eaten and drunk with him after his resurrection
from the dead.

Peter addressed the people in these words: "I take it you know what has been reported all over Judea about Jesus of Nazareth, beginning in Galilee with the baptism John preached; of the way God anointed him with the Holy Spirit and power. He went about doing good works and healing all who were in the grip of the devil, and God was with him. We are witnesses to all that he did in the land of the Jews and in Jerusalem. They killed him finally, 'hanging him on a tree,' only to have God raise him up on the third day and grant that he be seen, not by all, but only by such witnesses as had been chosen beforehand by God—by us who ate and drank with him after he rose from the dead. He commissioned us to preach to the people and to bear witness that he is the one set apart by God as judge of the living and the dead. To him all the prophets testify, saying that everyone who believes in him has forgiveness of sins through his name."

　　　　This is the Word of the Lord.

Responsorial Psalm　Ps 118, 1-2. 16-17. 22-23

℟. (24) This is the day the Lord has made;
　　let us rejoice and be glad.

Give thanks to the Lord, for he is good,
　　for his mercy endures forever.
Let the house of Israel say,
　　"His mercy endures forever."

℟. This is the day the Lord has made;
　　let us rejoice and be glad.

"The right hand of the Lord has struck with
　　power;
　　the right hand of the Lord is exalted.
I shall not die, but live,
　　and declare the works of the Lord.

℟. This is the day the Lord has made;
　　let us rejoice and be glad.

The stone which the builders rejected
　　has become the cornerstone.
By the Lord has this been done;

it is wonderful in our eyes.

℟. This is the day the Lord has made;
　　let us rejoice and be glad.

℟. Or: Alleluia.

READING II　　　　　　　　　　Col 3, 1-4

**A reading from the letter of Paul to the
Colossians**

Look for the things that are in heaven, where Christ is.

Since you have been raised up in company with Christ, set your heart on what pertains to higher realms where Christ is seated at God's right hand. Be intent on things above rather than on things of earth. After all, you have died! Your life is hidden now with Christ in God. When Christ our life appears, then you shall appear with him in glory.

　　　　This is the Word of the Lord.

OR

READING II　　　　　　　　　　1 Cor 5, 6-8

**A reading from the first letter of Paul to the
Corinthians**

Throw away the old yeast, that you may be new dough.

Do you not know that a little yeast has its effect all through the dough? Get rid of the old yeast to make of yourselves fresh dough, unleavened loaves, as it were; Christ our Passover has been sacrificed. Let us celebrate the feast not with the old yeast, that of corruption and wickedness, but with the unleavened bread of sincerity and truth.

　　　　This is the Word of the Lord.

Sequence　　　(Prose text)

To the Paschal Victim let Christians offer a sacrifice of praise.

　　The Lamb redeemed the sheep. Christ, sinless, reconciled sinners to the Father.

　　Death and life were locked together in a unique struggle. Life's captain died; now he reigns, never more to die.

　　Tell us, Mary, "What did you see on the way?"

　　"I saw the tomb of the now living Christ. I saw the glory of Christ, now risen.

　　"I saw angels who gave witness; the cloths

too which once had covered head and limbs.

"Christ my hope has arisen. He will go before his own into Galilee."

We know that Christ has indeed risen from the dead. Do you, conqueror and king, have mercy on us. Amen. Alleluia.

OR
(Poetic text)

Christians, to the Paschal Victim
Offer your thankful praises!
A Lamb the sheep redeems: Christ,
who only is sinless,
Reconciles sinners to the Father.
Death and life have contended in that combat
stupendous:
The Prince of life, who died, reigns immortal.

Speak, Mary, declaring
What you saw, wayfaring.
"The tomb of Christ, who is living,
The glory of Jesus' resurrection;
Bright angels attesting,
The shroud and napkin resting.
Yes, Christ my hope is arisen:
To Galilee he goes before you."

Christ indeed from death is risen, our new life
obtaining.
Have mercy, victor King, ever reigning!
Amen. Alleluia.

GOSPEL   Jn 20, 1-9
Alleluia   1 Cor 5, 7-8

℟. Alleluia. Christ has become our paschal
sacrifice;
let us feast with joy in the Lord. ℟. Alleluia.

✠ A reading from the holy gospel according
to John
The teaching of scripture is that he must rise from the dead.
Early in the morning on the first day of the
week, while it was still dark, Mary Magdalene
came to the tomb. She saw that the stone had
been moved away, so she ran off to Simon
Peter and the other disciple (the one Jesus
loved) and told them, "The Lord has been
taken from the tomb! We don't know where

they have put him!" At that, Peter and the
other disciple started out on their way toward
the tomb. They were running side by side, but
then the other disciple outran Peter and
reached the tomb first. He did not enter but
bent down to peer in, and saw the wrappings
lying on the ground. Presently, Simon Peter
came along behind him and entered the tomb.
He observed the wrappings on the ground and
saw the piece of cloth which had covered the
head not lying with the wrappings, but rolled
up in a place by itself. Then the disciple who
had arrived first at the tomb went in. He saw
and believed. (Remember, as yet they did not
understand the Scripture that Jesus had to rise
from the dead.)
     This is the gospel of the Lord.

The gospel from the Easter Vigil (see no. 42) may be read
in place of this.
At an afternoon Mass, another gospel may be read: Lk 24,
13-35. Stay with us now since it is almost evening (see no.
47).

---

44   SECOND SUNDAY OF EASTER **A**

READING I   Acts 2, 42-47
     A reading from the Acts of the Apostles
The faithful lived together and owned everything in common.
The brethren devoted themselves to the apos-
tles' instruction and the communal life, to the
breaking of bread and the prayers. A reverent
fear overtook them all, for many wonders and
signs were performed by the apostles. Those
who believed shared all things in common;
they would sell their property and goods, dividing everything on the basis of each one's need.
They went to the temple area together every
day, while in their homes they broke bread.
With exultant and sincere hearts they took
their meals in common, praising God and winning the approval of all the people. Day by day
the Lord added to their number those who
were being saved.
     This is the Word of the Lord.

Responsorial Psalm   Ps 118, 2-4. 13-15. 22-24

℟. (1) Give thanks to the Lord for he is good,
his love is everlasting.

Let the house of Israel say,
 "His mercy endures forever."
Let the house of Aaron say,
 "His mercy endures forever."
Let those who fear the Lord say,
 "His mercy endures forever."
℟. Give thanks to the Lord for he is good,
 his love is everlasting.
I was hard pressed and was falling,
 but the Lord helped me.
My strength and my courage is the Lord,
 and he has been my savior.
The joyful shout of victory
 in the tents of the just:
℟. Give thanks to the Lord for he is good,
 his love is everlasting.
The stone which the builders rejected
 has become the cornerstone.
By the Lord has this been done;
 it is wonderful in our eyes.
This is the day the Lord has made;
 let us be glad and rejoice in it.
℟. Give thanks to the Lord for he is good,
 his love is everlasting.
℟. Or: Alleluia.

READING II   1 Pt 1, 3-9

A reading from the first letter of Peter

He has given us a new birth as his sons, by raising Jesus
Christ from the dead.

Praised be the God and Father of our Lord
 Jesus Christ,
he who in his great mercy gave us new birth;
a birth unto hope which draws its life
from the resurrection of Jesus Christ from
 the dead;
a birth to an imperishable inheritance
incapable of fading or defilement,
which is kept in heaven for you
who are guarded with God's power through
 faith;
a birth to a salvation which stands ready
to be revealed in the last days.
 There is cause for rejoicing here. You may
for a time have to suffer the distress of many
trials; but this is so that your faith, which is
more precious than the passing splendor of
fire-tried gold, may by its genuineness lead to
praise, glory, and honor when Jesus Christ ap-

pears. Although you have never seen him, you
love him, and without seeing you believe in
him, and rejoice with inexpressible joy touched
with glory because you are achieving faith's
goal, your salvation.
 This is the Word of the Lord.

GOSPEL   Jn 20, 19-31
Alleluia Jn 20, 29

℟. Alleluia. You believe in me, Thomas, because you have seen me;
happy those who have not seen me, but still
 believe! ℟. Alleluia.

✠ A reading from the holy gospel according
                    to John

After eight days Jesus came in and stood among them.

On the evening of that first day of the week,
even though the disciples had locked the doors
of the place where they were for fear of the
Jews, Jesus came and stood before them.
"Peace be with you," he said. When he had said
this, he showed them his hands and his side. At
the sight of the Lord the disciples rejoiced.
"Peace be with you," he said again.
 "As the Father has sent me,
 so I send you."
Then he breathed on them and said:
 "Receive the Holy Spirit.
 If you forgive men's sins,
 they are forgiven them;
 if you hold them bound,
 they are held bound."
 It happened that one of the Twelve, Thomas
(the name means "Twin"), was absent when
Jesus came. The other disciples kept telling
him: "We have seen the Lord!" His answer
was, "I'll never believe it without probing the
nail-prints in his hands, without putting my
finger in the nail-marks and my hand into his
side."
 A week later, the disciples were once more
in the room, and this time Thomas was with
them. Despite the locked doors, Jesus came
and stood before them. "Peace be with you,"
he said; then, to Thomas: "Take your finger
and examine my hands. Put your hand into my
side. Do not persist in your unbelief, but believe!" Thomas said in response, "My Lord and

my God!" Jesus then said to him:

"You became a believer because you saw me.

Blest are they who have not seen and have believed."

Jesus performed many other signs as well—signs not recorded here—in the presence of his disciples. But these have been recorded to help you believe that Jesus is the Messiah, the Son of God, so that through this faith you may have life in his name.

This is the gospel of the Lord.

---

45   SECOND SUNDAY OF EASTER   B

READING I   Acts 4, 32-35

A reading from the Acts of the Apostles
The whole group was united heart and soul.

The community of believers were of one heart and one mind. None of them ever claimed anything as his own; rather everything was held in common. With power the apostles bore witness to the resurrection of the Lord Jesus, and great respect was paid to them all; nor was there anyone needy among them, for all who owned property or houses sold them and donated the proceeds. They used to lay them at the feet of the apostles to be distributed to everyone according to his need.

This is the Word of the Lord.

Responsorial Psalm   Ps 118, 2-4. 13-15. 22-24

℟. (1) Give thanks to the Lord for he is good, his love is everlasting.

Let the house of Israel say,
   "His mercy endures forever."
Let the house of Aaron say,
   "His mercy endures forever."
Let those who fear the Lord say,
   "His mercy endures forever."

℟. Give thanks to the Lord for he is good, his love is everlasting.

I was hard pressed and was falling,
   but the Lord helped me.

My strength and my courage is the Lord,
   and he has been my savior.
The joyful shout of victory
   in the tents of the just:

℟. Give thanks to the Lord for he is good, his love is everlasting.

The stone which the builders rejected
   has become the cornerstone.
By the Lord has this been done;
   it is wonderful in our eyes.
This is the day the Lord has made;
   let us be glad and rejoice in it.

℟. Give thanks to the Lord for he is good, his love is everlasting.

℟. Or: Alleluia.

READING II   1 Jn 5, 1-6

A reading from the first letter of John
Anyone begotten by God has already overcome the world.

Everyone who believes that Jesus is the Christ
   has been begotten by God.
Now, everyone who loves the father
   loves the child he has begotten.
We can be sure that we love God's children
   when we love God
   and do what he has commanded.
The love of God consists in this:
   that we keep his commandments—
   and his commandments are not burdensome.
Everyone begotten of God conquers the world,
   and the power that has conquered the world
   is this faith of ours.
Who, then, is conqueror of the world?
   The one who believes that Jesus is the Son of God.
Jesus Christ it is who came through water and blood—
   not in water only,
   but in water and in blood.
It is the Spirit who testifies to this,
   and the Spirit is truth.

This is the Word of the Lord.

GOSPEL　　　　　　　　　　Jn 20, 19-31
Alleluia　Jn 20, 29

℟. Alleluia. You believe in me, Thomas, because you have seen me;
happy those who have not seen me, but still believe! ℟. Alleluia.

✠ A reading from the holy gospel according to John

After eight days Jesus came in and stood among them.

On the evening of that first day of the week, even though the disciples had locked the doors of the place where they were for fear of the Jews, Jesus came and stood before them. "Peace be with you," he said. When he had said this, he showed them his hands and his side. At the sight of the Lord the disciples rejoiced. "Peace be with you," he said again.

"As the Father has sent me,
so I send you."

Then he breathed on them and said:
"Receive the Holy Spirit.
If you forgive men's sins,
they are forgiven them;
if you hold them bound,
they are held bound."

It happened that one of the Twelve, Thomas (the name means "Twin"), was absent when Jesus came. The other disciples kept telling him: "We have seen the Lord!" His answer was, "I'll never believe it without probing the nail-prints in his hands, without putting my finger in the nail-marks and my hand into his side."

A week later, the disciples were once more in the room, and this time Thomas was with them. Despite the locked doors, Jesus came and stood before them. "Peace be with you," he said; then, to Thomas: "Take your finger and examine my hands. Put your hand into my side. Do not persist in your unbelief, but believe!" Thomas said in response, "My Lord and my God!" Jesus then said to him:

"You became a believer because you saw me.
Blest are they who have not seen and have believed."

Jesus performed many other signs as well—signs not recorded here—in the presence of his disciples. But these have been recorded to help you believe that Jesus is the Messiah, the Son of God, so that through this faith you may have life in his name.

This is the gospel of the Lord.

46　　SECOND SUNDAY OF EASTER　Ⓒ

READING I　　　　　　　　　Acts 5, 12-16

A reading from the Acts of the Apostles

The numbers of men and women who came to believe in the Lord increased steadily.

Through the hands of the apostles, many signs and wonders occurred among the people. By mutual agreement they used to meet in Solomon's Portico. No one else dared to join them, despite the fact that the people held them in great esteem. Nevertheless more and more believers, men and women in great numbers, were continually added to the Lord. The people carried the sick into the streets and laid them on cots and mattresses, so that when Peter passed by at least his shadow might fall on one or another of them. Crowds from the towns around Jerusalem would gather, too, bringing their sick and those who were troubled by unclean spirits, all of whom were cured.

This is the Word of the Lord.

Responsorial Psalm　　Ps 118, 2-4. 13-15. 22-24

℟. (1) Give thanks to the Lord for he is good,
　　his love is everlasting.
Let the house of Israel say,
　　"His mercy endures forever."
Let the house of Aaron say,
　　"His mercy endures forever."
Let those who fear the Lord say,
　　"His mercy endures forever."
℟. Give thanks to the Lord for he is good,
　　his love is everlasting.
I was hard pressed and was falling,
　　but the Lord helped me.
My strength and my courage is the Lord,
　　and he has been my savior.

The joyful shout of victory
in the tents of the just:
℟. Give thanks to the Lord for he is good,
his love is everlasting.
The stone which the builders rejected
has become the cornerstone.
By the Lord has this been done;
it is wonderful in our eyes.
This is the day the Lord has made;
let us be glad and rejoice in it.
℟. Give thanks to the Lord for he is good,
his love is everlasting.
℟. Or: Alleluia.

READING II   Rv 1, 9-11. 12-13. 17-19

A reading from the book of Revelation
I was dead and now I am to live for ever and ever.

I, John, your brother, who share with you the distress and the kingly reign and the endurance we have in Jesus, found myself on the island called Patmos because I proclaimed God's word and bore witness to Jesus. On the Lord's day I was caught up in ecstasy, and I heard behind me a piercing voice like the sound of a trumpet, which said, "Write on a scroll what you now see." I turned around to see whose voice it was that spoke to me. When I did so I saw seven lampstands of gold, and among the lampstands One like a Son of Man wearing an ankle-length robe, with a sash of gold about his breast.

When I caught sight of him I fell down at his feet as though dead. He touched me with his right hand and said: "There is nothing to fear. I am the First and the Last and the One who lives. Once I was dead but now I live—forever and ever. I hold the keys of death and the nether world. Write down, therefore, whatever you see in visions—what you see now and will see in time to come."

This is the Word of the Lord.

GOSPEL   Jn 20, 19-31
Alleluia   Jn 20, 29

℟. Alleluia. You believe in me, Thomas, because you have seen me;
happy those who have not seen me, but still believe! ℟. Alleluia.

✠ A reading from the holy gospel according to John
After eight days Jesus came in and stood among them.

On the evening of that first day of the week, even though the disciples had locked the doors of the place where they were for fear of the Jews, Jesus came and stood before them. "Peace be with you," he said. When he had said this, he showed them his hands and his side. At the sight of the Lord the disciples rejoiced. "Peace be with you," he said again.
"As the Father has sent me,
so I send you."
Then he breathed on them and said:
"Receive the Holy Spirit.
If you forgive men's sins,
they are forgiven them;
if you hold them bound,
they are held bound."

It happened that one of the Twelve, Thomas (the name means "Twin"), was absent when Jesus came. The other disciples kept telling him: "We have seen the Lord!" His answer was, "I'll never believe it without probing the nail-prints in his hands, without putting my finger in the nail-marks and my hand into his side."

A week later, the disciples were once more in the room, and this time Thomas was with them. Despite the locked doors, Jesus came and stood before them. "Peace be with you," he said; then, to Thomas: "Take your finger and examine my hands. Put your hand into my side. Do not persist in your unbelief, but believe!" Thomas said in response, "My Lord and my God!" Jesus then said to him:
"You became a believer because you saw me.
Blest are they who have not seen and have believed."

Jesus performed many other signs as well—signs not recorded here—in the presence of his disciples. But these have been recorded to help you believe that Jesus is the Messiah, the Son of God, so that through this faith you may have life in his name.

This is the gospel of the Lord.

47   THIRD SUNDAY OF EASTER   A

READING I   Acts 2, 14. 22-28

A reading from the Acts of the Apostles

It was impossible for him to be held by the power of Hades.

[On the day of Pentecost] Peter stood up with the Eleven, raised his voice, and addressed them: "You who are Jews, indeed all of you staying in Jerusalem! Listen to what I have to say: Men of Israel, listen to me! Jesus the Nazorean was a man whom God sent to you with miracles, wonders and signs as his credentials. These God worked through him in your midst, as you well know. He was delivered up by the set purpose and plan of God; you even used pagans to crucify and kill him. God freed him from death's bitter pangs, however, and raised him up again, for it was impossible that death should keep its hold on him. David says of him:
'I have set the Lord ever before me,
    with him at my right hand I shall not be disturbed.
My heart has been glad and my tongue has rejoiced,
    my body will live on in hope,
For you will not abandon my soul to the nether world,
    nor will you suffer your faithful one to undergo corruption.
You have shown me the paths of life;
    you will fill me with joy in your presence.' "
    This is the Word of the Lord.

Responsorial Psalm   Ps 16, 1-2. 5. 7-8. 9-10. 11

℟. (11) Lord, you will show us the path of life.
Keep me, O God, for in you I take refuge;
    I say to the Lord, "My Lord are you."
O Lord, my allotted portion and my cup,
    you it is who hold fast my lot.
℟. Lord, you will show us the path of life.
I bless the Lord who counsels me;
    even in the night my heart exhorts me.
I set the Lord ever before me;
    with him at my right hand I shall not be disturbed.
℟. Lord, you will show us the path of life.

Therefore my heart is glad and my soul rejoices,
    my body, too, abides in confidence;
Because you will not abandon my soul to the nether world,
    nor will you suffer your faithful one to undergo corruption.
℟. Lord, you will show us the path of life.
You will show me the path to life,
    fullness of joys in your presence,
    the delights at your right hand forever.
℟. Lord, you will show us the path of life.
℟. Or: Alleluia.

READING II   1 Pt 1, 17-21

A reading from the first letter of Peter

The ransom that was paid to free you was the blood of the Lamb, Jesus Christ.

In prayer you call upon a Father who judges each one justly, on the basis of his actions. Since this is so, conduct yourselves reverently during your sojourn in a strange land. Realize that you were delivered from the futile way of life your fathers handed on to you, not by any diminishable sum of silver or gold but by Christ's blood beyond all price: the blood of a spotless, unblemished lamb chosen before the world's foundation and revealed for your sake in these last days. It is through him you are believers in God, the God who raised him from the dead and gave him glory. Your faith and hope, then, are centered in God.
    This is the Word of the Lord.

GOSPEL   Lk 24, 13-35
Alleluia   See Lk 24, 32

℟. Alleluia. **Lord Jesus, make your word plain to us,**
make our hearts burn with love when you speak. ℟. Alleluia.

✠ **A reading from the holy gospel according to Luke**

They had recognized him at the breaking of the bread.

Two disciples of Jesus that same day [the first day of the sabbath] were making their way to a village named Emmaus seven miles distant from Jerusalem, discussing as they went all that had happened. In the course of their lively exchange, Jesus approached and began to walk along with them. However, they were restrained from recognizing him. He said to them, "What are you discussing as you go your way?" They halted in distress, and one of them, Cleopas by name, asked him, "Are you the only resident of Jerusalem who does not know the things that went on there these past few days?" He said to them, "What things?" They said: "All those that had to do with Jesus of Nazareth, a prophet powerful in word and deed in the eyes of God and all the people; how our chief priests and leaders delivered him up to be condemned to death, and crucified him. We were hoping that he was the one who would set Israel free. Besides all this, today, the third day since these things happened, some women of our group have just brought us some astonishing news. They were at the tomb before dawn and failed to find his body, but returned with the tale that they had seen a vision of angels who declared he was alive. Some of our number went to the tomb and found it to be just as the women said; but him they did not see."

Then he said to them, "What little sense you have! How slow you are to believe all that the prophets have announced! Did not the Messiah have to undergo all this so as to enter into his glory?" Beginning, then, with Moses and all the prophets, he interpreted for them every passage of Scripture which referred to him. By now they were near the village to which they were going, and he acted as if he were going farther. But they pressed him: "Stay with us. It is nearly evening—the day is practically over." So he went in to stay with them.

When he had seated himself with them to eat, he took bread, pronounced the blessing, then broke the bread and began to distribute it to them. With that their eyes were opened and they recognized him; whereupon he vanished from their sight. They said to one another, "Were not our hearts burning inside us as he talked to us on the road and explained the Scriptures to us?" They got up immediately

and returned to Jerusalem, where they found the Eleven and the rest of the company assembled. They were greeted with, "The Lord has been raised! It is true! He has appeared to Simon." Then they recounted what had happened on the road and how they had come to know him in the breaking of bread.

This is the gospel of the Lord.

48   THIRD SUNDAY OF EASTER   B

READING I   Acts 3, 13-15. 17-19

A reading from the Acts of the Apostles

You have killed the prince of life; God, however, raised him from the dead.

Peter said to the people: "The 'God of Abraham, of Isaac, and of Jacob, the God of our fathers,' has glorified his Servant Jesus, whom you handed over and disowned in Pilate's presence when Pilate was ready to release him. You disowned the Holy and Just One and preferred instead to be granted the release of a murderer. You put to death the Author of life. But God raised him from the dead, and we are his witnesses.

"Yet I know, my brothers, that you acted out of ignorance, just as your leaders did. God has brought to fulfillment by this means what he announced long ago through all the prophets: that his Messiah would suffer. Therefore, reform your lives! Turn to God, that your sins may be wiped away!"

This is the Word of the Lord.

Responsorial Psalm   Ps 4, 2. 4. 7-8. 9

℟. (7) Lord, let your face shine on us.
When I call, answer me, O my just God,
    you who relieve me when I am in distress;
    Have pity on me, and hear my prayer!
℟. Lord, let your face shine on us.
Know that the Lord does wonders for his faithful one;
    the Lord will hear me when I call upon him.
℟. Lord, let your face shine on us.
O Lord, let the light of your countenance shine upon us!
    You put gladness into my heart.
℟. Lord, let your face shine on us.

As soon as I lie down, I fall peacefully asleep,
for you alone, O Lord,
bring security to my dwelling.
℟. Lord, let your face shine on us.
℟. Or: Alleluia.

READING II   1 Jn 2, 1-5

A reading from the first letter of John

Jesus Christ is the sacrifice that takes away our sins, and
those of the whole world.

My little ones,
I am writing this to keep you from sin.
But if anyone should sin,
we have, in the presence of the Father,
Jesus Christ, an intercessor who is just.
He is an offering for our sins,
and not for our sins only,
but for those of the whole world.
The way we can be sure of our knowledge of
him
is to keep his commandments.
The man who claims, "I have known him,"
without keeping his commandments,
is a liar; in such a one there is no truth.
But whoever keeps his word
truly has the love of God made perfect in
him.
This is the Word of the Lord.

GOSPEL   Lk 24, 35-48

Alleluia   See Lk 24, 32

℟. Alleluia. **Lord Jesus, make your word plain
to us,**
make our hearts burn with love when you
speak. ℟. Alleluia.

✠ A reading from the holy gospel according
to Luke

It was written that the Christ would suffer and on the third
day rise from the dead.

The disciples recounted what had happened on
the road to Emmaus and how they had come to
know Jesus in the breaking of bread.

While they were still speaking about all this,
he himself stood in their midst [and said to
them, "Peace to you."] In their panic and fright
they thought they were seeing a ghost. He said
to them, "Why are you disturbed? Why do such

ideas cross your mind? Look at my hands and
my feet; it is really I. Touch me, and see that a
ghost does not have flesh and bones as I do."
[As he said this he showed them his hands and
feet.] They were still incredulous for sheer joy
and wonder, so he said to them, "Have you
anything here to eat?" They gave him a piece
of cooked fish, which he took and ate in their
presence. Then he said to them, "Recall those
words I spoke to you when I was still with
you: everything written about me in the law of
Moses and the prophets and psalms had to be
fulfilled." Then he opened their minds to the
understanding of the Scriptures.

He said to them: "Thus it is likewise written
that the Messiah must suffer and rise from the
dead on the third day. In his name, penance
for the remission of sins is to be preached to
all the nations, beginning at Jerusalem. You
are witnesses of this."

This is the gospel of the Lord.

---

49   THIRD SUNDAY OF EASTER   C

READING I   Acts 5, 27-32. 40-41

A reading from the Acts of the Apostles

We are witnesses to all this, we and the Holy Spirit whom
God has given to those who obey him.

The high priest began the interrogation of the
apostles in this way: "We gave you strict
orders not to teach about that name, yet you
have filled Jerusalem with your teaching and
are determined to make us responsible for that
man's blood." To this, Peter and the apostles
replied: "Better for us to obey God than men!
The God of our fathers has raised up Jesus
whom you put to death, 'hanging him on a
tree.' He whom God has exalted at his right
hand as ruler and savior is to bring repentance to Israel and forgiveness of sins. We
testify to this. So too does the Holy Spirit,
whom God has given to those that obey him."
The Sanhedrin ordered the apostles not to
speak again about the name of Jesus, and
afterward dismissed them. The apostles for
their part left the Sanhedrin full of joy that

they had been judged worthy of ill-treatment
for the sake of the Name.

This is the Word of the Lord.

Responsorial Psalm   Ps 30, 2. 4. 5-6. 11-12. 13

R̸. (2) I will praise you, Lord,
   for you have rescued me.

I will extol you, O Lord, for you drew me clear
   and did not let my enemies rejoice over me.

O Lord, you brought me up from the nether
      world;
   you preserved me from among those going
      down into the pit.

R̸. I will praise you, Lord,
   for you have rescued me.

Sing praise to the Lord, you his faithful ones,
   and give thanks to his holy name.

For his anger lasts but a moment;
   a lifetime, his good will.

At nightfall, weeping enters in,
   but with the dawn, rejoicing.

R̸. I will praise you, Lord,
   for you have rescued me.

Hear, O Lord, and have pity on me;
   O Lord, be my helper.

You changed my mourning into dancing;
   O Lord, my God, forever will I give you
      thanks.

R̸. I will praise you, Lord,
   for you have rescued me.

R̸. Or: Alleluia.

READING II   Rv 5, 11-14

A reading from the book of Revelation

The Lamb that was sacrificed is worthy to be given power,
wealth, glory, and blessing.

I, John, had a vision, and I heard the voices of
many angels who surrounded the throne and
the living creatures and the elders. They were
countless in number, thousands and tens of
thousands, and they all cried out:
"Worthy is the Lamb that was slain
   to receive power and riches, wisdom and
      strength,
   honor and glory and praise!"
Then I heard the voices of every creature in
heaven and on earth and under the earth and

in the sea; everything in the universe cried
aloud:
"To the One seated on the throne, and to the
      Lamb,
   be praise and honor, glory and might,
   forever and ever!"
The four living creatures answered,
"Amen," and the elders fell down and worshiped.

This is the Word of the Lord.

GOSPEL   Jn 21, 1-19 or 21, 1-14
Alleluia

As above no. 47

✠ **A reading from the holy gospel according
to John**

Jesus stepped forward, took the bread and gave it to
them, and did the same with the fish.

(Long Form)

At the Sea of Tiberias Jesus showed himself
to the disciples [once again]. This is how the
appearance took place. Assembled were Simon
Peter, Thomas ("the Twin"), Nathanael (from
Cana in Galilee), Zebedee's sons, and two other
disciples. Simon Peter said to them, "I'm going
out to fish." "We'll join you," they replied, and
went off to get into their boat. All through the
night they caught nothing. Just after daybreak
Jesus was standing on the shore, though none
of the disciples knew it was Jesus. He said to
them, "Children, have you caught anything to
eat?" "Not a thing," they answered. "Cast your
net off to the starboard side," he suggested,
"and you will find something." So they made a
cast, and took so many fish they could not haul
the net in. Then the disciple Jesus loved cried
out to Peter, "It is the Lord!" On hearing it
was the Lord, Simon Peter threw on some
clothes—he was stripped—and jumped into
the water.

Meanwhile the other disciples came in the
boat, towing the net full of fish. Actually they
were not far from land—no more than a hundred yards.

When they landed, they saw a charcoal fire
there with a fish laid on it and some bread.

"Bring some of the fish you just caught," Jesus told them. Simon Peter went aboard and hauled ashore the net loaded with sizable fish —one hundred fifty-three of them! In spite of the great number, the net was not torn.

"Come and eat your meal," Jesus told them. Not one of the disciples presumed to inquire "Who are you?" for they knew it was the Lord. Jesus came over, took the bread and gave it to them, and did the same with the fish. This marked the third time that Jesus appeared to the disciples after being raised from the dead.

When they had eaten their meal, Jesus said to Simon Peter, "Simon, son of John, do you love me more than these?" "Yes, Lord," Peter said, "you know that I love you." At which Jesus said, "Feed my lambs."

A second time he put his question, "Simon, son of John, do you love me?" "Yes, Lord," Peter said, "you know that I love you." Jesus replied, "Tend my sheep."

A third time Jesus asked him, "Simon, son of John, do you love me?" Peter was hurt because he had asked a third time, "Do you love me?" So he said to him: "Lord, you know everything. You know well that I love you." Jesus told him, "Feed my sheep.

"I tell you solemnly:
as a young man
you fastened your belt
and went about as you pleased;
but when you are older
you will stretch out your hands,
and another will tie you fast
and carry you off against your will."

(What he said indicated the sort of death by which Peter was to glorify God.) When Jesus had finished speaking he said to him, "Follow me."

This is the gospel of the Lord.

OR
(Short Form)

At the Sea of Tiberias Jesus showed himself to the disciples once again. This is how the appearance took place. Assembled were Simon Peter, Thomas ("the Twin"), Nathanael (from Cana in Galilee), Zebedee's sons, and two other

disciples. Simon Peter said to them, "I'm going out to fish." "We'll join you," they replied, and went off to get into their boat. All through the night they caught nothing. Just after daybreak Jesus was standing on the shore, though none of the disciples knew it was Jesus. He said to them, "Children, have you caught anything to eat?" "Not a thing," they answered. "Cast your net off to the starboard side," he suggested, "and you will find something." So they made a cast, and took so many fish they could not haul the net in. Then the disciple Jesus loved cried out to Peter, "It is the Lord!" On hearing it was the Lord, Simon Peter threw on some clothes—he was stripped—and jumped into the water.

Meanwhile the other disciples came in the boat, towing the net full of fish. Actually they were not far from land—no more than a hundred yards.

When they landed, they saw a charcoal fire there with a fish laid on it and some bread. "Bring some of the fish you just caught, "Jesus told them. Simon Peter went aboard and hauled ashore the net loaded with sizable fish —one hundred fifty-three of them! In spite of the great number, the net was not torn.

"Come and eat your meal," Jesus told them. Not one of the disciples presumed to inquire "Who are you?" for they knew it was the Lord. Jesus came over, took the bread and gave it to them, and did the same with the fish. This marked the third time that Jesus appeared to the disciples after being raised from the dead.

This is the gospel of the Lord.

50 FOURTH SUNDAY OF EASTER A

READING I Acts 2, 14. 36-41

A reading from the Acts of the Apostles

God has made Jesus both Lord and Christ.

[On the day of Pentecost] Peter stood up with the Eleven, raised his voice, and addressed them: "Let the whole house of Israel know beyond any doubt that God has made both Lord and Messiah this Jesus whom you crucified." When they heard this, they were deeply shaken. They asked Peter and the other apostles, "What are we to do, brothers?" Peter answered: "You must reform and be baptized, each one of you, in the name of Jesus Christ, that your sins may be forgiven; then you will receive the gift of the Holy Spirit. It was to you and your children that the promise was made, and to all those still far off whom the Lord our God calls."

In support of his testimony he used many other arguments, and kept urging, "Save yourselves from this generation which has gone astray." Those who accepted his message were baptized; some three thousand were added that day.

This is the Word of the Lord.

Responsorial Psalm   Ps 23, 1-3. 3-4. 5. 6

℞. (1) The Lord is my shepherd;
  there is nothing I shall want.

**The Lord is my shepherd; I shall not want.
  In verdant pastures he gives me repose;
Beside restful waters he leads me;
  he refreshes my soul.**

℞. The Lord is my shepherd;
  there is nothing I shall want.

**He guides me in right paths
  for his name's sake.
Even though I walk in the dark valley
  I fear no evil; for you are at my side
With your rod and your staff
  that give me courage.**

℞. The Lord is my shepherd;
  there is nothing I shall want.

**You spread the table before me
  in the sight of my foes;
You anoint my head with oil;
  my cup overflows.**

℞. The Lord is my shepherd;
  there is nothing I shall want.

**Only goodness and kindness follow me
  all the days of my life;
And I shall dwell in the house of the Lord
  for years to come.**

℞. The Lord is my shepherd;
  there is nothing I shall want.

℞. Or: Alleluia.

READING II   1 Pt 2, 20-25

A reading from the first letter of Peter

You had gone astray but now you have come back to the shepherd and guardian of your souls.

If you put up with suffering for doing what is right, this is acceptable in God's eyes. It was for this you were called, since Christ suffered for you in just this way and left you an example, to have you follow in his footsteps. He did no wrong; no deceit was found in his mouth. When he was insulted he returned no insult. When he was made to suffer, he did not counter with threats. Instead, he delivered himself up to the One who judges justly. In his own body he brought your sins to the cross, so that all of us, dead to sin, could live in accord with God's will. By his wounds you were healed. At one time you were straying like sheep, but now you have returned to the shepherd, the guardian of your souls.

This is the Word of the Lord.

GOSPEL   Jn 10, 1-10

Alleluia Jn 10, 14

℞. Alleluia. **I am the good shepherd, says the Lord;
I know my sheep, and mine know me.** ℞. Alleluia.

✠ **A reading from the holy gospel according to John**

I am the gate of the sheepfold.

Jesus said:
  "Truly I assure you:
  **Whoever does not enter the sheepfold
    through the gate
  but climbs in some other way
  is a thief and a marauder.
  The one who enters through the gate
  is shepherd of the sheep;
  the keeper opens the gate for him.
  The sheep hear his voice
  as he calls his own by name
  and leads them out.
  When he has brought out [all] those that
    are his,
  he walks in front of them,**

and the sheep follow him
because they recognize his voice.
They will not follow a stranger;
such a one they will flee,
because they do not recognize a stranger's
voice."
Even though Jesus used this figure with them,
they did not grasp what he was trying to tell
them. He therefore said [to them again]:
"My solemn word is this:
I am the sheepgate.
All who came before me
were thieves and marauders
whom the sheep did not heed.

"I am the gate.
Whoever enters through me
will be safe.
He will go in and out,
and find pasture.
The thief comes
only to steal and slaughter and destroy.
I came
that they might have life
and have it to the full."
   This is the gospel of the Lord.

---

51   FOURTH SUNDAY OF EASTER   B

READING I   Acts 4, 8-12

   A reading from the Acts of the Apostles
   This is the only name by which we can be saved.

Peter, filled with the Holy Spirit, spoke up:
"Leaders of the people! Elders! If we must
answer today for a good deed done to a cripple
and explain how he was restored to health,
then you and all the people of Israel must realize that it was done in the name of Jesus
Christ the Nazorean whom you crucified and
whom God raised from the dead. In the power
of that name this man stands before you perfectly sound. This Jesus is 'the stone rejected
by you the builders which has become the
cornerstone.' There is no salvation in anyone
else, for there is no other name in the whole
world given to men by which we are to be
saved."
   This is the Word of the Lord.

Responsorial Psalm   Ps 118, 1. 8-9. 21-23. 26. 21. 29

℟. (22) The stone rejected by the builders has
   become the cornerstone.
Give thanks to the Lord, for he is good,
   for his mercy endures forever.
It is better to take refuge in the Lord
   than to trust in man.
It is better to take refuge in the Lord
   than to trust in princes.
℟. The stone rejected by the builders has become the cornerstone.
I will give thanks to you, for you have answered me
   and have been my savior.
The stone which the builders rejected
   has become the cornerstone.
By the Lord has this been done;
   it is wonderful in our eyes.
℟. The stone rejected by the builders has become the cornerstone.
Blessed is he who comes in the name of the
   Lord;
   we bless you from the house of the Lord.
I will give thanks to you, for you have answered me
   and have been my savior.
Give thanks to the Lord, for he is good;
   for his kindness endures forever.
℟. The stone rejected by the builders has become the cornerstone.
℟. Or: Alleluia.

READING II   1 Jn 3, 1-2

   A reading from the first letter of John
   We shall see God as he is.

See what love the Father has bestowed on us
   in letting us be called children of God!
Yet that is what we are.
   The reason the world does not recognize us
   is that it never recognized the Son.
Dearly beloved,
   we are God's children now;
   what we shall later be has not yet come to
   light.
We know that when it comes to light
   we shall be like him,
   for we shall see him as he is.
      This is the Word of the Lord.

GOSPEL   Jn 10, 11-18
Alleluia   Jn 10, 14

R̸. Alleluia. **I am the good shepherd, says the Lord;**
I know my sheep, and mine know me.
R̸. Alleluia.

✠ **A reading from the holy Gospel according to John**

The good shepherd lays down his life for his sheep.

Jesus said:
    "I am the good shepherd;
    the good shepherd lays down his life for
        the sheep.
    The hired hand, who is no shepherd
    nor owner of the sheep,
    catches sight of the wolf coming
    and runs away, leaving the sheep
    to be snatched and scattered by the wolf.
    That is because he works for pay;
    he has no concern for the sheep.

    "I am the good shepherd.
    I know my sheep
    and my sheep know me
    in the same way that the Father knows me
    and I know the Father;
    for these sheep I will give my life.
    I have other sheep
    that do not belong to this fold.
    I must lead them, too,
    and they shall hear my voice.
    There shall be one flock then, one shep-
        herd.
    The Father loves me for this:
    that I lay down my life
    to take it up again.
    No one takes it from me;
    I lay it down freely.
    I have power to lay it down,
    and I have power to take it up again.
    This command I received from my
        Father."
        This is the gospel of the Lord.

52   FOURTH SUNDAY OF EASTER   C
READING I   Acts 13, 14. 43-52
A reading from the Acts of the Apostles

Many became believers.

Paul and Barnabas travelled on from Perga and came to Antioch in Pisidia. On the sabbath day they entered the synagogue and sat down. Many Jews and devout Jewish converts became their followers and they spoke to them and urged them to hold fast to the grace of God.

The following sabbath, almost the entire city gathered to hear the word of God. When the Jews saw the crowds, they became very jealous and countered with violent abuse whatever Paul said. Paul and Barnabas spoke out fearlessly, nonetheless: "The word of God has to be declared to you first of all; but since you reject it and thus convict yourselves as unworthy of everlasting life, we now turn to the Gentiles. For thus were we instructed by the Lord: 'I have made you a light to the nations, a means of salvation to the ends of the earth.' " The Gentiles were delighted when they heard this and responded to the word of the Lord with praise. All who were destined for life everlasting believed in it. Thus the word of the Lord was carried throughout that area.

But some of the Jews stirred up their influential women sympathizers and the leading men of the town, and in that way got a persecution started against Paul and Barnabas. The Jews finally expelled them from their territory. So the two shook the dust from their feet in protest and went on to Iconium. Their disciples knew only how to be filled with joy and the Holy Spirit.
        This is the Word of the Lord.

Responsorial Psalm   Ps 100, 1-2. 3. 5

R̸. (3) We are his people:
    the sheep of his flock.
Sing joyfully to the Lord, all you lands;
    serve the Lord with gladness;
    come before him with joyful song.
R̸. We are his people:
    the sheep of his flock.

Know that the Lord is God;
  he made us, his we are;
  his people, the flock he tends.
℞. We are his people:
  the sheep of his flock.
The Lord is good:
  his kindness endures forever,
  and his faithfulness, to all generations.
℞. We are his people:
  the sheep of his flock.
℞. Or: Alleluia.

READING II   Rv 7, 9. 14-17

A reading from the book of Revelation
The Lamb who is at the throne will be their shepherd and
will lead them to springs of living water.

I, John, saw before me a huge crowd which no
one could count from every nation and race,
people and tongue. They stood before the throne
and the Lamb, dressed in long white robes and
holding palm branches in their hands.
   Then one of the elders said to me: "These are
the ones who have survived the great period of
trial; they have washed their robes and made
them white in the blood of the Lamb.
"It was this that brought them before God's
   throne:
   day and night they minister to him in his
      temple;
   he who sits on the throne will give them
      shelter.
Never again shall they know hunger or thirst,
   nor shall the sun or its heat beat down on
      them,
   for the Lamb on the throne will shepherd
      them.
He will lead them to springs of life-giving
   water,
   and God will wipe every tear from their
      eyes."
      This is the Word of the Lord.

GOSPEL   Jn 10, 27-30
Alleluia   Jn 10, 14

℞. Alleluia. **I am the good shepherd, says the
   Lord;**
I know my sheep, and mine know me.
℞. Alleluia.

✠ **A reading from the holy gospel according
               to John**
               I give my sheep eternal life.

Jesus said:
   "My sheep hear my voice.
   I know them,
   and they follow me.
   I give them eternal life,
   and they shall never perish.
   No one shall snatch them out of my hand.
   My Father is greater than all, in what he
      has given me,
   and there is no snatching out of his hand.
   The Father and I are one."
      This is the gospel of the Lord.

---

53   FIFTH SUNDAY OF EASTER   Ⓐ

READING I   Acts 6, 1-7

A reading from the Acts of the Apostles
They elected seven men filled with the Spirit and wisdom.

In those days, as the number of disciples grew,
the ones who spoke Greek complained that
their widows were being neglected in the daily
distribution of food, as compared with the
widows of those who spoke Hebrew. The
Twelve assembled the community of the disciples and said, "It is not right for us to neglect
the word of God in order to wait on the tables.
Look around among your own number,
brothers, for seven men acknowledged to be
deeply spiritual and prudent, and we shall appoint them to this task. This will permit us to
concentrate on prayer and the ministry of the
word." The proposal was unanimously accepted by the community. Following this they
selected Stephen, a man filled with faith and
a Holy Spirit; Philip, Prochorus, Nicanor,
Timon, Parmenas and Nicolaus of Antioch,

who had been a convert to Judaism. They presented these men to the apostles, who first prayed over them and then imposed hands on them.

The word of God continued to spread, while at the same time the number of the disciples in Jerusalem enormously increased. There were many priests among those who embraced the faith.

This is the Word of the Lord.

Responsorial Psalm   Ps 33, 1-2. 4-5. 18-19

℟. (22) Lord, let your mercy be on us,
as we place our trust in you.

Exult, you just, in the Lord;
praise from the upright is fitting.
Give thanks to the Lord on the harp;
with the ten-stringed lyre chant his praises.
℟. Lord, let your mercy be on us,
as we place our trust in you.

Upright is the word of the Lord,
and all his works are trustworthy.
He loves justice and right;
of the kindness of the Lord the earth is full.
℟. Lord, let your mercy be on us,
as we place our trust in you.

See, the eyes of the Lord are upon those who
fear him,
upon those who hope for his kindness,
To deliver them from death
and preserve them in spite of famine.
℟. Lord, let your mercy be on us,
as we place our trust in you.
℟. Or: Alleluia.

READING II   1 Pt 2, 4-9
A reading from the first letter of Peter
You are a chosen race, a royal priesthood.

Come to the Lord, a living stone, rejected by men but approved, nonetheless, and precious in God's eyes. You too are living stones, built as an edifice of spirit, into a holy priesthood, offering spiritual sacrifices acceptable to God through Jesus Christ. For Scripture has it:
"See, I am laying a cornerstone in Zion,
an approved stone, and precious.
He who puts his faith in it shall not be shaken."

The stone is of value for you who have faith.
For those without faith, it is rather,
"A stone which the builders rejected
that became a cornerstone."
It is likewise "an obstacle and a stumbling stone." Those who stumble and fall are the disbelievers in God's word; it belongs to their destiny to do so.

You, however, are "a chosen race, a royal priesthood, a consecrated nation, a people he claims for his own to proclaim the glorious works" of the One who called you from darkness into his marvelous light.

This is the Word of the Lord.

GOSPEL   Jn 14, 1-12
Alleluia Jn 14, 6

℟. Alleluia. I am the way, the truth, and the life, says the Lord;
no one comes to the Father, except through me.
℟. Alleluia.

✠ A reading from the holy gospel according
to John
I am the way, the truth and the life.

Jesus said to his disciples:
"Do not let your hearts be troubled.
Have faith in God
and faith in me.
In my Father's house there are many
dwelling places;
otherwise, how could I have told you
that I was going to prepare a place for
you?
I am indeed going to prepare a place for
you,
and then I shall come back to take you
with me,
that where I am you also may be.
You know the way that leads where I go."
"Lord," said Thomas, "we do not know where you are going. How can we know the way?"
Jesus told him:
"I am the way, and the truth, and the life;
no one comes to the Father but
through me.
If you really knew me, you would know
my Father also.

From this point on you know him; you
have seen him."

"Lord," Philip said to him, "show us the
Father and that will be enough for us."
"Philip," Jesus replied, "after I have been with
you all this time, you still do not know me?
"Whoever has seen me has seen the
Father.

How can you say, 'Show us the Father'?
Do you not believe that I am in the Father
and the Father is in me?
The words I speak are not spoken of
myself;
it is the Father who lives in me accomplishing his works.
Believe me that I am in the Father
and the Father is in me,
or else, believe because of the works I do.
I solemnly assure you,
the man who has faith in me
will do the works I do, and greater far
than these.
Why? Because I go to the Father."
This is the gospel of the Lord.

---

54   FIFTH SUNDAY OF EASTER   B

READING I   Acts 9, 26-31

A reading from the Acts of the Apostles

He explained how the Lord appeared to Saul and spoke to
him on his journey.

When Saul arrived back in Jerusalem he tried
to join the disciples there; but it turned out
that they were all afraid of him. They even
refused to believe that he was a disciple. Then
Barnabas took him in charge and introduced
him to the apostles. He explained to them how
on his journey Saul had seen the Lord, who had
conversed with him, and how Saul had been
speaking out fearlessly in the name of Jesus at
Damascus. Saul stayed on with them, moving
freely about Jerusalem and expressing himself
quite openly in the name of the Lord. He even
addressed the Greek-speaking Jews and debated with them. They for their part responded
by trying to kill him. When the brothers

learned of this, some of them took him down
to Caesarea and sent him off to Tarsus.

Meanwhile throughout all Judea, Galilee and
Samaria the church was at peace. It was being
built up and was making steady progress in the
fear of the Lord; at the same time it enjoyed the
increased consolation of the Holy Spirit.
This is the Word of the Lord.

Responsorial Psalm   Ps 22, 26-27. 28. 30. 31-32

℟. (26) I will praise you, Lord, in the assembly
of your people.
I will fulfill my vows before those who fear
the Lord.
The lowly shall eat their fill;
They who seek the Lord shall praise him:
"May your hearts be ever merry!"
℟. I will praise you, Lord, in the assembly of
your people.
All the ends of the earth
shall remember and turn to the Lord;
All the families of the nations
shall bow down before him.
To him alone shall bow down
all who sleep in the earth;
Before him shall bend
all who go down into the dust.
℟. I will praise you, Lord, in the assembly of
your people.
And to him my soul shall live;
my descendants shall serve him.
Let the coming generation be told of the Lord
that they may proclaim to a people yet to be
born
the justice he has shown.
℟. I will praise you, Lord, in the assembly of
your people.
℟. Or: Alleluia.

READING II   1 Jn 3, 18-24

A reading from the first letter of John

His commandments are these: that we believe and that we
love one another.

Little children,
let us love in deed and in truth
and not merely talk about it.
This is our way of knowing we are committed
to the truth

and are at peace before him
no matter what our consciences may charge
us with;
for God is greater than our hearts
and all is known to him.

Beloved,
if our consciences have nothing to charge us
with,
we can be sure that God is with us
and that we will receive at his hands
whatever we ask.

Why? Because we are keeping his commandments
and doing what is pleasing in his sight.

His commandment is this:
we are to believe in the name of his Son,
Jesus Christ,
and are to love one another as he commanded us.

Those who keep his commandments remain in
him
and he in them.
and this is how we know that he remains in us:
from the Spirit that he gave us.
This is the Word of the Lord.

GOSPEL   Jn 15, 1-8

Alleluia   Jn 15, 4. 5

℟. Alleluia. Live in me and let me live in you,
says the Lord;
my branches bear much fruit. ℟. Alleluia.

✠ A reading from the holy gospel according
to John
He who lives in me, and I in him, bears much fruit.

Jesus said to his disciples:
"I am the true vine
and my Father is the vinegrower.
He prunes away
every barren branch,
but the fruitful ones
he trims clean
to increase their yield.
You are clean already,
thanks to the word I have spoken to you.
Live on in me, as I do in you.
No more than a branch can bear fruit of
itself

apart from the vine,
can you bear fruit
apart from me.
I am the vine, you are the branches.
He who lives in me and I in him,
will produce abundantly,
for apart from me you can do nothing.
A man who does not live in me
is like a withered, rejected branch,
picked up to be thrown in the fire and
burnt.
If you live in me,
and my words stay part of you,
you may ask what you will—
it will be done for you.
My Father has been glorified
in your bearing much fruit
and becoming my disciples."
This is the gospel of the Lord.

---

55   FIFTH SUNDAY OF EASTER   **C**

READING I   Acts 14, 21-27

A reading from the Acts of the Apostles
They assembled the church and gave an account of all
that God had done with them.

After Paul and Barnabas had proclaimed the
good news in Derbe and made numerous disciples, they retraced their steps to Lystra and
Iconium first, then to Antioch. They gave their
disciples reassurances, and encouraged them
to persevere in the faith with this instruction:
"We must undergo many trials if we are to
enter into the reign of God." In each church
they installed elders and, with prayer and fasting, commended them to the Lord in whom
they had put their faith.

Then they passed through Pisidia and came
to Pamphylia. After preaching the message in
Perga, they went down to Attalia. From there
they sailed back to Antioch, where they had
first been commended to the favor of God for
the task they had now completed. On their
arrival, they called the congregation together
and related all that God had helped them accomplish, and how he had opened the door of
faith to the Gentiles.
This is the Word of the Lord.

Responsorial Psalm   Ps 145, 8-9. 10-11. 12-13

℟. (1) I will praise your name for ever, my king
  and my God.
The Lord is gracious and merciful,
  slow to anger and of great kindness.
The Lord is good to all
  and compassionate toward all his works.
℟. I will praise your name for ever, my king
  and my God.
Let all your works give you thanks, O Lord,
  and let your faithful ones bless you.
Let them discourse of the glory of your
  kingdom
  and speak of your might.
℟. I will praise your name for ever, my king
  and my God.
Let them make known to men your might
  and the glorious splendor of your kingdom.
Your kingdom is a kingdom for all ages,
  and your dominion endures through all
  generations.
℟. I will praise your name for ever, my king
  and my God.
℟. Or: Alleluia.

READING II   Rv 21, 1-5

A reading from the book of Revelation
He will wipe away all the tears from their eyes.

I, John, saw new heavens and a new earth.
The former heavens and the former earth
had passed away, and the sea was no longer.
I also saw a new Jerusalem, the holy city,
coming down out of heaven from God, beautiful as a bride prepared to meet her husband.
I heard a loud voice from the throne cry out:
"This is God's dwelling among men. He shall
dwell with them and they shall be his people,
and he shall be their God who is always with
them. He shall wipe every tear from their
eyes, and there shall be no more death or
mourning, crying out or pain, for the former
world has passed away."
  The One who sat on the throne said to me,
"See, I make all things new!"
  This is the Word of the Lord.

GOSPEL   Jn 13, 31-33. 34-35
Alleluia   Jn 13, 34

℟. Alleluia. **I give you a new commandment:
love one another as I have loved you.** ℟.
Alleluia.

✠ A reading from the holy gospel according
  to John
  I give you a new commandment: love one another.

Once Judas had left [the cenacle], Jesus said:
  "Now is the Son of Man glorified
  and God is glorified in him.
  [If God has been glorified in him,]
  God will, in turn, glorify him in himself,
  and will glorify him soon.
  My children, I am not to be with you much
    longer.
  I give you a new commandment:
  Love one another.
  Such as my love has been for you,
  so must your love be for each other.
  This is how all will know you for my dis-
    ciples:
  your love for one another."
    This is the gospel of the Lord.

---

56   SIXTH SUNDAY OF EASTER   🅰

READING I   Acts 8, 5-8. 14-17

A reading from the Acts of the Apostles
They laid hands on them, and they received the Holy Spirit.

Philip went down to the town of Samaria and
there proclaimed the Messiah. Without exception, the crowds that heard Philip and saw
the miracles he performed attended closely to
what he had to say. There were many who had
unclean spirits, which came out shrieking
loudly. Many others were paralytics or cripples, and these were cured. The rejoicing in
that town rose to fever pitch.
  When the apostles in Jerusalem heard that
Samaria had accepted the word of God, they
sent Peter and John to them. The two went
down to these people and prayed that they
might receive the Holy Spirit. It had not as

yet come down upon any of them since they had only been baptized in the name of the Lord Jesus. The pair upon arriving imposed hands on them and they received the Holy Spirit.

This is the Word of the Lord.

Responsorial Psalm   Ps 66, 1-3. 4-5. 6-7. 16. 20

℟. (1) Let all the earth cry out to God with joy.
Shout joyfully to God, all you on earth,
   sing praise to the glory of his name;
   proclaim his glorious praise.
Say to God, "How tremendous are your deeds!
℟. Let all the earth cry out to God with joy.
Let all on earth worship and sing praise to you,
   sing praise to your name!"
Come and see the works of God,
   his tremendous deeds among men.
℟. Let all the earth cry out to God with joy.
He has changed the sea into dry land;
   through the river they passed on foot;
   therefore let us rejoice in him.
He rules by his might forever.
℟. Let all the earth cry out to God with joy.
Hear now, all you who fear God, while I de-
   clare
   what he has done for me.
Blessed be God who refused me not
   my prayer or his kindness!
℟. Let all the earth cry out to God with joy.
℟. Or: Alleluia.

READING II   1 Pt 3, 15-18

A reading from the first letter of Peter

In the body he was put to death, in the spirit he was raised to life.

Venerate the Lord, that is, Christ, in your hearts. Should anyone ask you the reason for this hope of yours be ever ready to reply, but speak gently and respectfully. Keep your con-science clear so that, whenever you are de-famed, those who libel your way of life in Christ may be disappointed. If it should be God's will that you suffer, it is better to do so for good deeds than for evil ones.

This is why Christ died for sins once for all, a just man for the sake of the unjust: so that he could lead you to God. He was put to death

insofar as fleshly existence goes, but was given life in the realm of the spirit.

This is the Word of the Lord.

GOSPEL   Jn 14, 15-21

Alleluia   Jn 14, 23

℟. Alleluia. **If anyone loves me, he will hold to my words,
and my Father will love him, and we will come to him.** ℟. Alleluia.

✠ **A reading from the holy gospel according to John**

I shall ask the Father and he will give you another Advocate.

Jesus said to his disciples:
   "If you love me
   and obey the commands I give you,
   I will ask the Father
   and he will give you another Paraclete—
   to be with you always:
   the Spirit of truth,
   whom the world cannot accept,
   since it neither sees him nor recognizes
      him;
   but you can recognize him
   because he remains with you
   and will be within you.
   I will not leave you orphaned;
   I will come back to you.
   A little while now and the world will see
      me no more;
   but you see me
   as one who has life, and you will have life.
   On that day you will know
   that I am in my Father,
   and you in me, and I in you.
   He who obeys the commandments he has
      from me
   is the man who loves me;
   and he who loves me will be loved by my
      Father.
   I too will love him
   and reveal myself to him."
      This is the gospel of the Lord.

57   SIXTH SUNDAY OF EASTER   **B**

READING I   Acts 10, 25-26. 34-35. 44-48

A reading from the Acts of the Apostles

The Holy Spirit came down on all the listeners.

Peter entered the house of Cornelius who met him, dropped to his knees before Peter and bowed low. Peter said as he helped him to his feet, "Get up! I am only a man myself."

Peter proceeded to address [the relatives and friends of Cornelius] in these words: "I begin to see how true it is that God shows no partiality. Rather, the man of any nation who fears God and acts uprightly is acceptable to him."

Peter had not finished these words when the Holy Spirit descended upon all who were listening to Peter's message. The circumcised believers who had accompanied Peter were surprised that the gift of the Holy Spirit should have been poured out on the Gentiles also, whom they could hear speaking in tongues and glorifying God. Peter put the question at that point: "What can stop these people who have received the Holy Spirit, even as we have, from being baptized with water?" So he gave orders that they be baptized in the name of Jesus Christ. After this was done, they asked him to stay with them for a few days.

This is the Word of the Lord.

Responsorial Psalm   Ps 98, 1. 2-3. 3-4

℟. (2) The Lord has revealed to the nations his saving power.

Sing to the Lord a new song,
  for he has done wondrous deeds;
His right hand has won victory for him,
  his holy arm.

℟. The Lord has revealed to the nations his saving power.

The Lord has made his salvation known:
  in the sight of the nations he has revealed his justice.
He has remembered his kindness and his faithfulness
  toward the house of Israel.

℟. The Lord has revealed to the nations his saving power.

All the ends of the earth have seen
  the salvation by our God.
Sing joyfully to the Lord, all you lands;
  break into song; sing praise.

℟. The Lord has revealed to the nations his saving power.

℟. Or: Alleluia.

READING II   1 Jn 4, 7-10

A reading from the first letter of John

God is love.

Beloved,
  let us love one another
  because love is of God;
  everyone who loves is begotten of God
  and has knowledge of God.
The man without love has known nothing of God,
  for God is love.
God's love was revealed in our midst in this way:
  he sent his only Son to the world
  that we might have life through him.
Love, then, consists in this:
  not that we have loved God,
  but that he has loved us
  and has sent his Son as an offering for our sins.

This is the Word of the Lord.

GOSPEL   Jn 15, 9-17

Alleluia   Jn 14, 23

℟. Alleluia. If anyone loves me, he will hold to my words,
and my Father will love him, and we will come to him. ℟. Alleluia.

✠ A reading from the holy gospel according to John

A man can have no greater love than to lay down his life for his friends.

Jesus said to his disciples:
  "As the Father has loved me,
  so I have loved you.
  Live on in my love.
  You will live in my love
  if you keep my commandments,

even as I have kept my Father's commandments,
and live in his love.
All this I tell you
that my joy may be yours
and your joy may be complete.
This is my commandment:
love one another
as I have loved you.
There is no greater love than this:
to lay down one's life for one's friends.
You are my friends
if you do what I command you.
I no longer speak of you as slaves,
for a slave does not know what his master
   is about.
Instead, I call you friends
since I have made known to you all that I
   heard from my Father.
It was not you who chose me,
it was I who chose you
to go forth and bear fruit.
Your fruit must endure,
so that all you ask the Father in my name
he will give you.
The command I give you is this:
that you love one another."
   This is the gospel of the Lord.

---

58   SIXTH SUNDAY OF EASTER

READING I   Acts 15, 1-2. 22-29

A reading from the Acts of the Apostles

It seemed right to the Holy Spirit and to us not to burden
you beyond what is essential.

Some men came down to Antioch from Judea
and began to teach the brothers: "Unless you
are circumcised according to Mosaic practice,
you cannot be saved." This created dissension
and much controversy between them and Paul
and Barnabas. Finally it was decided that Paul,
Barnabas, and some others should go up to
see the apostles and elders in Jerusalem about
this question.

It was resolved by the apostles and the
elders, in agreement with the whole Jerusalem
church, that representatives be chosen from

among their number and sent to Antioch along
with Paul and Barnabas. Those chosen were
leading men of the community, Judas, known
as Barsabbas, and Silas. They were to deliver
this letter:

"The apostles and the elders, your brothers,
send greetings to the brothers of Gentile origin
in Antioch, Syria and Cilicia. We have heard
that some of our number without any instructions from us have upset you with their discussions and disturbed your peace of mind.
Therefore we have unanimously resolved to
choose representatives and send them to you,
along with our beloved Barnabas and Paul,
who have dedicated themselves to the cause of
our Lord Jesus Christ. Those whom we are
sending you are Judas and Silas, who will convey this message by word of mouth: 'It is the
decision of the Holy Spirit, and ours too, not to
lay on you any burden beyond that which is
strictly necessary, namely, to abstain from
meat sacrificed to idols, from blood, from the
meat of strangled animals, and from illicit
sexual union. You will be well advised to avoid
these things. Farewell.' "
   This is the Word of the Lord.

Responsorial Psalm   Ps 67, 2-3. 5. 6. 8

℟. (4) O God, let all the nations praise you!
May God have pity on us and bless us;
   may he let his face shine upon us.
So may your way be known upon earth;
   among all nations, your salvation.
℟. O God, let all the nations praise you!
May the nations be glad and exult
   because you rule the peoples in equity;
   the nations on the earth you guide.
℟. O God, let all the nations praise you!
May the peoples praise you, O God;
   may all the peoples praise you!
May God bless us,
   and may all the ends of the earth fear him!
℟. O God, let all the nations praise you!
℟. Or: Alleluia.

READING II   Rv 21, 10-14. 22-23

A reading from the book of Revelation

He showed me the holy city coming down out of heaven.

The angel carried me away in spirit to the top of a very high mountain and showed me the holy city Jerusalem coming down out of heaven from God. It gleamed with the splendor of God. The city had the radiance of a precious jewel that sparkled like a diamond. Its wall, massive and high, had twelve gates at which twelve angels were stationed. Twelve names were written on the gates, the names of the twelve tribes of Israel. There were three gates facing east, three north, three south, and three west. The wall of the city had twelve courses of stones as its foundation, on which were written the names of the twelve apostles of the Lamb.

I saw no temple in the city. The Lord, God the Almighty, is its temple—he and the Lamb. The city had no need of sun or moon, for the glory of God gave it light, and its lamp was the Lamb.

This is the Word of the Lord.

GOSPEL   Jn 14, 23-29

Alleluia   Jn 14, 23

R̯. Alleluia. **If anyone loves me, he will hold to my words,**
and my Father will love him, and we will come to him. R̯. Alleluia.

✠ **A reading from the holy gospel according to John**

The Holy Spirit will teach you everything and remind you of all I have said to you.

Jesus said to his disciples:
"Anyone who loves me
will be true to my word,
and my Father will love him;
we will come to him
and make our dwelling place with him
always.
He who does not love me does not keep
my words.
Yet the word you hear is not mine;
it comes from the Father who sent me.

This much have I told you while I was
still with you;
the Paraclete, the Holy Spirit
whom the Father will send in my name,
will instruct you in everything,
and remind you of all that I told you.
'Peace' is my farewell to you,
my peace is my gift to you;
I do not give it to you as the world gives
peace.
Do not be distressed or fearful.
You have heard me say,
'I go away for a while, and I come back
to you.'
If you truly loved me
you would rejoice to have me go to the
Father,
for the Father is greater than I.
I tell you this now, before it takes place,
so that when it takes place you may
believe."
This is the gospel of the Lord.

When the Lord's Ascension is celebrated on the following Sunday, the second reading and gospel given for the Seventh Sunday of Easter (see nos. 60-62) may be read on the Sixth Sunday.

59   **ASCENSION**   **A** **B** **C**

READING I   Acts 1, 1-11

The beginning of the Acts of the Apostles

Why are you standing here looking into the sky? Jesus has been taken into heaven.

In my first account, Theophilus, I dealt with all that Jesus did and taught until the day he was taken up to heaven, having first instructed the apostles he had chosen through the Holy Spirit. In the time after his suffering he showed them in many convincing ways that he was alive, appearing to them over the course of forty days and speaking to them about the reign of God. On one occasion when he met with them, he told them not to leave Jerusalem: "Wait, rather, for the fulfillment of my Father's promise, of which you have heard me speak. John baptized with water, but within a few days you will be baptized with the Holy Spirit."

While they were with him they asked, "Lord, are you going to restore the rule to Israel now?" His answer was: "The exact time it is not yours to know. The Father has reserved that to himself. You will receive power when the Holy Spirit comes down on you; then you are to be my witnesses in Jerusalem, throughout Judea and Samaria, yes, even to the ends of the earth." No sooner had he said this than he was lifted up before their eyes in a cloud which took him from their sight.

They were still gazing up into the heavens when two men dressed in white stood beside them. "Men of Galilee," they said, "why do you stand here looking up at the skies? This Jesus who has been taken from you will return, just as you saw him go up into the heavens."

This is the Word of the Lord.

Responsorial Psalm   Ps 47, 2-3. 6-7. 8-9

℟. (6) God mounts his throne to shouts of joy;
    a blare of trumpets for the Lord.

All you peoples, clap your hands,
    shout to God with cries of gladness,
For the Lord, the Most High, the awesome,
    is the great king over all the earth.

℟. God mounts his throne to shouts of joy;
    a blare of trumpets for the Lord.

God mounts his throne amid shouts of joy;
    the Lord, amid trumpet blasts.
Sing praise to God, sing praise;
    sing praise to our king, sing praise.

℟. God mounts his throne to shouts of joy;
    a blare of trumpets for the Lord.

For king of all the earth is God;
    sing hymns of praise.
God reigns over the nations,
    God sits upon his holy throne.

℟. God mounts his throne to shouts of joy;
    a blare of trumpets for the Lord.

℟. Or: Alleluia.

READING II   Eph 1, 17-23

A reading from the letter of Paul to the Ephesians

He made Jesus to sit at his right hand in heaven.

May the God of our Lord Jesus Christ, the Father of glory, grant you a spirit of wisdom and insight to know him clearly. May he enlighten your innermost vision that you may know the great hope to which he has called you, the wealth of his glorious heritage to be distributed among the members of the church, and the immeasurable scope of his power in us who believe. It is like the strength he showed in raising Christ from the dead and seating him at his right hand in heaven, high above every principality, power, virtue and domination, and every name that can be given in this age or the age to come.

He has put all things under Christ's feet and has made him thus exalted, head of the church, which is his body: the fullness of him who fills the univese in all its parts.

This is the Word of the Lord.

GOSPEL   Mt 28, 16-20

Alleluia   Mt 28, 19. 20

℟. Alleluia. **Go and teach all people my gospel. I am with you always, until the end of the world.** ℟. **Alleluia.**

✠ **The conclusion of the holy gospel according to Matthew**

All authority in heaven and on earth has been given to me.

The eleven disciples made their way to Galilee, to the mountain to which Jesus had summoned them. At the sight of him, those who had entertained doubts fell down in homage. Jesus came forward and addressed them in these words:

"Full authority has been given to me
    both in heaven and on earth;
go, therefore, and make disciples of all
    the nations.
Baptize them in the name
    'of the Father,
    and of the Son,

and of the Holy Spirit.'
Teach them to carry out everything I have
commanded you.
And know that I am with you always,
until the end of the world!"
This is the gospel of the Lord.

B

GOSPEL   Mk 16, 15-20
Alleluia   Mt 28, 19. 20

R̪. Alleluia. **Go and teach all people my gospel.
I am with you always, until the end of the
world.** R̪. Alleluia.

✠ The conclusion of the holy gospel according
to Mark

The Lord Jesus was taken up into heaven and is seated
at the right hand of God.

[Jesus appeared to the Eleven and] said to them:
"Go into the whole world and proclaim the good
news to all creation. The man who believes in it
and accepts baptism will be saved; the man who
refuses to believe in it will be condemned. Signs
like these will accompany those who have professed their faith: they will use my name to expel demons, they will speak entirely new languages, they will be able to handle serpents,
they will be able to drink deadly poison without
harm, and the sick upon whom they lay their
hands will recover." Then, after speaking to
them, the Lord Jesus was taken up into heaven
and took his seat at God's right hand. The Eleven went forth and preached everywhere. The
Lord continued to work with them throughout
and confirm the message through the signs
which accompanied them.
This is the gospel of the Lord.

C

GOSPEL   Lk 24, 46-53
Alleluia   Mt 28, 19. 20

R̪. Alleluia. **Go and teach all people my gospel.
I am with you always, until the end of the
world.** R̪. Alleluia.

✠ The conclusion of the holy gospel according
to Luke

He blessed them, withdrew from them, and was carried up
to heaven.

Jesus said to the Eleven: "Thus it is written that
the Messiah must suffer and rise from the dead
on the third day. In his name, penance for the remission of sins is to be preached to the nations,
beginning at Jerusalem. You are witnesses of
all this. See, I send down upon you the promise
of my Father. Remain here in the city until you
are clothed with power from on high."
He then led them out near Bethany, and with
hands upraised, blessed them. As he blessed,
he left them, and was taken up to heaven.
They fell down to do him reverence, then returned to Jerusalem filled with joy. There they
were to be found in the temple constantly,
speaking the praises of God.
This is the gospel of the Lord.

---

60   SEVENTH SUNDAY OF EASTER   **A**

READING I   Acts 1, 12-14
A reading from the Acts of the Apostles

All of them were joined together in the upper room,
continuously praying.

[After Jesus was taken up into the heavens,]
the apostles returned to Jerusalem from the
mount called Olivet near Jerusalem, a mere
sabbath's journey away. Entering the city, they
went to the upstairs room where they were
staying: Peter and John and James and Andrew; Philip and Thomas, Bartholomew and
Matthew; James son of Alpheus; Simon, the
Zealot party member, and Judas son of James.
Together they devoted themselves to constant
prayer. There were some women in their company and Mary the mother of Jesus, and his
brothers.
This is the Word of the Lord.

Responsorial Psalm   Ps 27, 1. 4. 7-8

R̪. (13) I believe that I shall see the good things
of the Lord in the land of the living.

The Lord is my light and my salvation;
  whom should I fear?
The Lord is my life's refuge;
  of whom should I be afraid?
R̂. I believe that I shall see the good things of
  the Lord in the land of the living.
One thing I ask of the Lord;
  this I seek:
To dwell in the house of the Lord
  all the days of my life,
That I may gaze on the loveliness of the Lord
  and contemplate his temple.
R̂. I believe that I shall see the good things of
  the Lord in the land of the living.
Hear, O Lord, the sound of my call;
  have pity on me, and answer me.
Of you my heart speaks; you my glance seeks.
R̂. I believe that I shall see the good things of
  the Lord in the land of the living.
R̂. Or: Alleluia.

READING II   1 Pt 4, 13-16

A reading from the first letter of Peter

It is a blessing for you when they insult you for bearing
the name of Christ.

Rejoice, insofar as you share Christ's sufferings. When his glory is revealed you will
rejoice exultantly. Happy are you when you
are insulted for the sake of Christ, for then
God's Spirit in its glory has come to rest on
you. See to it that none of you suffers for being
a murderer, a thief, a malefactor, or a destroyer of another's rights. If anyone suffers
for being a Christian, however, he ought not
be ashamed. He should rather glorify God in
virtue of that name.
              This is the Word of the Lord.

GOSPEL   Jn 17, 1-11
Alleluia   Jn 14, 18

R̂. Alleluia. **The Lord said: I will not leave
you orphans.
I will come back to you, and your hearts will
rejoice.** R̂. Alleluia.

✠ **A reading from the holy gospel according
to John**

Jesus raised his eyes to heaven and said: Father, glorify
your Son.

Jesus looked up to heaven and said:
  "Father, the hour has come!
Give glory to your Son
  that your Son may give glory to you,
  inasmuch as you have given him authority
    over all mankind,
  that he may bestow eternal life on those
    you gave him.
(Eternal life is this:
  to know you, the only true God,
  and him whom you have sent, Jesus
    Christ.)
I have given you glory on earth
  by finishing the work you gave me to do.
Do you now, Father, give me glory at your
    side,
  a glory I had with you before the world
    began.
I have made your name known
  to those you gave me out of the world.
These men you gave me were yours;
  they have kept your word.
Now they realize
  that all that you gave me comes from you.
I entrusted to them
  the message you entrusted to me,
  and they received it.
They have known that in truth I came
    from you,
  they have believed it was you who sent
    me.
"For these I pray—
  not for the world
but for these you have given me,
  for they are really yours.
(Just as all that belongs to me is yours,
  so all that belongs to you is mine.)
It is in them that I have been glorified.
I am in the world no more,
  but these are in the world
  as I come to you."
              This is the gospel of the Lord.

61　SEVENTH SUNDAY OF EASTER　B

READING I　　　　　　　　　Acts 1, 15-17. 20-26

A reading from the Acts of the Apostles

We must therefore choose someone who has been with us the whole time, and he can act with us as a witness to his resurrection.

In those days Peter stood up in the midst of the brothers—there must have been a hundred and twenty gathered together. "Brothers," he said, "the saying in Scripture uttered long ago by the Holy Spirit through the mouth of David was destined to be fulfilled in Judas, the one that guided those who arrested Jesus. He was one of our number and he had been given a share in this ministry of ours.

"It is written in the Book of Psalms, 'May another take his office.'

"It is entirely fitting, therefore, that one of those who was of our company while the Lord Jesus moved among us, from the baptism of John until the day he was taken up from us, should be named as witness with us to his resurrection." At that they nominated two, Joseph (called Barsabbas, also known as Justus) and Matthias. Then they prayed: "O Lord, you read the hearts of men. Make known to us which of these two you choose for this apostolic ministry, replacing Judas, who deserted the cause and went the way he was destined to go." They then drew lots between the two men. The choice fell to Matthias, who was added to the eleven apostles.

This is the Word of the Lord.

Responsorial Psalm　　　Ps 103, 1-2. 11-12. 19-20

℟. (19) The Lord has set his throne in heaven.
Bless the Lord, O my soul;
　and all my being, bless his holy name.
Bless the Lord, O my soul,
　and forget not all his benefits.
℟. The Lord has set his throne in heaven.
For as the heavens are high above the earth,
　so surpassing is his kindness toward those
　who fear him.
As far as the east is from the west,
　so far has he put our transgressions from us.

℟. The Lord has set his throne in heaven.
**The Lord has established his throne in heaven,
　and his kingdom rules over all.**
Bless the Lord, all you his angels,
　you mighty in strength, who do his bidding.
℟. The Lord has set his throne in heaven.
℟. Or: Alleluia.

READING II　　　　　　　　　1 Jn 4, 11-16

A reading from the first letter of John

The man who lives in love, lives in God, and God in him.

Beloved,
　if God has loved us so,
　we must have the same love for one another.
No one has ever seen God.
Yet if we love one another
　God dwells in us,
　and his love is brought to perfection in us.
The way we know we remain in him
　and he in us
　is that he has given us of his Spirit.
We have seen for ourselves, and can testify,
　that the Father has sent the Son as savior of
　the world.
When anyone acknowledges that Jesus is the
　Son of God,
　God dwells in him
　and he in God.
We have come to know and to believe
　in the love God has for us.
God is love,
　and he who abides in love
　abides in God,
　and God in him.
　　This is the Word of the Lord.

GOSPEL　　　　　　　　　　Jn 17, 11-19
Alleluia　Jn 14, 18

℟. Alleluia. **The Lord said: I will not leave you
　orphans.**
**I will come back to you, and your hearts shall
　rejoice.** ℟. Alleluia.

✠ A reading from the holy gospel according
to John

Father, may they be one in us!

Jesus looked up to heaven and prayed:
    "O Father most holy,
    protect them with your name which you
        have given me,
    [that they may be one, even as we are
        one.]
    As long as I was with them,
    I guarded them with your name which you
        gave me.
    I kept careful watch,
    and not one of them was lost,
    none but him who was destined to be
        lost—
    in fulfillment of Scripture.
    Now, however, I come to you;
    I say all this while I am still in the world
    that they may share my joy completely.
    I gave them your word,
    and the world has hated them for it;
    they do not belong to the world,
    [any more than I belong to the world.]
    I do not ask you to take them out of the
        world,
    but to guard them from the evil one.
    They are not of the world,
    any more than I am of the world.
    Consecrate them by means of truth—
    'Your word is truth.'
    As you have sent me into the world,
    so I have sent them into the world;
    I consecrate myself for their sakes now,
    that they may be consecrated in truth."

    This is the gospel of the Lord.

---

62   SEVENTH SUNDAY OF EASTER

READING I   Acts 7, 55-60

A reading from the Acts of the Apostles

I can see the heavens thrown open and the Son of Man
standing at the right hand of God.

Stephen, filled with the Holy Spirit, looked to
the sky above and saw the glory of God, and
Jesus standing at God's right hand. "Look!"

he exclaimed, "I see an opening in the sky,
and the Son of Man standing at God's right
hand." The onlookers were shouting aloud,
holding their hands over their ears as they did
so. Then they rushed at him as one man,
dragged him out of the city, and began to stone
him. The witnesses meanwhile were piling
their cloaks at the feet of a young man named
Saul. As Stephen was being stoned he could
be heard praying, "Lord Jesus, receive my
spirit." He fell to his knees and cried out in a
loud voice, "Lord, do not hold this sin against
them." And with that he died.

    This is the Word of the Lord.

Responsorial Psalm   Ps 97, 1-2. 6-7. 9

℟. (1. 9) The Lord is king, the most high over
    all the earth.

The Lord is king; let the earth rejoice;
    let the many isles be glad.
Justice and judgment are the foundation of his
    throne.

℟. The Lord is king, the most high over all the
    earth.

The heavens proclaim his justice,
    and all peoples see his glory.
All gods are prostrate before him.

℟. The Lord is king, the most high over all the
    earth.

You, O Lord, are the Most High over all the
    earth,
    exalted far above all gods.

℟. The Lord is king, the most high over all the
    earth.

℟. Or: Alleluia.

READING II   Rv 22, 12-14. 16-17. 20

A reading from the book of Revelation

Come, Lord Jesus!

I, John, heard a voice saying to me: "Remember, I am coming soon! I bring with me the reward that will be given to each man as his conduct deserves. I am the Alpha and the Omega,
the First and the Last, the Beginning and the
End! Happy are they who wash their robes so
as to have free access to the tree of life and enter the city through its gates!

"It is I, Jesus, who have sent my angel to give you this testimony about the churches. I am the Root and Offspring of David, the Morning Star shining bright."

The Spirit and the Bride say, "Come!" Let him who hears answer, "Come!" Let him who is thirsty come forward; let all who desire it accept the gift of life-giving water.

The One who gives this testimony says, "Yes, I am coming soon!" Amen! Come, Lord Jesus!

This is the Word of the Lord.

GOSPEL   Jn 17, 20-26

Alleluia Jn 14, 18

℟. Alleluia. **The Lord said: I will not leave you orphans.**

I will come back to you, and your hearts shall rejoice. ℟. Alleluia.

✠ A reading from the holy gospel according to John

Father, may they be one in us!

Jesus looked up to heaven and said:
"I do not pray for my disciples alone.
   I pray also for those who will believe in me
      through their word,
   that all may be one
   as you, Father, are in me, and I in you;
   I pray that they may be [one] in us,
   that the world may believe that you sent
      me.
   I have given them the glory you gave me
   that they may be one, as we are one—
   I living in them, you living in me—
   that their unity may be complete.
   So shall the world know that you sent me,
   and that you loved them as you loved me.
Father,
   all those you gave me
   I would have in my company
   where I am,
   to see this glory of mine
   which is your gift to me,
   because of the love you bore me before
      the world began.
Just Father,

the world has not known you,
   but I have known you;
   and these men have known that you sent
      me.
   To them I have revealed your name,
   and I will continue to reveal it
   so that your love for me may live in them,
   and I may live in them."

This is the gospel of the Lord.

---

63   **PENTECOST** Ⓐ Ⓑ Ⓒ
              Vigil

These readings may be used in Masses celebrated on Saturday afternoon, either before or after first Vespers of Pentecost Sunday.

READING I   Gn 11, 1-9

A reading from the book of Genesis

It was named Babel because there the Lord confused the language of the whole earth.

At that time the whole world spoke the same language, using the same words. While men were migrating in the east, they came upon a valley in the land of Shinar and settled there. They said to one another, "Come, let us mold bricks and harden them with fire." They used bricks for stone, and bitumen for mortar. Then they said, "Come, let us build ourselves a city and a tower with its top in the sky, and so make a name for ourselves; otherwise we shall be scattered all over the earth."

The Lord came down to see the city and the tower that the men had built. Then the Lord said: "If now, while they are one people, all speaking the same language, they have started to do this, nothing will later stop them from doing whatever they presume to do. Let us then go down and there confuse their language, so that one will not understand what another says." Thus the Lord scattered them from there all over the earth, and they stopped building the city. That is why it was called Babel, because there the Lord confused the speech of all the world. It was from that place that he scattered them all over the earth.

This is the Word of the Lord.

OR

READING I   Ex 19, 3-8. 16-20

A reading from the book of Exodus

The Lord God appeared before all the people on Mount Sinai.

Moses went up the mountain to God. Then the Lord called to him and said, "Thus shall you say to the house of Jacob; tell the Israelites: You have seen for yourselves how I treated the Egyptians and how I bore you up on eagle wings and brought you here to myself. Therefore, if you hearken to my voice and keep my covenant, you shall be my special possession, dearer to me than all other people, though all the earth is mine. You shall be to me a kingdom of priests, a holy nation. That is what you must tell the Israelites." So Moses went and summoned the elders of the people. When he set before them all that the Lord had ordered him to tell them, the people all answered together, "Everything the Lord has said, we will do."

On the morning of the third day there were peals of thunder and lightning, and a heavy cloud over the mountain, and a very loud trumpet blast, so that all the people in the camp trembled. But Moses led the people out of the camp to meet God, and they stationed themselves at the foot of the mountain. Mount Sinai was all wrapped in smoke, for the Lord came down upon it in fire. The smoke rose from it as though from a furnace, and the whole mountain trembled violently. The trumpet blast grew louder and louder, while Moses was speaking and God answering him with thunder.

When the Lord came down to the top of Mount Sinai, he summoned Moses to the top of the mountain.

This is the Word of the Lord.

OR

READING I   Ez 37, 1-14

A reading from the book of the prophet Ezekiel

Dry bones of Israel, I shall put my spirit in you, and you will live.

The hand of the Lord came upon me, and he led me out in the spirit of the Lord and set me in the center of the plain, which was now filled with bones. He made me walk among them in every direction so that I saw how many they were on the surface of the plain. How dry they were! He asked me: Son of man, can these bones come to life? "Lord God," I answered, "you alone know that." Then he said to me: Prophesy over these bones, and say to them: Dry bones, hear the word of the Lord! Thus says the Lord God to these bones: See! I will bring spirit into you, that you may come to life. I will put sinews upon you, make flesh grow over you, cover you with skin, and put spirit in you so that you may come to life and know that I am the Lord. I prophesied as I had been told, and even as I was prophesying I heard a noise; it was a rattling as the bones came together, bone joining bone. I saw the sinews and the flesh come upon them, and the skin cover them, but there was no spirit in them. Then he said to me: Prophesy to the spirit, prophesy, son of man, and say to the spirit: Thus says the Lord God: From the four winds come, O spirit, and breathe into these slain that they may come to life. I prophesied as he told me, and the spirit came into them; they came alive and stood upright, a vast army. Then he said to me: Son of man, these bones are the whole house of Israel. They have been saying, "Our bones are dried up, our hope is lost, and we are cut off." Therefore, prophesy and say to them: Thus says the Lord God: O my people, I will open your graves and have you rise from them, and bring you back to the land of Israel. Then you shall know that I am the Lord, when I open your graves and have you rise from them, O my people! I will put my spirit in you that you may live, and I will settle you upon your land; thus you shall know that I am the Lord. I have promised, and I will do it, says the Lord.

This is the Word of the Lord.

OR

READING I   Jl 3, 1-5

A reading from the book of the prophet Joel

I will pour out my spirit on all mankind.

Thus says the Lord:
I will pour out
   my spirit upon all mankind.
Your sons and daughters shall prophesy,
   your old men shall dream dreams,
   your young men shall see visions;
Even upon the servants and the handmaids,
   in those days, I will pour out my spirit.
And I will work wonders in the heavens and on
      the earth,
   blood, fire, and columns of smoke;
The sun will be turned to darkness,
   and the moon to blood,
At the coming of the Day of the Lord,
   the great and terrible day.
Then everyone shall be rescued
   who calls on the name of the Lord;
For on Mount Zion there shall be a remnant,
   as the Lord has said,
And in Jerusalem survivors
   whom the Lord shall call.
      This is the Word of the Lord.

Responsorial Psalm   Ps 104, 1-2. 24. 35. 27-28. 29. 30

R̷. (30) Lord, send out your Spirit,
   and renew the face of the earth.
Bless the Lord, O my soul!
   O Lord, my God, you are great indeed!
You are clothed with majesty and glory,
   robed in light as with a cloak.
R̷. Lord, send out your Spirit,
   and renew the face of the earth.
How manifold are your works, O Lord!
   In wisdom you have wrought them all—
   the earth is full of your creatures;
   Bless the Lord, O my soul! Alleluia.
R̷. Lord, send out your Spirit,
   and renew the face of the earth.
Creatures all look to you
   to give them food in due time.
When you give it to them, they gather it;
   when you open your hand, they are filled
   with good things.
R̷. Lord, send out your Spirit,
   and renew the face of the earth.

If you take away their breath, they perish
   and return to their dust.
When you send forth your spirit, they are
      created,
   and you renew the face of the earth.
R̷. Lord, send out your Spirit,
   and renew the face of the earth.
R̷. Or: Alleluia.

READING II   Rom 8, 22-27

A reading from the letter of Paul to the Romans

The Spirit himself pleads for us in a way that could never be put into words.

We know that all creation groans and is in agony even until now. Not only that, but we ourselves, although we have the Spirit as first fruits, groan inwardly while we await the redemption of our bodies. In hope we were saved. But hope is not hope if its object is seen; how is it possible for one to hope for what he sees? And hoping for what we cannot see means awaiting it with patient endurance.

The Spirit too helps us in our weakness, for we do not know how to pray as we ought; but the Spirit himself makes intercession for us with groanings which cannot be expressed in speech. He who searches hearts knows what the Spirit means, for the Spirit intercedes for the saints as God himself wills.
      This is the Word of the Lord.

GOSPEL   Jn 7, 37-39
Alleluia

R̷. Alleluia. **Come, Holy Spirit, fill the hearts of your faithful;**
and kindle in them the fire of your love. R̷. Alleluia.

✠ **A reading from the holy gospel according to John**

From his breast shall flow fountains of living waters.

On the last and greatest day of the festival, Jesus stood up and cried out:
   "If anyone thirsts, let him come to me;
   Let him drink who believes in me.
   Scripture has it:
   'From within him rivers of living water
      shall flow.' "

(Here he was referring to the Spirit, whom those that came to believe in him were to receive. There was, of course, no Spirit as yet, since Jesus had not yet been glorified.)
This is the gospel of the Lord.

---

64   PENTECOST SUNDAY 🅐🅑🅒

READING I   Acts 2, 1-11

A reading from the Acts of the Apostles

They were all filled with the Holy Spirit, and began to speak in different languages.

When the day of Pentecost came it found the brethren gathered in one place. Suddenly from up in the sky there came a noise like a strong, driving wind which was heard all through the house where they were seated. Tongues as of fire appeared which parted and came to rest on each of them. All were filled with the Holy Spirit. They began to express themselves in foreign tongues and make bold proclamation as the Spirit prompted them.

Staying in Jerusalem at the time were devout Jews of every nation under heaven. These heard the sound, and assembled in a large crowd. They were much confused because each one heard these men speaking his own language. The whole occurrence astonished them. They asked in utter amazement, "Are not all of these men who are speaking Galileans? How is it that each of us hears them in his native tongue? We are Parthians, Medes, and Elamites. We live in Mesopotamia, Judea and Cappadocia, Pontus, the province of Asia, Phrygia and Pamphylia, Egypt, and the regions of Libya around Cyrene. There are even visitors from Rome—all Jews, or those who have come over to Judaism; Cretans and Arabs too. Yet each of us hears them speaking in his own tongue about the marvels God has accomplished."
This is the Word of the Lord.

Responsorial Psalm   Ps 104, 1. 24. 29-30. 31. 34

℟. (30) Lord, send out your Spirit,
    and renew the face of the earth.

Bless the Lord, O my soul!
    O Lord, my God, you are great indeed!
How manifold are your works, O Lord!
    the earth is full of your creatures.
℟. Lord, send out your Spirit,
    and renew the face of the earth.
If you take away their breath, they perish
    and return to their dust.
When you send forth your spirit, they are created,
    and you renew the face of the earth.
℟. Lord, send out your Spirit,
    and renew the face of the earth.
May the glory of the Lord endure forever;
    may the Lord be glad in his works!
Pleasing to him be my theme;
    I will be glad in the Lord.
℟. Lord, send out your Spirit,
    and renew the face of the earth.
℟. Or: Alleluia.

READING II   1 Cor 12, 3-7. 12-13

A reading from the first letter of Paul to the Corinthians

In one Spirit we were all baptized, making one body.

No one can say: "Jesus is Lord," except in the Holy Spirit.

There are different gifts but the same Spirit; there are different ministries but the same Lord; there are different works but the same God who accomplishes all of them in every one. To each person the manifestation of the Spirit is given for the common good.

The body is one and has many members, but all the members, many though they are, are one body; and so it is with Christ. It was in one Spirit that all of us, whether Jew or Greek, slave or free, were baptized into one body. All of us have been given to drink of the one Spirit.
This is the Word of the Lord.

Sequence   (Prose text)

Come, Holy Spirit, and from heaven direct on man the rays of your light. Come, Father of the poor; come, giver of God's gifts; come, light of men's hearts.

Kindly Paraclete, in your gracious visits to

man's soul you bring relief and consolation. If it is weary with toil, you bring it ease; in the heat of temptation, your grace cools it; if sorrowful, your words console it.

Light most blessed, shine on the hearts of your faithful—even into their darkest corners; for without your aid man can do nothing good, and everything is sinful.

Wash clean the sinful soul, rain down your grace on the parched soul and heal the injured soul. Soften the hard heart, cherish and warm the ice-cold heart, and give direction to the wayward.

Give your seven holy gifts to your faithful, for their trust is in you. Give them reward for their virtuous acts; give them a death that ensures salvation; give them unending bliss. Amen. Alleluia.

OR
(Poetic text)

Come, Holy Spirit, come!
And from your celestial home
   Shed a ray of light divine!

Come, Father of the poor!
Come, source of all our store!
   Come, within our bosoms shine!

You, of comforters the best;
You, the soul's most welcome guest;
   Sweet refreshment here below;

In our labor, rest most sweet;
Grateful coolness in the heat;
   Solace in the midst of woe.

O most blessed Light divine,
Shine within these hearts of yours,
   And our inmost being fill!

Where you are not, man has naught,
Nothing good in deed or thought,
   Nothing free from taint of ill.

Heal our wounds, our strength renew;
On our dryness pour your dew;
   Wash the stains of guilt away:

Bend the stubborn heart and will;
Melt the frozen, warm the chill;
   Guide the steps that go astray.

On the faithful, who adore
And confess you, evermore
   In your sev'nfold gift descend;

Give them virtue's sure reward;
Give them your salvation, Lord;
   Give them joys that never end. Amen.
      Alleluia.

GOSPEL   Jn 20, 19-23
Alleluia

℟. Alleluia. **Come, Holy Spirit, fill the hearts of your faithful;**
and kindle in them the fire of your love. ℟. Alleluia.

✠ **A reading from the holy gospel according to John**

As the Father sent me, so I send you: Receive the Holy Spirit.

On the evening of that first day of the week, even though the disciples had locked the doors of the place where they were for fear of the Jews, Jesus came and stood before them. "Peace be with you," he said. When he had said this, he showed them his hands and his side. At the sight of the Lord the disciples rejoiced. "Peace be with you," he said again.
      "As the Father has sent me,
      so I send you."
Then he breathed on them and said:
      "Receive the Holy Spirit.
      If you forgive men's sins,
      they are forgiven them;
      if you hold them bound,
      they are held bound."
         This is the gospel of the Lord.

If it is customary or obligatory for the faithful to attend Mass on the Monday or even the Tuesday after Pentecost, the Mass of Pentecost Sunday may be repeated or the Mass of the Holy Spirit used in its place.

SEASON OF THE YEAR

The First Sunday of the Year is the feast of the Baptism of the Lord (see no. 21).

65   SECOND SUNDAY ▲
OF THE YEAR

READING I   Is 49, 3. 5-6

A reading from the book of the prophet Isaiah

I will make you the light of nations so that my salvation may reach to the end of the earth.

The Lord said to me: you are my servant,
    Israel, through whom I show my glory.

Now the Lord has spoken
    who formed me as his servant from the
        womb,
That Jacob may be brought back to him
    and Israel gathered to him;
And I am made glorious in the sight of the
        Lord,
    and my God is now my strength!
It is too little, he says, for you to be my servant,
    to raise up the tribes of Jacob,
    and restore the survivors of Israel;
I will make you a light to the nations,
    that my salvation may reach to the ends of
        the earth.
        This is the Word of the Lord.

Responsorial Psalm   Ps 40, 2. 4. 7-8. 8-9. 10

℟. (8. 9) Here am I, Lord;
    I come to do your will.
I have waited, waited for the Lord,
    and he stooped toward me and heard my cry.
And he put a new song into my mouth,
    a hymn to our God.
℟. Here am I, Lord;
    I come to do your will.
Sacrifice or oblation you wished not,
    but ears open to obedience you gave me.
Holocausts or sin-offerings you sought not;
    then said I, "Behold I come."
℟. Here am I, Lord;
    I come to do your will.
"In the written scroll it is prescribed for me,
    to do your will, O my God, is my delight,
And your law is within my heart!"
℟. Here am I, Lord;

I come to do your will.
I announced your justice in the vast assembly;
    I did not restrain my lips, as you, O Lord,
        know.
℟. Here am I, Lord;
    I come to do your will.

READING II   1 Cor 1, 1-3

**The beginning of the first letter of Paul to the
                    Corinthians**

The grace and peace of God our Father and the Lord Jesus Christ be with you.

Paul, called by God's will to be an apostle of
Christ Jesus, and Sosthenes our brother, send
greetings to the church of God which is in
Corinth; to you who have been consecrated
in Christ Jesus and called to be a holy people,
as to all those who, wherever they may be, call
on the name of our Lord Jesus Christ, their
Lord and ours. Grace and peace from God our
Father and the Lord Jesus Christ.
        This is the Word of the Lord.

GOSPEL   Jn 1, 29-34
Alleluia

See no. 164.

✠ **A reading from the holy gospel according
                    to John**

This is the Lamb of God that takes away the sins of the world.

When John caught sight of Jesus coming toward him, he exclaimed:
    "Look there! The Lamb of God
        who takes away the sin of the world!
It is he of whom I said:
    'After me is to come a man
        who ranks ahead of me,
        because he was before me.'
I confess I did not recognize him, though the
very reason I came baptizing with water was
that he might be revealed to Israel."
    John gave this testimony also:
    "I saw the Spirit descend
        like a dove from the sky,
        and it came to rest on him.
But, as I say, I did not recognize him. The
one who sent me to baptize with water told

me, 'When you see the Spirit descend and rest on someone, it is he who is to baptize with the Holy Spirit.' Now I have seen for myself and have testified, 'This is God's chosen One.' "
This is the gospel of the Lord.

66   SECOND SUNDAY
OF THE YEAR   **B**

READING I   1 Sm 3, 3-10. 19

A reading from the first book of Samuel
Speak, Lord, your servant is listening.

Samuel was sleeping in the temple of the Lord where the ark of God was. The Lord called to Samuel, who answered, "Here I am." He ran to Eli and said, "Here I am. You called me." "I did not call you," Eli said. "Go back to sleep." So he went back to sleep. Again the Lord called Samuel, who rose and went to Eli. "Here I am," he said. "You called me." But he answered, "I did not call you, my son. Go back to sleep." At that time Samuel was not familiar with the Lord, because the Lord had not revealed anything to him as yet. The Lord called Samuel again, for the third time. Getting up and going to Eli, he said, "Here I am. You called me." Then Eli understood that the Lord was calling the youth. So he said to Samuel, "Go to sleep, and if you are called, reply, 'Speak, Lord, for your servant is listening.' " When Samuel went to sleep in his place, the Lord came and revealed his presence, calling out as before, "Samuel, Samuel!" Samuel answered, "Speak, for your servant is listening."

Samuel grew up, and the Lord was with him, not permitting any word of his to be without effect.
This is the Word of the Lord.

Responsorial Psalm   Ps 40, 2. 4. 7-8. 8-9. 10

℟. (8. 9) Here am I, Lord;
I come to do your will.

I have waited, waited for the Lord,
    and he stooped toward me and heard my cry.
And he put a new song into my mouth,
    a hymn to our God.

℟. Here am I, Lord;
I come to do your will.

Sacrifice or oblation you wished not,
    but ears open to obedience you gave me.
Holocausts or sin-offerings you sought not;
    then said I, "Behold I come."

℟. Here am I, Lord;
I come to do your will.

"In the written scroll it is prescribed for me,
    to do your will, O my God, is my delight,
And your law is within my heart!"

℟. Here am I, Lord;
I come to do your will.

I announced your justice in the vast assembly;
    I did not restrain my lips, as you, O Lord, know.

℟. Here am I, Lord;
I come to do your will.

READING II   1 Cor 6, 13-15. 17-20

A reading from the first letter of Paul to the Corinthians
Your bodies are members of the body of Christ.

The body is not for immorality; it is for the Lord, and the Lord is for the body. God, who raised up the Lord, will raise us also by his power.

Do you not see that your bodies are members of Christ? Whoever is joined to the Lord becomes one spirit with him. Shun lewd conduct. Every other sin a man commits is outside his body, but the fornicator sins against his own body. You must know that your body is a temple of the Holy Spirit, who is within—the Spirit you have received from God. You are not your own. You have been purchased, and at what a price! So glorify God in your body.
    This is the Word of the Lord.

GOSPEL   Jn 1, 35-42
Alleluia

See no. 164.

✠ **A reading from the holy gospel according to John**
They saw where Jesus lived and they stayed with him.

John was in Bethany across the Jordan with two of his disciples. As he watched Jesus walk by he said, "Look! There is the Lamb of God!" The

two disciples heard what he said, and followed Jesus. When Jesus turned around and noticed them following him, he asked them, "What are you looking for?" They said to him, "Rabbi (which means Teacher), where do you stay?" "Come and see," he answered. So they went to see where he was lodged, and stayed with him that day. (It was about four in the afternoon.)

One of the two who had followed him after hearing John was Simon Peter's brother Andrew. The first thing he did was seek out his brother Simon and tell him, "We have found the Messiah!" (which means the Anointed). He brought him to Jesus, who looked at him and said, "You are Simon, son of John; your name shall be Cephas (which is rendered Peter)."

This is the gospel of the Lord.

**67   SECOND SUNDAY   C
            OF THE YEAR**

READING I   Is 62, 1-5

A reading from the book of the prophet Isaiah
As the bridegroom rejoices in his bride, so will your God rejoice in you.

For Zion's sake I will not be silent,
    for Jerusalem's sake I will not be quiet,
Until her vindication shines forth like the dawn
    and her victory like a burning torch.

Nations shall behold your vindication,
    and all kings your glory;
You shall be called by a new name
    pronounced by the mouth of the Lord.
You shall be a glorious crown in the hand of the
    Lord,
    a royal diadem held by your God.
No more shall men call you "Forsaken,"
    or your land "Desolate,"
But you shall be called "My Delight,"
    and your land "Espoused."
For the Lord delights in you,
    and makes your land his spouse.
As a young man marries a virgin,
    your Builder shall marry you;
And as a bridegroom rejoices in his bride,
    so shall your God rejoice in you.
        This is the Word of the Lord.

Responsorial Psalm   Ps 96, 1-2. 2-3. 7-8. 9-10

℞. (3) Proclaim his marvelous deeds to all the
    nations.
Sing to the Lord a new song;
    sing to the Lord, all you lands.
Sing to the Lord; bless his name.
℞. Proclaim his marvelous deeds to all the
    nations.
Announce his salvation, day after day.
    Tell his glory among the nations;
Among all peoples, his wondrous deeds.
℞. Proclaim his marvelous deeds to all the
    nations.
Give to the Lord, you families of nations,
    give to the Lord glory and praise;
    give to the Lord the glory due his name!
℞. Proclaim his marvelous deeds to all the
    nations.
Worship the Lord in holy attire.
    Tremble before him, all the earth;
Say among the nations: The Lord is king.
    He governs the peoples with equity.
℞. Proclaim his marvelous deeds to all the
    nations.

READING II   1 Cor 12, 4-11

**A reading from the first letter of Paul to the
                Corinthians**
One and the same Spirit distributes different gifts as he
                chooses.

There are different gifts but the same Spirit; there are different ministries but the same Lord; there are different works but the same God who accomplishes all of them in everyone. To each person the manifestation of the Spirit is given for the common good. To one the Spirit gives wisdom in discourse, to another the power to express knowledge. Through the Spirit one receives faith; by the same Spirit another is given the gift of healing, and still another miraculous powers. Prophecy is given to one; to another power to distinguish one spirit from another. One receives the gift of tongues, another that of interpreting the tongues. But it is one and the same Spirit who produces all these gifts, distributing them to each as he wills.

        This is the Word of the Lord.

GOSPEL　　　　　　　　　Jn 2, 1-12
Alleluia

See no. 164.

✠ A reading from the holy gospel according
　　　　　　to John

The first of the signs given by Jesus was at Cana in Galilee.

There was a wedding at Cana in Galilee, and
the mother of Jesus was there. Jesus and his
disciples had likewise been invited to the celebration. At a certain point the wine ran out,
and Jesus' mother told him, "They have no
more wine." Jesus replied, "Woman, how does
this concern of yours involve me? My hour has
not yet come." His mother instructed those
waiting on table, "Do whatever he tells you."
As prescribed for Jewish ceremonial washings,
there were at hand six stone water jars, each
one holding fifteen to twenty-five gallons. "Fill
those jars with water," Jesus ordered, at which
they filled them to the brim. "Now," he said,
"draw some out and take it to the waiter in
charge." They did as he instructed them. The
waiter in charge tasted the water made wine,
without knowing where it had come from; only
the waiters knew, since they had drawn the
water. Then the waiter in charge called the
groom over and remarked to him: "People usually serve the choice wine first; then when the
guests have been drinking awhile, a lesser vintage. What you have done is keep the choice
wine until now." Jesus performed this first of
his signs at Cana in Galilee. Thus did he reveal his glory, and his disciples believed in him.

　After this he went down to Capernaum,
along with his mother and brothers [and his
disciples] but they stayed there only a few
days.　　　　This is the gospel of the Lord.

68　　　**THIRD SUNDAY**　　　Ⓐ
　　　　　OF THE YEAR

READING I　　　　　　　Is 8, 23—9, 3·

A reading from the book of the prophet Isaiah

In the Galilean country, the people have seen a great light.

First he degraded the land of Zebulun and the
land of Naphtali; but in the end he has glorified

the seaward road, the land west of the Jordan,
the District of the Gentiles.
Anguish has taken wing, dispelled is darkness:
　for there is no gloom where but now there
　　was distress.
The people who walked in darkness
　have seen a great light;
Upon those who dwelt in the land of gloom
　a light has shone.
You have brought them abundant joy
　and great rejoicing,
As they rejoice before you as at the harvest,
　as men make merry when dividing spoils.
For the yoke that burdened them,
　the pole on their shoulder,
And the rod of their taskmaster
　you have smashed, as on the day of Midian.
　　　This is the Word of the Lord.

Responsorial Psalm　　　Ps 27, 1. 4. 13-14

℟. (1) The Lord is my light and my salvation.
The Lord is my light and my salvation;
　whom should I fear?
The Lord is my life's refuge;
　of whom should I be afraid?
℟. The Lord is my light and my salvation.
One thing I ask of the Lord;
　this I seek:
To dwell in the house of the Lord
　all the days of my life,
That I may gaze on the loveliness of the Lord
　and contemplate his temple.
℟. The Lord is my light and my salvation.
I believe that I shall see the bounty of the Lord
　in the land of the living.
Wait for the Lord with courage;
　be stouthearted, and wait for the Lord.
℟. The Lord is my light and my salvation.

READING II　　　　　　1 Cor 1, 10-13. 17

A reading from the first letter of Paul to the
　　　　　　Corinthians

I appeal to you, my brothers, make up the difference
between you.

I beg you; brothers, in the name of our Lord Jesus Christ, to agree in what you say. Let there be no factions; rather, be united in mind and judgment. I have been informed, my brothers, by certain members of Chloe's household that you are quarreling among yourselves. This is what I mean: One of you will say, "I belong to Paul," another, "I belong to Apollos," still another, "Cephas has my allegiance," and the fourth, "I belong to Christ." Has Christ, then, been divided into parts? Was it Paul who was crucified for you? Was it in Paul's name that you were baptized? Christ did not send me to baptize but to preach the gospel—not with wordy "wisdom," however, lest the cross of Christ be rendered void of its meaning!

This is the Word of the Lord.

GOSPEL   Mt 4, 12-23 or 4, 12-17
Alleluia   Mt 4, 23

R̝. Alleluia. **Jesus preached the Good News of the kingdom,**
and healed those who were sick. R̝. Alleluia.

✠ A reading from the holy gospel according
to Matthew

He went to Capernaum, that the prophecy of Isaiah be
fulfilled.

(Long Form)

When Jesus heard that John had been arrested, he withdrew to Galilee. He left Nazareth and went down to live in Capernaum by the sea near the territory of Zebulun and Naphtali, to fulfill what had been said through Isaiah the prophet:

"Land of Zebulun, land of Naphtali
along the sea beyond the Jordan,
heathen Galilee:
a people living in darkness
has seen a great light.
On those who inhabit a land overshadowed by death,
light has arisen."

From that time on Jesus began to proclaim this theme: "Reform your lives! The kingdom of heaven is at hand."

As he was walking along the Sea of Galilee he watched two brothers, Simon now known as Peter, and his brother Andrew, casting a net into the sea. They were fishermen. He said to them, "Come after me and I will make you fishers of men." They immediately abandoned their nets and became his followers. He walked along farther and caught sight of two other brothers, James, Zebedee's son, and his brother John. They too were in their boat, getting their nets in order with their father, Zebedee. He called them, and immediately they abandoned boat and father to follow him.

Jesus toured all of Galilee. He taught in their synagogues, proclaimed the good news of the kingdom, and cured the people of every disease and illness.

This is the gospel of the Lord.

OR

(Short Form)

When Jesus heard that John had been arrested, he withdrew to Galilee. He left Nazareth and went down to live in Capernaum by the sea near the territory of Zebulun and Naphtali, to fulfill what had been said through Isaiah the prophet:

"Land of Zebulun, land of Naphtali
along the sea beyond the Jordan,
heathen Galilee:
a people living in darkness
has seen a great light.
On those who inhabit a land overshadowed by death,
light has arisen."

From that time on Jesus began to proclaim this theme: "Reform your lives! The kingdom of heaven is at hand."

This is the gospel of the Lord.

---

69   **THIRD SUNDAY**   **B**
           OF THE YEAR

READING I   Jon 3, 1-5. 10

A reading from the book of the prophet Jonah

The Ninevites renounced their evil ways.

The word of the Lord came to Jonah saying: "Set out for the great city of Nineveh, and announce to it the message that I will tell you." So Jonah made ready and went to Nineveh.

according to the Lord's bidding. Now Nineveh was an enormously large city; it took three days to go through it. Jonah began his journey through the city, and had gone but a single day's walk announcing, "Forty days more and Nineveh shall be destroyed," when the people of Nineveh believed God; they proclaimed a fast and all of them, great and small, put on sackcloth.

When God saw by their actions how they turned from their evil way, he repented of the evil that he had threatened to do to them; he did not carry it out.

This is the Word of the Lord.

Responsorial Psalm   Ps 25, 4-5. 6-7. 8-9

℟. (4) Teach me your ways, O Lord.

Your ways, O Lord, make known to me;
  teach me your paths,
Guide me in your truth and teach me,
  for you are God my savior.
℟. Teach me your ways, O Lord.

Remember that your compassion, O Lord,
  and your kindness are from of old.
In your kindness remember me,
  because of your goodness, O Lord.
℟. Teach me your ways, O Lord.

Good and upright is the Lord;
  thus he shows sinners the way.
He guides the humble to justice,
  he teaches the humble his way.
℟. Teach me your ways, O Lord.

READING II   1 Cor 7, 29-31

A reading from the first letter of Paul to the Corinthians
The world as we know it is passing away.

I tell you, brothers, the time is short. From now on those with wives should live as though they had none; those who weep should live as though they were not weeping, and those who rejoice as though they were not rejoicing; buyers should conduct themselves as though they owned nothing, and those who make use of the world as though they were not using it, for the world as we know it is passing away.

This is the Word of the Lord.

GOSPEL   Mk 1, 14-20
Alleluia   Mk 1, 15

℟. Alleluia. **The kingdom of God is near: believe the Good News!** ℟. Alleluia.

✠ **A reading from the holy gospel according to Mark**
Repent, and believe the Good News.

After John's arrest, Jesus appeared in Galilee proclaiming God's good news: "This is the time of fulfillment. The reign of God is at hand! Reform your lives and believe in the good news!"

As he made his way along the Sea of Galilee, he observed Simon and his brother Andrew casting their nets into the sea; they were fishermen. Jesus said to them, "Come after me; I will make you fishers of men." They immediately abandoned their nets and became his followers. Proceeding a little farther along, he caught sight of James, Zebedee's son, and his brother John. They too were in their boat putting their nets in order. He summoned them on the spot. They abandoned their father Zebedee, who was in the boat with the hired men, and went off in his company.

This is the gospel of the Lord.

---

70   **THIRD SUNDAY**   **C**
OF THE YEAR

READING I   Neh 8, 2-4. 5-6. 8-10

A reading from the book of Nehemiah
They read from the book of Law and they understood what was read.

Ezra the priest brought the law before the assembly, which consisted of men, women, and those children old enough to understand. Standing at one end of the open place that was before the Water Gate, he read out of the book from daybreak till midday, in the presence of the men, the women, and those children old enough to understand; and all the people listened attentively to the book of the law. Ezra the scribe stood on a wooden platform that had been made for the occasion. Ezra opened the scroll so that all the people might see it (for he was standing higher up than any of the people); and, as he opened it, all the people rose. Ezra blessed the Lord, the great God, and all the people, their hands raised high, answered, "Amen, amen!" Then they bowed down and prostrated themselves before the Lord, their faces to the ground. Ezra read plainly from the book of the law of God, interpreting it so that all could understand what was read. Then [Nehemiah, that is, His Excellency, and] Ezra the priest-scribe [and the Levites who were instructing the people] said to all the people: "Today is holy to the Lord your God. Do not be sad, and do not weep"— for all the people were weeping as they heard the words of the law. He said further: "Go, eat rich foods and drink sweet drinks, and allot portions to those who had nothing prepared; for today is holy to our Lord. Do not be saddened this day, for rejoicing in the Lord must be your strength!"

This is the Word of the Lord.

Responsorial Psalm   Ps 19, 8. 9. 10. 15

℟. (Jn 6, 64) Your words, Lord, are spirit and life.

The law of the Lord is perfect,
  refreshing the soul;
The decree of the Lord is trustworthy,
  giving wisdom to the simple.

℟. Your words, Lord, are spirit and life.

The precepts of the Lord are right,
  rejoicing the heart;
The command of the Lord is clear,
  enlightening the eye.

℟. Your words, Lord, are spirit and life.

The fear of the Lord is pure,
  enduring forever;
The ordinances of the Lord are true,
  all of them just.

℟. Your words, Lord, are spirit and life.

Let the words of my mouth and the thought of
    my heart
  find favor before you,
O Lord, my rock and my redeemer.

℟. Your words, Lord, are spirit and life.

READING II   1 Cor 12, 12-30 or 12, 12-14. 27

A reading from the first letter of Paul to the Corinthians

Together you are Christ's body, but each of you is a different part of it.

(Long Form)

The body is one and has many members, but all the members, many though they are, are one body; and so it is with Christ. It was in one Spirit that all of us, whether Jew or Greek, slave or free, were baptized into one body. All of us have been given to drink of the one Spirit. Now the body is not one member, it is many. If the foot should say, "Because I am not a hand I do not belong to the body," would it then no longer belong to the body? If the ear should say, "Because I am not an eye I do not belong to the body," would it then no longer belong to the body? If the body were all eye, what would happen to our hearing? If it were all ear, what would happen to our smelling? As it is, God has set each member of the body in the place he wanted it to be. If all the members were alike, where would the body be? There are, indeed, many different members, but one body. The eye cannot say to the hand, "I do not need you," any more than the head can say to the feet, "I do not need you." Even those members of the body which seem less important are in fact indispensable. We honor the members we consider less honorable by clothing them with greater care, thus bestowing on the less presentable a propriety which the more presentable already have. God has so constructed the body as to give greater honor to the lowly members, that there may be no dissension in the body, but that all the members may be concerned for one another. If one member suffers, all the members suffer with it; if one member is honored, all the members share its joy.

You, then, are the body of Christ. Every one of you is a member of it. Furthermore, God has set up in the church first apostles, second prophets, third teachers, then miracle workers, healers, assistants, administrators, and those who speak in tongues. Are all apostles? Are all prophets? Are all teachers? Do all work miracles or have the gift of healing? Do all speak in tongues, all have the gift of interpretation of tongues?

This is the Word of the Lord.

OR (Short Form)

The body is one and has many members, but all the members, many though they are, are one body; and so it is with Christ. It was in one Spirit that all of us, whether Jew or Greek, slave or free, were baptized into one body. All of us have been given to drink of the one Spirit. Now the body is not one member, it is many.

You, then, are the body of Christ. Every one of you is a member of it.

This is the Word of the Lord.

GOSPEL　　　　　　　　Lk 1, 1-4; 4, 14-21
Alleluia　　Lk 4, 18-19

℟. Alleluia. **The Lord sent me to bring Good News to the poor,**
and freedom to prisoners. ℟. Alleluia.

✠ The beginning of the holy gospel according to Luke

The scriptures were fulfilled on this day.

Many have undertaken to compile a narrative of the events which have been fulfilled in our midst, precisely as those events were transmitted to us by the original eye-witnesses and ministers of the word. I too have carefully traced the whole sequence of events from the beginning, and have decided to set it in writing for you, Theophilus, so that Your Excellency may see how reliable the instruction was that you received.

Jesus returned in the power of the Spirit to Galilee, and his reputation spread throughout the region. He was teaching in their synagogues, and all were loud in his praise.

He came to Nazareth where he had been reared, and entering the synagogue on the sabbath as he was in the habit of doing, he stood up to do the reading. When the book of the prophet Isaiah was handed him, he unrolled the scroll and found the passage where it was written:

"The spirit of the Lord is upon me;
　therefore he has anointed me.
He has sent me to bring glad tidings to the poor,
　to proclaim liberty to captives,
Recovery of sight to the blind
　and release to prisoners,
To announce a year of favor from the Lord."

Rolling up the scroll he gave it back to the assistant and sat down. All in the synagogue had their eyes fixed on him. Then he began by saying to them, "Today this Scripture passage is fulfilled in your hearing."

This is the gospel of the Lord.

71　　　　**FOURTH SUNDAY**　　　🅰
　　　　　　　OF THE YEAR

READING I　　　　　　Zep 2, 3; 3, 12-13

A reading from the book of the prophet Zephaniah

In your midst I will leave a humble and a lowly people.

Seek the Lord, all you humble of the earth,
　who have observed his law;
Seek justice, seek humility;
　perhaps you may be sheltered
on the day of the Lord's anger.

But I will leave as a remnant in your midst
　a people humble and lowly,
Who shall take refuge in the name of the Lord:
　the remnant of Israel.
They shall do no wrong
　and speak no lies;
Nor shall there be found in their mouths
　a deceitful tongue;
They shall pasture and couch their flocks
　with none to disturb them.

This is the Word of the Lord.

Responsorial Psalm   Ps 146, 6-7. 8-9. 9-10

℟. (Mt 5, 3) Happy the poor in spirit;
    the kingdom of heaven is theirs!
The Lord keeps faith forever,
    secures justice for the oppressed,
    gives food to the hungry.
The Lord sets captives free.

℟. Happy the poor in spirit;
    the kingdom of heaven is theirs!
The Lord gives sight to the blind;
    the Lord raises up those that were bowed
    down.
The Lord loves the just;
    the Lord protects strangers.

℟. Happy the poor in spirit;
    the kingdom of heaven is theirs!
The fatherless and the widow the Lord sus-
    tains,
but the way of the wicked he thwarts.
The Lord shall reign forever;
    your God, O Zion, through all generations.
    Alleluia.

℟. Happy the poor in spirit;
    the kingdom of heaven is theirs!

℟. Or: Alleluia.

READING II   1 Cor 1, 26-31

**A reading from the first letter of Paul to the
Corinthians**

God has chosen what is weak by human reckoning.

Brothers, you are among those called. Consider
your own situation. Not many of you are wise,
as men account wisdom; not many are influential; and surely not many are well-born. God
chose those whom the world considers absurd
to shame the wise he singled out the weak of
this world to shame the strong. He chose the
world's lowborn and despised, those who count
for nothing, to reduce to nothing those who
were something; so that mankind can do no
boasting before God. God it is who has given
you life in Christ Jesus. He has made him our
wisdom and also our justice, our sanctification,
and our redemption. This is just as you find it
written, "Let him who would boast, boast in
the Lord."

This is the Word of the Lord.

GOSPEL   Mt 5, 1-12
Alleluia
See no. 164.

✠ A reading from the holy gospel according
        to Matthew

Happy are the poor in spirit.

When Jesus saw the crowds, he went up on
the mountainside. After he had sat down his
disciples gathered around him, and he began
to teach them:

"How blest are the poor in spirit: the reign
    of God is theirs.
Blest too are the sorrowing; they shall be
    consoled.
[Blest are the lowly; they shall inherit the
    land.]
Blest are they who hunger and thirst for
    holiness; they shall have their fill.
Blest are they who show mercy; mercy
    shall be theirs.
Blest are the single-hearted,
    for they shall see God.
Blest too the peacemakers; they shall be
    called sons of God.
Blest are those persecuted for holiness'
    sake; the reign of God is theirs.
Blest are you when they insult you and
    persecute you and utter every kind of
    slander against you because of me.
Be glad and rejoice, for your reward in
    heaven is great."
    This is the gospel of the Lord.

---

72   **FOURTH SUNDAY**
      OF THE YEAR

READING I   Dt 18, 15-20

A reading from the book of Deuteronomy

I will put my words into the prophet's mouth and he will
tell them all I command.

Moses spoke to the people, saying: "A prophet
like me will the Lord, your God, raise up for
you from among your own kinsmen; to him
you shall listen. This is exactly what you requested of the Lord, your God, at Horeb on the
day of the assembly, when you said, 'Let us not

again hear the voice of the Lord, our God, nor see this great fire any more, lest we die.' And the Lord said to me, 'This was well said. I will raise up for them a prophet like you from among their kinsmen, and will put my words into his mouth; he shall tell them all that I command him. If any man will not listen to my words which he speaks in my name, I myself will make him answer for it. But if a prophet presumes to speak in my name an oracle that I have not commanded him to speak, or speaks in the name of other gods, he shall die.' "

This is the Word of the Lord.

Responsorial Psalm   Ps 95, 1-2. 6-7. 7-9

R℣. (8) If today you hear his voice,
   harden not your hearts.
Come, let us sing joyfully to the Lord;
   let us acclaim the Rock of our salvation.
Let us greet him with thanksgiving;
   let us joyfully sing psalms to him.
R℣. If today you hear his voice,
   harden not your hearts.
Come, let us bow down in worship;
   let us kneel before the Lord who made us.
For he is our God,
   and we are the people he shepherds, the
   flock he guides.
R℣. If today you hear his voice,
   harden not your hearts.
Oh, that today you would hear his voice:
   "Harden not your hearts as at Meribah,
   as in the day of Massah in the desert,
Where your fathers tempted me;
   they tested me though they had seen my
   works.
R℣. If today you hear his voice,
   harden not your hearts.

READING II   1 Cor 7, 32-35

A reading from the first letter of Paul to the Corinthians

The unmarried woman dedicates herself to the things of the Lord, that she might be holy.

I should like you to be free of all worries. The unmarried man is busy with the Lord's affairs, concerned with pleasing the Lord; but the married man is busy with this world's demands and is occupied with pleasing his wife. This means he is divided. The virgin—indeed, any unmarried woman—is concerned with things of the Lord, in pursuit of holiness in body and spirit. The married woman, on the other hand, has the cares of this world to absorb her and is concerned with pleasing her husband. I am going into this with you for your own good. I have no desire to place restrictions on you, but I do want to promote what is good, what will help you to devote yourselves entirely to the Lord.

This is the Word of the Lord.

GOSPEL   Mk 1, 21-28
Alleluia

See no. 164.

✠ **A reading from the holy gospel according to Mark**

This is a new kind of teaching that speaks with authority.

[In the city of Capernaum,] Jesus entered the synagogue on the sabbath and began to teach. The people were spellbound by his teaching because he taught with authority and not like the scribes.

There appeared in their synagogue a man with an unclean spirit that shrieked: "What do you want of us, Jesus of Nazareth? Have you come to destroy us? I know who you are— the Holy One of God!" Jesus rebuked him sharply: "Be quiet! Come out of the man!" At that the unclean spirit convulsed the man violently and with a loud shriek came out of him. All who looked on were amazed. They began to ask one another: "What does this mean? A completely new teaching in a spirit of authority! He gives orders to unclean spirits and they obey him!" From that point on his reputation spread throughout the surrounding region of Galilee.

This is the gospel of the Lord.

73   FOURTH SUNDAY OF THE YEAR **C**

READING I   Jer 1, 4-5. 17-19

A reading from the book of the prophet Jeremiah

I have appointed you as a prophet to the nations.

In the days of Josiah the word of the Lord came to me thus:
Before I formed you in the womb I knew you,
  before you were born I dedicated you,
  a prophet to the nations I appointed you.

But do you gird your loins;
  stand up and tell them
  all that I command you.
Be not crushed on their account,
  as though I would leave you crushed before them;
For it is I this day
  who have made you a fortified city,
A pillar of iron, a wall of brass,
  against the whole land:
Against Judah's kings and princes,
  against its priests and people.
They will fight against you, but not prevail over you,
  for I am with you to deliver you, says the Lord.
          This is the Word of the Lord.

Responsorial Psalm   Ps 71, 1-2. 3-4. 5-6. 15-17

℞. (15) I will sing of your salvation.
In you, O Lord, I take refuge;
  let me never be put to shame.
In your justice rescue me, and deliver me;
  incline your ear to me, and save me.
℞. I will sing of your salvation.
Be my rock of refuge,
  a stronghold to give me safety,
  for you are my rock and my fortress.
O my God, rescue me from the hand of the wicked.
℞. I will sing of your salvation.
For you are my hope, O Lord;
  my trust, O God, from my youth.

On you I depend from birth;
  from my mother's womb you are my strength.
℞. I will sing of your salvation.
My mouth shall declare your justice,
  day by day your salvation.
O God, you have taught me from my youth,
  and till the present I proclaim your wondrous deeds.
℞. I will sing of your salvation.

READING II   1 Cor 12, 31—13, 13 or 13, 4-13

A reading from the first letter of Paul to the Corinthians

There are three things that last: faith, hope and love; and the greatest of these is love.

(Long Form)

Set your hearts on the greater gifts.

Now I will show you the way which surpasses all the others. If I speak with human tongues and angelic as well, but do not have love, I am a noisy gong, a clanging cymbal. If I have the gift of prophecy and, with full knowledge, comprehend all mysteries, if I have faith great enough to move mountains, but have not love, I am nothing. If I give everything I have to feed the poor and hand over my body to be burned, but have not love, I gain nothing.

Love is patient; love is kind. Love is not jealous, it does not put on airs, it is not snobbish. Love is never rude, it is not self-seeking, it is not prone to anger; neither does it brood over injuries. Love does not rejoice in what is wrong but rejoices with the truth. There is no limit to love's forbearance, to its trust, its hope, its power to endure.

Love never fails. Prophecies will cease, tongues will be silent, knowledge will pass away. Our knowledge is imperfect and our prophesying is imperfect. When the perfect comes, the imperfect will pass away. When I was a child I used to talk like a child, think like a child, reason like a child. When I became a man I put childish ways aside. Now we see indistinctly, as in a mirror; then we shall see

face to face. My knowledge is imperfect now; then I shall know even as I am known. There are in the end three things that last: faith, hope, and love, and the greatest of these is love.
This is the Word of the Lord.

OR
(Short Form)

Love is patient; love is kind. Love is not jealous, it does not put on airs, it is not snobbish. Love is never rude, it is not self-seeking, it is not prone to anger; neither does it brood over injuries. Love does not rejoice in what is wrong but rejoices with the truth. There is no limit to love's forbearance, to its trust, its hope, its power to endure.

Love never fails. Prophecies will cease, tongues will be silent, knowledge will pass away. Our knowledge is imperfect and our prophesying is imperfect. When the perfect comes, the imperfect will pass away. When I was a child I used to talk like a child, think like a child, reason like a child. When I became a man I put childish ways aside. Now we see indistinctly, as in a mirror; then we shall see face to face. My knowledge is imperfect now; then I shall know even as I am known. There are in the end three things that last: faith, hope, and love, and the greatest of these is love.
This is the Word of the Lord.

GOSPEL   Lk 4, 21-30
Alleluia

See no. 164.

✠ A reading from the holy gospel according to Luke
Jesus, like Elijah and Elisha, was not sent only to the Jews.

Jesus began speaking in the synagogue: "Today this Scripture passage is fulfilled in your hearing." All who were present spoke favorably of him; they marveled at the appealing discourse which came from his lips. They also asked, "Is not this Joseph's son?"

He said to them, "You will doubtless quote me the proverb, 'Physician, heal yourself,' and say, 'Do here in your own country the things we have heard you have done in Capernaum.' But in fact," he went on, "no prophet gains acceptance in his native place. Indeed, let me remind you, there were many widows in Israel in the days of Elijah when the heavens remained closed for three and a half years and a great famine spread over the land. It was to none of these that Elijah was sent, but to a widow of Zarephath near Sidon. Recall, too, the many lepers in Israel in the time of Elisha the prophet; yet not one was cured except Naaman the Syrian."

At these words the whole audience in the synagogue was filled with indignation. They rose up and expelled him from the town, leading him to the brow of the hill on which it was built, and intending to hurl him over the edge. But he went straight through their midst and walked away.
This is the gospel of the Lord.

---

74   FIFTH SUNDAY   **A**
            OF THE YEAR

READING I   Is 58, 7-10
A reading from the book of the prophet Isaiah
Your light will shine like the dawn.

Thus says the Lord:
Share your bread with the hungry,
    shelter the oppressed and the homeless;
Clothe the naked when you see them,
    and do not turn your back on your own.

Then your light shall break forth like the dawn,
    and your wound shall quickly be healed;
Your vindication shall go before you,
    and the glory of the Lord shall be your rear guard.
Then you shall call, and the Lord will answer,
    you shall cry for help, and he will say: Here I am!
If you remove from your midst oppression,
    false accusation and malicious speech;
If you bestow your bread on the hungry
    and satisfy the afflicted;

Then light shall rise for you in the darkness,
and the gloom shall become for you like midday.
This is the Word of the Lord.

Responsorial Psalm   Ps 112, 4-5. 6-7. 8-9

R̸. (4) The just man is a light in darkness to
the upright.
The Lord dawns through the darkness, a light
for the upright;
he is gracious and merciful and just.
Well for the man who is gracious and lends,
who conducts his affairs with justice.
R̸. The just man is a light in darkness to the
upright.
He shall never be moved;
the just man shall be in everlasting remembrance.
An evil report he shall not fear;
his heart is firm, trusting in the Lord.
R̸. The just man is a light in darkness to the
upright.
His heart is steadfast; he shall not fear.
Lavishly he gives to the poor;
His generosity shall endure forever;
his horn shall be exalted in glory.
R̸. The just man is a light in darkness to the
upright.
R̸. Or: Alleluia.

READING II   1 Cor 2, 1-5

A reading from the first letter of Paul to the
Corinthians

I have told you of the witness of the crucified Christ.

As for myself, brothers, when I came to you I
did not come proclaiming God's testimony
with any particular eloquence or "wisdom."
No, I determined that while I was with you I
would speak of nothing but Jesus Christ and
him crucified. When I came among you it was
in weakness and fear, and with much trepidation. My message and my preaching had none
of the persuasive force of "wise" argumentation, but the convincing power of the Spirit.
As a consequence, your faith rests not on the
wisdom of men but on the power of God.
This is the Word of the Lord.

GOSPEL   Mt 5, 13-16
Alleluia

See no. 164.

✠ A reading from the holy gospel according
to Matthew

You are the light of the world.

Jesus said to his disciples: "You are the salt
of the earth. But what if salt goes flat? How
can you restore its flavor? Then it is good for
nothing but to be thrown out and trampled
underfoot.
"You are the light of the world. A city set on
a hill cannot be hidden. Men do not light a lamp
and then put it under a bushel basket. They set
it on a stand where it gives light to all in the
house. In the same way, your light must shine
before men so that they may see goodness in
your acts and give praise to your heavenly
Father."
This is the gospel of the Lord.

---

75   FIFTH SUNDAY   **B**
              OF THE YEAR

READING I   Jb 7, 1-4. 6-7

A reading from the book of Job

I am filled with sorrows all day long.

Job spoke, saying:
Is not man's life on earth a drudgery?
Are not his days those of a hireling?
He is a slave who longs for the shade,
a hireling who waits for his wages.
So I have been assigned months of misery,
and troubled nights have been told off
for me.

If in bed I say, "When shall I arise?"
then the night drags on;
I am filled with restlessness until the dawn.

My days are swifter than a weaver's shuttle;
they come to an end without hope.
Remember that my life is like the wind;
I shall not see happiness again.
This is the Word of the Lord.

Responsorial Psalm   Ps 147, 1-2. 3-4. 5-6

℟. (3) Praise the Lord who heals the brokenhearted.

Praise the Lord, for he is good;
    sing praise to our God, for he is gracious;
    it is fitting to praise him.
The Lord rebuilds Jerusalem;
    the dispersed of Israel he gathers.

℟. Praise the Lord who heals the brokenhearted.

He heals the brokenhearted
    and binds up their wounds.
He tells the number of the stars;
    he calls each by name.

℟. Praise the Lord who heals the brokenhearted.

Great is our Lord and mighty in power;
    to his wisdom there is no limit.
The Lord sustains the lowly;
    the wicked he casts to the ground.

℟. Praise the Lord who heals the brokenhearted.

℟. Or: Alleluia.

READING II   1 Cor 9, 16-19. 22-23

A reading from the first letter of Paul to the
Corinthians

Punishment will come to me if I do not preach the gospel.

Preaching the gospel is not the subject of a
boast; I am under compulsion and have no
choice. I am ruined if I do not preach it! If I
do it willingly, I have my recompense; if un-
willingly, I am nonetheless entrusted with a
charge. And this recompense of mine? It is
simply this, that when preaching I offer the
gospel free of charge and do not make full use
of the authority the gospel gives me.

Although I am not bound to anyone, I made
myself the slave of all so as to win over as
many as possible. To the weak I became a
weak person with a view to winning the weak.
I have made myself all things to all men in
order to save at least some of them. In fact,
I do all that I do for the sake of the gospel in
the hope of having a share in its blessings.

This is the Word of the Lord.

GOSPEL   Mk 1, 29-39
Alleluia

See no. 164.

✠ **A reading from the holy gospel according**
to Mark

He cured many who suffered from diseases of one kind
or another.

Upon leaving the synagogue, Jesus entered the
house of Simon and Andrew with James and
John. Simon's mother-in-law lay ill with a
fever, and the first thing they did was to
tell him about her. He went over to her and
grasped her hand and helped her up, and the
fever left her. She immediately began to wait
on them.

After sunset, as evening drew on, they
brought him all who were ill and those pos-
sessed by demons. Before long the whole town
was gathered outside the door. Those whom
he cured, who were variously afflicted, were
many, and so were the demons he expelled.
But he would not permit the demons to speak,
because they knew him. Rising early the next
morning, he went off to a lonely place in the
desert; there he was absorbed in prayer. Simon
and his companions managed to track him
down; and when they found him, they told him,
"Everybody is looking for you!" He said to
them: "Let us move on to the neightboring vil-
lages so that I may proclaim the good news
there also. That is what I have come to do." So
he went into their synagogues preaching the
good news and expelling demons throughout
the whole of Galilee.

This is the gospel of the Lord.

---

76   **FIFTH SUNDAY**   **C**
    OF THE YEAR

READING I   Is 6, 1-2. 3-8

A reading from the book of the prophet Isaiah

Here am I! Send me.

In the year King Uzziah died, I saw the Lord
seated on a high and lofty throne, with the
train of his garment filling the temple. Sera-
phim were stationed above.

"Holy, holy, holy is the Lord of hosts!" they cried one to the other. "All the earth is filled with his glory!" At the sound of that cry, the frame of the door shook and the house was filled with smoke.

Then I said, "Woe is me, I am doomed! For I am a man of unclean lips, living among a people of unclean lips; yet my eyes have seen the King, the Lord of hosts!" Then one of the seraphim flew to me, holding an ember which he had taken with tongs from the altar.

He touched my mouth with it. "See," he said, "now that this has touched your lips, your wickedness is removed, your sin purged."

Then I heard the voice of the Lord saying, "Whom shall I send? Who will go for us?" "Here I am," I said; "send me!"

This is the Word of the Lord.

Responsorial Psalm   Ps 138, 1-2. 2-3. 4-5. 7-8

℟. (1) In the sight of the angels
   I will sing your praises, Lord.

I will give thanks to you, O Lord, with all my
   heart,
   [for you have heard the words of my mouth;]
   in the presence of the angels I will sing your
   praise;
I will worship at your holy temple
   and give thanks to your name.

℟. In the sight of the angels
   I will sing your praises, Lord.

Because of your kindness and your truth;
   for you have made great above all things
   your name and your promise.
When I called, you answered me;
   you built up strength within me.

℟. In the sight of the angels
   I will sing your praises, Lord.

All the kings of the earth shall give thanks to
   you, O Lord,
   when they hear the words of your mouth;
And they shall sing of the ways of the Lord:
   "Great is the glory of the Lord."

℟. In the sight of the angels
   I will sing your praises, Lord.

Your right hand saves me.
   The Lord will complete what he has done for
   me;
Your kindness, O Lord, endures forever;
   forsake not the work of your hands.

℟. In the sight of the angels
   I will sing your praises, Lord.

READING II   1 Cor 15, 1-11 or 15, 3-8. 11

**A reading from the first letter of Paul to the
Corinthians**
I preach what they preach, and this is what you believe.

(Long Form)

Brothers, I want to remind you of the gospel I preached to you, which you received and in which you stand firm. You are being saved by it at this very moment if you retain it as I preached it to you. Otherwise you have believed in vain. I handed on to you first of all what I myself received, that Christ died for our sins in accord with the Scriptures; that he was buried and, in accord with the Scriptures, rose on the third day; that he was seen by Cephas, then by the Twelve. After that he was seen by five hundred brothers at once, most of whom are still alive, although some have fallen asleep. Next he was seen by James; then by all the apostles. Last of all he was seen by me, as one born out of the normal course. I am the least of the apostles; in fact, because I persecuted the church of God, I do not even deserve the name. But by God's favor I am what I am. This favor of his to me has not proved fruitless. Indeed, I have worked harder than all the others, not on my own but through the favor of God. In any case, whether it be I or they, this is what we preach and this is what you believed.

This is the Word of the Lord.

OR

(Short Form)

Brothers, I handed on to you first of all what I myself received, that Christ died for our sins in accord with the Scriptures; that he was buried and, in accord with the Scriptures, rose on the third day; that he was seen by Cephas, then by the Twelve. After that he was seen by five hundred brothers at once, most of whom are still alive, although some have fallen asleep. Next he was seen by James; then by all the apostles. Last of all he was seen by me, as one born out of the normal course. In any case, whether it be I or they, this is what we preach and this is what you believed.

This is the Word of the Lord.

GOSPEL   Lk 5, 1-11
Alleluia
See no. 164.

✠ A reading from the holy gospel according to Luke
They left everything and followed him.

As the crowd pressed in on Jesus to hear the word of God, he saw two boats moored by the side of the lake; the fishermen had disembarked and were washing their nets. He got into one of the boats, the one belonging to Simon, and asked him to pull out a short distance from the shore; then, remaining seated, he continued to teach the crowds from the boat. When he had finished speaking he said to Simon, "Put out into deep water and lower your nets for a catch." Simon answered, "Master, we have been hard at it all night long and have caught nothing; but if you say so, I will lower the nets." Upon doing this they caught such a great number of fish that their nets were at the breaking point. They signaled to their mates in the other boat to come and help them. These came, and together they filled the two boats until they nearly sank.

At the sight of this, Simon Peter fell at the knees of Jesus saying, "Leave me, Lord. I am a sinful man." For indeed, amazement at the catch they had made seized him and all his shipmates, as well as James and John, Zebedee's sons, who were partners with Simon. Jesus said to Simon, "Do not be afraid. From now on you will be catching men." With that they brought their boats to land, left eveything, and became his followers.

This is the gospel of the Lord.

---

77   **SIXTH SUNDAY**   🅰
               OF THE YEAR

READING I   Sir 15, 15-20
A reading from the book of Sirach
He never commanded anyone to be godless.

If you choose you can keep the commandments;
  it is loyalty to do his will.
There are set before you fire and water;
  to whichever you choose, stretch forth your hand.
Before man are life and death,
  whichever he chooses shall be given him.
Immense is the wisdom of the Lord;
  he is mighty in power, and all-seeing.
The eyes of God see all he has made;
  he understands man's every deed.
No man does he command to sin,
  to none does he give strength for lies.

This is the Word of the Lord.

Responsorial Psalm   Ps 119, 1-2. 4-5. 17-18. 33-34

℟. (1) Happy are they who follow the law of the Lord!
Happy are they whose way is blameless,
  who walk in the law of the Lord.
Happy are they who observe his decrees,
  who seek him with all their heart.
℟. Happy are they who follow the law of the Lord!
You have commanded that your precepts
  be diligently kept.
Oh, that I might be firm in the ways
  of keeping your statutes!
℟. Happy are they who follow the law of the Lord!
Be good to your servant, that I may live
  and keep your words.
Open my eyes, that I may consider
  the wonders of your law.
℟. Happy are they who follow the law of the Lord!
Instruct me, O Lord, in the way of your statutes,
  that I may exactly observe them.

Give me discernment, that I may observe your
    law
and keep it with all my heart.
℟. Happy are they who follow the law of the
    Lord!

READING II   1 Cor 2, 6-10

**A reading from the first letter of Paul to the
                Corinthians**

God in his wisdom predestined our glory before the ages
                began.

There is, to be sure, a certain wisdom which we
express among the spiritually mature. It is not
a wisdom of this age, however, nor of the
rulers of this age who are men headed for
destruction. No, what we utter is God's wisdom: a mysterious, a hidden wisdom. God
planned it before all ages for our glory. None
of the rulers of this age knew the mystery;
if they had known it, they would never have
crucified the Lord of glory. Of this wisdom it
is written:
"Eye has not seen, ear has not heard,
    nor has it so much as dawned on man
    what God has prepared for those who love
        him."
Yet God has revealed this wisdom to us
through the Spirit. The Spirit scrutinizes all
matters, even the deep things of God.
        This is the Word of the Lord.

GOSPEL   Mt 5, 17-37 or 5, 20-22. 27-28. 33-34. 37
Alleluia

See no. 164.

✠ **A reading from the holy gospel according
            to Matthew**

Such was said to your ancestors; but I am speaking to you.

                (Long Form)

Jesus said to his disciples: "Do not think that
I have come to abolish the law and the
prophets. I have come, not to abolish them, but
to fulfill them. Of this much I assure you: until
heaven and earth pass away, not the smallest
letter of the law, not the smallest part of a
letter, shall be done away with until it all

comes true. That is why whoever breaks
the least significant of these commands and
teaches others to do so shall be called least in
the kingdom of God. Whoever fulfills and
teaches these commands shall be great in the
kingdom of God. I tell you, unless your holiness surpasses that of the scribes and Pharisees you shall not enter the kingdom of God.

"You have heard the commandment imposed on your forefathers, 'You shall not commit murder; every murderer will be liable to
judgment.' What I say to you is: everyone who
grows angry with his brother will be liable to
judgment; any man who uses abusive language
toward his brother shall be answerable to the
Sanhedrin, and if he holds him in contempt he
risks the fires of Gehenna. If you bring your gift
to the altar and there recall that your brother
has anything against you, leave your gift at the
altar, go first to be reconciled with with brother, and then come and offer your gift. Lose no
time; settle with your opponent while on your
way to court with him. Otherwise your opponent may hand you over to the judge, who will
hand you over to the guard, who will throw you
into prison. I warn you, you will not be released
until you have paid the last penny.

"You have heard the commandment, 'You
shall not commit adultery.' What I say to you
is: anyone who looks lustfully at a woman has
already committed adultery with her in his
thoughts. If your right eye is your trouble,
gouge it out and throw it away! Better to lose
part of your body than to have it all cast into
Gehenna. Again, if your right hand is your
trouble, cut it off and throw it away! Better to
lose part of your body than to have it all cast
into Gehenna.

"It was also said, 'Whenever a man divorces
his wife, he must give her a decree of divorce.'
What I say to you is: everyone who divorces his
wife—lewd conduct is a separate case—forces
her to commit adultery. The man who marries
a divorced woman likewise commits adultery.

"You have heard the commandment imposed on your forefathers, 'Do not take a false
oath; rather, make good to the Lord all your
pledges.' What I tell you is: do not swear at

all. Do not swear by heaven (it is God's throne), nor by the earth (it is his footstool), nor by Jerusalem (it is the city of the great King); do not swear by your head (you cannot make a single hair white or black). Say, 'Yes' when you mean 'Yes' and 'No' when you mean 'No.' Anything beyond that is from the evil one."

This is the gospel of the Lord.

OR
(Short Form)

Jesus said to his disciples: "I tell you, unless your holiness surpasses that of the scribes and Pharisees you shall not enter the kingdom of God.

"You have heard the commandment imposed on your forefathers, 'You shall not commit murder; every murderer will be liable to judgment.' What I say to you is: everyone who grows angry with his brother shall be liable to judgment.

"You have heard the commandment, 'You shall not commit adultery.' What I say to you is: anyone who looks lustfully at a woman has already committed adultery with her in his thoughts.

"You have heard the commandment imposed on your forefathers, 'Do not take a false oath; rather, make good to the Lord all your pledges.' What I tell you is: do not swear at all. Say, 'Yes' when you mean 'Yes' and 'No' when you mean 'No.' Anything beyond that is from the evil one."

This is the gospel of the Lord.

---

78   **SIXTH SUNDAY**   **B**
            OF THE YEAR

READING I   Lv 13, 1-2. 44-46

A reading from the book of Leviticus

As long as he is unclean, he must live alone, outside the camp.

The Lord said to Moses and Aaron, "If someone has on his skin a scab or pustule or blotch which appears to be the sore of leprosy, he

shall be brought to Aaron, the priest, or to one of the priests among his descendants. If the man is leprous and unclean, the priest shall declare him unclean by reason of the sore on his head.

"The one who bears the sore of leprosy shall keep his garments rent and his head bare, and shall muffle his beard; he shall cry out, 'Unclean, unclean!' As long as the sore is on him he shall declare himself unclean, since he is in fact unclean. He shall dwell apart, making his abode outside the camp."

This is the Word of the Lord.

Responsorial Psalm   Ps 32, 1-2. 5. 11

℞. (7) I turn to you, Lord, in time of trouble,
   and you fill me with the joy of salvation.
Happy is he whose fault is taken away,
   whose sin is covered.
Happy the man to whom the Lord imputes not guilt,
   in whose spirit there is no guile.
℞. I turn to you, Lord, in time of trouble,
   and you fill me with the joy of salvation.
Then I acknowledged my sin to you,
   my guilt I covered not.
I said, "I confess my faults to the Lord,"
   and you took away the guilt of my sin.
℞. I turn to you, Lord, in time of trouble,
   and you fill me with the joy of salvation.
Be glad in the Lord and rejoice, you just;
   exult, all you upright of heart.
℞. I turn to you, Lord, in time of trouble,
   and you fill me with the joy of salvation.

READING II   1 Cor 10, 31—11, 1

A reading from the first letter of Paul to the Corinthians

Be imitators of me, as I am of Christ.

Whether you eat or drink—whatever you do—you should do all for the glory of God. Give no offense to Jew or Greek or to the church of God, just as I try to please all in any way I can by seeking not my own advantage, but that of the many that they may be saved. Imitate me as I imitate Christ.

This is the Word of the Lord.

GOSPEL   Mk 1, 40-45
Alleluia

See no. 164.

A reading from the holy gospel according
to Mark

He sent the leper from him and he was cured.

A leper approached Jesus with a request,
kneeling down as he addressed him: "If you
will to do so, you can cure me." Moved with
pity, Jesus stretched out his hand, touched him,
and said: "I do will it. Be cured." The leprosy
left him then and there, and he was cured.
Jesus gave him a stern warning and sent him
on his way. "Not a word to anyone, now,"
he said. "Go off and present yourself to the
priest and offer for your cure what Moses
prescribed. That should be a proof for them."
The man went off and began to proclaim the
whole matter freely, making the story public.
As a result of this, it was no longer possible
for Jesus to enter a town openly. He stayed in
desert places; yet people kept coming to him
from all sides.

This is the gospel of the Lord.

---

79   SIXTH SUNDAY   C

OF THE YEAR

READING I   Jer 17, 5-8

A reading from the book of the prophet
Jeremiah

Unhappy is he who trusts in man; happy the man who
trusts in the Lord.

Thus says the Lord:
Cursed is the man who trusts in human beings,
    who seeks his strength in flesh,
    whose heart turns away from the Lord.
He is like a barren bush in the desert
    that enjoys no change of season,
But stands in a lava waste,
    a salt and empty earth.
Blessed is the man who trusts in the Lord,
    whose hope is the Lord.
He is like a tree planted beside the waters
    that stretches out its roots to the stream:

It fears not the heat when it comes,
    its leaves stay green;
In the year of drought it shows no distress,
    but still bears fruit.
        This is the Word of the Lord.

Responsorial Psalm   Ps 1, 1-2. 3. 4. 6

℟. (Ps 39, 5) Happy are they who hope in the
    Lord.
Happy the man who follows not
    the counsel of the wicked
Nor walks in the way of sinners,
    nor sits in the company of the insolent,
But delights in the law of the Lord
    and meditates on his law day and night.
℟. Happy are they who hope in the Lord.
He is like a tree
    planted near running water,
That yields its fruit in due season,
    and whose leaves never fade.
    [Whatever he does, prospers.]
℟. Happy are they who hope in the Lord.
Not so the wicked, not so;
    they are like chaff which the wind drives
        away.
For the Lord watches over the way of the just,
    but the way of the wicked vanishes.
℟. Happy are they who hope in the Lord.

READING II   1 Cor 15, 12. 16-20

A reading from the first letter of Paul to the
Corinthians

If Christ is not raised from the dead, your faith is in vain.

If Christ is preached as raised from the dead,
how is it that some of you say there is no
resurrection of the dead? If the dead are not
raised, then Christ was not raised; and if Christ
was not raised, your faith is worthless. You are
still in your sins, and those who have fallen
asleep in Christ are the deadest of the dead.
If our hopes in Christ are limited to this life
only, we are the most pitiable of men.

But as it is, Christ has been raised from the
dead, the first fruits of those who have fallen
asleep.
        This is the Word of the Lord.

GOSPEL   Lk 6, 17. 20-26
Alleluia

See no. 164.

✠ A reading from the holy gospel according
                    to Luke

Happy are the poor; their reward will be great.

When Jesus came down the mountain, he stopped at a level stretch where there were many of
his disciples; a large crowd of people was with
them from all Judea and Jerusalem and the
coast of Tyre and Sidon. Then, raising his eyes
to his disciples, he said:

"Blest are you poor; the reign of God is yours.
Blest are you who hunger;   filled you shall
be.
Blest are you who are weeping; you shall
laugh.

"Blest shall you be when men hate you,
when they ostracize you and insult you and
proscribe your name as evil because of the
Son of Man. On the day they do so, rejoice
and exult, for your reward shall be great in
heaven. Thus it was that their fathers treated
the prophets.

"But woe to you rich, for your consolation
is now.
Woe to you who are full; you shall go hungry.
Woe to you who laugh now; you shall
weep in your grief.
"Woe to you when all speak well of you.
Their fathers treated the false prophets in just
this way."

This is the gospel of the Lord.

---

80   **SEVENTH SUNDAY**   **A**
              OF THE YEAR

READING I   Lv 19, 1-2. 17-18

A reading from the book of Leviticus

You must love your neighbor, as yourself.

The Lord said to Moses, "Speak to the whole
Israelite community and tell them: Be holy, for
I, the Lord, your God, am holy.

"You shall not bear hatred for your brother

in your heart. Though you may have to reprove your fellow man, do not incur sin because of him. Take no revenge and cherish no
grudge against your fellow countrymen. You
shall love your neighbor as yourself. I am the
Lord."

This is the Word of the Lord.

Responsorial Psalm   Ps 103, 1-2. 3-4. 8. 10. 12-13

℟. (8) The Lord is kind and merciful.
Bless the Lord, O my soul;
     and all my being, bless his holy name.
Bless the Lord, O my soul,
     and forget not all his benefits.
℟. The Lord is kind and merciful.
He pardons all your iniquities,
     he heals all your ills.
He redeems your life from destruction,
     he crowns you with kindness and compas-
     sion.
℟. The Lord is kind and merciful.
Merciful and gracious is the Lord,
     slow to anger and abounding in kindness.
Not according to our sins does he deal with us,
     nor does he requite us according to our
     crimes.
℟. The Lord is kind and merciful.
As far as the east is from the west,
     so far has he put our transgressions from us.
As a father has compassion on his children,
     so the Lord has compassion on those who
     fear him.
℟. The Lord is kind and merciful.

READING II   1 Cor 3, 16-23

A reading from the first letter of Paul to the
                    Corinthians

All things are yours, but you belong to Christ and Christ
                belongs to God.

Are you not aware that you are the temple of
God, and that the Spirit of God dwells in you?
If anyone destroys God's temple, God will
destroy him. For the temple of God is holy,
and you are that temple.

Let no one delude himself. If any one of you
thinks he is wise in a worldly way, he had
better become a fool. In that way he will really

be wise, for the widom of this world is absurdity with God. Scripture says, "He catches the wise in their craftiness"; and again, "The Lord knows how empty are the thoughts of the wise." Let there be no boasting about men. All things are yours, whether it be Paul, or Apollos, or Cephas, or the world, or life, or death, or the present, or the future: all these are yours, and you are Christ's and Christ is God's.

This is the Word of the Lord.

GOSPEL

Alleluia

Mt 5, 38-48

See no. 164.

✠ A reading from the holy gospel according to Matthew

Love your enemies.

Jesus said to his disciples: "You have heard the commandment, 'An eye for an eye, a tooth for a tooth.' But what I say to you is: offer no resistance to injury. When a person strikes you on the right cheek, turn and offer him the other. If anyone wants to go to law over your shirt, hand him your coat as well. Should anyone press you into service for one mile, go with him two miles. Give to the man who begs from you. Do not turn your back on the borrower.

"You have heard the commandment, 'You shall love your countryman but hate your enemy.' My command to you is: love your enemies, pray for your persecutors. This will prove that you are sons of your heavenly Father, for his sun rises on the bad and the good, he rains on the just and the unjust. If you love those who love you, what merit is there in that? Do not tax collectors do as much? And if you greet your brothers only, what is so praiseworthy about that? Do not pagans do as much? In a word, you must be perfected as your heavenly Father is perfect."

This is the gospel of the Lord.

SEVENTH SUNDAY OF THE YEAR **B**

READING I   Is 43, 18-19. 21-22. 24-25

A reading from the book of the prophet Isaiah

On account of me your iniquities are blotted out.

Thus says the Lord:
Remember not the events of the past,
  the things of long ago consider not;
See, I am doing something new!
  Now it springs forth, do you not perceive it?
In the desert I make a way,
  in the wasteland, rivers.
The people whom I formed for myself,
  that they might announce my praise.
Yet you did not call upon me, O Jacob,
  for you grew weary of me, O Israel.
You burdened me with your sins,
  and wearied me with your crimes.
It is I, I, who wipe out,
  for my own sake, your offenses;
  your sins I remember no more.
  This is the Word of the Lord.

Responsorial Psalm   Ps 41, 2-3. 4-5. 13-14

℟. (5) Lord, heal my soul,
  for I have sinned against you.
Happy is he who has regard for the lowly and the poor;
  in the day of misfortune the Lord will deliver him.
The Lord will keep and preserve him;
  he will make him happy on the earth,
  and not give him over to the will of his enemies.
℟. Lord, heal my soul,
  for I have sinned against you.
The Lord will help him on his sickbed,
  he will take away all his ailment when he is ill.
Once I said, "O Lord, have pity on me;
  heal me, though I have sinned against you."
℟. Lord, heal my soul,
  for I have sinned against you.
But because of my integrity you sustain me
  and let me stand before you forever.

Blessed be the Lord, the God of Israel,
    from all eternity and forever. Amen. Amen.
℟. Lord, heal my soul,
    for I have sinned against you.

READING II   2 Cor 1, 18-22

A reading from the second letter of Paul to the Corinthians

Every promise of God finds its affirmative in Jesus.

As God keeps his word, I declare that my word
to you is not "yes" one minute and "no" the
next. Jesus Christ, whom Silvanus, Timothy,
and I preached to you as Son of God, was not
alternately "yes" and "no"; he was never anything but "yes." Whatever promises God has
made have been fulfilled in him; therefore it is
through him that we address our Amen to God
when we worship together. God is the one who
firmly establishes us along with you in Christ;
it is he who anointed us and has sealed us,
thereby depositing the first payment, the Spirit
in our hearts.

    This is the Word of the Lord.

GOSPEL   Mk 2, 1-12
Alleluia

See no. 164.

✠ **A reading from the holy gospel according
to Mark**

The Son of Man has authority on earth to forgive sins.

After a lapse of several days Jesus came back
to Capernaum and word got around that he
was at home. At that they began to gather in
great numbers. There was no longer any room
for them, even around the door. While he was
delivering God's word to them, some people
arrived bringing a paralyzed man to him. The
four who carried him were unable to bring
him to Jesus because of the crowd, so they
began to open up the roof over the spot where
Jesus was. When they had made a hole, they
let down the mat on which the paralytic was
lying. When Jesus saw their faith, he said to
the paralyzed man, "My son, your sins are
forgiven." Now some of the scribes were
sitting there asking themselves: "Why does the

25-6

man talk in that way? He commits blasphemy!
Who can forgive sins except God alone?" Jesus
was immediately aware of their reasoning,
though they kept it to themselves, and he said
to them: "Why do you harbor these thoughts?
Which is easier, to say to the paralytic, 'Your
sins are forgiven,' or to say, 'Stand up, pick up
your mat, and walk again'? That you may know
that the Son of Man has authority on earth to
forgive sins" (he said to the paralyzed man),
"I command you: Stand up! Pick up your mat
and go home." The man stood and picked up
his mat and went outside in the sight of everyone. They were awestruck; all gave praise to
God, saying, "We have never seen anything like
this!"

    This is the gospel of the Lord.

---

82   **SEVENTH SUNDAY**   Ⓒ
              OF THE YEAR

READING I   1 Sm 26, 2. 7-9. 12-13. 22-23

A reading from the first book of Samuel

The Lord has put you in my power, but I will not raise my
hand against you.

Saul went off down to the desert of Ziph with
three thousand picked men of Israel, to search
for David in the desert of Ziph. So David and
Abishai went among Saul's soldiers by night
and found Saul lying asleep within the barri-
cade, with his spear thrust into the ground
at his head and Abner and his men sleeping
around him.

    Abishai whispered to David: "God has de-
livered your enemy into your grasp this day.
Let me nail him to the ground with one thrust
of the spear; I will not need a second thrust!"
But David said to Abishai, "Do not harm him,
for who can lay hands on the Lord's anointed
and remain unpunished? So David took the
spear and the water jug from their place at
Saul's head, and they got away without anyone's seeing or knowing or awakening. All remained asleep, because the Lord had put them
into a deep slumber.

    Going across to an opposite slope, David
stood on a remote hilltop at a great distance

from Abner, son of Ner, and the troops. He said: "Here is the king's spear. Let an attendant come over to get it. The Lord will reward each man for his justice and faithfulness. Today, though the Lord delivered you into my grasp, I would not harm the Lord's anointed."
     This is the Word of the Lord.

Responsorial Psalm   Ps 103, 1-2. 3-4. 8. 10. 12-13

℟. (8) The Lord is kind and merciful.
Bless the Lord, O my soul;
     and all my being, bless his holy name.
Bless the Lord, O my soul,
     and forget not all his benefits.
℟. The Lord is kind and merciful.
He pardons all your iniquities,
     he heals all your ills.
He redeems your life from destruction,
     he crowns you with kindness and compassion.
℟. The Lord is kind and merciful.
Merciful and gracious is the Lord,
     slow to anger and abounding in kindness.
Not according to our sins does he deal with us,
     nor does he requite us according to our crimes.
℟. The Lord is kind and merciful.
As far as the east is from the west,
     so far has he put our transgressions from us.
As a father has compassion on his children,
     so the Lord has compassion on those who fear him.
℟. The Lord is kind and merciful.

READING II   1 Cor 15, 45-49

A reading from the first letter of Paul to the Corinthians

Just as we have carried the earthly image, we must carry the heavenly image.

Scripture has it that Adam, the first man, became a living soul; the last Adam has become a life-giving spirit. Notice the spiritual was not first; first came the natural and after that the spiritual. The first man was of earth, formed from dust, the second is from heaven. Earthly men are like the man of earth, heavenly men are like the man of heaven. Just as we resemble the man from earth, so shall we bear the likeness of the man from heaven.
     This is the Word of the Lord.

GOSPEL   Lk 6, 27-38
Alleluia
See no. 164.

✠ **A reading from the holy gospel according to Luke**

Be merciful as your Father is merciful.

Jesus said to his disciples: "To you who hear me, I say: Love your enemies, do good to those who hate you; bless those who curse you and pray for those who maltreat you. When someone slaps you on one cheek, turn and give him the other; when someone takes your coat, let him have your shirt as well. Give to all who beg from you. When a man takes what is yours, do not demand it back. Do to others what you would have them do to you. If you love those who love you, what credit is that to you? Even sinners love those who love them. If you do good to those who do good to you, how can you claim any credit? Sinners do as much. If you lend to those from whom you expect repayment, what merit is there in it for you? Even sinners lend to sinners, expecting to be repaid in full.
     "Love your enemy and do good; lend without expecting repayment. Then will your recompense be great. You will rightly be called sons of the Most High, since he himself is good to the ungrateful and the wicked.
     "Be compassionate, as your Father is compassionate. Do not judge, and you will not be judged. Do not condemn, and you will not be condemned. Pardon, and you shall be pardoned. Give, and it shall be given to you. Good measure pressed down, shaken together, running over, will they pour into the fold of your garment. For the measure you measure with will be measured back to you."
     This is the gospel of the Lord.

83   EIGHTH SUNDAY
OF THE YEAR   **A**

READING I   Is 49, 14-15

A reading from the book of the prophet Isaiah

Even these may forget, says the Lord, yet I will not forget
you.

Zion said, "The Lord has forsaken me;
  my Lord has forgotten me."
Can a mother forget her infant,
  be without tenderness for the child of her
    womb?
Even should she forget,
  I will never forget you.
        This is the Word of the Lord.

Responsorial Psalm   Ps 62, 2-3. 6-7. 8-9

℞. (6) Rest in God alone, my soul.
**Only in God is my soul at rest;
  from him comes my salvation.
He only is my rock and my salvation,
  my stronghold; I shall not be disturbed at
    all.**
℞. Rest in God alone, my soul.
**Only in God be at rest, my soul,
  for from him comes my hope.
He only is my rock and my salvation,
  my stronghold; I shall not be disturbed.**
℞. Rest in God alone, my soul.
**With God is my safety and my glory,
  he is the rock of my strength; my refuge is
    in God.
Trust in him at all times, O my people!
  Pour out your hearts before him.**
℞. Rest in God alone, my soul.

READING II   1 Cor 4, 1-5

**A reading from the first letter of Paul to the
    Corinthians**

The Lord will bring light to all that is hidden in the darkness

Men should regard us as servants of Christ
and administrators of the mysteries of God.
The first requirement of an administrator is
that he prove trustworthy. It matters little
to me whether you or any human court pass
judgment on me. I do not even pass judgment

on myself. Mind you, I have nothing on my
conscience. But that does not mean that I am
declaring myself innocent. The Lord is the one
to judge me, so stop passing judgment before
the time of his return. He will bring to light
what is hidden in darkness and manifest the
intentions of hearts. At that time, everyone will
receive his praise from God.
        This is the Word of the Lord.

GOSPEL   Mt 6, 24-34
Alleluia

See no. 164.

✠ **A reading from the holy gospel according
    to Matthew**

Do not worry about your life and what you are to eat or
to wear.

Jesus said to his disciples: "No man can serve
two masters. He will either hate one and love
the other or be attentive to one and despise
the other. You cannot give yourself to God
and money. I warn you, then: do not worry
about your livelihood, what you are to eat or
drink or use for clothing. Is not life more
than food? Is not the body more valuable than
clothes?

"Look at the birds in the sky. They do not
sow or reap, they gather nothing into barns;
yet your heavenly Father feeds them. Are not
you more important than they? Which of you
by worrying can add a moment to his lifespan?
As for clothes, why be concerned? Learn a
lesson from the way the wild flowers grow.
They do not work; they do not spin. Yet I assure you, not even Solomon in all his splendor
was arrayed like one of these. If God can
clothe in such splendor the grass of the field,
which blooms today and is thrown on the fire
tomorrow, will he not provide much more for
you, O weak in faith! Stop worrying, then,
over questions like, 'What are we to eat, or
what are we to drink, or what are we to wear?'
The unbelievers are always running after these
things. Your heavenly Father knows all that
you need. Seek first his kingship over you, his
way of holiness, and all these things will be
given you besides. Enough, then, of worrying

about tomorrow. Let tomorrow take care of
itself. Today has troubles enough of its own."
    This is the gospel of the Lord.

---

84   EIGHTH SUNDAY   B
OF THE YEAR

READING I   Hos 2, 16.17. 21-22
A reading from the book of the prophet Hosea
                I will betroth you to me for ever.
    Thus says the Lord:
    I will lead her into the desert
    and speak to her heart.
She shall respond there as in the days of her
    youth,
    when she came up from the land of Egypt.
I will espouse you to me forever:
    I will espouse you in right and in justice,
    in love and in mercy;
I will espouse you in fidelity,
    and you shall know the Lord.
        This is the Word of the Lord.

Responsorial Psalm   Ps 103, 1-2. 3-4. 8. 10. 12-13

℟. (8) The Lord is kind and merciful.
Bless the Lord, O my soul;
    and all my being, bless his holy name.
Bless the Lord, O my soul,
    and forget not all his benefits.
℟. The Lord is kind and merciful.
He pardons all your iniquities,
    he heals all your ills.
He redeems your life from destruction,
    he crowns you with kindness and compas-
    sion.
℟. The Lord is kind and merciful.
Merciful and gracious is the Lord,
    slow to anger and abounding in kindness.
Not according to our sins does he deal with us,
    nor does he requite us according to our
    crimes.
℟. The Lord is kind and merciful.
As far as the east is from the west,
    so far has he put our transgressions from us.

As a father has compassion on his children,
    so the Lord has compassion on those who
    fear him.
℟. The Lord is kind and merciful.

READING II   2 Cor 3, 1-6
A reading from the second letter of Paul to the
                    Corinthians
        You are a letter from Christ for us to deliver.
Do I need letters of recommendation to you or
from you as others might? You are my letter,
known and read by all men, written on your
hearts. Clearly you are a letter of Christ which
I have delivered, a letter written not with ink
but by the Spirit of the living God, not on ta-
blets of stone but on tablets of flesh in the heart.
    This great confidence in God is ours, through
Christ. It is not that we are entitled of ourselves
to take credit for anything. Our sole credit is
from God, who has made us qualified ministers
of a new covenant, a covenant not of a written
law but of spirit. The written law kills, but the
Spirit gives life.
        This is the Word of the Lord.

GOSPEL   Mk 2, 18-22
Alleluia

See no. 164.

✠ **A reading from the holy gospel according**
                    to Mark
            The bridegroom is still with them.
John's disciples and the Pharisees were ac-
customed to fast. People came to Jesus with
the objection, "Why do John's disciples and
those of the Pharisees fast while yours do not?"
Jesus replied: "How can the guests at a wed-
ding fast as long as the groom is still among
them? So long as the groom stays with them,
they cannot fast. The day will come, however,
when the groom will be taken away from
them; on that day they will fast. No one sews
a patch of unshrunken cloth on an old cloak.
If he should do so, the very thing he has used
to cover the hole would pull away—the new
from the old—and the tear would get worse.

Similarly, no man pours new wine into old wineskins. If he does so, the wine will burst the skins and both wine and skins will be lost. No, new wine is poured into new skins."

This is the gospel of the Lord.

---

85 EIGHTH SUNDAY OF THE YEAR **C**

READING I   Sir 27, 4-7

A reading from the book of Sirach

Do not praise a man before he has spoken.

When a sieve is shaken, the husks appear;
so do a man's faults when he speaks.
As the test of what the potter molds is in the
furnace,
so in his conversation is the test of a man.
The fruit of a tree shows the care it has had;
so too does a man's speech disclose the bent
of his mind.
Praise no man before he speaks,
for it is then that men are tested.

This is the Word of the Lord.

Responsorial Psalm   Ps 92, 2-3. 13-14. 15-16

℞. (2) Lord, it is good to give thanks to you.
It is good to give thanks to the Lord,
to sing praise to your name, Most High,
To proclaim your kindness at dawn
and your faithfulness throughout the night.
℞. Lord, it is good to give thanks to you.
The just man shall flourish like the palm tree,
like a cedar of Lebanon shall he grow.
They that are planted in the house of the Lord
shall flourish in the courts of our God.
℞. Lord, it is good to give thanks to you.
They shall bear fruit even in old age;
vigorous and sturdy shall they be,
Declaring how just is the Lord,
my Rock, in whom there is no wrong.
℞. Lord, it is good to give thanks to you.

READING II   1 Cor 15, 54-58

A reading from the first letter of Paul to the Corinthians

Victory has been given to us through Jesus Christ.

When the corruptible frame takes on incorruptibility and the mortal immortality, then will the saying of Scripture be fulfilled: "Death is swallowed up in victory." "O death, where is your victory? O death, where is your sting?" The sting of death is sin, and sin gets its power from the law. But thanks be to God who has given us the victory through our Lord Jesus Christ. Be steadfast and persevering, my beloved brothers, fully engaged in the work of the Lord. You know that your toil is not in vain when it is done in the Lord.

This is the Word of the Lord.

GOSPEL   Lk 6, 39-45
Alleluia

See no. 164.

✠ **A reading from the holy gospel according to Luke**

A man speaks from what is in his heart.

Jesus used images in speaking to the disciples: "Can a blind man act as guide to a blind man? Will they not both fall into a ditch? A student is not above his teacher; but every student when he has finished his studies will be on a par with his teacher.

"Why look at the speck in your brother's eye when you miss the plank in your own? How can you say to your brother, 'Brother, let me remove the speck from your eye,' yet fail yourself to see the plank lodged in your own? Hypocrite, remove the plank from your own eye first; then you will see clearly enough to remove the speck from your brother's eye.

"A good tree does not produce decayed fruit any more than a decayed tree produces good fruit. Each tree is known by its yield. Figs are not taken from thornbushes, nor grapes picked from brambles. A good man produces goodness from the good in his heart; an evil man produces evil out of his store of evil. Each man speaks from his heart's abundance."

This is the gospel of the Lord.

86   NINTH SUNDAY **A**
OF THE YEAR

READING I   Dt 11, 18. 26-28

A reading from the book of Deuteronomy
I set before you today a blessing and a curse.

Moses told the people, "Take these words of mine into your heart and soul. Bind them at your wrist as a sign, and let them be a pendant on your forehead.

"I set before you here, this day, a blessing and a curse: a blessing for obeying the commandments of the Lord, your God, which I enjoin on you today; a curse if you do not obey the commandments of the Lord, your God, but turn aside from the way I ordain for you today, to follow other gods, whom you have not known."

This is the Word of the Lord.

Responsorial Psalm   Ps 31, 2-3. 3-4. 17. 25

℟. (3) Lord, be my rock of safety.
In you, O Lord, I take refuge;
   let me never be put to shame.
In your justice rescue me,
   incline your ear to me,
   make haste to deliver me!
℟. Lord, be my rock of safety.
Be my rock of refuge,
   a stronghold to give me safety.
You are my rock and my fortress;
   for your name's sake you will lead and guide
   me.
℟. Lord, be my rock of safety.
Let your face shine upon your servant;
   save me in your kindness.
Take courage and be stouthearted,
   all you who hope in the Lord.
℟. Lord, be my rock of safety.

READING II   Rom 3, 21-25. 28

A reading from the letter of Paul to the Romans
A man is justified by faith, not by law.

Now the justice of God has been manifested apart from the law, even though both law and prophets bear witness to it—that justice of God which works through faith in Jesus Christ for all who believe. All men have sinned and hence are deprived of the glory of God. All men are now undeservedly justified by the gift of God, through the redemption wrought in Christ Jesus. Through his blood, God made him the means of expiation for all who believe.

For we hold that a man is justified by faith apart from observance of the law.

This is the Word of the Lord.

GOSPEL   Mt 7, 21-27
Alleluia

See no. 164.

✠ A reading from the holy gospel according to Matthew
A wise man builds his house on rock, not on sand.

Jesus said to his disciples: "None of those who cry out, 'Lord, Lord,' will enter the kingdom of God but only the one who does the will of my Father in heaven. When that day comes, many will plead with me, 'Lord, Lord, have we not prophesied in your name? Have we not exorcised demons by its power? Did we not do many miracles in your name as well?' Then I will declare to them solemnly, 'I never knew you. Out of my sight, you evildoers!'

"Anyone who hears my words and puts them into practice is like the wise man who built his house on rock. When the rainy season set in, the torrents came and the winds blew and buffeted his house. It did not collapse; it had been solidly set on rock. Anyone who hears my words but does not put them into practice is like the foolish man who built his house on sandy ground. The rains fell, the torrents came, the winds blew and lashed against his house. It collapsed under all this and was completely ruined."

This is the gospel of the Lord.

87   NINCH SUNDAY   B
OF THE YEAR

READING I   Dt 5, 12-15

A reading from the book of Deuteronomy

Remember that you were a servant in the land of Egypt
and that the Lord God brought you out.

"Take care to keep holy the sabbath day as
the Lord, your God, commanded you. Six days
you may labor and do all your work; but the
seventh day is the sabbath of the Lord, your
God. No work may be done then, whether by
you, or your son or daughter, or your male or
female slave, or your ox or ass or any of your
beasts, or the alien who lives with you. Your
male and female slave should rest as you do.
For remember that you too were once slaves
in Egypt, and the Lord, your God, brought you
from there with his strong hand and outstretched arm. That is why the Lord, your
God, has commanded you to observe the sabbath day."

This is the Word of the Lord.

Responsorial Psalm   Ps 81, 3-4. 5-6. 6-8. 10-11

℟. (2) Sing with joy to God our help.
Take up a melody, and sound the timbrel,
    the pleasant harp and the lyre.
Blow the trumpet at the new moon,
    at the full moon, on our solemn feast.
℟. Sing with joy to God our help.
For it is a statute in Israel,
    an ordinance of the God of Jacob,
Who made it a decree for Joseph
    when he came forth from the land of Egypt.
℟. Sing with joy to God our help.
An unfamiliar speech I hear:
    "I relieved his shoulder of the burden;
    his hands were freed from the basket.
In distress you called, and I rescued you."
℟. Sing with joy to God our help.
"There shall be no strange god among you
    nor shall you worship any alien god.
I, the Lord, am your God
    who led you forth from the land of Egypt."
℟. Sing with joy to God our help.

READING II   2 Cor 4, 6-11

**A reading from the second letter of Paul to the
Corinthians**

The life of Jesus is revealed in our body.

God, who said, "Let light shine out of darkness," has shone in our hearts, that we in turn
might make known the glory of God shining
on the face of Christ. This treasure we possess
in earthen vessels to make it clear that its
surpassing power comes from God and not
from us. We are afflicted in every way possible,
but we are not crushed; full of doubts, we never
despair. We are persecuted but never abandoned; we are struck down but never destroyed. Continually we carry about in our
bodies the dying of Jesus so that in our bodies
the life of Jesus may also be revealed. While
we live we are constantly being delivered to
death for Jesus' sake, so that the life of Jesus
may be revealed in our mortal flesh.

This is the Word of the Lord.

GOSPEL   Mk 2, 23-3, 6 or 2, 23-28
Alleluia

See no. 164.

✠ **A reading from the holy gospel according
to Mark**

The Son of Man is master even of the sabbath.

(Long Form)

It happened that Jesus was walking through
standing grain on the sabbath, and his disciples began to pull off heads of grain as they
went along. At this the Pharisees protested:
"Look! Why do they do a thing not permitted
on the sabbath?" He said to them: "Have you
never read what David did when he was in
need and he and his men were hungry? How
he entered God's house in the days of Abiathar
the high priest and ate the holy bread which
only the priests were permitted to eat? He
even gave it to his men." Then he said to
them: "The sabbath was made for man, not
man for the sabbath. That is why the Son
of Man is lord even of the sabbath."

He returned to the synagogue where there
was a man whose hand was shriveled up.

They kept an eye on Jesus to see whether he would heal him on the sabbath, hoping to be able to bring an accusation against him. He addressed the man with the shriveled hand: "Stand up here in front!" Then he said to them: "Is it permitted to do a good deed on the sabbath —or an evil one? To preserve life—or to destroy it?" At this they remained silent. He looked around at them angrily, for he was deeply grieved that they had closed their minds against him. Then he said to the man, "Stretch out your hand." The man did so and his hand was perfectly restored. When the Pharisees went outside, they immediately began to plot with the Herodians on how they might destroy him.
This is the gospel of the Lord.

OR

(Short Form)

It happened that Jesus was walking through standing grain on the sabbath, and his disciples began to pull off heads of grain as they went along. At this the Pharisees protested: "Look! Why do they do a thing not permitted on the sabbath?" He said to them: "Have you never read what David did when he was in need and he and his men were hungry? How he entered God's house in the days of Abiathar the high priest and ate the holy bread which only the priests were permitted to eat? He even gave it to his men." Then he said to them: "The sabbath was made for man, not man for the sabbath. That is why the Son of Man is lord even of the sabbath."
This is the gospel of the Lord.

---

88   NINTH SUNDAY   C
OF THE YEAR

READING II   1 Kgs 8, 41-43

A reading from the first book of Kings
When the stranger comes, hear him.

Solomon prayed in the temple, saying, "To the foreigner, likewise, who is not of your people Israel, but comes from a distant land to honor you (since men will learn of your great name and your mighty hand and your outstretched arm), when he comes and prays toward this temple, listen from your heavenly dwelling. Do all that the foreigner asks of you, that all the peoples of the earth may know your name, may fear you as do your people Israel, and may acknowledge that this temple which I have built is dedicated to your honor.
This is the Word of the Lord.

Responsorial Psalm   Ps 117, 1. 2

℟. (Mk 16, 15) Go out to all the world, and tell the Good News.
Praise the Lord, all you nations; glorify him, all you peoples!
For steadfast is his kindness toward us, and the fidelity of the Lord endures forever.
℟. Go out to all the world, and tell the Good News.
℟. Or: Alleluia.

READING II   Gal 1, 1-2. 6-10

The beginning of the letter of Paul to the Galatians
If I tried to please man, I could not be a servant of Christ.

Paul, an apostle sent not by men or by any man, but by Jesus Christ and God his Father who raised him from the dead—I and my brothers who are with me, send greetings to the churches in Galatia.

I am amazed that you are so soon deserting him who called you in accord with his gracious design in Christ, and are going over to another gospel. But there is no other. Some who wish to alter the gospel of Christ must have confused you. For if even we or an angel from heaven should preach to you a gospel not in accord with the one we delivered to you, let a curse be upon him! I repeat what I have just said: if anyone preaches a gospel to you other than the one you received, let a curse be upon him!

Whom would you say I am trying to please at this point—men or God? Is this how I seek to ingratiate myself with men? If I were trying

to win man's approval, I would surely not be
serving Christ!

This is the Word of the Lord.

GOSPEL   Lk 7, 1-10
Alleluia

See no. 164.

✠ **A reading from the holy gospel according
to Luke**

Nowhere in Israel have I found as much faith.

When Jesus had finished his discourse in the
hearing of the people, he entered Capernaum.
A centurion had a servant he held in high
regard, who was at that moment sick to the
point of death. When he heard about Jesus
he sent some Jewish elders to him, asking
him to come and save the life of his servant.
Upon approaching Jesus they petitioned him
earnestly. "He deserves this favor from you,"
they said, "because he loves our people, and
even built our synagogue for us." Jesus set
out with them. When he was only a short
distance from the house, the centurion sent
friends to tell him: "Sir, do not trouble yourself, for I am not worthy to have you enter
my house. That is why I did not presume
to come to you myself. Just give the order
and my servant will be cured. I too am a
man who knows the meaning of an order,
having soldiers under my command. I say to
one, 'On your way,' and off he goes; to another,
'Come here,' and he comes; to my slave, 'Do
this,' and he does it." Jesus showed amazement
on hearing this, and turned to the crowd which
was following him to say, "I tell you, I have
never found so much faith among the Israelites." When the deputation returned to the
house, they found the servant in perfect health.

This is the gospel of the Lord.

TENNTH SUNDAY **A**
OF THE YEAR

READING I   Hos 6, 3-6

A reading from the book of the prophet Hosea

What I want is love, not sacrifice, says the Lord.

"Let us know, let us strive to know the Lord;
as certain as the dawn is his coming,
and his judgment shines forth like the light
of day!
He will come to us like the rain,
like spring rain that waters the earth."

What can I do with you, Ephraim?
What can I do with you, Judah?
Your piety is like a morning cloud,
like the dew that early passes away.
For this reason I smote them through the
prophets,
I slew them by the words of my mouth;
For it is love that I desire, not sacrifice,
and knowledge of God rather than holo-
causts.

This is the Word of the Lord.

Responsorial Psalm   Ps 50, 1. 8. 12-13. 14-15

℟. (23) To the upright I will show the saving
power of God.
God the Lord has spoken and summoned the
earth,
from the rising of the sun to its setting.
"Not for your sacrifices do I rebuke you,
for your holocausts are before me always."
℟. To the upright I will show the saving
power of God.
"If I were hungry, I should not tell you,
for mine are the world and its fullness.
Do I eat the flesh of strong bulls,
or is the blood of goats my drink?"
℟. To the upright I will show the saving
power of God.
"Offer to God praise as your sacrifice
and fulfill your vows to the Most High;
Then call upon me in time of distress;
I will rescue you, and you shall glorify me."
℟. To the upright I will show the saving
power of God.

READING II   Rom 4, 18-25

A reading from the letter of Paul to the Romans

He drew strength from his faith while giving glory to God.

Abraham believed hoping against hope, and so became the father of many nations, just as it was once told him, "Numerous as this shall your descendants be." Without growing weak in faith he thought of his own body, which was as good as dead (for he was nearly a hundred years old), and of the dead womb of Sarah. Yet he never questioned or doubted God's promise; rather, he was strengthened in faith and gave glory to God, fully persuaded that God could do whatever he had promised. Thus his faith was credited to him as justice.

The words, "It was credited to him," were not written with him alone in view; they were intended for us too. For our faith will be credited to us also if we believe in him who raised Jesus our Lord from the dead, the Jesus who was handed over to death for our sins and raised up for our justification.

This is the Word of the Lord.

GOSPEL   Mt 9, 9-13

Alleluia

See no. 164.

✠ **A reading from the holy gospel according to Matthew**

I did not come to call the just, but sinners.

As Jesus moved about, he saw a man named Matthew at his post where taxes were collected. He said to him, "Follow me." Matthew got up and followed him, Now it happened that, while Jesus was at table in Matthew's home, many tax collectors and those known as sinners came to join Jesus and his disciples at dinner. The Pharisees saw this and complained to his disciples, "What reason can the Teacher have for eating with tax collectors and those who disregard the law?" Overhearing the remark, he said: "People who are in good health do not need a doctor; sick people do. Go and learn the meaning of the words, 'It is mercy I desire and not sacrifice.' I have come to call not the self-righteous, but sinners."

This is the gospel of the Lord.

TENTH SUNDAY
OF THE YEAR   **B**

READING I   Gn 3, 9-15

A reading from the book of Genesis

I will make you enemies of each other: your offspring and her offspring.

[After Adam had eaten of the tree] the Lord God called him and asked him, "Where are you?" He answered, "I heard you in the garden; but I was afraid, because I was naked, so I hid myself." Then he asked, "Who told you that you were naked? You have eaten, then, from the tree of which I had forbidden you to eat!" The man replied, "The woman whom you put here with me—she gave me fruit from the tree, and so I ate it." The Lord God then asked the woman, "Why did you do such a thing?" The woman answered, "The serpent tricked me into it, so I ate it."

Then the Lord God said to the serpent:
"Because you have done this, you shall be banned
    from all the animals
    and from all the wild creatures;
On your belly shall you crawl,
    and dirt shall you eat
    all the days of your life.
I will put enmity between you and the woman,
    and between your offspring and hers;
He will strike at your head,
    while you strike at his heel."

This is the Word of the Lord.

Responsorial Psalm   Ps 130, 1-2. 3-4. 5-6. 7-8

℟. (7) With the Lord there is mercy,
    and fullness of redemption.
Out of the depths I cry to you, O Lord;
    Lord, hear my voice!
Let your ears be attentive
    to my voice in supplication.
℟. With the Lord there is mercy,
    and fullness of redemption.
If you, O Lord, mark iniquities,
    Lord, who can stand?
But with you is forgiveness,
    that you may be revered.

℟. With the Lord there is mercy,
    and fullness of redemption.
I trust in the Lord;
    my soul trusts in his word.
More than sentinels wait for the dawn,
    let Israel wait for the Lord.
℟. With the Lord there is mercy,
    and fullness of redemption.
For with the Lord is kindness
    and with him is plenteous redemption;
And he will redeem Israel
    from all their iniquities.
℟. With the Lord there is mercy,
    and fullness of redemption.

READING II   2 Cor 4, 13–5, 1

A reading from the second letter of Paul to the
Corinthians

We believe, and therefore we speak.

We have that spirit of faith of which the Scripture says, "Because I believed, I spoke out."
We believe and so we speak, knowing that he who raised up the Lord Jesus will raise us up along with Jesus and place both us and you in his presence. Indeed, everything is ordered to your benefit, so that the grace bestowed in abundance may bring greater glory to God because they who give thanks are many.

We do not lose heart because our inner being is renewed each day, even though our body is being destroyed at the same time. The present burden of our trial is light enough and earns for us an eternal weight of glory beyond all comparison. We do not fix our gaze on what is seen but on what is unseen. What is seen is transitory; what is not seen lasts forever.

Indeed, we know that when the earthly tent in which we dwell is destroyed we have a dwelling provided for us by God, a dwelling in the heavens. not made by hands, but to last forever.

This is the Word of the Lord.

GOSPEL   Mk 3, 20-35
Alleluia
See no. 164.

✠ **A reading from the holy gospel according**
to Mark

It is the end of Satan.

Jesus came to the house with his disciples and again the crowd assembled, making it impossible for them to get any food whatever. When his family heard of this they came to take charge of him, saying, "He is out of his mind"; while the scribes who arrived from Jerusalem asserted, "He is possessed by Beelzebul," and "He expels demons with the help of the prince of demons." Summoning them, he then began to speak to them by way of examples: "How can Satan expel Satan? If a kingdom is torn by civil strife, that kingdom cannot last. If a household is divided according to loyalties, that household will not survive. Similarly, if Satan has suffered mutiny in his ranks and is torn by dissension, he cannot endure; he is finished. No one can enter a strong man's house and despoil his property unless he has first put him under restraint. Only then can he plunder his house.

"I give you my word, every sin will be forgiven mankind and all the blasphemies men utter, but whoever blasphemes against the Holy Spirit will never be forgiven. He carries the guilt of his sin without end." He spoke thus because they had said, "He is possessed by an unclean spirit."

His mother and his brothers arrived, and as they stood outside they sent word to him to come out. The crowd seated around him told him, "Your mother and your brothers and sisters are outside asking for you." He said in reply, "Who are my mother and my brothers?" And gazing around him at those seated in the circle he continued, "These are my mother and my brothers. Whoever does the will of God is brother and sister and mother to me."

This is the gospel of the Lord.

91 **TENTH SUNDAY** **C**
OF THE YEAR

READING I 1 Kgs 17, 17-24

A reading from the first book of Kings

Look, said Elijah, your son is living.

The son of the mistress of the house fell sick, and his sickness grew more severe until he stopped breathing. So she said to Elijah, "Why have you done this to me, O man of God? Have you come to me to call attention to my guilt and to kill my son?" "Give me your son," Elijah said to her. Taking him from her lap, he carried him to the upper room where he was staying, and laid him on his own bed. He called out to the Lord: "O Lord, my God, will you afflict even the widow with whom I am staying by killing her son?" Then he stretched himself out upon the child three times and called out to the Lord: "O Lord, my God, let the life breath return to the body of this child." The Lord heard the prayer of Elijah; the life breath returned to the child's body and he revived. Taking the child, Elijah brought him down into the house from the upper room and gave him to his mother. "See!" Elijah said to her, "your son is alive." "Now indeed I know that you are a man of God," the woman replied to Elijah. "The word of the Lord comes truly from your mouth."

This is the Word of the Lord.

Responsorial Psalm Ps 30, 2. 4. 5-6. 11. 12. 13

℞. (2) I will praise you, Lord,
for you have rescued me.

I will extol you, O Lord, for you drew me clear
and did not let my enemies rejoice over me.
O Lord, you brought me up from the nether world;
you preserved me from among those going down into the pit.

℞. I will praise you, Lord,
for you have rescued me.

Sing praise to the Lord, you his faithful ones,
and give thanks to his holy name.
For his anger lasts but a moment;
a lifetime, his good will.
At nightfall, weeping enters in,
but with the dawn, rejoicing.

℞. I will praise you, Lord,
for you have rescued me.

Hear, O Lord, and have pity on me;
O Lord, be my helper.
You changed my mourning into dancing;
O Lord, my God, forever will I give you thanks.

℞. I will praise you, Lord,
for you have rescued me.

READING II Gal 1, 11-19

A reading from the letter of Paul to the Galatians

God has revealed his Son in me, that I might preach the good news about him to the pagans.

I assure you, brothers, the gospel I proclaimed to you is no mere human invention. I did not receive it from any man, nor was I schooled in it. It came by revelation from Jesus Christ. You have heard, I know, the story of my former way of life in Judaism. You know that I went to extremes in persecuting the Church of God and tried to destroy it; I made progress in Jewish observances far beyond most of my contemporaries, in my excess of zeal to live out all the traditions of my ancestors.

But the time came when he who had set me apart before I was born and called me by his favor chose to reveal his Son through me, that I might spread among the Gentiles the good tidings concerning him. Immediately, without seeking human advisers or even going to Jerusalem to see those who were apostles before me, I went off to Arabia; later I returned to Damascus. Three years after that I went up to Jerusalem to get to know Cephas, with whom I stayed fifteen days. I did not meet any other apostles except James, the brother of the Lord.

This is the Word of the Lord.

GOSPEL
Lk 7, 11-17

Alleluia

See no. 164.

✠ A reading from the holy gospel according
to Luke

Young man, I say to you, arise.

Jesus went to a town called Naim, and his disciples and a large crowd accompanied him. As
he approached the gate of the town a dead man
was being carried out, the only son of a widowed mother. A considerable crowd of townsfolk were with her. The Lord was moved with
pity upon seeing her and said to her, "Do not
cry." Then he stepped forward and touched
the litter; at this, the bearers halted. He said,
"Young man, I bid you get up." The dead man
sat up and began to speak. Then Jesus gave
him back to his mother. Fear seized them all
and they began to praise God. "A great prophet
has risen among us," they said; and, "God has
visited his people." This was the report that
spread about him throughout Judea and the
surrounding country.

This is the gospel of the Lord.

92   ELEVENTH SUNDAY A
OF THE YEAR

READING I
Ex 19, 2-6

A reading from the book of Exodus

You will be a kingdom of priests, a consecrated nation.

The Israelites came to the desert of Sinai [and]
pitched camp.

While Israel was encamped here in front of
the mountain, Moses went up the mountain to
God. Then the Lord called to him and said,
"Thus shall you say to the house of Jacob; tell
the Israelites: You have seen for yourselves
how I treated the Egyptians and how I bore
you up on eagle wings, and brought you here to
myself. Therefore, if you hearken to my voice
and keep my covenant, you shall be my special
possession, dearer to me than all other people,
though all the earth is mine. You shall be to
me a kingdom of priests, a holy nation."

This is the Word of the Lord.

Responsorial Psalm
Ps 100, 1-2. 3. 5

℟. (3) We are his people:
the sheep of his flock.

Sing joyfully to the Lord, all you lands;
serve the Lord with gladness;
come before him with joyful song.

℟. We are his people:
the sheep of his flock.

Know that the Lord is God;
he made us, his we are;
his people, the flock he tends.

℟. We are his people:
the sheep of his flock.

The Lord is good:
his kindness endures forever,
and his faithfulness, to all generations.

℟. We are his people:
the sheep of his flock.

READING II
Rom 5, 6-11

A reading from the letter of Paul to the Romans

We have been reconciled to God through the death of his
Son; we are saved by his life.

At the appointed time, when we were still
powerless, Christ died for us godless men. It is
rare that anyone should lay down his life for a
just man, though it is barely possible that for a
good man someone may have the courage to
die. It is precisely in this that God proves his
love for us: that while we were still sinners,
Christ died for us. Now that we have been
justified by his blood, it is all the more certain
that we shall be saved by him from God's
wrath. For if, when we were God's enemies,
we were reconciled to him by the death of his
Son, it is all the more certain that we who have
been reconciled will be saved by his life. Not
only that; we go so far as to make God our
boast through our Lord Jesus Christ, through
whom we have now received reconciliation.

This is the Word of the Lord.

GOSPEL   Mt 9, 36–10, 8
Alleluia

See no. 164.

✠ A reading from the holy gospel according
to Matthew

He summoned his twelve disciples, and sent them out.

At the sight of the crowds, the heart of Jesus
was moved with pity. They were lying prostrate from exhaustion, like sheep without a
shepherd. He said to his disciples: "The harvest
is good but laborers are scarce. Beg the harvest
master to send out laborers to gather his harvest."

Then he summoned his twelve disciples and
gave them authority to expel unclean spirits
and cure sickness and disease of every kind.

The names of the twelve apostles are these:
first Simon, now known as Peter, and his
brother Andrew; James, Zebedee's son, and
his brother John; Philip and Bartholomew,
Thomas and Matthew the tax collector; James,
son of Alphaeus, and Thaddaeus; Simon the
Zealot party member, and Judas Iscariot, who
betrayed him. Jesus sent these men on mission
as the Twelve, after giving them the following
instructions:

"Do not visit pagan territory and do not
enter a Samaritan town. Go instead after the
lost sheep of the house of Israel. As you go,
make this announcement: 'The reign of God is
at hand!' Cure the sick, raise the dead, heal the
leprous, expel demons. The gift you have received, give as a gift."

This is the gospel of the Lord.

---

93   **ELEVENTH SUNDAY**   **B**
OF THE YEAR

READING I   Ez 17, 22-24

A reading from the book of the prophet Ezekiel

I have made the small tree great.

Thus says the Lord God:
I, too, will take from the crest of the cedar,
from its topmost branches tear off a tender
shoot,

And plant it on a high and lofty mountain;
on the mountain heights of Israel I will
plant it.
It shall put forth branches and bear fruit,
and become a majestic cedar.
Birds of every kind shall dwell beneath it,
every winged thing in the shade of its
boughs.
And all the trees of the field shall know
that I, the Lord,
Bring low the high tree,
lift high the lowly tree,
Wither up the green tree,
and make the withered tree bloom.
As I, the Lord, have spoken, so will I do.
This is the Word of the Lord.

Responsorial Psalm   Ps 92, 2-3. 13-14: 15-16

℟. (2) Lord, it is good to give thanks to you.
It is good to give thanks to the Lord,
to sing praise to your name, Most High,
To proclaim your kindness at dawn
and your faithfulness throughout the night.
℟. Lord, it is good to give thanks to you.
The just man shall flourish like the palm tree,
like a cedar of Lebanon shall he grow.
They that are planted in the house of the Lord
shall flourish in the courts of our God.
℟. Lord, it is good to give thanks to you.
They shall bear fruit even in old age;
vigorous and sturdy shall they be,
Declaring how just is the Lord,
my Rock, in whom there is no wrong.
℟. Lord, it is good to give thanks to you.

READING II   2 Cor 5, 6-10

A reading from the second letter of Paul to the
Corinthians

Whether we are living in the body or exiled from it, we
are intent on pleasing the Lord.

We continue to be confident. We know that
while we dwell in the body we are away from
the Lord. We walk by faith, not by sight. I repeat, we are full of confidence, and would much
rather be away from the body and at home with
the Lord. This being so, we make it our aim to

please him whether we are with him or away from him. The lives of all of us are to be revealed before the tribunal of Christ so that each one may receive his recompense, good or bad, according to his life in the body.

This is the Word of the Lord.

GOSPEL　　　　　　　　　　　　Mk 4, 26-34
Alleluia

See no. 164.

✠ A reading from the holy gospel according to Mark

The mustard seed, the smallest of all the seeds, grows into the biggest shrub of all.

Jesus said to the crowd: "This is how it is with the reign of God. A man scatters seed on the ground. He goes to bed and gets up day after day. Through it all the seed sprouts and grows without his knowing how it happens. The soil produces of itself first the blade, then the ear, finally the ripe wheat in the ear. When the crop is ready he 'wields the sickle, for the time is ripe for harvest.' "

He went on to say: "What comparison shall we use for the reign of God? What image will help to present it? It is like mustard seed which, when planted in the soil, is the smallest of all the earth's seeds, yet once it is sown, springs up to become the largest of shrubs, with branches big enough for the birds of the sky to build nests in its shade." By means of many such parables he taught them the message in a way they could understand. To them he spoke only by way of parable, while he kept explaining things privately to his disciples.

This is the gospel of the Lord.

94　　ELEVENTH SUNDAY　　C
OF THE YEAR

READING I　　　　　　　　　2 Sm 12, 7-10. 13

A reading from the second book of Samuel

The Lord God forgave your sin; you will not die.

Nathan said to David: "Thus says the Lord God of Israel: 'I anointed you king of Israel. I rescued you from the hand of Saul. I gave you

your lord's house and your lord's wives for your own. I gave you the house of Israel and of Judah. And if this were not enough, I could count up for you still more. Why have you spurned the Lord and done evil in his sight? You have cut down Uriah the Hittite with the sword; you took his wife as your own, and him you killed with the sword of the Ammonites. Now, therefore, the sword shall never depart from your house, because you have despised me and have taken the wife of Uriah to be your wife.' " Then David said to Nathan, "I have sinned against the Lord." Nathan answered David: "The Lord on his part has forgiven your sin: you shall not die."

This is the Word of the Lord.

Responsorial Psalm　　　　Ps 32, 1-2. 5. 7. 11

℟. (5) Lord, forgive the wrong I have done.
Happy is he whose fault is taken away,
　　whose sin is covered.
Happy the man to whom the Lord imputes not guilt,
　　in whose spirit there is no guile.
℟. Lord, forgive the wrong I have done.
I acknowledged my sin to you,
　　my guilt I covered not.
I said, "I confess my faults to the Lord,"
　　and you took away the guilt of my sin.
℟. Lord, forgive the wrong I have done.
You are my shelter; from distress you will preserve me;
　　with glad cries of freedom you will ring me round.
℟. Lord, forgive the wrong I have done.
Be glad in the Lord and rejoice, you just;
　　exult, all you upright of heart.
℟. Lord, forgive the wrong I have done.

READING II　　　　　　　　　Gal 2, 16. 19-21

A reading from the letter of Paul to the Galatians

I live now, not with my own life but with the life of Christ who lives in me.

Knowing that a man is not justified by legal observance but by faith in Jesus Christ, we too have believed in him in order to be justified by faith in Christ, not by observance of the law; for by works of the law no one will be justified. It was through the law that I died to the law, to live for God. I have been crucified with Christ, and the life I live now is not my own; Christ is living in me. I still live my human life, but it is a life of faith in the Son of God, who loved me and gave himself for me. I will not treat God's gracious gift as pointless. If justice is available through the law, then Christ died to no purpose!

This is the Word of the Lord.

GOSPEL   Lk 7, 36–8, 3 or 7, 36-50

Alleluia

See no. 164.

✠ A reading from the holy gospel according to Luke

Her many sins were forgiven her, because she has shown great love.

(Long Form)

There was a certain Pharisee who invited Jesus to dine with him. Jesus went to the Pharisee's home and reclined to eat. A woman known in the town to be a sinner learned that he was dining in the Pharisee's home. She brought in a vase of perfumed oil and stood behind him at his feet, weeping so that her tears fell upon his feet. Then she wiped them with her hair, kissing them and perfuming them with the oil. When his host, the Pharisee, saw this, he said to himself, "If this man were a prophet, he would know who and what sort of woman this is that touches him—that she is a sinner." In answer to his thoughts, Jesus said to him, "Simon, I have something to propose to you." "Teacher," he said, "speak."

"Two men owed money to a certain money-lender; one owed a total of five hundred coins, the other fifty. Since neither was able to repay, he wrote off both debts. Which of them was more grateful to him?" Simon answered, "He, I presume, to whom he remitted the larger sum." Jesus said to him, "You are right."

Turning then to the woman, he said to Simon: "You see this woman? I came to your home and you provided me with no water for my feet. She has washed my feet with her tears and wiped them with her hair. You gave me no kiss, but she has not ceased kissing my feet since I entered. You did not anoint my head with oil, but she has anointed my feet with perfume. I tell you, that is why her many sins are forgiven—because of her great love. Little is forgiven the one whose love is small."

He said to her then, "Your sins are forgiven," at which his fellow guests began to ask among themselves, "Who is this that he even forgives sins?" Meanwhile he said to the woman, "Your faith has been your salvation. Go now in peace."

After this he journeyed through towns and villages preaching and proclaiming the good news of the kingdom of God. The Twelve accompanied him, and also some women who had been cured of evil spirits and maladies: Mary called the Magdalene, from whom seven devils had gone out, Joanna, the wife of Herod's steward Chuza, Susanna, and many others who were assisting them out of their means.

This is the gospel of the Lord.

OR

(Short Form)

There was a certain Pharisee who invited Jesus to dine with him. Jesus went to the Pharisee's home and reclined to eat. A woman known in the town to be a sinner learned that he was dining in the Pharisee's home. She brought in a vase of perfumed oil and stood behind him at his feet, weeping so that her tears fell upon his feet. Then she wiped them with her hair, kissing them and perfuming them with the oil. When his host, the Pharisee, saw this, he said to himself, "If this man were a prophet, he would know who and what sort of woman this is that touches him—that she is a sinner." In answer to his thoughts, Jesus said to him, "Simon, I have something to propose to you." "Teacher," he said, "speak."

"Two men owed money to a certain money-lender; one owed a total of five hundred coins, the other fifty. Since neither was able to repay, he wrote off both debts. Which of them was more grateful to him?" Simon answered, "He,

I presume, to whom he remitted the larger sum." Jesus said to him, "You are right."

Turning then to the woman, he said to Simon: "You see this woman? I came to your home and you provided me with no water for my feet. She has washed my feet with her tears and wiped them with her hair. You gave me no kiss, but she has not ceased kissing my feet since I entered. You did not anoint my head with oil, but she has anointed my feet with perfume. I tell you, that is why her many sins are forgiven—because of her great love. Little is forgiven the one whose love is small."

He said to her then, "Your sins are forgiven," at which his fellow guests began to ask among themselves, "Who is this that he even forgives sins?" Meanwhile he said to the woman, "Your faith has been your salvation. Go now in peace."

This is the gospel of the Lord.

---

95   **TWELFTH SUNDAY**   **A**
            OF THE YEAR

READING I   Jer 20, 10-13

A reading from the book of the prophet Jeremiah

He has delivered the soul of the needy from the hands of evil men.

Jeremiah said:
"Yes, I hear the whisperings of many:
    'Terror on every side!
    Denounce! let us denounce him!'
All those who were my friends
    are on the watch for any misstep of mine.
'Perhaps he will be trapped; then we can prevail,
    and take our vengeance on him.'
But the Lord is with me, like a mighty champion:
    my persecutors will stumble, they will not triumph.
In their failure they will be put to utter shame,
    to lasting, unforgettable confusion.
O Lord of hosts, you who test the just,
    who probe mind and heart,

Let me witness the vengeance you take on them,
    for to you I have entrusted my cause.
Sing to the Lord,
    praise the Lord,
For he has rescued the life of the poor
    from the power of the wicked!"

        This is the Word of the Lord.

Responsorial Psalm   Ps 69, 8-10. 14. 17. 33-35

℟. (14) Lord, in your great love, answer me.
For your sake I bear insult,
    and shame covers my face.
I have become an outcast to my brothers,
    a stranger to my mother's sons,
Because zeal for your house consumes me,
    and the insults of those who blaspheme you fall upon me.
℟. Lord, in your great love, answer me.
I pray to you, O Lord,
    for the time of your favor, O God!
In your great kindness answer me
    with your constant help.
Answer me, O Lord, for bounteous is your kindness;
    in your great mercy turn toward me.
℟. Lord, in your great love, answer me.
"See, you lowly ones, and be glad;
    you who seek God, may your hearts be merry!
For the Lord hears the poor,
    and his own who are in bonds he spurns not.
Let the heavens and the earth praise him,
    the seas and whatever moves in them!"
℟. Lord, in your great love, answer me.

READING II   Rom 5, 12-15

A reading from the letter of Paul to the Romans

God's gift to us is nothing like our sin against him.

Just as through one man sin entered the world and with sin death, death thus coming to all men inasmuch as all sinned—before the law there was sin in the world, even though sin is not imputed when there is no law—I say, from Adam to Moses death reigned, even over those who had not sinned by breaking a precept as did Adam, that type of the man to come.

But the gift is not like the offense. For if by the offense of the one man all died, much more did the grace of God and the gracious gift of the one man, Jesus Christ, abound for all.

This is the Word of the Lord.

GOSPEL   Mt 10, 26-33

Alleluia

See no. 164.

✠ A reading from the holy gospel according to Matthew

Do not fear those who can kill the body.

Jesus said to his apostles: "Do not let men intimidate you. Nothing is concealed that will not be revealed, and nothing hidden that will not become known. What I tell you in darkness, speak in the light. What you hear in private, proclaim from the housetops.

"Do not fear those who deprive the body of life but cannot destroy the soul. Rather, fear him who can destroy both body and soul in Gehenna. Are not two sparrows sold for next to nothing? Yet not a single sparrow falls to the ground without your Father's consent. As for you, every hair of your head has been counted; so do not be afraid of anything. You are worth more than an entire flock of sparrows. Whoever acknowledges me before men I will acknowledge before my Father in heaven. Whoever disowns me before men I will disown before my Father in heaven."

This is the gospel of the Lord.

---

96   **TWELFTH SUNDAY**   **B**

OF THE YEAR

READING I   Jb 38, 1. 8-11

A reading from the book of Job

Here I have set the boundaries of the sea.

The Lord addressed Job out of the storm and said:

Who shut within doors the sea,
    when it burst forth from the womb;
When I made the clouds its garment
    and thick darkness its swaddling bands?

When I set limits for it
    and fastened the bar of its door,
And said: Thus far shall you come but no
    farther,
    and here shall your proud waves be stilled!

This is the Word of the Lord.

Responsorial Psalm   Ps 107, 23-24. 25-26. 28-29. 30-31

℟. (1) Give thanks to the Lord,
    his love is everlasting.

They who sailed the sea in ships,
    trading on the deep waters,
These saw the works of the Lord
    and his wonders in the abyss.

℟. Give thanks to the Lord,
    his love is everlasting.

His command raised up a storm wind
    which tossed its waves on high.
They mounted up to heaven; they sank to the
    depths;
    their hearts melted away in their plight.

℟. Give thanks to the Lord,
    his love is everlasting.

They cried to the Lord in their distress;
    from their straits he rescued them,
He hushed the storm to a gentle breeze,
    and the billows of the sea were stilled.

℟. Give thanks to the Lord,
    his love is everlasting.

They rejoiced that they were calmed,
    and he brought them to their desired haven.
Let them give thanks to the Lord for his kindness
    and his wondrous deeds to the children of
    men.

℟. Give thanks to the Lord,
    his love is everlasting.

℟. Or: Alleluia.

READING II   2 Cor 5, 14-17

**A reading from the second letter of Paul to the
    Corinthians**

All things are made new.

The love of Christ impels us who have reached the conviction that since one died for all, all died. He died for all so that those who live might live no longer for themselves, but for him who for their sakes died and was raised up.

Because of this we no longer look on anyone in terms of mere human judgment. If at one time we so regarded Christ, we no longer know him by this standard. This means that if anyone is in Christ, he is a new creation. The old order has passed away; now all is new!

This is the Word of the Lord.

GOSPEL   Mk 4, 35-41
Alleluia

See no. 164.

✠ **A reading from the holy gospel according to Mark**

Who can this be? Even the wind and the sea obey him.

One day as evening drew on Jesus said to his disciples, "Let us cross over to the farther shore." Leaving the crowd, they took him away in the boat in which he was sitting, while the other boats accompanied him. It happened that a bad squall blew up. The waves were breaking over the boat and it began to ship water badly. Jesus was in the stern through it all, sound asleep on a cushion. They finally woke him and said to him, "Teacher, doesn't it matter to you that we are going to drown?" He awoke and rebuked the wind and said to the sea: "Quiet! Be still!" The wind fell off and everything grew calm. Then he said to them, "Why are you so terrified? Why are you lacking in faith?" A great awe overcame them at this. They kept saying to one another, "Who can this be that the wind and the sea obey him?"

This is the gospel of the Lord.

---

97   **TWELFTH SUNDAY**   **C**
            OF THE YEAR

READING I   Zec 12, 10-11

A reading from the book of the prophet Zechariah

They will look on the one whom they have pierced
(Jn 19, 37).

I will pour out on the house of David and on the inhabitants of Jerusalem a spirit of grace and petition; and they shall look on him whom they have thrust through, and they shall mourn for him as one mourns for an only son, and they shall grieve over him as one grieves over a first-born.

On that day the mourning in Jerusalem shall be as great as the mourning of Hadadrimmon in the plain of Megiddo.

This is the Word of the Lord.

Responsorial Psalm   Ps 63, 2. 3-4. 5-6. 8-9

℟. (2) My soul is thirsting for you, O Lord my God.

O God, you are my God whom I seek;
  for you my flesh pines and my soul thirsts
  like the earth, parched, lifeless and without water.

℟. My soul is thirsting for you, O Lord my God.

Thus have I gazed toward you in the sanctuary
  to see your power and your glory,
For your kindness is a greater good than life;
  my lips shall glorify you.

℟. My soul is thirsting for you, O Lord my God.

Thus will I bless you while I live;
  lifting up my hands, I will call upon your name.
As with the riches of a banquet shall my soul be satisfied,
  and with exultant lips my mouth shall praise you.

℟. My soul is thirsting for you, O Lord my God.

You are my help,
  and in the shadow of your wings I shout for joy.

My soul clings fast to you;
   your right hand upholds me.
℞. My soul is thirsting for you, O Lord my
   God.

READING II   Gal 3, 26-29

A reading from the letter of Paul to the Galatians

You who have been baptized have put on Christ.

Each one of you is a son of God because of
your faith in Christ Jesus. All of you who have
been baptized into Christ have clothed yourselves with him. There does not exist among
you Jew or Greek, slave or freeman, male or
female. All are one in Christ Jesus. Furthermore, if you belong to Christ you are the descendants of Abraham, which means you inherit all that was promised.
   This is the Word of the Lord.

GOSPEL   Lk 9, 18-24
Alleluia
See no. 164.

✠ A reading from the holy gospel according
   to Luke

*You are the Messiah sent by God. It is necessary for the
Son of Man to suffer much.*

One day when Jesus was praying in seclusion
and his disciples were with him, he put the
question to them, "Who do the crowds say that
I am?" "John the Baptizer," they replied, "and
some say Elijah, while others claim that one of
the prophets of old has returned from the
dead." "But you—who do you say that I am?"
he asked them. Peter said in reply, "The Messiah of God." He strictly forbade them to tell
this to anyone. "The Son of Man," he said,
"must first endure many sufferings, be rejected
by the elders, the high priests and the scribes,
and be put to death, and then be raised up on
the third day."
   Jesus said to all: "Whoever wishes to be my
follower must deny his very self, take up his
cross each day, and follow in my steps. Whoever would save his life will lose it, and whoever
loses his life for my sake will save it."
   This is the gospel of the Lord.

---

98   **THIRTEENTH SUNDAY**   A
          OF THE YEAR

READING I   2 Kgs 4, 8-11. 14-16

A reading from the second book of Kings

That is the holy man of God, let him remain there.

One day Elisha came to Shunem, where there
was a woman of influence, who urged him to
dine with her. Afterward, whenever he passed
by, he used to stop there to dine. So she said to
her husband, "I know that he is a holy man of
God. Since he visits us often, let us arrange a
little room on the roof and furnish it for him
with a bed, table, chair, and lamp, so that when
he comes to us he can stay there." Sometime
later Elisha arrived and stayed in the room
overnight.
   Later Elisha asked, "Can something be done
for her?" "Yes!" Gehazi answered. "She has no
son, and her husband is getting on in years."
"Call her," said Elisha. When she had been
called, and stood at the door, Elisha promised,
"This time next year you will be fondling a
baby son."
   This is the Word of the Lord.

Responsorial Psalm   Ps 89, 2-3. 16-17. 18-19

℞. (2) For ever I will sing the goodness of the
   Lord.
The favors of the Lord I will sing forever;
   through all generations my mouth shall pro-
   claim your faithfulness.
For you have said, "My kindness is established
   forever";
   in heaven you have confirmed your faithful-
   ness.
℞. For ever I will sing the goodness of the
   Lord.
Happy the people who know the joyful shout;
   in the light of your countenance, O Lord,
   they walk.
At your name they rejoice all the day,
   and through your justice they are exalted.
℞. For ever I will sing the goodness of the
   Lord.
For you are the splendor of their strength,
   and by your favor our horn is exalted.

For to the Lord belongs our shield,
and to the Holy One of Israel, our king.
℟. For ever I will sing the goodness of the
Lord.

READING II   Rom 6, 3-4. 8-11
A reading from the letter of Paul to the Romans
Having been buried with him through baptism, we shall
walk in a new life.

Are you not aware that we who were baptized
into Christ Jesus were baptized into his death?
Through baptism into his death we were buried
with him, so that, just as Christ was raised
from the dead by the glory of the Father, we
too might live a new life. If we have died with
Christ, we believe that we are also to live with
him. We know that Christ, once raised from
the dead, will never die again; death has no
more power over him. His death was death to
sin, once for all; his life is life for God. In the
same way, you must consider yourselves dead
to sin but alive for God in Christ Jesus.
            This is the Word of the Lord.

GOSPEL   Mt 10, 37-42
Alleluia
See no. 164.

✠ **A reading from the holy gospel according
to Matthew**
Anyone who does not accept his cross is not worthy of me.
Anyone who welcomes you, welcomes me.

Jesus said to his apostles: "Whoever loves father or mother, son or daughter, more than me
is not worthy of me. He who will not take up his
cross and come after me is not worthy of me.
He who seeks only himself brings himself to
ruin, whereas he who brings himself to nought
for me discovers who he is.

"He who welcomes you welcomes me, and
he who welcomes me welcomes him who sent
me. He who welcomes a prophet because he
bears the name of prophet receives a prophet's
reward; he who welcomes a holy man because
he is known as holy receives a holy man's reward. And I promise you that whoever gives a
cup of cold water to one of these lowly ones

because he is a disciple will not want for his
reward."
            This is the gospel of the Lord.

---

99   **THIRTEENTH SUNDAY**   **B**
            OF THE YEAR
READING I   Wis 1, 13-15; 2, 23-24
A reading from the book of Wisdom
It was the devil's envy that brought death into the world.
God did not make death,
nor does he rejoice in the destruction of the
living.
For he fashioned all things that they might
have being;
and the creatures of the world are whole-
some,
And there is not a destructive drug among
them
nor any domain of the nether world on earth,
For justice is undying.

For God formed man to be imperishable;
the image of his own nature he made him.
But by the envy of the devil, death entered the
world,
and they who are in his possession experience it.
            This is the Word of the Lord.

Responsorial Psalm   Ps 30, 2. 4. 5-6. 11. 12. 13
℟. (2) I will praise you, Lord,
for you have rescued me.
I will extol you, O Lord, for you drew me clear
and did not let my enemies rejoice over me.
O Lord, you brought me up from the nether
world;
you preserved me from among those going
down into the pit.
℟. I will praise you, Lord,
for you have rescued me.
Sing praise to the Lord, you his faithful ones,
and give thanks to his holy name.
For his anger lasts but a moment;
a lifetime, his good will.
At nightfall, weeping enters in,
but with the dawn, rejoicing.

℟. I will praise you, Lord,
  for you have rescued me.
Hear, O Lord, and have pity on me;
  O Lord, be my helper.
You changed my mourning into dancing;
  O Lord, my God, forever will I give you
  thanks.
℟. I will praise you, Lord,
  for you have rescued me.

READING II   2 Cor 8, 7. 9. 13-15

A reading from the second letter of Paul to the Corinthians

Your abundance should supply their want.

**Just as you are rich in every respect, in faith
and discourse, in knowledge, in total concern,
and in our love for you, you may also abound in
your work of charity.**

You are well acquainted with the favor
shown you by our Lord Jesus Christ: how for
your sake he made himself poor though he was
rich, so that you might become rich by his poverty. The relief of others ought not to impoverish you; there should be a certain equality. Your
plenty at the present time should supply their
need so that their surplus may in turn one day
supply your need, with equality as the result.
It is written, "He who gathered much had no
excess and he who gathered little had no lack."
  This is the Word of the Lord.

GOSPEL   Mk 5, 21-43 or 5, 21-24. 35-43
Alleluia

See no. 164.

✠ **A reading from the holy gospel according
to Mark**

Young girl, I say to you, arise.

(Long Form)

When Jesus had crossed back to the other side
of the Sea of Galilee in the boat, a large crowd
gathered around him and he stayed close to the
lake. One of the officials of the synagogue, a
man named Jairus, came near. Seeing Jesus, he
fell at his feet and made this earnest appeal:
"My little daughter is critically ill. Please

come and lay your hands on her so that she
may get well and live." The two went off
together and a large crowd followed, pushing
against Jesus.

There was a woman in the area who had
been afflicted with a hemorrhage for a dozen
years. She had received treatment at the hands
of doctors of every sort and exhausted her
savings in the process, yet she got no relief; on
the contrary, she only grew worse. She had
heard about Jesus and came up behind him in
the crowd and put her hand to his cloak. "If I
just touch his clothing," she thought, "I shall
get well." Immediately her flow of blood dried
up and the feeling that she was cured of her
affliction ran through her whole body. Jesus
was immediately conscious that healing power
had gone out from him. Wheeling about in the
crowd, he began to ask, "Who touched my
clothing?" His disciples said to him, "You can
see how this crowd hems you in, yet you ask,
'Who touched me?' Despite this, he kept looking around to see the woman who had done it.
Fearful and beginning to tremble now as she
realized what had happened, the woman came
and fell in front of him and told him the whole
truth. He said to her, "Daughter, it is your faith
that has cured you. Go in peace and be free of
this illness."

He had not finished speaking when people
from the official's house arrived saying, "Your
daughter is dead. Why bother the Teacher
further?" Jesus disregarded the report that had
been brought and said to the official: "Fear is
useless. What is needed is trust." He would not
permit anyone to follow him except Peter,
James, and James's brother John. As they approached the house of the synagogue leader,
Jesus was struck by the noise of people wailing
and crying loudly on all sides. He entered and
said to them: "Why do you make this din with
your wailing? The child is not dead. She is
asleep." At this they began to ridicule him.
Then he put them all out.

Jesus took the child's father and mother and
his own companions and entered the room
where the child lay. Taking her hand he said to
her, "Talitha, koum," which means, "Little girl,

get up." The girl, a child of twelve, stood up immediately and began to walk around. At this the family's astonishment was complete. He enjoined them strictly not to let anyone know about it, and told them to give her something to eat.

This is the gospel of the Lord.

OR

(Short Form)

When Jesus had crossed back to the other side of the Sea of Galilee in the boat, a large crowd gathered around him and he stayed close to the lake. One of the officials of the synagogue, a man named Jairus, came near. Seeing Jesus, he fell at his feet and made this earnest appeal: "My little daughter is critically ill. Please come and lay your hands on her so that she may get well and live." The two went off together and a large crowd followed, pushing against Jesus.

People from the official's house arrived, saying, "Your daughter is dead. Why bother the Teacher further?" Jesus disregarded the report that had been brought and said to the official: "Fear is useless. What is needed is trust." He would not permit anyone to follow him except Peter, James, and James's brother John. As they approached the house of the synagogue leader, Jesus was struck by the noise of people wailing and crying loudly on all sides. He entered and said to them: "Why do you make this din with your wailing? The child is not dead. She is asleep." At this they began to ridicule him. Then he put them all out.

Jesus took the child's father and mother and his own companions and entered the room where the child lay. Taking her hand he said to her, "Talitha, koum," which means, "Little girl, get up." The girl, a child of twelve, stood up immediately and began to walk around. At this the family's astonishment was complete. He enjoined them strictly not to let anyone know about it, and told them to give her something to eat.

This is the gospel of the Lord.

**100   THIRTEENTH SUNDAY   C
OF THE YEAR**

READING I   1 Kgs 19, 16. 19-21

A reading from the first book of Kings

Elisha rose and followed Elijah and became his servant.

The Lord said to Elijah: "You shall anoint Elisha, son of Shaphat of Abel-meholah, as prophet to succeed you."

Elijah set out, and came upon Elisha, son of Shaphat, as he was plowing with twelve yoke of oxen; he was following the twelfth. Elijah went over to him and threw his cloak over him. Elisha left the oxen, ran after Elijah, and said, "Please, let me kiss my father and mother goodbye, and I will follow you." "Go back!" Elijah answered. "Have I done anything to you?" Elisha left him and, taking the yoke of oxen, slaughtered them; he used the plowing equipment for fuel to boil their flesh, and gave it to his people to eat. Then he left and followed Elijah as his attendant.

This is the Word of the Lord.

Responsorial Psalm   Ps 16, 1-2. 5. 7-8. 9-10. 11

℟. (5) You are my inheritance, O Lord.
Keep me, O God, for in you I take refuge;
    I say to the Lord, "My Lord are you.
O Lord, my allotted portion and my cup,
    you it is who hold fast my lot.
℟. You are my inheritance, O Lord.
I bless the Lord who counsels me;
    even in the night my heart exhorts me.
I set the Lord ever before me;
    with him at my right hand I shall not be disturbed.
℟. You are my inheritance, O Lord.
Therefore my heart is glad and my soul rejoices,
    my body, too, abides in confidence;
Because you will not abandon my soul to the nether world,
    nor will you suffer your faithful one to undergo corruption.
℟. You are my inheritance, O Lord.
You will show me the path to life,
    fullness of joys in your presence,
    the delights at your right hand forever.

℟. You are my inheritance, O Lord.

READING II   Gal 5, 1. 13-18
A reading from the letter of Paul to the Galatians

My brothers, you were called to freedom.

It was for liberty that Christ freed us. So stand firm, and do not take on yourselves the yoke of slavery a second time!

My brothers, remember that you have been called to live in freedom—but not a freedom that gives free rein to the flesh. Out of love, place yourselves at one another's service. The whole law has found its fulfillment in this one saying: "You shall love your neighbor as yourself." If you go on biting and tearing one another to pieces, take care! You will end up in mutual destruction!

My point is that you should live in accord with the spirit and you will not yield to the cravings of the flesh. The flesh lusts against the spirit and the spirit against the flesh; the two are directly opposed. This is why you do not do what your will intends. If you are guided by the spirit, you are not under the law.

This is the Word of the Lord.

GOSPEL   Lk 9, 51-62
Alleluia

See no. 164.

✠ **A reading from the holy gospel according to Luke**

Jesus resolutely set his face toward Jerusalem. I will follow you wherever you will go.

As the time approached when Jesus was to be taken from this world, he firmly resolved to proceed toward Jerusalem, and sent messengers on ahead of him. These entered a Samaritan town to prepare for his passing through, but the Samaritans would not welcome him because he was on his way to Jerusalem. When his disciples James and John saw this, they said, "Lord, would you not have us call down fire from heaven to destroy them?" He turned toward them only to reprimand them. Then they set off for another town.

As they were making their way along, someone said to him, "I will be your follower wherever you go." Jesus said to him, "The foxes have lairs, the birds of the sky have nests, but the Son of Man has nowhere to lay his head." To another he said, "Come after me." The man replied, "Let me bury my father first." Jesus said to him, "Let the dead bury their dead; come away and proclaim the kingdom of God." Yet another said, "I will be your follower, Lord, but first let me take leave of my people at home." Jesus answered him, "Whoever puts his hand to the plow but keeps looking back is unfit for the reign of God."

This is the gospel of the Lord.

---

101   FOURTEENTH SUNDAY 🅐
OF THE YEAR

READING I   Zec 9, 9-10
A reading from the book of the prophet Zechariah

See how humbly your king comes to you!

Rejoice heartily, O daughter Zion,
  shout for joy, O daughter Jerusalem!
See, your king shall come to you;
  a just savior is he,
Meek, and riding on an ass,
  on a colt, the foal of an ass.
He shall banish the chariot from Ephraim,
  and the horse from Jerusalem;
The warrior's bow shall be banished,
  and he shall proclaim peace to the nations.
His dominion shall be from sea to sea,
  and from the River to the ends of the earth.
        This is the Word of the Lord.

Responsorial Psalm   Ps 145, 1-2. 8-9. 10-11. 13-14

℟. (1) I will praise your name for ever,
  my king and my God.
I will extol you, O my God and King,
  and I will bless your name forever and ever.
Every day will I bless you,
  and I will praise your name forever and ever.
℟. I will praise your name for ever,
  my king and my God.

The Lord is gracious and merciful,
  slow to anger and of great kindness.
The Lord is good to all
  and compassionate toward all his works.
℟. I will praise your name for ever,
  my king and my God.
Let all your works give you thanks, O Lord,
  and let your faithful ones bless you.
Let them discourse of the glory of your kingdom
  and speak of your might.
℟. I will praise your name for ever,
  my king and my God.
The Lord is faithful in all his words
  and holy in all his works.
The Lord lifts up all who are falling
  and raises up all who are bowed down.
℟. I will praise your name for ever,
  my king and my God.
℟. Or: Alleluia.

READING II   Rom 8, 9. 11-13

A reading from the letter of Paul to the Romans
*If by the spirit you put an end to the misdeeds of the body,
you will live.*

You are not in the flesh; you are in the spirit,
since the Spirit of God dwells in you. If anyone
does not have the Spirit of Christ, he does not
belong to Christ. If the Spirit of him who raised
Jesus from the dead dwells in you, then he who
raised Christ from the dead will bring your
mortal bodies to life also through his Spirit
dwelling in you.

  We are debtors, then, my brothers—but not
to the flesh, so that we should live according
to the flesh. If you live according to the flesh,
you will die; but if by the spirit you put to
death the evil deeds of the body, you will live.
    This is the Word of the Lord.

GOSPEL   Mt 11, 25-30
Alleluia

See no. 164, e.g., no. 2.

✠ **A reading from the holy gospel according
to Matthew**
I am gentle and humble of heart.

On one occasion Jesus spoke thus: "Father,
Lord of heaven and earth, to you I offer praise;
for what you have hidden from the learned and
the clever you have revealed to the merest
children. Father, it is true. You have graciously
willed it so. Everything has been given over to
me by my Father. No one knows the Son but
the Father, and no one knows the Father but
the Son—and anyone to whom the Son wishes
to reveal him.

  "Come to me, all you who are weary and find
life burdensome, and I will refresh you. Take
my yoke upon your shoulders and learn from
me, for I am gentle and humble of heart. Your
souls will find rest, for my yoke is easy and my
burden light."
    This is the gospel of the Lord.

102   FOURTEENTH SUNDAY   B
OF THE YEAR

READING I   Ez 2, 2-5

A reading from the book of the prophet Ezekiel
*The head of the house was annoyed; he knew there was a
prophet in their midst.*

Spirit entered into me and set me on my feet,
and I heard the one who was speaking say to
me: Son of man, I am sending you to the
Israelites, rebels who have rebelled against
me; they and their fathers have revolted
against me to this very day. Hard of face and
obstinate of heart are they to whom I am sending you. But you shall say to them: Thus says
the Lord God! And whether they heed or resist—for they are a rebellious house—they
shall know that a prophet has been among
them.
    This is the Word of the Lord.

Responsorial Psalm   Ps 123, 1-2. 2. 3-4

℟. (2) Our eyes are fixed on the Lord,
  pleading for his mercy.
To you I lift up my eyes
  who are enthroned in heaven—

As the eyes of servants
   are on the hands of their masters.
℞. Our eyes are fixed on the Lord,
   pleading for his mercy.
As the eyes of a maid
   are on the hands of her mistress,
So are our eyes on the Lord, our God,
   till he have pity on us.
℞. Our eyes are fixed on the Lord,
   pleading for his mercy.
Have pity on us, O Lord, have pity on us,
   for we are more than sated with contempt;
Our souls are more than sated
   with the mockery of the arrogant,
   with the contempt of the proud.
℞. Our eyes are fixed on the Lord,
   pleading for his mercy.

READING II   2 Cor 12, 7-10

A reading from the second letter of Paul to the Corinthians
I will glory in my infirmities so that the power of Christ
may dwell in me.

As to the extraordinary revelations, in order
that I might not become conceited I was given
a thorn in the flesh, an angel of Satan to beat
me and keep me from getting proud. Three
times I begged the Lord that this might leave
me. He said to me, "My grace is enough for
you, for in weakness power reaches perfection." And so I willingly boast of my weaknesses instead, that the power of Christ may
rest upon me.
   Therefore I am content with weakness, with
mistreatment, with distress, with persecutions
and difficulties for the sake of Christ; for when
I am powerless, it is then than I am strong.
   This is the Word of the Lord.

GOSPEL   Mk 6, 1-6
Alleluia
See no. 164.

✠ **A reading from the holy gospel according
to Mark**
A prophet is despised only in his own country.

Jesus went to his own part of the country followed by his disciples. When the sabbath came
he began to teach in the synagogue in a way
that kept his large audience amazed. They
said: "Where did he get all this? What kind of
wisdom is he endowed with? How is it such
miraculous deeds are accomplished by his
hands? Isn't this the carpenter, the son of
Mary, a brother of James and Joses and Judas
and Simon? Aren't his sisters our neighbors
here?" They found him too much for them.
Jesus' response to all this was: "No prophet
is without honor except in his native place,
among his own kindred, and in his own house."
He could work no miracle there, apart from
curing a few who were sick by laying hands
on them, so much did their lack of faith distress him. He made the rounds of the neighboring villages instead, and spent his time
teaching.
   This is the gospel of the Lord.

---

103   FOURTEENTH SUNDAY   C
OF THE YEAR

READING I   Is 66, 10-14
A reading from the book of the prophet Isaiah
I will send toward Jerusalem peace like a river.

Rejoice with Jerusalem and be glad because of
   her,
   all you who love her;
Exult, exult with her,
   all you who were mourning over her!
Oh, that you may suck fully
   of the milk of her comfort,
That you may nurse with delight
   at her abundant breasts!
   For thus says the Lord:
Lo, I will spread prosperity over her like a
   river,
   and the wealth of the nations like an over-
      flowing torrent.
As nurslings, you shall be carried in her arms,
   and fondled in her lap;
As a mother comforts her son,
   so will I comfort you;
   in Jerusalem you shall find your comfort.
When you see this, your heart shall rejoice,

and your bodies flourish like the grass;
The Lord's power shall be known to his
 servants.
   This is the Word of the Lord.

Responsorial Psalm   Ps 66, 1-3. 4-5. 6-7. 16. 20

℟. (1) Let all the earth cry out to God with joy.
Shout joyfully to God, all you on earth,
 sing praise to the glory of his name;
 proclaim his glorious praise.
Say to God, "How tremendous are your deeds!"
℟. Let all the earth cry out to God with joy.
"Let all on earth worship and sing praise to
 you,
 sing praise to your name!"
Come and see the works of God,
 his tremendous deeds among men.
℟. Let all the earth cry out to God with joy.
He has changed the sea into dry land;
 through the river they passed on foot;
 therefore let us rejoice in him.
He rules by his might forever.
℟. Let all the earth cry out to God with joy.
Hear now, all you who fear God, while I
 declare
 what he has done for me.
Blessed be God who refused me not
 my prayer or his kindness!
℟. Let all the earth cry out to God with joy.

READING II   Gal 6, 14-18

A reading from the letter of Paul to the Galatians

The marks I carry on my body are those of Jesus Christ.

May I never boast of anything but the cross
of our Lord Jesus Christ! Through it, the world
has been crucified to me and I to the world.
It means nothing whether one is circumcised or
not. All that matters is that one is created anew.
Peace and mercy on all who follow this rule of
life, and on the Israel of God.

Henceforth, let no man trouble me, for I
bear the brand marks of Jesus in my body.

Brothers, may the favor of our Lord Jesus
Christ be with your spirit. Amen.
   This is the Word of the Lord.

GOSPEL   Lk 10, 1-12. 17-20 or 10, 1-9
Alleluia
See no. 164.

✠ A reading from the holy gospel according
    to Luke
Your peace will rest upon him.

(Long Form)

The Lord appointed a further seventy-two and
sent them in pairs before him to every town
and place he intended to visit. He said to
them: "The harvest is rich but the workers
are few; therefore ask the harvest-master to
send workers to his harvest. Be on your way,
and remember: I am sending you as lambs in
the midst of wolves. Do not carry a walking
staff or traveling bag; wear no sandals and
greet no one along the way. On entering any
house, first say, 'Peace to this house.' If there
is a peaceable man there, your peace will rest
on him; if not, it will come back to you. Stay
in the one house eating and drinking what they
have, for the laborer is worth his wage. Do
not move from house to house.

"Into whatever city you go, after they welcome you, eat what they set before you, and
cure the sick there. Say to them, 'The reign of
God is at hand.' If the people of any town you
enter do not welcome you, go into its streets
and say, 'We shake the dust of this town from
our feet as testimony against you. But know
that the reign of God is near.' I assure you, on
that day the fate of Sodom will be less severe
than that of such a town.''

The seventy-two returned in jubilation saying, "Master, even the demons are subject to
us in your name." He said in reply: "I watched
Satan fall from the sky like lightning. See what
I have done; I have given you power to tread
on snakes and scorpions and all the forces of
the enemy, and nothing shall ever injure you.
Nevertheless, do not rejoice so much in the
fact that the devils are subject to you as that
your names are inscribed in heaven."
   This is the gospel of the Lord.

OR
(Short Form)

The Lord appointed a further seventy-two and sent them in pairs before him to every town and place he intended to visit. He said to them: "The harvest is rich but the workers are few; therefore ask the harvest-master to send workers to his harvest. Be on your way, and remember: I am sending you as lambs in the midst of wolves. Do not carry a walking staff or traveling bag; wear no sandals and greet no one along the way. On entering any house, first say, 'Peace to this house.' If there is a peaceable man there, your peace will rest on him; if not, it will come back to you. Stay in the one house eating and drinking what they have, for the laborer is worth his wage. Do not move from house to house.

"Into whatever city you go, after they welcome you, eat what they set before you, and cure the sick there. Say to them, 'The reign of God is at hand.'"

This is the gospel of the Lord.

---

104 FIFTEENTH SUNDAY A
OF THE YEAR

READING I Is 55, 10-11

A reading from the book of the prophet Isaiah
The rain makes the earth fruitful.

Just as from the heavens
  the rain and snow come down
And do not return there
  till they have watered the earth,
  making it fertile and fruitful,
Giving seed to him who sows
  and bread to him who eats,
So shall my word be
  that goes forth from my mouth;
It shall not return to me void,
  but shall do my will,
  achieving the end for which I sent it.
This is the Word of the Lord.

Responsorial Psalm Ps 65, 10. 11. 12-13. 14

℟. (Lk 8, 8) The seed that falls on good ground
  will yield a fruitful harvest.

You have visited the land and watered it;
  greatly have you enriched it.
God's watercourses are filled;
  you have prepared the grain.
℟. The seed that falls on good ground
  will yield a fruitful harvest.

Thus have you prepared the land: drenching its furrows,
  breaking up its clods,
Softening it with showers,
  blessing its yield.
℟. The seed that falls on good ground
  will yield a fruitful harvest.

You have crowned the year with your bounty,
  and your paths overflow with a rich harvest;
The untilled meadows overflow with it,
  and rejoicing clothes the hills.
℟. The seed that falls on good ground
  will yield a fruitful harvest.

The fields are garmented with flocks
  and the valleys blanketed with grain.
They shout and sing for joy.
℟. The seed that falls on good ground
  will yield a fruitful harvest.

READING II Rom 8, 18-23

A reading from the letter of Paul to the Romans
All creation is waiting for God to reveal his sons.

I consider the sufferings of the present to be as nothing compared with the glory to be revealed in us. Indeed, the whole created world eagerly awaits the revelation of the sons of God. Creation was made subject to futility, not of its own accord buy by him who once subjected it; yet not without hope, because the world itself will be freed from its slavery to corruption and share in the glorious freedom of the children of God. Yes, we know that all creation groans and is in agony even until now. Not only that, but we ourselves, although we have the Spirit as first fruits, groan inwardly while we await the redemption of our bodies.
This is the Word of the Lord.

GOSPEL
Alleluia

Mt 13, 1-23 or 13, 1-9

See no. 164.

✠ A reading from the holy gospel according to Matthew

A sower went out to sow.

(Long Form)

Jesus, on leaving the house on a certain day, sat down by the lakeshore. Such great crowds gathered around him that he went and took his seat in a boat while the crowd stood along the shore. He addressed them at length in parables, speaking in this fashion:

"One day a farmer went out sowing. Part of what he sowed landed on a footpath, where birds came and ate it up. Part of it fell on rocky ground, where it had little soil. It sprouted at once since the soil had no depth, but when the sun rose and scorched it, it began to wither for lack of roots. Again, part of the seed fell among thorns, which grew up and choked it. Part of it, finally, landed on good soil and yielded grain at a hundred- or sixty- or thirty-fold. Let everyone heed what he hears!"

When the disciples got near him, they asked him, "Why do you speak to them in parables?" He answered: "To you has been given a knowledge of the mysteries of the reign of God, but it has not been given to the others. To the man who has, more will be given until he grows rich; the man who has not, will lose what little he has.

"I use parables when I speak to them because they look but do not see, they listen but do not hear or understand. Isaiah's prophecy is fulfilled in them which says:

'Listen as you will, you shall not understand,
look intently as you will, you shall not see.
Sluggish indeed is this people's heart.
They have scarcely heard with their ears,
they have firmly closed their eyes;
otherwise they might see with their eyes,
and hear with their ears,
and understand with their hearts,

and turn back to me,
and I should heal them.'

"But blest are your eyes because they see and blest are your ears because they hear. I assure you, many a prophet and many a saint longed to see what you see but did not see it, to hear what you hear but did not hear it.

"Mark well, then, the parable of the sower. The seed along the path is the man who hears the message about God's reign without understanding it. The evil one approaches him to steal away what was sown in his mind. The seed that fell on patches of rock is the man who hears the message and at first receives it with joy. But he has no roots, so he lasts only for a time. When some setback or persecution involving the message occurs, he soon falters. What was sown among briers is the man who hears the message, but then worldly anxiety and the lure of money choke it off. Such a one produces no yield. But what was sown on good soil is the man who hears the message and takes it in. He it is who bears a yield of a hundred- or sixty- or thirty-fold."

This is the gospel of the Lord.

OR

(Short Form)

Jesus, on leaving the house on a certain day, sat down by the lakeshore. Such great crowds gathered around him that he went and took his seat in a boat while the crowd stood along the shore. He addressed them at length in parables, speaking in this fashion:

"One day a farmer went out sowing. Part of what he sowed landed on a footpath, where birds came and ate it up. Part of it fell on rocky ground, where it had little soil. It sprouted at once since the soil had no depth, but when the sun rose and scorched it, it began to wither for lack of roots. Again, part of the seed fell among thorns, which grew up and choked it. Part of it, finally, landed on good soil and yielded grain a hundred- or sixty- or thirty-fold. Let everyone heed what he hears!"

This is the gospel of the Lord.

105   FIFTEENTH SUNDAY   **B**
OF THE YEAR

READING I   Am 7, 12-15
A reading from the book of the prophet Amos

Go, prophesy to my people.

Amaziah (priest of Bethel) said to Amos, "Off with you, visionary, flee to the land of Judah! There earn your bread by prophesying, but never again prophesy in Bethel; for it is the king's sanctuary and a royal temple." Amos answered Amaziah, "I was no prophet, nor have I belonged to a company of prophets; I was a shepherd and a dresser of sycamores. The Lord took me from following the flock, and said to me, Go, prophesy to my people Israel."

This is the Word of the Lord.

Responsorial Psalm   Ps 85, 9-10. 11-12. 13-14

℟. (8) Lord, let us see your kindness,
   and grant us your salvation.
I will hear what God proclaims;
   the Lord—for he proclaims peace to his people.
Near indeed is his salvation to those who fear him,
   glory dwelling in our land.
℟. Lord, let us see your kindness,
   and grant us your salvation.
Kindness and truth shall meet;
   justice and peace shall kiss.
Truth shall spring out of the earth,
   and justice shall look down from heaven.
℟. Lord, let us see your kindness,
   and grant us your salvation.
The Lord himself will give his benefits;
   our land shall yield its increase.
Justice shall walk before him,
   and salvation, along the way of his steps.
℟. Lord, let us see your kindness,
   and grant us your salvation.

READING II   Eph 1, 3-14 or 1, 3-10
A reading from the letter of Paul to the Ephesians

Before the world was made, he chose us in Christ.

(Long Form)

Praised be the God and Father of our Lord Jesus Christ, who has bestowed on us in Christ every spiritual blessing in the heavens! God chose us in him before the world began, to be holy and blameless in his sight, to be full of love; he likewise predestined us through Christ Jesus to be his adopted sons—such was his will and pleasure—that all might praise the divine favor he has bestowed on us in his beloved.

It is in Christ and through his blood that we have been redeemed and our sins forgiven, so immeasurably generous is God's favor to us. God has given us the wisdom to understand fully the mystery, the plan he was pleased to decree in Christ, to be carried out in the fullness of time: namely, to bring all things in the heavens and on earth into one under Christ's headship.

In him we were chosen; for in the decree of God, who administers everything according to his will and counsel, we were predestined to praise his glory by being the first to hope in Christ. In him you too were chosen; when you heard the glad tidings of salvation, the word of truth, and believed in it, you were sealed with the Holy Spirit who had been promised. He is the pledge of our inheritance, the first payment against the full redemption of a people God has made his own to praise his glory.

This is the Word of the Lord.

OR
(Short Form)

Praised be the God and Father of our Lord Jesus Christ, who has bestowed on us in Christ every spiritual blessing in the heavens! God chose us in him before the world began, to be holy and blameless in his sight, to be full of love; he likewise predestined us through Christ Jesus to be his adopted sons—such was his will and pleasure—that all might praise the divine favor he has bestowed on us in his beloved.

It is in Christ and through his blood that we have been redeemed and our sins forgiven, so immeasurably generous is God's favor to us. God has given us the wisdom to understand fully the mystery, the plan he was pleased to decree in Christ, to be carried out in the fullness of time: namely, to bring all things in the heavens and on earth into one under Christ's headship.

This is the Word of the Lord.

GOSPEL   Mk 6, 7-13
Alleluia

See no. 164.

✠ **A reading from the holy gospel according to Mark**

He called the Twelve, and began to send them out.

Jesus summoned the Twelve and began to send them out two by two, giving them authority over unclean spirits. He instructed them to take nothing on the journey but a walking stick—no food, no traveling bag, not a coin in the purses in their belts. They were, however, to wear sandals. "Do not bring a second tunic," he said, and added: "Whatever house you find yourself in, stay there until you leave the locality. If any place will not receive you or hear you, shake its dust from your feet in testimony against them as you leave." With that they went off, preaching the need of repentance. They expelled many demons, anointed the sick with oil, and worked many cures.

This is the gospel of the Lord.

---

106   **FIFTEENTH SUNDAY**   **C**
            OF THE YEAR

READING I   Dt 30, 10-14
A reading from the book of Deuteronomy

Let the instruction of the Lord God be near you.

Moses said to the people: "If only you heed the voice of the Lord, your God, and keep his commandments and statutes that are written in this book of the law, when you return to the Lord, your God, with all your heart and all your soul.

"For this command which I enjoin on you today is not too mysterious and remote for you. It is not up in the sky, that you should say, 'Who will go up in the sky to get it for us and tell us of it, that we may carry it out?' Nor is it across the sea, that you should say, 'Who will cross the sea to get it for us and tell us of it, that we may carry it out?' No, it is something very near to you, already in your mouths and in your hearts; you have only to carry it out."

This is the Word of the Lord.

Responsorial Psalm   Ps 69, 14. 17. 30-31. 33-34. 36. 37

℟. (33) Turn to the Lord in your need, and you will live.

I pray to you, O Lord,
    for the time of your favor, O God!
In your great kindness answer me
    with your constant help.

Answer me, O Lord, for bounteous is your kindness:
    in your great mercy turn toward me.

℟. Turn to the Lord in your need, and you will live.

I am afflicted and in pain;
    let your saving help, O God, protect me.
I will praise the name of God in song,
    and I will glorify him with thanksgiving.

℟. Turn to the Lord in your need, and you will live.

"See, you lowly ones, and be glad;
    you who seek God, may your hearts be merry!
For the Lord hears the poor,
    and his own who are in bonds he spurns not."

℞. Turn to the Lord in your need, and you will
    live.
For God will save Zion
    and rebuild the cities of Judah.
The descendants of his servants shall inherit it,
    and those who love his name shall inhabit it.
℞. Turn to the Lord in your need, and you will
    live.

READING II   Col 1, 15-20
A reading from the letter of Paul to the
Colossians
In him were created all things.

Christ Jesus is the image of the invisible God,
the first-born of all creatures. In him everything in heaven and on earth was created,
things visible and invisible, whether thrones or
dominations, principalities or powers; all were
created through him, and for him. He is before all else that is. In him everything continues in being. It is he who is head of the body,
the church; he who is the beginning, the first-
born of the dead, so that primacy may be his
in everything. It pleased God to make absolute
fullness reside in him and, by means of him, to
reconcile everything in his person, everything,
I say, both on earth and in the heavens, making
peace through the blood of his cross.

     This is the Word of the Lord.

GOSPEL   Lk 10, 25-37
Alleluia

See no. 164.

✠ A reading from the holy gospel according
    to Luke
Who is my neighbor?

On one occasion a lawyer stood up to pose this
problem to Jesus: "Teacher, what must I do to
inherit everlasting life?" Jesus answered him:
"What is written in the law? How do you read
it?" He replied:
    "You shall love the Lord your God
      with all your heart,
      with all your soul,
      with all your strength,
      and with all your mind;
      and your neighbor as yourself."

Jesus said, "You have answered correctly. Do
this and you shall live." But because he wished
to justify himself he said to Jesus, "And who
is my neighbor?" Jesus replied: "There was a
man going down from Jerusalem to Jericho
who fell in with robbers. They stripped him,
beat him, and then went off leaving him half-
dead. A priest happened to be going down the
same road; he saw him but continued on. Likewise there was a Levite who came the same
way; he saw him and went on. But a Samaritan
who was journeying along came on him and
was moved to pity at the sight. He approached
him and dressed his wounds, pouring in oil and
wine as a means to heal. He then hoisted him
on his own beast and brought him to an inn,
where he cared for him. The next day he took
out two silver pieces and gave them to the innkeeper with the request: 'Look after him, and if
there is any further expense I will repay you on
my way back.'

    "Which of these three, in your opinion, was
neighbor to the man who fell in with the
robbers?" The answer came, "The one who
treated him with compassion." Jesus said to
him, "Then go and do the same."

     This is the gospel of the Lord.

107   SIXTEENTH SUNDAY   Ⓐ
OF THE YEAR

READING I   Wis 12, 13. 16-19
A reading from the book of Wisdom
In the place of sin, you give repentance.

There is no god besides you who have the care
    of all,
    that you need show you have not unjustly
      condemned.
For your might is the source of justice;
    your mastery over all things makes you le-
      nient to all.
For you show your might when the perfection
    of your power is disbelieved;
    and in those who know you, you rebuke
      temerity.
But though you are master of might, you judge
    with clemency,

and with much lenience you govern us;
for power, whenever you will, attends you.
And you taught your people, by these deeds,
that those who are just must be kind;
And you gave your sons good ground for hope
that you would permit repentance for their
sins.
This is the Word of the Lord.

Responsorial Psalm   Ps 86, 5-6. 9-10. 15-16

R̝. (5) Lord, you are good and forgiving.

You, O Lord, are good and forgiving,
    abounding in kindness to all who call upon
    you.
Hearken, O Lord, to my prayer
    and attend to the sound of my pleading.
R̝. Lord, you are good and forgiving.

All the nations you have made shall come
    and worship you, O Lord,
    and glorify your name.
For you are great, and you do wondrous deeds;
    you alone are God.
R̝. Lord, you are good and forgiving.

You, O Lord, are a God merciful and gracious,
    slow to anger, abounding in kindness and
    fidelity.
Turn toward me, and have pity on me;
    give your strength to your servant.
R̝. Lord, you are good and forgiving.

READING II   Rom 8, 26-27

A reading from the letter of Paul to the Romans
The Spirit himself pleads for us in a way that could never
be put into words.

The Spirit too helps us in our weakness, for we
do not know how to pray as we ought; but the
Spirit himself makes intercession for us with
groanings which cannot be expressed in
speech. He who searches hearts knows what
the Spirit means, for the Spirit intercedes for
the saints as God himself wills.
This is the Word of the Lord.

GOSPEL   Mt 13, 24-43 or 13, 24-30
Alleluia

See no. 164.

✠ **A reading from the holy gospel according
to Matthew**
Let them grow together until the harvest.

(Long Form)

Jesus proposed to the crowd another parable:
"The reign of God may be likened to a man
who sowed good seed in his field. While everyone was asleep, his enemy came and sowed
weeds through his wheat, and then made off.
When the crop began to mature and yield
grain, the weeds made their appearance as
well. The owner's slaves came to him and
said, 'Sir, did you not sow good seed in your
field? Where are the weeds coming from?'
He answered, 'I see an enemy's hand in this.'
His slaves said to him, 'Do you want us to
go out and pull them up?' 'No,' he replied,
'pull up the weeds and you might take the
wheat along with them. Let them grow together until harvest; then at harvest time I
will order the harvesters, First collect the
weeds and bundle them up to burn, then gather
the wheat into my barn.' "

He proposed still another parable: "The
reign of God is like a mustard seed which
someone took and sowed in his field. It is
the smallest seed of all, yet when full-grown
it is the largest of plants. It becomes so big
a shrub that the birds of the sky come and
build their nests in its branches."

He offered them still another image: "The
reign of God is like yeast which a woman
took and kneaded into three measures of flour.
Eventually the whole mass of dough began
to rise." All these lessons Jesus taught the
crowds in the form of parables. He spoke
to them in parables only, to fulfill what had
been said through the prophet:

"I will open my mouth in parables,
    I will announce what has lain hidden since
        the creation of the world."

Then, dismissing the crowds, he went home.
His disciples came to him with the request,
"Explain to us the parable of the weeds in
the field." He said in answer: "The farmer
sowing good seed is the Son of Man; the
field is the world, the good seed the citizens

of the kingdom. The weeds are the followers of the evil one and the enemy who sowed them is the devil. The harvest is the end of the world, while the harvesters are the angels. Just as weeds are collected and burned, so it will be at the end of the world. The Son of Man will dispatch his angels to collect from his kingdom all who draw others to apostasy, and all evildoers. The angels will hurl them into the fiery furnace where they will wail and grind their teeth. Then the saints will shine like the sun in their Father's kingdom. Let everyone heed what he hears!"

This is the gospel of the Lord.

OR
(Short Form)

Jesus proposed to the crowd another parable: "The reign of God may be likened to a man who sowed good seed in his field. While everyone was asleep, his enemy came and sowed weeds through his wheat and then made off. When the crop began to mature and yield grain, the weeds made their appearance as well. The owner's slaves came to him and said, 'Sir, did you not sow good seed in your field? Where are the weeds coming from?' He answered, 'I see an enemy's hand in this.' His slaves said to him, 'Do you want us to go out and pull them up?' 'No,' he replied, 'pull up the weeds and you might take the wheat along with them. Let them grow together until harvest; then at harvest time I will order the harvesters, First collect the weeds and bundle them up to burn, then gather the wheat into my barn.' "

This is the gospel of the Lord.

---

108   **SIXTEENTH SUNDAY**   **B**
             OF THE YEAR

READING I   Jer 23, 1-6

A reading from the book of the prophet Jeremiah

The remnant of the flock I will gather to me, and bring them back to their pastures.

Woe to the shepherds who mislead and scatter the flock of my pasture, says the Lord. There-

fore, thus says the Lord, the God of Israel, against the shepherds who shepherd my people: You have scattered my sheep and driven them away. You have not cared for them, but I will take care to punish your evil deeds. I myself will gather the remnant of my flock from all the lands to which I have driven them and bring them back to their meadow; there they shall increase and multiply. I will appoint shepherds for them who will shepherd them so that they need no longer fear and tremble; and none shall be missing, says the Lord.

Behold, the days are coming, says the Lord,
    when I will raise up a righteous shoot to
    David;
As king he shall reign and govern wisely,
    he shall do what is just and right in the land.
In his days Judah shall be saved,
    Israel shall dwell in security.
This is the name they give him:
    "The Lord our justice."

This is the Word of the Lord.

Responsorial Psalm   Ps 23, 1-3. 3-4. 5. 6

R̸. (1) The Lord is my shepherd;
    there is nothing I shall want.
The Lord is my shepherd; I shall not want.
    In verdant pastures he gives me repose;
Beside restful waters he leads me;
    he refreshes my soul.
R̸. The Lord is my shepherd;
    there is nothing I shall want.
He guides me in right paths
    for his name's sake.
Even though I walk in the dark valley
    I fear no evil; for you are at my side
With your rod and your staff
    that give me courage.
R̸. The Lord is my shepherd;
    there is nothing I shall want.
You spread the table before me
    in the sight of my foes;
You anoint my head with oil;
    my cup overflows.
R̸. The Lord is my shepherd;
    there is nothing I shall want.
Only goodness and kindness follow me
    all the days of my life;

And I shall dwell in the house of the Lord
   for years to come.
℟. The Lord is my shepherd;
      there is nothing I shall want.

READING II   Eph 2, 13-18

A reading from the letter of Paul to the Ephesians
Christ is the peace between us.

In Christ Jesus you who once were far off have
been brought near through the blood of Christ.
It is he who is our peace, and who made the
two of us one by breaking down the barrier of
hostility that kept us apart. In his own flesh he
abolished the law with its commands and precepts, to create in himself one new man from us
who had been two, and to make peace, reconciling both of us to God in one body through his
cross which put that enmity to death. He came
and "announced the good news of peace to you
who were far off, and to those who were near";
through him we both have access in one Spirit
to the Father.
               This is the Word of the Lord.

GOSPEL   Mk 6, 30-34
Alleluia
See no. 164.

✠ A reading from the holy gospel according
   to Mark
They were as sheep without a shepherd.

The apostles returned to Jesus and reported to
him all that they had done and what they
had taught. He said to them, "Come by yourselves to an out-of-the-way place and rest a
little." People were coming and going in great
numbers, making it impossible for them to so
much as eat. So Jesus and the apostles went
off in the boat by themselves to a deserted
place. People saw them leaving, and many got
to know about it. People from all the towns
hastened on foot to the place, arriving ahead of
them.
   Upon disembarking Jesus saw a vast crowd.
He pitied them, for they were like sheep without a shepherd; and he began to teach them at
great length.
               This is the gospel of the Lord.

READING I   Gn 18, 1-10

A reading from the book of Genesis
Lord, do not bypass your servant.

The Lord appeared to Abraham by the terebinth of Mamre, as he sat in the entrance of his
tent, while the day was growing hot. Looking
up, he saw three men standing nearby. When
he saw them, he ran from the entrance of the
tent to greet them; and bowing to the ground,
he said: "Sir, if I may ask you this favor, please
do not go on past your servant. Let some water
be brought, that you may bathe your feet, and
then rest yourselves under the tree. Now that
you have come this close to your servant, let
me bring you a little food, that you may refresh
yourselves; and afterward you may go on your
way." "Very well," they replied, "do as you
have said."
   Abraham hastened into the tent and told
Sarah, "Quick, three seahs of fine flour! Knead
it and make rolls." He ran to the herd, picked
out a tender, choice steer, and gave it to a servant, who quickly prepared it. Then he got
some curds and milk, as well as the steer that
had been prepared, and set these before them;
and he waited on them under the tree while
they ate.
   "Where is your wife Sarah?" they asked
him. "There in the tent," he replied. One of
them said, "I will surely return to you about
this time next year, and Sarah will then have a
son."
               This is the Word of the Lord.

Responsorial Psalm   Ps 15, 2-3. 3-4. 5

℟. (1) He who does justice will live in the
         presence of the Lord.
He who walks blamelessly and does justice;
   who thinks the truth in his heart
   and slanders not with his tongue.

℟. He who does justice will live in the presence
of the Lord.
Who harms not his fellow man,
nor takes up a reproach against his neighbor;
By whom the reprobate is despised,
while he honors those who fear the Lord.
℟. He who does justice will live in the presence
of the Lord.
Who lends not his money at usury
and accepts no bribe against the innocent.
He who does these things
shall never be disturbed.
℟. He who does justice will live in the presence
of the Lord.

READING II   Col 1, 24-28

A reading from the letter of Paul to the
Colossians
The mystery hidden for centuries has now been revealed to
his saints.

Even now I find my joy in the suffering I endure
for you. In my own flesh I fill up what is lacking
in the sufferings of Christ for the sake of his
body, the church. I became a minister of this
church through the commission God gave me
to preach among you his word in its fullness,
that mystery hidden from ages and generations
past but now revealed to his holy ones. God
has willed to make known to them the glory
beyond price which this mystery brings to the
Gentiles—the mystery of Christ in you, your
hope of glory. This is the Christ we proclaim
while we admonish all men and teach them in
the full measure of wisdom, hoping to make
every man complete in Christ.
This is the Word of the Lord.

GOSPEL   Lk 10, 38-42

Alleluia

See no. 164.

✠ **A reading from the holy gospel according**
to Luke
Jesus speaks with Martha and Mary.

Jesus entered a village where a woman named
Martha welcomed him to her home. She had a
sister named Mary, who seated herself at the
Lord's feet and listened to his words. Martha,
who was busy with all the details of hospitality, came to him and said, "Lord, are you not
concerned that my sister has left me all alone
to do the household tasks? Tell her to help me."
The Lord in reply said to her: "Martha,
Martha, you are anxious and upset about many
things; one thing only is required. Mary has
chosen the better portion and she shall not be
deprived of it."
This is the gospel of the Lord.

---

110   **SEVENTEENTH SUNDAY**   **A**
OF THE YEAR

READING I   1 Kgs 3, 5. 7-12

A reading from the first book of Kings
He sought to give you wisdom.

The Lord appeared to Solomon in a dream at
night. God said, "Ask something of me and I
will give it to you." Solomon answered: "O
Lord, my God, you have made me, your servant, king to succeed my father David; but I
am a mere youth, not knowing at all how to
act. I serve you in the midst of the people
whom you have chosen, a people so vast that it
cannot be numbered or counted. Give your
servant, therefore, an understanding heart to
judge your people and to distinguish right from
wrong. For who is able to govern this vast
people of yours?"
The Lord was pleased that Solomon made
this request. So God said to him: "Because you
have asked for this—not for a long life for
yourself, nor for riches, nor for the life of your
enemies, but for understanding so that you
may know what is right—I do as you requested. I give you a heart so wise and understanding that there has never been anyone like
you up to now, and after you there will come
no one to equal you."
This is the Word of the Lord.

Responsorial Psalm

Ps 119, 57. 72. 76-77. 127-128. 129-130

℟. (97) Lord, I love your commands.

I have said, O Lord, that my part
    is to keep your words.
The law of your mouth is to me more precious
    than thousands of gold and silver pieces.

℟. Lord, I love your commands.

Let your kindness comfort me
    according to your promise to your servants.
Let your compassion come to me that I may
    live,
    for your law is my delight.

℟. Lord, I love your commands.

For I love your command
    more than gold, however fine.
For in all your precepts I go forward;
    every false way I hate.

℟. Lord, I love your commands.

Wonderful are your decrees;
    therefore I observe them.
The revelation of your words sheds light,
    giving understanding to the simple.

℟. Lord, I love your commands.

READING II   Rom 8, 28-30

A reading from the letter of Paul to the Romans

He predestined us to become true images of his Son.

We know that God makes all things work together for the good of those who love him, who
have been called according to his decree. Those
whom he foreknew he predestined to share the
image of his Son, that the Son might be the
first-born of many brothers. Those he predestined he likewise called; those he called he also
justified; and those he justified he in turn
glorified.

      This is the Word of the Lord.

GOSPEL   Mt 13, 44-52 or 13, 44-46

Alleluia

See no. 164.

✠ **A reading from the holy gospel according
to Matthew**

He sells everything he owns, and buys the field.

(Long Form)

Jesus said to the crowd: "The reign of God is
like a buried treasure which a man found in a
field. He hid it again, and rejoicing at his find
went and sold all he had and bought that field.
Or again, the kingdom of heaven is like a merchant's search for fine pearls. When he found
one really valuable pearl, he went back and put
up for sale all that he had and bought it.

    "The reign of God is also like a dragnet
thrown into the lake, which collected all sorts
of things. When it was full they hauled it
ashore and sat down to put what was worthwhile into containers. What was useless they
threw away. That is how it will be at the end
of the world. Angels will go out and separate
the wicked from the just and hurl the wicked
into the fiery furnace, where they will wail and
grind their teeth.

    "Have you understood all this?" "Yes," they
answered; to which he replied, "Every scribe
who is learned in the reign of God is like the
head of a household who can bring from his
store both the new and the old."

      This is the gospel of the Lord.

OR
(Short Form)

Jesus said to the crowd: "The reign of God is
like a buried treasure which a man found in a
field. He hid it again, and rejoicing at his find
went and sold all he had and bought that field.
Or again, the kingdom of heaven is like a merchant's search for fine pearls. When he found
one really valuable pearl, he went back and put
up for sale all that he had and bought it."

      This is the gospel of the Lord.

111 SEVENTEENTH SUNDAY OF THE YEAR **B**

READING I 2 Kgs 4, 42-44

A reading from the second book of Kings

They will eat, and have some left over.

A man came from Baal-shalishah bringing to Elisha, the man of God, twenty barley loaves made from the firstfruits, and fresh grain in the ear. "Give it to the people to eat," Elisha said. But his servant objected, "How can I set this before a hundred men?" "Give it to the people to eat," Elisha insisted. "For thus says the Lord, 'They shall eat and there shall be some left over.' " And when they had eaten, there was some left over, as the Lord had said.

This is the Word of the Lord.

Responsorial Psalm Ps 145, 10-11. 15-16. 17-18

℞. (16) The hand of the Lord feeds us;
    he answers all our needs.

Let all your works give you thanks, O Lord,
    and let your faithful ones bless you.
Let them discourse of the glory of your kingdom
    and speak of your might.

℞. The hand of the Lord feeds us;
    he answers all our needs.

The eyes of all look hopefully to you,
    and you give them their food in due season;
You open your hand
    and satisfy the desire of every living thing.

℞. The hand of the Lord feeds us;
    he answers all our needs.

The Lord is just in all his ways
    and holy in all his works.
The Lord is near to all who call upon him,
    to all who call upon him in truth.

℞. The hand of the Lord feeds us;
    he answers all our needs.

READING II Eph 4, 1-6

A reading from the letter of Paul to the Ephesians

There is one body, one Lord, one faith, one baptism.

I plead with you as a prisoner for the Lord, to live a life worthy of the calling you have received, with perfect humility, meekness, and patience, bearing with one another lovingly. Make every effort to preserve the unity which has the Spirit as its origin and peace as its binding force. There is but one body and one Spirit, just as there is but one hope given all of you by your call. There is one Lord, one faith, one baptism; one God and Father of all, who is over all, and works through all, and is in all.

This is the Word of the Lord.

GOSPEL Jn 6, 1-15

Alleluia

See no. 164.

✠ **A reading from the holy gospel according to John**

He distributed to those who were seated as much as they wanted.

Jesus crossed the Sea of Galilee [to the shore] of Tiberias; a vast crowd kept following him because they saw the signs he was performing for the sick. Jesus then went up the mountain and sat down there with his disciples. The Jewish feast of Passover was near; when Jesus looked up and caught sight of a vast crowd coming toward him, he said to Philip, "Where shall we buy bread for these people to eat?" (He knew well what he intended to do but he asked this to test Philip's response.) Philip replied, "Not even with two hundred days' wages could we buy loaves enough to give each of them a mouthful!"

One of Jesus' disciples, Andrew, Simon Peter's brother, remarked to him, "There is a lad here who has five barley loaves and a couple of dried fish, but what good is that for so many?" Jesus said, "Get the people to recline." Even though the men numbered about five thousand, there was plenty of grass for them to find a place on the ground. Jesus then took the loaves of bread, gave thanks, and passed them around to those reclining there; he did the same with the dried fish, as much as they wanted. When they had had enough, he told his disciples, "Gather up the crusts that are left over so that nothing will go to waste." At this, they gathered twelve baskets full of pieces left over by those who had been fed with the five barley loaves.

When the people saw the sign he had performed they began to say, "This is undoubtedly the Prophet who is to come into the world." At that, Jesus realized that they would come and carry him off to make him king, so he fled back to the mountain alone.

This is the gospel of the Lord.

---

112   SEVENTEENTH SUNDAY   C
OF THE YEAR

READING I   Gn 18, 20-32

A reading from the book of Genesis
Lord, do not be angry if I speak.

The Lord said: "The outcry against Sodom and Gomorrah is so great, and their sin so grave, that I must go down and see whether or not their actions fully correspond to the cry against them that comes to me. I mean to find out."

While the two men walked on farther toward Sodom, the Lord remained standing before Abraham. Then Abraham drew nearer to him and said: "Will you sweep away the innocent with the guilty? Suppose there were fifty innocent people in the city; would you wipe out the place, rather than spare it for the sake of the fifty innocent people within it? Far be it from you to do such a thing, to make the innocent die with the guilty, so that the innocent and the guilty would be treated alike! Should not the judge of all the world act with justice?" The Lord replied, "If I find fifty innocent people in the city of Sodom, I will spare the whole place for their sake." Abraham spoke up again: "See how I am presuming to speak to my Lord, though I am but dust and ashes! What if there are five less than fifty innocent people? Will you destroy the whole city because of those five?" "I will not destroy it," he answered, "if I find forty-five there." But Abraham persisted, saying, "What if only forty are found there?" He replied, "I will forbear doing it for the sake of the forty." Then he said, "Let not my Lord grow impatient if I go on. What if only thirty are found there?" He replied, "I will forbear doing it if I can find but thirty there." Still he went on, "Since I have thus dared to speak to my Lord. what if there are no more than twenty?" "I will not destroy it," he answered, "for the sake of the twenty." But he still persisted: "Please, let not my Lord grow angry if I speak up this last time. What if there are at least ten there?" "For the sake of those ten," he replied, "I will not destroy it."

This is the Word of the Lord.

Responsorial Psalm   Ps 138, 1-2. 2-3. 6-7. 7-8

℟. (3) Lord, on the day I called for help, you answered me.

I will give thanks to you, O Lord, with all my heart,
[for you have heard the words of my mouth;]
in the presence of the angels I will sing your praise;
I will worship at your holy temple
and give thanks to your name.

℟. Lord, on the day I called for help, you answered me.

Because of your kindness and your truth;
for you have made great above all things your name and your promise.
When I called you answered me;
you built up strength within me.

℟. Lord, on the day I called for help, you answered me.

The Lord is exalted, yet the lowly he sees, and the proud he knows from afar.
Though I walk amid distress, you preserve me;
against the anger of my enemies you raise your hand.

℟. Lord, on the day I called for help, you answered me.

Your right hand saves me.
The Lord will complete what he has done for me;
Your kindness, O Lord, endures forever;
forsake not the work of your hands.

℟. Lord, on the day I called for help, you answered me.

READING II   Col 2, 12-14
A reading from the letter of Paul to the Colossians

He has made you alive with Christ for he has forgiven all our sins.

In baptism you were not only buried with him but also raised to life with him because you believed in the power of God who raised him from the dead. Even when you were dead in sin and your flesh was uncircumcised, God gave you new life in company with Christ. He pardoned all our sins. He canceled the bond that stood against us with all its claims, snatching it up and nailing it to the cross.
This is the Word of the Lord.

GOSPEL   Lk 11, 1-13
Alleluia
See no. 164.

✠ A reading from the holy gospel according to Luke
Ask, and it will be given to you.

One day Jesus was praying in a certain place. When he had finished, one of his disciples asked him, "Lord, teach us to pray as John taught his disciples." He said to them, "When you pray, say:
"Father,
hallowed be your name,
your kingdom come.
Give us each day our daily bread.
Forgive us our sins
for we too forgive all who do us wrong;
and subject us not to the trial."
Jesus said to them: "If one of you knows someone who comes to him in the middle of the night and says to him, 'Friend, lend me three loaves, for a friend of mine has come in from a journey and I have nothing to offer him'; and he from inside should reply, 'Leave me alone. The door is shut now and my children and I are in bed. I can't get up to look after your needs'—I tell you, even though he does not get up and take care of the man because of friendship, he will find himself doing

so because of his persistence and give him as much as he needs.
"So I say to you, 'Ask and you shall receive; seek and you shall find, knock and it shall be opened to you.'
"For whoever asks, receives; whoever seeks, finds; whoever knocks, is admitted. What father among you will give his son a snake if he asks for a fish, or hand him a scorpion if he asks for an egg? If you, with all your sins, know how to give your children good things, how much more will the heavenly Father give the Holy Spirit to those who ask him."
This is the gospel of the Lord.

---

113   EIGHTEENTH SUNDAY   A
OF THE YEAR
READING I   Is 55, 1-3
A reading from the book of the prophet Isaiah
Hasten and eat.

All you who are thirsty,
come to the water!
You who have no money,
come, receive grain and eat;
Come, without paying and without cost,
drink wine and milk!
Why spend your money for what is not bread;
your wages for what fails to satisfy?
Heed me, and you shall eat well,
you shall delight in rich fare.
Come to me heedfully,
listen, that you may have life.
I will renew with you the everlasting covenant,
the benefits assured to David.
This is the Word of the Lord.

Responsorial Psalm   Ps 145, 8-9. 15-16. 17-18

℟. (16) The hand of the Lord feeds us;
he answers all our needs.
The Lord is gracious and merciful,
slow to anger and of great kindness.
The Lord is good to all
and compassionate toward all his works.
℟. The hand of the Lord feeds us;
he answers all our needs.

The eyes of all look hopefully to you,
　and you give them their food in due season;
You open your hand
　and satisfy the desire of every living thing.
℞. The hand of the Lord feeds us;
　he answers all our needs.
The Lord is just in all his ways
　and holy in all his works.
The Lord is near to all who call upon him,
　to all who call upon him in truth.
℞. The hand of the Lord feeds us;
　he answers all our needs.

READING II　　　　　　　Rom 8, 35. 37-39

A reading from the letter of Paul to the Romans
No creature can separate us from the love of God, which
is in Christ.

Who will separate us from the love of Christ?
Trial, or distress, or persecution, or hunger, or
nakedness, or danger, or the sword? Yet in all
this we are more than conquerors because of
him who has loved us. For I am certain that
neither death nor life, neither angels nor principalities, neither the present nor the future, nor
powers, neither height nor depth nor any other
creature, will be able to separate us from the
love of God that comes to us in Christ Jesus, our
Lord.

　　　　This is the Word of the Lord.

GOSPEL　　　　　　　　　Mt 14, 13-21
Alleluia

See no. 164.

✠ A reading from the holy gospel according
　　　　to Matthew
They all ate and were satisfied.

When Jesus heard [of the death of John the
Baptizer], he withdrew by boat to a deserted
place by himself. The crowds heard of it and
followed him on foot from the towns. When he
disembarked and saw the vast throng, his heart
was moved with pity, and he cured their sick.
As evening drew on, his disciples came to him
with the suggestion: "This is a deserted place
and it is already late. Dismiss the crowds so
that they may go to the villages and buy some
food for themselves." Jesus said to them:

"There is no need for them to disperse. Give
them something to eat yourselves." "We have
nothing here," they replied, "but five loaves
and a couple of fish." "Bring them here," he
said. Then he ordered the crowds to sit down
on the grass. He took the five loaves and two
fish, looked up to heaven, blessed and broke
them and gave the loaves to the disciples, who
in turn gave them to the people. All those present ate their fill. The fragments which remained,
when gathered up, filled twelve baskets. Those
who ate were about five thousand, not counting
women and children.
　　　　This is the gospel of the Lord.

114　　EIGHTEENTH SUNDAY　　**B**
　　　　　OF THE YEAR

READING I　　　　　　　Ex 16, 2-4. 12-15

A reading from the book of Exodus
I will rain bread from heaven upon you.

The whole Israelite community grumbled
against Moses and Aaron. The Israelites said to
them, "Would that we had died at the Lord's
hand in the land of Egypt, as we sat by our
fleshpots and ate our fill of bread! But you had
to lead us into this desert to make the whole
community die of famine!"

　　Then the Lord said to Moses, "I will now
rain down bread from heaven for you. Each
day the people are to go out and gather their
daily portion; thus will I test them, to see
whether they follow my instructions or not.

　　"I have heard the grumbling of the Israelites.
Tell them: In the evening twilight you shall eat
flesh, and in the morning you shall have your
fill of bread, so that you may know that I, the
Lord, am your God."

　　In the evening quail came up and covered
the camp. In the morning a dew lay all about
the camp, and when the dew evaporated, there
on the surface of the desert were fine flakes
like hoarfrost on the ground. On seeing it, the
Israelites asked one another, "What is this?"
for they did not know what it was. But Moses
told them, "This is the bread which the Lord
has given you to eat."
　　　　This is the Word of the Lord.

Responsorial Psalm   Ps 78, 3-4. 23-24. 25. 54

℞. (24) The Lord gave them bread from heaven.

What we have heard and know,
   and what our fathers have declared to us,
We will declare to the generation to come
   the glorious deeds of the Lord and his strength
   and the wonders that he wrought.

℞. The Lord gave them bread from heaven.

He commanded the skies above
   and the doors of heaven he opened;
He rained manna upon them for food
   and gave them heavenly bread.

℞. The Lord gave them bread from heaven.

The bread of the mighty was eaten by men;
   even a surfeit of provisions he sent them.
And he brought them to his holy land,
   to the mountains his right hand had won.

℞. The Lord gave them bread from heaven.

READING II   Eph 4, 17. 20-24

A reading from the letter of Paul to the Ephesians

Put on the new man that has been created in God's image.

I declare and solemnly attest in the Lord that you must no longer live as the pagans do— their minds empty. That is not what you learned when you learned Christ! I am supposing, of course, that he has been preached and taught to you in accord with the truth that is in Jesus: namely, that you must lay aside your former way of life and the old self which deteriorates through illusion and desire, and acquire a fresh, spiritual way of thinking. You must put on that new man created in God's image, whose justice and holiness are born of truth.

This is the Word of the Lord.

GOSPEL   Jn 6, 24-35
Alleluia

See no. 164.

✠ **A reading from the holy gospel according to John**

He who comes to me will never be hungry; he who believes in me will never thirst.

When the crowd saw that neither Jesus nor his disciples were at the place where Jesus had eaten the bread, they too embarked in the boats and went to Capernaum looking for Jesus.

When they found him on the other side of the lake, they said to him, "Rabbi, when did you come here?" Jesus answered them:
   "I assure you,
   you are not looking for me because you have seen signs
   but because you have eaten your fill of the loaves.
   You should not be working for perishable food
   but for food that remains unto life eternal,
   food which the Son of Man will give you;
   it is on him that God the Father has set his seal."

At this they said to him, "What must we do to perform the works of God?" Jesus replied:
   "This is the work of God:
   have faith in the One he sent."

"So that we can put faith in you," they asked him, "what sign are you going to perform for us to see? What is the 'work' you do? Our ancestors had manna to eat in the desert; according to Scripture, 'He gave them bread from the heavens to eat.' " Jesus said to them:
   "I solemnly assure you,
   it was not Moses who gave you bread from the heavens;
   it is my Father who gives you the real heavenly bread.
   God's bread comes down from heaven
   and gives life to the world."

"Sir, give us this bread always," they besought him.

Jesus explained to them:
   "I myself am the bread of life.
   No one who comes to me shall ever be hungry,
   no one who believes in me shall thirst again."

This is the gospel of the Lord.

115 EIGHTEENTH SUNDAY OF THE YEAR **C**

READING I Eccl 1, 2; 2, 21-23

A reading from the book of Ecclesiastes

What do all his labors profit a man?

Vanity of vanities, says Qoheleth,
vanity of vanities! All things are vanity!
Here is a man who has labored with wisdom
and knowledge and skill, and to another, who
has not labored over it, he must leave his property. This also is vanity and a great misfortune.
For what profit comes to a man from all the toil
and anxiety of heart with which he has labored
under the sun? All his days sorrow and grief
are his occupation; even at night his mind is
not at rest. This also is vanity.
    This is the Word of the Lord.

Responsorial Psalm Ps 95, 1-2. 6-7. 8-9

℟. (8) If today you hear his voice,
    harden not your hearts.

Come, let us sing joyfully to the Lord;
    let us acclaim the Rock of our salvation.
Let us greet him with thanksgiving;
    let us joyfully sing psalms to him.

℟. If today you hear his voice,
    harden not your hearts.

Come, let us bow down in worship;
    let us kneel before the Lord who made us.
For he is our God,
    and we are the people he shepherds, the
        flock he guides.

℟. If today you hear his voice,
    harden not your hearts.

Oh, that today you would hear his voice:
    "Harden not your hearts as at Meribah,
    as in the day of Massah in the desert,
Where your fathers tempted me;
    they tested me though they had seen my
        works."

℟. If today you hear his voice,
    harden not your hearts.

READING II Col 3, 1-5. 9-11

A reading from the letter of Paul to the Colossians

Seek the things that are above where Christ is.

Since you have been raised up in company
with Christ, set your heart on what pertains to
higher realms where Christ is seated at God's
right hand. Be intent on things above rather
than on things of earth. After all, you have
died! Your life is hidden now with Christ in
God. When Christ our life appears, then you
shall appear with him in glory.
    Put to death whatever in your nature is
rooted in earth: fornication, uncleanness, passion, evil desires, and that lust which is idolatry. Stop lying to one another. What you
have done is put aside your old self with its
past deeds and put on a new man, one who
grows in knowledge as he is formed anew
in the image of his Creator. There is no Greek
or Jew here, circumcised or uncircumcised,
foreigner, Scythian, slave, or freeman. Rather,
Christ is everything in all of you.
    This is the Word of the Lord.

GOSPEL Lk 12, 13-21
Alleluia

See no. 164.

✠ **A reading from the holy gospel according to Luke**

Why are you preparing these things?

Someone in the crowd said to Jesus, "Teacher,
tell my brother to give me my share of our inheritance." He replied, "Friend, who has set me
up as your judge or arbiter?" Then he said to
the crowd, "Avoid greed in all its forms. A man
may be wealthy, but his possessions do not
guarantee him life."
    He told them a parable in these words:
"There was a rich man who had a good harvest. 'What shall I do?' he asked himself. 'I
have no place to store my harvest. I know!' he
said. 'I will pull down my grain bins and build
larger ones. All my grain and my goods will go
there. Then I will say to myself: You have
blessings in reserve for years to come. Relax!

Eat heartily, drink well. Enjoy yourself.' But God said to him, 'You fool! This very night your life shall be required of you. To whom will all this piled-up wealth of yours go?' That is the way it works with the man who grows rich for himself instead of growing rich in the sight of God."

This is the gospel of the Lord.

116   NINETEENTH SUNDAY **A**
OF THE YEAR

READING I   1 Kgs 19, 9. 11-13
A reading from the first book of Kings
Go out and stand on the mountain before the Lord God.
Elijah came to a cave [from the mountain of God, Horeb], where he took shelter. Then the Lord said, "Go outside and stand on the mountain before the Lord; the Lord will be passing by." A strong and heavy wind was rending the mountains and crushing rocks before the Lord —but the Lord was not in the wind. After the wind there was an earthquake—but the Lord was not in the earthquake. After the earthquake there was fire—but the Lord was not in the fire. After the fire there was a tiny whispering sound. When he heard this, Elijah hid his face in his cloak and went and stood at the entrance of the cave.

This is the Word of the Lord.

Responsorial Psalm   Ps 85, 9. 10. 11-12. 13-14
℟. (7. 8) Lord, let us see your kindness,
    and grant us your salvation.
I will hear what God proclaims;
    the Lord—for he proclaims peace.
Near indeed is his salvation to those who fear
    him,
    glory dwelling in our land.
℟. Lord, let us see your kindness,
    and grant us your salvation.
Kindness and truth shall meet;
    justice and peace shall kiss.
Truth shall spring out of the earth,
    and justice shall look down from heaven.

℟. Lord, let us see your kindness,
    and grant us your salvation.
The Lord himself will give his benefits;
    our land shall yield its increase.
Justice shall walk before him,
    and salvation, along the way of his steps.
℟. Lord, let us see your kindness,
    and grant us your salvation.

READING II   Rom 9, 1-5
A reading from the letter of Paul to the Romans
I would willingly be condemned if it would help my brother.
I speak the truth in Christ: I do not lie. My conscience bears me witness in the Holy Spirit that there is great grief and constant pain in my heart. Indeed, I could even wish to be separated from Christ for the sake of my brothers, my kinsmen the Israelites. Theirs were the adoption, the glory, the covenants, the lawgiving, the worship, and the promises; theirs were the patriarchs, and from them came the Messiah (I speak of his human origins). Blessed forever be God who is over all! Amen.

This is the Word of the Lord.

GOSPEL   Mt 14, 22-33
Alleluia
See no. 164.

✠ **A reading from the holy gospel according to Matthew**
Command me to come to you over the waters.
[After the crowds had their fill] Jesus insisted that his disciples get into the boat and precede him to the other side. When he had sent them away, he went up on the mountain by himself to pray, remaining there alone as evening drew on. Meanwhile the boat, already several hundred yards out from shore, was being tossed about in the waves raised by strong head winds. At about three in the morning, he came walking toward them on the lake. When the disciples saw him walking on the water, they were terrified. "It is a ghost!" they said, and in their fear they began to cry out. Jesus hastened to reassure them: "Get hold of yourselves! It is I. Do not be afraid!" Peter spoke up and said,

"Lord, if it is really you, tell me to come to you across the water." "Come!" he said. So Peter got out of the boat and began to walk on the water, moving toward Jesus. But when he perceived how strong the wind was, becoming frightened he began to sink, and cried out, "Lord, save me!" Jesus at once stretched out his hand and caught him. "How little faith you have!" he exclaimed. "Why did you falter?" Once they had climbed into the boat, the wind died down. Those who were in the boat showed him reverence, declaring, "Beyond doubt you are the Son of God!"

This is the gospel of the Lord.

---

117   **NINETEENTH SUNDAY**   **B**
              OF THE YEAR

READING I   1 Kgs 19, 4-8

A reading from the first book of Kings

Strengthened by the food, he walked to the mountain of the Lord.

Elijah went a day's journey into the desert, until he came to a broom tree and sat beneath it. He prayed for death: "This is enough, O Lord! Take my life, for I am no better than my fathers." He lay down and fell asleep under the broom tree, but then an angel touched him and ordered him to get up and eat. He looked and there at his head was a hearth cake and a jug of water. After he ate and drank, he lay down again, but the angel of the Lord came back a second time, touched him, and ordered, "Get up and eat, else the journey will be too long for you!" He got up, ate and drank; then strengthened by that food, he walked forty days and forty nights to the mountain of God, Horeb.

This is the Word of the Lord.

Responsorial Psalm   Ps 34, 2-3. 4-5. 6-7. 8-9

R̸. (9) Taste and see the goodness of the Lord.
I will bless the Lord at all times;
   his praise shall be ever in my mouth.
Let my soul glory in the Lord;
   the lowly will hear me and be glad.
R̸. Taste and see the goodness of the Lord.
Glorify the Lord with me,

let us together extol his name.
I sought the Lord, and he answered me
   and delivered me from all my fears.
R̸. Taste and see the goodness of the Lord.
Look to him that you may be radiant with joy,
   and your faces may not blush with shame.
When the afflicted man called out, the Lord heard,
   and from all his distress he saved him.
R̸. Taste and see the goodness of the Lord.
The angel of the Lord encamps
   around those who fear him, and delivers them.
Taste and see how good the Lord is;
   happy the man who takes refuge in him.
R̸. Taste and see the goodness of the Lord.

READING II   Eph 4, 30-5, 2

A reading from the letter of Paul to the Ephesians

Walk in love, just as Christ.

Do nothing to sadden the Holy Spirit with whom you were sealed against the day of redemption. Get rid of all bitterness, all passion and anger, harsh words, slander, and malice of every kind. In place of these, be kind to one another, compassionate, and mutually forgiving, just as God has forgiven you in Christ.

Be imitators of God as his dear children. Follow the way of love, even as Christ loved you. He gave himself for us as an offering to God, a gift of pleasing fragrance.

This is the Word of the Lord.

GOSPEL   Jn 6, 41-51
Alleluia

See no. 164.

✠ **A reading from the holy gospel according to John**

I am the living bread that came down from heaven.

The Jews started to murmur in protest because Jesus claimed, "I am the bread that came down from heaven." They kept saying: "Is this not Jesus, the son of Joseph? Do we not know his father and mother? How can he claim to have come down from heaven?"

"Stop your murmuring," Jesus told them.
"No one can come to me
unless the Father who sent me draws him;
I will raise him up on the last day.
It is written in the prophets:
'They shall all be taught by God.'
Everyone who has heard the Father
and learned from him
comes to me.
Not that anyone has seen the Father—
only the one who is from God
has seen the Father.
Let me firmly assure you,
he who believes has eternal life.
I am the bread of life.
Your ancestors ate manna in the desert,
but they died.
This is the bread that comes down from
heaven,
for a man to eat and never die.
I myself am the living bread
come down from heaven.
If anyone eats this bread
he shall live forever;
the bread I will give
is my flesh, for the life of the world."
This is the gospel of the Lord.

118   **NINETEENTH SUNDAY**   **C**
OF THE YEAR

READING I   Wis 18, 6-9
A reading from the book of Wisdom
Just as you struck our enemies, you made us glorious by
calling us to you.

That night was known beforehand to our
fathers,
  that, with sure knowledge of the oaths in
  which they put their faith, they might
  have courage.
Your people awaited
  the salvation of the just and the destruction
  of their foes.
For when you punished our adversaries,
  in this you glorified us whom you had summoned.
For in secret the holy children of the good were
  offering sacrifice

and putting into effect with one accord the
divine institution.
This is the Word of the Lord.

Responsorial Psalm   Ps 33, 1. 12. 18-19. 20-22
℞. (12) Happy the people the Lord has chosen
to be his own.
Exult, you just, in the Lord;
  praise from the upright is fitting.
Happy the nation whose God is the Lord,
  the people he has chosen for his own inheritance.
℞. Happy the people the Lord has chosen to
be his own.
See, the eyes of the Lord are upon those who
fear him,
  upon those who hope for his kindness,
To deliver them from death
  and preserve them in spite of famine.
℞. Happy the people the Lord has chosen to be
his own.
Our soul waits for the Lord,
  who is our help and our shield.
May your kindness, O Lord, be upon us
  who have put our hope in you.
℞. Happy the people the Lord has chosen to be
his own.

READING II   Heb 11, 1-2. 8-19 or 11, 1-2. 8-12
A reading from the letter to the Hebrews
We will look for the city designed and built by God.
(Long Form)

Faith is confident assurance concerning what
we hope for, and conviction about things we do
not see. Because of faith the men of old were
approved by God. By faith Abraham obeyed
when he was called, and went forth to the place
he was to receive as a heritage; he went forth,
moreover, not knowing where he was going.
By faith he sojourned in the promised land as in
a foreign country, dwelling in tents with Isaac
and Jacob, heirs of the same promise; for he
was looking forward to the city with foundations, whose designer and maker is God. By
faith Sarah received power to conceive though
she was past the age, for she thought that the
One who had made the promise was worthy of

trust. As a result of this faith, there came forth from one man, who was himself as good as dead, descendants as numerous as the stars in the sky and the sands of the seashore.

All of these died in faith. They did not obtain what had been promised but saw and saluted it from afar. By acknowledging themselves to be strangers and foreigners on the earth, they showed that they were seeking a homeland. If they had been thinking back to the place from which they had come, they would have had the opportunity of returning there. But they were searching for a better, a heavenly home. Wherefore God is not ashamed to be called their God, for he has prepared a city for them. By faith Abraham, when put to the test, offered up Isaac; he who had received the promises was ready to sacrifice his only son, of whom it was said, "Through Isaac shall your descendants be called." He reasoned that God was able to raise from the dead, and so he received Isaac back as a symbol.

This is the Word of the Lord.

OR
(Short Form)

Faith is confident assurance concerning what we hope for, and conviction about things we do not see. Because of faith the men of old were approved by God. By faith Abraham obeyed when he was called, and went forth to the place he was to receive as a heritage; he went forth, moreover, not knowing where he was going. By faith he sojourned in the promised land as in a foreign country, dwelling in tents with Isaac and Jacob, heirs of the same promise; for he was looking forward to the city with foundations, whose designer and maker is God. By faith Sarah received power to conceive though she was past the age, for she thought that the One who had made the promise was worthy of trust. As a result of this faith, there came forth from one man, who was himself as good as dead, descendants as numerous as the stars in the sky and the sands of the seashore.

This is the Word of the Lord.

GOSPEL Lk 12, 32-48 or 12, 35-40
Alleluia
See no. 164.

✠ A reading from the holy gospel according to Luke
See that you are prepared.

(Long Form)

Jesus said to his disciples: "Do not live in fear, little flock. It has pleased your Father to give you the kingdom. Sell what you have and give alms. Get purses for yourselves that do not wear out, a never-failing treasure with the Lord which no thief comes near nor any moth destroys. Wherever your treasure lies, there your heart will be.

"Let your belts be fastened around your waists and your lamps be burning ready. Be like men awaiting their master's return from a wedding, so that when he arrives and knocks, you will open for him without delay. It will go well with those servants whom the master finds wide-awake on his return. I tell you, he will put on an apron, seat them at table, and proceed to wait on them. Should he happen to come at midnight or before sunrise and find them prepared, it will go well with them. You know as well as I that if the head of the house knew when the thief was coming he would not let him break into his house. Be on guard, therefore. The Son of Man will come when you least expect him."

Peter said, "Do you intend this parable for us, Lord, or do you mean it for the whole world?" The Lord said, "Who in your opinion is that faithful, farsighted steward whom the master will set over his servants to dispense their ration of grain in season? That servant is fortunate whom his master finds busy when he returns. Assuredly, his master will put him in charge of all his property. But if the servant says to himself, 'My master is taking his time about coming,' and begins to abuse the housemen and servant girls, to eat and drink and get drunk, that servant's master will come back on a day when he does not expect him, at a time he does not know. He will punish him severely and rank him among those undeserving of trust. The slave who knew his master's wishes but did not prepare to fulfill them will get a severe beating, whereas the one who did not know them and who nonetheless deserved to be flogged will get off with fewer stripes. When much has been given a man, much will be required of him. More will be asked of a man to whom more has been entrusted.

This is the gospel of the Lord.

OR
(Short Form)

Jesus said to his disciples: "Let your belts be fastened around your waists and your lamps be burning ready. Be like men awaiting their master's return from a wedding, so that when he arrives and knocks, you will open for him without delay. It will go well with those servants whom the master finds wide-awake on his return. I tell you, he will put on an apron, seat them at table, and proceed to wait on them. Should he happen to come at midnight or before sunrise and find them prepared, it will go well with them. You know as well as I that if the head of the house knew when the thief was coming he would not let him break into his house. Be on guard, therefore. The Son of Man will come when you least expect him."

This is the gospel of the Lord.

---

119   **TWENTIETH SUNDAY**   **A**
               OF THE YEAR

READING I   Is 56, 1. 6-7

A reading from the book of the prophet Isaiah

My sons who come to me I will lead to my holy mountain.

Thus says the Lord:
Observe what is right, do what is just;
　for my salvation is about to come,
　my justice, about to be revealed.

The foreigners who join themselves to the
　Lord,
　ministering to him,
Loving the name of the Lord,
　and becoming his servants—

All who keep the sabbath free from profanation
　and hold to my covenant,
Them I will bring to my holy mountain
　and make joyful in my house of prayer;
Their holocausts and sacrifices
　will be acceptable on my altar,
For my house shall be called
　a house of prayer for all peoples.

This is the Word of the Lord.

Responsorial Psalm   Ps 67, 2-3. 5. 6. 8

℟. (4) O God, let all the nations praise you!
May God have pity on us and bless us;
　may he let his face shine upon us.
So may your way be known upon earth;
　among all nations, your salvation.

℟.O God, let all the nations praise you!
May the nations be glad and exult
　because you rule the peoples in equity;
　the nations on the earth you guide.

℟.O God, let all the nations praise you!
May the peoples praise you, O God;
　may all the peoples praise you!
May God bless us,
　and may all the ends of the earth fear him!

℟.O God, let all the nations praise you!

READING II   Rom 11, 13-15. 29-32

A reading from the letter of Paul to the Romans

The gifts and call of God are irrevocable.

I say this now to you Gentiles: Inasmuch as I am the apostle of the Gentiles, I glory in my ministry, trying to rouse my fellow Jews to envy and save some of them. For if their rejection has meant reconciliation for the world, what will their acceptance mean? Nothing less than life from the dead!

God's gifts and his call are irrevocable. Just as you were once disobedient to God and now have received mercy through their disobedience, so they have become disobedient—since God wished to show you mercy—that they too may receive mercy. God has imprisoned all in disobedience that he might have mercy on all.

This is the Word of the Lord.

GOSPEL   Mt 15, 21-28
Alleluia
See no. 164.

✠ A reading from the holy gospel according
to Matthew

Woman, your faith is great.

Jesus withdrew to the district of Tyre and
Sidon. It happened that a Canaanite woman
living in that locality presented herself, crying
out to him, "Lord, Son of David, have pity on
me! My daughter is terribly troubled by a demon." He gave her no word of response. His
disciples came up and began to entreat him,
"Get rid of her. She keeps shouting after us."
"My mission is only to the lost sheep of the
house of Israel," Jesus replied. She came forward then and did him homage with the plea,
"Help me, Lord!" But he answered, "It is not
right to take the food of sons and daughters
and throw it to the dogs." "Please, Lord," she
insisted, "even the dogs eat the leavings that
fall from their masters' tables." Jesus then said
in reply, "Woman, you have great faith! Your
wish will come to pass." That very moment her
daughter got better.

This is the gospel of the Lord.

---

120   TWENTIETH SUNDAY   **B**
OF THE YEAR

READING I   Prv 9, 1-6
A reading from the book of Proverbs
Come and eat my bread, drink the wine I have prepared.

Wisdom has built her house,
    she has set up her seven columns;
She has dressed her meat, mixed her wine,
    yes, she has spread her table.
She has sent out her maidens; she calls
    from the heights out over the city:
"Let whoever is simple turn in here;
    to him who lacks understanding, I say,
Come, eat of my food,
    and drink of the wine I have mixed!
Forsake foolishness that you may live;
    advance in the way of understanding.

This is the Word of the Lord.

Responsorial Psalm   Ps 34, 2-3. 10-11. 12-13. 14-15

℟. (9) Taste and see the goodness of the Lord.

I will bless the Lord at all times;
    his praise shall be ever in my mouth.
Let my soul glory in the Lord;
    the lowly will hear me and be glad.

℟. Taste and see the goodness of the Lord.

Fear the Lord, you his holy ones,
    for nought is lacking to those who fear him.
The great grow poor and hungry;
    but those who seek the Lord want for no
    good thing.

℟. Taste and see the goodness of the Lord.

Come, children, hear me;
    I will teach you the fear of the Lord.
Which of you desires life,
    and takes delight in prosperous days?

℟. Taste and see the goodness of the Lord.

Keep your tongue from evil
    and your lips from speaking guile;
Turn from evil, and do good;
    seek peace, and follow after it.

℟. Taste and see the goodness of the Lord.

READING II   Eph 5, 15-20
A reading from the letter of Paul to the
Ephesians
Be watchful that you may know the will of God.

Keep careful watch over your conduct. Do not
act like fools, but like thoughtful men. Make
the most of the present opportunity, for these
are evil days. Do not continue in ignorance, but
try to discern the will of the Lord. Avoid getting
drunk on wine that leads to debauchery. Be
filled with the Spirit, addressing one another in
psalms and hymns and inspired songs. Sing
praise to the Lord with all your hearts. Give
thanks to God the Father always and for everything in the name of our Lord Jesus Christ.

This is the Word of the Lord.

GOSPEL
Jn 6, 51-58
Alleluia

See no. 164, or no. 168.

✠ **A reading from the holy gospel according to John**

My flesh is real food and my blood is real drink.

Jesus said to the crowds:
"I myself am the living bread
come down from heaven.
If anyone eats this bread
he shall live forever;
the bread I will give
is my flesh, for the life of the world."
At this the Jews quarreled among themselves, saying, "How can he give us his flesh to eat?" Thereupon Jesus said to them:
"Let me solemnly assure you,
if you do not eat the flesh of the Son
of Man
and drink his blood,
you have no life in you.
He who feeds on my flesh
and drinks my blood
has life eternal,
and I will raise him up on the last day.
For my flesh is real food
and my blood real drink.
The man who feeds on my flesh
and drinks my blood
remains in me, and I in him.
Just as the Father who has life sent me
and I have life because of the Father,
so the man who feeds on me
will have life because of me.
This is the bread that came down from
heaven.
Unlike your ancestors who ate and died
nonetheless,
the man who feeds on this bread shall live
forever."
This is the gospel of the Lord.

**121   TWENTIETH SUNDAY
OF THE YEAR   C**

READING I
Jer 38, 4-6. 8-10
**A reading from the book of the prophet
Jeremiah**

You bore me to be a man of strife for the whole world.

The princes said to the king: "Jeremiah ought to be put to death; he demoralizes the soldiers who are left in this city, and all the people, by speaking such things to them; he is not interested in the welfare of our people, but in their ruin." King Zedekiah answered: "He is in your power"; for the king could do nothing with them. And so they took Jeremiah and threw him into the cistern of Prince Malchiah, which was in the quarters of the guard, letting him down with ropes. There was no water in the cistern, only mud, and Jeremiah sank into the mud.

Ebed-melech went to the Gate of Benjamin from the palace and said to the king: "My lord king, these men have been at fault in all they have done to the prophet Jeremiah, casting him into the cistern. He will die of famine on the spot, for there is no more food in the city." Then the king ordered Ebed-melech the Cushite to take three men along with him, and draw the prophet Jeremiah out of the cistern before he should die.

This is the Word of the Lord.

Responsorial Psalm
Ps 40, 2. 3. 4. 18

℟. (14) Lord, come to my aid!
I have waited, waited for the Lord,
and he stooped toward me.
℟. Lord, come to my aid!
The Lord heard my cry.
He drew me out of the pit of destruction,
out of the mud of the swamp;
He set my feet upon a crag;
he made firm my steps.
℟. Lord, come to my aid!
And he put a new song into my mouth,
a hymn to our God.
Many shall look on in awe
and trust in the Lord.

Ry. Lord, come to my aid!
Though I am afflicted and poor,
   yet the Lord thinks of me.
You are my help and my deliverer;
   O my God, hold not back!
Ry. Lord, come to my aid!

READING II   Heb 12, 1-4

A reading from the letter to the Hebrews

Let us bear patiently the struggle placed upon us.

Since we for our part are surrounded by a cloud of witnesses; let us lay aside every encumbrance of sin which clings to us and persevere in running the race which lies ahead; let us keep our eyes fixed on Jesus, who inspires and perfects our faith. For the sake of the joy which lay before him he endured the cross, heedless of its shame. He has taken his seat at the right of the throne of God. Remember how he endured the opposition of sinners; hence do not grow despondent or abandon the struggle.

    This is the Word of the Lord.

GOSPEL   Lk 12, 49-53
Alleluia

See no. 164.

✠ **A reading from the holy gospel according to Luke**

I have come not to give peace, but discord.

Jesus said to his disciples: "I have come to light a fire on the earth. How I wish the blaze were ignited! I have a baptism to receive. What anguish I feel till it is over! Do you think I have come to establish peace on the earth? I assure you, the contrary is true; I have come for division. From now on, a household of five will be divided three against two and two against three; father will be split against son and son against father, mother against daughter and daughter against mother, mother-in-law against daughter-in-law, daughter-in-law against mother-in-law."

    This is the gospel of the Lord.

---

122   **TWENTY-FIRST SUNDAY**   **A**
                 OF THE YEAR

READING I   Is 22, 15. 19-23

A reading from the book of the prophet Isaiah

I place the key of the house of David upon his shoulder.

Thus says the Lord, the God of hosts:
   Up, go to that official,
   Shebna, master of the palace:
"I will thrust you from your office
   and pull you down from your station.

On that day I will summon my servant
   Eliakim, son of Hilkiah;
I will clothe him with your robe,
   and gird him with your sash,
   and give over to him your authority.
He shall be a father to the inhabitants of
   Jerusalem,
   and to the house of Judah.
I will place the key of the House of David
   on his shoulder;
   when he opens, no one shall shut,
   when he shuts, no one shall open.
I will fix him like a peg in a sure spot,
   to be a place of honor for his family."
    This is the Word of the Lord.

Responsorial Psalm   Ps 138, 1-2. 2-3. 6. 8

Ry. (8) Lord, your love is eternal;
   do not forsake the work of your hands.
I will give thanks to you, O Lord, with all
   my heart,
   [for you have heard the words of my mouth;]
   in the presence of the angels I will sing
   your praise;
I will worship at your holy temple.
Ry. Lord, your love is eternal;
   do not forsake the work of your hands.
I will give thanks to your name,
   because of your kindness and your truth:
When I called, you answered me;
   you built up strength within me.
Ry. Lord, your love is eternal;
   do not forsake the work of your hands.

The Lord is exalted, yet the lowly he sees,
  and the proud he knows from afar.
Your kindness, O Lord, endures forever;
  forsake not the work of your hands.
℟. Lord, your love is eternal;
  do not forsake the work of your hands.

READING II   Rom 11, 33-36
A reading from the letter of Paul to the Romans

From him, through him, and in him are all things.

How deep are the riches and the wisdom and
the knowledge of God! How inscrutable his
judgments, how unsearchable his ways! For
"who has known the mind of the Lord? Or
who has been his counselor? Who has given him
anything so as to deserve return?" For from
him and through him and for him all things are.
To him be glory forever. Amen.
            This is the Word of the Lord.

GOSPEL   Mt 16, 13-20
Alleluia

See no. 164.

✠ **A reading from the holy gospel according
        to Matthew**

You are Peter, to you I will give the keys of the kingdom
of heaven.

When Jesus came to the neighborhood of
Caesarea Philippi, he asked his disciples this
question: "Who do people say that the Son of
Man is?" They replied, "Some say John the
Baptizer, others Elijah, still others Jeremiah
or one of the prophets." "And you," he said
to them, "who do you say that I am?" "You
are the Messiah," Simon Peter answered, "the
Son of the living God!" Jesus replied, "Blest are
you, Simon son of John! No mere man has revealed this to you, but my heavenly Father. I
for my part declare to you, you are 'Rock,' and
on this rock I will build my church, and the
jaws of death shall not prevail against it. I will
entrust to you the keys of the kingdom of heav-
en. Whatever you declare bound on earth shall
be bound in heaven; whatever you declare
loosed on earth shall be loosed in heaven." Then

he strictly ordered his disciples not to tell anyone that he was the Messiah.
        This is the gospel of the Lord.

---

123   **TWENTY-FIRST SUNDAY
                OF THE YEAR**   **B**

READING I   Jos 24, 1-2. 15-17. 18
A reading from the book of Joshua

We will serve the Lord God, because he is our God.

Joshua gathered together all the tribes of Israel at Shechem, summoning their elders, their
leaders, their judges and their officers. When
they stood in ranks before God, Joshua addressed all the people: "If it does not please
you to serve the Lord, decide today whom
you will serve, the gods your fathers served
beyond the River or the gods of the Amorites
in whose country you are dwelling. As for
me and my household, we will serve the Lord."
    But the people answered, "Far be it from
us to forsake the Lord for the service of other
gods. For it was the Lord, our God, who
brought us and our fathers up out of the land
of Egypt, out of a state of slavery. He performed those great miracles before our very
eyes and protected us along our entire journey
and among all the peoples through whom we
passed. Therefore we also will serve the Lord,
for he is our God."
        This is the Word of the Lord.

Responsorial Psalm
                        Ps 34, 2-3. 16-17. 18-19. 20-21. 22-23
℟. (9) Taste and see the goodness of the Lord.
I will bless the Lord at all times;
  his praise shall be ever in my mouth.
Let my soul glory in the Lord;
  the lowly will hear me and be glad.
℟. Taste and see the goodness of the Lord.
The Lord has eyes for the just,
  and ears for their cry.
The Lord confronts the evildoers,
  to destroy remembrance of them from the
  earth.

R̷. Taste and see the goodness of the Lord.
When the just cry out, the Lord hears them,
   and from all their distress he rescues them.
The Lord is close to the brokenhearted;
   and those who are crushed in spirit he saves.
R̷. Taste and see the goodness of the Lord.
Many are the troubles of the just man,
   but out of them all the Lord delivers him;
He watches over all his bones;
   not one of them shall be broken.
R̷. Taste and see the goodness of the Lord.
Vice slays the wicked,
   and the enemies of the just pay for their
   guilt.
But the Lord redeems the lives of his ser-
   vants;
   no one incurs guilt who takes refuge in him.
R̷. Taste and see the goodness of the Lord.

READING II   Eph 5, 21-32

A reading from the letter of Paul to the
Ephesians
This is the great mystery, it applies to Christ and the
Church.
Defer to one another out of reverence for
Christ.
   Wives should be submissive to their hus-
bands as if to the Lord because the husband
is head of his wife just as Christ is head of
his body, the church, as well as its savior.
As the church submits to Christ, so wives
should submit to their husbands in everything.
   Husbands, love your wives, as Christ loved
the church. He gave himself up for her to make
her holy, purifying her in the bath of water by
the power of the word, to present to himself a
glorious church, holy and immaculate, without
stain or wrinkle or anything of that sort. Hus-
bands should love their wives as they do their
own bodies. He who loves his wife loves him-
self. Observe that no one ever hates his own
flesh; no, he nourishes it and takes care of it as
Christ cares for the church—for we are mem-
bers of his body.
   "For this reason a man shall leave his father
   and mother,
and shall cling to his wife,
and the two shall be made into one."

This is a great foreshadowing; I mean that it
refers to Christ and the church.
   This is the Word of the Lord.

GOSPEL   Jn 6, 60-69
Alleluia
See no. 164.

✠ **A reading from the holy gospel according**
   to John
Lord, whom shall we go to? You have the words of eternal life
Many of the disciples of Jesus remarked, "This
sort of talk is hard to endure! How can anyone
take it seriously?" Jesus was fully aware that
his disciples were murmuring in protest at
what he had said. "Does it shake your faith?"
he asked them.
   "What, then, if you were to see the Son
   of Man
ascend to where he was before . . . ?
It is the spirit that gives life;
   the flesh is useless.
The words I spoke to you
   are spirit and life.
Yet among you there are some who do
   not believe."
(Jesus knew from the start, of course, the
ones who refused to believe, and the one who
would hand him over.) He went on to say:
   "This is why I have told you
   that no one can come to me
unless it is granted him by the Father."
From this time on, many of his disciples broke
away and would not remain in his company
any longer. Jesus then said to the Twelve, "Do
you want to leave me too?" Simon Peter an-
swered him, "Lord, to whom shall we go?
You have the words of eternal life. We have
come to believe; we are convinced that you
are God's holy one."
   This is the gospel of the Lord.

124   **TWENTY-FIRST SUNDAY**   **C**
           OF THE YEAR

READING I   Is 66, 18-21

A reading from the book of the prophet Isaiah

They will gather all of your brothers from all nations.

I come to gather nations of every language; they shall come and see my glory. I will set a sign among them; from them I will send fugitives to the nations: to Tarshish, Put and Lud, Mosoch, Tubal and Javan, to the distant coastlands that have never heard of my fame, or seen my glory; and they shall proclaim my glory among the nations. They shall bring all your brethren from all the nations as an offering to the Lord, on horses and in chariots, in carts, upon mules and dromedaries, to Jerusalem, my holy mountain, says the Lord, just as the Israelites bring their offering to the house of the Lord in clean vessels. Some of these I will take as priests and Levites, says the Lord.

This is the Word of the Lord.

Responsorial Psalm   Ps 117, 1. 2

℟. (Mk 16, 15) Go out to all the world
    and tell the Good News.
**Praise the Lord, all you nations;
    glorify him, all you peoples!**
℟. Go out to all the world
    and tell the Good News.
**For steadfast is his kindness toward us,
    and the fidelity of the Lord endures forever.**
℟. Go out to all the world
    and tell the Good News.
℟. Or: Alleluia.

READING II   Heb 12, 5-7. 11-13

A reading from the letter to the Hebrews

The Lord disciplines those he loves.

You have forgotten the encouraging words addressed to you as sons:
"My sons, do not disdain the discipline of the
    Lord
    nor lose heart when he reproves you;
For, whom the Lord loves, he disciplines;
    he scourges every son he receives."

Endure your trials as the discipline of God, who deals with you as sons. For what son is there whom his father does not discipline? At the time it is administered, all discipline seems a cause for grief and not for joy, but later it brings forth the fruit of peace and justice to those who are trained in its school. So strengthen your drooping hands and your weak knees. Make straight the paths you walk on, that your halting limbs may not be dislocated but healed.

This is the Word of the Lord.

GOSPEL   Lk 13, 22-30
Alleluia

See no. 164.

✠ A reading from the holy gospel according
        to Luke

Men from the east and from the west will come to take their place in the kingdom of God.

Jesus went through cities and towns teaching —all the while making his way toward Jerusalem. Someone asked him, "Lord, are they few in number who are to be saved?" He replied: "Try to come in through the narrow door. Many, I tell you, will try to enter and be unable. When once the master of the house has risen to lock the door and you stand outside knocking and saying, 'Sir, open for us,' he will say in reply, 'I do not know where you come from.' Then you will begin to say, 'We ate and drank in your company. You taught in our streets.' But he will answer, 'I tell you, I do not know where you come from. Away from me, you evildoers!'

"There will be wailing and grinding of teeth when you see Abraham, Isaac, Jacob, and all the prophets safe in the kingdom of God, and you yourselves rejected. People will come from the east and the west, from the north and the south, and will take their place at the feast in the kingdom of God. Some who are last will be first and some who are first will be last."

This is the gospel of the Lord.

125   TWENTY-SECOND SUNDAY OF THE YEAR   **A**

READING I   Jer 20, 7-9

A reading from the book of the prophet Jeremiah

The word of the Lord has meant derision for me.

You duped me, O Lord, and I let myself be duped;
  you were too strong for me, and you triumphed.
All the day I am an object of laughter;
  everyone mocks me.
Whenever I speak, I must cry out,
  violence and outrage is my message;
The word of the Lord has brought me
  derision and reproach all the day.
I say to myself, I will not mention him,
  I will speak in his name no more.
But then it becomes like fire burning in my heart,
  imprisoned in my bones;
I grow weary holding it in,
  I cannot endure it.
        This is the Word of the Lord.

Responsorial Psalm   Ps 63, 2. 3-4. 5-6. 8-9

℟. (2) My soul is thirsting for you, O Lord my God.

O God, you are my God whom I seek;
  for you my flesh pines and my soul thirsts
  like the earth, parched, lifeless and without water.
℟. My soul is thirsting for you, O Lord my God.
Thus have I gazed toward you in the sanctuary
  to see your power and your glory,
For your kindness is a greater good than life;
  my lips shall glorify you.
℟. My soul is thirsting for you, O Lord my God.
Thus will I bless you while I live;
  lifting up my hands, I will call upon your name.
As with the riches of a banquet shall my soul be satisfied,

and with exultant lips my mouth shall praise you.
℟. My soul is thirsting for you, O Lord my God.
You are my help,
  and in the shadow of your wings I shout for joy.
My soul clings fast to you;
  your right hand upholds me.
℟. My soul is thirsting for you, O Lord my God.

READING II   Rom 12, 1-2

A reading from the letter of Paul to the Romans

May you present your bodies as a living sacrifice.

Brothers, I beg you through the mercy of God to offer your bodies as a living sacrifice holy and acceptable to God, your spiritual worship. Do not conform yourselves to this age, but be transformed by the renewal of your mind, so that you may judge what is God's will, what is good, pleasing and perfect.
        This is the Word of the Lord.

GOSPEL   Mt 16, 21-27
Alleluia

See no. 164.

✠ **A reading from the holy gospel according to Matthew**

If any man wishes to come after me, let him deny himself.

From then on Jesus [the Messiah] started to indicate to his disciples that he must go to Jerusalem to suffer greatly there at the hands of the elders, the chief priests, and the scribes, and to be put to death, and raised up on the third day. At this, Peter took him aside and began to remonstrate with him. "May you be spared, Master! God forbid that any such thing ever happen to you!" Jesus turned on Peter and said, "Get out of my sight, you satan! You are trying to make me trip and fall. You are not judging by God's standards but by man's."

Jesus then said to his disciples: "If a man wishes to come after me, he must deny his very self, take up his cross, and begin to follow in my footsteps. Whoever would save his life will lose it, but whoever loses his life for my sake will find it. What profit would a man show if he were to gain the whole world and ruin himself in the process? What can a man offer in exchange for his very self? The Son of Man will come with his Father's glory accompanied by his angels. When he does, he will repay each man according to his conduct.

This is the gospel of the Lord.

---

126   TWENTY-SECOND SUNDAY   B
OF THE YEAR

READING I   Dt 4, 1-2. 6-8

A reading from the book of Deuteronomy

You may add nothing to the word which I speak to you—keep the commands of the Lord.

Moses told the people: "Now, Israel, hear the statutes and decrees which I am teaching you to observe, that you may live, and may enter in and take possession of the land which the Lord, the God of your fathers, is giving you. In your observance of the commandments of the Lord, your God, which I enjoin upon you, you shall not add to what I command you nor subtract from it. Observe them carefully, for thus will you give evidence of your wisdom and intelligence to the nations, who will hear of all these statutes and say, 'This great nation is truly a wise and intelligent people.' For what great nation is there that has gods so close to it as the Lord, our God, is to us whenever we call upon him? Or what great nation has statutes and decrees that are as just as this whole law which I am setting before you today?"

This is the Word of the Lord.

Responsorial Psalm   Ps 15, 2-3. 3-4. 4-5

℟. (1) He who does justice will live in the presence of the Lord.

He who walks blamelessly and does justice;
  who thinks the truth in his heart
  and slanders not with his tongue.

℟. He who does justice will live in the presence of the Lord.

Who harms not his fellow man,
  nor takes up a reproach against his neighbor;
By whom the reprobate is despised,
  while he honors those who fear the Lord.

℟. He who does justice will live in the presence of the Lord.

Who lends not his money at usury
  and accepts no bribe against the innocent.
He who does these things
  shall never be disturbed.

℟. He who does justice will live in the presence of the Lord.

READING II   Jas 1, 17-18. 21-22. 27

A reading from the letter of James

Be doers of the word.

Every worthwhile gift, every genuine benefit comes from above, descending from the Father of the heavenly luminaries, who cannot change and who is never shadowed over. He wills to bring us to birth with a word spoken in truth so that we may be a kind of firstfruits of his creatures.

Humbly welcome the word that has taken root in you, with its power to save you. Act on this word. If all you do is listen to it, you are deceiving yourselves.

Looking after orphans and widows in their distress and keeping oneself unspotted by the world make for pure worship without stain before our God and Father.

This is the Word of the Lord.

GOSPEL   Mk 7, 1-8. 14-15. 21-23
Alleluia

See no. 164.

✠ **A reading from the holy gospel according to Mark**

You forget the commandments of God and hold on to the traditions of men.

The Pharisees and some of the experts in the law who had come from Jerusalem gathered around Jesus. They had observed a few of his disciples eating meals without having purified —that is to say, washed—their hands. The Pharisees, and in fact all Jews, cling to the custom of their ancestors and never eat without scrupulously washing their hands. Moreover, they never eat anything from the market without first sprinkling it. There are many other traditions they observe—for example, the washing of cups and jugs and kettles. So the Pharisees and the scribes questioned him: "Why do your disciples not follow the tradition of our ancestors, but instead take food without purifying their hands?" He said to them: "How accurately Isaiah prophesied about you hypocrites when he wrote,

'This people pays me lip service
but their heart is far from me.
Empty is the reverence they do me
because they teach as dogmas mere human precepts.'

You disregard God's commandment and cling to what is human tradition."

He summoned the crowd again and said to them: "Hear me, all of you, and try to understand. Nothing that enters a man from outside can make him impure; that which comes out of him, and only that, constitutes impurity. Let everyone heed what he hears!"

"Wicked designs come from the deep recesses of the heart: acts of fornication, theft, murder, adulterous conduct, greed, maliciousness, deceit, sensuality, envy, blasphemy, arrogance, an obtuse spirit. All these evils come from within and render a man impure."

This is the gospel of the Lord.

---

127   TWENTY-SECOND SUNDAY   C
OF THE YEAR

READING I   Sir 3, 17-18. 20. 28-29
A reading from the book of Sirach
Humble yourself and you will find favor with the Lord.

My son, conduct your affairs with humility,
and you will be loved more than a giver of gifts.
Humble yourself the more, the greater you are,
and you will find favor with God.
What is too sublime for you, seek not,
into things beyond your strength search not.

The mind of a sage appreciates proverbs,
and an attentive ear is the wise man's joy.
Water quenches a flaming fire,
and alms atone for sins.
This is the Word of the Lord.

Responsorial Psalm   Ps 68, 4-5. 6-7. 10-11
℟. (11) God, in your goodness, you have made
a home for the poor.
The just rejoice and exult before God;
they are glad and rejoice.
Sing to God, chant praise to his name;
whose name is the Lord.
℟. God, in your goodness, you have made a
home for the poor.
The father of orphans and the defender of
widows
is God in his holy dwelling.
God gives a home to the forsaken;
he leads forth prisoners to prosperity.
℟. God, in your goodness, you have made a
home for the poor.
A bountiful rain you showered down, O God,
upon your inheritance;
you restored the land when it languished;
Your flock settled in it;
in your goodness, O God, you provided it
for the needy.
℟. God, in your goodness, you have made a
home for the poor.

READING II   Heb 12, 18-19. 22-24
A reading from the letter to the Hebrews
You have come to Mount Zion and to the city of the living God.

You have not drawn near to an untouchable mountain and a blazing fire, and gloomy darkness and storm and trumpet blast, and a voice speaking words such that those who heard begged that they be not addressed to them. No, you have drawn near to Mount Zion and the city of the living God, the heavenly Jerusalem, to myriads of angels in festal gathering, to the assembly of the first-born enrolled in heaven, to God the judge of all, to the spirits of just men made perfect, to Jesus, the mediator of a new covenant.
This is the Word of the Lord.

GOSPEL Lk 14, 1. 7-14
Alleluia
See no. 164.

✠ A reading from the holy gospel according to Luke
The man who exalts himself shall be humbled and he who humbles himself shall be exalted.

When Jesus came on a sabbath to eat a meal in the house of one of the leading Pharisees, they observed him closely.

He went on to address a parable to the guests, noticing how they were trying to get the places of honor at the table: "When you are invited by someone to a wedding party, do not sit in the place of honor in case some greater dignitary has been invited. Then the host might come and say to you, 'Make room for this man,' and you would have to proceed shamefacedly to the lowest place. What you should do when you have been invited is go and sit in the lowest place, so that when your host approaches you he will say, 'My friend, come up higher.' This will win you the esteem of your fellow guests. For everyone who exalts himself shall be humbled and he who humbles himself shall be exalted."

He said to the one who had invited him: "Whenever you give a lunch or dinner, do not invite your friends or brothers or relatives or wealthy neighbors. They might invite you in return and thus repay you. No, when you have a reception, invite beggars and the crippled, the lame and the blind. You should be pleased that they cannot repay you, for you will be repaid in the resurrection of the just."
This is the gospel of the Lord.

---

128 TWENTY-THIRD SUNDAY OF THE YEAR **A**

READING I Ez 33, 7-9

A reading from the book of the prophet Ezekiel
If you have not warned the wicked man, then I will hold you responsible for his death.

You, son of man, I have appointed watchman for the house of Israel; when you hear me say

anything, you shall warn them for me. If I tell the wicked man that he shall surely die, and you do not speak out to dissuade the wicked man from his way, he [the wicked man] shall die for his guilt, but I will hold you responsible for his death. But if you warn the wicked man, trying to turn him from his way, and he refuses to turn from his way, he shall die for his guilt, but you shall save yourself.
This is the Word of the Lord.

Responsorial Psalm Ps 95, 1-2. 6-7. 8-9

℟. (7. 8) If today you hear his voice,
 harden not your hearts.
Come, let us sing joyfully to the Lord;
 let us acclaim the Rock of our salvation.
Let us greet him with thanksgiving;
 let us joyfully sing psalms to him.
℟. If today you hear his voice,
 harden not your hearts.
Come, let us bow down in worship;
 let us kneel before the Lord who made us.
For he is our God,
 and we are the people he shepherds, the flock he guides.
℟. If today you hear his voice,
 harden not your hearts.
Oh, that today you would hear his voice:
 "Harden not your hearts as at Meribah,
 as in the day of Massah in the desert,
Where your fathers tempted me;
 they tested me though they had seen my works."
℟. If today you hear his voice,
 harden not your hearts.

READING II Rom 13, 8-10

A reading from the letter of Paul to the Romans
Love is the fulfillment of the law.

Owe no debt to anyone except the debt that binds us to love one another. He who loves his neighbor has fulfilled the law. The commandments, "You shall not commit adultery; you shall not murder; you shall not steal; you shall not covet," and any other commandment there may be are all summed up in this, "You shall love your neighbor as yourself." Love never does any wrong to the neighbor, hence love is the fulfillment of the law.

This is the Word of the Lord.

GOSPEL   Mt 18, 15-20
Alleluia
See no. 164.

✠ A reading from the holy gospel according to Matthew

If he listens to you, you have won back your brother.

Jesus said to his disciples: "If your brother should commit some wrong against you, go and point out his fault, but keep it between the two of you. If he listens to you, you have won your brother over. If he does not listen, however, summon another, so that every case may stand on the word of two or three witnesses. If he ignores them, refer it to the church. If he ignores even the church, then treat him as you would a Gentile or a tax collector. I assure you, whatever you declare bound on earth shall be held bound in heaven, and whatever you declare loosed on earth shall be held loosed in heaven.

"Again I tell you, if two of you join your voices on earth to pray for anything whatever, it shall be granted you by my Father in heaven. Where two or three are gathered in my name, there am I in their midst."

This is the gospel of the Lord.

---

129   **TWENTY-THIRD SUNDAY**   **B**
                OF THE YEAR

READING I   Is 35, 4-7

A reading from the book of the prophet Isaiah

Then the ears of the deaf shall be opened and the tongues of the dumb speak.

Say to those whose hearts are frightened:
  Be strong, fear not!
Here is your God,
  he comes with vindication;
With divine recompense
  he comes to save you.
Then will the eyes of the blind be opened,
  the ears of the deaf be cleared;

Then will the lame leap like a stag,
  then the tongue of the dumb will sing.

Streams will burst forth in the desert,
  and rivers in the steppe.
The burning sands will become pools,
  and the thirsty ground, springs of water.

This is the Word of the Lord.

Responsorial Psalm   Ps 146, 7. 8-9. 9-10

℞. (2) Praise the Lord, my soul!
The God of Jacob keeps faith forever,
  secures justice for the oppressed,
  gives food to the hungry.
The Lord sets captives free.
℞. Praise the Lord, my soul!
The Lord gives sight to the blind;
  the Lord raises up those that were bowed down.
The Lord loves the just;
  the Lord protects strangers.
℞. Praise the Lord, my soul!
The fatherless and the widow the Lord sustains,
  but the way of the wicked he thwarts.
The Lord shall reign forever;
  your God, O Zion, through all generations.
    Alleluia.
℞. Praise the Lord, my soul!
℞. Or: Alleluia.

READING II   Jas 2, 1-5

A reading from the letter of James

Has not God chosen the poor of the world to inherit the kingdom?

My brothers, your faith in our Lord Jesus Christ glorified must not allow of favoritism. Suppose there should come into your assembly a man fashionably dressed, with gold rings on his fingers, and at the same time a poor man dressed in shabby clothes. Suppose further you were to take notice of the well-dressed man and say, "Sit right here, please;" whereas you were to say to the poor man, "You can stand!" or "Sit over there by my footrest." Have you not in a case like this discriminated in your hearts?

Have you not set yourselves up as judges who hand down corrupt decisions?

Listen, dear brothers. Did not God choose those who are poor in the eyes of the world to be rich in faith and heirs of the kingdom he promised to those who love him?

This is the Word of the Lord.

GOSPEL   Mk 7, 31-37
Alleluia
See no. 164.

✠ **A reading from the holy gospel according to Mark**
He has made the deaf hear and the dumb speak.

Jesus left Tyrian territory and returned by way of Sidon to the Sea of Galilee, into the district of the Ten Cities. Some people brought him a deaf man who had a speech impediment and begged him to lay his hand on him. Jesus took him off by himself away from the crowd. He put his fingers into the man's ears and, spitting, touched his tongue; then he looked up to heaven and emitted a groan. He said to him, "Ephphatha!" (that is, "Be opened!") At once the man's ears were opened; he was freed from the impediment, and began to speak plainly. Then he enjoined them strictly not to tell anyone; but the more he ordered them not to, the more they proclaimed it. Their amazement went beyond all bounds: "He has done everything well! He makes the deaf hear and the mute speak!"

This is the gospel of the Lord.

**130   TWENTY-THIRD SUNDAY C
           OF THE YEAR**

READING I   Wis 9, 13-18

· **A reading from the book of Wisdom**
Who can comprehend the will of God?

For what man knows God's counsel,
    or who can conceive what the Lord intends?
For the deliberations of mortals are timid,
    and unsure are our plans.

For the corruptible body burdens the soul
    and the earthen shelter weighs down the mind that has many concerns.
And scarce do we guess the things on earth,
    and what is within our grasp we find with difficulty;
but when things are in heaven, who can search them out?
Or who ever knew your counsel, except you had given Wisdom
and sent your holy spirit from on high?
And thus were the paths of those on earth made straight.

This is the Word of the Lord.

Responsorial Psalm   Ps 90, 3-4. 5-6. 12-13. 14-17

℟. (1) In every age, O Lord, you have been our refuge.
You turn man back to dust,
    saying, "Return, O children of men."
For a thousand years in your sight
    are as yesterday, now that it is past,
    or as a watch of the night.

℟. In every age, O Lord, you have been our refuge.
You make an end of them in their sleep;
    the next morning they are like the changing grass,
Which at dawn springs up anew,
    but by evening wilts and fades.

℟. In every age, O Lord, you have been our refuge.
Teach us to number our days aright,
    that we may gain wisdom of heart.
Return, O Lord! How long?
    Have pity on your servants!

℟. In every age, O Lord, you have been our refuge.
Fill us at daybreak with your kindness,
    that we may shout for joy and gladness all our days.
And may the gracious care of the Lord our God be ours;
    prosper the work of our hands for us!
[Prosper the work of our hands!]

℟. In every age, O Lord, you have been our refuge.

READING II   Phlm 9-10. 12-17

A reading from the letter of Paul to Philemon

Receive him, not as a slave anymore, but as a very dear brother.

I, Paul, ambassador of Christ and now a prisoner for him, appeal to you for my child, whom I have begotten during my imprisonment. It is he I am sending to you—and that means I am sending my heart!

I had wanted to keep him with me, that he might serve me in your place while I am in prison for the gospel; but I did not want to do anything without your consent, that kindness might not be forced on you but freely bestowed. Perhaps he was separated from you for a while for this reason: that you might possess him forever, no longer as a slave but as more than a slave, a beloved brother, especially dear to me; and how much more than a brother to you, since now you will know him both as a man and in the Lord.

If then you regard me as a partner, welcome him as you would me.

This is the Word of the Lord.

GOSPEL   Lk 14, 25-33
Alleluia

See no. 164.

✠ **A reading from the holy gospel according to Luke**

The man who does not renounce his possessions cannot be my disciple.

On one occasion when a great crowd was with Jesus, he turned to them and said, "If anyone comes to me without turning his back on his father and mother, his wife and his children, his brothers and sisters, indeed his very self, he cannot be my follower. Anyone who does not take up his cross and follow me cannot be my disciple. If one of you decides to build a tower, will he not first sit down and calculate the outlay to see if he has enough money to complete the project? He will do that for fear of laying the foundation and then not being able to complete the work; at which all

who saw it would then jeer at him, saying, 'That man began to build what he could not finish.'

"Or if a king is about to march on another king to do battle with him, will he not sit down first and consider whether, with ten thousand men, he can withstand an enemy coming against him with twenty thousand? If he cannot, he will send a delegation while the enemy is still at a distance, asking for terms of peace. In the same way, none of you can be my disciple if he does not renounce all his possessions.''

This is the gospel of the Lord.

---

131   TWENTY-FOURTH SUNDAY   Ⓐ
OF THE YEAR

READING I   Sir 27, 30—28, 7

A reading from the book of Sirach

Forgive your neighbor's faults, and when you pray, your sins will be forgiven.

Wrath and anger are hateful things,
    yet the sinner hugs them tight.
The vengeful will suffer the Lord's vengeance,
    for he remembers their sins in detail.
Forgive your neighbor's injustice;
    then when you pray, your own sins will be
    forgiven.

Should a man nourish anger against his fellows
    and expect healing from the Lord?
Should a man refuse mercy to his fellows,
    yet seek pardon for his own sins?
If he who is but flesh cherishes wrath,
    who will forgive his sins?
Remember your last days, set enmity aside;
    remember death and decay, and cease from
    sin!
Think of the commandments, hate not your
    neighbor;
    of the Most High's covenant, and overlook
    faults.

This is the Word of the Lord.

Responsorial Psalm Ps 103, 1-2. 3-4. 9-10.11-12

℟. (8) The Lord is kind and merciful;
   slow to anger, and rich in compassion.

Bless the Lord, O my soul;
   and all my being, bless his holy name.
Bless the Lord, O my soul,
   and forget not all his benefits.

℟. The Lord is kind and merciful;
   slow to anger, and rich in compassion.

He pardons all your iniquities,
   he heals all your ills.
He redeems your life from destruction,
   he crowns you with kindness and compassion.

℟. The Lord is kind and merciful;
   slow to anger, and rich in compassion.

He will not always chide,
   nor does he keep his wrath forever.
Not according to our sins does he deal with us,
   nor does he requite us according to our crimes.

℟. The Lord is kind and merciful;
   slow to anger, and rich in compassion.

For as the heavens are high above the earth,
   so surpassing is his kindness toward those who fear him.
As far as the east is from the west,
   so far has he put our transgressions from us.

℟. The Lord is kind and merciful;
   slow to anger, and rich in compassion.

READING II   Rom 14, 7-9

A reading from the letter of Paul to the Romans
   Whether alive or dead, we belong to the Lord.

None of us lives as his own master and none of us dies as his own master. While we live we are responsible to the Lord, and when we die we die as his servants. Both in life and in death we are the Lord's. That is why Christ died and came to life again, that he might be Lord of both the dead and the living.
   This is the Word of the Lord.

GOSPEL   Mt 18, 21-35
Alleluia
See no. 164.

✠ **A reading from the holy gospel according to Matthew**
   I tell you that you forgive not seven times but seventy times seven.

Peter came up and asked Jesus, "Lord, when my brother wrongs me, how often must I forgive him? Seven times?" "No," Jesus replied, "not seven times; I say, seventy times seven times. That is why the reign of God may be said to be like a king who decided to settle accounts with his officials. When he began his auditing, one was brought in who owed him a huge amount. As he had no way of paying it, his master ordered him to be sold, along with his wife, his children, and all his property, in payment of the debt. At that the official prostrated himself in homage and said, 'My lord, be patient with me and I will pay you back in full.' Moved with pity, the master let the official go and wrote off the debt. But when that same official went out he met a fellow servant who owed him a mere fraction of what he himself owed. He seized him and throttled him. 'Pay back what you owe,' he demanded. His fellow servant dropped to his knees and began to plead with him, 'Just give me time and I will pay you back in full.' But he would hear none of it. Instead, he had him put in jail until he paid back what he owed. When his fellow servants saw what had happened they were badly shaken, and went to their master to report the whole incident. His master sent for him and said, 'You worthless wretch! I canceled your entire debt when you pleaded with me. Should you not have dealt mercifully with your fellow servant, as I dealt with you?' Then in anger the master handed him over to the torturers until he paid back all that he owed. My heavenly Father will treat you in exactly the same way unless each of you forgives his brother from his heart."
   This is the gospel of the Lord.

132   TWENTY-FOURTH SUNDAY   **B**
OF THE YEAR

READING I   Is 50, 4-9

A reading from the book of the prophet Isaiah
I gave my body to those who struck me.

The Lord God opens my ear that I may hear
And I have not rebelled,
  have not turned back.
I gave my back to those who beat me,
  my cheeks to those who plucked my beard;
My face I did not shield
  from buffets and spitting.

The Lord God is my help,
  therefore I am not disgraced;
I have set my face like flint,
  knowing that I shall not be put to shame.
He is near who upholds my right;
  if anyone wishes to oppose me,
  let us appear together.
Who disputes my right?
  Let him confront me.
See, the Lord God is my help;
  who will prove me wrong?
    This is the Word of the Lord.

Responsorial Psalm   Ps 116, 1-2. 3-4, 5-6. 8-9

℟. (9) I will walk in the presence of the Lord,
  in the land of the living.
I love the Lord because he has heard
  my voice in supplication,
Because he has inclined his ear to me
  the day I called.
℟. I will walk in the presence of the Lord,
  in the land of the living.
The cords of death encompassed me;
  the snares of the nether world seized
    upon me;
  I fell into distress and sorrow,
And I called upon the name of the Lord,
  "O Lord, save my life!"
℟. I will walk in the presence of the Lord,
  in the land of the living.
Gracious is the Lord and just;
  yes, our God is merciful.
The Lord keeps the little ones;
  I was brought low, and he saved me.

℟. I will walk in the presence of the Lord,
  in the land of the living.
For he has freed my soul from death,
  my eyes from tears, my feet from stumbling.
I shall walk before the Lord
  in the lands of the living.
℟. I will walk in the presence of the Lord,
  in the land of the living.
℟. Or: Alleluia.

READING II   Jas 2, 14-18

A reading from the letter of James
Faith without good works is dead.

My brothers, what good is it to profess faith
without practicing it? Such faith has no power
to save one, has it? If a brother or sister has
nothing to wear and no food for the day, and
you say to them, "Good-bye and good luck!
Keep warm and well fed," but do not meet
their bodily needs, what good is that? So it is
with the faith that does nothing in practice.
It is thoroughly lifeless.

To such a person one might say, "You have
faith and I have works—is that it?" Show me
your faith without works, and I will show you
the faith that underlies my works!
    This is the Word of the Lord.

GOSPEL   Mk 8, 27-35
Alleluia

See no. 164.

✠ **A reading from the holy gospel according**
  to Mark
You are the Christ . . . the Son of Man was destined to
suffer much.

Jesus and his disciples set out for the villages
around Caesarea Philippi. On the way he asked
his disciples this question: "Who do people say
that I am?" They replied, "Some, John the
Baptizer, others, Elijah, still others, one of
the prophets." "And you," he went on to ask,
"who do you say that I am?" Peter answered
him, "You are the Messiah!" Then he strictly
ordered them not to tell anyone about him.

He then began to teach them that the Son of
Man had to suffer much, be rejected by the
elders, the chief priests, and the scribes, be put

to death, and rise three days later. He said this quite openly. Peter then took him aside and began to remonstrate with him. At this he turned around and, eyeing the disciples, reprimanded Peter in turn: "Get out of my sight, you satan! You are not judging by God's standards but by man's!"

He summoned the crowd with his disciples and said to them: "If a man wishes to come after me, he must deny his very self, take up his cross, and follow in my steps. Whoever would save his life will lose it, but whoever loses his life for my sake and the gospel's will save it."

This is the gospel of the Lord.

---

133   TWENTY-FOURTH SUNDAY   C
OF THE YEAR

READING I   Ex 32, 7-11. 13-14

A reading from the book of Exodus
The Lord relented and did not send the evil he had threatened.

The Lord said to Moses, "Go down at once to your people, whom you brought out of the land of Egypt, for they have become depraved. They have soon turned aside from the way I pointed out to them, making for themselves a molten calf and worshiping it, sacrificing to it and crying out, 'This is your God, O Israel, who brought you out of the land of Egypt!' I see how stiff-necked this people is," continued the Lord to Moses. "Let me alone, then, that my wrath may blaze up against them to consume them. Then I will make of you a great nation."

But Moses implored the Lord, his God, saying, "Why, O Lord, should your wrath blaze up against your own people, whom you brought out of the land of Egypt with such great power and with so strong a hand? Remember your servants Abraham, Isaac and Israel, and how you swore to them by your own self, saying, 'I will make your descendants as numerous as the stars in the sky; and all this land that I promised, I will give your descendants as their perpetual heritage.' " So

the Lord relented in the punishment he had threatened to inflict on his people.

This is the Word of the Lord.

Responsorial Psalm   Ps 51, 3-4. 12-13. 17. 19

℟. (Lk 15, 18) I will rise and go to my father.
Have mercy on me, O God, in your goodness;
    in the greatness of your compassion wipe
        out my offense.
Thoroughly wash me from my guilt
    and of my sin cleanse me.
℟. I will rise and go to my father.
A clean heart create for me, O God,
    and a steadfast spirit renew within me.
Cast me not out from your presence,
    and your holy spirit take not from me.
℟. I will rise and go to my father.
O Lord, open my lips,
    and my mouth shall proclaim your praise.
My sacrifice, O God, is a contrite spirit;
    a heart contrite and humbled, O God, you
        will not spurn.
℟. I will rise and go to my father.

READING II   1 Tm 1, 12-17

A reading from the first letter of Paul to
Timothy
Christ came to save sinners.

I thank Christ Jesus our Lord, who has strengthened me, that he has made me his servant and judged me faithful. I was once a blasphemer, a persecutor, a man filled with arrogance; but because I did not know what I was doing in my unbelief, I have been treated mercifully, and the grace of our Lord has been granted me in overflowing measure, along with the faith and love which are in Christ Jesus. You can depend on this as worthy of full acceptance: that Christ Jesus came into the world to save sinners. Of these I myself am the worst. But on that very account I was dealt with mercifully, so that in me, as an extreme case, Jesus Christ might display all his patience, and that I might become an example to those who would later have faith in him and gain everlasting life. To the King of ages, the immortal, the invisible, the only God, be honor and glory forever and ever! Amen.

This is the Word of the Lord.

GOSPEL   Lk 15, 1-32 or 15, 1-10
Alleluia

See no. 164.

✠ **A reading from the holy gospel according to Luke**

There will be joy in heaven over one sinner who does penance.

(Long Form)

The tax collectors and sinners were all gathering around to hear Jesus, at which the Pharisees and the scribes murmured, "This man welcomes sinners and eats with them." Then he addressed this parable to them: "Who among you, if he has a hundred sheep and loses one of them, does not leave the ninety-nine in the wasteland and follow the lost one until he finds it? And when he finds it, he puts it on his shoulders in jubilation. Once arrived home, he invites friends and neighbors in and says to them, 'Rejoice with me because I have found my lost sheep.' I tell you, there will likewise be more joy in heaven over one repentant sinner than over ninety-nine righteous people who have no need to repent.

"What woman, if she has ten silver pieces and loses one, does not light a lamp and sweep the house in a diligent search until she has retrieved what she lost? And when she finds it, she calls in her friends and neighbors to say, 'Rejoice with me! I have found the silver piece I lost.' I tell you, there will be the same kind of joy before the angels of God over one repentant sinner."

Jesus said to them: "A man had two sons. The younger of them said to his father, 'Father, give me the share of the estate that is coming to me.' So the father divided up the property. Some days later this younger son collected all his belongings and went off to a distant land, where he squandered his money on dissolute living. After he had spent everything, a great famine broke out in that country and he was in dire need. So he attached himself to one of the

properted class of the place, who sent him to his farm to take care of the pigs. He longed to fill his belly with the husks that were fodder for the pigs, but no one made a move to give him anything. Coming to his senses at last, he said: 'How many hired hands at my father's place have more than enough to eat, while here I am starving! I will break away and return to my father, and say to him, "Father, I have sinned against God and against you; I no longer deserve to be called your son. Treat me like one of your hired hands." ' With that he set off for his father's house. While he was still a long way off, his father caught sight of him and was deeply moved. He ran out to meet him, threw his arms around his neck, and kissed him. The son said to him, 'Father, I have sinned against God and against you; I no longer deserve to be called your son.' The father said to his servants: 'Quick! bring out the finest robe and put it on him; put a ring on his finger and shoes on his feet. Take the fatted calf and kill it. Let us eat and celebrate because this son of mine was dead and has come back to life. He was lost and is found.' Then the celebration began.

"Meanwhile the elder son was out on the land. As he neared the house on his way home, he heard the sound of music and dancing. He called one of the servants and asked him the reason for the dancing and the music. The servant answered, 'Your brother is home, and your father has killed the fatted calf because he has him back in good health.' The son grew angry at this and would not go in; but his father came out and began to plead with him.

"He said in reply to his father: 'For years now I have slaved for you. I never disobeyed one of your orders, yet you never gave me so much as a kid goat to celebrate with my friends. Then, when this son of yours returns after having gone through your property with loose women, you kill the fatted calf for him.'

" 'My son,' replied the father, 'you are with me always, and everything I have is yours. But we had to celebrate and rejoice! This brother of yours was dead, and has come back to life. He was lost, and is found.' "

This is the gospel of the Lord.

OR
(Short Form)

The tax collectors and sinners were all gathering around to hear Jesus, at which the Pharisees and the scribes murmured, "This man welcomes sinners and eats with them." Then he addressed this parable to them: "Who among you, if he has a hundred sheep and loses one of them, does not leave the ninety-nine in the wasteland and follow the lost one until he finds it? And when he finds it, he puts it on his shoulders in jubilation. Once arrived home, he invites friends and neighbors in and says to them, 'Rejoice with me because I have found my lost sheep.' I tell you, there will likewise be more joy in heaven over one repentant sinner than over ninety-nine righteous people who have no need to repent.

"What woman, if she has ten silver pieces and loses one, does not light a lamp and sweep the house in a diligent search until she has retrieved what she lost? And when she finds it, she calls in her friends and neighbors to say, 'Rejoice with me! I have found the silver piece I lost.' I tell you, there will be the same kind of joy before the angels of God over one repentant sinner."

This is the gospel of the Lord.

---

134   TWENTY-FIFTH SUNDAY **A**
OF THE YEAR

READING I   Is 55, 6-9

A reading from the book of the prophet Isaiah

My thoughts are not your thoughts.

Seek the Lord while he may be found,
  call him while he is near.
Let the scoundrel forsake his way,
  and the wicked man his thoughts;
Let him turn to the Lord for mercy;
  to our God, who is generous in forgiving.
For my thoughts are not your thoughts,
  nor are your ways my ways, says the Lord.
As high as the heavens are above the earth,
  so high are my ways above your ways
  and my thoughts above your thoughts.

This is the Word of the Lord.

Responsorial Psalm   Ps 145, 2-3. 8-9. 17-18

℟. (18) The Lord is near to all who call him.
Every day will I bless you,
  and I will praise your name forever and ever.
Great is the Lord and highly to be praised;
  his greatness is unsearchable.
℟. The Lord is near to all who call upon him.
The Lord is gracious and merciful,
  slow to anger and of great kindness.
The Lord is good to all
  and compassionate toward all his works.
℟. The Lord is near to all who call upon him.
The Lord is just in all his ways
  and holy in all his works.
The Lord is near to all who call upon him,
  to all who call upon him in truth.
℟. The Lord is near to all who call upon him.

READING II   Phil 1, 20-24. 27

A reading from the letter of Paul to the Philippians

For me to live is Christ.

Christ will be exalted through me, whether I live or die. For, to me, "life" means Christ; hence dying is so much gain. If, on the other hand, I am to go on living in the flesh, that means productive toil for me—and I do not know which to prefer. I am strongly attracted by both: I long to be freed from this life and to be with Christ, for that is the far better thing; yet it is more urgent that I remain alive for your sakes. Conduct yourselves, then, in a way worthy of the gospel of Christ.

This is the Word of the Lord.

GOSPEL   Mt 20, 1-16
Alleluia

See no. 164.

✠ **A reading from the holy gospel according to Matthew**

Why are you jealous because I am generous?

Jesus told his disciples this parable: "The reign of God is like the case of the owner of an estate who went out at dawn to hire workmen for his vineyard. After reaching an agreement with them for the usual daily wage, he sent them out to his vineyard. He came out about midmorning and saw other men standing around the marketplace without work, so he said to them, 'You too go along to my vineyard and I will pay you whatever is fair.' At that they went away. He came out again around noon and midafternoon and did the same. Finally, going out in late afternoon he found still others standing around. To these he said, 'Why have you been standing here idle all day?' 'No one has hired us,' they told him. He said, 'You go to the vineyard too.' When evening came the owner of the vineyard said to his foreman, 'Call the workmen and give them their pay, but begin with the last group and end with the first.' When those hired late in the afternoon came up they received a full day's pay, and when the first group appeared they supposed they would get more; yet they received the same daily wage. Thereupon they complained to the owner, 'This last group did only an hour's work, but you have put them on the same basis as us who have worked a full day in the scorching heat.' 'My friend,' he said to one in reply, 'I do you no injustice. You agreed on the usual wage, did you not? Take your pay and go home. I intend to give this man who was hired last the same pay as you. I am free to do as I please with my money, am I not? Or are you envious because I am generous?' Thus the last shall be first and the first shall be last."

This is the gospel of the Lord.

---

135   **TWENTY-FIFTH SUNDAY**   **B**
OF THE YEAR

READING I   Wis 2, 12. 17-20

A reading from the book of Wisdom

Let us condemn him to a most shameful death.

[The wicked say:]
Let us beset the just one, because he is obnoxious to us;
  he sets himself against our doings,
Reproaches us for transgressions of the law
  and charges us with violations of our training.
Let us see whether his words be true;
  let us find out what will happen to him.
For if the just one be the son of God, he will defend him
  and deliver him from the hand of his foes.
With revilement and torture let us put him to the test
  that we may have proof of his gentleness and try his patience.
Let us condemn him to a shameful death;
  for according to his own words, God will take care of him.

This is the Word of the Lord.

Responsorial Psalm   Ps 54, 3-4. 5. 6-8

℟. (6) The Lord upholds my life.
O God, by your name save me,
  and by your might defend my cause.
O God, hear my prayer;
  hearken to the words of my mouth.
℟. The Lord upholds my life.
For haughty men have risen up against me,
  and fierce men seek my life;
  they set not God before their eyes.
℟. The Lord upholds my life.
Behold, God is my helper;
  the Lord sustains my life.
Freely will I offer you sacrifice;
  I will praise your name, O Lord, for its goodness.
℟. The Lord upholds my life.

READING II   Jas 3, 16—4, 3

A reading from the letter of James

Justice is the harvest of peacemakers from seeds sown in a spirit of peace.

Where there are jealousy and strife, there also are inconstancy and all kinds of vile behavior. Wisdom from above, by contrast, is first of all innocent. It is also peaceable, lenient, docile, rich in sympathy and the kindly deeds that are its fruit, impartial and sincere. The harvest of justice is sown in peace for those who cultivate peace.

Where do the conflicts and disputes among you originate? Is it not your inner cravings that make war within your members? What you desire you do not obtain, and so you resort to murder. You envy and you cannot acquire, so you quarrel and fight. You do not obtain because you do not ask. You ask and you do not receive because you ask wrongly, with a view to squandering what you receive on your pleasures.

This is the Word of the Lord.

GOSPEL   Mk 9, 30-37
Alleluia

See no. 164.

✠ **A reading from the holy gospel according to Mark**

The Son of Man will be delivered into the hands of men . . . If anyone wishes to be first, he must make himself the servant of all.

Jesus and his disciples came down the mountain and began to go through Galilee, but he did not want anyone to know about it. He was teaching his disciples in this vein: "The Son of Man is going to be delivered into the hands of men who will put him to death; three days after his death he will rise." Though they failed to understand his words, they were afraid to question him.

They returned to Capernaum and Jesus, once inside the house, began to ask them, "What were you discussing on the way home?" At this they fell silent, for on the way they had been arguing about who was the most important. So he sat down and called the Twelve around him and said, "If anyone wishes to

rank first, he must remain the last one of all and the servant of all." Then he took a little child, stood him in their midst, and putting his arms around him, said to them, "Whoever welcomes a child such as this for my sake welcomes me. And whoever welcomes me welcomes, not me, but him who sent me."

This is the gospel of the Lord.

---

136   **TWENTY-FIFTH SUNDAY**   **C**
                    OF THE YEAR

READING I   Am 8, 4-7

A reading from the book of the prophet Amos

The Lord God spoke against those who buy the poor for money.

Hear this, you who trample upon the needy
  and destroy the poor of the land!
"When will the new moon be over," you ask,
  "that we may sell our grain,
  and the sabbath, that we may display the
    wheat?
We will diminish the ephah,
  add to the shekel,
  and fix our scales for cheating!
We will buy the lowly man for silver,
  and the poor man for a pair of sandals;
  even the refuse of the wheat we will sell!"
The Lord has sworn by the pride of Jacob:
  Never will I forget a thing they have done!
    This is the Word of the Lord.

Responsorial Psalm   Ps 113, 1-2. 4-6. 7-8

℟. (1.7) Praise the Lord who lifts up the poor.
Praise, you servants of the Lord,
  praise the name of the Lord.
Blessed be the name of the Lord
  both now and forever.
℟. Praise the Lord who lifts up the poor.
High above all nations is the Lord;
  above the heavens is his glory.
Who is like the Lord, our God, who is en-
    throned on high
  and looks upon the heavens and the earth
    below?
℟. Praise the Lord who lifts up the poor.

He raises up the lowly from the dust;
  from the dunghill he lifts up the poor
To seat them with princes,
  with the princes of his own people.
℟. Praise the Lord who lifts up the poor.
℟. Or: Alleluia.

READING II   1 Tm 2, 1-8
A reading from the letter of Paul to Timothy
Let prayers be offered to God for everyone, for he wishes
that all men be saved.

First of all, I urge that petitions, prayers, intercessions, and thanksgivings be offered for all
men, especially for kings and those in authority, that we may be able to lead undisturbed
and tranquil lives in perfect piety and dignity.
Prayer of this kind is good, and God our savior
is pleased with it, for he wants all men to be
saved and come to know the truth. And the
truth is this:
  "God is one.
One also is the mediator between God and
    men,
  the man Christ Jesus,
who gave himself as a ransom for all."
This truth was attested at the fitting time. I
have been made its herald and apostle (believe me, I am not lying but speak the truth),
the teacher of the nations in the true faith.
  It is my wish, then, that in every place the
men shall offer prayers with blameless hands
held aloft, and be free from anger and dissension.
             This is the Word of the Lord.

GOSPEL   Lk 16, 1-13 or 16, 10-13
Alleluia

See no. 164.

✠ **A reading from the holy gospel according
to Luke**
You cannot be slaves both of God and of money.

(Long Form)

Jesus said to his disciples: "A rich man had a
manager who was reported to him for dissipating his property. He summoned him and
said, 'What is this I hear about you? Give me an

account of your service, for it is about to come
to an end.' The manager thought to himself,
'What shall I do next? My employer is sure to
dismiss me. I cannot dig ditches. I am ashamed
to go begging. I have it! Here is a way to make
sure that people will take me into their homes
when I am let go.'
  "So he called in each of his master's debtors,
and said to the first, 'How much do you owe
my master?' The man replied, 'A hundred jars
of oil.' The manager said, 'Take your invoice,
sit down quickly, and make it fifty.' Then he
said to a second, 'How much do you owe?'
The answer came, 'A hundred measures of
wheat,' and the manager said, 'Take your invoice and make it eighty.'
  "The owner then gave his devious employee
credit for being enterprising! Why? Because
the worldly take more initiative than the other-
worldly when it comes to dealing with their
own kind.
  "What I say to you is this: Make friends for
yourselves through your use of this world's
goods, so that when they fail you, a lasting
reception will be yours. If you can trust a man
in little things, you can also trust him in
greater; while anyone unjust in a slight matter
is also unjust in greater. If you cannot be
trusted with elusive wealth, who will trust you
with lasting? And if you have not been trustworthy with someone else's money, who will
give you what is your own?
  "No servant can serve two masters. Either
he will hate the one and love the other or be
attentive to the one and despise the other.
You cannot give yourself to God and money."
             This is the gospel of the Lord.

OR
(Short Form)

Jesus said to his disciples: "If you can trust a
man in little things, you can also trust him in
greater; while anyone unjust in a slight matter
is also unjust in greater. If you cannot be
trusted with elusive wealth, who will trust you
with lasting? And if you have not been trustworthy with someone else's money, who will
give you what is your own?

"No servant can serve two masters. Either he will hate the one and love the other or be attentive to the one and despise the other. You cannot give yourself to God and money."
    This is the gospel of the Lord.

---

137   TWENTY-SIXTH SUNDAY   **A**
       OF THE YEAR

READING I   Ez 18, 25-28
    A reading from the book of the prophet Ezekiel
When the sinner decides to turn against his sinfulness, he deserves to live.

You say, "The Lord's way is not fair!" Hear now, house of Israel: Is it my way that is unfair, or rather, are not your ways unfair? When a virtuous man turns away from virtue to commit iniquity, and dies, it is because of the iniquity he committed that he must die. But if a wicked man, turning from the wickedness he has committed, does what is right and just, he shall preserve his life; since he has turned away from all the sins which he committed, he shall surely live, he shall not die.
    This is the Word of the Lord.

Responsorial Psalm   Ps 125, 4-5. 6-7. 8-9

℞. (6) Remember your mercies, O Lord.
Your ways, O Lord, make known to me;
    teach me your paths,
Guide me in your truth and teach me,
    for you are God my savior.
℞. Remember your mercies, O Lord.
Remember that your compassion, O Lord,
    and your kindness are from of old.
The sins of my youth and my frailties remember not;
    in your kindness remember me,
    because of your goodness, O Lord.
℞. Remember your mercies, O Lord.
Good and upright is the Lord;
    thus he shows sinners the way.
He guides the humble to justice,
    he teaches the humble his way.
℞. Remember your mercies, O Lord.

READING II   Phil 2, 1-11 or 2, 1-5
    A reading from the letter of Paul to the Philippians
In your minds be as Jesus Christ.

(Long Form)

In the name of the encouragement you owe me in Christ, in the name of the solace that love can give, of fellowship in spirit, compassion, and pity, I beg you: make my joy complete by your unanimity, possessing the one love, united in spirit and ideals. Never act out of rivalry or conceit; rather, let all parties think humbly of others as superior to themselves, each of you looking to others' interests rather than his own.
Your attitude must be Christ's:
    Though he was in the form of God,
    he did not deem equality with God
    something to be grasped at.
Rather, he emptied himself
    and took the form of a slave,
    being born in the likeness of men.
He was known to be of human estate
    and it was thus that he humbled himself,
    obediently accepting even death,
    death on a cross!
Because of this,
    God highly exalted him
    and bestowed on him the name
    above every other name,
So that at Jesus' name
    every knee must bend
    in the heavens, on the earth,
    and under the earth,
    and every tongue proclaim
    to the glory of God the Father:
JESUS CHRIST IS LORD!
    This is the Word of the Lord.

OR
(Short Form)

In the name of the encouragement you owe me in Christ, in the name of the solace that love can give, of fellowship in spirit, compassion, and pity, I beg you: make my joy complete by your unanimity, possessing the one love, united in spirit and ideals. Never act out of rivalry or conceit; rather, let all parties think humbly of others as superior to themselves, each of you looking to others' interests rather than his own.

Your attitude must be Christ's.

This is the Word of the Lord.

GOSPEL   Mt 21, 28-32
Alleluia

See no. 164.

✠ A reading from the holy gospel according to Matthew

He went out moved by regret. The tax collectors and prostitutes will precede you into the kingdom of God.

Jesus said to the chief priests and elders of the people: "What do you think of this case? There was a man who had two sons. He approached the elder and said, 'Son, go out and work in the vineyard today.' The son replied, 'I am on my way, sir'; but he never went. Then the man came to his second son and said the same thing. This son said in reply, 'No, I will not'; but afterward he regretted it and went. Which of the two did what the father wanted?" They said, "The second." Jesus said to them, "Let me make it clear that tax collectors and prostitutes are entering the kingdom of God before you. When John came preaching a way of holiness, you put no faith in him; but the tax collectors and the prostitutes did believe in him. Yet even when you saw that, you did not repent and believe in him."

This is the gospel of the Lord.

---

138   TWENTY-SIXTH SUNDAY   B
OF THE YEAR

READING I   Nm 11, 25-29
A reading from the book of Numbers

Are you jealous on my account? Who decrees that all men may prophesy?

The Lord came down in the cloud and spoke to Moses. Taking some of the spirit that was on him, he bestowed it on the seventy elders;

and as the spirit came to rest on them, they prophesied.

Now two men, one named Eldad and the other Medad, were not in the gathering but had been left in the camp. They too had been on the list, but had not gone out to the tent; yet the spirit came to rest on them also, and they prophesied in the camp. So, when a young man quickly told Moses, "Eldad and Medad are prophesying in the camp," Joshua, son of Nun, who from his youth had been Moses' aide, said, "Moses, my lord, stop them." But Moses answered him, "Are you jealous for my sake? Would that all the people of the Lord were prophets! Would that the Lord might bestow his spirit on them all!"

This is the Word of the Lord.

Responsorial Psalm   Ps 19, 8. 10. 12-13. 14

℟. (9) The precepts of the Lord give joy to the heart.

The law of the Lord is perfect,
refreshing the soul;
The decree of the Lord is trustworthy,
giving wisdom to the simple.

℟. The precepts of the Lord give joy to the heart.

The fear of the Lord is pure,
enduring forever;
The ordinances of the Lord are true,
all of them just.

℟. The precepts of the Lord give joy to the heart.

Though your servant is careful of them,
very diligent in keeping them,
Yet who can detect failings?
Cleanse me from my unknown faults!

℟. The precepts of the Lord give joy to the heart.

From wanton sin especially, restrain your servant;
let it not rule over me.
Then shall I be blameless and innocent
of serious sin.

℟. The precepts of the Lord give joy to the heart.

READING II   Jas 5, 1-6

A reading from the letter of James
Your wealth is rotting.

You rich, weep and wail over your impending miseries. Your wealth has rotted, your fine wardrobe has grown moth-eaten, your gold and silver have corroded, and their corrosion shall be a testimony against you; it will devour your flesh like a fire. See what you have stored up for yourselves against the last days. Here, crying aloud, are the wages you withheld from the farmhands who harvested your fields. The shouts of the harvesters have reached the ears of the Lord of hosts. You lived in wanton luxury on the earth; you fattened yourselves for the day of slaughter. You condemned, even killed, the just man; he does not resist you.

This is the Word of the Lord.

GOSPEL   Mk 9, 38-43. 45. 47-48
Alleluia

See no. 164.

✠ **A reading from the holy gospel according to Mark**
Anyone who is not against us is for us. If your hand should cause you to sin, cut it off.

John said to Jesus, "Teacher, we saw a man using your name to expel demons and we tried to stop him because he is not of our company." Jesus said in reply: "Do not try to stop him. No man who performs a miracle using my name can at once speak ill of me. Anyone who is not against us is with us. Any man who gives you a drink of water because you belong to Christ will not, I assure you, go without his reward. But it would be better if anyone who leads astray one of these simple believers were to be plunged in the sea with a great millstone fastened around his neck.

"If your hand is your difficulty, cut it off! Better for you to enter life maimed than to keep both hands and enter Gehenna, with its unquenchable fire. If your foot is your undoing, cut it off! Better for you to enter life crippled than to be thrown into Gehenna with

both feet. If your eye is your downfall, tear it out! Better for you to enter the kingdom of God with one eye than to be thrown with both eyes into Gehenna, where 'the worm dies not and the fire is never extinguished.' "

This is the gospel of the Lord.

---

139   **TWENTY-SIXTH SUNDAY**
                OF THE YEAR

READING I   Am 6, 1. 4-7

A reading from the book of the prophet Amos
You who give yourself to licentiousness and revelry will be exiled.

Woe to the complacent in Zion!
Lying upon beds of ivory,
    stretched comfortably on their couches,
They eat lambs taken from the flock,
    and calves from the stall!
Improvising to the music of the harp,
    like David, they devise their own accompaniment.
They drink wine from bowls
    and anoint themselves with the best oils;
    yet they are not made ill by the collapse of Joseph!
Therefore, now they shall be the first to go into exile,
    and their wanton revelry shall be done away with.

This is the Word of the Lord.

Responsorial Psalm   Ps 146, 7. 8-9. 9-10

℟. (2) Praise the Lord, my soul!
Happy he who keeps faith forever,
    secures justice for the oppressed,
    gives food to the hungry.
The Lord sets captives free.
℟. Praise the Lord, my soul!
The Lord gives sight to the blind.
    The Lord raises up those that were bowed down;
The Lord loves the just.
    The Lord protects strangers.
℟. Praise the Lord, my soul!
The fatherless and the widow he sustains,
    but the way of the wicked he thwarts.

The Lord shall reign forever;
  your God, O Sion, through all generations.
  Alleluia.
R̅. Praise the Lord, my soul!
R̅. Or: Alleluia.

READING II   1 Tm 6, 11-16

A reading from the first letter of Paul to Timothy

Obey the commandments until the coming of the Lord.

Man of God that you are, seek after integrity, piety, faith, love, steadfastness, and a gentle spirit. Fight the good fight of faith. Take firm hold on the everlasting life to which you were called when, in the presence of many witnesses, you made your noble profession of faith. Before God, who gives life to all, and before Christ Jesus, who in bearing witness made his noble profession before Pontius Pilate, I charge you to keep God's command without blame or reproach until our Lord Jesus Christ shall appear. This appearance God will bring to pass at his chosen time. He is the blessed and only ruler, the King of kings and Lord of lords who alone has immortality and who dwells in inapproachable light, whom no human being has ever seen or can see. To him be honor and everlasting rule! Amen.

    This is the Word of the Lord.

GOSPEL   Lk 16, 19-31

Alleluia

See no. 164.

✠ A reading from the holy gospel according to Luke

During your life good things came your way just as bad things came the way of Lazarus. Now he is being comforted while you are in agony.

Jesus said to the Pharisees: "Once there was a rich man who dressed in purple and linen and feasted splendidly every day. At his gate lay a beggar named Lazarus who was covered with sores. Lazarus longed to eat the scraps that fell from the rich man's table. The dogs even came and licked his sores. Eventually the beggar died. He was carried by angels to the bosom of Abraham. The rich man likewise died and was buried. From the abode of the dead where he was in torment, he raised his eyes and saw Abraham afar off, and Lazarus resting in his bosom.

  "He called out, 'Father Abraham, have pity on me. Send Lazarus to dip the tip of his finger in water to refresh my tongue, for I am tortured in these flames.' 'My child,' replied Abraham, 'remember that you were well off in your lifetime, while Lazarus was in misery. Now he has found consolation here, but you have found torment. And that is not all. Between you and us there is fixed a great abyss, so that those who might wish to cross from here to you cannot do so, nor can anyone cross from your side to us.'

  " 'Father, I ask you, then,' the rich man said, 'send him to my father's house where I have five brothers. Let him be a warning to them so that they may not end in this place of torment.' Abraham answered, 'They have Moses and the prophets. Let them hear them.' 'No, Father Abraham,' replied the rich man. 'But if someone would only go to them from the dead, then they would repent.' Abraham said to him, 'If they do not listen to Moses and the prophets, they will not be convinced even if one should rise from the dead.' "

    This is the gospel of the Lord.

140   TWENTY-SEVENTH SUNDAY OF THE YEAR   🅰

READING I   Is 5, 1-7

A reading from the book of the prophet Isaiah

The vineyard of the Lord God of hosts is the house of Israel.

Let me now sing of my friend,
  my friend's song concerning his vineyard.
My friend had a vineyard
  on a fertile hillside;
He spaded it, cleared it of stones,
  and planted the choicest vines;
Within it he built a watchtower,
  and hewed out a wine press.
Then he looked for the crop of grapes,
  but what it yielded was wild grapes.

Now, inhabitants of Jerusalem and men of
  Judah,

judge between me and my vineyard:
What more was there to do for my vineyard
    that I had not done?
Why, when I looked for the crop of grapes,
    did it bring forth wild grapes?
Now, I will let you know
    what I mean to do to my vineyard:
Take away its hedge, give it to grazing,
    break through its wall, let it be trampled!
Yes, I will make it a ruin:
    it shall not be pruned or hoed,
    but overgrown with thorns and briers;
I will command the clouds
    not to send rain upon it.
The vineyard of the Lord of hosts is the house
    of Israel,
    and the men of Judah are his cherished
    plant;
He looked for judgment, but see, bloodshed!
    for justice, but hark, the outcry!
            This is the Word of the Lord.

Responsorial Psalm   Ps 80, 9. 12. 13-14. 15-16. 19-20

℟. (Is 5, 7) The vineyard of the Lord is the
    house of Israel.
A vine from Egypt you transplanted;
    you drove away the nations and planted it.
It put forth its foliage to the Sea,
    its shoots as far as the River.
℟. The vineyard of the Lord is the house of
    Israel.
Why have you broken down its walls,
    so that every passer-by plucks its fruit,
The boar from the forest lays it waste,
    and the beasts of the field feed upon it?
℟. The vineyard of the Lord is the house of
    Israel.
Once again, O Lord of hosts,
    look down from heaven, and see;
Take care of this vine,
    and protect what your right hand has
    planted
    [the son of man whom you yourself made
    strong].
℟. The vineyard of the Lord is the house of
    Israel.

Then we will no more withdraw from you;
    give us new life, and we will call upon your
    name.
O Lord of hosts, restore us;
    if your face shine upon us, then we shall be
    safe.
℟. The vineyard of the Lord is the house of
    Israel.

READING II   Phil 4, 6-9
    **A reading from the letter of Paul to the
                    Philippians**
            The God of peace be with you.

Dismiss all anxiety from your minds. Present
your needs to God in every form of prayer
and in petitions full of gratitude. Then God's
own peace, which is beyond all understanding,
will stand guard over your hearts and minds,
in Christ Jesus.

    Finally, my brothers, your thoughts should
be wholly directed to all that is true, all that
deserves respect, all that is honest, pure, admirable, decent, virtuous, or worthy of praise.
Live according to what you have learned and
accepted, what you have heard me say and
seen me do. Then will the God of peace be
with you.
            This is the Word of the Lord.

GOSPEL   Mt 21, 33-43
Alleluia
See no. 175.

✠ A reading from the holy gospel according
            to Matthew
    He leased his vineyard to other farmers.

Jesus said to the chief priests and elders of
the people: "Listen to another parable. There
was a property owner who planted a vineyard, put a hedge around it, dug out a vat, and
erected a tower. Then he leased it out to tenant
farmers and went on a journey. When vintage
time arrived he dispatched his slaves to the
tenants to obtain his share of the grapes. The
tenants responded by seizing the slaves. They
beat one, killed another, and stoned a third. A
second time he dispatched even more slaves
than before, but they treated them the same

way. Finally he sent his son to them, thinking, 'They will respect my son.' When they saw the son, the tenants said to one another, 'Here is the one who will inherit everything. Let us kill him and then we shall have his inheritance!' With that they seized him, dragged him outside the vineyard, and killed him. What do you suppose the owner of the vineyard will do to those tenants when he comes?" They replied, "He will bring that wicked crowd to a bad end and lease his vineyard out to others who will see to it that he has grapes at vintage time." Jesus said to them, "Did you never read in the Scriptures,

'The stone which the builders rejected
has become the keystone of the structure.
It was the Lord who did this
and we find it marvelous to behold'?
For this reason, I tell you, the kingdom of God will be taken away from you and given to a people that will yield a rich harvest."
This is the gospel of the Lord.

---

141   **TWENTY-SEVENTH SUNDAY**   **B**
OF THE YEAR

READING I   Gn 2, 18-24

A reading from the book of Genesis
They were two in one flesh.

The Lord God said: "It is not good for the man to be alone. I will make a suitable partner for him." So the Lord God formed out of the ground various wild animals and various birds of the air, and he brought them to the man to see what he would call them; whatever the man called each of them would be its name. The man gave names to all the cattle, all the birds of the air, and all wild animals; but none proved to be the suitable partner for the man.

So the Lord God cast a deep sleep on the man, and while he was asleep, he took out one of his ribs and closed up its place with flesh. The Lord God then built up into a woman the rib that he had taken from the man. When he brought her to the man, the man said:
"This one, at last, is bone of my bones
and flesh of my flesh;

This one shall be called 'woman,'
for out of 'her man' this one has been taken."
That is why a man leaves his father and mother and clings to his wife, and the two of them become one body.
This is the Word of the Lord.

Responsorial Psalm   Ps 128, 1-2. 3. 4-5. 6

℟. (5) May the Lord bless us
all the days of our lives.
Happy are you who fear the Lord,
who walk in his ways!
For you shall eat the fruit of your handiwork;
happy shall you be, and favored.
℟. May the Lord bless us
all the days of our lives.
Your wife shall be like a fruitful vine
in the recesses of your home;
Your children like olive plants
around your table.
℟. May the Lord bless us
all the days of our lives.
Behold, thus is the man blessed
who fears the Lord.
The Lord bless you from Zion:
may you see the prosperity of Jerusalem
all the days of your life.
℟. May the Lord bless us
all the days of our lives.
May you see your children's children.
Peace be upon Israel!
℟. May the Lord bless us
all the days of our lives.

READING II   Heb 2, 9-11

A reading from the letter to the Hebrews
He who sanctifies and those who are sanctified have one origin.

Jesus was made for a little while lower than the angels, that through God's gracious will he might taste death for the sake of all men. Indeed, it was fitting that, when bringing many sons to glory, God, for whom and through whom all things exist, should make their leader in the work of salvation perfect through suffering. He who consecrates and those who

are consecrated have one and the same Father.
Therefore, he is not ashamed to call them
brothers.

This is the Word of the Lord.

GOSPEL   Mk 10, 2-16 or 10, 2-12
Alleluia

See no. 164.

✠ A reading from the holy gospel according
to Mark

What God has joined together, man must not divide.

(Long Form)

Some Pharisees came up and as a test began
to ask Jesus whether it was permissible for a
husband to divorce his wife. In reply he said,
"What command did Moses give you?" They
answered, "Moses permitted divorce and the
writing of a decree of divorce." But Jesus told
them: "He wrote that commandment for you
because of your stubbornness. At the beginning of creation God made them male and
female; for this reason a man shall leave his
father and mother and the two shall become
as one. They are no longer two but one flesh.
Therefore let no man separate what God has
joined." Back in the house again, the disciples
began to question him about this. He told them,
"Whoever divorces his wife and marries another commits adultery against her; and the
woman who divorces her husband and marries
another commits adultery."

People were bringing their little children to
him to have him touch them, but the disciples
were scolding them for this. Jesus became indignant when he noticed it and said to them:
"Let the children come to me and do not hinder
them. It is to just such as these that the kingdom of God belongs. I assure you that whoever does not accept the kingdom of God like
a little child shall not enter into it." Then he
embraced them and blessed them, placing his
hands on them.

This is the gospel of the Lord.

OR
(Short Form)

Some Pharisees came up and as a test began
to ask Jesus whether it was permissible for a
husband to divorce his wife. In reply he said,
"What command did Moses give you?" They
answered, "Moses permitted divorce and the
writing of a decree of divorce." But Jesus told
them: "He wrote that commandment for you
because of your stubbornness. At the beginning of creation God made them male and
female; for this reason a man shall leave his
father and mother and the two shall become
as one. They are no longer two but one flesh.
Therefore let no man separate what God has
joined." Back in the house again, the disciples
began to question him about this. He told them,
"Whoever divorces his wife and marries another commits adultery against her; and the
woman who divorces her husband and marries
another commits adultery."

This is the gospel of the Lord.

142   **TWENTY-SEVENTH SUNDAY** **C**
OF THE YEAR

READING I   Hb 1, 2-3; 2, 2-4
A reading from the book of the prophet
Habakkuk

The just man will live by his faithfulness.

How long, O Lord? I cry for help
but you do not listen!
I cry out to you, "Violence!"
but you do not intervene.
Why do you let me see ruin;
why must I look at misery?
Destruction and violence are before me;
there is strife, and clamorous discord.
Then the Lord answered me and said:
Write down the vision
Clearly upon the tablets,
so that one can read it readily.
For the vision still has its time,
presses on to fulfillment, and will not dis-
appoint;

If it delays, wait for it,
　it will surely come, it will not be late.
The rash man has no integrity;
　but the just man, because of his faith, shall
　　live.
　　　This is the Word of the Lord.

Responsorial Psalm   Ps 95, 1-2. 6-7. 8-9

℟. (7. 8) If today you hear his voice,
　harden not your hearts.
Come, let us sing joyfully to the Lord;
　let us acclaim the Rock of our salvation.
Let us greet him with thanksgiving;
　let us joyfully sing psalms to him.
℟. If today you hear his voice,
　harden not your hearts.
Come, let us bow down in worship;
　let us kneel before the Lord who made us.
For he is our God,
　and we are the people he shepherds, the
　　flock he guides.
℟. If today you hear his voice,
　harden not your hearts.
Oh, that today you would hear his voice:
　"Harden not your hearts as at Meribah,
　as in the day of Massah in the desert,
Where your fathers tempted me;
　they tested me though they had seen my
　　works.
℟. If today you hear his voice,
　harden not your hearts.

READING II   2 Tm 1, 6-8. 13-14

A reading from the second letter of Paul to
Timothy

Never be ashamed of witnessing the Lord.

I remind you to stir into flame the gift of God
bestowed when my hands were laid on you.
The Spirit God has given us is no cowardly
spirit, but rather one that makes us strong,
loving and wise. Therefore, never be ashamed
of your testimony to our Lord, nor of me, a
prisoner for his sake; but with the strength
which comes from God bear your share of the
hardship which the gospel entails.
　Take as a model of sound teaching what you
have heard me say, in faith and love in Christ

Jesus. Guard the rich deposit of faith with the
help of the Holy Spirit who dwells within us.
　　　This is the Word of the Lord.

GOSPEL   Lk 17, 5-10
Alleluia

See no. 164.

✠ A reading from the holy gospel according
to Luke

If you had faith!

The apostles said to the Lord, "Increase our
faith," and he answered: "If you had faith the
size of a mustard seed, you could say to this
sycamore, 'Be uprooted and transplanted into
the sea,' and it would obey you.
　"If one of you had a servant plowing or herding sheep and he came in from the fields, would
you say to him, 'Come and sit down at table'?
Would you not rather say, 'Prepare my supper.
Put on your apron and wait on me while I eat
and drink. You can eat and drink afterward'?
Would he be grateful to the servant who was
only carrying out his orders? It is quite the
same with you who hear me. When you have
done all you have been commanded to do,
say, 'We are useless servants. We have done no
more than our duty.' "
　　　This is the gospel of the Lord.

---

143   TWENTY-EIGHTH SUNDAY   A
OF THE YEAR

READING I   Is 25, 6-10

A reading from the book of the prophet Isaiah

The Lord will prepare a feast and will wipe away the tears
from every cheek

On this mountain the Lord of hosts
　will provide for all peoples
A feast of rich food and choice wines,
　juicy, rich food and pure, choice wines.
On this mountain he will destroy
　the veil that veils all peoples,
The web that is woven over all nations;
　he will destroy death forever.
The Lord God will wipe away
　the tears from all faces;

The reproach of his people he will remove
   from the whole earth; for the Lord has
   spoken.

On that day it will be said:
"Behold our God, to whom we looked to save
   us!
   This is the Lord for whom we looked;
   let us rejoice and be glad that he has saved
   us!"
For the hand of the Lord will rest on this
   mountain.
                 This is the Word of the Lord.

Responsorial Psalm   Ps 23, 1-3. 3-4. 5. 6

℟. (6) I shall live in the house of the Lord
   all the days of my life.
The Lord is my shepherd; I shall not want.
   In verdant pastures he gives me repose;
Beside restful waters he leads me;
   he refreshes my soul.
℟. I shall live in the house of the Lord
   all the days of my life.
He guides me in right paths
   for his name's sake.
Even though I walk in the dark valley
   I fear no evil; for you are at my side
With your rod and your staff
   that give me courage.
℟. I shall live in the house of the Lord
   all the days of my life.
You spread the table before me
   in the sight of my foes;
You anoint my head with oil;
   my cup overflows.
℟. I shall live in the house of the Lord
   all the days of my life.
Only goodness and kindness follow me
   all the days of my life;
And I shall dwell in the house of the Lord
   for years to come.
℟. I shall live in the house of the Lord
   all the days of my life.

READING II   Phil 4, 12-14. 19-20
**A reading from the letter of Paul to the
Philippians**
I am able to do all things in him who strengthens me.

I am experienced in being brought low, yet I
know what it is to have an abundance. I have
learned how to cope with every circumstance
—how to eat well or go hungry, to be well
provided for or do without. In him who is the
source of my strength I have strength for
everything.
   Nonetheless, it was kind of you to want to
share in my hardships.
   My God in turn will supply your needs fully,
in a way worthy of his magnificent riches in
Christ Jesus. All glory to our God and Father
for unending ages! Amen.
            This is the Word of the Lord.

GOSPEL   Mt 22, 1-14 or 22, 1-10
Alleluia
See no. 164.

✠ **A reading from the holy gospel according
to Matthew**
Whomsoever you find invite to the wedding.

(Long Form)
Jesus began to address the chief priests and
elders of the people, once more using parables.
"The reign of God may be likened to a king
who gave a wedding banquet for his son. He
dispatched his servants to summon the invited
guests to the wedding, but they refused to
come. A second time he sent other servants,
saying: 'Tell those who were invited, See, I
have my dinner prepared! My bullocks and
corn-fed cattle are killed; everything is ready.
Come to the feast.' Some ignored the invitation
and went their way, one to his farm, another
to his business. The rest laid hold of his servants, insulted them, and killed them. At this
the king grew furious and sent his army to
destroy those murderers and burn their city.
Then he said to his servants: 'The banquet is
ready, but those who were invited were unfit
to come. That is why you must go out into the
byroads and invite to the wedding anyone you

come upon.' The servants then went out into the byroads and rounded up everyone they met, bad as well as good. This filled the wedding hall with banqueters.

"When the king came in to meet the guests, however, he caught sight of a man not properly dressed for a wedding feast. 'My friend,' he said, 'how is it you came in here not properly dressed?' The man had nothing to say. The king then said to the attendants, 'Bind him hand and foot and throw him out into the night to wail and grind his teeth.' The invited are many, the elect are few."

This is the gospel of the Lord.

OR
(Short Form)

Jesus began to address the chief priests and elders of the people, once more using parables. "The reign of God may be likened to a king who gave a wedding banquet for his son. He dispatched his servants to summon the invited guests to the wedding, but they refused to come. A second time he sent other servants, saying: 'Tell those who were invited, See, I have my dinner prepared! My bullocks and corn-fed cattle are killed; everything is ready. Come to the feast.' Some ignored the invitation and went their way, one to his farm, another to his business. The rest laid hold of his servants, insulted them, and killed them. At this the king grew furious and sent his army to destroy those murderers and burn their city. Then he said to his servants: 'The banquet is ready, but those who were invited were unfit to come. That is why you must go out into the byroads and invite to the wedding anyone you come upon.' The servants then went out into the byroads and rounded up everyone they met, bad as well as good. This filled the wedding hall with banqueters."

This is the gospel of the Lord.

---

144   **TWENTY-EIGHTH SUNDAY**   **B**
           OF THE YEAR

READING I   Wis 7, 7-11

A reading from the book of Wisdom
In comparison to wisdom, I held riches as nothing.

I prayed, and prudence was given me;
  I pleaded, and the spirit of Wisdom came to
  me.
I preferred her to scepter and throne,
And deemed riches nothing in comparison with
  her,
  nor did I liken any priceless gem to her;
Because all gold, in view of her, is a little sand,
  and before her, silver is to be accounted
  mire.
Beyond health and comeliness I loved her,
And I chose to have her rather than the light,
  because the splendor of her never yields to
  sleep.
Yet all good things together came to me in her
  company,
  and countless riches at her hands.

This is the Word of the Lord.

Responsorial Psalm   Ps 90, 12-13. 14-15. 16-17

℟. (14) Fill us with your love, O Lord,
  and we will sing for joy!
Teach us to number our days aright,
  that we may gain wisdom of heart.
Return, O Lord! How long?
  Have pity on your servants!
℟. Fill us with your love, O Lord,
  and we will sing for joy!
Fill us at daybreak with your kindness,
  that we may shout for joy and gladness all
  our days.
Make us glad, for the days when you afflicted us,
  for the years when we saw evil.
℟. Fill us with your love, O Lord,
  and we will sing for joy!
Let your work be seen by your servants
  and your glory by their children;
And may the gracious care of the Lord our
  God be ours;
  prosper the work of our hands for us!

[Prosper the work of our hands!]
R/. Fill us with your love, O Lord,
     and we will sing for joy!

READING II   Heb 4, 12-13

A reading from the letter to the Hebrews
The word of God discerns the thoughts and intentions of
the heart.

God's word is living and effective, sharper than
any two-edged sword. It penetrates and divides soul and spirit, joints and marrow; it
judges the reflections and thoughts of the
heart. Nothing is concealed from him; all lies
bare and exposed to the eyes of him to whom
we must render an account.
     This is the Word of the Lord.

GOSPEL   Mk 10, 17-30 or 10, 17-27
Alleluia
See no. 164.

✠ A reading from the holy gospel according
     to Mark
Go and sell whatever you have and come follow me.

(Long Form)

As Jesus was setting out on a journey a man
came running up, knelt down before him and
asked, "Good Teacher, what must I do to share
in everlasting life?" Jesus answered, "Why do
you call me good? No one is good but God
alone. You know the commandments:
     'You shall not kill;
     You shall not commit adultery;
     You shall not steal;
     You shall not bear false witness;
     You shall not defraud;
     Honor your father and your mother.' "
He replied, "Teacher, I have kept all these
since my childhood." Then Jesus looked at
him with love and told him, "There is one thing
more you must do. Go and sell what you have
and give to the poor; you will then have treasure in heaven. After that come and follow me."
At these words the man's face fell. He went
away sad, for he had many possessions. Jesus
looked around and said to his disciples, "How
hard it is for the rich to enter the kingdom of

God!" The disciples could only marvel at his
words. So Jesus repeated what he had said:
"My sons, how hard it is to enter the kingdom
of God! It is easier for a camel to pass through
a needle's eye than for a rich man to enter the
kingdom of God."
     They were completely overwhelmed at this,
and exclaimed to one another, "Then who can
be saved?" Jesus fixed his gaze on them and
said, "For man it is impossible but not for God.
With God all things are possible."
     Peter was moved to say to him: "We have
put aside everything to follow you!" Jesus answered: "I give you my word, there is no one
who has given up home, brothers or sisters,
mother or father, children or property, for me
and for the gospel who will not receive in this
present age a hundred times as many homes,
brothers and sisters, mothers, children and
property—and persecution besides—and in the
age to come, everlasting life."
     This is the gospel of the Lord.

OR
(Short Form)

As Jesus was setting out on a journey a man
came running up, knelt down before him and
asked, "Good Teacher, what must I do to share
in everlasting life?" Jesus answered, "Why do
you call me good? No one is good but God
alone. You know the commandments:
     'You shall not kill;
     You shall not commit adultery;
     You shall not steal;
     You shall not bear false witness;
     You shall not defraud;
     Honor your father and your mother.' "
He replied, "Teacher, I have kept all these since
my childhood." Then Jesus looked at him with
love and told him, "There is one thing more
you must do. Go and sell what you have and
give to the poor; you will then have treasure
in heaven. After that come and follow me."
At these words the man's face fell. He went
away sad, for he had many possessions. Jesus
looked around and said to his disciples, "How
hard it is for the rich to enter the kingdom of
God!" The disciples could only marvel at his

words. So Jesus repeated what he had said: "My sons, how hard it is to enter the kingdom of God! It is easier for a camel to pass through a needle's eye than for a rich man to enter the kingdom of God."

They were completely overwhelmed at this, and exclaimed to one another, "Then who can be saved?" Jesus fixed his gaze on them and said, "For man it is impossible but not for God. With God all things are possible."

This is the gospel of the Lord.

---

145   TWENTY-EIGHTH SUNDAY   C
OF THE YEAR

READING I   2 Kgs 5, 14-17

A reading from the second book of Kings

He returned to Naaman and acknowledged the Lord to this man of God.

Naaman went down and plunged into the Jordan seven times at the word of Elisha, the man of God. His flesh became again like the flesh of a little child, and he was clean [of his leprosy].

He returned with his whole retinue to the man of God. On his arrival he stood before him and said, "Now I know that there is no God in all the earth, except in Israel. Please accept a gift from your servant."

"As the Lord lives whom I serve, I will not take it," Elisha replied; and despite Naaman's urging, he still refused. Naaman said: "If you will not accept, please let me, your servant, have two mule-loads of earth, for I will no longer offer holocaust or sacrifice to any other god except to the Lord."

This is the Word of the Lord.

Responsorial Psalm   Ps 98, 1. 2-3. 3-4

R̂. (2) The Lord has revealed to the nations his saving power.

Sing to the Lord a new song,
  for he has done wondrous deeds;
His right hand has won victory for him,
  his holy arm.

R̂. The Lord has revealed to the nations his saving power.

The Lord has made his salvation known:
  in the sight of the nations he has revealed his justice.
He has remembered his kindness and his faithfulness
  toward the house of Israel.

R̂. The Lord has revealed to the nations his saving power.

All the ends of the earth have seen
  the salvation by our God.
Sing joyfully to the Lord, all you lands:
  break into song; sing praise.

R̂. The Lord has revealed to the nations his saving power.

READING II   2 Tm 2, 8-13

A reading from the second letter of Paul to Timothy

If we hold firm, we shall reign with Christ.

Remember that Jesus Christ, a descendant of David, was raised from the dead. This is the gospel I preach; in preaching it I suffer as a criminal, even to the point of being thrown into chains—but there is no chaining the word of God! Therefore I bear with all of this for the sake of those whom God has chosen, in order that they may obtain the salvation to be found in Christ Jesus and with it eternal glory.

You can depend on this:
If we have died with him
  we shall also live with him;
If we hold out to the end
  we shall also reign with him.
But if we deny him he will deny us. If we are unfaithful he will still remain faithful; for he cannot deny himself.

This is the Word of the Lord.

GOSPEL   Lk 17, 11-19
Alleluia

See no. 164.

✠ **A reading from the holy gospel according to Luke**

It seems that no one has returned to give thanks to God except this stranger.

On his journey to Jerusalem Jesus passed along the borders of Samaria and Galilee. As he was entering a village, ten lepers met him. Keeping their distance, they raised their voices and said, "Jesus, Master, have pity on us!" When he saw them, he responded, "Go and show yourselves to the priests." On their way there they were cured. One of them, realizing that he had been cured, came back praising God in a loud voice. He threw himself on his face at the feet of Jesus and spoke his praises. This man was a Samaritan.

Jesus took the occasion to say, "Were not all ten made whole? Where are the other nine? Was there no one to return and give thanks to God except this foreigner?" He said to the man, "Stand up and go your way; your faith has been your salvation."

This is the gospel of the Lord.

---

146   TWENTY-NINTH SUNDAY   **A**
OF THE YEAR

READING I   Is 45, 1. 4-6

A reading from the book of the prophet Isaiah
I have taken the hand of Cyrus to subdue nations before
his countenance.

Thus says the Lord to his anointed, Cyrus,
    whose right hand I grasp,
Subduing nations before him,
    and making kings run in his service,
Opening doors before him
    and leaving the gates unbarred:
For the sake of Jacob, my servant,
    of Israel, my chosen one,

I have called you by your name,
    giving you a title, though you knew me not.
I am the Lord and there is no other,
    there is no God besides me.
It is I who arm you, though you know me not,
    so that toward the rising and the setting of
        the sun
    men may know that there is none besides
        me.
I am the Lord, there is no other.
            This is the word of the Lord.

Responsorial Psalm   Ps 96, 1. 3. 4-5. 7-8. 9-10

℞. (7) Give the Lord glory and honor.
Sing to the Lord a new song;
    sing to the Lord, all you lands.
Tell his glory among the nations;
    among all peoples, his wondrous deeds.
℞. Give the Lord glory and honor.
For great is the Lord and highly to be praised;
    awesome is he, beyond all gods.
For all the gods of the nations are things of
        nought,
    but the Lord made the heavens.
℞. Give the Lord glory and honor.
Give to the Lord, you families of nations,
    give to the Lord glory and praise;
    give to the Lord the glory due his name!
Bring gifts, and enter his courts.
℞. Give the Lord glory and honor.
Worship the Lord in holy attire;
    tremble before him, all the earth;
Say among the nations: The Lord is king,
    he governs the peoples with equity.
℞. Give the Lord glory and honor.

READING II   1 Thes 1, 1-5

The beginning of the first letter of Paul to the
Thessalonians
We are mindful of your faith, hope, and love.

Paul, Silvanus, and Timothy, to the church of Thessalonians who belong to God the Father and the Lord Jesus Christ. Grace and peace be yours.

We keep thanking God for all of you and we remember you in our prayers, for we constantly are mindful before our God and Father of the way you are proving your faith, and laboring in love, and showing constancy in hope in our Lord Jesus Christ. We know, too, brothers beloved of God, how you were chosen. Our preaching of the gospel proved not a mere matter of words for you but one of power; it was carried on in the Holy Spirit and out of complete conviction.

This is the Word of the Lord.

GOSPEL   Mt 22, 15-21
Alleluia
See no. 164.

✠ A reading from the holy gospel according to Matthew

Give to Caesar the things that belong to Caesar and to God the things that are God's.

The Pharisees went off and began to plot how they might trap Jesus in speech. They sent their disciples to him, accompanied by Herodian sympathizers, who said: "Teacher, we know you are a truthful man and teach God's way sincerely. You court no one's favor and do not act out of human respect. Give us your opinion, then, in this case. Is it lawful to pay tax to the emperor or not?" Jesus recognized their bad faith and said to them, "Why are you trying to trip me up, you hypocrites? Show me the coin used for the tax." When they handed him a small Roman coin he asked them, "Whose head is this, and whose inscription?" "Caesar's," they replied. At that he said to them, "Then give to Caesar what is Caesar's, but give to God what is God's."

This is the gospel of the Lord.

---

147   TWENTY-NINTH SUNDAY   **B**
OF THE YEAR

READING I   Is 53, 10-11

A reading from the book of the prophet Isaiah

If he offers his life in atonement, he shall see his heirs and have a long life.

[But the Lord was pleased
    to crush him in infirmity.]
If he gives his life as an offering for sin,
    he shall see his descendants in a long life,
    and the will of the Lord shall be accomplished through him.

Because of his affliction
    he shall see the light in fullness of days;
Through his suffering, my servant shall justify many,
    and their guilt he shall bear.
        This is the Word of the Lord.

Responsorial Psalm   Ps 33, 4-5. 18-19. 20. 22

℟. (22) Lord, let your mercy be on us,
    as we place our trust in you.
Upright is the word of the Lord,
    and all his works are trustworthy.
He loves justice and right;
    of the kindness of the Lord the earth is full.
℟. Lord, let your mercy be on us,
    as we place our trust in you.
See, the eyes of the Lord are upon those who fear him,
    upon those who hope for his kindness,
To deliver them from death
    and preserve them in spite of famine.
℟. Lord, let your mercy be on us,
    as we place our trust in you.
Our soul waits for the Lord,
    who is our help and our shield.
May your kindness, O Lord, be upon us
    who have put our hope in you.
℟. Lord, let your mercy be on us,
    as we place our trust in you.

READING II   Heb 4, 14-16

A reading from the letter to the Hebrews

Let us be confident in approaching the throne of grace.

We have a great high priest who has passed through the heavens, Jesus, the Son of God; let us hold fast to our profession of faith. For we do not have a high priest who is unable to sympathize with our weakness, but one who was tempted in every way that we are, yet never sinned. So let us confidently approach the throne of grace to receive mercy and favor and to find help in time of need.

This is the Word of the Lord.

GOSPEL   Mk 10, 35-45 or 10, 42-45
Alleluia
See no. 164.

✠ A reading from the holy gospel according to Mark

The Son of Man came to give his life as a ransom for many.

(Long Form)

Zebedee's sons, James and John, approached Jesus. "Teacher," they said, "we want you to grant our request." "What is it?" he asked. They replied, "See to it that we sit, one at your right and the other at your left, when you come into your glory." Jesus told them, "You do not know what you are asking. Can you drink the cup I shall drink or be baptized in the same bath of pain as I?" "We can," they told him. Jesus said in response, "From the cup I drink of you shall drink; the bath I am immersed in you shall share. But sitting at my right or my left is not mine to give; that is for those for whom it has been reserved." The other ten, on hearing this, became indignant at James and John. Jesus called them together and said to them: "You know how among the Gentiles those who seem to exercise authority lord it over them; their great ones make their importance felt. It cannot be like that with you. Anyone among you who aspires to greatness must serve the rest; whoever wants to rank first among you must serve the needs of all. The Son of Man has not come to be served but to serve—to give his life in ransom for the many."

This is the gospel of the Lord.

OR
(Short Form)

Jesus called the Twelve together and said to them: "You know how among the Gentiles those who seem to exercise authority lord it over them; their great ones make their importance felt. It cannot be like that with you. Anyone among you who aspires to greatness must serve the rest; whoever wants to rank first among you must serve the needs of all. The Son of Man has not come to be served but to serve—to give his life in ransom for the many."

This is the gospel of the Lord.

---

148   **TWENTY-NINTH SUNDAY**   **C**
         OF THE YEAR

READING I   Ex 17, 8-13

A reading from the book of Exodus

As long as Moses kept his arms raised, Israel had the advantage.

Amalek came and waged war against Israel. Moses, therefore, said to Joshua, "Pick out certain men, and tomorrow go out and engage Amalek in battle. I will be standing on top of the hill with the staff of God in my hand." So Joshua did as Moses told him: he engaged Amalek in battle after Moses had climbed to the top of the hill with Aaron and Hur. As long as Moses kept his hands raised up, Israel had the better of the fight, but when he let his hands rest, Amalek had the better of the fight. Moses' hands, however, grew tired; so they put a rock in place for him to sit on. Meanwhile Aaron and Hur supported his hands, one on one side and one on the other, so that his hands remained steady till sunset. And Joshua mowed down Amalek and his people with the edge of the sword.

This is the Word of the Lord.

Responsorial Psalm   Ps 121, 1-2. 3-4. 5-6. 7-8

R̶̸. (2) Our help is from the Lord
    who made heaven and earth.

I lift up my eyes toward the mountains;
    whence shall help come to me?
My help is from the Lord,
    who made heaven and earth.

R̶̸. Our help is from the Lord
    who made heaven and earth.

May he not suffer your foot to slip;
    may he slumber not who guards you:
Indeed he neither slumbers nor sleeps,
    the guardian of Israel.

R̶̸. Our help is from the Lord
    who made heaven and earth.

The Lord is your guardian; the Lord is your shade;
    he is beside you at your right hand.
The sun shall not harm you by day,
    nor the moon by night.

℟. Our help is from the Lord
  who made heaven and earth.
The Lord will guard you from all evil;
  he will guard your life.
The Lord will guard your coming and your
  going,
  both now and forever.
℟. Our help is from the Lord
  who made heaven and earth.

READING II   2 Tm 3, 14–4, 2

**A reading from the second letter of Paul to
Timothy**

This is how the man of God becomes equipped and ready
for every good work.

You must remain faithful to what you have
learned and believed, because you know who
your teachers were. Likewise, from your infancy you have known the sacred Scriptures,
the source of the wisdom which through faith
in Jesus Christ leads to salvation. All Scripture
is inspired of God and is useful for teaching—
for reproof, correction, and training in holiness
so that the man of God may be fully competent
and equipped for every good work.

In the presence of God and of Christ Jesus,
who is coming to judge the living and the dead,
and by his appearing and his kingly power, I
charge you to preach the word, to stay with
this task whether convenient or inconvenient
—correcting, reproving, appealing—constantly
teaching and never losing patience.

This is the Word of the Lord.

GOSPEL   Lk 18, 1-8
Alleluia

See no. 164.

✠ A reading from the holy gospel according
to Luke

God will see those who cry to him vindicated.

Jesus told his disciples a parable on the necessity of praying always and not losing heart:
"Once there was a judge in a certain city who
respected neither God nor man. A widow in
that city kept coming to him saying, 'Give me
my rights against my opponent.' For a time he
refused, but finally he thought, 'I care little

for God or man, but this widow is wearing me
out. I am going to settle in her favor or she
will end by doing me violence.'" The Lord said,
"Listen to what the corrupt judge has to say.
Will not God then do justice to his chosen who
call out to him day and night? Will he delay
long over them, do you suppose? I tell you, he
will give them swift justice. But when the Son
of Man comes, will he find any faith on the
earth?"

This is the gospel of the Lord.

---

149   THIRTIETH SUNDAY   **A**
OF THE YEAR

READING I   Ex 22, 20-26

A reading from the book of Exodus

If you are harsh with the widow or the orphan, my anger
will rage against you.

"You shall not molest or oppress an alien, for
you were once aliens yourselves in the land of
Egypt. You shall not wrong any widow or
orphan. If ever you wrong them and they cry
out to me, I will surely hear their cry. My
wrath will flare up, and I will kill you with the
sword; then your own wives will be widows,
and your children orphans.

"If you lend money to one of your poor
neighbors among my people, you shall not act
like an extortioner toward him by demanding
interest from him. If you take your neighbor's
cloak as a pledge, you shall return it to him
before sunset; for this cloak of his is the only
covering he has for his body. What else has he
to sleep in? if he cries out to me, I will hear
him; for I am compassionate."

This is the Word of the Lord.

Responsorial Psalm   Ps 18, 2-3. 3-4. 47. 51

℟. (2) I love you, Lord, my strength.
I love you, O Lord, my strength,
  O Lord, my rock, my fortress, my deliverer.
℟. I love you, Lord, my strength.
My God, my rock of refuge,
  my shield, the horn of my salvation, my
  stronghold!

Praised be the Lord, I exclaim,
and I am safe from my enemies.
℟. I love you, Lord, my strength.
The Lord live! And blessed be my Rock!
Extolled be God my savior.
You who gave great victories to your king
and showed kindness to your anointed.
℟. I love you, Lord, my strength.

READING II   1 Thes 1, 5-10

A reading from the first letter of Paul to the Thessalonians

You turned away from idols to serve God and to await his Son.

You know as well as we do what we proved to be like when, while still among you, we acted on your behalf. You, in turn, became imitators of us and of the Lord, receiving the word despite great trials, with the joy that comes from the Holy Spirit. Thus you became a model for all the believers of Macedonia and Achaia. The word of the Lord has echoed forth from you resoundingly. This is true not only in Macedonia and Achaia; throughout every region your faith in God is celebrated, which makes it needless for us to say anything more. The people of those parts are reporting what kind of reception we had from you and how you turned to God from idols, to serve him who is the living and true God and to await from heaven the Son he raised from the dead—Jesus, who delivers us from the wrath to come.

This is the Word of the Lord.

GOSPEL   Mt 22, 34-40
Alleluia

See no. 164.

✠ A reading from the holy gospel according to Matthew

You shall love the Lord your God and your neighbor as yourself.

When the Pharisees heard that Jesus had silenced the Sadducees, they assembled in a body; and one of them, a lawyer, in an attempt to trip him up, asked him, "Teacher, which commandment of the law is the greatest?" Jesus said to him:

" 'You shall love the Lord your God
with your whole heart,
with your whole soul,
and with all your mind.'
This is the greatest and first commandment. The second is like it:
'You shall love your neighbor as yourself.'
On these two commandments the whole law is based, and the prophets as well."
This is the gospel of the Lord.

---

150   **THIRTIETH SUNDAY**   **B**
           OF THE YEAR

READING I   Jer 31, 7-9

A reading from the book of the prophet Jeremiah

I shall lead them back in mercy—both the blind and the lame.

Thus says the Lord:
Shout with joy for Jacob,
exult at the head of the nations;
proclaim your praise and say:
The Lord has delivered his people,
the remnant of Israel.
Behold, I will bring them back
from the land of the north;
I will gather them from the ends of the world,
with the blind and the lame in their midst,
The mothers and those with child;
they shall return as an immense throng.
They departed in tears,
but I will console them and guide them;
I will lead them to brooks of water,
on a level road, so that none shall stumble.
For I am a father to Israel,
Ephraim is my first-born.
This is the Word of the Lord.

Responsorial Psalm   Ps 126, 1-2. 2-3. 4-5. 6

℟. (3) The Lord has done great things for us;
we are filled with joy.
When the Lord brought back the captives of Zion,
we were like men dreaming.
Then our mouth was filled with laughter,
and our tongue with rejoicing.

℞. The Lord has done great things for us;
we are filled with joy.
Then they said among the nations,
"The Lord has done great things for them."
The Lord has done great things for us;
we are glad indeed.
℞. The Lord has done great things for us;
we are filled with joy.
Restore our fortunes, O Lord,
like the torrents in the southern desert.
Those that sow in tears
shall reap rejoicing.
℞. The Lord has done great things for us;
we are filled with joy.
Although they go forth weeping,
carrying the seed to be sown,
They shall come back rejoicing,
carrying their sheaves.
℞. The Lord has done great things for us;
we are filled with joy.

READING II   Heb 5, 1-6

A reading from the letter to the Hebrews
You are a priest forever according to the order of
Melchizedek

Every high priest is taken from among men and
made their representative before God, to offer
gifts and sacrifices for sins. He is able to deal
patiently with erring sinners, for he is himself
beset by weakness and so must make sin of-
ferings for himself as well as for the people.
One does not take this honor on his own initia-
tive, but only when called by God as Aaron
was. Even Christ did not glorify himself with
the office of high priest; he received it from the
One who said to him,
"You are my son;
today I have begotten you";
just as he says in another place,
"You are a priest forever,
according to the order of Melchizedek."
This is the Word of the Lord.

GOSPEL   Mk 10, 46-52
Alleluia

See no. 164.

✠ **A reading from the holy gospel according**
to Mark
Master, grant that I may see.

As Jesus was leaving Jericho with his disciples
and a sizable crowd, there was a blind beggar
Bartimaeus ("son of Timaeus") sitting by the
roadside. On hearing that it was Jesus of Naza-
reth, he began to call out, "Jesus, Son of David,
have pity on me!" Many people were scolding
him to make him keep quiet, but he shouted all
the louder, "Son of David, have pity on me!"
Then Jesus stopped and said, "Call him over."
So they called the blind man over, telling him as
they did so, "You have nothing whatever to fear
from him! Get up! He is calling you!" He threw
aside his cloak, jumped up and came to Jesus.
Jesus asked him, "What do you want me to
do for you?" "Rabboni," the blind man said, "I
want to see." Jesus said in reply, "Be on your
way! Your faith has healed you." Immediately
he received his sight and started to follow him
up the road.
This is the gospel of the Lord.

---

151   **THIRTIETH SUNDAY**
             OF THE YEAR

READING I   Sir 35, 12-14. 16-18

A reading from the book of Sirach
The prayer of the humble man will penetrate the heavens.

The Lord is a God of justice,
who knows no favorites.
Though not unduly partial toward the weak,
yet he hears the cry of the oppressed.
He is not deaf to the wail of the orphan,
nor to the widow when she pours out her
complaint.

He who serves God willingly is heard;
his petition reaches the heavens.
The prayer of the lowly pierces the clouds;
it does not rest till it reaches its goal,
Nor will it withdraw till the Most High re-
sponds,
judges justly and affirms the right.
This is the Word of the Lord.

Responsorial Psalm   Ps 34, 2-3. 17-18. 19. 23

℟. (7) The Lord hears the cry of the poor.
I will bless the Lord at all times;
    his praise shall be ever in my mouth.
Let my soul glory in the Lord;
    the lowly will hear me and be glad.
℟. The Lord hears the cry of the poor.
The Lord confronts the evildoers,
    to destroy remembrance of them from the
    earth.
When the just cry out, the Lord hears them,
    and from all their distress he rescues them.
℟. The Lord hears the cry of the poor.
The Lord is close to the brokenhearted;
    and those who are crushed in spirit he saves.
The Lord redeems the lives of his servants;
    no one incurs guilt who takes refuge in him.
℟. The Lord hears the cry of the poor.

READING II   2 Tm 4, 6-8. 16-18

**A reading from the second letter of Paul to
Timothy**

All that remains is the crown of righteousness reserved
for me.

I am already being poured out like a libation.
The time of my dissolution is near. I have
fought the good fight, I have finished the race, I
have kept the faith. From now on a merited
crown awaits me; on that Day the Lord, just
judge that he is, will award it to me—and not
only to me but to all who have looked for his
appearing with eager longing.
    At the first hearing of my case in court, no
one took my part. In fact, everyone abandoned
me. May it not be held against them! But the
Lord stood by my side and gave me strength,
so that through me the preaching task might
be completed and all the nations might hear
the gospel. That is how I was saved from the
lion's jaws. The Lord will continue to rescue
me from all attempts to do me harm and will
bring me safe to his heavenly kingdom. To him
be glory forever and ever. Amen.
    This is the Word of the Lord.

GOSPEL   Lk 18, 9-14
Alleluia

See no. 164.

✠ **A reading from the holy gospel according
to Luke**

The publican returned home justified; the pharisee did not.

Jesus spoke this parable addressed to those
who believed in their own self-righteousness
while holding everyone else in contempt: "Two
men went up to the temple to pray; one was a
Pharisee, the other a tax collector. The Pharisee with head unbowed prayed in this fashion:
'I give you thanks, O God, that I am not like the
rest of men—grasping, crooked, adulterous—
or even like this tax collector. I fast twice a
week. I pay tithes on all I possess.' The other
man, however, kept his distance, not even daring to raise his eyes to heaven. All he did was
beat his breast and say, 'O God, be merciful to
me, a sinner.' Believe me, this man went home
from the temple justified but the other did not.
For everyone who exalts himself shall be humbled while he who humbles himself shall be exalted."
    This is the gospel of the Lord.

---

152   **THIRTY-FIRST SUNDAY**   Ⓐ
                 OF THE YEAR

READING I   Mal 1, 14–2, 2. 8-10

**A reading from the book of the prophet
Malachi**

You have strayed from the way, you have caused many to
stumble by your teaching.

A great King am I, says the Lord of hosts,
    and my name will be feared among the na-
    tions.
If you do not lay it to heart,
    to give glory to my name, says the Lord of
    hosts,
I will send a curse upon you
    and of your blessing I will make a curse.
Yes, I have already cursed it,
    because you do not lay it to heart.
You have turned aside from the way,
    and have caused many to falter by your in-
    struction;

You have made void the covenant of Levi,
   says the Lord of hosts.
I, therefore, have made you contemptible
   and base before all the people,
Since you do not keep my ways,
   but show partiality in your decisions.

Have we not all the one Father?
Has not the one God created us?
Why then do we break faith with each other,
   violating the covenant of our fathers?
   This is the Word of the Lord.

Responsorial Psalm   Ps 131, 1. 2. 3

℟. In you, Lord, I have found my peace.
O Lord, my heart is not proud,
   nor are my eyes haughty;
I busy not myself with great things,
   nor with things too sublime for me.
℟. In you, Lord, I have found my peace.
Nay rather, I have stilled and quieted
   my soul like a weaned child.
Like a weaned child on its mother's lap,
   [so is my soul within me.]
℟. In you, Lord, I have found my peace.
O Israel, hope in the Lord,
   both now and forever.

READING II   1 Thes 2, 7-9. 13

A reading from the first letter of Paul to the Thessalonians
We were eager to hand over to you not only the good news
but our lives as well

While we were among you we were as gentle
as any nursing mother fondling her little ones.
So well disposed were we toward you, in fact,
that we wanted to share with you not only
God's tidings but our very lives, you had become so dear to us. You must recall, brothers,
our efforts and our toil: how we worked day
and night all the time we preached God's good
tidings to you in order not to impose on you in
any way. That is why we thank God constantly
that in receiving his message from us you took
it, not as the word of men, but as it truly is, the
word of God at work within you who believe.
   This is the Word of the Lord.

GOSPEL   Mt 23, 1-12
Alleluia
See no. 164.

✠ **A reading from the holy gospel according
to Matthew**
They do not practice what they preach.

Jesus told the crowds and his disciples: "The
scribes and the Pharisees have succeeded
Moses as teachers; therefore, do everything
and observe everything they tell you. But do
not follow their example. Their words are bold
but their deeds are few. They bind up heavy
loads, hard to carry, to lay on other men's
shoulders, while they themselves will not lift a
finger to budge them. All their works are performed to be seen. They widen their phylacteries and wear huge tassels. They are fond of
places of honor at banquets and the front seats
in synagogues, of marks of respect in public
and of being called 'Rabbi.' As to you, avoid the
title 'Rabbi.' One among you is your teacher,
the rest are learners. Do not call anyone on
earth your father. Only one is your father, the
One in heaven. Avoid being called teachers.
Only one is your teacher, the Messiah. The
greatest among you will be the one who serves
the rest. Whoever exalts himself shall be humbled, but whoever humbles himself shall be exalted."
   This is the gospel of the Lord.

---

153   **THIRTY-FIRST SUNDAY**   **B**
             OF THE YEAR

READING I   Dt 6, 2-6
A reading from the book of Deuteronomy
Hear, Israel, you shall love the Lord with all your heart

Moses told the people: Fear the Lord, your
God, and keep, throughout the days of your
lives, all his statutes and commandments
which I enjoin on you, and thus have long life.
Hear then, Israel, and be careful to observe
them, that you may grow and prosper the
more, in keeping with the promise of the Lord,
the God of your fathers, to give you a land
flowing with milk and honey. "Hear, O Israel!

The Lord is our God, the Lord alone! Therefore, you shall love the Lord, your God, with all your heart, and with all your soul, and with all your strength. Take to heart these words which I enjoin on you today."
This is the Word of the Lord.

Responsorial Psalm   Ps 18, 2-3. 3-4. 47. 51

R̸. (2) I love you, Lord, my strength.
I love you, O Lord, my strength,
   O Lord, my rock, my fortress, my deliverer.
R̸. I love you, Lord, my strength.
My God, my rock of refuge,
   my shield, the horn of my salvation, my stronghold!
Praised be the Lord, I exclaim,
   and I am safe from my enemies.
R̸. I love you, Lord, my strength.
The Lord live! And blessed be my Rock!
   Extolled be God my savior.
You who gave great victories to your king
   and showed kindness to your anointed.
R̸. I love you, Lord, my strength.

READING II   Heb 7, 23-28

A reading from the letter to the Hebrews
This one, because he remains for ever, has an eternal priesthood.

Under the old covenant there were many priests because they were prevented by death from remaining in office; but Jesus, because he remains forever, has a priesthood which does not pass away. Therefore he is always able to save those who approach God through him, since he forever lives to make intercession for them.
   It was fitting that we should have such a high priest: holy, innocent, undefiled, separated from sinners, higher than the heavens. Unlike the other high priests, he has no need to offer sacrifice day after day, first for his own sins and then for those of the people; he did that once for all when he offered himself. For the law sets up as high priests men who are weak, but the word of the oath which came after the law appoints as priest the Son, made perfect forever.
This is the Word of the Lord.

GOSPEL   Mk 12, 28-34
Alleluia
See no. 164.

✠ A reading from the holy gospel according to Mark
This is the first commandment, and the second is similar to it.

One of the scribes came up to Jesus, and asked him, "Which is the first of all the commandments?" Jesus replied: "This is the first:
   'Hear, O Israel! The Lord our God is Lord alone!
   Therefore you shall love the Lord your God
   with all your heart,
   with all your soul,
   with all your mind,
   and with all your strength.'
This is the second,
   'You shall love your neighbor as yourself.'
There is no other commandment greater than these." The scribe said to him: "Excellent, Teacher! You are right in saying, 'He is the One, there is no other than he.' Yes, 'to love him with all our heart, with all our thoughts and with all our strength, and to love our neighbor as ourselves' is worth more than any burnt offering or sacrifice." Jesus approved the insight of this answer and told him, "You are not far from the reign of God." And no one had the courage to ask him any more questions.
   This is the gospel of the Lord.

---

154   **THIRTY-FIRST SUNDAY
OF THE YEAR**   C

READING I   Wis 11, 22–12, 1

A reading from the book of Wisdom
You have mercy on all things because you love everything that exists.

Before the Lord the whole universe is as a grain from a balance
   or a drop of morning dew come down upon the earth.

But you have mercy on all, because you can do
  all things;
  and you overlook the sins of men that they
    may repent.
For you love all things that are
  and loathe nothing that you have made;
  for what you hated, you would not have
    fashioned.
And how could a thing remain, unless you
  willed it;
  or be preserved, had it not been called forth
    by you?
But you spare all things, because they are
  yours, O Lord and lover of souls,
  for your imperishable spirit is in all things!
    This is the Word of the Lord.

Responsorial Psalm   Ps 145, 1-2. 8-9. 10-11. 13. 14

℟. (1) I will praise your name for ever, my
  king and my God.
I will extol you, O my God and King,
  and I will bless your name forever and ever.
Every day will I bless you,
  and I will praise your name forever and ever.
℟. I will praise your name for ever, my King
  and my God.
The Lord is gracious and merciful,
  slow to anger and of great kindness.
The Lord is good to all
  and compassionate toward all his works.
℟. I will praise your name for ever, my King
  and my God.
Let all your works give you thanks, O Lord,
  and let your faithful ones bless you.
Let them discourse of the glory of your kingdom
  and speak of your might.
℟. I will praise your name for ever, my King
  and my God.
The Lord is faithful in all his words
  and holy in all his works.
The Lord lifts up all who are falling
  and raises up all who are bowed down.
℟. I will praise your name for ever, my King
  and my God.

READING II   2 Thes 1, 11–2, 2
**A reading from the second letter of Paul to the
Thessalonians**
The name of our Lord Jesus Christ will be glorified in you
and you in him.

We pray for you always that our God may
make you worthy of his call, and fulfill by his
power every honest intention and work of
faith. In this way the name of our Lord Jesus
may be glorified in you and you in him, in accord with the gracious gift of our God and of
the Lord Jesus Christ.

On the question of the coming of our Lord
Jesus Christ and our being gathered to him, we
beg you, brothers, not to be so easily agitated
or terrified, whether by an oracular utterance
or rumor or a letter alleged to be ours, into believing that the day of the Lord is here.
    This is the Word of the Lord.

GOSPEL   Lk 19, 1-10
Alleluia
See no. 164.

✠ **A reading from the holy gospel according
to Luke**
The Son of Man came to seek and to find that which was
lost.

Jesus, upon entering Jericho, passed through
the city. There was a man there named Zacchaeus, the chief tax collector and a wealthy
man. He was trying to see what Jesus was like,
but being small of stature, was unable to do so
because of the crowd. He first ran on in front,
then climbed a sycamore tree which was along
Jesus' route, in order to see him. When Jesus
came to the spot he looked up and said, "Zacchaeus, hurry down. I mean to stay at your
house today." He quickly descended, and welcomed him with delight. When this was
observed, everyone began to murmur, "He has
gone to a sinner's house as a guest." Zacchaeus
stood his ground and said to the Lord: "I give
half my belongings, Lord, to the poor. If I have
defrauded anyone in the least, I pay him back
fourfold." Jesus said to him: "Today salvation
has come to this house, for this is what it

means to be a son of Abraham. The Son of Man has come to search out and save what was lost."

This is the gospel of the Lord.

---

155 THIRTY-SECOND SUNDAY OF THE YEAR **A**

READING I Wis 6, 12-16

A reading from the book of Wisdom
Wisdom is found by those who look for it.

Resplendent and unfading is Wisdom,
 and she is readily perceived by those who love her,
 and found by those who seek her.
She hastens to make herself known in anticipation of men's desire;
 he who watches for her at dawn shall not be disappointed,
 for he shall find her sitting by his gate.
For taking thought of her is the perfection of prudence,
 and he who for her sake keeps vigil shall quickly be free from care;
Because she makes her own rounds, seeking those worthy of her,
 and graciously appears to them in the ways,
 and meets them with all solicitude.

This is the Word of the Lord.

Responsorial Psalm Ps 63, 2. 3-4. 5-6. 7-8

℟. (2) My soul is thirsting for you, O Lord my God.

O God, you are my God whom I seek;
 for you my flesh pines and my soul thirsts
 like the earth, parched, lifeless and without water.
℟. My soul is thirsting for you, O Lord my God.

Thus have I gazed toward you in the sanctuary
 to see your power and your glory,
For your kindness is a greater good than life;
 my lips shall glorify you.
℟. My soul is thirsting for you, O Lord my God.

Thus will I bless you while I live;
 lifting up my hands, I will call upon your name.
As with the riches of a banquet shall my soul be satisfied,
 and with exultant lips my mouth shall praise you.
℟. My soul is thirsting for you, O Lord my God.

I will remember you upon my couch,
 and through the night-watches I will meditate on you:
You are my help,
 and in the shadow of your wings I shout for joy.
℟. My soul is thirsting for you, O Lord my God.

READING II 1 Thes 4, 13-18 or 4, 13-14

A reading from the first letter of Paul to the Thessalonians
Those who died as Christians, God will bring to life with Jesus.

(Long Form)

We would have you be clear about those who sleep in death, brothers; otherwise you might yield to grief like those who have no hope. For if we believe that Jesus died and rose, God will bring forth with him from the dead those also who have fallen asleep believing in him. We say to you, as if the Lord himself had said it, that we who live, who survive until his coming, will in no way have an advantage over those who have fallen asleep. No, the Lord himself will come down from heaven at the word of command, at the sound of the archangel's voice and God's trumpet; and those who have died in Christ will rise first. Then we, the living, the survivors, will be caught up with them in the clouds to meet the Lord in the air. Thenceforth we shall be with the Lord unceasingly. Console one another with this message.

This is the Word of the Lord.

OR
(Short Form)

We would have you be clear about those who sleep in death, brothers; otherwise you might yield to grief like those who have no hope. For if we believe that Jesus died and rose, God will bring forth with him from the dead those also who have fallen asleep believing in him.

This is the Word of the Lord.

GOSPEL   Mt 25, 1-13
Alleluia

See no. 164, at the end.

✠ A reading from the holy gospel according to Matthew

Look, the bridegroom comes. Go out to meet him.

Jesus told this parable to his disciples: "The reign of God can be likened to ten bridesmaids who took their torches and went out to welcome the groom. Five of them were foolish, while the other five were sensible. The foolish ones, in taking their torches, brought no oil along, but the sensible ones took flasks of oil as well as their torches. The groom delayed his coming, so they all began to nod, then to fall asleep. At midnight someone shouted, 'The groom is here! Come out and greet him!' At the outcry all the virgins woke up and got their torches ready. The foolish ones said to the sensible, 'Give us some of your oil. Our torches are going out.' But the sensible ones replied, 'No, there may not be enough for you and us. You had better go to the dealers and buy yourselves some.' While they went off to buy it the groom arrived, and the ones who were ready went in to the wedding with him. Then the door was barred. Later the other bridesmaids came back. 'Master, master!' they cried. 'Open the door for us.' But he answered, 'I tell you, I do not know you.' The moral is: keep your eyes open, for you know not the day or the hour."

This is the gospel of the Lord.

---

156   THIRTY-SECOND SUNDAY   B
OF THE YEAR

READING I   1 Kgs 17, 10-16
A reading from the first book of Kings

The widow made a little scone from her flour meal and brought it to Elijah.

Elijah [the prophet] went to Zarephath. As he arrived at the entrance of the city, a widow was gathering sticks there; he called out to her, "Please bring me a small cupful of water to drink." She left to get it, and he called out after her, "Please bring along a bit of bread." "As the Lord, your God, lives," she answered, "I have nothing baked; there is only a handful of flour in my jar and a little oil in my jug. Just now I was collecting a couple of sticks, to go in and prepare something for myself and my son; when we have eaten it, we shall die." "Do not be afraid," Elijah said to her. "Go and do as you propose. But first make me a little cake and bring it to me. Then you can prepare something for yourself and your son. For the Lord, the God of Israel, says, 'The jar of flour shall not go empty, nor the jug of oil run dry, until the day when the Lord sends rain upon the earth.'" She left and did as Elijah had said. She was able to eat for a year, and he and her son as well; the jar of flour did not go empty, nor the jug of oil run dry, as the Lord had foretold through Elijah.

This is the Word of the Lord.

Responsorial Psalm   Ps 146, 7. 8-9. 9-10

℟. (2) Praise the Lord, my soul!
The Lord keeps faith forever,
    secures justice for the oppressed,
    gives food to the hungry.
The Lord sets captives free.
℟. Praise the Lord, my soul!
The Lord gives sight to the blind.
    The Lord raises up those that were bowed
        down;
The Lord loves the just.
    The Lord protects strangers.
℟. Praise the Lord, my soul!
The fatherless and the widow he sustains,
    but the way of the wicked he thwarts.

The Lord shall reign forever;
  your God, O Zion, through all generations.
    Alleluia.
℞. Praise the Lord, my soul!
℞. Or: Alleluia.

READING II   Heb 9, 24-28
A reading from the letter to the Hebrews

Christ offered himself only once to take the faults of many
on himself.

Christ did not enter into a sanctuary made by
hands, a mere copy of the true one; he entered
heaven itself that he might appear before God
now on our behalf. Not that he might offer
himself there again and again, as the high
priest enters year after year into the sanctuary
with blood that is not his own; were that so, he
would have had to suffer death over and over
from the creation of the world. But now he has
appeared, at the end of the ages to take away
sins once for all by his sacrifice. Just as it is
appointed that men die once, and after death be
judged, so Christ was offered up once to take
away the sins of many; he will appear a second
time not to take away sin but to bring salvation
to those who eagerly await him.
        This is the Word of the Lord.

GOSPEL   Mk 12, 38-44 or 12, 41-44
Alleluia

See no. 164, at the end.

✠ **A reading from the holy gospel according
to Mark**

This poor widow has put more in than all who contributed.

(Long Form)

In the course of his teaching Jesus said: "Be on
guard against the scribes, who like to parade
around in their robes and accept marks of respect in public, front seats in the synagogues,
and places of honor at banquets. These men
devour the savings of widows and recite long
prayers for appearance' sake; it is they who
will receive the severest sentence."
        Taking a seat opposite the treasury, he ob-
served the crowd putting money into the collection box. Many of the wealthy put in sizable

amounts; but one poor widow came and put in
two small copper coins worth about a cent. He
called his disciples over and told them: "I want
you to observe that this poor widow contributed more than all the others who donated to
the treasury. They gave from their surplus
wealth, but she gave from her want, all that she
had to live on."
        This is the gospel of the Lord.

OR
(Short Form)

Taking a seat opposite the treasury, Jesus observed the crowd putting money into the collection box. Many of the wealthy put in sizable
amounts; but one poor widow came and put in
two small copper coins worth about a cent. He
called his disciples over and told them: "I want
you to observe that this poor widow contributed more than all the others who donated to
the treasury. They gave from their surplus
wealth, but she gave from her want, all that she
had to live on."
        This is the gospel of the Lord.

---

157   THIRTY-SECOND SUNDAY   [C]
OF THE YEAR

READING I   2 Mc 7, 1-2. 9-14
A reading from the second book of Maccabees

The king of the world will receive us into life eternal at
the resurrection.

It happened that seven brothers with their
mother were arrested and tortured with whips
and scourges by the king, to force them to eat
pork in violation of God's law. One of the
brothers, speaking for the others, said: "What
do you expect to achieve by questioning us?
We are ready to die rather than transgress the
laws of our ancestors."
        At the point of death the second brother
said: "You accursed fiend, you are depriving us
of this present life, but the King of the world
will raise us up to live again forever. It is for
his laws that we are dying."
        After him the third suffered their cruel sport.
He put out his tongue at once when told to do
so, and bravely held out his hands, as he spoke

these noble words: "It was from Heaven that I received these; for the sake of his laws I disdain them; from him I hope to receive them again." Even the king and his attendants marveled at the young man's courage, because he regarded his sufferings as nothing.

After he had died, they tortured and maltreated the fourth brother in the same way. When he was near death, he said, "It is my choice to die at the hands of men with the God-given hope of being restored to life by him; but for you, there will be no resurrection to life."
This is the Word of the Lord.

Responsorial Psalm   Ps 17, 1. 5-6. 8. 15

℟. (15) Lord, when your glory appears,
     my joy will be full.

Hear, O Lord, a just suit;
attend to my outcry;
hearken to my prayer from lips without
deceit.

℟. Lord, when your glory appears,
     my joy will be full.

My steps have been steadfast in your paths,
my feet have not faltered.
I call upon you, for you will answer me, O God;
incline your ear to me; hear my word.

℟. Lord, when your glory appears,
     my joy will be full.

Keep me as the apple of your eye,
hide me in the shadow of your wings.
But I in justice shall behold your face;
on waking I shall be content in your presence.

℟. Lord, when your glory appears,
     my joy will be full.

READING II   2 Thes 2, 16–3, 5

A reading from the second letter of Paul to the Thessalonians

May the Lord strengthen you in everything good that you do or say.

May our Lord Jesus Christ himself, may God our Father who loved us and in his mercy gave us eternal consolation and hope, console your hearts and strengthen them for every good work and word.

For the rest, brothers, pray for us that the word of the Lord may make progress and be hailed by many others, even as it has been by you. Pray that we may be delivered from confused and evil men. For not everyone has faith; the Lord, however, keeps faith; he it is who will strengthen you and guard you against the evil one. In the Lord we are confident that you are doing and will continue to do whatever we enjoin. May the Lord rule your hearts in the love of God and the constancy of Christ.
This is the Word of the Lord.

GOSPEL   Lk 20, 27-38 or 20, 27. 34-38
Alleluia

See no. 164, at the end.

✠ **A reading from the holy gospel according to Luke**

He is not a God of the dead but of the living.

(Long Form)
Some Sadducees came forward (the ones who claim there is no resurrection) to pose this problem to Jesus: "Master, Moses prescribed that if a man's brother dies leaving a wife and no child, the brother should marry the widow and raise posterity to his brother. Now there were seven brothers. The first one married and died childless. Next, the second brother married the widow, then the third, and so on. All seven died without leaving her any children. Finally the widow herself died. At the resurrection, whose wife will she be? Remember, seven married her.

Jesus said to them: "The children of this age marry and are given in marriage, but those judged worthy of a place in the age to come and of resurrection from the dead do not. They become like angels and are no longer liable to death. Sons of the resurrection, they are sons of God. Moses in the passage about the bush showed that the dead rise again when he called the Lord the God of Abraham, and the God of Isaac, and the God of Jacob. God is not the God of the dead but of the living. All are alive for him."

This is the gospel of the Lord.

OR
(Short Form)

Some Sadducees came forward (the ones who claim there is no resurrection).

Jesus said to them: "The children of this age marry and are given in marriage, but those judged worthy of a place in the age to come and of resurrection from the dead do not. They become like angels and are no longer liable to death. Sons of the resurrection, they are sons of God. Moses in the passage about the bush showed that the dead rise again when he called the Lord the God of Abraham, and the God of Isaac, and the God of Jacob. God is not the God of the dead but of the living. All are alive for him."

This is the gospel of the Lord.

158   **THIRTY-THIRD SUNDAY**   **A**
OF THE YEAR

READING I   Prv 31, 10-13. 19-20. 30-31

A reading from the book of Proverbs
Give her a share in what she has worked for.

When one finds a worthy wife,
    her value is far beyond pearls.
Her husband, entrusting his heart to her,
    has an unfailing prize.
She brings him good, and not evil,
    all the days of her life.
She obtains wool and flax
    and makes cloth with skillful hands.
She puts her hands to the distaff,
    and her fingers ply the spindle.
She reaches out her hands to the poor,
    and extends her arms to the needy.
Charm is deceptive and beauty fleeting;
    the woman who fears the Lord is to be
    praised.
Give her a reward of her labors,
    and let her works praise her at the city gates.
This is the Word of the Lord.

Responsorial Psalm   Ps 128, 1-2. 3. 4-5

℟. (1) Happy are those who fear the Lord.
Happy are you who fear the Lord,
    who walk in his ways!

For you shall eat the fruit of your handiwork;
    happy shall you be, and favored.
℟. Happy are those who fear the Lord.
Your wife shall be like a fruitful vine
    in the recesses of your home;
Your children like olive plants
    around your table.
℟. Happy are those who fear the Lord.
Behold, thus is the man blessed
    who fears the Lord.
The Lord bless you from Zion:
    may you see the prosperity of Jerusalem
    all the days of your life.
℟. Happy are those who fear the Lord.

READING II   1 Thes 5, 1-6

**A reading from the first letter of Paul to the
Thessalonians**
The day of the Lord is going to come like a thief in the
night.

As regards specific times and moments, brothers, we do not need to write you; you know very well that the day of the Lord is coming like a thief in the night. Just when people are saying, "Peace and security," ruin will fall on them with the suddenness of pains overtaking a woman in labor, and there will be no escape. You are not in the dark, brothers, that the day might catch you off guard, like a thief. No, all of you are children of light and of the day. We belong neither to darkness nor to night; therefore let us not be asleep like the rest, but awake and sober!
This is the Word of the Lord.

GOSPEL   Mt 25, 14-30 or 25, 14-15. 19-20
Alleluia

See no. 164, at the end.

✠ **A reading from the holy gospel according
to Matthew**
Because you have been faithful over a few things, enter into
the joy of the Lord.

(Long Form)

Jesus told this parable to his disciples: "A man was going on a journey. He called in his servants and handed his funds over to them according to each man's abilities. To one he disbursed five thousand silver pieces, to a second two thousand, and to a third a thousand. Then he went away. Immediately the man who received the five thousand went to invest it and made another five. In the same way, the man who received the two thousand doubled his figure. The man who received the thousand went off instead and dug a hole in the ground, where he buried his master's money. After a long absence, the master of those servants came home and settled accounts with them. The man who had received the five thousand came forward bringing the additional five. 'My lord,' he said, 'you let me have five thousand. See, I have made five thousand more.' His master said to him, 'Well done! You are an industrious and reliable servant. Since you were dependable in a small matter I will put you in charge of larger affairs. Come, share your master's joy!' The man who had received the two thousand then stepped forward. 'My lord,' he said, 'you entrusted me with two thousand and I have made two thousand more.' His master said to him, 'Cleverly done! You too are an industrious and reliable servant. Since you were dependable in a small matter I will put you in charge of larger affairs. Come, share your master's joy!'

"Finally the man who had received the thousand stepped forward. 'My lord,' he said, 'I knew you were a hard man. You reap where you did not sow and gather where you did not scatter, so out of fear I went off and buried your thousand silver pieces in the ground. Here is your money back.' His master exclaimed: 'You worthless, lazy lout! You know I reap where I did not sow and gather where I did not scatter. All the more reason to deposit my money with the bankers, so that on my return I could have had it back with interest. You, there! Take the thousand away from him and give it to the man with the ten thousand. Those who have, will get more until they grow rich, while those who have not, will lose even the little they have. Throw this worthless servant into the darkness outside, where he can wail and grind his teeth.' "

This is the gospel of the Lord.

OR
(Short Form)

Jesus told this parable to his disciples: "A man was going on a journey. He called in his servants and handed his funds over to them according to each man's abilities. To one he disbursed five thousand silver pieces, to a second two thousand, and to a third a thousand. After a long absence, the master of those servants came home and settled accounts with them. The man who had received the five thousand came forward bringing the additional five. 'My lord,' he said, 'you let me have five thousand. See, I have made five thousand more.' "

This is the gospel of the Lord.

**159   THIRTY-THIRD SUNDAY   B
OF THE YEAR**

READING I   Dn 12, 1-3

A reading from the book of the prophet Daniel

When that time comes your own people will be spared.

At that time there shall arise
  Michael, the great prince,
  guardian of your people;
It shall be a time unsurpassed in distress
  since nations began until that time.
At that time your people shall escape,
  everyone who is found written in the book.
Many of those who sleep
  in the dust of the earth shall awake;
Some shall live forever,
  others shall be an everlasting horror and disgrace.
But the wise shall shine brightly
  like the splendor of the firmament,
And those who lead the many to justice
  shall be like the stars forever.

This is the Word of the Lord.

Responsorial Psalm   Ps 16, 5. 8. 9-10. 11

Ry. (1) Keep me safe, O God;
  you are my hope.

O Lord, my allotted portion and my cup,
  you it is who hold fast my lot.
I set the Lord ever before me;

with him at my right hand I shall not be disturbed.
℟. Keep me safe, O God;
   you are my hope.
Therefore my heart is glad and my soul rejoices,
   my body, too, abides in confidence;
Because you will not abandon my soul to the
      nether world,
   nor will you suffer your faithful one to undergo corruption.
℟. Keep me safe, O God;
   you are my hope.
You will show me the path to life,
   fullness of joys in your presence,
   the delights at your right hand forever.
℟. Keep me safe, O God;
   you are my hope.

READING II   Heb 10, 11-14. 18
A reading from the letter to the Hebrews
By a single offering he has achieved the eternal perfection
of all those who are sanctified.

Every other priest stands ministering day by
day, and offering again and again those same
sacrifices which can never take away sins. But
Jesus offered one sacrifice for sins and took his
seat forever at the right hand of God; now he
waits until his enemies are placed beneath his
feet. By one offering he has forever perfected
those who are being sanctified. Once sins have
been forgiven, there is no further offering for
sin.
           This is the Word of the Lord.

GOSPEL   Mk 13, 24-32
Alleluia

See no. 164, at the end.

✠ **A reading from the holy gospel according
            to Mark**
He shall gather his elect from the four winds.

Jesus said to his disciples: "During that period
after trials of every sort the sun will be darkened, the moon will not shed its light, stars
will fall out of the skies, and the heavenly hosts
will be shaken. Then men will see the Son of
Man coming in the clouds with great power
and glory. He will dispatch his messengers and
assemble his chosen from the four winds, from
the farthest bounds of earth and sky. Learn a
lesson from the fig tree. Once the sap of its
branches runs high and it begins to sprout
leaves, you know that summer is near. In the
same way, when you see these things happening, you will know that he is near, even at the
door. I assure you, this generation will not pass
away until all these things take place. The
heavens and the earth will pass away, but my
words will not.
   "As to the exact day or hour, no one knows
it, neither the angels in heaven nor even the
Son, but only the Father."
           This is the gospel of the Lord.

**160   THIRTY-THIRD SUNDAY   C
              OF THE YEAR**

READING I   Mal 3, 19-20
**A reading from the book of the prophet
                    Malachi**
The sun of righteousness will shine on you.

Lo, the day is coming, blazing like an oven,
   when all the proud and all evildoers will be
      stubble,
And the day that is coming will set them on
      fire,
   leaving them neither root nor branch,
   says the Lord of hosts.
But for you who fear my name, there will arise
   the sun of justice with its healing rays.
           This is the Word of the Lord.

Responsorial Psalm   Ps 98, 5-6. 7-8. 9
℟. (9) The Lord comes to rule the earth with
      justice.
Sing praise to the Lord with the harp,
   with the harp and melodious song.
With trumpets and the sound of the horn
   sing joyfully before the King, the Lord.
℟. The Lord comes to rule the earth with
      justice.
Let the sea and what fills it resound,
   the world and those who dwell in it;
Let the rivers clap their hands,
   the mountains shout with them for joy.

℟. The Lord comes to rule the earth with justice.

Before the Lord, for he comes,
  for he comes to rule the earth,
He will rule the world with justice
  and the peoples with equity.

℟. The Lord comes to rule the earth with justice.

READING II   2 Thes 3, 7-12

A reading from the second letter of Paul to the Thessalonians

If anyone refuses to work then do not let him eat.

You know how you ought to imitate us. We did not live lives of disorder when we were among you, nor depend on anyone for food. Rather, we worked day and night, laboring to the point of exhaustion so as not to impose on any of you. Not that we had no claim on you, but that we might present ourselves as an example for you to imitate. Indeed, when we were with you we used to lay down the rule that anyone who would not work should not eat.

We hear that some of you are unruly, not keeping busy but acting like busybodies. We enjoin all such, and we urge them strongly in the Lord Jesus Christ to earn the food they eat by working quietly.

This is the Word of the Lord.

GOSPEL   Lk 21, 5-19
Alleluia

See no. 164, at the end.

✠ **A reading from the holy gospel according to Luke**

Your endurance will win you your life.

Some were speaking of how the temple was adorned with precious stones and votive offerings. Jesus said, "These things you are contemplating—the day will come when not one stone will be left on another, but it will all be torn down." They asked him, "When will this occur, Teacher? And what will be the sign it is going to happen?" He said, "Take care not to be misled. Many will come in my name, say-ing, 'I am he' and 'The time is at hand.' Do not follow them. Neither must you be perturbed when you hear of wars and insurrections. These things are bound to happen first, but the end does not follow immediately."

He said to them further: "Nation will rise against nation and kingdom against kingdom. There will be great earthquakes, plagues and famines in various places—and in the sky fearful omens and great signs. But before any of this, they will manhandle and persecute you, sum-moning you to synagogues and prisons, bring-ing you to trial before kings and governors, all because of my name. You will be brought to give witness on account of it. I bid you resolve not to worry about your defense beforehand, for I will give you words and a wisdom which none of your adversaries can take exception to or contradict. You will be delivered up even by your parents, brothers, relatives and friends, and some of you will be put to death. All will hate you because of me, yet not a hair of your head will be harmed. By patient endurance you will save your lives."

This is the gospel of the Lord.

---

161   **THIRTY-FOURTH OR LAST**   **A**
      SUNDAY OF THE YEAR
      CHRIST THE KING

READING I   Ez 34, 11-12. 15-17

A reading from the book of the prophet Ezekiel

You, my flock, I judge between sheep and sheep, between rams and he-goats.

Thus says the Lord God: I myself will look after and tend my sheep. As a shepherd tends his flock when he finds himself among his scat-tered sheep, so will I tend my sheep. I will res-cue them from every place where they were scattered when it was cloudy and dark. I my-self will pasture my sheep; I myself will give them rest, says the Lord God. The lost I will seek out, the strayed I will bring back, the in-jured I will bind up, the sick I will heal [but the sleek and the strong I will destroy], shepherd-ing them rightly.

As for you, my sheep, says the Lord God, I will judge between one sheep and another, between rams and goats.
This is the Word of the Lord

Responsorial Psalm   Ps 23, 1-2. 2-3. 5-6

℞. (1) The Lord is my shepherd;
there is nothing I shall want.
The Lord is my shepherd; I shall not want.
In verdant pastures he gives me repose.
℞. The Lord is my shepherd;
there is nothing I shall want.
Beside restful waters he leads me;
he refreshes my soul.
He guides me in right paths
for his name's sake.
℞. The Lord is my shepherd;
there is nothing I shall want.
You spread the table before me
in the sight of my foes;
You anoint my head with oil;
my cup overflows.
Only goodness and kindness follow me
all the days of my life;
And I shall dwell in the house of the Lord
for years to come.
℞. The Lord is my shepherd;
there is nothing I shall want.

READING II   1 Cor 15, 20-26. 28

A reading from the first letter of Paul to the Corinthians
He will hand over the kingdom to God the Father, so that God may be all in all.

Christ has been raised from the dead, the first fruits of those who have fallen asleep. Death came through a man; hence the resurrection of the dead comes through a man also. Just as in Adam all die, so in Christ all will come to life again, but each one in proper order: Christ the first-fruits and then, at his coming, all those who belong to him. After that will come the end, when, after having destroyed every sovereignty, authority, and power, he will hand over the kingdom to God the Father. Christ must reign until God has put all enemies under his feet, and the last enemy to be destroyed is death. When, finally, all has been subjected to the Son,

he will then subject himself to the One who made all things subject to him, so that God may be all in all.
This is the Word of the Lord.

GOSPEL   Mt 25, 31-46
Alleluia   Mk 11, 10

℞. Alleluia. **Blessed is he who inherits the kingdom of David our father;**
blessed is he who comes in the name of the Lord. ℞. Alleluia.

✠ **A reading from the holy gospel according to Matthew**
He will sit upon his seat of glory and he will separate men one from another.

Jesus said to his disciples: "When the Son of Man comes in his glory, escorted by all the angels of heaven, he will sit upon his royal throne, and all the nations will be assembled before him. Then he will separate them into two groups, as a shepherd separates sheep from goats. The sheep he will place on his right hand, the goats on his left. The king will say to those on his right: 'Come. You have my Father's blessing! Inherit the kingdom prepared for you from the creation of the world. For I was hungry and you gave me food, I was thirsty and you gave me drink. I was a stranger and you welcomed me, naked and you clothed me. I was ill and you comforted me, in prison and you came to visit me.' Then the just will ask him: 'Lord, when did we see you hungry and feed you or see you thirsty and give you drink? When did we welcome you away from home or clothe you in your nakedness? When did we visit you when you were ill or in prison?' The king will answer them: 'I assure you, as often as you did it for one of my least brothers, you did it for me.'
"Then he will say to those on his left: 'Out of my sight, you condemned, into that everlasting fire prepared for the devil and his angels! I was hungry and you gave me no food, I was thirsty and you gave me no drink. I was away from home and you gave me no welcome, naked and you gave me no clothing. I was ill

and in prison and you did not come to comfort me.' Then they in turn will ask: 'Lord, when did we see you hungry or thirsty or away from home or naked or ill or in prison and not attend you in your needs?' He will answer them: 'I assure you, as often as you neglected to do it to one of these least ones, you neglected to do it to me.' These will go off to eternal punishment and the just to eternal life."

This is the gospel of the Lord.

---

162   **THIRTY-FOURTH OR LAST**   **B**

SUNDAY OF THE YEAR

CHRIST THE KING

READING I   Dn 7, 13-14

A reading from the book of the prophet Daniel

His sovereignty is eternal.

As the visions during the night continued, I saw
One like a son of man coming,
    on the clouds of heaven;
When he reached the Ancient One
    and was presented before him,
He received dominion, glory, and kingship;
nations and peoples of every language serve him.
His dominion is an everlasting dominion
    that shall not be taken away,
    his kingship shall not be destroyed.

       This is the Word of the Lord.

Responsorial Psalm   Ps 93, 1. 1-2. 5

℟. (1) The Lord is king;
    he is robed in majesty.
The Lord is king, in splendor robed;
    robed is the Lord and girt about with strength.
℟. The Lord is king;
    he is robed in majesty.
And he has made the world firm,
    not to be moved.
Your throne stands firm from of old;
    from everlasting you are, O Lord.
℟. The Lord is king;
    he is robed in majesty.

Your decrees are worthy of trust indeed;
    holiness befits your house,
    O Lord, for length of days.
℟. The Lord is king;
    he is robed in majesty.

READING II   Rv 1, 5-8

A reading from the book of Revelation

The ruler of the kings of the earth . . . made us a line of kings, priests to serve his God.

Jesus Christ is the faithful witness, the first-born from the dead and ruler of the kings of earth. To him who loves us and freed us from our sins by his own blood, who has made us a royal nation of priests in the service of his God and Father—to him be glory and power forever and ever! Amen.
See, he comes amid the clouds!
    Every eye shall see him,
    even of those who pierced him.
All the peoples of the earth
    shall lament him bitterly.
    So it is to be! Amen!
The Lord God says, "I am the Alpha and the Omega, the One who is and who was and who is to come, the Almighty!"

       This is the Word of the Lord.

GOSPEL   Jn 18, 33-37

Alleluia   Mk 11, 10

℟. Alleluia. Blessed is he who inherits the kingdom of David our father;
blessed is he who comes in the name of the Lord. ℟. Alleluia.

✠ **A reading from the holy gospel according to John**

You say that I am a king.

Pilate said to Jesus: "Are you the king of the Jews?" Jesus answered, "Are you saying this on your own, or have others been telling you about me?" "I am no Jew!" Pilate retorted. "It is your own people and the chief priests who have handed you over to me. What have you done?" Jesus answered:

"My kingdom does not belong to this world.
If my kingdom were of this world,

my subjects would be fighting
  to save me from being handed over to the
    Jews.
  As it is, my kingdom is not here."
At this Pilate said to him, "So, then, you are a
king?" Jesus replied:
  "It is you who say I am a king.
  The reason I was born,
    the reason why I came into the world,
  is to testify to the truth.
  Anyone committed to the truth hears my
    voice."
    This is the gospel of the Lord.

---

163   **THIRTY-FOURTH OR LAST**   **C**
          SUNDAY OF THE YEAR
          CHRIST THE KING
READING I   2 Sm 5, 1-3
A reading from the second book of Samuel
      They anointed David king of Israel.
All the tribes of Israel came to David in Hebron and said: "Here we are, your bone and
your flesh. In days past, when Saul was our
king, it was you who led the Israelites out and
brought them back. And the Lord said to you,
'You shall shepherd my people Israel and shall
be commander of Israel.'" When all the elders
of Israel came to David in Hebron, King David
made an agreement with them there before the
Lord, and they anointed him king of Israel.
      This is the Word of the Lord.

Responsorial Psalm   Ps 122, 1-2. 3-4. 4-5

℟. (1) I rejoiced when I heard them say:
  let us go to the house of the Lord.
I rejoiced because they said to me,
  "We will go up to the house of the Lord."
And now we have set foot
  within your gates, O Jerusalem.
℟. I rejoiced when I heard them say:
  let us go to the house of the Lord.
Jerusalem, built as a city
  with compact unity.
To it the tribes go up,
  the tribes of the Lord.
℟. I rejoiced when I heard them say:
  let us go to the house of the Lord.

According to the decree for Israel,
  to give thanks to the name of the Lord.
In it are set up judgment seats,
  seats for the house of David.
℟. I rejoiced when I heard them say:
  let us go to the house of the Lord.

READING II   Col 1, 12-20
**A reading from the letter of Paul to the
              Colossians**
      He has taken us into the kingdom of his beloved Son.
**Give thanks to the Father for having made you
worthy to share the lot of the saints in light. He
rescued us from the power of darkness and
brought us into the kingdom of his beloved
Son. Through him we have redemption, the forgiveness of our sins.**
    **He is the image of the invisible God, the first-
born of all creatures. In him everything in
heaven and on earth was created, things visible
and invisible, whether thrones or dominations,
principalities or powers; all were created
through him, and for him. He is before all
else that is. In him everything continues in
being. It is he who is head of the body, the
church; he who is the beginning, the first-born
of the dead, so that primacy may be his in
everything. It pleased God to make absolute
fullness reside in him and, by means of him, to
reconcile everything in his person, everything,
I say, both on earth and in the heavens, making
peace through the blood of his cross.**
      This is the Word of the Lord.

GOSPEL   Lk 23, 35-43
Alleluia   Mk 11, 10
℟. Alleluia. **Blessed is he who inherits the
  kingdom of David our father;**
blessed is he who comes in the name of the
  Lord. ℟. Alleluia.

✠ **A reading from the holy gospel according
              to Luke**
      Lord, remember me when you come into your kingdom.
**The people stood there watching, and the lead-
ers kept jeering at Jesus, saying, "He saved**

others; let him save himself if he is the Messiah of God, the chosen one." The soldiers also made fun of him, coming forward to offer him their sour wine and saying, "If you are the king of the Jews, save yourself." There was an inscription over his head:

"THIS IS THE KING OF THE JEWS."
One of the criminals hanging in crucifixion blasphemed him, "Aren't you the Messiah? Then save yourself and us." But the other one rebuked him: "Have you no fear of God, seeing you are under the same sentence? We deserve it, after all. We are only paying the price for what we've done, but this man has done nothing wrong." He then said, "Jesus, remember me when you enter upon your reign." And Jesus replied, "I assure you: this day you will be with me in paradise."

This is the gospel of the Lord.

164 ALLELUIA

FOR SUNDAYS OF THE YEAR

1   1 Sm 3, 9; Jn 6, 69

℞. Alleluia. **Speak, O Lord, your servant is listening;**
you have the words of everlasting life. ℞. Alleluia.

2   Mt 11, 25

℞. Alleluia. **Blessed are you, Father, Lord of heaven and earth;**
you have revealed to little ones the mysteries of the kingdom. ℞. Alleluia.

3   Lk 19, 38

℞. Alleluia. **Blessed is the king who comes in the name of the Lord:**
peace on earth, and glory in heaven! ℞. Alleluia.

4   Jn 1, 14. 12

℞. Alleluia. **The Word of God became a man and lived among us.**
He enabled those who accepted him to become the children of God. ℞. Alleluia.

5   Jn 6, 64. 69

℞. Alleluia. **Your words, O Lord, are spirit and life,**
you have the words of everlasting life. ℞. Alleluia.

6   Jn 8, 12

℞. Alleluia. **I am the light of the world, says the Lord;**
the man who follows me will have the light of life. ℞. Alleluia.

7   Jn 10, 27

℞. Alleluia. **My sheep listen to my voice, says the Lord;**
I know them, and they follow me. ℞. Alleluia.

8   Jn 14, 5

℞. Alleluia. **I am the way, the truth, and the life, says the Lord;**
no one comes to the Father, except through me. ℞. Alleluia.

9   Jn 14, 23

℞. Alleluia. **If anyone loves me, he will hold to my words,**
and my Father will love him, and we will come to him. ℞. Alleluia.

10   Jn 15, 15

℞. Alleluia. **I call you my friends, says the Lord,**
for I have made known to you all that the Father has told me. ℞. Alleluia.

11   Jn 17, 17

℞. Alleluia. **Your word, O Lord. is truth;**
make us holy in the truth. ℞. Alleluia.

12   See Acts 16, 14

℞. Alleluia. **Open our hearts, O Lord,**
to listen to the words of your Son. ℞. Alleluia.

13   See Eph 1, 17-18

℞. Alleluia. **May the Father of our Lord Jesus Christ enlighten the eyes of our hearts**
that we might see how great is the hope to which we are called. ℞. Alleluia.

FOR THE LAST SUNDAYS

14   Mt 24, 42. 44

℞. Alleluia. **Be watchful and ready:**
you know not when the Son of Man is coming. ℞. Alleluia.

15   Lk 21, 36

℞. Alleluia. **Be watchful, pray constantly, that you may be worthy to stand before the Son of Man.** ℞. Alleluia.

16   Rv 2, 10

℞. Alleluia. **Be faithful until death, says the Lord,**
and I will give you the crown of life. ℞. Alleluia.

See also No. 509.

SOLEMNITIES OF THE LORD DURING THE
SEASON OF THE YEAR

165 SUNDAY AFTER PENTECOST Ⓐ
TRINITY SUNDAY

READING I
Ex 34, 4-6. 8-9

A reading from the book of Exodus
The Lord God, ruler of all, merciful and loving.

Early in the morning Moses went up Mount Sinai as the Lord had commanded him, taking along the two stone tablets.

Having come down in a cloud, the Lord stood with him there and proclaimed his name, "Lord." Thus the Lord passed before him and cried out, "The Lord, the Lord, a merciful and gracious God, slow to anger and rich in kindness and fidelity." Moses at once bowed down to the ground in worship. Then he said, "If I find favor with you, O Lord, do come along in our company. This is indeed a stiff-necked people; yet pardon our wickedness and sins, and receive us as your own."
    This is the Word of the Lord.

Responsorial Psalm   Dn 3, 52. 53. 54. 55. 56

℟. (52) Glory and praise for ever!

Blessed are you, O Lord, the God of our fathers,
    praiseworthy and exalted above all forever;
And blessed is your holy and glorious name,
    praiseworthy and exalted above all for all
    ages.
℟. Glory and praise for ever!

Blessed are you in the temple of your holy
    glory,
praiseworthy and glorious above all forever.
℟. Glory and praise for ever!

Blessed are you on the throne of your kingdom,
    praiseworthy and exalted above all forever.

℟. Glory and praise for ever!
Blessed are you who look into the depths
    from your throne upon the cherubim,
    praiseworthy and exalted above all forever.
℟. Glory and praise for ever!
Blessed are you in the firmament of heaven,
    praiseworthy and glorious forever.
℟. Glory and praise for ever!

READING II
2 Cor 13, 11-13

**A reading from the second letter of Paul to the
Corinthians**
The grace of our Lord Jesus Christ and the love of God
and the fellowship of the Holy Spirit be with you all.

Brothers, mend your ways. Encourage one another. Live in harmony and peace, and the God of love and peace will be with you. Greet one another with a holy kiss. All the holy ones send greetings to you. The grace of the Lord Jesus Christ, and the love of God, and the fellowship of the Holy Spirit be with you all!
    This is the Word of the Lord.

GOSPEL
Jn 3, 16-18

Alleluia   See Rv 1, 8

℟. Alleluia. **Glory to the Father, the Son and
    the Holy Spirit:**
to God who is, who was, and who is to come.
℟. Alleluia.

✠ **A reading from the holy gospel according
    to John**
God sent his Son to save the world through him.

Jesus said to Nicodemus:
    "Yes, God so loved the world
        that he gave his only Son,
        that whoever believes in him may not die
        but may have eternal life.
    God did not send the Son into the world
        to condemn the world,

but that the world might be saved through him.

Whoever believes in him avoids condemnation,

but whoever does not believe is already condemned

for not believing in the name of God's only Son."

This is the gospel of the Lord.

---

166 SUNDAY AFTER PENTECOST **B**
TRINITY SUNDAY

READING I Dt 4, 32-34. 39-40

A reading from the book of Deuteronomy

The Lord himself is God in heaven above and on earth below: there is no other.

Moses said to the people: "Ask now of the days of old, before your time, ever since God created man upon the earth; ask from one end of the sky to the other: Did anything so great ever happen before? Was it ever heard of? Did a people ever hear the voice of God speaking from the midst of fire, as you did, and live? Or did any god venture to go and take a nation for himself from the midst of another nation, by testings, by signs and wonders, by war, with his strong hand and outstretched arm, and by great terrors, all of which the Lord, your God, did for you in Egypt before your very eyes? This is why you must now know, and fix in your heart, that the Lord is God in the heavens above and on earth below, and that there is no other. You must keep his statutes and commandments which I enjoin on you today, that you and your children after you may prosper, and that you may have long life on the land which the Lord, your God, is giving you forever."

This is the Word of the Lord.

Responsorial Psalm Ps 33, 4-5. 6. 9. 18-19. 20. 22

℟. (12) Happy the people the Lord has chosen to be his own.

Upright is the word of the Lord,
and all his works are trustworthy.
He loves justice and right;
of the kindness of the Lord the earth is full.

℟. Happy the people the Lord has chosen to be his own.

By the word of the Lord the heavens were made;
by the breath of his mouth all their host.
For he spoke, and it was made;
he commanded, and it stood forth.

℟. Happy the people the Lord has chosen to be his own.

See, the eyes of the Lord are upon those who fear him,
upon those who hope for his kindness,
To deliver them from death
and preserve them in spite of famine.

℟. Happy the people the Lord has chosen to be his own.

Our soul waits for the Lord,
who is our help and our shield.
May your kindness, O Lord, be upon us
who have put our hope in you.

℟. Happy the people the Lord has chosen to be his own.

READING II Rom 8, 14-17

A reading from the letter of Paul to the Romans

You have received the Spirit that makes you God's own children, and in that Spirit we call God: Father, our Father!

All who are led by the Spirit of God are sons of God. You did not receive a spirit of slavery leading you back into fear, but a spirit of adoption through which we cry out, "Abba!" (that is, "Father"). The Spirit himself gives witness with our spirit that we are children of God. But if we are children, we are heirs as well: heirs of God, heirs with Christ, if only we suffer with him so as to be glorified with him.

This is the Word of the Lord.

GOSPEL   Mt 28, 16-20
Alleluia   See Rv 1, 8

℟. Alleluia. **Glory to the Father, the Son and
the Holy Spirit:**
to God who is, who was, and who is to come.
℟. Alleluia.

✠ **A reading from the holy gospel according
to Matthew**
Baptize them in the name of the Father, and of the Son, and
of the Holy Spirit.

**The eleven disciples made their way to Gali-
lee, to the mountain to which Jesus had summoned them. At the sight of him, those who
had entertained doubts fell down in homage.
Jesus came forward and addressed them in
these words:**
   **"Full authority has been given to me
   both in heaven and on earth;
   go, therefore, and make disciples of all the
      nations.
   Baptize them in the name
   'of the Father
   and of the Son,
   and of the Holy Spirit.'
   Teach them to carry out everything I have
      commanded you.
   And know that I am with you always, un-
      til the end of the world!"**
This is the gospel of the Lord.

---

167   SUNDAY AFTER PENTECOST   C
TRINITY SUNDAY

READING I   Prv 8, 22-31
   A reading from the book of Proverbs
   Wisdom was born before the earth was made.

Thus says the Wisdom of God:
**"The Lord begot me, the first-born of his ways,
   the forerunner of his prodigies of long ago;
From of old I was poured forth,
   at the first, before the earth.
When there were no depths I was brought
      forth,
   when there were no fountains or springs of
      water;**

**Before the mountains were settled into place,
   before the hills, I was brought forth;
While as yet the earth and the fields were not
      made,
   nor the first clods of the world.
"When he established the heavens I was there,
   when he marked out the vault over the face
      of the deep;
When he made firm the skies above,
   when he fixed fast the foundations of the
      earth;
When he set for the sea its limit,
   so that the waters should not transgress his
      command;
Then was I beside him as his craftsman,
   and I was his delight day by day,
Playing before him all the while,
   playing on the surface of his earth;
   and I found delight in the sons of men."**
   This is the Word of the Lord.

Responsorial Psalm   Ps 8, 4-5. 6-7. 8-9

℟. (2) O Lord, our God,
   how wonderful your name in all the earth!
**When I behold your heavens, the work of your
      fingers,
   the moon and the stars which you set in
      place—
What is man that you should be mindful of
      him,
   or the son of man that you should care for
      him?**
℟. O Lord, our God,
   how wonderful your name in all the earth!
**You have made him little less than the angels,
   and crowned him with glory and honor.
You have given him rule over the works of
      your hands,
   putting all things under his feet:**
℟. O Lord, our God,
   how wonderful your name in all the earth!
**All sheep and oxen,
   yes, and the beasts of the field,
The birds of the air, the fishes of the sea,
   and whatever swims the paths of the seas.**
℟. O Lord, our God,
   how wonderful your name in all the earth!

READING II   Rom 5, 1-5

A reading from the letter of Paul to the Romans

To God through Christ in the love which is poured out
through the Spirit.

Now that we have been justified by faith, we
are at peace with God through our Lord Jesus
Christ. Through him we have gained access by
faith to the grace in which we now stand, and
we boast of our hope for the glory of God. But
not only that—we even boast of our afflictions!
We know that affliction makes for endurance,
and endurance for tested virtue, and tested virtue for hope. And this hope will not leave us
disappointed, because the love of God has been
poured out in our hearts through the Holy
Spirit who has been given to us.
        This is the Word of the Lord.

GOSPEL   Jn 16, 12-15

Alleluia   See Rv 1, 8

℟. Alleluia. **Glory to the Father, the Son and
the Holy Spirit:
to God who is, who was, and who is to come.**
    ℟. Alleluia.

✠ **A reading from the holy gospel according
to John**

Whatever the Father has is mine. The Spirit will receive
what I give and tell you about it.

Jesus said to his disciples:
    "I have much more to tell you,
    but you cannot bear it now.
    When he comes, however,
    being the Spirit of truth
    he will guide you to all truth.
    He will not speak on his own,
    but will speak only what he hears,
    and will announce to you the things to
        come.
    In doing this he will give glory to me,
    because he will have received from me
    what he will announce to you.
    All that the Father has belongs to me.
    That is why I said that what he will an-
        nounce to you
    he will have from me."
        This is the gospel of the Lord.

168   **THURSDAY**   **A**
        AFTER TRINITY SUNDAY
            CORPUS CHRISTI

READING I   Dt 8, 2-3. 14-16

A reading from the book of Deuteronomy

He gave you food which you and your fathers did not know.

Moses said to the people: "Remember how for
forty years now the Lord, your God, has directed all your journeying in the desert, so as to
test you by affliction and find out whether or
not it was your intention to keep his commandments. He therefore let you be afflicted
with hunger, and then fed you with manna, a
food unknown to you and your fathers, in order to show you that not by bread alone does
man live, but by every word that comes forth
from the mouth of the Lord.

    "Remember, the Lord, your God, who brought
you out of the land of Egypt, that place of
slavery; who guided you through the vast and
terrible desert with its saraph serpents and
scorpions, its parched and waterless ground;
who brought forth water for you from the
flinty rock and fed you in the desert with
manna, a food unknown to your fathers."
        This is the Word of the Lord.

Responsorial Psalm   Ps 147, 12-13. 14-15. 19-20

℟. (12) Praise the Lord, Jerusalem.
**Glorify the Lord, O Jerusalem;
    praise your God, O Zion.
For he has strengthened the bars of your gates;
    he has blessed your children within you.**
    ℟. Praise the Lord, Jerusalem.
**He has granted peace in your borders;
    with the best of wheat he fills you.
He sends forth his command to the earth;
    swiftly runs his word!**
    ℟. Praise the Lord, Jerusalem.
**He has proclaimed his word to Jacob,
    his statutes and his ordinances to Israel.
He has not done thus for any other nation;
    his ordinances he has not made known to
        them. Alleluia.**
    ℟. Praise the Lord, Jerusalem.
    ℟. Or: Alleluia.

READING II   1 Cor 10, 16-17
A reading from the first letter of Paul to the Corinthians

Though we are, many, we form a single body because we share this one loaf.

Is not the cup of blessing we bless a sharing in the blood of Christ? And is not the bread we break a sharing in the body of Christ? Because the loaf of bread is one, we, many though we are, are one body for we all partake of the one loaf.

This is the Word of the Lord

The following sequence, Lauda, Sion is optional before the Alleluia verse.

Sequence   (Prose Text)

Zion, praise your Savior. Praise your leader and shepherd in hymns and canticles. Praise him as much as you can, for he is beyond all praising and you will never be able to praise him as he merits.

But today a theme worthy of particular praise is put before us—the living and life-giving bread that, without any doubt, was given to the Twelve at table during the holy supper.

Therefore let our praise be full and resounding and our soul's rejoicing full of delight and beauty, for this is the festival day to commemorate the first institution of this table.

At this table of the new King, the new law's new Pasch puts an end to the old Pasch. The new displaces the old, reality the shadow and light the darkness. Christ wanted what he did at the supper to be repeated in his memory.

And so we, in accordance with his holy directions, consecrate bread and wine to be salvation's Victim. Christ's followers know by faith that bread is changed into his flesh and wine into his blood.

Man cannot understand this, cannot perceive it; but a lively faith affirms that the change, which is outside the natural course of things, takes place. Under the different species, which are now signs only and not their own reality, there lie hid wonderful realities. His body is our food, his blood our drink.

And yet Christ remains entire under each species. The communicant receives the complete Christ—uncut, unbroken and undivided. Whether one receive or a thousand, the one receives as much as the thousand. Nor is Christ diminished by being received.

The good and the wicked alike receive him, but with the unlike destiny of life or death. To the wicked it is death, but life to the good. See how different is the result, though each receives the same.

Last of all, if the sacrament is broken, have no doubt. Remember there is as much in a fragment as in an unbroken host. There is no division of the reality, but only a breaking of the sign; nor does the breaking diminish the condition or size of the One hidden under the sign.

Behold, the bread of angels is become the pilgrim's food; truly it is bread for the sons, and is not to be cast to dogs. It was prefigured in type when Isaac was brought as an offering, when a lamb was appointed for the Pasch and when manna was given to the Jews of old.

Jesus, good shepherd and true bread, have mercy on us; feed us and guard us. Grant that we find happiness in the land of the living. You know all things, can do all things, and feed us here on earth. Make us your guests in heaven, co-heirs with you and companions of heaven's citizens. Amen. Alleluia.

OR
(Poetic Text)

Laud, O Zion, your salvation,
Laud with hymns of exultation,
   Christ, your king and shepherd true:

Bring him all the praise you know,
He is more than you bestow,
   Never can you reach his due.

Special theme for glad thanksgiving
Is the quick'ning and the living
   Bread today before you set:

From his hands of old partaken,
As we know, by faith unshaken,
   Where the Twelve at supper met.

Full and clear ring out your chanting,
Joy nor sweetest grace be wanting,
   From your heart let praises burst:

For today the feast is holden,
When the institution olden
   Of that supper was rehearsed.

Here the new law's new oblation,
By the new king's revelation,
   Ends the form of ancient rite:

Now the new the old effaces,
Truth away the shadow chasees,
   Light dispels the gloom of night.

What he did at supper seated,
Christ ordained to be repeated,
   His memorial ne'er to cease:

And his rule for guidance taking,
Bread and wine we hallow, making
   Thus our sacrifice of peace.

This the truth each Christian learns,
Bread into his flesh he turns,
   To his precious blood the wine:

Sight has fail'd, nor thought conceives,
But a dauntless faith believes,
   Resting on a pow'r divine.

Here beneath these signs are hidden
Priceless things to sense forbidden;
   Signs, not things are all we see:

Blood is poured and flesh is broken.
Yet in either wondrous token
   Christ entire we know to be.

Whoso of this food partakes,
Does not rend the Lord nor breaks;
   Christ is whole to all that taste:

Thousands are, as one, receivers,
One, as thousands of believers,
   Eats of him who cannot waste.

Bad and good the feast are sharing,
Of what divers dooms preparing,
   Endless death, or endless life.

Life to these, to those damnation,
See how like participation
   Is with unlike issues rife.

When the sacrament is broken,
Doubt not, but believe 'tis spoken,
   That each sever'd outward token
     doth the very whole contain.

Nought the precious gift divides,
Breaking but the sign betides
   Jesus still the same abides,
     still unbroken does remain.

Lo! the angel's food is given
To the pilgrim who has striven;
   See the children's bread from heaven,
     which on dogs may not be spent.

Truth the ancient types fulfilling,
Isaac bound, a victim willing,
   Paschal lamb, its life blood spilling,
     manna to the fathers sent.

Very bread, good shepherd, tend us,
Jesu, of your love befriend us,
   You refresh us, you defend us,
     Your eternal goodness send us
In the land of life to see.

You who all things can and know,
Who on earth such food bestows,
   Grant us with your saints, though lowest,
   Where the heav'nly feast you show,
Fellow heirs and guests to be. Amen. Alleluia.

GOSPEL   Jn 6, 51-58
Alleluia   Jn 6, 51-52

℟. Alleluia. I am the living bread from heaven,
   says the Lord;
if anyone eats this bread he will live for ever.
   ℟. Alleluia.

✠ **A reading from the holy gospel according
to John**

My flesh is real food and my blood is real drink.

Jesus said to the crowds of Jews:
   "I myself am the living bread
   come down from heaven.
   If anyone eats this bread
   he shall live forever;
   the bread I will give
   is my flesh, for the life of the world."
At this the Jews quarreled among themselves, saying, "How can he give us his flesh to eat?" Thereupon Jesus said to them:
   "Let me solemnly assure you,
   if you do not eat the flesh of the Son of
     Man
   and drink his blood,

you have no life in you.
He who feeds on my flesh
and drinks my blood
has life eternal,
and I will raise him up on the last day.
For my flesh is real food
and my blood real drink.
The man who feeds on my flesh
and drinks my blood
remains in me, and I in him.
Just as the Father who has life sent me
and I have life because of the Father,
so the man who feeds on me
will have life because of me.
This is the bread that came down from
    heaven.
Unlike your ancestors who ate and died
    nonetheless,
the man who feeds on this bread shall live
    forever."
    This is the gospel of the Lord.

---

169   **THURSDAY**   **B**
       AFTER TRINITY SUNDAY
           CORPUS CHRISTI

READING I   Ex 24, 3-8

A reading from the book of Exodus
This is the blood of the covenant that the Lord has made
                     with you.

When Moses came to the people and related all
the words and ordinances of the Lord, they all
answered with one voice, "We will do everything that the Lord has told us." Moses then
wrote down all the words of the Lord and, rising
early the next day, he erected at the foot of the
mountain an altar and twelve pillars for the
twelve tribes of Israel. Then, having sent certain young men of the Israelites to offer holocausts and sacrifice young bulls as peace offerings to the Lord, Moses took half of the blood
and put it in large bowls; the other half
he splashed on the altar. Taking the book of the
covenant, he read it aloud to the people, who
answered, "All that the Lord has said, we will
heed and do." Then he took the blood and

sprinkled it on the people, saying, "This is the
blood of the covenant which the Lord has made
with you in accordance with all these words of
his."
    This is the Word of the Lord.

Responsorial Psalm   Ps 116, 12-13. 15-16. 17-18

℟. (13) I will take the cup of salvation,
    and call on the name of the Lord.
How shall I make a return to the Lord
    for all the good he has done for me?
The cup of salvation I will take up,
    and I will call upon the name of the Lord.
℟. I will take the cup of salvation,
    and call on the name of the Lord.
Precious in the eyes of the Lord
    is the death of his faithful ones.
I am your servant, the son of your handmaid;
    you have loosed my bonds.
℟. I will take the cup of salvation,
    and call on the name of the Lord.
To you will I offer sacrifice of thanksgiving,
    and I will call upon the name of the Lord.
My vows to the Lord I will pay
    in the presence of all his people.
℟. I will take the cup of salvation,
    and call on the name of the Lord
℟. Or: Alleluia.

READING II   Heb 9, 11-15

A reading from the letter of Paul to the
                  Hebrews
The blood of Christ will purify our inner selves.

When Christ came as high priest of the good
things which came to be, he entered once for all
into the sanctuary, passing through the greater
and more perfect tabernacle not made by hands,
that is, not belonging to this creation. He entered not with the blood of goats and calves but
with his own blood, and achieved eternal redemption. For if the blood of goats and bulls
and the sprinkling of a heifer's ashes can
sanctify those who are defiled so that their
flesh is cleansed, how much more will the
blood of Christ, who through the eternal spirit
offered himself up unblemished to God, cleanse

our consciences from dead works to worship the living God!

This is why he is mediator of a new covenant: since his death has taken place for deliverance from transgressions committed under the first covenant, those who are called may receive the promised eternal inheritance.
This is the Word of the Lord.

The sequence, Lauda, Sion, pp. 265-266, is optional before the Alleluia verse.

GOSPEL   Mk 14, 12-16. 22-26
Alleluia   Jn 6, 51-52

℟. Alleluia. **I am the living bread from heaven, says the Lord;**
if anyone eats this bread he will live forever.
℟. Alleluia.

✠ A reading from the holy gospel according to Mark
This is my body. This is my blood.

On the first day of Unleavened Bread, when it was customary to sacrifice the paschal lamb, the disciples said to Jesus, "Where do you wish us to go to prepare the Passover supper for you?" He sent two of his disciples with these instructions: "Go into the city and you will come upon a man carrying a water jar. Follow him. Whatever house he enters, say to the owner, 'The Teacher asks, Where is my guestroom where I may eat the Passover with my disciples?' Then he will show you an uptairs room, spacious, furnished, and all in order. That is the place you are to get ready for us." The disciples went off. When they reached the city they found it just as he had told them, and they prepared the Passover supper.

During the meal he took bread, blessed and broke it, and gave it to them. "Take this," he said, "this is my body." He likewise took a cup, gave thanks and passed it to them, and they all drank from it. He said to them: "This is my blood, the blood of the covenant, to be poured out on behalf of many. I solemnly assure you, I will never again drink of the fruit of the vine until the day when I drink it new in the reign of God."

After singing songs of praise they walked out to the Mount of Olives.
This is the gospel of the Lord.

---

170   **THURSDAY**   **C**
AFTER TRINITY SUNDAY
CORPUS CHRISTI

READING I   Gn 14, 18-20
A reading from the book of Genesis
Melchizedek brought bread and wine.

Melchizedek, king of Salem, brought out bread and wine, and being a priest of God Most High, he blessed Abram with these words:
"Blessed be Abram by God Most High,
   the creator of heaven and earth;
And blessed be God Most High,
   who delivered your foes into your hand."
This is the Word of the Lord.

Responsorial Psalm   Ps 110, 1. 2. 3. 4

℟. (4) You are a priest for ever,
   in the line of Melchizedek.
The Lord said to my Lord: "Sit at my right hand
   till I make your enemies your footstool."
℟. You are a priest for ever,
   in the line of Melchizedek.
The scepter of your power the Lord will stretch forth from Zion:
   "Rule in the midst of your enemies."
℟. You are a priest for ever,
   in the line of Melchizedek.
"Yours is princely power in the day of your birth, in holy splendor;
   before the daystar, like the dew, I have begotten you."
℟. You are a priest for ever,
   in the line of Melchizedek.
The Lord has sworn, and he will not repent:
   "You are a priest forever, according to the order of Melchizedek."
℟. You are a priest for ever,
   in the line of Melchizedek.

READING II   1 Cor 11, 23-26

A reading from the first letter of Paul to the Corinthians

Every time you eat this bread and drink this cup, you are proclaiming the death of the Lord.

I received from the Lord what I handed on to you, namely, that the Lord Jesus on the night in which he was betrayed took bread, and after he had given thanks, broke it and said, "This is my body, which is for you. Do this in remembrance of me." In the same way, after the supper, he took the cup, saying, "This cup is the new covenant in my blood. Do this, whenever you drink it, in remembrance of me." Every time, then, you eat this bread and drink this cup, you proclaim the death of the Lord until he comes!

This is the Word of the Lord.

The sequence, Lauda, Sion, pp. 265-266, is optional before the Alleluia verse.

GOSPEL   Lk 9, 11-17

Alleluia   John 6, 51-52

℞. Alleluia. **I am the living bread from heaven, says the Lord;**
if anyone eats this bread he will live for ever.
℞. Alleluia.

✠ **A reading from the holy gospel according to Luke**

They all ate and were filled.

Jesus spoke to the crowds of the reign of God, and he healed all who were in need of healing.

As sunset approached the Twelve came and said to him, "Dismiss the crowd so that they can go into the villages and farms in the neighborhood and find themselves lodging and food, for this is certainly an out-of-the-way place." He answered them, "Why do you not give them something to eat yourselves?" They replied, "We have nothing but five loaves and two fishes. Or shall we ourselves go and buy food for all these people?" (There were about five thousand men.) Jesus said to his disciples, "Have them sit down in groups of fifty or so." They followed his instructions and got them all seated. Then, taking the five loaves and the two fishes, Jesus raised his eyes to heaven,

pronounced a blessing over them, broke them, and gave them to his disciples for distribution to the crowd. They all ate until they had enough. What they had left, over and above, filled twelve baskets.

This is the gospel of the Lord.

171

A

FRIDAY OF THE SECOND SUNDAY AFTER PENTECOST SACRED HEART

READING I   Dt 7, 6-11

A reading from the book of Deuteronomy

The Lord loves you and has chosen you.

Moses said to the people: "You are a people sacred to the Lord, your God; he has chosen you from all the nations on the face of the earth to be a people peculiarly his own. It was not because you are the largest of all nations that the Lord set his heart on you and chose you, for you are really the smallest of all nations. It was because the Lord loved you and because of his fidelity to the oath he had sworn to your fathers, that he brought you out with his strong hand from the place of slavery, and ransomed you from the hand of Pharaoh, king of Egypt. Understand, then, that the Lord, your God, is God indeed, the faithful God who keeps his merciful covenant down to the thousandth generation toward those who love him and keep his commandments, but who repays with destruction the person who hates him; he does not dally with such a one, but makes him personally pay for it. You shall therefore carefully observe the commandments, the statutes and the decrees which I enjoin on you today."

This is the Word of the Lord.

Responsorial Psalm   Ps 103, 1-2. 3-4. 6-7. 8. 10

℞. (17) The Lord's kindness is everlasting to those who fear him.
Bless the Lord, O my soul;
and all my being, bless his holy name.
Bless the Lord, O my soul,
and forget not all his benefits.

℟. The Lord's kindness is everlasting
to those who fear him.
**He pardons all your iniquities,
he heals all your ills.
He redeems your life from destruction,
he crowns you with kindness and compassion.**
℟. The Lord's kindness is everlasting
to those who fear him.
**Merciful and gracious is the Lord,
slow to anger and abounding in kindness.
Not according to our sins does he deal with us,
nor does he requite us according to our crimes.**
℟. The Lord's kindness is everlasting
to those who fear him.

READING II   1 Jn 4, 7-16

A reading from the first letter of John
God loved us first.

**Beloved,
let us love one another
because love is of God;
everyone who loves is begotten of God
and has knowledge of God.
The man without love has known nothing of God,
for God is love.
God's love was revealed in our midst in this way:
he sent his only Son to the world
that we might have life through him.
Love, then, consists in this:
not that we have loved God,
but that he has loved us
and has sent his Son as an offering for our sins.
Beloved,
if God has loved us so,
we must have the same love for one another.
No one has ever seen God.
Yet if we love one another
God dwells in us,
and his love is brought to perfection in us.
The way we know we remain in him
and he in us
is that he has given us of his Spirit.
We have seen for ourselves, and can testify,**

**that the Father has sent the Son as savior
of the world.
When anyone acknowledges that Jesus is
the Son of God,
God dwells in him
and he in God.
We have come to know and to believe in
the love God has for us.
This is the Word of the Lord.**

GOSPEL   Mt 11, 25-30
Alleluia   Mt 11, 29

℟. Alleluia. **Take my yoke upon you;
learn from me, for I am gentle and lowly in
heart.** ℟. Alleluia.

✠ **A reading from the holy gospel according
to Matthew**
I am gentle and humble of heart.

**At that time Jesus said: "Father, Lord of
heaven and earth, to you I offer praise; for
what you have hidden from the learned and
the clever you have revealed to the merest
children. Father, it is true. You have graciously
willed it so. Everything has been given over to
me by my Father. No one knows the Son but
the Father, and no one knows the Father but
the Son—and anyone to whom the Son wishes
to reveal him.
"Come to me, all you who are weary and
find life burdensome, and I will refresh you.
Take my yoke upon your shoulders and learn
from me, for I am gentle and humble of heart.
Your souls will find rest, for my yoke is easy
and my burden light."
This is the gospel of the Lord.**

FRIDAY OF THE SECOND SUNDAY
AFTER PENTECOST
172   SACRED HEART   **B**

READING I   Hos 11, 1. 3-4. 8-9

A reading from the book of the prophet Hosea
Israel, how could I give you up? My heart turns against it.

**When Israel was a child I loved him,
out of Egypt I called my son.
Yet it was I who taught Ephraim to walk,**

who took them in my arms;
I drew them with human cords,
 with bands of love;
I fostered them like one
 who raises an infant to his cheeks;
Yet, though I stooped to feed my child,
 they did not know that I was their healer.

My heart is overwhelmed,
 my pity is stirred.
I will not give vent to my blazing anger,
 I will not destroy Ephraim again;
For I am God and not man,
 the Holy One present among you;
I will not let the flames consume you.
 This is the Word of the Lord.

Responsorial Psalm   Is 12, 2-3. 4. 5-6

℟. (3) You will draw water joyfully from the
 springs of salvation.
God indeed is my savior;
 I am confident and unafraid.
My strength and my courage is the Lord,
 and he has been my savior.
With joy you will draw water
 at the fountain of salvation.
℟. You will draw water joyfully from the
 springs of salvation.
Give thanks to the Lord, acclaim his name;
 among the nations make known his deeds,
 proclaim how exalted is his name.
℟. You will draw water joyfully from the
 springs of salvation.
Sing praise to the Lord for his glorious achieve-
 ment;
 let this be known throughout all the earth.
Shout with exultation, O city of Zion,
 for great in your midst
 is the Holy One of Israel!
℟. You will draw water joyfully from the
 springs of salvation.

READING II   Eph 3, 8-12. 14-19

A reading from the letter of Paul to the
Ephesians
To know the love of Christ is better than all knowledge

To me, the least of all believers, was given the
grace to preach to the Gentiles the unfathom-
able riches of Christ and to enlighten all men
on the mysterious design which for ages was
hidden in God, the Creator of all. Now, therefore, through the church, God's manifold wisdom is made known to the principalities and
powers of heaven, in accord with his age-old
purpose, carried out in Christ Jesus our Lord.
In Christ and through faith in him we can speak
freely to God, drawing near him with confidence.

That is why I kneel before the Father from
whom every family in heaven and on earth
takes its name; and I pray that he will bestow
on you gifts in keeping with the riches of his
glory. May he strengthen you inwardly
through the working of his Spirit. May Christ
dwell in your hearts through faith, and may
charity be the root and foundation of your
life. Thus you will be able to grasp fully, with
all the holy ones, the breadth and length and
height and depth of Christ's love, and experience this love which surpasses all knowledge,
so that you may attain to the fullness of God
himself.
 This is the Word of the Lord.

GOSPEL   Jn 19, 31-37
Alleluia   Mt 11, 29

℟. Alleluia. **Take my yoke upon you;**
for I am gentle and lowly in heart. ℟. Alleluia.

OR

Alleluia   1 Jn 4, 10
℟. Alleluia. **God first loved us**
 and sent his Son to take away our Sins. ℟. Alleluia.

✠ **A reading from the holy gospel according**
 to John
One of the soldiers pierced his side with a lance, and
immediately there came out blood and water.

Since it was the Preparation Day the Jews
did not want to have the bodies left on the
cross during the sabbath, for that sabbath was
a solemn feast day. They asked Pilate that
the legs be broken and the bodies be taken
away. Accordingly, the soldiers came and broke
the legs of the men crucified with Jesus, first
of the one, then of the other. When they came

to Jesus and saw that he was already dead, they did not break his legs. One of the soldiers thrust a lance into his side, and immediately blood and water flowed out. (This testimony has been given by an eyewitness, and his testimony is true. He tells what he knows is true, so that you may believe.) These events took place for the fulfillment of Scripture:

"Break none of his bones."

There is still another Scripture passage which says:

"They shall look on him whom they have pierced."

This is the gospel of the Lord.

FRIDAY OF THE SECOND SUNDAY
AFTER PENTECOST

173   SACRED HEART   C

READING I   Ez 34, 11-16

A reading from the book of the prophet Ezekiel
I will watch over my sheep and tend them.

Thus says the Lord God: I myself will look after and tend my sheep. As a shepherd tends his flock when he finds himself among his scattered sheep, so will I tend my sheep. I will rescue them from every place where they were scattered when it was cloudy and dark. I will lead them out from among the peoples and gather them from the foreign lands; I will bring them back to their own country and pasture them upon the mountains of Israel [in the land's ravines and all its inhabited places]. In good pastures will I pasture them, and on the mountain heights of Israel shall be their grazing ground. There they shall lie down on good grazing ground, and in rich pastures shall they be pastured on the mountains of Israel. I myself will pasture my sheep; I myself will give them rest, says the Lord God. The lost I will seek out, the strayed I will bring back, the injured I will bind up, the sick I will heal [but the sleek and the strong I will destroy], shepherding them rightly.

This is the Word of the Lord.

Responsorial Psalm   Ps 23, 1-3. 3-4. 5. 6

℟. (1) The Lord is my shepherd;
    there is nothing I shall want.

The Lord is my shepherd; I shall not want.
    In verdant pastures he gives me repose;
Beside restful waters he leads me;
    he refreshes my soul.

℟. The Lord is my shepherd;
    there is nothing I shall want.

He guides me in right paths
    for his name's sake.
Even though I walk in the dark valley
    I fear no evil; for you are at my side
With your rod and your staff
    that give me courage.

℟. The Lord is my shepherd;
    there is nothing I shall want.

You spread the table before me
    in the sight of my foes;
You anoint my head with oil;
    my cup overflows.

℟. The Lord is my shepherd;
    there is nothing I shall want.

Only goodness and kindness follow me
    all the days of my life;
And I shall dwell in the house of the Lord
    for years to come.

℟. The Lord is my shepherd;
    there is nothing I shall want.

READING II   Rom 5, 5-11

A reading from the letter of Paul to the Romans
God has entrusted his love to us.

The love of God has been poured out in our hearts through the Holy Spirit who has been given to us. At the appointed time, when we were still powerless, Christ died for us godless men. It is rare that anyone should lay down his life for a just man, though it is barely possible that for a good man someone may have the courage to die. It is precisely in this that God proves his love for us: that while we were still sinners, Christ died for us. Now that we have been justified by his blood, it is all the more certain that we shall be saved by him from God's wrath. For if, when we were God's enemies, we were reconciled to him by the death of his Son, it is all the more certain that we who have been reconciled will be saved by his life. Not only that; we go so far as to make God our boast through our Lord Jesus Christ, through whom we have now received reconciliation.

This is the Word of the Lord.

GOSPEL　　　　　　　　　　　　　**Lk 15, 3-7**
Alleluia　Mt 11, 29

℟. Alleluia. **Take my yoke upon you; learn from me, for I am gentle and lowly in heart.** ℟. Alleluia.

OR

Alleluia　1 Jn 4, 10

℟. Alleluia. **God first loved us and sent his Son to take away our sins.** ℟. Alleluia.

OR

Alleluia　Jn 10, 14

℟. Alleluia. **I am the good shepherd, says the Lord; I know my sheep, and mine know me.** ℟. Alleluia.

✠ **A reading from the holy gospel according to Luke**

Share my joy: I have found my lost sheep!

Jesus addressed this parable to the Pharisees and the scribes: "Who among you, if he has a hundred sheep and loses one of them, does not leave the ninety-nine in the wasteland and follow the lost one until he finds it? And when he finds it, he puts it on his shoulders in jubilation. Once arrived home, he invites friends and neighbors in and says to them, 'Rejoice with me because I have found my lost sheep.' I tell you, there will likewise be more joy in heaven over one repentant sinner than over ninety-nine righteous people who have no need to repent."

This is the gospel of the Lord.

COMMON TEXTS
FOR SUNG RESPONSORIAL PSALMS

The psalm is usually taken from the lectionary, since these texts are related to and depend upon the respective readings. At other times to make the people's response easier, texts of psalms and responses are selected for the several parts of the year or for the different kinds of celebrations for saints. These may be used in place of the text corresponding to the reading whenever the psalm is sung. (General Instruction, Roman Missal, no. 36.)

174 **RESPONSES**

Advent Season

Come, O Lord, and set us free.

Christmas Season

Lord, today we have seen your glory.

Lenten Season

Remember your love and your faithfulness, Lord.

Easter Season

Alleluia (two or three times)

Season of the Year

a) for use with a psalm of praise:

Praise the Lord for he is good.

OR

**We praise you, O Lord,
for all your works are wonderful.**

OR

Sing to the Lord a new song.

b) with a psalm of petition:

The Lord is near to all who call on him.

OR

Hear us, Lord, and save us.

OR

The Lord is kind and merciful.

175 **PSALMS**

Advent Season

Ps 25: 4-5. 8-9. 10. 14

℟. (1) To you, O Lord, I lift my soul.
Your ways, O Lord, make known to me;
  teach me your paths,
Guide me in your truth and teach me,
  for you are God my savior.
℟. To you, O Lord, I lift my soul.
Good and upright is the Lord;
  thus he shows sinners the way.
He guides the humble to justice,
  he teaches the humble his way.
℟. To you, O Lord, I lift my soul.
All the paths of the Lord are kindness and constancy
  toward those who keep his covenant and his decrees.
The friendship of the Lord is with those who fear him,
  and his covenant, for their instruction.
℟. To you, O Lord, I lift my soul.

Ps 85, 9-10. 11-12. 13-14

℟. (8) Lord, let us see your kindness.
I will hear what God proclaims;
  the Lord—for he proclaims peace to his people.
Near indeed is his salvation to those who fear him,
  glory dwelling in our land.
℟. Lord, let us see your kindness.
Kindness and truth shall meet;
  justice and peace shall kiss.
Truth shall spring out of the earth,
  and justice shall look down from heaven.
℟. Lord, let us see your kindness.
The Lord himself will give his benefits;
  our land shall yield its increase.
Justice shall walk before him,
  and salvation, along the way of his steps.
℟. Lord, let us see your kindness.

Christmas Season

Ps 98, 1. 2-3. 3-4. 5-6

℟. (3) All the ends of the earth have seen the saving power of God.

Sing to the Lord a new song,
   for he has done wondrous deeds;
His right hand has won victory for him,
   his holy arm.
℟. All the ends of the earth have seen the saving power of God.

The Lord has made his salvation known:
   in the sight of the nations he has revealed his justice.
He has remembered his kindness and his faithfulness
   toward the house of Israel.
℟. All the ends of the earth have seen the saving power of God.

All the ends of the earth have seen
   the salvation by our God.
Sing joyfully to the Lord, all you lands;
   break into song; sing praise.
℟. All the ends of the earth have seen the saving power of God.

Sing praise to the Lord with the harp,
   with the harp and melodious song.
With trumpets and the sound of the horn
   sing joyfully before the King, the Lord.
℟. All the ends of the earth have seen the saving power of God.

Epiphany

Ps 72, 1-2. 7-8. 10-11. 12-13

℟. (11) Lord, every nation on earth will adore you.

O God, with your judgment endow the king,
   and with your justice, the king's son;
He shall govern your people with justice
   and your afflicted ones with judgment.
℟. Lord, every nation on earth will adore you.

Justice shall flower in his days,
   and profound peace, till the moon be no more.
May he rule from sea to sea,
   and from the River to the ends of the earth.
℟. Lord, every nation on earth will adore you.

The kings of Tarshish and the Isles shall offer gifts;
   the kings of Arabia and Seba shall bring tribute.
All kings shall pay him homage,
   all nations shall serve him.
℟. Lord, every nation on earth will adore you.

For he shall rescue the poor man when he cries out,
   and the afflicted when he has no one to help him.
He shall have pity for the lowly and the poor;
   the lives of the poor he shall save.
℟. Lord, every nation on earth will adore you.

Lenten Season

Ps 51, 3-4. 5-6. 12-13. 14. 17

℟. (3) Be merciful, O Lord, for we have sinned.

Have mercy on me, O God, in your goodness;
   in the greatness of your compassion wipe out my offense.
Thoroughly wash me from my guilt
   and of my sin cleanse me.
℟. Be merciful, O Lord, for we have sinned.

For I acknowledge my offense,
   and my sin is before me always:
"Against you only have I sinned,
   and done what is evil in your sight."
℟. Be merciful, O Lord, for we have sinned.

A clean heart create for me, O God,
   and a steadfast spirit renew within me.
Cast me not out from your presence,
   and your holy spirit take not from me.
℟. Be merciful, O Lord, for we have sinned.

Give me back the joy of your salvation,
   and a willing spirit sustain in me.
O Lord, open my lips,
   and my mouth shall proclaim your praise.
℟. Be merciful, O Lord, for we have sinned.

Ps 91, 1-2. 10-11. 12-13. 14. 16

℟. (15) Be with me, Lord, when I am in trouble.

You who dwell in the shelter of the Most High,
   who abide in the shadow of the Almighty,
Say to the Lord, "My refuge and my fortress,
   my God, in whom I trust."
℟. Be with me, Lord, when I am in trouble.

No evil shall befall you,
  nor shall affliction come near your tent,
For to his angels he has given command about
    you,
  that they guard you in all your ways.
℞. Be with me, Lord, when I am in trouble.
Upon their hands they shall bear you up,
  lest you dash your foot against a stone.
You shall tread upon the asp and the viper;
  you shall trample down the lion and the
    dragon.
℞. Be with me, Lord, when I am in trouble.
Because he clings to me, I will deliver him;
  I will set him on high because he acknowl-
    edges my name.
With length of days I will gratify him
  and will show him my salvation.
℞. Be with me, Lord, when I am in trouble.

Ps 130, 1-2. 3-4. 4-6. 7-8

℞. (7) With the Lord there is mercy,
  and fullness of redemption.
Out of the depths I cry to you, O Lord;
  Lord, hear my voice!
Let your ears be attentive
  to my voice in supplication.
℞. With the Lord there is mercy,
  and fullness of redemption.
If you, O Lord, mark iniquities,
  Lord, who can stand?
But with you is forgiveness,
  that you may be revered.
℞. With the Lord there is mercy,
  and fullness of redemption.
I trust in the Lord;
  my soul trusts in his word.
My soul waits for the Lord
  more than sentinels wait for the dawn.
Let Israel wait for the Lord.
℞. With the Lord there is mercy,
  and fullness of redemption.
For with the Lord is kindness
  and with him is plenteous redemption;
And he will redeem Israel
  from all their iniquities.
℞. With the Lord there is mercy,
  and fullness of redemption.

Holy Week

Ps 22, 8-9. 17-18. 19-20. 23-24

℞. (2) My God, my God, why have you
  abandoned me?
All who see me scoff at me;
  they mock me with parted lips, they wag
    their heads:
"He relied on the Lord; let him deliver him,
  let him rescue him, if he loves him."
℞. My God, my God, why have you abandoned
  me?
Indeed, many dogs surround me,
  a pack of evildoers closes in upon me;
They have pierced my hands and my feet;
  I can count all my bones.
℞. My God, my God, why have you abandoned
  me?
They divide my garments among them,
  and for my vesture they cast lots.
But you, O Lord, be not far from me;
  O my help, hasten to aid me.
℞. My God, my God, why have you abandoned
  me?
I will proclaim your name to my brethren;
  in the midst of the assembly I will praise
    you:
"You who fear the Lord, praise him;
  all you descendants of Jacob, give glory to
    him."
℞. My God, my God, why have you abandoned
  me?

Easter Vigil

Ps 136: a) 1-3. 4-6. 7-9. 24-26
     b) 1. 3. 16. 21-23. 24-26

a)

℞. His love is everlasting.
Give thanks to the Lord, for he is good,
  for his mercy endures forever;
Give thanks to the God of gods,
  for his mercy endures forever;
Give thanks to the Lord of lords,
  for his mercy endures forever.
℞. His love is everlasting.
Who alone does great wonders,
  for his mercy endures forever;

Who made the heavens in wisdom,
  for his mercy endures forever;
Who spread out the earth upon the waters,
  for his mercy endures forever.
℟. His love is everlasting.
Who made the great lights,
  for his mercy endures forever;
The sun to rule over the day,
  for his mercy endures forever;
The moon and the stars to rule over the night,
  for his mercy endures forever.
℟. His love is everlasting.
And freed us from our foes,
  for his mercy endures forever;
Who gives food to all flesh,
  for his mercy endures forever.
Give thanks to the God of heaven,
  for his mercy endures forever.
℟. His love is everlasting.

b)

℟. His love is everlasting.
Give thanks to the Lord, for he is good,
  for his mercy endures forever;
Give thanks to the Lord of lords,
  for his mercy endures forever;
Who led his people through the wilderness,
  for his mercy endures forever.
℟. His love is everlasting.
And made their land a heritage,
  for his mercy endures forever;
The heritage of Israel his servant,
  for his mercy endures forever;
Who remembered us in our abjection,
  for his mercy endures forever;
℟. His love is everlasting.
And freed us from our foes,
  for his mercy endures forever;
Who gives food to all flesh,
  for his mercy endures forever.
Give thanks to the God of heaven,
  for his mercy endures forever.
℟. His love is everlasting.

Easter Season

Ps 118, 1-2. 16-17. 22-23

℟. (24) This is the day the Lord has made;
  let us rejoice and be glad.
Give thanks to the Lord, for he is good,
  for his mercy endures forever.
Let the house of Israel say,
  "His mercy endures forever."
℟. This is the day the Lord has made;
  let us rejoice and be glad.
The right hand of the Lord has struck with
  power:
  the right hand of the Lord is exalted.
I shall not die, but live,
  and declare the works of the Lord.
℟. This is the day the Lord has made;
  let us rejoice and be glad.
The stone which the builders rejected
  has become the cornerstone.
By the Lord has this been done;
  it is wonderful in our eyes.
℟. This is the day the Lord has made;
  let us rejoice and be glad.

Ps 66, 1-3. 4-5. 6-7. 16. 20

℟. (1) Let all the earth cry out to God with joy.
Shout joyfully to God, all you on earth,
  sing praise to the glory of his name;
  proclaim his glorious praise.
Say to God, "How tremendous are your deeds!
℟. Let all the earth cry out to God with joy.
"Let all on earth worship and sing praise to
  you,
  sing praise to your name!"
Come and see the works of God,
  his tremendous deeds among men.
℟. Let all the earth cry out to God with joy.
He has changed the sea into dry land;
  through the river they passed on foot;
  therefore let us rejoice in him.
He rules by his might forever.
℟. Let all the earth cry out to God with joy.
Hear now, all you who fear God, while I
  declare
  what he has done for me.
Blessed be God who refused me not
  my prayer or his kindness!
℟. Let all the earth cry out to God with joy.

Ascension

Ps 47, 2-3. 6-7. 8-9

℞. (6) God mounts his throne to shouts of joy.
All you peoples, clap your hands,
  shout to God with cries of gladness,
For the Lord, the Most High, the awesome,
  is the great king over all the earth.
℞. God mounts his throne to shouts of joy.
God mounts his throne amid shouts of joy;
  the Lord, amid trumpet blasts.
Sing praise to God, sing praise;
  sing praise to our king, sing praise.
℞. God mounts his throne to shouts of joy.
For king of all the earth is God;
  sing hymns of praise.
God reigns over the nations,
  God sits upon his holy throne.
℞. God mounts his throne to shouts of joy.

Pentecost

Ps 104, 1. 24. 29-30. 31. 34

℞. (30) Lord, send out your Spirit,
  and renew the face of the earth.
Bless the Lord, O my soul!
  O Lord, my God, you are great indeed!
How manifold are your works, O Lord!
  the earth is full of your creatures.
℞. Lord, send out your Spirit,
  and renew the face of the earth.
If you take away their breath, they perish
  and return to their dust.
When you send forth your spirit, they are
  created,
  and you renew the face of the earth.
℞. Lord, send out your Spirit,
  and renew the face of the earth.
May the glory of the Lord endure forever;
  may the Lord be glad in his works!
Pleasing to him be my theme;
  I will be glad in the Lord.
℞. Lord, send out your Spirit,
  and renew the face of the earth.

Season of the Year

Ps 19, 8. 9. 10. 11

℞. (Jn 6, 69) Lord, you have the words of
  everlasting life.
The law of the Lord is perfect,
  refreshing the soul;
The decree of the Lord is trustworthy,
  giving wisdom to the simple.
℞. Lord, you have the words of everlasting
  life.
The precepts of the Lord are right,
  rejoicing the heart;
The command of the Lord is clear,
  enlightening the eye.
℞. Lord, you have the words of everlasting
  life.
The fear of the Lord is pure,
  enduring forever;
The ordinances of the Lord are true,
  all of them just.
℞. Lord, you have the words of everlasting
  life.
They are more precious than gold,
  than a heap of purest gold;
Sweeter also than syrup
  or honey from the comb.
℞. Lord, you have the words of everlasting
  life.

Ps 27, 1. 4. 13-14

℞. (1) The Lord is my light and my salvation.
The Lord is my light and my salvation;
  whom should I fear?
The Lord is my life's refuge;
  of whom should I be afraid?
℞. The Lord is my light and my salvation.
One thing I ask of the Lord;
  this I seek:
To dwell in the house of the Lord
  all the days of my life,
That I may gaze on the loveliness of the Lord
  and contemplate his temple.
℞. The Lord is my light and my salvation.
I believe that I shall see the bounty of the Lord
  in the land of the living.
Wait for the Lord with courage;
  be stouthearted, and wait for the Lord.
℞. The Lord is my light and my salvation.

Ps 34, 2-3. 4-5. 6-7. 8-9

℟. (2) I will bless the Lord at all times.
I will bless the Lord at all times;
  his praise shall be ever in my mouth.
Let my soul glory in the Lord;
  the lowly will hear me and be glad.
℟. I will bless the Lord at all times.
Glorify the Lord with me,
  let us together extol his name.
I sought the Lord, and he answered me
  and delivered me from all my fears.
℟. I will bless the Lord at all times.
Look to him that you may be radiant with joy,
  and your faces may not blush with shame.
When the afflicted man called out, the Lord
  heard,
  and from all his distress he saved him.
℟. I will bless the Lord at all times.
The angel of the Lord encamps
  around those who fear him, and delivers
  them.
Taste and see how good the Lord is;
  happy the man who takes refuge in him.
℟. I will bless the Lord at all times.
℟. Or: (9) Taste and see the goodness of the
  Lord.

Ps 63, 2. 3-4. 5-6. 8-9

℟. (2) My soul is thirsting for you, O Lord my
  God.
O God, you are my God whom I seek;
  for you my flesh pines and my soul thirsts
  like the earth, parched, lifeless and without
  water.
℟. My soul is thirsting for you, O Lord my
  God.
Thus have I gazed toward you in the sanctuary
  to see your power and your glory,
For your kindness is a greater good than life;
  my lips shall glorify you.
℟. My soul is thirsting for you, O Lord my
  God.
Thus will I bless you while I live;
  lifting up my hands, I will call upon your
  name.
As with the riches of a banquet shall my soul
  be satisfied,

and with exultant lips my mouth shall praise
  you.
℟. My soul is thirsting for you, O Lord my
  God.
That you are my help,
  and in the shadow of your wings I shout for
  joy.
My soul clings fast to you;
  your right hand upholds me.
℟. My soul is thirsting for you, O Lord my
  God.

Ps 95, 1-2. 6-7. 8-9

℟. (8) If today you hear his voice,
  harden not your hearts.
Come, let us sing joyfully to the Lord;
  let us acclaim the Rock of our salvation.
Let us greet him with thanksgiving;
  let us joyfully sing psalms to him.
℟. If today you hear his voice,
  harden not your hearts.
Come, let us bow down in worship;
  let us kneel before the Lord who made us.
For he is our God,
  and we are the people he shepherds, the
  flock he guides.
℟. If today you hear his voice,
  harden not your hearts.
Oh, that today you would hear his voice:
  "Harden not your hearts as at Meribah,
  as in the day of Massah in the desert,
Where your fathers tempted me."
℟. If today you hear his voice,
  harden not your hearts.

Ps 100, 2. 3. 5

℟. (3) We are his people:
  the sheep of his flock.
Sing joyfully to the Lord, all you lands;
  serve the Lord with gladness;
  come before him with joyful song.
℟. We are his people:
  the sheep of his flock.
Know that the Lord is God;
  he made us, his we are;
  his people, the flock he tends.
℟. We are his people:
  the sheep of his flock.

The Lord is good:
   his kindness endures forever,
   and his faithfulness, to all generations.
℞. We are his people:
   the sheep of his flock.

Ps 103, 1-2. 3-4. 8. 10. 12-13

℞. (8) The Lord is kind and merciful.
Bless the Lord, O my soul;
   and all my being, bless his holy name.
Bless the Lord, O my soul,
   and forget not all his benefits.
℞. The Lord is kind and merciful.
He pardons all your iniquities,
   he heals all your ills.
He redeems your life from destruction,
   he crowns you with kindness and compassion.
℞. The Lord is kind and merciful.
Merciful and gracious is the Lord,
   slow to anger and abounding in kindness.
Not according to our sins does he deal with us,
   nor does he requite us according to our crimes.
℞. The Lord is kind and merciful.
As far as the east is from the west,
   so far has he put our transgressions from us.
As a father has compassion on his children,
   so the Lord has compassion on those who fear him.
℞. The Lord is kind and merciful.

Ps 145, 1-2. 8-9. 10-11. 13-14

℞. (1) I will praise your name for ever, my king and my God.
I will extol you, O my God and King,
   and I will bless your name forever and ever.
Every day will I bless you,
   and I will praise your name forever and ever.
℞. I will praise your name for ever, my king and my God.
The Lord is gracious and merciful,
   slow to anger and of great kindness.
The Lord is good to all
   and compassionate toward all his works.

℞. I will praise your name for ever, my king and my God.
Let all your works give you thanks, O Lord,
   and let your faithful ones bless you.
Let them discourse of the glory of your kingdom
   and speak of your might.
℞. I will praise your name for ever, my King and my God.
The Lord is faithful in all his words
   and holy in all his works.
The Lord lifts up all who are falling
   and raises up all who are bowed down.
℞. I will praise your name for ever, my King and my God.

Last Weeks of the Year

Ps 122, 1-2. 3-4. 4-5. 6-7. 8-9

℞. (See 1) Let us go rejoicing to the house of the Lord.
I rejoiced because they said to me,
   "We will go up to the house of the Lord."
And now we have set foot
   within your gates, O Jerusalem.
℞. Let us go rejoicing to the house of the Lord.
Jerusalem, built as a city
   with compact unity.
To it the tribes go up,
   the tribes of the Lord.
℞. Let us go rejoicing to the house of the Lord.
According to the decree for Israel,
   to give thanks to the name of the Lord.
In it are set up judgment seats,
   seats for the house of David.
℞. Let us go rejoicing to the house of the Lord.
Pray for the peace of Jerusalem!
   May those who love you prosper!
May peace be within your walls,
   prosperity in your buildings.
℞. Let us go rejoicing to the house of the Lord.
Because of my relatives and friends
   I will say, "Peace be within you!"
Because of the house of the Lord, our God,
   I will pray for your good.
℞. Let us go rejoicing to the house of the Lord.

PROPER OF SEASONS

WEEKDAY READINGS

ADVENT SEASON

176 MONDAY OF THE FIRST WEEK
OF ADVENT

READING I   Is 2, 1-5

In year A, when this reading is used on the First Sunday of Advent, the reading below (Is 4, 2-6) replaces it:

A reading from the book of the prophet Isaiah

The Lord will gather many nations in an everlasting peace in the kingdom of heaven.

This is what Isaiah, son of Amoz, saw concerning Judah and Jerusalem.

In days to come,
The mountain of the Lord's house
  shall be established as the highest mountain
  and raised above the hills.
All nations shall stream toward it;
  many peoples shall come and say:
"Come, let us climb the Lord's mountain,
  to the house of the God of Jacob,
That he may instruct us in his ways,
  and we may walk in his paths."
For from Zion shall go forth instruction,
  and the word of the Lord from Jerusalem.
He shall judge between the nations,
  and impose terms on many peoples.
They shall beat their swords into plowshares
  and their spears into pruning hooks;
One nation shall not raise the sword against
    another,
  nor shall they train for war again.
O house of Jacob, come,
  let us walk in the light of the Lord!
    This is the Word of the Lord.

READING I   (for Year A)   Is 4, 2-6

A reading from the book of the prophet Isaiah

There will be unlimited joy for those who are saved.

On that day,
The branch of the Lord will be luster and glory,
  and the fruit of the earth will be honor and
    splendor
for the survivors of Israel.

He who remains in Zion
  and he that is left in Jerusalem
Will be called holy:
  every one marked down for life in Jeru-
    salem.
When the Lord washes away
  the filth of the daughters of Zion,
And purges Jerusalem's blood from her midst
  with a blast of searing judgment,
Then will the Lord create,
  over the whole site of Mount Zion
  and over her place of assembly,
A smoking cloud by day
  and a light of flaming fire by night.
For over all, his glory will be shelter and pro-
    tection:
  shade from the parching heat of day,
  refuge and cover from storm and rain.
    This is the Word of the Lord.

Responsorial Psalm   Ps 122, 1-2. 3-4. (4-5. 6-7) 8-9

℞. (1) I rejoiced when I heard them say:
  let us go to the house of the Lord.
I rejoiced because they said to me,
  "We will go up to the house of the Lord."
And now we have set foot
  within your gates, O Jerusalem.

℞. I rejoiced when I heard them say:
  let us go to the house of the Lord.
Jerusalem, built as a city
  with compact unity.
To it the tribes go up,
  the tribes of the Lord.

℞. I rejoiced when I heard them say:
  let us go to the house of the Lord.
According to the decree for Israel,
  to give thanks to the name of the Lord.
In it are set up judgment seats,
  seats for the house of David.

℞. I rejoiced when I heard them say:
  let us go to the house of the Lord.
Pray for the peace of Jerusalem!
  May those who love you prosper!

May peace be within your walls,
   prosperity in your buildings.
Ry. I rejoiced when I heard them say:
   let us go to the house of the Lord.
Because of my relatives and friends
   I will say, "Peace be within you!"
Because of the house of the Lord, our God,
   I will pray for your good.
Ry. I rejoiced when I heard them say:
   let us go to the house of the Lord.

GOSPEL   Mt 8, 5-11
Alleluia

See no. 193.

✠ A reading from the holy gospel according
          to Matthew

Many will come from the east and west and take their place
          in the kingdom of heaven.

As Jesus entered Capernaum, a centurion approached him with this request: "Sir, my serving boy is at home in bed paralyzed, suffering painfully." He said to him, "I will come and cure him." "Sir," the centurion said in reply, "I am not worthy to have you under my roof. Just give an order and my boy will get better. I am a man under authority myself and I have troops assigned to me. If I give one man the order, 'Dismissed,' off he goes. If I say to another, 'Come here,' he comes. If I tell my slave, 'Do this,' he does it." Jesus showed amazement on hearing this and remarked to his followers, "I assure you, I have never found this much faith in Israel. Mark what I say! Many will come from the east and the west and will find a place at the banquet in the kingdom of God with Abraham, Isaac, and Jacob."
          This is the gospel of the Lord.

─────────────────────────────

177   **TUESDAY OF THE FIRST WEEK**
          OF ADVENT

READING I   Is 11, 1-10
A reading from the book of the prophet Isaiah
          The Spirit of the Lord God rests upon him.
   On that day,
A shoot shall sprout from the stump of Jesse,

and from his roots a bud shall blossom.
The spirit of the Lord shall rest upon him:
   a spirit of wisdom and of understanding,
A spirit of counsel and of strength,
   a spirit of knowledge and of fear of the Lord,
   and his delight shall be the fear of the Lord.
Not by appearance shall he judge,
   nor by hearsay shall he decide,
But he shall judge the poor with justice,
   and decide aright for the land's afflicted.
He shall strike the ruthless with the rod of his
          mouth,
   and with the breath of his lips he shall slay
          the wicked.
Justice shall be the band around his waist,
   and faithfulness a belt upon his hips.

Then the wolf shall be a guest of the lamb,
   and the leopard shall lie down with the kid;
The calf and the young lion shall browse
          together,
   with a little child to guide them.
The cow and the bear shall be neighbors,
   together their young shall rest;
   the lion shall eat hay like the ox.
The baby shall play by the cobra's den,
   and the child lay his hand on the adder's lair.
There shall be no harm or ruin on all my holy
          mountain;
   for the earth shall be filled with knowledge
          of the Lord,
   as water covers the sea.

   On that day,
The root of Jesse,
   set up as a signal for the nations,
The Gentiles shall seek out,
   for his dwelling shall be glorious.
          This is the Word of the Lord.

Responsorial Psalm   Ps 72, 1. 7-8. 12-13. 17

Ry. (7) Justice shall flourish in his time,
   and fullness of peace for ever.
O God, with your judgment endow the king,
   and with your justice, the king's son;
He shall govern your people with justice
   and your afflicted ones with judgment.
Ry. Justice shall flourish in his time,
   and fullness of peace for ever.

Justice shall flower in his days,
    and profound peace, till the moon be no
    more.
May he rule from sea to sea,
    and from the River to the ends of the earth.
℞. Justice shall flourish in his time,
    and fullness of peace for ever.
He shall rescue the poor man when he cries
    out,
    and the afflicted when he has no one to help
    him.
He shall have pity for the lowly and the poor;
    the lives of the poor he shall save.
℞. Justice shall flourish in his time,
    and fullness of peace for ever.
May his name be blessed forever;
    as long as the sun his name shall remain.
In him shall all the tribes of the earth be
    blessed;
    all the nations shall proclaim his happiness.
℞. Justice shall flourish in his time,
    and fullness of peace for ever.

GOSPEL   Lk 10, 21-24
Alleluia

See no. 193.

✠ A reading from the holy gospel according
         to Luke
       Jesus is filled with the Holy Spirit.

Jesus rejoiced in the Holy Spirit and said: "I
offer you praise, O Father, Lord of heaven and
earth, because what you have hidden from the
learned and the clever you have revealed to the
merest children.

   "Yes, Father, you have graciously willed it
so.

   "Everything has been given over to me by
my Father. No one knows the Son except the
Father and no one knows the Father except
the Son—and anyone to whom the Son wishes
to reveal him."

   Turning to his disciples he said to them
privately: "Blest are the eyes that see what you
see. I tell you, many prophets and kings wished
to see what you see but did not see it, and to
hear what you hear but did not hear it."
        This is the gospel of the Lord.

178 WEDNESDAY OF THE FIRST WEEK
OF ADVENT

READING I   Is 25, 6-10

A reading from the book of the prophet Isaiah
*The Lord God has invited us to rejoice with him, and he
will wipe away the tears from every face.*

On this mountain the Lord of hosts
    will provide for all peoples
A feast of rich food and choice wines,
    juicy, rich food and pure, choice wines.
On this mountain he will destroy
    the veil that veils all peoples,
The web that is woven over all nations;
    he will destroy death forever.
The Lord God will wipe away
    the tears from all faces;
The reproach of his people he will remove
    from the whole earth; for the Lord has
    spoken.

   On that day it will be said:
"Behold our God, to whom we looked to save
    us!
    This is the Lord for whom we looked;
    let us rejoice and be glad that he has saved
    us!"
For the hand of the Lord will rest on this
    mountain.
        This is the Word of the Lord.

Responsorial Psalm   Ps 23, 1-3. 3-4. 5. 6

℞. (6) I shall live in the house of the Lord
    all the days of my life.
The Lord is my shepherd; I shall not want.
    In verdant pastures he gives me repose;
Beside restful waters he leads me;
    he refreshes my soul.
℞. I shall live in the house of the Lord
    all the days of my life.
He guides me in right paths
    for his name's sake.
Even though I walk in the dark valley
    I fear no evil; for you are at my side
With your rod and your staff
    that give me courage.
℞. I shall live in the house of the Lord
    all the days of my life.

You spread the table before me
  in the sight of my foes;
You anoint my head with oil;
  my cup overflows.
℞. I shall live in the house of the Lord
  all the days of my life.
Only goodness and kindness follow me
  all the days of my life;
And I shall dwell in the house of the Lord
  for years to come.
℞. I shall live in the house of the Lord
  all the days of my life.

GOSPEL   Mt 15, 29-37
Alleluia

See no. 193.

✠ A reading from the holy gospel according
    to Matthew
Jesus healed many and multiplied the bread.

Jesus went along the Sea of Galilee. He went
up onto the mountainside and sat down there.
Large crowds of people came to him bringing
with them cripples, the deformed, the blind,
the mute, and many others besides. They laid
them at his feet and he cured them. The result
was great astonishment in the crowds as they
beheld the mute speaking, the deformed made
sound, cripples walking about, and the blind
seeing. They glorified the God of Israel.
    Jesus called his disciples to him and said:
"My heart is moved with pity for the crowd.
By now they have been with me three days,
and have nothing to eat. I do not wish to send
them away hungry, for fear they may collapse
on the way." His disciples said to him, "How
could we ever get enough bread in this deserted
spot to satisfy such a crowd?" But Jesus asked
them, "How many loaves of bread do you
have?" "Seven," they replied, "and a few small
fish." Then he directed the crowd to seat themselves on the ground. He took the seven loaves
and the fish, and after giving thanks he broke
them and gave them to the disciples, who in
turn gave them to the crowds. All ate until
they were full. When they gathered up the
fragments left over, these filled seven hampers.
    This is the gospel of the Lord.

179 THURSDAY OF THE FIRST WEEK
OF ADVENT

READING I   Is 26, 1-6
A reading from the book of the prophet Isaiah
Let the upright nations, the custodians of truth, come in.

On that day they will sing this song in the land
of Judah:
"A strong city have we;
  he sets up walls and ramparts to protect us.
Open up the gates
  to let in a nation that is just,
  one that keeps faith.
A nation of firm purpose you keep in peace;
  in peace, for its trust in you."

Trust in the Lord forever!
  For the Lord is an eternal rock.
He humbles those in high places,
  and the lofty city he brings down;
He tumbles it to the ground,
  levels it with the dust.
It is trampled underfoot by the needy,
  by the footsteps of the poor.
    This is the Word of the Lord.

Responsorial Psalm   Ps 118, 1. 8-9. 19-21. 25-27

℞. (26) Blessed is he who comes in the name of
  the Lord.
Give thanks to the Lord, for he is good,
  for his mercy endures forever.
It is better to take refuge in the Lord
  than to trust in man.
It is better to take refuge in the Lord
  than to trust in princes.
℞. Blessed is he who comes in the name of the
  Lord.
Open to me the gates of justice;
  I will enter them and give thanks to the Lord.
This gate is the Lord's;
  the just shall enter it.
I will give thanks to you, for you have
  answered me
  and have been my savior.
℞. Blessed is he who comes in the name of the
  Lord.

O Lord, grant salvation!
   O Lord, grant prosperity!
Blessed is he who comes in the name of the Lord;
   we bless you from the house of the Lord.
The Lord is God, and he has given us light.

℟. Blessed is he who comes in the name of the Lord.

℟. Or: Alleluia.

GOSPEL   Mt 7, 21. 24-27

Alleluia

See no. 193.

✠ A reading from the holy gospel according
            to Matthew
He who does the will of the Father will enter the kingdom
of heaven.

Jesus said to his disciples: "None of those who cry out, 'Lord, Lord,' will enter the kingdom of God but only the one who does the will of my Father in heaven.

"Anyone who hears my words and puts them into practice is like the wise man who built his house on rock. When the rainy season set in, the torrents came and the winds blew and buffeted his house. It did not collapse; it had been solidly set on rock. Anyone who hears my words but does not put them into practice is like the foolish man who built his house on sandy ground. The rains fell, the torrents came, the winds blew and lashed against his house. It collapsed under all this and was completely ruined."

    This is the gospel of the Lord.

---

180   FRIDAY OF THE FIRST WEEK
OF ADVENT

READING I   Is 29, 17-24

A reading from the book of the prophet Isaiah
In that day, the eyes of the blind will see.

Thus says the Lord God:
But a very little while,
   and Lebanon shall be changed into an orchard,

and the orchard be regarded as a forest!
On that day the deaf shall hear
   the words of a book;
And out of gloom and darkness,
   the eyes of the blind shall see.
The lowly will ever find joy in the Lord,
   and the poor rejoice in the Holy One of Israel.
For the tyrant will be no more
   and the arrogant will have gone;
All who are alert to do evil will be cut off,
   those whose mere word condemns a man,
Who ensnare his defender at the gate,
   and leave the just man with an empty claim.
Therefore thus says the Lord,
   the God of the house of Jacob,
   who redeemed Abraham:
Now Jacob shall have nothing to be ashamed of,
   nor shall his face grow pale.
When his children see
   the work of my hands in his midst,
They shall keep my name holy;
   they shall reverence the Holy One of Jacob,
   and be in awe of the God of Israel.
Those who err in spirit shall acquire understanding,
   and those who find fault shall receive instruction.
    This is the Word of the Lord.

Responsorial Psalm   Ps 27, 1. 4. 13-14

℟. (1) The Lord is my light and my salvation.
The Lord is my light and my salvation;
   whom should I fear?
The Lord is my life's refuge;
   of whom should I be afraid?

℟. The Lord is my light and my salvation.
One thing I ask of the Lord;
   this I seek:
To dwell in the house of the Lord
   all the days of my life,
That I may gaze on the loveliness of the Lord
   and contemplate his temple.

℟. The Lord is my light and my salvation.
I believe that I shall see the bounty of the Lord
   in the land of the living.

Wait for the Lord with courage;
  be stouthearted, and wait for the Lord.
℞. The Lord is my light and my salvation.
℞. Or: Alleluia.

GOSPEL   Mt 9, 27-31
Alleluia
See no. 193.

✠ A reading from the holy gospel according
            to Matthew
Their belief in Jesus brought a cure to the two blind men.

As Jesus moved on from Capernaum, two blind
men came after him crying out, "Son of David,
have pity on us!" When he got to the house,
the blind men caught up with him. Jesus said
to them, "Are you confident I can do this?"
"Yes, Lord," they told him. At that he touched
their eyes and said, "Because of your faith it
shall be done to you"; and they recovered their
sight. Then Jesus warned them sternly, "See
to it that no one knows of this." But they
went off and spread word of him through the
whole area.
            This is the gospel of the Lord.

---

181   SATURDAY OF THE FIRST WEEK
            OF ADVENT

READING I   Is 30, 19-21. 23-26
A reading from the book of the prophet Isaiah
If you have mercy the Lord God will be gracious to you
            when he hears your cry.

Thus says the Lord God,
  the Holy One of Israel:
O people of Zion, who dwell in Jerusalem,
  no more will you weep;
He will be gracious to you when you cry out,
  as soon as he hears he will answer you.
The Lord will give you the bread you need
  and the water for which you thirst.
No longer will your Teacher hide himself,
  but with your own eyes you shall see your
      Teacher,
While from behind, a voice shall sound in your
      ears:
"This is the way; walk in it,"

when you would turn to the right or to the
      left.
He will give rain for the seed
  that you sow in the ground,
And the wheat that the soil produces
  will be rich and abundant.
On that day your cattle will graze
  in spacious meadows;
The oxen and the asses that till the ground
  will eat silage tossed to them
  with shovel and pitchfork.
Upon every high mountain and lofty hill
  there will be streams of running water.
On the day of the great slaughter,
  when the towers fall,
The light of the moon will be like that of the
      sun
  and the light of the sun will be seven times
      greater
[like the light of seven days].
On the day the Lord binds up the wounds of his
      people,
  he will heal the bruises left by his blows.
            This is the Word of the Lord.

Responsorial Psalm   Ps 147, 1-2. 3-4. 5-6
℞. (Is 30, 18) Happy are all who long for the
      coming of the Lord.
Praise the Lord, for he is good;
  sing praise to our God, for he is gracious;
  it is fitting to praise him.
The Lord rebuilds Jerusalem;
  the dispersed of Israel he gathers.
℞. Happy are all who long for the coming of
      the Lord.
He heals the brokenhearted
  and binds up their wounds.
He tells the number of the stars;
  he calls each by name.
℞. Happy are all who long for the coming of
      the Lord.
Great is our Lord and mighty in power:
  to his wisdom there is no limit.
The Lord sustains the lowly;
  the wicked he casts to the ground.
℞. Happy are all who long for the coming of
      the Lord.
℞. Or: Alleluia.

GOSPEL   Mt 9, 35—10, 1. 6-8
Alleluia

See no. 193.

✠ A reading from the holy gospel according
   to Matthew

When Jesus saw the crowds he felt sorry for them.

Jesus toured all the towns and villages. He
taught in their synagogues, he proclaimed the
good news of God's reign, and he cured every
sickness and disease. At the sight of the
crowds, his heart was moved with pity. They
were lying prostrate from exhaustion, like
sheep without a shepherd. He said to his disciples: "The harvest is good but laborers are
scarce. Beg the harvest master to send out laborers to gather his harvest."

Then he summoned his twelve disciples and
gave them authority to expel unclean spirits and
to cure sickness and disease of every kind. He
gave them these instructions: "Go instead after
the lost sheep of the house of Israel. As you go,
make this announcement: 'The reign of God is
at hand!' Cure the sick, raise the dead, heal the
leprous, expel demons. The gift you have received, give as a gift."

This is the gospel of the Lord.

**182 MONDAY OF THE SECOND WEEK
OF ADVENT**

READING I   Is 35, 1-10

A reading from the book of the prophet Isaiah

God will come and save you.

The desert and the parched land will exult;
   the steppe will rejoice and bloom.
They will bloom with abundant flowers,
   and rejoice with joyful song.
The glory of Lebanon will be given to them,
   the splendor of Carmel and Sharon;
They will see the glory of the Lord,
   the splendor of our God.

Strengthen the hands that are feeble,
   make firm the knees that are weak,
Say to those whose hearts are frightened:
   Be strong, fear not!

Here is your God,
   he comes with vindication;
With divine recompense
   he comes to save you.
Then will the eyes of the blind be opened,
   the ears of the deaf be cleared;
Then will the lame leap like a stag,
   then the tongue of the dumb will sing.

Streams will burst forth in the desert,
   and rivers in the steppe.
The burning sands will become pools,
   and the thirsty ground, springs of water;
The abode where jackals lurk
   will be a marsh for the reed and papyrus.
A highway will be there,
   called the holy way;
No one unclean may pass over it,
   nor fools go astray on it.
No lion will be there,
   nor beast of prey go up to be met upon it.
It is for those with a journey to make,
   and on it the redeemed will walk.
Those whom the Lord has ransomed will return
   and enter Zion singing,
   crowned with everlasting joy;
They will meet with joy and gladness,
   sorrow and mourning will flee.
                  This is the Word of the Lord.

Responsorial Psalm   Ps 85, 9-10. 11-12. 13-14

℟. (Is 35, 4) Our God will come to save us!
I will hear what the Lord God proclaims;
   the Lord—for he proclaims peace to his people.
Near indeed is his salvation to those who fear
   him,
   glory dwelling in our land.
℟. Our God will come to save us!
Kindness and truth shall meet;
   justice and peace shall kiss.
Truth shall spring out of the earth,
   and justice shall look down from heaven.
℟. Our God will come to save us!
The Lord himself will give his benefits;
   our land shall yield its increase.
Justice shall walk before him,
   and salvation, along the way of his steps.
℟. Our God will come to save us!

GOSPEL   Lk 5, 17-26
Alleluia
See no. 193.

✠ **A reading from the holy gospel according to Luke**

We have seen wonderful things this day.

One day Jesus was teaching, and the power of the Lord made him heal. Sitting close by were Pharisees and teachers of the law who had come from every village of Galilee and from Judea and Jerusalem. Some men came along carrying a paralytic on a mat. They were trying to bring him in and lay him before Jesus; but they found no way of getting him through because of the crowd, so they went up on the roof. There they let him down with his mat through the tiles into the middle of the crowd before Jesus. Seeing their faith, Jesus said, "My friend, your sins are forgiven you."

The scribes and the Pharisees began a discussion, saying: "Who is this man who utters blasphemies? Who can forgive sins but God alone?" Jesus, however, knew their reasoning and answered them by saying: "Why do you harbor these thoughts? Which is easier: to say, 'Your sins are forgiven you,' or to say, 'Get up and walk'? In any case, to make it clear to you that the Son of Man has authority on earth to forgive sins"—he then addressed the paralyzed man: "I say to you, get up! Take your mat with you, and return to your house."

At once the man stood erect before them. He picked up the mat he had been lying on and went home praising God. At this they were all seized with astonishment. Full of awe, they gave praise to God, saying, "We have seen incredible things today!"

This is the gospel of the Lord.

---

183   TUESDAY OF THE SECOND WEEK OF ADVENT

READING I   Is 40, 1-11

A reading from the book of the prophet Isaiah

God consoles his people.

Comfort, give comfort to my people,
  says your God.

Speak tenderly to Jerusalem, and proclaim to her
  that her service is at an end,
  her guilt is expiated;
Indeed, she has received from the hand of the Lord
  double for all her sins.

A voice cries out:
In the desert prepare the way of the Lord!
  Make straight in the wasteland a highway for our God!
Every valley shall be filled in,
  every mountain and hill shall be made low;
The rugged land shall be made a plain,
  the rough country, a broad valley.
Then the glory of the Lord shall be revealed,
  and all mankind shall see it together;
  for the mouth of the Lord has spoken.

A voice says, "Cry out!"
  I answer, "What shall I cry out?"
"All mankind is grass,
  and all their glory like the flower of the field.
The grass withers, the flower wilts,
  when the breath of the Lord blows upon it.
[So then, the people is the grass.]
Though the grass withers and the flower wilts,
  the word of our God stands forever."

Go up onto a high mountain,
  Zion, herald of glad tidings;
Cry out at the top of your voice,
  Jerusalem, herald of good news!
Fear not to cry out
  and say to the cities of Judah:
  Here is your God!
Here comes with power
  the Lord God,
  who rules by his strong arm;
Here is his reward with him,
  his recompense before him.
Like a shepherd he feeds his flock;
  in his arms he gathers the lambs,
Carrying them in his bosom,
  and leading the ewes with care.

This is the Word of the Lord.

Responsorial Psalm Ps 96, 1-2. 3. 10. 11-12. 13

℟. (Is 40, 9-10) The Lord our God comes in
   strength.

Sing to the Lord a new song;
   sing to the Lord, all you lands.
Sing to the Lord; bless his name;
   announce his salvation, day after day.

℟. The Lord our God comes in strength.

Tell his glory among the nations;
   among all peoples, his wondrous deeds.
Say among the nations: The Lord is king;
   he governs the peoples with equity.

℟. The Lord our God comes in strength.

Let the heavens be glad and the earth rejoice;
   let the sea and what fills it resound;
   let the plains be joyful and all that is in them!
Then shall all the trees of the forest exult.

℟. The Lord our God comes in strength.

They shall exult before the Lord, for he comes;
   for he comes to rule the earth.
He shall rule the world with justice
   and the peoples with his constancy.

℟. The Lord our God comes in strength.

GOSPEL Mt 18, 12-14
Alleluia

See no. 193.

✠ A reading from the holy gospel according
   to Matthew
God does not will that the little ones be lost.

Jesus said to his disciples: "What is your
thought on this: A man owns a hundred sheep
and one of them wanders away; will he not
leave the ninety-nine out on the hills and go in
search of the stray? If he succeeds in finding it,
believe me he is happier about this one than
about the ninety-nine that did not wander
away. Just so, it is no part of your heavenly
Father's plan that a single one of these little
ones shall ever come to grief."
   This is the gospel of the Lord.

**184 WEDNESDAY OF THE SECOND
   WEEK OF ADVENT**

READING I Is 40, 25-31
A reading from the book of the prophet Isaiah
The Lord God is almighty and gives strength to the weary.

To whom can you liken me as an equal?
   says the Holy One.
Lift up your eyes on high
   and see who has created these things:
He leads out their army and numbers them,
   calling them all by name.
By his great might and the strength of his
      power
   not one of them is missing!
Why, O Jacob, do you say,
   and declare, O Israel,
"My way is hidden from the Lord,
   and my right is disregarded by my God"?
Do you not know
   or have you not heard?
The Lord is the eternal God,
   creator of the ends of the earth.
He does not faint nor grow weary,
   and his knowledge is beyond scrutiny.
He gives strength to the fainting;
   for the weak he makes vigor abound.
Though young men faint and grow weary,
   and youths stagger and fall,
They that hope in the Lord will renew their
      strength,
   they will soar as with eagles' wings;
They will run and not grow weary,
   walk and not grow faint.
      This is the Word of the Lord.

Responsorial Psalm Ps 103, 1-2. 3-4. 8. 10

℟. (1) O bless the Lord, my soul.
Bless the Lord, O my soul;
   and all my being, bless his holy name.
Bless the Lord, O my soul,
   and forget not all his benefits.

℟. O bless the Lord, my soul.

He pardons all your iniquities,
   he heals all your ills.
He redeems your life from destruction,
   he crowns you with kindness and compas-
      sion.

℟. O bless the Lord, my soul.
Merciful and gracious is the Lord,
   slow to anger and abounding in kindness.
Not according to our sins does he deal with us,
   nor does he requite us according to our
   crimes.
℟. O bless the Lord, my soul.

GOSPEL   Mt 11, 28-30
Alleluia

See no. 193.

✠ **A reading from the holy gospel according**
   to Matthew
Come to me, all you who are overburdened.

Jesus said: "Come to me, all you who are
weary and find life burdensome, and I will re-
fresh you. Take my yoke upon your shoulders
and learn from me, for I am gentle and humble
of heart. Your souls will find rest, for my yoke
is easy and my burden light."
   This is the gospel of the Lord.

---

185   THURSDAY OF THE SECOND
WEEK OF ADVENT

READING I   Is 41, 13-20

A reading from the book of the prophet Isaiah
   I am your redeemer, the Holy One of Israel.

I am the Lord, your God,
   who grasp your right hand;
It is I who say to you, "Fear not,
   I will help you."
Fear not, O worm Jacob,
   O maggot Israel;
I will help you, says the Lord;
   your redeemer is the Holy One of Israel.
I will make of you a threshing sledge,
   sharp, new, and double-edged,
To thresh the mountains and crush them,
   to make the hills like chaff.
When you winnow them, the wind shall carry
   them off
   and the storm shall scatter them.

But you shall rejoice in the Lord,
   and glory in the Holy One of Israel.

The afflicted and the needy seek water in vain,
   their tongues are parched with thirst.
I, the Lord, will answer them;
   I, the God of Israel, will not forsake them.
I will open up rivers on the bare heights,
   and fountains in the broad valleys;
I will turn the desert into a marshland,
   and the dry ground into springs of water.
I will plant in the desert the cedar,
   acacia, myrtle, and olive;
I will set in the wasteland the cypress,
   together with the plane tree and the pine,
That all may see and know,
   observe and understand,
That the hand of the Lord has done this,
   the Holy One of Israel has created it.
      This is the Word of the Lord.

Responsorial Psalm   Ps 145, 1. 9. 10-11. 12-13

℟. (8) The Lord is kind and merciful;
   slow to anger, and rich in compassion.
I will extol you, O my God and King,
   and I will bless your name forever and ever.
The Lord is good to all
   and compassionate toward all his works.
℟. The Lord is kind and merciful;
   slow to anger, and rich in compassion.
Let all your works give you thanks, O Lord,
   and let your faithful ones bless you.
Let them discourse of the glory of your king-
   dom
   and speak of your might.
℟. The Lord is kind and merciful;
   slow to anger, and rich in compassion.
Let them make known to men your might
   and the glorious splendor of your kingdom.
Your kingdom is a kingdom for all ages,
   and your dominion endures through all gen-
   erations.
℟. The Lord is kind and merciful;
   slow to anger, and rich in compassion.

GOSPEL   Mt 11, 11-15
Alleluia

See no. 193.

✠ A reading from the holy gospel according
to Matthew

No greater than John the Baptizer has been born.

Jesus said to the crowds: "I solemnly assure
you, history has not known a man born of
woman greater than John the Baptizer. Yet the
least born into the kingdom of God is greater
than he. From John the Baptizer's time until
now the kingdom of God has suffered violence,
and the violent take it by force. All the prophets as well as the law spoke prophetically until
John. If you are prepared to accept it, he is Elijah, the one who was certain to come. Heed
carefully what you hear!"
This is the gospel of the Lord.

**186   FRIDAY OF THE SECOND WEEK
OF ADVENT**

READING I   Is 48, 17-19

A reading from the book of the prophet Isaiah

If only you had listened to my commandments.

Thus says the Lord, your redeemer,
the Holy One of Israel:
I, the Lord, your God,
teach you what is for your good,
and lead you on the way you should go.
If you would hearken to my commandments,
your prosperity would be like a river,
and your vindication like the waves of the
sea;
Your descendants would be like the sand,
and those born of your stock like its grains,
Their name never cut off
or blotted out from my presence.
This is the Word of the Lord.

Responsorial Psalm   Ps 1, 1-2. 3. 4. 6

℟. (Jn 8, 12) Those who follow you, Lord, will
have the light of life.
Happy the man who follows not
the counsel of the wicked

Nor walks in the way of sinners,
nor sits in the company of the insolent,
But delights in the law of the Lord
and meditates on his law day and night.
℟. Those who follow you, Lord, will have the
light of life.
He is like a tree
planted near running water,
That yields its fruit in due season,
and whose leaves never fade.
[Whatever he does, prospers.]
℟. Those who follow you, Lord, will have the
light of life.
Not so the wicked, not so;
they are like chaff which the wind drives
away.
For the Lord watches over the way of the just,
but the way of the wicked vanishes.
℟. Those who follow you, Lord, will have the
light of life.

GOSPEL   Mt 11, 16-19
Alleluia

See no. 193.

✠ A reading from the holy gospel according
to Matthew

They listened to neither John nor the Son of Man.

Jesus said to the crowds: "What comparison
can I use to describe this breed? They are like
children squatting in the town squares, calling
to their playmates:
'We piped you a tune but you did not
dance!
We sang you a dirge but you did not wail!'
In other words, John appeared neither eating
nor drinking, and people say, 'He is mad!' The
Son of Man appeared eating and drinking, and
they say, 'This one is a glutton and drunkard, a
lover of tax collectors and those outside the
law!' Yet time will prove where wisdom lies."
This is the gospel of the Lord.

---

187 **SATURDAY OF THE SECOND WEEK OF ADVENT**

READING I Sir 48, 1-4. 9-11

A reading from the book of Sirach
Elijah came to them.

Like a fire there appeared the prophet Elijah
  whose words were as a flaming furnace.
Their staff of bread he shattered,
  in his zeal he reduced them to straits;
By God's word he shut up the heavens
  and three times brought down fire.
How awesome are you, Elijah!
  Whose glory is equal to yours?
You were taken aloft in a whirlwind,
  in a chariot with fiery horses.
You are destined, it is written, in time to come
  to put an end to wrath before the day of the
    Lord,
To turn back the hearts of fathers toward their
    sons,
  and to re-establish the tribes of Jacob.
Blessed is he who shall have seen you before he
    dies.
  This is the Word of the Lord.

Responsorial Psalm Ps 80, 2-3. 15-16. 18-19

R⃒. (4) Lord, make us turn to you,
  let us see your face and we shall be saved.
O shepherd of Israel, hearken,
  from your throne upon the cherubim, shine
    forth.
Rouse your power,
  and come to save us.
R⃒. Lord, make us turn to you,
  let us see your face and we shall be saved.
Once again, O Lord of hosts,
  look down from heaven, and see;
Take care of this vine,
  and protect what your right hand has
    planted
  [the son of man whom you yourself made
    strong].
R⃒. Lord, make us turn to you,
  let us see your face and we shall be saved.

May your help be with the man of your right
    hand,
  with the son of man whom you yourself
    made strong.
Then we will no more withdraw from you;
  give us new life, and we will call upon your
    name.
R⃒. Lord, make us turn to you,
  let us see your face and we shall be saved.

GOSPEL Mt 17, 10-13
Alleluia
See no. 193.

✠ **A reading from the holy gospel according
to Matthew**
Elijah has already come and they did not know him.

As they were coming down the mountainside,
the disciples put this question to Jesus: "Why
do the scribes claim that Elijah must come
first?" In reply he said: "Elijah is indeed coming, and he will restore everything. I assure
you, though, that Elijah has already come, but
they did not recognize him and they did as they
pleased with him. The Son of Man will suffer at
their hands in the same way." The disciples
then realized that he had been speaking to
them about John the Baptizer.
  This is the gospel of the Lord.

188 **MONDAY OF THE THIRD WEEK
OF ADVENT**

If today is December 17 or 18, omit these readings and
use those given for the Weekdays of Advent, nos. 194 or
195.

READING I Nm 24, 2-7. 15-17

A reading from the book of Numbers
A star from Jacob will arise.

When Balaam raised his eyes and saw Israel
encamped, tribe by tribe, the spirit of God
came upon him, and he gave voice to his oracle:

The utterance of Balaam, son of Beor,
  the utterance of the man whose eye is true,
The utterance of one who hears what God says,
  and knows what the Most High knows,

Of one who sees what the Almighty sees,
  enraptured, and with eyes unveiled:
How goodly are your tents, O Jacob;
  your encampments, O Israel!
They are like gardens beside a stream,
  like the cedars planted by the Lord.
His wells shall yield free-flowing waters,
  he shall have the sea within reach;
His king shall rise higher,
  and his royalty shall be exalted.

Balaam again gave voice to his oracle:

The utterance of Balaam, son of Beor,
  the utterance of the man whose eye is true,
The utterance of one who hears what God says,
  and knows what the Most High knows,
Of one who sees what the Almighty sees,
  enraptured and with eyes unveiled.
I see him, though not now;
  I behold him, though not near:
A star shall advance from Jacob,
  and a staff shall rise from Israel.
          This is the Word of the Lord.

Responsorial Psalm   Ps 25, 4-5. 6-7. 8-9

R̸. (4) Teach me your ways, O Lord.
Your ways, O Lord, make known to me;
  teach me your paths,
Guide me in your truth and teach me,
  for you are God my savior.
R̸. Teach me your ways, O Lord.
Remember that your compassion, O Lord,
  and your kindness are from of old.
In your kindness remember me,
  because of your goodness, O Lord.
R̸. Teach me your ways, O Lord.
Good and upright is the Lord;
  thus he shows sinners the way.
He guides the humble to justice,
  he teaches the humble his way.
R̸. Teach me your ways, O Lord.

GOSPEL   Mt 21, 23-27
Alleluia
See no. 193.

✠ A reading from the holy gospel according
           to Matthew
John's baptism: where did it come from?
After Jesus had entered the temple precincts
and while he was teaching, the chief priests
and elders of the people came up to him and
said: "On what authority are you doing these
things? Who has given you this power?" Jesus
answered: "I too will ask a question. If you answer it for me, then I will tell you on what
authority I do the things I do. What was the
origin of John's baptism? Was it divine or
merely human?" They thought to themselves,
"If we say 'divine,' he will ask us, 'Then why
did you not put faith in it?'; while if we say,
'merely human,' we shall have reason to fear
the people, who all regard John as a prophet."
So their answer to Jesus was, "We do not
know." He said in turn, "Then neither will I tell
you on what authority I do the things I do."
        This is the gospel of the Lord.

---

189   TUESDAY OF THE THIRD WEEK
OF ADVENT

**If today is December 17 or 18, omit these readings and use
those given for the Weekdays of Advent, nos. 194 or 195.**

READING I   Zep 3, 1-2. 9-13
A reading from the book of the prophet
Zephaniah
Messianic salvation is promised to all of the poor.
Woe to the city, rebellious and polluted,
  to the tyrannical city!
She hears no voice,
  accepts no correction;
In the Lord she has not trusted,
  to her God she has not drawn near.

I will change and purify
  the lips of the peoples,

That they all may call upon the name of the
   Lord,
   to serve him with one accord;
From beyond the rivers of Ethiopia
   and as far as the recesses of the North,
   they shall bring me offerings.

On that day
You need not be ashamed
   of all your deeds,
   your rebellious actions against me;
For then will I remove from your midst
   the proud braggarts,
And you shall no longer exalt yourself
   on my holy mountain.
But I will leave as a remnant in your midst
   a people humble and lowly,
Who shall take refuge in the name of the Lord:
   the remnant of Israel.
They shall do no wrong
   and speak no lies;
Nor shall there be found in their mouths
   a deceitful tongue;
They shall pasture and couch their flocks
   with none to disturb them.
            This is the Word of the Lord.

Responsorial Psalm   Ps 34, 2-3. 6-7. 17-18. 19. 23

℟. (7) The Lord hears the cry of the poor.
I will bless the Lord at all times;
   his praise shall be ever in my mouth.
Let my soul glory in the Lord;
   the lowly will hear me and be glad.
℟. The Lord hears the cry of the poor.
Look to him that you may be radiant with joy,
   and your faces may not blush with shame.
When the afflicted man called out, the Lord
   heard,
   and from all his distress he saved him.
℟. The Lord hears the cry of the poor.
The Lord confronts the evildoers,
   to destroy remembrance of them from the
   earth.
When the just cry out, the Lord hears them,
   and from all their distress he rescues them.
℟. The Lord hears the cry of the poor.
The Lord is close to the brokenhearted;
   and those who are crushed in spirit he saves.

The Lord redeems the lives of his servants;
   no one incurs guilt who takes refuge in him.
℟. The Lord hears the cry of the poor.

GOSPEL   Mt 21, 28-32
Alleluia
See no. 193.

✠ A reading from the holy gospel according
            to Matthew
        John came and sinners believed in him.

Jesus said to the chief priests and elders of the
people: "What do you think of this case? There
was a man who had two sons. He approached
the elder and said, 'Son, go out and work in the
vineyard today.' The son replied, 'I am on my
way, sir'; but he never went. Then the man
came to his second son and said the same thing.
This son said in reply, 'No, I will not'; but afterward he regretted it and went. Which of the
two did what the father wanted?" They said,
"The second." Jesus said to them, "Let me
make it clear that tax collectors and prostitutes
are entering the kingdom of God before you.
When John came preaching a way of holiness,
you put no faith in him; but the tax collectors
and the prostitutes did believe in him. Yet even
when you saw that, you did not repent and believe in him."
        This is the gospel of the Lord.

**190   WEDNESDAY OF THE THIRD
            WEEK OF ADVENT**

If today is December 17 or 18, omit these readings and use
those given for the Weekdays of Advent, nos. 194 or 195.

READING I   Is 45, 6-8. 18. 21-25

A reading from the book of the prophet Isaiah
        Let the clouds rain down.

I am the Lord, there is no other;
   I form the light, and create the darkness,
I make well-being and create woe;
   I, the Lord, do all these things.
Let justice descend, O heavens, like dew from
      above,
   like gentle rain let the skies drop it down.

Let the earth open and salvation bud forth;
  let justice also spring up!
I, the Lord, have created this.

    For thus says the Lord,
The creator of the heavens,
  who is God,
The designer and maker of the earth
  who established it,
Not creating it to be a waste,
  but designing it to be lived in:
I am the Lord, and there is no other.

Who announced this from the beginning
  and foretold it from of old?
Was it not I, the Lord,
  besides whom there is no other God?
  There is no just and saving God but me.

Turn to me and be safe,
  all you ends of the earth,
  for I am God; there is no other!
By myself I swear,
  uttering my just decree
  and my unalterable word:
To me every knee shall bend;
  by me every tongue shall swear,
Saying, "Only in the Lord
  are just deeds and power.
Before him in shame shall come
  all who vent their anger against him.
In the Lord shall be the vindication and the
    glory
  of all the descendants of Israel."
    This is the Word of the Lord.

Responsorial Psalm   Ps 85, 9-10. 11-12. 13-14

℟. (Is 45, 8) Let the clouds rain down the Just
  One,
  and the earth bring forth a savior.
I will hear what God proclaims;
  the Lord—for he proclaims peace to his people.
Near indeed is his salvation to those who fear
  him,
  glory dwelling in our land.
℟. Let the clouds rain down the Just One,
  and the earth bring forth a savior.

Kindness and truth shall meet;
  justice and peace shall kiss.
Truth shall spring out of the earth,
  and justice shall look down from heaven.
℟. Let the clouds rain down the Just One,
  and the earth bring forth a savior.
The Lord himself will give his benefits;
  our land shall yield its increase.
Justice shall walk before him,
  and salvation, along the way of his steps.
℟. Let the clouds rain down the Just One,
  and the earth bring forth a savior.

GOSPEL   Lk 7, 18-23
Alleluia

See no. 193.

✠ **A reading from the holy gospel according**
                    to Luke
Go back and tell John what you have seen and heard.

Summoning two of his disciples, John sent
them to ask the Lord, "Are you 'He who is to
come' or are we to expect someone else?"
When the men came to him they said, "John
the Baptizer sends us to you with this question:
'Are you "He who is to come" or do we look
for someone else?' " (At that time he was curing many of their diseases, afflictions, and evil
spirits; he also restored sight to many who
were blind.) Jesus gave this response: "Go and
report to John what you have seen and heard.
The blind recover their sight, cripples walk,
lepers are cured, the deaf hear, dead men are
raised to life, and the poor have the good news
preached to them. Blest is that man who finds
no stumbling-block in me."
        This is the gospel of the Lord.

191 THURSDAY OF THE THIRD WEEK
OF ADVENT

If today is December 17 or 18, omit these readings and use those given for the Weekdays of Advent, nos. 194 or 195.

READING I   Is 54, 1-10
A reading from the book of the prophet Isaiah

Like a forsaken wife, the Lord has called you back.

Raise a glad cry, you barren one who did not
    bear,
    break forth in jubilant song, you who were
    not in labor,
For more numerous are the children of the de-
    serted wife
    than the children of her who has a husband,
    says the Lord.
Enlarge the space for your tent,
    spread out your tent cloths unsparingly;
    lengthen your ropes and make firm your
    stakes.
For you shall spread abroad to the right and to
    the left;
    your descendants shall dispossess the na-
    tions
    and shall people the desolate cities.

Fear not, you shall not be put to shame;
    you need not blush, for you shall not be dis-
    graced.
The shame of your youth you shall forget,
    the reproach of your widowhood no longer
    remember.
For he who has become your husband is your
    Maker;
    his name is the Lord of hosts;
Your redeemer is the Holy One of Israel,
    called God of all the earth.

The Lord calls you back,
    like a wife forsaken and grieved in spirit,
A wife married in youth and then cast off,
    says your God.
For a brief moment I abandoned you,
    but with great tenderness I will take you
    back.
In an outburst of wrath, for a moment
    I hid my face from you;
But with enduring love I take pity on you,
    says the Lord, your redeemer.

This is for me like the days of Noah,
    when I swore that the waters of Noah
    should never again deluge the earth;
So I have sworn not to be angry with you,
    or to rebuke you.
Though the mountains leave their place
    and the hills be shaken,
My love shall never leave you
    nor my covenant of peace be shaken,
    says the Lord, who has mercy on you.
    This is the Word of the Lord.

Responsorial Psalm   Ps 30, 2. 4. 5-6. 11-12. 13

℟. (2) I will praise you, Lord,
    for you have rescued me.
I will extol you, O Lord, for you drew me clear
    and did not let my enemies rejoice over me.
O Lord, you brought me up from the nether
    world;
    you preserved me from among those going
    down into the pit.
℟. I will praise you, Lord,
    for you have rescued me.
Sing praise to the Lord, you his faithful ones,
    and give thanks to his holy name.
For his anger lasts but a moment;
    a lifetime, his good will.
At nightfall, weeping enters in,
    but with the dawn, rejoicing.
℟. I will praise you, Lord,
    for you have rescued me.
Hear, O Lord, and have pity on me;
    O Lord, be my helper.
You changed my mourning into dancing;
    O Lord, my God, forever will I give you
    thanks.
℟. I will praise you, Lord,
    for you have rescued me.

GOSPEL   Lk 7, 24-30
Alleluia
See no. 193.

✠ **A reading from the holy gospel according
to Luke**

John is the messenger who prepares the way of the Lord.

When the messengers of John had set off,
Jesus began to speak about him to the crowds.

"What did you go out to see in the desert—a reed swayed by the wind? What, really, did you go out to see—someone dressed luxuriously? Remember, those who dress in luxury and eat in splendor are to be found in royal palaces. Then what did you go out to see—a prophet? He is that, I assure you, and something more. This is the man of whom Scripture says,

'I send my messenger ahead of you
    to prepare your way before you.'

I assure you, there is no man born of woman greater than John. Yet the least born into the kingdom of God is greater than he."

The entire populace that had heard Jesus, even the tax collectors, gave praise to God, for they had received from John the baptismal bath he administered. The Pharisees and the lawyers, on the other hand, by failing to receive his baptism defeated God's plan in their regard.

This is the gospel of the Lord.

---

192   FRIDAY OF THE THIRD WEEK
OF ADVENT

If today is December 17 or 18, omit these readings and use those given for the Weekdays of Advent, nos. 194 or 195.

READING I   Is 56, 1-3. 6-8

A reading from the book of the prophet Isaiah
My house will be called a house of prayer for all people.

Thus says the Lord:
Observe what is right, do what is just;
    for my salvation is about to come,
    my justice, about to be revealed.
Happy is the man who does this,
    the son of man who holds to it;
Who keeps the sabbath free from profanation,
    and his hand from any evildoing.
Let not the foreigner say,
    when he would join himself to the Lord,
    "The Lord will surely exclude me from his
        people."

The foreigners who join themselves to the
    Lord,
    ministering to him,

Loving the name of the Lord,
    and becoming his servants—
All who keep the sabbath free from profana-
    tion
    and hold to my covenant,
Them I will bring to my holy mountain
    and make joyful in my house of prayer;
Their holocausts and sacrifices
    will be acceptable on my altar,
For my house shall be called
    a house of prayer for all peoples.
Thus says the Lord God,
    who gathers the dispersed of Israel:
Others will I gather to him
    besides those already gathered.
    This is the Word of the Lord.

Responsorial Psalm   Ps 67, 2-3. 5. 7-8

℟. (4) O God, let all the nations praise you!
May God have pity on us and bless us;
    may he let his face shine upon us.
So may your way be known upon earth;
    among all nations, your salvation.
℟. O God, let all the nations praise you!
May the nations be glad and exult
    because you rule the peoples in equity;
    the nations on the earth you guide.
℟. O God, let all the nations praise you!
The earth has yielded its fruits;
    God, our God, has blessed us.
May God bless us,
    and may all the ends of the earth fear him!
℟. O God, let all the nations praise you!

GOSPEL   Jn 5, 33-36
Alleluia

See no. 193.

✠ A reading from the holy gospel according
    to John
John was a burning and shining lamp.

Jesus said to the Jews:
"You have sent to John,
    who has testified to the truth.
    (Not that I myself accept such human
        testimony—
    I refer to these things only for your salva-
        tion.)

He was the lamp, set aflame and burning bright,
and for awhile you exulted willingly in his light.
Yet I have testimony greater than John's,
namely, the works the Father has given me to accomplish.
These very works which I perform testify on my behalf
that the Father has sent me."
This is the gospel of the Lord.

---

193   **ALLELUIA**

FOR THE WEEKDAYS OF ADVENT

UP TO DECEMBER 16

1   See Ps 79, 4

Ry. Alleluia. **Come and save us, Lord our God;**
let us see your face, and we shall be saved.
Ry. Alleluia.

2   Ps 85, 8

Ry. Alleluia. **Lord, let us see your kindness,**
and grant us your salvation. Ry. Alleluia.

3   Is 33, 22

Ry. Alleluia. **The Lord will judge us by his law;**
he is our King and Savior. Ry. Alleluia.

4   Is 40, 9. 10

Ry. Alleluia. **Raise your voice and tell the Good News:**
the Lord our God comes in strength. Ry. Alleluia.

5   Is 45, 8

Ry. Alleluia. **Let the clouds rain down the Just One,**
and the earth bring forth a Savior. Ry. Alleluia.

6   Is 55, 6

Ry. Alleluia. **Seek the Lord while he can be found.**
Call on him while he is near. Ry. Alleluia.

7   Lk 3, 4. 6

Ry. Alleluia. **Prepare the way for the Lord,**
make straight his paths:
all mankind shall see the salvation of God.
Ry. Alleluia.

8

Ry. Alleluia. **Come, O Lord, do not delay:**
forgive the sins of your people. Ry. Alleluia.

9

Ry. Alleluia. **Behold, our Lord shall come with power,**
he will enlighten the eyes of his servants. Ry. Alleluia.

10

Ry. Alleluia. **Come, Lord, bring to us your peace;**
let us rejoice before you with a perfect heart.
Ry. Alleluia.

11

Ry. Alleluia. **Behold, the king will come, the Lord of earth:**
and he will set us free. Ry. Alleluia.

12

Ry. Alleluia. **The day of the Lord is near:**
he comes to save us. Ry. Alleluia.

13

Ry. Alleluia. **The Lord will come; go out to meet him!**
He is the prince of peace. Ry. Alleluia.

14

Ry. Alleluia. **The Lord is coming to save his people;**
happy are those prepared to meet him. Ry. Alleluia.

WEEKDAYS OF ADVENT

DECEMBER 17 TO DECEMBER 24

These readings are for use between December 17 and 24. If a Sunday occurs during this time, the weekday reading for that day is omitted, but may be used on another day during the week, especially to avoid duplicating the Sunday reading.

194   **DECEMBER 17**

READING I   Gn 49, 2. 8-10

A reading from the book of Genesis

The scepter shall not pass from Judah.

Jacob called his sons and said to them:
"Assemble and listen, sons of Jacob,
    listen to Israel, your father.

"You, Judah, shall your brothers praise
    —your hand on the neck of your enemies;
    the sons of your father shall bow down to
    you.
Judah, like a lion's whelp,
    you have grown up on prey, my son.
He crouches like a lion recumbent,
    the king of beasts—who would dare rouse
    him?
The scepter shall never depart from Judah,
    or the mace from between his legs,
While tribute is brought to him,
    and he receives the peoples' homage."
        This is the Word of the Lord.

Responsorial Psalm   Ps 72, 3-4. 7-8. 17

℟. (7) Justice shall flourish in his time,
    and fullness of peace forever.

O God, with your judgment endow the king,
    and with your justice, the king's son;
He shall govern your people with justice
    and your afflicted ones with judgment.
℟. Justice shall flourish in his time,
    and fullness of peace for ever.

The mountains shall yield peace for the people,
    and the hills justice.
He shall defend the afflicted among the people,
    save the children of the poor.
℟. Justice shall flourish in his time,
    and fullness of peace for ever.

Justice shall flower in his days,
    and profound peace, till the moon be no
    more.
May he rule from sea to sea,
    and from the River to the ends of the earth.
℟. Justice shall flourish in his time,
    and fullness of peace for ever.

May his name be blessed forever;
    as long as the sun his name shall remain.
In him shall all the tribes of the earth be
    blessed;
    all the nations shall proclaim his happiness.
℟. Justice shall flourish in his time,
    and fullness of peace for ever.

GOSPEL   Mt 1, 1-17
Alleluia

See no. 202.

✠ The beginning of the holy gospel according
            to Matthew

A genealogy of Jesus Christ, son of David.

A family record of Jesus Christ, son of David,
son of Abraham. Abraham was the father of
Isaac, Isaac the father of Jacob, Jacob the
father of Judah and his brothers.
    Judah was the father of Perez and Zerah,
        whose mother was Tamar.
    Perez was the father of Hezron,
    Hezron the father of Ram.
    Ram was the father of Amminadab,
    Amminadab the father of Nahshon,
    Nahshon the father of Salmon.
    Salmon was the father of Boaz, whose
        mother was Rahab,
    Boaz was the father of Obed, whose
        mother was Ruth.
    Obed was the father of Jesse,
    Jesse the father of King David.
    David was the father of Solomon, whose
        mother had been the wife of Uriah.
    Solomon was the father of Rehoboam,
    Rehoboam the father of Abijah,
    Abijah the father of Asa.
    Asa was the father of Jehoshaphat,
    Jehoshaphat the father of Joram,
    Joram the father of Uzziah.
    Uzziah was the father of Jotham,

Jotham the father of Ahaz,
Ahaz the father of Hezekiah.
Hezekiah was the father of Manasseh,
Manasseh the father of Amos,
Amos the father of Josiah.
Josiah became the father of Jechoniah and
   his brothers at the time of the Baby-
   lonian exile.
After the Babylonian exile
Jechoniah was the father of Shealtiel,
Shealtiel the father of Zerubbabel.
Zerubbabel was the father of Abiud,
Abiud the father of Eliakim,
Eliakim the father of Azor.
Azor was the father of Zadok,
Zadok the father of Achim,
Achim the father of Eliud.
Eliud was the father of Eleazar,
Eleazar the father of Matthan,
Matthan the father of Jacob.
Jacob was the father of Joseph the hus-
   band of Mary.
It was of her that Jesus who is called the
   Messiah was born.
Thus the total number of generations is:
   from Abraham to David, fourteen gen-
   erations;
   from David to the Babylonian captivity,
   fourteen generations;
   from the Babylonian captivity to the
   Messiah, fourteen generations.
This is the gospel of the Lord.

---

195   DECEMBER 18

READING I   Jer 23, 5-8

**A reading from the book of the prophet
Jeremiah**
I will raise a virtuous branch for David.

Behold, the days are coming, says the Lord,
   when I will raise up a righteous shoot to
   David;
As king he shall reign and govern wisely,
   he shall do what is just and right in the land.
In his days Judah shall be saved,
   Israel shall dwell in security.
This is the name they give him:
   "The Lord our justice."

Therefore, the days will come, says the Lord,
when they shall no longer say, "As the Lord
lives, who brought the Israelites out of the land
of Egypt"; but rather, "As the Lord lives, who
brought the descendants of the house of Israel
up from the land of the north"—and from all
the lands to which I banished them; they shall
again live on their own land.
   This is the Word of the Lord.

Responsorial Psalm   Ps 72, 1- 12-13. 18-19

℟. Justice shall flourish in his time,
   and fullness of peace for ever.
O God, with your judgment endow the king,
   and with your justice, the king's son;
He shall govern your people with justice
   and your afflicted ones with judgment.
℟. Justice shall flourish in his time,
   and fullness of peace for ever.
For he shall rescue the poor man when he cries
   out,
   and the afflicted when he has no one to help
   him.
He shall have pity for the lowly and the poor;
   the lives of the poor he shall save.
℟. Justice shall flourish in his time,
   and fullness of peace for ever.
Blessed be the Lord, the God of Israel,
   who alone does wondrous deeds.
And blessed forever be his glorious name;
   may the whole earth be filled with his glory.
   Amen. Amen.
℟. Justice shall flourish in his time,
   and fullness of peace for ever.

GOSPEL   Mt 1, 18-24
Alleluia
See no. 202.

✠ **A reading from the holy gospel according
to Matthew**
Jesus was born of Mary, the betrothed of Joseph, a son
of David.

Now this is how the birth of Jesus Christ came
about. When his mother Mary was engaged to
Joseph, but before they lived together, she was
found with child through the power of the Holy

Spirit. Joseph her husband, an upright man un-willing to expose her to the law, decided to divorce her quietly. Such was his intention when suddenly the angel of the Lord appeared in a dream and said to him: "Joseph, son of David, have no fear about taking Mary as your wife. It is by the Holy Spirit that she has conceived this child. She is to have a son and you are to name him Jesus because he will save his people from their sins." All this happened to fulfill what the Lord had said through the prophet:

"The virgin shall be with child
and give birth to a son,
and they shall call him Emmanuel,"

a name which means "God is with us." When Joseph awoke he did as the angel of the Lord had directed him and received her into his home as his wife. He had no relations with her at any time before she bore a son, whom he named Jesus.

This is the gospel of the Lord.

---

196   **DECEMBER 19**

READING I   Jgs 13, 2-7. 24-25

A reading from the book of Judges

The birth of Samuel was announced by an angel.

There was a certain man from Zorah, of the clan of the Danites, whose name was Manoah. His wife was barren and had borne no children. An angel of the Lord appeared to the woman and said to her, "Though you are barren and have had no children, yet you will conceive and bear a son. Now, then, be careful to take no wine or strong drink and to eat nothing un-clean. As for the son you will conceive and bear, no razor shall touch his head, for this boy is to be consecrated to God from the womb. It is he who will begin the deliverance of Israel from the power of the Philistines."

The woman went and told her husband, "A man of God came to me; he had the appearance of an angel of God, terrible indeed. I did not ask him where he came from, nor did he tell me his name. But he said to me, 'You will be with child and will bear a son. So take neither wine nor

strong drink, and eat nothing unclean. For the boy shall be consecrated to God from the womb, until the day of his death.'"

The woman bore a son and named him Samson. The boy grew up and the Lord blessed him. The spirit of the Lord began to be with him.

This is the Word of the Lord.

Responsorial Psalm   Ps 71, 3-4. 5-6. 16-17

℟. (8) Fill me with your praise
and I will sing your glory!

Be my rock of refuge,
a stronghold to give me safety,
for you are my rock and my fortress.

O my God, rescue me from the hand of the wicked.

℟. Fill me with your praise
and I will sing your glory!

For you are my hope, O Lord;
my trust, O God, from my youth.

On you I depend from birth;
from my mother's womb you are my strength.

℟. Fill me with your praise
and I will sing your glory!

I will treat of the mighty works of the Lord;
O God, I will tell of your singular justice.

O God, you have taught me from my youth,
and till the present I proclaim your won-drous deeds.

℟. Fill me with your praise
and I will sing your glory!

GOSPEL   Lk 1, 5-25

Alleluia

See no. 202.

✠ **A reading from the holy gospel according to Luke**

The birth of John the Baptizer was announced by Gabriel.

In the days of Herod, king of Judea, there was a priest named Zechariah of the priestly class of Abijah; his wife was a descendant of Aaron named Elizabeth. Both were just in the eyes of God, blamelessly following all the command-ments and ordinances of the Lord. They were childless, for Elizabeth was sterile; moreover, both were advanced in years.

Once, when it was the turn of Zechariah's class and he was fulfilling his functions as a priest before God, it fell to him by lot according to priestly usage to enter the sanctuary of the Lord and offer incense. While the full assembly of people was praying outside at the incense hour, an angel of the Lord appeared to him, standing at the right of the altar of incense. Zechariah was deeply disturbed upon seeing him, and overcome by fear.

The angel said to him: "Do not be frightened, Zechariah; your prayer has been heard. Your wife Elizabeth shall bear a son whom you shall name John. Joy and gladness will be yours, and many will rejoice at his birth; for he will be great in the eyes of the Lord. He will never drink wine or strong drink, and he will be filled with the Holy Spirit from his mother's womb. Many of the sons of Israel will he bring back to the Lord their God. God himself will go before him, in the spirit and power of Elijah, to turn the hearts of fathers to their children and the rebellious to the wisdom of the just, and to prepare for the Lord a people well-disposed."

Zechariah said to the angel: "How am I to know this? I am an old man; my wife too is advanced in age."

The angel replied: "I am Gabriel, who stand in attendance before God. I was sent to speak to you and bring you this good news. But now you will be mute—unable to speak—until the day when these things take place, because you have not trusted my words. They will all come true in due season." Meanwhile, the people were waiting for Zechariah, wondering at his delay in the temple. When he finally came out he was unable to speak to them, and they realized that he had seen a vision inside. He kept making signs to them, for he remained speechless.

Then, when his period of priestly service was over, he went home.

Afterward, his wife Elizabeth conceived. She went into seclusion for five months, saying, "In these days the Lord is acting on my behalf; he has seen fit to remove my reproach among men."

This is the gospel of the Lord.

197   DECEMBER 20

READING I   Is 7, 10-14

A reading from the book of the prophet Isaiah
The virgin shall conceive.

The Lord spoke to Ahaz: Ask for a sign from the Lord, your God; let it be deep as the nether world, or high as the sky! But Ahaz answered, "I will not ask! I will not tempt the Lord!" Then he said: Listen, O house of David! Is it not enough for you to weary men, must you also weary my God? Therefore the Lord himself will give you this sign: the virgin shall be with child, and bear a son, and shall name him Immanuel [because "God is with us"].

This is the Word of the Lord.

Responsorial Psalm   Ps 24, 1-2. 3-4. 5-6

℞. (7.10) Let the Lord enter;
    he is king of glory.
The Lord's are the earth and its fullness;
    the world and those who dwell in it.
For he founded it upon the seas
    and established it upon the rivers.
℞. Let the Lord enter;
    he is king of glory.
Who can ascend the mountain of the Lord?
    or who may stand in his holy place?
He whose hands are sinless, whose heart is clean,
    who desires not what is vain.
℞. Let the Lord enter;
    he is king of glory.
He shall receive a blessing from the Lord,
    a reward from God his savior.
Such is the race that seeks for him,
    that seeks the face of the God of Jacob.
℞. Let the Lord enter;
    he is king of glory.

GOSPEL   Lk 1, 26-38
Alleluia

See no. 202.

✠ **A reading from the holy gospel according to Luke**
You are to conceive and bear a son.

In the sixth month, the angel Gabriel was sent from God to a town of Galilee named Nazareth, to a virgin betrothed to a man named Joseph, of the house of David. The virgin's name was Mary. Upon arriving, the messenger said to her: "Rejoice, O highly favored daughter! The Lord is with you. Blessed are you among women." She was deeply troubled by his words, and wondered what his greeting meant. The messenger went on to say to her: "Do not fear, Mary. You have found favor with God. You shall conceive and bear a son and give him the name Jesus. Great will be his dignity and he will be called Son of the Most High. The Lord God will give him the throne of David his father. He will rule over the house of Jacob forever and his reign will be without end."

Mary said to the angel, "How can this be since I do not know man?" The angel answered her: "The Holy Spirit will come upon you and the power of the Most High will overshadow you; hence, the holy offspring to be born will be called Son of God. Know that Elizabeth your kinswoman has conceived a son in her old age; she who was thought to be sterile is now in her sixth month, for nothing is impossible with God."

Mary said: "I am the maidservant of the Lord. Let it be done to me as you say." With that the angel left her.

This is the gospel of the Lord.

---

198   **DECEMBER 21**

READING I   Sg 2, 8-14

A reading from the Song of Solomon

I hear my beloved, see how he comes leaping on the mountains.

Hark! my lover—here he comes
　springing across the mountains,
　leaping across the hills.
My lover is like a gazelle
　or a young stag.
Here he stands behind our wall,
　gazing through the windows,
　peering through the lattices.
My lover speaks; he says to me,
　"Arise, my beloved, my beautiful one,
　and come!

"For see, the winter is past,
　the rains are over and gone.
The flowers appear on the earth,
　the time of pruning the vines has come,
　and the song of the dove is heard in our land.
The fig tree puts forth its figs,
　and the vines, in bloom, give forth fragrance.
Arise, my beloved, my beautiful one,
　and come!

"O my dove in the clefts of the rock,
　in the secret recesses of the cliff,
Let me see you,
　let me hear your voice,
For your voice is sweet,
　and you are lovely."

This is the Word of the Lord.

OR

READING I   Zep 3, 14-18

A reading from the book of the prophet Zephaniah

The Lord, the King, is among his people.

Shout for joy, O daughter Zion!
　sing joyfully, O Israel!
Be glad and exult with all your heart,
　O daughter Jerusalem!
The Lord has removed the judgment against you,
　he has turned away your enemies;
The King of Israel, the Lord, is in your midst,
　you have no further misfortune to fear.
On that day, it shall be said to Jerusalem:
　Fear not, O Zion, be not discouraged!
The Lord, your God, is in your midst,
　a mighty savior;
He will rejoice over you with gladness,
　and renew you in his love.
He will sing joyfully because of you,
　as one sings at festivals.

This is the Word of the Lord.

Responsorial Psalm   Ps 33, 2-3. 11-12. 20-21

℟. (1.3) Cry out with joy in the Lord, you holy ones;
　sing a new song to him.

Give thanks to the Lord on the harp;
  with the ten-stringed lyre chant his praises.
Sing to him a new song;
  pluck the strings skillfully, with shouts of
    gladness.
℟. Cry out with joy in the Lord, you holy ones;
  sing a new song to him.
The plan of the Lord stands forever;
  the design of his heart, through all gener-
    ations.
Happy the nation whose God is the Lord,
  the people he has chosen for his own in-
    heritance.
℟. Cry out with joy in the Lord, you holy ones;
  sing a new song to him.
Our soul waits for the Lord,
  who is our help and our shield,
For in him our hearts rejoice;
  in his holy name we trust.
℟. Cry out with joy in the Lord, you holy ones;
  sing a new song to him.

GOSPEL

Alleluia

Lk 1, 39-45

See no. 202.

✠ A reading from the holy gospel according
    to Luke

*Why should I be honored with a visit from the mother
    of my Lord?*

Mary set out, proceeding in haste into the hill
country to a town of Judah, where she entered
Zechariah's house and greeted Elizabeth.
When Elizabeth heard Mary's greeting, the
baby stirred in her womb. Elizabeth was filled
with the Holy Spirit, and cried out in a loud
voice: "Blessed are you among women and
blessed is the fruit of your womb. But who am
I that the mother of my Lord should come to
me? The moment your greeting sounded in my
ears, the baby stirred in my womb for joy.
Blessed is she who trusted that the Lord's
words to her would be fulfilled."
  This is the gospel of the Lord.

199   **DECEMBER 22**

READING I

1 Sm 1, 24-28

A reading from the first book of Samuel

Anna gave thanks for the birth of Samuel.

Anna brought Samuel with her, along with a
three-year-old bull, an ephah of flour, and a
skin of wine, and presented him at the temple
of the Lord in Shiloh. After the boy's father
had sacrificed the young bull, Hannah, his
mother, approached Eli and said: "Pardon, my
lord! As you live, my lord, I am the woman
who stood near you here, praying to the Lord.
I prayed for this child, and the Lord granted
my request. Now I, in turn, give him to the
Lord; as long as he lives, he shall be dedicated
to the Lord." She left him there.
  This is the Word of the Lord.

Responsorial Psalm   1 Sm 2, 1. 4-5. 6-7. 8

℟. (1) My heart rejoices in the Lord, my
  Savior.
My heart exults in the Lord,
  my horn is exalted in my God.
I have swallowed up my enemies;
  I rejoice in my victory.
℟. My heart rejoices in the Lord, my Savior.
The bows of the mighty are broken,
  while the tottering gird on strength.
The well-fed hire themselves out for bread,
  while the hungry batten on spoil.
The barren wife bears seven sons,
  while the mother of many languishes.
℟. My heart rejoices in the Lord, my Savior.
The Lord puts to death and gives life;
  he casts down to the nether world;
  he raises up again.
The Lord makes poor and makes rich,
  he humbles, he also exalts.
℟. My heart rejoices in the Lord, my Savior.
He raises the needy from the dust;
  from the ash heap he lifts up the poor,
To seat them with nobles
  and make a glorious throne their heritage.
℟. My heart rejoices in the Lord, my Savior.

GOSPEL
Lk 1, 46-56

Alleluia
See no. 202.

✠ A reading from the holy gospel according to Luke

He who has done great things for me is powerful.

Mary said:
"My being proclaims the greatness of the Lord,
  my spirit finds joy in God my savior,
For he has looked upon his servant in her lowliness;
all ages to come shall call me blessed.
God who is mighty has done great things for me,
  holy is his name;
His mercy is from age to age
  on those who fear him.
"He has shown might with his arm;
  he has confused the proud in their inmost thoughts.
He has deposed the mighty from their thrones
  and raised the lowly to high places.
The hungry he has given every good thing,
  while the rich he has sent empty away.
He has upheld Israel his servant,
  ever mindful of his mercy;
Even as he promised our fathers,
  promised Abraham and his descendants forever."
Mary remained with Elizabeth about three months and then returned home.
This is the gospel of the Lord.

---

200 **DECEMBER 23**

READING I
Mal 3, 1-4. 23-24

A reading from the book of the prophet Malachi

I shall send you the prophet Elijah as a sign that the day of the Lord is near.

Lo, I am sending my messenger
to prepare the way before me;
And suddenly there will come to the temple
the Lord whom you seek,

And the messenger of the covenant whom you desire.
Yes, he is coming, says the Lord of hosts.
But who will endure the day of his coming?
And who can stand when he appears?
For he is like the refiner's fire,
  or like the fuller's lye.
He will sit refining and purifying [silver],
  and he will purify the sons of Levi,
Refining them like gold or like silver
  that they may offer due sacrifice to the Lord.
Then the sacrifice of Judah and Jerusalem
  will please the Lord,
  as in the days of old, as in years gone by.
Lo, I will send you
  Elijah, the prophet,
Before the day of the Lord comes,
  the great and terrible day,
To turn the hearts of the fathers to their children,
  and the hearts of the children to their fathers,
Lest I come and strike
  the land with doom.
This is the Word of the Lord.

Responsorial Psalm
Ps 25, 4-5. 8-9. 10. 14

℞. (Lk 21, 28) Lift up your heads and see;
  your redemption is near at hand.

Your ways, O Lord, make known to me;
  teach me your paths,
Guide me in your truth and teach me,
  for you are God my savior.
℞. Lift up your heads and see;
  your redemption is near at hand.

Good and upright is the Lord;
  thus he shows sinners the way.
He guides the humble to justice,
  he teaches the humble his way.
℞. Lift up your heads and see;
  your redemption is near at hand.

All the paths of the Lord are kindness and constancy
  toward those who keep his covenant and his decrees.
The friendship of the Lord is with those who fear him,
  and his covenant, for their instruction.

℟. Lift up your heads and see;
  your redemption is near at hand.

GOSPEL   Lk 1, 57-66
Alleluia

See no. 202.

✠ A reading from the holy gospel according
  to Luke

The birth of John the Baptizer.

When Elizabeth's time for delivery arrived, she gave birth to a son. Her neighbors and relatives, upon hearing that the Lord had extended his mercy to her, rejoiced with her. When they assembled for the circumcision of the child on the eighth day, they intended to name him after his father Zechariah. At this his mother intervened, saying, "No, he is to be called John."

They pointed out to her, "None of your relatives has this name." Then, using signs, they asked the father what he wished him to be called.

He signaled for a writing tablet and wrote the words, "His name is John." This astonished them all. At that moment his mouth was opened and his tongue loosed, and he began to speak in praise of God.

Fear descended on all in the neighborhood; throughout the hill country of Judea these happenings began to be recounted to the last detail. All who heard stored these things in their hearts, saying, "What will this child be?" and, "Was not the hand of the Lord upon him?"
This is the gospel of the Lord.

---

201   **DECEMBER 24**

Mass in the Morning

READING I   2 Sm 7, 1-5. 8-11. 16

A reading from the second book of Samuel

The kingdom of David will be established for ever in the sight of the Lord.

When King David was settled in his palace, and the Lord had given him rest from his enemies on every side, he said to Nathan the prophet, "Here I am living in a house of cedar, while the ark of God dwells in a tent!" Nathan answered the king, "Go, do whatever you have in mind, for the Lord is with you." But that night the Lord spoke to Nathan and said: "Go, tell my servant David, 'Thus says the Lord: Should you build me a house to dwell in? The Lord of hosts has this to say: It was I who took you from the pasture and from the care of the flock to be commander of my people Israel. I have been with you wherever you went, and I have destroyed all your enemies before you. And I will make you famous like the great ones of the earth. I will fix a place for my people Israel; I will plant them so that they may dwell in their place without further disturbance. Neither shall the wicked continue to afflict them as they did of old, since the time I first appointed judges over my people Israel. I will give you rest from all your enemies. The Lord also reveals to you that he will establish a house for you. Your house and your kingdom shall endure forever before me; your throne shall stand firm forever.' "
This is the Word of the Lord.

Responsorial Psalm   Ps 89, 2-3. 4-5. 27. 29

℟. (2) For ever I will sing the goodness of the Lord.

The favors of the Lord I will sing forever;
  through all generations my mouth shall proclaim your faithfulness.
For you have said, "My kindness is established forever";
  in heaven you have confirmed your faithfulness.

℟. For ever I will sing the goodness of the Lord.

"I have made a covenant with my chosen one,
  I have sworn to David my servant:
Forever will I confirm your posterity
  and establish your throne for all generations."

℟. For ever I will sing the goodness of the Lord.

He shall say of me, "You are my father,
  my God, the Rock, my savior."
Forever I will maintain my kindness toward him,
  and my covenant with him stands firm.

℟. For ever I will sing the goodness of the Lord.

GOSPEL   Lk 1, 67-79
Alleluia

See no. 202.

✠ A reading from the holy gospel according to Luke

From on high the rising sun will visit us.

Zechariah, the father of John, filled with the Holy Spirit, uttered this prophecy:

"Blessed be the Lord the God of Israel
  because he has visited and ransomed his people.
He has raised a horn of saving strength for us
  in the house of David his servant,
As he promised through the mouths of his holy ones,
  the prophets of ancient times:
Salvation from our enemies
  and from the hands of all our foes.
He has dealt mercifully with our fathers
  and remembered the holy covenant he made,
The oath he swore to Abraham our father
  he would grant us:
that, rid of fear and delivered from the enemy,
We should serve him devoutly, and through all our days,
  be holy in his sight.
And you, O child, shall be called
  prophet of the Most High;
For you shall go before the Lord
  to prepare straight paths for him,
Giving his people a knowledge of salvation
  in freedom from their sins.
All this is the work of the kindness of our God;
  he, the Dayspring, shall visit us in his mercy
To shine on those who sit in darkness and in the shadow of death,
  to guide our feet into the way of peace."
This is the gospel of the Lord.

---

202   **ALLELUIA**
FOR THE WEEKDAYS OF ADVENT
FROM DECEMBER 17 TO DECEMBER 24

1

℟. Alleluia. **Come,**
Wisdom of our God Most High,
guiding creation with power and love:
teach us to walk in the paths of knowledge:
  ℟. Alleluia.

2

℟. Alleluia. **Come,**
Leader of ancient Israel,
giver of the Law to Moses on Sinai:
rescue us with your mighty power! ℟. Alleluia.

3

℟. Alleluia. **Come,**
Flower of Jesse's stem,
sign of God's love for all his people:
save us without delay! ℟. Alleluia.

4

℟. Alleluia. **Come,**
Key of David,
opening the gates of God's eternal Kingdom:
free the prisoners of darkness! ℟. Alleluia.

5

℟. Alleluia. **Come,**
Radiant Dawn,
splendor of eternal light, sun of justice:
shine on those lost in the darkness of death!
  ℟. Alleluia.

6

℟. Alleluia. **Come,**
King of all nations,
source of your Church's unity and faith:
save all mankind, your own creation! ℟. Alleluia.

7

℟. Alleluia. **Come,**
Emmanuel,
God's presence among us, our King, our Judge:
save us, Lord our God! ℟. Alleluia.

203

DECEMBER 29

The Fifth Day in the Octave of Christmas

READING I   1 Jn 2, 3-11

A reading from the first letter of John

He who loves his brother lives in the light.

The way we can be sure of our knowledge of
    Jesus
  is to keep his commandments.
The man who claims, "I have known him,"
  without keeping his commandments,
  is a liar; in such a one there is no truth.
But whoever keeps his word
  truly has the love of God made perfect in
    him.
The way we can be sure we are in union with
    him
  is if one who claims to abide in him
  conducts himself just as he did.

Dearly beloved,
  it is no new commandment that I write to
    you,
  but an old one which you had from the start.
The commandment, now old, is the word you
    have already heard.
On second thought, the commandment that I
    write you is new,
  as it is realized in him and you,
  for the darkness is over
  and the real light begins to shine.
The man who claims to be in light,
  hating his brother all the while,
  is in darkness even now.
The man who continues in the light
  is the one who loves his brother;
  there is nothing in him to cause a fall.
But the man who hates his brother is in
    darkness.
He walks in shadows,
  not knowing where he is going,
  since the dark has blinded his eyes.
        This is the Word of the Lord.

Responsorial Psalm   Ps 96, 1-2. 2-3. 5-6
Let heaven and earth exult in joy.

Sing to the Lord a new song;
  sing to the Lord, all you lands.
Sing to the Lord; bless his name.
  Let heaven and earth exult in joy.
Announce his salvation, day after day
  tell his glory among the nations;
Among all peoples, his wondrous deeds.
  Let heaven and earth exult in joy.
The Lord made the heavens.
  Splendor and majesty go before him;
Praise and grandeur are in his sanctuary.
℟. Let heaven and earth exult in joy.

GOSPEL   Lk 2, 22-35
Alleluia
See no. 212.

✠ A reading from the holy gospel according
              to Luke

I have seen a light, the glory of your people Israel.

When the day came to purify them according
to the law of Moses, the couple brought Jesus
up to Jerusalem so that he could be presented
to the Lord, for it is written in the law of the
Lord, "Every first-born male shall be consecrated to the Lord." They came to offer in
sacrifice "a pair of turtledoves or two young
pigeons," in accord with the dictate in the law
of the Lord.
    There lived in Jerusalem a certain man
named Simeon. He was just and pious, and
awaited the consolation of Israel, and the Holy
Spirit was upon him. It was revealed to him by
the Holy Spirit that he would not experience
death until he had seen the Anointed of the
Lord. He came to the temple now, inspired by
the Spirit; and when the parents brought in the
child Jesus to perform for him the customary
ritual of the law, he took him in his arms and
blessed God in these words:
    "Now, Master, you can dismiss your ser-
vant in peace;
  you have fulfilled your word.
    For my eyes have witnessed your saving
    deed
    displayed for all the peoples to see:
  A revealing light to the Gentiles,
    the glory of your people Israel."

The child's father and mother were marveling at what was being said about him. Simeon blessed them and said to Mary his mother: "This child is destined to be the downfall and the rise of many in Israel, a sign that will be opposed—and you yourself shall be pierced with a sword—so that the thoughts of many hearts may be laid bare."

This is the gospel of the Lord.

---

204   DECEMBER 30

The Sixth Day in the Octave of Christmas

READING I   1 Jn 2, 12-17

A reading from the first letter of John
He who does the will of God remains for ever.

Little ones, I address you,
　for through his Name your sins have been
　　forgiven.
Fathers, I address you,
　for you have known him who is from the
　　beginning.
Young men, I address you,
　for you have conquered the evil one.
I address you, children,
　for you have known the Father.
I address you, fathers,
　for you have known him who is from the beginning.
I address you, young men,
　for you are strong,
　and the word of God remains in you,
　and you have conquered the evil one.

Have no love for the world,
　nor the things that the world affords.
If anyone loves the world,
　the Father's love has no place in him,
　for nothing that the world affords
　comes from the Father.
Carnal allurements,
　enticements for the eye,
　the life of empty show—
　all these are from the world.
And the world with its seductions is passing
　away
　but the man who does God's will
　endures forever.

This is the Word of the Lord.

Responsorial Psalm   Ps 96, 7-8. 8-9. 10

℟. (11) Let heaven and earth exult in joy.
Give to the Lord, you families of nations,
　give to the Lord glory and praise;
　give to the Lord the glory due his name!
℟. Let heaven and earth exult in joy.
Bring gifts, and enter his courts;
　worship the Lord in holy attire.
　Tremble before him, all the earth.
℟. Let heaven and earth exult in joy.
Say among the nations: The Lord is king.
　He has made the world firm, not to be
　　moved;
　he governs the peoples with equity.
℟. Let heaven and earth exult in joy.

GOSPEL   Lk 2, 36-40
Alleluia

See no. 212.

✠ **A reading from the holy gospel according
to Luke**
She spoke of the child to all who looked for the deliverance
of Israel.

There was a certain prophetess, Anna by name, daughter of Phanuel of the tribe of Asher. She had seen many days, having lived seven years with her husband after her marriage and then as a widow until she was eighty-four. She was constantly in the temple, worshiping day and night in fasting and prayer. Coming on the scene at this moment, she gave thanks to God and talked about the child to all who looked forward to the deliverance of Jerusalem.

When the pair had fulfilled all the prescriptions of the law of the Lord, they returned to Galilee and their own town of Nazareth. The child grew in size and strength, filled with wisdom, and the grace of God was upon him.

This is the gospel of the Lord.

205   DECEMBER 31

The Seventh Day in the Octave of Christmas

READING I   1 Jn 2, 18-21

A reading from the first letter of John

You have been appointed by the Holy One, and have all knowledge.

Children, it is the final hour;
    just as you heard that the Antichrist was
        coming,
    so now many such antichrists have appeared.
It was from our ranks that they took their
        leave—
    not that they really belonged to us;
    for if they had belonged to us,
    they would have stayed with us.
It only served to show that none of them was
        ours.

But you have the anointing that comes from
        the Holy One,
    so that all knowledge is yours.
My reason for having written you
    is not that you do not know the truth
    but that you do,
    and that no lie has anything in common with
        the truth.
            This is the Word of the Lord.

Responsorial Psalm   Ps 96, 1-2. 11-12. 13

R̊. (11) Let heaven and earth exult in joy.
Sing to the Lord a new song;
    sing to the Lord, all you lands.
Sing to the Lord; bless his name;
    announce his salvation, day after day.
R̊. Let heaven and earth exult in joy.
Let the heavens be glad and the earth rejoice;
    let the sea and what fills it resound;
Let the plains be joyful and all that is in them!
    Then shall all the trees of the forest exult
        before the Lord.
R̊. Let heaven and earth exult in joy.
The Lord comes,
    he comes to rule the earth.
He shall rule the world with justice
    and the peoples with his constancy.
R̊. Let heaven and earth exult in joy.

GOSPEL   Jn 1, 1-18
Alleluia

See no. 212.

✠ **The beginning of the holy gospel according
            to John**
The Word was made flesh.

In the beginning was the Word;
    the Word was in God's presence,
    and the Word was God.
He was present to God in the beginning.
Through him all things came into being,
    and apart from him nothing came to be.
Whatever came to be in him, found life,
    life for the light of men.
The light shines on in darkness,
    a darkness that did not overcome it.
There was a man named John sent by God,
who came as a witness to testify to the light,
so that through him all men might believe—
but only to testify to the light, for he himself
was not the light. The real light which gives
light to every man was coming into the world.
    He was in the world,
    and through him the world was made,
    yet the world did not know who he was.
    To his own he came,
    yet his own did not accept him.
    Any who did accept him
    he empowered to become children of God.
These are they who believe in his name—who
were begotten not by blood, nor by carnal
desire, nor by man's willing it, but by God.
    The Word became flesh
    and made his dwelling among us,
    and we have seen his glory:
    the glory of an only Son coming from the
        Father,
    filled with enduring love.
John testified to him by proclaiming: "This is
he of whom I said, 'The one who comes after
me ranks ahead of me, for he was before me.' "
    Of his fullness
    we have all had a share—
    love following upon love.
For while the law was a gift through Moses,
this enduring love came through Jesus Christ.
No one has ever seen God. It is God the only

Son, ever at the Father's side, who has revealed him.
                This is the gospel of the Lord.

---

206   JANUARY 2

READING I   1 Jn 2, 22-28

A reading from the first letter of John

What you were taught in the beginning remains alive in
                                    you.

Who is the liar?
He who denies that Jesus is the Christ.
He is the antichrist,
    denying the Father and the Son.
Anyone who denies the Son
    has no claim on the Father,
    but he who acknowledges the Son
    can claim the Father as well.

As for you,
    let what you heard from the beginning
    remain in your hearts.
If what you heard from the beginning
    does remain in your hearts,
    then you in turn will remain in the Son and
        in the Father.
He himself made us a promise
    and the promise is no less than this:
    eternal life.
I have written you these things
    about those who try to deceive you.
As for you,
    the anointing you received from him
    remains in your hearts.
This means you have no need
    for anyone to teach you.
Rather, as his anointing teaches you about all
        things
    and is true—free from any lie—
    remain in him
    as that anointing taught you.
Remain in him now, little ones,
    so that when he reveals himself,
    we may be fully confident
    and not retreat in shame at his coming.
            This is the Word of the Lord.

Responsorial Psalm   Ps 98, 1. 2-3. 3-4

℟. (3) All the ends of the earth have seen the
    saving power of God.

Sing to the Lord a new song,
    for he has done wondrous deeds;
His right hand has won victory for him,
    his holy arm.
℟. All the ends of the earth have seen the
    saving power of God.
The Lord has made his salvation known:
    in the sight of the nations he has revealed his
        justice.
He has remembered his kindness and his faith-
        fulness
    toward the house of Israel.
℟. All the ends of the earth have seen the
    saving power of God.
All the ends of the earth have seen
    the salvation by our God.
Sing joyfully to the Lord, all you lands;
    break into song; sing praise.
℟. All the ends of the earth have seen the
    saving power of God.

GOSPEL   Jn 1, 19-28
Alleluia

See no. 212.

✠ **A reading from the holy gospel according**
                to John

There is one to come after me who was created before me.

The testimony John gave when the Jews sent
priests and Levites from Jerusalem to ask
"Who are you?" was the absolute statement,
"I am not the Messiah." They questioned him
further, "Who, then? Elijah?" "I am not Elijah,"
he answered. "Are you the Prophet?" "No,"
he replied.
    Finally they said to him: "Tell us who you
are, so that we can give some answer to those
who sent us. What do you have to say for
yourself?" He said, quoting the prophet Isaiah,
"I am
    'a voice in the desert, crying out:
    Make straight the way of the Lord!' "
Those whom the Pharisees had sent pro-
ceeded to question him further: "If you are not
the Messiah, nor Elijah, nor the Prophet, why
do you baptize?" John answered them: "I bap-
tize with water. There is one among you whom
you do not recognize—the one who is to come

after me—the strap of whose sandal I am not worthy to unfasten.''

This happened in Bethany, across the Jordan, where John was baptizing.

This is the gospel of the Lord.

In countries where Epiphany is celebrated on the Sunday between January 2 and January 8, the readings assigned to the days January 7 to January 12 are used after Epiphany and the following readings are omitted (see nos. 213–218).

207   **JANUARY 3**

READING I   1 Jn 2, 29–3, 6

A reading from the first letter of John
He who lives in God does not sin.

If you consider the holiness that is God's,
  you can be sure that everyone who acts in
    holiness
  has been begotten by him.

See what love the Father has bestowed on us
  in letting us be called children of God!
Yet that is what we are.

The reason the world does not recognize us
  is that it never recognized the Son.
Dearly beloved,
  we are God's children now;
  what we shall later be has not yet come to
    light.
We know that when it comes to light
  we shall be like him,
  for we shall see him as he is.
Everyone who has this hope based on him
  keeps himself pure, as he is pure.
Everyone who sins acts lawlessly,
  for sin is lawlessness.
You know well that the reason he revealed
    himself
  was to take away sins;
  in him there is nothing sinful.
The man who remains in him does not sin.
The man who sins has not seen him nor known
    him.
          This is the Word of the Lord.

Responsorial Psalm   Ps 98, 1. 3-4. 5-6

℟. (3) All the ends of the earth have seen the
  saving power of God.

Sing to the Lord a new song,
  for he has done wondrous deeds;
His right hand has won victory for him,
  his holy arm.

℟. All the ends of the earth have seen the
  saving power of God.

All the ends of the earth have seen
  the salvation by our God.
Sing joyfully to the Lord, all you lands;
  break into song; sing praise.

℟. All the ends of the earth have seen the
  saving power of God.

Sing praise to the Lord with the harp,
  with the harp and melodious song.
With trumpets and the sound of the horn
  sing joyfully before the King, the Lord.

℟. All the ends of the earth have seen the
  saving power of God.

GOSPEL   Jn 1, 29-34
Alleluia

See no. 212.

✠ **A reading from the holy gospel according
            to John**
This is the Lamb of God

When John caught sight of Jesus coming
toward him, he exclaimed:
    "Look there! The Lamb of God
    who takes away the sin of the world!
It is he of whom I said:
    'After me is to come a man
    who ranks ahead of me,
    because he was before me.'
I confess I did not recognize him, though the
very reason I came baptizing with water was
that he might be revealed to Israel.''

John gave this testimony also:
    "I saw the Spirit descend
    like a dove from the sky,
    and it came to rest on him.
But I did not recognize him. The one who
    me to baptize with water told me, 'When
you see the Spirit descend and rest on someone, it is he who is to baptize with the Holy

Spirit.' Now I have seen for myself and have testified, 'This is God's chosen One.' "

This is the gospel of the Lord.

---

208   **JANUARY 4**

READING I   1 Jn 3, 7-10

A reading from the first letter of John

No one who has been begotten by God sins.

Little ones,

let no one deceive you;

the man who acts in holiness is holy indeed,

even as the Son is holy.

The man who sins belongs to the devil,

because the devil is a sinner from the beginning.

It was to destroy the devil's works

that the Son of God revealed himself.

No one begotten of God acts sinfully

because he remains of God's stock;

he cannot sin

because he is begotten of God.

That is the way to see who are God's children,

and who are the devil's.

No one whose actions are unholy belongs to God,

nor anyone who fails to love his brother.

This is the Word of the Lord.

Responsorial Psalm   Ps 98, 1. 7-8. 9

℟. (3) All the ends of the earth have seen the saving power of God.

Sing to the Lord a new song,

for he has done wondrous deeds;

His right hand has won victory for him,

his holy arm.

℟. All the ends of the earth have seen the saving power of God.

Let the sea and what fills it resound,

the world and those who dwell in it;

Let the rivers clap their hands,

the mountains shout with them for joy before the Lord.

℟. All the ends of the earth have seen the saving power of God.

The Lord comes;

he comes to rule the earth;

He will rule the world with justice

and the peoples with equity.

℟. All the ends of the earth have seen the saving power of God.

GOSPEL   Jn 1, 35-42

Alleluia

See no. 212.

✠ **A reading from the holy gospel according to John**

We have found the Messiah.

John was at Bethany across the Jordan with two of his disciples. As he watched Jesus walk by he said, "Look! There is the Lamb of God!" The two disciples heard what he said, and followed Jesus. When Jesus turned around and noticed them following him, he asked them, "What are you looking for?" They said to him, "Rabbi (which means Teacher), where do you stay?" "Come and see," he answered. So they went to see where he was lodged, and stayed with him that day. (It was about four in the afternoon.)

One of the two who had followed him after hearing John was Simon Peter's brother Andrew. The first thing he did was seek out his brother Simon and tell him, "We have found the Messiah" (which means the Anointed)! He brought him to Jesus, who looked at him and said: "You are Simon, son of John; your name shall be Cephas (which is rendered Peter)."

This is the gospel of the Lord.

---

209   **JANUARY 5**

READING I   1 Jn 3, 11-21

A reading from the first letter of Paul

We have passed from death to life, because we love our brothers.

This, remember, is the message

you heard from the beginning:

we should love one another.

We should not follow the example of Cain
who belonged to the evil one
and killed his brother.
Why did he kill him?
Because his own deeds were wicked
while his brother's were just.
No need, then, brothers, to be surprised
if the world hates you.
That we have passed from death to life we
know
because we love the brothers.
The man who does not love is among the
living dead.
Anyone who hates his brother is a murderer,
and you know that eternal life
abides in no murderer's heart.
The way we came to understand love
was that he laid down his life for us;
we too must lay down our lives for our
brothers.
I ask you, how can God's love survive in a man
who has enough of this world's goods
yet closes his heart to his brother
when he sees him in need?
Little children,
let us love in deed and in truth
and not merely talk about it.
This is our way of knowing we are committed
to the truth
and are at peace before him
no matter what our consciences may charge
us with;
for God is greater than our hearts
and all is known to him.

Beloved,
if our consciences have nothing to charge
us with,
we can be sure that God is with us.
This is the Word of the Lord.

Responsorial Psalm　Ps 100, 1-2. 3. 4. 5

℟. (1) Let all the earth cry out to God with joy.
Sing joyfully to the Lord, all you lands;
serve the Lord with gladness;
come before him with joyful song.
℟. Let all the earth cry out to God with joy.

Know that the Lord is God;
he made us, his we are;
his people, the flock he tends.
℟. Let all the earth cry out to God with joy.
Enter his gates with thanksgiving,
his courts with praise;
Give thanks to him; bless his name.
℟. Let all the earth cry out to God with joy.
The Lord is good:
the Lord, whose kindness endures forever,
and his faithfulness, to all generations.
℟. Let all the earth cry out to God with joy.

GOSPEL　Jn 1, 43-51
Alleluia
See no. 212.

✠ A reading from the holy gospel according
to John
You are the Son of God, the king of Israel.

Jesus wanted to set out for Galilee, but first
he came upon Philip. "Follow me," Jesus said
to him. Now Philip was from Bethsaida, the
same town as Andrew and Peter. Philip sought
out Nathanael and told him, "We have found
the one Moses spoke of in the law—the
prophets too—Jesus, son of Joseph, from
Nazareth." Nathanael's response to that was,
"Can anything good come from Nazareth?"
and Philip replied, "Come, see for yourself."
When Jesus saw Nathanael coming toward
him, he remarked: "This man is a real Israelite.
There is no guile in him." "How do you know
me?" Nathanael asked him. "Before Philip
called you," Jesus answered, "I saw you under
the fig tree." "Rabbi," said Nathanael, "you
are the Son of God; you are the king of Israel."
Jesus responded: "Do you believe just because
I told you I saw you under the fig tree? You
will see much greater things than that."
　　He went on to tell them, "I solemnly assure
you, you shall see the sky opened and the
angels of God ascending and descending on the
Son of Man."
　　This is the gospel of the Lord.

210   **JANUARY 6**

In countries where Epiphany is celebrated on January 7
or January 8.

READING I   1 Jn 5, 5-13

A reading from the first letter of John
There are three witnesses: the Spirit and the water and
the blood.

Who, then, is conqueror of the world?
The one who believes that Jesus is the Son
    of God.

Jesus Christ it is who came through water and
    blood—
    not in water only,
    but in water and in blood.
It is the Spirit who testifies to this,
    and the Spirit is truth.
Thus there are three that testify,
    the Spirit and the water and the blood—
    and these three are of one accord.
Do we not accept human testimony?
The testimony of God is much greater:
    it is the testimony God has given
    on his own Son's behalf.
Whoever believes in the Son of God
    possesses that testimony within his heart.
Whoever does not believe God
    has made God a liar
    by refusing to believe in the testimony
    he has given on his own Son's behalf.
The testimony is this:
    God gave us eternal life,
    and this life is in his Son.
Whoever possesses the Son
    possesses life;
    whoever does not possess the Son of God
    does not possess life.

I have written this to you to make you
realize that you possess eternal life—you who
believe in the name of the Son of God.
    This is the Word of the Lord.

Responsorial Psalm   Ps 147, 12-13. 14-15. 19-20

℟. (12) Praise the Lord, Jerusalem.
Glorify the Lord, O Jerusalem;
    praise your God, O Zion.

For he has strengthened the bars of your gates;
    he has blessed your children within you.
℟. Praise the Lord, Jerusalem.
He has granted peace in your borders;
    with the best of wheat he fills you.
He sends forth his command to the earth;
    swiftly runs his word!
℟. Praise the Lord, Jerusalem.
He has proclaimed his word to Jacob,
    his statutes and his ordinances to Israel.
He has not done thus for any other nation;
    his ordinances he has not made known to
    them. Alleluia.
℟. Praise the Lord, Jerusalem.
℟. Or: Alleluia.

GOSPEL   Mk 1, 7-11
Alleluia

See no. 212 or no. 21.

✠ A reading from the holy gospel according
    to Mark
You are my beloved Son in whom I am well pleased.

The theme of John's preaching was: "One more
powerful than I is to come after me. I am
not fit to stoop and untie his sandal straps. I
have baptized you in water; he will baptize you
in the Holy Spirit."
    During that time, Jesus came from Nazareth
in Galilee and was baptized in the Jordan by
John. Immediately on coming up out of the
water he saw the sky rent in two and the Spirit
descending on him like a dove. Then a voice
came from the heavens: "You are my beloved
Son. On you my favor rests."
    This is the gospel of the Lord.

___

211   **JANUARY 7**

In countries where Epiphany is celebrated on January 7
or January 8.

READING I   1 Jn 5, 14-21

A reading from the first letter of John
If we ask for anything, he will hear us.

We have this confidence in God: that he hears
us whenever we ask for anything according
to his will. And since we know that he hears

us whenever we ask, we know that what we have asked him for is ours. Anyone who sees his brother sinning, if the sin is not deadly, should petition God and thus life will be given to the sinner. This is only for those whose sin is not deadly. There is such a thing as deadly sin; I do not say that one should pray about that. True, all wrong doing is sin, but not all sin is deadly.

We know that no one begotten of God commits sin; rather, God protects the one begotten by him, and so the evil one cannot touch him. We know that we belong to God, while the whole world is under the evil one. We know, too, that the Son of God has come and has given us discernment to recognize the One who is true. And we are in the One who is true, for we are in his Son Jesus Christ. He is the true God and eternal life.

My little children, be on your guard against idols.

This is the Word of the Lord.

Responsorial Psalm   Ps 149, 1-2. 3-4. 5. 6. 9

℟. (4) The Lord takes delight in his people.
Sing to the Lord a new song
    of praise in the assembly of the faithful.
Let Israel be glad in their maker,
    let the children of Zion rejoice in their king.
℟. The Lord takes delight in his people.
Let them praise his name in the festive dance,
    let them sing praise to him with timbrel
        and harp.
For the Lord loves his people,
    and he adorns the lowly with victory.
℟. The Lord takes delight in his people.
Let the faithful exult in glory;
    let them sing for joy upon their couches;
    let the high praises of God be in their throats.
This is the glory of all his faithful. Alleluia.
℟. The Lord takes delight in his people.
℟. Or: Alleluia.

GOSPEL   Jn 2, 1-12
Alleluia
See no. 212.

✠ A reading from the holy gospel according
            to John
This was the first of the signs given by Jesus, at Cana in
                    Galilee.

There was a wedding at Cana in Galilee, and the mother of Jesus was there. Jesus and his disciples had likewise been invited to the celebration. At a certain point the wine ran out, and Jesus' mother told him, "They have no more wine." Jesus replied, "Woman, how does this concern of yours involve me? My hour has not yet come." His mother instructed those waiting on table, "Do whatever he tells you." As prescribed for Jewish ceremonial washings, there were at hand six stone water jars, each one holding fifteen to twenty-five gallons. "Fill those jars with water," Jesus ordered, at which they filled them to the brim. "Now," he said, "draw some out and take it to the waiter in charge." They did as he instructed them. The waiter in charge tasted the water made wine, without knowing where it had come from; only the waiters knew, since they had drawn the water. Then the waiter in charge called the groom over and remarked to him: "People usually serve the choice wine first; then when the guests have been drinking awhile, a lesser vintage. What you have done is keep the choice wine until now." Jesus performed this first of his signs at Cana in Galilee. Thus did he reveal his glory, and his disciples believed in him.

After this he went down to Capernaum, along with his mother and brothers [and his disciples] but they stayed there only a few days.

This is the gospel of the Lord.

212	**ALLELUIA**

SEASON OF CHRISTMAS

BEFORE EPIPHANY

1	Jn 1, 14. 12

℟. Alleluia. The Word of God became a man
and lived among us.
He enabled those who accepted him
to become the children of God. ℟. Alleluia.

2	Heb 1, 1-2

℟. Alleluia. In the past God spoke to our
fathers through the prophets;
now he speaks to us through his Son. ℟.
Alleluia.

3

℟. Alleluia. A holy day has dawned upon us.
Come, you nations, and adore the Lord.
Today a great light has come upon the earth.
℟. Alleluia.

___

The readings assigned from January 7 to January 12 are
used on the days which follow Epiphany, even if this is
transferred to Sunday, up to the following Saturday.
Nevertheless on Monday after the Sunday on which the
Baptism of the Lord is celebrated (i.e. the Sunday after
January 6), the readings of the season of the year begin,
and any readings left over from those assigned for January
7 to January 12 are omitted.

213	**JANUARY 7 OR MONDAY**

AFTER EPIPHANY

READING I	1 Jn 3, 22–4, 6

A reading from the first letter of John
Test every spirit to see if it comes from God.

Whatever we ask we shall receive at God's
hands.
Why? Because we are keeping his commandments
and doing what is pleasing in his sight.
His commandment is this:
we are to believe in the name of his Son,
Jesus Christ,
and are to love one another as he commanded us.

Those who keep his commandments remain in
him
and he in them.
And this is how we know that he remains in us:
from the Spirit that he gave us.
Beloved,
do not trust every spirit,
but put the spirits to a test
to see if they belong to God,
because many false prophets have appeared
in the world.
This is how you can recognize God's spirit:
every spirit that acknowledges Jesus Christ
come in the flesh
belongs to God,
while every spirit that fails to acknowledge
him
does not belong to God.
Such is the spirit of the Antichrist
which, as you have heard, is to come;
in fact, it is in the world already.
You are of God, you little ones,
and thus you have conquered the false prophets.
For there is in you One greater
than there is in the world.
Those others belong to the world;
that is why theirs is the language of the
world
and why the world listens to them.
We belong to God
and anyone who has knowledge of God gives
us a hearing,
while anyone who is not of God refuses to
hear us.
Thus do we distinguish the spirit of truth
from the spirit of deception.
This is the Word of the Lord.

Responsorial Psalm	Ps 2, 7-8. 10-11

℟. (8) I will give you all the nations for your
heritage.
The Lord said to me, "You are my son;
this day I have begotten you.
Ask of me and I will give you
the nations for an inheritance
and the ends of the earth for your possession."

℞. I will give you all the nations for your
    heritage.
And now, O kings, give heed;
    take warning, you rulers of the earth.
Serve the Lord with fear, and rejoice before
    him;
    with trembling, pay homage to him.
℞. I will give you all the nations for your
    heritage.

GOSPEL   Mt 4, 12-17. 23-25
Alleluia

See no. 219.

✠ A reading from the holy gospel according
        to Matthew

The kingdom of heaven is close at hand.

When Jesus heard that John had been arrested,
he withdrew to Galilee. He left Nazareth and
went down to live in Capernaum by the sea
near the territory of Zebulun and Naphtali, to
fulfill what had been said through Isaiah the
prophet:

> "Land of Zebulun, land of Naphtali
>   along the sea beyond the Jordan,
> heathen Galilee:
> a people living in darkness
> has seen a great light.
> On those who inhabit a land overshad-
>   owed by death,
>   light has arisen."

From that time on Jesus began to proclaim this
theme: "Reform your lives! The kingdom of
heaven is at hand."
    Jesus toured all of Galilee. He taught in their
synagogues, proclaimed the good news of the
kingdom, and cured the people of every disease
and illness. As a consequence of this, his reputation traveled the length of Syria. They
carried to him all those afflicted with various
diseases and racked with pain: the possessed,
the lunatics, the paralyzed. He cured them
all. The great crowds that followed him came
from Galilee, the Ten Cities, Jerusalem and
Judea, and from across the Jordan.
        This is the gospel of the Lord.

214   JANUARY 8 OR TUESDAY
AFTER EPIPHANY

READING I   1 Jn 4, 7-10
A reading from the first letter of John

God is Love.

Beloved,
    let us love one another
    because love is of God;
    everyone who loves is begotten of God
    and has knowledge of God.
The man without love has known nothing of
        God,
    for God is love.
God's love was revealed in our midst in this
        way:
    he sent his only Son to the world
    that we might have life through him.
Love, then, consists in this:
    not that we have loved God,
    but that he has loved us
    and has sent his Son as an offering for our
        sins.
        This is the Word of the Lord.

Responsorial Psalm   Ps 72, 1-2. 3-4. 7-8

℞. (11) Lord, every nation on earth will adore
    you.
O God, with your judgment endow the king,
    and with your justice, the king's son;
He shall govern your people with justice
    and your afflicted ones with judgment.
℞. Lord, every nation on earth will adore you.
The mountains shall yield peace for the people,
    and the hills justice.
He shall defend the afflicted among the people,
    save the children of the poor.
℞. Lord, every nation on earth will adore you.
Justice shall flower in his days,
    and profound peace, till the moon be no
        more.
May he rule from sea to sea,
    and from the River to the ends of the earth.
℞. Lord, every nation on earth will adore you.

GOSPEL   Mk 6, 34-44
Alleluia

See no. 219.

✠ A reading from the holy gospel according
to Mark

When Jesus fed the large crowd from the loaves, he showed
himself as a prophet.

Jesus saw a vast crowd. He pitied them, for
they were like sheep without a shepherd; and
he began to teach them at great length. It
was now getting late and his disciples came to
him with a suggestion: "This is a deserted
place and it is already late. Why do you not
dismiss them so that they can go to the crossroads and villages around here and buy themselves something to eat?" "You give them
something to eat," Jesus replied. At that they
said, "Are we to go and spend two hundred
days' wages for bread to feed them?" "How
many loaves have you?" Jesus asked. "Go and
see." When they learned the number they
answered, "Five, and two fish." He told them
to make the people sit down on the green
grass in groups or parties. The people took
their places in hundreds and fifties, neatly
arranged like flower beds. Then, taking the
five loaves and two fish, Jesus raised his eyes
to heaven, pronounced a blessing, broke the
loaves, and gave them to the disciples to distribute. He divided the two fish among all of
them and they ate until they had their fill.
They gathered up enough leftovers to fill
twelve baskets, besides what remained of the
fish. Those who had eaten the loaves numbered
five thousand men.

This is the gospel of the Lord.

215   **JANUARY 9 OR WEDNESDAY
AFTER EPIPHANY**

READING I   1 Jn 4, 11-18

A reading from the first letter of John

If we love one another God will live in us.

Beloved,
if God has loved us so,
we must have the same love for one another.

No one has ever seen God.
Yet if we love one another
God dwells in us,
and his love is brought to perfection in us.
The way we know we remain in him
and he in us
is that he has given us of his Spirit.
We have seen for ourselves, and can testify,
that the Father has sent the Son as savior
of the world.
When anyone acknowledges that Jesus is
the Son of God,
God dwells in him
and he in God.
We have come to know and to believe
in the love God has for us.

God is love,
and he who abides in love
abides in God,
and God in him.
Our love is brought to perfection in this,
that we should have confidence on the day of
judgment;
for our relation to this world is just like his.
Love has no room for fear;
rather, perfect love casts out all fear.
And since fear has to do with punishment,
love is not yet perfect in one who is afraid.
This is the Word of the Lord.

Responsorial Psalm   Ps 72, 1-2. 10. 12-13

℟. (11) Lord, every nation on earth will adore
you.
O God, with your judgment endow the king,
and with your justice, the king's son;
He shall govern your people with justice
and your afflicted ones with judgment.
℟. Lord, every nation on earth will adore you.
The kings of Tarshish and the Isles shall offer
gifts;
the kings of Arabia and Seba shall bring
tribute.
℟. Lord, every nation on earth will adore you.
For he shall rescue the poor man when he cries
out,
and the afflicted when he has no one to help
him.

He shall have pity for the lowly and the poor;
  the lives of the poor he shall save.
R̷. Lord, every nation on earth will adore you.

GOSPEL   Mk 6, 45-52
Alleluia

See no. 219.

✠ A reading from the holy gospel according
              to Mark

He shall have pity for the lowly and the poor;
the lives of the poor he shall save.

✠ A reading from the holy gospel according
to Mark
They saw Jesus walking on the waters.

[After the five thousand men were satiated]
Jesus insisted that his disciples get into the boat
and precede him to the other side toward Bethsaida, while he dismissed the crowd. When he
had taken leave of them, he went off to the
mountain to pray. As evening drew on, the
boat was far out on the lake while he was
alone on the land. Then, seeing them tossed
about as they tried to row with the wind
against them, he came walking toward them
on the water; the time was between three and
six in the morning. He meant to pass them
by. When they saw him walking on the lake,
they thought it was a ghost and they began to
cry out. They had all seen him and were terrified. He hastened to reassure them: "Get hold
of yourselves! It is I. Do not be afraid!" He
got into the boat with them and the wind
died down. They were taken aback by these
happenings, for they had not understood about
the loaves. On the contrary, their minds were
completely closed to the meaning of the events.
      This is the gospel of the Lord.

---

216   JANUARY 10 OR THURSDAY
                AFTER EPIPHANY

READING I   1 Jn 4, 19–5, 4

A reading from the first letter of John
He who loves God must also love his brother.

Beloved,
We, for our part, love God,
  because he first loved us.
If anyone says, "My love is fixed on God,"
  yet hates his brother,
he is a liar.

One who has no love for the brother he has
    seen
  cannot love the God he has not seen.
The commandment we have from him is this:
Whoever loves God must also love his brother.
Everyone who believes that Jesus is the
    Christ
  has been begotten of God.
Now, everyone who loves the father
  loves the child he has begotten.
We can be sure that we love God's children
    when we love God
  and do what he has commanded.
The love of God consists in this:
  that we keep his commandments—
  and his commandments are not burdensome.
Everyone begotten of God conquers the world,
  and the power that has conquered the world
  is this faith of ours.
      This is the Word of the Lord.

Responsorial Psalm   Ps 72, 1-2. 14-15. 17

R̷. (11) Lord, every nation on earth will adore
    you.
O God, with your judgment endow the king,
  and with your justice, the king's son;
He shall govern your people with justice
  and your afflicted ones with judgment.
R̷. Lord, every nation on earth will adore you.
From fraud and violence he shall redeem the
    poor,
  and precious shall their blood be in his sight.
May they be prayed for continually;
  day by day shall they bless him.
R̷. Lord, every nation on earth will adore you.
May his name be blessed forever;
  as long as the sun his name shall remain.
In him shall all the tribes of the earth be
    blessed;
  all the nations shall proclaim his happiness.
R̷. Lord, every nation on earth will adore you.

GOSPEL   Lk 4, 14-22
Alleluia

See no. 219.

✠ A reading from the holy gospel according
     to Luke

Today the scriptures are being fulfilled.

Jesus returned in the power of the Spirit to
Galilee, and his reputation spread throughout
the region. He was teaching in their synagogues, and all were loud in his praise.

He came to Nazareth where he had been
reared, and entering the synagogue on the sabbath as he was in the habit of doing, he stood
up to do the reading. When the book of the
prophet Isaiah was handed him he unrolled the
scroll and found the passage where it was
written:

"The spirit of the Lord is upon me;
     therefore he has anointed me.
He has sent me to bring glad tidings to the
     poor,
to proclaim liberty to captives,
Recovery of sight to the blind
     and release to prisoners,
To announce a year of favor from the
     Lord."

Rolling up the scroll he gave it back to the
assistant and sat down. All in the synagogue
had their eyes fixed on him. Then he began by
saying to them, "Today this Scripture passage
is fulfilled in your hearing." All who were present spoke favorably of him; they marveled at
the appealing discourse which came from his
lips.

        This is the gospel of the Lord.

---

217   **JANUARY 11 OR FRIDAY**
         AFTER EPIPHANY

READING I   1 Jn 5, 5-13

   A reading from the first letter of John

There are three witnesses: the Spirit and the water and
the blood.

Who, then, is conqueror of the world?
The one who believes that Jesus is the Son of
     God.

Jesus Christ it is who came through water and
     blood—
     not in water only,
     but in water and in blood.
It is the Spirit who testifies to this,
     and the Spirit is truth.
Thus there are three that testify,
     the Spirit and the water and the blood—
     and these three are of one accord.
Do we not accept human testimony?
The testimony of God is much greater:
     it is the testimony God has given
     on his own Son's behalf.
Whoever believes in the Son of God
     possesses that testimony within his heart.
Whoever does not believe God
     has made God a liar
     by refusing to believe in the testimony
he has given on his own Son's behalf.
The testimony is this:
God gave us eternal life,
     and this life is in his Son.
Whoever possesses the Son
     possesses life;
     whoever does not possess the Son of God
     does not possess life.
I have written this to you to make you re-
alize that you possess eternal life—you who
believe in the name of the Son of God.

        This is the Word of the Lord.

Responsorial Psalm   Ps 147, 12-13. 14-15. 19-20

℟. (12) Praise the Lord, Jerusalem.
Glorify the Lord, O Jerusalem;
     praise your God, O Sion.
For he has strengthened the bars of your gates;
     he has blessed your children within you.
℟. Praise the Lord, Jerusalem.
He has granted peace in your borders;
     with the best of wheat he fills you.
He sends forth his command to the earth;
     swiftly runs his word!
℟. Praise the Lord, Jerusalem.
He has proclaimed his word to Jacob,
     his statutes and his ordinances to Israel.
He has not done thus for any other nation;
     his ordinances he has not made known to
     them.

℟. Praise the Lord, Jerusalem.
℟. Or: Alleluia.

GOSPEL   Lk 5, 12-16
Alleluia

See no. 219.

✠ A reading from the holy gospel according
to Luke
The man afflicted with leprosy implored Jesus.

On one occasion in a certain town, a man full
of leprosy came to Jesus. Seeing Jesus, he
bowed down to the ground and said to him,
"Lord, if you will to do so, you can cure me."
Jesus stretched out his hand to touch him and
said, "I do will it. Be cured." Immediately the
leprosy left him. Jesus then instructed the man:
"Tell no one, but go and show yourself to the
priest. Offer for your healing what Moses prescribed; that should be a proof for them." His
reputation spread more and more, and great
crowds gathered to hear him and to be cured of
their maladies. He often retired to deserted
places and prayed.
This is the gospel of the Lord.

---

218   JANUARY 12 OR SATURDAY
AFTER EPIPHANY

READING I   1 Jn 5, 14-21

A reading from the first letter of John
If we ask him for anything, he will hear us.

We have this confidence in God: that he hears
us whenever we ask for anything according to
his will. And since we know that he hears us
whenever we ask, we know that what we have
asked him for is ours. Anyone who sees his
brother sinning, if the sin is not deadly, should
petition God, and thus life will be given to the
sinner. This is only for those whose sin is not
deadly. There is such a thing as a deadly sin;
I do not say that one should pray about that.
True, all wrongdoing is sin, but not all sin is
deadly.

We know that no one begotten of God commits sin; rather, God protects the one begotten

by him, and so the evil one cannot touch him.
We know that we belong to God, while the
whole world is under the evil one. We know,
too, that the Son of God has come and has
given us discernment to recognize the One who
is true. And we are in the One who is true, for
we are in his Son Jesus Christ. He is the true
God and eternal life.

My little children, be on your guard against
idols.
This is the Word of the Lord.

Responsorial Psalm   Ps 149, 1-2. 3-4. 5-6. 9

℟. (4) The Lord takes delight in his people.
Sing to the Lord a new song
    of praise in the assembly of the faithful.
Let Israel be glad in their maker,
    let the children of Zion rejoice in their king.
℟. The Lord takes delight in his people.
Let them praise his name in the festive dance,
    let them sing praise to him with timbrel and
        harp.
For the Lord loves his people,
    and he adorns the lowly with victory.
℟. The Lord takes delight in his people.
Let the faithful exult in glory;
    let them sing for joy upon their couches;
Let the high praises of God be in their throats.
    This is the glory of all his faithful.
℟. The Lord takes delight in his people.
℟. Or: Alleluia.

GOSPEL   Jn 3, 22-30
Alleluia

See no. 219.

✠ A reading from the holy gospel according
to John
The friend of the bridegroom is glad when he hears the
bridegroom's voice.

Jesus and his disciples came into Judean territory, and he spent some time with them there
baptizing. John too was baptizing at Aenon
near Salim where water was plentiful, and
people kept coming to be baptized. (John, of
course, had not yet been thrown into prison.)
A controversy about purification arose between John's disciples and a certain Jew. So

they came to John, saying, "Rabbi, the man who was with you across the Jordan—the one about whom you have been testifying—is baptizing now, and everyone is flocking to him." John answered:

"No one can lay hold on anything
unless it is given him from on high.

You yourselves are witnesses to the fact that I said: 'I am not the Messiah; I am sent before him.'

"It is the groom who has the bride.
The groom's best man
just waits there listening for him
and is overjoyed to hear his voice.
That is my joy, and it is complete.
He must increase,
while I must decrease."
    This is the gospel of the Lord.

---

219   ALLELUIA

FOR WEEKDAYS AFTER EPIPHANY

1   Mt 4, 16

R̸. Alleluia. **A people in darkness have seen a great light;**
a radiant dawn shines on those lost in faith. R̸. Alleluia.

2   Mt 4, 23

R̸. Alleluia. **Jesus preached the Good News of the Kingdom**
and healed all who were sick. R̸. Alleluia.

3   Lk 4, 18-19

R̸. Alleluia. **The Lord sent me to bring Good News to the poor,**
and freedom to prisoners. R̸. Alleluia.

4   Lk 7, 16

R̸. Alleluia. **A great prophet has risen among us;**
God has visited his people. R̸. Alleluia.

5   See 1 Tm 3, 16

R̸. Alleluia. **Glory to Christ who is proclaimed to the world;**
glory from all who believe in him! R̸. Alleluia.

---

220   **LENTEN SEASON**

ASH WEDNESDAY

READING I   Jl 2, 12-18

A reading from the book of the prophet Joel
Let your hearts be broken, and not your garments torn.

Even now, says the Lord,
    return to me with your whole heart,
    with fasting, and weeping, and mourning;
Rend your hearts, not your garments,
    and return to the Lord, your God.
For gracious and merciful is he,
    slow to anger, rich in kindness,
    and relenting in punishment.
Perhaps he will again relent
    and leave behind him a blessing,
Offerings and libations
    for the Lord, your God.

Blow the trumpet in Zion!
    proclaim a fast,
    call an assembly;
Gather the people,
    notify the congregation;
Assemble the elders,
    gather the children
    and the infants at the breast;
Let the bridegroom quit his room,
    and the bride her chamber.
Between the porch and the altar
    let the priests, the ministers of the Lord, weep,
And say, "Spare, O Lord, your people,
    and make not your heritage a reproach,
    with the nations ruling over them!
Why should they say among the peoples,
    'Where is their God?' "
    Then the Lord was stirred to concern for his land and took pity on his people.
        This is the Word of the Lord.

Responsorial Psalm   Ps 51, 3-4. 5-6. 12-13. 14. 17

R̸. (3) Be merciful, O Lord, for we have sinned.
Have mercy on me, O God, in your goodness;
    in the greatness of your compassion wipe
        out my offense.
Thoroughly wash me from my guilt
    and of my sin cleanse me.

R̯. Be merciful, O Lord, for we have sinned.
For I acknowledge my offense,
  and my sin is before me always:
"Against you only have I sinned,
  and done what is evil in your sight."
R̯. Be merciful, O Lord, for we have sinned.
A clean heart create for me, O God,
  and a steadfast spirit renew within me.
Cast me not out from your presence,
  and your holy spirit take not from me.
R̯. Be merciful, O Lord, for we have sinned.
Give me back the joy of your salvation,
  and a willing spirit sustain in me.
O Lord, open my lips,
  and my mouth shall proclaim your praise.
R̯. Be merciful, O Lord, for we have sinned.

READING II   2 Cor 5, 20—6, 2

A reading from the second letter of Paul to the Corinthians
Be reconciled to God, now is the acceptable time.

We are ambassadors for Christ, God as it were appealing through us. We implore you, in Christ's name: be reconciled to God! For our sakes God made him who did not know sin to be sin, so that in him we might become the very holiness of God.

As your fellow workers we beg you not to receive the grace of God in vain. For he says, "In an acceptable time I have heard you; on a day of salvation I have helped you." Now is the acceptable time! Now is the day of salvation!
This is the Word of the Lord.

GOSPEL   Mt 6, 1-6. 16-18
Verse before the Gospel
See no. 224.

✠ A reading from the holy gospel according to Matthew
Your Father, who sees all that is done in secret, will reward you.

Jesus said to his disciples: "Be on guard against performing religious acts for people to see. Otherwise expect no recompense from your heavenly Father. When you give alms, for example, do not blow a horn before you in synagogues and streets like hypocrites looking for applause. You can be sure of this much, they are already repaid. In giving alms you are not to let your left hand know what your right hand is doing. Keep your deeds of mercy secret, and your Father who sees in secret will repay you.

"When you are praying, do not behave like the hypocrites who love to stand and pray in synagogues or on street corners in order to be noticed. I give you my word, they are already repaid. Whenever you pray, go to your room, close your door, and pray to your Father in private. Then your Father, who sees what no man sees, will repay you.

"When you fast, you are not to look glum as the hypocrites do. They change the appearance of their faces so that others may see they are fasting. I assure you, they are already repaid. When you fast, see to it that you groom your hair and wash your face. In that way no one can see you are fasting but your Father who is hidden; and your Father who sees what is hidden will repay you."
This is the gospel of the Lord.

If the blessing and distribution of ashes takes place apart from Mass, it is appropriate that the liturgy of the word precede it, using texts assigned to the Mass of Ash Wednesday.

221   **THURSDAY
AFTER ASH WEDNESDAY**

READING I   Dt 30, 15-20
A reading from the book of Deuteronomy
I set before you life or death, blessing or curse.

Moses said to the people: "Today I have set before you life and prosperity, death and doom. If you obey the commandments of the Lord, your God, which I enjoin on you today, loving him, and walking in his ways, and keeping his commandments, statutes and decrees, you will live and grow numerous, and the Lord, your God, will bless you in the land you are entering to occupy. If, however, you turn away your hearts and will not listen, but are led astray and adore and serve other gods, I tell you now that you will certainly perish; you will not have a long life on the land which you are crossing the Jordan to enter and occupy. I call heaven and earth today to witness against you: I have set before you life and death, the blessing and the curse. Choose life, then, that you and your descendants may live, by loving the Lord, your God, heeding his voice, and holding fast to him. For that will mean life for you, a long life for you to live on the land which the Lord swore he would give to your fathers Abraham, Isaac and Jacob."

This is the Word of the Lord.

Responsorial Psalm   Ps 1, 1-2. 3. 4. 6

℟. (Ps 39, 5) Happy are they who hope in the Lord.

Happy the man who follows not
  the counsel of the wicked
Nor walks in the way of sinners,
  nor sits in the company of the insolent,
But delights in the law of the Lord
  and meditates on his law day and night.

℟. Happy are they who hope in the Lord.

He is like a tree
  planted near running water,
That yields its fruit in due season,
  and whose leaves never fade.
[Whatever he does, prospers.]

℟. Happy are they who hope in the Lord.

Not so the wicked, not so;
  they are like chaff which the wind drives
    away.
For the Lord watches over the way of the just,
  but the way of the wicked vanishes.

℟. Happy are they who hope in the Lord.

GOSPEL   Lk 9, 22-25
Verse before the Gospel

See no. 224.

✠ A reading from the holy gospel according
                to Luke

He who loses his life for my sake, that man will find
                    salvation.

Jesus said to his disciples: "The Son of Man must first endure many sufferings, be rejected by the elders, the high priests and the scribes, and be put to death, and then be raised up on the third day."

Jesus said to all: "Whoever wishes to be my follower must deny his very self, take up his cross each day, and follow in my steps. Whoever would save his life will lose it, and whoever loses his life for my sake will save it. What profit does he show who gains the whole world and destroys himself in the process?"

This is the gospel of the Lord.

---

222   **FRIDAY**
            AFTER ASH WEDNESDAY

READING I   Is 58, 1-9

A reading from the book of the prophet Isaiah

Is this not the sort of fast that pleases me?

Cry out full-throated and unsparingly,
  lift up your voice like a trumpet blast;
Tell my people their wickedness,
  and the house of Jacob their sins.
They seek me day after day,
  and desire to know my ways,
Like a nation that has done what is just
  and not abandoned the law of their God;
They ask me to declare what is due them,
  pleased to gain access to God.
"Why do we fast, and you do not see it?
  afflict ourselves, and you take no note of it?"
Lo, on your fast day you carry out your own
        pursuits,
  and drive all your laborers.
Yes, your fast ends in quarreling and fighting,
  striking with wicked claw.
Would that today you might fast
  so as to make your voice heard on high!
Is this the manner of fasting I wish,
  of keeping a day of penance:
That a man bow his head like a reed,
  and lie in sackcloth and ashes?
Do you call this a fast,
  a day acceptable to the Lord?
This, rather, is the fasting that I wish:
  releasing those bound unjustly,
  untying the thongs of the yoke;
Setting free the oppressed,
  breaking every yoke;
Sharing your bread with the hungry,

sheltering the oppressed and the homeless;
Clothing the naked when you see them,
    and not turning your back on your own.

Then your light shall break forth like the dawn,
    and your wound shall quickly be healed.
Your vindication shall go before you,
    and the glory of the Lord shall be your rear
    guard.
Then you shall call, and the Lord will answer,
    you shall cry for help, and he will say: Here
    I am!
If you remove from your midst oppression,
    false accusation and malicious speech.
        This is the Word of the Lord.

Responsorial Psalm   Ps 51, 3-4. 5-6. 18-19

℞. (19) A broken, humbled heart, O God, you
    will not scorn.

Have mercy on me, O God, in your goodness;
    in the greatness of your compassion wipe
    out my offense.
Thoroughly wash me from my guilt
    and of my sin cleanse me.

℞. A broken, humbled heart, O God, you will
    not scorn.

For I acknowledge my offense,
    and my sin is before me always:
"Against you only have I sinned,
    and done what is evil in your sight."

℞. A broken, humbled heart, O God, you will
    not scorn.

For you are not pleased with sacrifices;
    should I offer a holocaust, you would not ac-
    cept it.
My sacrifice, O God, is a contrite spirit;
    a heart contrite and humbled, O God, you
    will not spurn.

℞. A broken, humbled heart, O God, you will
    not scorn.

GOSPEL   Mt 9, 14-15

Verse before the Gospel

See no. 224.

✠ A reading from the holy gospel according
        to Matthew

When the bridegroom is taken from them, then they will fast.

When Jesus had crossed over into the territory

of the Gerasenes, John's disciples came to him
with the objection, "Why is it that while we
and the Pharisees fast, your disciples do not?"
Jesus said to them: "How can wedding guests
go in mourning so long as the groom is with
them? When the day comes that the groom is
taken away, then they will fast."
        This is the gospel of the Lord.

---

223   **SATURDAY**
        AFTER ASH WEDNESDAY

READING I   Is 58, 9-14

A reading from the book of the prophet Isaiah

You will glory to the Lord God by not going your own way.

    Thus says the Lord:
If you remove from your midst oppression,
    false accusation and malicious speech;
If you bestow your bread on the hungry
    and satisfy the afflicted;
Then light shall rise for you in the darkness,
    and the gloom shall become for you like
    midday;
Then the Lord will guide you always
    and give you plenty even on the parched
    land.
He will renew your strength,
    and you shall be like a watered garden,
    like a spring whose water never fails.
The ancient ruins shall be rebuilt for your sake,
    and the foundations from ages past you shall
    raise up;
"Repairer of the breach," they shall call you,
    "Restorer of ruined homesteads."

If you hold back your foot on the sabbath
    from following your own pursuits on my
    holy day;
If you call the sabbath a delight,
    and the Lord's holy day honorable;
If you honor it by not following your ways,
    seeking your own interests, or speaking with
    malice—
Then you shall delight in the Lord,
    and I will make you ride on the heights of the
    earth;

I will nourish you with the heritage of Jacob,
  your father,
for the mouth of the Lord has spoken.
  This is the Word of the Lord.

Responsorial Psalm   Ps 86, 1-2. 3-4. 5-6

℟. (11) Teach me your way, O Lord, that I
  may be faithful in your sight.
Incline your ear, O Lord; answer me,
  for I am afflicted and poor.
Keep my life, for I am devoted to you;
  save your servant who trusts in you.
℟. Teach me your way, O Lord, that I may be
  faithful in your sight.
You are my God; have pity on me, O Lord,
  for to you I call all the day.
Gladden the soul of your servant,
  for to you, O Lord, I lift up my soul.
℟. Teach me your way, O Lord, that I may be
  faithful in your sight.
For you, O Lord, are good and forgiving,
  abounding in kindness to all who call upon
  you.
Hearken, O Lord, to my prayer
  and attend to the sound of my pleading.
℟. Teach me your way, O Lord, that I may be
  faithful in your sight.

GOSPEL   Lk 5, 27-32
Verse before the Gospel

See no. 224.

✠ **A reading from the holy gospel according
  to Luke**

I have not come to call the just, but sinners to repentance.

Jesus saw a tax collector named Levi sitting at
his customs post. He said to him, "Follow me."
Leaving everything behind, Levi stood up and
became his follower. After that Levi gave a
great reception for Jesus in his house, in
which he was joined by a large crowd of tax
collectors and others at dinner. The Pharisees
and the scribes of their party said to his disciples, "Why do you eat and drink with tax collectors and non-observers of the law?" Jesus
said to them, "The healthy do not need a doctor; sick people do. I have not come to invite

the self-righteous to a change of heart, but sinners."
  This is the gospel of the Lord.

---

224   VERSES BEFORE THE GOSPEL
FOR THE WEEKDAYS OF LENT

1   Ps 51, 12. 14

Create a clean heart in me, O God;
give back to me the joy of your salvation.

2   Ps 95, 8

If today you hear his voice,
harden not your hearts.

3   Ps 130, 5. 7

I hope in the Lord, I trust in his word;
with him there is mercy and fullness of redemption.

4   Ez 18, 31

Rid yourselves of all your sins;
and make a new heart and a new spirit.

5   Ez 33, 11

I do not wish the sinner to die, says the Lord,
but to turn to me and live.

6   Jl 2, 12-13

With all your heart turn to me
for I am tender and compassionate.

7   Am 5, 14

Seek good and not evil
so that you may live,
and the Lord will be with you.

8   Mt 4, 4

Man does not live on bread alone,
but on every word that comes from the mouth
  of God.

9   Mt 4, 17

Repent, says the Lord,
the kingdom of heaven is at hand.

10   See Lk 8, 15

Happy are they who have kept the word with a
  generous heart,
and yield a harvest through perseverance.

11   Lk 15, 18

I will rise and go to my father and tell him:
Father, I have sinned against heaven and
  against you.

12   Jn 3, 16

God loved the world so much, he gave us his
  only Son,
that all who believe in him might have eternal life.

13   Jn 6, 64. 69

Your words, Lord, are spirit and life;
you have the message of eternal life.

14   Jn 8, 12

I am the light of the world, says the Lord:
he who follows me will have the light of life.

15   Jn 11, 25. 26

I am the resurrection and the life, said the
  Lord:
he who believes in me will not die forever.

16   2 Cor 6, 2

This is the favorable time,
this is the day of salvation.

17

The seed is the word of God, Christ is the
  sower;
all who come to him will live for ever.

---

225   **MONDAY OF THE FIRST
              WEEK OF LENT**

READING I   Lv 19, 1-2. 11-18

A reading from the book of Leviticus
Judge your neighbor justly.

The Lord said to Moses, "Speak to the whole
Israelite community and tell them: Be holy, for
I, the Lord, your God, am holy.

"You shall not steal. You shall not lie or
speak falsely to one another. You shall not
swear falsely by my name, thus profaning the
name of your God. I am the Lord.

"You shall not defraud or rob your neighbor.
You shall not withhold overnight the wages of
your day laborer. You shall not curse the deaf,
or put a stumbling block in front of the blind,
but you shall fear your God. I am the Lord.

"You shall not act dishonestly in rendering
judgment. Show neither partiality to the weak
nor deference to the mighty, but judge your
fellow men justly. You shall not go about
spreading slander among your kinsmen; nor
shall you stand by idly when your neighbor's
life is at stake. I am the Lord.

"You shall not bear hatred for your brother
in your heart. Though you may have to reprove
your fellow man, do not incur sin because of
him. Take no revenge and cherish no grudge
against your fellow countrymen. You shall
love your neighbor as yourself. I am the Lord."
    This is the Word of the Lord.

Responsorial Psalm   Ps 19, 8. 9. 10. 15

℟. (Jn 6, 63) Your words, Lord, are spirit and
  life.
The law of the Lord is perfect,
  refreshing the soul;
The decree of the Lord is trustworthy,
  giving wisdom to the simple.
℟. Your words, Lord, are spirit and life.
The precepts of the Lord are right,
  rejoicing the heart;
The command of the Lord is clear,
  enlightening the eye.
℟. Your words, Lord, are spirit and life.

The fear of the Lord is pure,
   enduring forever;
The ordinances of the Lord are true,
   all of them just.
℞. Your words, Lord, are spirit and life.
Let the words of my mouth and the thought of
   my heart
   find favor before you,
   O Lord, my rock and my redeemer.
℞. Your words, Lord, are spirit and life.

GOSPEL   Mt 25, 31-46
Verse before the Gospel
See no. 224.

✠ **A reading from the holy gospel according
to Matthew**
Whatever you do for one of the least of these brothers of
mine, you do to me.

Jesus said to his disciples: "When the Son of
Man comes in his glory, escorted by all the angels of heaven, he will sit upon his royal throne
and all the nations will be assembled before
him. Then he will separate them into two
groups, as a shepherd separates sheep from
goats. The sheep he will place on his right
hand, the goats on his left. The king will say to
those on his right: 'Come, you have my Father's blessing! Inherit the kingdom prepared
for you from the creation of the world. For I
was hungry and you gave me food, I was
thirsty and you gave me drink. I was a stranger
and you welcomed me, naked and you clothed
me. I was ill and you comforted me, in prison
and you came to visit me.' Then the just will
ask him: 'Lord, when did we see you hungry
and feed you or see you thirsty and give you
drink? When did we welcome you away from
home or clothe you in your nakedness? When
did we visit you when you were ill or in
prison?' The king will answer them: 'I assure
you, as often as you did it for one of my least
brothers, you did it for me.'

"Then he will say to those on his left: 'Out of
my sight, you condemned, into that everlasting
fire prepared for the devil and his angels! I was
hungry and you gave me no food, I was thirsty
and you gave me no drink. I was away from

home and you gave me no welcome, naked and
you gave me no clothing. I was ill and in prison
and you did not come to comfort me.' Then
they in turn will ask: 'Lord, when did we see
you hungry or thirsty or away from home or
naked or ill or in prison and not attend you in
your needs?' He will answer them: 'I assure
you, as often as you neglected to do it to one of
these least ones, you neglected to do it to me.'
These will go off to eternal punishment and the
just to eternal life."
   This is the gospel of the Lord.

---

226   TUESDAY OF THE FIRST
WEEK OF LENT

READING I   Is 55, 10-11
A reading from the book of the prophet Isaiah
My word carries out my will.

For just as from the heavens
   the rain and snow come down
And do not return there
   till they have watered the earth,
   making it fertile and fruitful,
Giving seed to him who sows
   and bread to him who eats,
So shall my word be
   that goes forth from my mouth;
It shall not return to me void,
   but shall do my will,
   achieving the end for which I sent it.
   This is the Word of the Lord

Responsorial Psalm   Ps 34, 4-5. 6-7. 16-17. 18-19
℞. (18) From all their afflictions
   God will deliver the just.
Glorify the Lord with me,
   let us together extol his name.
I sought the Lord, and he answered me
   and delivered me from all my fears.
℞. From all their afflictions
   God will deliver the just.
Look to him that you may be radiant with joy,
   and your faces may not blush with shame.
When the afflicted man called out, the Lord
   heard,
   and from all his distress he saved him.

℟. From all their afflictions
   God will deliver the just.
The Lord has eyes for the just,
   and ears for their cry.
The Lord confronts the evildoers,
   to destroy remembrance of them from the
   earth.
℟. From all their afflictions
   God will deliver the just.
When the just cry out, the Lord hears them,
   and from all their distress he rescues them.
The Lord is close to the brokenhearted;
   and those who are crushed in spirit he saves.
℟. From all their afflictions
   God will deliver the just.

GOSPEL   Mt 6, 7-15
Verse before the Gospel

See no. 224.

✠ **A reading from the holy gospel according**
   to Matthew

This is how you should pray.

Jesus said to his disciples: "In your prayer do
not rattle on like the pagans. They think they
will win a hearing by the sheer multiplication
of words. Do not imitate them. Your Father
knows what you need before you ask him. This
is how you are to pray:
   'Our Father in heaven,
   hallowed be your name,
   your kingdom come,
   your will be done
   on earth as it is in heaven.
   Give us today our daily bread,
   and forgive us the wrong we have done
   as we forgive those who wrong us.
   Subject us not to the trial
   but deliver us from the evil one.'
   "If you forgive the faults of others, your
heavenly Father will forgive you yours. If you
do not forgive others, neither will your Father
forgive you."
      This is the gospel of the Lord.

---

227   WEDNESDAY OF THE FIRST
        WEEK OF LENT

READING I   Jon 3, 1-10
A reading from the book of the prophet Jonah

Nineveh was converted from its evil ways.

The word of the Lord came to Jonah: "Set out
for the great city of Nineveh, and announce to
it the message that I will tell you." So Jonah
made ready and went to Nineveh, according to
the Lord's bidding. Now Nineveh was an enormously large city; it took three days to go
through it. Jonah began his journey through
the city, and had gone but a single day's walk
announcing, "Forty days more and Nineveh
shall be destroyed," when the people of Nineveh believed God; they proclaimed a fast and
all of them, great and small, put on sackcloth.

   When the news reached the king of Nineveh,
he rose from his throne, laid aside his robe,
covered himself with sackcloth, and sat in the
ashes. Then he had this proclaimed throughout
Nineveh, by decree of the king and his nobles:
"Neither man nor beast, neither cattle nor
sheep, shall taste anything; they shall not eat,
nor shall they drink water. Man and beast shall
be covered with sackcloth and call loudly to
God; every man shall turn from his evil way
and from the violence he has in hand. Who
knows, God may relent and forgive, and withhold his blazing wrath, so that we shall not
ᵖerish." When God saw by their actions how
they turned from their evil way, he repented of
the evil that he had threatened to do to them;
he did not carry it out.
      This is the Word of the Lord.

Responsorial Psalm   Ps 51, 3-4. 12-13. 18-19
℟. (19) A broken, humbled heart,
   O God, you will not scorn.
Have mercy on me, O God, in your goodness;
   in the greatness of your compassion wipe
   out my offense.
Thoroughly wash me from my guilt
   and of my sin cleanse me.
℟. A broken, humbled heart,
   O God, you will not scorn.

A clean heart create for me, O God,
  and a steadfast spirit renew within me.
Cast me not out from your presence,
  and your holy spirit take not from me.
℞. A broken, humbled heart,
  O God, you will not scorn.
For you are not pleased with sacrifices;
  should I offer a holocaust, you would not accept it.
My sacrifice, O God, is a contrite spirit;
  a heart contrite and humbled, O God, you
  will not spurn.
℞. A broken, humbled heart,
  O God, you will not scorn.

GOSPEL   Lk 11, 29-32
Verse before the Gospel
See no. 224.

✠ A reading from the holy gospel according
to Luke

No sign will be given to this generation except the sign
of Jonah.

While the crowds pressed around Jesus, he began to speak to them in these words: "This is an evil age. It seeks a sign. But no sign will be given it except the sign of Jonah. Just as Jonah was a sign for the Ninevites, so will the Son of Man be a sign for the present age. The queen of the south will rise at the judgment along with the men of this generation, and she will condemn them. She came from the farthest corner of the world to listen to the wisdom of Solomon, but you have a greater than Solomon here. At the judgment, the citizens of Nineveh will rise along with the present generation, and they will condemn it. For at the preaching of Jonah they reformed, but you have a greater than Jonah here."
   This is the gospel of the Lord.

---

228   **THURSDAY OF THE FIRST
WEEK OF LENT**

READING I   Est C, 12. 14-16. 23-25
A reading from the book of Esther

I have no help other than you, Lord.

Queen Esther, seized with mortal anguish, had recourse to the Lord. She prayed to the Lord, the God of Israel, saying: "My Lord, our King, you alone are God. Help me, who am alone and have no help but you, for I am taking my life in my hand. As a child I was wont to hear from the people of the land of my forefathers that you, O Lord, chose Israel from among all peoples, and our fathers from among all their ancestors, as a lasting heritage, and that you fulfilled all your promises to them.
   "Be mindful of us, O Lord. Manifest yourself in the time of our distress and give me courage, King of gods and Ruler of every power. Put in my mouth persuasive words in the presence of the lion, and turn his heart to hatred for our enemy, so that he and those who are in league with him may perish. Save us by your power, and help me, who am alone and have no one but you, O Lord. You know all things."
   This is the Word of the Lord.

Responsorial Psalm   Ps 138, 1-2. 2-3. 7-8
℞. (3) Lord, on the day I called for help,
  you answered me.
I will give thanks to you, O Lord, with all my
  heart,
  [for you have heard the words of my mouth;]
  in the presence of the angels I will sing your
  praise;
I will worship at your holy temple
  and give thanks to your name,
℞. Lord, on the day I called for help,
  you answered me.
Because of your kindness and your truth;
  for you have made great above all things
  your name and your promise.
When I called, you answered me;
  you built up strength within me.
℞. Lord, on the day I called for help,
  you answered me.

Your right hand saves me.
The Lord will complete what he has done for
   me;
Your kindness, O Lord, endures forever;
   forsake not the work of your hands.
R̸. Lord, on the day I called for help,
   you answered me.

GOSPEL   Mt 7, 7-12
Verse before the Gospel

See no. 224.

✠ A reading from the holy gospel according
   to Matthew

He who asks, always receives.

Jesus said to his disciples: "Ask, and you will
receive. Seek, and you will find. Knock, and it
will be opened to you. For the one who asks,
receives. The one who seeks, finds. The one
who knocks, enters. Would one of you hand his
son a stone when he asks for a loaf, or a poison-
ous snake when he asks for a fish? If you, with
all your sins, know how to give your children
what is good, how much more will your heavenly Father give good things to anyone who
asks him!

   "Treat others the way you would have them
treat you: this sums up the law and the prophets."

   This is the gospel of the Lord.

**229   FRIDAY OF THE FIRST
           WEEK OF LENT**

READING I   Ez 18, 21-28

A reading from the book of the prophet Ezekiel

If a wicked man turns away from his sins, he shall live.

If the wicked man turns away from all the sins
he committed, if he keeps all my statutes and
does what is right and just, he shall surely live,
he shall not die. None of the crimes he committed shall be remembered against him; he shall
live because of the virtue he has practiced. Do
I indeed derive any pleasure from the death of
the wicked? says the Lord God. Do I not rather
rejoice when he turns from his evil way that he
may live?

And if the virtuous man turns from the path
of virtue to do evil, the same kind of abominable things that the wicked man does, can he
do this and still live? None of his virtuous deeds
shall be remembered, because he has broken
faith and committed sin; because of this, he
shall die. You say, "The Lord's way is not fair!"
Hear now, house of Israel: Is it my way that is
unfair, or rather, are not your ways unfair?
When a virtuous man turns away from virtue
to commit iniquity, and dies, it is because of
the iniquity he committed that he must die.
But if a wicked man, turning from the wickedness he has committed, does what is right and
just, he shall preserve his life; since he has
turned away from all the sins which he committed, he shall surely live, he shall not die.

   This is the Word of the Lord.

Responsorial Psalm   Ps 130, 1-2. 3-4. 4-6. 7-8

R̸. (3) If you, O Lord, laid bare our guilt
   who could endure it?
Out of the depths I cry to you, O Lord;
   Lord, hear my voice!
Let your ears be attentive
   to my voice in supplication.
R̸. If you, O Lord, laid bare our guilt
   who could endure it?
If you, O Lord, mark iniquities,
   Lord, who can stand?
But with you is forgiveness,
   that you may be revered.
R̸. If you, O Lord, laid bare our guilt
   who could endure it?
I trust in the Lord;
   my soul trusts in his word.
My soul waits for the Lord
   more than sentinels wait for the dawn.
Let Israel wait for the Lord.
R̸. If you, O Lord, laid bare our guilt
   who could endure it?
For with the Lord is kindness
   and with him is plenteous redemption;
And he will redeem Israel
   from all their iniquities.
R̸. If you, O Lord, laid bare our guilt
   who could endure it?

GOSPEL Mt 5, 20-26
Verse before the Gospel
See no. 224.

✠ A reading from the holy gospel according
to Matthew

Go first and be reconciled with your brother.

Jesus said to his disciples: "Unless your holiness surpasses that of the scribes and Pharisees you shall not enter the kingdom of God. You have heard the commandment imposed on your forefathers, 'You shall not commit murder; every murderer shall be liable to judgment.' What I say to you is: everyone who grows angry with his brother shall be liable to judgment, any man who uses abusive language toward his brother shall be answerable to the Sanhedrin, and if he holds him in contempt he risks the fires of Gehenna. If you bring your gift to the altar and there recall that your brother has anything against you, leave your gift at the altar, go first to be reconciled with your brother, and then come and offer your gift. Lose no time; settle with your opponent while on your way to court with him. Otherwise your opponent may hand you over to the judge, who will hand you over to the guard, who will throw you into prison. I warn you, you will not be released until you have paid the last penny."
    This is the gospel of the Lord.

**230   SATURDAY OF THE FIRST
WEEK OF LENT**

READING I Dt 26, 16-19
A reading from the book of Deuteronomy
You will be a people consecrated to the Lord God.

Moses spoke to the people, saying: "This day the Lord, your God, commands you to observe these statutes and decrees. Be careful, then, to observe them with all your heart and with all your soul. Today you are making this agreement with the Lord: he is to be your God and you are to walk in his ways and observe his statutes, commandments and decrees, and to

hearken to his voice. And today the Lord is making this agreement with you: you are to be a people peculiarly his own, as he promised you; and provided you keep all his commandments, he will then raise you high in praise and renown and glory above all other nations he has made, and you will be a people sacred to the Lord, your God, as he promised."
    This is the Word of the Lord.

Responsorial Psalm Ps 119, 1-2. 4-5. 7-8

℟. (1) Happy are they who follow the law of the Lord.

Happy are they whose way is blameless,
    who walk in the law of the Lord.
Happy are they who observe his decrees,
    who seek him with all their heart.

℟. Happy are they who follow the law of the Lord.

You have commanded that your precepts
    be diligently kept.
Oh, that I might be firm in the ways
    of keeping your statutes!

℟. Happy are they who follow the law of the Lord.

I will give you thanks with an upright heart,
    when I have learned your just ordinances.
I will keep your statutes;
    do not utterly forsake me.

℟. Happy are they who follow the law of the Lord.

GOSPEL Mt 5, 43-48
Verse before the Gospel
See no. 224.

✠ A reading from the holy gospel according
to Matthew

Be perfect as your heavenly Father is perfect.

Jesus said to his disciples: "You have heard the commandment, 'You shall love your countryman but hate your enemy.' My command to you is: love your enemies, pray for your persecutors. This will prove that you are sons of your heavenly Father, for his sun rises on the bad and the good, he rains on the just and the unjust. If you love those who love you, what merit is there in that? Do not tax collectors do as much? And if you greet your brothers only, what is so praiseworthy about that? Do not pagans do as much? In a word, you must be perfected as your heavenly Father is perfect."

This is the gospel of the Lord.

---

231 MONDAY OF THE SECOND WEEK OF LENT

READING I   Dn 9, 4-10

A reading from the book of the prophet Daniel
We have sinned, we have done wrong.

"Lord, great and awesome God, you who keep your merciful covenant toward those who love you and observe your commandments! We have sinned, been wicked and done evil; we have rebelled and departed from your commandments and your laws. We have not obeyed your servants the prophets, who spoke in your name to our kings, our princes, our fathers, and all the people of the land. Justice, O Lord, is on your side; we are shamefaced even to this day: the men of Judah, the residents of Jerusalem, and all Israel, near and far, in all the countries to which you have scattered them because of their treachery toward you. O Lord, we are shamefaced, like our kings, our princes, and our fathers, for having sinned against you. But yours, O Lord, our God, are compassion and forgiveness! Yet we rebelled against you and paid no heed to your command, O Lord, our God, to live by the law you gave us through your servants the prophets."

This is the Word of the Lord.

Responsorial Psalm   Ps 79, 8. 9. 11. 13

℟. (Ps 103, 10) Lord, do not deal with us as our sins deserve.

Remember not against us the iniquities of the past;
     may your compassion quickly come to us,
     for we are brought very low.

℟. Lord, do not deal with us as our sins deserve.

Help us, O God our savior,
     because of the glory of your name;
Deliver us and pardon our sins
     for your name's sake.

℟. Lord, do not deal with us as our sins deserve.

Let the prisoners' sighing come before you;
     with your great power free those doomed to death.
Then we, your people and the sheep of your pasture,
     will give thanks to you forever;
     through all generations we will declare your praise.

℟. Lord, do not deal with us as our sins deserve.

GOSPEL   Lk 6, 36-38
Verse before the Gospel

See no. 224.

✠ **A reading from the holy gospel according to Luke**
Forgive, and you will be forgiven.

Jesus said to his disciples: "Be compassionate, as your Father is compassionate. Do not judge, and you will not be judged. Do not condemn, and you will not be condemned. Pardon, and you shall be pardoned. Give, and it shall be given to you. Good measure pressed down, shaken together, running over, will they pour into the fold of your garment. For the measure you measure with will be measured back to you."

This is the gospel of the Lord.

---

232 TUESDAY OF THE SECOND WEEK OF LENT

READING I   Is 1, 10. 16-20

A reading from the book of the prophet Isaiah
Learn to do good, search for justice.

Hear the word of the Lord,
     princes of Sodom!
Listen to the instruction of our God,
     people of Gomorrah!

Wash yourselves clean!
Put away your misdeeds from before my eyes;
    cease doing evil; learn to do good.
Make justice your aim: redress the wronged,
    hear the orphan's plea, defend the widow.
Come now, let us set things right,
    says the Lord:
Though your sins be like scarlet,
    they may become white as snow;
Though they be crimson red,
    they may become white as wool.
If you are willing, and obey,
    you shall eat the good things of the land;
But if you refuse and resist,
    the sword shall consume you:
    for the mouth of the Lord has spoken!
    This is the Word of the Lord.

Responsorial Psalm   Ps 50, 8-9. 16-17. 21. 23

℟. (23) To the upright
    I will show the saving power of God.
Not for your sacrifices do I rebuke you,
    for your holocausts are before me always.
I take from your house no bullock,
    no goats out of your fold.
℟. To the upright
    I will show the saving power of God.
Why do you recite my statutes,
    and profess my covenant with your mouth,
Though you hate discipline
    and cast my words behind you?
℟. To the upright
    I will show the saving power of God.
When you do these things, shall I be deaf to it?
    Or think you that I am like yourself?
    I will correct you by drawing them up before
        your eyes.
He that offers praise as a sacrifice glorifies me;
    and to him that goes the right way I will
        show the salvation of God.
℟. To the upright
    I will show the saving power of God.

GOSPEL   Mt 23, 1-12
Verse before the Gospel

See no. 224.

✠ A reading from the holy gospel according
        to Matthew
They do not practice what they preach.

Jesus told the crowds and his disciples: "The
scribes and the Pharisees have succeeded
Moses as teachers; therefore, do everything
and observe everything they tell you. But do
not follow their example. Their words are bold
but their deeds are few. They bind up heavy
loads, hard to carry, to lay on other men's
shoulders, while they themselves will not lift a
finger to budge them. All their works are performed to be seen. They widen their phylacteries and wear huge tassels. They are fond of
places of honor at banquets and the front seats
in synagogues, of marks of respect in public
and of being called 'Rabbi.' As to you, avoid
the title 'Rabbi.' One among you is your
teacher, the rest are learners. Do not call anyone on earth your father. Only one is your father, the One in heaven. Avoid being called
teachers. Only one is your teacher, the Messiah. The greatest among you will be the one
who serves the rest. Whoever exalts himself
shall be humbled, but whoever humbles himself shall be exalted."
    This is the gospel of the Lord.

---

233   **WEDNESDAY OF THE SECOND
            WEEK OF LENT**

READING I   Jer 18, 18-20
    A reading from the book of the prophet
                Jeremiah
Come, let us persecute him.

The men of Judah and the citizens of Jerusalem said, "Let us contrive a plot against Jeremiah. It will not mean the loss of instruction
from the priests, nor of counsel from the wise,
nor of messages from the prophets. And so, let
us destroy him by his own tongue; let us carefully note his every word."
Heed me, O Lord,
    and listen to what my adversaries say.
Must good be repaid with evil
    that they should dig a pit to take my life?

Remember that I stood before you
  to speak in their behalf,
  to turn away your wrath from them.
      This is the Word of the Lord.

Responsorial Psalm   Ps 31, 5-6. 14. 15-16

℟. (17) Save me, O Lord, in your steadfast
  love.
You will free me from the snare they set for
  me,
  for you are my refuge.
Into your hands I commend my spirit;
  you will redeem me, O Lord, O faithful God.
℟. Save me, O Lord, in your steadfast love.
I hear the whispers of the crowd, that frighten
  me from every side,
  as they consult together against me, plotting
  to take my life.
℟. Save me, O Lord, in your steadfast love.
But my trust is in you, O Lord;
  I say, "You are my God."
In your hands is my destiny; rescue me
  from the clutches of my enemies and my
  persecutors.
℟. Save me, O Lord, in your steadfast love.

GOSPEL   Mt 20, 17-28
Verse before the Gospel

See no. 224.

✠ **A reading from the holy gospel according
      to Matthew**
      They condemned him to death.

As Jesus was starting to go up to Jerusalem, he
took the Twelve aside on the road and said to
them: "We are going up to Jerusalem now.
There the Son of Man will be handed over to
the chief priests and scribes, who will condemn
him to death. They will turn him over to the
Gentiles, to be made sport of and flogged and
crucified. But on the third day he will be raised
up."
    The mother of Zebedee's sons came up to
him accompanied by her sons, to do him homage and ask of him a favor. "What is it you
want?" he said. She answered, "Promise me
that these sons of mine will sit, one at your

right hand and the other at your left, in your
kingdom." In reply Jesus said, "You do not
know what you are asking. Can you drink of
the cup I am to drink of?" "We can," they said.
He told them, "From the cup I drink of you
shall drink. Sitting at my right hand or my left
is not mine to give. That is for those for whom
it has been reserved by my Father." The other
ten, on hearing this, became indignant at the
two brothers. Jesus then called them together
and said: "You know how those who exercise
authority among the Gentiles lord it over them;
their great ones make their importance felt. It
cannot be like that with you. Anyone among
you who aspires to greatness must serve the
rest, and whoever wants to rank first among
you, must serve the needs of all. Such is the
case with the Son of Man who has come, not
to be served by others but to serve, to give his
own life as a ransom for the many."
    This is the gospel of the Lord.

234   **THURSDAY OF THE SECOND
             WEEK OF LENT**

READING I   Jer 17, 5-10

**A reading from the book of the prophet
             Jeremiah**
A curse on him who trusts in man; a blessing on him who
             trusts in the Lord God.

Thus says the Lord:
Cursed is the man who trusts in human beings,
  who seeks his strength in flesh,
  whose heart turns away from the Lord.
He is like a barren bush in the desert
  that enjoys no change of season,
But stands in a lava waste,
  a salt and empty earth.
Blessed is the man who trusts in the Lord,
  whose hope is the Lord.
He is like a tree planted beside the waters
  that stretches out its roots to the stream:
It fears not the heat when it comes,
  its leaves stay green;
In the year of drought it shows no distress,
  but still bears fruit.

More tortuous than all else is the human heart,
    beyond remedy; who can understand it?
I, the Lord, alone probe the mind
    and test the heart,
To reward everyone according to his ways,
    according to the merit of his deeds.
        This is the Word of the Lord.

Responsorial Psalm   Ps 1, 1-2. 3. 4. 6

℟. (Ps 40, 5) Happy are they who hope in the
    Lord.
Happy the man who follows not
    the counsel of the wicked
Nor walks in the way of sinners,
    nor sits in the company of the insolent,
But delights in the law of the Lord
    and meditates on his law day and night.
℟. Happy are they who hope in the Lord.
He is like a tree
    planted near running water,
That yields its fruit in due season,
    and whose leaves never fade.
    [Whatever he does, prospers.]
℟. Happy are they who hope in the Lord.
Not so, the wicked, not so;
    they are like chaff which the wind drives
    away.
For the Lord watches over the way of the just,
    but the way of the wicked vanishes.
℟. Happy are they who hope in the Lord.

GOSPEL   Lk 16, 19-31
Verse before the Gospel
See no. 224.

✠ A reading from the holy gospel according
    to Luke.
Good things came to you and bad things to Lazarus; now
    he is comforted while you are in agony.

Jesus said to the Pharisees: "Once there was a
rich man who dressed in purple and linen and
feasted splendidly every day. At his gate lay a
beggar named Lazarus, who was covered with
sores. Lazarus longed to eat the scraps that fell
from the rich man's table. The dogs even came
and licked his sores. Eventually the beggar
died. He was carried by angels to the bosom of
Abraham. The rich man likewise died and was
buried. From the abode of the dead where he
was in torment, he raised his eyes and saw
Abraham afar off, and Lazarus resting in his
bosom.

"He called out, 'Father Abraham, have pity
on me. Send Lazarus to dip the tip of his finger
in water to refresh my tongue, for I am tortured in these flames.' 'My child,' replied
Abraham, 'remember that you were well off in
your lifetime, while Lazarus was in misery.
Now he has found consolation here, but you
have found torment. And that is not all. Between you and us there is fixed a great
abyss, so that those who might wish to cross
from here to you cannot do so, nor can anyone
cross from your side to us.'

" 'Father, I ask you, then,' the rich man said,
'send him to my father's house where I have
five brothers. Let him be a warning to them so
that they may not end in this place of torment.'
Abraham answered, 'They have Moses and the
prophets. Let them hear them.' 'No, Father
Abraham,' replied the rich man. 'But if someone would only go to them from the dead, then
they would repent.' Abraham said to him, 'If
they do not listen to Moses and the prophets,
they will not be convinced even if one should
rise from the dead.' "
        This is the gospel of the Lord.

235   **FRIDAY OF THE SECOND
        WEEK OF LENT**

READING I   Gn 37, 3-4. 12-13. 17-28
    A reading from the book of Genesis
    Here comes the man of dreams; let us kill him.

Israel loved Joseph best of all his sons, for he
was the child of his old age; and he had made
him a long tunic. When his brothers saw that
their father loved him best of all his sons, they
hated him so much that they would not even
greet him.

One day, when his brothers had gone to pasture their father's flocks at Shechem, Israel
said to Joseph, "Your brothers, you know, are
tending our flocks at Shechem. Get ready; I
will send you to them."

So Joseph went after his brothers and caught up with them in Dothan. They noticed him from a distance, and before he came up to them, they plotted to kill him. They said to one another: "Here comes that master dreamer! Come on, let us kill him and throw him into one of the cisterns here; we could say that a wild beast devoured him. We shall then see what comes of his dreams."

When Reuben heard this, he tried to save him from their hands, saying: "We must not take his life. Instead of shedding blood," he continued, "just throw him into that cistern there in the desert; but don't kill him outright." His purpose was to rescue him from their hands and restore him to his father. So when Joseph came up to them, they stripped him of the long tunic he had on; then they took him and threw him into the cistern, which was empty and dry.

They then sat down to their meal. Looking up, they saw a caravan of Ishmaelites coming from Gilead, their camels laden with gum, balm, and resin to be taken down to Egypt. Judah said to his brothers: "What is to be gained by killing our brother and concealing his blood? Rather, let us sell him to these Ishmaelites, instead of doing away with him ourselves. After all, he is our brother, our own flesh." His brothers agreed. They sold Joseph to the Ishmaelites for twenty pieces of silver.

This is the Word of the Lord.

Responsorial Psalm   Ps 105, 16-17. 18-19. 20-21

℟. (5) Remember the marvels the Lord has done.
When the Lord called down a famine on the land
 and ruined the crop that sustained them,
He sent a man before them,
 Joseph, sold as a slave.
℟. Remember the marvels the Lord has done.
They had weighed him down with fetters,
 and he was bound with chains,
Till his prediction came to pass
 and the word of the Lord proved him true.
℟. Remember the marvels the Lord has done.

The king sent and released him,
 the ruler of the peoples set him free.
He made him lord of his house
 and ruler of all his possessions.
℟. Remember the marvels the Lord has done.

GOSPEL   Mt 21, 33-43. 45-46
Verse before the Gospel

See no. 224.

✠ A reading from the holy gospel according to Matthew
This is the heir; let us kill him.

Jesus said to the chief priests and elders of the people: "Listen to this parable. There was a property owner who planted a vineyard, put a hedge around it, dug out a vat, and erected a tower. Then he leased it out to tenant farmers and went on a journey. When vintage time arrived he dispatched his slaves to the tenants to obtain his share of the grapes. The tenants responded by seizing the slaves. They beat one, killed another, and stoned a third. A second time he dispatched even more slaves than before, but they treated them the same way. Finally he sent his son to them, thinking, 'They will respect my son.' When they saw the son, the tenants said to one another, 'Here is the one who will inherit everything. Let us kill him and then we shall have his inheritance!' With that they seized him, dragged him outside the vineyard, and killed him. What do you suppose the owner of the vineyard will do to those tenants when he comes?" They replied, "He will bring that wicked crowd to a bad end and lease his vineyard out to others, who will see to it that he has grapes at vintage time." Jesus said to them, "Did you never read in the Scriptures,
'The stone which the builders rejected
 has become the keystone of the structure.
It was the Lord who did this
 and we find it marvelous to behold'?
For this reason, I tell you, the kingdom of God will be taken away from you and given to a nation that will yield a rich harvest."

When the chief priests and the Pharisees heard these parables, they realized he was speaking about them. Although they sought to arrest him they had reason to fear the crowds who regarded him as a prophet.

This is the gospel of the Lord.

---

236   SATURDAY OF THE SECOND WEEK OF LENT

READING I   Mi 7, 14-15. 18-20

A reading from the book of the prophet Micah

Once again tread down all our sins to the bottom of the sea.

Shepherd your people with your staff,
  the flock of your inheritance,
That dwells apart in a woodland,
  in the midst of Carmel.
Let them feed in Bashan and Gilead,
  as in the days of old;
As in the days when you came from the land
  of Egypt,
  show us wonderful signs.

Who is there like you, the God who removes
  guilt
  and pardons sin for the remnant of his inheritance;
Who does not persist in anger forever,
  but delights rather in clemency,
And will again have compassion on us,
  treading underfoot our guilt?
You will cast into the depths of the sea
  all our sins;
You will show faithfulness to Jacob,
  and grace to Abraham,
As you have sworn to our fathers
  from days of old.

This is the Word of the Lord.

Responsorial Psalm   Ps 103, 1-2. 3-4. 9-10. 11-12

℞. (8) The Lord is kind and merciful.
Bless the Lord, O my soul;
  and all my being, bless his holy name.
Bless the Lord, O my soul,
  and forget not all his benefits.
℞. The Lord is kind and merciful.
He pardons all your iniquities,
  he heals all your ills.

He redeems your life from destruction,
  he crowns you with kindness and compassion.
℞. The Lord is kind and merciful.
He will not always chide,
  nor does he keep his wrath forever.
Not according to our sins does he deal with us,
  nor does he requite us according to our
  crimes.
℞. The Lord is kind and merciful.
For as the heavens are high above the earth,
  so surpassing is his kindness toward those
  who fear him.
As far as the east is from the west,
  so far has he put our transgressions from us.
℞. The Lord is kind and merciful.

GOSPEL   Lk 15, 1-3. 11-32

Verse before the Gospel

See no. 224.

✠ **A reading from the holy gospel according to Luke**

Your brother here was dead, and has come to life.

The tax collectors and sinners were all gathering around Jesus to hear him, at which the Pharisees and the scribes murmured, "This man welcomes sinners and eats with them."

At this Jesus addressed this parable to them: "A man had two sons. The younger of them said to his father, 'Father, give me the share of the estate that is coming to me.' So the father divided up the property. Some days later this younger son collected all his belongings and went off to a distant land, where he squandered his money on dissolute living. After he had spent everything, a great famine broke out in that country and he was in dire need. So he attached himself to one of the propertied class of the place, who sent him to his farm to take care of the pigs. He longed to fill his belly with the husks that were fodder for pigs, but no one made a move to give him anything. Coming to his senses at last, he said: 'How many hired hands at my father's place have more than enough to eat, while here I am starving! I will break away and return to my father, and say to him, "Father, I have sinned against God and against you; I no longer deserve to be called your son. Treat me like one of your hired hands." ' With that he set off for his father's house. While he was still a long way off, his father caught sight of him and was deeply moved. He ran out to meet him, threw his arms around his neck, and kissed him. The son said to him, 'Father, I have sinned against God and against you; I no longer deserve to be called your son.' The father said to his servants: 'Quick! bring out the finest robe and put it on him; put a ring on his finger and shoes on his feet. Take the fatted calf and kill it. Let us eat and celebrate because this son of mine was dead and has come back to life. He was lost and is found.' Then the celebration began.

"Meanwhile the elder son was out on the land. As he neared the house on his way home, he heard the sound of music and dancing. He called one of the servants and asked him the reason for the dancing and the music. The servant answered, 'Your brother is home, and your father has killed the fatted calf because he has him back in good health.' The son grew angry at this and would not go in; but his father came out and began to plead with him.

"He said to his father in reply: 'For years now I have slaved for you. I never disobeyed one of your orders, yet you never gave me so much as a kid goat to celebrate with my friends. Then, when this son of yours returns after having gone through your property with loose women, you kill the fatted calf for him.'

" 'My son,' replied the father, 'you are with me always, and everything I have is yours. But we must celebrate and rejoice! This brother of yours was dead, and has come back to life. He was lost, and is found.' "

This is the gospel of the Lord.

237   OPTIONAL MASS FOR THE THIRD WEEK OF LENT

This Mass may be used on any day of this week, especially in years B and C when the gospel of the Samaritan woman is not read on the Third Sunday of Lent.

READING I   Ex 17, 1-7

A reading from the book of Exodus

He showed him water, that the people might drink.

From the desert of Sin the whole Israelite community journeyed by stages, as the Lord directed, and encamped at Rephidim.

Here there was no water for the people to drink. They quarreled, therefore, with Moses and said, "Give us water to drink." Moses replied, "Why do you quarrel with me? Why do you put the Lord to a test?" Here, then, in their thirst for water, the people grumbled against Moses, saying, "Why did you ever make us leave Egypt? Was it just to have us die here of thirst with our children and our livestock?" So Moses cried out to the Lord, "What shall I do with this people? A little more and they will stone me!" The Lord answered Moses, "Go over there in front of the people, along with some of the elders of Israel, holding in your hand, as you go, the staff with which you struck the river. I will be standing there in front of you on the rock in Horeb. Strike the rock, and the water will flow from it for the people to drink." This Moses did, in the presence of the elders of Israel.

This is the Word of the Lord.

Responsorial Psalm   Ps 95, 1-2. 6-7. 8-9

℞. (7. 8) If today you hear his voice,
    harden not your hearts.
Come, let us sing joyfully to the Lord;
    let us acclaim the Rock of our salvation.
Let us greet him with thanksgiving;
    let us joyfully sing psalms to him.
℞. If today you hear his voice,
    harden not your hearts.
Come, let us bow down in worship;
    let us kneel before the Lord who made us.

For he is our God,
  and we are the people he shepherds, the
  flock he guides.
℟. If today you hear his voice,
  harden not your hearts.
Oh, that today you would hear his voice:
  "Harden not your hearts as at Meribah,
  as in the day of Massah in the desert,
Where your fathers tempted me;
  they tested me though they had seen my
  works."
℟. If today you hear his voice,
  harden not your hearts.

GOSPEL   Jn 4, 5-42
Verse before the Gospel
See no. 224.

✠ A reading from the holy gospel according
                to John
The water that I shall give will become a spring of
                    eternal life.

The journey of Jesus brought him to a
Samaritan town named Shechem near the plot
of land which Jacob had given to his son
Joseph. This was the site of Jacob's well. Jesus,
tired from his journey, sat down at the well.
  The hour was about noon. When a Samaritan woman came to draw water, Jesus said
to her, "Give me a drink." (His disciples had
gone off to the town to buy provisions.) The
Samaritan woman said to him, "You are a Jew.
How can you ask me, a Samaritan and a
woman, for a drink?" (Recall that Jews have
nothing to do with Samaritans.) Jesus replied:
  "If only you recognized God's gift,
  and who it is that is asking you for a drink,
  you would have asked him instead,
  and he would have given you living
  water."
"Sir," she challenged him, "you don't have a
bucket and this well is deep. Where do you
expect to get this flowing water? Surely you
don't pretend to be greater than our ancestor
Jacob, who gave us this well and drank from
it with his sons and his flocks?" Jesus replied:
  "Everyone who drinks this water
  will be thirsty again.

But whoever drinks the water I give him
  will never be thirsty;
  no, the water I give
  shall become a fountain within him,
  leaping up to provide eternal life."
The woman said to him, "Give me this water,
sir, so that I won't grow thirsty and have to
keep coming here to draw water."
  He told her, "Go, call your husband, and then
come back here." "I have no husband," replied
the woman. "You are right in saying you have
no husband!" Jesus exclaimed. "The fact is,
you have had five, and the man you are living
with now is not your husband. What you said
is true enough."
  "Sir," answered the woman, "I can see you
are a prophet. Our ancestors worshiped on this
mountain, but you people claim that Jerusalem
is the place where men ought to worship God."
Jesus told her:
  "Believe me, woman,
  an hour is coming
  when you will worship the Father
  neither on this mountain
  nor in Jerusalem.
  You people worship what you do not
  understand,
  while we understand what we worship;
  after all, salvation is from the Jews.
  Yet an hour is coming, and is already here,
  when authentic worshipers
  will worship the Father in Spirit and truth.
  Indeed, it is just such worshipers
  the Father seeks.
  God is Spirit,
  and those who worship him
  must worship in Spirit and truth."
The woman said to him: "I know there is a
Messiah coming. (This term means Anointed.)
When he comes, he will tell us everything."
Jesus replied, "I who speak to you am he."
  His disciples, returning at this point, were
surprised that Jesus was speaking with a
woman. No one put a question, however, such
as "What do you want of him?" or "Why are
you talking with her?" The woman then left
her water jar and went off into the town. She
said to the people, "Come and see someone

who told me everything I ever did! Could this not be the Messiah?" With that they set out from the town to meet him.

Meanwhile the disciples were urging him, "Rabbi, eat something." But he told them:
"I have food to eat
of which you do not know."
At this the disciples said to one another, "You do not suppose anyone has brought him something to eat?" Jesus explained to them:
"Doing the will of him who sent me
and bringing his work to completion
is my food.
Do you not have a saying:
'Four months more
and it will be harvest!'?
Listen to what I say:
Open your eyes and see!
The fields are shining for harvest!
The reaper already collects his wages
and gathers a yield for eternal life,
that sower and reaper may rejoice together.
Here we have the saying verified:
'One man sows; another reaps.'
I sent you to reap
what you had not worked for.
Others have done the labor,
and you have come into their gain."

Many Samaritans from that town believed in him on the strength of the woman's word of testimony: "He told me everything I ever did." The result was that, when these Samaritans came to him, they begged him to stay with them awhile. So he stayed there two days, and through his own spoken word many more came to faith. As they told the woman: "No longer does our faith depend on your story. We have heard for ourselves, and we know that this really is the Savior of the world."

This is the gospel of the Lord.

---

238   **MONDAY OF THE THIRD
WEEK OF LENT**

READING I   2 Kgs 5, 1-15

A reading from the second book of Kings

There were many lepers in Israel, but none were made clean, except Naaman the Syrian.

Naaman, the army commander of the king of Aram, was highly esteemed and respected by his master, for through him the Lord had brought victory to Aram. But valiant as he was, the man was a leper. Now the Arameans had captured from the land of Israel in a raid a little girl, who became the servant of Naaman's wife. "If only my master would present himself to the prophet in Samaria," she said to her mistress, "he would cure him of his leprosy." Naaman went and told his lord just what the slave girl from the land of Israel had said. "Go," said the king of Aram. "I will send along a letter to the king of Israel." So Naaman set out, taking along ten silver talents, six thousand gold pieces, and ten festal garments. To the king of Israel he brought the letter, which read: "With this letter I am sending my servant Naaman to you, that you may cure him of his leprosy."

When he read the letter, the king of Israel tore his garments and exclaimed: "Am I a god with power over life and death, that this man should send someone to me to be cured of leprosy? Take note! You can see he is only looking for a quarrel with me!" When Elisha, the man of God, heard that the king of Israel had torn his garments, he sent word to the king: "Why have you torn your garments? Let him come to me and find out that there is a prophet in Israel."

Naaman came with his horses and chariots and stopped at the door of Elisha's house. The prophet sent him the message: "Go and wash seven times in the Jordan, and your flesh will heal, and you will be clean." But Naaman went away angry, saying, "I thought that he would surely come out and stand there to invoke the Lord his God, and would move his hand over the spot, and thus cure the leprosy. Are not the rivers of Damascus, the

Abana and the Pharpar, better than all the waters of Israel? Could I not wash in them and be cleansed?" With this, he turned about in anger and left.

But his servants came up and reasoned with him. "My father," they said, "if the prophet had told you to do something extraordinary, would you not have done it? All the more now, since he said to you, 'Wash and be clean,' should you do as he said." So Naaman went down and plunged into the Jordan seven times at the word of the man of God. His flesh became again like the flesh of a little child, and he was clean.

He returned with his whole retinue to the man of God. On his arrival he stood before him and said, "Now I know that there is no God in all the earth, except in Israel."

This is the Word of the Lord.

Responsorial Psalm   Pss 42, 2. 3; 43, 3. 4

℟. (Ps 42, 3) My soul is thirsting for the living God:
  when shall I see him face to face?
As the hind longs for the running waters,
  so my soul longs for you, O God.
℟. My soul is thirsting for the living God:
  when shall I see him face to face?
Athirst is my soul for God, the living God.
  When shall I go and behold the face of God?
℟. My soul is thirsting for the living God:
  when shall I see him face to face?
Send forth your light and your fidelity;
  they shall lead me on
And bring me to your holy mountain,
  to your dwelling-place.
℟. My soul is thirsting for the living God:
  when shall I see him face to face?
Then will I go in to the altar of God,
  the God of my gladness and joy;
Then will I give you thanks upon the harp,
  O God, my God!
℟. My soul is thirsting for the living God:
  when shall I see him face to face?

GOSPEL   Lk 4, 24-30
Verse before the Gospel

See no. 224.

✠ A reading from the holy gospel according to Luke

Like Elijah and Elisha Jesus was not sent only to the Jews.

When Jesus had come to Nazareth, he said to the people in the synagogue: "No prophet gains acceptance in his native place. Indeed, let me remind you, there were many widows in Israel in the days of Elijah when the heavens remained closed for three and a half years and a great famine spread over the land. It was to none of these that Elijah was sent, but to a widow of Zarephath near Sidon. Recall, too, the many lepers in Israel in the time of Elisha the prophet; yet not one was cured except Naaman the Syrian."

At these words the whole audience in the synagogue was filled with indignation. They rose up and expelled him from the town, leading him to the brow of the hill on which it was built and intending to hurl him over the edge. But he went straight through their midst and walked away.

This is the gospel of the Lord.

---

239   TUESDAY OF THE THIRD WEEK OF LENT

READING I   Dn 3, 25. 34-43

A reading from the book of the prophet Daniel

We ask you to receive us with humble and contrite hearts.

Azariah stood up in the fire and prayed aloud: "For your name's sake, O Lord, do not deliver us up forever,
  or make void your covenant.
Do not take away your mercy from us,
  for the sake of Abraham, your beloved,
  Isaac your servant, and Israel your holy one,
To whom you promised to multiply their offspring
  like the stars of heaven,
  or the sand on the shore of the sea.
For we are reduced, O Lord, beyond any other nation,
  brought low everywhere in the world this day
  because of our sins.
We have in our day no prince, prophet, or leader,

no holocaust, sacrifice, oblation, or incense,
no place to offer first fruits, to find favor
with you.
But with contrite heart and humble spirit
let us be received;
As though it were holocausts of rams and
bullocks,
or thousands of fat lambs,
So let our sacrifice be in your presence today
as we follow you unreservedly;
for those who trust in you cannot be put
to shame.
And now we follow you with our whole heart,
we fear you and we pray to you.
Do not let us be put to shame,
but deal with us in your kindness and great
mercy.
Deliver us by your wonders,
and bring glory to your name, O Lord."
This is the Word of the Lord.

Responsorial Psalm   Ps 25, 4-5. 6-7. 8-9

R̰. (6) Remember your mercies, O Lord.
Your ways, O Lord, make known to me;
teach me your paths,
Guide me in your truth and teach me,
for you are God my savior.
R̰. Remember your mercies, O Lord.
Remember that your compassion, O Lord,
and your kindness are from of old.
In your kindness remember me,
because of your goodness, O Lord.
R̰. Remember your mercies, O Lord.
Good and upright is the Lord;
thus he shows sinners the way.
He guides the humble to justice,
he teaches the humble his way.
R̰. Remember your mercies, O Lord.

GOSPEL   Mt 18, 21-35
Verse before the Gospel

See no. 224.

✠ **A reading from the holy gospel according**
to Matthew
Unless each of you forgive your brother, the Father will
not forgive you.
Peter came up and asked Jesus, "Lord, when
my brother wrongs me, how often must I for-
give him? Seven times?" "No," Jesus replied,

"not seven times; I say, seventy times seven
times. That is why the reign of God may
be said to be like a king who decided to settle
accounts with his officials. When he began
his auditing, one was brought in who owed
him a huge amount. As he had no way of
paying it, his master ordered him to be sold,
along with his wife, his children, and all his
property, in payment of the debt. At that the
official prostrated himself in homage and said,
'My lord, be patient with me and I will pay you
back in full.' Moved with pity, the master let
the official go and wrote off the debt. But when
that same official went out he met a fellow servant who owed him a mere fraction of what he
himself owed. He seized him and throttled him.
'Pay back what you owe,' he demanded. His fellow servant dropped to his knees and began to
plead with him, 'Just give me time and I will
pay you back in full.' But he would hear none
of it. Instead, he had him put in jail until he paid
back what he owed. When his fellow servants
saw what had happened they were badly shaken,
and went to their master to report the whole
incident. His master sent for him and said, 'You
worthless wretch! I canceled your entire debt
when you pleaded with me. Should you not
have dealt mercifully with your fellow servant,
as I dealt with you?' Then in anger the master
handed him over to the torturers until he paid
back all that he owed. My heavenly Father will
treat you in exactly the same way unless each
of you forgives his brother from his heart."
This is the gospel of the Lord.

---

240   WEDNESDAY OF THE THIRD
WEEK OF LENT

READING I   Dt 4, 1. 5-9
A reading from the book of Deuteronomy
Keep the commandments and your work will be complete.
These are the words which Moses spoke to the
people: "Now, Israel, hear the statutes and
decrees which I am teaching you to observe,
that you may live, and may enter in and take
possession of the land which the Lord, the
God of your fathers, is giving you. Therefore,
I teach you the statutes and decrees as the
Lord, my God, has commanded me, that you

may observe them in the land you are entering to occupy. Observe them carefully, for thus will you give evidence of your wisdom and intelligence to the nations, who will hear of all these statutes and say, 'This great nation is truly a wise and intelligent people.' For what great nation is there that has gods so close to it as the Lord, our God, is to us whenever we call upon him? Or what great nation has statutes and decrees that are as just as this whole law which I am setting before you today?

"However, take care and be earnestly on your guard not to forget the things which your own eyes have seen, nor let them slip from your memory as long as you live, but teach them to your children and to your children's children."

This is the Word of the Lord.

Responsorial Psalm   Ps 147, 12-13. 15-16. 19-20

℟. (12) Praise the Lord, Jerusalem.

Glorify the Lord, O Jerusalem;
    praise your God, O Zion.
For he has strengthened the bars of your gates;
    he has blessed your children within you.

℟. Praise the Lord, Jerusalem.

He sends forth his command to the earth;
    swiftly runs his word!
He spreads snow like wool;
    frost he strews like ashes.

℟. Praise the Lord, Jerusalem.

He has proclaimed his word to Jacob,
    his statutes and his ordinances to Israel.
He has not done thus for any other nation;
    his ordinances he has not made known to
    them.

℟. Praise the Lord, Jerusalem.

GOSPEL   Mt 5, 17-19
Verse before the Gospel

See no. 224.

✠ A reading from the holy gospel according to Matthew

The man who keeps and teaches the law will be called great.

Jesus said to his disciples: "Do not think that I have come to abolish the law and the prophets. I have come, not to abolish them, but to fulfill

them. Of this much I assure you: until heaven and earth pass away, not the smallest letter of the law, not the smallest part of a letter shall be done away with until it all comes true. That is why whoever breaks the least significant of these commands and teaches others to do so shall be called least in the kingdom of God. Whoever fulfills and teaches these commands shall be great in the kingdom of God."

This is the gospel of the Lord.

241   **THURSDAY OF THE THIRD WEEK OF LENT**

READING I   Jer 7, 23-28

A reading from the book of the prophet Jeremiah

This is the nation that will not listen to the voice of the Lord God.

Thus says the Lord: This is what I commanded my people: Listen to my voice; then I will be your God and you shall be my people. Walk in all the ways that I command you, so that you may prosper.

But they obeyed not, nor did they pay heed. They walked in the hardness of their evil hearts and turned their backs, not their faces, to me. From the day that your fathers left the land of Egypt even to this day, I have sent you untiringly all my servants the prophets. Yet they have not obeyed me nor paid heed; they have stiffened their necks and done worse than their fathers. When you speak all these words to them, they will not listen to you either; when you call to them, they will not answer you. Say to them: This is the nation which does not listen to the voice of the Lord, its God, or take correction. Faithfulness has disappeared; the word itself is banished from their speech.

This is the Word of the Lord.

Responsorial Psalm   Ps 95, 1-2. 6-7. 8-9

℟. (7. 8) If today you hear his voice,
    harden not your hearts.
Come, let us sing joyfully to the Lord;
    let us acclaim the Rock of our salvation.
Let us greet him with thanksgiving;
    let us joyfully sing psalms to him.

℟. If today you hear his voice,
    harden not your hearts.
Come, let us bow down in worship;
    let us kneel before the Lord who made us.
For he is our God,
    and we are the people he shepherds, the
    flock he guides.
℟. If today you hear his voice,
    harden not your hearts.
Oh, that today you would hear his voice:
    "Harden not your hearts as at Meribah,
    as in the day of Massah in the desert,
Where your fathers tempted me;
    they tested me though they had seen my
    works."
℟. If today you hear his voice,
    harden not your hearts.

GOSPEL   Lk 11, 14-23
Verse before the Gospel
See no. 224.

✠ A reading from the holy gospel according
    to Luke
He who is not with me is against me.

Jesus was casting out a devil which was mute,
and when the devil was cast out the dumb man
spoke. The crowds were amazed at this. Some
of them said, "It is by Beelzebul, the prince
of devils, that he casts out devils." Others, to
test him, were demanding of him a sign from
heaven.

Because he knew their thoughts, he said to
them: "Every kingdom divided against itself
is laid waste. Any house torn by dissension
falls. If Satan is divided against himself, how
can his kingdom last?—since you say it is
by Beelzebul that I cast out devils. If I cast
out devils by Beelzebul, by whom do your
people cast them out? In such case, let them act
as your judges. But if it is by the finger of God
that I cast out devils, then the reign of God is
upon you.

"When a strong man fully armed guards his
courtyard, his possessions go undisturbed. But
when someone stronger than he comes and
overpowers him, such a one carries off the
arms on which he was relying and divides the

spoils. The man who is not with me is against
me. The man who does not gather with me
scatters."
    This is the gospel of the Lord.

---

242 FRIDAY OF THE THIRD WEEK OF LENT

READING I   Hos 14 2-10
A reading from the book of the prophet Hosea
We will not say to the work of our hands: Our God.

Return, O Israel, to the Lord, your God;
    you have collapsed through your guilt.
Take with you words,
    and return to the Lord;
Say to him, "Forgive all iniquity,
    and receive what is good, that we may
    render
    as offerings the bullocks from our stalls.
Assyria will not save us,
    nor shall we have horses to mount;
We shall say no more, 'Our god,'
    to the work of our hands;
    for in you the orphan finds compassion."

I will heal their defection,
    I will love them freely;
    for my wrath is turned away from them.
I will be like the dew for Israel:
    he shall blossom like the lily;
He shall strike root like the Lebanon cedar,
    and put forth his shoots.
His splendor shall be like the olive tree
    and his fragrance like the Lebanon cedar.
Again they shall dwell in his shade
    and raise grain;
They shall blossom like the vine,
    and his fame shall be like the wine of
    Lebanon.

Ephraim! What more has he to do with idols?
    I have humbled him, but I will prosper him.
"I am like a verdant cypress tree"—
    Because of me you bear fruit!

Let him who is wise understand these things;
    let him who is prudent know them.
Straight are the paths of the Lord,
    in them the just walk,
    but sinners stumble in them.
    This is the Word of the Lord.

Responsorial Psalm   Ps 81, 6-8. 8-9. 10-11. 14. 17

℞. (11. 9) I am the Lord, your God:
 hear my voice.

An unfamiliar speech I hear:
 "I relieved his shoulder of the burden;
 his hands were freed from the basket.
In distress you called, and I rescued you.

℞. I am the Lord, your God:
 hear my voice.

Unseen, I answered you in thunder;
 I tested you at the waters of Meribah.
Hear, my people, and I will admonish you;
 O Israel, will you not hear me?

℞. I am the Lord, your God:
 hear my voice.

There shall be no strange god among you
 nor shall you worship any alien god.
I, the Lord, am your God
 who led you forth from the land of Egypt.

℞. I am the Lord, your God:
 hear my voice.

If only my people would hear me,
 and Israel walk in my ways,
I would feed them with the best of wheat,
 and with honey from the rock I would fill
 them."

℞. I am the Lord, your God:
 hear my voice.

GOSPEL   Mk 12, 28-34
Verse before the Gospel
See no. 224.

✠ A reading from the holy gospel according
 to Mark
The Lord your God is one Lord and you must love him.

One of the scribes came up to Jesus and asked
him, "Which is the first of all the commandments?" Jesus replied: "This is the first:
 'Hear, O Israel! The Lord our God is Lord
 alone!
 Therefore you shall love the Lord your
 God
 with all your heart,
 with all your soul,
 with all your mind,
 and with all your strength.'

This is the second,
 'You shall love your neighbor as yourself.'
There is no other commandment greater than
these." The scribe said to him: "Excellent,
Teacher! you are right in saying, 'He is the One,
there is no other than he.' Yes, 'to love him with
all our heart, with all our thoughts and with all
our strength, and to love our neighbor as ourselves' is worth more than any burnt offering
or sacrifice." Jesus approved the insight of this
answer and told him, "You are not far from
the reign of God." And no one had the courage
to ask him any more questions.

 This is the gospel of the Lord.

---

243   SATURDAY OF THE THIRD
WEEK OF LENT

READING I   Hos 6, 1-6
A reading from the book of the prophet Hosea
What I want is love, not sacrifice.

In their affliction, they shall look for me:
 "Come, let us return to the Lord,
For it is he who has rent, but he will heal us;
 he has struck us, but he will bind our
 wounds.
He will revive us after two days;
 on the third day he will raise us up,
 to live in his presence.
Let us know, let us strive to know the Lord;
 as certain as the dawn is his coming,
 and his judgment shines forth like the light
 of day!
He will come to us like the rain,
 like spring rain that waters the earth."

What can I do with you, Ephraim?
 What can I do with you, Judah?
Your piety is like a morning cloud,
 like the dew that early passes away.
For this reason I smote them through the
 prophets,
 I slew them by the words of my mouth;
For it is love that I desire, not sacrifice,
 and knowledge of God rather than holo-
 causts.

 This is the Word of the Lord.

Responsorial Psalm   Ps 51, 3-4. 18-19. 20-21

℟. (Hos 6, 6) It is steadfast love, not sacrifice,
that God desires.

Have mercy on me, O God, in your goodness;
in the greatness of your compassion wipe
out my offense.
Thoroughly wash me from my guilt
and of my sin cleanse me.
℟. It is steadfast love, not sacrifice,
that God desires.

For you are not pleased with sacrifices;
should I offer a holocaust, you would not
accept it.
My sacrifice, O God, is a contrite spirit;
a heart contrite and humbled, O God, you
will not spurn.
℟. It is steadfast love, not sacrifice,
that God desires.

Be bountiful, O Lord, to Zion in your kindness
by rebuilding the walls of Jerusalem;
Then shall you be pleased with due sacrifices,
burnt offerings and holocausts.
℟. It is steadfast love, not sacrifice,
that God desires.

GOSPEL   Lk 18, 9-14
Verse before the Gospel

See no. 224.

✠ A reading from the holy gospel according
to Luke
The publican went home justified, not the pharisee.

Jesus spoke this parable addressed to those
who believed in their own self-righteousness
while holding everyone else in contempt: "Two
men went up to the temple to pray; one was
a Pharisee, the other a tax collector. The
Pharisee with head unbowed prayed in this
fashion: 'I give you thanks, O God, that I am
not like the rest of men—grasping, crooked,
adulterous—or even like this tax collector. I
fast twice a week. I pay tithes on all I possess.'
The other man, however, kept his distance,
not even daring to raise his eyes to heaven.
All he did was beat his breast and say, 'O God,
be merciful to me, a sinner.' Believe me, this
man went home from the temple justified but

the other did not. For everyone who exalts
himself shall be humbled while he who
humbles himself shall be exalted."
This is the gospel of the Lord.

**244   OPTIONAL MASS
FOR THE FOURTH WEEK OF LENT**

This Mass may be used on any day of this week, especially
in years B and C when the gospel of the man born blind
is not read on the Fourth Sunday of Lent.

READING I   Mi 7, 7-9

A reading from the book of the prophet Micah
Though I live in darkness, the Lord God is my light.

I will look to the Lord,
I will put my trust in God my savior;
my God will hear me!

Rejoice not over me, O my enemy!
though I have fallen, I will arise;
though I sit in darkness, the Lord is my light.
The wrath of the Lord I will endure·
because I have sinned against him,
Until he takes up my cause,
and establishes my right.
He will bring me forth to the light;
I will see his justice.
This is the Word of the Lord.

Responsorial Psalm   Ps 27, 1. 7-8. 8-9. 13-14

℟. (1) The Lord is my light and my salvation.
The Lord is my light and my salvation;
whom should I fear?
The Lord is my life's refuge;
of whom should I be afraid?
℟. The Lord is my light and my salvation.
Hear, O Lord, the sound of my call;
have pity on me, and answer me.
Of you my heart speaks; you my glance seeks.
℟. The Lord is my light and my salvation.
Your presence, O Lord, I seek.
Hide not your face from me;
Do not in anger repel your servant.
You are my helper: cast me not off.
℟. The Lord is my light and my salvation.

I believe that I shall see the bounty of the Lord
  in the land of the living.
Wait for the Lord with courage;
  be stouthearted, and wait for the Lord.
℟. The Lord is my light and my salvation.

GOSPEL   Jn 9, 1-41
Verse before the Gospel

See no. 224.

✠ A reading from the holy gospel according
                    to John

I went to the pool of Siloam, and when I washed I could see.

As Jesus walked along, he saw a man who had
been blind from birth. His disciples asked him,
"Rabbi, was it his sin or his parents' that
caused him to be born blind?" "Neither," answered Jesus:

  "It was no sin, either of this man
    or of his parents.
  Rather, it was to let God's works show
    forth in him.
  We must do the deeds of him who sent me
    while it is day.
  The night comes on
    when no one can work.
  While I am in the world
    I am the light of the world."

With that Jesus spat on the ground, made mud
with his saliva, and smeared the man's eyes
with the mud. Then he told him, "Go, wash in
the pool of Siloam." (This name means "One
who has been sent.") So the man went off
and washed, and came back able to see.

  His neighbors and the people who had been
accustomed to see him begging began to ask,
"Isn't this the fellow who used to sit and beg?"
Some were claiming it was he; others maintained it was not but someone who looked
like him. The man himself said, "I'm the one,
all right." They said to him then, "How were
your eyes opened?" He answered, "That man
they call Jesus made mud and smeared it on
my eyes, telling me to go to Siloam and wash.
When I did go and wash, I was able to see."
"Where is he?" they asked. He replied, "I have
no idea."

  Next, they took the man who had been born
blind to the Pharisees. (Note that it was on a
sabbath that Jesus had made the mud paste
and opened his eyes.) The Pharisees, in turn,
began to inquire how he had recovered his
sight. He told them, "He put mud on my eyes.
I washed it off, and now I can see." This
prompted some of the Pharisees to assert,
"This man cannot be from God because he
does not keep the sabbath." Others objected,
"If a man is a sinner, how can he perform signs
like these?" They were sharply divided over
him. Then they addressed the blind man again:
"Since it was your eyes he opened, what do
you have to say about him?" "He is a prophet,"
he replied.

  The Jews refused to believe that he had
really been born blind and had begun to see,
until they summoned the parents of this man
who now could see. "Is this your son?" they
asked, "and if so, do you attest that he was
blind at birth? How do you account for the fact
that he now can see?" The parents answered,
"We know this is our son, and we know he was
blind at birth. But how he can see now, or who
opened his eyes, we have no idea. Ask him.
He is old enough to speak for himself." (His
parents answered in this fashion because they
were afraid of the Jews, who had already
agreed among themselves that anyone who
acknowledged Jesus as the Messiah would be
put out of the synagogue. That was why his
parents said, "He is of age—ask him.")

  A second time they summoned the man who
had been born blind and said to him, "Give
glory to God! First of all, we know this man is
a sinner." "I would not know whether he is a
sinner or not," he answered. "I know this
much: I was blind before; now I can see." They
persisted: "Just what did he do to you? How
did he open your eyes?" "I have told you once,
but you would not listen to me," he answered
them. "Why do you want to hear it all over
again? Do not tell me you want to become
his disciples too?" They retorted scornfully:
"You are the one who is that man's disciple.
We are disciples of Moses. We know that God
spoke to Moses, but we have no idea where this

man comes from." He came back at them, "Well, this is news! You do not know where he comes from, yet he opened my eyes. We know that God does not hear sinners, but that if someone is devout and obeys his will he listens to him. It is unheard of that anyone ever gave sight to a person blind from birth. If this man were not from God, he could never have done such a thing." "What!" they exclaimed, "You are steeped in sin from your birth, and you are giving us lectures?" With that they threw him out bodily.

When Jesus heard of his expulsion, he sought him out and asked him, "Do you believe in the Son of Man?" He answered, "Who is he, sir, that I may believe in him?" "You have seen him," Jesus replied. "He is speaking to you now." ["I do believe, Lord," he said, and bowed down to worship him. Then Jesus said:]

"I came into this world to divide it,
    to make the sightless see
    and the seeing blind."

Some of the Pharisees around him picked this up, saying, "You are not counting us in with the blind, are you?" To which Jesus replied:

"If you were blind
    there would be no sin in that.
'But we see,' you say,
    and your sin remains."
        This is the gospel of the Lord.

---

245   **MONDAY OF THE FOURTH
WEEK OF LENT**

READING I   Is 65, 17-21

A reading from the book of the prophet Isaiah
No more will the sound of weeping or the sound of cries
be heard.

Lo, I am about to create new heavens
    and a new earth;
The things of the past shall not be remembered
    or come to mind.
Instead, there shall always be rejoicing and
        happiness
    in what I create;
For I create Jerusalem to be a joy
    and its people to be a delight;

I will rejoice in Jerusalem
    and exult in my people.
No longer shall the sound of weeping be heard
        there,
    or the sound of crying;
No longer shall there be in it
    an infant who lives but a few days,
    or an old man who does not round out his
        full lifetime;
He dies a mere youth who reaches but a
        hundred years,
    and he who fails of a hundred shall be
        thought accursed.

They shall live in the houses they build,
    and eat the fruit of the vineyards they plant.
        This is the Word of the Lord.

Responsorial Psalm   Ps 30, 2. 4. 5-6. 11-13

℟. (2) I will praise you, Lord, for you have
    rescued me.
I will extol you, O Lord, for you drew me clear
    and did not let my enemies rejoice over me.
O Lord, you brought me up from the nether
        world;
    you preserved me from among those going
        down into the pit.
℟. I will praise you, Lord, for you have
    rescued me.
Sing praise to the Lord, you his faithful ones,
    and give thanks to his holy name.
For his anger lasts but a moment;
    a lifetime, his good will.
At nightfall, weeping enters in,
    but with the dawn, rejoicing.
℟. I will praise you, Lord, for you have
    rescued me.
Hear, O Lord, and have pity on me;
    O Lord, be my helper.
You changed my mourning into dancing;
    O Lord, my God, forever will I give you
        thanks.
℟. I will praise you, Lord, for you have
    rescued me.

GOSPEL   Jn 4, 43-54
Verse before the Gospel

See no. 224.

✠ A reading from the holy gospel according to John

Go, your son will live.

Jesus left [Samaria] for Galilee. (He himself had testified that no one esteems a prophet in his own country.) When he arrived in Galilee, the people there welcomed him. They themselves had been at the feast and had seen all that he had done in Jerusalem on that occasion.

He went to Cana in Galilee once more, where he had made the water wine. At Capernaum there happened to be a royal official whose son was ill. When he heard that Jesus had come back from Judea to Galilee, he went to him and begged him to come down and restore health to his son, who was near death. Jesus replied, "Unless you people see signs and wonders, you do not believe." "Sir," the royal official pleaded with him, "come down before my child dies." Jesus told him, "Return home. Your son will live." The man put his trust in the word Jesus spoke to him, and started for home.

He was on his way there when his servants met him with the news that his boy was going to live. When he asked them at what time the boy had shown improvement, they told him, "The fever left him yesterday afternoon about one." It was at that very hour, the father realized, that Jesus had told him, "Your son is going to live." He and his whole household thereupon became believers. This was the second sign that Jesus performed on returning from Judea to Galilee.

This is the gospel of the Lord.

---

246   **TUESDAY OF THE FOURTH WEEK OF LENT**

READING I   Ez 47, 1-9. 12
A reading from the book of the prophet Ezekiel

I saw water coming forth from the temple, and all those were saved to whom that water came

The angel brought me back to the entrance of the temple of the Lord, and I saw water flowing out from beneath the threshold of the temple toward the east, for the façade of the temple was toward the east; the water flowed down from the southern side of the temple, south of the altar. He led me outside by the north gate, and around to the outer gate facing the east, where I saw water trickling from the southern side. Then when he had walked off to the east with a measuring cord in his hand, he measured off a thousand cubits and had me wade through the water, which was ankle-deep. He measured off another thousand and once more had me wade through the water, which was now knee-deep. Again he measured off a thousand and had me wade; the water was up to my waist. Once more he measured off a thousand, but there was now a river through which I could not wade; for the water had risen so high it had become a river that could not be crossed except by swimming. He asked me, "Have you seen this, son of man?" Then he brought me to the bank of the river, where he had me sit. Along the bank of the river I saw very many trees on both sides. He said to me, "This water flows into the eastern district down upon the Arabah, and empties into the sea, the salt waters, which it makes fresh. Wherever the river flows, every sort of living creature that can multiply shall live, and there shall be abundant fish, for wherever this water comes the sea shall be made fresh. Along both banks of the river, fruit trees of every kind shall grow; their leaves shall not fade, nor their fruit fail. Every month they shall bear fresh fruit, for they shall be watered by the flow from the sanctuary. Their fruit shall serve for food, and their leaves for medicine."

This is the Word of the Lord.

Responsorial Psalm Ps 46, 2-3. 5-6. 8-9

R̶̸. (8) The mighty Lord is with us;
the God of Jacob is our refuge.
God is our refuge and our strength,
an ever-present help in distress.
Therefore we fear not, though the earth be
shaken
and mountains plunge into the depths of the
sea.
R̶̸. The mighty Lord is with us;
the God of Jacob is our refuge.
There is a stream whose runlets gladden the
city of God,
the holy dwelling of the Most High.
God is in its midst; it shall not be disturbed;
God will help it at the break of dawn.
R̶̸. The mighty Lord is with us;
the God of Jacob is our refuge.
The Lord of hosts is with us;
our stronghold is the God of Jacob.
Come! behold the deeds of the Lord,
the astounding things he has wrought on
earth.
R̶̸. The mighty Lord is with us;
the God of Jacob is our refuge.

GOSPEL Jn 5, 1-3. 5-16
Verse before the Gospel

See no. 224.

✠ A reading from the holy gospel according
to John
He was cured at once by that man.

On the occasion of a Jewish feast, Jesus went
up to Jerusalem. Now in Jerusalem by the
Sheep Pool there is a place with the Hebrew
name Bethesda. Its five porticoes were
crowded with sick people lying there blind,
lame or disabled [waiting for the movement
of the waters]. There was one man who had
been sick for thirty-eight years. Jesus, who
knew he had been sick a long time, said when
he saw him lying there, "Do you want to be
healed?" "Sir," the sick man answered, "I don't
have anyone to plunge me into the pool once
the water has been stirred up. By the time I
get there, someone else has gone in ahead of
me." Jesus said to him, "Stand up! Pick up your

mat and walk!" The man was immediately
cured; he picked up his mat and began to walk.
The day was a sabbath. Consequently, some
of the Jews began telling the man who had
been cured, "It is the sabbath, and you are not
allowed to carry that mat around." He explained: "It was the man who cured me who
told me, 'Pick up your mat and walk.'" "This
person who told you to pick it up and walk,"
they asked, "who is he?" The man who had
been restored to health had no idea who it was.
The crowd in that place was so great that
Jesus had been able to slip away.
Later on, Jesus found him in the temple
precincts and said to him: "Remember, now,
you have been cured. Give up your sins so that
something worse may not overtake you." The
man went off and informed the Jews that
Jesus was the one who had cured him.
It was because Jesus did things such as this
on the sabbath that they began to persecute
him.
This is the gospel of the Lord.

**247 WEDNESDAY OF THE FOURTH
WEEK OF LENT**

READING I Is 49, 8-15
A reading from the book of the prophet Isaiah
I have given you as covenant of the people to establish
the land.
Thus says the Lord:
In a time of favor I answer you,
on the day of salvation I help you,
To restore the land
and allot the desolate heritages,
Saying to the prisoners: Come out!
To those in darkness: Show yourselves!
Along the ways they shall find pasture,
on every bare height shall their pastures be.
They shall not hunger or thirst,
nor shall the scorching wind or the sun
strike them;
For he who pities them leads them
and guides them beside springs of water.
I will cut a road through all my mountains,
and make my highways level.

See, some shall come from afar,
  others from the north and the west,
  and some from the land of Syene.

Sing out, O heavens, and rejoice, O earth,
  break forth into song, you mountains.
For the Lord comforts his people
  and shows mercy to his afflicted.

But Zion said, "The Lord has forsaken me;
  my Lord has forgotten me."
Can a mother forget her infant,
  be without tenderness for the child of her
    womb?
Even should she forget,
  I will never forget you.
      This is the word of the Lord.

Responsorial Psalm   Ps 145, 8-9. 13-14. 17-18

℞. (8) The Lord is kind and merciful.
The Lord is gracious and merciful,
  slow to anger and of great kindness.
The Lord is good to all
  and compassionate toward all his works.
℞. The Lord is kind and merciful.
The Lord is faithful in all his words
  and holy in all his works.
The Lord lifts up all who are falling
  and raises up all who are bowed down.
℞. The Lord is kind and merciful.
The Lord is just in all his ways
  and holy in all his works.
The Lord is near to all who call upon him,
  to all who call upon him in truth.
℞. The Lord is kind and merciful.

GOSPEL   Jn 5, 17-30
Verse before the Gospel

See no. 224.

✠ A reading from the holy gospel according
  to John

As the Father raises the dead and gives them life, so the
Son gives life to those he chooses.

Jesus said to the Jews:
  "My Father is at work until now,
    and I am at work as well."
The reason why the Jews were even more

determined to kill him was that he not only
was breaking the sabbath but, worse still, was
speaking of God as his own Father, thereby
making himself God's equal.
  This was Jesus' answer:
    "I solemnly assure you,
      the Son cannot do anything by himself—
    he can do only what he sees the Father
      doing.
    For whatever the Father does,
      the Son does likewise.
    For the Father loves the Son
    and everything the Father does he shows
      him.
    Yes, to your great wonderment,
    he will show him even greater works than
      these.
    Indeed, just as the Father raises the dead
      and grants life,
    so the Son grants life to those to whom he
      wishes.
    The Father himself judges no one,
      but has assigned all judgment to the Son,
    so that all men may honor the Son
    just as they honor the Father.
    He who refuses to honor the Son
    refuses to honor the Father who sent him.
    I solemnly assure you,
      the man who hears my word
    and has faith in him who sent me
    possesses eternal life.
    He does not come under condemnation,
    but has passed from death to life.
    I solemnly assure you,
    an hour is coming, has indeed come,
    when the dead shall hear the voice of
      God's Son,
    and those who have heeded it shall live.
    Indeed, just as the Father possesses life
      in himself,
    so has he granted it to the Son to have life
      in himself.
    The Father has given over to him power to
      pass judgment
    because he is Son of Man;
    no need for you to be surprised at this,
    for an hour is coming
    in which all those in the tombs

shall hear his voice and come forth.
Those who have done right shall rise to
    live;
the evildoers shall rise to be damned.
I cannot do anything of myself.
I judge as I hear,
and my judgment is honest
because I am not seeking my own will
but the will of him who sent me."
This is the gospel of the Lord.

248   **THURSDAY OF THE FOURTH
        WEEK OF LENT**

READING I   Ex 32, 7-14
    A reading from the book of Exodus
Relent, Lord, and do not bring disaster on your people.

The Lord said to Moses, "Go down at once to
your people, whom you brought out of the land
of Egypt, for they have become depraved. They
have soon turned aside from the way I pointed
out to them, making for themselves a molten
calf and worshiping it, sacrificing to it and
crying out, 'This is your God, O Israel, who
brought you out of the land of Egypt!' I see
how stiff-necked this people is," continued the
Lord to Moses. "Let me alone, then, that my
wrath may blaze up against them to consume
them. Then I will make of you a great nation."
    But Moses implored the Lord, his God, say-
ing, "Why, O Lord, should your wrath blaze
up against your own people, whom you
brought out of the land of Egypt with such
great power and with so strong a hand? Why
should the Egyptians say, 'With evil intent he
brought them out, that he might kill them in
the mountains and exterminate them from the
face of the earth'? Let your blazing wrath die
down; relent in punishing your people. Remember your servants Abraham, Isaac and
Israel, and how you swore to them by your
own self, saying, 'I will make your descendants
as numerous as the stars in the sky; and all
this land that I promised, I will give your
descendants as their perpetual heritage.' " So
the Lord relented in the punishment he had
threatened to inflict on his people.
    This is the Word of the Lord.

Responsorial Psalm   Ps 106, 19-20. 21 22. 23

℟. (4) Lord, remember us,
    for the love you bear your people.
Our fathers made a calf in Horeb
    and adored a molten image;
They exchanged their glory
    for the image of a grass-eating bullock.
℟. Lord, remember us,
    for the love you bear your people.
They forgot the God who had saved them,
    who had done great deeds in Egypt,
Wondrous deeds in the land of Ham,
    terrible things at the Red Sea.
℟. Lord, remember us,
    for the love you bear your people.
Then he spoke of exterminating them,
    but Moses, his chosen one,
Withstood him in the breach
    to turn back his destructive wrath.
℟. Lord, remember us,
    for the love you bear your people.

GOSPEL   . Jn 5, 31-47
Verse before the Gospel
See no. 224.

✠ **A reading from the holy gospel according
        to John**
It is Moses who will be your accuser in whom you hoped.

Jesus said to the Jews:
    "If I witness on my own behalf,
    you cannot verify my testimony;
    but there is another who is testifying on
        my behalf,
    and the testimony he renders me
    I know can be verified.
    You have sent to John,
    who has testified to the truth.
    (Not that I myself accept such human
        testimony—
    I refer to these things only for your sal-
        vation.)
    He was the lamp, set aflame and burning
        bright,
    and for a while you exulted willingly in
        his light.
    Yet I have testimony greater than John's,

namely, the works the Father has given
me to accomplish.
These very works which I perform
testify on my behalf
that the Father has sent me.
Moreover, the Father who sent me
has himself given testimony on my behalf.
His voice you have never heard,
his form you have never seen,
neither do you have his word abiding in
your hearts
because you do not believe
the one he has sent.
Search the Scriptures
in which you think you have eternal life—
they also testify on my behalf.
Yet you are unwilling to come to me
to possess that life.

"It is not that I accept human praise—
it is simply that I know you,
and you do not have the love of God in
your hearts.
I have come in my Father's name,
yet you do not accept me.
But let someone come in his own name
and him you will accept.
How can people like you believe,
when you accept praise from one another
yet do not seek the glory that comes from
the One [God]?
Do not imagine that I will be your accuser
before the Father;
the one to accuse you is Moses
on whom you have set your hopes.
If you believed Moses
you would then believe me,
for it was about me that he wrote.
But if you do not believe what he wrote,
how can you believe what I say?"
    This is the gospel of the Lord.

249   **FRIDAY OF THE FOURTH
WEEK OF LENT**

READING I   Wis 2, 1. 12-22

A reading from the book of Wisdom
Let us condemn him to a shameful death.

The wicked said among themselves, thinking
not aright:
"Let us beset the just one, because he is obnoxious to us;
  he sets himself against our doings,
Reproaches us for transgressions of the law
  and charges us with violations of our
  training.
He professes to have knowledge of God
  and styles himself a child of the Lord.
To us he is the censure of our thoughts;
  merely to see him is a hardship for us,
Because his life is not like other men's,
  and different are his ways.
He judges us debased;
  he holds aloof from our paths as from things
  impure.
He calls blest the destiny of the just
  and boasts that God is his Father.
Let us see whether his words be true;
  let us find out what will happen to him.
For if the just one be the son of God, he will
  defend him
  and deliver him from the hand of his foes.
With revilement and torture let us put him to
  the test
  that we may have proof of his gentleness
  and try his patience.
Let us condemn him to a shameful death;
  for according to his own words, God will
  take care of him."
These were their thoughts, but they erred;
  for their wickedness blinded them,
And they knew not the hidden counsels of God;
  neither did they count on a recompense of
  holiness
  nor discern the innocent souls' reward.
    This is the Word of the Lord.

Responsorial Psalm   Ps 34, 17-18. 19-20. 21. 23

℟. (19) The Lord is near to broken hearts.

The Lord confronts the evildoers,
   to destroy remembrance of them from the
      earth.
When the just cry out, the Lord hears them,
   and from all their distress he rescues them.
R̷. The Lord is near to broken hearts.
The Lord is close to the brokenhearted;
   and those who are crushed in spirit he saves.
Many are the troubles of the just man,
   but out of them all the Lord delivers him.
R̷. The Lord is near to broken hearts.
He watches over all his bones;
   not one of them shall be broken.
The Lord redeems the lives of his servants;
   no one incurs guilt who takes refuge in him.
R̷. The Lord is near to broken hearts.

GOSPEL   Jn 7, 1-2. 10. 25-30
Verse before the Gospel

See no. 224.

✠ A reading from the holy gospel according
      to John

They would have arrested him but his hour had not come.

Jesus moved about within Galilee. He had decided not to travel in Judea because some of
the Jews were looking for a chance to kill him.
The Jewish feast of Booths drew near. Once his
brothers had gone up to the festival he too
went up, but as if in secret and not for all to
see.

   Some of the people of Jerusalem remarked,
"Is this not the one they want to kill? Here he
is speaking in public and they don't say a word
to him! Perhaps even the authorities have decided that this is the Messiah. Still, we know
where this man is from. When the Messiah
comes, no one is supposed to know his
origins."

   At this, Jesus, who was teaching in the
temple area, cried out:
   "So you know me,
      and you know my origins?
   The truth is, I have not come of myself.
   I was sent by One who has the right to
      send,
   and him you do not know.
   I know him

because it is from him I come:
   he sent me."
At this they tried to seize him, but no one laid
a finger on him because his hour had not
yet come.
   This is the gospel of the Lord.

---

250   SATURDAY OF THE FOURTH
WEEK OF LENT

READING I   Jer 11, 18-20
A reading from the book of the prophet
Jeremiah

I am like the trustful lamb, being led to the slaughter.

I knew their plot because the Lord informed
me; at that time you, O Lord, showed me their
doings. Yet I, like a trusting lamb led to
slaughter, had not realized that they were
hatching plots against me: "Let us destroy the
tree in its vigor; let us cut him off from the land
of the living, so that his name will be spoken no
more."

But, you, O Lord of hosts, O just Judge,
   searcher of mind and heart,
Let me witness the vengeance you take on
   them,
   for to you I have entrusted my cause!
      This is the Word of the Lord.

Responsorial Psalm   Ps 7, 2-3. 9-10. 11-12

R̷. (2) Lord, my God, I take shelter in you.
O Lord, my God, in you I take refuge;
   save me from all my pursuers and rescue me,
Lest I become like the lion's prey,
   to be torn to pieces, with no one to
      rescue me.
R̷. Lord, my God, I take shelter in you.
Do me justice, O Lord, because I am just,
   and because of the innocence that is mine.
Let the malice of the wicked come to an end,
   but sustain the just,
   O searcher of heart and soul, O just God.
R̷. Lord, my God, I take shelter in you.
A shield before me is God,
   who saves the upright of heart;

A just judge is God,
 a God who punishes day by day.
℞. Lord, my God, I take shelter in you.

GOSPEL   Jn 7, 40-53
Verse before the Gospel
See no. 224.

✠ A reading from the holy gospel according
    to John
Would the Christ be from Galilee?

Some in the crowd who heard the words of
Jesus began to say, "This must be the Prophet."
Others were claiming, "He is the Messiah."
But an objection was raised: "Surely the Messiah is not to come from Galilee? Does not
Scripture say that the Messiah, being of David's
family, is to come from Bethlehem, the village
where David lived?" In this fashion the crowd
was sharply divided over him. Some of them
even wanted to apprehend him. However, no
one laid hands on him.

When the temple guards came, the chief
priests and Pharisees asked them, "Why did
you not bring him in?" "No man ever spoke like
that before," the guards replied. "Do not tell us
you too have been taken in!" the Pharisees
retorted. "You do not see any of the Sanhedrin
believing in him, do you? Or the Pharisees?
Only this lot, that knows nothing about the law
—and they are lost anyway!" One of their own
number, Nicodemus (the man who had come
to him), spoke up to say, "Since when does our
law condemn any man without first hearing
him and knowing the facts?" "Do not tell us
you are a Galilean too," they taunted him.
"Look it up. You will not find the Prophet coming from Galilee."

Then each went off to his own house.
This is the gospel of the Lord.

---

251   **OPTIONAL MASS**
  FOR THE FIFTH WEEK OF LENT

This Mass may be used on any day of this week in years
B and C when the gospel of Lazarus is not read on the
Fifth Sunday of Lent.

READING I   2 Kgs 4, 18-21. 32-37
 A reading from the second book of Kings
The man of God stretched himself over him, and the child's
    flesh grew warm.

The day came when the child of the Shunammite woman was old enough to go out to his
father among the reapers. "My head hurts!" he
complained to his father. "Carry him to his
mother," the father said to a servant. The servant picked him up and carried him to his
mother; he stayed with her until noon, when he
died in her lap. The mother took him upstairs
and laid him on the bed of the man of God. Closing the door on him, she went out.

When Elisha reached the house, he found the
boy lying dead. He went in, closed the door on
them both, and prayed to the Lord. Then he lay
upon the child on the bed, placing his mouth
upon the child's mouth, his eyes upon the eyes,
and his hands upon the hands. As Elisha
stretched himself over the child, the body became warm. He arose, paced up and down the
room, and then once more lay down upon the
boy, who now sneezed seven times and opened
his eyes. Elisha summoned Gehazi and said,
"Call the Shunammite." She came at his call,
and Elisha said to her, "Take your son." She
came in and fell at his feet in gratitude; then
she took her son and left the room.

    This is the Word of the Lord.

Responsorial Psalm Ps 17, 1. 6-7. 8. 15
℞. (15) Lord, when your glory appears,
 my joy will be full.
Hear, O Lord, a just suit;
 attend to my outcry;
  hearken to my prayer from lips without
  deceit.
℞. Lord, when your glory appears,
 my joy will be full.

I call upon you, for you will answer me, O
   God;
   incline your ear to me; hear my word.
Show your wondrous kindness,
   O savior of those who flee
   from their foes to refuge at your right hand.
Ry. Lord, when your glory appears,
   my joy will be full.
Hide me in the shadow of your wings.
   I in justice shall behold your face;
   on waking, I shall be content in your pres-
      ence.
Ry. Lord, when your glory appears,
   my joy will be full.

GOSPEL   Jn 11, 1-45
Verse before the Gospel
See no. 224.

✠ A reading from the holy gospel according
                 to John
          I am the resurrection and the life.

There was a certain man named Lazarus who
was sick. He was from Bethany, the village of
Mary and her sister Martha. (This Mary whose
brother Lazarus was sick was the one who
anointed the Lord with perfume and dried his
feet with her hair.) The sisters sent word to
Jesus to inform him, "Lord, the one you love is
sick." Upon hearing this, Jesus said:
   "This sickness is not to end in death;
   rather it is for God's glory,
   that through it the Son of God may be
      glorified."
Jesus loved Martha and her sister and Lazarus
very much. Yet, after hearing that Lazarus was
sick, he stayed on where he was for two days
more. Finally he said to his disciples, "Let us
go back to Judea." "Rabbi," protested the disciples, "with the Jews only recently trying to
stone you, you are going back up there again?"
Jesus answered:
   "Are there not twelve hours of daylight?
   If a man goes walking by day he does not
      stumble,
   because he sees the world bathed in light.
   But if he goes walking at night he will
      stumble,
   since there is no light in him."

After uttering these words, he added, "Our beloved Lazarus has fallen asleep, but I am going
there to wake him." At this the disciples objected, "Lord, if he is asleep his life will be
saved." Jesus had been speaking about his
death, but they thought he meant sleep in the
sense of slumber. Finally Jesus said plainly,
"Lazarus is dead. For your sakes I am glad I
was not there, that you may come to believe.
In any event, let us go to him." Then Thomas
(the name means "Twin") said to his fellow
disciples, "Let us go along, to die with him."
   When Jesus arrived at Bethany, he found
that Lazarus had already been in the tomb four
days. The village was not far from Jerusalem—
just under two miles—and many Jewish people
had come out to console Martha and Mary over
their brother. When Martha heard that Jesus
was coming she went to meet him, while Mary
sat at home. Martha said to Jesus, "Lord, if you
had been here, my brother would never have
died. Even now, I am sure that God will give
you whatever you ask of him." "Your brother
will rise again," Jesus assured her. "I know he
will rise again," Martha replied, "in the resurrection on the last day." Jesus told her:
   "I am the resurrection and the life:
   whoever believes in me,
   though he should die, will come to life;
   and whoever is alive and believes in me
   will never die.
Do you believe this?" "Yes, Lord," she replied.
"I have come to believe that you are the Messiah, the Son of God: he who is to come into
the world."
   When she had said this she went back and
called her sister Mary. "The Teacher is here,
asking for you," she whispered. As soon as
Mary heard this, she got up and started out in
his direction. (Actually Jesus had not yet come
into the village but was still at the spot where
Martha had met him.) The Jews who were in
the house with Mary consoling her saw her get
up quickly and go out, so they followed her,
thinking she was going to the tomb to weep
there. When Mary came to the place where
Jesus was, seeing him, she fell at his feet and
said to him, "Lord, if you had been here my
brother would never have died." When Jesus

saw her weeping, and the Jewish folk who had accompanied her also weeping, he was troubled in spirit, moved by the deepest emotions. "Where have you laid him?" he asked. "Lord, come and see," they said. Jesus began to weep, which caused the Jews to remark, "See how much he loved him!" But some said, "He opened the eyes of that blind man. Why could he not have done something to stop this man from dying?" Once again troubled in spirit, Jesus approached the tomb.

It was a cave with a stone laid across it. "Take away the stone," Jesus directed. Martha, the dead man's sister, said to him, "Lord, it has been four days now; surely there will be a stench!" Jesus replied, "Did I not assure you that if you believed you would see the glory of God?" They then took away the stone and Jesus looked upward and said:

"Father, I thank you for having heard me.
I know that you always hear me
but I have said this for the sake of the crowd,
that they may believe that you sent me."

Having said this, he called loudly, "Lazarus, come out!" The dead man came out, bound hand and foot with linen strips, his face wrapped in a cloth. "Untie him," Jesus told them, "and let him go free."

This caused many of the Jews who had come to visit Mary, and had seen what Jesus did, to put their faith in him.

This is the gospel of the Lord.

252　MONDAY OF THE FIFTH WEEK OF LENT

READING I　Dn 13, 1-9. 15-17. 19-30. 33-62 or 13, 41-62

A reading from the book of the prophet Daniel

Be aware of death, since we know not the hour when it comes.

(Long Form)

In Babylon there lived a man named Joakim, who married a very beautiful and God-fearing woman, Susanna, the daughter of Hilkiah; her pious parents had trained their daughter according to the law of Moses. Joakim was very rich; he had a garden near his house, and the Jews had recourse to him often because he was the most respected of them all.

That year, two elders of the people were appointed judges, of whom the Lord said, "Wickedness has come out of Babylon: from the elders who were to govern the people as judges." These men, to whom all brought their cases, frequented the house of Joakim. When the people left at noon, Susanna used to enter her husband's garden for a walk. When the old men saw her enter every day for her walk, they began to lust for her. They suppressed their consciences; they would not allow their eyes to look to heaven, and did not keep in mind just judgments.

One day, while they were waiting for the right moment, she entered the garden as usual, with two maids only. She decided to bathe, for the weather was warm. Nobody else was there except the two elders, who had hidden themselves and were watching her. "Bring me oil and soap," she said to the maids, "and shut the garden doors while I bathe."

As soon as the maids had left, the two old men got up and hurried to her. "Look," they said, "the garden doors are shut, and no one can see us; give in to our desire, and lie with us. If you refuse, we will testify against you that you dismissed your maids because a young man was here with you."

"I am completely trapped," Susanna groaned. "If I yield, it will be my death; if I refuse, I cannot escape your power. Yet it is better for me to fall into your power without guilt than to sin before the Lord." Then Susanna shrieked, and the old men also shouted at her, as one of them ran to open the garden doors. When the people in the house heard the cries from the garden, they rushed in by the side gate to see what had happened to her. At the accusations by the old men, the servants felt very much ashamed, for never had any such thing been said about Susanna.

When the people came to her husband Joakim the next day, the two wicked elders also came, fully determined to put Susanna to death. Before all the people they ordered:

"Send for Susanna, the daughter of Hilkiah, the wife of Joakim." When she was sent for, she came with her parents, children and all her relatives. All her relatives and the onlookers were weeping.

In the midst of the people the two elders rose up and laid their hands on her head. Through her tears she looked up to heaven, for she trusted in the Lord wholeheartedly. The elders made this accusation: "As we were walking in the garden alone, this woman entered with two girls and shut the doors of the garden, dismissing the girls. A young man, who was hidden there, came and lay with her. When we, in a corner of the garden, saw this crime, we ran toward them. We saw them lying together, but the man we could not hold, because he was stronger than we; he opened the doors and ran off. Then we seized this one and asked who the young man was, but she refused to tell us. We testify to this." The assembly believed them, since they were elders and judges of the people, and they condemned her to death.

But Susanna cried aloud: "O eternal God, you know what is hidden and are aware of all things before they come to be: you know that they have testified falsely against me. Here I am about to die, though I have done none of the things with which these wicked men have charged me."

The Lord heard her prayer. As she was being led to execution, God stirred up the holy spirit of a young boy named Daniel, and he cried aloud: "I will have no part in the death of this woman." All the people turned and asked him, "What is this you are saying?" He stood in their midst and continued, "Are you such fools, O Israelites! To condemn a woman of Israel without examination and without clear evidence? Return to court, for they have testified falsely against her."

Then all the people returned in haste. To Daniel the elders said, "Come, sit with us and inform us, since God has given you the prestige of old age." But he replied, "Separate these two far from one another that I may examine them."

After they were separated one from the other, he called one of them and said: "How you have grown evil with age! Now have your past sins come to term: passing unjust sentences, condemning the innocent, and freeing the guilty, although the Lord says, 'The innocent and the just you shall not put to death.' Now, then, if you were a witness, tell me under what tree you saw them together." "Under a mastic tree," he answered. "Your fine lie has cost you your head," said Daniel; "for the angel of God shall receive the sentence from him and split you in two." Putting him to one side, he ordered the other one to be brought. "Offspring of Canaan, not of Judah," Daniel said to him, "beauty has seduced you, lust has subverted your conscience. This is how you acted with the daughters of Israel, and in their fear they yielded to you; but a daughter of Judah did not tolerate your wickedness. Now, then, tell me under what tree you surprised them together." "Under an oak," he said. "Your fine lie has cost you also your head," said Daniel; "for the angel of God waits with a sword to cut you in two so as to make an end of you both."

The whole assembly cried aloud, blessing God who saves those that hope in him. They rose up against the two elders, for by their own words Daniel had convicted them of perjury. According to the law of Moses, they inflicted on them the penalty they had plotted to impose on their neighbor: they put them to death. Thus was innocent blood spared that day.

This is the Word of the Lord.

OR
(Short Form)

The assembly condemned Susanna to death. But Susanna cried aloud: "O eternal God, you know what is hidden and are aware of all things before they come to be: you know that they have testified falsely against me. Here I am about to die, though I have done none of the things with which these wicked men have charged me."

The Lord heard her prayer. As she was being led to execution, God stirred up the holy spirit of a young boy named Daniel, and he cried aloud: "I will have no part in the death of this woman." All the people turned and asked him, "What is this you are saying?" He stood in their midst and continued, "Are you such fools, O Israelites! To condemn a woman of Israel without examination and without clear evidence? Return to court, for they have testified falsely against her."

Then all the people returned in haste. To Daniel the elders said, "Come, sit with us and inform us, since God has given you the prestige of old age." But he replied, "Separate these two far from one another that I may examine them."

After they were separated one from the other, he called one of them and said: "How you have grown evil with age! Now have your past sins come to term: passing unjust sentences, condemning the innocent, and freeing the guilty, although the Lord says, 'The innocent and the just you shall not put to death.' Now, then, if you were a witness, tell me under what tree you saw them together." "Under a mastic tree," he answered. "Your fine lie has cost you your head," said Daniel; "for the angel of God shall receive the sentence from him and split you in two." Putting him to one side, he ordered the other one to be brought. "Offspring of Canaan, not of Judah," Daniel said to him, "beauty has seduced you, lust has subverted your conscience. This is how you acted with the daughters of Israel, and in their fear they yielded to you; but a daughter of Judah did not tolerate your wickedness. Now, then, tell me under what tree you surprised them together." "Under an oak," he said. "Your fine lie has cost you also your head," said Daniel; "for the angel of God waits with a sword to cut you in two so as to make an end of you both."

The whole assembly cried aloud, blessing God who saves those that hope in him. They rose up against the two elders, for by their own words Daniel had convicted them of perjury. According to the law of Moses, they inflicted on them the penalty they had plotted to impose on their neighbor: they put them to death. Thus was innocent blood spared that day.

This is the Word of the Lord.

Responsorial Psalm   Ps 23, 1-3. 3-4. 5. 6

℟. (4) Though I walk in the valley of darkness,
   I fear no evil, for you are with me.
**The Lord is my shepherd; I shall not want.
   In verdant pastures he gives me repose.
Beside restful waters he leads me;
   he refreshes my soul.**
℟. Though I walk in the valley of darkness,
   I fear no evil, for you are with me.
**He guides me in right paths
   for his name's sake.
Even though I walk in the dark valley
   I fear no evil; for you are at my side
With your rod and your staff
   that give me courage.**
℟. Though I walk in the valley of darkness,
   I fear no evil, for you are with me.
**You spread the table before me
   in the sight of my foes;
You anoint my head with oil;
   my cup overflows.**
℟. Though I walk in the valley of darkness,
   I fear no evil, for you are with me.
**Only goodness and kindness follow me
   all the days of my life;
And I shall dwell in the house of the Lord
   for years to come.**
℟. Though I walk in the valley of darkness,
   I fear no evil, for you are with me.

GOSPEL   Jn 8, 1-11
Verse before the Gospel

See no. 224.

✠ A reading from the holy gospel according
to John
*If there is one of you who has not sinned, let him be the
first to throw a stone*

Jesus went out to the Mount of Olives. At daybreak he reappeared in the temple area; and when the people started coming to him, he sat down and began to teach them. The scribes and the Pharisees led a woman forward who had been caught in adultery. They made her stand there in front of everyone. "Teacher," they said to him, "this woman has been caught in the act of adultery. In the law, Moses ordered such women to be stoned. What do you have to say about the case?" (They were posing this question to trap him, so that they could have something to accuse him of.) Jesus simply bent down and started tracing on the ground with his finger. When they persisted in their questioning, he straightened up and said to them, "Let the man among you who has no sin be the first to cast a stone at her." A second time he bent down and wrote on the ground. Then the audience drifted away one by one, beginning with the elders. This left him alone with the woman, who continued to stand there before him. Jesus finally straightened up again and said to her, "Woman, where did they all disappear to? Has no one condemned you?" "No one, sir," she answered. Jesus said, "Nor do I condemn you. You may go. But from now on, avoid this sin."

This is the gospel of the Lord.

In year C, when this gospel is read on the preceding Sunday, the following text (Jn 8, 12-20) is used:

I am the light of the world.

Jesus said to the Jews:
"I am the light of the world.
No follower of mine shall ever walk in darkness;
no, he shall possess the light of life."
This caused the Pharisees to break in with: "You are your own witness. Such testimony cannot be valid." Jesus answered:
"What if I am my own witness?
My testimony is valid nonetheless,
because I know where I came from
and where I am going;
you know neither the one nor the other.
You pass judgment according to appearances
but I pass judgment on no man.
Even if I do judge,
that judgment of mine is valid
because I am not alone:
I have at my side the One who sent me, the Father.
It is laid down in your law
that evidence given by two persons is valid.

I am one of those testifying in my behalf,
the Father who sent me is the other."
They pressed him: "And where is this 'Father' of yours?" Jesus replied:
"You know neither me nor my Father.
If you knew me, you would know my Father too."
He spoke these words while teaching at the temple treasury. Still, he went unapprehended, because his hour had not yet come.

This is the gospel of the Lord.

253   **TUESDAY OF THE FIFTH WEEK OF LENT**

READING I   Nm 21, 4-9

A reading from the book of Numbers
Whoever looks at the fiery serpent shall live.

From Mount Hor the Israelites set out on the Red Sea road, to by-pass the land of Edom. But with their patience worn out by the journey, the people complained against God and Moses, "Why have you brought us up from Egypt to die in this desert, where there is no food or water? We are disgusted with this wretched food!"

In punishment the Lord sent among the people saraph serpents, which bit the people so that many of them died. Then the people came to Moses and said, "We have sinned in complaining against the Lord and you. Pray the Lord to take the serpents from us." So Moses prayed for the people, and the Lord said to Moses, "Make a saraph and mount it on a pole, and if anyone who has been bitten looks at it, he will recover." Moses accordingly made a bronze serpent and mounted it on a pole, and whenever anyone who had been bitten by a serpent looked at the bronze serpent, he recovered.

This is the Word of the Lord.

Responsorial Psalm   Ps 102, 2-3. 16-18. 19-21

℟. (2) O Lord, hear my prayer,
and let my cry come to you.

O Lord, hear my prayer,
and let my cry come to you.

Hide not your face from me
   in the day of my distress.
Incline your ear to me;
   in the day when I call, answer me speedily.
℞. O Lord, hear my prayer,
   and let my cry come to you.

The nations shall revere your name, O Lord,
   and all the kings of the earth your glory,
When the Lord has rebuilt Zion
   and appeared in his glory;
When he has regarded the prayer of the desti-
     tute,
   and not despised their prayer.
℞. O Lord, hear my prayer,
   and let my cry come to you.

Let this be written for the generation to come,
   and let his future creatures praise the Lord:
"The Lord looked down from his holy height,
   from heaven he beheld the earth,
To hear the groaning of the prisoners,
   to release those doomed to die."
℞. O Lord, hear my prayer,
   and let my cry come to you.

GOSPEL   Jn 8, 21-30
Verse before the Gospel
See no. 224.

✠ **A reading from the holy gospel according
to John**

*When you have lifted up the Son of Man, then you will
know that I am he.*

Jesus said to the Pharisees:
   "I am going away. You will look for me
but you will die in your sins.
   Where I am going you cannot come."
At this some of the Jews began to ask, "Does
he mean he will kill himself when he claims,
'Where I am going you cannot come'? He went
on:
   "You belong to what is below;
   I belong to what is above.
   You belong to this world—
   a world which cannot hold me.
   That is why I said you would die in your
     sins.
   You will surely die in your sins
   unless you come to believe that I AM."

"Who are you, then?" they asked him. Jesus
answered:
   "What I have been telling you from the be-
     ginning.
   I could say much about you in condemna-
     tion,
   but no, I only tell the world
   what I have heard from him,
   the truthful One, who sent me."
They did not grasp that he was speaking to
them of the Father. Jesus continued:
   "When you lift up the Son of Man,
   you will come to realize that I AM
   and that I do nothing by myself.
   I say only what the Father has taught me.
   The One who sent me is with me.
   He has not deserted me
   since I always do what pleases him."
Because he spoke this way, many came to believe in him.
      This is the gospel of the Lord.

---

254   WEDNESDAY OF THE FIFTH
WEEK OF LENT

READING I   Dn 3, 14-20. 91-92. 95
A reading from the book of the prophet Daniel

He has sent his angel to rescue his servants.

King Nebuchadnezzar said: "Is it true, Shadrach, Meshach, and Abednego, that you will
not serve my god, or worship the golden statue
that I set up? Be ready now to fall down and
worship the statue I had made, whenever you
hear the sound of the trumpet, flute, lyre, harp,
psaltery, bagpipe, and all the other musical instruments; otherwise, you shall be instantly
cast into the white-hot furnace; and who is the
God that can deliver you out of my hands?"
Shadrach, Meshach, and Abednego answered
King Nebuchadnezzar, "There is no need for us
to defend ourselves before you in this matter.
If our God, whom we serve, can save us from
the white-hot furnace and from your hands, O
king, may he save us! But even if he will not,
know, O king, that we will not serve your god
or worship the golden statue which you set
up."

Nebuchadnezzar's face became livid with utter rage against Shadrach, Meshach, and Abednego. He ordered the furnace to be heated seven times more than usual and had some of the strongest men in his army bind Shadrach, Meshach, and Abednego and cast them into the white-hot furnace.

Nebuchadnezzar rose in haste and asked his nobles, "Did we not cast three men bound into the fire?" "Assuredly, O king," they answered. "But," he replied, "I see four men unfettered and unhurt, walking in the fire, and the fourth looks like a son of God." Nebuchadnezzar exclaimed, "Blessed be the God of Shadrach, Meshach, and Abednego, who sent his angel to deliver the servants that trusted in him; they disobeyed the royal command and yielded their bodies rather than serve or worship any god except their own God."

This is the Word of the Lord.

Responsorial Psalm Dn 3, 52. 53. 54. 55. 56

℟. (52) Glory and praise for ever!

Blessed are you, O Lord, the God of our fathers,
praiseworthy and exalted above all forever;
And blessed is your holy and glorious name,
praiseworthy and exalted above all for all ages.

℟. Glory and praise for ever!

Blessed are you in the temple of your holy glory,
praiseworthy and glorious above all forever.

℟. Glory and praise for ever!

Blessed are you on the throne of your kingdom,
praiseworthy and exalted above all forever.

℟. Glory and praise for ever!

Blessed are you who look into the depths
from your throne upon the cherubim,
praiseworthy and exalted above all forever.

℟. Glory and praise for ever!

Blessed are you in the firmament of heaven,
praiseworthy and glorious forever.

℟. Glory and praise for ever!

GOSPEL Jn 8, 31-42

Verse before the Gospel

See no. 224.

✠ **A reading from the holy gospel according to John**

If the Son makes you free, you will be free indeed.

Jesus said to those Jews who believed in him:
"If you live according to my teaching,
you are truly my disciples;
then you will know the truth,
and the truth will set you free."
"We are descendants of Abraham," was their answer. "Never have we been slaves to anyone. What do you mean by saying, 'You will be free'?" Jesus answered them:
"I give you my assurance,
everyone who lives in sin
is the slave of sin.
(No slave has a permanent place in the family,
but the son has a place there forever.)
That is why, if the son frees you,
you will really be free.
I realize you are of Abraham's stock.
Nonetheless, you are trying to kill me
because my word finds no hearing among you.
I tell what I have seen in the Father's presence;
you do what you have heard from your father."
They retorted, "Our father is Abraham." Jesus told them:
"If you were Abraham's children,
you would be following Abraham's example.
The fact is, you are trying to kill me,
a man who has told you the truth
which I have heard from God.
Abraham did nothing like that.
Indeed you are doing your father's works!"
They cried, "We are no illegitimate breed! We have but one father and that is God himself."
Jesus answered:
"Were God your father
you would love me,
for I came forth from God, and am here.
I did not come of my own will;
it was he who sent me."
This is the gospel of the Lord.

**255   THURSDAY OF THE FIFTH
WEEK OF LENT**

READING I   Gn 17, 3-9

A reading from the book of Genesis

He will be the father of a multitude of nations.

When Abram prostrated himself, God spoke to him: "My covenant with you is this: you are to become the father of a host of nations. No longer shall you be called Abram; your name shall be Abraham, for I am making you the father of a host of nations. I will render you exceedingly fertile; I will make nations of you; kings shall stem from you. I will maintain my covenant with you and your descendants after you throughout the ages as an everlasting pact, to be your God and the God of your descendants after you. I will give to you and to your descendants after you the land in which you are now staying, the whole land of Canaan, as a permanent possession; and I will be their God."

God also said to Abraham: "On your part, you and your descendants after you must keep my covenant throughout the ages."

This is the word of the Lord.

Responsorial Psalm   Ps 105, 4-5. 6-7. 8-9

℟. (8) The Lord remembers his covenant for ever.

Look to the Lord in his strength;
    seek to serve him constantly.
Recall the wondrous deeds that he has wrought,
    his portents, and the judgments he has uttered.
℟. The Lord remembers his covenant for ever.

You descendants of Abraham, his servants,
    sons of Jacob, his chosen ones!
He, the Lord, is our God;
    throughout the earth his judgments prevail.
℟. The Lord remembers his covenant for ever.

He remembers forever his covenant
    which he made binding for a thousand generations—
Which he entered into with Abraham
    and by his oath to Isaac.
℟. The Lord remembers his covenant for ever.

GOSPEL   Jn 8, 51-59
Verse before the Gospel

See no. 224.

✠ **A reading from the holy gospel according
to John**

Your father, Abraham, rejoiced because he saw my day.

Jesus said to the Jews:
    "I solemnly assure you,
    if a man is true to my word
    he shall never see death."
"Now we are sure you are possessed," the Jews retorted. "Abraham is dead. The prophets are dead. Yet you claim, 'A man shall never know death if he keeps my word.' Surely you do not pretend to be greater than our father Abraham, who died! Or the prophets, who died! Whom do you make yourself out to be?"
Jesus answered:
    "If I glorify myself,
    that glory comes to nothing.
    He who gives me glory is the Father,
    the very one you claim for your God,
    even though you do not know him.
    But I know him.
    Were I to say I do not know him,
    I would be no better than you—a liar!
    Yes, I know him well,
    and I keep his word.
    Your father Abraham rejoiced
    that he might see my day.
    He saw it and was glad."
At this the Jews objected: "You are not yet fifty! How can you have seen Abraham?" Jesus answered them:
    "I solemnly declare it:
    before Abraham came to be, I AM."
At that they picked up rocks to throw at Jesus, but he hid himself and slipped out of the temple precincts.

This is the gospel of the Lord.

256   FRIDAY OF THE FIFTH WEEK OF LENT

READING I   Jer 20, 10-13

A reading from the book of the prophet Jeremiah

The Lord God is with me, a mighty hero.

I hear the whisperings of many:
  "Terror on every side!
  Denounce! let us denounce him!"
All those who were my friends
  are on the watch for any misstep of mine.
"Perhaps he will be trapped; then we can prevail,
  and take our vengeance on him."
But the Lord is with me, like a mighty champion;
  my persecutors will stumble, they will not triumph.
In their failure they will be put to utter shame,
  to lasting, unforgettable confusion.
O Lord of hosts, you who test the just,
  who probe mind and heart,
Let me witness the vengeance you take on them,
  for to you I have entrusted my cause.
Sing to the Lord,
  praise the Lord,
For he has rescued the life of the poor
  from the power of the wicked!
    This is the Word of the Lord.

Responsorial Psalm   Ps 18, 2-3. 3-4. 5-6. 7

℟. (7) In my distress I called upon the Lord,
  and he heard my voice.
I love you, O Lord, my strength,
  O Lord, my rock, my fortress, my deliverer.
℟. In my distress I called upon the Lord,
  and he heard my voice.
My God, my rock of refuge,
  my shield, the horn of my salvation, my stronghold!
Praised be the Lord, I exclaim,
  and I am safe from my enemies.
℟. In my distress I called upon the Lord,
  and he heard my voice.

The breakers of death surged round about me,
  the destroying floods overwhelmed me;
The cords of the nether world enmeshed me,
  the snares of death overtook me.
℟. In my distress I called upon the Lord,
  and he heard my voice.
In my distress I called upon the Lord
  and cried out to my God;
From his temple he heard my voice,
  and my cry to him reached his ears.
℟. In my distress I called upon the Lord,
  and he heard my voice.

GOSPEL   Jn 10, 31-42
Verse before the Gospel

See no. 224.

✠ **A reading from the holy gospel according to John**

They wanted to arrest him but he eluded them.

When the Jews reached for rocks to stone him,
Jesus protested to them, "Many good deeds
have I shown you from the Father. For which
of these do you stone me?" "It is not for any
'good deed' that we are stoning you," the Jews
retorted, "but for blaspheming. You who are
only a man are making yourself God." Jesus
answered:
    "Is it not written in your law,
    'I have said, You are gods'?
    If it calls those men gods
    to whom God's word was addressed—
    and Scripture cannot lose its force—
    do you claim that I blasphemed
    when, as he whom the Father consecrated
    and sent into the world,
    I said, 'I am God's Son'?
    If I do not perform my Father's works,
    put no faith in me.
    But if I do perform them,
    even though you put no faith in me,
    put faith in these works,
    so as to realize what it means
    that the Father is in me
    and I in him."
At these words they again tried to arrest him,
but he eluded their grasp.

Then he went back across the Jordan to the place where John had been baptizing earlier, and while he stayed there many people came to him. "John may never have performed a sign," they commented, "but whatever John said about this man was true." In that place, many came to believe in him.

This is the gospel of the Lord.

---

257 SATURDAY OF THE FIFTH WEEK OF LENT

READING I   Ez 37, 21-28

A reading from the book of the prophet Ezekiel

I will make them into one nation.

Thus speaks the Lord God: I will take the Israelites from among the nations to which they have come, and gather them from all sides to bring them back to their land. I will make them one nation upon the land, in the mountains of Israel, and there shall be one prince for them all. Never again shall they be two nations, and never again shall they be divided into two kingdoms.

No longer shall they defile themselves with their idols, their abominations, and all their transgressions. I will deliver them from all their sins of apostasy, and cleanse them so that they may be my people and I may be their God. My servant David shall be prince over them, and there shall be one shepherd for them all; they shall live by my statutes and carefully observe my decrees. They shall live on the land which I gave to my servant Jacob, the land where their fathers lived; they shall live on it forever, they, and their children, and their children's children, with my servant David their prince forever. I will make with them a covenant of peace; it shall be an everlasting covenant with them, and I will multiply them, and put my sanctuary among them forever. My dwelling shall be with them; I will be their God, and they shall be my people. Thus the nations shall know that it is I, the Lord, who make Israel holy, when my sanctuary shall be set up among them forever.

This is the Word of the Lord.

Responsorial Psalm   Jer 31, 10. 11-12. 13

℟. (10) The Lord will guard us,
  like a shepherd guarding his flock.

Hear the word of the Lord, O nations,
  proclaim it on distant coasts, and say:
He who scattered Israel, now gathers them together,
  he guards them as a shepherd his flock.

℟. The Lord will guard us,
  like a shepherd guarding his flock.

The Lord shall ransom Jacob,
  he shall redeem him from the hand of his conqueror.
Shouting, they shall mount the heights of Zion,
  they shall come streaming to the Lord's blessings:
The grain, the wine, and the oil,
  the sheep and the oxen.

℟. The Lord will guard us,
  like a shepherd guarding his flock.

Then the virgins shall make merry and dance,
  and young men and old as well.
I will turn their mourning into joy,
  I will console and gladden them after their sorrows.

℟. The Lord will guard us,
  like a shepherd guarding his flock.

GOSPEL   Jn 11, 45-57

Verse before the Gospel

See no. 224.

✠ **A reading from the holy gospel according to John**

He gathered together in unity the scattered children of God.

Many of the Jews who had come to visit Mary, and had seen what Jesus did, put their faith in him. Some others, however, went to the Pharisees and reported what Jesus had done. The result was that the chief priests and the Pharisees called a meeting of the Sanhedrin. "What are we to do," they said, "with this man performing all sorts of signs? If we let him go on like this, the whole world will believe in him. Then the Romans will come in and sweep away our sanctuary and our nation." One of their number named Caiaphas, who was high priest that year, addressed them at this point:

"You have no understanding whatever! Can you not see that it is better for you to have one man die [for the people] than to have the whole nation destroyed?" (He did not say this on his own. It was rather as high priest for that year that he prophesied that Jesus would die for the nation—and not for this nation only, but to gather into one all the dispersed children of God.)

From that day onward there was a plan afoot to kill him. In consequence, Jesus no longer moved about freely in Jewish circles. He withdrew instead to a town called Ephraim in the region near the desert, where he stayed with his disciples.

The Jewish Passover was near, which meant that many people from the country went up to Jerusalem for Passover purification. They were on the lookout for Jesus, various people in the temple vicinity saying to each other, "What do you think? Is he likely to come for the feast?" (The chief priests and the Pharisees had given orders that anyone who knew where he was should report it, so that they could apprehend him.)

This is the gospel of the Lord.

---

258   MONDAY OF HOLY WEEK

READING I   Is 42, 1-7

A reading from the book of the prophet Isaiah
He will not cry out, nor make his voice heard in the streets
(First song of the servant of Yahweh).

Here is my servant whom I uphold,
  my chosen one with whom I am pleased,
Upon whom I have put my spirit;
  he shall bring forth justice to the nations,
Not crying out, not shouting,
  not making his voice heard in the street.
A bruised reed he shall not break,
  and a smoldering wick he shall not quench,
Until he establishes justice on the earth;
  the coastlands will wait for his teaching.

Thus says God, the Lord,
  who created the heavens and stretched them out,
  who spreads out the earth with its crops,

Who gives breath to its people
  and spirit to those who walk on it:
I, the Lord, have called you for the victory of justice,
  I have grasped you by the hand;
I formed you, and set you
  as a covenant of the people,
  a light for the nations,
To open the eyes of the blind,
  to bring out prisoners from confinement,
  and from the dungeon, those who live in darkness.

This is the Word of the Lord.

Responsorial Psalm   Ps 27, 1. 2. 3. 13-14

℞. (1) The Lord is my light and my salvation.
The Lord is my light and my salvation;
  whom should I fear?
The Lord is my life's refuge;
  of whom should I be afraid?
℞. The Lord is my light and my salvation.
When evildoers come at me
  to devour my flesh,
My foes and my enemies
  themselves stumble and fall.
℞. The Lord is my light and my salvation.
Though an army encamp against me,
  my heart will not fear;
Though war be waged upon me,
  even then will I trust.
℞. The Lord is my light and my salvation.
I believe that I shall see the bounty of the Lord
  in the land of the living.
Wait for the Lord with courage;
  be stouthearted, and wait for the Lord.
℞. The Lord is my light and my salvation.

GOSPEL   Jn 12, 1-11
Verse before the Gospel

  Let us greet our king;
  he alone showed mercy for our sins.

✠ **A reading from the holy gospel according to John**
Let her keep it for the day of my burial.

Six days before Passover Jesus came to Bethany, the village of Lazarus whom Jesus had raised from the dead. There they gave him a banquet, at which Martha served. Lazarus was one of those at table with him. Mary brought a pound of costly perfume made from genuine aromatic nard, with which she anointed Jesus' feet. Then she dried his feet with her hair, and the house was filled with the ointment's fragrance. Judas Iscariot, one of his disciples (the one about to hand him over), protested: "Why was this perfume not sold? It could have brought three hundred silver pieces, and the money have been given to the poor." (He did not say this out of concern for the poor, but because he was a thief. He held the purse, and used to help himself to what was deposited there.) To this Jesus replied, "Leave her alone. Let her keep it against the day they prepare me for burial. The poor you always have with you, but me you will not always have."

The great crowd of Jews discovered he was there and came out, not only because of Jesus but also to see Lazarus, whom he had raised from the dead. The fact was, the chief priests planned to kill Lazarus too, because many Jews were going over to Jesus and believing in him on account of Lazarus.

This is the gospel of the Lord.

---

259   TUESDAY OF HOLY WEEK

READING I   Is 49, 1-6

A reading from the book of the prophet Isaiah
I have made you the light of nations so that my salvation may reach to the ends of the earth (Second song of the servant of Yahweh).

Hear me, O coastlands,
  listen, O distant peoples.
The Lord called me from birth,
  from my mother's womb he gave me my name.
He made of me a sharp-edged sword
  and concealed me in the shadow of his arm.
He made me a polished arrow,
  in his quiver he hid me.
You are my servant, he said to me,
  Israel, through whom I show my glory.

Though I thought I had toiled in vain,
  and for nothing, uselessly, spent my strength,
Yet my reward is with the Lord,
  my recompense is with my God.
For now the Lord has spoken
  who formed me as his servant from the womb,
That Jacob may be brought back to him
  and Israel gathered to him;
And I am made glorious in the sight of the Lord,
  and my God is now my strength!
It is too little, he says, for you to be my servant,
  to raise up the tribes of Jacob,
  and restore the survivors of Israel;
I will make you a light to the nations,
  that my salvation may reach to the ends of the earth.

This is the Word of the Lord.

Responsorial Psalm   Ps 71, 1-2. 3-4. 5-6. 15. 17

℟. (15) I will sing of your salvation.
In you, O Lord, I take refuge;
  let me never be put to shame.
In your justice rescue me, and deliver me;
  incline your ear to me, and save me.
℟. I will sing of your salvation.
Be my rock of refuge,
  a stronghold to give me safety,
  for you are my rock and my fortress.
O my God, rescue me from the hand of the wicked.
℟. I will sing of your salvation.
For you are my hope, O Lord;
  my trust, O God, from my youth.
On you I depend from birth;
  from my mother's womb you are my strength.
℟. I will sing of your salvation.
My mouth shall declare your justice,
  day by day your salvation,
  though I know not their extent.
O God, you have taught me from my youth,
  and till the present I proclaim your wondrous deeds.
℟. I will sing of your salvation.

GOSPEL   Jn 13, 21-33. 36-38
Verse before the Gospel

Hail to our king, obedient to his Father;
he went to his crucifixion like a gentle
lamb.

✠ A reading from the holy gospel according
to John

One of you will betray me; before the cock crows, you will
have disowned me three times.

Jesus, reclining with his disciples, grew deeply
troubled. He went on to give this testimony:
"I tell you solemnly,
    one of you will betray me."
The disciples looked at one another, puzzled as
to whom he could mean. One of them, the disciple whom Jesus loved, reclined close to him
as they ate. Simon Peter signaled him to ask
Jesus whom he meant. He leaned back against
Jesus' chest and said to him, "Lord, who is he?"
Jesus answered, "The one to whom I give the
bit of food I dip in the dish." He dipped the
morsel, then took it and gave it to Judas, son
of Simon Iscariot. Immediately after, Satan
entered his heart. Jesus addressed himself to
him, "Be quick about what you are to do."
(Naturally, none of those reclining at table
understood why Jesus said this to him. A few
had the idea that, since Judas held the common
purse, Jesus was telling him to buy what was
needed for the feast, or to give something to
the poor.) No sooner had Judas eaten the
morsel than he went out. It was night.
    Once Judas had left, Jesus said:
"Now is the Son of Man glorified
    and God is glorified in him.
[If God has been glorified in him,]
God will, in turn, glorify him in himself,
    and will glorify him soon.
My children, I am not to be with you much
    longer.
You will look for me,
    but I say to you now
    what I once said to the Jews:
'Where I am going, you cannot come.'"
    "Lord," Simon Peter said to him, "where do
you mean to go?" Jesus answered:

"I am going where you cannot follow me
    now;
    later on you shall come after me."
"Lord," Peter said to him, "why can I not
follow you now? I will lay down my life for
you!" "You will lay down your life for me, will
you?" Jesus answered. "I tell you truly, the
cock will not crow before you have three times
disowned me!"
    This is the gospel of the Lord.

---

260   WEDNESDAY OF HOLY WEEK
READING I   Is 50, 4-9

A reading from the book of the prophet Isaiah
I did not cover my face against insult and spittle (Third
song of the servant of Yahweh).

The Lord God has given me
    a well-trained tongue,
That I might know how to speak to the weary
    a word that will rouse them.
Morning after morning
    he opens my ear that I may hear;
And I have not rebelled,
    have not turned back.
I gave my back to those who beat me,
    my cheeks to those who plucked my beard;
My face I did not shield
    from buffets and spitting.

The Lord God is my help,
    therefore I am not disgraced;
I have set my face like flint,
    knowing that I shall not be put to shame.
He is near who upholds my right;
    if anyone wishes to oppose me,
    let us appear together.
Who disputes my right?
    Let him confront me.
See, the Lord God is my help.
    This is the Word of the Lord.

Responsorial Psalm   Ps 69, 8-10. 21-22. 31. 33-34

℟. (14) Lord, in your great love, answer me.
For your sake I bear insult,
    and shame covers my face.

I have become an outcast to my brothers,
a stranger to my mother's sons,
Because zeal for your house consumes me,
and the insults of those who blaspheme you
fall upon me.
R̸. Lord, in your great love, answer me.
Insult has broken my heart, and I am weak,
I looked for sympathy, but there was none;
for comforters, and I found none.
Rather they put gall in my food,
and in my thirst they gave me vinegar to
drink.
R̸. Lord, in your great love, answer me.
I will praise the name of God in song,
and I will glorify him with thanksgiving:
"See, you lowly ones, and be glad;
you who seek God, may your hearts be
merry!
For the Lord hears the poor,
and his own who are in bonds he spurns
not."
R̸. Lord, in your great love, answer me.

GOSPEL   Mt 26, 14-25
Verse before the Gospel

As above, nos. 258–259.

✠ A reading from the holy gospel according
to Matthew

The Son of Man is going the way scripture says, but alas for
that man by whom the Son of Man is betrayed.

One of the Twelve whose name was Judas
Iscariot went off to the chief priests and said,
"What are you willing to give me if I hand him
over to you?" They paid him thirty pieces of
silver, and from that time on he kept looking
for an opportunity to hand him over.

On the first day of the feast of Unleavened
Bread, the disciples came up to Jesus and said,
'Where do you wish us to prepare the Passover supper for you?" He said, "Go to this man
in the city and tell him, 'The Teacher says,
My appointed time draws near. I am to celebrate the Passover with my disciples in your
house.' "

The disciples then did as Jesus had ordered,
and prepared the Passover supper.

When it grew dark he reclined at table with
the Twelve. In the course of the meal he said,
"I give you my word, one of you is about to
betray me." Distressed at this, they began to
say to him one after another, "Surely it is not
I, Lord?" He replied: "The man who has dipped
his hand into the dish with me is the one who
will hand me over. The Son of Man is departing, as Scripture says of him, but woe to that
man by whom the Son of Man is betrayed.
Better for him if he had never been born."

Then Judas, his betrayer, spoke: "Surely it
is not I, Rabbi?" Jesus answered, "It is you who
have said it."

This is the gospel of the Lord.

EASTER SEASON
261   **MONDAY OF THE OCTAVE
OF EASTER**

READING I   Acts 2, 14. 22-32
A reading from the Acts of the Apostles

God raised this man Jesus to life, and all of us are witnesses to it.

[On the day of Pentecost] Peter stood up with
the Eleven, raised his voice, and addressed
them: "You who are Jews, indeed all of you
staying in Jerusalem! Listen to what I have to
say.

"Jesus the Nazorean was a man whom God
sent to you with miracles, wonders and signs
as his credentials. These God worked through
him in your midst, as you well know. He was
delivered up by the set purpose and plan of
God; you even made use of pagans to crucify
and kill him. God freed him from death's bitter
pangs, however, and raised him up again, for it
was impossible that death should keep its hold
on him. David says of him:
'I have set the Lord ever before me,
with him at my right hand I shall not be
disturbed.
My heart has been glad and my tongue has
rejoiced,
my body will live on in hope,
for you will not abandon my soul to the nether
world,
nor will you suffer your faithful one to
undergo corruption.

You have shown me the paths of life;
  you will fill me with joy in your presence.'
  "Brothers, I can speak confidently to you about our father David. He died and was buried, and his grave is in our midst to this day. He was a prophet and knew that God had sworn to him that one of 'his descendants would sit upon his throne.' He said that he was 'not abandoned to the nether world,' nor did his body 'undergo corruption,' thus proclaiming beforehand the resurrection of the Messiah. This is the Jesus God has raised up, and we are his witnesses."
  This is the Word of the Lord.

Responsorial Psalm   Ps 16, 1-2. 5. 7-8. 9-10. 11

R̸. (1) Keep me safe, O God;
  you are my hope.
Keep me, O God, for in you I take refuge;
  I say to the Lord, "My Lord are you."
O Lord, my allotted portion and my cup,
  you it is who hold fast my lot.
R̸. Keep me safe, O God;
  you are my hope.
I bless the Lord who counsels me;
  even in the night my heart exhorts me.
I set the Lord ever before me;
  with him at my right hand I shall not be disturbed.
R̸. Keep me safe, O God;
  you are my hope.
Therefore my heart is glad and my soul rejoices,
  my body, too, abides in confidence;
Because you will not abandon my soul to the nether world,
  nor will you suffer your faithful one to undergo corruption.
R̸. Keep me safe, O God;
  you are my hope.
You will show me the path to life,
  fullness of joys in your presence,
  the delights at your right hand forever.
R̸. Keep me safe, O God;
  you are my hope.
R̸. Or: Alleluia.

GOSPEL   Mt 28, 8-15
Alleluia   Ps 118, 24

R̸. Alleluia. **This is the day the Lord has made; let us rejoice and be glad.** R̸. Alleluia.

✠ **A reading from the holy gospel according to Matthew**
Tell my brothers that they must leave for Galilee; they will see me there

The women hurried away from the tomb half-overjoyed, half-fearful, and ran to carry the good news to his disciples. Suddenly, without warning, Jesus stood before them and said, "Peace!" The women came up and embraced his feet and did him homage. At this Jesus said to them, "Do not be afraid! Go and carry the news to my brothers that they are to go to Galilee, where they will see me."
  As the women were returning, some of the guard went into the city and reported to the chief priests all that had happened. They, in turn, convened with the elders and worked out their strategy, giving the soldiers a large bribe with the instructions: "You are to say, 'His disciples came during the night and stole him while we were asleep.' If any word of this gets to the procurator, we will straighten it out with him and keep you out of trouble." The soldiers pocketed the money and did as they had been instructed. This is the story that circulates among the Jews to this very day.
  This is the gospel of the Lord.

262   **TUESDAY OF THE OCTAVE OF EASTER**

READING I   Acts 2, 36-41

A reading from the Acts of the Apostles
You must repent and everyone must be baptized in the name of Jesus.

[On the day of Pentecost] Peter said to the Jews: "Let the whole house of Israel know beyond any doubt that God has made both Lord and Messiah this Jesus whom you crucified."
  When they heard this, they were deeply shaken. They asked Peter and the other apostles, "What are we to do, brothers?" Peter

answered: "You must reform and be baptized, each one of you, in the name of Jesus Christ, that your sins may be forgiven; then you will receive the gift of the Holy Spirit. It was to you and your children that the promise was made, and to all those still far off whom the Lord our God calls."

In support of his testimony he used many other arguments, and kept urging, "Save yourselves from this generation which has gone astray." Those who accepted his message were baptized; some three thousand were added that day.

This is the Word of the Lord.

Responsorial Psalm   Ps 33, 4-5. 18-19. 20. 22

℞. (5) The earth is full of the goodness of the Lord.

Upright is the word of the Lord,
  and all his works are trustworthy.
He loves justice and right;
  of the kindness of the Lord the earth is full.
℞. The earth is full of the goodness of the Lord.

See, the eyes of the Lord are upon those who fear him,
  upon those who hope for his kindness,
To deliver them from death
  and preserve them in spite of famine.
℞. The earth is full of the goodness of the Lord.

Our soul waits for the Lord,
  who is our help and our shield.
May your kindness, O Lord, be upon us
  who have put our hope in you.
℞. The earth is full of the goodness of the Lord.
℞. Or: Alleluia.

GOSPEL   Jn 20, 11-18
Alleluia   Ps 118, 24

℞. Alleluia. This is the day the Lord has made; let us rejoice and be glad. ℞. Alleluia.

✠ A reading from the holy gospel according to John
I have seen the Lord and he said these things to me.

Mary stood weeping beside the tomb. Even as she wept, she stooped to peer inside, and there she saw two angels in dazzling robes. One was seated at the head and the other at the foot of the place where Jesus' body had lain. "Woman," they asked her, "why are you weeping?" She answered them, "Because the Lord has been taken away, and I do not know where they have put him." She had no sooner said this than she turned around and caught sight of Jesus standing there. But she did not know him. "Woman," he asked her, "why are you weeping? Who is it you are looking for?" She supposed he was the gardener, so she said, "Sir, if you are the one who carried him off, tell me where you have laid him and I will take him away." Jesus said to her, "Mary!" She turned to him and said [in Hebrew], "Rabboni!" (meaning "Teacher"). Jesus then said: "Do not cling to me, for I have not yet ascended to the Father. Rather, go to my brothers and tell them, 'I am ascending to my Father and your Father, to my God and your God!'" Mary Magdalene went to the disciples. "I have seen the Lord!" she announced. Then she reported what he had said to her.

This is the gospel of the Lord.

263   **WEDNESDAY OF THE OCTAVE OF EASTER**

READING I   Acts 3, 1-10

A reading from the Acts of the Apostles
I will give you what I have: in the name of Jesus, arise and walk.

Once, when Peter and John were going up to the temple for prayer at the three o'clock hour, a man crippled from birth was being carried in. They would bring him every day and put him at the temple gate called "the Beautiful" to beg from the people as they entered. When he saw Peter and John on their way in, he begged them for an alms. Peter fixed his gaze on the man; so did John. "Look at us!" Peter said. The cripple gave them his whole attention, hoping to get something. Then Peter said: "I have neither silver nor gold, but what I have I give you! In the name of Jesus Christ the Nazorean, walk!" Then Peter took him by the right hand and pulled him up. Immediately the beggar's feet and ankles became strong; he jumped up, stood for a moment, then began to walk around. He went into the temple with them—walking, jumping about, and praising God. When the people saw him moving and giving praise to God, they recognized him as that beggar who used to sit at the Beautiful Gate of the temple. They were struck with astonishment—utterly stupefied at what had happened to him.

This is the Word of the Lord.

Responsorial Psalm　Ps 105, 1-2. 3-4. 6-7. 8-9

R̶⁊. (5) The earth is full of the goodness of the Lord.

Give thanks to the Lord, invoke his name;
　make known among the nations his deeds.
Sing to him, sing his praise,
　proclaim all his wondrous deeds.
R̶⁊.The earth is full of the goodness of the Lord.

Glory in his holy name;
　rejoice, O hearts that seek the Lord!
Look to the Lord in his strength;
　seek to serve him constantly.
R̶⁊.The earth is full of the goodness of the Lord.

You descendants of Abraham, his servants,
　sons of Jacob, his chosen ones!
He, the Lord, is our God;
　throughout the earth his judgments prevail.
R̶⁊.The earth is full of the goodness of the Lord.

He remembers forever his covenant
　which he made binding for a thousand generations—
Which he entered into with Abraham
　and by his oath to Isaac.
R̶⁊.The earth is full of the goodness of the Lord.
R̶⁊. Or:Alleluia.

GOSPEL　Lk 24, 13-35

Alleluia　Ps 118, 24

R̶⁊.Alleluia. **This is the day the Lord has made; let us rejoice and be glad.** R̶⁊.Alleluia.

✠ **A reading from the holy gospel according to Luke**

They recognized him at the breaking of the bread.

Two of the disciples of Jesus that same day [the first day of the week] were making their way to a village named Emmaus seven miles
distant from Jerusalem, discussing as they went all that had happened. In the course of their lively exchange, Jesus approached and began to walk along with them. However, they were restrained from recognizing him. He said to them, "What are you discussing as you go your way?" They halted in distress, and one of them, Cleopas by name, asked him, "Are you the only resident of Jerusalem who does not know the things that went on there these past few days?" He said to them, "What things?" They said: "All those that had to do with Jesus of Nazareth, a prophet powerful in word and deed in the eyes of God and all the people; how our chief priests and leaders delivered him up to be condemned to death, and crucified him. We were hoping that he was the one who would set Israel free. Besides all this, today, the third day since these things happened, some women of our group have just brought us some astonishing news. They were at the tomb before dawn and failed to find his body, but returned with the tale that they had seen a vision of angels who declared he was alive. Some of our number went to the tomb and found it to be just as the women said; but him they did not see."

Then he said to them, "What little sense you have! How slow you are to believe all that the prophets have announced! Did not the Messiah have to undergo all this so as to enter into his glory?" Beginning, then, with Moses and all the prophets, he interpreted for them every passage of Scripture which referred to him. By now they were near the village to which they were going, and he acted as if he were going farther. But they pressed him: "Stay with us. It is nearly evening—the day is practically over." So he went in to stay with them.

When he had seated himself with them to eat, he took bread, pronounced the blessing, then broke the bread and began to distribute it to them. With that their eyes were opened and they recognized him; whereupon he vanished from their sight. They said to one another, "Were not our hearts burning inside us as he talked to us on the road and explained the Scriptures to us?" They got up immediately and returned to Jerusalem, where they found the Eleven and the rest of the company assembled. They were greeted with, "The Lord has been raised! It is true! He has appeared to Simon." Then they recounted what had happened on the road and how they had come to know him in the breaking of bread.

This is the gospel of the Lord.

---

264 THURSDAY OF THE OCTAVE OF EASTER

READING I   Acts 3, 11-26

A reading from the Acts of the Apostles

You have killed the prince of life; God however has raised him from the dead.

As the lame man who had been cured stood clinging to Peter and John, the whole crowd rushed over to them excitedly in Solomon's Portico. When Peter saw this, he addressed the people as follows: "Fellow Israelites, why does this surprise you? Why do you stare at us as if we had made this man walk by some power or holiness of our own? The 'God of Abraham, of Isaac, and of Jacob, the God of our fathers,' has glorified his Servant Jesus, whom you handed over and disowned in Pilate's presence when Pilate was ready to release him. You disowned the Holy and Just One and preferred instead to be granted the release of a murderer. You put to death the Author of life. But God raised him from the dead, and we are his witnesses. It is his name, and trust in this name, that has strengthened the limbs of this man whom you see and know well. Such faith has given him perfect health, as all of you can observe.

"Yet I know, my brothers, that you acted out of ignorance, just as your leaders did. God has brought to fulfillment by this means what he announced long ago through the prophets: that his Messiah would suffer. Therefore, reform your lives! Turn to God, that your sins may be wiped away! Thus may a season of refreshment be granted you by the Lord when he sends you Jesus, already designated as your Messiah. Jesus must remain in heaven until the time of universal restoration which God spoke of long ago through his holy prophets. For Moses said:

"'The Lord God will raise up for you a prophet like me from among your own kinsmen: you shall listen to him in everything he says to you. Anyone who does not listen to that prophet shall be ruthlessly cut off from the people.'

"Moreover, all the prophets who have spoken, from Samuel onward, have announced the events of these days. You are the children of those prophets, you are the heirs of the covenant God made with your fathers when he said to Abraham, 'In your offspring, all the families of the earth shall be blessed.' When God raised up his servant, he sent him to you first to bless you by turning you from your evil ways."

This is the Word of the Lord.

Responsorial Psalm   Ps 8, 2. 5. 6-7. 8-9

℟. (2) O Lord, our God,
how wonderful your name in all the earth!
O Lord, our Lord,
how glorious is your name over all the earth!
What is man that you should be mindful of
him,
or the son of man that you should care for
him?
℟. O Lord, our God,
how wonderful your name in all the earth!
You have made him little less than the angels,
and crowned him with glory and honor.
You have given him rule over the works of
your hands,
putting all things under his feet:
℟. O Lord, our God,
how wonderful your name in all the earth!
All sheep and oxen,
yes, and the beasts of the field,
The birds of the air, the fishes of the sea,
and whatever swims the paths of the seas.
℟. O Lord, our God,
how wonderful your name in all the earth!
℟. Or: Alleluia.

GOSPEL   Lk 24 35-48
Alleluia   Ps 118, 24

℟. Alleluia. This is the day the Lord has made;
let us rejoice and be glad. ℟. Alleluia.

✠ A reading from the holy gospel according
to Luke

It was necessary that Christ suffer and rise from the dead
on the third day.

The disciples recounted what had happened on
the road to Emmaus and how they had come
to know Jesus in the breaking of bread.

While they were still speaking about all this,
Jesus himself stood in their midst [and said to
them, "Peace to you."] In their panic and fright
they thought they were seeing a ghost. He said
to them, "Why are you disturbed? Why do such
ideas cross your mind? Look at my hands and
my feet; it is really I. Touch me, and see that
a ghost does not have flesh and bones as I do."
[As he said this he showed them his hands and
feet.] They were still incredulous for sheer joy
and wonder, so he said to them, "Have you
anything here to eat?" They gave him a piece
of cooked fish, which he took and ate in their
presence. Then he said to them, "Recall those
words I spoke to you when I was still with
you: everything written about me in the law of
Moses and the prophets and psalms had to be
fulfilled." Then he opened their minds to the
understanding of the Scriptures.

He said to them: "Thus it is written that the
Messiah must suffer and rise from the dead
on the third day. In his name, penance for the
remission of sins is to be preached to all the
nations, beginning at Jerusalem. You are witnesses of all this."

This is the gospel of the Lord.

265   **FRIDAY OF THE OCTAVE
OF EASTER**

READING I   Acts 4, 1-12

A reading from the Acts of the Apostles

There is no other name by which we can be saved.

While Peter and John were still addressing
the crowd, [after the lame man was healed]
the priests, the captain of the temple guard,
and the Sadducees came up to them, angry
because they were teaching the people and
proclaiming the resurrection of the dead in the
person of Jesus. It was evening by now, so they
arrested them and put them in jail for the
night. Despite this, many of those who had
heard the speech believed; the number of the
men came to about five thousand.

When the leaders, the elders, and the scribes
assembled the next day in Jerusalem, Annas
the high priest, Caiaphas, John, Alexander,
and all who were of the high-priestly class
were there. They brought Peter and John before them and began the interrogation in this
fashion: "By what power or in whose name
have men of your stripe done this?"

Then Peter, filled with the Holy Spirit, spoke
up: "Leaders of the people! Elders! If we must
answer today for a good deed done to a cripple
and explain how he was restored to health,
then you and all the people of Israel must
realize that it was done in the name of Jesus
Christ the Nazorean whom you crucified and
whom God raised from the dead. In the power
of that name this man stands before you perfectly sound. This Jesus is 'the stone rejected
by you the builders which has become the
cornerstone.' There is no salvation in anyone
else, for there is no other name in the whole
world given to men by which we are to be
saved."

This is the Word of the Lord.

Responsorial Psalm   Ps 118, 1-2, 4, 22-24, 25-27

℟. (22) The stone rejected by the builders has
become the cornerstone.

Give thanks to the Lord, for he is good,
for his mercy endures forever.
Let the house of Israel say,
"His mercy endures forever."
Let those who fear the Lord say,
"His mercy endures forever."

℟. The stone rejected by the builders has become the cornerstone.

The stone which the builders rejected
has become the cornerstone.

By the Lord has this been done;
  it is wonderful in our eyes.
This is the day the Lord has made;
  let us be glad and rejoice in it.
℞. The stone rejected by the builders has be-
  come the cornerstone.
O Lord, grant salvation!
  O Lord, grant prosperity!
Blessed is he who comes in the name of the
  Lord;
  we bless you from the house of the Lord.
  The Lord is God, and he has given us light.
℞. The stone rejected by the builders has be-
  come the cornerstone.
℞. Or: Alleluia.

GOSPEL   Jn 21, 1-14
Alleluia   Ps 118, 24

℞. Alleluia. This is the day the Lord has made;
let us rejoice and be glad. ℞. Alleluia.

✠ A reading from the holy gospel according
to John

*Jesus came and took the bread and gave it to them, and
the same with the fish.*

Jesus showed himself to the disciples [once
again] at the Sea of Tiberias. This is how the
appearance took place. Assembled were Simon
Peter, Thomas ("the Twin"), Nathanael (from
Cana in Galilee), Zebedee's sons, and two other
disciples. Simon Peter said to them, "I am going
out to fish." "We will join you," they replied,
and went off to get into their boat. All through
the night they caught nothing. Just after daybreak Jesus was standing on the shore, though
none of the disciples knew it was Jesus. He
said to them, "Children, have you caught anything to eat?" "Not a thing," they answered.
"Cast your net off to the starboard side," he
suggested, "and you will find something." So
they made a cast, and took so many fish that
they could not haul the net in. Then the disciple
Jesus loved cried out to Peter, "It is the Lord!"
On hearing it was the Lord, Simon Peter threw
on some clothes—he was stripped—and
jumped into the water.
  Meanwhile the other disciples came in the
boat, towing the net full of fish. Actually they

were not far from land—no more than a
hundred yards.
  When they landed, they saw a charcoal fire
there with a fish laid on it and some bread.
"Bring some of the fish you just caught," Jesus
told them. Simon Peter went aboard and
hauled ashore the net loaded with sizable
fish—one hundred fifty-three of them! In spite
of the great number, the net was not torn.
  "Come and eat your meal," Jesus told them.
Not one of the disciples presumed to inquire
"Who are you?" for they knew it was the
Lord. Jesus came over, took the bread and gave
it to them, and did the same with the fish.
This marked the third time that Jesus appeared
to the disciples after being raised from the
dead.

This is the gospel of the Lord.

---

266   **SATURDAY OF THE OCTAVE**
                 OF EASTER

READING I   Acts 4, 13-21
A reading from the Acts of the Apostles

We cannot stop preaching what we have seen and heard.

The priests and elders were amazed as they
observed the self-assurance of Peter and John
and realized that the speakers were unedu-
cated men of no standing. Then they recognized these men as having been with Jesus.
When they saw the man who had been cured
standing there with them, they could think of
nothing to say, so they ordered them out of
the court while they held a consultation.
"What shall we do with these men? Everyone
who lives in Jerusalem knows what a remarkable show of power took place through them.
We cannot deny it. To stop this from spreading further among the people we must give
them a stern warning never to mention that
man's name to anyone again." So they called
them back and made it clear that under no
circumstances were they to speak the name
of Jesus or teach about him. Peter and John
answered, "Judge for yourselves whether it is
right in God's sight for us to obey you rather
than God. Surely we cannot help speaking of

what we have heard and seen." At that point they were dismissed with further warnings. The court could find no way to punish them because of the people, all of whom were praising God for what had happened.

This is the Word of the Lord.

Responsorial Psalm Ps 118, 1. 14-15. 16-18. 19-21

R̥. (21) I praise you, Lord,
for you have answered me.

Give thanks to the Lord, for he is good,
for his mercy endures forever.
My strength and my courage is the Lord,
and he has been my savior.
The joyful shout of victory
in the tents of the just.

R̥. I praise you, Lord,
for you have answered me.

The right hand of the Lord is exalted;
"The right hand of the Lord has struck with power."
I shall not die, but live,
and declare the works of the Lord.
Though the Lord has indeed chastised me,
yet he has not delivered me to death.

R̥. I praise you, Lord,
for you have answered me.

Open to me the gates of justice;
I will enter them and give thanks to the Lord.
This gate is the Lord's;
the just shall enter it.
I will give thanks to you, for you have answered me
and have been my savior.

R̥. I praise you, Lord,
for you have answered me.

R̥. Or: Alleluia.

GOSPEL Mk 16, 9-15
Alleluia Ps 118, 24

R̥. Alleluia. This is the day the Lord has made; let us rejoice and be glad. R̥. Alleluia.

✠ A reading from the holy gospel according to Mark

Go out to the whole world and proclaim the Good News to all creation.

Jesus rose from the dead early on the first day of the week. He first appeared to Mary Magdalene, out of whom he had cast seven demons. She went to announce the good news to his followers, who were now grieving and weeping. But when they heard that he was alive and had been seen by her, they refused to believe it. Later on, as two of them were walking along on their way to the country, he was revealed to them completely changed in appearance. These men retraced their steps and announced the good news to the others; but the others put no more faith in them than in Mary Magdalene. Finally, as they were at table, Jesus was revealed to the Eleven. He took them to task for their disbelief and their stubbornness, since they had put no faith in those who had seen him after he had been raised.

Then he told them: "Go into the whole world and proclaim the good news to all creation."

This is the gospel of the Lord.

267 **MONDAY OF THE SECOND WEEK OF EASTER**

READING I Acts 4, 23-31

A reading from the Acts of the Apostles

When they had prayed they were filled with the Holy Spirit and began to proclaim the word of God boldly.

Peter and John, after being released, went back to their own people and told them what the priests and elders had said. All raised their voices in prayer to God on hearing the story: "Sovereign Lord, 'who made heaven and earth, and sea and all that is in them,' you have said by the Holy Spirit through the lips of our father David your servant:

'Why did the Gentiles rage,
the peoples conspire in folly?
The kings of the earth were aligned,
the princes gathered together
against the Lord and against his anointed.'

Indeed, they gathered in this very city against your holy Servant, Jesus, 'whom you anointed' —Herod and Pontius Pilate in league with 'the Gentiles' and 'the peoples' of Israel. They have brought about the very things which in your powerful providence you planned long ago. But now, O Lord, look at the threats they are leveling against us. Grant to your servants, even as they speak your words, complete assurance by stretching forth your hand in cures and signs and wonders to be worked in the name of Jesus, your holy Servant."

The place where they were gathered shook as they prayed. They were filled with the Holy Spirit and continued to speak God's word with confidence.

This is the Word of the Lord.

Responsorial Psalm   Ps 2, 1-3. 4-6. 7-9

℟. (12) Happy are all who put their trust in the Lord.
Why do the nations rage
  and the peoples utter folly?
The kings of the earth rise up,
  and the princes conspire together
against the Lord and against his anointed:
"Let us break their fetters
  and cast their bonds from us!"
℟. Happy are all who put their trust in the Lord.
He who is throned in heaven laughs;
  the Lord derides them.
Then in anger he speaks to them;
  he terrifies them in his wrath:
"I myself have set up my king
  on Zion, my holy mountain."
I will proclaim the decree of the Lord.
℟. Happy are all who put their trust in the Lord.
The Lord said to me, "You are my son;
  this day I have begotten you.
Ask of me and I will give you
  the nations for an inheritance
  and the ends of the earth for your possession.
You shall rule them with an iron rod;
  you shall shatter them like an earthen dish."
℟. Happy are all who put their trust in the Lord.
℟. Or: Alleluia.

GOSPEL   Jn 3, 1-8
Alleluia
See no. 303.

✠ A reading from the holy gospel according to John
Unless a man has been born again, he cannot see the kingdom of God.

A certain Pharisee named Nicodemus, a member of the Jewish Sanhedrin, came to Jesus at night. "Rabbi," he said, "we know you are a teacher come from God, for no man can perform signs and wonders such as you perform unless God is with him." Jesus gave him this answer:
"I solemnly assure you,
no one can see the rule of God
unless he is begotten from above."
"How can a man be born again once he is old?" retorted Nicodemus. "Can he return to his mother's womb and be born all over again?" Jesus replied:
"I solemnly assure you,
no one can enter into God's kingdom
without being begotten of water and
  Spirit.
Flesh begets flesh,
Spirit begets spirit.
Do not be surprised that I tell you
you must all be begotten from above.
The wind blows where it will.
You hear the sound it makes
but you do not know where it comes from,
or where it goes.
So it is with everyone begotten of the
  Spirit."
This is the gospel of the Lord.

268   TUESDAY OF THE SECOND WEEK OF EASTER

READING I   Acts 4, 32-37

A reading from the Acts of the Apostles
Be of one heart and one mind.

The community of believers were of one heart and one mind. None of them ever claimed anything as his own; rather, everything was held in common. With power the apostles bore witness to the resurrection of the Lord Jesus, and great respect was paid to them all; nor was there anyone needy among them, for all who owned property or houses sold them and donated the proceeds. They used to lay them at the feet of the apostles to be distributed to everyone according to his need.

There was a certain Levite from Cyprus named Joseph, to whom the apostles gave the name Barnabas (meaning "son of encouragement"). He sold a farm that he owned and made a donation of the money, laying it at the apostles' feet.

This is the Word of the Lord.

Responsorial Psalm   Ps 93, 1. 1-2. 5

R̼. (1) The Lord is king;
    he is robed in majesty.

The Lord is king, in splendor robed;
    robed is the Lord and girt about with
      strength.

R̼. The Lord is king;
    he is robed in majesty.

And he has made the world firm,
    not to be moved.
Your throne stands firm from of old;
    from everlasting you are, O Lord.

R̼. The Lord is king;
    he is robed in majesty.

Your decrees are worthy of trust indeed:
    holiness befits your house,
    O Lord, for length of days.

R̼. The Lord is king;
    he is robed in majesty.

R̼. Or: Alleluia.

GOSPEL   Jn 3, 7-15

Alleluia

See no. 303.

✠ A reading from the holy gospel according to John

No one has gone to heaven, except the one who came from heaven, the Son of Man.

Jesus said to Nicodemus:
"I solemnly assure you,

do not be surprised that I tell you
you must all be begotten from above.
The wind blows where it will.
You hear the sound it makes
but you do not know where it comes from,
or where it goes.
So it is with everyone begotten of the
    Spirit."

"How can such a thing happen?" asked Nicodemus. Jesus responded: "You hold the office of teacher of Israel and still you do not understand these matters?

"I solemnly assure you,
we are talking about what we know,
we are testifying to what we have seen.
You are the ones who do not accept our
    testimony.
If you do not believe
when I tell you about earthly things,
how are you to believe
when I tell you about those of heaven?
No one has gone up to heaven
except the One who came down from
    there—
the Son of Man [who is in heaven].
Just as Moses lifted up the serpent in the
    desert,
so must the Son of Man be lifted up,
that all who believe
may have eternal life in him."

This is the gospel of the Lord.

**269   WEDNESDAY OF THE SECOND
            WEEK OF EASTER**

READING I   Acts 5, 17-26

A reading from the Acts of the Apostles

The men you have put into prisons are in the temple preaching to the people.

The high priest and all his supporters (that is, the party of the Sadducees), filled with jealousy, arrested the apostles and threw them into the public jail. During the night, however, an angel of the Lord opened the gates of the jail, led them forth, and said, "Go out now and take your place in the temple precincts and preach to the people all about this new life." Accordingly they went into the temple at dawn and resumed their teaching.

When the high priest and his supporters arrived they convoked the Sanhedrin, the full council of the elders of Israel. They sent word to the jail that the prisoners were to be brought in. But when the temple guard got to the jail they could not find them, and they hurried back with the report, "We found the jail securely locked and the guards at their posts outside the gates, but when we opened it we found no one inside."

On hearing this report, the captain of the temple guard and the high priests did not know what to make of the affair. Someone then came up to them, pointing out, "Look, there! Those men you put in jail are standing over there in the temple, teaching the people." At that, the captain went off with the guard and brought them in, but without any show of force, for fear of being stoned by the crowd.
This is the Word of the Lord.

Responsorial Psalm   Ps 34, 2-3. 4-5. 6-7. 8-9

R̷. (7) The Lord hears the cry of the poor.
I will bless the Lord at all times;
   his praise shall be ever in my mouth.
Let my soul glory in the Lord;
   the lowly will hear me and be glad.
R̷. The Lord hears the cry of the poor.
Glorify the Lord with me,
   let us together extol his name.
I sought the Lord, and he answered me
   and delivered me from all my fears.
R̷. The Lord hears the cry of the poor.
Look to him that you may be radiant with joy,
   and your faces may not blush with shame.
When the afflicted man called out, the Lord heard,
   and from all his distress he saved him.
R̷. The Lord hears the cry of the poor.
The angel of the Lord encamps
   around those who fear him, and delivers them.
Taste and see how good the Lord is;
   happy the man who takes refuge in him.
R̷. The Lord hears the cry of the poor.
R̷. Or: Alleluia.

25-13

GOSPEL   Jn 3, 16-21
Alleluia
See no. 303.

✠ **A reading from the holy gospel according to John**
God sent his Son into the world that we might be saved through him.

Jesus said to Nicodemus:
"Yes, God so loved the world
   that he gave his only Son,
that whoever believes in him may not die
   but may have eternal life.
God did not send the Son into the world
   to condemn the world,
but that the world might be saved through him.
Whoever believes in him avoids condemnation,
but whoever does not believe is already condemned
for not believing in the name of God's only Son.
The judgment in question is this:
the light came into the world,
but men loved darkness rather than light
   because their deeds were wicked.
Everyone who practices evil
   hates the light;
he does not come near it
   for fear his deeds will be exposed.
But he who acts in truth
   comes into the light,
to make clear
   that his deeds are done in God."
This is the gospel of the Lord.

---

270   THURSDAY OF THE SECOND WEEK OF EASTER

READING I   Acts 5, 27-33

A reading from the Acts of the Apostles
We are witnesses of these words, and so is the Holy Spirit.

When the attendants had led the apostles in and made them stand before the Sanhedrin, the high priest began the interrogation in this way:

"We gave you strict orders not to teach about that name, yet you have filled Jerusalem with your teaching and are determined to make us responsible for that man's blood." To this, Peter and the apostles replied: "Better for us to obey God than men! The God of our fathers has raised up Jesus whom you put to death, 'hanging him on a tree.' He whom God has exalted at his right hand as ruler and savior is to bring repentance to Israel and forgiveness of sins. We testify to this. So too does the Holy Spirit, whom God has given to those that obey him."

When the Sanhedrin heard this, they were stung to fury and wanted to kill them.

This is the Word of the Lord.

Responsorial Psalm   Ps 34, 2. 9. 17-18. 19-20

R̂. (7) The Lord hears the cry of the poor.
I will bless the Lord at all times;
   his praise shall be ever in my mouth.
Taste and see how good the Lord is;
   happy the man who takes refuge in him.
R̂. The Lord hears the cry of the poor.
The Lord confronts the evildoers,
   to destroy remembrance of them from the earth.
When the just cry out, the Lord hears them,
   and from all their distress he rescues them.
R̂. The Lord hears the cry of the poor.
The Lord is close to the brokenhearted;
   and those who are crushed in spirit he saves.
Many are the troubles of the just man,
   but out of them all the Lord delivers him.
R̂. The Lord hears the cry of the poor.
R̂. Or: Alleluia.

GOSPEL   Jn 3, 31-36
Alleluia

See no. 303.

✠ A reading from the holy gospel according to John

The Father loves the Son, and gave all things into his hands.

Jesus said to Nicodemus:

"The One who comes from above is above all;
   the one who is of the earth is earthly,

and he speaks on an earthly plane.
The One who comes from heaven [who is above all]
testifies to what he has seen and heard,
but no one accepts his testimony.
Whoever does accept this testimony
certifies that God is truthful.
For the One whom God has sent
speaks the words of God;
he does not ration his gift of the Spirit.
The Father loves the Son
and has given everything over to him.

Whoever believes in the Son
has life eternal.
Whoever disobeys the Son
will not see life,
but must endure the wrath of God."

This is the gospel of the Lord.

---

271   FRIDAY OF THE SECOND WEEK OF EASTER

READING I   Acts 5, 34-42

A reading from the Acts of the Apostles

They went out rejoicing that they had the honor of suffering humiliation for the sake of the name of Jesus.

A certain member of the Sanhedrin stood up and had the apostles ordered out of court for a few minutes, and then said to the assembly, "Fellow Israelites, think twice about what you are going to do with these men. Not long ago a certain Theudas came on the scene and tried to pass himself off as someone of importance. About four hundred men joined him. However he was killed, and all those who had been so easily convinced by him were disbanded. In the end it came to nothing. Next came Judas the Galilean at the time of the census. He too built up quite a following, but likewise died, and all his followers were dispersed. The present case is similar. My advice is that you have nothing to do with these men. Let them alone. If their purpose or activity is human in its origins it will destroy itself. If, on the other hand, it comes from God, you will not be able to destroy them without fighting God himself."

This speech persuaded them. In spite of it, however, the Sanhedrin called in the apostles and had them whipped. They ordered them not to speak again about the name of Jesus, and afterward dismissed them. The apostles for their part left the Sanhedrin full of joy that they had been judged worthy of ill-treatment for the sake of the Name. Day after day, both in the temple and at home, they never stopped teaching and proclaiming the good news of Jesus the Messiah.

This is the Word of the Lord.

Responsorial Psalm   Ps 27, 1. 4. 13-14

℟. (4) One thing I seek:
to dwell in the house of the Lord.
The Lord is my light and my salvation;
whom should I fear?
The Lord is my life's refuge;
of whom should I be afraid?

℟. One thing I seek:
to dwell in the house of the Lord.

One thing I ask of the Lord;
this I seek:
To dwell in the house of the Lord
all the days of my life,
That I may gaze on the loveliness of the Lord
and contemplate his temple.

℟. One thing I seek:
to dwell in the house of the Lord.

I believe that I shall see the bounty of the Lord
in the land of the living.
Wait for the Lord with courage;
be stouthearted, and wait for the Lord.

℟. One thing I seek:
to dwell in the house of the Lord.

℟. Or: Alleluia.

GOSPEL   Jn 6, 1-15
Alleluia
See no. 303.

✠ A reading from the holy gospel according to John

He gave the food to those who were sitting around, as much as they wanted.

Jesus crossed the Sea of Galilee [to the shore] of Tiberias; a vast crowd kept following him because they saw the signs he was performing for the sick. Jesus then went up the mountain and sat down there with his disciples. The Jewish feast of Passover was near; when Jesus looked up and caught sight of a vast crowd coming toward him, he said to Philip, "Where shall we buy bread for these people to eat?" (He knew well what he intended to do but he asked this to test Philip's response.) Philip replied, "Not even with two hundred days' wages could we buy loaves enough to give each of them a mouthful."

One of Jesus' disciples, Andrew, Simon Peter's brother, remarked to him, "There is a lad here who has five barley loaves and a couple of dried fish, but what good is that for so many?" Jesus said, "Get the people to recline." Even though the men numbered about five thousand, there was plenty of grass for them to find a place on the ground. Jesus then took the loaves of bread, gave thanks, and passed them around to those reclining there; he did the same with the dried fish, as much as they wanted. When they had had enough, he told his disciples, "Gather up the crusts that are left over so that nothing will go to waste." At this, they gathered twelve baskets full of pieces left over by those who had been fed with the five barley loaves.

When the people saw the sign he had performed they began to say, "This is undoubtedly the Prophet who is to come into the world." At that, Jesus realized that they would come and carry him off to make him king, so he fled back to the mountain alone.

This is the gospel of the Lord.

272   **SATURDAY OF THE SECOND WEEK OF EASTER**

READING I   Acts 6, 1-7

A reading from the Acts of the Apostles

They chose seven men who were filled with the Holy Spirit.

In those days as the number of disciples grew, the ones who spoke Greek complained that their widows were being neglected in the daily distribution of food, as compared with the widows of those who spoke Hebrew. The Twelve assembled the community of the disciples and said, "It is not right for us to neglect the word of God in order to wait on the tables. Look around among your own number, brothers, for seven men acknowledged to be deeply spiritual and prudent, and we shall appoint them to this task. This will permit us to concentrate on prayer and the ministry of the word." The proposal was unanimously accepted by the community. Following this they selected Stephen, a man filled with faith and the Holy Spirit; Philip, Prochorus, Nicanor, Timon, Parmenas and Nicolaus of Antioch, who had been a convert to Judaism. They presented these men to the apostles, who first prayed over them and then imposed hands on them.

The word of God continued to spread, while at the same time the number of the disciples in Jerusalem enormously increased. There were many priests among those who embraced the faith.

This is the Word of the Lord.

Responsorial Psalm   Ps 33, 1-2. 4-5. 18-19

℟. (22) Lord, let your mercy be on us,
    as we place our trust in you.

Exult, you just, in the Lord;
    praise from the upright is fitting.
Give thanks to the Lord on the harp;
    with the ten-stringed lyre chant his praises.
℟. Lord, let your mercy be on us,
    as we place our trust in you.

Upright is the word of the Lord,
    and all his works are trustworthy.
He loves justice and right;
    of the kindness of the Lord the earth is full.
℟. Lord, let your mercy be on us,
    as we place our trust in you.

See, the eyes of the Lord are upon those who
        fear him,
    upon those who hope for his kindness,
To deliver them from death
    and preserve them in spite of famine.

℟. Lord, let your mercy be on us,
    as we place our trust in you.
℟. Or: Alleluia.

GOSPEL   Jn 6, 16-21
Alleluia

See no. 303.

✠ A reading from the holy gospel according
        to John

They saw Jesus, walking upon the water.

As evening drew on, the disciples of Jesus came down to the lake. They embarked, intending to cross the lake toward Capernaum. By this time it was dark, and Jesus had still not joined them; moreover, with a strong wind blowing, the sea was becoming rough. Finally, when they had rowed three or four miles, they sighted Jesus approaching the boat, walking on the water. They were frightened, but he told them, "It is I; do not be afraid." They wanted to take him into the boat, but suddenly it came aground on the shore they had been approaching.

This is the gospel of the Lord.

---

273   **MONDAY OF THE THIRD
            WEEK OF EASTER**

READING I   Acts 6, 8-15

A reading from the Acts of the Apostles

They could not withstand the wisdom and the Spirit with
        which he spoke.

Stephen, filled with grace and power, worked great wonders and signs among the people. Certain members of the so-called "Synagogue of Roman Freedmen" (that is, the Jews from Cyrene, Alexandria, Cilicia and Asia) would undertake to engage Stephen in debate, but they proved no match for the wisdom and spirit with which he spoke. They persuaded some men to make the charge that they had heard him speaking blasphemies against Moses and God, and in this way they incited the people, the elders, and the scribes. All together they confronted him, seized him, and led him off to the Sanhedrin. There they brought in false witnesses, who said: "This man never stops making statements against the holy place and the law. We have heard him claim that Jesus the Nazorean will destroy this place and change the customs which Moses handed down to us." The members of the Sanhedrin who sat there stared at him intently. Throughout, Stephen's face seemed like that of an angel.

This is the Word of the Lord.

Responsorial Psalm   Ps 119, 23-24. 26-27. 29-30

℟. (1) Happy are those of blameless life.
Though princes meet and talk against me,
   your servant meditates on your statutes.
Yes, your decrees are my delight;
   they are my counselors.
℟. Happy are those of blameless life.
I declared my ways, and you answered me;
   teach me your statutes.
Make me understand the way of your precepts,
   and I will meditate on your wondrous deeds.
℟. Happy are those of blameless life.
Remove from me the way of falsehood,
   and favor me with your law.
The way of truth I have chosen;
   I have set your ordinances before me.
℟. Happy are those of blameless life.
℟. Or: Alleluia.

GOSPEL   Jn 6, 22-29
Alleluia

See no. 303.

✠ A reading from the holy gospel according to John
Do not work for food which cannot last, but for food which endures to eternal life.

The crowd remained on the other side of the lake. The next day they realized that there had been only one boat there and that Jesus had not left in it with his disciples; rather, they had set out by themselves. Then some boats came out from Tiberias near the place where they had eaten the bread after the Lord had given thanks. Once the crowd saw that neither Jesus

nor his disciples were there, they too embarked in the boats and went to Capernaum looking for Jesus.

When they found him on the other side of the lake, they said to him, "Rabbi, when did you come here?" Jesus answered them:
   "I assure you,
   you are not looking for me because you
      have seen signs
   but because you have eaten your fill of the
      loaves.
   You should not be working for perishable
      food
   but for food that remains unto life eternal,
   food which the Son of Man will give you;
   it is on him that God the Father has set his
      seal."
At this they said to him, "What must we do to perform the works of God?" Jesus replied:
   "This is the work of God:
   have faith in the One whom he sent."
     This is the gospel of the Lord.

---

274   **TUESDAY OF THE THIRD
WEEK OF EASTER**

READING I   Acts 7, 51–8, 1
A reading from the Acts of the Apostles
Jesus, Lord, receive my spirit.

Stephen said to the people and elders and scribes: "You stiff-necked people, uncircumcised in heart and ears, you are always opposing the Holy Spirit just as your fathers did before you. Was there ever any prophet whom your fathers did not persecute? In their day, they put to death those who foretold the coming of the Just One; now you in your turn have become his betrayers and murderers. You who received the law through the ministry of angels have not observed it."

Those who listened to his words were stung to the heart; they ground their teeth in anger at him. Stephen meanwhile, filled with the Holy Spirit, looked to the sky above and saw the glory of God, and Jesus standing at God's right hand. "Look!" he exclaimed, "I see an opening in the sky, and the Son of Man standing at God's right hand." The onlookers were shouting aloud, holding their hands over their ears as they did so. Then they rushed at him as one man, dragged him out of the city, and began to stone him. The witnesses meanwhile were piling their cloaks at the feet of a young man named Saul. As Stephen was being stoned he could be heard praying, "Lord Jesus, receive my spirit." He fell to his knees and cried out in a loud voice, "Lord, do not hold this sin against them." And with that he died.

Saul, for his part, concurred in the act of killing.

This is the word of the Lord.

Responsorial Psalm   Ps 31, 3-4. 6. 7. 8. 17. 21

℟. (6) Into your hands, O Lord,
I entrust my spirit.
Be my rock of refuge,
a stronghold to give me safety.
You are my rock and my fortress;
for your name's sake you will lead and guide me.
℟. Into your hands, O Lord,
I entrust my spirit.
Into your hands I commend my spirit;
you will redeem me, O Lord, O faithful God.
My trust is in the Lord;
I will rejoice and be glad of your kindness.
℟. Into your hands, O Lord,
I entrust my spirit.
Let your face shine upon your servant;
save me in your kindness.
You hide them in the shelter of your presence
from the plottings of men.
℟. Into your hands, O Lord,
I entrust my spirit.
℟. Or: Alleluia.

GOSPEL   Jn 6, 30-35
Alleluia

See no. 303.

✠ **A reading from the holy gospel according to John**
It was not Moses, but my Father who gave you bread from heaven.

The crowd said to Jesus: "What sign are you going to perform for us to see so that we can put faith in you? What is the 'work' you do? Our ancestors had manna to eat in the desert; according to Scripture, 'He gave them bread from the heavens to eat.' " Jesus said to them:
"I solemnly assure you,
it was not Moses who gave you bread
from the heavens;
it is my Father who gives you the real
heavenly bread.
God's bread
comes down from heaven
and gives life to the world."
"Sir, give us this bread always," they besought him.
Jesus explained to them:
"I myself am the bread of life.
No one who comes to me shall ever be hungry,
no one who believes in me shall thirst again."
This is the gospel of the Lord.

---

275   WEDNESDAY OF THE THIRD WEEK OF EASTER

READING I   Acts 8, 1-8

A reading from the Acts of the Apostles
They went from place to place preaching the Good News.
A certain day saw the beginning of a great persecution of the church in Jerusalem. All except the apostles scattered throughout the countryside of Judea and Samaria. Devout men buried Stephen, bewailing him loudly as they did so. After that, Saul began to harass the church. He entered house after house, dragged men and women out, and threw them into jail.

The members of the church who had been dispersed went about preaching the word. Philip, for example, went down to the town of Samaria and there proclaimed the Messiah. Without exception, the crowds that heard Philip and saw the miracles he performed attended closely to what he had to say. There were many who had unclean spirits, which came out shrieking loudly. Many others were paralytics or cripples, and these were cured. The rejoicing in that town rose to fever pitch. **This is the Word of the Lord.**

Responsorial Psalm   Ps 66, 1-3. 4-5. 6-7

℞. (1) Let all the earth cry out to God with joy.
Shout joyfully to God, all you on earth,
   sing praise to the glory of his name;
   proclaim his glorious praise.
Say to God, "How tremendous are your
   deeds!
℞. Let all the earth cry out to God with joy.
Let all on earth worship and sing praise to you,
   sing praise to your name!"
Come and see the works of God,
   his tremendous deeds among men.
℞. Let all the earth cry out to God with joy.
He has changed the sea into dry land;
   through the river they passed on foot;
   therefore let us rejoice in him.
He rules by his might forever.
℞. Let all the earth cry out to God with joy.
℞. Or: Alleluia.

GOSPEL   Jn 6, 35-40
Alleluia

See no. 303.

✠ **A reading from the holy gospel according to John**

This is the will of my Father, that whoever sees the Son will have eternal life.

Jesus explained to the crowd:
   "I myself am the bread of life.
   No one who comes to me shall ever be
   hungry,
   no one who believes in me shall thirst
   again.
   But as I told you—
   though you have seen me, you still do not
   believe.
   All that the Father gives me shall come to
   me;
   no one who comes will I ever reject,
   because it is not to do my own will
   that I have come down from heaven,
   but to do the will of him who sent me.

   It is the will of him who sent me
   that I should lose nothing of what he has
   given me;
   rather, that I should raise it up on the last
   day.
   Indeed, this is the will of my Father,
   that everyone who looks upon the Son
   and believes in him
   shall have eternal life.
   Him I will raise up on the last day."
   This is the gospel of the Lord.

276   THURSDAY OF THE THIRD
WEEK OF EASTER

READING I   Acts 8, 26-40
A reading from the Acts of the Apostles

If you believe with your whole heart, then you may be baptized.

An angel of the Lord addressed himself to Philip: "Head south toward the road which goes from Jerusalem to Gaza, the desert route." Philip began the journey. It happened that an Ethiopian eunuch, a court official in charge of the entire treasury of Candace (a name meaning queen) of the Ethiopians, had come on a pilgrimage to Jerusalem and was returning home. He was sitting in his carriage reading the prophet Isaiah. The Spirit said to Philip, "Go and catch up with that carriage." Philip ran ahead and heard the man reading the prophet Isaiah. He said to him, "Do you really grasp what you are reading?" "How can I," the man replied, "unless someone explains it to me?" With that, he invited Philip to get in and sit down beside him. This was the passage of Scripture he was reading:
"Like a sheep he was led to the slaughter,
   like a lamb before its shearer he was silent
   and opened not his mouth.
In his humiliation he was deprived of justice.
   Who will ever speak of his posterity,
   for he is deprived of his life on earth?"
The eunuch said to Philip, "Tell me, if you will, of whom the prophet says this—himself or someone else?" Philip launched out with this Scripture passage as his starting point, telling

him the good news of Jesus. As they moved along the road they came to some water, and the eunuch said, "Look, there is some water right there. What is to keep me from being baptized?" He ordered the carriage stopped, and Philip went down into the water with the eunuch and baptized him. When they came out of the water, the Spirit of the Lord snatched Philip away and the eunuch saw him no more. Nevertheless the man went on his way rejoicing. Philip found himself at Azotus next, and he went about announcing the good news in all the towns until he reached Caesarea.

This is the Word of the Lord.

Responsorial Psalm   Ps 66, 8-9. 16-17. 20

R̸. (1) Let all the earth cry out to God with joy.
Bless our God, you peoples,
    loudly sound his praise;
He has given life to our souls,
    and has not let our feet slip.
R̸. Let all the earth cry out to God with joy.
Hear now, all you who fear God, while I declare
    what he has done for me.
When I appealed to him in words,
    praise was on the tip of my tongue.
R̸. Let all the earth cry out to God with joy.
Blessed be God who refused me not
    my prayer or his kindness!
R̸. Let all the earth cry out to God with joy.
R̸. Or: Alleluia.

GOSPEL   Jn 6, 44-51
Alleluia

See no. 303.

✠ A reading from the holy gospel according to John

I am the living bread which comes down from heaven.

Jesus said to the crowds:
    "No one can come to me
    unless the Father who sent me draws him;
    I will raise him up on the last day.
    It is written in the prophets:
    'They shall all be taught by God.'
    Everyone who has heard the Father

and learned from him
comes to me.
Not that anyone has seen the Father—
only the one who is from God
has seen the Father.
Let me firmly assure you,
he who believes has eternal life.
I am the bread of life.
Your ancestors ate manna in the desert,
    but they died.
This is the bread that comes down from
    heaven,
for a man to eat and never die.
I myself am the living bread
come down from heaven.
If anyone eats this bread
he shall live forever;
the bread I will give
is my flesh, for the life of the world."
    This is the gospel of the Lord.

277   **FRIDAY OF THE THIRD**
    WEEK OF EASTER

READING I   Acts 9, 1-20

A reading from the Acts of the Apostles

This man is my chosen instrument to bring my name before the gentiles.

Saul, breathing murderous threats against the Lord's disciples, went to the high priest and asked him for letters to the synagogues in Damascus which would empower him to arrest and bring to Jerusalem anyone he might find, man or woman, living according to the new way. As he traveled along and was approaching Damascus, a light from the sky suddenly flashed about him. He fell to the ground and at the same time heard a voice saying, "Saul, Saul, why do you persecute me?" "Who are you, sir?" he asked. The voice answered, "I am Jesus, the one you are persecuting. Get up and go into the city, where you will be told what to do." The men who were traveling with him stood there speechless. They had heard the voice but could see no one. Saul got up from the ground unable to see, even though his eyes were open. They had to take him by the hand and lead him into Damascus. For three days he continued blind, during which time he neither ate nor drank.

There was a disciple in Damascus named Ananias to whom the Lord had appeared in a vision. "Ananias!" he said. "Here I am, Lord," came the answer. The Lord said to him, "Go at once to Straight Street, and at the house of Judas ask for a certain Saul of Tarsus. He is there praying." (Saul saw in a vision a man named Ananias coming to him and placing his hands on him so that he might recover his sight.) But Ananias protested: "Lord, I have heard from many sources about this man and all the harm he has done to your holy people in Jerusalem. He is here now with authorization from the chief priests to arrest any who invoke your name." The Lord said to him: "You must go! This man is the instrument I have chosen to bring my name to the Gentiles and their kings and to the people of Israel. I myself shall indicate to him how much he will have to suffer for my name." With that Ananias left. When he entered the house he laid his hands on Saul and said, "Saul, my brother, I have been sent by the Lord Jesus who appeared to you on the way here, to help you recover your sight and be filled with the Holy Spirit." Immediately something like scales fell from his eyes and he regained his sight. He got up and was baptized, and his strength returned to him after he had taken food.

Saul stayed some time with the disciples in Damascus, and soon began to proclaim in the synagogues that Jesus was the Son of God.
This is the Word of the Lord.

Responsorial Psalm   Ps 117, 1. 2

R̶. (Mk 16, 15) Go out to all the world,
    and tell the Good News.
Praise the Lord, all you nations;
    glorify him, all you peoples!
R̶. Go out to all the world,
    and tell the Good News.
For steadfast is his kindness toward us,
    and the fidelity of the Lord endures forever.
R̶. Go out to all the world,
    and tell the Good News.
R̶. Or: Alleluia.

GOSPEL   Jn 6, 52-59
Alleluia

See no. 303.

✠ A reading from the holy gospel according
to John

My flesh is real food and my blood is real drink.

The Jews quarreled among themselves, saying, "How can this man give us his flesh to eat?" Thereupon Jesus said to them:
"Let me solemnly assure you,
    if you do not eat the flesh of the Son of
      Man
    and drink his blood,
    you have no life in you.
He who feeds on my flesh
    and drinks my blood
    has life eternal,
and I will raise him up on the last day.
For my flesh is real food
    and my blood real drink.
The man who feeds on my flesh
    and drinks my blood
    remains in me, and I in him.
Just as the Father who has life sent me
    and I have life because of the Father,
so the man who feeds on me
    will have life because of me.
This is the bread that came down from
    heaven.
Unlike your ancestors who ate and died
    nonetheless,
the man who feeds on this bread shall live
    forever."
He said this in a synagogue instruction at Capernaum.
This is the gospel of the Lord.

---

278   **SATURDAY OF THE THIRD
WEEK OF EASTER**

READING I   Acts 9, 31-42

A reading from the Acts of the Apostles

The Church became established and in the presence of the Holy Spirit grew in numbers.

Throughout all Judea, Galilee and Samaria the church was at peace. It was being built up and was making steady progress in the fear of the Lord; at the same time it enjoyed the increased consolation of the Holy Spirit.

Once when Peter was making numerous journeys, he went—among other places—to God's holy people living in Lydda. There he found a man named Aeneas, a paralytic who had been bedridden for eight years. Peter said to him, "Aeneas, Jesus Christ cures you! Get up and make your bed." The man got up at once. All the inhabitants of Lydda and Sharon, upon seeing him, were converted to the Lord.

Now in Joppa there was a certain woman convert named Tabitha (in Greek Dorcas, meaning a gazelle). Her life was marked by constant good deeds and acts of charity. At about that time she fell ill and died. They washed her body and laid it out in an upstairs room. Since Lydda was near Joppa, the disciples who had heard that Peter was there sent two men to him with the urgent request, "Please come over to us without delay." Peter set out with them as they asked. Upon his arrival they took him upstairs to the room. All the widows came to him in tears and showed him the various garments Dorcas had made when she was still with them. Peter first made everyone go outside; then he knelt down and prayed. Turning to the dead body, he said, "Tabitha, stand up." She opened her eyes, then looked at Peter and sat up. He gave her his hand and helped her to her feet. The next thing he did was to call in those who were believers and the widows to show them that she was alive. This became known all over Joppa, and because of it, many came to believe in the Lord.
This is the Word of the Lord.

Responsorial Psalm   Ps 116, 12-13. 14-15. 16-17

℟. (12) What return can I make to the Lord
for all that he gives to me?
How shall I make a return to the Lord
for all the good he has done for me?
The cup of salvation I will take up,
and I will call upon the name of the Lord.
℟. What return can I make to the Lord
for all that he gives to me?

My vows to the Lord I will pay
in the presence of all his people.
Precious in the eyes of the Lord
is the death of his faithful ones.
℟. What return can I make to the Lord
for all that he gives to me?
O Lord, I am your servant;
I am your servant, the son of your handmaid;
you have loosed my bonds.
To you will I offer sacrifice of thanksgiving,
and I will call upon the name of the Lord.
℟. What return can I make to the Lord
for all that he gives to me?
℟. Or: Alleluia.

GOSPEL   Jn 6, 60-69
Alleluia
See no. 303.

✠ A reading from the holy gospel according
to John
To whom shall we go? You have the words of eternal life.

Many of the disciples of Jesus remarked, "This sort of talk is hard to endure! How can anyone take it seriously?" Jesus was fully aware that his disciples were murmuring in protest at what he had said. "Does it shake your faith?" he asked them.
"What, then, if you were to see the Son of Man
ascend to where he was before . . . ?
It is the spirit that gives life;
the flesh is useless.
The words I spoke to you
are spirit and life.
Yet among you there are some who do not believe."
(Jesus knew from the start, of course, the ones who refused to believe, and the one who would hand him over.) He went on to say:
"This is why I have told you
that no one can come to me
unless it is granted him by the Father."
From this time on, many of his disciples broke away and would not remain in his company any longer. Jesus then said to the Twelve, "Do you want to leave me too?" Simon Peter answered him, "Lord, to whom shall we go? You

have the words of eternal life. We have come to believe; we are convinced that you are God's holy one."

This is the gospel of the Lord.

---

279   **MONDAY OF THE FOURTH WEEK OF EASTER**

READING I   Acts 11, 1-18

A reading from the Acts of the Apostles

God can give even the gentiles the repentance that leads to eternal life.

The apostles and the brothers heard that Gentiles, too, had accepted the word of God. As a result, when Peter went up to Jerusalem some among the circumcised took issue with him, saying, "You entered the house of uncircumcised men and ate with them." Peter then explained the whole affair to them step by step from the beginning: "I was at prayer in the city of Joppa when, in a trance, I saw a vision. An object like a big canvas came down; it was lowered down to me from the sky by its four corners. As I stared at it I could make out four-legged creatures of the earth, wild beasts and reptiles, and birds of the sky. I listened as a voice said to me, 'Get up, Peter! Slaughter, then eat.' I replied: 'Not for a moment, sir! Nothing unclean or impure has ever entered my mouth!' A second time the voice from the heavens spoke out: 'What God has purified you are not to call unclean.' This happened three times; then the canvas with everything in it was drawn up again into the sky.

"Immediately after that, the three men who had been sent to me from Caesarea came to the house where we were staying. The Spirit instructed me to accompany them without hesitation. These six brothers came along with me, and we entered the man's house. He informed us that he had seen an angel standing in his house and that the angel had said: 'Send someone to Joppa and fetch Simon, known also as Peter. In the light of what he will tell you, you shall be saved, and all your household.' As I began to address them the Holy Spirit came upon them, just as it had upon us at the beginning.

Then I remembered what the Lord had said: ' John baptized with water but you will be baptized with the Holy Spirit.' If God was giving them the same gift he gave us when we first believed in the Lord Jesus Christ, who was I to interfere with him?" When they heard this they stopped objecting, and instead began to glorify God in these words: "If this be so, then God has granted life-giving repentance even to the Gentiles."

This is the Word of the Lord.

Responsorial Psalm   Pss 42, 2-3; 43, 3. 4

℟. (Ps 41, 3) My soul is thirsting for the living God.

As the hind longs for the running waters,
    so my soul longs for you, O God.
Athirst is my soul for God, the living God.
    When shall I go and behold the face of God?
℟. My soul is thirsting for the living God.
Send forth your light and your fidelity;
    they shall lead me on
And bring me to your holy mountain,
    to your dwelling-place.
℟. My soul is thirsting for the living God.
Then will I go in to the altar of God,
    the God of my gladness and joy;
Then will I give you thanks upon the harp,
    O God, my God!
℟. My soul is thirsting for the living God.
℟. Or: Alleluia.

GOSPEL   Jn 10, 1-10
Alleluia

See no. 303.

✠ A reading from the holy gospel according to John

I am the gate of the sheepfold.

Jesus said:
    "Truly I assure you:
    Whoever does not enter the sheepfold
        through the gate
    but climbs in some other way
    is a thief and a marauder.
    The one who enters through the gate
    is shepherd of the sheep;

the keeper opens the gate for him.
The sheep hear his voice
as he calls his own by name
and leads them out.
When he has brought out [all] those that
     are his,
he walks in front of them,
and the sheep follow him
because they recognize his voice.
They will not follow a stranger;
such a one they will flee,
because they do not recognize a stranger's
     voice."

Even though Jesus used this figure with them,
they did not grasp what he was trying to tell
them. He therefore said [to them again]:
     "My solemn word is this:
I am the sheepgate.
All who came before me
were thieves and marauders
whom the sheep did not heed.

"I am the gate.
Whoever enters through me
will be safe.
He will go in and out,
and find pasture.
The thief comes
only to steal and slaughter and destroy.
I came
that they might have life
and have it to the full."
     This is the gospel of the Lord.

OR

In year A, when this gospel is read on the preceding Sunday,
the following text (Jn 10, 11-18) is used:

The good shepherd lays down his life for the sheep.

Jesus said:
     "I am the good shepherd;
the good shepherd lays down his life for
     the sheep.
The hired hand who is no shepherd
nor owner of the sheep
catches sight of the wolf coming
and runs away, leaving the sheep
to be snatched and scattered by the wolf.
That is because he works for pay;
he has no concern for the sheep.

"I am the good shepherd;
I know my sheep
and my sheep know me
in the same way that the Father knows me
and I know the Father;
for these sheep I will give my life.
I have other sheep
that do not belong to this fold.
I must lead them, too,
and they shall hear my voice.
There shall be one flock then, one shep-
     herd.
The Father loves me for this:
that I lay down my life
to take it up again.
No one takes it from me;
I lay it down freely.
I have power to lay it down,
and I have power to take it up again.
This command I received from my Fa-
     ther."
     This is the gospel of the Lord.

280   TUESDAY OF THE FOURTH
WEEK OF EASTER

READING I   Acts 11, 19-26

A reading from the Acts of the Apostles

They preached to the Greeks proclaiming the Lord Jesus.

Those in the community who had been dispersed by the persecution that arose because of
Stephen went as far as Phoenicia, Cyprus and
Antioch, making the message known to none
but Jews. However, some men of Cyprus and
Cyrene among them who had come to Antioch
began to talk even to the Greeks, announcing
the good news of the Lord Jesus to them. The
hand of the Lord was with them and a great
number of them believed and were converted
to the Lord. News of this eventually reached
the ears of the church in Jerusalem, resulting
in Barnabas' being sent to Antioch. On his arrival he rejoiced to see the evidence of God's
favor. He encouraged them all to remain firm
in their commitment to the Lord, since he
himself was a good man filled with the Holy

Spirit and faith. Thereby large numbers were added to the Lord. Then Barnabas went off to Tarsus to look for Saul; once he had found him, he brought him back to Antioch. For a whole year they met with the church and instructed great numbers. It was in Antioch that the disciples were called Christians for the first time. This is the Word of the Lord.

Responsorial Psalm　　　　　　　　Ps 87, 1-3. 4-5. 6-7

℟. (Ps 117, 1) All you nations, praise the Lord.
His foundation upon the holy mountains
　the Lord loves:
The gates of Zion,
　more than any dwelling of Jacob.
Glorious things are said of you,
　O city of God!

℟. All you nations, praise the Lord.
I tell of Egypt and Babylon
　among those that know the Lord;
Of Philistia, Tyre, Ethiopia:
　"This man was born there."
And of Zion they shall say:
　"One and all were born in her;
And he who has established her
　is the Most High Lord."

℟. All you nations, praise the Lord.
They shall note, when the peoples are enrolled:
　"This man was born there."
And all shall sing, in their festive dance:
　"My home is within you."

℟. All you nations, praise the Lord.
℟. Or: Alleluia.

GOSPEL　　　　　　　　　　　　　Jn 10, 22-30
Alleluia

See no. 303.

✠ A reading from the holy gospel according
　to John

My Father and I are one.

It was winter, and the time came for the feast of the Dedication in Jerusalem. Jesus was walking in the temple area, in Solomon's Portico, when the Jews gathered around him and said, "How long are you going to keep us

in suspense? If you really are the Messiah, tell us so in plain words." Jesus answered:
　"I did tell you, but you do not believe.
　The works I do in my Father's name
　give witness in my favor,
　but you refuse to believe
　because you are not my sheep.
　My sheep hear my voice.
　I know them,
　and they follow me.
　I give them eternal life,
　and they shall never perish.
　No one shall snatch them out of my hand.
　My Father is greater than all, in what he
　　has given me,
　and there is no snatching out of his hand.
　The Father and I are one."
This is the gospel of the Lord.

281　**WEDNESDAY OF THE FOURTH
　　　　WEEK OF EASTER**

READING I　　　　　　　　　　Acts 12, 24—13, 5
　A reading from the Acts of the Apostles

I want Saul and Barnabas set aside.

The word of the Lord continued to spread and increase.

Barnabas and Saul returned to Jerusalem upon completing the relief mission, taking with them John Mark.

There were in the church at Antioch certain prophets and teachers: Barnabas, Symeon known as Niger, Lucius of Cyrene, Manaen (who had been brought up with Herod the tetrarch), and Saul. On one occasion, while they were engaged in the liturgy of the Lord and were fasting, the Holy Spirit spoke to them: "Set apart Barnabas and Saul for me to do the work for which I have called them." Then, after they had fasted and prayed, they imposed hands on them and sent them off.

These two, sent forth by the Holy Spirit, went down to the port of Seleucia and set sail from there for Cyprus. On their arrival in Salamis they proclaimed the word of God in the Jewish synagogues.

This is the Word of the Lord.

Responsorial Psalm   Ps 67, 2-3. 5. 6. 8

℟. (4) O God, let all the nations praise you!
May God have pity on us and bless us;
   may he let his face shine upon us.
So may your way be known upon earth;
   among all nations, your salvation.
℟. O God, let all the nations praise you!
May the nations be glad and exult
   because you rule the peoples in equity;
   the nations on the earth you guide.
℟. O God, let all the nations praise you!
May the peoples praise you, O God;
   may all the peoples praise you!
May God bless us,
   and may all the ends of the earth fear him!
℟. O God, let all the nations praise you!
℟. Or: Alleluia.

GOSPEL   Jn 12, 44-50
Alleluia

See no. 303.

✠ A reading from the holy gospel according
to John
I the light have come into the world.

Jesus proclaimed aloud:
"Whoever puts faith in me
believes not so much in me
as in him who sent me;
and whoever looks on me
is seeing him who sent me.
I have come to the world as its light,
to keep anyone who believes in me
from remaining in the dark.
If anyone hears my words and does not
   keep them,
I am not the one to condemn him,
for I did not come to condemn the world
but to save it.
Whoever rejects me and does not accept
   my words
already has his judge,
namely, the word I have spoken—
it is that which will condemn him on the
   last day.
For I have not spoken on my own;

no, the Father who sent me
has commanded me
what to say and how to speak.
Since I know that his commandment means
   eternal life,
whatever I say
is spoken just as he instructed me."
   This is the gospel of the Lord.

**282   THURSDAY OF THE FOURTH
WEEK OF EASTER**

READING I   Acts 13, 13-25

A reading from the Acts of the Apostles
God has raised up one of David's descendants, Jesus, as
Savior.

From Paphos, Paul and his companions put out
to sea and sailed to Perga in Pamphylia. There
John left them and returned to Jerusalem. They
continued to travel on from Perga and came to
Antioch in Pisidia. On the sabbath day they entered the synagogue and sat down. After the
reading of the law and of the prophets, the
leading men of the synagogue sent this message to them: "Brothers, if you have any exhortation to address to the people please speak
up."
   So Paul arose, motioned to them for silence,
and began: "Fellow Israelites and you others
who reverence our God, listen to what I have to
say! The God of the people Israel once chose
our fathers. He made this people great during
their sojourn in the land of Egypt, and 'with an
outstretched arm' he led them out of it. For
forty years 'he put up with them in the desert';
then he destroyed 'seven nations' in the land of
Canaan to give them that country as their heritage at the end of some four hundred and fifty
years. Later on he set up judges to rule them
until the time of the prophet Samuel. When
they asked for a king, God gave them Saul son
of Kish, of the tribe of Benjamin, who ruled for
forty years. Then God removed him and raised
up David as their king; on his behalf God testified, 'I have found David son of Jesse to be a
man after my own heart who will fulfill my
every wish.'
   "According to his promise, God has brought
forth from this man's descendants Jesus, a

savior for Israel. John heralded the coming of Jesus by proclaiming a baptism of repentance to all the people of Israel. As John's career was coming to an end, he would say, 'What you suppose me to be I am not. Rather, look for the one who comes after me. I am not worthy to unfasten the sandals on his feet.' "

This is the Word of the Lord.

Responsorial Psalm   Ps 89, 2-3. 21-22. 25. 27

℞. (2) For ever I will sing the goodness of the Lord.

The favors of the Lord I will sing forever;
    through all generations my mouth shall proclaim your faithfulness.
For you have said, "My kindness is established forever";
    in heaven you have confirmed your faithfulness.

℞. For ever I will sing the goodness of the Lord.

I have found David, my servant;
    with my holy oil I have anointed him,
That my hand may be always with him,
    and that my arm may make him strong.

℞. For ever I will sing the goodness of the Lord.

My faithfulness and my kindness shall be with him,
    and through my name shall his horn be exalted.
"He shall say of me, 'You are my father,
    my God, the Rock, my savior.' "

℞. For ever I will sing the goodness of the Lord.

℞. Or: Alleluia.

GOSPEL   Jn 13, 16-20
Alleluia

See no. 303.

✠ A reading from the holy gospel according to John

Whoever receives the one I send, receives me.

[After Jesus had washed the feet of the disciples he said:]

"I solemnly assure you,
    no slave is greater than his master;

no messenger outranks the one who sent him.
Once you know all these things,
blest will you be if you put them into practice.
What I say is not said of all,
for I know the kind of men I chose.
My purpose here is the fulfillment of Scripture:
'He who partook of bread with me
has raised his heel against me.'
I tell you this now, before it takes place,
so that when it takes place you may believe
that I AM.
I solemnly assure you,
he who accepts anyone I send
accepts me,
and in accepting me
accepts him who sent me."

This is the gospel of the Lord.

---

283   FRIDAY OF THE FOURTH WEEK OF EASTER

READING I   Acts 13, 26-33

A reading from the Acts of the Apostles

God has fulfilled his promise by raising Jesus from the dead.

[When Paul came to Antioch in Pisidia, he said in the synagogue:] "My brothers, children of the family of Abraham and you others who reverence our God, it was to us that this message of salvation was sent forth. The inhabitants of Jerusalem and their rulers failed to recognize him, and in condemning him they fulfilled the words of the prophets which we read sabbath after sabbath. Even though they found no charge against him which deserved death, they begged Pilate to have him executed. Once they had thus brought about all that had been written of him, they took him down from the tree and laid him in a tomb. Yet God raised him from the dead, and for many days thereafter Jesus appeared to those who had come up with him from Galilee to Jerusalem. These are his witnesses now before the people.

"We ourselves announce to you the good news that what God promised our fathers he has fulfilled for us, their children, in raising up Jesus, according to what is written in the second psalm, 'You are my son; this day I have begotten you.' "

This is the Word of the Lord.

Responsorial Psalm   Ps 2, 6-7. 8-9. 10-11

℟. (7) You are my Son;
  this day have I begotten you.

"I myself have set up my king
  on Zion, my holy mountain."
I will proclaim the decree of the Lord:
  The Lord said to me, "You are my son;
  this day I have begotten you."

℟. You are my Son;
  this day have I begotten you.

"Ask of me and I will give you
  the nations for an inheritance
  and the ends of the earth for your possession.
You shall rule them with an iron rod;
  you shall shatter them like an earthen dish."

℟. You are my Son;
  this day have I begotten you.

And now, O kings, give heed;
  take warning, you rulers of the earth.
Serve the Lord with fear, and rejoice before him;
  with trembling pay homage to him.

℟. You are my Son;
  this day have I begotten you.

℟. Or: Alleluia.

GOSPEL   Jn 14, 1-6
Alleluia
See no. 303.

✠ A reading from the holy gospel according to John
I am the way, the truth, and the life.

Jesus said to his disciples,
  "Do not let your hearts be troubled.
  Have faith in God
  and faith in me.
  In my Father's house there are many
  dwelling places;

otherwise, how could I have told you
  that I was going to prepare a place for you?
I am indeed going to prepare a place for you,
  and then I shall come back to take you with me,
  that where I am you also may be.
You know the way that leads where I go."
"Lord," said Thomas, "we do not know where you are going. How can we know the way?" Jesus told him:
  "I am the way, and the truth, and the life;
  no one comes to the Father but through me."

This is the gospel of the Lord.

284   SATURDAY OF THE FOURTH WEEK OF EASTER

READING I   Acts 13, 44-52
A reading from the Acts of the Apostles
Now he must turn to the gentiles.

On another sabbath, almost the entire city gathered to hear the word of God. When the Jews saw the crowds, they became very jealous and countered with violent abuse whatever Paul said. Paul and Barnabas spoke out fearlessly, nonetheless: "The word of God has to be declared to you first of all; but since you reject it and thus convict yourselves as unworthy of everlasting life, we now turn to the Gentiles. For thus were we instructed by the Lord: 'I have made you a light to the nations, a means of salvation to the ends of the earth.' " The Gentiles were delighted when they heard this and responded to the word of the Lord with praise. All who were destined for life everlasting believed in it. Thus the word of the Lord was carried throughout that area.

But some of the Jews stirred up their influential women sympathizers and the leading men of the town, and in that way got a persecution started against Paul and Barnabas. The Jews finally expelled them from their territory. So the two shook the dust from their feet in protest and went on to Iconium. The disciples

could not but be filled with joy and the Holy
Spirit.
　　　This is the Word of the Lord.

Responsorial Psalm　　　　Ps 98, 1. 2-3. 3-4

R̶̸. (3) All the ends of the earth have seen the
　　saving power of God.
Sing to the Lord a new song,
　　for he has done wondrous deeds;
His right hand has won victory for him,
　　his holy arm.
R̶̸. All the ends of the earth have seen the sav-
　　ing power of God.
The Lord has made his salvation known:
　　in the sight of the nations he has revealed his
　　justice.
He has remembered his kindness and his faith-
　　fulness
　　toward the house of Israel.
R̶̸. All the ends of the earth have seen the sav-
　　ing power of God.
All the ends of the earth have seen
　　the salvation by our God.
Sing joyfully to the Lord, all you lands;
　　break into song; sing praise.
R̶̸. All the ends of the earth have seen the sav-
　　ing power of God.
R̶̸. Or: Alleluia.

GOSPEL　　　　　　　　　　Jn 14, 7-14
Alleluia
See no. 303.

✠ **A reading from the holy gospel according**
　　　　to John
He who sees me, also sees the Father.
Jesus said to his disciples,
　　"If you really knew me, you would know
　　　my Father also.
　　From this point on you know him; you
　　　have seen him."
　"Lord," Philip said to him, "show us the Fa-
ther and that will be enough for us." "Philip,"
Jesus replied, "after I have been with you all
this time, you still do not know me?
　"Whoever has seen me has seen the Fa-
ther.

How can you say, 'Show us the Father'?
Do you not believe that I am in the Father
and the Father is in me?
The words I speak are not spoken of my-
　self;
it is the Father who lives in me accom-
　plishing his works.
Believe me that I am in the Father
and the Father is in me, or else, believe be-
　cause of the works I do.
I solemnly assure you,
　the man who has faith in me
will do the works I do,
and greater far than these.
Why? Because I go to the Father,
and whatever you ask in my name
I will do,
so as to glorify the Father in the Son.
Anything you ask me in my name
I will do."
　　　This is the gospel of the Lord.

285　　　**MONDAY OF THE FIFTH**
　　　　　WEEK OF EASTER

READING I　　　　　　　　Acts 14, 5-18
　　A reading from the Acts of the Apostles
We have come with Good News to make you turn from these
　　　　vain things to the living God.
A move was made [in Iconium] by Gentiles and
Jews, together with their leaders, to abuse and
stone Paul and Barnabas. When they learned of
this, they fled to the Lycaonian towns of Lys-
tra and Derbe and to the surrounding country,
where they continued to proclaim the good
news.
　At Lystra there was a man who was lame
from birth; he used to sit crippled, never hav-
ing walked in his life. On one occasion he was
listening to Paul preaching, and Paul looked
directly at him and saw that he had the faith
to be saved. He called out to him in a loud
voice, "Stand up! On your feet!" The man
jumped up and began to walk around. When
the crowds saw what Paul had done, they cried
out in Lycaonian, "Gods have come to us in the
form of men!" They named Barnabas Zeus;
Paul they called Hermes, since he was the

spokesman. Even the priest of the temple of Zeus, which stood outside the town, brought oxen and garlands to the gates because he wished to offer sacrifice to them with the crowds.

When the apostles Barnabas and Paul heard of this, they tore their garments and rushed out into the crowd. "Friends, why do you do this?" they shouted frantically. "We are only men, human like you. We are bringing you the good news that will convert you from just such follies as these to the living God, 'the one who made heaven and earth and the sea and all that is in them.' In past ages he let the Gentiles go their way. Yet in bestowing his benefits, he has not hidden himself completely, without a clue. From the heavens he sends down rain and rich harvests; your spirits he fills with food and delight." Yet even with a speech such as this, they could scarcely stop the crowds from offering sacrifice to them.

This is the Word of the Lord.

Responsorial Psalm   Ps 115, 1-2. 3-4. 15-16

℟. (1) Not to us, O Lord,
   but to your name give the glory.

Not to us, O Lord, not to us
   but to your name give glory
   because of your kindness, because of your
      truth.
Why should the pagans say,
   "Where is their God?"

℟. Not to us, O Lord,
   but to your name give the glory.

Our God is in heaven;
   whatever he wills, he does.
Their idols are silver and gold,
   the handiwork of men.

℟. Not to us, O Lord,
   but to your name give the glory.

May you be blessed by the Lord,
   who made heaven and earth.
Heaven is the heaven of the Lord,
   but the earth he has given to the children of
      men.

℟. Not to us, O Lord,
   but to your name give the glory.

℟. Or: Alleluia.

GOSPEL   Jn 14, 21-26
Alleluia
See no. 303.

✠ **A reading from the holy gospel according
to John**

The Holy Spirit whom the Father will send will teach you
all things.

Jesus said to his disciples:
   "He who obeys the commandments he has
      from me
   is the man who loves me;
   and he who loves me will be loved by my
      Father.
   I too will love him
   and reveal myself to him."
Judas (not Judas Iscariot) said to him, "Lord,
why is it that you will reveal yourself to us and
not to the world?" Jesus answered:
   "Anyone who loves me
   will be true to my word,
   and my Father will love him;
   we will come to him
   and make our dwelling place with him.
   He who does not love me does not keep my
      words.
   Yet the word you hear is not mine;
   it comes from the Father who sent me.
   This much have I told you while I was still
      with you;
   the Paraclete, the Holy Spirit
   whom the Father will send in my name,
   will instruct you in everything,
   and remind you of all that I told you."
   This is the gospel of the Lord.

**286   TUESDAY OF THE FIFTH
WEEK OF EASTER**

READING I   Acts 14, 19-28

A reading from the Acts of the Apostles

They assembled the Church and gave an account of all that
God had done with them.

**In those days some Jews from Antioch and
Iconium arrived and won the people over. They
stoned Paul and dragged him out of the town,**

leaving him there for dead. His disciples quickly formed a circle about him, and before long he got up and went back into the town. The next day he left with Barnabas for Derbe. After they had proclaimed the good news in that town and made numerous disciples, they retraced their steps to Lystra and Iconium first, then to Antioch. They gave their disciples reassurances, and encouraged them to persevere in the faith with this instruction: "We must undergo many trials if we are to enter into the reign of God." In each church they installed elders and, with prayer and fasting, commended them to the Lord in whom they had put their faith.

Then they passed through Pisidia and came to Pamphylia. After preaching the message in Perga, they went down to Attalia. From there they sailed back to Antioch, where they had first been commended to the favor of God for the task they had now completed. On their arrival, they called the congregation together and related all that God had helped them accomplish, and how he had opened the door of faith to the Gentiles. Then they spent some time there with the disciples.

This is the Word of the Lord.

Responsorial Psalm   Ps 145, 10-11. 12-13. 21

℟. (12) Your friends tell the glory of your kingship, Lord.

Let all your works give you thanks, O Lord,
   and let your faithful ones bless you.
Let them discourse of the glory of your kingdom
   and speak of your might.

℟. Your friends tell the glory of your kingship, Lord.

Making known to men your might
   and the glorious splendor of your kingdom.
Your kingdom is a kingdom for all ages,
   and your dominion endures through all generations.

℟. Your friends tell the glory of your kingship, Lord.

May my mouth speak the praise of the Lord,
   and may all flesh bless his holy name
     forever and ever.

℟. Your friends tell the glory of your kingship, Lord.

℟. Or: Alleluia.

GOSPEL   Jn 14, 27-31
Alleluia
See no. 303.

✠ A reading from the holy gospel according to John

My peace I give to you

Jesus said to his disciples:
  "'Peace' is my farewell to you,
    my peace is my gift to you;
  I do not give it to you as the world gives peace.
  Do not be distressed or fearful.
  You have heard me say,
  'I go away for a while and I come back to you.'
  If you truly loved me
  you would rejoice to have me go to the Father,
  for the Father is greater than I.
  I tell you this now, before it takes place,
  so that when it takes place you may believe.
  I shall not go on speaking to you longer;
  the Prince of this world is at hand.
  He has no hold on me,
  but the world must know that I love the Father
  and do as the Father has commanded."
  This is the gospel of the Lord.

---

287   WEDNESDAY OF THE FIFTH WEEK OF EASTER

READING I   Acts 15, 1-6
A reading from the Acts of the Apostles

They arranged to go to the apostles and elders in Jerusalem and consider the problem with them.

Some men came down to Antioch from Judea and began to teach the brothers: "Unless you are circumcised according to Mosaic practice, you cannot be saved." This created dissension and much controversy between them and Paul and Barnabas. Finally it was decided that Paul, Barnabas, and some others should go up to see the apostles and elders in Jerusalem about this question.

The church saw them off and they made their way through Phoenicia and Samaria, telling everyone about the conversion of the Gentiles as they went. Their story caused great joy among the brothers. When they arrived in Jerusalem they were welcomed by that church, as well as by the apostles and the elders, to whom they reported all that God had helped them accomplish. Some of the converted Pharisees then got up and demanded that such Gentiles be circumcised and told to keep the Mosaic law.

The apostles and the elders accordingly convened to look into the matter.
This is the Word of the Lord.

Responsorial Psalm   Ps 122, 1-2. 3-4. 4-5

R̰. (1) I rejoiced when I heard them say:
let us go to the house of the Lord.
I rejoiced because they said to me,
"We will go up to the house of the Lord."
And now we have set foot
within your gates, O Jerusalem.
R̰. I rejoiced when I heard them say:
let us go to the house of the Lord.
Jerusalem, built as a city
with compact unity.
To it the tribes go up,
the tribes of the Lord.
R̰. I rejoiced when I heard them say:
let us go to the house of the Lord.
According to the decree for Israel,
to give thanks to the name of the Lord.
In it are set up judgment seats,
seats for the house of David.
R̰. I rejoiced when I heard them say:
let us go to the house of the Lord.
R̰. Or: Alleluia.

GOSPEL   Jn 15, 1-8
Alleluia

See no. 303.

✠ **A reading from the holy gospel according to John**

Whoever remains in me and I in him, this man bears much fruit.

Jesus said to his disciples:
"I am the true vine
and my Father is the vinegrower.
He prunes away
every barren branch,
but the fruitful ones
he trims clean
to increase their yield.
You are clean already,
thanks to the word I have spoken to you.
Live on in me, as I do in you.
No more than a branch can bear fruit of
itself
apart from the vine,
can you bear fruit
apart from me.
I am the vine, you are the branches.
He who lives in me and I in him,
will produce abundantly,
for apart from me you can do nothing.
A man who does not live in me
is like a withered, rejected branch,
picked up to be thrown in the fire and
burnt.
If you live in me,
and my words stay part of you,
you may ask what you will—
it will be done for you.
My Father has been glorified
in your bearing much fruit
and becoming my disciples."
This is the gospel of the Lord.

---

288   THURSDAY OF THE FIFTH WEEK OF EASTER

READING I   Acts 15, 7-21

A reading from the Acts of the Apostles

I judge that we should not make things more difficult for those gentiles who have turned to God.

After much discussion, Peter took the floor and said to the apostles and the elders: "Brothers, you know well enough that from the early

days God selected me from your number to be the one from whose lips the Gentiles would hear the message of the gospel and believe. God, who reads the hearts of men, showed his approval by granting the Holy Spirit to them just as he did to us. He made no distinction between them and us, but purified their hearts by means of faith also. Why, then, do you put God to the test by trying to place on the shoulders of these converts a yoke which neither we nor our fathers were able to bear? Our belief is rather that we are saved by the favor of the Lord Jesus and so are they." At that the whole assembly fell silent. They listened to Barnabas and Paul as the two described all the signs and wonders God had worked among the Gentiles through them.

When they concluded their presentation, James spoke up: "Brothers, listen to me. Symeon has told you how God first concerned himself with taking from among the Gentiles a people to bear his name. The words of the prophets agree with this, where it says in Scripture, 'Hereafter I will return and rebuild the fallen hut of David: from its ruins I will rebuild it and set it up again, so that all the rest of mankind and all the nations that bear my name may seek out the Lord. Thus says the Lord who accomplishes these things known to him from of old.' It is my judgment, therefore, that we ought not to cause God's Gentile converts any difficulties. We should merely write to them to abstain from anything contaminated by idols, from illicit sexual union, from the meat of strangled animals, and from eating blood. After all, for generations now Moses has been proclaimed in every town and has been read aloud in the synagogues on every sabbath."

This is the Word of the Lord.

Responsorial Psalm   Ps 96, 1-2. 2-3. 10

R̝. (3) Proclaim his marvelous deeds
   to all the nations.

Sing to the Lord a new song;
   sing to the Lord, all you lands.
Sing to the Lord; bless his name.
R̝. Proclaim his marvelous deeds
   to all the nations.

Announce his salvation, day after day.
   Tell his glory among the nations;
   among all peoples, his wondrous deeds.
R̝. Proclaim his marvelous deeds
   to all the nations.

Say among the nations: The Lord is king.
   He has made the world firm, not to be
      moved;
   he governs the peoples with equity.
R̝. Proclaim his marvelous deeds
   to all the nations.
R̝. Or: Alleluia.

GOSPEL   Jn 15, 9-11
Alleluia
See no. 303.

✠ A reading from the holy gospel according
               to John
   Remain in my love that your joy may be increased.

Jesus said to his disciples:
   "As the Father has loved me,
   so I have loved you.
   Live on in my love.
   You will live in my love
   if you keep my commandments,
   even as I have kept my Father's commandments,
   and live in his love.
   All this I tell you
   that my joy may be yours
   and your joy may be complete."
      This is the gospel of the Lord.

---

289   **FRIDAY OF THE FIFTH**
              WEEK OF EASTER

READING I   Acts 15, 22-31

   A reading from the Acts of the Apostles
   It has been decided by the Holy Spirit and ourselves not
      to burden you beyond what is essential.

It was resolved by the apostles and elders, in agreement with the whole Jerusalem church, that representatives be chosen from among their number and sent to Antioch along with Paul and Barnabas. Those chosen were leading men of the community, Judas, known as Barsabbas, and Silas. They were to deliver this letter:

"The apostles and the elders, your brothers, send greetings to the brothers of Gentile origin in Antioch, Syria and Cilicia. We have heard that some of our number without any instructions from us have upset you with their discussions and disturbed your peace of mind. Therefore we have unanimously resolved to choose representatives and send them to you, along with our beloved Barnabas and Paul, who have dedicated themselves to the cause of our Lord Jesus Christ. Those whom we are sending you are Judas and Silas, who will convey this message by word of mouth: 'It is the decision of the Holy Spirit, and ours too, not to lay on you any burden beyond that which is strictly necessary, namely, to abstain from meat sacrificed to idols, from blood, from the meat of strangled animals, and from illicit sexual union. You will be well advised to avoid these things. Farewell.' "

Thus were the representatives sent on their way to Antioch; and upon their arrival there they called the assembly together to deliver the letter. When it was read there was great delight at the encouragement it gave.

This is the Word of the Lord.

Responsorial Psalm   Ps 57, 8-9. 10-12

℟. (10) I will praise you among the nations, O Lord.

My heart is steadfast, O God; my heart is steadfast;
  I will sing and chant praise.
Awake, O my soul; awake, lyre and harp!
  I will wake the dawn.

℟. I will praise you among the nations, O Lord.

I will give thanks to you among the peoples, O Lord,
  I will chant your praise among the nations.
Be exalted above the heavens, O God;
  above all the earth be your glory!

℟. I will praise you among the nations, O Lord.
℟. Or: Alleluia.

GOSPEL   Jn 15, 12-17
Alleluia

See no. 303.

✠ **A reading from the holy gospel according to John**

This I command you, that you love one another.

Jesus said to his disciples,
  "This is my commandment:
  love one another
  as I have loved you.
  There is no greater love than this:
  to lay down one's life for one's friends.
  You are my friends
  if you do what I command you.
  I no longer speak of you as slaves,
  for a slave does not know what his master
    is about.
  Instead I call you friends,
  since I have made known to you all that I
    heard from my Father.
  It was not you who chose me,
  it was I who chose you
  to go forth and bear fruit.
  Your fruit must endure,
  so that all you ask the Father in my name
  he will give you.
  The command I give you is this,
  that you love one another."

  This is the gospel of the Lord.

290   **SATURDAY OF THE FIFTH
WEEK OF EASTER**

READING I   Acts 16, 1-10

A reading from the Acts of the Apostles

Come to Macedonia and help us.

Paul arrived at Derbe; then he came to Lystra, where there was a disciple named Timothy, whose mother was a Jew and a believer, and whose father was a Greek. Since the brothers in Lystra and Iconium spoke highly of him, Paul was anxious to have him come along on the journey. Paul had him circumcised because of the Jews of that region, for they all knew that it was only his father who was

Greek. As they made their way from town to town, they transmitted to the people for observance the decisions which the apostles and elders had made in Jerusalem.

Through all this, the congregations grew stronger in faith and daily increased in numbers.

They next traveled through Phrygia and Galatian territory because they had been prevented by the Holy Spirit from preaching the message in the province of Asia. When they came to Mysia they tried to go on into Bithynia, but again the Spirit of Jesus would not allow them. Crossing through Mysia instead, they came down to Troas. There one night Paul had a vision. A man of Macedonia stood before him and invited him, "Come over to Macedonia and help us."

After this vision, we immediately made efforts to get across to Macedonia, concluding that God had summoned us to proclaim the good news there.

This is the Word of the Lord.

Responsorial Psalm   Ps 100, 1-2. 3. 5

℟. (2) Let all the earth cry out to God with joy.
Sing joyfully to the Lord, all you lands;
   serve the Lord with gladness;
   come before him with joyful song.
℟. Let all the earth cry out to God with joy.
Know that the Lord is God;
   he made us, his we are;
   his people, the flock he tends.
℟. Let all the earth cry out to God with joy.
The Lord is good:
   his kindness endures forever,
   and his faithfulness, to all generations.
℟. Let all the earth cry out to God with joy.
℟. Or: Alleluia.

GOSPEL   Jn 15, 18-21
Alleluia

See no. 303.

✠ A reading from the holy gospel according to John
You do not belong to the world because I have chosen you out of it.

Jesus said to his disciples:
   "If you find that the world hates you,
   know it has hated me before you.
   If you belonged to the world,
   it would love you as its own;
   the reason it hates you
   is that you do not belong to the world.
   But I chose you out of the world.
   Remember what I told you:
   no slave is greater than his master.
   They will harry you
   as they harried me.
   They will respect your words
   as much as they respected mine.
   All this they will do to you because of my name,
   for they know nothing of him who sent me."
     This is the gospel of the Lord.

291   **MONDAY OF THE SIXTH WEEK OF EASTER**

READING I   Acts 16, 11-15
A reading from the Acts of the Apostles
The Lord opened her heart to accept those things which Paul taught.

We put out to sea from Troas and set a course straight for Samothrace, and the next day on to Neapolis; from there we went to Philippi, a leading city in the district of Macedonia and a Roman colony. We spent some time in that city. Once, on the sabbath, we went outside the city gate to the bank of the river, where we thought there would be a place of prayer. We sat down and spoke to the women who were gathered there. One who listened was a woman named Lydia, a dealer in purple goods from the town of Thyatira. She already reverenced God, and the Lord opened her heart to accept what Paul was saying. After she and her household had been baptized, she extended us an invitation: "If you are convinced that I believe in the Lord, come and stay at my house." She managed to prevail on us.

This is the Word of the Lord.

Responsorial Psalm   Ps 149, 1-2. 3-4. 5-6. 9

℟. (4) The Lord takes delight in his people.
Sing to the Lord a new song
  of praise in the assembly of the faithful.
Let Israel be glad in their maker,
  let the children of Zion rejoice in their king.
℟. The Lord takes delight in his people.
Let them praise his name in the festive dance,
  let them sing praise to him with timbrel and
    harp.
For the Lord loves his people,
  and he adorns the lowly with victory.
℟. The Lord takes delight in his people.
Let the faithful exult in glory;
  let them sing for joy upon their couches.
Let the high praises of God be in their throats.
  This is the glory of all his faithful. Alleluia.
℟. The Lord takes delight in his people.
℟. Or: Alleluia.

GOSPEL   Jn 15, 26—16, 4
Alleluia

See no. 303.

✠ A reading from the holy gospel according
to John
The Spirit of truth will bear witness to me.

Jesus said to his disciples:
  "When the Paraclete comes,
  the Spirit of truth who comes from the
    Father—
  and whom I myself will send from the
    Father—
  he will bear witness on my behalf.
  You must bear witness as well,
  for you have been with me from the be-
    ginning.
  I have told you all this
  to keep your faith from being shaken.
  Not only will they expel you from syna-
    gogues;
  a time will come
  when anyone who puts you to death
  will claim to be serving God!
  All this they will do [to you]
  because they know neither the Father nor
    me.

But I have told you these things
  that when their hour comes
  you may remember my telling you of
    them."
  This is the gospel of the Lord.

**292   TUESDAY OF THE SIXTH
WEEK OF EASTER**

READING I   Acts 16, 22-34
A reading from the Acts of the Apostles
Believe in the Lord Jesus, and you will be saved, and your
household too.

The crowd [of Philippians] joined in the attack
on Paul and Silas, and the magistrates stripped
them and ordered them to be flogged. After receiving many lashes they were thrown into
prison, and the jailer was given instructions to
guard them well. Upon receipt of these instructions he put them in maximum security, going
so far as to chain their feet to a stake.
  About midnight, while Paul and Silas were
praying and singing hymns to God as their
fellow prisoners listened, a severe earthquake
suddenly shook the place, rocking the prison to
its foundations. Immediately all the doors flew
open and everyone's chains were pulled loose.
The jailer woke up to see the prison gates wide
open. Thinking that the prisoners had escaped,
he drew his sword to kill himself; but Paul
shouted to him, "Do not harm yourself! We are
all still here." The jailer called for a light, then
rushed in and fell trembling at the feet of Paul
and Silas. After a brief interval he led them out
and said, "Men, what must I do to be saved?"
Their answer was, "Believe in the Lord Jesus
and you will be saved, and all your household."
They proceeded to announce the word of God
to him and to everyone in his house. At that
late hour of the night he took them in and
bathed their wounds; then he and his whole
household were baptized. He led them up into
his house, spread a table before them, and joyfully celebrated with his whole family his
newfound faith in God.
  This is the Word of the Lord.

Responsorial Psalm   Ps 138, 1-2. 2-3. 7-8

R̷. (7) Your right hand has saved me, O Lord.
I will give thanks to you, O Lord, with all my
  heart,
[for you have heard the words of my mouth;]
In the presence of the angels I will sing your
  praise;
  I will worship at your holy temple,
  and give thanks to your name.

R̷. Your right hand has saved me, O Lord.
Because of your kindness and your truth,
  you have made great above all things
  your name and your promise.
When I called, you answered me;
  you built up strength within me.

R̷. Your right hand has saved me, O Lord.
Your right hand saves me.
  The Lord will complete what he has done
  for me;
Your kindness, O Lord, endures forever;
  forsake not the work of your hands.

R̷. Your right hand has saved me, O Lord.
R̷. Or: Alleluia.

GOSPEL   Jn 16, 5-11
Alleluia

See no. 303.

✠ A reading from the holy gospel according
  to John

Unless I go away, the Advocate will not come to you.

Jesus said to his disciples,
  "Now that I go back to him who sent me,
  not one of you asks me, 'Where are you
  going?'
  Because I have had all this to say to you,
  you are overcome with grief.
  Yet I tell you the sober truth:
  It is much better for you that I go.
  If I fail to go,
  the Paraclete will never come to you,
  whereas if I go,
  I will send him to you.
  When he comes,
  he will prove the world wrong
  about sin,
  about justice,
  about condemnation.

About sin—
  in that they refuse to believe in me;
about justice—
  from the fact that I go to the Father
  and you can see me no more;
about condemnation—
  for the prince of this world has been condemned."
  This is the gospel of the Lord.

**293   WEDNESDAY OF THE SIXTH
        WEEK OF EASTER**

READING I   Acts 17, 15. 22-18, 1
  A reading from the Acts of the Apostles

The God I proclaim to you, you already worship without
                    knowing it.

Paul was taken as far as Athens by an escort,
who then returned with instructions for Silas
and Timothy to join him as soon as possible.
  Then Paul stood up in the Areopagus and
delivered this address: "Men of Athens, I note
that in every respect you are scrupulously religious. As I walked around looking at your
shrines, I even discovered an altar inscribed,
'To a God Unknown.' Now, what you are
thus worshiping in ignorance I intend to make
known to you. For the God who made the
world and 'all that is in it,' the Lord of heaven
and earth, does not dwell in sanctuaries made
by human hands; no more does he receive
man's service as if he were in need of it.
Rather, it is he 'who gives' to all life and
'breath' and everything else. From one stock
he made every nation of mankind to dwell on
the face of the earth. It is he who set limits to
their epochs and 'fixed the boundaries' of their
regions. They were to seek God, yes, to grope
for him and perhaps eventually to find him—
though he is not really far from any one of us.
'In him we live and move and have our being,'
as some of your own poets have put it, 'for we
too are his offspring.' If we are in fact God's
offspring, we ought not to think of divinity
as something like a statue of gold or silver or
stone, a product of man's genius and his art.
God may well have overlooked bygone periods

when men did not know him; but now he calls on all men everywhere to reform their lives. He has set the day on which he is going to 'judge the world with justice' through a man he has appointed—one whom he has endorsed in the sight of all by raising him from the dead."

When they heard about the raising of the dead, some sneered, while others said, "We must hear you on this topic some other time." At that point, Paul left them. A few did join him, however, to become believers. Among these were Dionysius, a member of the court of the Areopagus, a woman named Damaris, and a few others.

After that, Paul left Athens and went to Corinth.

This is the Word of the Lord.

Responsorial Psalm   Ps 148, 1-2. 11-12. 12-14. 14

R̠. Heaven and earth are filled with your glory.
Praise the Lord from the heavens,
    praise him in the heights;
Praise him, all you his angels,
    praise him, all you his hosts.
R̠. Heaven and earth are filled with your glory.
Let the kings of the earth and all peoples,
    the princes and all the judges of the earth,
Young men too, and maidens,
    old men and boys,
R̠. Heaven and earth are filled with your glory.
Praise the name of the Lord,
    for his name alone is exalted;
His majesty is above earth and heaven.
R̠. Heaven and earth are filled with your glory.
He has lifted up the horn of his people;
    be this his praise from all his faithful ones,
From the children of Israel, the people close to
    him. Alleluia.
R̠. Heaven and earth are filled with your glory.
R̠. Or: Alleluia.

GOSPEL   Jn 16, 12-15
Alleluia

See no. 303.

✠ A reading from the holy gospel according to John

The spirit of truth will lead you to the complete truth.
Jesus said to his disciples,
    "I have much more to tell you,
    but you cannot bear it now.
When he comes, however,
    being the Spirit of truth
    he will guide you to all truth.
He will not speak on his own,
    but will speak only what he hears,
    and will announce to you the things to
        come.
In doing this he will give glory to me,
    because he will have received from me
    what he will announce to you.
All that the Father has belongs to me.
That is why I said that what he will
    announce to you
he will have from me."
    This is the gospel of the Lord.

**294   THURSDAY OF THE SIXTH
            WEEK OF EASTER**

In countries where the celebration of the Ascension is transferred to the Seventh Sunday of Easter, the following readings are used on this Thursday.

READING I   Acts 18, 1-8

A reading from the Acts of the Apostles

He lived with them and they worked together and debated in the synagogue.

Paul left Athens and went to Corinth. There he found a Jew named Aquila, a native of Pontus recently arrived from Italy with his wife Priscilla. An edict of Claudius had ordered all Jews to leave Rome. Paul went to visit the pair, whose trade he had in common with them. He took up lodgings with them and they worked together as tentmakers. Every sabbath, in the synagogue, Paul led discussions in which he persuaded certain Jews and Greeks.

When Silas and Timothy came down from Macedonia, Paul was absorbed in preaching and giving evidence to the Jews that Jesus was the Messiah. When they opposed him and insulted him, he would shake out his garments in protest and say to them: "Your blood be on your own heads. I am not to blame! From now on, I will turn to the Gentiles."

Later, Paul withdrew and went to the house of a Gentile named Titus Justus, who reverenced God; his house was next door to the synagogue. A leading man of the synagogue, Crispus, along with his whole household, put his faith in the Lord. Many of the Corinthians, too, who heard Paul believed and were baptized.

This is the Word of the Lord.

Responsorial Psalm   Ps 98, 1. 2-3. 3-4

℟. (2) The Lord has revealed to the nations his saving power.
Sing to the Lord a new song,
  for he has done wondrous deeds;
His right hand has won victory for him,
  his holy arm.
℟. The Lord has revealed to the nations his saving power.
The Lord has made his salvation known:
  in the sight of the nations he has revealed his justice.
He has remembered his kindness and his faithfulness
  toward the house of Israel.
℟. The Lord has revealed to the nations his saving power.
All the ends of the earth have seen
  the salvation by our God.
Sing joyfully to the Lord, all you lands;
  break into song; sing praise.
℟. The Lord has revealed to the nations his saving power.
℟. Or: Alleluia.

GOSPEL   Jn 16, 16-20
Alleluia

See no. 303.

✠ **A reading from the holy gospel according to John**
You will be sorrowful but your sorrow will be turned into joy.
Jesus said to his disciples:
  "Within a short time you will lose sight of me,
    but soon after that you shall see me again."

At this some of his disciples asked one another, "What can he mean, 'Within a short time you will lose sight of me, but soon after that you will see me?' And did he not say that he is going back to the Father?" They kept asking, "What does he mean by this 'short time'? We do not know what he is talking about." Since Jesus was aware that they wanted to question him, he said: "You are asking one another about my saying, 'Within a short time you will lose sight of me, but soon after that you will see me.'
  "I tell you truly:
  you will weep and mourn
  while the world rejoices;
  you will grieve for a time,
  but your grief will be turned into joy."
This is the gospel of the Lord.

295   **FRIDAY OF THE SIXTH WEEK OF EASTER**

READING I   Acts 18, 9-18
A reading from the Acts of the Apostles
Many people in this city are with me.

[When Paul was in Corinth] one night in a vision the Lord said to him: "Do not be afraid. Go on speaking and do not be silenced, for I am with you. No one will attack you or harm you. There are many of my people in this city." Paul ended by settling there for a year and a half, teaching them the word of God.

During Gallio's proconsulship in Achaia, the Jews rose in a body against Paul and brought him before the bench. "This fellow," they charged, "is influencing people to worship God in ways that are against the law." Paul was about to speak in self-defense when Gallio said to the Jews: "If it were a crime or a serious fraud, I would give you Jews a patient and reasonable hearing. But since this is a dispute about terminology and titles and your own law, you must see to it yourselves. I refuse to judge such matters." With that, he dismissed them from the court. Then they all pounced on Sosthenes, a leading man of the synagogue, and beat him in full view of the bench; but Gallio paid no attention to it.

Paul stayed on in Corinth for quite a while; but eventually he took leave of the brothers and sailed for Syria, in the company of Priscilla and Aquila. At the port of Cenchreae he shaved his head because of a vow he had taken.

This is the Word of the Lord.

Responsorial Psalm   Ps 47, 2-3. 4-5. 6-7

℟. (8) God is king of all the earth.
All you peoples, clap your hands,
    shout to God with cries of gladness,
For the Lord, the Most High, the awesome,
    is the great king over all the earth.
℟. God is king of all the earth.
He brings peoples under us;
    nations under our feet.
He chooses for us our inheritance,
    the glory of Jacob, whom he loves.
℟. God is king of all the earth.
God mounts his throne amid shouts of joy;
    the Lord, amid trumpet blasts.
Sing praise to God, sing praise;
    sing praise to our king, sing praise.
℟. God is king of all the earth.
℟. Or: Alleluia.

GOSPEL   Jn 16, 20-23
Alleluia

See no. 303 or no. 304.

✠ A reading from the holy gospel according
        to John
Your joy no man will take from you.

Jesus said to his disciples:
"I tell you truly:
    you will weep and mourn
    while the world rejoices;
    you will grieve for a time,
    but your grief will be turned into joy.
When a woman is in labor
    she is sad that her time has come.
When she has borne her child,
    she no longer remembers her pain
    for joy that a man has been born into the
    world.

In the same way, you are sad for a time,
    but I shall see you again;
    then your hearts will rejoice
    with a joy no one can take from you.
On that day you will have no questions
    to ask me."

This is the gospel of the Lord.

**296   SATURDAY OF THE SIXTH
                WEEK OF EASTER**

READING I   Acts 18, 23-28
A reading from the acts of the Apostles
Apollos demonstrated from the scriptures that Jesus was
                    Christ.

After spending some time in Antioch, Paul set out again, traveling systematically through the Galatian country and Phrygia to reassure all his disciples.

A Jew named Apollos, a native of Alexandria and a man of eloquence, arrived by ship at Ephesus. He was both an authority on Scripture and instructed in the new way of the Lord. Apollos was a man full of spiritual fervor. He spoke and taught accurately about Jesus, although he knew only of John's baptism. He too began to express himself fearlessly in the synagogue. When Priscilla and Aquila heard him, they took him home and explained to him God's new way in greater detail. He wanted to go on to Achaia, and so the brothers encouraged him by writing the disciples there to welcome him. When he arrived, he greatly strengthened those who through God's favor had become believers. He was vigorous in his public refutation of the Jewish party as he went about establishing from the Scriptures that Jesus is the Messiah.

This is the Word of the Lord.

Responsorial Psalm   Ps 47, 2-3. 8-9. 10

℟. (8) God is king of all the earth.
All you peoples, clap your hands,
    shout to God with cries of gladness,
For the Lord, the Most High, the awesome,
    is the great king over all the earth.

℟. God is king of all the earth.
For king of all the earth is God;
  sing hymns of praise.
God reigns over the nations,
  God sits upon his holy throne.
℟. God is king of all the earth.
The princes of the peoples are gathered to-
  gether
  with the people of the God of Abraham.
For God's are the guardians of the earth;
  he is supreme.
℟. God is king of all the earth.
℟. Or: Alleluia.

GOSPEL   Jn 16, 23-28
Alleluia

See no. 303 or no. 304.

✠ **A reading from the holy gospel according**
  to John
My Father loves you because you have loved me and
believed in me.

Jesus said to his disciples,
  "I give you my assurance,
  whatever you ask the Father,
  he will give you in my name.
  Until now you have not asked for any-
    thing in my name.
  Ask and you shall receive,
  that your joy may be full.
  I have spoken these things to you in veiled
    language.
  A time will come when I shall no longer
    do so,
  but shall tell you about the Father in plain
    speech.
  On that day you will ask in my name
  and I do not say that I will petition the
    Father for you.
  The Father already loves you,
  because you have loved me
  and have believed that I came from God.
  [I did indeed come from the Father;]
  I came into the world.
  Now I am leaving the world
  to go to the Father."
    This is the gospel of the Lord.

READING I   Acts 19, 1-8

A reading from the Acts of the Apostles
Did you receive the Holy Spirit when you became believers?

While Apollos was in Corinth, Paul passed
through the interior of the country and came to
Ephesus. There he found some disciples to
whom he put the question, "Did you receive
the Holy Spirit when you became believers?"
They answered, "We have not so much as
heard that there is a Holy Spirit." "Well, how
were you baptized?" he persisted. They replied,
"With the baptism of John." Paul then explained, "John's baptism was a baptism of
repentance. He used to tell the people about the
one who would come after him in whom they
were to believe—that is, Jesus." When they
heard this, they were baptized in the name of
the Lord Jesus. As Paul laid his hands on them,
the Holy Spirit came down on them and they
began to speak in tongues and to utter prophecies. There were in the company about twelve
men in all.

Paul entered the synagogue, and over a period of three months debated fearlessly, with
persuasive arguments, about the kingdom of
God.
    This is the Word of the Lord.

Responsorial Psalm   Ps 68, 2-3. 4-5. 6-7

℟. (33) Sing to God, O kingdoms of the earth.
God arises; his enemies are scattered,
  and those who hate him flee before him.
As smoke is driven away, so are they driven;
  as wax melts before the fire.
℟. Sing to God, O kingdoms of the earth.
But the just rejoice and exult before God;
  they are glad and rejoice.
Sing to God, chant praise to his name;
  his name is the Lord; exult before him.
℟. Sing to God, O kingdoms of the earth.
The father of orphans and the defender of
  widows
  is God in his holy dwelling.
God gives a home to the forsaken;
  he leads forth prisoners to prosperity.

℟. Sing to God, O kingdoms of the earth.
℟. Or: Alleluia.

GOSPEL   Jn 16, 29-33
Alleluia
See no. 304.

✠ A reading from the holy gospel according
to John

Be brave, I have conquered the world.

The disciples said to Jesus:
"At last you are speaking plainly without
talking in veiled language! We are convinced
that you know everything. There is no need for
anyone to ask you questions. We do indeed believe you came from God."
Jesus answered them:
"Do you really believe?
An hour is coming—has indeed already
come—
when you will be scattered and each will
go his way,
leaving me quite alone.
(Yet I can never be alone;
the Father is with me.)
I tell you all this
that in me you may find peace.
You will suffer in the world.
But take courage!
I have overcome the world."
This is the gospel of the Lord.

---

298   **TUESDAY OF THE SEVENTH
WEEK OF EASTER**

READING I   Acts 20, 17-27

A reading from the Acts of the Apostles

I have run the race and borne witness to the world, a task
I accepted from the Lord Jesus.

Paul sent word from Miletus to Ephesus, summoning the elders of that church. When they
came to him he delivered this address: "You
know how I lived among you from the first day
I set foot in the province of Asia—how I served
the Lord in humility through the sorrows and
trials that came my way from the plottings of
certain Jews. Never did I shrink from telling
you what was for your own good, or from
teaching you in public or in private. With Jews
and Greeks alike I insisted solemnly on repentance before God and on faith in our Lord
Jesus. But now, as you see, I am on my way to
Jerusalem, compelled by the Spirit and not
knowing what will happen to me there—except that the Holy Spirit has been warning me
from city to city that chains and hardships
await me. I put no value on my life if only I
can finish my race and complete the service to
which I have been assigned by the Lord Jesus,
bearing witness to the gospel of God's grace. I
know as I speak these words that none of you
among whom I went about preaching the kingdom will ever see my face again. Therefore I
solemnly declare this day that I take the blame
for no man's conscience, for I have never
shrunk from announcing to you God's design
in its entirety."
This is the Word of the Lord.

Responsorial Psalm   Ps 68, 10-11. 20-21

℟. (33) Sing to God, O kingdoms of the earth.
A bountiful rain you showered down, O God,
upon your inheritance;
you restored the land when it languished;
Your flock settled in it;
in your goodness, O God, you provided it for
the needy.
℟. Sing to God, O kingdoms of the earth.
Blessed day by day be the Lord,
who bears our burdens; God, who is our salvation.
God is a saving God for us;
the Lord, my Lord, controls the passageways
of death.
℟. Sing to God, O kingdoms of the earth.
℟. Or: Alleluia.

GOSPEL   Jn 17, 1-11
Alleluia
See no. 304.

✠ A reading from the holy gospel according
to John

Father, glorify your Son.

Jesus looked up to heaven and said:
"Father, the hour has come!
Give glory to your Son
that your Son may give glory to you,
inasmuch as you have given him authority
    over all mankind,
that he may bestow eternal life on those
    you gave him.
(Eternal life is this:
to know you, the only true God,
and him whom you have sent, Jesus
    Christ.)
I have given you glory on earth
by finishing the work you gave me to do.
Do you now, Father, give me glory at your
    side,
a glory I had with you before the world
    began.
I have made your name known
to those you gave me out of the world.
These men you gave me were yours;
they have kept your word.
Now they realize
that all that you gave me comes from you.
I entrusted to them
the message you entrusted to me,
and they received it.
They have known that in truth I came
    from you,
they have believed it was you who sent
    me.

"For these I pray—
not for the world
but for these you have given me,
for they are really yours.
(Just as all that belongs to me is yours,
so all that belongs to you is mine.)
It is in them that I have been glorified.
I am in the world no more,
but these are in the world
as I come to you."
    This is the gospel of the Lord.

**299   WEDNESDAY OF THE SEVENTH
WEEK OF EASTER**

READING I   Acts 20, 28-38

A reading from the Acts of the Apostles

I commend you to God, who has power to build you up and to give you an inheritance.

Paul spoke to the elders of the church of Ephesus: "Keep watch over yourselves, and over the whole flock the Holy Spirit has given you to guard. Shepherd the church of God, which he has acquired at the price of his own blood. I know that when I am gone, savage wolves will come among you who will not spare the flock. From your own number, men will present themselves distorting the truth and leading astray any who follow them. Be on guard, therefore. Do not forget that for three years, night and day, I never ceased warning you individually even to the point of tears. I commend you now to the Lord, and to that gracious word of his which can enlarge you, and give you a share among all who are consecrated to him. Never did I set my heart on anyone's silver or gold or envy the way he dressed. You yourselves know that these hands of mine have served both my needs and those of my companions. I have always pointed out to you that it is by such hard work that you must help the weak. You need to recall the words of the Lord Jesus himself, who said, 'There is more happiness in giving than receiving.' "

After this discourse, Paul knelt down with them all and prayed. They began to weep without restraint, throwing their arms around him and kissing him, for they were deeply distressed to hear that they would never see his face again. Then they escorted him to the ship.
    This is the Word of the Lord.

Responsorial Psalm   Ps 68, 29-30. 33-35. 35-36

℟. (33) Sing to God, O kingdoms of the earth.
Show forth, O God, your power,
    **the power, O God, with which you took our
    part;**
**For your temple in Jerusalem
    let the kings bring you gifts.**
℟. Sing to God, O kingdoms of the earth.

You kingdoms of the earth, sing to God,
    chant praise to the Lord
    who rides on the heights of the ancient
        heavens.
Behold, his voice resounds, the voice of power:
    "Confess the power of God!"
℟. Sing to God, O kingdoms of the earth.
Over Israel is his majesty;
    his power is in the skies.
Awesome in his sanctuary is God, the God of
        Israel;
    he gives power and strength to his people.
℟. Sing to God, O kingdoms of the earth.
℟. Or: Alleluia.

GOSPEL   Jn. 17, 11-19
Alleluia

See no. 304.

✠ A reading from the holy gospel according
            to John

            May they be one as we are one.

Jesus looked up to heaven and prayed:
    "O Father most holy,
    protect them with your name which you
        have given me,
    [that they may be one, even as we are
        one.]
    As long as I was with them,
    I guarded them with your name which you
        gave me.
    I kept careful watch,
    and not one of them was lost,
    none but him who was destined to be
        lost—
    in fulfillment of Scripture.
    Now, however, I come to you;
    I say all this while I am still in the world
    that they may share my joy completely.
    I gave them your word,
    and the world has hated them for it;
    they do not belong to the world,
    [any more than I belong to the world].
    I do not ask you to take them out of the
        world,
    but to guard them from the evil one.
    They are not of the world,
    any more than I am of the world.

Consecrate them by means of truth—
    'Your word is truth.'
As you have sent me into the world,
    so I have sent them into the world;
I consecrate myself for their sakes now,
    that they may be consecrated in truth."
    This is the gospel of the Lord.

**300   THURSDAY OF THE SEVENTH
            WEEK OF EASTER**

READING I   Acts 22, 30; 23, 6-11

A reading from the Acts of the Apostles
            You must testify at Rome.

The commander released Paul from prison, intending to look carefully into the charge which
the Jews were bringing against him. He summoned the chief priests and the whole Sanhedrin to a meeting; then he brought Paul down
and made him stand before them.

    Paul, it should be noted, was aware that
some of them were Sadducees and some Pharisees. Consequently he spoke out before the
Sanhedrin: "Brothers, I am a Pharisee and was
born a Pharisee. I find myself on trial now because of my hope in the resurrection of the
dead." At these words, a dispute arose between
Pharisees and Sadducees which divided the
whole assembly. (The Sadducees, of course,
maintain that there is no resurrection and that
there are neither angels nor spirits, while the
Pharisees believe in all these things.) A loud
uproar ensued. Finally, some scribes of the
Pharisee party arose and declared emphati-
cally: "We do not find this man guilty of any
crime. If a spirit or an angel has spoken to him.
. . ." At this, the dispute grew worse and the
commander feared they would tear Paul to
pieces. He therefore ordered his troops to go
down and rescue Paul from their midst and
take him back to headquarters. That night the
Lord appeared at Paul's side and said: "Keep
up your courage! Just as you have given testimony to me here in Jerusalem, so must you do
in Rome."

    This is the Word of the Lord.

Responsorial Psalm   Ps 16, 1-2. 5. 7-8. 9-10. 11

℟. (1) Keep me safe, O God;
    you are my hope.
Keep me, O God, for in you I take refuge;
    I say to the Lord, "My Lord are you."
O Lord, my allotted portion and my cup,
    you it is who hold fast my lot.
℟. Keep me safe, O God;
    you are my hope.
I bless the Lord who counsels me;
    even in the night my heart exhorts me.
I set the Lord ever before me;
    with him at my right hand I shall not be dis-
        turbed.
℟. Keep me safe, O God;
    you are my hope.
Therefore my heart is glad and my soul re-
        joices,
    my body, too, abides in confidence;
Because you will not abandon my soul to the
        nether world,
    nor will you suffer your faithful one to un-
        dergo corruption.
℟. Keep me safe, O God;
    you are my hope.
You will show me the path to life,
    fullness of joys in your presence,
    the delights at your right hand forever.
℟. Keep me safe, O God;
    you are my hope.
℟. Or: Alleluia.

GOSPEL   Jn 17, 20-26
Alleluia

See no. 304.

✠ A reading from the holy gospel according
                to John
May they be joined as one.

Jesus looked up to heaven and said:
    "I do not pray for my disciples alone.
    I pray also for those who will believe in me
        through their word,
        that all may be one
        as you, Father, are in me, and I in you;
    I pray that they may be [one] in us,
        that the world may believe that you sent
            me.

I have given them the glory you gave me
    that they may be one, as we are one—
I living in them, you living in me—
    that their unity may be complete.
So shall the world know that you sent me,
    and that you loved them as you loved me.
Father,
    all those you gave me
    I would have in my company
    where I am,
    to see this glory of mine
    which is your gift to me,
    because of the love you bore me before the
        world began.
Just Father,
    the world has not known you,
    but I have known you;
    and these men have known that you sent
        me.
To them I have revealed your name,
    and I will continue to reveal it
    so that your love for me may live in them,
    and I may live in them."
    This is the gospel of the Lord.

**301   FRIDAY OF THE SEVENTH
            WEEK OF EASTER**

READING I   Acts 25, 13-21

A reading from the Acts of the Apostles
Jesus was dead, whom Paul claimed to be alive.

King Agrippa and Bernice arrived in Caesarea
and paid Festus a courtesy call. Since they
were to spend several days there, Festus referred Paul's case to the king. "There is a prisoner here," he said, "whom Felix left behind in
custody. While I was in Jerusalem the chief
priests and the elders of the Jews presented
their case against this man and demanded his
condemnation. I replied that it was not the
Roman practice to hand an accused man over
before he had been confronted with his accusers and given a chance to defend himself
against their charges. When they came here
with me, I did not delay the matter. The very
next day I took my seat on the bench and ordered the man brought in. His accusers surrounded him but they did not charge him with

any of the crimes I expected. Instead they differed with him over issues in their own religion, and about a certain Jesus who had died but who Paul claimed is alive. Not knowing how to decide the case, I asked whether the prisoner was willing to go to Jerusalem and stand trial there on these charges. Paul appealed to be kept here until there would be an imperial investigation of his case, so I issued orders that he be kept in custody until I could send him to the emperor."
This is the Word of the Lord.

Responsorial Psalm   Ps 103, 1-2. 11-12. 19-20

R⁊. (19) The Lord has set his throne in heaven.
Bless the Lord, O my soul;
    and all my being, bless his holy name.
Bless the Lord, O my soul,
    and forget not all his benefits;
R⁊. The Lord has set his throne in heaven.
For as the heavens are high above the earth,
    so surpassing is his kindness toward those
        who fear him.
As far as the east is from the west,
    so far has he put our transgressions from us.
R⁊. The Lord has set his throne in heaven.
The Lord has established his throne in heaven,
    and his kingdom rules over all.
Bless the Lord, all you his angels,
    you mighty in strength, who do his bidding.
R⁊. The Lord has set his throne in heaven.
R⁊. Or: Alleluia.

GOSPEL   Jn 21, 15-19
Alleluia

See no. 304.

✠ A reading from the holy gospel according
to John
Feed my lambs, feed my sheep.

When [Jesus manifested himself to his disciples and] they had eaten their meal, he said to Simon Peter, "Simon, son of John, do you love me more than these?" "Yes, Lord," Peter said, "you know that I love you." At which Jesus said, "Feed my lambs."
    A second time he put his question, "Simon, son of John, do you love me?" "Yes, Lord,"

Peter said, "you know that I love you." Jesus replied, "Tend my sheep."
    A third time Jesus asked him, "Simon, son of John, do you love me?" Peter was hurt because he had asked a third time, "Do you love me?" So he said to him: "Lord, you know everything. You know well that I love you." Jesus told him, "Feed my sheep."
    "I tell you solemnly:
    as a young man
    you fastened your belt
    and went about as you pleased;
    but when you are older
    you will stretch out your hands,
    and another will tie you fast
    and carry you off against your will."
(What he said indicated the sort of death by which Peter was to glorify God.) When Jesus had finished speaking he said to him, "Follow me."
    This is the gospel of the Lord.

---

302   **SATURDAY OF THE SEVENTH
WEEK OF EASTER**
Mass in the Early Morning

READING I   Acts 28, 16-20. 30-31

A reading from the Acts of the Apostles
He remained at Rome, proclaiming the kingdom of God.

Upon entry into Rome, Paul was allowed to take a lodging of his own, although a soldier was assigned to keep guard over him.
    Three days later Paul invited the prominent men of the Jewish community to visit him. When they had gathered he said: "My brothers, I have done nothing against our people or our ancestral customs; yet in Jerusalem I was handed over to the Romans as a prisoner. The Romans tried my case and wanted to release me because they found nothing against me deserving of death. When the Jews objected, I was forced to appeal to the emperor, though I had no cause to make accusations against my own people. This is the reason, then, why I have asked to see you and speak with you. I wear these chains solely because I share the hope of Israel."

For two full years Paul stayed on in his rented lodgings, welcoming all who came to him. With full assurance, and without any hindrance whatever, he preached the reign of God and taught about the Lord Jesus Christ.
This is the Word of the Lord.

Responsorial Psalm   Ps 11, 4. 5. 7

℟. (7) The just will gaze on your face, O Lord.
The Lord is in his holy temple;
   the Lord's throne is in heaven.
His eyes behold,
   his searching glance is on mankind.
℟. The just will gaze on your face, O Lord.
The Lord searches the just and the wicked;
   the lover of violence he hates.
For the Lord is just, he loves just deeds;
   the upright shall see his face.
℟. The just will gaze on your face, O Lord.
℟. Or: Alleluia.

GOSPEL   Jn 21, 20-25
Alleluia

See no. 304.

✠ A reading from the holy gospel according to John
This is the disciple who has written these facts and his testimony is true.

As Peter followed Jesus, he turned around and noticed that the disciple whom Jesus loved was following (the one who had leaned against Jesus' chest during the supper and said, "Lord, which one will hand you over?"). Seeing him, Peter was prompted to ask Jesus, "But Lord, what about him?" "Suppose I want him to stay until I come," Jesus replied, "how does that concern you? Your business is to follow me." This is how the report spread among the brothers that this disciple was not going to die. Jesus never told him, as a matter of fact, that the disciple was not going to die; all he said was, "Suppose I want him to stay until I come. [How does that concern you]?"

It is this same disciple who is the witness to these things; it is he who wrote them down and his testimony, we know, is true. There are still many other things that Jesus did, yet if they were written about in detail, I doubt there would be room enough in the entire world to hold the books to record them.
This is the gospel of the Lord.

---

303   **ALLELUIA**

FOR WEEKDAYS OF THE EASTER SEASON UP TO THE ASCENSION

1

℟. Alleluia. **Christ had to suffer and to rise from the dead,**
and so enter into his glory. ℟. Alleluia.

2

℟. Alleluia. **I am the good shepherd, says the Lord;**
I know my sheep and mine know me. ℟. Alleluia.

3

℟. Alleluia. **My sheep listen to my voice, says the Lord;**
I know them and they follow me. ℟. Alleluia.

4

℟. Alleluia. **You believe in me, Thomas, because you have seen me;**
happy those who have not seen me, but still believe! ℟. Alleluia.

5

℟. Alleluia. **Christ now raised from the dead will never die again;**
death no longer has power over him. ℟. Alleluia.

6

℟. Alleluia. **If then you have been raised with Christ, seek the things that are above,**
where Christ is seated at the right hand of God. ℟. Alleluia.

7

℟. Alleluia. **Jesus Christ, you are the faithful witness, first-born from the dead;**
you have loved us and washed away our sins in your blood. ℟. Alleluia.

8

℟. Alleluia. **Christ has risen and shines upon us,**
whom he has redeemed by his blood. ℟. Alleluia.

9

℟. Alleluia. **Nailed to the cross for our sake,**
the Lord is now risen from the grave. ℟. Alleluia.

10

℟. Alleluia. **Christ is risen, and makes all things new;**
he has shown pity to all mankind. ℟. Alleluia.

11

℟. Alleluia. **We know that Christ is truly risen from the dead;**
victorious king, deal kindly with us. ℟. Alleluia.

304   **ALLELUIA**

FOR WEEKDAYS OF THE EASTER SEASON AFTER THE ASCENSION

1

℟. Alleluia. **Go and teach all people my gospel;**
I am with you always, until the end of the world. ℟. Alleluia.

2

℟. Alleluia. **The Father will send you the Holy Spirit, says the Lord,**
to be with you for ever. ℟. Alleluia.

3

℟. Alleluia. **The Lord said: I will not leave you orphans.**
I will come back to you, and your hearts will rejoice. ℟. Alleluia.

4

℟. Alleluia. **The Holy Spirit will teach you all things,**
and remind you of all I have said to you. ℟. Alleluia.

5

℟. Alleluia. **I will send you the Spirit of truth, says the Lord;**
he will lead you to the whole truth. ℟. Alleluia.

6

℟. Alleluia. **I went from the Father and came into the world;**
and now I leave the world to return to the Father. ℟. Alleluia.

7

℟. Alleluia. **If then you have been raised with Christ, seek the things that are above,**
where Christ is seated at the right hand of God. ℟. Alleluia.

SEASON OF THE YEAR

305 MONDAY OF THE FIRST WEEK OF THE YEAR

Year I

READING I   Heb 1, 1-6

The beginning of the letter to the Hebrews

God has spoken to us through his Son.

In times past, God spoke in fragmentary and varied ways to our fathers through the prophets; in this, the final age, he has spoken to us through his Son, whom he has made heir of all things and through whom he first created the universe. This Son is the reflection of the Father's being, and he sustains all things by his powerful word. When he had cleansed us from our sins, he took his seat at the right hand of the Majesty in heaven, as far superior to the angels as the name he has inherited is superior to theirs.

To which of the angels did God ever say,
   "You are my son; today I have begotten you"?
Or again,
   "I will be his father, and he shall be my son"?
And again when he leads his first-born into the world, he says,
   "Let all the angels of God worship him."
   This is the Word of the Lord.

Responsorial Psalm   Ps 97, 1-2. 6-7. 9

℟. (7) Let all his angels worship him.
The Lord is king; let the earth rejoice;
   let the many isles be glad.
Justice and judgment are the foundation of his throne.
℟. Let all his angels worship him.
The heavens proclaim his justice,
   and all peoples see his glory.
All gods are prostrate before him.
℟. Let all his angels worship him.

Because you, O Lord, are the Most High over all the earth,
   exalted far above all gods.
℟. Let all his angels worship him.

Year II

READING I   1 Sm 1, 1-8

The beginning of the first book of Samuel

Hannah was tormented by her rival because God had made her barren.

There was a certain man from Ramathaim, Elkanah by name, a Zuphite from the hill country of Ephraim. He was the son of Jeroham, son of Elihu, son of Tohu, son of Zuph, an Ephraimite. He had two wives, one named Hannah, the other Peninnah; Peninnah had children, but Hannah was childless. This man regularly went on pilgrimage from his city to worship the Lord of hosts and to sacrifice to him at Shiloh, where the two sons of Eli, Hophni and Phinehas, were ministering as priests of the Lord. When the day came for Elkanah to offer sacrifice, he used to give a portion each to his wife Peninnah and to all her sons and daughters, but a double portion to Hannah because he loved her, though the Lord had made her barren. Her rival, to upset her, turned it into a constant reproach to her that the Lord had left her barren. This went on year after year; each time they made their pilgrimage to the sanctuary of the Lord, Peninnah would reproach her, and Hannah would weep and refuse to eat. Her husband Elkanah used to ask her: "Hannah, why do you weep, and why do you refuse to eat? Why do you grieve? Am I not more to you than ten sons?"
   This is the Word of the Lord.

Responsorial Psalm   Ps 116, 12-13. 14-17. 18-19

℟. (17) To you, Lord, I will offer a sacrifice of praise.
How shall I make a return to the Lord
   for all the good he has done for me?
The cup of salvation I will take up,
   and I will call upon the name of the Lord.
℟. To you, Lord, I will offer a sacrifice of praise.

My vows to the Lord I will pay
  in the presence of all his people.
Precious in the eyes of the Lord
  is the death of his faithful ones.
O Lord, I am your servant;
  I am your servant, the son of your handmaid;
  you have loosed my bonds.
To you will I offer sacrifice of thanksgiving,
  and I will call upon the name of the Lord.
℟. To you, Lord, I will offer a sacrifice of
  praise.
My vows to the Lord I will pay
  in the presence of all his people,
In the courts of the house of the Lord,
  in your midst, O Jerusalem.
℟. To you, Lord, I will offer a sacrifice of
  praise.
℟. Or: Alleluia.

Years I and II

GOSPEL   Mk 1, 14-20
Alleluia

See no. 509.

✠ **A reading from the holy gospel according
  to Mark**

Repent and believe the Good News.

After John's arrest, Jesus appeared in Galilee
proclaiming the good news of God: "This is
the time of fulfillment. The reign of God is at
hand! Reform your lives and believe in the
good news!"
  As he made his way along the Sea of Galilee,
he observed Simon and his brother Andrew
casting their nets into the sea; they were
fishermen. Jesus said to them, "Come after me;
I will make you fishers of men." They immediately abandoned their nets and became his
followers. Proceeding a little farther along,
he caught sight of James, Zebedee's son, and
his brother John. They too were in their boat
putting their nets in order. He summoned them
on the spot. They abandoned their father
Zebedee, who was in the boat with the hired
men, and went off in his company.
  This is the gospel of the Lord.

306   **TUESDAY OF THE FIRST
        WEEK OF THE YEAR**

Year I

READING I   Heb 2, 5-12

  A reading from the letter to the Hebrews

He perfected the author of our salvation through suffering.

For God did not make the world to come—that
world of which we speak—subject to angels.
Somewhere this is testified to, in the passage
that says:
"What is man that you should be mindful of
  him,
  or the son of man that you should care for
  him?
You made him for a little while lower than the
  angels;
  you crowned him with glory and honor,
  and put all things under his feet."
In subjecting all things to him, God left nothing
unsubjected. At present we do not see all
things thus subject, but we do see Jesus
crowned with glory and honor because he
suffered death: Jesus, who was made for a
little while lower than the angels, that through
God's gracious will he might taste death for
the sake of all men. Indeed, it was fitting that
when bringing many sons to glory, God, for
whom and through whom all things exist,
should make their leader in the work of salvation perfect through suffering. He who consecrates and those who are consecrated have
one and the same Father. Therefore he is not
ashamed to call them brothers, saying,
"I will announce your name to my brothers,
  I will sing your praise in the midst of the
  assembly."
    This is the Word of the Lord.

Responsorial Psalm   Ps 8, 2. 5. 6-7. 8-9

℟. (7) You gave your Son authority over all
  your creation.
O Lord, our Lord,
  how glorious is your name over all the earth!
What is man that you should be mindful of
  him,
  or the son of man that you should care for
  him?

℟. You gave your Son authority over all your
   creation.
**You have made him little less than the angels,
   and crowned him with glory and honor.
You have given him rule over the works of
   your hands,
   putting all things under his feet:**
℟. You gave your Son authority over all your
   creation.
**All sheep and oxen,
   yes, and the beasts of the field,
The birds of the air, the fishes of the sea,
   and whatever swims the paths of the seas.**
℟. You gave your Son authority over all your
   creation.

Year II

READING I   1 Sm 1, 9-20
A reading from the first book of Samuel
The Lord God remembered Hannah and she gave birth to
Samuel.

**Hannah rose after a meal at Shiloh, and pre-
sented herself before the Lord; at the time,
Eli the priest was sitting on a chair near the
doorpost of the Lord's temple. In her bitterness
she prayed to the Lord, weeping copiously,
and she made a vow, promising: "O Lord of
hosts, if you look with pity on the misery of
your handmaid, if you remember me and do
not forget me, if you give your handmaid a
male child, I will give him to the Lord for as
long as he lives; neither wine nor liquor shall
he drink, and no razor shall ever touch his
head." As she remained long at prayer before
the Lord, Eli watched her mouth, for Hannah
was praying silently; though her lips were
moving, her voice could not be heard. Eli,
thinking her drunk, said to her, "How long will
you make a drunken show of yourself? Sober
up from your wine!" "It isn't that, my lord,"
Hannah answered. "I am an unhappy woman.
I have had neither wine nor liquor; I was only
pouring out my troubles to the Lord. Do not
think your handmaid a ne'er-do-well; my
prayer has been prompted by my deep sorrow
and misery." Eli said, "Go in peace, and may
the God of Israel grant you what you have
asked of him." She replied, "Think kindly of**

your maidservant," and left. She went to her
quarters, ate and drank with her husband, and
no longer appeared downcast. Early the next
morning they worshiped before the Lord, and
then returned to their home in Ramah.
    When Elkanah had relations with his wife
Hannah, the Lord remembered her. She conceived, and at the end of her term bore a son
whom she called Samuel, since she had asked
the Lord for him.
            This is the Word of the Lord.

Responsorial Psalm   1 Sm 2, 1. 4-5. 6-7. 8

℟. (1) My heart rejoices in the Lord, my
   Savior.
**My heart exults in the Lord,
   my horn is exalted in my God.
I have swallowed up my enemies;
   I rejoice in my victory.**
℟. My heart rejoices in the Lord, my Savior.
**The bows of the mighty are broken,
   while the tottering gird on strength.
The well-fed hire themselves out for bread,
   while the hungry batten on spoil.
The barren wife bears seven sons,
   while the mother of many languishes.**
℟. My heart rejoices in the Lord, my Savior.
**The Lord puts to death and gives life;
   he casts down to the nether world;
   he raises up again.
The Lord makes poor and makes rich,
   he humbles, he also exalts.**
℟. My heart rejoices in the Lord, my Savior.
**He raises the needy from the dust;
   from the ash heap he lifts up the poor,
To seat them with nobles
   and make a glorious throne their heritage.**
℟. My heart rejoices in the Lord, my Savior.

Years I and II

GOSPEL   Mk 1, 21-28
Alleluia
See no. 509.

✠ **A reading from the holy gospel according
               to Mark**
Here was a teaching with authority behind it.

**[In the city of Capernaum,] Jesus entered
the synagogue on the sabbath and began to**

teach. The people were spellbound by his teaching because he taught with authority and not like the scribes.

There appeared in their synagogue a man with an unclean spirit that shrieked: "What do you want of us, Jesus of Nazareth? Have you come to destroy us? I know who you are— the holy One of God!" Jesus rebuked him sharply: "Be quiet! Come out of the man!" At that the unclean spirit convulsed the man violently and with a loud shriek came out of him. All who looked on were amazed. They began to ask one another: "What does this mean? A completely new teaching in a spirit of authority! He gives orders to unclean spirits and they obey!" From that point on his reputation spread throughout the surrounding region of Galilee.

This is the gospel of the Lord.

307　**WEDNESDAY OF THE FIRST WEEK OF THE YEAR**

Year I

READING I　Heb 2, 14-18

A reading from the letter to the Hebrews

He became like all the brothers that he might share their suffering.

Since the children are men of blood and flesh, Jesus likewise had a full share in ours, that by his death he might rob the devil, the prince of death, of his power, and free those who through fear of death had been slaves their whole life long. Surely he did not come to help angels, but rather the children of Abraham; therefore he had to become like his brothers in every way, that he might be a merciful and faithful high priest before God on their behalf, to expiate the sins of the people. Since he was himself tested through what he suffered, he is able to help those who are tempted.

This is the Word of the Lord.

Responsorial Psalm　Ps 105, 1-2. 3-4. 6-7. 8-9

R̸. (8) The Lord remembers his covenant for ever.

Give thanks to the Lord, invoke his name;
　make known among the nations his deeds.
Sing to him, sing his praise,
　proclaim all his wondrous deeds.
R̸. The Lord remembers his covenant for ever.
Glory in his holy name;
　rejoice, O hearts that seek the Lord!
Look to the Lord in his strength;
　seek to serve him constantly.
R̸. The Lord remembers his covenant for ever.
You descendants of Abraham, his servants,
　sons of Jacob, his chosen ones!
He, the Lord, is our God;
　throughout the earth his judgments prevail.
R̸. The Lord remembers his covenant for ever.
He remembers forever his covenant
　which he made binding for a thousand generations—
Which he entered into with Abraham
　and by his oath to Isaac.
R̸. The Lord remembers his covenant for ever.
R̸. Or: Alleluia.

Year II

READING I　1 Sm 3, 1-10. 19-20

A reading from the first book of Samuel

Speak, Lord God, your servant is listening

During the time young Samuel was minister to the Lord under Eli, a revelation of the Lord was uncommon and vision infrequent. One day Eli was asleep in his usual place. His eyes had lately grown so weak that he could not see. The lamp of God was not yet extinguished, and Samuel was sleeping in the temple of the Lord where the ark of God was. The Lord called to Samuel, who answered, "Here I am." He ran to Eli and said, "Here I am. You called me." "I did not call you," Eli said. "Go back to sleep." So he went back to sleep. Again the Lord called Samuel, who rose and went to Eli. "Here I am," he said. "You called me." But he answered, "I did not call you, my son. Go back to sleep." At that time Samuel was not familiar with the Lord, because the Lord had not revealed anything to him as yet. The Lord called Samuel again, for the third time. Getting up and going to Eli, he said, "Here I am. You called me." Then Eli understood that the Lord was calling the youth. So he said to Samuel, "Go to sleep, and if you are called, reply, 'Speak, Lord, for your servant is listening.' " When Samuel went to sleep in his place, the Lord came and revealed his presence, calling out as before, "Samuel, Samuel!" Samuel answered, "Speak, for your servant is listening."

Samuel grew up, and the Lord was with him, not permitting any word of his to be without effect. Thus all Israel from Dan to Beer-sheba came to know that Samuel was an accredited prophet of the Lord.

This is the word of the Lord.

Responsorial Psalm   Ps 40, 2-5. 7-8. 8-9. 10

℞. (8. 9) Here am I, Lord; I come to do your will.

I have waited, waited for the Lord,
    and he stooped toward me.
Happy the man who makes the Lord his trust;
    who turns not to idolatry
    or to those who stray after falsehood.
℞. Here am I, Lord; I come to do your will.
Sacrifice or oblation you wished not,
    but ears open to obedience you gave me.
Holocausts or sin-offerings you sought not;
    then said I, "Behold I come."
℞. Here am I, Lord; I come to do your will.
"In the written scroll it is prescribed for me
    to do your will, O my God, is my delight,
And your law is within my heart!"
℞. Here am I, Lord; I come to do your will.
I announced your justice in the vast assembly;
    I did not restrain my lips, as you, O Lord,
    know.
℞. Here am I, Lord; I come to do your will.

GOSPEL   **Years I and II**
Alleluia   Mk 1, 29-39

See no. 509.

✠ A reading from the holy gospel according
    to Mark
He healed many who were suffering from diseases.

Upon leaving the synagogue, Jesus entered the house of Simon and Andrew with James and John. Simon's mother-in-law lay ill with a fever, and the first thing they did was to tell him about her. He went over to her and grasped her hand and helped her up, and the fever left her. She immediately began to wait on them.

After sunset, as evening drew on, they brought him all who were ill and those possessed by demons. Before long the whole town was gathered outside the door. Those whom he cured, who were variously afflicted, were many, and so were the demons he expelled. But he would not permit the demons to speak, because they knew him. Rising early the next morning, he went off to a lonely place in the desert; there he was absorbed in prayer. Simon and his companions managed to track him down, and when they found him, they told him, "Everybody is looking for you!" He said to them: "Let us move on to the neighboring villages so that I may proclaim the good news there also. That is what I have come to do." So he went into their synagogues preaching the good news and expelling demons throughout the whole of Galilee.

This is the gospel of the Lord.

---

308   **THURSDAY OF THE FIRST
WEEK OF THE YEAR**

Year I

READING I   Heb 3, 7-14
A reading from the letter to the Hebrews
If only you would listen to him today, and not harden your
hearts.

As the Holy Spirit says:
"Today, if you should hear his voice,
    harden not your hearts as at the revolt
    in the day of testing in the desert,
When your fathers tested and tried me,
    and saw my works for forty years.
Because of this I was angered with that generation
    and I said, 'They have always been of erring
    heart,
    and have never known my ways.'
Thus I swore in my anger,

'They shall never enter into my rest.' "
Take care, my brothers, lest any of you have an evil and unfaithful spirit and fall away from the living God. Encourage one another daily while it is still "today," so that no one grows hardened by the deceit of sin. We have become partners of Christ if only we maintain to the end that confidence with which we began.

This is the Word of the Lord.

Responsorial Psalm   Ps 95, 6-7. 8-9. 10-11

℞. (8) If today you hear his voice,
   harden not your hearts.
Come, let us bow down in worship;
   let us kneel before the Lord who made us.
For he is our God,
   and we are the people he shepherds, the
   flock he guides.
℞. If today you hear his voice,
   harden not your hearts.
Oh, that today you would hear his voice:
   "Harden not your hearts as at Meribah,
   as in the day of Massah in the desert,
Where your fathers tempted me;
   they tested me though they had seen my
   works."
℞. If today you hear his voice,
   harden not your hearts.
Forty years I loathed that generation,
   and I said: They are a people of erring
   heart,
   and they know not my ways.
Therefore I swore in my anger:
   They shall not enter into my rest."
℞. If today you hear his voice,
   harden not your hearts.

Year II

READING I   1 Sm 4, 1-11

A reading from the first book of Samuel
Israel was defeated and the ark of God was captured.

The Philistines gathered for an attack on Israel. Israel went out to engage them in battle and camped at Ebenezer, while the Philistines camped at Aphek. The Philistines then drew up in battle formation against Israel. After a fierce struggle Israel was defeated by the Philistines, who slew about four thousand men on the battlefield. When the troops retired to the camp, the elders of Israel said, "Why has the Lord permitted us to be defeated today by the Philistines? Let us fetch the ark of the Lord from Shiloh that it may go into battle among us and save us from the grasp of our enemies."

So the people sent to Shiloh and brought from there the ark of the Lord of hosts, who is enthroned upon the cherubim. The two sons of Eli, Hophni and Phinehas, were with the ark of God. When the ark of the Lord arrived in the camp, all Israel shouted so loudly that the earth resounded. The Philistines, hearing the noise of shouting, asked, "What can this loud shouting in the camp of the Hebrews mean?" On learning that the ark of the Lord had come into the camp, the Philistines were frightened. They said, "Gods have come to their camp." They said also, "Woe to us! This has never happened before. Woe to us! Who can deliver us from the power of these mighty gods? These are the gods that struck the Egyptians with various plagues and with pestilence. Take courage and be manly, Philistines; otherwise you will become slaves to the Hebrews, as they were your slaves. So fight manfully!" The Philistines fought and Israel was defeated; every man fled to his own tent. It was a disastrous defeat, in which Israel lost thirty thousand foot soldiers. The ark of God was captured, and Eli's two sons, Hophni and Phinehas, were among the dead.

This is the Word of the Lord.

Responsorial Psalm   Ps 44, 10-11. 14-15. 25-26

℞. (27) Save us, Lord, in your mercy.
Yet now you have cast us off and put us in
   disgrace,
   and you go not forth with our armies.
You have let us be driven back by our foes;
   those who hated us plundered us at will.
℞. Save us, Lord, in your mercy.
You made us the reproach of our neighbors,
   the mockery and the scorn of those around
   us.

You made us a byword among the nations,
　a laughingstock among the peoples.
Ry. Save us, Lord, in your mercy.
Why do you hide your face,
　forgetting our woe and our oppression?
For our souls are bowed down to the dust,
　our bodies are pressed to the earth.
Ry. Save us, Lord, in your mercy.

Years I and II

GOSPEL　　　　　　　　　　　　　　Mk 1, 40-45
Alleluia

See no. 509.

✠ A reading from the holy gospel according
　　　　　　to Mark

The leper went away from him, cleansed.

A leper approached Jesus with a request,
kneeling down as he addressed him: "If you
will to do so, you can cure me." Moved with
pity, Jesus stretched out his hand, touched him,
and said: "I do will it. Be cured." The leprosy
left him then and there, and he was cured.
Jesus gave him a stern warning and sent him
on his way. "Not a word to anyone, now,"
he said. "Go off and present yourself to the
priest and offer for your cure what Moses
prescribed. That should be a proof for them."
The man went off and began to proclaim the
whole matter freely, making the story public.
As a result of this, it was no longer possible
for Jesus to enter a town openly. He stayed in
desert places; yet people kept coming to him
from all sides.
　　　　　This is the gospel of the Lord.

309　　　**FRIDAY OF THE FIRST
　　　　　WEEK OF THE YEAR**

Year I

READING I　　　　　　　　　　　Heb 4, 1-5. 11
A reading from the letter to the Hebrews

We must be eager to reach the place of rest.

While the promise of entrance into his rest
still holds, we ought to be fearful of disobeying
lest any one of you be judged to have lost his
chance of entering. We have indeed heard the
good news, as they did. But the word which
they heard did not profit them, for they did not
receive it in faith. It is we, who have believed,
who enter into that rest, just as God said:
　"Thus I swore in my anger,
　'They shall never enter into my rest.' "
Yet God's work was finished when he created
the world, for in reference to the seventh day
Scripture somewhere says, "And God rested
from all his work on the seventh day," and
again, in the place we referred to, God says,
"They shall never enter into my rest." Let us
strive to enter into that rest, so that no one
may fall in imitation of the example of Israel's
unbelief.
　　　　　This is the Word of the Lord.

Responsorial Psalm　　　Ps 78, 3. 4. 6-7. 8

Ry. (7) Do not forget the works of the Lord!
What we have heard and know,
　　and what our fathers have declared to us,
　　we will declare to the generation to come
The glorious deeds of the Lord and his strength
　　and the wonders that he wrought.
Ry. Do not forget the works of the Lord!
That they too may rise and declare to their sons
　　that they should put their hope in God,
And not forget the deeds of God
　　but keep his commands.
Ry. Do not forget the works of the Lord!
And not be like their fathers,
　　a generation wayward and rebellious,
A generation that kept not its heart steadfast
　　nor its spirit faithful toward God.
Ry. Do not forget the works of the Lord!

Year II

READING I　　　　　　　　　1 Sm 8, 4-7. 10-22
A reading from the first book of Samuel

You will cry out because of your king, but the Lord will not
answer you because you have chosen him yourselves.

All the elders of Israel came in a body to
Samuel at Ramah and said to him, "Now that
you are old, and your sons do not follow your
example, appoint a king over us, as other
nations have, to judge us."

Samuel was displeased when they asked for a king to judge them. He prayed to the Lord, however, who said in answer: "Grant the people's every request. It is not you they reject, they are rejecting me as their king."

Samuel delivered the message of the Lord in full to those who were asking him for a king. He told them: "The rights of the king who will rule you will be as follows: He will take your sons and assign them to his chariots and horses, and they will run before his chariot. He will also appoint from among them his commanders of groups of a thousand and of a hundred soldiers. He will set them to do his plowing and his harvesting, and to make his implements of war and the equipment of his chariots. He will use your daughters as ointment-makers, as cooks, and as bakers. He will take the best of your fields, vineyards, and olive groves, and give them to his officials. He will tithe your crops and your vineyards, and give the revenue to his eunuchs and his slaves. He will take your male and female servants, as well as your best oxen and your asses, and use them to do his work. He will tithe your flocks and you yourselves will become his slaves. When this takes place, you will complain against the king whom you have chosen, but on that day the Lord will not answer you."

The people, however, refused to listen to Samuel's warning and said, "Not so! There must be a king over us. We too must be like other nations, with a king to rule us and to lead us in warfare and fight our battles." When Samuel had listened to all the people had to say, he repeated it to the Lord, who then said to him, "Grant their request and appoint a king to rule them."

This is the Word of the Lord.

Responsorial Psalm　　　　Ps 89, 16-17. 18-19

℟. (2) For ever I will sing the goodness of the Lord.
Happy the people who know the joyful shout;
　in the light of your countenance, O Lord,
　they walk.

At your name they rejoice all the day,
　and through your justice they are exalted.
℟. For ever I will sing the goodness of the Lord.
For you are the splendor of their strength,
　and by your favor our horn is exalted.
For to the Lord belongs our shield,
　and to the Holy One of Israel, our king.
℟. For ever I will sing the goodness of the Lord.

Years I and II

GOSPEL　　　　　　　　　　Mk 2, 1-12
Alleluia

See no. 509.

✠ **A reading from the holy gospel according to Mark**
The Son of Man has authority on earth to forgive sins.

Jesus came back to Capernaum after a lapse of several days and word got around that he was at home. At that they began to gather in great numbers. There was no longer any room for them, even around the door. While he was delivering God's word to them, some people arrived bringing a paralyzed man to him. The four who carried him were unable to bring him to Jesus because of the crowd, so they began to open up the roof over the spot where Jesus was. When they had made a hole, they let down the mat on which the paralytic was lying. When Jesus saw their faith, he said to the paralyzed man, "My son, your sins are forgiven." Now some of the scribes were sitting there asking themselves: "Why does the man talk in that way? He commits blasphemy! Who can forgive sins except God alone?" Jesus was immediately aware of their reasoning, though they kept it to themselves, and he said to them: "Why do you harbor these thoughts? Which is easier, to say to the paralytic, 'Your sins are forgiven,' or to say, 'Stand up, pick up your mat, and walk again'? That you may know that the Son of Man has authority on earth to forgive sins" (he said to the paralyzed man), "I command you: Stand up! Pick up your mat and go home." The man stood and picked up his mat and went outside in the sight of everyone. They were awestruck; all gave praise to God, saying, "We have never seen anything like this!"

This is the gospel of the Lord.

---

310   **SATURDAY OF THE FIRST WEEK OF THE YEAR**

Year I

READING I   Heb 4, 12-16

A reading from the letter to the Hebrews
Let us approach the throne of grace with confidence.

God's word is living and effective, sharper than any two-edged sword. It penetrates and divides soul and spirit, joints and marrow; it judges the reflections and thoughts of the heart. Nothing is concealed from him; all lies bare and exposed to the eyes of him to whom we must render an account.

Since, then, we have a great high priest who has passed through the heavens, Jesus, the Son of God, let us hold fast to our profession of faith. For we do not have a high priest who is unable to sympathize with our weakness, but one who was tempted in every way that we are, yet never sinned. So let us confidently approach the throne of grace to receive mercy and favor and to find help in time of need.

This is the Word of the Lord.

Responsorial Psalm   Ps 19, 8. 9. 10. 15

℟. (Jn 6, 64) Your words, Lord, are spirit and life.

The law of the Lord is perfect,
   refreshing the soul;
The decree of the Lord is trustworthy,
   giving wisdom to the simple.

℟. Your words, Lord, are spirit and life.

The precepts of the Lord are right,
   rejoicing the heart;
The command of the Lord is clear,
   enlightening the eye.

℟. Your words, Lord, are spirit and life.

The fear of the Lord is pure,
   enduring forever;
The ordinances of the Lord are true,
   all of them just.

℟. Your words, Lord, are spirit and life.

Let the words of my mouth and the thought of
   my heart
   find favor before you,
O Lord, my rock and my redeemer.

℟. Your words, Lord, are spirit and life.

Year II

READING I   1 Sm 9, 1-4. 17-19; 10, 1

A reading from the first book of Samuel
This is the man of whom the Lord God spoke, Saul who will rule his people.

There was a stalwart man from Benjamin named Kish, who was the son of Abiel, son of Zeror, son of Becorath, son of Aphiah, a Benjaminite. He had a son named Saul, who was a handsome young man. There was no other Israelite handsomer than Saul; he stood head and shoulders above the people.

Now the asses of Saul's father, Kish, had wandered off. Kish said to his son Saul, "Take one of the servants with you and go out and hunt for the asses." Accordingly they went through the hill country of Ephraim, and through the land of Shalishah. Not finding them there they continued through the land of Shaalim without success. They also went through the land of Benjamin, but they failed to find the animals.

When Samuel caught sight of Saul, the Lord assured him, "This is the man of whom I told you; he is to govern my people."

Saul met Samuel in the gateway and said, "Please tell me where the seer lives." Samuel answered Saul: "I am the seer. Go up ahead of me to the high place and eat with me today. In the morning, before dismissing you, I will tell you whatever you wish."

From a flask Samuel had with him, he poured oil on Saul's head; he also kissed him, saying: "The Lord anoints you commander over his heritage. You are to govern the Lord's people Israel, and to save them from the grasp of their enemies round about."

This is the Word of the Lord.

Responsorial Psalm   Ps 21, 2-3. 4-5. 6-7

℟. (2) Lord, your strength gives joy to the
     king.

O Lord, in your strength the king is glad;
in your victory how greatly he rejoices!
You have granted him his heart's desire;
you refused not the wish of his lips.

℟. Lord, your strength gives joy to the king.

For you welcomed him with goodly blessings,
you placed on his head a crown of pure gold.
He asked life of you: you gave him
length of days forever and ever.

℟. Lord, your strength gives joy to the king.

Great is his glory in your victory;
majesty and splendor you conferred upon
him.
For you made him a blessing forever;
you gladdened him with the joy of your
presence.

℟. Lord, your strength gives joy to the king.

Years I and II

GOSPEL   Mk 2, 13-17
Alleluia

See no. 509.

✠ **A reading from the holy gospel according**
to Mark

I have not come to call the just, but sinners.

While Jesus went walking along the lakeshore,
people kept coming to him in crowds and he
taught them. As he moved on he saw Levi the
son of Alphaeus at his tax collector's post,
and said to him, "Follow me." Levi got up and
became his follower. While Jesus was reclin-
ing to eat in Levi's house, many tax collectors
and those known as sinners joined him and his
disciples at dinner. The number of those who
followed him was large. When the scribes who
belonged to the Pharisee party saw that he was
eating with tax collectors and offenders
against the law, they complained to his dis-
ciples, "Why does he eat with such as these?"
Overhearing the remark, Jesus said to them,
"People who are healthy do not need a doctor;
sick people do. I have come to call sinners, not
the self-righteous."

This is the gospel of the Lord.

311   MONDAY OF THE SECOND
WEEK OF THE YEAR

Year I

READING I   Heb 5, 1-10
A reading from the letter to the Hebrews

Since he is the Son of God, he becomes for all who obey
him the source of salvation.

Every high priest is taken from among men
and made their representative before God, to
offer gifts and sacrifices for sins. He is able
to deal patiently with erring sinners, for he is
himself beset by weakness and so must make
sin offerings for himself as well as for the
people. One does not take this honor on his
own initiative, but only when called by God
as Aaron was. Even Christ did not glorify
himself with the office of high priest; he re-
ceived it from the One who said to him,

"You are my son;
today I have begotten you";
just as he says in another place,
"You are a priest forever,
according to the order of Melchizedek."
In the days when he was in the flesh, he
offered prayers and supplications with loud
cries and tears to God, who was able to save
him from death, and he was heard because of
his reverence. Son though he was, he learned
obedience from what he suffered; and when
perfected, he became the source of eternal sal-
vation for all who obey him, designated by
God as high priest according to the order of
Melchizedek.

This is the Word of the Lord.

Responsorial Psalm   Ps 110, 1. 2. 3. 4

℟. (4) You are a priest for ever, in the line of
     Melchizedek.

The Lord said to my Lord: "Sit at my right
hand
till I make your enemies your footstool."

℟. You are a priest for ever, in the line of
   Melchizedek.

The scepter of your power the Lord will stretch
forth from Zion:
"Rule in the midst of your enemies."

℟. You are a priest for ever, in the line of Melchizedek.

"Yours is princely power in the day of your birth, in holy splendor;
  before the daystar, like the dew, I have begotten you."

℟. You are a priest for ever, in the line of Melchizedek.

The Lord has sworn, and he will not repent:
  "You are a priest forever, according to the order of Melchizedek."

℟. You are a priest for ever, in the line of Melchizedek.

Year II

READING I   1 Sm 15, 16-23

A reading from the first book of Samuel

Obedience is better than sacrifice. Since you have rejected the voice of the Lord God, he has rejected you as king.

Samuel said to Saul: "Stop! Let me tell you what the Lord said to me last night." "Speak!" he replied. Samuel then said: "Though little in your own esteem, are you not leader of the tribes of Israel? The Lord anointed you king of Israel and sent you on a mission, saying, 'Go and put the sinful Amalekites under a ban of destruction. Fight against them until you have exterminated them.' Why, then, have you disobeyed the Lord? You have pounced on the spoil, thus displeasing the Lord." Saul answered Samuel: "I did indeed obey the Lord and fulfill the mission on which the Lord sent me. I have brought back Agag, and I have destroyed Amalek under the ban. But from the spoil the men took sheep and oxen, the best of what had been banned, to sacrifice to the Lord their God in Gilgal."
  But Samuel said:
"Does the Lord so delight in holocausts and sacrifices
  as in obedience to the command of the Lord?
Obedience is better than sacrifice,
  and submission than the fat of rams.
For a sin like divination is rebellion,
  and presumption is the crime of idolatry.
Because you have rejected the command of the Lord,
  he, too, has rejected you as ruler."
This is the Word of the Lord.

Responsorial Psalm   Ps 50, 8-9. 16-17. 21. 23

℟. (23) To the upright I will show
  the saving power of God.

Not for your sacrifices do I rebuke you,
  for your holocausts are before me always.
I take from your house no bullock,
  no goats out of your fold.

℟. To the upright I will show
  the saving power of God.

Why do you recite my statutes,
  and profess my covenant with your mouth,
Though you hate discipline
  and cast my words behind you?

℟. To the upright I will show
  the saving power of God.

When you do these things, shall I be deaf to it?
  Or do you think that I am like yourself?
  I will correct you by drawing them up before your eyes.
He that offers praise as a sacrifice glorifies me;
  and to him that goes the right way I will
  show the salvation of God.

℟. To the upright I will show
  the saving power of God.

Years I and II

GOSPEL   Mk 2, 18-22
Alleluia

See no. 509.

✠ A reading from the holy gospel according to Mark

The bridegroom is still with them.

John's disciples and the Pharisees were accustomed to fast. People came to Jesus with the objection, "Why do John's disciples and those of the Pharisees fast while yours do not?" Jesus replied: "How can the guests at a wedding fast as long as the groom is still among them? So long as the groom stays with them, they cannot fast. The day will come, however, when the groom will be taken away from them; on that day they will fast. No one sews a patch of unshrunken cloth on an old cloak. If he should do so, the very thing he has used to cover the hole would pull away—the new from the old—and the tear would get worse. Similarly, no man pours new wine into old

wineskins. If he does so, the wine will burst the skins and both wine and skins will be lost. No, new wine is poured into new skins."
This is the gospel of the Lord.

---

312   **TUESDAY OF THE SECOND WEEK OF THE YEAR**

Year I

READING I   Heb 6, 10-20

A reading from the letter to the Hebrews

We have a source of strength to take firm grip of the hope that is held out to us.

God is not unjust; he will not forget your work and the love you have shown him by your service, past and present, to his holy people. Our desire is that each of you show the same zeal till the end, fully assured of that for which you hope. Do not grow lazy, but imitate those who, through faith and patience, are inheriting the promises.

When God made his promise to Abraham, he swore by himself, having no one greater to swear by, and said, "I will indeed bless you, and multiply you." And so, after patient waiting, Abraham obtained what God had promised. Men swear by someone greater than themselves; an oath gives firmness to a promise and puts an end to all argument. God, wishing to give the heirs of his promise even clearer evidence that his purpose would not change, guaranteed it by oath, so that, by two things that are unchangeable, in which, he could not lie, we who have taken refuge in him might be strongly encouraged to seize the hope which is placed before us. Like a sure and firm anchor, that hope extends beyond the veil through which Jesus, our forerunner, has entered on our behalf, being made high priest forever according to the order of Melchizedek.
This is the Word of the Lord.

Responsorial Psalm   Ps 111, 1-2. 4-5. 9-10

℟. (5) The Lord will remember his covenant for ever.
I will give thanks to the Lord with all my heart
   in the company and assembly of the just.

Great are the works of the Lord,
   exquisite in all their delights.
℟. The Lord will remember his covenant for ever.

He has won renown for his wondrous deeds;
   gracious and merciful is the Lord.
He has given food to those who fear him;
   he will forever be mindful of his covenant.
℟. The Lord will remember his covenant for ever.

He has sent deliverance to his people;
   he has ratified his covenant forever;
   holy and awesome is his name.
His praise endures forever.
℟. The Lord will remember his covenant for ever.
℟. Or: Alleluia.

Year II

READING I   1 Sm 16, 1-13

A reading from the first book of Samuel

Samuel anointed David where he stood with his brothers, and the spirit of the Lord God was with him.

The Lord said to Samuel: "How long will you grieve for Saul, whom I have rejected as king of Israel? Fill your horn with oil, and be on your way. I am sending you to Jesse of Bethlehem, for I have chosen my king from among his sons." But Samuel replied: "How can I go? Saul will hear of it and kill me." To this the Lord answered: "Take a heifer along and say, 'I have come to sacrifice to the Lord.' Invite Jesse to the sacrifice, and I myself will tell you what to do; you are to anoint for me the one I point out to you."

Samuel did as the Lord had commanded him. When he entered Bethlehem, the elders of the city came trembling to meet him and inquired, "Is your visit peaceful, O seer?" He replied: "Yes! I have come to sacrifice to the Lord. So cleanse yourselves and join me today for the banquet." He also had Jesse and his sons cleanse themselves and invited them to the sacrifice. As they came, he looked at Eliab and thought, "Surely the Lord's anointed is here before him." But the Lord said to Samuel: "Do not judge from his appearance or from his lofty stature, because I have rejected him. Not as man sees does God see, because man sees the appearance but the Lord looks into the heart." Then Jesse called Abinadab and presented him before Samuel, who said, "The Lord has not chosen him." Next Jesse presented Shammah, but Samuel said, "The Lord has not chosen this one either." In the same way Jesse presented seven sons before Samuel, but Samuel said to Jesse, "The Lord has not chosen any one of these." Then Samuel asked Jesse, "Are these all the sons you have?" Jesse replied, "There is still the youngest, who is tending the sheep." Samuel said to Jesse, "Send for him; we will not begin the sacrificial banquet until he arrives here." Jesse sent and had the young man brought to them. He was ruddy, a youth handsome to behold and making a splendid appearance. The Lord said, "There—anoint him, for this is he!" Then Samuel, with the horn of oil in hand, anointed him in the midst of his brothers; and from that day on, the spirit of the Lord rushed upon David. When Samuel took his leave, he went to Ramah.

This is the Word of the Lord.

Responsorial Psalm   Ps 89, 20. 21-22. 27-28

℟. (21) I have found David, my servant.
Once you spoke in a vision,
  and to your faithful ones you said:
"On a champion I have placed a crown;
  over the people I have set a youth."
℟. I have found David, my servant.
I have found David, my servant;
  with my holy oil I have anointed him,
That my hand may be always with him,
  and that my arm may make him strong.
℟. I have found David, my servant.
He shall say of me, "You are my father,
  my God, the Rock, my savior."
And I will make him the first-born,
  highest of the kings of the earth.
℟. I have found David, my servant.

Years I and II

GOSPEL   Mk 2, 23-28
Alleluia

See no. 509.

✠ **A reading from the holy gospel according to Mark**
The sabbath was made for man, not man for the sabbath.

It happened that the Lord was walking through standing grain on the sabbath, and his disciples began to pull off heads of grain as they went along. At this the Pharisees protested: "Look! Why do they do a thing not permitted on the sabbath?" He said to them: "Have you never read what David did when he was in need and he and his men were hungry? How he entered God's house in the days of Abiathar the high priest and ate the holy bread which only the priests were permitted to eat? He even gave it to his men." Then he said to them: "The sabbath was made for man, not man for the sabbath. That is why the Son of Man is lord even of the sabbath."

This is the gospel of the Lord.

313   **WEDNESDAY OF THE SECOND WEEK OF THE YEAR**

Year I

READING I   Heb 7, 1-3. 15-17

A reading from the letter to the Hebrews
You are a priest for ever of the order of Melchizedek.

Melchizedek, king of Salem and priest of the Most High God, met Abraham returning from his defeat of the kings and blessed him. And Abraham apportioned to him one tenth of all his booty. His name means "king of justice"; he was also king of Salem, that is, "king of peace." Without father, mother or ancestry, without beginning of days or end of life, like the Son of God he remains a priest forever.

The matter is clearer still if another priest is appointed according to the likeness of Melchizedek: one who has become a priest, not in virtue of a law expressed in a commandment concerning physical descent, but in virtue of the power of a life which cannot be destroyed. Scripture testifies: "You are a priest forever according to the order of Melchizedek."

This is the Word of the Lord.

Responsorial Psalm

℟. (4) You are a priest for ever,
in the line of Melchizedek.

The Lord said to my Lord: "Sit at my right
hand
till I make your enemies your footstool."

℟. You are a priest for ever,
in the line of Melchizedek.

The scepter of your power the Lord will stretch
forth from Zion:
"Rule in the midst of your enemies."

℟. You are a priest for ever,
in the line of Melchizedek.

"Yours is princely power in the day of your
birth, in holy splendor;
before the daystar, like the dew, I have begotten you."

℟. You are a priest for ever,
in the line of Melchizedek.

The Lord has sworn, and he will not repent:
"You are a priest forever, according to the
order of Melchizedek."

℟. You are a priest for ever,
in the line of Melchizedek.

Year II

READING I   1 Sm 17, 32-33. 37. 40-51

A reading from the first book of Samuel

David triumphed over the Philistine with a sling and a stone.

Then David spoke to Saul: "Let your majesty
not lose courage. I am at your service to go and
fight this Philistine." But Saul answered
David, "You cannot go up against this Philistine and fight with him, for you are only a
youth, while he has been a warrior from his
youth."

David continued: "The Lord, who delivered
me from the claws of the lion and the bear, will
also keep me safe from the clutches of this
Philistine." Saul answered David, "Go! the
Lord will be with you."

Then, staff in hand, David selected five
smooth stones from the wadi and put them in
the pocket of his shepherd's bag. With his sling
also ready to hand, he approached the Philistine.

With his shield-bearer marching before him,
the Philistine also advanced closer and closer
to David. When he had sized David up, and
seen that he was youthful, and ruddy, and
handsome in appearance, he held him in contempt. The Philistine said to David, "Am I a
dog that you come against me with a staff?"
Then the Philistine cursed David by his gods
and said to him, "Come here to me, and I will
leave your flesh for the birds of the air and the
beasts of the field." David answered him:

"You come against me with sword and spear
and scimitar, but I come against you in the
name of the Lord of hosts, the God of the armies
of Israel that you have insulted. Today the
Lord shall deliver you into my hand; I will
strike you down and cut off your head. This
very day I will leave your corpse and the
corpses of the Philistine army for the birds of
the air and the beasts of the field; thus the
whole land shall learn that Israel has a God. All
this multitude, too, shall learn that it is not by
sword or spear that the Lord saves. For the
battle is the Lord's, and he shall deliver you
into our hands."

The Philistine then moved to meet David at
close quarters, while David ran quickly toward
the battle line in the direction of the Philistine.
David put his hand into the bag and took out a
stone, hurled it with the sling, and struck the
Philistine on the forehead. The stone embedded
itself in his brow, and he fell prostrate on the
ground. [Thus David overcame the Philistine
with sling and stone; he struck the Philistine
mortally, and did it without a sword.] Then
David ran and stood over him; with the Philistine's own sword [which he drew from its
sheath] he dispatched him and cut off his head.

This is the Word of the Lord.

Responsorial Psalm   Ps 144, 1. 2. 9-10

℟. (1) Blessed be the Lord, my Rock!

Blessed be the Lord, my rock,
who trains my hands for battle, my fingers
for war.

℟. Blessed be the Lord, my Rock!

My refuge and my fortress,
my stronghold, my deliverer,

My shield, in whom I trust,
  who subdues peoples under me.
℟. Blessed be the Lord, my Rock!
O God, I will sing a new song to you;
  with a ten-stringed lyre I will chant your
  praise,
You who give victory to kings,
  and deliver David, your servant.
℟. Blessed be the Lord, my Rock!

Years I and II

GOSPEL   Mk 3, 1-6
Alleluia

See no. 509.

✠ A reading from the holy gospel according
                    to Mark

Is it against the law on the sabbath day to do good—to
              save life or to kill?

Jesus returned to the synagogue where there
was a man whose hand was shriveled up. The
Pharisees kept an eye on Jesus to see whether
he would heal him on the sabbath, hoping to be
able to bring an accusation against him. He addressed the man with the shriveled hand:
"Stand up here in front!" Then he said to them:
"Is it permitted to do a good deed on the sabbath—or an evil one? To preserve life—or to
destroy it?" At this they remained silent. He
looked around at them angrily, for he was
deeply grieved that they had closed their minds
against him. Then he said to the man, "Stretch
out your hand." The man did so and his hand
was perfectly restored. When the Pharisees
went outside, they immediately began to plot
with the Herodians on how they might destroy
him.
            This is the gospel of the Lord.

---

314   **THURSDAY OF THE SECOND
            WEEK OF THE YEAR**

Year I

READING I   Heb 7, 25–8, 6
    A reading from the letter to the Hebrews

He lives for ever to intercede for all who came to God
                 through him.

Jesus is always able to save those who approach God through him, since he forever lives
to make intercession for them.

It was fitting that we should have such a
high priest: holy, innocent, undefiled, separated from sinners, higher than the heavens.
Unlike the other high priests, he has no need to
offer sacrifice day after day, first for his own
sins and then for those of the people; he did
that once for all when he offered himself. For
the law sets up as high priests men who are
weak, but the word of the oath which came
after the law appoints as priest the Son, made
perfect forever.

The main point in what we are saying is this:
we have such a high priest, who has taken his
seat at the right hand of the throne of the
Majesty in heaven, minister of the sanctuary
and of that true tabernacle set up not by man
but by the Lord. Now every high priest is appointed to offer gifts and sacrifices; hence the
necessity for this one to have something to
offer. If he were on earth he would not be a
priest, for there are priests already offering the
gifts which the law prescribes. They offer worship in a sanctuary which is only a copy and
shadow of the heavenly one, for Moses, when
about to erect the tabernacle, was warned,
"See that you make everything according to
the pattern shown you on the mountain." Jesus
has obtained a more excellent ministry now,
just as he is mediator of a better covenant,
founded on better promises.
          This is the Word of the Lord.

Responsorial Psalm   Ps 40, 7-8. 8-9. 10. 17
℟. (8. 9) Here am I, Lord;
    I come to do your will.
Sacrifice or oblation you wished not,
    but ears open to obedience you gave me.
Holocausts or sin-offerings you sought not;
    then said I, "Behold I come."
℟. Here am I, Lord;
    I come to do your will.
"In the written scroll it is prescribed for me,
    to do your will, O my God, is my delight,
And your law is within my heart!"

℞. Here am I, Lord;
  I come to do your will.
I announced your justice in the vast assembly;
  I did not restrain my lips, as you, O Lord,
    know.
℞. Here am I, Lord;
  I come to do your will.
May all who seek you
  exult and be glad in you,
And may those who love your salvation
  say ever, "The Lord be glorified."
℞. Here am I, Lord;
  I come to do your will.

Year II

READING I   1 Sm 18, 6-9; 19, 1-7

A reading from the first book of Samuel
My father Saul is looking for a way to kill you.

At the approach of Saul and David (on David's
return after slaying the Philistine), women
came out from each of the cities of Israel to
meet King Saul, singing and dancing, with
tambourines, joyful songs, and sistrums. The
women played and sang:
  "Saul has slain his thousands,
    and David his ten thousands."
Saul was very angry and resentful of the song,
for he thought: "They give David ten thousands, but only thousands to me. All that remains for him is the kingship." [And from that
day on, Saul was jealous of David.]

Saul discussed his intention of killing David
with his son Jonathan and with all his servants. But Saul's son Jonathan, who was very
fond of David, told him: "My father Saul is trying to kill you. Therefore, please be on your
guard tomorrow morning; get out of sight and
remain in hiding. I, however, will go out and
stand beside my father in the countryside
where you are, and will speak to him about
you. If I learn anything, I will let you know."

Jonathan then spoke well of David to his father Saul, saying to him: "Let not your majesty
sin against his servant David, for he has committed no offense against you, but has helped
you very much by his deeds. When he took his
life in his hands and slew the Philistine, and the
Lord brought about a great victory for all Israel

through him, you were glad to see it. Why,
then, should you become guilty of shedding innocent blood by killing David without cause?"
Saul heeded Jonathan's plea and swore, "As
the Lord lives, he shall not be killed." So Jonathan summoned David and repeated the whole
conversation to him. Jonathan then brought
David to Saul, and David served him as before.

This is the Word of the Lord.

Responsorial Psalm   Ps 56, 2-3. 9-10. 10-12. 13-14

℞. (5) In God I trust;
  I shall not fear.
Have pity on me, O God, for men trample upon
    me;
  all the day they press their attack against
    me.
My adversaries trample upon me all the day;
  yes, many fight against me.
℞. In God I trust;
  I shall not fear.
My wanderings you have counted;
  my tears are stored in your flask;
  are they not recorded in your book?
Then do my enemies turn back,
  when I call upon you.
℞. In God I trust;
  I shall not fear.
Now I know that God is with me.
  In God, in whose promise I glory,
In God I trust without fear;
  what can flesh do against me?
℞. In God I trust;
  I shall not fear.
I am bound, O God, by vows to you;
  your thank offerings I will fulfill.
For you have rescued me from death,
  my feet, too, from stumbling;
  that I may walk before God in the light of the
    living.
℞. In God I trust;
  I shall not fear.

Years I and II

GOSPEL   Mk 3, 7-12
Alleluia
See no. 509.

✠ A reading from the holy gospel according
to Mark

*The unclean spirits shouted, you are the Son of God, but
he warned them not to make him known.*

Jesus withdrew toward the lake with his disciples. A great crowd followed him from Galilee,
and an equally great multitude came to him
from Judea, Jerusalem, Idumea, Transjordan,
and the neighborhood of Tyre and Sidon, because they had heard what he had done. In
view of their numbers, he told his disciples to
have a fishing boat ready for him so that he
could avoid the press of the crowd against him.
Because he had cured many, all who had afflictions kept pushing toward him to touch him.
Unclean spirits would catch sight of him, fling
themselves down at his feet, and shout, "You
are the Son of God!", while he kept ordering
them sternly not to reveal who he was.

    This is the gospel of the Lord.

---

315   FRIDAY OF THE SECOND
WEEK OF THE YEAR

Year I

READING I   Heb 8, 6-13

A reading from the letter to the Hebrews

He is mediator of a better covenant.

Jesus our high priest has obtained a more excellent ministry now just as he is mediator of a
better covenant, founded on better promises.

    If that first covenant had been faultless,
there would have been no place for a second
one. But God, finding fault with them, says:
"Days are coming, says the Lord,
    when I will make a new covenant with the
      house of Israel
    and with the house of Judah.
It will not be like the covenant I made with
      their fathers
    the day I took them by the hand
    to lead them forth from the land of Egypt;
For they broke my covenant
    and I grew weary of them, says the Lord.
But this is the covenant I will make with the
      house of Israel

after those days, says the Lord:
I will place my laws in their minds
    and I will write them upon their hearts;
I will be their God
    and they shall be my people.
And they shall not teach their fellow citizens
    or their brothers, saying, 'Know the Lord,'
for all shall know me, from least to greatest.
I will forgive their evildoing,
    and their sins I will remember no more."
When he says, "a new covenant," he declares
the first one obsolete. And what has become
obsolete and has grown old is close to disap-
pearing.

    This is the Word of the Lord.

Responsorial Psalm   Ps 85, 8. 10. 11-12. 13-14

℟. (11) Kindness and truth shall meet.
Show us, O Lord, your kindness,
    and grant us your salvation.
Near indeed is his salvation to those who fear
      him,
    glory dwelling in our land.
℟. Kindness and truth shall meet.
Kindness and truth shall meet;
    justice and peace shall kiss.
Truth shall spring out of the earth,
    and justice shall look down from heaven.
℟. Kindness and truth shall meet.
The Lord himself will give his benefits;
    our land shall yield its increase.
Justice shall walk before him,
    and salvation, along the way of his steps.
℟. Kindness and truth shall meet.

Year II

READING I   1 Sm 24, 3-21

A reading from the first book of Samuel

*I shall not raise my hand against him, for he is the anointed
of the Lord God.*

Saul took three thousand picked men from all
Israel and went in search of David and his men
in the direction of the wild goat crags. When
he came to the sheepfolds along the way, he
found a cave, which he entered to ease nature.
David and his men were occupying the inmost
recesses of the cave.

David's servants said to him, "This is the day of which the Lord said to you, 'I will deliver your enemy into your grasp; do with him as you see fit.' " So David moved up and stealthily cut off an end of Saul's mantle. Afterward, however, David regretted that he had cut off an end of Saul's mantle. He said to his men, "The Lord forbid that I should do such a thing to my master, the Lord's anointed, as to lay a hand on him, for he is the Lord's anointed." With these words David restrained his men and would not permit them to attack Saul. Saul then left the cave and went on his way. David also stepped out of the cave, calling to Saul, "My lord the king!" When Saul looked back, David bowed to the ground in homage and asked Saul:

"Why do you listen to those who say, 'David is trying to harm you'? You see for yourself today that the Lord just now delivered you into my grasp in the cave. I had some thought of killing you, but I took pity on you instead. I decided, 'I will not raise a hand against my lord, for he is the Lord's anointed and a father to me.' Look here at this end of your mantle which I hold. Since I cut off an end of your mantle and did not kill you, see and be convinced that I plan no harm and no rebellion. I have done you no wrong, though you are hunting me down to take my life. The Lord will judge between me and you, and the Lord will exact justice from you in my case. I shall not touch you. The old proverb says, 'From the wicked comes forth wickedness.' So I will take no action against you. Against whom are you on campaign, O king of Israel? Whom are you pursuing? A dead dog, or a single flea! The Lord will be the judge; he will decide between me and you. May he see this, and take my part, and grant me justice beyond your reach!"

When David finished saying these things to Saul, Saul answered, "Is that your voice, my son David?" And he wept aloud. Saul then said to David: "You are in the right rather than I; you have treated me generously, while I have done you harm. Great is the generosity you showed me today, when the Lord delivered me into your grasp and you did not kill me. For if a man meets his enemy, does he send him away unharmed? May the Lord reward you generously for what you have done this day. And now, I know that you shall surely be king and that sovereignty over Israel shall come into your possession."

This is the Word of the Lord.

Responsorial Psalm   Ps 57, 2. 3-4. 6. 11

℟. (2) Have mercy on me, God, have mercy.
Have pity on me, O God; have pity on me,
    for in you I take refuge.
In the shadow of your wings I take refuge,
    till harm pass by.
℟. Have mercy on me, God, have mercy.
I call to God the Most High,
    to God, my benefactor.
May he send from heaven and save me;
    may he make those a reproach who trample
        upon me;
    may God send his kindness and his faithful-
        ness.
℟. Have mercy on me, God, have mercy.
Be exalted above the heavens, O God;
    above all the earth be your glory!
For your kindness towers to the heavens,
    and your faithfulness to the skies.
℟. Have mercy on me, God, have mercy.

Years I and II

GOSPEL   Mk 3, 13-19
Alleluia
See no. 509.

✠ **A reading from the holy gospel according to Mark**

He called those he wanted and they went with him.

Jesus went up the mountain and summoned the men he himself had decided on, who came and joined him. He named twelve as his companions whom he would send to preach the good news; they were likewise to have authority to expel demons. He appointed the Twelve as follows: Simon to whom he gave the name Peter; James, son of Zebedee; and John, the brother of James (he gave these two the name Boanerges, or "sons of thunder"); Andrew, Philip, Bartholomew, Matthew, Thomas,

James son of Alphaeus; Thaddaeus, Simon of the Zealot party, and Judas Iscariot, who betrayed him.

> **This is the gospel of the Lord.**

---

316   SATURDAY OF THE SECOND WEEK OF THE YEAR

Year I

READING I   Heb 9, 2-3. 11-14

A reading from the letter to the Hebrews

Through his own blood he has entered into a more perfect covenant.

A tabernacle was constructed, the outer one, in which were the lampstand, and the table, and the showbread; this was called the holy place. Behind the second veil was the tabernacle called the holy of holies.

But when Christ came as high priest of the good things which came to be, he entered once for all into the sanctuary, passing through the greater and more perfect tabernacle not made by hands, that is, not belonging to this creation. He entered not with the blood of goats and calves but with his own blood, and achieved eternal redemption. For if the blood of goats and bulls and the sprinkling of a heifer's ashes can sanctify those who are defiled so that their flesh is cleansed, how much more will the blood of Christ, who through the eternal spirit offered himself up unblemished to God, cleanse our consciences from dead works to worship the living God!

> **This is the Word of the Lord.**

Responsorial Psalm   Ps 47, 2-3. 6-7. 8-9

℟. (6) God mounts his throne to shouts of joy;
    a blare of trumpets for the Lord.
All you peoples, clap your hands,
    shout to God with cries of gladness,
For the Lord, the Most High, the awesome,
    is the great king over all the earth.
℟. God mounts his throne to shouts of joy;
    a blare of trumpets for the Lord.
God mounts his throne amid shouts of joy;
    the Lord, amid trumpet blasts.
Sing praise to God, sing praise;
    sing praise to our king, sing praise.

℟. God mounts his throne to shouts of joy;
    a blare of trumpets for the Lord.
For king of all the earth is God:
    sing hymns of praise.
God reigns over the nations,
    God sits upon his holy throne.
℟. God mounts his throne to shouts of joy;
    a blare of trumpets for the Lord.

Year II

READING I   2 Sm 1, 1-4. 11-12. 19. 23-27

A reading from the second book of Samuel

How the heroes were killed in the battle!

David returned from his defeat of the Amalekites and spent two days in Ziklag. On the third day a man came from Saul's camp, with his clothes torn and dirt on his head. Going to David, he fell to the ground in homage. David asked him, "Where do you come from?" He replied, "I have escaped from the Israelite camp." "Tell me what happened," David bade him. He answered that the soldiers had fled the battle and that many of them had fallen and were dead, among them Saul and his son Jonathan.

David seized his garments and rent them, and all the men who were with him did likewise. They mourned and wept and fasted until evening for Saul and his son Jonathan, and for the soldiers of the Lord of the clans of Israel, because they had fallen by the sword.

David chanted this elegy for Saul and his son Jonathan:
"Alas! the glory of Israel, Saul,
    slain upon your heights;
    how can the warriors have fallen!

"Saul and Jonathan, beloved and cherished,
    separated neither in life nor in death,
    swifter than eagles, stronger than lions!
Women of Israel, weep over Saul,
    who clothed you in scarlet and in finery,
    who decked your attire with ornaments of
    gold.

"How can the warriors have fallen—
    in the thick of the battle,
    slain upon your heights!

"I grieve for you, Jonathan my brother!
    most dear have you been to me;
More precious have I held love for you
    than love for women.

"How can the warriors have fallen,
    the weapons of war have perished!"
    This is the Word of the Lord.

Responsorial Psalm   Ps 80, 2-3. 5-7

℟. (4) Let us see your face, Lord,
    and we shall be saved.
O shepherd of Israel, hearken,
    O guide of the flock of Joseph!
From your throne upon the cherubim, shine
    forth
    before Ephraim, Benjamin and Manasseh.
Rouse your power,
    and come to save us.

℟. Let us see your face, Lord,
    and we shall be saved.

O Lord of hosts, how long will you burn with
    anger
    while your people pray?
You have fed them with the bread of tears
    and given them tears to drink in ample mea-
    sure.
You have left us to be fought over by our neigh-
    bors,
    and our enemies mock us.

℟. Let us see your face, Lord,
    and we shall be saved.

Years I and II

GOSPEL   Mk 3, 20-21
Alleluia

See no. 509.

✠ A reading from the holy gospel according
    to Mark
The people said that he was out of his mind.
Jesus returned to the house with his disciples
and again the crowd assembled, making it impossible for them to get any food whatever.
When his family heard of this they came to
take charge of him, saying, "He is out of his
mind."
    This is the gospel of the Lord.

**317   MONDAY OF THE THIRD
            WEEK OF THE YEAR**

Year I

READING I   Heb 9, 15. 24-28
    A reading from the letter to the Hebrews
He offered himself to take the faults of many away; he
will appear a second time to those who are awaiting him.
Christ is mediator of a new covenant: since his
death has taken place for deliverance from
transgressions committed under the first covenant, those who are called may receive the
promised eternal inheritance.
    For Christ did not enter into a sanctuary
made by hands, a mere copy of the true one; he
entered heaven itself that he might appear before God now on our behalf. Not that he might
offer himself there again and again, as the high
priest enters year after year into the sanctuary
with blood that is not his own; were that so, he
would have had to suffer death over and over
from the creation of the world. But now he has
appeared at the end of the ages to take away
sins once for all by his sacrifice. Just as it is
appointed that men die once, and after death
be judged, so Christ was offered up once to
take away the sins of many; he will appear a
second time not to take away sin but to bring
salvation to those who eagerly await him.
    This is the Word of the Lord.

Responsorial Psalm   Ps 98, 1. 2-3. 3-4. 5-6

℟. (1) Sing to the Lord a new song,
    for he has done marvelous deeds.
Sing to the Lord a new song,
    for he has done wondrous deeds;
His right hand has won victory for him,
    his holy arm.

℟. Sing to the Lord a new song,
    for he has done marvelous deeds.
The Lord has made his salvation known:
    in the sight of the nations he has revealed
    his justice.
He has remembered his kindness and his faith-
    fulness
    toward the house of Israel.

℟. Sing to the Lord a new song,
   for he has done marvelous deeds.
**All the ends of the earth have seen
   the salvation by our God.
Sing joyfully to the Lord, all you lands;
   break into song; sing praise.**
℟. Sing to the Lord a new song,
   for he has done marvelous deeds.
**Sing praise to the Lord with the harp,
   with the harp and melodious song.
With trumpets and the sound of the horn
   sing joyfully before the King, the Lord.**
℟. Sing to the Lord a new song,
   for he has done marvelous deeds.

Year II

READING I   2 Sm 5, 1-7. 10
A reading from the second book of Samuel
   It is the leader of my people Israel.

**All the tribes of Israel came to David in Hebron
and said: "Here we are, your bone and your
flesh. In days past, when Saul was our king, it
was you who led the Israelites out and brought
them back. And the Lord said to you, 'You shall
shepherd my people Israel and shall be commander of Israel.' " When all the elders of
Israel came to David in Hebron, King David
made an agreement with them there before the
Lord, and they anointed him king of Israel.
David was thirty years old when he became
king, and he reigned for forty years: seven
years and six months in Hebron over Judah,
and thirty-three years in Jerusalem over all
Israel and Judah.**
   **Then the king and his men set out for Jerusa-
lem against the Jebusites who inhabited the
region. David was told, "You cannot enter
here: the blind and the lame will drive you
away!" which was their way of saying, "David
cannot enter here." But David did take the
stronghold of Zion, which is the City of David.**
   **David grew steadily more powerful, for the
Lord of hosts was with him.**
      This is the Word of the Lord.

Responsorial Psalm   Ps 89, 20. 21-22. 25-26
℟. (25) My faithfulness and love shall be with
   him.

**Once you spoke in a vision,
   and to your faithful ones you said:
"On a champion I have placed a crown;
   over the people I have set a youth.**
℟. My faithfulness and love shall be with him.
**I have found David, my servant;
   with my holy oil I have anointed him,
That my hand may be always with him,
   and that my arm may make him strong.**
℟. My faithfulness and love shall be with him.
**My faithfulness and my kindness shall be with
   him,
   and through my name shall his horn be
      exalted.
I will set his hand upon the sea,
   his right hand upon the rivers.**
℟. My faithfulness and love shall be with him.

Years I and II

GOSPEL   Mk 3, 22-30
Alleluia
See no. 509.

✠ **A reading from the holy gospel according
                  to Mark**
   It is the end of Satan.

**The scribes who arrived from Jerusalem said of
Jesus, "He is possessed by Beelzebul," and "He
expels demons with the help of the prince of
demons." Summoning them, Jesus began to
speak to them by way of examples: "How
can Satan expel Satan? If a kingdom is torn by
civil strife, that kingdom cannot last. If a
household is divided according to loyalties,
that household will not survive. Similarly, if
Satan has suffered mutiny in his ranks and is
torn by dissension, he cannot endure; he is
finished. No one can enter a strong man's
house and despoil his property unless he has
first put him under restraint. Only then can he
plunder his house.**
   **"I give you my word, every sin will be for-
given mankind and all the blasphemies men
utter, but whoever blasphemes against the
Holy Spirit will never be forgiven. He carries
the guilt of his sin without end." He spoke thus
because they had said, "He is possessed by an
unclean spirit."**
      This is the gospel of the Lord.

**318   TUESDAY OF THE THIRD
WEEK OF THE YEAR**

Year I

READING I   Heb 10, 1-10

A reading from the letter to the Hebrews
God, I am coming to do your will.

Since the law had only a shadow of the good
things to come, and no real image of them, it
was never able to perfect the worshipers by the
same sacrifices offered continually year after
year. Were matters otherwise, the priests would
have stopped offering them, for the worshipers, once cleansed, would have had no sin on
their conscience. But through those sacrifices
there came only a yearly recalling of sins, because it is impossible for the blood of bulls and
goats to take sins away. Wherefore, on coming
into the world, Jesus said:
  "Sacrifice and offering you did not desire,
    but a body you have prepared for me;
  Holocausts and sin offerings you took no
    delight in.
  Then I said, 'As is written of me in the
    book,
  I have come to do your will, O God.'"
First he says,
  "Sacrifices and offerings, holocausts and
    sin offerings
  you neither desired nor delighted in."
(These are offered according to the prescrip-
tions of the law.) Then he says,
  "I have come to do your will."
In other words, he takes away the first cove-
nant to establish the second.
  By this "will," we have been sanctified
through the offering of the body of Jesus Christ
once for all.
    This is the Word of the Lord.

Responsorial Psalm   Ps 40, 2. 4. 7-8. 10. 11

℟. (8. 9) Here am I, Lord;
  I come to do your will.

I have waited, waited for the Lord,
  and he stooped toward me.
And he put a new song into my mouth,
  a hymn to our God.

℟. Here am I, Lord;
  I come to do your will.
Sacrifice or oblation you wished not,
  but ears open to obedience you gave me.
Holocausts or sin-offerings you sought not;
  then said I, "Behold I come."

℟. Here am I, Lord;
  I come to do your will.

I announced your justice in the vast assembly;
  I did not restrain my lips, as you, O Lord,
    know.

℟. Here am I, Lord;
  I come to do your will.

Your justice I kept not hid within my heart;
  your faithfulness and your salvation I have
    spoken of;
I have made no secret of your kindness and
  your truth
  in the vast assembly.

℟. Here am I, Lord;
  I come to do your will.

Year II

READING I   2 Sm 6, 12-15. 17-19

A reading from the second book of Samuel
David and all the house of Israel led the ark of the Lord
God in jubilation.

David went to bring up the ark of God from the
house of Obed-edom into the City of David
amid festivities. As soon as the bearers of the
ark of the Lord had advanced six steps, he sacrificed an ox and a fatling. Then David, girt
with a linen apron, came dancing before the
Lord with abandon, as he and all the Israelites
were bringing up the ark of the Lord with
shouts of joy and to the sound of the horn. The
ark of the Lord was brought in and set in its
place within the tent David had pitched for it.
Then David offered holocausts and peace offerings before the Lord. When he finished making
these offerings, he blessed the people in the
name of the Lord of hosts. He then distributed
among all the people, to each man and each
woman in the entire multitude of Israel, a loaf
of bread, a cut of roast meat, and a raisin cake.
With this, all the people left for their homes.
    This is the Word of the Lord.

Responsorial Psalm   Ps 24, 7. 8. 9. 10

℟. (8) Who is this king of glory?
   It is the Lord!
Lift up, O gates, your lintels;
   reach up, you ancient portals,
   that the king of glory may come in!
℟. Who is this king of glory?
   It is the Lord!
Who is this king of glory?
   The Lord, strong and mighty,
   the Lord, mighty in battle.
℟. Who is this king of glory?
   It is the Lord!
Lift up, O gates, your lintels;
   reach up, you ancient portals,
   that the king of glory may come in!
℟. Who is this king of glory?
   It is the Lord!
Who is this king of glory?
   the Lord of hosts; he is the king of glory.
℟. Who is this king of glory?
   It is the Lord!

Years I and II

GOSPEL   Mk 3, 31-35
Alleluia

See no. 509.

✠ A reading from the holy gospel according
   to Mark

*Here are my mother and my brothers: anyone who does
the will of God.*

The mother of Jesus and his brothers arrived,
and as they stood outside they sent word to
him to come out. The crowd seated around him
told him, "Your mother and your brothers and
sisters are outside asking for you." He said in
reply, "Who are my mother and my brothers?"
And gazing around him at those seated in the
circle he continued, "These are my mother and
my brothers. Whoever does the will of God is
brother and sister and mother to me."
   This is the gospel of the Lord.

319   **WEDNESDAY OF THE THIRD
         WEEK OF THE YEAR**

Year I

READING I   Heb 10, 11-18
A reading from the letter to the Hebrews

*He has achieved the eternal perfection of all whom he is
sanctifying.*

Every other priest stands ministering day by
day, and offering again and again those same
sacrifices which can never take away sins. But
Jesus offered one sacrifice for sins and took his
seat forever at the right hand of God; now he
waits until his enemies are placed beneath his
feet. By one offering he has forever perfected
those who are being sanctified. The Holy Spirit
attests this to us, for after saying,
   "This is the covenant I will make with
      them
         after those days, says the Lord:
   I will put my laws in their hearts
      and I will write them on their minds,"
he also says,
   "Their sins and their transgressions
      I will remember no more."
Once these have been forgiven, there is no
further offering for sin.
   This is the Word of the Lord.

Responsorial Psalm   Ps 110, 1. 2. 3. 4

℟. (4) You are a priest for ever,
   in the line of Melchizedek.
The Lord said to my Lord: "Sit at my right
      hand
   till I make your enemies your footstool."
℟. You are a priest for ever,
   in the line of Melchizedek.
The scepter of your power the Lord will stretch
      forth from Zion:
   "Rule in the midst of your enemies."
℟. You are a priest for ever,
   in the line of Melchizedek.
"Yours is princely power in the day of your
      birth, in holy splendor;
   before the daystar, like the dew, I have be-
      gotten you."
℟. You are a priest for ever,
   in the line of Melchizedek.
The Lord has sworn, and he will not repent:
   "You are a priest forever, according to the
      order of Melchizedek."
℟. You are a priest for ever,
   in the line of Melchizedek.

Year II

READING I
2 Sm 7, 4-17

A reading from the second book of Samuel

I will preserve the offspring of your body after you and make his sovereignty secure.

The Lord spoke to Nathan and said: "Go, tell my servant David, 'Thus says the Lord: Should you build me a house to dwell in? I have not dwelt in a house from the day on which I led the Israelites out of Egypt to the present, but I have been going about in a tent under cloth. In all my wanderings everywhere among the Israelites, did I ever utter a word to any one of the judges whom I charged to tend my people Israel, to ask: Why have you not built me a house of cedar?'

"Now then, speak thus to my servant David, 'The Lord of hosts has this to say: It was I who took you from the pasture and from the care of the flock to be commander of my people Israel. I have been with you wherever you went, and I have destroyed all your enemies before you. And I will make you famous like the great ones of the earth. I will fix a place for my people Israel; I will plant them so that they may dwell in their place without further disturbance. Neither shall the wicked continue to afflict them as they did of old, since the time I first appointed judges over my people Israel. I will give you rest from all your enemies. The Lord also reveals to you that he will establish a house for you. And when your time comes and you rest with your ancestors, I will raise up your heir after you, sprung from your loins, and I will make his kingdom firm. It is he who shall build a house for my name. And I will make his royal throne firm forever. I will be a father to him, and he shall be a son to me. And if he does wrong, I will correct him with the rod of men and with human chastisements; but I will not withdraw my favor from him as I withdrew it from your predecessor Saul, whom I removed from my presence. Your house and your kingdom shall endure forever before me; your throne shall stand firm forever.' "

Nathan reported all these words and this entire vision to David.

This is the Word of the Lord.

Responsorial Psalm
Ps 89, 4-5. 27-28. 29-30

℟. (29) For ever I will keep my love for him.

I have made a covenant with my chosen one,
   I have sworn to David my servant:
Forever will I confirm your posterity
   and establish your throne for all generations.

℟. For ever I will keep my love for him.

He shall say of me, "You are my father,
   my God, the Rock, my savior."
And I will make him the first-born,
   highest of the kings of the earth.

℟. For ever I will keep my love for him.

Forever I will maintain my kindness toward him,
   and my covenant with him stands firm.
I will make his posterity endure forever
   and his throne as the days of heaven.

℟. For ever I will keep my love for him.

Years I and II

GOSPEL
Mk 4, 1-20

Alleluia

See no. 509.

✠ **A reading from the holy gospel according to Mark**

The sower goes out to sow.

On one occasion Jesus began to teach beside the lake. Such a huge crowd gathered around him that he went and sat in a boat on the water, while the crowd remained on the shore nearby. He began to instruct them at great length, by the use of parables, and in the course of his teaching said: "Listen carefully to this. A farmer went out sowing. Some of what he sowed landed on the footpath, where the birds came along and ate it. Some of the seed landed on rocky ground where it had little soil; it sprouted immediately because the soil had no depth. Then, when the sun rose and scorched it, it began to wither for lack of roots. Again, some landed among thorns, which grew up and choked it off, and there was no yield of grain. Some seed, finally, landed on good soil and yielded grain that sprang up to produce at a rate of thirty and sixty and a hundredfold." Having spoken this parable, he added: "Let him who has ears to hear me, hear!"

Now when he was away from the crowd, those present with the Twelve questioned him about the parables. He told them: "To you the mystery of the reign of God has been confided. To the others outside it is all presented in parables, so that they will look intently and not see, listen carefully and not understand, lest perhaps they repent and be forgiven."

He said to them: "You do not understand this parable? How then are you going to understand other figures like it? What the sower is sowing is the word. Those on the path are the ones to whom, as soon as they hear the word, Satan comes to carry off what was sown in them. Similarly, those sown on rocky ground are people who on listening to the word accept it joyfully at the outset. Being rootless, they last only a while. When some pressure or persecution overtakes them because of the word, they falter. Those sown among thorns are another class. They have listened to the word, but anxieties over life's demands, and the desire for wealth, and cravings of other sorts come to choke it off; it bears no yield. But those sown on good soil are the ones who listen to the word, take it to heart, and yield thirty- and sixty- and a hundred-fold."

This is the gospel of the Lord.

---

320   **THURSDAY OF THE THIRD WEEK OF THE YEAR**

Year I

READING I   Heb 10, 19-25

A reading from the letter to the Hebrews

Let us be filled with faith, firm in the hope we profess and encourage each other in love

Brothers, since the blood of Jesus assures our entrance into the sanctuary by the new and living path he has opened up for us through the veil (the "veil" means his flesh), and since we have a great priest who is over the house of God, let us draw near in utter sincerity and absolute confidence, our hearts sprinkled clean from the evil which lay on our conscience and our bodies washed in pure water. Let us hold unswervingly to our profession which gives us

hope, for he who made the promise deserves our trust. We must consider how to rouse each other to love and good deeds. We should not absent ourselves from the assembly, as some do, but encourage one another; and this all the more because you see that the Day draws near.

This is the Word of the Lord.

Responsorial Psalm   Ps 24, 1-2. 3-4. 5-6

℟. (6) Lord, this is the people that longs to see your face.

The Lord's are the earth and its fullness;
    the world and those who dwell in it.
For he founded it upon the seas
    and established it upon the rivers.

℟. Lord, this is the people that longs to see your face.

Who can ascend the mountain of the Lord?
    or who may stand in his holy place?
He whose hands are sinless, whose heart is clean,
    who desires not what is vain.

℟. Lord, this is the people that longs to see your face.

He shall receive a blessing from the Lord,
    a reward from God his savior.
Such is the race that seeks for him,
    that seeks the face of the God of Jacob.

℟. Lord, this is the people that longs to see your face.

Year II

READING I   2 Sm 7, 18-19. 24-29

A reading from the second book of Samuel

Who am I, Lord God, and what is my house?

After Nathan had spoken to David, the king went in and sat before the Lord and said, "Who am I, Lord God, and who are the members of my house, that you have brought me to this point? Yet even this you see as too little, Lord God; you have also spoken of the house of your servant for a long time to come: this too you have shown to man, Lord God!

"You have established for yourself your people Israel as yours forever, and you, Lord, have become their God. And now, Lord God, confirm for all time the prophecy you have made concerning your servant and his house, and do as you have promised. Your name will be forever great, when men say, 'The Lord of hosts is God of Israel,' and the house of your servant David stands firm before you. It is you, Lord of hosts, God of Israel, who said in a revelation to your servant, 'I will build a house for you.' Therefore your servant now finds the courage to make this prayer to you. And now, Lord God, you are God and your words are truth; you have made this generous promise to your servant. Do, then, bless the house of your servant that it may be before you forever; for you, Lord God, have promised, and by your blessing the house of your servant shall be blessed forever."

    This is the Word of the Lord.

Responsorial Psalm Ps 132, 1-2. 3-5. 11. 12. 13-14

℟. (Lk 1, 32) **God will give him the throne of David, his father.**

Remember, O Lord, for David
  all his anxious care:
How he swore to the Lord,
  vowed to the Mighty One of Jacob.
℟. God will give him the throne of David, his father.

"I will not enter the house I live in,
  nor lie on the couch where I sleep;
I will give my eyes no sleep
  my eyelids no rest,
Till I find a place for the Lord,
  a dwelling for the Mighty One of Jacob."
℟. God will give him the throne of David, his father.

The Lord swore to David
  a firm promise from which he will not withdraw:
"Your own offspring
  I will set upon your throne.
℟. God will give him the throne of David, his father.

If your sons keep my covenant
  and the decrees which I shall teach them,
Their sons, too, forever
  shall sit upon your throne."
℟. God will give him the throne of David, his father.

For the Lord has chosen Zion;
  he prefers her for his dwelling.
"Zion is my resting place forever;
  in her will I dwell, for I prefer her."
℟. God will give him the throne of David, his father.

Years I and II

GOSPEL   Mk 4, 21-25
Alleluia

See no. 509.

✠ **A reading from the holy gospel according to Mark**

Come and place your lamp on a stand. The man who has will receive even more.

Jesus said to the crowd: "Is a lamp acquired to be put under a bushel basket or hidden under a bed? Is it not meant to be put on a stand? Things are hidden only to be revealed at a later time; they are covered so as to be brought out into the open. Let him who has ears to hear me, hear!" He said to them another time: "Listen carefully to what you hear. In the measure you give you shall receive, and more besides. To those who have, more will be given; from those who have not, what little they have will be taken away."

    This is the gospel of the Lord.

---

321   **FRIDAY OF THE THIRD**
        WEEK OF THE YEAR

Year I

READING I   Heb 10, 32-39

    A reading from the letter to the Hebrews

Do not throw your confidence away. It will have a great reward.

Recall the days gone by when you endured a great contest of suffering after you had been enlightened. At times you were publicly exposed to insult and trial; at other times you associated yourselves with those who were being so dealt with. You even joined in the sufferings of those who were in prison and joyfully assented to the confiscation of your goods, knowing that you had better and more permanent

possessions. Do not, then, surrender your confidence; it will have great reward. You need patience to do God's will and receive what he has promised.

> For, just "a brief moment,
>   and he who is to come will come; he will
>   not delay.
> My just man will live by faith,"
>   and "if he draws back
> I take no pleasure in him."

We are not among those who draw back and perish, but among those who have faith and live.

This is the Word of the Lord.

Responsorial Psalm Ps 37, 3-4. 5-6. 23-24. 39-40

℞. (39) The salvation of the just comes from the Lord.

Trust in the Lord and do good,
  that you may dwell in the land and enjoy
    security.
Take delight in the Lord,
  and he will grant you your heart's requests.

℞. The salvation of the just comes from the Lord.

Commit to the Lord your way;
  trust in him, and he will act.
He will make justice dawn for you like the
    light;
  bright as the noonday shall be your vindication.

℞. The salvation of the just comes from the Lord.

By the Lord are the steps of a man made firm,
  and he approves his way.
Though he fall, he does not lie prostrate,
  for the hand of the Lord sustains him.

℞. The salvation of the just comes from the Lord.

The salvation of the just is from the Lord;
  he is their refuge in time of distress.
And the Lord helps them and delivers them;
  he delivers them from the wicked and saves
    them,
  because they take refuge in him.

℞. The salvation of the just comes from the Lord.

Year II

READING I   2 Sm 11, 1-4. 5-10. 13-17

A reading from the second book of Samuel

He looked down on her and carried the wife of Uriah to be his own wife.

At the turn of the year, when kings go out on campaign, David sent out Joab along with his officers and the army of Israel, and they ravaged the Ammonites and besieged Rabbah. David, however, remained in Jerusalem. One evening David rose from his siesta and strolled about on the roof of the palace. From the roof he saw a woman bathing, who was very beautiful. David had inquiries made about the woman and was told, "She is Bathsheba, daughter of Eliam, and wife of [Joab's armorbearer] Uriah the Hittite." Then David sent messengers and took her. When she came to him, he had relations with her. The woman conceived, and sent the information to David, "I am with child."

David therefore sent a message to Joab, "Send me Uriah the Hittite." So Joab sent Uriah to David. When he came, David questioned him about Joab, the soldiers, and how the war was going, and Uriah answered that all was well. David then said to Uriah, "Go down to your house and bathe your feet." Uriah left the palace, and a portion was sent out after him from the king's table. But Uriah slept at the entrance of the royal palace with the other officers of his lord, and did not go down to his own house. David was told that Uriah had not gone home. On the day following, David summoned him, and he ate and drank with David, who made him drunk. But in the evening he went out to sleep on his bed among his lord's servants, and did not go down to his home. The next morning David wrote a letter to Joab which he sent by Uriah. In it he directed: "Place Uriah up front, where the fighting is fierce. Then pull back and leave him to be struck down dead." So while Joab was besieging the city, he assigned Uriah to a place where he knew the defenders were strong. When the men of the city made a sortie against Joab, some officers of David's army fell, and among them Uriah the Hittite died.

This is the Word of the Lord.

Responsorial Psalm　　Ps 51, 3-4. 5-6. 6-7. 10-11

℟. (3) Be merciful, O Lord, for we have sinned.
Have mercy on me, O God, in your goodness;
　in the greatness of your compassion wipe
　out my offense.
Thoroughly wash me from my guilt
　and of my sin cleanse me.
℟. Be merciful, O Lord, for we have sinned.
For I acknowledge my offense,
　and my sin is before me always:
"Against you only have I sinned,
　and done what is evil in your sight."
℟. Be merciful, O Lord, for we have sinned.
That you may be justified in your sentence,
　vindicated when you condemn.
Indeed, in guilt was I born,
　and in sin my mother conceived me.
℟. Be merciful, O Lord, for we have sinned.
Let me hear the sounds of joy and gladness;
　the bones you have crushed shall rejoice.
Turn away your face from my sins,
　and blot out all my guilt.
℟. Be merciful, O Lord, for we have sinned.

Years I and II
GOSPEL　　　　　　　　Mk 4, 26-34
Alleluia

See no. 509.

✠ A reading from the holy gospel according
　　　　to Mark
A man scatters seed and while he sleeps it grows even
　　　though he does not know how.

Jesus said to the crowd: "This is how it is with
the reign of God. A man scatters seed on the
ground. He goes to bed and gets up day after
day. Through it all the seed sprouts and grows
without his knowing how it happens. The soil
produces of itself first the blade, then the ear,
finally the ripe wheat in the ear. When the crop
is ready he 'wields the sickle, for the time is
ripe for harvest.' "

　He went on to say: "What comparison shall
we use for the reign of God? What image will
help to present it? It is like mustard seed
which, when planted in the soil, is the smallest
of all the earth's seeds, yet once it is sown,
springs up to become the largest of shrubs,
with branches big enough for the birds of the
sky to build nests in its shade." By means of
many such parables he taught them the message in a way they could understand. To them
he spoke only by way of parable, while he kept
explaining things privately to his disciples.
　This is the gospel of the Lord.

322　**SATURDAY OF THE THIRD
　　　WEEK OF THE YEAR**

Year I

READING I　　　　　　Heb 11, 1-2. 8-19

A reading from the letter to the Hebrews
They looked forward to a city founded, designed, and built
　　　　　　　by God.

Faith is confident assurance concerning what
we hope for, and conviction about things we do
not see. Because of faith the men of old were
approved by God. By faith Abraham obeyed
when he was called and went forth to the place
he was to receive as a heritage; he went forth,
moreover, not knowing where he was going.
By faith he sojourned in the promised land as
in a foreign country, dwelling in tents with
Isaac and Jacob, heirs of the same promise; for
he was looking forward to the city with foundations, whose designer and maker is God. By
faith Sarah received power to conceive though
she was past the age, for she thought that the
One who had made the promise was worthy of
trust. As a result of this faith, there came forth
from one man, who was himself as good as
dead, descendants as numerous as the stars in
the sky and the sands of the seashore.

　All of these died in faith. They did not obtain
what had been promised but saw and saluted it
from afar. By acknowledging themselves to be
strangers and foreigners on the earth, they
showed that they were seeking a homeland. If
they had been thinking back to the place from
which they had come, they would have had the
opportunity of returning there. But they were
searching for a better, a heavenly home.
Wherefore God is not ashamed to be called
their God, for he has prepared a city for them.

By faith Abraham, when put to the test, offered up Isaac; he who had received the promises was ready to sacrifice his only son, of whom it was said, "Through Isaac shall your descendants be called." He reasoned that God was able to raise from the dead, and so he received Isaac back as a symbol.

This is the Word of the Lord.

Responsorial Psalm   Lk 1, 69-70. 71-72. 73-75

℟. (68) Blessed be the Lord God of Israel, for he has visited his people.

He has raised a horn of saving strength for us in the house of David his servant,

As he promised through the mouths of his holy ones,
   the prophets of ancient times:

℟. Blessed be the Lord God of Israel, for he has visited his people.

Salvation from our enemies
   and from the hands of all our foes.

He has dealt mercifully with our fathers
   and remembered the holy covenant.

℟. Blessed be the Lord God of Israel, for he has visited his people.

The oath he swore to Abraham our father he would grant us:
   that, rid of fear and delivered from the enemy,

We should serve him devoutly, and through all our days,
   be holy in his sight.

℟. Blessed be the Lord God of Israel, for he has visited his people.

Year II

READING I   2 Sm 12, 1-7. 10-17

A reading from the second book of Samuel

I have sinned against the Lord God.

The Lord sent Nathan to David, and when he came to him, he said: "Judge this case for me! In a certain town there were two men, one rich, the other poor. The rich man had flocks and herds in great numbers. But the poor man had nothing at all except one little ewe lamb that he had bought. He nourished her, and she grew up with him and his children. She shared the little food he had and drank from his cup and slept in his bosom. She was like a daughter to him. Now, the rich man received a visitor, but he would not take from his own flocks and herds to prepare a meal for the wayfarer who had come to him. Instead he took the poor man's ewe lamb and made a meal of it for his visitor." David grew very angry with that man and said to Nathan: "As the Lord lives, the man who has done this merits death! He shall restore the ewe lamb fourfold because he has done this and has had no pity."

Then Nathan said to David: "You are the man!

"Now, therefore, the sword shall never depart from your house, because you have despised me and have taken the wife of Uriah to be your wife. Thus says the Lord: 'I will bring evil upon you out of your own house. I will take your wives while you live to see it, and will give them to your neighbor. He shall lie with your wives in broad daylight. You have done this deed in secret, but I will bring it about in the presence of all Israel, and with the sun looking down.' "

Then David said to Nathan, "I have sinned against the Lord." Nathan answered David: "The Lord on his part has forgiven your sin: you shall not die. But since you have utterly spurned the Lord by this deed, the child born to you must surely die." Then Nathan returned to his house.

The Lord struck the child that the wife of Uriah had borne to David, and it became desperately ill. David besought God for the child. He kept a fast, retiring for the night to lie on the ground clothed in sackcloth. The elders of his house stood beside him urging him to rise from the ground; but he would not, nor would he take food with them.

This is the word of the Lord.

Responsorial Psalm   Ps 51, 12-13. 14-15. 16-17

℟. (12) Create a clean heart in me, O God.

A clean heart create for me, O God,
   and a steadfast spirit renew within me.

Cast me not out from your presence,
   and your holy spirit take not from me.

℟. Create a clean heart in me, O God.

Give me back the joy of your salvation,
 and a willing spirit sustain in me.
I will teach transgressors your ways,
 and sinners shall return to you.
R̸. Create a clean heart in me, O God.
Free me from blood guilt, O God, my saving
 God;
 then my tongue shall revel in your justice.
O Lord, open my lips,
 and my mouth shall proclaim your praise.
R̸. Create a clean heart in me, O God.

Years I and II

GOSPEL
Mk 4, 35-41
Alleluia
See no. 509.

✠ A reading from the holy gospel according
 to Mark
Who can this be? Even the wind and the sea obey him.

One day as evening drew on Jesus said to his
disciples, "Let us cross over to the farther
shore." Leaving the crowd, they took him away
in the boat in which he was sitting, while the
other boats accompanied him. It happened that
a bad squall blew up. The waves were breaking
over the boat and it began to ship water badly.
Jesus was in the stern through it all, sound
asleep on a cushion. They finally woke him and
said to him, "Teacher, doesn't it matter to you
that we are going to drown?" He awoke and rebuked the wind and said to the sea: "Quiet!
Be still!" The wind fell off and everything grew
calm. Then he said to them, "Why are you so
terrified? Why are you lacking in faith?" A
great awe overcame them at this. They kept
saying to one another, "Who can this be that
the wind and the sea obey him?"
 This is the gospel of the Lord.

---

323 **MONDAY OF THE FOURTH
 WEEK OF THE YEAR**

Year I

READING I
Heb 11, 32-40
 A reading from the letter to the Hebrews
Through faith they conquered kingdoms. God will provide
for us something better.

What more shall I recount? I have no time to
tell of Gideon, Barak, Samson, Jephthah, of
David and Samuel and the prophets, who by
faith conquered kingdoms, did what was just,
obtained the promises; they broke the jaws of
lions, put out raging fires, escaped the devouring sword; though weak they were made powerful, became strong in battle, and turned back
foreign invaders. Women received back their
dead through resurrection. Others were tortured and did not receive deliverance, in order
to obtain a better resurrection. Still others endured mockery, scourging, even chains and imprisonment. They were stoned, sawed in two,
put to death at sword's point; they went about
garbed in the skins of sheep or goats, needy, afflicted, tormented. The world was not worthy
of them. They wandered about in deserts and on
mountains, they dwelt in caves and in holes of
the earth. Yet despite the fact that all of these
were approved because of their faith, they did
not obtain what had been promised. God had
made a better plan, a plan which included us.
Without us, they were not to be made perfect.
 This is the Word of the Lord.

Responsorial Psalm   Ps 31, 20. 21. 22. 23. 24
R̸. (25) Let your hearts take comfort,
 all who hope in the Lord.
How great is the goodness, O Lord,
 which you have in store for those who fear
 you,
And which, toward those who take refuge in
 you,
 you show in the sight of men.
R̸. Let your hearts take comfort,
 all who hope in the Lord.

You hide them in the shelter of your presence
  from the plottings of men;
You screen them within your abode
  from the strife of tongues.
℞. Let your hearts take comfort,
  all who hope in the Lord.
Blessed be the Lord whose wondrous kindness
he has shown me in a fortified city.
℞. Let your hearts take comfort,
  all who hope in the Lord.
Once I said in my anguish,
  "I am cut off from your sight";
Yet you heard the sound of my pleading
  when I cried out to you.
℞. Let your hearts take comfort,
  all who hope in the Lord.
Love the Lord, all you his faithful ones!
  The Lord keeps those who are constant,
  but more than requites those who act
    proudly.
℞. Let your hearts take comfort,
  all who hope in the Lord.

Year II

READING I   2 Sm 15, 13-14. 30; 16, 5-13

A reading from the second book of Samuel

Let us fly from the face of Absalom. Shimei was sent to bring the curse by precept of the Lord God.

An informant came to David with the report,
"The Israelites have transferred their loyalty to
Absalom." At this, David said to all his servants who were with him in Jerusalem: "Up!
Let us take flight, or none of us will escape
from Absalom. Leave quickly, lest he hurry
and overtake us, then visit disaster upon us
and put the city to the sword."

As David went up the Mount of Olives, he
wept without ceasing. His head was covered,
and he was walking barefoot. All those who
were with him also had their heads covered
and were weeping as they went.

As David was approaching Bahurim, a man
named Shimei, the son of Gera of the same clan
as Saul's family, was coming out of the place,
cursing as he came. He threw stones at David
and at all the king's officers, even though all
the soldiers, including the royal guard, were on
David's right and on his left. Shimei was saying as he cursed: "Away, away, you murderous
and wicked man! The Lord has requited you
for all the bloodshed in the family of Saul, in
whose stead you became king, and the Lord
has given over the kingdom to your son Absalom. And now you suffer ruin because you are
a murderer." Abishai, son of Zeruiah, said to
the king: "Why should this dead dog curse my
lord the king? Let me go over, please, and lop
off his head." But the king replied: "What business is it of mine or of yours, sons of Zeruiah,
that he curses? Suppose the Lord has told him
to curse David; who then will dare to say, 'Why
are you doing this?'" Then the king said to
Abishai and to all his servants: "If my own son,
who came forth from my loins, is seeking my
life, how much more might this Benjaminite do
so! Let him alone and let him curse, for the
Lord has told him to. Perhaps the Lord will
look upon my affliction and make it up to me
with benefits for the curses he is uttering this
day." David and his men continued on the
road.

This is the Word of the Lord.

Responsorial Psalm   Ps 3, 2-3. 4-5. 6-7

℞. (7) Lord, rise up and save me.
O Lord, how many are my adversaries!
  Many rise up against me!
Many are saying of me,
  "There is no salvation for him in God."
℞. Lord, rise up and save me.
But you, O Lord, are my shield;
  my glory, you lift up my head!
When I call out to the Lord,
  he answers me from his holy mountain.
℞. Lord, rise up and save me.
When I lie down in sleep,
  I wake again, for the Lord sustains me.
I fear not the myriads of people
  arrayed against me on every side.
Rise up, O Lord!
  Save me, my God!
℞. Lord, rise up and save me.

GOSPEL   **Years I and II**
Alleluia   Mk 5, 1-20
See no. 509.

✠ A reading from the holy gospel according
to Mark
Unclean spirits came out of the man.

Jesus and his disciples came to Gerasene territory on the other side of the lake. As he got out
of the boat, he was immediately met by a man
from the tombs who had an unclean spirit. The
man had taken refuge among the tombs; he
could no longer be restrained even with a
chain. In fact, he had frequently been secured
with handcuffs and chains, but had pulled the
chains apart and smashed the fetters. No one
had proved strong enough to tame him. Unin-
terruptedly night and day, amid the tombs and
on the hillsides, he screamed and gashed himself with stones. Catching sight of Jesus at a
distance, he ran up and did him homage,
shrieking in a loud voice, "Why meddle with
me, Jesus, Son of God Most High? I implore
you in God's name, do not torture me!" (Jesus
had been saying to him, "Unclean spirit, come
out of the man!") "What is your name?" Jesus
asked him. "Legion is my name," he answered. "There are hundreds of us." He
pleaded hard with Jesus not to drive them
away from that neighborhood.

It happened that a large herd of swine was
feeding there on the slope of the mountain.
"Send us into the swine," they begged him.
"Let us enter them." He gave the word, and
with it the unclean spirits came out and entered the swine. The herd of about two thousand went rushing down the bluff into the
lake, where they began to drown. The swine-
herds ran off and brought the news to field and
village, and the people came to see what had
happened. As they approached Jesus, they
caught sight of the man who had been possessed by Legion sitting fully clothed and perfectly sane, and they were seized with fear.
The spectators explained what had happened
to the possessed man, and told them about the
swine. Before long they were begging him to
go away from their district. As Jesus was getting into the boat, the man who had been possessed was pressing to accompany him. Jesus
did not grant his request, but told him instead:
"Go home to your family and make it clear to
them how much the Lord in his mercy has done
for you." At that the man went off and began
to proclaim throughout the Ten Cities what
Jesus had done for him. They were all amazed
at what they heard.

This is the gospel of the Lord.

---

324   **TUESDAY OF THE FOURTH
WEEK OF THE YEAR**

Year I
READING I   Heb 12, 1-4

A reading from the letter to the Hebrews
Through patience we are led to perfection.

Since we for our part are surrounded by a
cloud of witnesses, let us lay aside every encumbrance of sin which clings to us and persevere in running the race which lies ahead; let
us keep our eyes fixed on Jesus, who inspires
and perfects our faith. For the sake of the joy
which lay before him he endured the cross,
heedless of its shame. He has taken his seat at
the right of the throne of God. Remember how
he endured the opposition of sinners; hence do
not grow despondent or abandon the struggle.
In your fight against sin you have not yet resisted to the point of shedding blood.

This is the Word of the Lord.

Responsorial Psalm   Ps 22, 26-27. 28. 30. 31-32

℟. (27) They will praise you, Lord, who long
for you.
I will fulfill my vows before those who fear
him.
The lowly shall eat their fill;
They who seek the Lord shall praise him:
"May your hearts be ever merry!"
℟. They will praise you, Lord, who long for you.

All the ends of the earth
   shall remember and turn to the Lord;
All the families of the nations
   shall bow down before him.
To him alone shall bow down
   all who sleep in the earth;
Before him shall bend
   all who go down into the dust.
℟.They will praise you, Lord, who long for you.

And to him my soul shall live.
   My descendants shall serve him.
Let the coming generation be told of the Lord
   that they may proclaim to a people yet to be
     born
   the justice he has shown.
℟.They will praise you, Lord, who long for you.

Year II

READING I　　　2 Sm 18, 9-10. 14. 24-25. 30–19, 3

A reading from the second book of Samuel
My son Absalom, would that I had died in your place.

Absalom unexpectedly came up against David's servants. He was mounted on a mule, and, as the mule passed under the branches of a large terebinth, his hair caught fast in the tree. He hung between heaven and earth while the mule he had been riding ran off. Someone saw this and reported to Joab that he had seen Absalom hanging from a terebinth. And taking three pikes in hand, Joab thrust for the heart of Absalom.

Now David was sitting between the two gates, and a lookout mounted to the roof of the gate above the city wall, where he looked about and saw a man running all alone. The lookout shouted to inform the king, who said, "If he is alone, he has good news to report." The king said, "Step aside and remain in attendance here." So he stepped aside and remained there. When the Cushite came in, he said, "Let my lord the king receive the good news that this day the Lord has taken your part, freeing you from the grasp of all who rebelled against you." But the king asked the Cushite, "Is young Absalom safe?" The Cushite replied, "May the enemies of my lord the king and all

who rebel against you with evil intent be as that young man!"

The king was shaken, and went up to the room over the city gate to weep. He said as he wept, "My son Absalom! My son, my son Absalom! If only I had died instead of you, Absalom, my son, my son!"

Joab was told that the king was weeping and mourning for Absalom; and that day's victory was turned into mourning for the whole army when they heard that the king was grieving for his son.

This is the Word of the Lord.

Responsorial Psalm　　　Ps 86, 1-2. 3-4. 5-6

℟. (1) Listen, Lord, and answer me.
Incline your ear, O Lord; answer me,
   for I am afflicted and poor.
Keep my life, for I am devoted to you;
   save your servant who trusts in you.
℟. Listen, Lord, and answer me.

You are my God; have pity on me, O Lord,
   for to you I call all the day.
Gladden the soul of your servant,
   for to you, O Lord, I lift up my soul.
℟. Listen, Lord, and answer me.

For you, O Lord, are good and forgiving,
   abounding in kindness to all who call upon
     you.
Hearken, O Lord, to my prayer
   and attend to the sound of my pleading.
℟. Listen, Lord, and answer me.

Years I and II

GOSPEL　　　Mk 5, 21-43
Alleluia
See no. 509.

✠ **A reading from the holy gospel according
to Mark**
Young woman, I say to you, arise.

When Jesus had crossed back to the other side of the Sea of Galilee in the boat, a large crowd gathered around him and he stayed close to the lake. One of the officials of the synagogue, a man named Jairus, came near. Seeing Jesus, he fell at his feet and made this earnest appeal: "My little daughter is critically ill. Please come and lay your hands on her so that she may get well and live." The two went off together and a large crowd followed, pushing against Jesus.

There was a woman in the area who had been afflicted with a hemorrhage for a dozen years. She had received treatment at the hands of doctors of every sort and exhausted her savings in the process, yet she got no relief; on the contrary, she only grew worse. She had heard about Jesus and came up behind him in the crowd and put her hand to his cloak. "If I just touch his clothing," she thought, "I shall get well." Immediately her flow of blood dried up and the feeling that she was cured of her affliction ran through her whole body. Jesus was immediately conscious that healing power had gone out from him. Wheeling about in the crowd, he began to ask, "Who touched my clothing?" His disciples said to him, "You can see how this crowd hems you in, yet you ask, 'Who touched me?' Despite this, he kept looking around to see the woman who had done it. Fearful and beginning to tremble now as she realized what had happened, the woman came and fell in front of him and told him the whole truth. He said to her, "Daughter, it is your faith that has cured you. Go in peace and be free of this illness."

He had not finished speaking when people from the official's house arrived saying, "Your daughter is dead. Why bother the Teacher further?" Jesus disregarded the report that had been brought and said to the official: "Fear is useless. What is needed is trust." He would not permit anyone to follow him except Peter, James, and James' brother John. As they approached the house of the synagogue leader, Jesus was struck by the noise of people wailing and crying loudly on all sides. He entered and said to them: "Why do you make this din with your wailing? The child is not dead. She is asleep." At this they began to ridicule him. Then he put them all out.

Jesus took the child's father and mother and his own companions and entered the room where the child lay. Taking her hand he said to her, "Talitha, koum," which means, "Little girl, get up." The girl, a child of twelve, stood up

immediately and began to walk around. At this the family's astonishment was complete. He enjoined them strictly not to let anyone know about it, and told them to give her something to eat.

This is the gospel of the Lord.

325   WEDNESDAY OF THE FOURTH WEEK OF THE YEAR

Year I

READING I   Heb 12, 4-7. 11-15

A reading from the letter to the Hebrews
The Lord disciplines those he loves.

In your fight against sin you have not yet resisted to the point of shedding blood. Moreover, you have forgotten the encouraging words addressed to you as sons:

"My sons, do not disdain the discipline of the Lord
nor lose heart when he reproves you;
For, whom the Lord loves, he disciplines;
he scourges every son he receives."

Endure your trials as the discipline of God, who deals with you as sons. For what son is there whom his father does not discipline? At the time it is administered, all discipline seems a cause for grief and not for joy, but later it brings forth the fruit of peace and justice to those who are trained in its school. So strengthen your drooping hands and your weak knees. Make straight the paths you walk on, that your halting limbs may not be dislocated but healed.

Strive for peace with all men, and for that holiness without which no one can see the Lord. See to it that no one falls away from the grace of God; that no bitter root springs up through which many may become defiled.

This is the Word of the Lord.

Responsorial Psalm   Ps 103, 1-2. 13-14. 17-18

℟. (17) The Lord's kindness is everlasting to those who fear him.
Bless the Lord, O my soul;
    and all my being, bless his holy name.
Bless the Lord, O my soul,
    and forget not all his benefits.

Ry. The Lord's kindness is everlasting to those who fear him.

As a father has compassion on his children,
so the Lord has compassion on those who
fear him,
For he knows how we are formed;
he remembers that we are dust.

Ry. The Lord's kindness is everlasting to those who fear him.

But the kindness of the Lord is from eternity
to eternity toward those who fear him,
And his justice toward children's children
among those who keep his covenant.

Ry. The Lord's kindness is everlasting to those who fear him.

Year II

READING I   2 Sm 24, 2. 9-17

A reading from the second book of Samuel

I have sinned, but these people, this flock, what have they done?

King David said to Joab and the leaders of the army who were with him, "Tour all the tribes in Israel from Dan to Beer-sheba and register the people, that I may know their number."

Joab then reported to the king the number of people registered: in Israel, eight hundred thousand men fit for military service; in Judah, five hundred thousand.

Afterward, however, David regretted having numbered the people, and said to the Lord: "I have sinned grievously in what I have done. But now, Lord, forgive the guilt of your servant, for I have been very foolish." When David rose in the morning, the Lord had spoken to the prophet Gad, David's seer, saying: "Go and say to David, 'This is what the Lord says: I offer you three alternatives; choose one of them and I will inflict it on you.'" Gad then went to David to inform him. He asked: "Do you want a three years' famine to come upon your land, or to flee from your enemy three months while he pursues you, or to have a three days' pestilence in your land? Now consider and decide what I must reply to him who sent me." David answered Gad: "I am in very serious difficulty. Let us fall by the hand of God, for he is most merciful; but let me

not fall by the hand of man." Thus David chose the pestilence. Now it was the time of the wheat harvest when the plague broke out among the people. [The Lord then sent a pestilence over Israel from morning until the time appointed, and seventy thousand of the people from Dan to Beer-sheba died.] But when the angel stretched forth his hand toward Jerusalem to destroy it, the Lord regretted the calamity and said to the angel causing the destruction among the people, "Enough now! Stay your hand." The angel of the Lord was then standing at the threshing floor of Araunah the Jebusite. When David saw the angel who was striking the people, he said to the Lord: "It is I who have sinned; it is I, the shepherd, who have done wrong. But these are sheep; what have they done? Punish me and my kindred."

This is the Word of the Lord.

Responsorial Psalm   Ps 32, 1-2. 5. 6. 7

Ry. (5) Lord, forgive the wrong I have done.

Happy is he whose fault is taken away,
whose sin is covered.
Happy the man to whom the Lord imputes not
guilt,
in whose spirit there is no guile.

Ry. Lord, forgive the wrong I have done.

Then I acknowledged my sin to you,
my guilt I covered not.
I said, "I confess my faults to the Lord,"
and you took away the guilt of my sin.

Ry. Lord, forgive the wrong I have done.

For this shall every faithful man pray to you
in time of stress.
Though deep waters overflow,
they shall not reach him.

Ry. Lord, forgive the wrong I have done.

You are my shelter; from distress you will
preserve me;
with glad cries of freedom you will ring me
round.

Ry. Lord, forgive the wrong I have done.

Years I and II

GOSPEL   Mk 6, 1-6

Alleluia

See no. 509.

✠ **A reading from the holy gospel according to Mark**

A prophet is without honor in his own country.

Jesus went to his own part of the country followed by his disciples. When the sabbath came he began to teach in the synagogue in a way that kept his large audience amazed. They said: "Where did he get all this? What kind of wisdom is he endowed with? How is it such miraculous deeds are accomplished by his hands? Isn't this the carpenter, the son of Mary, a brother of James and Joses and Judas and Simon? Aren't his sisters our neighbors here?" They found him too much for them. Jesus' response to all this was: "No prophet is without honor except in his native place, among his own kindred, and in his own house." He could work no miracle there, apart from curing a few who were sick by laying hands on them, so much did their lack of faith distress him. He made the rounds of the neighboring villages instead, and spent his time teaching.

This is the gospel of the Lord.

---

326   THURSDAY OF THE FOURTH WEEK OF THE YEAR

Year I

READING I   Heb 12, 18-19. 21-24

A reading from the letter to the Hebrews

You have come to Mount Zion and the city of the living God.

You have not drawn near to an untouchable mountain and a blazing fire, and gloomy darkness and storm and trumpet blast, and a voice speaking words such that those who heard begged that they be not addressed to them. Indeed, so fearful was the spectacle that Moses said, "I am terrified and trembling." No, you have drawn near to Mount Zion and the city of the living God, the heavenly Jerusalem, to myriads of angels in festal gathering, to the assembly of the first-born enrolled in heaven, to God the judge of all, to the spirits of just men made perfect, to Jesus, the mediator of a new covenant, and to the sprinkled blood which speaks more eloquently than that of Abel.

This is the Word of the Lord.

Responsorial Psalm   Ps 48, 2-3. 3-4. 9. 10-11

℟. (10) God, in your temple, we ponder your love.

Great is the Lord and wholly to be praised
  in the city of our God.
His holy mountain, fairest of heights,
  is the joy of all the earth.

℟. God, in your temple, we ponder your love.

Mount Zion, "the recesses of the North,"
  is the city of the great King.
God is with her castles;
  renowned is he as a stronghold.

℟. God, in your temple, we ponder your love.

As we had heard, so have we seen
  in the city of the Lord of hosts,
In the city of our God;
  God makes it firm forever.

℟. God, in your temple, we ponder your love.

O God, we ponder your kindness
  within your temple.
As your name, O God, so also your praise
  reaches to the ends of the earth.
Of justice your right hand is full.

℟. God, in your temple, we ponder your love.

Year II

READING I   1 Kgs 2, 1-4. 10-12

A reading from the first book of Kings

I am going the way of all the earth; be strong, Solomon, and show yourself a man.

When the time of David's death drew near, he gave these instructions to his son Solomon: "I am going the way of all mankind. Take courage and be a man. Keep the mandate of the Lord, your God, following his ways and observing his statutes, commands, ordinances, and decrees as they are written in the law of Moses, that you may succeed in whatever you do, wherever you turn, and the Lord may fulfill the promise he made on my behalf when he said, 'If your sons so conduct themselves that they remain faithful to me with their whole heart and with their whole soul, you shall always have someone of your line on the throne of Israel.' "

David rested with his ancestors and was buried in the City of David. The length of David's reign over Israel was forty years: he reigned seven years in Hebron and thirty-three years in Jerusalem.

Solomon was seated on the throne of his father David, with his sovereignty firmly established.

This is the Word of the Lord.

Responsorial Psalm   1 Chr 29, 10. 11. 11-12. 12

℟. (12) Lord, you are exalted over all.
Blessed may you be, O Lord,
   God of Israel our father,
   from eternity to eternity.
℟. Lord, you are exalted over all.
Yours, O Lord, are grandeur and power,
   majesty, splendor, and glory.
℟. Lord, you are exalted over all.
Yours, O Lord, is the sovereignty;
   you are exalted as head over all.
   Riches and honor are from you,
℟. Lord, you are exalted over all.
And you have dominion over all.
   In your hand are power and might;
It is yours to give grandeur and strength to all.
℟. Lord, you are exalted over all.

Years I and II

GOSPEL   Mk 6, 7-13
Alleluia

See no. 509.

✠ A reading from the holy gospel according
to Mark

He summoned the Twelve and sent them out in pairs.

Jesus summoned the Twelve and began to send them out two by two, giving them authority over unclean spirits. He instructed them to take nothing on the journey but a walking stick—no food, no traveling bag, not a coin in the purses in their belts. They were, however, to wear sandals. "Do not bring a second tunic," he said, and added: "Whatever house you find yourself in, stay there until you leave the locality. If any place will not receive you or hear you, shake its dust from your feet in testimony against them as you leave." With that they went off, preaching the need of repentance. They expelled many demons, anointed the sick with oil, and worked many cures.

This is the gospel of the Lord.

---

327   **FRIDAY OF THE FOURTH
           WEEK OF THE YEAR**

Year I

READING I   Heb 13, 1-8
   A reading from the letter to the Hebrews
Jesus Christ is the same today as yesterday and as he will
be for ever.

Love your fellow Christians always. Do not neglect to show hospitality, for by that means some have entertained angels without knowing it. Be as mindful of prisoners as if you were sharing their imprisonment, and of the ill-treated as yourselves, for you may yet suffer as they do. Let marriage be honored in every way and the marriage bed be kept undefiled, for God will judge fornicators and adulterers. Do not love money but be content with what you have, for God has said, "I will never desert you, nor will I forsake you." Thus we may say with confidence:
   "The Lord is my helper,
      I will not be afraid;
   What can man do to me?"
Remember your leaders who spoke the word of God to you; consider how their lives ended, and imitate their faith. Jesus Christ is the same yesterday, today, and forever.

This is the Word of the Lord.

Responsorial Psalm   Ps 27, 1. 3. 5. 8-9

℟. (1) The Lord is my light and my salvation.
The Lord is my light and my salvation;
   whom should I fear?
The Lord is my life's refuge;
   of whom should I be afraid?
℟. The Lord is my light and my salvation.
Though an army encamp against me,
   my heart will not fear;
Though war be waged upon me,
   even then will I trust.

℞. The Lord is my light and my salvation.
For he will hide me in his abode
in the day of trouble;
He will conceal me in the shelter of his tent,
he will set me high upon a rock.
℞. The Lord is my light and my salvation.
Your presence, O Lord, I seek.
Hide not your face from me;
Do not in anger repel your servant.
You are my helper: cast me not off.
℞. The Lord is my light and my salvation.

Year II

READING I   Sir 47, 2-11

A reading from the book of Sirach

David praised the Lord God with all his heart and loved him.

Like the choice fat of the sacred offerings,
so was David in Israel.
He made sport of lions as though they were
kids,
and of bears, like lambs of the flock.
As a youth he slew the giant
and wiped out the people's disgrace,
When his hand let fly the slingstone
that crushed the pride of Goliath.
Since he called upon the Most High God,
who gave strength to his right arm
To defeat the skilled warrior
and raise up the might of his people,
Therefore the women sang his praises
and ascribed to him tens of thousands.
When he assumed the royal crown, he battled
and subdued the enemy on every side.
He destroyed the hostile Philistines
and shattered their power till our own day.
With his every deed he offered thanks
to God Most High, in words of praise.
With his whole being he loved his Maker
and daily had his praises sung;
He added beauty to the feasts
and solemnized the seasons of each year
With string music before the altar,
providing sweet melody for the psalms
So that when the Holy Name was praised,
before daybreak the sanctuary would re-
sound.
The Lord forgave him his sins
and exalted his strength forever;

He conferred on him the rights of royalty
and established his throne in Israel.
This is the Word of the Lord.

Responsorial Psalm   Ps 18, 31. 47. 50. 51

℞. (47) Blessed be God my salvation!
God's way is unerring,
the promise of the Lord is fire-tried;
he is a shield to all who take refuge in him.
℞. Blessed be God my salvation!
The Lord live! And blessed be my Rock!
Extolled be God my savior.
Therefore will I proclaim you, O Lord, among
the nations,
and I will sing praise to your name.
℞. Blessed be God my salvation!
You who gave great victories to your king
and showed kindness to your anointed,
to David and his posterity forever.
℞. Blessed be God my salvation!

Years I and II

GOSPEL   Mk 6, 14-29
Alleluia

See no. 509.

✠ **A reading from the holy gospel according**
to Mark

It is John whose head I have cut off. He has risen from the dead.

King Herod came to hear of Jesus whose repu-
tation had become widespread and people
were saying, "John the Baptizer has been
raised from the dead; that is why such miracu-
lous powers are at work in him." Others were
saying, "He is Elijah"; still others, "He is a
prophet equal to any of the prophets." On hear-
ing of Jesus, Herod exclaimed, "John, whose
head I had cut off, has been raised up!" Herod
was the one who had ordered John arrested,
chained, and imprisoned on account of He-
rodias, the wife of his brother Philip, whom he
had married. That was because John had told
Herod, "It is not right for you to live with your
brother's wife." Herodias harbored a grudge
against him for this and wanted to kill him but
was unable to do so. Herod feared John, know-
ing him to be an upright and holy man, and

kept him in custody. When he heard him speak he was very much disturbed; yet he felt the attraction of his words. Herodias had her chance one day when Herod held a birthday dinner for his court circle, military officers, and the leading men of Galilee. Herodias' own daughter came in at one point and performed a dance which delighted Herod and his guests. The king told the girl, "Ask for anything you want and I will give it to you." He went so far as to swear to her: "I will grant you whatever you ask, even to half my kingdom!" She went out and said to her mother, "What shall I ask for?" The mother answered, "The head of John the Baptizer." At that the girl hurried back to the king's presence and made her request: "I want you to give me, at once, the head of John the Baptizer on a platter." The king bitterly regretted the request; yet because of his oath and the presence of the guests, he did not want to refuse her. He promptly dispatched an executioner, ordering him to bring back the Baptizer's head. The man went and beheaded John in the prison. He brought in the head on a platter and gave it to the girl, and the girl gave it to her mother. Later, when his disciples heard about this, they came and carried his body away and laid it in a tomb.

This is the gospel of the Lord.

---

328   **SATURDAY OF THE FOURTH WEEK OF THE YEAR**

Year I

READING I   Heb 13, 15-17. 20-21

A reading from the letter to the Hebrews

May the God of peace who brought back from the dead the great shepherd, lead you in all good things.

Through Jesus let us continually offer God a sacrifice of praise, that is, the fruit of lips which acknowledge his name.

Do not neglect good deeds and generosity; God is pleased by sacrifices of that kind. Obey your leaders and submit to them, for they keep watch over you as men who must render an account. So act that they may fulfill their task

with joy, not with sorrow, for that would be harmful to you.

May the God of peace, who brought up from the dead the great Shepherd of the sheep in the blood of the eternal covenant, Jesus our Lord, furnish you with all that is good, that you may do his will. Through Jesus Christ may he carry out in you all that is pleasing to him. To Christ be glory forever! Amen.

This is the Word of the Lord.

Responsorial Psalm   Ps 23, 1-3. 3-4. 5. 6

℞. (1) The Lord is my shepherd;
    there is nothing I shall want.

The Lord is my shepherd; I shall not want.
    In verdant pastures he gives me repose;
Beside restful waters he leads me;
    he refreshes my soul.

℞. The Lord is my shepherd;
    there is nothing I shall want.

He guides me in right paths
    for his name's sake.
Even though I walk in the dark valley
    I fear no evil; for you are at my side
With your rod and your staff
    that give me courage.

℞. The Lord is my shepherd;
    there is nothing I shall want.

You spread the table before me
    in the sight of my foes;
You anoint my head with oil;
    my cup overflows.

℞. The Lord is my shepherd;
    there is nothing I shall want.

Only goodness and kindness follow me
    all the days of my life;
And I shall dwell in the house of the Lord
    for years to come.

℞. The Lord is my shepherd;
    there is nothing I shall want.

Year II

READING I   1 Kgs 3, 4-13

A reading from the first book of Kings

Give your servant an understanding heart to govern your people.

Solomon went to Gibeon to sacrifice there, because that was the most renowned high place. Upon its altar Solomon offered a thousand holocausts. In Gibeon the Lord appeared to Solomon in a dream at night. God said, "Ask something of me and I will give it to you." Solomon answered: "You have shown great favor to your servant, my father David, because he behaved faithfully toward you, with justice and an upright heart; and you have continued this great favor toward him, even today, seating a son of his on his throne. O Lord, my God, you have made me, your servant, king to succeed my father David; but I am a mere youth, not knowing at all how to act. I serve you in the midst of the people whom you have chosen, a people so vast that it cannot be numbered or counted. Give your servant, therefore, an understanding heart to judge your people and to distinguish right from wrong. For who is able to govern this vast people of yours?"

The Lord was pleased that Solomon made this request. So God said to him: "Because you have asked for this—not for a long life for yourself, nor for riches, nor for the life of your enemies, but for understanding so that you may know what is right—I do as you requested. I give you a heart so wise and understanding that there has never been anyone like you up to now, and after you there will come no one to equal you. In addition, I give you what you have not asked for, such riches and glory that among kings there is not your like."

This is the Word of the Lord.

Responsorial Psalm Ps 119, 9. 10. 11. 12. 13. 14

R℣. (12) Lord, teach me your decrees.
How shall a young man be faultless in his way?
    By keeping to your words.
R℣. Lord, teach me your decrees.
With all my heart I seek you;
    let me not stray from your commands.
R℣. Lord, teach me your decrees.
Within my heart I treasure your promise,
    that I may not sin against you.
R℣. Lord, teach me your decrees.
Blessed are you, O Lord;
    teach me your statutes.
R℣. Lord, teach me your decrees.

With my lips I declare
    all the ordinances of your mouth.
R℣. Lord, teach me your decrees.
In the way of your decrees I rejoice,
    as much as in all riches.
R℣. Lord, teach me your decrees.

Years I and II

GOSPEL   Mk 6, 30-34
Alleluia

See no. 509.

✠ A reading from the holy gospel according
        to Mark

They were sheep without a shepherd.

The apostles returned to Jesus and reported to him all that they had done and what they had taught. He said to them, "Come by yourselves to an out-of-the-way place and rest a little." People were coming and going in great numbers, making it impossible for them to so much as eat. So Jesus and the apostles went off in the boat by themselves to a deserted place. People saw them leaving, and many got to know about it. People from all the towns hastened on foot to the place, arriving ahead of them. Upon disembarking Jesus saw a vast crowd. He pitied them, for they were like sheep without a shepherd; and he began to teach them at great length.

This is the gospel of the Lord.

329   **MONDAY OF THE FIFTH
            WEEK OF THE YEAR**

Year I

READING I   Gn 1, 1-19
    The beginning of the book of Genesis

God spoke, and it was done.

In the beginning, when God created the heavens and the earth, the earth was a formless wasteland, and darkness covered the abyss, while a mighty wind swept over the waters.

Then God said, "Let there be light," and there was light. God saw how good the light was. God then separated the light from the darkness. God called the light "day," and the darkness he called "night." Thus evening came, and morning followed—the first day.

Then God said, "Let there be a dome in the middle of the waters, to separate one body of water from the other." And so it happened: God made the dome, and it separated the water above the dome from the water below it. God called the dome "the sky." Evening came, and morning followed—the second day.

Then God said, "Let the water under the sky be gathered into a single basin, so that the dry land may appear." And so it happened: the water under the sky was gathered into its basin, and the dry land appeared. God called the dry land "the earth," and the basin of the water he called "the sea." God saw how good it was. Then God said, "Let the earth bring forth vegetation: every kind of plant that bears seed and every kind of fruit tree on earth that bears fruit with its seed in it." And so it happened: the earth brought forth every kind of plant that bears seed and every kind of fruit tree on earth that bears fruit with its seed in it. God saw how good it was. Evening came, and morning followed—the third day.

Then God said: "Let there be lights in the dome of the sky, to separate day from night. Let them mark the fixed times, the days and the years, and serve as luminaries in the dome of the sky, to shed light upon the earth." And so it happened: God made the two great lights, the greater one to govern the day, and the lesser one to govern the night; and he made the stars. God set them in the dome of the sky, to shed light upon the earth, to govern the day and the night, and to separate the light from the darkness. God saw how good it was. Evening came, and morning followed—the fourth day.

This is the Word of the Lord.

Responsorial Psalm   Ps 104, 1-2. 5-6. 10. 12. 24. 35

℞. (31) May the Lord be glad in his works.
Bless the Lord, O my soul!
O Lord, my God, you are great indeed!
You are clothed with majesty and glory,
    robed in light as with a cloak.
℞. May the Lord be glad in his works.

You fixed the earth upon its foundation,
    not to be moved forever;
With the ocean, as with a garment, you covered it;
    above the mountains the waters stood.
℞. May the Lord be glad in his works.
You send forth springs into the watercourses
    that wind among the mountains.
Beside them the birds of heaven dwell;
    from among the branches they send forth
    their song.
℞. May the Lord be glad in his works.
How manifold are your works, O Lord!
    In wisdom you have wrought them all—
    the earth is full of your creatures;
    Bless the Lord, O my soul! Alleluia.
℞. May the Lord be glad in his works.

Year II

READING I   1 Kgs 8, 1-7. 9-13

A reading from the first book of Kings

They carried the ark of the covenant to the Holy of Holies and a cloud filled the house of God.

The elders of Israel and all the leaders of the tribes, the princes in the ancestral houses of the Israelites, came to King Solomon in Jerusalem, to bring up the ark of the Lord's covenant from the City of David [which is Zion]. All the men of Israel assembled before King Solomon during the festival in the month of Ethanim (the seventh month). When all the elders of Israel had arrived, the priests took up the ark; they carried the ark of the Lord and the meeting tent with all the sacred vessels that were in the tent. (The priests and Levites carried them.)

King Solomon and the entire community of Israel present for the occasion sacrificed before the ark sheep and oxen too many to number or count. The priests brought the ark of the covenant of the Lord to its place beneath the wings of the cherubim in the sanctuary, the holy of holies of the temple. The cherubim had their wings spread out over the place of the ark, sheltering the ark and its poles from above. There was nothing in the ark but the two stone tablets which Moses had put there at Horeb, when the Lord made a covenant with the Israelites at their departure from the land of Egypt.

When the priests left the holy place, the cloud filled the temple of the Lord so that the priests could no longer minister because of the cloud, since the Lord's glory had filled the temple of the Lord. Then Solomon said, "The Lord intends to dwell in the dark cloud; I have truly built you a princely house, a dwelling where you may abide forever."

This is the Word of the Lord.

Responsorial Psalm   Ps 132, 6-7. 8-10

R̝. (8) Lord, go up to the place of your rest!
Behold, we heard of it in Ephratha;
    we found it in the fields of Jaar.
Let us enter into his dwelling,
    let us worship at his footstool.
R̝. Lord, go up to the place of your rest!
Advance, O Lord, to your resting place
    you and the ark of your majesty.
May your priests be clothed with justice;
    let your faithful ones shout merrily for joy.
For the sake of David your servant,
    reject not the plea of your anointed.
R̝. Lord, go up to the place of your rest!

Years I and II

GOSPEL   Mk 6, 53-56
Alleluia

See no. 509.

✠ A reading from the holy gospel according to Mark

All those who touched him were cured.

Jesus and his disciples, after crossing the lake, came ashore at Gennesaret and tied up there. As they were leaving the boat, people immediately recognized him. The crowds scurried about the adjacent area and began to bring in the sick on bedrolls to the place where they heard he was. Wherever he put in an appearance, in villages, in towns, or at crossroads, they laid the sick in the marketplaces and begged him to let them touch just the tassel of his cloak. All who touched him got well.

This is the gospel of the Lord.

330   **TUESDAY OF THE FIFTH WEEK OF THE YEAR**

Year I

READING I   Gn 1, 20-2, 4
A reading from the book of Genesis

Let us make man in our own image and likeness.

Then God said, "Let the water teem with an abundance of living creatures, and on the earth let birds fly beneath the dome of the sky." And so it happened: God created the great sea monsters and all kinds of swimming creatures with which the water teems, and all kinds of winged birds. God saw how good it was, and God blessed them, saying, "Be fertile, multiply, and fill the water of the seas; and let the birds multiply on the earth." Evening came, and morning followed—the fifth day.

Then God said, "Let the earth bring forth all kinds of living creatures: cattle, creeping things, and wild animals of all kinds." And so it happened: God made all kinds of wild animals, all kinds of cattle, and all kinds of creeping things of the earth. God saw how good it was. Then God said: "Let us make man in our image, after our likeness. Let them have dominion over the fish of the sea, the birds of the air, and the cattle, and over all the wild animals and all the creatures that crawl on the ground."

God created man in his image;
    in the divine image he created him;
    male and female he created them.

God blessed them, saying: "Be fertile and multiply; fill the earth and subdue it. Have dominion over the fish of the sea, the birds of the air, and all the living things that move on the earth." God also said: "See, I give you every seed-bearing plant all over the earth and every tree that has seed-bearing fruit on it to be your food; and to all the animals of the land, all the birds of the air, and all the living creatures that crawl on the ground, I give all the green plants for food." And so it happened. God looked at everything he had made, and he found it very good. Evening came, and morning followed—the sixth day.

Thus the heavens and the earth and all their array were completed. Since on the seventh day God was finished with the work he had been doing, he rested on the seventh day from all the work he had undertaken. So God blessed the seventh day and made it holy, because on it he rested from all the work he had done in creation.

Such is the story of the heavens and the earth at their creation.

This is the Word of the Lord.

Responsorial Psalm   Ps 8, 4-5. 6-7. 8-9

℟. (2) O Lord, our God,
   how wonderful your name in all the earth!
When I behold your heavens, the work of your fingers,
   the moon and the stars which you set in place—
What is man that you should be mindful of him,
   or the son of man that you should care for him?
℟. O Lord, our God,
   how wonderful your name in all the earth!
You have made him little less than the angels, and crowned him with glory and honor.
You have given him rule over the works of your hands,
   putting all things under his feet.
℟. O Lord, our God,
   how wonderful your name in all the earth!
All sheep and oxen,
   yes, and the beasts of the field,
The birds of the air, the fishes of the sea,
   and whatever swims the paths of the seas.
℟. O Lord, our God,
   how wonderful your name in all the earth!

Year II

READING I   1 Kgs 8, 22-23. 27-30

A reading from the first book of Kings
You have said, my name shall be there, to hear the prayers of your people Israel.

Solomon stood before the altar of the Lord in the presence of the whole community of Israel, and stretching forth his hands toward heaven, he said, "Lord, God of Israel, there is no God like you in heaven above or on earth below;

you keep your covenant of kindness with your servants who are faithful to you with their whole heart.

"Can it indeed be that God dwells among men on earth? If the heavens and the highest heavens cannot contain you, how much less this temple which I have built! Look kindly on the prayer and petition of your servant, O Lord, my God, and listen to the cry of supplication which I, your servant, utter before you this day. May your eyes watch night and day over this temple, the place where you have decreed you shall be honored; may you heed the prayer which I, your servant, offer in this place. Listen to the petitions of your servant and of your people Israel which they offer in this place. Listen from your heavenly dwelling and grant pardon."

This is the Word of the Lord.

Responsorial Psalm   Ps 84, 3. 4. 5. 10. 11

℟. (2) How lovely is your dwelling-place, Lord, mighty God!
My soul yearns and pines
   for the courts of the Lord.
My heart and my flesh
   cry out for the living God.
℟. How lovely is your dwelling-place, Lord, mighty God!
Even the sparrow finds a home,
   and the swallow a nest
   in which she puts her young—
Your altars, O Lord of hosts,
   my king and my God!
℟. How lovely is your dwelling-place, Lord, mighty God!
Happy they who dwell in your house!
   continually they praise you.
O God, behold our shield,
   and look upon the face of your anointed.
℟. How lovely is your dwelling-place, Lord, mighty God!
I had rather one day in your courts
   than a thousand elsewhere;
I had rather lie at the threshold of the house of my God
   than dwell in the tents of the wicked.
℟. How lovely is your dwelling-place, Lord, mighty God!

GOSPEL
Years I and II

Mk 7, 1-13

Alleluia

See no. 509.

✠ A reading from the holy gospel according to Mark

You put aside the commandments of God to hold on to human traditions.

The Pharisees and some of the experts in the law who had come from Jerusalem gathered around Jesus. They had observed a few of his disciples eating meals without having purified —that is to say, washed—their hands. The Pharisees, and in fact all Jews, cling to the custom of their ancestors and never eat without scrupulously washing their hands. Moreover, they never eat anything from the market without first sprinkling it. There are many other traditions they observe—for example, the washing of cups and jugs and kettles. So the Pharisees and the scribes questioned him: "Why do your disciples not follow the tradition of our ancestors, but instead take food without purifying their hands?" He said to them: "How accurately Isaiah prophesied about you hypocrites when he wrote,

'This people pays me lip service
   but their heart is far from me.
Empty is the reverence they do me
   because they teach as dogmas mere human precepts.'

You disregard God's commandment and cling to what is human tradition."

He went on to say: "You have made a fine art of setting aside God's commandment in the interests of keeping your traditions! For example, Moses said, 'Honor your father and your mother'; and in another place, 'Whoever curses father or mother shall be put to death.' Yet you declare, 'If a person says to his father or mother, Any support you might have had from me is korban' (that is, dedicated to God), you allow him to do nothing more for his father or mother. That is the way you nullify God's word in favor of the traditions you have handed on. And you have many other such practices besides."

This is the gospel of the Lord.

---

331   WEDNESDAY OF THE FIFTH WEEK OF THE YEAR

Year I

READING I   Gn 2, 5-9. 15-17

A reading from the book of Genesis

The Lord God planted a garden in Eden, and there he put the man he had formed.

At the time when the Lord God made the earth and the heavens—while as yet there was no field shrub on earth and no grass of the field had sprouted, for the Lord God had sent no rain upon the earth and there was no man to till the soil, but a stream was welling up out of the earth and was watering all the surface of the ground—the Lord God formed man out of the clay of the ground and blew into his nostrils the breath of life, and so man became a living being.

Then the Lord God planted a garden in Eden, in the east, and he placed there the man whom he had formed. Out of the ground the Lord God made various trees grow that were delightful to look at and good for food, with the tree of life in the middle of the garden and the tree of the knowledge of good and bad.

The Lord God then took the man and settled him in the garden of Eden, to cultivate and care for it. The Lord God gave man this order: "You are free to eat from any of the trees of the garden except the tree of the knowledge of good and bad. From that tree you shall not eat; the moment you eat from it you are surely doomed to die."

This is the Word of the Lord.

Responsorial Psalm   Ps 104, 1-2. 27-28. 29-30

℟. (1) Oh, bless the Lord, my soul!

Bless the Lord, O my soul!
   O Lord, my God, you are great indeed!
You are clothed with majesty and glory,
   robed in light as with a cloak.
℟. Oh, bless the Lord, my soul!

All creatures look to you
   to give them food in due time.
When you give it to them, they gather it;
   when you open your hand, they are filled
      with good things.

℟. Oh, bless the Lord, my soul!
If you take away their breath, they perish
and return to their dust.
When you send forth your spirit, they are
created,
and you renew the face of the earth.
℟. Oh, bless the Lord, my soul!

Year II

READING I   1 Kgs 10, 1-10
A reading from the first book of Kings
The Queen of Sheba saw all the wisdom of Solomon.

The queen of Sheba, having heard of Solomon's
fame, came to test him with subtle questions.
She arrived in Jerusalem with a very numerous
retinue, and with camels bearing spices, a large
amount of gold, and precious stones. She came
to Solomon and questioned him on every subject in which she was interested. King Solomon
explained everything she asked about, and
there remained nothing hidden from him that
he could not explain to her.

When the queen of Sheba witnessed Solomon's great wisdom, the palace he had built,
the food at his table, the seating of his ministers, the attendance and garb of his waiters,
his banquet service, and the holocausts he offered in the temple of the Lord, she was breath-
less. "The report I heard in my country about
your deeds and your wisdom is true," she told
the king. "Though I did not believe the report
until I came and saw with my own eyes, I have
discovered that they were not telling me the
half. Your wisdom and prosperity surpass the
report I heard. Happy are your men, happy
these servants of yours, who stand before you
always and listen to your wisdom. Blessed be
the Lord, your God, whom it has pleased to
place you on the throne of Israel. In his enduring love for Israel, the Lord has made you king
to carry out judgment and justice." Then she
gave the king one hundred and twenty gold
talents, a very large quantity of spices, and
precious stones. Never again did anyone bring
such an abundance of spices as the queen of
Sheba gave to King Solomon.
This is the word of the Lord.

Responsorial Psalm   Ps 37, 5-6. 30-31. 39-40
℟. (30) **The mouth of the just man murmurs**
wisdom.
Commit to the Lord your way;
trust in him, and he will act.
He will make justice dawn for you like the
light;
bright as the noonday shall be your vindica-
tion.
℟. The mouth of the just man murmurs wisdom.
The mouth of the just man tells of wisdom
and his tongue utters what is right.
The law of his God is in his heart,
and his steps do not falter.
℟. The mouth of the just man murmurs wisdom.
The salvation of the just is from the Lord;
he is their refuge in time of distress.
And the Lord helps them and delivers them;
he delivers them from the wicked and saves
them,
because they take refuge in him.
℟. The mouth of the just man murmurs wisdom.

Years I and II

GOSPEL   Mk 7, 14-23
Alleluia
See no. 509.

✠ **A reading from the holy gospel according**
to Mark
It is the things that come out of a man that make him
unclean.

Jesus summoned the crowd and said to them:
"Hear me, all of you, and try to understand.
Nothing that enters a man from outside can
make him impure; that which comes out of
him, and only that, constitutes impurity. Let
everyone heed what he hears!"

When he got home, away from the crowd,
his disciples questioned him about the proverb.
"Are you, too, incapable of understanding?" he
asked them. "Do you not see that nothing that
enters a man from outside can make him impure? It does not penetrate his being, but enters
his stomach only and passes into the latrine."
Thus did he render all foods clean. He went on:

"What emerges from within a man, that and nothing else is what makes him impure. Wicked designs come from the deep recesses of the heart: acts of fornication, theft, murder, adulterous conduct, greed, maliciousness, deceit, sensuality, envy, blasphemy arrogance, an obtuse spirit. All these evils come from within and render a man impure."

This is the gospel of the Lord.

---

332   THURSDAY OF THE FIFTH WEEK OF THE YEAR

Year I

READING I   Gn 2, 18-25

A reading from the book of Genesis

The Lord God led her to Adam, and they became two in one body.

The Lord God said: "It is not good for the man to be alone. I will make a suitable partner for him." So the Lord God formed out of the ground various wild animals and various birds of the air, and he brought them to the man to see what he would call them; whatever the man called each of them would be its name. The man gave names to all the cattle, all the birds of the air, and all the wild animals; but none proved to be the suitable partner for the man.

So the Lord God cast a deep sleep on the man, and while he was asleep, he took out one of his ribs and closed up its place with flesh. The Lord God then built up into a woman the rib that he had taken from the man. When he brought her to the man, the man said:

"This one, at last, is bone of my bones
    and flesh of my flesh;
This one shall be called 'woman,'
    for out of 'her man' this one has been taken."

That is why a man leaves his father and mother and clings to his wife, and the two of them become one body.

The man and his wife were both naked, yet they felt no shame.

This is the word of the Lord.

Responsorial Psalm   Ps 128, 1-2. 3. 4-5

R̸. (1) Happy are those who fear the Lord.
Happy are you who fear the Lord,
    who walk in his ways!
For you shall eat the fruit of your handiwork;
    happy shall you be, and favored.
R̸. Happy are those who fear the Lord.
Your wife shall be like a fruitful vine
    in the recesses of your home;
Your children like olive plants
    around your table.
R̸. Happy are those who fear the Lord.
Behold, thus is the man blessed
    who fears the Lord.
The Lord bless you from Zion:
    may you see the prosperity of Jerusalem
    all the days of your life.
R̸. Happy are those who fear the Lord.

Year II

READING I   1 Kgs 11, 4-13

A reading from the first book of Kings

Since you did not keep my covenant I will tear the kingdom away from you and I will leave your son one tribe for the sake of my servant, David.

When Solomon was old his wives had turned his heart to strange gods, and his heart was not entirely with the Lord, his God, as the heart of his father David had been. By adoring Astarte, the goddess of the Sidonians, and Milcom, the idol of the Ammonites, Solomon did evil in the sight of the Lord; he did not follow him unreservedly as his father David had done. Solomon then built a high place to Chemosh, the idol of Moab, and to Molech, the idol of the Ammonites, on the hill opposite Jerusalem. He did the same for all his foreign wives who burned incense and sacrificed to their gods. The Lord, therefore, became angry with Solomon, because his heart was turned away from the Lord, the God of Israel, who had appeared to him twice (for though the Lord had forbidden him this very act of following strange gods, Solomon had not obeyed him).

So the Lord said to Solomon: "Since this is what you want, and you have not kept my covenant and my statutes which I enjoined on you,

I will deprive you of the kingdom and give it to your servant. I will not do this during your lifetime, however, for the sake of your father David; it is your son whom I will deprive. Nor will I take away the whole kingdom. I will leave your son one tribe for the sake of my servant David and of Jerusalem, which I have chosen."

This is the Word of the Lord.

Responsorial Psalm   Ps 106, 3-4. 35-36. 37. 40

℟. (4) Lord, remember us,
   for the love you bear your people.
**Happy are they who observe what is right,
   who do always what is just.
Remember us, O Lord, as you favor your people;
   visit us with your saving help.**
℟. Lord, remember us,
   for the love you bear your people.
**But they mingled with the nations
   and learned their works.
They served their idols,
   which became a snare for them.**
℟. Lord, remember us,
   for the love you bear your people.
**They sacrificed their sons
   and their daughters to demons.
And the Lord grew angry with his people,
   and abhorred his inheritance.**
℟. Lord, remember us,
   for the love you bear your people.

Years I and II

GOSPEL   Mk 7, 24-30
Alleluia

See no. 509.

✠ A reading from the holy gospel according
to Mark

The dogs under the table can eat the children's scraps.

Jesus went to the territory of Tyre and Sidon. He retired to a certain house and wanted no one to recognize him; however, he could not escape notice. Soon a woman, whose small daughter had an unclean spirit, heard about him. She approached him and crouched at his feet. The woman who was Greek—a Syro-Phoenician by birth—began to beg him to expel the demon from her daughter. He told her: "Let the sons of the household satisfy themselves at table first. It is not right to take the food of the children and throw it to the dogs." "Please, Lord," she replied, "even the dogs under the table eat the family's leavings." Then he said to her, "For such a reply, be off now! The demon has already left your daughter." When she got home, she found the child lying in bed and the demon gone.**

This is the gospel of the Lord.

**333   FRIDAY OF THE FIFTH
WEEK OF THE YEAR**

Year I

READING I   Gn 3, 1-8
A reading from the book of Genesis

You will be like God, knowing good and evil.

Now the serpent was the most cunning of all the animals that the Lord God had made. The serpent asked the woman, "Did God really tell you not to eat from any of the trees in the garden?" The woman answered the serpent: "We may eat of the fruit of the trees in the garden; it is only about the fruit of the tree in the middle of the garden that God said, 'You shall not eat it or even touch it, lest you die.'" But the serpent said to the woman: "You certainly will not die! No, God knows well that the moment you eat of it you will be like gods who know what is good and what is bad." The woman saw that the tree was good for food, pleasing to the eyes, and desirable for gaining wisdom. So she took some of its fruit and ate it; and she also gave some to her husband, who was with her, and he ate it. Then the eyes of both of them were opened, and they realized that they were naked; so they sewed fig leaves together and made loincloths for themselves.

   When they heard the sound of the Lord God moving about in the garden at the breezy time of the day, the man and his wife hid themselves from the Lord God among the trees of the garden.

This is the Word of the Lord.

Responsorial Psalm   Ps 32, 1-2. 5. 6. 7

℟. (1) Happy are those whose sins are forgiven.

Happy is he whose fault is taken away,
    whose sin is covered.
Happy the man to whom the Lord imputes not
    guilt,
    in whose spirit there is no guile.

℟. Happy are those whose sins are forgiven.

Then I acknowledged my sin to you,
    my guilt I covered not.
I said, "I confess my faults to the Lord,"
    and you took away the guilt of my sin..

℟. Happy are those whose sins are forgiven.

For this shall every faithful man pray to you
    in time of stress.
Though deep waters overflow,
    they shall not reach him.

℟. Happy are those whose sins are forgiven.

You are my shelter; from distress you will pre-
    .serve me;
    with glad cries of freedom you will ring me
    round.

℟. Happy are those whose sins are forgiven.

Year II

READING I   1 Kgs 11, 29-32; 12, 19

A reading from the first book of Kings

All Israel has been separated from the house of David.

At that time Jeroboam left Jerusalem, and the
prophet Ahijah the Shilonite met him on the
road. The two were alone in the area, and the
prophet was wearing a new cloak. Ahijah took
off his new cloak, tore it into twelve pieces,
and said to Jeroboam:

"Take ten pieces for yourself; the Lord, the
God of Israel, says: 'I will tear away the kingdom from Solomon's grasp and will give you
ten of the tribes. One tribe shall remain to him
for the sake of David my servant, and of Jerusalem, the city I have chosen out of the tribes
of Israel.'"

Israel went into rebellion against David's
house to this day.

This is the Word of the Lord.

Responsorial Psalm   Ps 81, 10-11. 12-13. 14-15

℟. (11. 9) I am the Lord, your God:
    hear my voice.

There shall be no strange god among you
    nor shall you worship any alien god.
I, the Lord, am your God
    who led you forth from the land of Egypt.

℟. I am the Lord, your God:
    hear my voice.

But my people heard not my voice,
    and Israel obeyed me not;
So I gave them up to the hardness of their
    hearts;
    they walked according to their own coun-
    sels.

℟. I am the Lord, your God:
    hear my voice.

If only my people would hear me,
    and Israel walk in my ways,
Quickly would I humble their enemies;
    against their foes I would turn my hand.

℟. I am the Lord, your God:
    hear my voice.

Years I and II

GOSPEL   Mk 7, 31-37
Alleluia

See no. 509

✠ **A reading from the holy gospel according
to Mark**

He makes the deaf hear and the dumb speak.

Jesus left Tyrian territory and returned by way
of Sidon to the Sea of Galilee, into the district
of the Ten Cities. Some people brought him a
deaf man who had a speech impediment and
begged him to lay his hand on him. Jesus took
him off by himself away from the crowd. He
put his fingers into the man's ears and, spitting, touched his tongue; then he looked up to
heaven and emitted a groan. He said to him,
"Ephphatha!" (that is, "Be opened!") At once
the man's ears were opened; he was freed from
the impediment, and began to speak plainly.
Then he enjoined them strictly not to tell anyone; but the more he ordered them not to,
the more they proclaimed it. Their amazement

went beyond all bounds: "He has done everything well! He makes the deaf hear and the mute speak!"

This is the gospel of the Lord.

---

334   SATURDAY OF THE FIFTH WEEK OF THE YEAR

Year I

READING I   Gn 3, 9-24

A reading from the book of Genesis

God expelled them from the garden of Eden to toil the earth.

The Lord God called to Adam and asked him, "Where are you?" He answered, "I heard you in the garden; but I was afraid, because I was naked, so I hid myself." Then he asked, "Who told you that you were naked? You have eaten, then, from the tree of which I had forbidden you to eat!" The man replied, "The woman whom you put here with me—she gave me fruit from the tree, and so I ate it." The Lord God then asked the woman, "Why did you do such a thing?" The woman answered, "The serpent tricked me into it, so I ate it."

Then the Lord God said to the serpent: "Because you have done this, you shall be banned
     from all the animals
     and from all the wild creatures;
On your belly shall you crawl,
     and dirt shall you eat
     all the days of your life.
I will put enmity between you and the woman,
     and between your offspring and hers;
He will strike at your head,
     while you strike at his heel."
To the woman he said:
"I will intensify the pangs of your childbearing;
     in pain shall you bring forth children.
Yet your urge shall be for your husband,
     and he shall be your master."
To the man he said: "Because you listened to your wife and ate from the tree of which I had forbidden you to eat,
"Cursed be the ground because of you!

In toil shall you eat its yield
     all the days of your life.
Thorns and thistles shall it bring forth to you,
     as you eat of the plants of the field.
By the sweat of your face
     shall you get bread to eat,
Until you return to the ground,
     from which you were taken;
For you are dirt,
     and to dirt you shall return."

The man called his wife Eve, because she became the mother of all the living.

For the man and his wife the Lord God made leather garments, with which he clothed them. Then the Lord God said: "See! The man has become like one of us, knowing what is good and what is bad! Therefore, he must not be allowed to put out his hand to take fruit from the tree of life also, and thus eat of it and live forever." The Lord God therefore banished him from the garden of Eden, to till the ground from which he had been taken. When he expelled the man, he settled him east of the garden of Eden; and he stationed the cherubim and the fiery revolving sword, to guard the way to the tree of life.

This is the Word of the Lord.

Responsorial Psalm   Ps 90, 2. 3-4. 5-6. 12-13

℞. (1) In every age, O Lord, you have been our
     refuge.
Before the mountains were begotten
     and the earth and the world were brought
     forth,
     from everlasting to everlasting you are God.
℞. In every age, O Lord, you have been our
     refuge.
You turn man back to dust,
     saying, "Return, O children of men."
For a thousand years in your sight
     are as yesterday, now that it is past,
     or as a watch of the night.
℞. In every age, O Lord, you have been our
     refuge.
You make an end of them in their sleep;
     the next morning they are like the changing
     grass,
Which at dawn springs up anew,
     but by evening wilts and fades.

℟. In every age, O Lord, you have been our refuge.

Teach us to number our days aright,
that we may gain wisdom of heart.

Return, O Lord! How long?

Have pity on your servants!

℟. In every age, O Lord, you have been our refuge.

Year II

READING I   1 Kgs 12, 26-32; 13, 33-34

A reading from the first book of Kings

Jeroboam made two golden calves.

Jeroboam thought to himself: "The kingdom will return to David's house. If now this people go up to offer sacrifices in the temple of the Lord in Jerusalem, the hearts of this people will return to their master, Rehoboam, king of Judah, and they will kill me." After taking counsel, the king made two calves of gold and said to the people: "You have been going up to Jerusalem long enough. Here is your God, O Israel, who brought you up from the land of Egypt." And he put one in Bethel, the other in Dan. This led to sin, because the people frequented these calves in Bethel and in Dan. He also built temples on the high places and made priests from among the people who were not Levites. Jeroboam established a feast in the eighth month on the fifteenth day of the month to duplicate in Bethel the pilgrimage feast of Judah, with sacrifices to the calves he had made; and he stationed in Bethel priests of the high places he had built.

Jeroboam did not give up his evil ways after this event, but again made priests for the high places from among the common people. Whoever desired it was consecrated and became a priest of the high places. This was a sin on the part of the house of Jeroboam for which it was to be cut off and destroyed from the earth.

This is the Word of the Lord.

Responsorial Psalm   Ps 106, 6-7. 19-20. 21-22

℟. (4) Lord, remember us,
for the love you bear your people.

We have sinned, we and our fathers;
we have committed crimes; we have done wrong.

Our fathers in Egypt
considered not your wonders.

℟. Lord, remember us,
for the love you bear your people.

They made a calf in Horeb
and adored a molten image;

They exchanged their glory
for the image of a grass-eating bullock.

℟. Lord, remember us,
for the love you bear your people.

They forgot the God who had saved them,
who had done great deeds in Egypt,

Wondrous deeds in the land of Ham,
terrible things at the Red Sea.

℟. Lord, remember us,
for the love you bear your people.

Years I and II

GOSPEL   Mk 8, 1-10
Alleluia
See no. 509

✠ A reading from the holy gospel according to Mark

They ate and were filled.

A large crowd assembled, and they were without anything to eat. Jesus called the disciples over to him and said: "My heart is moved with pity for the crowd. By now they have been with me three days and have nothing to eat. If I send them home hungry, they will collapse on the way. Some of them have come a great distance." His disciples replied, "How can anyone give these people sufficient bread in this deserted spot?" Still he asked them, "How many loaves do you have?" "Seven," they replied. Then he directed the crowd to take their places on the ground. Taking the seven loaves he gave thanks, broke them, and gave them to his disciples to distribute, and they handed them out to the crowd. They also had a few small fishes; asking a blessing on the fish, he told them to distribute these also. The people in the crowd ate until they had their fill; then they gathered up seven wicker baskets of leftovers. Those who had eaten numbered about four thousand.

He dismissed them and got into the boat with his disciples to go to the neighborhood of Dalmanutha.

This is the gospel of the Lord.

---

335   **MONDAY OF THE SIXTH WEEK OF THE YEAR**

Year I

READING I   Gn 4, 1-15. 25

A reading from the book of Genesis
Cain set on his brother and killed him.

The man had relations with his wife Eve, and she conceived and bore Cain, saying, "I have produced a man with the help of the Lord." Next she bore his brother Abel. Abel became a keeper of flocks, and Cain a tiller of the soil. In the course of time Cain brought an offering to the Lord from the fruit of the soil, while Abel, for his part, brought one of the best firstlings of his flock. The Lord looked with favor on Abel and his offering, but on Cain and his offering he did not. Cain greatly resented this and was crestfallen. So the Lord said to Cain: "Why are you so resentful and crestfallen? If you do well, you can hold up your head; but if not, sin is a demon lurking at the door: his urge is toward you, yet you can be his master."

Cain said to his brother Abel, "Let us go out in the field." When they were in the field, Cain attacked his brother Abel and killed him. Then the Lord asked Cain, "Where is your brother Abel?" He answered, "I do not know. Am I my brother's keeper?" The Lord then said: "What have you done! Listen: your brother's blood cries out to me from the soil! Therefore you shall be banned from the soil that opened its mouth to receive your brother's blood from your hand. If you till the soil, it shall no longer give you its produce. You shall become a restless wanderer on the earth." Cain said to the Lord: "My punishment is too great to bear. Since you have now banished me from the soil, and I must avoid your presence and become a restless wanderer on the earth, anyone may kill me at sight." "Not so!" the Lord said to him. "If anyone kills Cain, Cain shall be avenged sevenfold." So the Lord put a mark on Cain, lest anyone should kill him at sight.

Adam again had relations with his wife, and she gave birth to a son whom she called Seth. "God has granted me more offspring in place of Abel," she said, "because Cain slew him."

This is the Word of the Lord.

Responsorial Psalm   Ps 50, 1. 8. 16-17. 20-21

℟. (14) Offer to God a sacrifice of praise.
God the Lord has spoken and summoned the earth,
    from the rising of the sun to its setting.
Not for your sacrifices do I rebuke you,
    for your holocausts are before me always.
℟. Offer to God a sacrifice of praise.
"Why do you recite my statutes,
    and profess my covenant with your mouth
Though you hate discipline
    and cast my words behind you?
℟. Offer to God a sacrifice of praise.
You sit speaking against your brother;
    against your mother's son you spread rumors.
When you do these things, shall I be deaf to it?
    Or think you that I am like yourself?
    I will correct you by drawing them up before your eyes.
℟. Offer to God a sacrifice of praise.

Year II

READING I   Jas 1, 1-11

The beginning of the letter of James
Your faith is put to the test to make you patient, so that you will become perfect and complete.

To the twelve tribes in the dispersion, James, a servant of God and of the Lord Jesus Christ, sends greeting.

My brothers, count it pure joy when you are involved in every sort of trial. Realize that when your faith is tested this makes for endurance. Let endurance come to its perfection so that you may be fully mature and lacking in nothing.

If any of you is without wisdom, let him ask it from the God who gives generously and ungrudgingly to all, and it will be given him.

Yet he must ask in faith, never doubting, for the doubter is like the surf tossed and driven by the wind. A person like this, devious and erratic in all that he does, must not expect to receive anything from the Lord.

Let the brother in humble circumstances take pride in his eminence and the rich man be proud of his lowliness, for he will disappear "like the flower of the field." When the sun comes up with its scorching heat it parches the meadow, the field flowers droop, and with that the meadow's loveliness is gone. Just so will the rich man wither away amid his many projects.

This is the Word of the Lord.

Responsorial Psalm Ps 119, 67. 68. 71. 72. 75. 76

℟. (77) Be kind to me, Lord, and I shall live.
Before I was afflicted I went astray,
   but now I hold to your promise.
℟. Be kind to me, Lord, and I shall live.
You are good and bountiful;
   teach me your statutes.
℟. Be kind to me, Lord, and I shall live.
It is good for me that I have been afflicted,
   that I may learn your statutes.
℟. Be kind to me, Lord, and I shall live.
The law of your mouth is to me more precious
   than thousands of gold and silver pieces.
℟. Be kind to me, Lord, and I shall live.
I know, O Lord, that your ordinances are just,
   and in your faithfulness you have afflicted me.
℟. Be kind to me, Lord, and I shall live.
Let your kindness comfort me
   according to your promise to your servants.
℟. Be kind to me, Lord, and I shall live.

Years I and II

GOSPEL   Mk 8, 11-13
Alleluia

See no. 509.

✠ **A reading from the holy gospel according to Mark**

Why does this generation demand a sign?

The Pharisees came forward and began to argue with Jesus. They were looking for some heavenly sign from him as a test. With a sigh from the depths of his spirit he said, "Why does this age seek a sign? I assure you, no such sign will be given it!" Then he left them, got into the boat again, and went off to the other shore.

This is the gospel of the Lord.

336   **TUESDAY OF THE SIXTH WEEK OF THE YEAR**

Year I

READING I   Gn 6, 5-8; 7, 1-5. 10
A reading from the book of Genesis

I will rid man, my own creation, from the face of the earth.

When the Lord saw how great was man's wickedness on earth, and how no desire that his heart conceived was ever anything but evil, he regretted that he had made man on the earth, and his heart was grieved.

So the Lord said: "I will wipe out from the earth the men whom I have created, and not only the men, but also the beasts and the creeping things and the birds of the air, for I am sorry that I made them." But Noah found favor with the Lord.

Then the Lord said to Noah: "Go into the ark, you and all your household, for you alone in this age have I found to be truly just. Of every clean animal, take with you seven pairs, a male and its mate; and of the unclean animals, one pair, a male and its mate; likewise, of every clean bird of the air, seven pairs, a male and a female, and of all the unclean birds, one pair, a male and a female. Thus you will keep their issue alive over all the earth. Seven days from now I will bring rain down on the earth for forty days and forty nights, and so I will wipe out from the surface of the earth every moving creature that I have made." Noah did just as the Lord had commanded him.

As soon as the seven days were over, the waters of the flood came upon the earth.

This is the Word of the Lord.

Responsorial Psalm   Ps 29, 1-2. 3-4. 3. 9-10

℟. (11) The Lord will bless his people with peace.

Give to the Lord, you sons of God,
  give to the Lord glory and praise,
Give to the Lord the glory due his name;
  adore the Lord in holy attire.

℟. The Lord will bless his people with peace.

The voice of the Lord is over the waters,
  the Lord, over vast waters.
The voice of the Lord is mighty;
  the voice of the Lord is majestic.

℟. The Lord will bless his people with peace.

The God of glory thunders,
  and in his temple all say, "Glory!"
The Lord is enthroned above the flood;
  the Lord is enthroned as king forever.

℟. The Lord will bless his people with peace.

Year II

READING I   Jas 1, 12-18

A reading from the letter of James

God tempts no one.

Happy the man who holds out to the end through trial! Once his worth has been proved, he will receive the crown of life the Lord has promised to those who love him. No one who is tempted is free to say, "I am being tempted by God." Surely God who is untouched by evil tempts no one. Rather the tug and lure of his own passion tempts every man. Once passion has conceived it gives birth to sin, and when sin reaches maturity it begets death.

Make no mistake about this, my dear brothers. Every worthwhile gift, every genuine benefit comes from above, descending from the Father of the heavenly luminaries, who cannot change and who is never shadowed over. He wills to bring us to birth with a word spoken in truth so that we may be a kind of firstfruits of his creatures.

This is the Word of the Lord.

Responsorial Psalm   Ps 94, 12-13. 14-15. 18-19

℟. (12) Happy the man you teach, O Lord.

Happy the man whom you instruct, O Lord,
  whom by your law you teach,
Giving him rest from evil days.

℟. Happy the man you teach, O Lord.

For the Lord will not cast off his people,
  nor abandon his inheritance;
But judgment shall again be with justice,
  and all the upright of heart shall follow it.

℟. Happy the man you teach, O Lord.

When I say, "My foot is slipping,"
  your kindness, O Lord, sustains me;
When cares abound within me,
  your comfort gladdens my soul.

℟. Happy the man you teach, O Lord.

Years I and II

GOSPEL   Mk 8, 14-21

Alleluia

See no. 509.

✠ **A reading from the holy gospel according to Mark**

Be on guard against the "yeast" of the Pharisees and the "yeast" of Herod.

The disciples had forgotten to bring any bread along; except for one loaf they had none with them in the boat. So when Jesus instructed them, "Keep your eyes open! Be on your guard against the yeast of the Pharisees and the yeast of Herod," they concluded among themselves that it was because they had no bread. Aware of this he said to them, "Why do you suppose that it is because you have no bread? Do you still not see or comprehend? Are your minds completely blinded? Have you eyes but no sight? Ears but no hearing? Do you remember when I broke the five loaves for the five thousand, how many baskets of fragments you gathered up." They answered, "Twelve." "When I broke the seven loaves for the four thousand, how many full hampers of fragments did you collect?" They answered, "Seven." He said to them again, "Do you still not understand?"

This is the gospel of the Lord.

337   WEDNESDAY OF THE SIXTH WEEK OF THE YEAR

Year I

READING I   Gn 8, 6-13. 20-22

A reading from the book of Genesis

He saw that the waters covered the face of the earth.

At the end of forty days Noah opened the hatch he had made in the ark, and he sent out a raven, to see if the waters had lessened on the earth. It flew back and forth until the waters dried off from the earth. Then he sent out a dove, to see if the waters had lessened on the earth. But the dove could find no place to alight and perch, and it returned to him in the ark, for there was water all over the earth. Putting out his hand, he caught the dove and drew it back to him inside the ark. He waited seven days more and again sent the dove out from the ark. In the evening the dove came back to him, and there in its bill was a plucked-off olive leaf! So Noah knew that the waters had lessened on the earth. He waited still another seven days and then released the dove once more; and this time it did not come back.

In the six hundred and first year of Noah's life, in the first month, on the first day of the month, the water began to dry up on the earth. Noah then removed the covering of the ark and saw that the surface of the ground was drying up.

Noah built an altar to the Lord, and choosing from every clean animal and every clean bird, he offered holocausts on the altar. When the Lord smelled the sweet odor, he said to himself: "Never again will I doom the earth because of man, since the desires of man's heart are evil from the start; nor will I ever again strike down all living beings, as I have done.

As long as the earth lasts,
    seedtime and harvest,
    cold and heat,
Summer and winter,
    and day and night
    shall not cease."

This is the Word of the Lord.

Responsorial Psalm   Ps 116, 12-13. 14-15. 18-19

℟. (17) To you, Lord, I will offer a sacrifice of praise.

How shall I make a return to the Lord
    for all the good he has done for me?
The cup of salvation I will take up,
    and I will call upon the name of the Lord.

℟. To you, Lord, I will offer a sacrifice of praise.

My vows to the Lord I will pay
    in the presence of all his people.
Precious in the eyes of the Lord
    is the death of his faithful ones.

℟. To you, Lord, I will offer a sacrifice of praise.

My vows to the Lord I will pay
    in the presence of all his people,
In the courts of the house of the Lord,
    in your midst, O Jerusalem.

℟. To you, Lord, I will offer a sacrifice of praise.

℟. Or: Alleluia.

Year II

READING I   Jas 1, 19-27

A reading from the letter of James

Be doers of the word and not just listeners.

Keep this in mind, dear brothers.

Let every man be quick to hear, slow to speak, slow to anger; for a man's anger does not fulfill God's justice. Strip away all that is filthy, every vicious excess. Humbly welcome the word that has taken root in you, with its power to save you. Act on this word. If all you do is listen to it, you are deceiving yourselves.

A man who listens to God's word but does not put it into practice is like a man who looks into a mirror at the face he was born with; he looks at himself, then goes off and promptly forgets what he looked like. There is, on the other hand, the man who peers into freedom's ideal law and abides by it. He is no forgetful listener, but one who carries out the law in practice. Happy will this man be in whatever he does.

If a man who does not control his tongue

imagines that he is devout, he is self-deceived; his worship is pointless. Looking after orphans and widows in their distress and keeping oneself unspotted by the world make for pure worship without stain before our God and Father.
This is the Word of the Lord.

Responsorial Psalm   Ps 15, 2-3. 3-4. 5

℟. (1) He who does justice shall live on the Lord's holy mountain.

He who walks blamelessly and does justice;
  who thinks the truth in his heart
  and slanders not with his tongue.
℟. He who does justice shall live on the Lord's holy mountain.

Who harms not his fellow man,
  nor takes up a reproach against his neighbor;
By whom the reprobate is despised,
  while he honors those who fear the Lord.
℟. He who does justice shall live on the Lord's holy mountain.

Who lends not his money at usury
  and accepts no bribe against the innocent.
He who does these things
  shall never be disturbed.
℟. He who does justice shall live on the Lord's holy mountain.

Years I and II

GOSPEL   Mk 8, 22-26
Alleluia

See no. 509.

✠ **A reading from the holy gospel according to Mark**
He restored sight to the blind man and he could see everything clearly.

When Jesus and his disciples arrived at Bethsaida, some people brought him a blind man and begged him to touch him. Jesus took the blind man's hand and led him outside the village. Putting spittle on his eyes he laid his hands on him and asked, "Can you see anything?" The man opened his eyes and said, "I can see people but they look like walking trees!" Then a second time Jesus laid hands on his eyes, and he saw perfectly; his sight was restored and he could see everything clearly.

Jesus sent him home with the admonition, "Do not even go into the village."
This is the gospel of the Lord.

---

338   **THURSDAY OF THE SIXTH WEEK OF THE YEAR**

Year I

READING I   Gn 9, 1-13
A reading from the book of Genesis
I set my bow in the clouds and it shall be a sign of the covenant between me and the earth.

God blessed Noah and his sons and said to them: "Be fertile and multiply and fill the earth. Dread fear of you shall come upon all the animals of the earth and all the birds of the air, upon all the creatures that move about on the ground and all the fishes of the sea; into your power they are delivered. Every creature that is alive shall be yours to eat; I give them all to you as I did the green plants. Only flesh with its lifeblood still in it you shall not eat. For your own lifeblood, too, I will demand an accounting: from every animal I will demand it, and from man in regard to his fellow man I will demand an accounting for human life.

  If anyone sheds the blood of man,
    by man shall his blood be shed;
  For in the image of God
    has man been made.

Be fertile, then, and multiply; abound on the earth and subdue it."
  God said to Noah and to his sons with him: "See, I am now establishing my covenant with you and your descendants after you and with every living creature that was with you: all the birds, and the various tame and wild animals that were with you and came out of the ark. I will establish my covenant with you, that never again shall all bodily creatures be destroyed by the waters of a flood; there shall not be another flood to devastate the earth." God added: "This is the sign that I am giving for all ages to come, of the covenant between me and you and every living creature with you: I set my bow in the clouds to serve as a sign of the covenant between me and the earth."
This is the Word of the Lord.

Responsorial Psalm   Ps 102, 16-18. 19-21. 29. 22-23

℟. (20) From heaven the Lord looks down on
  the earth.
The nations shall revere your name, O Lord,
  and all the kings of the earth your glory,
When the Lord has rebuilt Zion
  and appeared in his glory;
When he has regarded the prayer of the destitute,
  and not despised their prayer.
℟. From heaven the Lord looks down on the
  earth.
Let this be written for the generation to come,
  and let his future creatures praise the Lord:
"The Lord looked down from his holy height,
  from heaven he beheld the earth,
To hear the groaning of the prisoners,
  to release those doomed to die."
℟. From heaven the Lord looks down on the
  earth.
The children of your servants shall abide,
  and their posterity shall continue in your
  presence,
That the name of the Lord may be declared in
  Zion,
  and his praise, in Jerusalem,
When the peoples gather together,
  and the kingdoms, to serve the Lord.
℟. From heaven the Lord looks down on the
  earth.

Year II

READING I   Jas 2, 1-9

A reading from the letter of James
Did not God choose the poor? You, however, do not respect
them.

My brothers, your faith in our Lord Jesus
Christ glorified must not allow of favoritism.
Suppose there should come into your assembly
a man fashionably dressed, with gold rings on
his fingers, and at the same time a poor man
dressed in shabby clothes. Suppose further you
were to take notice of the well-dressed man and
say, "Sit right here, please;" whereas you were
to say to the poor man, "You can stand!" or
"Sit over there by my footrest." Have you not

in a case like this discriminated in your hearts?
Have you not set yourselves up as judges who
hand down corrupt decisions?
  Listen, dear brothers. Did not God choose
those who are poor in the eyes of the world to
be rich in faith and heirs of the kingdom he
promised to those who love him? Yet you
treated the poor man shamefully. Are not the
rich exploiting you? They are the ones who
hale you into the courts and who blaspheme
that noble name which has made you God's
own.
  You are acting rightly, however, if you fulfill the law of the kingdom. Scripture has it,
"You shall love your neighbor as yourself."
But if you show favoritism you commit sin and
are convicted by the law as transgressors.
  This is the Word of the Lord.

Responsorial Psalm   Ps 34, 2-3. 4-5. 6-7

℟. (7) The Lord hears the cry of the poor.
I will bless the Lord at all times;
  his praise shall be ever in my mouth.
Let my soul glory in the Lord;
  the lowly will hear me and be glad.
℟. The Lord hears the cry of the poor.
Glorify the Lord with me,
  let us together extol his name.
I sought the Lord, and he answered me
  and delivered me from all my fears.
℟. The Lord hears the cry of the poor.
Look to him that you may be radiant with joy,
  and your faces may not blush with shame.
When the afflicted man called out, the Lord
  heard,
  and from all his distress he saved him.
℟. The Lord hears the cry of the poor.

Years I and II

GOSPEL   Mk 8, 27-33

Alleluia

See no. 509.

✠ **A reading from the holy gospel according
to Mark**
You are the Christ. The Son of Man must suffer many things.

Jesus and his disciples set out for the villages
around Caesarea Philippi. On the way he asked

his disciples this question: "Who do people say that I am?" They replied, "Some, John the Baptizer, others, Elijah, still others, one of the prophets." "And you," he went on to ask, "who do you say that I am?" Peter answered him, "You are the Messiah!" Then he strictly ordered them not to tell anyone about him.

He then began to teach them that the Son of Man had to suffer much, be rejected by the elders, the chief priests, and the scribes, be put to death, and rise three days later. He said this quite openly. Peter then took him aside and began to remonstrate with him. At this he turned around and, eyeing the disciples, reprimanded Peter in turn: "Get out of my sight, you satan! You are not judging by God's standards but by man's!"

This is the gospel of the Lord.

339　　**FRIDAY OF THE SIXTH WEEK OF THE YEAR**

Year I

READING I　　　　　　　　　Gn 11, 1-9

A reading from the book of Genesis
Let us go down and confuse their language.

The whole world spoke the same language, using the same words. While men were migrating in the east, they came upon a valley in the land of Shinar and settled there. They said to one another, "Come, let us mold bricks and harden them with fire." They used bricks for stone, and bitumen for mortar. Then they said, "Come, let us build ourselves a city and a tower with its top in the sky, and so make a name for ourselves; otherwise we shall be scattered all over the earth."

The Lord came down to see the city and the tower that the men had built. Then the Lord said: "If now, while they are one people, all speaking the same language, they have started to do this, nothing will later stop them from doing whatever they presume to do. Let us then go down and there confuse their language, so that one will not understand what another says." Thus the Lord scattered them from there all over the earth, and they stopped building

the city. That is why it was called Babel, because there the Lord confused the speech of all the world. It was from that place that he scattered them all over the earth.

This is the Word of the Lord.

Responsorial Psalm　　Ps 33, 10-11. 12-13. 14-15

℟. (12) Happy the people the Lord has chosen to be his own.

The Lord brings to nought the plans of nations;
　he foils the designs of peoples.
But the plan of the Lord stands forever;
　the design of his heart, through all generations.

℟. Happy the people the Lord has chosen to be his own.

Happy the nation whose God is the Lord,
　the people he has chosen for his own inheritance.
From heaven the Lord looks down;
　he sees all mankind.

℟. Happy the people the Lord has chosen to be his own.

From his fixed throne he beholds
　all who dwell on the earth,
He who fashioned the heart of each,
　he who knows all their works.

℟. Happy the people the Lord has chosen to be his own.

Year II

READING I　　　　　　　　　Jas 2, 14-24. 26

A reading from the letter of James
A body dies when it is separated from the spirit, and in the same way faith is dead if it is separated from good works.

My brothers, what good is it to profess faith without practicing it? Such faith has no power to save one, has it? If a brother or sister has nothing to wear and no food for the day, and you say to them, "Good-bye and good luck! Keep warm and be well fed," but do not meet their bodily needs, what good is that? So it is with the faith that does nothing in practice. It is thoroughly lifeless.

To such a person one might say, "You have faith and I have works—is that it?" Show me your faith without works, and I will show you the faith that underlies my works! Do you believe that God is one? You are quite right. The demons believe that and shudder. Do you want proof, you ignoramus, that without works faith is idle? Was not our father Abraham justified by his works when he offered his son Isaac on the altar? There you see proof that faith was both assisting his works and implemented by his works. You also see how the Scripture was fulfilled which says, "Abraham believed God, and it was credited to him as justice"; for this he received the title, "God's friend."

You must perceive that a person is justified by his works and not by faith alone. Be assured, then, that faith without works is as dead as a body without breath.

This is the Word of the Lord.

Responsorial Psalm   Ps 112, 1-2. 3-4. 5-6

R̸. (1) Happy are those who do what the Lord commands.

Happy the man who fears the Lord,
    who greatly delights in his commands.
His posterity shall be mighty upon the earth;
    the upright generation shall be blessed.

R̸. Happy are those who do what the Lord commands.

Wealth and riches shall be in his house;
    his generosity shall endure forever.
He dawns through the darkness, a light for the
    upright;
    he is gracious and merciful and just.

R̸. Happy are those who do what the Lord commands.

Well for the man who is gracious and lends,
    who conducts his affairs with justice;
He shall never be moved;
    the just man shall be in everlasting remembrance.

R̸. Happy are those who do what the Lord commands.

Years I and II

GOSPEL   Mk 8, 34—9, 1
Alleluia
See no. 509.

✠ A reading from the holy gospel according to Mark
He who loses his life for my sake and the sake of the gospel will save it.

Jesus summoned the crowd with his disciples and said to them: "If a man wishes to come after me, he must deny his very self, take up his cross and follow in my steps. Whoever would save his life will lose it, but whoever loses his life for my sake and the gospel's will save it. What profit does a man show who gains the whole world and destroys himself in the process? What can a man offer in exchange for his life? If any one in this faithless and corrupt age is ashamed of me and my doctrine, the Son of Man will be ashamed of him when he comes with the holy angels in his Father's glory."

He also said to them: "I assure you, among those standing here there are some who will not taste death until they see the reign of God established in power."

This is the gospel of the Lord.

340   **SATURDAY OF THE SIXTH
        WEEK OF THE YEAR**

Year I

READING I   Heb 11, 1-7

A reading from the letter to the Hebrews
By faith we understand that the world was created by God.

Faith is confident assurance concerning what we hope for, and conviction about things we do not see. Because of faith the men of old were approved by God. Through faith we perceive that the worlds were created by the word of God, and that what is visible came into being through the invisible. By faith Abel offered God a sacrifice greater than Cain's. Because of this he was attested to be just, God himself having borne witness to him on account of his gifts; therefore, although Abel is dead, he still speaks. By faith Enoch was taken away without dying, and "he was seen no more because God took him." Scripture testifies that, before he was taken up, he was pleasing to God—but without faith, it is impossible to please him. Anyone who comes to God must believe that he exists, and that he rewards those who seek him. By faith Noah, warned about things not yet seen, revered God and built an ark that his household might be saved. He thereby condemned the world and inherited the justice which comes through faith.

This is the Word of the Lord.

Responsorial Psalm   Ps 145, 2-3. 4-5. 10-11

℟. (1) I will praise your name for ever, Lord.
Every day will I bless you,
    and I will praise your name forever and ever.
Great is the Lord and highly to be praised;
    his greatness is unsearchable.
℟. I will praise your name for ever, Lord.
Generation after generation praises your
        works
    and proclaims your might.
They speak of the splendor of your glorious
        majesty
    and tell of your wondrous works.
℟. I will praise your name for ever, Lord.
Let all your works give you thanks, O Lord,
    and let your faithful ones bless you.
Let them discourse of the glory of your king-
        dom
    and speak of your might.
℟. I will praise your name for ever, Lord.

Year II

READING I   Jas 3, 1-10
A reading from the letter of James
No human being can tame the tongue.

Not many of you should become teachers, my brothers; you should realize that those of us who do so will be called to the stricter account. All of us fall short in many respects. If a person is without fault in speech he is a man in the fullest sense, because he can control his entire body. When we put bits into the mouths of horses to make them obey us, we guide the rest of their bodies. It is the same with ships: however large they are, and despite the fact that they are driven by fierce winds, they are directed by very small rudders on whatever course the steersman's impulse may select. The tongue is something like that. It is a small member, yet it makes great pretensions.

See how tiny the spark is that sets a huge forest ablaze! The tongue is such a flame. It exists among our members as a whole universe of malice. The tongue defiles the entire body. Its flames encircle our course from birth, and its fire is kindled by hell. Every form of life, four-footed or winged, crawling or swimming, can be tamed, and has been tamed, by mankind; the tongue no man can tame. It is a restless evil, full of deadly poison. We use it to say, "Praised be the Lord and Father"; then we use it to curse men, though they are made in the likeness of God. Blessing and curse come out of the same mouth. This ought not to be, my brothers!

This is the Word of the Lord.

Responsorial Psalm   Ps 12, 2-3. 4-5. 7-8

℟. (8) You will protect us, Lord.
Help, O Lord! for no one now is dutiful;
    faithfulness has vanished from among men.
Everyone speaks falsehood to his neighbor;
    with smooth lips they speak, and double
        heart.
℟. You will protect us, Lord.
May the Lord destroy all smooth lips,
    every boastful tongue,
Those who say, "We are heroes with our
        tongues;
    our lips are our own; who is lord over us?"
℟. You will protect us, Lord.
The promises of the Lord are sure,
    like tried silver, freed from dross, sevenfold
        refined.
You, O Lord, will keep us
    and preserve us always from this generation.
℟. You will protect us, Lord.

Years I and II

GOSPEL   Mk 9, 2-13
Alleluia
See no. 509.

✠ **A reading from the holy gospel according
to Mark**
He was transfigured in their presence.

Jesus took Peter, James, and John off by themselves with him and led them up a high mountain. He was transfigured before their eyes and his clothes became dazzlingly white—whiter than the work of any bleacher could make them. Elijah appeared to them along with Moses; the two were in conversation with Jesus. Then Peter spoke to Jesus: "Rabbi, how good it is for us to be here. Let us erect three booths on this site, one for you, one for Moses, and one for Elijah." He hardly knew what to say, for they were all overcome with awe. A cloud came, overshadowing them, and out of the cloud a voice: "This is my Son, my beloved. Listen to him." Suddenly looking around they no longer saw anyone with them—only Jesus.

As they were coming down the mountain, he strictly enjoined them not to tell anyone what they had seen, before the Son of Man had risen from the dead. They kept this word of his to themselves, though they continued to discuss what "to rise from the dead" meant. Finally they put to him this question: "Why do the scribes claim that Elijah must come first?" He told them: "Elijah will indeed come first and restore everything. Yet why does Scripture say of the Son of Man that he must suffer much and be despised? Let me assure you, Elijah has already come. They did entirely as they pleased with him, as the Scriptures say of him."

This is the gospel of the Lord.

341   **MONDAY OF THE SEVENTH WEEK OF THE YEAR**

Year I

READING I   Sir 1, 1-10

The beginning of the book of Sirach

Before all other things, wisdom was created.

All wisdom comes from the Lord
    and with him it remains forever.
The sand of the seashore, the drops of rain,
    the days of eternity: who can number these?
Heaven's height, earth's breadth,
    the depths of the abyss: who can explore these?
Before all things else wisdom was created;
    and prudent understanding, from eternity.

To whom has wisdom's root been revealed?
    Who knows her subtleties?
There is but one, wise and truly awe-inspiring,
    seated upon his throne:
It is the Lord; he created her,
    has seen her and taken note of her.
He has poured her forth upon all his works,
    upon every living thing according to his bounty;
    he has lavished her upon his friends.

Fear of the Lord is glory and splendor,
    gladness and a festive crown.
Fear of the Lord warms the heart,
    giving gladness and joy and length of days.
        This is the Word of the Lord.

Responsorial Psalm   Ps 93, 1. 1-2. 5

℟. (1) The Lord is king; he is robed in majesty.
The Lord is king, in splendor robed;
    robed is the Lord and girt about with strength.
℟. The Lord is king; he is robed in majesty.
And he has made the world firm,
    not to be moved.
Your throne stands firm from of old;
    from everlasting you are, O Lord.
℟. The Lord is king; he is robed in majesty.
Your decrees are worthy of trust indeed:
    holiness befits your house,
    O Lord, for length of days.
℟. The Lord is king; he is robed in majesty.

Year II

READING I   Jas 3, 13-18

A reading from the letter of James

If there is disharmony in your hearts, you cannot give glory.

If one of you is wise and understanding, let him show this in practice through a humility filled with good sense. Should you instead nurse bitter jealousy and selfish ambition in your hearts, at least refrain from arrogant and false claims against the truth. Wisdom like this does not come from above. It is earthbound, a kind of animal, even devilish, cunning. Where there are jealousy and strife, there also are inconstancy and all kinds of vile behavior. Wisdom from above, by contrast, is first of all innocent. It is also peaceable, lenient, docile, rich in sympathy and the kindly deeds that are its fruits, impartial and sincere. The harvest of justice is sown in peace for those who cultivate peace.

This is the Word of the Lord.

Responsorial Psalm   Ps 19, 8. 9. 10. 15

R̷. (9) The precepts of the Lord give joy to the heart.

The law of the Lord is perfect,
    refreshing the soul;
The decree of the Lord is trustworthy,
    giving wisdom to the simple.

R̷. The precepts of the Lord give joy to the heart.

The precepts of the Lord are right,
    rejoicing the heart;
The command of the Lord is clear,
    enlightening the eye.

R̷. The precepts of the Lord give joy to the heart.

The fear of the Lord is pure,
    enduring forever;
The ordinances of the Lord are true,
    all of them just.

R̷. The precepts of the Lord give joy to the heart.

Let the words of my mouth and the thought of
    my heart
    find favor before you,
O Lord, my rock and my redeemer.

R̷. The precepts of the Lord give joy to the heart.

Years I and II

GOSPEL   Mk 9, 14-29
Alleluia

See no. 509.

✠ **A reading from the holy gospel according to Mark**
     I believe, Lord, help my unbelief.

[As Jesus came down the mountain with Peter, James and John] and approached the disci-ples, they saw a large crowd standing around, and scribes in lively discussion with them. Immediately on catching sight of Jesus, the whole crowd was overcome with awe. They ran up to greet him. He asked them, "What are you discussing among yourselves?" "Teacher," a man in the crowd replied, "I have brought my son to you because he is possessed by a mute spirit. Whenever it seizes him it throws him down; he foams at the mouth and grinds his teeth and becomes rigid. Just now I asked your disciples to expel him, but they were unable to do so." He replied by saying to the crowd, "What an unbelieving lot you are! How long must I remain with you? How long can I endure you? Bring him to me." When they did so the spirit caught sight of Jesus and immediately threw the boy into convulsions. As he fell to the ground he began to roll around and foam at the mouth. Then Jesus questioned the father: "How long has this been happening to him?" "From childhood," the father replied. "Often it throws him into the fire and into water. You would think it would kill him. If out of the kindness of your heart you can do anything to help us, please do!" Jesus said, " 'If you can?' Everything is possible to a man who trusts." The boy's father immediately exclaimed, "I do believe! Help my lack of trust!" Jesus, on seeing a crowd rapidly gathering, reprimanded the unclean spirit by saying to him, "Mute and deaf spirit, I command you: Get out of him and never enter him again!" Shouting, and throwing the boy into convulsions, it came out of him; the boy became like a corpse, which caused many to say, "He is dead." But Jesus took him by the hand and helped him to his feet. When Jesus arrived at the house his disciples began to ask him privately, "Why is it that we could not expel it?" He told them, "This kind you can drive out only by prayer."

This is the gospel of the Lord.

342   TUESDAY OF THE SEVENTH WEEK OF THE YEAR

Year I

READING I   Sir 2, 1-11

A reading from the book of Sirach
Prepare yourself for the trials.

My son, when you come to serve the Lord,
   prepare yourself for trials.
Be sincere of heart and steadfast,
   undisturbed in time of adversity.
Cling to him, forsake him not;
   thus will your future be great.
Accept whatever befalls you,
   in crushing misfortune be patient;
For in fire gold is tested,
   and worthy men in the crucible of humiliation.
Trust God and he will help you;
   make straight your ways and hope in him.

You who fear the Lord, wait for his mercy,
   turn not away lest you fall.
You who fear the Lord, trust him,
   and your reward will not be lost.
You who fear the Lord, hope for good things,
   for lasting joy and mercy.
Study the generations long past and understand;
   has anyone hoped in the Lord and been disappointed?
Has anyone persevered in his fear and been forsaken?
   has anyone called upon him and been rebuffed?
Compassionate and merciful is the Lord;
   he forgives sins, he saves in time of trouble.
      This is the Word of the Lord.

Responsorial Psalm   Ps 37, 3-4. 18-19. 27-28. 39-40

℟. (5) Commit your life to the Lord,
   and he will help you.
Trust in the Lord and do good,
   that you may dwell in the land and enjoy security.
Take delight in the Lord,
   and he will grant you your heart's requests.

℟. Commit your life to the Lord,
   and he will help you.
The Lord watches over the lives of the wholehearted;
   their inheritance lasts forever.
They are not put to shame in an evil time;
   in days of famine they have plenty.

℟. Commit your life to the Lord,
   and he will help you.
Turn from evil and do good,
   that you may abide forever;
For the Lord loves what is right,
   and forsakes not his faithful ones.

℟. Commit your life to the Lord,
   and he will help you.
The salvation of the just is from the Lord;
   he is their refuge in time of distress.
And the Lord helps them and delivers them;
   he delivers them from the wicked and saves them,
   because they take refuge in him.

℟. Commit your life to the Lord,
   and he will help you.

Year II

READING I   Jas 4, 1-10

A reading from the letter of James
You desire something you cannot have, and so you kill.

Where do the conflicts and disputes among you originate? Is it not your inner cravings that make war within your members? What you desire you do not obtain, and so you resort to murder. You envy and you cannot acquire, so you quarrel and fight. You do not obtain because you do not ask. You ask and you do not receive because you ask wrongly, with a view to squandering what you receive on your pleasures. O you unfaithful ones, are you not aware that love of the world is enmity to God? A man is marked out as God's enemy if he chooses to be the world's friend. Do you suppose it is to no purpose that Scripture says, "The spirit he has implanted in us tends toward jealousy"? Yet he bestows a greater gift, for the sake of which it is written,

   "God resists the proud
      but bestows his favor on the lowly."

Therefore submit to God; resist the devil and he will take flight. Draw close to God, and he will draw close to you. Cleanse your hands, you sinners; purify your hearts, you backsliders. Begin to lament, to mourn, and to weep; let your laughter be turned into mourning and your joy into sorrow. Be humbled in the sight of the Lord and he will raise you on high.

This is the Word of the Lord.

Responsorial Psalm   Ps 55, 7-8. 9-10. 10-11. 23

℟. (23) Throw your cares on the Lord,
    and he will support you.

And I say, "Had I but wings like a dove,
    I would fly away and be at rest.
Far away I would flee;
    I would lodge in the wilderness.

℟. Throw your cares on the Lord,
    and he will support you.

"I would hasten to find shelter
    from the violent storm and the tempest."
Engulf them, O Lord; divide their counsels.

℟. Throw your cares on the Lord,
    and he will support you.

In the city I see violence and strife,
    day and night they prowl about upon its
    walls.

℟. Throw your cares on the Lord,
    and he will support you.

Cast your care upon the Lord,
    and he will support you;
    never will he permit the just man to be disturbed.

℟. Throw your cares on the Lord,
    and he will support you.

Years I and II

GOSPEL   Mk 9, 30-37
Alleluia

See no. 509.

✠ A reading from the holy gospel according to Mark

The Son of Man will be betrayed. If anyone wishes to be first he must be last.

Jesus and his disciples came down the mountain and began a journey through Galilee, but he did not want anyone to know about it. He was teaching his disciples in this vein: "The Son of Man is going to be delivered into the hands of men who will put him to death; three days after his death he will rise." Though they failed to understand his words, they were afraid to question him.

They returned to Capernaum and Jesus, once inside the house, began to ask them, "What were you discussing on the way home?" At this they fell silent, for on the way they had been arguing about who was the most important. So he sat down and called the Twelve around him and said, "If anyone wishes to rank first, he must remain the last one of all and the servant of all." Then he took a little child, stood him in their midst, and putting his arms around him, said to them, "Whoever welcomes a child such as this for my sake welcomes me. And whoever welcomes me welcomes, not me, but him who sent me."

This is the gospel of the Lord.

---

343   **WEDNESDAY OF THE SEVENTH WEEK OF THE YEAR**

Year I

READING I   Sir 4, 11-19

A reading from the book of Sirach

Those who love wisdom, love God.

Wisdom instructs her children
    and admonishes those who seek her.
He who loves her loves life;
    those who seek her out win her favor.
He who holds her fast inherits glory;
    wherever he dwells, the Lord bestows blessings.
Those who serve her serve the Holy One;
    those who love her the Lord loves.
He who obeys her judges nations;
    he who hearkens to her dwells in her inmost chambers.
If one trusts her, he will possess her;
    his descendants too will inherit her.
She walks with him as a stranger,
    and at first she puts him to the test;
Fear and dread she brings upon him
    and tries him with her discipline;

With her precepts she puts him to the proof,
   until his heart is fully with her.
Then she comes back to bring him happiness
   and reveal her secrets to him.
But if he fails her, she will abandon him
   and deliver him into the hands of despoilers.
   This is the word of the Lord.

Responsorial Psalm

Ps 119, 165. 168. 171. 172. 174. 175

R⁄. (165) O Lord, great peace have they who
   love your law.
Those who love your law have great peace,
   and for them there is no stumbling block.
R⁄. O Lord, great peace have they who love
   your law.
I keep your precepts and your decrees,
   for all my ways are before you.
R⁄. O Lord, great peace have they who love
   your law.
My lips pour forth your praise,
   because you teach me your statutes.
R⁄. O Lord, great peace have they who love
   your law.
May my tongue sing of your promise,
   for all your commands are just.
R⁄. O Lord, great peace have they who love
   your law.
I long for your salvation, O Lord,
   and your law is my delight.
R⁄. O Lord, great peace have they who love
   your law.
Let my soul live to praise you,
   and may your ordinances help me.
R⁄. O Lord, great peace have they who love
   your law.

Year II

READING I   Jas 4, 13-17

A reading from the letter of James
What about your life? You should say: If it is the Lord's will.

Come now, you who say, "Today or tomorrow we shall go to such and such a town, spend
a year there, trade, and come off with a profit!"
You have no idea what kind of life will be
yours tomorrow. You are a vapor that appears
briefly and vanishes. Instead of saying, "If the

Lord wills it, we shall live to do this or that,"
all you can do is make arrogant and preten-
tious claims. All such boasting is reprehensible.
When a man knows the right thing to do and
does not do it, he sins.
   This is the Word of the Lord.

Responsorial Psalm   Ps 49, 2-3. 6-7. 8-10. 11

R⁄. (Mt 5, 3) Happy the poor in spirit;
   the kingdom of heaven is theirs!
Hear this, all you peoples;
   hearken, all who dwell in the world,
Of lowly birth or high degree,
   rich and poor alike.
R⁄. Happy the poor in spirit;
   the kingdom of heaven is theirs!
Why should I fear in evil days
   when my wicked ensnarers ring me round?
They trust in their wealth;
   the abundance of their riches is their boast.
R⁄. Happy the poor in spirit;
   the kingdom of heaven is theirs!
Yet in no way can a man redeem himself,
   or pay his own ransom to God;
Too high is the price to redeem one's life; he
      would never have enough
   to remain alive always and not see destruc-
      tion.
R⁄. Happy the poor in spirit;
   the kingdom of heaven is theirs!
For he can see that wise men die,
   and likewise the senseless and the stupid
      pass away,
   leaving to others their wealth.
R⁄. Happy the poor in spirit;
   the kingdom of heaven is theirs!

Years I and II

GOSPEL   Mk 9, 38-40
Alleluia

See no. 509.

✠ **A reading from the holy gospel according
to Mark**
Anyone who is not against us, is for us.

John said to Jesus, "Teacher, we saw a man
using your name to expel demons and we tried
to stop him because he is not of our company."

Jesus said in reply: "Do not try to stop him. No one can perform a miracle in my name and at the same time speak ill of me. Anyone who is not against us is with us."
>   This is the gospel of the Lord.

---

344   THURSDAY OF THE SEVENTH WEEK OF THE YEAR

Year I

READING I   Sir 5, 1-8

A reading from the book of Sirach
Do not delay your return to the Lord.

Rely not on your wealth;
>   say not: "I have the power."
Rely not on your strength
>   in following the desires of your heart.
Say not: "Who can prevail against me?"
>   for the Lord will exact the punishment.
Say not: "I have sinned, yet what has befallen me?"
>   for the Lord bides his time.
Of forgiveness be not overconfident,
>   adding sin upon sin.
Say not: "Great is his mercy;
>   my many sins he will forgive."
For mercy and anger alike are with him;
>   upon the wicked alights his wrath.
Delay not your conversion to the Lord,
>   put it not off from day to day.
>   This is the word of the Lord.

Responsorial Psalm   Ps 1, 1-2. 3. 4. 6

℟ (Ps 40, 5) Happy are they who hope in the Lord.
Happy the man who follows not
>   the counsel of the wicked
Nor walks in the way of sinners,
>   nor sits in the company of the insolent,
But delights in the law of the Lord
>   and meditates on his law day and night.
℟. Happy are they who hope in the Lord.
He is like a tree
>   planted near running water,
That yields its fruit in due season,
>   and whose leaves never fade.

[Whatever he does, prospers.]
℟. Happy are they who hope in the Lord.
Not so the wicked, not so;
>   they are like chaff which the wind drives away.
For the Lord watches over the way of the just,
>   but the way of the wicked vanishes.
℟. Happy are they who hope in the Lord.

Year II

READING I   Jas 5, 1-6

A reading from the letter of James
The hired workers you cheated cry out, and their cries reach the ears of the Lord.

You rich, weep and wail over your impending miseries. Your wealth has rotted, your fine wardrobe has grown moth-eaten, your gold and silver have corroded, and their corrosion shall be a testimony against you; it will devour your flesh like a fire. See what you have stored up for yourselves against the last days.

Here, crying aloud, are the wages you withheld from the farmhands who harvested your fields. The shouts of the harvesters have reached the ears of the Lord of hosts. You lived in wanton luxury on the earth; you fattened yourselves for the day of slaughter. You condemned, even killed, the just man; he does not resist you.
>   This is the Word of the Lord.

Responsorial Psalm   Ps 49, 14-15. 15-16. 17-18. 19-20

℟. (Mt 5, 3) Happy the poor in spirit;
>   the kingdom of heaven is theirs!
This is the way of those whose trust is folly,
>   the end of those contented with their lot:
Like sheep they are herded into the nether world;
>   death is their shepherd, and the upright rule over them.
℟. Happy the poor in spirit;
>   the kingdom of heaven is theirs!
Quickly their form is consumed;
>   the nether world is their palace.
But God will redeem me
>   from the power of the nether world by receiving me.

℞. Happy the poor in spirit;
  the kingdom of heaven is theirs!
Fear not when a man grows rich,
  when the wealth of his house becomes great,
For when he dies, he shall take none of it;
  his wealth shall not follow him down.
℞. Happy the poor in spirit;
  the kingdom of heaven is theirs!
Though in his lifetime he counted himself
  blessed,
  "They will praise you for doing well for
  yourself,"
He shall join the circle of his forebears
  who shall never more see light.
℞. Happy the poor in spirit;
  the kingdom of heaven is theirs!

Years I and II

GOSPEL Mk 9, 41-50
Alleluia
See no. 509.

✠ **A reading from the holy gospel according**
  to Mark
It is better to enter into life crippled, than to have two hands
and go to hell.

Jesus said to his disciples: "Any man who
gives you a drink of water because you belong
to Christ will not, I assure you, go without his
reward. But it would be better if anyone who
leads astray one of these simple believers were
to be plunged in the sea with a great millstone
fastened around his neck.
  "If your hand is your difficulty, cut it off!
Better for you to enter life maimed than to keep
both hands and enter Gehenna with its un-
quenchable fire. If your foot is your undoing,
cut it off! Better for you to enter life crippled
than to be thrown into Gehenna with both feet.
If your eye is your downfall, tear it out! Better
for you to enter the kingdom of God with one
eye than to be thrown with both eyes into Ge-
henna, where 'the worm dies not and the fire is
never extinguished.' Everyone will be salted
with fire. Salt is excellent in its place; but if salt
becomes tasteless, how can you season it? Keep
salt in your hearts and you will be at peace
with one another."
  This is the gospel of the Lord.

345   FRIDAY OF THE SEVENTH
WEEK OF THE YEAR

Year I

READING I Sir 6, 5-17
  A reading from the book of Sirach
  A faithful friend is beyond comparison.
A kind mouth multiplies friends,
  and gracious lips prompt friendly greetings.
Let your acquaintances be many,
  but one in a thousand your confidant.
When you gain a friend, first test him,
  and be not too ready to trust him.
For one sort of friend is a friend when it suits
  him,
  but he will not be with you in time of dis-
  tress.
Another is a friend who becomes an enemy,
  and tells of the quarrel to your shame.
Another is a friend, a boon companion,
  who will not be with you when sorrow
  comes.
When things go well, he is your other self,
  and lords it over your servants;
But if you are brought low, he turns against
  you
  and avoids meeting you.
Keep away from your enemies;
  be on your guard with your friends.
A faithful friend is a sturdy shelter;
  he who finds one finds a treasure.
A faithful friend is beyond price,
  no sum can balance his worth.
A faithful friend is a life-saving remedy,
  such as he who fears God finds;
For he who fears God behaves accordingly,
  and his friend will be like himself.
    This is the Word of the Lord.

Responsorial Psalm Ps 119, 12. 16. 18. 27. 34. 35

℞. (35) Guide me, Lord, in the way of your
  commands.
Blessed are you, O Lord;
  teach me your statutes.
℞. Guide me, Lord, in the way of your commands.

In your statutes I will delight;
   I will not forget your words.
R/. Guide me, Lord, in the way of your commands.
Open my eyes, that I may consider
   the wonders of your law.
R/. Guide me, Lord, in the way of your commands.
Make me understand the way of your precepts,
   and I will meditate on your wondrous deeds.
R/. Guide me, Lord, in the way of your commands.
Give me discernment, that I may observe your law
   and keep it with all my heart.
R/. Guide me, Lord, in the way of your commands.
Lead me in the path of your commands,
   for in it I delight.
R/. Guide me, Lord, in the way of your commands.

Year II

READING I   Jas 5, 9-12

A reading from the letter of James
The judge is waiting at the gates.

Do not grumble against one another, my brothers, lest you be condemned. See! The judge stands at the gate. As your models in suffering hardships and in patience, brothers, take the prophets who spoke in the name of the Lord. Those who have endured we call blessed. You have heard of the steadfastness of Job, and have seen what the Lord, who is compassionate and merciful, did in the end.

   Above all else, my brothers, you must not swear an oath, any oath at all, either "by heaven" or "by earth." Rather, let it be "yes" if you mean yes and "no" if you mean no. In this way you will not incur condemnation.
      This is the Word of the Lord.

Responsorial Psalm   Ps 103, 1-2. 3-4. 8-9. 11-12

R/. (8) The Lord is kind and merciful.
Bless the Lord, O my soul;
   and all my being, bless his holy name.

Bless the Lord, O my soul,
   and forget not all his benefits.
R/. The Lord is kind and merciful.
He pardons all your iniquities,
   he heals all your ills.
He redeems your life from destruction,
   he crowns you with kindness and compassion.
R/. The Lord is kind and merciful.
Merciful and gracious is the Lord,
   slow to anger and abounding in kindness.
He will not always chide,
   nor does he keep his wrath forever.
R/. The Lord is kind and merciful.
For as the heavens are high above the earth,
   so surpassing is his kindness toward those who fear him.
As far as the east is from the west,
   so far has he put our transgressions from us.
R/. The Lord is kind and merciful.

Years I and II

GOSPEL   Mk 10, 1-12
Alleluia
See no. 509.

✠ A reading from the holy gospel according to Mark
What God has joined together, man must not divide.

Jesus came to the districts of Judea and across the Jordan. Once more crowds gathered around him and as usual he began to teach them. Then some Pharisees came up and as a test began to ask Jesus whether it was permissible for a husband to divorce his wife. In reply he said, "What command did Moses give you?" They answered, "Moses permitted divorce and the writing of a decree of divorce." But Jesus told them: "He wrote that commandment for you because of your stubbornness. At the beginning of creation God made them male and female; for this reason a man shall leave his father and mother and the two shall become as one. They are no longer two but one flesh. Therefore, let no man separate what God has joined." Back in the house again, the disciples began to question him about this. He told them, "Whoever divorces his wife and marries another commits adultery against her; and the

woman who divorces her husband and marries another commits adultery."
        This is the gospel of the Lord.

---

346   **SATURDAY OF THE SEVENTH
        WEEK OF THE YEAR**

Year I

READING I   Sir 17, 1-15
        A reading from the book of Sirach
        The Lord made man in his own image.

The Lord from the earth created man,
    and in his own image he made him.
Limited days of life he gives him
    and makes him return to earth again.
He endows man with a strength of his own,
    and with power over all things else on earth.
He puts the fear of him in all flesh,
    and gives him rule over beasts and birds.
He forms men's tongues and eyes and ears,
    and imparts to them an understanding heart.
With wisdom and knowledge he fills them;
    good and evil he shows them.
He looks with favor upon their hearts,
    and shows them his glorious works,
That they may describe the wonders of his
        deeds
    and praise his holy name.
He has set before them knowledge,
    a law of life as their inheritance;
An everlasting covenant he has made with
        them,
    his commandments he has revealed to them.
His majestic glory their eyes beheld,
    his glorious voice their ears heard.
He says to them, "Avoid all evil";
    each of them he gives precepts about his
        fellow men.
Their ways are ever known to him,
    they cannot be hidden from his eyes.
Over every nation he places a ruler,
    but the Lord's own portion is Israel.
All their actions are clear as the sun to him,
    his eyes are ever upon their ways.
        This is the Word of the Lord.

Responsorial Psalm   Ps 103, 13-14. 15-16. 17-18

℟. (17) The Lord's kindness is everlasting
    to those who fear him.

As a father has compassion on his children,
    so the Lord has compassion on those who
        fear him,
For he knows how we are formed;
    he remembers that we are dust.
℟. The Lord's kindness is everlasting
    to those who fear him.

Man's days are like those of grass;
    like a flower of the field he blooms;
The wind sweeps over him and he is gone,
    and his place knows him no more.
℟. The Lord's kindness is everlasting
    to those who fear him.

But the kindness of the Lord is from eternity
    to eternity toward those who fear him,
And his justice toward children's children
    among those who keep his covenant.
℟. The Lord's kindness is everlasting
    to those who fear him.

Year II

READING I   Jas 5, 13-20
        A reading from the letter of James
        The prayer of a just man has great power.

If anyone among you is suffering hardship, he must pray. If a person is in good spirits, he should sing a hymn of praise. Is there anyone sick among you? He should ask for the elders of the church. They in turn are to pray over him, anointing him with oil in the Name [of the Lord]. This prayer uttered in faith will reclaim the one who is ill, and the Lord will restore him to health. If he has commited any sins, forgiveness will be his. Hence, declare your sins to one another, and pray for one another, that you may find healing.

    The fervent petition of a holy man is powerful indeed. Elijah was only a man like us, yet he prayed earnestly that it would not rain and no rain fell on the land for three years and six months. When he prayed again, the sky burst forth with rain and the land produced its crop.

    My brothers, the case may arise among you of someone straying from the truth, and of another bringing him back. Remember this: the person who brings a sinner back from his way will save his soul from death and cancel a multitude of sins.

This is the Word of the Lord.

Responsorial Psalm   Ps 141, 1-2. 3. 8

℞. (2) Let my prayer come like incense before you.

O Lord, to you I call; hasten to me;
  hearken to my voice when I call upon you.
Let my prayer come like incense before you;
  the lifting up of my hands, like the evening sacrifice.

℞. Let my prayer come like incense before you.

O Lord, set a watch before my mouth,
  a guard at the door of my lips.
For toward you, O God, my Lord, my eyes are turned;
  in you I take refuge; strip me not of life.

℞. Let my prayer come like incense before you.

Years I and II

GOSPEL   Mk 10, 13-16
Alleluia
See no. 509.

✠ A reading from the holy gospel according to Mark

He who does not accept the kingdom of heaven like a child will never enter it.

People were bringing their little children to Jesus to have him touch them, but the disciples were scolding them for this. Jesus became indignant when he noticed it and said to them: "Let the children come to me and do not hinder them. It is to just such as these that the kingdom of God belongs. I assure you that whoever does not accept the kingdom of God like a little child shall not enter into it." Then he embraced them and blessed them, placing his hands on them.

This is the gospel of the Lord.

347   **MONDAY OF THE EIGHTH
       WEEK OF THE YEAR**

Year I

READING I   Sir 17, 19-27
A reading from the book of Sirach

Turn to the Lord, plead before his face and lessen your offense.

But to the penitent he provides a way back,
  he encourages those who are losing hope!
Return to the Lord and give up sin,
  pray to him and make your offenses few.
Turn again to the Most High and away from sin,
  hate intensely what he loathes;
Who in the nether world can glorify the Most High
  in place of the living who offer their praise?
No more can the dead give praise than those who have never lived;
  they glorify the Lord who are alive and well.
How great the mercy of the Lord,
  his forgiveness of those who return to him!
The like cannot be found in men,
  for not immortal is any son of man.
Is anything brighter than the sun? Yet it can be eclipsed.
  How obscure then the thoughts of flesh and blood!
God watches over the hosts of highest heaven,
  while all men are dust and ashes.

This is the Word of the Lord.

Responsorial Psalm   Ps 32, 1-2. 5. 6. 7

℞. (11) Let the just exult and rejoice in the Lord.

Happy is he whose fault is taken away,
  whose sin is covered.
Happy the man to whom the Lord imputes not guilt,
  in whose spirit there is no guile.

℞. Let the just exult and rejoice in the Lord.

Then I acknowledged my sin to you,
  my guilt I covered not.
I said, "I confess my faults to the Lord,"
  and you took away the guilt of my sin.

℞. Let the just exult and rejoice in the Lord.

For this shall every faithful man pray to you
in time of stress.
Though deep waters overflow,
they shall not reach him.
℟. Let the just exult and rejoice in the Lord.
You are my shelter; from distress you will preserve me;
with glad cries of freedom you will ring me
round.
℟. Let the just exult and rejoice in the Lord.

Year II

READING I   1 Pt 1, 3-9

A reading from the first letter of Peter

You did not see Christ, yet you love him, and because you
believe you are filled with a joy that cannot be described.

Praised be the God and Father of our Lord
Jesus Christ,
he who in his great mercy gave us new birth;
a birth unto hope which draws its life
from the resurrection of Jesus Christ from
the dead;
a birth to an imperishable inheritance
incapable of fading or defilement,
which is kept in heaven for you
who are guarded with God's power through
faith;
a birth to a salvation which stands ready
to be revealed in the last days.
There is cause for rejoicing here. You may
for a time have to suffer the distress of many
trials; but this is so that your faith, which is
more precious than the passing splendor of
fire-tried gold, may by its genuineness lead to
praise, glory and honor when Jesus Christ appears. Although you have never seen him, you
love him, and without seeing him, you now believe in him and rejoice with inexpressible joy
touched with glory because you are achieving
faith's goal, your salvation.
This is the Word of the Lord.

Responsorial Psalm   Ps 111, 1-2. 5-6. 9. 10

℟. (5) The Lord will remember his covenant
for ever.
I will give thanks to the Lord with all my heart
in the company and assembly of the just.

Great are the works of the Lord,
exquisite in all their delights.
℟. The Lord will remember his covenant for
ever.
He has given food to those who fear him;
he will forever be mindful of his covenant.
He has made known to his people the power of
his works,
giving them the inheritance of the nations.
℟. The Lord will remember his covenant for
ever.
He has sent deliverance to his people;
he has ratified his covenant forever;
holy and awesome is his name.
His praise endures forever.
℟. The Lord will remember his covenant for
ever.
℟. Or: Alleluia.

Years I and II

GOSPEL   Mk 10, 17-27
Alleluia

See no. 509.

✠ **A reading from the holy gospel according
to Mark**

Go, sell everything you have and follow me.

As Jesus was setting out on a journey a man
came running up, knelt down before him and
asked, "Good Teacher, what must I do to share
in everlasting life?" Jesus answered, "Why do
you call me good? No one is good but God
alone. You know the commandments:
'You shall not kill;
You shall not commit adultery;
You shall not steal;
You shall not bear false witness;
You shall not defraud;
Honor your father and your mother.' "

He replied, "Teacher, I have kept all these since
my childhood." Then Jesus looked at him with
love and told him, "There is one thing more you
must do. Go and sell what you have and give to
the poor; you will then have treasure in
heaven. After that, come and follow me." At
these words the man's face fell. He went away
sad, for he had many possessions. Jesus looked
around and said to his disciples, "How hard it
is for the rich to enter the kingdom of God!"

The disciples could only marvel at his words. So Jesus repeated what he had said: "My sons, how hard it is to enter the kingdom of God! It is easier for a camel to pass through a needle's eye than for a rich man to enter the kingdom of God."

They were completely overwhelmed at this, and exclaimed to one another, "Then who can be saved?" Jesus fixed his gaze on them and said, "For man it is impossible but not for God. With God all things are possible."

This is the gospel of the Lord.

---

348 TUESDAY OF THE EIGHTH WEEK OF THE YEAR

Year I

READING I   Sir 35, 1-12

A reading from the book of Sirach

A man offers sacrifice by following the law.

To keep the law is a great oblation,
    and he who observes the commandments sacrifices a peace offering.
In works of charity one offers fine flour,
    and when he gives alms he presents his sacrifice of praise.
To refrain from evil pleases the Lord,
    and to avoid injustice is an atonement.
Appear not before the Lord empty-handed,
    for all that you offer is in fulfillment of the precepts.
The just man's offering enriches the altar
    and rises as a sweet odor before the Most High.
The just man's sacrifice is most pleasing,
    nor will it ever be forgotten.
In generous spirit pay homage to the Lord,
    be not sparing of freewill gifts.
With each contribution show a cheerful countenance,
    and pay your tithes in a spirit of joy.
Give to the Most High as he has given to you,
    generously, according to your means.

For the Lord is one who always repays,
    and he will give back to you sevenfold.

But offer no bribes, these he does not accept!
    Trust not in sacrifice of the fruits of extortion,
For he is a God of justice,
    who knows no favorites.

This is the Word of the Lord.

Responsorial Psalm   Ps 50, 5-6. 7-8. 14. 23

℟. (23) To the upright I will show the saving power of God.
"Gather my faithful ones before me,
    those who have made a covenant with me by sacrifice."
And the heavens proclaim his justice;
    for God himself is the judge.

℟. To the upright I will show the saving power of God.

"Hear, my people, and I will speak;
    Israel, I will testify against you;
    God, your God, am I.
Not for your sacrifices do I rebuke you,
    for your holocausts are before me always.

℟. To the upright I will show the saving power of God.

"Offer to God praise as your sacrifice
    and fulfill your vows to the Most High.
He that offers praise as a sacrifice glorifies me;
    and to him that goes the right way I will show the salvation of God."

℟. To the upright I will show the saving power of God.

Year II

READING I   1 Pt 1, 10-16

A reading from the first letter of Peter

They prophesied about the grace which was to come to you, so be watchful and perfect in hope.

This is the salvation which the prophets carefully searched out and examined. They prophesied the divine favor that was destined to be yours. They investigated the times and the circumstances which the Spirit of Christ within them was pointing to, for he predicted the sufferings destined for Christ and the glories that would follow. They knew by revelation that they were providing, not for themselves but for you, what has now been proclaimed to you by those who preach the gospel to you, in the power of the Holy Spirit sent from heaven. Into these matters angels long to search.

So "gird the loins" of your understanding; live soberly; set all your hope on the gift to be conferred on you when Jesus Christ appears. As obedient sons, do not yield to the desires that once shaped you in your ignorance. Rather, become holy yourselves in every aspect of your conduct, after the likeness of the holy One who called you; remember, Scripture says, "Be holy, for I am holy."

    This is the Word of the Lord.

Responsorial Psalm   Ps 98, 1. 2-3. 3-4

℟. (2) The Lord has made known his salvation.
Sing to the Lord a new song,
    for he has done wondrous deeds;
His right hand has won victory for him,
    his holy arm.
℟. The Lord has made known his salvation.
The Lord has made his salvation known:
    in the sight of the nations he has revealed his justice.
He has remembered his kindness and his faithfulness
    toward the house of Israel.
℟. The Lord has made known his salvation.
All the ends of the earth have seen
    the salvation by our God.
Sing joyfully to the Lord, all you lands;
    break into song; sing praise.
℟. The Lord has made known his salvation.

GOSPEL   Years I and II

                              Mk 10, 28-31
Alleluia
See no. 509.

✠ A reading from the holy gospel according
            to Mark
Our offerings are acceptable in this present time of persecution and in the world to come, eternal life.

Peter was moved to say to Jesus: "We have put aside everything to follow you!" Jesus answered: "I give you my word, there is no one who has given up home, brothers or sisters,

mother or father, children or property, for me and for the gospel who will not receive in this present age a hundred times as many homes, brothers and sisters, mothers, children and property—and persecution besides—and in the age to come, everlasting life. Many who are first shall come last, and the last shall come first."

    This is the gospel of the Lord.

---

349   **WEDNESDAY OF THE EIGHTH
        WEEK OF THE YEAR**

                                 Year I

READING I   Sir 36, 1. 5-6. 10-17
A reading from the book of Sirach
The nations have acknowledged that there is no God
                but you.
Come to our aid, O God of the universe,
    and put all the nations in dread of you!
Thus they will know, as we know,
    that there is no God but you.
Give new signs and work new wonders.

Gather all the tribes of Jacob,
    that they may inherit the land as of old,
Show mercy to the people called by your name;
    Israel, whom you named your first-born.
Take pity on your holy city,
    Jerusalem, your dwelling place.
Fill Zion with your majesty,
    your temple with your glory.

Give evidence of your deeds of old;
    fulfill the prophecies spoken in your name,
Reward those who have hoped in you,
    and let your prophets be proved true.
Hear the prayer of your servants,
    for you are ever gracious to your people;
Thus it will be known to the very ends of the earth
    that you are the eternal God.
    This is the Word of the Lord.

Responsorial Psalm   Ps 79, 8. 9. 11. 13

℟. (Sir 36, 16) Show us, O Lord, the light of
    your kindness.
Remember not against us the iniquities of the
    past;

may your compassion quickly come to us,
for we are brought very low.
℞. Show us, O Lord, the light of your kindness.
Help us, O God our savior,
because of the glory of your name;
Deliver us and pardon our sins
for your name's sake.
℞. Show us, O Lord, the light of your kindness.
Let the prisoners' sighing come before you;
with your great power free those doomed to
death.
Then we, your people and the sheep of your
pasture,
will give thanks to you forever;
through all generations we will declare your
praise.
℞. Show us, O Lord, the light of your kindness.

Year II

READING I   1 Pt 1, 18-25
A reading from the first letter of Peter
You have been ransomed in the precious blood of Christ,
a spotless lamb.

Realize that you were delivered from the futile
way of life your fathers handed on to you, not
by any diminishable sum of silver or gold but
by Christ's blood beyond all price: the blood of
a spotless, unblemished lamb chosen before the
world's foundation and revealed for your sake
in these last days. It is through him that you
are believers in God, the God who raised him
from the dead and gave him glory. Your faith
and hope, then, are centered in God.

By obedience to the truth you have purified
yourselves for a genuine love of your brothers;
therefore, love one another constantly from the
heart. Your rebirth has come, not from a de-
structible but from an indestructible seed,
through the living and enduring word of God.
For,
"All mankind is grass,
and the glory of men is like the flower of
the field.
The grass withers, the flower wilts,
but the word of the Lord endures forever."
Now this "word" is the gospel which was
preached to you.
This is the Word of the Lord.

Responsorial Psalm   Ps 147, 12-13. 14-15. 19-20
℞. (12) Praise the Lord, Jerusalem.
Glorify the Lord, O Jerusalem;
praise your God, O Zion.
For he has strengthened the bars of your gates;
he has blessed your children within you.
℞. Praise the Lord, Jerusalem.
He has granted peace in your borders;
with the best of wheat he fills you.
He sends forth his command to the earth;
swiftly runs his word!
℞. Praise the Lord, Jerusalem.
He has proclaimed his word to Jacob,
his statutes and his ordinances to Israel.
He has not done thus for any other nation;
his ordinances he has not made known to
them. Alleluia.
℞. Praise the Lord, Jerusalem.
℞. Or: Alleluia.

Years I and II

GOSPEL   Mk 10, 32-45
Alleluia

See no. 509.

✠ **A reading from the holy gospel according
to Mark**
Now we are going up to Jerusalem, and the Son of Man will
be handed over.

The disciples were on the road going up to
Jerusalem, with Jesus walking in the lead.
Their mood was one of wonderment, while
that of those who followed was fear. Taking
the Twelve aside once more, he began to tell
them what was going to happen to him. "We
are on our way up to Jerusalem, where the
Son of Man will be handed over to the chief
priests and the scribes. They will condemn him
to death and hand him over to the Gentiles,
who will mock him and spit at him, flog him,
and finally kill him. But three days later he
will rise."

Zebedee's sons, James and John, approached
him. "Teacher," they said, "we want you to
grant our request." "What is it?" he asked.
They replied, "See to it that we sit, one at
your right and the other at your left, when you
come into your glory." Jesus told them, "You
do not know what you are asking. Can you

drink the cup I shall drink or be baptized in the same bath of pain as I?" "We can," they told him. Jesus said in response, "From the cup I drink of you shall drink; the bath I am immersed in you shall share. But sitting at my right or my left is not mine to give; that is for those for whom it has been reserved." The other ten, on hearing this, became indignant at James and John. Jesus called them together and said to them: "You know how among the Gentiles those who seem to exercise authority lord it over them; their great ones make their importance felt. It cannot be like that with you. Anyone among you who aspires to greatness must serve the rest; whoever wants to rank first among you must serve the needs of all. The Son of Man has not come to be served but to serve—to give his life in ransom for the many."

This is the gospel of the Lord.

---

350   THURSDAY OF THE EIGHTH WEEK OF THE YEAR

Year I

READING I   Sir 42, 15-25

A reading from the book of Sirach

The work of the Lord is filled with his glory.

Now will I recall God's works;
  what I have seen, I will describe.
At God's word were his works brought into being;
  they do his will as he has ordained for them.
As the rising sun is clear to all,
  so the glory of the Lord fills all his works;
Yet even God's holy ones must fail
  in recounting the wonders of the Lord,
Though God has given these, his hosts, the strength
  to stand firm before his glory.
He plumbs the depths and penetrates the heart;
  their innermost being he understands.
The Most High possesses all knowledge,
  and sees from of old the things that are to come:
He makes known the past and the future,
  and reveals the deepest secrets.

No understanding does he lack;
  no single thing escapes him.
Perennial is his almighty wisdom;
  he is from all eternity one and the same,
With nothing added, nothing taken away;
  no need of a counselor for him!
How beautiful are all his works!
  even to the spark and the fleeting vision!
The universe lives and abides forever;
  to meet each need, each creature is preserved.
All of them differ, one from another,
  yet none of them has he made in vain,
For each in turn, as it comes, is good;
  can one ever see enough of their splendor?

This is the Word of the Lord.

Responsorial Psalm   Ps 33, 2-3. 4-5. 6-7. 8-9

℞. (6) By the word of the Lord the heavens were made.

Give thanks to the Lord on the harp;
  with the ten-stringed lyre chant his praises.
Sing to him a new song;
  pluck the strings skillfully, with shouts of gladness.

℞. By the word of the Lord the heavens were made.

For upright is the word of the Lord,
  and all his works are trustworthy.
He loves justice and right;
  of the kindness of the Lord the earth is full.

℞. By the word of the Lord the heavens were made.

By the word of the Lord the heavens were made;
  by the breath of his mouth all their host.
He gathers the waters of the sea as in a flask;
  in cellars he confines the deep.

℞. By the word of the Lord the heavens were made.

Let all the earth fear the Lord;
  let all who dwell in the world revere him.
For he spoke, and it was made;
  he commanded, and it stood forth.

℞. By the word of the Lord the heavens were made.

Year II

READING I   1 Pt 2, 2-5. 9-12

A reading from the first letter of Peter

You are a chosen race, a royal priesthood, sing the praises of God who called you out of darkness.

Be as eager for milk as newborn babies—pure milk of the spirit to make you grow unto salvation, now that "you have tasted that the Lord is good."

Come to him, a living stone, rejected by men but approved, nonetheless, and precious in God's eyes. You too are living stones, built as an edifice of spirit, into a holy priesthood, offering spiritual sacrifices acceptable to God through Jesus Christ.

You, however, are "a chosen race, a royal priesthood, a consecrated nation, a people he claims for his own to proclaim the glorious works" of the One who called you from darkness into his marvelous light. Once you were "no people," but now you are God's people; once there was "no mercy for you," but now you have found mercy.

Beloved, you are strangers and in exile; hence I urge you not to indulge your carnal desires. By their nature they wage war on the soul. Though the pagans may slander you as troublemakers, conduct yourselves blamelessly among them. By observing your good works they may give glory to God on the day of visitation.

This is the Word of the Lord.

Responsorial Psalm   Ps 100, 2. 3. 4. 5

℟. (2) Come with joy into the presence of the Lord.

Sing joyfully to the Lord, all you lands;
     serve the Lord with gladness;
     come before him with joyful song.
℟. Come with joy into the presence of the Lord.

Know that the Lord is God;
     he made us, his we are;
     his people, the flock he tends.
℟. Come with joy into the presence of the Lord.

Enter his gates with thanksgiving,
     his courts with praise;
Give thanks to him;
     bless his name.
℟. Come with joy into the presence of the Lord.

The Lord is good:
     his kindness endures forever,
     and his faithfulness, to all generations.
℟. Come with joy into the presence of the Lord.

Years I and II

GOSPEL   Mk 10, 46-52
Alleluia

See no. 509.

✠ A reading from the holy gospel according to Mark

Master, let me see again.

As Jesus was leaving Jericho with his disciples and a sizable crowd, there was a blind beggar Bartimaeus ("son of Timaeus") sitting by the roadside. On hearing that it was Jesus of Nazareth, he began to call out, "Jesus, Son of David, have pity on me!" Many people were scolding him to make him keep quiet, but he shouted all the louder, "Son of David, have pity on me!" Then Jesus stopped and said, "Call him over." So they called the blind man over, telling him as they did so, "You have nothing whatever to fear from him! Get up! He is calling you!" He threw aside his cloak, jumped up and came to Jesus. Jesus asked him, "What do you want me to do for you?" "Rabboni," the blind man said, "I want to see." Jesus said in reply, "Be on your way! Your faith has healed you." Immediately he received his sight and started to follow him up the road.

This is the gospel of the Lord.

351   **FRIDAY OF THE EIGHTH
WEEK OF THE YEAR**

Year I

READING I   Sir 44, 1. 9-13

A reading from the book of Sirach

Our ancestors were merciful men, and their name will live
for generations.

Now will I praise those godly men,
    our ancestors, each in his own time.
But of others there is no memory,
    for when they ceased, they ceased.
And they are as though they had not lived,
    they and their children after them.
Yet these also were godly men
    whose virtues have not been forgotten;
Their wealth remains in their families,
    their heritage with their descendants;
Through God's covenant with them their
    family endures,
    their posterity, for their sake.
And for all time their progeny will endure,
    their glory will never be blotted out.
        This is the Word of the Lord.

Responsorial Psalm   Ps 149, 1-2. 3-4. 5-6. 9

℟. (4) The Lord takes delight in his people.
Sing to the Lord a new song
    of praise in the assembly of the faithful.
Let Israel be glad in their maker,
    let the children of Zion rejoice in their king.
℟. The Lord takes delight in his people.
Let them praise his name in the festive dance,
    let them sing praise to him with timbrel and
    harp.
For the Lord loves his people,
    and he adorns the lowly with victory.
℟. The Lord takes delight in his people.
Let the faithful exult in glory;
    let them sing for joy upon their couches;
    let the high praises of God be in their throats.
This is the glory of all his faithful. Alleluia.
℟. The Lord takes delight in his people.

Year II

READING I   1 Pt 4, 7-13

A reading from the first letter of Peter

Be good stewards of the many graces you have received.

The consummation of all is close at hand. Therefore do not be perturbed; remain calm so that
you will be able to pray. Above all, let your
love for one another be constant, for love
covers a multitude of sins. Be mutually hospitable without complaining. As generous distributors of God's manifold grace, put your gifts
at the service of one another, each in the
measure he has received. The one who speaks
is to deliver God's message. The one who
serves is to do it with the strength provided
by God. Thus, in all of you God is to be
glorified through Jesus Christ: to him be glory
and dominion throughout the ages. Amen.

Do not be surprised, beloved, that a trial by
fire is occurring in your midst. It is a test for
you, but it should not catch you off guard.
Rejoice instead, insofar as you share Christ's
sufferings. When his glory is revealed, you will
rejoice exultantly.
        This is the Word of the Lord.

Responsorial Psalm   Ps 96, 10. 11-12. 13

℟. (13) The Lord comes to judge the earth.
Say among the nations: The Lord is king.
    He has made the world firm, not to be
    moved;
    he governs the peoples with equity.
℟. The Lord comes to judge the earth.
Let the heavens be glad and the earth rejoice;
    let the sea and what fills it resound;
    let the plains be joyful and all that is in them!
℟. The Lord comes to judge the earth.
They shall exult before the Lord, for he comes;
    for he comes to rule the earth.
He shall rule the world with justice
    and the peoples with his constancy.
℟. The Lord comes to judge the earth.

GOSPEL

Years I and II

Mk 11, 11-26

Alleluia

See no. 509.

✠ A reading from the holy gospel according to Mark

My house will be called a house of prayer for all people. Have faith in God.

Jesus entered Jerusalem [amid acclamations from the crowd] and went into the temple precincts. He inspected everything there, but since it was already late in the afternoon, he went out to Bethany accompanied by the Twelve.

The next day when they were leaving Bethany he felt hungry. Observing a fig tree some distance off, covered with foliage, he went over to see if he could find anything on it. When he reached it he found nothing but leaves; it was not the time for figs. Then addressing it he said, "Never again shall anyone eat of your fruit!" His disciples heard all this.

When they reached Jerusalem he entered the temple precincts and began to drive out those who were engaged in buying and selling. He overturned the money-changers' tables and the stalls of the men selling doves; moreover, he would not permit anyone to carry things through the temple area.

Then he began to teach them: "Does not Scripture have it,

'My house shall be called a house of prayer for all peoples'?

but you have turned it into a den of thieves." The chief priests and the scribes heard of this and began to look for a way to destroy him. They were at the same time afraid of him because the whole crowd was under the spell of his teaching. When evening drew on, Jesus and his disciples went out of the city. Early next morning, as they were walking along, they saw the fig tree withered to its roots. Peter remembered and said to him, "Rabbi, look! The fig tree you cursed has withered up." In reply Jesus told them: "Put your trust in God. I solemnly assure you, whoever says to this mountain, 'Be lifted up and thrown into the sea,' and has no inner doubts but believes that what he says will happen, shall have it done for him. I give you my word, if you are ready to believe that you will receive whatever you ask for in prayer, it shall be done for you. When you stand to pray, forgive anyone against whom you have a grievance so that your heavenly Father may in turn forgive you your faults."

This is the gospel of the Lord.

---

352   SATURDAY OF THE EIGHTH WEEK OF THE YEAR

Year I

READING I

Sir 51, 12-20

A reading from the book of Sirach

Give me wisdom and I will give you glory.

I thank him and I praise him;
  I bless the name of the Lord.
When I was young and innocent,
  I sought wisdom.
She came to me in her beauty,
  and until the end I will cultivate her.
As the blossoms yielded to ripening grapes,
  the heart's joy,
My feet kept to the level path
  because from earliest youth I was familiar with her.
In the short time I paid heed,
  I met with great instruction.
Since in this way I have profited,
  I will give my teacher grateful praise.
I became resolutely devoted to her—
  the good I persistently strove for.
I burned with desire for her,
  never turning back.
I became preoccupied with her,
  never weary of extolling her.
My hand opened her gate
  and I came to know her secrets.
For her I purified even the soles of my feet;
  in cleanness I attained to her.
At first acquaintance with her, I gained understanding
  such that I will never forsake her.
This is the Word of the Lord.

Responsorial Psalm　Ps 19, 8. 9. 10. 11

℟. (9) The precepts of the Lord give joy to
the heart.

The law of the Lord is perfect,
　refreshing the soul;
The decree of the Lord is trustworthy,
　giving wisdom to the simple.

℟. The precepts of the Lord give joy to the
heart.

The precepts of the Lord are right,
　rejoicing the heart;
The command of the Lord is clear,
　enlightening the eye.

℟. The precepts of the Lord give joy to the
heart.

The fear of the Lord is pure,
　enduring forever;
The ordinances of the Lord are true,
　all of them just.

℟. The precepts of the Lord give joy to the
heart.

They are more precious than gold,
　than a heap of purest gold;
Sweeter also than syrup
　or honey from the comb.

℟. The precepts of the Lord give joy to the
heart.

Year II

READING I　Jude 17. 20-25

A reading from the letter of Jude

Glory be to him who can keep you from falling and bring
you safe to his presence.

Remember, beloved, the prophetic words of
the apostles of our Lord Jesus Christ. Praying
in the Holy Spirit, persevere in God's love, and
welcome the mercy of our Lord Jesus Christ
which leads to life eternal. Correct those who
are confused; the others you must rescue,
snatching them from the fire. Even with those
you pity, be on your guard; abhor so much as
their flesh-stained clothing.

　There is One who can protect you from a
fall and make you stand unblemished and
exultant in the presence of his glory. Glory be
to this only God our Savior, through Jesus
Christ our Lord. Majesty, too, be his, might

and power from ages past, now and for ages
to come. Amen.
　This is the Word of the Lord.

Responsorial Psalm　Ps 63, 2. 3-4. 5-6

℟. (2) My soul is thirsting for you, O Lord
my God.

O God, you are my God whom I seek;
　for you my flesh pines and my soul thirsts
　like the earth, parched, lifeless and without
　water.

℟. My soul is thirsting for you, O Lord my
God.

Thus have I gazed toward you in the sanctuary
　to see your power and your glory,
For your kindness is a greater good than life;
　my lips shall glorify you.

℟. My soul is thirsting for you, O Lord my
God.

Thus will I bless you while I live;
　lifting up my hands, I will call upon your
　name.
As with the riches of a banquet shall my soul
　be satisfied,
　and with exultant lips my mouth shall praise
　you.

℟. My soul is thirsting for you, O Lord my
God.

Years I and II

GOSPEL　Mk 11, 27-33
Alleluia

See no. 509.

✠ A reading from the holy gospel according
to Mark

By what authority have you done this?

Jesus and his disciples returned once more to
Jerusalem. As he was walking in the temple
precincts the chief priests, the scribes, and the
elders approached him and said to him, "On
what authority are you doing these things?
Who has given you the power to do them?"
Jesus said to them, "I will ask you a question.
If you give me an answer, I will tell you on
what authority I do the things I do. Tell me,
was John's baptism of divine origin or merely
from men?" They thought to themselves, "If

we say 'divine,' he will ask, 'Then why did you not put faith in it?' But can we say, 'merely human'?" (They had reason to fear the people, who all regarded John as a true prophet.) So their answer to Jesus was, "We do not know." In turn, Jesus said to them, "Then neither will I tell you on what authority I do the things I do."

This is the gospel of the Lord.

---

353   MONDAY OF THE NINTH WEEK OF THE YEAR

Year I

READING I   Tb 1, 1. 2; 2, 1-9

The beginning of the book of Tobit

Tobiah feared the Lord more than the king.

This book tells the story of Tobit of the tribe of Naphtali, who during the reign of Shalmaneser, king of Assyria, was taken captive from Thisbe, which is south of Kedesh Naphtali in upper Galilee, above and to the west of Asser, north of Phogor.

On our festival of Pentecost, the feast of Weeks, a fine dinner was prepared for me, and I reclined to eat. The table was set for me, and when many different dishes were placed before me, I said to my son Tobiah: "My son, go out and try to find a poor man from among our kinsmen exiled here in Nineveh. If he is a sincere worshiper of God, bring him back with you, so that he can share this meal with me. Indeed, son, I shall wait for you to come back."

Tobiah went out to look for some poor kinsman of ours. When he returned he exclaimed, "Father!" I said to him, "What is it, son?" He answered, "Father, one of our people has been murdered! His body lies in the market place where he was just strangled!" I sprang to my feet, leaving the dinner untouched; and I carried the dead man from the street and put him in one of the rooms, so that I might bury him after sunset. Returning to my own quarters, I washed myself and ate my food in sorrow. I was reminded of the oracle pronounced by the prophet Amos against Bethel:

"Your festivals shall be turned into mourning, And all your songs into lamentation."

And I wept. Then at sunset I went out, dug a grave, and buried him.

The neighbors mocked me, saying to one another: "Will this man never learn! Once before he was hunted down for execution because of this very thing; yet now that he has escaped, here he is again burying the dead!"

That same night I bathed, and went to sleep next to the wall of my courtyard. Because of the heat I left my face uncovered.

This is the Word of the Lord.

Responsorial Psalm   Ps 112, 1-2. 3-4. 5-6

℟. (1) Happy the man who fears the Lord.
Happy the man who fears the Lord,
  who greatly delights in his commands.
His posterity shall be mighty upon the earth;
  the upright generation shall be blessed.
℟. Happy the man who fears the Lord.
Wealth and riches shall be in his house;
  his generosity shall endure forever.
The Lord dawns through the darkness, a light
    for the upright;
  he is gracious and merciful and just.
℟. Happy the man who fears the Lord.
Well for the man who is gracious and lends,
  who conducts his affairs with justice;
He shall never be moved;
  the just man shall be in everlasting remem-
    brance.
℟. Happy the man who fears the Lord.
℟. Or: Alleluia.

Year II

READING I   2 Pt 1, 2-7

A reading from the second letter of Peter

In making these gifts he has enabled us to share the divine nature.

May grace be yours and peace in abundance through your knowledge of God and of Jesus, our Lord.

That divine power of his has freely bestowed on us everything necessary for a life of genuine piety through knowledge of him who called us by his own glory and power. By virtue of them he has bestowed on us the great and precious things he promised, so that through these you who have fled a world corrupted by lust might become sharers of the divine nature. This is reason enough for you to make every effort to undergird your virtue with faith, your discernment with virtue, and your self-control with discernment. This self-control, in turn, to piety, and piety to care for your brother, and care for your brother, to love.

This is the Word of the Lord.

Responsorial Psalm   Ps 91, 1-2. 14-15. 15-16

℟. (2) In you, my God, I place my trust.
You who dwell in the shelter of the Most High,
    who abide in the shadow of the Almighty,
Say to the Lord, "My refuge and my fortress,
    my God, in whom I trust."
℟. In you, my God, I place my trust.

Because he clings to me, I will deliver him;
    I will set him on high because he acknowl-
    edges my name.
He shall call upon me, and I will answer him;
    I will be with him in distress.
℟. In you, my God, I place my trust.

I will deliver him and glorify him;
    with length of days I will gratify him
    and will show him my salvation.
℟. In you, my God, I place my trust.

Years I and II

GOSPEL   Mk 12, 1-12
Alleluia
See no. 509.

✠ A reading from the holy gospel according
    to Mark
*They seized the beloved son, killed him, and threw him out
of the vineyard.*

Jesus began to address the chief priests, the scribes and the elders once more in parables: "A man planted a vineyard, put a hedge around it, dug out a vat, and erected a tower. Then he leased it to tenant farmers and went on a journey. In due time he dispatched a man in his service to the tenants to obtain from them his

share of produce from the vineyard. But they seized him, beat him, and sent him off empty-handed. The second time he sent them another servant; him too they beat over the head and treated shamefully. He sent yet another and they killed him. So too with many others: some they beat; some they killed. He still had one to send—the son whom he loved. He sent him to them as a last resort, thinking, 'They will have to respect my son.' But those tenants said to one another, 'Here is the one who will inherit everything. Come, let us kill him, and the inheritance will be ours.' Then they seized and killed him and dragged him outside the vineyard. What do you suppose the owner of the vineyard will do? He will come and destroy those tenants and turn his vineyard over to others. Are you not familiar with this passage of Scripture:

    'The stone rejected by the builders
        has become the keystone of the struc-
        ture.
    It was the Lord who did it
        and we find it marvelous to behold'?"

They wanted to arrest him at this, yet they had reason to fear the crowd. (They knew well enough that he meant the parable for them.) Finally they left him and went off.

This is the gospel of the Lord.

354   **TUESDAY OF THE NINTH
        WEEK OF THE YEAR**

                                        Year I
READING I   Tb 2, 9-14
    A reading from the book of Tobit
Even though he was blind he did not turn against God.

One night I (Tobit) [fatigued from burying the dead] went to sleep next to the wall of my courtyard. Because of the heat I left my face uncovered. I did not know there were birds perched on the wall above me, till their warm droppings settled in my eyes, causing cataracts. I went to see some doctors for a cure, but the more they anointed my eyes with various salves, the worse the cataracts became, until I could see no more. For four years

I was deprived of eyesight, and all my kinsmen were grieved at my condition. Ahiqar, however, took care of me for two years, until he left for Elymais.

At that time my wife Anna worked for hire at weaving cloth, the kind of work women do. When she sent back the goods to their owners, they would pay her. Late in winter she finished the cloth and sent it back to the owners. They paid her the full salary, and also gave her a young goat for the table. On entering my house the goat began to bleat. I called to my wife and said: "Where did this goat come from? Perhaps it was stolen! Give it back to its owners; we have no right to eat stolen food!" But she said to me, "It was given to me as a bonus over and above my wages." Yet I would not believe her, and told her to give it back to its owners. I became very angry with her over this. So she retorted: "Where are your charitable deeds now? Where are your virtuous acts? See! Your true character is finally showing itself!"

This is the Word of the Lord.

Responsorial Psalm   Ps 112, 1-2. 7-8. 9

℟. (7) The heart of the just man is secure, trusting in the Lord.

Happy the man who fears the Lord, who greatly delights in his commands.
His posterity shall be mighty upon the earth; the upright generation shall be blessed.

℟. The heart of the just man is secure, trusting in the Lord.

An evil report he shall not fear; his heart is firm, trusting in the Lord.
His heart is steadfast; he shall not fear till he looks down upon his foes.

℟. The heart of the just man is secure, trusting in the Lord.

Lavishly he gives to the poor; his generosity shall endure forever; his horn shall be exalted in glory.

℟. The heart of the just man is secure, trusting in the Lord.

℟. Or: Alleluia.

READING I   2 Pt 3, 12-15. 17-18

A reading from the second letter of Peter

We are waiting for the new heavens and the new earth.

Look for the coming of the day of God and try to hasten it! Because of it, the heavens will be destroyed in flames and the elements will melt away in a blaze. What we await are new heavens and a new earth where, according to his promise, the justice of God will reside.

So, beloved, while waiting for this, make every effort to be found without stain or defilement, and at peace in his sight. Consider that our Lord's patience is directed toward salvation.

You are forewarned, beloved brothers. Be on your guard lest you be led astray by the error of the wicked, and forfeit the security you enjoy. Grow rather in grace, and in the knowledge of our Lord and Savior Jesus Christ. Glory be to him now and to the day of eternity! Amen.

This is the Word of the Lord.

Responsorial Psalm   Ps 90, 2. 3-4. 10. 14. 16

℟. (1) In every age, O Lord, you have been our refuge.

Before the mountains were begotten and the earth and the world were brought forth,
from everlasting to everlasting you are God.

℟. In every age, O Lord, you have been our refuge.

You turn man back to dust, saying, "Return, O children of men."
For a thousand years in your sight are as yesterday, now that it is past, or as a watch of the night.

℟. In every age, O Lord, you have been our refuge.

Seventy is the sum of our years, or eighty, if we are strong,
And most of them are fruitless toil, for they pass quickly and we drift away.

℟ In every age, O Lord, you have been our refuge.

Fill us at daybreak with your kindness,
  that we may shout for joy and gladness all
  our days.
Let your work be seen by your servants
  and your glory by their children.
℟. In every age, O Lord, you have been our
  refuge.

GOSPEL   Mk 12, 13-17
Alleluia

See no. 509.

✠ A reading from the holy gospel according
          to Mark

Give to Caesar what belongs to Caesar and to God what
          belongs to God.

**Some Pharisees and Herodians were sent after
Jesus to catch him in his speech. The two
groups came and said to him: "Teacher, we
know you are a truthful man, unconcerned
about anyone's opinion. It is evident you do not
act out of human respect but teach God's way
of life sincerely. Is it lawful to pay the tax
to the emperor or not? Are we to pay or not to
pay?" Knowing their hypocrisy he said to
them, "Why are you trying to trip me up?
Bring me a coin and let me see it." When
they brought one, he said to them, "Whose
head is this and whose inscription is it?"
"Caesar's," they told him. At that Jesus said
to them, "Give to Caesar what is Caesar's but
give to God what is God's." Their amazement
at him knew no bounds.**
          This is the gospel of the Lord.

---

355   **WEDNESDAY OF THE NINTH
        WEEK OF THE YEAR**

READING I   Tb 3, 1-11. 16
      A reading from the book of Tobit
Their prayers were heard by the Lord and found favor in
          his sight.

**Grief-stricken in spirit, Tobit groaned and
wept aloud. Then with sobs he began to pray:
"You are righteous, O Lord,
  and all your deeds are just;**

All your ways are mercy and truth;
  you are the judge of the world.
And now, O Lord, may you be mindful of me,
  and look with favor upon me.
Punish me not for my sins,
  nor for my inadvertent offenses,
  nor for those of my fathers.

"They sinned against you,
  and disobeyed your commandments.
So you handed us over to plundering, exile,
  and death,
  till we were an object lesson, a byword,
  a reproach
  in all the nations among whom you scattered
  us.

"Yes, your judgments are many and true
  in dealing with me as my sins
  and those of my fathers deserve.
For we have not kept your commandments,
  nor have we trodden the paths of truth before you.

"So now, deal with me as you please,
  and command my life breath to be taken
  from me,
  that I may go from the face of the earth
  into dust.
It is better for me to die than to live,
  because I have heard insulting calumnies,
  and I am overwhelmed with grief.

"Lord, command me to be delivered from such
  anguish;
  let me go to the everlasting abode;
  Lord, refuse me not.
For it is better for me to die
  than to endure so much misery in life,
  and to hear these insults!"

On the same day, at Ecbatana in Media, it
so happened that Raguel's daughter Sarah also
had to listen to abuse, from one of her father's
maids. For she had been married to seven husbands, but the wicked demon Asmodeus killed
them off before they could have intercourse
with her, as it is prescribed for wives. So the
maid said to her: "You are the one who
strangles your husbands! Look at you! You
have already been married seven times, but
you have had no joy with any one of your

husbands. Why do you beat us? Because your husbands are dead? Then why not join them! May we never see a son or daughter of yours!"

That day she was deeply grieved in spirit. She went in tears to an upstairs room in her father's house with the intention of hanging herself. But she reconsidered, saying to herself: "No! People would level this insult against my father: 'You had only one beloved daughter, but she hanged herself because of ill fortune!' And thus would I cause my father in his old age to go down to the nether world laden with sorrow. It is far better for me not to hang myself, but to beg the Lord to have me die, so that I need no longer live to hear such insults."

At that time, then, she spread out her hands, and facing the window, poured out her prayer.

At that very time, the prayer of these two suppliants was heard in the glorious presence of Almighty God. So Raphael was sent to heal them both.

This is the Word of the Lord.

Responsorial Psalm   Ps 25, 2-4. 4-5. 6-7. 8-9

R̶. (1) To you, O Lord, I lift my soul.

O Lord, my God
In you I trust; let me not be put to shame, let not my enemies exult over me.
No one who waits for you shall be put to shame;
those shall be put to shame who heedlessly break faith.
R̶. To you, O Lord, I lift my soul.
Your ways, O Lord, make known to me;
teach me your paths,
Guide me in your truth and teach me,
for you are God my savior.
R̶. To you, O Lord, I lift my soul.
Remember that your compassion, O Lord,
and your kindness are from of old.
In your kindness remember me,
because of your goodness, O Lord.
R̶. To you, O Lord, I lift my soul.
Good and upright is the Lord;
thus he show sinners the way.

He guides the humble to justice,
he teaches the humble his way.
R̶. To you, O Lord, I lift my soul.

Year II

READING I   2 Tm 1, 1-3. 6-12
The beginning of the second letter of Paul to Timothy
Rekindle the gift God gave you when I laid my hands on you.

Paul, by the will of God an apostle of Christ Jesus sent to proclaim the promise of life in him, to Timothy, my dear child whom I love. May grace, mercy, and peace from God the Father and from Christ Jesus our Lord be with you.

I thank God, the God of my forefathers whom I worship with a clear conscience, whenever I remember you in my prayers—as indeed I do constantly, night and day.

For this reason, I remind you to stir into flame the gift of God bestowed when my hands were laid on you. The Spirit God has given us is no cowardly spirit but rather one that makes us strong, loving and wise. Therefore, never be ashamed of your testimony to our Lord, nor of me, a prisoner for his sake, but with the strength which comes from God bear your share of the hardship which the gospel entails.

God has saved us and has called us to a holy life, not because of any merit of ours but according to his own design—the grace held out to us in Christ Jesus before the world began but now made manifest through the appearance of our Savior. He has robbed death of its power and has brought life and immortality into clear light through the gospel. In the service of this gospel I have been appointed preacher and apostle and teacher, and for its sake I undergo present hardships. But I am not ashamed, for I know him in whom I have believed, and I am confident that he is able to guard what has been entrusted to me until that final Day.

This is the Word of the Lord.

Responsorial Psalm   Ps 123, 1-2. 2

℟. (1) To you, O Lord, I lift up my eyes.

To you I lift up my eyes
   who are enthroned in heaven.
Behold, as the eyes of servants
   are on the hands of their masters,

℟. To you, O Lord, I lift up my eyes.

As the eyes of a maid
   are on the hands of her mistress,
So are our eyes on the Lord, our God,
   till he have pity on us.

℟. To you, O Lord, I lift up my eyes.

Years I and II

GOSPEL   Mk 12, 18-27
Alleluia

See no. 509.

✠ A reading from the holy gospel according
to Mark

He is the God not of the dead, but of the living.

Then some Sadducees who hold there is no
resurrection came to Jesus with a question:
"Teacher, we were left this in writing by
Moses: 'If anyone's brother dies leaving a wife
but no child, his brother must take the wife
and produce offspring for his brother.' There
were these seven brothers. The eldest took a
wife and died, leaving no children. The second
took the woman, and he too died childless. The
same thing happened to the third; in fact none
of the seven left any children behind. Last of
all, the woman also died. At the resurrection,
when they all come back to life, whose wife
will she be? All seven married her." Jesus
said: "You are badly misled, because you fail to
understand the Scriptures or the power of God.
When people rise from the dead, they neither
marry nor are given in marriage but live like
angels in heaven. As to the raising of the dead,
have you not read in the book of Moses, in the
passage about the burning bush, how God told
him,

   'I am the God of Abraham, the God of
      Isaac,
     the God of Jacob'?

He is the God of the living, not of the dead.
You are very much mistaken."

     This is the gospel of the Lord.

Year I

READING I   Tb 6, 11; 7, 1. 9-14; 8, 4-7

A reading from the book of Tobit

The Lord made you come to me that we might be joined
together.

The angel Raphael spoke thus to Tobiah, "Tonight we must stay with Raguel, who is a
relative of yours. He has a daughter named
Sarah." So he brought him to the house of
Raguel, whom they found seated by his courtyard gate. They greeted him first. He said to
them, "Greetings to you too, brothers! Good
health to you and welcome!"

Afterward, Raguel slaughtered a ram from
the flock and gave them a cordial reception.
When they had bathed and reclined to eat,
Tobiah said to Raphael, "Brother Azariah, ask
Raguel to let me marry my kinswoman Sarah."
Raguel overheard the words; so he said to the
boy: "Eat and drink and be merry tonight, for
no man is more entitled to marry my daughter
Sarah than you, brother. Besides, not even I
have the right to give her to anyone but you,
because you are my closest relative. But I
will explain the situation to you very frankly.
I have given her in marriage to seven men,
all of whom were kinsmen of ours, and all
died on the very night they approached her.
But now, son, eat and drink. I am sure the Lord
will look after you both." Tobiah answered,
"I will eat or drink nothing until you set aside
what belongs to me."

Raguel said to him: "I will do it. She is yours
according to the decree of the Book of Moses.
Your marriage to her has been decided in
heaven! Take your kinswoman; from now on
you are her love, and she is your beloved. She
is yours today and ever after. And tonight,
son, may the Lord of heaven prosper you both.
May he grant you mercy and peace." Then
Raguel called his daughter Sarah, and she came
to him. He took her by the hand and gave her
to Tobiah with the words: "Take her according
to the law. According to the decree written in
the Book of Moses she is your wife. Take her

and bring her back safely to your father. And may the God of heaven grant both of you peace and prosperity." He then called her mother and told her to bring a scroll, so that he might draw up a marriage contract stating that he gave Sarah to Tobiah as his wife according to the decree of the Mosaic law. Her mother brought the scroll, and he drew up the contract, to which they affixed their seals. Afterward they began to eat and drink.

Tobiah arose from bed and said to his wife, "My love, get up. Let us pray and beg our Lord to have mercy on us and to grant us deliverance." She got up, and they started to pray and beg that deliverance might be theirs. He began with these words:

"Blessed are you, O God of our fathers;
  praised be your name forever and ever.
Let the heavens and all your creation
  praise you forever.
You made Adam and you gave him his wife Eve
  to be his help and support;
  and from these two the human race descended.
You said, 'It is not good for the man to be alone;
  let us make him a partner like himself.'
Now, Lord, you know that I take this wife of mine
  not because of lust,
  but for a noble purpose.
Call down your mercy on me and on her,
  and allow us to live together to a happy old age."

  This is the Word of the Lord.

Responsorial Psalm   Ps 128, 1-2. 3. 4-5

℟. (1) Happy are those who fear the Lord.
Happy are you who fear the Lord,
  who walk in his ways!
For you shall eat the fruit of your handiwork;
  happy shall you be, and favored.
℟. Happy are those who fear the Lord.
Your wife shall be like a fruitful vine
  in the recesses of your home;
Your children like olive plants
  around your table.

℟. Happy are those who fear the Lord.
Behold, thus is the man blessed
  who fears the Lord.
The Lord bless you from Zion:
  may you see the prosperity of Jerusalem
  all the days of your life.
℟. Happy are those who fear the Lord.

Year II

READING I   2 Tm 2, 8-15
A reading from the second letter of Paul to Timothy
The word of God is not chained. If we have died with him, we shall live with him.

Remember that Jesus Christ, a descendant of David, was raised from the dead. This is the gospel I preach; in preaching it I suffer as a criminal, even to the point of being thrown into chains—but there is no chaining the word of God! Therefore I bear with all of this for the sake of those whom God has chosen, in order that they may obtain the salvation to be found in Christ Jesus and with it eternal glory.

  You can depend on this:
    If we have died with him
      we shall also live with him;
    If we hold out to the end
      we shall reign with him.
But if we deny him he will deny us. If we are unfaithful he will still remain faithful, for he cannot deny himself.

Keep reminding people of these things and charge them before God to stop disputing about mere words. This does no good and can be the ruin of those who listen. Try hard to make yourself worthy of God's approval, a workman who has no cause to be ashamed, following a straight course in preaching the truth.

  This is the Word of the Lord.

Responsorial Psalm   Ps 25, 4-5. 8-9. 10. 14

℟. (4) Teach me your ways, O Lord.
Your ways, O Lord, make known to me;
  teach me your paths,
Guide me in your truth and teach me,
  for you are God my savior.

Rℤ. Teach me your ways, O Lord.
Good and upright is the Lord;
  thus he shows sinners the way.
He guides the humble to justice,
  he teaches the humble his way.
Rℤ. Teach me your ways, O Lord.
All the paths of the Lord are kindness and
  constancy
  toward those who keep his covenant and his
  decrees.
The friendship of the Lord is with those who
  fear him,
  and his covenant, for their instruction.
Rℤ. Teach me your ways, O Lord.

Years I and II

GOSPEL   Mk 12, 28-34
Alleluia

See no. 509.

✠ **A reading from the holy gospel according**
                    to Mark
This is the first commandment. The second is similar to it.

One of the scribes came up to ask Jesus,
"Which is the first of all the commandments?"
Jesus replied: "This is the first:
  'Hear, O Israel! The Lord our God is Lord
    alone!
  Therefore you shall love the Lord your
    God
  with all your heart,
  with all your soul,
  with all your mind,
  and with all your strength.'
This is the second,
  'You shall love your neighbor as yourself.'
There is no other commandment greater than
these." The scribe said to him: "Excellent,
Teacher! You are right in saying, 'He is the
One, there is no other than he.' Yes, 'to love
him with all our heart, with all our thoughts
and with all our strength, and to love our
neighbor as ourselves' is worth more than any
burnt offering or sacrifice." Jesus approved
the insight of this answer and told him, "You
are not far from the reign of God." And no one
had the courage to ask him any more questions.
            This is the gospel of the Lord.

357   **FRIDAY OF THE NINTH**
      WEEK OF THE YEAR

Year I

READING I   Tb 11, 5-15
      A reading from the book of Tobit
You have scourged me and now you have saved me, Lord;
            I can see my son.

**Anna sat watching the road by which her son
was to come. When she saw him coming, she
exclaimed to his father, "Tobit, your son is
coming, and the man who traveled with him!"
  Raphael said to Tobiah before he reached his
father: "I am certain that his eyes will be
opened. Smear the fish gall on them. This
medicine will make the cataracts shrink and
peel off from his eyes; then your father will
again be able to see the light of day."
  Then Anna ran up to her son, threw her arms
around him, and said to him, "Now that I have
seen you again, son, I am ready to die!" And
she sobbed aloud. Tobit got up and stumbled
out through the courtyard gate. Tobiah went
up to him with the fish gall in his hand, and
holding him firmly, blew into his eyes. "Courage, father," he said. Next he smeared the
medicine on his eyes, and it made them smart.
Then, beginning at the corners of Tobit's eyes,
Tobiah used both hands to peel off the cataracts. When Tobit saw his son, he threw his
arms around him and wept. He exclaimed, "I
can see you, son, the light of my eyes!" Then he
said:**
"Blessed be God,
  and praised be his great name,
  and blessed be all his holy angels.
May his holy name be praised
  throughout all the ages,
Because it was he who scourged me,
  and it is he who has had mercy on me.
  Behold, I now see my son Tobiah!"
            This is the Word of the Lord.

Responsorial Psalm   Ps 146, 2. 7. 8-9. 9-10

Rℤ. (2) Praise the Lord, my soul!
Praise the Lord, O my soul;
  I will praise the Lord all my life;
  I will sing praise to my God while I live.

℟. Praise the Lord, my soul!
The Lord keeps faith forever,
   secures justice for the oppressed,
   gives food to the hungry.
The Lord sets captives free.
℟. Praise the Lord, my soul!
The Lord gives sight to the blind.
   The Lord raises up those that were bowed
   down;
   The Lord loves the just.
   The Lord protects strangers.
℟. Praise the Lord, my soul!
The fatherless and the widow he sustains,
   but the way of the wicked he thwarts.
The Lord shall reign forever;
   your God, O Zion, through all generations.
   Alleluia.
℟. Praise the Lord, my soul!
℟. Or: Alleluia.

Year II

READING I
2 Tm 3, 10-17

**A reading from the second letter of Paul to
Timothy**

He who tries to live for Christ will be persecuted.

**You have followed closely my teaching and
my conduct. You have observed my resolution,
fidelity, patience, love, and endurance, through
persecutions and sufferings in Antioch, Iconium, and Lystra. You know what persecutions
I have had to bear, and you know how the Lord
saved me from them all. Anyone who wants to
live a godly life in Christ Jesus can expect to be
persecuted. But all the while evil men and char-
latans will go from bad to worse, deceiving
others, themselves deceived. You, for your
part, must remain faithful to what you have
learned and believed, because you know who
your teachers were. Likewise, from your infancy you have known the sacred Scriptures, the
source of the wisdom which through faith in
Jesus Christ leads to salvation. All Scripture is
inspired of God and is useful for teaching—for
reproof, correction, and training in holiness so
that the man of God may be fully competent and
equipped for every good work.**

   This is the Word of the Lord.

Responsorial Psalm
Ps 119, 157. 160. 161. 165. 166. 168

℟. (165) O Lord, great peace have they who
   love your law.

Though my persecutors and my foes are many,
   I turn not away from your decrees.
℟. O Lord, great peace have they who love
   your law.

Permanence is your word's chief trait;
   each of your just ordinances is everlasting.
℟. O Lord, great peace have they who love
   your law.

Princes persecute me without cause
   but my heart stands in awe of your word.
℟. O Lord, great peace have they who love
   your law.

Those who love your law have great peace,
   and for them there is no stumbling block.
℟. O Lord, great peace have they who love
   your law.

I wait for your salvation, O Lord,
   and your commands I fulfill.
℟. O Lord, great peace have they who love
   your law.

I keep your precepts and your decrees,
   for all my ways are before you.
℟. O Lord, great peace have they who love
   your law.

Years I and II

GOSPEL
Mk 12, 35-37

Alleluia

See no. 509.

✠ **A reading from the holy gospel according
to Mark**

How can the scribes maintain that Christ is the son of
David?

**As Jesus was teaching in the temple precincts
he went on to say: "How can the scribes claim,
'The Messiah is David's son'? David himself,
inspired by the Holy Spirit, said,**

   **'The Lord said to my Lord: Sit at my right
   hand**
      **until I make your enemies your foot-
      stool.'**
**If David himself addresses him as 'Lord,' in
what sense can he be his son?" The majority
of the crowd heard this with delight.**

   This is the gospel of the Lord.

358   SATURDAY OF THE NINTH WEEK OF THE YEAR

Year I

READING I   Tb 12, 1. 5-15. 20

A reading from the book of Tobit
I will return to him who sent me; bless the Lord.

Tobit called his son Tobiah and said to him, "Son, see to it that you give what is due to the man who made the journey with you; give him a bonus too." So Tobiah called Raphael and said, "Take as your wages half of all that you have brought back, and go in peace."

Raphael called the two men aside privately and said to them: "Thank God! Give him the praise and the glory. Before all the living, acknowledge the many good things he has done for you, by blessing and extolling his name in song. Before all men, honor and proclaim God's deeds, and do not be slack in praising him. A king's secret it is prudent to keep, but the works of God are to be declared and made known. Praise them with due honor. Do good, and evil will not find its way to you. Prayer and fasting are good, but better than either is almsgiving accompanied by righteousness. A little with righteousness is better than abundance with wickedness. It is better to give alms than to store up gold; for almsgiving saves one from death and expiates every sin. Those who regularly give alms shall enjoy a full life; but those habitually guilty of sin are their own worst enemies.

"I will now tell you the whole truth; I will conceal nothing at all from you. I have already said to you, 'A king's secret it is prudent to keep, but the works of God are to be made known with due honor.' I can now tell you that when you, Tobit, and Sarah prayed, it was I who presented and read the record of your prayer before the Glory of the Lord; and I did the same thing when you used to bury the dead. When you did not hesitate to get up and leave your dinner in order to go and bury the dead, I was sent to put you to the test. At the same time, however, God commissioned me to heal you and your daughter-in-law Sarah. I am Raphael, one of the seven angels who enter and serve before the Glory of the Lord.

"So now get up from the ground and praise God. Behold, I am about to ascend to him who sent me; write down all these things that have happened to you."

This is the Word of the Lord.

Responsorial Psalm   Tb 13, 2. 6

℟. (1) Blessed be God, who lives for ever.
God scourges and then has mercy;
  he casts down to the depths of the nether world,
  and he brings up from the great abyss.
No one can escape his hand.
℟. Blessed be God, who lives for ever.
So now consider what he has done for you,
  and praise him with full voice.
Bless the Lord of righteousness,
  and exalt the King of the ages.
℟. Blessed be God, who lives for ever.
In the land of my exile I praise him,
  and show his power and majesty to a sinful nation.
℟. Blessed be God, who lives for ever.
Turn back, you sinners! do the right before him:
  perhaps he may look with favor upon you
  and show you mercy.
℟. Blessed be God, who lives for ever.

Year II

READING I   2 Tm 4, 1-8

A reading from the second letter of Paul to Timothy
Proclaim the Good News. I am already being destroyed and the Lord will give me the crown of righteousness.

In the presence of God and of Christ Jesus, who is coming to judge the living and the dead, and by his appearing and his kingly power, I charge you to preach the word, to stay with this task whether convenient or inconvenient—correcting, reproving, appealing—constantly teaching and never losing patience. For the time will come when people will not tolerate sound doctrine, but, following their own desires, will surround themselves with teachers who tickle their ears. They will stop listening to the truth and will wander off to fables. As for you, be steady and self-possessed; put up with hardship, perform your work as an evangelist, fulfill your ministry.

For my part I am already being poured out like a libation. The time of my dissolution is near. I have fought the good fight, I have finished the race, I have kept the faith. From now on a merited crown awaits me; on that Day the Lord, just judge that he is, will award it to me—and not only to me but to all who have looked for his appearing with eager longing.

This is the Word of the Lord.

Responsorial Psalm   Ps 71, 8-9. 14-15. 16-17. 22

℟. (15) I will sing of your salvation.
My mouth shall be filled with your praise,
   with your glory day by day.
Cast me not off in my old age;
   as my strength fails, forsake me not.
℟. I will sing of your salvation.

But I will always hope
   and praise you ever more and more.
My mouth shall declare your justice,
   day by day your salvation.
℟. I will sing of your salvation.

I will treat of the mighty works of the Lord;
   O God, I will tell of your singular justice.
O God, you have taught me from my youth,
   and till the present I proclaim your wondrous deeds.
℟. I will sing of your salvation.

So will I give you thanks with music on the lyre,
   for your faithfulness, O my God!
I will sing your praises with the harp,
   O Holy One of Israel!
℟. I will sing of your salvation.

GOSPEL   **Years I and II**   Mk 12, 38-44
Alleluia
See no. 509.

✠ A reading from the holy gospel according to Mark

This poor widow has given more than all others.

In the course of his teaching Jesus said: "Be on guard against the scribes, who like to parade around in their robes and accept marks of respect in public, front seats in the synagogues, and places of honor at banquets. These men devour the savings of widows and recite long prayers for appearance' sake; it is they who will receive the severest sentence."

Taking a seat opposite the treasury, he observed the crowd putting money into the collection box. Many of the wealthy put in sizable amounts; but one poor widow came and put in two small copper coins worth about a cent. He called his disciples over and told them: "I want you to observe that this poor widow contributed more than all the others who donated to the treasury. They gave from their surplus wealth, but she gave from her want, all that she had to live on."

This is the gospel of the Lord.

---

359   **MONDAY OF THE TENTH WEEK OF THE YEAR**

Year I

READING I   2 Cor 1, 1-7

The beginning of the second letter of Paul to the Corinthians

God comforts us that we might comfort others in their sorrow.

Paul, by God's will an apostle of Jesus Christ, and Timothy his brother, to the church of God that is at Corinth and to all the holy ones of the church who live in Achaia. Grace and peace from God our Father and the Lord Jesus Christ.

Praised be God, the Father of our Lord Jesus Christ, the Father of mercies and the God of all consolation! He comforts us in all our afflictions and thus enables us to comfort those who are in any trouble, with the same consolation we have received from him. As we have shared much in the suffering of Christ, so through Christ do we share abundantly in his consolation. If we are afflicted it is for your encouragement and salvation, and when we are consoled it is for your consolation, so that you may endure patiently the same sufferings we endure. Our hope for you is firm because we know that just as you share in the sufferings, so you will share in the consolation.

    This is the Word of the Lord.

Responsorial Psalm   Ps 34, 2-3. 4-5. 6-7. 8-9

℞. (9) Taste and see the goodness of the Lord.
I will bless the Lord at all times;
  his praise shall be ever in my mouth.
Let my soul glory in the Lord;
  the lowly will hear me and be glad.
℞. Taste and see the goodness of the Lord.
Glorify the Lord with me,
  let us together extol his name.
I sought the Lord, and he answered me
  and delivered me from all my fears.
℞. Taste and see the goodness of the Lord.
Look to him that you may be radiant with joy,
  and your faces may not blush with shame.
When the afflicted man called out, the Lord heard,
  and from all his distress he saved him.
℞. Taste and see the goodness of the Lord.
The angel of the Lord encamps
  around those who fear him, and delivers them.
Taste and see how good the Lord is;
  happy the man who takes refuge in him.
℞. Taste and see the goodness of the Lord.

Year II

READING I   1 Kgs 17, 1-6

  A reading from the first book of Kings
    Elijah stands before the Lord God of Israel.

Elijah the Tishbite, from Tishbe in Gilead, said to Ahab: "As the Lord, the God of Israel, lives, whom I serve, during these years there shall be no dew or rain except at my word." The Lord then said to Elijah: "Leave here, go east and hide in the Wadi Cherith, east of the Jordan. You shall drink of the stream, and I have commanded ravens to feed you there." So he left and did as the Lord had commanded. He went and remained by the Wadi Cherith, east of the Jordan. Ravens brought him bread
and meat in the morning, and bread and meat in the evening, and he drank from the stream.
    This is the Word of the Lord.

Responsorial Psalm   Ps 121, 1-2. 3-4. 5-6. 7-8

℞. (2) Our help is from the Lord
  who made heaven and earth.
I lift up my eyes toward the mountains;
  whence shall help come to me?
My help is from the Lord,
  who made heaven and earth.
℞. Our help is from the Lord
  who made heaven and earth.
May he not suffer your foot to slip;
  may he slumber not who guards you:
Indeed he neither slumbers nor sleeps,
  the guardian of Israel.
℞. Our help is from the Lord
  who made heaven and earth.
The Lord is your guardian; the Lord is your shade;
  he is beside you at your right hand.
The sun shall not harm you by day,
  nor the moon by night.
℞. Our help is from the Lord
  who made heaven and earth.
The Lord will guard you from all evil;
  he will guard your life.
The Lord will guard your coming and your going,
  both now and forever.
℞. Our help is from the Lord
  who made heaven and earth.

Years I and II

GOSPEL   Mt 5, 1-12
Alleluia

See no. 509.

✠ **A reading from the holy gospel according to Matthew**
    Happy are the poor in spirit.

When Jesus saw the crowds he went up on the mountainside. After he had sat down his disciples gathered around him, and he began to teach them:
    "How blest are the poor in spirit: the reign of God is theirs.

Blest too are the sorrowing; they shall be consoled.
[Blest are the lowly; they shall inherit the land.]
Blest are they who hunger and thirst for holiness;
they shall have their fill.
Blest are they who show mercy; mercy shall be theirs.
Blest are the single-hearted for they shall see God.
Blest too the peacemakers; they shall be called sons of God.
Blest are those persecuted for holiness' sake; the reign of God is theirs.
Blest are you when they insult you and persecute you and utter every kind of slander against you because of me.
Be glad and rejoice, for your reward in heaven is great;
they persecuted the prophets before you in the very same way."
This is the gospel of the Lord.

---

360   **TUESDAY OF THE TENTH WEEK OF THE YEAR**

Year I

READING I   2 Cor 1, 18-22

A reading from the second letter of Paul to the Corinthians

The Son of God, Jesus Christ was not yes and no, in him it is always yes.

As God keeps his word, I declare that my word to you is not "yes" one minute and "no" the next. Jesus Christ, whom Silvanus, Timothy, and I preached to you as Son of God, was not alternately "yes" and "no"; he was never anything but "yes." Whatever promises God has made have been fulfilled in him; therefore it is through him that we address our Amen to God when we worship together. God is the one who firmly establishes us along with you in Christ; it is he who anointed us and has sealed us, thereby depositing the first payment, the Spirit in our hearts.
This is the Word of the Lord.

Responsorial Psalm

Ps 119, 129. 130. 131. 132. 133. 135

R̶. (135) Lord, let your face shine on me.
Wonderful are your decrees;
therefore I observe them.
R̶. Lord, let your face shine on me.
The revelation of your words sheds light,
giving understanding to the simple.
R̶. Lord, let your face shine on me.
I gasp with open mouth
in my yearning for your commands.
R̶. Lord, let your face shine on me.
Turn to me in pity
as you turn to those who love your name.
R̶. Lord, let your face shine on me.
Steady my footsteps according to your promise,
and let no iniquity rule over me.
R̶. Lord, let your face shine on me.
Let your countenance shine upon your servant,
and teach me your statutes.
R̶. Lord, let your face shine on me.

Year II

READING I   1 Kgs 17, 7-16

A reading from the first book of Kings

The jar of meal shall not be spent according to the word of the Lord spoken through Elijah.

The brook [where Elijah was hiding] ran dry, because no rain had fallen in the land. So the Lord said to him: "Move on to Zarephath of Sidon and stay there. I have designated a widow there to provide for you." He left and went to Zarephath. As he arrived at the entrance of the city, a widow was gathering sticks there; he called out to her, "Please bring me a small cupful of water to drink." She left to get it, and he called out after her, "Please bring along a bit of bread." "As the Lord, your God, lives," she answered, "I have nothing baked; there is only a handful of flour in my jar and a little oil in my jug. Just now I was collecting a couple of sticks, to go in and prepare something for myself and my son; when we have eaten it, we shall die." "Do not be afraid," Elijah said to her. "Go and do as you propose. But first make me a little cake and bring it to me. Then you can prepare something for yourself and your son. For the Lord, the God of Israel, says, 'The jar of flour shall not go empty, nor the jug of oil run dry, until the day when the Lord sends rain upon the earth.' " She left and did as Elijah had said. She was able to eat for a year, and he and her son as well; the jar of flour did not go empty, nor the jug of oil run dry, as the Lord had foretold through Elijah.

This is the Word of the Lord.

Responsorial Psalm   Ps 4, 2-3. 4-5. 7-8

℞. (7) Lord, let your face shine on us.

When I call, answer me, O my just God,
   you who relieve me when I am in distress;
   have pity on me, and hear my prayer!

Men of rank, how long will you be dull of heart?
   Why do you love what is vain and seek after falsehood?

℞. Lord, let your face shine on us.

Know that the Lord does wonders for his faithful one;
   the Lord will hear me when I call upon him.

Tremble, and sin not;
   reflect, upon your beds, in silence.

℞. Lord, let your face shine on us.

O Lord, let the light of your countenance shine upon us!
   You put gladness into my heart,
   more than when grain and wine abound.

℞. Lord, let your face shine on us.

GOSPEL   Years I and II   Mt 5, 13-16

Alleluia

See no. 509.

✠ A reading from the holy gospel according to Matthew

You are the light of the world.

Jesus said to his disciples: "You are the salt of the earth. But what if salt goes flat? How can you restore its flavor? Then it is good for nothing but to be thrown out and trampled under-foot.

"You are the light of the world. A city set on a hill cannot be hidden. Men do not light a lamp and then put it under a bushel basket. They set it on a stand where it gives light to all in the house. In the same way, your light must shine before men so that they may see goodness in your acts and give praise to your heavenly Father."

This is the gospel of the Lord.

361   **WEDNESDAY OF THE TENTH WEEK OF THE YEAR**

Year I

READING I   2 Cor 3, 4-11

A reading from the second letter of Paul to the Corinthians

He made us ministers of the new covenant, a covenant of spirit not of letters.

This great confidence in God is ours, through Christ. It is not that we are entitled of ourselves to take credit for anything. Our sole credit is from God, who has made us qualified ministers of a new covenant, a covenant not of a written law but of spirit. The written law kills, but the Spirit gives life.

If the ministry of death, carved in writing on stone, was inaugurated with such glory that the Israelites could not look on Moses' face because of the glory that shone on it (even though it was a fading glory), how much greater will be the glory of the ministry of the Spirit? If the ministry of the covenant that condemned had glory, greater by far is the glory of the ministry that justifies. Indeed, when you compare that limited glory with this surpassing glory, the former should be declared no glory at all. If what was destined to pass away was given in glory, greater by far is the glory that endures.

This is the Word of the Lord.

Responsorial Psalm   Ps 99, 5. 6. 7. 8. 9

℞. (9) Holy is the Lord our God.

Extol the Lord, our God,
   and worship at his footstool;
   holy is he!

℟. Holy is the Lord our God.

Moses and Aaron were among his priests,
  and Samuel, among those who called upon
    his name;
  they called upon the Lord, and he answered
    them.

℟. Holy is the Lord our God.

From the pillar of cloud he spoke to them;
  they heard his decrees and the law he gave
    them.

℟. Holy is the Lord our God.

O Lord, our God, you answered them;
  a forgiving God you were to them,
  though requiting their misdeeds.

℟. Holy is the Lord our God.

Extol the Lord, our God,
  and worship at his holy mountain;
  for holy is the Lord, our God.

℟. Holy is the Lord our God.

Year II

READING I   1 Kgs 18, 20-39

A reading from the first book of Kings

Let this people know that you are the Lord God and are
winning back their hearts.

**Ahab sent to all the Israelites and had the
prophets assemble on Mount Carmel.**

Elijah appealed to all the people and said,
"How long will you straddle the issue? If the
Lord is God, follow him; if Baal, follow him."
The people, however, did not answer him. So
Elijah said to the people, "I am the only surviv-
ing prophet of the Lord, and there are four hundred and fifty prophets of Baal. Give us two
young bulls. Let them choose one, cut it into
pieces, and place it on the wood, but start no
fire. I shall prepare the other and place it on
the wood, but shall start no fire. You shall call
on your gods, and I will call on the Lord.
The God who answers with fire is God."
All the people answered, "Agreed!"

Elijah then said to the prophets of Baal,
"Choose one young bull and prepare it first, for
there are more of you. Call upon your gods, but
do not start the fire." Taking the young bull
that was turned over to them, they prepared it
and called on Baal from morning to noon, saying, "Answer us, Baal!" But there was no

sound, and no one answering. And they hopped
around the altar they had prepared. When it
was noon, Elijah taunted them: "Call louder,
for he is a god and may be meditating, or may
have retired, or may be on a journey. Perhaps
he is asleep and must be awakened." They
called out louder and slashed themselves with
swords and spears, as was their custom, until
blood gushed over them. Noon passed and they
remained in a prophetic state until the time for
offering sacrifice. But there was not a sound;
no one answered, and no one was listening.

Then Elijah said to all the people, "Come
here to me." When they had done so, he repaired the altar of the Lord which had been
destroyed. He took twelve stones, for the number of tribes of the sons of Jacob, to whom the
Lord had said, "Your name shall be Israel." He
built an altar in honor of the Lord with the
stones, and made a trench around the altar
large enough for two seahs of grain. When he
had arranged the wood, he cut up the young
bull and laid it on the wood. "Fill four jars with
water," he said, "and pour it over the holocaust
and over the wood." "Do it again," he said, and
they did it again. "Do it a third time," he said,
and they did it a third time. The water flowed
around the altar, and the trench was filled with
the water.

At the time for offering sacrifice, the prophet
Elijah came forward and said, "Lord, God of
Abraham, Isaac, and Israel, let it be known this
day that you are God in Israel and that I am
your servant and have done all these things by
your command. Answer me, Lord! Answer me,
that this people may know that you, Lord, are
God and that you have brought them back to
their senses." The Lord's fire came down and
consumed the holocaust, wood, stones, and
dust, and it lapped up the water in the trench.
Seeing this, all the people fell prostrate and
said, "The Lord is God! The Lord is God!"

This is the Word of the Lord.

Responsorial Psalm   Ps 16, 1-2. 4. 5. 8. 11

℟. (1) Keep me safe, O God;
  you are my hope.

Keep me, O God, for in you I take refuge;
  I say to the Lord, "My Lord are you."
℟. Keep me safe, O God;
  you are my hope.
They multiply their sorrows
  who court other gods.
Blood libations to them I will not pour out,
  nor will I take their names upon my lips.
℟. Keep me safe, O God;
  you are my hope.
O Lord, my allotted portion and my cup,
  you it is who hold fast my lot.
I set the Lord ever before me;
  with him at my right hand I shall not be
  disturbed.
℟. Keep me safe, O God;
  you are my hope.
You will show me the path to life,
  fullness of joys in your presence,
  the delights at your right hand forever.
℟. Keep me safe, O God;
  you are my hope..

Years I and II

GOSPEL   Mt 5, 17-19
Alleluia

See no. 509.

✠ A reading from the holy gospel according
  to Mark

I have come not to abolish the law, but to complete it.

Jesus said to his disciples: "Do not think that I
have come to abolish the law and the prophets.
I have come, not to abolish them, but to fulfill
them. Of this much I assure you: until heaven
and earth pass away, not the smallest letter of
the law, not the smallest part of a letter, shall
be done away with until it all comes true.
That is why whoever breaks the least significant of these commands and teaches others to
do so shall be called least in the kingdom of
God. Whoever fulfills and teaches these commands shall be great in the kingdom of God."
  This is the gospel of the Lord.

362   **THURSDAY OF THE TENTH
          WEEK OF THE YEAR**

Year I

READING I   2 Cor 3, 15—4, 1. 3-6
A reading from the second letter of Paul to the
            Corinthians

God has shone in our minds to radiate the light of God's
glory.

Even now, when Moses is read a veil covers
the understanding of the Israelites. "But whenever Israel turns to the Lord, the veil will be
removed." The Lord is the Spirit, and where
the Spirit of the Lord is, there is freedom. All
of us, gazing on the Lord's glory with unveiled
faces, are being transformed from glory to
glory into his very image by the Lord who is
the Spirit.
  Because we possess this ministry through
God's mercy, we do not give in to discouragement. If our gospel can be called "veiled" in
any sense, it is such only for those who are
headed toward destruction. Their unbelieving
minds have been blinded by the god of the present age so that they do not see the splendor
of the gospel showing forth the glory of Christ,
the image of God. It is not ourselves we preach
but Christ Jesus as Lord, and ourselves as your
servants for Jesus' sake. For God, who said,
"Let light shine out of darkness," has shone in
our hearts, that we in turn might make known
the glory of God shining on the face of Christ.
  This is the Word of the Lord.

Responsorial Psalm   Ps 85, 9-10. 11-12. 13-14
℟. (10) The glory of the Lord will dwell in our
      land.
I will hear what God proclaims;
  the Lord—for he proclaims peace to his people.
Near indeed is his salvation to those who fear
  him,
  glory dwelling in our land.
℟. The glory of the Lord will dwell in our land.
Kindness and truth shall meet;
  justice and peace shall kiss.

Truth shall spring out of the earth,
  and justice shall look down from heaven.
℞. The glory of the Lord will dwell in our land.
The Lord himself will give his benefits;
  our land shall yield its increase.
Justice shall walk before him,
  and salvation, along the way of his steps.
℞. The glory of the Lord will dwell in our land.

READING I   Year II   1 Kgs 18, 41-46

A reading from the first book of Kings

Elijah prayed and the rain fell in torrents (Jas 5, 18).

Elijah said to Ahab, "Go up, eat and drink, for there is the sound of a heavy rain." So Ahab went up to eat and drink, while Elijah climbed to the top of Carmel, crouched down to the earth, and put his head between his knees. "Climb up and look out to sea," he directed his servant, who went up and looked, but reported, "There is nothing." Seven times he said, "Go, look again!" And the seventh time the youth reported, "There is a cloud as small as a man's hand rising from the sea." Elijah said, "Go and say to Ahab, 'Harness up and leave the mountain before the rain stops you.' " In a trice, the sky grew dark with clouds and wind, and a heavy rain fell. Ahab mounted his chariot and made for Jezreel. But the hand of the Lord was on Elijah, who girded up his clothing and ran before Ahab as far as the approaches to Jezreel.

This is the Word of the Lord.

Responsorial Psalm   Ps 65, 10. 10-11. 12-13

℞. (2) It is right to praise you in Zion, O God.
You have visited the land and watered it;
  greatly have you enriched it.
God's watercourses are filled;
  you have prepared the grain.
℞. It is right to praise you in Zion, O God.
Thus have you prepared the land: drenching its
    furrows,
  breaking up its clods,
Softening it with showers,
  blessing its yield.
℞. It is right to praise you in Zion, O God.

You have crowned the year with your bounty,
  and your paths overflow with a rich harvest;
The untilled meadows overflow with it,
  and rejoicing clothes the hills.
℞. It is right to praise you in Zion, O God.

GOSPEL   Years I and II   Mt 5, 20-26
Alleluia

See no. 509.

✠ **A reading from the holy gospel according to Matthew**

He who is angry with his brother will be judged for it.

Jesus said to his disciples: "I tell you, unless your holiness surpasses that of the scribes and Pharisees you shall not enter the kingdom of God.

"You have heard the commandment imposed on your forefathers, 'You shall not commit murder; every murderer shall be liable to judgment.' What I say to you is: everyone who grows angry with his brother shall be liable to judgment; any man who uses abusive language toward his brother shall be answerable to the Sanhedrin, and if he holds him in contempt he risks the fires of Gehenna. If you bring your gift to the altar and there recall that your brother has anything against you, leave your gift at the altar, go first to be reconciled with your brother, and then come and offer your gift. Lose no time; settle with your opponent while on your way to court with him. Otherwise your opponent may hand you over to the judge, who will hand you over to the guard, who will throw you into prison. I warn you, you will not be released until you have paid the last penny."

This is the gospel of the Lord.

**363   FRIDAY OF THE TENTH
WEEK OF THE YEAR**

Year I

READING I   2 Cor 4, 7-15

**A reading from the second letter of Paul to the
Corinthians**

He who raised the Lord Jesus to life will raise us with him
in our turn.

The treasure [of the knowledge of the glory of
God] we possess in earthen vessels to make it
clear that its surpassing power comes from
God and not from us. We are afflicted in every
way possible, but we are not crushed; full of
doubts, we never despair. We are persecuted
but never abandoned; we are struck down but
never destroyed. Continually we carry about in
our bodies the dying of Jesus, so that in our
bodies the life of Jesus also may be revealed.
While we live we are constantly being delivered to death for Jesus' sake, so that the life
of Jesus may be revealed in our mortal flesh.
Death is at work in us, but life in you. We have
that spirit of faith of which the Scripture says,
"Because I believed, I spoke out." We believe
and so we speak, knowing that he who raised
up the Lord Jesus will raise us up along with
Jesus and place both us and you in his presence. Indeed, everything is ordered to your
benefit, so that the grace bestowed in abundance may bring greater glory to God because
they who give thanks are many.
This is the Word of the Lord.

Responsorial Psalm   Ps 116, 10-11. 15-16. 17-18

℟. (17) To you, Lord, I will offer a sacrifice of
praise.
I believed, even when I said,
"I am greatly afflicted";
I said in my alarm,
"No man is dependable."
℟. To you, Lord, I will offer a sacrifice of
praise.
Precious in the eyes of the Lord
is the death of his faithful ones.
O Lord, I am your servant;

I am your servant, the son of your handmaid;
you have loosed my bonds.
℟. To you, Lord, I will offer a sacrifice of
praise.
To you will I offer sacrifice of thanksgiving,
and I will call upon the name of the Lord.
My vows to the Lord I will pay
in the presence of all his people.
℟. To you, Lord, I will offer a sacrifice of
praise.
℟. Or: Alleluia.

Year II

READING I   1 Kgs 19, 9. 11-16

A reading from the first book of Kings

Stand on the mountain before the Lord God.

Elijah came [from the mountain of God,
Horeb] to a cave, where he took shelter. But
the word of the Lord came to him and said, "Go
outside and stand on the mountain before the
Lord; the Lord will be passing by." A strong
and heavy wind was rending the mountains
and crushing rocks before the Lord—but the
Lord was not in the wind. After the wind there
was an earthquake—but the Lord was not in
the earthquake. After the earthquake there
was fire—but the Lord was not in the fire. After the fire there was a tiny whispering sound.
When he heard this Elijah hid his face in his
cloak and went and stood at the entrance of
the cave. A voice said to him, "Elijah, why are
you here?" He replied, "I have been most zealous for the Lord, the God of hosts. But the
Israelites have forsaken your covenant, torn
down your altars, and put your prophets to the
sword. I alone am left, and they seek to take
my life." "Go, take the road back to the desert
near Damascus," the Lord said to him. "When
you arrive, you shall anoint Hazael as king of
Aram. Then you shall anoint Jehu, son of
Nimshi, as king of Israel, and Elisha, son of
Shaphat of Abel-meholah, as prophet to succeed you."
This is the Word of the Lord.

Responsorial Psalm   Ps 27, 7-8. 8-9. 13-14

℟. (8) I long to see your face, O Lord.

Hear, O Lord, the sound of my call;
   have pity on me, and answer me.
Of you my heart speaks; you my glance seeks.
℟. I long to see your face, O Lord.
Your presence, O Lord, I seek.
   Hide not your face from me;
Do not in anger repel your servant.
You are my helper: cast me not off.
℟. I long to see your face, O Lord.
I believe that I shall see the bounty of the Lord
   in the land of the living.
Wait for the Lord with courage;
   be stouthearted, and wait for the Lord.
℟. I long to see your face, O Lord.

Years I and II

GOSPEL   Mt 5, 27-32
Alleluia
See no. 509.

✠ A reading from the holy gospel according
           to Matthew
If a man looks at a woman lustfully, he has already sinned.

Jesus said to his disciples: "You have heard the commandment, 'You shall not commit adultery.' What I say to you is: anyone who looks lustfully at a woman has already committed adultery with her in his thoughts. If your right eye is your trouble, gouge it out and throw it away! Better to lose part of your body than to have it all cast into Gehenna. Again, if your right hand is your trouble, cut it off and throw it away! Better to lose part of your body than to have it all cast into Gehenna.

"It was also said, 'Whenever a man divorces his wife, he must give her a decree of divorce.' What I say to you is: everyone who divorces his wife—lewd conduct is a separate case—forces her to commit adultery. The man who marries a divorced woman likewise commits adultery."

This is the gospel of the Lord.

Year I

READING I   2 Cor 5, 14-21
**A reading from the second letter of Paul to the
Corinthians**
For our sake God made the sinless one into sin.

The love of Christ impels us who have reached the conviction that since one died for all, all died. He died for all so that those who live might live no longer for themselves, but for him who for their sakes died and was raised up.

Because of this we no longer look on anyone in terms of mere human judgment. If at one time we so regarded Christ, we no longer know him by this standard. This means that if anyone is in Christ, he is a new creation. The old order has passed away; now all is new! All this has been done by God, who has reconciled us to himself through Christ and has given us the ministry of reconciliation. I mean that God, in Christ, was reconciling the world to himself, not counting men's transgressions against them, and that he has entrusted the message of reconciliation to us. This makes us ambassadors for Christ, God as it were appealing through us. We implore you, in Christ's name: be reconciled to God! For our sakes God made him who did not know sin to be sin, so that in him we might become the very holiness of God.

This is the Word of the Lord.

Responsorial Psalm   Ps 103, 1-2. 3-4. 8-9. 11-12

℟. (8) The Lord is kind and merciful.
Bless the Lord, O my soul;
   and all my being, bless his holy name.
Bless the Lord, O my soul,
   and forget not all his benefits.
℟. The Lord is kind and merciful.
He pardons all your iniquities,
   he heals all your ills.
He redeems your life from destruction,
   he crowns you with kindness and compassion.
℟. The Lord is kind and merciful.

Merciful and gracious is the Lord,
    slow to anger and abounding in kindness.
He will not always chide,
    nor does he keep his wrath forever.
℟. The Lord is kind and merciful.
For as the heavens are high above the earth,
    so surpassing is his kindness toward those
    who fear him.
As far as the east is from the west,
    so far has he put our transgressions from us.
℟. The Lord is kind and merciful.

Year II

READING I   1 Kgs 19, 19-21

A reading from the first book of Kings

Elisha rose and followed Elijah and became his servant.

Elijah set out, and came upon Elisha, son of
Shaphat, as he was plowing with twelve yoke
of oxen; he was following the twelfth. Elijah
went over to him and threw his cloak over him.
Elisha left the oxen, ran after Elijah, and said,
"Please, let me kiss my father and mother
goodbye, and I will follow you." "Go back!"
Elijah answered. "Have I done anything to
you?" Elisha left him and, taking the yoke of
oxen, slaughtered them; he used the plowing
equipment for fuel to boil their flesh, and gave
it to his people to eat. Then he left and followed
Elijah as his attendant.
        This is the Word of the Lord.

Responsorial Psalm   Ps 16, 1-2. 5. 7-8. 9-10

℟. (5) You are my inheritance, O Lord.
Keep me, O God, for in you I take refuge;
    I say to the Lord, "My Lord are you."
O Lord, my allotted portion and my cup,
    you it is who hold fast my lot.
℟. You are my inheritance, O Lord.
I bless the Lord who counsels me;
    even in the night my heart exhorts me.
I set the Lord ever before me;
    with him at my right hand I shall not be
    disturbed.
℟. You are my inheritance, O Lord.
Therefore my heart is glad and my soul re-
    joices,
    my body, too, abides in confidence;

Because you will not abandon my soul to the
    nether world,
    nor will you suffer your faithful one to un-
    dergo corruption.
℟. You are my inheritance, O Lord.

Years I and II

GOSPEL   Mt 5, 33-37
Alleluia

See no. 509.

✠ **A reading from the holy gospel according
        to Matthew**

I say to you do not swear at all.

Jesus said to his disciples: "You have heard the
commandment imposed on your forefathers,
'Do not take a false oath; rather, make good to
the Lord all your pledges.' What I tell you is:
do not swear at all. Do not swear by heaven (it
is God's throne), nor by the earth (it is his footstool), nor by Jerusalem (it is the city of the
great King); do not swear by your head (you
cannot make a single hair white or black). Say,
'Yes' when you mean 'Yes' and 'No' when you
mean 'No.' Anything beyond that is from the
evil one."
        This is the gospel of the Lord.

---

365   **MONDAY OF THE ELEVENTH
            WEEK OF THE YEAR**

Year I

READING I   2 Cor 6, 1-10

**A reading from the second letter of Paul to the
                Corinthians**

We have shown that we are the servants of God.

As your fellow workers we beg you not to receive the grace of God in vain. For he says, "In
an acceptable time I have heard you; on a day
of salvation I have helped you." Now is the
acceptable time! Now is the day of salvation!
    We avoid giving anyone offense so that our
ministry may not be blamed. On the contrary,
in all that we do we strive to present ourselves·
as ministers of God, acting with patient endurance amid trials, difficulties, distresses, beatings, imprisonments, and riots; as men familiar

with hard work, sleepless nights, and fastings; conducting ourselves with innocence, knowledge, and patience, in the Holy Spirit, in sincere love; as men with the message of truth and the power of God, wielding the weapons of righteousness with right hand and left, whether honored or dishonored, spoken of well or ill. We are called imposters, yet we are truthful; nobodies who in fact are well known; dead, yet here we are alive; punished, but not put to death; sorrowful, though we are always rejoicing; poor, yet we enrich many. We seem to have nothing, yet everything is ours!

This is the Word of the Lord.

Responsorial Psalm   Ps 98, 1. 2-3. 3-4

℟. (2) The Lord has made known his salvation.
Sing to the Lord a new song,
    for he has done wondrous deeds;
His right hand has won victory for him,
    his holy arm.
℟. The Lord has made known his salvation.
The Lord has made his salvation known:
    in the sight of the nations he has revealed his
        justice.
He has remembered his kindness and his faithfulness
    toward the house of Israel.
℟. The Lord has made known his salvation.
All the ends of the earth have seen
    the salvation by our God.
Sing joyfully to the Lord, all you lands;
    break into song; sing praise.
℟. The Lord has made known his salvation.

Year II

READING I   1 Kgs 21, 1-16

A reading from the first book of Kings
Naboth has been stoned to death.

Naboth the Jezreelite had a vineyard in Jezreel next to the palace of Ahab, king of Samaria. Ahab said to Naboth, "Give me your vineyard to be my vegetable garden, since it is close by, next to my house. I will give you a better vineyard in exchange, or, if you prefer, I will give you its value in money." "The Lord forbid," Naboth answered him, "that I should give you

my ancestral heritage." Ahab went home disturbed and angry at the answer Naboth the Jezreelite had made to him: "I will not give you my ancestral heritage." Lying down on his bed, he turned away from food and would not eat.

His wife Jezebel came to him and said to him, "Why are you so angry that you will not eat?" He answered her, "Because I spoke to Naboth the Jezreelite and said to him, 'Sell me your vineyard, or, if you prefer, I will give you a vineyard in exchange.' But he refused to let me have his vineyard." "A fine ruler over Israel you are indeed!" his wife Jezebel said to him. "Get up. Eat and be cheerful. I will obtain the vineyard of Naboth the Jezreelite for you."

So she wrote letters in Ahab's name and, having sealed them with his seal, sent them to the elders and to the nobles who lived in the same city with Naboth. This is what she wrote in the letters: "Proclaim a fast and set Naboth at the head of the people. Next, get two scoundrels to face him and accuse him of having cursed God and king. Then take him out and stone him to death." His fellow citizens—the elders and the nobles who dwelt in his city—did as Jezebel had ordered them in writing, through the letters she had sent them. They proclaimed a fast and placed Naboth at the head of the people. Two scoundrels came in and confronted him with the accusation, "Naboth has cursed God and king." And they led him out of the city and stoned him to death. Then they sent the information to Jezebel that Naboth had been stoned to death.

When Jezebel learned that Naboth had been stoned to death, she said to Ahab, "Go on, take possession of the vineyard of Naboth the Jezreelite which he refused to sell you, because Naboth is not alive, but dead." On hearing that Naboth was dead, Ahab started off on his way down to the vineyard of Naboth the Jezreelite, to take possession of it.

This is the Word of the Lord.

Responsorial Psalm   Ps 5, 2-3. 5-6. 7

℟. (2) Lord, listen to my groaning.
Hearken to my words, O Lord,
    attend to my sighing.

Heed my call for help,
my king and my God!
R̂. Lord, listen to my groaning.
At dawn I bring my plea expectantly before
you.
For you, O God, delight not in wickedness;
no evil man remains with you;
The arrogant may not stand in your sight.
R̂. Lord, listen to my groaning.
You hate all evildoers.
You destroy all who speak falsehood;
The bloodthirsty and the deceitful
the Lord abhors.
R̂. Lord, listen to my groaning.

Years I and II

GOSPEL   Mt 5, 38-42
Alleluia

See no. 509.

✠ A reading from the holy gospel according
to Matthew
I say to you, offer the wicked man no resistance.

Jesus said to his disciples: "You have heard the
commandment, 'An eye for an eye, a tooth for
a tooth.' But what I say to you is: offer no resistance to injury. When a person strikes you
on the right cheek, turn and offer him the
other. If anyone wants to go to law over your
shirt, hand him your coat as well. Should anyone press you into service for one mile, go with
him two miles. Give to the man who begs from
you. Do not turn your back on the borrower."
This is the gospel of the Lord.

366   **TUESDAY OF THE ELEVENTH**
WEEK OF THE YEAR

Year I

READING I   2 Cor 8, 1-9

A reading from the second letter of Paul to the
Corinthians
Christ became poor for our sake.

Brothers, I should like you to know of the grace
of God conferred on the churches of Macedonia. In the midst of severe trial their overflowing joy and deep poverty have produced

an abundant generosity. According to their
means—indeed I can testify even beyond their
means—and voluntarily, they begged us insistently for the favor of sharing in this service to
members of the church. Beyond our hopes they
first gave themselves to God and then to us by
the will of God. That is why I have exhorted
Titus, who had already begun this work of
charity among you, to bring it to successful
completion: that just as you are rich in every
respect, in faith and discourse, in knowledge,
in total concern, and in our love for you, you
may also abound in this charity.

I am not giving an order but simply testing
your generous love against the concern which
others show. You are well acquainted with the
favor shown you by our Lord Jesus Christ:
how for your sake he made himself poor
though he was rich, so that you might become
rich by his poverty.
This is the Word of the Lord.

Responsorial Psalm   Ps 146, 2. 5-6. 7. 8-9

R̂. (2) Praise the Lord, my soul!
I will praise the Lord all my life;
I will sing praise to my God while I live.
R̂. Praise the Lord, my soul!
Happy he whose help is the God of Jacob,
whose hope is in the Lord, his God,
Who made heaven and earth,
the sea and all that is in them.
R̂. Praise the Lord, my soul!
Who keeps faith forever,
secures justice for the oppressed,
gives food to the hungry.
The Lord sets captives free.
R̂. Praise the Lord, my soul!
The Lord gives sight to the blind.
The Lord raises up those that were bowed
down;
The Lord loves the just.
The Lord protects strangers.
R̂. Praise the Lord, my soul!
R̂. Or: Alleluia.

READING I

1 Kgs 21, 17-29

A reading from the first book of Kings

Israel was led into sin.

[After the death of Naboth] the Lord said to Elijah the Tishbite: "Start down to meet Ahab, king of Israel, who rules in Samaria. He will be in the vineyard of Naboth, of which he has come to take possession. This is what you shall tell him, 'The Lord says: After murdering, do you also take possession? For this, the Lord says: In the place where the dogs licked up the blood of Naboth, the dogs shall lick up your blood, too.' " "Have you found me out, my enemy?" Ahab said to Elijah. "Yes," he answered. "Because you have given yourself up to doing evil in the Lord's sight, I am bringing evil upon you: I will destroy you and will cut off every male in Ahab's line, whether slave or freeman, in Israel. I will make your house like that of Jeroboam, son of Nebat, and like that of Baasha, son of Ahijah, because of how you have provoked me by leading Israel into sin." (Against Jezebel, too, the Lord declared, "The dogs shall devour Jezebel in the district of Jezreel.") "When one of Ahab's line dies in the city, dogs will devour him; when one of them dies in the field, the birds of the sky will devour him." Indeed, no one gave himself up to the doing of evil in the sight of the Lord as did Ahab, urged on by his wife Jezebel. He became completely abominable by following idols, just as the Amorites had done, whom the Lord drove out before the Israelites.

When Ahab heard these words, he tore his garments and put on sackcloth over his bare flesh. He fasted, slept in the sackcloth, and went about subdued. Then the Lord said to Elijah the Tishbite, "Have you seen that Ahab has humbled himself before me? Since he has humbled himself before me, I will not bring the evil in his time. I will bring the evil upon his house during the reign of his son."

This is the Word of the Lord.

Responsorial Psalm

Ps 51, 3-4. 5-6. 11. 16

℟. (3) Be merciful, O Lord, for we have sinned.

Have mercy on me, O God, in your goodness;
  in the greatness of your compassion wipe
  out my offense.
Thoroughly wash me from my guilt
  and of my sin cleanse me.

℟. Be merciful, O Lord, for we have sinned.

For I acknowledge my offense,
  and my sin is before me always:
"Against you only have I sinned,
  and done what is evil in your sight."

℟. Be merciful, O Lord, for we have sinned.

Turn away your face from my sins,
  and blot out all my guilt.
Free me from blood guilt, O God, my saving
  God;
  then my tongue shall revel in your justice.

℟. Be merciful, O Lord, for we have sinned.

GOSPEL

Mt 5, 43-48

Alleluia

See no. 509.

✠ **A reading from the holy gospel according
    to Matthew**

Love your enemies.

Jesus said to his disciples: "You have heard the commandment, 'You shall love your countryman but hate your enemy.' My command to you is: love your enemies, pray for your persecutors. This will prove that you are sons of your heavenly Father, for his sun rises on the bad and the good, he rains on the just and the unjust. If you love those who love you, what merit is there in that? Do not tax collectors do as much? And if you greet your brothers only, what is so praiseworthy about that? Do not pagans do as much? In a word, you must be perfected as your heavenly Father is perfect."

This is the gospel of the Lord.

**367   WEDNESDAY OF THE ELEVENTH
WEEK OF THE YEAR**

READING I   2 Cor 9, 6-11

**A reading from the second letter of Paul to the
Corinthians**

God loves a cheerful giver.

Let me say this much: He who sows sparingly
will reap sparingly, and he who sows bountifully will reap bountifully. Everyone must give
according to what he has inwardly decided;
not sadly, not grudgingly, for God loves a
cheerful giver. God can multiply his favors
among you so that you may always have
enough of everything and even a surplus for
good works, as it is written:
"He scattered abroad and gave to the poor,
   his justice endures forever."
He who supplies seed for the sower and bread
for the eater will provide in abundance; he will
multiply the seed you sow and increase your
generous yield. In every way your liberality is
enriched; through us it results in thanks offered to God.
           This is the Word of the Lord.

Responsorial Psalm   Ps 112, 1-2. 3-4. 9

℟. (1) Happy the man who fears the Lord.
Happy the man who fears the Lord,
   who greatly delights in his commands.
His posterity shall be mighty upon the earth;
   the upright generation shall be blessed.
℟. Happy the man who fears the Lord.
Wealth and riches shall be in his house;
   his generosity shall endure forever.
The Lord dawns through the darkness, a light
   for the upright;
   he is gracious and merciful and just.
℟. Happy the man who fears the Lord.
Lavishly he gives to the poor;
   his generosity shall endure forever;
   his horn shall be exalted in glory.
℟. Happy the man who fears the Lord.
℟. Or: Alleluia.

READING I   2 Kgs 2, 1. 6-14

A reading from the second book of Kings

A chariot of fire appeared and Elijah went up to heaven.

When the Lord was about to take Elijah up to
heaven in a whirlwind, [they went together to
Jericho]. Elijah said to Elisha, "Please stay
here; the Lord has sent me on to the Jordan."
"As the Lord lives, and as you yourself live,"
Elisha replied, "I will not leave you." And so
the two went on together. Fifty of the guild
prophets followed, and when the two stopped
at the Jordan, stood facing them at a distance.
Elijah took his mantle, rolled it up and struck
the water, which divided, and both crossed
over on dry ground.
   When they had crossed over, Elijah said to
Elisha, "Ask for whatever I may do for you,
before I am taken from you." Elisha answered,
"May I receive a double portion of your spirit?"
"You have asked something that is not easy,"
he replied. "Still, if you see me taken up from
you, your wish will be granted; otherwise not."
As they walked on conversing, a flaming
chariot and flaming horses came between
them, and Elijah went up to heaven in a whirlwind. When Elisha saw it happen he cried out,
"My father! my father! Israel's chariots and
drivers!" But when he could no longer see him,
Elisha gripped his own garment and tore it in
two.
   Then he picked up Elijah's mantle which had
fallen from him, and went back and stood at
the bank of the Jordan. Wielding the mantle
which had fallen from Elijah, he struck the
water in his turn and said, "Where is the Lord,
the God of Elijah?" When Elisha struck the
water it divided and he crossed over.
           This is the Word of the Lord.

Responsorial Psalm   Ps 31, 20. 21. 24

℟. (25) Let your hearts take comfort,
   all who hope in the Lord.
How great is the goodness, O Lord,
   **which you have in store for those who fear
   you,**

And which, toward those who take refuge in
    you,
    you show in the sight of men.
℞. Let your hearts take comfort,
    all who hope in the Lord.
You hide them in the shelter of your presence
    from the plottings of men;
You screen them within your abode
    from the strife of tongues.
℞. Let your hearts take comfort,
    all who hope in the Lord.
Love the Lord, all you his faithful ones!
    The Lord keeps those who are constant,
    but more than requites those who act
    proudly.
℞. Let your hearts take comfort,
    all who hope in the Lord.

Years I and II

GOSPEL   Mt 6, 1-6. 16-18
Alleluia

See no. 509.

✠ A reading from the holy gospel according
    to Matthew
Your Father who sees all that is done in secret will reward
you.

Jesus said to his disciples: "Be on guard
against performing religious acts for people to
see. Otherwise expect no recompense from
your heavenly Father. When you give alms, for
example, do not blow a horn before you in
synagogues and streets like hypocrites looking
for applause. You can be sure of this much,
they are already repaid. In giving alms you are
not to let your left hand know what your right
hand is doing. Keep your deeds of mercy secret, and your Father who sees in secret will
repay you.

    "When you are praying, do not behave like
the hypocrites who love to stand and pray in
synagogues or on street corners in order to be
noticed. I give you my word, they are already
repaid. Whenever you pray, go to your room,
close your door, and pray to your Father in
private.

    "When you fast, you are not to look glum as
the hypocrites do. They change the appearance
of their faces so that others may see they are

fasting. I assure you, they are already repaid.
When you fast, see to it that you groom your
hair and wash your face. In that way no one
can see you are fasting but your Father who is
hidden; and your Father who sees what is
hidden will repay you."
    This is the gospel of the Lord.

---

368   **THURSDAY OF THE ELEVENTH
           WEEK OF THE YEAR**

Year I

READING I   2 Cor 11, 1-11
**A reading from the second letter of Paul to the
    Corinthians**
I preached the gospel of God to you freely.

You must endure a little of my folly. Put up
with me, I beg you! I am jealous of you with the
jealousy of God himself, since I have given you
in marriage to one husband, presenting you as
a chaste virgin to Christ. My fear is that, just as
the serpent seduced Eve by his cunning, your
thoughts may be corrupted and you may fall
away from your sincere and complete devotion
to Christ. I say this because when someone
comes preaching another Jesus than the one
we preached, or when you receive a different
spirit than the one you have received, or a
gospel other than the gospel you accepted,
you seem to endure it quite well. I consider
myself inferior to the "super apostles" in nothing. I may be unskilled in speech but I know
that I am not lacking in knowledge. We have
made this evident to you in every conceivable
way.

    Could I have done wrong when I preached
the gospel of God to you free of charge, hum-
bling myself with a view to exalting you? I
robbed other churches, I accepted support from
them in order to minister to you. When I was
with you and in want I was a burden to none
of you, for the brothers who came from Macedonia supplied my needs. In every way possible I kept myself from being burdensome to
you, and I shall continue to do so. I swear by
the Christ who is in me that this boast of mine

will not cease in the regions of Achaia! Why?
Because I do not love you? God knows I do.
This is the Word of the Lord.

Responsorial Psalm   Ps 111, 1-2. 3-4. 7-8

℟. (7) Your works, O Lord, are justice and
truth.
I will give thanks to the Lord with all my heart
in the company and assembly of the just.
Great are the works of the Lord,
exquisite in all their delights.
℟. Your works, O Lord, are justice and truth.
Majesty and glory are his work,
and his justice endures forever.
He has won renown for his wondrous deeds;
gracious and merciful is the Lord.
℟. Your works, O Lord, are justice and truth.
The works of his hands are faithful and just;
sure are all his precepts,
Reliable forever and ever,
wrought in truth and equity.
℟. Your works, O Lord, are justice and truth.
℟. Or: Alleluia.

Year II

READING I   Sir 48, 1-14

A reading from the book of Sirach

Elijah was shrouded in a whirlwind, and Elisha was filled
with his spirit.

Like a fire there appeared the prophet Elijah
whose words were as a flaming furnace.
Their staff of bread he shattered,
in his zeal he reduced them to straits;
By God's word he shut up the heavens
and three times brought down fire.
How awesome are you, Elijah!
Whose glory is equal to yours?
You brought a dead man back to life
from the nether world, by the will of the
Lord.
You sent kings down to destruction,
and nobles, from their beds of sickness.
You heard threats at Sinai,
at Horeb avenging judgments.
You anointed kings who should inflict ven-
geance,
and a prophet as your successor.

You were taken aloft in a whirlwind,
in a chariot with fiery horses.
You are destined, it is written, in time to come
to put an end to wrath before the day of the
Lord,
To turn back the hearts of fathers toward their
sons,
and to re-establish the tribes of Jacob.
Blessed is he who shall have seen you before
he dies,
O Elijah, enveloped in the whirlwind!

Then Elisha, filled with a twofold portion of his
spirit,
wrought many marvels by his mere word.
During his lifetime he feared no one,
nor was any man able to intimidate his will.
Nothing was beyond his power;
beneath him flesh was brought back into life.
In life he performed wonders,
and after death, marvelous deeds.
This is the Word of the Lord.

Responsorial Psalm   Ps 97, 1-2. 3-4. 5-6. 7

℟. (12) Let good men rejoice in the Lord.
The Lord is king; let the earth rejoice;
let the many isles be glad.
Clouds and darkness are round about him,
justice and judgment are the foundation of
his throne.
℟. Let good men rejoice in the Lord.
Fire goes before him
and consumes his foes round about.
His lightnings illumine the world;
the earth sees and trembles.
℟. Let good men rejoice in the Lord.
The mountains melt like wax before the Lord,
before the Lord of all the earth.
The heavens proclaim his justice,
and all peoples see his glory.
℟. Let good men rejoice in the Lord.
All who worship graven things are put to
shame,
who glory in the things of nought;
all gods are prostrate before him.
℟. Let good men rejoice in the Lord.

GOSPEL   Mt 6, 7-15
Alleluia

See no. 509.

✠ A reading from the holy gospel according
to Matthew

You should pray like this: Our Father . . .

Jesus said to his disciples: "In your prayer do
not rattle on like the pagans. They think they
will win a hearing by the sheer multiplication
of words. Do not imitate them. Your Father
knows what you need before you ask him.
This is how you are to pray:

'Our Father in heaven,
hallowed be your name,
your kingdom come,
your will be done
on earth as it is in heaven.
Give us today our daily bread,
and forgive us the wrong we have done
as we forgive those who wrong us.
Subject us not to the trial
but deliver us from the evil one.'

"If you forgive the faults of others, your heavenly Father will forgive you yours. If you do
not forgive others, neither will your Father forgive you."

This is the gospel of the Lord.

369   **FRIDAY OF THE ELEVENTH
WEEK OF THE YEAR**

Year I

READING I   2 Cor 11, 18. 21-30

**A reading from the second letter of Paul to the
Corinthians**

Besides all the other important things, there is my daily
preoccupation, my anxiety for all the churches.

Since many are bragging about their human
distinctions, I too will boast. To my shame I
must confess that we have been too weak to do
such things. But what anyone else dares to
claim—I speak with absolute foolishness now
—I, too, will dare. Are they Hebrews? So am I!
Are they Israelites? So am I! Are they the seed
of Abraham? So am I! Are they ministers of
Christ? Now I am really talking like a fool—I
am more: with my many more labors and imprisonments, with far worse beatings and frequent brushes with death. Five times at the
hands of the Jews I received forty lashes less
one; three times I was beaten with rods; I was
stoned once, shipwrecked three times; I passed
a day and a night on the sea. I traveled continually, endangered by floods, robbers, my
own people, the Gentiles; imperiled in the city,
in the desert, at sea, by false brothers; enduring labor, hardship, many sleepless nights; in
hunger and thirst and frequent fastings, in cold
and nakedness. Leaving other sufferings un-
mentioned, there is that daily tension pressing
on me, my anxiety for all the churches. Who is
weak that I am not affected by it? Who is scan-
dalized that I am not aflame with indignation?
This is the Word of the Lord.

Responsorial Psalm   Ps 34, 2-3. 4-5. 6-7

℟. (18) From all their afflictions God will deliver the just.

I will bless the Lord at all times;
his praise shall be ever in my mouth.
Let my soul glory in the Lord;
the lowly will hear me and be glad.

℟. From all their afflictions God will deliver
the just.

Glorify the Lord with me,
let us together extol his name.
I sought the Lord, and he answered me
and delivered me from all my fears.

℟. From all their afflictions God will deliver
the just.

Look to him that you may be radiant with joy,
and your faces may not blush with shame.
When the afflicted man called out, the Lord
heard,
and from all his distress he saved him.

℟. From all their afflictions God will deliver
the just.

READING I   2 Kgs 11, 1-4. 9-18. 20

A reading from the second book of Kings

Jehoash was anointed king and they shouted: Long live
the king.

When Athaliah, the mother of Ahaziah, saw
that her son was dead, she began to kill off the
whole royal family. But Jehosheba, daughter of
King Jehoram and sister of Ahaziah, took
Jehoash, his son, and spirited him away, along
with his nurse, from the bedroom where the
princes were about to be slain. She concealed
him from Athaliah, and so he did not die. For
six years he remained hidden in the temple of
the Lord, while Athaliah ruled the land.

But in the seventh year, Jehoiada summoned
the captains of the Carians and of the guards.
He had them come to him in the temple of the
Lord, exacted from them a sworn commitment,
and then showed them the king's son.

The captains did just as Jehoiada the priest
commanded. Each one with his men, both
those going on duty for the sabbath and those
going off duty that week, came to Jehoiada the
priest. He gave the captains King David's
spears and shields, which were in the temple of
the Lord. And the guards, with drawn weapons, lined up from the southern to the northern
limit of the enclosure, surrounding the altar
and the temple on the king's behalf. Then
Jehoiada led out the king's son and put the
crown and the insignia upon him. They proclaimed him king and anointed him, clapping
their hands and shouting, "Long live the king!"

Athaliah heard the noise made by the people,
and appeared before them in the temple of the
Lord. When she saw the king standing by the
pillar, as was the custom, and the captains and
trumpeters near him, with all the people of the
land rejoicing and blowing trumpets, she tore
her garments and cried out, "Treason, treason!" Then Jehoiada the priest instructed the
captains in command of the force: "Bring her
outside through the ranks. If anyone follows
her," he added, "let him die by the sword." He
had given orders that she should not be slain in
the temple of the Lord. She was led out forcibly
to the horse gate of the royal palace, where
she was put to death.

Then Jehoiada made a covenant between the
Lord as one party and the king and the people as the other, by which they would be the
Lord's people; and another covenant, between
the king and the people. Thereupon all the people of the land went to the temple of Baal and
demolished it. They shattered its altars and
images completely, and slew Mattan, the priest
of Baal, before the altars. Jehoiada appointed a
detachment for the temple of the Lord. All the
people of the land rejoiced and the city was
quiet, now that Athaliah had been slain with
the sword at the royal palace.

This is the Word of the Lord.

Responsorial Psalm   Ps 132, 11. 12. 13-14. 17-18

℟. (13) The Lord has chosen Zion for his
     dwelling.

The Lord swore to David
  a firm promise from which he will not with-
     draw:
"Your own offspring
  I will set upon your throne.

℟. The Lord has chosen Zion for his dwelling.

If your sons keep my covenant
  and the decrees which I shall teach them,
Their sons, too, forever
  shall sit upon your throne.

℟. The Lord has chosen Zion for his dwelling.

For the Lord has chosen Zion;
  he prefers her for his dwelling.
"Zion is my resting place forever;
  in her will I dwell, for I prefer her.

℟. The Lord has chosen Zion for his dwelling.

In her will I make a horn to sprout forth for
     David;
  I will place a lamp for my anointed.
His enemies I will clothe with shame,
  but upon him my crown shall shine."

℟. The Lord has chosen Zion for his dwelling.

GOSPEL   Mt 6, 19-23
Alleluia

See no. 509.

✠ A reading from the holy gospel according
to Matthew

Where your treasure is, there will your heart be also.

Jesus said to his disciples: "Do not lay up for
yourselves an earthly treasure. Moths and rust
corrode; thieves break in and steal. Make it
your practice instead to store up heavenly
treasure, which neither moths nor rust corrode
nor thieves break in and steal. Remember,
where your treasure is, there your heart is also.
The eye is the body's lamp. If your eyes are
good, your body will be filled with light; if your
eyes are bad, your body will be in darkness.
And if your light is darkness, how deep the
darkness will be!"

This is the gospel of the Lord.

---

370   **SATURDAY OF THE ELEVENTH
WEEK OF THE YEAR**

Year I

READING I   2 Cor 12, 1-10

**A reading from the second letter of Paul to the
Corinthians**

Gladly will I boast of my weaknesses.

I must go on boasting, however useless it may
be, and speak of visions and revelations of the
Lord. I know a man in Christ who, fourteen
years ago—whether he was in or outside his
body I cannot say, only God can say—a man
who was snatched up to the third heaven. I
know that this man—whether in or outside
his body I do not know, God knows—was
snatched up to Paradise to hear words which
cannot be uttered, words which no man may
speak. About this man I will boast; but I will
do no boasting about myself unless it be about
my weaknesses. And even if I were to boast
it would not be folly in me because I would
only be telling the truth.

But I refrain, lest anyone think more of me
than what he sees in me or hears from my
lips. As to the extraordinary revelations, in
order that I might not become conceited I was
given a thorn in the flesh, an angel of Satan to
beat me and keep me from getting proud. Three

times I begged the Lord that this might leave
me. He said to me, "My grace is enough for
you, for in weakness power reaches perfection." And so I willingly boast of my weaknesses instead, that the power of Christ may
rest upon me.

Therefore I am content with weakness, with
mistreatment, with distress, with persecutions
and difficulties for the sake of Christ; for when
I am powerless, it is then that I am strong.

This is the Word of the Lord.

Responsorial Psalm   Ps 34, 8-9. 10-11. 12-13

℟. (9) Taste and see the goodness of the Lord.
The angel of the Lord encamps
    around those who fear him, and delivers
    them.
Taste and see how good the Lord is;
    happy the man who takes refuge in him.
℟. Taste and see the goodness of the Lord.
Fear the Lord, you his holy ones,
    for nought is lacking to those who fear him.
The great grow poor and hungry;
    but those who seek the Lord want for no
    good thing.
℟. Taste and see the goodness of the Lord.
Come, children, hear me;
    I will teach you the fear of the Lord.
Which of you desires life,
    and takes delight in prosperous days?
℟. Taste and see the goodness of the Lord.

Year II

READING I   2 Chr 24, 17-25

A reading from the second book of Chronicles

They killed Zechariah in the court of the temple.

After the death of Jehoiada, the princes of
Judah came and paid homage to the king, and
the king then listened to them. They forsook
the temple of the Lord, the God of their fathers,
and began to serve the sacred poles and the
idols; and because of this crime of theirs, wrath
came upon Judah and Jerusalem. Although
prophets were sent to them to convert them to
the Lord, the people would not listen to their
warnings. Then the spirit of God possessed
Zechariah, son of Jehoiada the priest. He took

his stand above the people and said to them: "God says, 'Why are you transgressing the Lord's commands, so that you cannot prosper? Because you have abandoned the Lord, he has abandoned you.' " But they conspired against him, and at the king's order they stoned him to death in the court of the Lord's temple. Thus King Joash was unmindful of the devotion shown him by Jehoiada, Zechariah's father, and slew his son. And as he was dying, he said, "May the Lord see and avenge."

At the turn of the year a force of Arameans came up against Joash. They invaded Judah and Jerusalem, did away with all the princes of the people, and sent all their spoil to the king of Damascus. Though the Aramean force came with few men, the Lord surrendered a very large force into their power, because Judah had abandoned the Lord, the God of their fathers. So punishment was meted out to Joash.

This is the Word of the Lord.

Responsorial Psalm   Ps 89, 4-5. 29-30. 31-32. 33-34

℟. (29) For ever I will keep my love for him.
I have made a covenant with my chosen one,
    I have sworn to David my servant:
Forever will I confirm your posterity
    and establish your throne for all generations.
℟. For ever I will keep my love for him.
Forever I will maintain my kindness toward him,
    and my covenant with him stands firm.
I will make his posterity endure forever
    and his throne as the days of heaven.
℟. For ever I will keep my love for him.
If his sons forsake my law
    and walk not according to my ordinances,
If they violate my statutes
    and keep not my commands,
℟. For ever I will keep my love for him.
I will punish their crime with a rod
    and their guilt with stripes.
Yet my kindness I will not take from him,
    nor will I belie my faithfulness.
℟. For ever I will keep my love for him.

GOSPEL   Mt 6, 24-34
Alleluia
See no. 509.

✠ A reading from the holy gospel according to Matthew
Do not worry about tomorrow.

Jesus said to his disciples: "No man can serve two masters. He will either hate one and love the other or be attentive to one and despise the other. You cannot give yourself to God and money. I warn you, then: do not worry about your livelihood, what you are to eat or drink or use for clothing. Is life not more than food? Is not the body more valuable than clothes?

"Look at the birds in the sky. They do not sow or reap, they gather nothing into barns; yet your heavenly Father feeds them. Are not you more important than they? Which of you by worrying can add a moment to his life-span? As for clothes, why be concerned? Learn a lesson from the way the wild flowers grow. They do not work; they do not spin. Yet I assure you, not even Solomon in all his splendor was arrayed like one of these. If God can clothe in such splendor the grass of the field, which blooms today and is thrown on the fire tomorrow, will he not provide much more for you, O weak in faith! Stop worrying, then, over questions like, 'What are we to eat, or what are we to drink, or what are we to wear?' The unbelievers are always running after these things. Your heavenly Father knows all that you need. Seek first his kingship over you, his way of holiness, and all these things will be given you besides. Enough, then, of worrying about tomorrow. Let tomorrow take care of itself. Today has troubles enough of its own."

This is the gospel of the Lord.

371   **MONDAY OF THE TWELFTH**
        WEEK OF THE YEAR

Year I

READING I   Gn 12, 1-9

A reading from the book of Genesis
Abraham went out as God told him.

The Lord said to Abram: "Go forth from the
land of your kinsfolk and from your father's
house to a land that I will show you.
"I will make of you a great nation,
    and I will bless you;
I will make your name great,
    so that you will be a blessing.
I will bless those who bless you
    and curse those who curse you.
All the communities of the earth
    shall find blessing in you."

Abram went as the Lord directed him, and
Lot went with him. Abram was seventy-five
years old when he left Haran. Abram took his
wife Sarai, his brother's son Lot, all the possessions that they had accumulated, and the
persons they had acquired in Haran, and they
set out for the land of Canaan. When they came
to the land of Canaan, Abram passed through
the land as far as the sacred place at Shechem,
by the terebinth of Moreh. (The Canaanites
were then in the land.)

The Lord appeared to Abram and said, "To
your descendants I will give this land." So
Abram built an altar there to the Lord who had
appeared to him. From there he moved on to
the hill country east of Bethel, pitching his
tent with Bethel to the west and Ai to the east.
He built an altar there to the Lord and invoked
the Lord by name. Then Abram journeyed on
by stages to the Negeb.

This is the Word of the Lord.

Responsorial Psalm   Ps 33, 12-13. 18-19. 20. 22

℟. (12) Happy the people the Lord has chosen
    to be his own.
Happy the nation whose God is the Lord,
    the people he has chosen for his own in-
heritance.

From heaven the Lord looks down;
    he sees all mankind.
℟. Happy the people the Lord has chosen to
    be his own.
See, the eyes of the Lord are upon those who
    fear him,
upon those who hope for his kindness,
To deliver them from death
    and preserve them in spite of famine.
℟. Happy the people the Lord has chosen to
    be his own.
Our soul waits for the Lord,
    who is our help and our shield.
May your kindness, O Lord, be upon us
    who have put our hope in you.
℟. Happy the people the Lord has chosen to
    be his own.

Year II

READING I   2 Kgs 17, 5-8. 13-15. 18

A reading from the second book of Kings
The Lord God thrust Israel away from him and there was
none left but the tribe of Judah.

Shalmaneser, king of Assyria, occupied the
whole land and attacked Samaria, which he
besieged for three years. In the ninth year of
Hoshea, the king of Assyria took Samaria, and
deported the Israelites to Assyria, setting
them in Halah, at the Habor, a river of Gozan,
and in the cities of the Medes.

This came about because the Israelites
sinned against the Lord, their God, who had
brought them up from the land of Egypt, from
under the domination of Pharaoh, king of
Egypt, and because they venerated other gods.
They followed the rites of the nations whom
the Lord had cleared out of the way of the
Israelites [and the kings of Israel whom they
set up].

And though the Lord warned Israel and
Judah by every prophet and seer, "Give up
your evil ways and keep my commandments
and statutes, in accordance with the entire law
which I enjoined on your fathers and which I
sent you by my servants the prophets," they
did not listen, but were as stiff-necked as their
fathers, who had not believed in the Lord, their
God. They rejected his statutes, the covenant

which he had made with their fathers, and the warnings which he had given them, till, in his great anger against Israel, the Lord put them away out of his sight. Only the tribe of Judah was left.

This is the Word of the Lord.

Responsorial Psalm   Ps 60, 3. 4-5. 12-13

℟. (7) Help us with your right hand, O Lord, and answer us.

O God, you have rejected us and broken our defenses;
  you have been angry; rally us!

℟. Help us with your right hand, O Lord, and answer us.

You have rocked the country and split it open;
  repair the cracks in it, for it is tottering.

You have made your people feel hardships;
  you have given us stupefying wine.

℟. Help us with your right hand, O Lord, and answer us.

Have not you, O God, rejected us,
  so that you go not forth, O God, with our armies?

Give us aid against the foe,
  for worthless is the help of men.

℟. Help us with your right hand, O Lord, and answer us.

Years I and II

GOSPEL   Mt 7, 1-5

Alleluia

See no. 509.

✠ A reading from the holy gospel according to Matthew
Take the beam out of your own eye first.

Jesus said to his disciples: "If you want to avoid judgment, stop passing judgment. Your verdict on others will be the verdict passed on you. The measure with which you measure will be used to measure you. Why look at the speck in your brother's eye when you miss the plank in your own? How can you say to your brother, 'Let me take that speck out of your eye,' while all the time the plank remains in your own? You hypocrite! Remove the plank from your own eye first; then you will see clearly to take the speck from your brother's eye."

This is the gospel of the Lord.

---

372   **TUESDAY OF THE TWELFTH WEEK OF THE YEAR**

Year I

READING I   Gn 13, 2. 5-18

A reading from the book of Genesis
Let there be no dispute between me and you, for we are brothers.

Abram was very rich in livestock, silver, and gold.

Lot, who went with Abram, also had flocks and herds and tents, so that the land could not support them if they stayed together; their possessions were so great that they could not dwell together. There were quarrels between the herdsmen of Abram's livestock and those of Lot's. (At this time the Canaanites and the Perizzites were occupying the land.)

So Abram said to Lot: "Let there be no strife between you and me, or between your herdsmen and mine, for we are kinsmen. Is not the whole land at your disposal? Please separate from me. If you prefer the left, I will go to the right; if you prefer the right, I will go to the left." Lot looked about and saw how well watered the whole Jordan Plain was as far as Zoar, like the Lord's own garden, or like Egypt. (This was before the Lord had destroyed Sodom and Gomorrah.) Lot, therefore, chose for himself the whole Jordan Plain and set out eastward. Thus they separated from each other; Abram stayed in the land of Canaan, while Lot settled among the cities of the Plain, pitching his tents near Sodom. Now the inhabitants of Sodom were very wicked in the sins they committed against the Lord.

After Lot had left, the Lord said to Abram: "Look about you, and from where you are, gaze to the north and south, east and west; all the land that you see I will give to you and your descendants forever. I will make your descendants like the dust of the earth; if anyone could count the dust of the earth, your descendants too might be counted. Set forth and walk about in the land, through its length and breadth, for to you I will give it." Abram moved his tents and went on to settle near the terebinth of Mamre, which is at Hebron. There he built an altar to the Lord.

This is the Word of the Lord.

Responsorial Psalm   Ps 15, 2-3. 3-4. 5

℟. (1) He who does justice will live in the presence of the Lord.

He who walks blamelessly and does justice;
  who thinks the truth in his heart
  and slanders not with his tongue.

℟. He who does justice will live in the presence of the Lord.

Who harms not his fellow man,
  nor takes up a reproach against his neighbor;
By whom the reprobate is despised,
  while he honors those who fear the Lord.

℟. He who does justice will live in the presence of the Lord.

Who lends not his money at usury
  and accepts no bribe against the innocent.
He who does these things
  shall never be disturbed.

℟. He who does justice will live in the presence of the Lord.

Year II

READING I   2 Kgs 19, 9-11. 14-21. 31-35. 36

A reading from the second book of Kings

I will protect this city and save it for my own sake and for the sake of David.

Sennacherib, king of Assyria, sent envoys to Hezekiah with this message: "Thus shall you say to Hezekiah, king of Judah: 'Do not let your God on whom you rely deceive you by saying that Jerusalem will not be handed over to the king of Assyria. You have heard what the kings of Assyria have done to all other countries: they doomed them! Will you, then, be saved?' "

Hezekiah took the letter from the hand of the messengers and read it; then he went up to the temple of the Lord, and spreading it out before him, he prayed in the Lord's presence: "O Lord, God of Israel, enthroned upon the cherubim! You alone are God over all the kingdoms of the earth. You have made the heavens and the earth. Incline your ear, O Lord, and listen! Open your eyes, O Lord, and see! Hear the words of Sennacherib which he sent to taunt the living God. Truly, O Lord, the kings of Assyria have laid waste the nations and their lands, and cast their gods into the fire; they destroyed them because they were not gods, but the work of human hands, wood and stone. Therefore, O Lord, our God, save us from the power of this man, that all the kingdoms of the earth may know that you alone, O Lord, are God."

Then Isaiah, son of Amoz, sent this message to Hezekiah: "Thus says the Lord, the God of Israel, in answer to your prayer for help against Sennacherib, king of Assyria: I have listened! This is the word the Lord has spoken concerning him:

" 'She despises you, laughs you to scorn,
  the virgin daughter Zion!
Behind you she wags her head,
  daughter Jerusalem.

For out of Jerusalem shall come a remnant,
  and from Mount Zion, survivors.
  The zeal of the Lord of hosts shall do this.'

"Therefore, thus says the Lord concerning the king of Assyria: 'He shall not reach this city, nor shoot an arrow at it, nor come before it with a shield, nor cast up siegeworks against it. He shall return by the same way he came, without entering the city, says the Lord. I will shield and save this city for my own sake, and for the sake of my servant David.' "

That night the angel of the Lord went forth and struck down one hundred and eighty-five thousand men in the Assyrian camp. So Sennacherib, the king of Assyria, broke camp, and went back home to Nineveh.

This is the Word of the Lord.

Responsorial Psalm   Ps 48, 2-3. 3-4. 10-11

℟. (9) God upholds his city for ever.

Great is the Lord and wholly to be praised
  in the city of our God.

His holy mountain, fairest of heights,
  is the joy of all the earth.
℟. God upholds his city for ever.
Mount Zion, "the recesses of the North,"
  is the city of the great King.
God is with her castles;
  renowned is he as a stronghold.
℟. God upholds his city for ever.
O God, we ponder your kindness
  within your temple.
As your name, O God, so also your praise
  reaches to the ends of the earth.
Of justice your right hand is full.
℟. God upholds his city for ever.

Years I and II

GOSPEL   Mt 7, 6. 12-14
Alleluia
See no. 509.

✠ A reading from the holy gospel according
  to Matthew
Always treat others as you would like them to treat you.
Jesus said to his disciples: "Do not give what is
holy to dogs or toss your pearls before swine.
They will trample them under foot, at best,
and perhaps even tear you to shreds.

"Treat others the way you would have them
treat you: this sums up the law and the
prophets.

"Enter through the narrow gate. The gate
that leads to damnation is wide, the road is
clear, and many choose to travel it. But how
narrow is the gate that leads to life, how rough
the road, and how few there are who find it!"
  This is the gospel of the Lord.

---

373   **WEDNESDAY OF THE TWELFTH**
      WEEK OF THE YEAR

Year I

READING I   Gn 15, 1-12. 17-18
A reading from the book of Genesis
Abraham put his faith in the Lord God, who counted this
as making him justified.
The word of the Lord came to Abram in a
vision:

"Fear not, Abram!
  I am your shield;
  I will make your reward very great."
But Abram said, "O Lord God, what good will
your gifts be, if I keep on being childless and
have as my heir the steward of my house,
Eliezer?" Abram continued, "See, you have
given me no offspring, and so one of my servants will be my heir." Then the word of the
Lord came to him: "No, that one shall not be
your heir; your own issue shall be your heir."
He took him outside and said: "Look up at the
sky and count the stars, if you can. Just so,"
he added, "shall your descendants be." Abram
put his faith in the Lord, who credited it to
him as an act of righteousness.

He then said to him, "I am the Lord who
brought you from Ur of the Chaldeans to give
you this land as a possession." "O Lord God,"
he asked, "how am I to know that I shall possess it?" He answered him, "Bring me a three-
year-old heifer, a three-year-old she-goat, a
three-year-old ram, a turtledove, and a young
pigeon." He brought him all these, split them
in two, and placed each half opposite the other;
but the birds he did not cut up. Birds of prey
swooped down on the carcasses, but Abram
stayed with them. As the sun was about to set,
a trance fell upon Abram, and a deep, terrifying darkness enveloped him.

When the sun had set and it was dark, there
appeared a smoking brazier and a flaming
torch, which passed between those pieces. It
was on that occasion that the Lord made a
covenant with Abram, saying: "To your descendants I give this land, from the Wadi of
Egypt to the Great River [the Euphrates]."
  This is the Word of the Lord.

Responsorial Psalm   Ps 105, 1-2. 3-4. 6-7. 8-9
℟. (8) The Lord remembers his covenant for
  ever.
Give thanks to the Lord, invoke his name;
  make known among the nations his deeds.
Sing to him, sing his praise,
  proclaim all his wondrous deeds.
℟. The Lord remembers his covenant for ever.

Glory in his holy name;
   rejoice, O hearts that seek the Lord!
Look to the Lord in his strength;
   seek to serve him constantly.
R̄. The Lord remembers his covenant for ever.
You descendants of Abraham, his servants,
   sons of Jacob, his chosen ones!
He, the Lord, is our God;
   throughout the earth his judgments prevail.
R̄. The Lord remembers his covenant for ever.
He remembers forever his covenant
   which he made binding for a thousand
   generations—
Which he entered into with Abraham
   and by his oath to Isaac.
R̄. The Lord remembers his covenant for ever.
R̄. Or: Alleluia.

Year II

READING I   2 Kgs 22, 8-13; 23, 1-3
A reading from the second book of Kings
The king read out everything that was in the covenant
found in the temple of the Lord, and he made a covenant
in the presence of the Lord.

The high priest Hilkiah informed the scribe
Shaphan, "I have found the book of the law
in the temple of the Lord." Hilkiah gave the
book to Shaphan, who read it. Then the scribe
Shaphan went to the king and reported, "Your
servants have smelted down the metals available in the temple and have consigned them to
the master workmen in the temple of the
Lord." The scribe Shaphan also informed the
king that the priest Hilkiah had given him a
book, and then read it aloud to the king. When
the king had heard the contents of the book of
the law, he tore his garments and issued this
command to Hilkiah the priest, Ahikam, son of
Shaphan, Achbor, son of Micaiah, the scribe
Shaphan, and the king's servant Asaiah: "Go,
consult the Lord for me, for the people, for all
Judah, about the stipulations of this book that
has been found, for the anger of the Lord has
been set furiously ablaze against us, because
our fathers did not obey the stipulations of this
book, nor fulfill our written obligations."
   The king then had all the elders of Judah and
of Jerusalem summoned together before him.

The king went up to the temple of the Lord
with all the men of Judah and all the inhabitants of Jerusalem: priests, prophets, and all
the people, small and great. He had the entire
contents of the book of the covenant that had
been found in the temple of the Lord, read out
to them. Standing by the column, the king
made a covenant before the Lord that they
would follow him and observe his ordinances,
statutes and decrees with their whole hearts
and souls, thus reviving the terms of the covenant which were written in this book. And all
the people stood as participants in the covenant.

   This is the Word of the Lord.

Responsorial Psalm Ps 119, 33. 34. 35. 36. 37. 40
R̄. (33) Teach me the way of your decrees,
   O Lord.
Instruct me, O Lord, in the way of your stat-
   utes,
   that I may exactly observe them.
R̄. Teach me the way of your decrees, O Lord.
Give me discernment, that I may observe your
   law
   and keep it with all my heart.
R̄. Teach me the way of your decrees, O Lord.
Lead me in the path of your commands,
   for in it I delight.
R̄. Teach me the way of your decrees, O Lord.
Incline my heart to your decrees
   and not to gain.
R̄. Teach me the way of your decrees, O Lord.
Turn away my eyes from seeing what is vain:
   by your way give me life.
R̄. Teach me the way of your decrees, O Lord.
Behold, I long for your precepts;
   in your justice give me life.
R̄. Teach me the way of your decrees, O Lord.

Years I and II

GOSPEL   Mt 7, 15-20
Alleluia
See no. 509.

✠ A reading from the holy gospel according
to Matthew

By their fruits you will know them.

Jesus said to his disciples: "Be on your guard
against false prophets, who come to you in
sheep's clothing but underneath are wolves on
the prowl. You will know them by their deeds.
Do you ever pick grapes from thornbushes,
or figs from prickly plants? Never! Any sound
tree bears good fruit, while a decayed tree
bears bad fruit. A sound tree cannot bear bad
fruit any more than a decayed tree can bear
good fruit. Every tree that does not bear good
fruit is cut down and thrown into the fire. You
can tell a tree by its fruit."

This is the gospel of the Lord.

---

374   THURSDAY OF THE TWELFTH WEEK OF THE YEAR

Year I

READING I   Gn 16, 1-12. 15-16 or 16, 6-12. 15-16

A reading from the book of Genesis

Hagar bore Abraham a son and he called him Ishmael.

(Long Form)

Abram's wife Sarai had borne him no children.
She had, however, an Egyptian maid-servant
named Hagar. Sarai said to Abram: "The Lord
has kept me from bearing children. Have intercourse, then, with my maid; perhaps I shall
have sons through her." Abram heeded Sarai's
request. Thus, after Abram had lived ten years
in the land of Canaan, his wife Sarai took her
maid, Hagar the Egyptian, and gave her to her
husband Abram to be his concubine. He had
intercourse with her, and she became pregnant. When she became aware of her pregnancy, she looked on her mistress with disdain.
So Sarai said to Abram: "You are responsible
for this outrage against me. I myself gave my
maid to your embrace; but ever since she became aware of her pregnancy, she has been
looking on me with disdain. May the Lord
decide between you and me!" Abram told
Sarai: "Your maid is in your power. Do to her
whatever you please." Sarai then abused her
so much that Hagar ran away from her.

The Lord's messenger found her by a spring
in the wilderness, the spring on the road to
Shur, and he asked, "Hagar, maid of Sarai,
where have you come from and where are you
going?" She answered, "I am running away
from my mistress, Sarai." But the Lord's
messenger told her: "Go back to your mistress
and submit to her abusive treatment. I will
make your descendants so numerous," added
the Lord's messenger, "that they will be too
many to count. Besides," the Lord's messenger
said to her:

"You are now pregnant and shall bear a son;
    you shall name him Ishmael,
For the Lord has heard you,
    God has answered you.
He shall be a wild ass of a man,
    his hand against everyone,
    and everyone's hand against him;
In opposition to all his kin
    shall he encamp."

Hagar bore Abram a son, and Abram named
the son whom Hagar bore him Ishmael.
Abram was eighty-six years old when Hagar
bore him Ishmael.

This is the Word of the Lord.

OR
(Short Form)

Abram told Sarai: "Your maid is in your
power. Do to her whatever you please." Sarai
then abused her so much that Hagar ran away
from her. The Lord's messenger found her by
a spring in the wilderness, the spring on the
road to Shur, and he asked, "Hagar, maid of
Sarai, where have you come from and where
are you going?" She answered, "I am running
away from my mistress, Sarai." But the Lord's
messenger told her: "Go back to your mistress
and submit to her abusive treatment. I will
make your descendants so numerous," added
the Lord's messenger, "that they will be too
many to count. Besides," the Lord's messenger
said to her:

"You are now pregnant and shall bear a son;
    you shall name him Ishmael,
For the Lord has heard you,
    God has answered you.

He shall be a wild ass of a man,
  his hand against everyone,
  and everyone's hand against him;
In opposition to all his kin
  shall he encamp."
Hagar bore Abram a son, and Abram named
the son whom Hagar bore him Ishmael. Abram
was eighty-six years old when Hagar bore him
Ishmael.
    This is the Word of the Lord.

Responsorial Psalm   Ps 106, 1-2. 3-4. 4-5

℟. (1) Give thanks to the Lord for he is good.
Give thanks to the Lord, for he is good,
  for his kindness endures forever.
Who can tell the mighty deeds of the Lord,
  or proclaim all his praises?
℟. Give thanks to the Lord for he is good.
Who can tell the mighty deeds of the Lord,
  or proclaim all his praises?
Happy are they who observe what is right,
  who do always what is just.
Remember us, O Lord, as you favor your
  people.
℟. Give thanks to the Lord for he is good.
Visit me with your saving help,
  that I may see the prosperity of your chosen
  ones,
Rejoice in the joy of your people,
  and glory with your inheritance.
℟. Give thanks to the Lord for he is good.
℟. Or: Alleluia.

Year II

READING I   2 Kgs 24, 8-17

A reading from the second book of Kings

Jehoiachin and all his leaders surrendered to the king of
Babylon and were prisoners in Babylon.

Jehoiachin was eighteen years old when he
began to reign, and he reigned three months in
Jerusalem. His mother's name was Nehushta,
daughter of Elnathan of Jerusalem. He did evil
in the sight of the Lord, just as his forebears
had done.
    At that time the officials of Nebuchadnezzar,
king of Babylon, attacked Jerusalem, and the
city came under siege. Nebuchadnezzar, king
of Babylon, himself arrived at the city while
his servants were besieging it. Then Jehoiachin, king of Judah, together with his mother,
his ministers, officers, and functionaries, surrendered to the king of Babylon, who, in the
eighth year of his reign, took him captive. He
carried off all the treasures of the temple of
the Lord and those of the palace, and broke up
all the gold utensils that Solomon, king of
Israel, had provided in the temple of the Lord,
as the Lord had foretold. He deported all
Jerusalem: all the officers and men of the
army, ten thousand in number, and all the
craftsmen and smiths. None were left among
the people of the land except the poor. He
deported Jehoiachin to Babylon, and also led
captive from Jerusalem to Babylon the king's
mother and wives, his functionaries, and the
chief men of the land. The king of Babylon
also led captive to Babylon all seven thousand
men of the army, and a thousand craftsmen
and smiths, all of them trained soldiers. In
place of Jehoiachin, the king of Babylon appointed his uncle Mattaniah king, and changed
his name to Zedekiah.
    This is the Word of the Lord.

Responsorial Psalm   Ps 79, 1-2. 3-5. 8. 9

℟. (9) For the glory of your name,
  O Lord, deliver us.
O God, the nations have come into your in-
  heritance;
  they have defiled your holy temple,
  they have laid Jerusalem in ruins.
They have given the corpses of your servants
  as food to the birds of heaven,
  the flesh of your faithful ones to the beasts
  of the earth.
℟. For the glory of your name,
  O Lord, deliver us.
They have poured out their blood like water
  round about Jerusalem,
  and there is no one to bury them.
We have become the reproach of our neigh-
  bors,
  the scorn and derision of those around us.
O Lord, how long? Will you be angry forever?
  Will your jealousy burn like fire?

℟. For the glory of your name,
  O Lord, deliver us.
Remember not against us the iniquities of the
  past;
  may your compassion quickly come to us,
  for we are brought very low.
℟. For the glory of your name,
  O Lord, deliver us.
Help us, O God our savior,
  because of the glory of your name;
Deliver us and pardon our sins
  for your name's sake.
℟. For the glory of your name,
  O Lord, deliver us.

Years I and II

GOSPEL   Mt 7, 21-29
Alleluia
See no. 509.

✠ **A reading from the holy gospel according**
             to Matthew
The house built on rock is compared to the house built on
sand.
**Jesus said to his disciples: "None of those who
cry out, 'Lord, Lord,' will enter the kingdom
of God but only the one who does the will of
my Father in heaven. When that day comes,
many will plead with me, 'Lord, Lord, have we
not prophesied in your name? Have we not
exorcised demons by its power? Did we not do
many miracles in your name as well?' Then I
will declare to them solemnly, 'I never knew
you. Out of my sight, you evildoers!'**

**"Anyone who hears my words and puts
them into practice is like the wise man who
built his house on rock. When the rainy season set in, the torrents came and the winds
blew and buffeted his house. It did not collapse; it had been solidly set on rock. Anyone
who hears my words but does not put them
into practice is like the foolish man who built
his house on sandy ground. The rains fell, the
torrents came, the winds blew and lashed
against his house. It collapsed under all this
and was completely ruined."**

**Jesus finished this discourse and left the
crowds spellbound at his teaching. The reason**

was that he taught with authority and not like
their scribes.
    This is the gospel of the Lord.

---

375   **FRIDAY OF THE TWELFTH**
             WEEK OF THE YEAR

Year I

READING I   Gn 17, 1. 9-10. 15-22
    A reading from the book of Genesis
All your males must be circumcised as a sign of my cove-
nant. I will give you a son by Sarah.
**When Abram was ninety-nine years old, the
Lord appeared to him and said: "I am God the
Almighty. Walk in my presence and be blame-
less."**

    **God also said to Abraham: "On your part,
you and your descendants after you must keep
my covenant throughout the ages. This is my
covenant with you and your descendants after
you that you must keep: every male among
you shall be circumcised."**

    **God further said to Abraham: "As for your
wife Sarai, do not call her Sarai; her name shall
be Sarah. I will bless her, and I will give you a
son by her. Him also will I bless; he shall give
rise to nations, and rulers of peoples shall issue
from him." Abraham prostrated himself and
laughed as he said to himself, "Can a child be
born to a man who is a hundred years old?
Or can Sarah give birth at ninety?" Then
Abraham said to God, "Let but Ishmael live on
by your favor!" God replied: "Nevertheless,
your wife Sarah is to bear you a son, and you
shall call him Isaac. I will maintain my covenant with him as an everlasting pact, to be his
God and the God of his descendants after him.
As for Ishmael, I am heeding you: I hereby
bless him. I will make him fertile and will
multiply him exceedingly. He shall become the
father of twelve chieftains, and I will make of
him a great nation. But my covenant I will
maintain with Isaac, whom Sarah shall bear
to you by this time next year." When he had
finished speaking with him, God departed from
Abraham.**

    This is the Word of the Lord.

Responsorial Psalm   Ps 128, 1-2. 3. 4-5

℟. (4) See how the Lord blesses those who fear
    him.

Happy are you who fear the Lord,
    who walk in his ways!
For you shall eat the fruit of your handiwork;
    happy shall you be, and favored.

℟. See how the Lord blesses those who fear
    him.

Your wife shall be like a fruitful vine
    in the recesses of your home;
Your children like olive plants
    around your table.

℟. See how the Lord blesses those who fear
    him.

Behold, thus is the man blessed
    who fears the Lord.
The Lord bless you from Zion:
    may you see the prosperity of Jerusalem
    all the days of your life.

℟. See how the Lord blesses those who fear
    him.

Year II

READING I   2 Kgs 25, 1-12

A reading from the second book of Kings
The land of Judah was taken away.

In the tenth month of the ninth year of
Zedekiah's reign, on the tenth day of the
month, Nebuchadnezzar, king of Babylon, and
his whole army advanced against Jerusalem,
encamped around it, and built siege walls on
every side. The siege of the city continued
until the eleventh year of Zedekiah. On the
ninth day of the fourth month, when famine
had gripped the city, and the people had no
more bread, the city walls were breached. Then
the king and all the soldiers left the city by
night through the gate between the two walls
which was near the king's garden. Since the
Chaldeans had the city surrounded, they went
in the direction of the Arabah. But the
Chaldean army pursued the king and overtook
him in the desert near Jericho, abandoned by
his whole army.

The king was therefore arrested and brought
to Riblah to the king of Babylon, who pronounced sentence on him. He had Zedekiah's
sons slain before his eyes. Then he blinded
Zedekiah, bound him with fetters, and had him
brought to Babylon.

On the seventh day of the fifth month (this
was in the nineteenth year of Nebuchadnezzar,
king of Babylon), Nebuzaradan, captain of the
bodyguard, came to Jerusalem as the representative of the king of Babylon. He burned the
house of the Lord, the palace of the king, and
all the houses of Jerusalem; every large building was destroyed by fire. Then the Chaldean
troops who were with the captain of the guard
tore down the walls that surrounded Jerusalem.

Then Nebuzaradan, captain of the guard, led
into exile the last of the people remaining in
the city, and those who had deserted to the
king of Babylon, and the last of the artisans.
But some of the country's poor, Nebuzaradan,
captain of the guard, left behind as vine-
dressers and farmers.

This is the Word of the Lord.

Responsorial Psalm   Ps 137, 1-2. 3. 4-5. 6

℟. (6) Let my tongue be silenced,
    if I ever forget you!

By the streams of Babylon
    we sat and wept
    when we remembered Zion.
On the aspens of that land
    we hung up our harps.

℟. Let my tongue be silenced,
    if I ever forget you!

Though there our captors asked of us
    the lyrics of our songs,
And our despoilers urged us to be joyous:
    "Sing for us the songs of Zion!"

℟. Let my tongue be silenced,
    if I ever forget you!

How could we sing a song of the Lord
    in a foreign land?
If I forget you, Jerusalem,
    may my right hand be forgotten!

℟. Let my tongue be silenced,
    if I ever forget you!

May my tongue cleave to my palate
  if I remember you not,
If I place not Jerusalem
  ahead of my joy.
R⁷. Let my tongue be silenced,
  if I ever forget you!

Years I and II

GOSPEL   Mt 8, 1-4
Alleluia
See no. 509.

✠ A reading from the holy gospel according
    to Matthew
If you will, you can cure me.

When Jesus came down from the mountain,
great crowds followed him. Suddenly a leper
came forward and did him homage, saying to
him, "Sir, if you will to do so, you can cure
me." Jesus stretched out his hand and touched
him and said, "I do will it. Be cured." Immediately the man's leprosy disappeared. Then
Jesus said to him: "See to it that you tell no
one. Go and show yourself to the priest and
offer the gift Moses prescribed. That should
be the proof they need."
        This is the gospel of the Lord.

376   **SATURDAY OF THE TWELFTH
        WEEK OF THE YEAR**

Year I

READING I   Gn 18, 1-15
A reading from the book of Genesis
Is anything too difficult for the Lord God? I will visit you
    again and Sarah will have a son.

The Lord appeared to Abraham by the terebinth of Mamre, as he sat in the entrance of his
tent, while the day was growing hot. Looking
up, he saw three men standing nearby. When
he saw them, he ran from the entrance of the
tent to greet them; and bowing to the ground,
he said: "Sir, if I may ask you this favor, please
do not go on past your servant. Let some water
be brought, that you may bathe your feet, and
then rest yourselves under the tree. Now that
you have come this close to your servant, let

me bring you a little food, that you may refresh
yourselves; and afterward you may go on your
way." "Very well," they replied, "do as you
have said."

Abraham hastened into the tent and told
Sarah, "Quick, three seahs of fine flour! Knead
it and make rolls." He ran to the herd, picked
out a tender, choice steer, and gave it to a servant, who quickly prepared it. Then he got
some curds and milk, as well as the steer that
had been prepared, and set these before them;
and he waited on them under the tree while
they ate.

"Where is your wife Sarah?" they asked
him. "There in the tent," he replied. One of
them said, "I will surely return to you about
this time next year, and Sarah will then have a
son." Sarah was listening at the entrance of the
tent, just behind him. Now Abraham and Sarah
were old, advanced in years, and Sarah had
stopped having her womanly periods. So Sarah
laughed to herself and said, "Now that I am so
withered and my husband is so old, am I still
to have sexual pleasure?" But the Lord said to
Abraham: "Why did Sarah laugh and say,
'Shall I really bear a child, old as I am?' Is anything too marvelous for the Lord to do? At the
appointed time, about this time next year, I
will return to you, and Sarah will have a son."
Because she was afraid, Sarah dissembled, saying, "I didn't laugh." But he said, "Yes you did."
        This is the Word of the Lord.

Responsorial Psalm   Lk 1, 46-47. 48-49. 50. 53. 54-55

R⁷. (54) The Lord has remembered his mercy.
My being proclaims the greatness of the Lord,
  my spirit finds joy in God my savior.
R⁷. The Lord has remembered his mercy.
For he has looked upon his servant in her lowli-
    ness;
  all ages to come shall call me blessed.
God who is mighty has done great things for
    me,
  holy is his name.
R⁷. The Lord has remembered his mercy.
His mercy is from age to age
  on those who fear him.

The hungry he has given every good thing,
  while the rich he has sent away empty.
R̞. The Lord has remembered his mercy.
He has upheld Israel his servant,
  ever mindful of his mercy;
Even as he promised our fathers,
  promised Abraham and his descendants for-
    ever.
R̞. The Lord has remembered his mercy.

Year II

READING I   Lam 2, 2. 10-14. 18-19

A reading from the book of Lamentations
The sons of Zion cried out to the Lord from the walls.

The Lord has consumed without pity
  all the dwellings of Jacob;
He has torn down in his anger
  the fortresses of daughter Judah;
He has brought to the ground in dishonor
  her king and her princes.

On the ground in silence sit
  the old men of daughter Zion;
They strew dust on their heads
  and gird themselves with sackcloth;
The maidens of Jerusalem
  bow their heads to the ground.

Worn out from weeping are my eyes,
  within me all is in ferment;
My gall is poured out on the ground
  because of the downfall of the daughter of
    my people,
As child and infant faint away
  in the open spaces of the town.

They ask their mothers,
  "Where is the cereal?"—in vain,
As they faint away like the wounded
  in the streets of the city,
And breathe their last
  in their mothers' arms.

To what can I liken or compare you,
  O daughter Jerusalem?
What example can I show you for your com-
    fort,
  virgin daughter Zion?
For great as the sea is your downfall;
  who can heal you?

Your prophets had for you
  false and specious visions;
They did not lay bare your guilt,
  to avert your fate;
They beheld for you in vision
  false and misleading portents.

Cry out to the Lord;
  moan, O daughter Zion!
Let your tears flow like a torrent
  day and night;
Let there be no respite for you,
  no repose for your eyes.

Rise up, shrill in the night,
  at the beginning of every watch;
Pour out your heart like water
  in the presence of the Lord;
Lift up your hands to him
  for the lives of your little ones
[Who faint from hunger
  at the corner of every street].
        This is the Word of the Lord.

Responsorial Psalm   Ps 74, 1-2. 3-5. 5-7. 20-21

R̞. (19) Lord, forget not the life of your poor
  ones.
Why, O God, have you cast us off forever?
  Why does your anger smolder against the
    sheep of your pasture?
Remember your flock which you built up of
    old,
  the tribe you redeemed as your inheritance,
  Mount Zion, where you took up your abode.
R̞. Lord, forget not the life of your poor ones.
Turn your steps toward the utter ruins;
  toward all the damage the enemy has done
    in the sanctuary.
Your foes roar triumphantly in your shrine;
  they have set up their tokens of victory.
They are like men coming up with axes to a
    clump of trees.
R̞. Lord, forget not the life of your poor ones.
With chisel and hammer they hack at all the
    paneling of the sanctuary.
  They set your sanctuary on fire;
The place where your name abides they have
    razed and profaned.
R̞. Lord, forget not the life of your poor ones.

Look to your covenant,
   for the hiding places in the land and the
   plains are full of violence.
May the humble not retire in confusion;
   may the afflicted and the poor praise your
   name.
℞. Lord, forget not the life of your poor ones.

Years I and II

GOSPEL   Mt 8, 5-17
Alleluia

See no. 509.

✠ A reading from the holy gospel according
   to Matthew

Many will come from east and west and take their places
with Abraham, Isaac, and Jacob at the feast.

As Jesus entered Capernaum, a centurion approached him with this request: "Sir, my serving boy is at home in bed paralyzed, suffering
painfully." He said to him, "I will come and
cure him." "Sir," the centurion said in reply,
"I am not worthy to have you under my roof.
Just give an order and my boy will get better.
I am a man under authority myself and I have
troops assigned to me. If I give one man the
order, 'Dismissed,' off he goes. If I say to another, 'Come here,' he comes. If I tell my slave,
'Do this,' he does it." Jesus showed amazement
on hearing this and remarked to his followers,
"I assure you, I have never found this much
faith in Israel. Mark what I say! Many will
come from the east and the west and will find
a place at the banquet in the kingdom of God
with Abraham, Isaac, and Jacob, while the
natural heirs of the kingdom will be driven out
into the dark. Wailing will be heard there, and
the grinding of teeth." To the centurion Jesus
said, "Go home. It shall be done because you
trusted." That very moment the boy got better.
   Jesus entered Peter's house and found Peter's mother-in-law in bed with a fever. He
took her by the hand and the fever left her. She
got up at once and began to wait on him.
   As evening drew on, they brought him many
who were possessed. He expelled the spirits by
a simple command and cured all who were
afflicted, thereby fulfilling what had been said
through Isaiah the prophet:

"It was our infirmities he bore,
our sufferings he endured."
   This is the gospel of the Lord.

377   MONDAY OF THE
THIRTEENTH WEEK OF THE YEAR

Year I

READING I   Gn 18, 16-33
   A reading from the book of Genesis

Are you going to destroy the just man with the sinner?

The men set out from the valley of Mamre and
looked down toward Sodom; Abraham was
walking with them, to see them on their way.
The Lord reflected: "Shall I hide from Abraham what I am about to do, now that he is to
become a great and populous nation, and all
the nations of the earth are to find blessing in
him? Indeed, I have singled him out that he
may direct his sons and his posterity to keep
the way of the Lord by doing what is right and
just, so that the Lord may carry into effect for
Abraham the promises he made about him."
Then the Lord said: "The outcry against
Sodom and Gomorrah is so great, and their sin
so grave, that I must go down and see whether
or not their actions fully correspond to the cry
against them that comes to me. I mean to find
out."
   While the two men walked on farther toward Sodom, the Lord remained standing before Abraham. Then Abraham drew nearer to
him and said: "Will you sweep away the innocent with the guilty? Suppose there were
fifty innocent people in the city; would you
wipe out the place, rather than spare it for the
sake of the fifty innocent people within it? Far
be it from you to do such a thing, to make the
innocent die with the guilty, so that the innocent and the guilty would be treated alike!
Should not the judge of all the world act with
justice?" The Lord replied, "If I find fifty innocent people in the city of Sodom, I will spare
the whole place for their sake." Abraham
spoke up again: "See how I am presuming to
speak to my Lord, though I am but dust and

ashes! What if there are five less than fifty innocent people? Will you destroy the whole city because of those five?" "I will not destroy it," he answered, "if I find forty-five there." But Abraham persisted, saying, "What if only forty are found there?" He replied, "I will forbear doing it for the sake of the forty." Then he said, "Let not my Lord grow impatient if I go on. What if only thirty are found there?" He replied, "I will forbear doing it if I can find but thirty there." Still he went on, "Since I have thus dared to speak to my Lord, what if there are no more than twenty?" "I will not destroy it," he answered, "for the sake of the twenty." But he still persisted: "Please, let not my Lord grow angry if I speak up this last time. What if there are at least ten there?" "For the sake of those ten," he replied, "I will not destroy it."

The Lord departed as soon as he had finished speaking with Abraham, and Abraham returned home.

This is the Word of the Lord.

Responsorial Psalm   Ps 103, 1-2. 3-4. 8-9. 10-11

℟. (8) The Lord is kind and merciful.
Bless the Lord, O my soul;
and all my being, bless his holy name.
Bless the Lord, O my soul,
and forget not all his benefits.
℟. The Lord is kind and merciful.
He pardons all your iniquities,
he heals all your ills.
He redeems your life from destruction,
he crowns you with kindness and compassion.
℟. The Lord is kind and merciful.
Merciful and gracious is the Lord,
slow to anger and abounding in kindness.
He will not always chide,
nor does he keep his wrath forever.
℟. The Lord is kind and merciful.
Not according to our sins does he deal with us,
nor does he requite us according to our crimes.
For as the heavens are high above the earth,

so surpassing is his kindness toward those who fear him.
℟. The Lord is kind and merciful.

Year II

READING I   Am 2, 6-10. 13-16
A reading from the book of the prophet Amos
They trample the head of the poor into the dust of the earth.
Thus says the Lord:
For three crimes of Israel, and for four,
I will not revoke my word;
Because they sell the just man for silver,
and the poor man for a pair of sandals.
They trample the heads of the weak
into the dust of the earth,
and force the lowly out of the way.
Son and father go to the same prostitute,
profaning my holy name.
Upon garments taken in pledge
they recline beside any altar;
And the wine of those who have been fined
they drink in the house of their god.

Yet it was I who destroyed the Amorites before them,
who were as tall as the cedars,
and as strong as the oak trees.
I destroyed their fruit above,
and their roots beneath.
It was I who brought you up from the land of Egypt,
and who led you through the desert for forty years,
to occupy the land of the Amorites.

Beware, I will crush you into the ground
as a wagon crushes when laden with sheaves.
Flight shall perish from the swift,
and the strong man shall not retain his strength;
The warrior shall not save his life,
nor the bowman stand his ground;
The swift of foot shall not escape,
nor the horseman save his life.
And the most stouthearted of warriors
shall flee naked on that day, says the Lord.
This is the Word of the Lord.

Responsorial Psalm Ps 50, 16-17. 18-19. 20-21. 22-23

℟. (22) Remember this, you who never think
of God.

Why do you recite my statutes,
and profess my covenant with your mouth,
Though you hate discipline
and cast my words behind you?

℟. Remember this, you who never think of
God.

When you see a thief, you keep pace with him,
and with adulterers you throw in your lot.
To your mouth you give free rein for evil,
you harness your tongue to deceit.

℟. Remember this, you who never think of
God.

You sit speaking against your brother;
against your mother's son you spread ru-
mors.
When you do these things, shall I be deaf to it?
Or do you think that I am like yourself?
I will correct you by drawing them up before
your eyes.

℟. Remember this, you who never think of
God.

Consider this, you who forget God,
lest I rend you and there be no one to rescue
you.
He that offers praise as a sacrifice glorifies me;
and to him that goes the right way I will
show the salvation of God.

℟. Remember this, you who never think of
God.

Years I and II

GOSPEL Mt 8, 18-22
Alleluia

See no. 509.

✠ A reading from the holy gospel according
to Matthew

Follow me.

Jesus, seeing the people crowd around him,
gave orders to cross the lake to the other shore.
A scribe approached him and said, "Teacher,
wherever you go I will come after you." Jesus
said to him, "The foxes have lairs, the birds in
the sky have nests, but the Son of Man has nowhere to lay his head." Another, a disciple,
said to him, "Lord, let me go and bury my father first." But Jesus told him, "Follow me, and
let the dead bury their dead."

This is the gospel of the Lord.

---

378 **TUESDAY OF THE**
THIRTEENTH WEEK OF THE YEAR

Year I

READING I Gn 19, 15-29

A reading from the book of Genesis

The Lord God rained brimstone and fire on Sodom and
Gomorrah.

As dawn was breaking, the angels urged Lot
on, saying, "On your way! Take with you your
wife and your two daughters who are here, or
you will be swept away in the punishment of
Sodom." When he hesitated, the men, by the
Lord's mercy, seized his hand and the hands of
his wife and his two daughters and led them to
safety outside the city. As soon as they had
been brought outside, he was told: "Flee for
your life! Don't look back or stop anywhere on
the Plain. Get off to the hills at once, or you
will be swept away." "Oh, no, my lord!" replied Lot. "You have already thought enough
of your servant to do me the great kindness of
intervening to save my life. But I cannot flee to
the hills to keep the disaster from overtaking
me, and so I shall die. Look, this town ahead is
near enough to escape to. It's only a small
place. Let me flee there—it's a small place, isn't
it?—that my life may be saved." "Well, then,"
he replied, "I will also grant you the favor you
now ask. I will not overthrow the town you
speak of. Hurry, escape there! I cannot do
anything until you arrive there." That is why
the town is called Zoar.

The sun was just rising over the earth as Lot
arrived in Zoar; at the same time the Lord
rained down sulphurous fire upon Sodom and
Gomorrah [from the Lord out of heaven]. He
overthrew those cities and the whole Plain, together with the inhabitants of the cities and
the produce of the soil. But Lot's wife looked
back, and she was turned into a pillar of salt.

Early the next morning Abraham went to the place where he had stood in the Lord's presence. As he looked down toward Sodom and Gomorrah and the whole region of the Plain, he saw dense smoke over the land rising like fumes from a furnace.

Thus it came to pass: when God destroyed the Cities of the Plain, he was mindful of Abraham by sending Lot away from the upheaval by which God overthrew the cities where Lot had been living.

This is the Word of the Lord.

Responsorial Psalm   Ps 26, 2-3. 9-10. 11-12

℞. (3) O Lord, your kindness is before my eyes.
Search me, O Lord, and try me;
  test my soul and my heart.
For your kindness is before my eyes,
  and I walk in your truth.

℞. O Lord, your kindness is before my eyes.
Gather not my soul with those of sinners,
  nor with men of blood my life.
On their hands are crimes,
  and their right hands are full of bribes.

℞. O Lord, your kindness is before my eyes.
But I walk in integrity;
  redeem me, and have pity on me.
My foot stands on level ground;
  in the assemblies I will bless the Lord.

℞. O Lord, your kindness is before my eyes.

Year II

READING I   Am 3, 1-8; 4, 11-12

A reading from the book of the prophet Amos
The Lord God spoke: who will refuse to prophesy?

Hear this word, O men of Israel, that the Lord pronounces over you, over the whole family that I brought up from the land of Egypt:
You alone have I favored,
  more than all the families of the earth;
Therefore I will punish you
  for all your crimes.

Do two walk together
  unless they have agreed?
Does a lion roar in the forest
  when it has no prey?

Does a young lion cry out from its den
  unless it has seized something?
Is a bird brought to earth by a snare
  when there is no lure for it?
Does a snare spring up from the ground
  without catching anything?
If the trumpet sounds in a city,
  will the people not be frightened?
If evil befalls a city,
  has not the Lord caused it?
Indeed, the Lord God does nothing
  without revealing his plan
  to his servants, the prophets.

The lion roars—
  who will not be afraid!
The Lord God speaks—
  who will not prophesy!
I brought upon you such upheaval
  as when God overthrew Sodom and Gomorrah:
  you were like a brand plucked from the fire;
Yet you returned not to me,
  says the Lord.

So now I will deal with you in my own way,
  O Israel!
  and since I will deal thus with you,
  prepare to meet your God, O Israel.
  This is the Word of the Lord.

Responsorial Psalm   Ps 5, 4-6. 6-7. 8

℞. (9) Lead me in your justice, Lord.
  At dawn I bring my plea expectantly before you.
For you, O God, delight not in wickedness;
  no evil man remains with you;
  the arrogant may not stand in your sight.

℞. Lead me in your justice, Lord.
You hate all evildoers;
  you destroy all who speak falsehood;
The bloodthirsty and the deceitful
  the Lord abhors.

℞. Lead me in your justice, Lord.
But I, because of your abundant kindness,
  will enter your house;
I will worship at your holy temple
  in fear of you, O Lord.

℞. Lead me in your justice, Lord.

GOSPEL   Mt 8, 23-27
Alleluia

See no. 509.

✠ **A reading from the holy gospel according to Matthew**

He commanded the wind and the sea, and all was calm again.

Jesus got into a boat and his disciples followed him. Without warning a violent storm came up on the lake, and the boat began to be swamped by the waves. Jesus was sleeping soundly, so they made their way toward him and woke him: "Lord, save us! We are lost!" He said to them: "Where is your courage? How little faith you have!" Then he stood up and took the winds and the sea to task. Complete calm ensued; the men were dumbfounded. "What sort of man is this," they said, "that even the winds and the sea obey him?"

This is the gospel of the Lord.

---

379   WEDNESDAY OF THE THIRTEENTH WEEK OF THE YEAR

Year I

READING I   Gn 21, 5. 8-20

A reading from the book of Genesis

The slave girl's son will not share the inheritance with my son Isaac.

Abraham was a hundred years old when his son Isaac was born to him. Isaac grew, and on the day of the child's weaning, Abraham held a great feast.

Sarah noticed the son whom Hagar the Egyptian had borne to Abraham playing with her son Isaac; so she demanded of Abraham: "Drive out that slave and her son! No son of that slave is going to share the inheritance with my son Isaac!" Abraham was greatly distressed, especially on account of his son Ishmael. But God said to Abraham: "Do not be distressed about the boy or about your slave woman. Heed the demands of Sarah, no matter what she is asking of you; for it is through Isaac that descendants shall bear your name.

As for the son of the slave woman, I will make a great nation of him also, since he too is your offspring."

Early the next morning Abraham got some bread and a skin of water and gave them to Hagar. Then, placing the child on her back, he sent her away. As she roamed aimlessly in the wilderness of Beer-sheba, the water in the skin was used up. So she put the child down under a shrub, and then went and sat down opposite him, about a bowshot away; for she said to herself, "Let me not watch the child die." As she sat opposite him, he began to cry. God heard the boy's cry, and God's messenger called to Hagar from heaven: "What is the matter, Hagar? Don't be afraid; God has heard the boy's cry in this plight of his. Arise, lift up the boy and hold him by the hand; for I will make of him a great nation." Then God opened her eyes, and she saw a well of water. She went and filled the skin with water, and then let the boy drink.

God was with the boy as he grew up.

This is the Word of the Lord.

Responsorial Psalm   Ps 34, 7-8. 10-11. 12-13

℟. (7) The Lord hears the cry of the poor.
When the afflicted man called out, the Lord heard,
and from all his distress he saved him.
The angel of the Lord encamps
around those who fear him, and delivers them.
℟. The Lord hears the cry of the poor.
Fear the Lord, you his holy ones,
for nought is lacking to those who fear him.
The great grow poor and hungry;
but those who seek the Lord want for no good thing.
℟. The Lord hears the cry of the poor.
Come, children, hear me;
I will teach you the fear of the Lord.
Which of you desires life,
and takes delight in prosperous days?
℟. The Lord hears the cry of the poor.

Year II

READING I   Am 5, 14-15. 21-24

A reading from the book of the prophet Amos

Take away your sacrifices, but let your justice flow like an unfailing stream.

Seek good and not evil,
    that you may live;
Then truly will the Lord, the God of hosts,
    be with you as you claim!
Hate evil and love good,
    and let justice prevail at the gate;
Then it may be that the Lord, the God of hosts,
    will have pity on the remnant of Joseph.

I hate, I spurn your feasts, says the Lord,
    I take no pleasure in your solemnities;
Your cereal offerings I will not accept,
    nor consider your stall-fed peace offerings.
Away with your noisy songs!
    I will not listen to the melodies of your
    harps.
But if you would offer me holocausts,
    then let justice surge like water,
    and goodness like an unfailing stream.

          This is the Word of the Lord.

Responsorial Psalm   Ps 50, 7. 8-9. 10-11. 12-13. 16-17

℞. (23) To the upright I will show the saving
    power of God.

Hear, my people, and I will speak;
    Israel, I will testify against you;
    God, your God, am I.
℞. To the upright I will show the saving power
    of God.

Not for your sacrifices do I rebuke you,
    for your holocausts are before me always.
I take from your house no bullock,
    no goats out of your fold.
℞. To the upright I will show the saving power
    of God.

For mine are all the animals of the forests,
    beasts by the thousand on my mountains.
I know all the birds of the air,
    and whatever stirs in the plains, belongs to
    me.
℞. To the upright I will show the saving power
    of God.

If I were hungry, I should not tell you,
    for mine are the world and its fullness.
Do I eat the flesh of strong bulls,
    or is the blood of goats my drink?
℞. To the upright I will show the saving power
    of God.
Why do you recite my statutes,
    and profess my covenant with your mouth,
Though you hate discipline
    and cast my words behind you?
℞. To the upright I will show the saving power
    of God.

Years I and II

GOSPEL   Mt 8, 28-34

Alleluia

See no. 509.

✠ **A reading from the holy gospel according
            to Matthew**

He came before the appointed time to torture the demons.

As Jesus approached the Gadarene boundary,
he encountered two men coming out of the
tombs. They were possessed by demons and
were so savage that no one could travel along
the road. With a sudden shriek they cried:
"Why meddle with us, Son of God? Have you
come to torture us before the appointed time?"
Some distance away a large herd of swine
was feeding. The demons kept appealing to
him, "If you expel us, send us into the herd of
swine." He answered, "Out with you!" At that
they came forth and entered the swine. The
whole herd went rushing down the bluff into
the sea and were drowned.

    The swineherds took to their heels, and upon
their arrival in the town related everything
that had happened, including the story about
the two possessed men. The upshot was that
the entire town came out to meet Jesus. When
they caught sight of him, they begged him to
leave their neighborhood.

          This is the gospel of the Lord.

380   THURSDAY OF THE THIRTEENTH WEEK OF THE YEAR

Year I

READING I   Gn 22, 1-19

A reading from the book of Genesis
The sacrifice of Abraham, our father in faith.

God put Abraham to the test. He called to him, "Abraham!" "Ready!" he replied. Then God said: "Take your son Isaac, your only one, whom you love, and go to the land of Moriah. There you shall offer him up as a holocaust on a height that I will point out to you." Early the next morning Abraham saddled his donkey, took with him his son Isaac, and two of his servants as well, and with the wood that he had cut for the holocaust, set out for the place of which God had told him.

On the third day Abraham got sight of the place from afar. Then he said to his servants: "Both of you stay here with the donkey, while the boy and I go on over yonder. We will worship and then come back to you." Thereupon Abraham took the wood for the holocaust and laid it on his son Isaac's shoulders, while he himself carried the fire and the knife. As the two walked on together, Isaac spoke to his father Abraham. "Father!" he said. "Yes, son," he replied. Isaac continued, "Here are the fire and the wood, but where is the sheep for the holocaust?" "Son," Abraham answered, "God himself will provide the sheep for the holocaust." Then the two continued going forward.

When they came to the place of which God had told him, Abraham built an altar there and arranged the wood on it. Next he tied up his son Isaac, and put him on top of the wood on the altar. Then he reached out and took the knife to slaughter his son. But the Lord's messenger called to him from heaven, "Abraham, Abraham!" "Yes, Lord," he answered. "Do not lay your hand on the boy," said the messenger. "Do not do the least thing to him. I know now how devoted you are to God, since you did not withhold from me your own beloved son." As Abraham looked about, he spied a ram caught by its horns in the thicket. So he went and took the ram and offered it up as a holocaust in place of his son. Abraham named the site Yahweh-yireh; hence people now say, "On the mountain the Lord will see."

Again the Lord's messenger called to Abraham from heaven and said: "I swear by myself, declares the Lord, that because you acted as you did in not withholding from me your beloved son, I will bless you abundantly and make your descendants as countless as the stars of the sky and the sands of the seashore; your descendants shall take possession of the gates of their enemies, and in your descendants all the nations of the earth shall find blessing— all this because you obeyed my command."

Abraham then returned to his servants, and they set out together for Beer-sheba, where Abraham made his home.

This is the Word of the Lord.

Responsorial Psalm   Ps 115, 1-2. 3-4. 5-6. 8-9

℟. (9) I will walk in the presence of the Lord, in the land of the living.

Not to us, O Lord, not to us
   but to your name give glory
   because of your kindness, because of your truth.
Why should the pagans say,
   "Where is their God?"

℟. I will walk in the presence of the Lord, in the land of the living.

Our God is in heaven;
   whatever he wills, he does.
Their idols are silver and gold,
   the handiwork of men.

℟. I will walk in the presence of the Lord, in the land of the living.

They have mouths but speak not;
   they have eyes but see not;
They have ears but hear not;
   they have noses but smell not.

℟. I will walk in the presence of the Lord, in the land of the living.

Their makers shall be like them,
   everyone that trusts in them.
The house of Israel trusts in the Lord;
   he is their help and their shield.

℟. I will walk in the presence of the Lord, in the land of the living.

℟. Or: Alleluia.

READING I
Year II

Am 7, 10-17

A reading from the book of the prophet Amos

Go prophesy to my people.

Amaziah, the priest of Bethel, sent word to Jeroboam, king of Israel: "Amos has conspired against you here within Israel; the country cannot endure all his words. For this is what Amos says:

Jeroboam shall die by the sword,
    and Israel shall surely be exiled from its
    land."

To Amos, Amaziah said: "Off with you, visionary, flee to the land of Judah! There earn your bread by prophesying, but never again prophesy in Bethel; for it is the king's sanctuary and a royal temple." Amos answered Amaziah, "I was no prophet, nor have I belonged to a company of prophets; I was a shepherd and a dresser of sycamores. The Lord took me from following the flock, and said to me, Go, prophesy to my people Israel. Now hear the word of the Lord!"

You say: prophesy not against Israel,
    preach not against the house of Isaac.
    Now thus says the Lord:
Your wife shall be made a harlot in the
    city,
    and your sons and daughters shall fall
    by the sword;
Your land shall be divided by measuring
    line,
    and you yourself shall die in an unclean
    land;
Israel shall be exiled far from its land.
This is the Word of the Lord.

Responsorial Psalm
Ps 19, 8, 9. 10. 11

℟. (10) The judgments of the Lord are true,
    and all of them are just.
The law of the Lord is perfect,
    refreshing the soul;
The decree of the Lord is trustworthy,
    giving wisdom to the simple.
℟. The judgments of the Lord are true,
    and all of them are just.

The precepts of the Lord are right,
    rejoicing the heart;
The command of the Lord is clear,
    enlightening the eye.
℟. The judgments of the Lord are true,
    and all of them are just.
The fear of the Lord is pure,
    enduring forever;
The ordinances of the Lord are true,
    all of them just.
℟. The judgments of the Lord are true,
    and all of them are just.
They are more precious than gold,
    than a heap of purest gold;
Sweeter also than syrup
    or honey from the comb.
℟. The judgments of the Lord are true,
    and all of them are just.

Years I and II

GOSPEL
Mt 9, 1-8

Alleluia

See no. 509.

✠ A reading from the holy gospel according
    to Matthew

They praised God for giving such power to men.

Jesus entered a boat, made the crossing, and came back to his own town. There the people at once brought to him a paralyzed man lying on a mat. When Jesus saw their faith he said to the paralytic, "Have courage, son, your sins are forgiven." At that some of the scribes said to themselves, "The man blasphemes." Jesus was aware of what they were thinking and said: "Why do you harbor evil thoughts? Which is less trouble to say, 'Your sins are forgiven' or 'Stand up and walk'? To help you realize that the Son of Man has authority on earth to forgive sins"—he then said to the paralyzed man—"Stand up! Roll up your mat, and go home." The man stood up and went toward his home. At the sight, a feeling of awe came over the crowd, and they praised God for giving such authority to men.

This is the gospel of the Lord.

381   FRIDAY OF THE THIRTEENTH WEEK OF THE YEAR

Year I

READING I   Gn 23, 1-4. 19; 24, 1-8. 62-67

A reading from the book of Genesis

Isaac loved Rebekah—he made her his wife, and was consoled for the loss of his mother.

The span of Sarah's life was one hundred and twenty-seven years. She died in Kiriatharba (that is, Hebron) in the land of Canaan, and Abraham performed the customary mourning rites for her. Then he left the side of his dead one and addressed the Hittites: "Although I am a resident alien among you, sell me from your holdings a piece of property for a burial ground, that I may bury my dead wife."

After this transaction, Abraham buried his wife Sarah in the cave of the field of Machpelah, facing Mamre (that is, Hebron) in the land of Canaan.

Abraham had now reached a ripe old age, and the Lord had blessed him in every way. Abraham said to the senior servant of his household, who had charge of all his possessions: "Put your hand under my thigh, and I will make you swear by the Lord, the God of heaven and the God of earth, that you will not procure a wife for my son from the daughters of the Canaanites among whom I live, but that you will go to my own land and to my kindred to get a wife for my son Isaac." The servant asked him: "What if the woman is unwilling to follow me to this land? Should I then take your son back to the land from which you migrated?" "Never take my son back there for any reason," Abraham told him. "The Lord, the God of heaven, who took me from my father's house and the land of my kin, and who confirmed by oath the promise he then made to me, 'I will give this land to your descendants' —he will send his messenger before you, and you will obtain a wife for my son there. If the woman is unwilling to follow you, you will be released from this oath. But never take my son back there!"

[A long time later, Isaac went] to live in the region of the Negeb. One day toward evening he went out . . . in the field, and as he looked around, he noticed that camels were approaching. Rebekah, too, was looking about, and when she saw him, she alighted from her camel and asked the servant, "Who is the man out there, walking through the fields toward us?" "That is my master," replied the servant. Then she covered herself with her veil.

The servant recounted to Isaac all the things he had done. Then Isaac took Rebekah into his tent; he married her, and thus she became his wife. In his love for her Isaac found solace after the death of his mother Sarah.

This is the Word of the Lord.

Responsorial Psalm   Ps 106, 1-2. 3-4. 4-5

℟. (1) Give thanks to the Lord for he is good.
Give thanks to the Lord, for he is good,
    for his kindness endures forever.
Who can tell the mighty deeds of the Lord,
    or proclaim all his praises?
℟. Give thanks to the Lord for he is good.
Happy are they who observe what is right,
    who do always what is just.
Remember me, O Lord, as you favor your
    people.
℟. Give thanks to the Lord for he is good.
Visit me with your saving help,
    that I may see the prosperity of your chosen
    ones,
Rejoice in the joy of your people,
    and glory with your inheritance.
℟. Give thanks to the Lord for he is good.
℟. Or: Alleluia.

Year II

READING I   Am 8, 4-6. 9-12

A reading from the book of the prophet Amos

I will send famine on the earth, not of bread but of hearing the word of God.

Hear this, you who trample upon the needy
    and destroy the poor of the land!
"When will the new moon be over," you ask,
    "that we may sell our grain,
    and the sabbath, that we may display the
    wheat?
We will diminish the ephah,

add to the shekel,
and fix our scales for cheating!"
We will buy the lowly man for silver,
and the poor man for a pair of sandals;
even the refuse of the wheat we will sell!"

On that day, says the Lord God,
I will make the sun set at midday
and cover the earth with darkness in broad
daylight.
I will turn your feasts into mourning
and all your songs into lamentations.
I will cover the loins of all with sackcloth
and make every head bald.
I will make them mourn as for an only son,
and bring their day to a bitter end.

Yes, days are coming, says the Lord God,
when I will send famine upon the land:
Not a famine of bread, or thirst for water,
but for hearing the word of the Lord.
Then shall they wander from sea to sea
and rove from the north to the east
In search of the word of the Lord,
but they shall not find it.
        This is the Word of the Lord.

Responsorial Psalm Ps 119, 2. 10. 20. 30. 40. 131

R̷. (Mt 4, 46) Man does not live on bread alone,
but on every word that comes from the
mouth of God.
Happy are they who observe his decrees,
who seek him with all their heart.
R̷. Man does not live on bread alone,
but on every word that comes from the
mouth of God.
With all my heart I seek you;
let me not stray from your commands.
R̷. Man does not live on bread alone,
but on every word that comes from the
mouth of God.
My soul is consumed with longing
for your ordinances at all times.
R̷. Man does not live on bread alone,
but on every word that comes from the
mouth of God.
The way of truth I have chosen;
I have set your ordinances before me.

R̷. Man does not live on bread alone,
but on every word that comes from the
the mouth of God.
Behold, I long for your precepts;
in your justice give me life.
R̷. Man does not live by bread alone,
but by every word that comes from the
mouth of God.
I gasp with open mouth
in my yearning for your commands.
R̷. Man does not live on bread alone,
but on every word that comes from the
mouth of God.

Years I and II

GOSPEL   Mt 9, 9-13
Alleluia
See no. 509.

✠ **A reading from the holy gospel according
to Matthew**

It is not the healthy who need the doctor; what I want is
mercy, not sacrifice.

As Jesus moved about, he saw a man named
Matthew at his post where taxes were collected. He said to him, "Follow me." Matthew
got up and followed him. Now it happened
that, while Jesus was at table in Matthew's
home, many tax collectors and those known as
sinners came to join Jesus and his disciples at
dinner. The Pharisees saw this and complained
to his disciples, "What reason can the Teacher
have for eating with tax collectors and those
who disregard the law?" Overhearing the remark, he said: "People who are in good health
do not need a doctor; sick people do. Go and
learn the meaning of the words, 'It is mercy I
desire and not sacrifice.' I have come to call,
not the self-righteous, but sinners."
        This is the gospel of the Lord.

382   **SATURDAY OF THE**
        THIRTEENTH WEEK OF THE YEAR

Year I

READING I   Gn 27, 1-5. 15-29

A reading from the book of Genesis

Jacob took his brother's place and by fraud received the blessing.

When Isaac was so old that his eyesight had failed him, he called his older son Esau and said to him, "Son!" "Yes, father!" he replied. Isaac then said, "As you can see, I am so old that I may now die at any time. Take your gear, therefore—your quiver and bow—and go out into the country to hunt some game for me. With your catch prepare an appetizing dish for me, such as I like, and bring it to me to eat, so that I may give you my special blessing before I die."

Rebekah had been listening while Isaac was speaking to his son Esau, who went out into the country to carry out his father's orders.

Rebekah then took the best clothes of her older son Esau that she had in the house, and gave them to her younger son Jacob to wear; and with the skins of the kids she covered up his hands and the hairless parts of his neck. Then she handed her son Jacob the appetizing dish and the bread she had prepared.

Bringing them to his father, Jacob said, "Father!" "Yes?" replied Isaac. "Which of my sons are you?" Jacob answered his father: "I am Esau, your first-born. I did as you told me. Please sit up and eat some of my game, so that you may give me your special blessing." But Isaac asked, "How did you succeed so quickly, son?" He answered, "The Lord, your God, let things turn out well with me." Isaac then said to Jacob, "Come closer, son, that I may feel you, to learn whether you really are my son Esau or not." So Jacob moved up closer to his father. When Isaac felt him, he said, "Although the voice is Jacob's, the hands are Esau's." (He failed to identify him because his hands were hairy, like those of his brother Esau; so in the end he gave him his blessing.) Again he asked him, "Are you really my son Esau?" "Certainly," he replied. Then Isaac said, "Serve me your game, son, that I may eat of it and then give you my blessing." Jacob served it to him, and Isaac ate; he brought him wine, and he drank. Finally his father Isaac said to him, "Come closer, son, and kiss me." As Jacob went up and kissed him, Isaac smelled the fragrance of his clothes. With that, he blessed him, saying,

"Ah, the fragrance of my son
    is like the fragrance of a field
    that the Lord has blessed!

"May God give to you
    of the dew of the heavens
And of the fertility of the earth
    abundance of grain and wine.

"Let peoples serve you,
    and nations pay you homage;
Be master of your brothers,
    and may your mother's sons bow down to
        you.
Cursed be those who curse you,
    and blessed be those who bless you."
            This is the Word of the Lord.

Responsorial Psalm   Ps 135, 1-2. 3-4. 5-6

℟. (3) Praise the Lord for he is good!
Praise the name of the Lord;
    Praise, you servants of the Lord
Who stand in the house of the Lord,
    in the courts of the house of our God.
℟. Praise the Lord for he is good!
Praise the Lord, for the Lord is good;
    sing praise to his name, which we love;
For the Lord has chosen Jacob for himself,
    Israel for his own possession.
℟. Praise the Lord for he is good!
For I know that the Lord is great;
    our Lord is greater than all gods.
All that the Lord wills he does
    in heaven and on earth,
    in the seas and in all the deeps.
℟. Praise the Lord for he is good!
℟. Or: Alleluia.

READING I   Am 9, 11-15

A reading from the book of the prophet Amos

I will restore my people Israel and plant them in their own country.

Thus says the Lord:
On that day I will raise up
    the fallen hut of David;
I will wall up its breaches,
    raise up its ruins,
    and rebuild it as in the days of old,
That they may conquer what is left of Edom
    and all the nations that shall bear my name,
    say I, the Lord, who will do this.
Yes, days are coming,
    says the Lord,
When the plowman shall overtake the reaper,
    and the vintager, him who sows the seed;
The juice of grapes shall drip down the mountains,
    and all the hills shall run with it.
I will bring about the restoration of my people Israel;
    they shall rebuild and inhabit their ruined cities,
Plant vineyards and drink the wine,
    set out gardens and eat the fruits.
I will plant them upon their own ground;
    never again shall they be plucked
From the land I have given them,
    say I, the Lord, your God.
            This is the Word of the Lord.

Responsorial Psalm   Ps 85, 9. 11-12. 13-14

R℣. (9) The Lord speaks of peace to his people.
I will hear what God proclaims;
    the Lord—for he proclaims peace
To his people, and to his faithful ones,
    and to those who put in him their hope.
R℣. The Lord speaks of peace to his people.
Kindness and truth shall meet;
    justice and peace shall kiss.
Truth shall spring out of the earth,
    and justice shall look down from heaven.
R℣. The Lord speaks of peace to his people.
The Lord himself will give his benefits;
    our land shall yield its increase.

Justice shall walk before him,
    and salvation, along the way of his steps.
R℣. The Lord speaks of peace to his people.

GOSPEL   Mt 9, 14-17
Alleluia

See no. 509.

✠ **A reading from the holy gospel according to Matthew**

The wedding guests would never mourn while the bridegroom is still with them.

John's disciples came to Jesus with the objection, "Why is it that while we and the Pharisees fast, your disciples do not?" Jesus said to them: "How can wedding guests go in mourning so long as the groom is with them? When the day comes that the groom is taken away, then they will fast. Nobody sews a piece of unshrunken cloth on an old cloak; the very thing he has used to cover the hole will pull, and the rip only get worse. People do not pour new wine into old wineskins. If they do, the skins burst, the wine spills out, and the skins are ruined. No, they pour new wine into new wineskins, and in that way both are preserved."
            This is the gospel of the Lord.

---

383   **MONDAY OF THE**
          FOURTEENTH WEEK OF THE YEAR

READING I   Gn 28, 10-22
            A reading from the book of Genesis

He saw a ladder standing there, angels of God going up and coming down, and God speaking.

Jacob departed from Beer-sheba and proceeded toward Haran. When he came upon a certain shrine, as the sun had already set, he stopped there for the night. Taking one of the stones at the shrine, he put it under his head and lay down to sleep at that spot. Then he had a dream: a stairway rested on the ground, with its top reaching to the heavens; and God's messengers were going up and down on it. And there was the Lord standing beside him and saying:

"I, the Lord, am the God of your forefather Abraham and the God of Isaac; the land on which you are lying I will give to you and your descendants. These shall be as plentiful as the dust of the earth, and through them you shall spread out east and west, north and south. In you and your descendants all the nations of the earth shall find blessing. Know that I am with you; I will protect you wherever you go, and bring you back to this land. I will never leave you until I have done what I promised you."

When Jacob awoke from his sleep, he exclaimed, "Truly, the Lord is in this spot, although I did not know it!" In solemn wonder he cried out: "How awesome is this shrine! This is nothing else but an abode of God, and that is the gateway to heaven!" Early the next morning Jacob took the stone that he had put under his head, set it up as a memorial stone, and poured oil on top of it. He called that site Bethel, whereas the former name of the town had been Luz.

Jacob then made this vow: "If God remains with me, to protect me on this journey I am making and to give me enough bread to eat and clothing to wear, and I come back safe to my father's house, the Lord shall be my God. This stone that I have set up as a memorial stone shall be God's abode.

This is the Word of the Lord.

Responsorial Psalm   Ps 91, 1-2. 3-4. 14-15

℟. (2) In you, my God, I place my trust.
You who dwell in the shelter of the Most High,
    who abide in the shadow of the Almighty,
Say to the Lord, "My refuge and my fortress,
    my God, in whom I trust."
℟. In you, my God, I place my trust.
For he will rescue you from the snare of the fowler,
    from the destroying pestilence.
With his pinions he will cover you,
    and under his wings you shall take refuge.
℟. In you, my God, I place my trust.
Because he clings to me, I will deliver him;
    I will set him on high because he acknowledges my name.

He shall call upon me, and I will answer him;
    I will be with him in distress.
℟. In you, my God, I place my trust.

READING I   Hos 2, 16. 17-18. 21-22
A reading from the book of the prophet Hosea
I will betroth you to myself for ever.

Thus says the Lord:
I will allure her;
    I will lead her into the desert
    and speak to her heart.
She shall respond there as in the days of her youth,
    when she came up from the land of Egypt.

On that day, says the Lord,
She shall call me "My husband,"
    and never again "My baal."

I will espouse you to me forever:
    I will espouse you in right and in justice,
    in love and in mercy;
I will espouse you in fidelity,
    and you shall know the Lord.

This is the Word of the Lord.

Responsorial Psalm   Ps 145, 2-3. 4-5. 6-7. 8-9

℟. (8) The Lord is kind and merciful.
Every day will I bless you,
    and I will praise your name forever and ever.
Great is the Lord and highly to be praised;
    his greatness is unsearchable.
℟. The Lord is kind and merciful.
Generation after generation praises your works
    and proclaims your might.
They speak of the splendor of your glorious majesty
    and tell of your wondrous works.
℟. The Lord is kind and merciful.
They discourse of the power of your terrible deeds
    and declare your greatness.
They publish the fame of your abundant goodness
    and joyfully sing of your justice.
℟. The Lord is kind and merciful.

The Lord is gracious and merciful,
    slow to anger and of great kindness.
The Lord is good to all
    and compassionate toward all his works.
℟. The Lord is kind and merciful.

Years I and II

GOSPEL   Mt 9, 18-26
Alleluia

See no. 509.

✠ A reading from the holy gospel according
    to Matthew

My daughter has just died, but come to her and she will live.
As Jesus was speaking, a synagogue leader
came up, did him reverence and said: "My
daughter has just died. Please come and lay
your hand on her and she will come back to
life." Jesus stood up and followed him, and
his disciples did the same. As they were going,
a woman who had suffered from hemorrhages
for twelve years came up behind him and
touched the tassel on his cloak. "If only I
can touch his cloak," she thought, "I shall get
well." Jesus turned around and saw her and
said, "Courage, daughter! Your faith has restored you to health." That very moment the
woman got well.

When Jesus arrived at the synagogue leader's house and saw the flute players and the
crowd who were making a din, he said, "Leave,
all of you! The little girl is not dead. She is
asleep." At this they began to ridicule him.
When the crowd had been put out he entered
and took her by the hand, and the little girl got
up. News of this circulated throughout the
district.

    This is the gospel of the Lord.

---

384   **TUESDAY OF THE
FOURTEENTH WEEK OF THE YEAR**

Year I

READING I   Gn 32, 23-33

A reading from the book of Genesis

Your name shall be called Israel, because you have been
strong against God.
**In the course of the night, Jacob arose, took
his two wives, with the two maidservants and**

his eleven children, and crossed the ford of the
Jabbok. After he had taken them across the
stream and had brought over all his possessions, Jacob was left there alone. Then some
man wrestled with him until the break of
dawn. When the man saw that he could not
prevail over him, he struck Jacob's hip at its
socket, so that the hip socket was wrenched as
they wrestled. The man then said, "Let me go,
for it is daybreak." But Jacob said, "I will not
let you go until you bless me." "What is your
name?" the man asked. He answered, "Jacob."
Then the man said, "You shall no longer be
spoken of as Jacob, but as Israel, because you
have contended with divine and human beings
and have prevailed." Jacob then asked him,
"Do tell me your name, please." He answered,
"Why should you want to know my name?"
With that, he bade him farewell. Jacob named
the place Peniel, "Because I have seen God face
to face," he said, "yet my life has been spared."

At sunrise, as he left Penuel, Jacob limped
along because of his hip. That is why, to this
day, the Israelites do not eat the sciatic muscle
that is on the hip socket, inasmuch as Jacob's
hip socket was struck at the sciatic muscle.

    This is the Word of the Lord.

Responsorial Psalm   Ps 17, 1. 2-3. 6-7. 8. 15

℟. (15) In my justice, I shall see your face, O
    Lord.
**Hear, O Lord, a just suit;
    attend to my outcry;
    hearken to my prayer from lips without
      deceit.**
℟. In my justice, I shall see your face, O Lord.
**From you let my judgment come;
    your eyes behold what is right.
Though you test my heart, searching it in the
    night,
    though you try me with fire, you shall find
      no malice in me.**
℟. In my justice, I shall see your face, O Lord.
**I call upon you, for you will answer me, O God;
    incline your ear to me; hear my word.
Show your wondrous kindness,
    O savior of those who flee.**
℟. In my justice, I shall see your face, O Lord.

Hide me in the shadow of your wings.
  I in justice shall behold your face;
On waking, I shall be content in your presence.
℟. In my justice, I shall see your face, O Lord.

Year II

READING I   Hos 8, 4-7. 11-13

A reading from the book of the prophet Hosea
They sow the wind and reap the whirlwind.

They made kings [in Israel] but not by my
    authority;
  they established princes, but without my
    approval.
With their silver and gold they made
  idols for themselves, to their own destruc-
    tion.
Cast away your calf, O Samaria!
  my wrath is kindled against them;
How long will they be unable to attain
  innocence in Israel?
The work of an artisan,
  no god at all,
Destined for the flames—
  such is the calf of Samaria!
When they sow the wind,
  they shall reap the whirlwind;
The stalk of grain that forms no ear
  can yield no flour;
Even if it could,
  strangers would swallow it.

When Ephraim made many altars to expiate
    sin,
  his altars became occasions of sin.
Though I write for him my many ordinances,
  they are considered as a stranger's.
Though they offer sacrifice,
  immolate flesh and eat it,
  the Lord is not pleased with them.
He shall still remember their guilt
  and punish their sins;
  they shall return to Egypt.
      This is the Word of the Lord.

Responsorial Psalm   Ps 115, 3-4. 5-6. 7-8. 9-10

℟. (9) The house of Israel trusts in the Lord.

Our God is in heaven;
  whatever he wills, he does.
Their idols are silver and gold,
  the handiwork of men.
℟. The house of Israel trusts in the Lord.
They have mouths but speak not;
  they have eyes but see not;
They have ears but hear not;
  they have noses but smell not.
℟. The house of Israel trusts in the Lord.
They have hands but feel not;
  they have feet but walk not.
Their makers shall be like them,
  everyone that trusts in them.
℟. The house of Israel trusts in the Lord.
℟. Or: Alleluia.

Years I and II

GOSPEL   Mt 9, 32-38
Alleluia
See no. 509.

✠ **A reading from the holy gospel according
      to Matthew**
The harvest is rich but the laborers are few.

Some people brought Jesus a mute who was
possessed by a demon. Once the demon was
expelled the mute began to speak, to the great
surprise of the crowds. "Nothing like this has
ever been seen in Israel!" they exclaimed. But
the Pharisees were saying, "He casts out demons through the prince of demons."

   Jesus continued his tour of all the towns and
villages. He taught in their synagogues, he proclaimed the good news of God's reign, and he
cured every sickness and disease. At the sight
of the crowds, his heart was moved with pity.
They were lying prostrate from exhaustion,
like sheep without a shepherd. He said to his
disciples: "The harvest is good but laborers
are scarce. Beg the harvest master to send out
laborers to gather his harvest."
      This is the gospel of the Lord.

385   WEDNESDAY OF THE
FOURTEENTH WEEK OF THE YEAR

READING I   Gn 41, 55-57; 42, 5-7. 17-24

A reading from the book of Genesis

We have merited this misery because we have sinned
against our brother

When hunger came to be felt throughout the land of Egypt and the people cried to Pharaoh for bread, Pharaoh directed all the Egyptians to go to Joseph and do whatever he told them. When the famine had spread throughout the land, Joseph opened all the cities that had grain and rationed it to the Egyptians, since the famine had gripped the land of Egypt. In fact, all the world came to Joseph to obtain rations of grain, for famine had gripped the whole world.

The sons of Israel were among those who came to Egypt to procure rations. It was Joseph, as governor of the country, who dispensed the rations to all the people. When Joseph's brothers came and knelt down before him with their faces to the ground, he recognized them as soon as he saw them. But he concealed his own identity from them and spoke sternly to them.

With that, he locked them up in the guardhouse for three days.

On the third day Joseph said to them: "Do this, and you shall live; for I am a God-fearing man. If you have been honest, only one of your brothers need be confined in this prison, while the rest of you may go and take home provisions for your starving families. But you must come back to me with your youngest brother. Your words will thus be verified, and you will not die." To this they agreed.

To one another, however, they said: "Alas, we are being punished because of our brother. We saw the anguish of his heart when he pleaded with us, yet we paid no heed; that is why this anguish has now come upon us." "Didn't I tell you," broke in Reuben, "not to do wrong to the boy? But you wouldn't listen! Now comes the reckoning for his blood." They did not know, of course, that Joseph understood what they said, since he spoke with them through an interpreter. But turning away from them, he wept.

This is the Word of the Lord.

Responsorial Psalm   Ps 33, 2-3. 10-11. 18-19

℟. (22) Lord, let your mercy be on us,
   as we place our trust in you.

Give thanks to the Lord on the harp;
   with the ten-stringed lyre chant his praises.
Sing to him a new song;
   pluck the strings skillfully, with shouts of
      gladness.

℟. Lord, let your mercy be on us,
   as we place our trust in you.

The Lord brings to nought the plans of nations;
   he foils the designs of peoples.
But the plan of the Lord stands forever;
   the design of his heart, through all generations.

℟. Lord, let your mercy be on us,
   as we place our trust in you.

But see, the eyes of the Lord are upon those
      who fear him,
   upon those who hope for his kindness,
To deliver them from death
   and preserve them in spite of famine.

℟. Lord, let your mercy be on us,
   as we place our trust in you.

READING I   Hos 10, 1-3. 7-8. 12

A reading from the book of the prophet Hosea

It is the time to go seeking the Lord God.

Israel is a luxuriant vine
   whose fruit matches its growth.
The more abundant his fruit,
   the more altars he built;
The more productive his land,
   the more sacred pillars he set up.
Their heart is false,
   now they pay for their guilt;
God shall break down their altars
   and destroy their sacred pillars.
If they would say,
   "We have no king"—

Since they do not fear the Lord,
   what can the king do for them?

The king of Samaria shall disappear,
   like foam upon the waters.
The high places of Aven shall be destroyed,
   the sin of Israel;
     thorns and thistles shall overgrow their
     altars.
Then they shall cry out to the mountains,
   "Cover us!"
   and to the hills, "Fall upon us!"

"Sow for yourselves justice,
   reap the fruit of piety;
Break up for yourselves a new field,
   for it is time to seek the Lord,
     till he come and rain down justice upon
     you."
       This is the Word of the Lord.

Responsorial Psalm   Ps 105, 2-3. 4-5. 6-7

℞. (4) Seek always the face of the Lord.
Sing to him, sing his praise,
   proclaim all his wondrous deeds.
Glory in his holy name;
   rejoice, O hearts that seek the Lord!
℞. Seek always the face of the Lord.
Look to the Lord in his strength;
   seek to serve him constantly.
Recall the wondrous deeds that he has
   wrought,
   his portents, and the judgments he has
   uttered.
℞. Seek always the face of the Lord.
You descendants of Abraham, his servants,
   sons of Jacob, his chosen ones!
He, the Lord, is our God;
   throughout the earth his judgments prevail.
℞. Seek always the face of the Lord.
℞. Or: Alleluia.

Years I and II

GOSPEL   Mt 10, 1-7
Alleluia

See no. 509.

✠ **A reading from the holy gospel according
to Matthew**
Go to the lost sheep of the house of Israel.

Jesus summoned his twelve disciples and gave
them authority to expel unclean spirits and to
cure sickness and disease of every kind.

   The names of the twelve apostles are these:
first Simon, now known as Peter, and his
brother Andrew; James, Zebedee's son, and
his brother John; Philip and Bartholomew,
Thomas and Matthew the tax collector; James,
son of Alphaeus, and Thaddaeus; Simon the
Zealot Party member, and Judas Iscariot, who
betrayed him. Jesus sent these men on mission
as the Twelve, after giving them the following
instructions:

   "Do not visit pagan territory and do not
enter a Samaritan town. Go instead after the
lost sheep of the house of Israel. As you go,
make this announcement: 'The reign of God is
at hand!' "
       This is the gospel of the Lord.

---

386   **THURSDAY OF THE
FOURTEENTH WEEK OF THE YEAR**

Year I

READING I   Gn 44, 18-21. 23-29; 45, 1-5
A reading from the book of Genesis
God sent me before you into Egypt to preserve your lives.

Judah approached Joseph and said: "I beg you,
my lord, let your servant speak earnestly to my
lord, and do not become angry with your servant, for you are the equal of Pharaoh. My lord
asked your servants, 'Have you a father, or
another brother?' So we said to my lord, 'We
have an aged father, and a young brother, the
child of his old age. This one's full brother is
dead, and since he is the only one by that
mother who is left, his father dotes on him.'
Then you told your servants, 'Bring him down
to me that my eyes may look on him. Unless
your youngest brother comes back with you,
you shall not come into my presence again.'
When we returned to your servant our father,
we reported to him the words of my lord.

"Later, our father told us to come back and buy some food for the family. So we reminded him, 'We cannot go down there; only if our youngest brother is with us can we go, for we may not see the man if our youngest brother is not with us.' Then your servant our father said to us, 'As you know, my wife bore me two sons. One of them, however, disappeared, and I had to conclude that he must have been torn to pieces by wild beasts; I have not seen him since. If you now take this one away from me too, and some disaster befalls him, you will send my white head down to the nether world in grief.' "

Joseph could no longer control himself in the presence of all his attendants, so he cried out, "Have everyone withdraw from me!" Thus no one else was about when he made himself known to his brothers. But his sobs were so loud that the Egyptians heard him, and so the news reached Pharaoh's palace. "I am Joseph," he said to his brothers. "Is my father still in good health?" But his brothers could give him no answer, so dumbfounded were they at him.

"Come closer to me," he told his brothers. When they had done so, he said: "I am your brother Joseph, whom you once sold into Egypt. But now do not be distressed, and do not reproach yourselves for having sold me here. It was really for the sake of saving lives that God sent me here ahead of you."

This is the Word of the Lord.

Responsorial Psalm   Ps 105, 16-17. 18-19. 20-21

℟. (5) Remember the marvels the Lord has done.
When he called down a famine on the land
and ruined the crop that sustained them,
He sent a man before them,
Joseph, sold as a slave.
℟. Remember the marvels the Lord has done.
They had weighed him down with fetters,
and he was bound with chains,
Till his prediction came to pass
and the word of the Lord proved him true.
℟. Remember the marvels the Lord has done.
The king sent and released him,
the ruler of the peoples set him free.

He made him lord of his house
and ruler of all his possessions.
℟. Remember the marvels the Lord has done.
℟. Or: Alleluia.

Year II

READING I   Hos 11, 1. 3-4. 8-9

A reading from the book of the prophet Hosea
My heart recoils within me.
When Israel was a child I loved him,
out of Egypt I called my son.
It was I who taught Ephraim to walk,
who took them in my arms;
I drew them with human cords,
with bands of love;
I fostered them like one
who raises an infant to his cheeks;
Yet, though I stooped to feed my child,
they did not know that I was their healer.

My heart is overwhelmed,
my pity is stirred.
I will not give vent to my blazing anger,
I will not destroy Ephraim again;
For I am God and not man,
the Holy One present among you;
I will not let the flames consume you.
This is the Word of the Lord.

Responsorial Psalm   Ps 80, 2. 3. 15-16

℟. (4) Let us see your face, Lord,
and we shall be saved.
O shepherd of Israel, hearken,
from your throne upon the cherubim, shine
forth,
Rouse your power.
℟. Let us see your face, Lord,
and we shall be saved.
Once again, O Lord of hosts,
look down from heaven, and see:
Take care of this vine,
and protect what your right hand has
planted
[the son of man whom you yourself made
strong].
℟. Let us see your face, Lord,
and we shall be saved.

GOSPEL
Alleluia

See no. 509.

✠ **A reading from the holy gospel according to Matthew**

You received without charge, give without charge.

Jesus said to his disciples: "As you go, make this announcement: 'The reign of God is at hand!' Cure the sick, raise the dead, heal the leprous, expel demons. The gift you have received, give as a gift. Provide yourselves with neither gold nor silver nor copper in your belts; no traveling bag, no change of shirt, no sandals, no walking staff. The workman, after all, is worth his keep.

"Look for a worthy citizen in every town or village you come to and stay with him until you leave. As you enter his home bless it. If the home is deserving, your blessing will descend on it. If it is not, your blessing will return to you. If anyone does not receive you or listen to what you have to say, leave that house or town, and once outside it shake its dust from your feet. I assure you, it will go easier for the region of Sodom and Gomorrah on the day of judgment than it will for that town."

This is the gospel of the Lord.

**387   FRIDAY OF THE
FOURTEENTH WEEK OF THE YEAR**

Year I

READING I   Gn 46, 1-7. 28-30

A reading from the book of Genesis

Now I can die, because I have seen you again.

Israel set out with all that was his. When he arrived at Beer-sheba, he offered sacrifices to the God of his father Isaac. There God, speaking to Israel in a vision by night, called, "Jacob! Jacob!" "Here I am," he answered. Then he said: "I am God, the God of your father. Do not be afraid to go down to Egypt, for there I will make you a great nation. Not only will I go down to Egypt with you; I will also bring you back here, after Joseph has closed your eyes."

So Jacob departed from Beer-sheba, and the sons of Israel put their father and their wives and children on the wagons that Pharaoh had sent for his transport. They took with them their livestock and the possessions they had acquired in the land of Canaan. Thus Jacob and all his descendants migrated to Egypt. His sons and his grandsons, his daughters and his granddaughters—all his descendants—he took with him to Egypt.

Israel had sent Judah ahead to Joseph, so that he might meet him in Goshen. On his arrival in the region of Goshen, Joseph hitched the horses to his chariot and rode to meet his father Israel in Goshen. As soon as he saw him, he flung himself on his neck and wept a long time in his arms. And Israel said to Joseph, "At last I can die, now that I have seen for myself that Joseph is still alive."

This is the Word of the Lord.

Responsorial Psalm   Ps 37, 3-4. 18-19. 27-28. 39-40

℟. (39) The salvation of the just comes from the Lord.

Trust in the Lord and do good,
    that you may dwell in the land and enjoy security.
Take delight in the Lord,
    and he will grant you your heart's requests.

℟. The salvation of the just comes from the Lord.

The Lord watches over the lives of the wholehearted;
    their inheritance lasts forever.
They are not put to shame in an evil time;
    in days of famine they have plenty.

℟. The salvation of the just comes from the Lord.

Turn from evil and do good,
    that you may abide forever;
For the Lord loves what is right,
    and forsakes not his faithful ones.
Criminals are destroyed,
    and the posterity of the wicked is cut off.

℟. The salvation of the just comes from the Lord.

The salvation of the just is from the Lord;
    he is their refuge in time of distress.

And the Lord helps them and delivers them;
  he delivers them from the wicked and saves
    them,
  because they take refuge in him.
℟. The salvation of the just comes from the
  Lord.

Year II

READING I Hos 14, 2-10

A reading from the book of the prophet Hosea
We will say no more: Our God, to the work of our hands.

Return, O Israel, to the Lord, your God;
  you have collapsed through your guilt.
Take with you words,
  and return to the Lord;
Say to him, "Forgive all iniquity,
  and receive what is good, that we may
    render
  as offerings the bullocks from our stalls.
Assyria will not save us,
  nor shall we have horses to mount;
We shall say no more, 'Our god,'
  to the work of our hands;
  for in you the orphan finds compassion."

I will heal their defection,
  I will love them freely;
  for my wrath is turned away from them.
I will be like the dew for Israel:
  he shall blossom like the lily;
He shall strike root like the Lebanon cedar,
  and put forth his shoots.
His splendor shall be like the olive tree
  and his fragrance like the Lebanon cedar.
Again they shall dwell in his shade
  and raise grain;
They shall blossom like the vine,
  and his fame shall be like the wine of
    Lebanon.

Ephraim! What more has he to do with idols?
  I have humbled him, but I will prosper him.
"I am like a verdant cypress tree"—
  Because of me you bear fruit!

Let him who is wise understand these things;
  let him who is prudent know them.

Straight are the paths of the Lord,
  in them the just walk,

but sinners stumble in them.
  This is the Word of the Lord.

Responsorial Psalm Ps 51, 3-4. 8-9. 12-13. 14. 17

℟. (17) My mouth will declare your praise.
Have mercy on me, O God, in your goodness;
  in the greatness of your compassion wipe
    out my offense.
Thoroughly wash me from my guilt
  and of my sin cleanse me.
℟. My mouth will declare your praise.
Behold, you are pleased with sincerity of heart,
  and in my inmost being you teach me
    wisdom.
Cleanse me of sin with hyssop, that I may be
    purified;
  wash me, and I shall be whiter than snow.
℟. My mouth will declare your praise.
A clean heart create for me, O God,
  and a steadfast spirit renew within me.
Cast me not out from your presence,
  and your holy spirit take not from me.
℟. My mouth will declare your praise.
Give me back the joy of your salvation,
  and a willing spirit sustain in me.
O Lord, open my lips,
  and my mouth shall proclaim your praise.
℟. My mouth will declare your praise.

Years I and II

GOSPEL Mt 10, 16-23
Alleluia

See no. 509.

✠ A reading from the holy gospel according
  to Matthew
It is not you who speak, but the Spirit speaking in you.

Jesus said to his disciples: "I am sending you
out like sheep among wolves. You must be
clever as snakes and innocent as doves. Be on
your guard with respect to others. They will
hale you into court, they will flog you in their
synagogues. You will be brought to trial before
rulers and kings, to give witness before them
and the Gentiles on my account. When they
hand you over, do not worry about what you
will say or how you will say it. When the hour
comes, you will be given what you are to say.

You yourselves will not be the speakers; the Spirit of your Father will be speaking in you.

"Brother will hand over brother to death, and the father his child; children will turn against parents and have them put to death. You will be hated by all on account of me. But whoever holds out till the end will escape death. When they persecute you in one town, flee to the next. I solemnly assure you, you will not have covered the towns of Israel before the Son of Man comes."

This is the gospel of the Lord.

---

388   **SATURDAY OF THE FOURTEENTH WEEK OF THE YEAR**

Year I

READING I   Gn 49, 29-33; 50, 15-24

A reading from the book of Genesis

God will visit you and bring about the deliverance of many people.

Jacob gave this charge to his sons: "Since I am about to be taken to my kindred, bury me with my fathers in the cave that lies in the field of Ephron the Hittite, the cave in the field of Machpelah, facing on Mamre, in the land of Canaan, the field that Abraham bought from Ephron the Hittite for a burial ground. There Abraham and his wife Sarah are buried, and so are Isaac and his wife Rebekah, and there, too, I buried Leah—the field and the cave in it that had been purchased from the Hittites."

When Jacob had finished giving these instructions to his sons, he drew his feet into the bed, breathed his last, and was taken to his kindred.

Now that their father was dead, Joseph's brothers became fearful and thought, "Suppose Joseph has been nursing a grudge against us and now plans to pay us back in full for all the wrong we did him!" So they approached Joseph and said: "Before your father died, he gave us these instructions: 'You shall say to Joseph, Jacob begs you to forgive the criminal wrongdoing of your brothers, who treated you so cruelly.' Please, therefore, forgive the crime that we, the servants of your father's God,

committed." When they spoke these words to him, Joseph broke into tears. Then his brothers proceeded to fling themselves down before him and said, "Let us be your slaves!" But Joseph replied to them: "Have no fear. Can I take the place of God? Even though you meant harm to me, God meant it for good, to achieve his present end, the survival of many people. Therefore have no fear. I will provide for you and for your children." By thus speaking kindly to them, he reassured them.

Joseph remained in Egypt, together with his father's family. He lived a hundred and ten years. He saw Ephraim's children to the third generation, and the children of Manasseh's son Machir were also born on Joseph's knees.

Joseph said to his brothers: "I am about to die. God will surely take care of you and lead you out of this land to the land that he promised on oath to Abraham, Isaac and Jacob."

This is the Word of the Lord.

Responsorial Psalm   Ps 105, 1-2. 3-4. 6-7

℟. (33) Turn to the Lord in your need
    and you will live.

Give thanks to the Lord, invoke his name;
    make known among the nations his deeds.
Sing to him, sing his praise,
    proclaim all his wondrous deeds.

℟. Turn to the Lord in your need
    and you will live.

Glory in his holy name;
    rejoice, O hearts that seek the Lord!
Look to the Lord in his strength;
    seek to serve him constantly.

℟. Turn to the Lord in your need
    and you will live.

You descendants of Abraham, his servants,
    sons of Jacob, his chosen ones!
He, the Lord, is our God;
    throughout the earth his judgments prevail.

℟. Turn to the Lord in your need
    and you will live.

Year II

READING I   Is 6, 1-8

A reading from the book of the prophet Isaiah

What a wretched state I am in, my eyes have looked at the
king, the Lord God.

In the year King Uzziah died, I saw the Lord
seated on a high and lofty throne, with the
train of his garment filling the temple. Seraphim were stationed above; each of them had
six wings: with two they veiled their faces,
with two they veiled their feet, and with two
they hovered aloft.

"Holy, holy, holy is the Lord of hosts!" they
cried one to the other. "All the earth is filled
with his glory!" At the sound of that cry, the
frame of the door shook and the house was
filled with smoke.

Then I said, "Woe is me, I am doomed!
For I am a man of unclean lips, living among a
people of unclean lips; yet my eyes have seen
the King, the Lord of hosts!" Then one of the
seraphim flew to me, holding an ember which
he had taken with tongs from the altar.

He touched my mouth with it. "See," he said,
"now that this has touched your lips, your
wickedness is removed, your sin purged."

Then I heard the voice of the Lord saying,
"Whom shall I send? Who will go for us?"
"Here I am," I said; "send me!"

This is the Word of the Lord.

Responsorial Psalm   Ps 93, 1. 1-2. 5

℟. (1) The Lord is king;
    he is robed in majesty.

The Lord is king, in splendor robed;
    robed is the Lord and girt about with
    strength.
℟. The Lord is king;
    he is robed in majesty.

And he has made the world firm,
    not to be moved.
Your throne stands firm from of old;
    from everlasting you are, O Lord.
℟. The Lord is king;
    he is robed in majesty.

Your decrees are worthy of trust indeed;
    holiness befits your house,
    O Lord, for length of days.

℟. The Lord is king;
    he is robed in majesty.

Years I and II

GOSPEL   Mt 10, 24-33

Alleluia

See no. 509.

✠ **A reading from the holy gospel according
    to Matthew**

Do not be afraid of those who can kill the body.

Jesus said to his apostles: "No pupil outranks
his teacher, no slave his master. The pupil
should be glad to become like his teacher, the
slave like his master. If they call the head of
the house Beelzebul, how much more the members of his household! Do not let them intimidate you. Nothing is concealed that will
not be revealed, and nothing hidden that will
not become known. What I tell you in darkness, speak in the light. What you hear in
private, proclaim from housetops.

"Do not fear those who deprive the body of
life but cannot destroy the soul. Rather, fear
him who can destroy both body and soul in
Gehenna. Are not two sparrows sold for next
to nothing? Yet not a single sparrow falls to
the ground without your Father's consent. As
for you, every hair of your head has been
counted; so do not be afraid of anything. You
are worth more than an entire flock of sparrows. Whoever acknowledges me before men
I will acknowledge before my Father in
heaven. Whoever disowns me before men I will
disown before my Father in heaven."

This is the gospel of the Lord.

389   **MONDAY OF THE
          FIFTEENTH WEEK OF THE YEAR**

Year I

READING I   Ex 1, 8-14. 22

A reading from the book of Exodus

We must move against Israel lest they become greater in
number.

A new king, who knew nothing of Joseph,
came to power in Egypt. He said to his subjects, "Look how numerous and powerful the

Israelite people are growing, more so than we ourselves! Come, let us deal shrewdly with them to stop their increase; otherwise, in time of war they too may join our enemies to fight against us, and so leave our country."

Accordingly, taskmasters were set over the Israelites to oppress them with forced labor. Thus they had to build for Pharaoh the supply cities of Pithom and Raamses. Yet the more they were oppressed, the more they multiplied and spread. The Egyptians, then, dreaded the Israelites and reduced them to cruel slavery, making life bitter for them with hard work in mortar and brick and all kinds of field work— the whole cruel fate of slaves.

Pharaoh then commanded all his subjects, "Throw into the river every boy that is born to the Hebrews, but you may let all the girls live."

This is the Word of the Lord.

Responsorial Psalm   Ps 124, 1-3. 4-6. 7-8

R̂. (8) Our help is in the name of the Lord.
Had not the Lord been with us—
     let Israel say,
     had not the Lord been with us—
When men rose up against us,
     then would they have swallowed us alive,
When their fury was inflamed against us.
R̂. Our help is in the name of the Lord.
Then would the waters have overwhelmed us;
The torrent would have swept over us;
     over us then would have swept
     the raging waters.
Blessed be the Lord, who did not leave us
     a prey to their teeth.
R̂. Our help is in the name of the Lord.
We were rescued like a bird
     from the fowlers' snare;
Broken was the snare,
     and we were freed.
Our help is in the name of the Lord,
     who made heaven and earth.
R̂. Our help is in the name of the Lord.

READING I   Is 1, 10-17

A reading from the book of the prophet Isaiah
Make yourselves clean, take your evil out of my sight.
Hear the word of the Lord,
     princes of Sodom!
Listen to the instruction of our God,
     people of Gomorrah!
What care I for the number of your sacrifices?
     says the Lord.
I have had enough of whole-burnt rams
     and fat of fatlings;
In the blood of calves, lambs and goats
     I find no pleasure.

When you come in to visit me,
     who asks these things of you?
Trample my courts no more!
     Bring no more worthless offerings;
     your incense is loathsome to me.
New moon and sabbath, calling of assemblies,
     octaves with wickedness: these I cannot
     bear.
Your new moons and festivals I detest;
     they weigh me down, I tire of the load.
When you spread out your hands,
     I close my eyes to you;
Though you pray the more,
     I will not listen.
Your hands are full of blood!
     Wash yourselves clean!
Put away your misdeeds from before my eyes;
     cease doing evil; learn to do good.
Make justice your aim: redress the wronged,
     hear the orphan's plea, defend the widow.
     This is the Word of the Lord.

Responsorial Psalm   Ps 50, 8-9. 16-17. 21. 23

R̂. (23) To the upright I will show the saving
     power of God.
Not for your sacrifices do I rebuke you,
     for your holocausts are before me always.
I take from your house no bullock,
     no goats out of your fold.
R̂. To the upright I will show the saving power
     of God.
Why do you recite my statutes,
     and profess my covenant with your mouth

Though you hate discipline
  and cast my words behind you?
℟. To the upright I will show the saving power
    of God.
When you do these things, shall I be deaf to it?
  Or do you think that I am like yourself?
I will correct you by drawing them up before
    your eyes.
He that offers praise as a sacrifice glorifies me;
  and to him that goes the right way I will
    show the salvation of God.
℟. To the upright I will show the saving power
    of God.

GOSPEL
Alleluia

Years I and II

Mt 10, 34–11, 1

See no. 509.

✠ A reading from the holy gospel according
        to Matthew

I have not come to bring peace, but the sword.

Jesus said to his apostles: "Do not suppose that
my mission on earth is to spread peace. My
mission is to spread, not peace, but division. I
have come to set a man at odds with his father,
a daughter with her mother, a daughter-in-law
with her mother-in-law: in short, to make a
man's enemies those of his own household.
Whoever loves father or mother, son or daughter more than me, is not worthy of me. He who
will not take up his cross and come after me is
not worthy of me. He who seeks only himself
brings himself to ruin, whereas he who brings
himself to nought for me discovers who he is.

"He who welcomes you welcomes me, and
he who welcomes me welcomes him who sent
me. He who welcomes a prophet because he
bears the name of prophet receives a prophet's
reward; he who welcomes a holy man because
he is known as holy receives a holy man's reward. And I promise you that whoever gives a
cup of cold water to one of these lowly ones
because he is a disciple will not want for his
reward."

When Jesus had finished instructing his
twelve disciples, he left that locality to teach
and preach in their towns.

    This is the gospel of the Lord.

---

390   **TUESDAY OF THE
FIFTEENTH WEEK OF THE YEAR**

Year I

READING I   Ex 2, 1-15

A reading from the book of Exodus

He was called by the name Moses because he was taken
from the water. Afterwards he grew up to lead his brothers.

A certain man of the house of Levi married a
Levite woman, who conceived and bore a son.
Seeing that he was a goodly child, she hid him
for three months. When she could hide him no
longer, she took a papyrus basket, daubed it
with bitumen and pitch, and putting the child
in it, placed it among the reeds on the river
bank. His sister stationed herself at a distance
to find out what would happen to him.

Pharaoh's daughter came down to the river
to bathe, while her maids walked along the
river bank. Noticing the basket among the
reeds, she sent her handmaid to fetch it. On
opening it, she looked and lo, there was a baby
boy, crying! She was moved with pity for him
and said, "It is one of the Hebrews' children."
Then his sister asked Pharaoh's daughter,
"Shall I go and call one of the Hebrew women
to nurse the child for you?" "Yes, do so," she
answered. So the maiden went and called the
child's own mother. Pharaoh's daughter said to
her, "Take this child and nurse it for me, and
I will repay you." The woman therefore took
the child and nursed it. When the child grew,
she brought him to Pharaoh's daughter, who
adopted him as her son and called him Moses;
for she said, "I drew him out of the water."

On one occasion, after Moses had grown up,
when he visited his kinsmen and witnessed
their forced labor, he saw an Egyptian striking
a Hebrew, one of his own kinsmen. Looking
about and seeing no one, he slew the Egyptian
and hid him in the sand. The next day he went
out again, and now two Hebrews were fighting! So he asked the culprit, "Why are you
striking your fellow Hebrew?" But he replied,
"Who has appointed you ruler and judge over
us? Are you thinking of killing me as you killed
the Egyptian?" Then Moses became afraid and
thought, "The affair must certainly be known."

Pharaoh, too, heard of the affair and sought to put him to death. But Moses fled from him and stayed in the land of Midian.
This is the Word of the Lord.

Responsorial Psalm   Ps 69, 3. 14. 30-31. 33-34

℟. (33) Turn to the Lord in your need, and you will live.
I am sunk in the abysmal swamp
   where there is no foothold;
I have reached the watery depths;
   the flood overwhelms me.
℟. Turn to the Lord in your need, and you will
   live.
But I pray to you, O Lord,
   for the time of your favor, O God!
In your great kindness answer me
   with your constant help.
℟. Turn to the Lord in your need, and you will
   live.
But I am afflicted and in pain;
   let your saving help, O God, protect me.
I will praise the name of God in song,
   and I will glorify him with thanksgiving;
℟. Turn to the Lord in your need, and you will
   live.
See, you lowly ones, and be glad;
   you who seek God, may your hearts be
      merry!
For the Lord hears the poor,
   and his own who are in bonds he spurns not.
℟. Turn to the Lord in your need, and you will
   live.

Year II

READING I   Is 7, 1-9
A reading from the book of the prophet Isaiah
If you do not stand by me, you will perish.
In the days of Ahaz, king of Judah, son of Jotham, son of Uzziah, Rezin, king of Aram, and Pekah, king of Israel, son of Remaliah, went up to attack Jerusalem, but they were not able to conquer it. When word came to the house of David that Aram was encamped in Ephraim, the heart of the king and the heart of the people trembled, as the trees of the forest tremble in the wind.

Then the Lord said to Isaiah: Go out to meet Ahaz, you and your son Shear-jashub, at the end of the conduit of the upper pool, on the highway of the fuller's field, and say to him: Take care you remain tranquil and do not fear; let not your courage fail before these two stumps of smoldering brands [the blazing anger of Rezin and the Arameans, and of the son of Remaliah], because of the mischief that Aram [Ephraim and the son of Remaliah] plots against you, saying, "Let us go up and tear Judah asunder, make it our own by force, and appoint the son of Tabeel king there."
   Thus says the Lord:
   This shall not stand, it shall not be!
Damascus is the capital of Aram,
   and Rezin the head of Damascus;
Samaria is the capital of Ephraim,
   and Remaliah's son the head of Samaria,
But within sixty years and five,
   Ephraim shall be crushed, no longer a nation.
Unless your faith is firm
   you shall not be firm!
   This is the Word of the Lord.

Responsorial Psalm   Ps 48, 2-3. 3-4. 5-6. 7-8

℟. (9) God upholds his city for ever.
Great is the Lord and wholly to be praised
   in the city of our God.
His holy mountain, fairest of heights,
   is the joy of all the earth.
℟. God upholds his city for ever.
Mount Zion, "the recesses of the North,"
   is the city of the great King.
God is with her castles;
   renowned is he as a stronghold.
℟. God upholds his city for ever.
For lo! the kings assemble,
   they come on together;
They also see, and at once are stunned,
   terrified, routed.
℟. God upholds his city for ever.
Quaking seizes them there;
   anguish, like a woman's in labor,
As though a wind from the east
   were shattering ships of Tarshish.
℟. God upholds his city for ever.

GOSPEL
Alleluia

Mt 11, 20-24

See no. 509.

✠ A reading from the holy gospel according
to Matthew

It will not go as hard with Tyre and Sidon and the land of
Sodom on Judgment Day as with you.

Jesus began to reproach the towns where most
of his miracles had been worked, with their
failure to reform: "It will go ill with you, Chorazin! And just as ill with you, Bethsaida! If the
miracles worked in you had taken place in
Tyre and Sidon, they would have reformed in
sackcloth and ashes long ago. I assure you, it
will go easier for Tyre and Sidon than for you
on the day of judgment. As for you, Capernaum,

'Are you to be exalted to the skies?
You shall go down to the realm of death!'
If the miracles worked in you had taken place
in Sodom, it would be standing today. I assure
you, it will go easier for Sodom than for you on
the day of judgment."

This is the gospel of the Lord.

---

391   **WEDNESDAY OF THE**
FIFTEENTH WEEK OF THE YEAR

READING I   Ex 3, 1-6. 9-12

A reading from the book of Exodus

The Lord appeared to Moses in the form of fire in the midst
of a bush.

Moses was tending the flock of his father-in-
law Jethro, the priest of Midian. Leading the
flock across the desert, he came to Horeb, the
mountain of God. There an angel of the Lord
appeared to him in fire flaming out of a bush.
As he looked on, he was surprised to see that
the bush, though on fire, was not consumed. So
Moses decided, "I must go over to look at this
remarkable sight, and see why the bush is not
burned."

When the Lord saw him coming over to look
at it more closely, God called out to him from
the bush, "Moses! Moses!" He answered,

"Here I am." God said, "Come no nearer! Remove the sandals from your feet, for the place
where you stand is holy ground. I am the God
of your father," he continued, "the God of
Abraham, the God of Isaac, the God of Jacob."
Moses hid his face, for he was afraid to look at
God.

The Lord said, "So indeed the cry of the Israelites has reached me, and I have truly noted
that the Egyptians are oppressing them. Come,
now! I will send you to Pharaoh to lead my
people, the Israelites, out of Egypt."

But Moses said to God, "Who am I that I
should go to Pharaoh and lead the Israelites out
of Egypt?" He answered, "I will be with you;
and this shall be your proof that it is I who have
sent you: when you bring my people out of
Egypt, you will worship God on this very
mountain."

This is the Word of the Lord.

Responsorial Psalm   Ps 103, 1-2. 3-4. 6-7

℟. (8) The Lord is kind and merciful.
Bless the Lord, O my soul;
    and all my being, bless his holy name.
Bless the Lord, O my soul,
    and forget not all his benefits.
℟. The Lord is kind and merciful.
He pardons all your iniquities,
    he heals all your ills.
He redeems your life from destruction,
    he crowns you with kindness and compas-
    sion.
℟. The Lord is kind and merciful.
The Lord secures justice
    and the rights of all the oppressed.
He has made known his ways to Moses,
    and his deeds to the children of Israel.
℟. The Lord is kind and merciful.

READING I   Is 10, 5-7. 13-16

A reading from the book of the prophet Isaiah

Does the axe claim more credit than the one who wields it?

Thus says the Lord:
Woe to Assyria! My rod in anger,
    my staff in wrath.
Against an impious nation I send him,

and against a people under my wrath I order him
To seize plunder, carry off loot,
　and tread them down like the mud of the streets.
But this is not what he intends,
　nor does he have this in mind;
Rather, it is in his heart to destroy,
　to make an end of nations not a few.

For he says:
"By my own power I have done it,
　and by my wisdom, for I am shrewd.
I have moved the boundaries of peoples,
　their treasures I have pillaged,
　and, like a giant, I have put down the enthroned.
My hand has seized like a nest
　the riches of nations;
As one takes eggs left alone,
　so I took in all the earth;
No one fluttered a wing,
　or opened a mouth, or chirped!"
Will the axe boast against him who hews with it?
　When will the saw exalt itself above him who wields it?
As if a rod could sway him who lifts it,
　or a staff him who is not wood!
Therefore the Lord, the Lord of hosts,
　will send among his fat ones leanness,
And instead of his glory there will be kindling
　like the kindling of fire.
　　This is the Word of the Lord.

Responsorial Psalm　　Ps 94, 5-6. 7-8. 9-10. 14-15

℟. (14) The Lord will not abandon his people.
Your people, O Lord, they trample down,
　your inheritance they afflict.
Widow and stranger they slay,
　the fatherless they murder.
℟. The Lord will not abandon his people.
And they say, "The Lord sees not;
　the God of Jacob perceives not."
Understand, you senseless ones among the people;
　and, you fools, when will you be wise?
℟. The Lord will not abandon his people.

Shall he who shaped the ear not hear?
　or he who formed the eye not see?
Shall he who instructs nations not chastise,
　he who teaches men knowledge?
℟. The Lord will not abandon his people.
For the Lord will not cast off his people,
　nor abandon his inheritance;
But judgment shall again be with justice,
　and all the upright of heart shall follow it.
℟. The Lord will not abandon his people.

Years I and II

GOSPEL　　　　　　　　　　　　Mt 11, 25-27
Alleluia

See no. 509.

✠ **A reading from the holy gospel according to Matthew**

The Lord hides these things from the wise and reveals them to children.

On one occasion Jesus spoke thus: "Father, Lord of heaven and earth, to you I offer praise; for what you have hidden from the learned and the clever you have revealed to the merest children. Father, it is true. You have graciously willed it so. Everything has been given over to me by my Father. No one knows the Son but the Father, and no one knows the Father but the Son—and anyone to whom the Son wishes to reveal him."
　　This is the gospel of the Lord.

392　　　　**THURSDAY OF THE**
　　　FIFTEENTH WEEK OF THE YEAR

Year I

READING I　　　　　　　　　　Ex 3, 11-20

A reading from the book of Exodus

I am who am. I am has sent me to you.

Moses, hearing the voice from the burning bush, said to God, "Who am I that I should go to Pharaoh and lead the Israelites out of Egypt?" He answered, "I will be with you; and this shall be your proof that it is I who have sent you: when you bring my people out of Egypt, you will worship God on this very mountain."
　　"But," said Moses to God, "when I go to the

Israelites and say to them, 'The God of your fathers has sent me to you,' if they ask me, 'What is his name?' what am I to tell them?" God replied, "I am who am." Then he added, "This is what you shall tell the Israelites: I AM sent me to you."

God spoke further to Moses, "Thus shall you say to the Israelites: The Lord, the God of your fathers, the God of Abraham, the God of Isaac, the God of Jacob, has sent me to you.

"This is my name forever;
this is my title for all generations.

"Go and assemble the elders of the Israelites, and tell them: The Lord, the God of your fathers, the God of Abraham, Isaac and Jacob, has appeared to me and said: I am concerned about you and about the way you are being treated in Egypt; so I have decided to lead you up out of the misery of Egypt into the land of the Canaanites, Hittites, Amorites, Perizzites, Hivites and Jebusites, a land flowing with milk and honey.

"Thus they will heed your message. Then you and the elders of Israel shall go to the king of Egypt and say to him: The Lord, the God of the Hebrews, has sent us word. Permit us, then, to go a three days' journey in the desert, that we may offer sacrifice to the Lord, our God.

"Yet I know that the king of Egypt will not allow you to go unless he is forced. I will stretch out my hand, therefore, and smite Egypt by doing all kinds of wondrous deeds there. After that he will send you away."

This is the Word of the Lord.

Responsorial Psalm Ps 105, 1. 5. 8-9. 24-25. 26-27

℟. (8) The Lord remembers his covenant for ever.

Give thanks to the Lord, invoke his name;
make known among the nations his deeds.
Recall the wondrous deeds that he has wrought,
his portents, and the judgments he has uttered.

℟. The Lord remembers his covenant for ever.

He remembers forever his covenant

which he made binding for a thousand generations—
Which he entered into with Abraham
and by his oath to Isaac.

℟. The Lord remembers his covenant for ever.

He greatly increased his people
and made them stronger than their foes,
Whose hearts he changed, so that they hated his people,
and dealt deceitfully with his servants.

℟. The Lord remembers his covenant for ever.

He sent Moses his servant;
Aaron, whom he had chosen.
They wrought his signs among them,
and wonders in the land of Ham.

℟. The Lord remembers his covenant for ever.
℟. Or: Alleluia.

Year II

READING I Is 26, 7-9. 12. 16-19

A reading from the book of the prophet Isaiah
Come to life and rejoice, all you who lie in the dust.

The way of the just is smooth;
the path of the just you make level.
Yes, for your way and your judgments, O Lord,
we look to you;
Your name and your title
are the desire of our souls.
My soul yearns for you in the night,
yes, my spirit within me keeps vigil for you;
When your judgment dawns upon the earth,
the world's inhabitants learn justice.

O Lord, you mete out peace to us,
for it is you who have accomplished all we have done.
O Lord, oppressed by your punishment,
we cried out in anguish under your chastising.
As a woman about to give birth
writhes and cries out in her pains,
so were we in your presence, O Lord.
We conceived and writhed in pain,
giving birth to wind;
Salvation we have not achieved for the earth,
the inhabitants of the world cannot bring it forth.
But your dead shall live, their corpses shall rise;
awake and sing, you who lie in the dust.

For your dew is a dew of light,
    and the land of shades gives birth.
        This is the Word of the Lord.

Responsorial Psalm   Ps 102, 13-14. 15. 16-18. 19-21

℟. (20) From heaven the Lord looks down on
    the earth.
You, O Lord, abide forever,
    and your name through all generations.
You will arise and have mercy on Zion,
    for it is time to pity her.
For her stones are dear to your servants,
    and her dust moves them to pity.
℟. From heaven the Lord looks down on the
    earth.

And the nations shall revere your name, O
    Lord,
    and all the kings of the earth your glory,
When the Lord has rebuilt Zion
    and appeared in his glory;
When he has regarded the prayer of the desti-
    tute,
    and not despised their prayer.
℟. From heaven the Lord looks down on the
    earth.

Let this be written for the generation to come,
    and let his future creatures praise the Lord:
"The Lord looked down from his holy height,
    from heaven he beheld the earth,
To hear the groaning of the prisoners,
    to release those doomed to die."
℟. From heaven the Lord looks down on the
    earth.

Years I and II

GOSPEL   Mt 11, 28-30
Alleluia

See no. 509.

✠ **A reading from the holy gospel according**
            to Matthew

I am gentle and humble in heart.

Jesus spoke thus: "Come to me, all you who
are weary and find life burdensome, and I will
refresh you. Take my yoke upon your shoulders and learn from me, for I am gentle and
humble of heart. Your souls will find rest, for
my yoke is easy and my burden light."
        This is the gospel of the Lord.

---

393   **FRIDAY OF THE**
              FIFTEENTH WEEK OF THE YEAR

Year I

READING I   Ex 11, 10—12, 14
    A reading from the book of Exodus

The lamb must be slain in the evening; when I see the blood
I will pass over it.

Moses and Aaron performed various wonders
in Pharaoh's presence, but the Lord made Pharaoh obstinate, and he would not let the Israelites leave his land.

The Lord said to Moses and Aaron in the
land of Egypt, "This month shall stand at the
head of your calendar; you shall reckon it the
first month of the year. Tell the whole community of Israel: On the tenth of this month
every one of your families must procure for
itself a lamb, one apiece for each household. If
a family is too small for a whole lamb, it shall
join the nearest household in procuring one
and shall share in the lamb in proportion to the
number of persons who partake of it. The
lamb must be a year-old male and without
blemish. You may take it from either the sheep
or the goats. You shall keep it until the fourteenth day of this month, and then, with the
whole assembly of Israel present, it shall be
slaughtered during the evening twilight. They
shall take some of its blood and apply it to
the two doorposts and the lintel of every house
in which they partake of the lamb. That same
night they shall eat its roasted flesh with unleavened bread and bitter herbs. It shall not be
eaten raw or boiled, but roasted whole, with its
head and shanks and inner organs. None of
it must be kept beyond the next morning;
whatever is left over in the morning shall be
burned up.

"This is how you are to eat it: with your
loins girt, sandals on your feet and your staff
in hand, you shall eat like those who are in
flight. It is the Passover of the Lord. For on this
same night I will go through Egypt, striking
down every first-born of the land, both man
and beast, and executing judgment on all the
gods of Egypt—I, the Lord! But the blood will
mark the houses where you are. Seeing the

blood, I will pass over you; thus, when I strike the land of Egypt, no destructive blow will come upon you.

"This day shall be a memorial feast for you, which all your generations shall celebrate with pilgrimage to the Lord, as a perpetual institution."

This is the Word of the Lord.

Responsorial Psalm   Ps 116, 12-13. 15-16. 17-18

℟. (13) I will take the cup of salvation,
    and call on the name of the Lord.
How shall I make a return to the Lord
    for all the good he has done for me?
The cup of salvation I will take up,
    and I will call upon the name of the Lord.
℟. I will take the cup of salvation,
    and call on the name of the Lord.
Precious in the eyes of the Lord
    is the death of his faithful ones.
I am your servant, the son of your handmaid;
    you have loosed my bonds.
℟. I will take the cup of salvation,
    and call on the name of the Lord.
To you will I offer sacrifice of thanksgiving,
    and I will call upon the name of the Lord.
My vows to the Lord I will pay
    in the presence of all his people.
℟. I will take the cup of salvation,
    and call on the name of the Lord.
℟. Or: Alleluia.

Year II

READING I   Is 38, 1-6. 21-22. 7-8

A reading from the book of the prophet Isaiah
   I have heard your prayer and seen your tears.

In those days, when Hezekiah was mortally ill, the prophet Isaiah, son of Amoz, came and said to him: "Thus says the Lord: Put your house in order, for you are about to die; you shall not recover." Then Hezekiah turned his face to the wall and prayed to the Lord: "O Lord, remember how faithfully and wholeheartedly I conducted myself in your presence, doing what was pleasing to you!" And Hezekiah wept bitterly.

Then the word of the Lord came to Isaiah: "Go, tell Hezekiah: Thus says the Lord, the God of your father David: I have heard your prayer and seen your tears. I will heal you: in three days you shall go up to the Lord's temple; I will add fifteen years to your life. I will rescue you and this city from the hand of the king of Assyria; I will be a shield to this city."

Isaiah then ordered a poultice of figs to be taken and applied to the boil, that he might recover. Then Hezekiah asked, "What is the sign that I shall go up to the temple of the Lord?"

[Isaiah answered:] "This will be the sign for you from the Lord that he will do what he has promised: See, I will make the shadow cast by the sun on the stairway to the terrace of Ahaz go back the ten steps it has advanced." So the sun came back the ten steps it had advanced.

This is the Word of the Lord.

Responsorial Psalm   Is 38, 10. 11. 12. 16

℟. (17) You saved my life, O Lord;
    I shall not die.
Once I said,
    "In the noontime of life I must depart!
To the gates of the nether world I shall be consigned
    for the rest of my years."
℟. You saved my life, O Lord;
    I shall not die.
I said, "I shall see the Lord no more
    in the land of the living.
No longer shall I behold my fellow men
    among those who dwell in the world."
℟. You saved my life, O Lord;
    I shall not die.
My dwelling, like a shepherd's tent,
    is struck down and borne away from me;
You have folded up my life, like a weaver
    who severs the last thread.
℟. You saved my life, O Lord;
    I shall not die.
Those live whom the Lord protects;
    yours is the life of my spirit.
You have given me health and life.
℟. You saved my life, O Lord;
    I shall not die.

GOSPEL   Years I and II

Alleluia   Mt 12, 1-8

See no. 509.

✠ A reading from the holy gospel according
to Matthew

The Son of Man is master of the Sabbath.

Once on a sabbath Jesus walked through the
standing grain. His disciples felt hungry, so
they began to pull off the heads of grain and
eat them. When the Pharisees spied this, they
protested: "See here! Your disciples are doing
what is not permitted on the sabbath." He replied: "Have you not read what David did
when he and his men were hungry, how he
entered God's house and ate the holy bread, a
thing forbidden to him and his men or anyone
other than priests? Have you not read in the
law how the priests on temple duty can break
the sabbath rest without incurring guilt? I assure you, there is something greater than the
temple here. If you understood the meaning of
the text, 'It is mercy I desire and not sacrifice,'
you would not have condemned these innocent
men. The Son of Man is indeed the Lord of the
sabbath."

This is the gospel of the Lord.

---

394   **SATURDAY OF THE
FIFTEENTH WEEK OF THE YEAR**

Year I

READING I   Ex 12, 37-42

A reading from the book of Exodus

The night is here when the Lord will lead Israel out of the
land of Egypt.

The Israelites set out from Rameses for Suc-
coth, about six hundred thousand men on foot,
not counting the children. A crowd of mixed
ancestry also went up with them, besides their
livestock, very numerous flocks and herds.
Since the dough they had brought out of Egypt
was not leavened, they baked it into unleavened loaves. They had been rushed out of
Egypt and had no opportunity even to prepare
food for the journey.

The time the Israelites had stayed in Egypt

was four hundred and thirty years. At the end
of four hundred and thirty years, all the hosts
of the Lord left the land of Egypt on this very
date. This was a night of vigil for the Lord, as
he led them out of the land of Egypt; so on this
same night all the Israelites must keep a vigil
for the Lord throughout their generations.

This is the Word of the Lord.

Responsorial Psalm   Ps 136, 1. 23-24. 10-12. 13-15

℟. His love is everlasting.

Give thanks to the Lord, for he is good,
    for his mercy endures forever;
Who remembered us in our abjection,
    for his mercy endures forever;
And freed us from our foes,
    for his mercy endures forever.

℟. His love is everlasting.

Who smote the Egyptians in their first-born,
    for his mercy endures forever;
And brought out Israel from their midst,
    for his mercy endures forever;
With a mighty hand and an outstretched arm,
    for his mercy endures forever.

℟. His love is everlasting.

Who split the Red Sea in twain,
    for his mercy endures forever;
And led Israel through its midst,
    for his mercy endures forever;
But swept Pharaoh and his army into the Red
    Sea,
    for his mercy endures forever.

℟. His love is everlasting.

℟. Or: Alleluia.

Year II

READING I   Mi 2, 1-5

A reading from the book of the prophet Micah

They seized the fields and houses that they coveted.

Woe to those who plan iniquity,
    and work out evil on their couches;
In the morning light they accomplish it
    when it lies within their power.
They covet fields, and seize them;
    houses, and they take them;
They cheat an owner of his house,
    a man of his inheritance.

Therefore thus says the Lord:
Behold, I am planning against this race an evil
   from which you shall not withdraw your
   necks;
Nor shall you walk with head high,
   for it will be a time of evil.

On that day a satire shall be sung over you,
   and there shall be a plaintive chant:
"Our ruin is complete,
   our fields are portioned out among our captors,
The fields of my people are measured out,
   and no one can get them back!"
Thus you shall have no one
   to mark out boundaries by lot
   in the assembly of the Lord.
      This is the Word of the Lord.

Responsorial Psalm   Ps 10, 1-2. 3-4. 7-8. 14

℟. (12) Do not forget the poor, O Lord!
Why, O Lord, do you stand aloof?
   Why hide in times of distress?
Proudly the wicked harass the afflicted,
   who are caught in the devices the wicked
   have contrived.
℟. Do not forget the poor, O Lord!
For the wicked man glories in his greed,
   and the covetous blasphemes, sets the Lord
   at nought.
The wicked man boasts, "He will not avenge
   it";
"There is no God," sums up his thoughts.
℟. Do not forget the poor, O Lord!
His mouth is full of cursing, guile and deceit;
   under his tongue are mischief and iniquity.
He lurks in ambush near the villages;
   in hiding he murders the innocent;
   his eyes spy upon the unfortunate.
℟. Do not forget the poor, O Lord!
You do see, for you behold misery and sorrow,
   taking them in your hands.
On you the unfortunate man depends;
   of the fatherless you are the helper.
℟. Do not forget the poor, O Lord!

GOSPEL   **Years I and II**
Alleluia   Mt 12, 14-21

See no. 509.

✠ **A reading from the holy gospel according
to Matthew**

He did not show himself to them that what had been said
would be fulfilled.

When the Pharisees were outside they began to
plot against Jesus to find a way to destroy him.
Jesus was aware of this, and so he withdrew
from that place.
   Many people followed him and he cured
them all, though he sternly ordered them not to
make public what he had done. This was to fulfill what had been said through Isaiah the
prophet:
      "Here is my servant whom I have chosen,
      my loved one in whom I delight.
      I will endow him with my spirit
      and he will proclaim justice to the Gen-
      tiles.
      He will not contend or cry out,
      nor will his voice be heard in the streets.
      The bruised reed he will not crush;
      The smoldering wick he will not quench
      until judgment is made victorious.
      In his name, the Gentiles will find hope."
         This is the gospel of the Lord.

---

395   **MONDAY OF THE
SIXTEENTH WEEK OF THE YEAR**

Year I

READING I   Ex 14, 5-18

A reading from the book of Exodus

They will know that I am the Lord God when I glorify myself
at the expense of Pharaoh.

When it was reported to the king of Egypt that
the people had fled, Pharaoh and his servants
changed their minds about them. "What have
we done!" they exclaimed. "Why, we have released Israel from our service!" So Pharaoh
made his chariots ready and mustered his soldiers—six hundred first-class chariots and all
the other chariots of Egypt, with warriors on
them all. So obstinate had the Lord made Pharaoh that he pursued the Israelites even while

they were marching away in triumph. The Egyptians, then, pursued them; Pharaoh's whole army, his horses, chariots and charioteers, caught up with them as they lay encamped by the sea, at Pi-hahiroth, in front of Baal-zephon.

Pharaoh was already near when the Israelites looked up and saw that the Egyptians were on the march in pursuit of them. In great fright they cried out to the Lord. And they complained to Moses, "Were there no burial places in Egypt that you had to bring us out here to die in the desert? Why did you do this to us? Why did you bring us out of Egypt? Did we not tell you this in Egypt, when we said, 'Leave us alone. Let us serve the Egyptians'? Far better for us to be the slaves of the Egyptians than to die in the desert." But Moses answered the people, "Fear not! Stand your ground, and you will see the victory the Lord will win for you today. These Egyptians whom you see today you will never see again. The Lord himself will fight for you; you have only to keep still."

Then the Lord said to Moses, "Why are you crying out to me? Tell the Israelites to go forward. And you, lift up your staff and, with hand outstretched over the sea, split the sea in two, that the Israelites may pass through it on dry land. But I will make the Egyptians so obstinate that they will go in after them. Then I will receive glory through Pharaoh and all his army, his chariots and charioteers. The Egyptians shall know that I am the Lord, when I receive glory through Pharaoh and his chariots and charioteers."

This is the Word of the Lord.

Responsorial Psalm　　　Ex 15, 1-2. 3-4. 5-6

R̲̅. (1) Let us sing to the Lord;
　he has covered himself in glory.
I will sing to the Lord, for he is gloriously triumphant;
　horse and chariot he has cast into the sea.
My strength and my courage is the Lord,
　and he has been my savior.
He is my God, I praise him;
　the God of my father, I extol him.

R̲̅. Let us sing to the Lord;
　he has covered himself in glory.
The Lord is a warrior,
　Lord is his name!
Pharaoh's chariots and army he hurled into the sea;
　the elite of his officers were submerged in the Red Sea.
R̲̅. Let us sing to the Lord;
　he has covered himself in glory.
The flood waters covered them,
　they sank into the depths like a stone.
Your right hand, O Lord, magnificent in power,
　your right hand, O Lord, has shattered the enemy.
R̲̅. Let us sing to the Lord;
　he has covered himself in glory.

Year II

READING I　　　　　　　　Mi 6, 1-4. 6-8
A reading from the book of the prophet Micah
I will explain to you, man, what it is the Lord God asks of you.

Hear what the Lord says:
Arise, present your plea before the mountains,
　and let the hills hear your voice!
Hear, O mountains, the plea of the Lord,
　pay attention, O foundations of the earth!
For the Lord has a plea against his people,
　and he enters into trial with Israel.

O my people, what have I done to you,
　or how have I wearied you? Answer me!
For I brought you up from the land of Egypt,
　from the place of slavery I released you;
And I sent before you Moses,
　Aaron, and Miriam.

With what shall I come before the Lord,
　and bow before God most high?
Shall I come before him with holocausts,
　with calves a year old?
Will the Lord be pleased with thousands of rams,
　with myriad streams of oil?
Shall I give my first-born for my crime,
　the fruit of my body for the sin of my soul?
You have been told, O man, what is good,
　and what the Lord requires of you:

Only to do the right and to love goodness,
   and to walk humbly with your God.
      This is the Word of the Lord.

Responsorial Psalm   Ps 50, 5-6. 8-9. 16-17. 21. 23

℞. (23) To the upright I will show the saving
   power of God.

"Gather my faithful ones before me,
   those who have made a covenant with me by
      sacrifice."
And the heavens proclaim his justice;
   for God himself is the judge.

℞. To the upright I will show the saving power
   of God.

Not for your sacrifices do I rebuke you,
   for your holocausts are before me always.
I take from your house no bullock,
   no goats out of your fold.

℞. To the upright I will show the saving power
   of God.

"Why do you recite my statutes,
   and profess my covenant with your mouth,
Though you hate discipline
   and cast my words behind you?

℞. To the upright I will show the saving power
   of God.

When you do these things, shall I be deaf to
   it?
   Or do you think that I am like yourself?
I will correct you by drawing them up before
   your eyes.
He that offers praise as a sacrifice glorifies me;
   and to him that goes the right way I will
      show the salvation of God."

℞. To the upright I will show the saving power
   of God.

Years I and II

GOSPEL   Mt 12, 38-42
Alleluia

See no. 509.

✠ A reading from the holy gospel according
               to Matthew

On Judgment Day the Queen of the South will rise up with
          this generation and condemn it.

Some of the scribes and Pharisees then spoke
up, saying, "Teacher, we want to see you work

some signs." Jesus answered: "An evil and unfaithful age is eager for a sign! No sign will be
given it but that of the prophet Jonah. Just as
Jonah spent three days and three nights in the
belly of the whale, so will the Son of Man
spend three days and three nights in the bowels
of the earth. At the judgment, the citizens of
Nineveh will rise with the present generation
and be the ones to condemn it. At the preaching of Jonah they reformed their lives; but you
have a greater than Jonah here. At the judgment, the queen of the South will rise with the
present generation and be the one to condemn
it. She came from the farthest corner of the
earth to listen to the wisdom of Solomon; but
you have a greater than Solomon here."
      This is the gospel of the Lord.

---

396   TUESDAY OF THE
       SIXTEENTH WEEK OF THE YEAR

Year I

READING I   Ex 14, 21–15, 1
       A reading from the book of Exodus

The sons of Israel went on dry ground right into the sea.

Moses stretched out his hand over the sea, and
the Lord swept the sea with a strong east wind
throughout the night and so turned it into dry
land. When the water was thus divided, the
Israelites marched into the midst of the sea on
dry land, with the water like a wall to their
right and to their left.

The Egyptians followed in pursuit; all Pharaoh's horses and chariots and charioteers
went after them right into the midst of the sea.
In the night watch just before dawn the Lord
cast through the column of the fiery cloud
upon the Egyptian force a glance that threw it
into a panic; and he so clogged their chariot
wheels that they could hardly drive. With that
the Egyptians sounded the retreat before Israel,
because the Lord was fighting for them against
the Egyptians.

Then the Lord told Moses, "Stretch out your
hand over the sea, that the water may flow
back upon the Egyptians, upon their chariots

and their charioteers." So Moses stretched out his hand over the sea, and at dawn the sea flowed back to its normal depth. The Egyptians were fleeing head on toward the sea, when the Lord hurled them into its midst. As the water flowed back, it covered the chariots and the charioteers of Pharaoh's whole army which had followed the Israelites into the sea. Not a single one of them escaped. But the Israelites had marched on dry land through the midst of the sea, with the water like a wall to their right and to their left. Thus the Lord saved Israel on that day from the power of the Egyptians. When Israel saw the Egyptians lying dead on the seashore and beheld the great power that the Lord had shown against the Egyptians, they feared the Lord and believed in him and in his servant Moses.

Then Moses and the Israelites sang this song to the Lord:

    I will sing to the Lord, for he is gloriously
        triumphant;
        horse and chariot he has cast into the
        sea.
        This is the Word of the Lord.

Responsorial Psalm   Ex 15, 8-9. 10. 12. 17

℟. (1) Let us sing to the Lord;
   he has covered himself in glory.
At the breath of your anger the waters piled
   up,
   the flowing waters stood like a mound,
   the flood waters congealed in the midst of
   the sea.
The enemy boasted, "I will pursue and overtake them;
   I will divide the spoils and have my fill of
   them;
   I will draw my sword; my hand shall despoil
   them!"
℟. Let us sing to the Lord;
   he has covered himself in glory.
When your wind blew, the sea covered them;
   like lead they sank in the mighty waters.
When you stretched out your right hand,
   the earth swallowed them!
℟. Let us sing to the Lord;
   he has covered himself in glory.

And you brought them in and planted them on
   the mountain of your inheritance—
   the place where you made your seat, O Lord,
   the sanctuary, O Lord, which your hands
   established.
℟. Let us sing to the Lord;
   he has covered himself in glory.

Year II

READING I   Mi 7, 14-15. 18-20

A reading from the book of the prophet Micah
He will cast our faults to the bottom of the sea.

Shepherd your people with your staff,
   the flock of your inheritance,
That dwells apart in a woodland,
   in the midst of Carmel.
Let them feed in Bashan and Gilead,
   as in the days of old;
As in the days when you came from the land
   of Egypt,
   show us wonderful signs.
Who is there like you, the God who removes
   guilt
   and pardons sin for the remnant of his inheritance;
Who does not persist in anger forever,
   but delights rather in clemency,
And will again have compassion on us,
   treading underfoot our guilt?
You will cast into the depths of the sea
   all our sins;
You will show faithfulness to Jacob,
   and grace to Abraham,
As you have sworn to our fathers
   from days of old.
        This is the Word of the Lord.

Responsorial Psalm   Ps 85, 2-4. 5-6. 7-8

℟. (8) Lord, let us see your kindness.
You have favored, O Lord, your land;
   you have restored the well-being of Jacob.
You have forgiven the guilt of your people;
   you have covered all their sins.
You have withdrawn all your wrath;
   you have revoked your burning anger.
℟. Lord, let us see your kindness.

Restore us, O God our savior,
    and abandon your displeasure against us.
Will you be ever angry with us,
    prolonging your anger to all generations?
℞. Lord, let us see your kindness.
Will you not instead give us life;
    and shall not your people rejoice in you?
Show us, O Lord, your kindness,
    and grant us your salvation.
℞. Lord, let us see your kindness.

GOSPEL   Years I and II
Alleluia   Mt 12, 46-50
See no. 509.

✠ A reading from the holy gospel according
            to Matthew
*Extending his hands toward the disciples, he said: Here are
my mother and my brothers.*

Jesus was addressing the crowds when his
mother and his brothers appeared outside to
speak with him. Someone said to him, "Your
mother and your brothers are standing out
there and they wish to speak to you." He said
to the one who had told him, "Who is my
mother? Who are my brothers?" Then extending his hands to his disciples, he said, "There
are my mother and my brothers. Whoever does
the will of my heavenly Father is brother and
sister and mother to me."
        This is the gospel of the Lord.

397   **WEDNESDAY OF THE
        SIXTEENTH WEEK OF THE YEAR**

                                    Year I
READING I   Ex 16, 1-5. 9-15
    A reading from the book of Exodus
    I am the bread for you that comes down from heaven.

The whole Israelite community, having set out
from Elim, came into the desert of Sin, which
is between Elim and Sinai, on the fifteenth day
of the second month after their departure from
the land of Egypt. Here in the desert the whole
Israelite community grumbled against Moses
and Aaron. The Israelites said to them, "Would

that we had died at the Lord's hand in the land
of Egypt, as we sat by our fleshpots and ate our
fill of bread! But you had to lead us into this
desert to make the whole community die of
famine!"
    Then the Lord said to Moses, "I will now
rain down bread from heaven for you. Each
day the people are to go out and gather their
daily portion; thus will I test them, to see
whether they follow my instructions or not. On
the sixth day, however, when they prepare
what they bring in, let it be twice as much as
they gather on the other days."
    Then Moses said to Aaron, "Tell the whole
Israelite community: Present yourselves before the Lord, for he has heard your grumbling." When Aaron announced this to the
whole Israelite community, they turned toward the desert and lo, the glory of the Lord
appeared in the cloud! The Lord spoke to
Moses and said, "I have heard the grumbling
of the Israelites. Tell them: In the evening
twilight you shall eat flesh, and in the morning
you shall have your fill of bread, so that you
may know that I, the Lord, am your God."
    In the evening quail came up and covered
the camp. In the morning a dew lay all about
the camp, and when the dew evaporated, there
on the surface of the desert were fine flakes
like hoarfrost on the ground. On seeing it, the
Israelites asked one another, "What is this?"
for they did not know what it was. But Moses
told them, "This is the bread which the Lord
has given you to eat."
        This is the Word of the Lord.

Responsorial Psalm   Ps 78, 18-19. 23-24. 25-26. 27-28
℞. (24) The Lord gave them bread from
        heaven.
They tempted God in their hearts
    by demanding the food they craved.
Yes, they spoke against God, saying,
    "Can God spread a table in the desert?"
℞. The Lord gave them bread from heaven.
Yet he commanded the skies above
    and the doors of heaven he opened;
He rained manna upon them for food
    and gave them heavenly bread.

℟. The Lord gave them bread from heaven
The bread of the mighty was eaten by men;
even a surfeit of provisions he sent them.
He stirred up the east wind in the heavens,
and by his power brought on the south wind.
℟. The Lord gave them bread from heaven.
And he rained meat upon them like dust,
and, like the sand of the sea, winged fowl,
Which fell in the midst of their camp
round about their tents.
℟. The Lord gave them bread from heaven.

Year II

READING I   Jer 1, 1. 4-10

The beginning of the book of the prophet Jeremiah

I have appointed you as a prophet to the nations.

The words of Jeremiah, son of Hilkiah, of a priestly family in Anathoth, in the land of Benjamin.
The word of the Lord came to me thus:
Before I formed you in the womb I knew
you,
before you were born I dedicated you,
a prophet to the nations I appointed you.
"Ah, Lord God!" I said,
"I know not how to speak; I am too young."
But the Lord answered me,
Say not, "I am too young."
To whomever I send you, you shall go;
whatever I command you, you shall speak.
Have no fear before them,
because I am with you to deliver you, says
the Lord.
Then the Lord extended his hand and touched my mouth, saying,
See, I place my words in your mouth!
This day I set you
over nations and over kingdoms,
To root up and to tear down,
to destroy and to demolish,
to build and to plant.
This is the Word of the Lord.

Responsorial Psalm   Ps 71, 1-2. 3-4. 5-6. 15. 17

℟. (15) I will sing of your salvation.
In you, O Lord, I take refuge;

let me never be put to shame.
In your justice rescue me, and deliver me;
incline your ear to me, and save me.
℟. I will sing of your salvation.
Be my rock of refuge,
a stronghold to give me safety,
for you are my rock and my fortress.
O my God, rescue me from the hand of the
wicked.
℟. I will sing of your salvation.
For you are my hope, O Lord;
my trust, O God, from my youth.
On you I depend from birth;
from my mother's womb you are my
strength.
℟. I will sing of your salvation.
My mouth shall declare your justice,
day by day your salvation.
O God, you have taught me from my youth,
and till the present I proclaim your wondrous deeds.
℟. I will sing of your salvation.

Years I and II

GOSPEL
Alleluia   Mt 13, 1-9

See no. 509.

✠ A reading from the holy gospel according
to Matthew

He increased the harvest a hundredfold.

On leaving the house, Jesus sat down by the lakeshore. Such great crowds gathered around him that he went and took his seat in a boat while the crowd stood along the shore. He addressed them at length in parables, speaking in this fashion:
"One day a farmer went out sowing. Part of what he sowed landed on a footpath, where birds came and ate it up. Part of it fell on rocky ground, where it had little soil. It sprouted at once since the soil had no depth, but when the sun rose and scorched it, it began to wither for lack of roots. Again, part of the seed fell among thorns, which grew up and choked it. Part of it, finally, landed on good soil and yielded grain a hundred or sixty ,or thirty-fold. Let evervone heed what he hears!"
This is the gospel of the Lord.

398 THURSDAY OF THE SIXTEENTH WEEK OF THE YEAR

Year I

READING I   Ex 19, 1-2. 9-11. 16-20

A reading from the book of Exodus

The Lord descended on Mount Sinai before all the people.

In the third month after their departure from the land of Egypt, on its first day, the Israelites came to the desert of Sinai. After the journey from Rephidim to the desert of Sinai, they pitched camp. While Israel was encamped here in front of the mountain, the Lord told Moses, "I am coming to you in a dense cloud, so that when the people hear me speaking with you, they may always have faith in you also." When Moses, then, had reported to the Lord the response of the people, the Lord added, "Go to the people and have them sanctify themselves today and tomorrow. Make them wash their garments and be ready for the third day; for on the third day the Lord will come down on Mount Sinai before the eyes of all the people."

On the morning of the third day there were peals of thunder and lightning, and a heavy cloud over the mountain, and a very loud trumpet blast, so that all the people in the camp trembled. But Moses led the people out of the camp to meet God, and they stationed themselves at the foot of the mountain. Mount Sinai was all wrapped in smoke, for the Lord came down upon it in fire. The smoke rose from it as though from a furnace, and the whole mountain trembled violently. The trumpet blast grew louder and louder, while Moses was speaking and God answering him with thunder.

When the Lord came down to the top of Mount Sinai, he summoned Moses to the top of the mountain.

This is the Word of the Lord.

Responsorial Psalm   Dn 3, 52. 53. 54. 55. 56

℟. (52) Glory and praise for ever!

Blessed are you, O Lord, the God of our fathers,
praiseworthy and exalted above all forever;
And blessed is your holy and glorious name,
praiseworthy and exalted above all for all ages.
℟. Glory and praise for ever!

Blessed are you in the temple of your holy glory,
praiseworthy and glorious above all forever.
℟. Glory and praise for ever!

Blessed are you on the throne of your kingdom,
praiseworthy and exalted above all forever.
℟. Glory and praise for ever!

Blessed are you who look into the depths from your throne upon the cherubim,
praiseworthy and exalted above all forever.
℟. Glory and praise for ever!

Blessed are you in the firmament of heaven,
praiseworthy and glorious forever.
℟. Glory and praise for ever!

Year II

READING I   Jer 2, 1-3. 7-8. 12-13

A reading from the book of the prophet Jeremiah

They have abandoned me, the fountain of living water, to dig broken cisterns for themselves.

This word of the Lord came to me: Go, cry out this message for Jerusalem to hear!
I remember the devotion of your youth,
how you loved me as a bride,
Following me in the desert,
in a land unsown.
Sacred to the Lord was Israel,
the first fruits of his harvest;
Should anyone presume to partake of them,
evil would befall him, says the Lord.

When I brought you into the garden land
to eat its goodly fruits,
You entered and defiled my land,
you made my heritage loathsome.
The priests asked not,
"Where is the Lord?"
Those who dealt with the law knew me not;
the shepherds rebelled against me.
The prophets prophesied by Baal,
and went after useless idols.

Be amazed at this, O heavens,
  and shudder with sheer horror, says the Lord.
Two evils have my people done:
  they have forsaken me, the source of living
    waters;
They have dug themselves cisterns,
  broken cisterns, that hold no water.
    This is the Word of the Lord.

Responsorial Psalm   Ps 36, 6-7. 8-9. 10-11

℟. (10) You are the source of life, O Lord.
O Lord, your kindness reaches to heaven;
  your faithfulness, to the clouds.
Your justice is like the mountains of God;
  your judgments, like the mighty deep.
℟. You are the source of life, O Lord.
How precious is your kindness, O God!
  The children of men take refuge in the
    shadow of your wings.
They have their fill of the prime gifts of your
    house;
  from your delightful stream you give them
    to drink.
℟. You are the source of life, O Lord.
For with you is the fountain of life,
  and in your light we see light.
Keep up your kindness toward your friends,
  your just defense of the upright of heart.
℟. You are the source of life, O Lord.

Years I and II

GOSPEL   Mt 13, 10-17
Alleluia

See no. 509.

✠ **A reading from the holy gospel according**
    to Matthew

To you it is given to know the mysteries of the kingdom of
  heaven, but to them it has not been given.

When the disciples approached Jesus, they
asked him, "Why do you speak to them in
parables?" He answered: "To you has been
given a knowledge of the mysteries of the reign
of God, but it has not been given to the others.
To the man who has, more will be given until
he grows rich; the man who has not, will lose
what little he has.

"I use parables when I speak to them because they look but do not see, they listen but
do not hear or understand. Isaiah's prophecy is
fulfilled in them which says:
  'Listen as you will, you shall not under-
    stand,
  look intently as you will, you shall not see.
  Sluggish indeed is this people's heart.
  They have scarcely heard with their ears,
    they have firmly closed their eyes;
  otherwise they might see with their eyes,
    and hear with their ears,
    and understand with their hearts,
    and turn back to me,
    and I should heal them.'
"But blest are your eyes because they see
and blest are your ears because they hear. I
assure you, many a prophet and many a saint
longed to see what you see but did not see it,
to hear what you hear but did not hear it."
    This is the gospel of the Lord.

399   **FRIDAY OF THE**
        SIXTEENTH WEEK OF THE YEAR

Year I

READING I   Ex 20, 1-17
  A reading from the book of Exodus
    The law was given through Moses.
God delivered all these commandments:
"I, the Lord, am your God, who brought you
out of the land of Egypt, that place of slavery.
You shall not have other gods besides me. You
shall not carve idols for yourselves in the shape
of anything in the sky above or on the earth
below or in the waters beneath the earth; you
shall not bow down before them or worship
them. For I, the Lord, your God, am a jealous
God, inflicting punishment for their fathers'
wickedness on the children of those who hate
me, down to the third and fourth generation;
but bestowing mercy down to the thousandth
generation, on the children of those who love
me and keep my commandments.
"You shall not take the name of the Lord,
your God, in vain. For the Lord will not leave

unpunished him who takes his name in vain.

"Remember to keep holy the sabbath day. Six days you may labor and do all your work, but the seventh day is the sabbath of the Lord, your God. No work may be done then either by you, or your son or daughter, or your male or female slave, or your beast, or by the alien who lives with you. In six days the Lord made the heavens and the earth, the sea and all that is in them; but on the seventh day he rested. That is why the Lord has blessed the sabbath day and made it holy.

"Honor your father and your mother, that you may have a long life in the land which the Lord, your God, is giving you.

"You shall not kill.

"You shall not commit adultery.

"You shall not steal.

"You shall not bear false witness against your neighbor.

"You shall not covet your neighbor's house. You shall not covet your neighbor's wife, nor his male or female slave, nor his ox or ass, nor anything else that belongs to him."

This is the Word of the Lord.

Responsorial Psalm   Ps 19, 8. 9. 10. 11

℞. (Jn 6, 69) Lord, you have the words of everlasting life.
The law of the Lord is perfect,
  refreshing the soul;
The decree of the Lord is trustworthy,
  giving wisdom to the simple.
℞. Lord, you have the words of everlasting
  life.
The precepts of the Lord are right,
  rejoicing the heart;
The command of the Lord is clear,
  enlightening the eye;
℞. Lord, you have the words of everlasting
  life.
The fear of the Lord is pure,
  enduring forever;
The ordinances of the Lord are true,
  all of them just.
℞. Lord, you have the words of everlasting
  life.

They are more precious than gold,
  than a heap of purest gold;
Sweeter also than syrup
  or honey from the comb.
℞. Lord, you have the words of everlasting
  life.

Year II

READING I   Jer 3, 14-17

**A reading from the book of the prophet
Jeremiah**

I will give you shepherds after my own heart. When that
time comes, Jerusalem shall be called.

Return, rebellious children, says the Lord,
  for I am your Master;
I will take you, one from a city, two from a
  clan,
  and bring you to Zion.
I will appoint over you shepherds after my own
  heart,
  who will shepherd you wisely and pru-
  dently.
When you multiply and become fruitful in the
  land,
  says the Lord,
They will in those days no longer say,
  "The ark of the covenant of the Lord!"
They will no longer think of it, or remember it,
  or miss it, or make another.
At that time they will call Jerusalem the
Lord's throne; there all nations will be gathered together to honor the name of the Lord
at Jerusalem, and they will walk no longer in
their hardhearted wickedness.

This is the Word of the Lord.

Responsorial Psalm   Jer 31, 10. 11-12. 13

℞. (10) The Lord will guard us,
  like a shepherd guarding his flock.
Hear the word of the Lord, O nations,
  proclaim it on distant coasts, and say:
He who scattered Israel, now gathers them
  together,
  he guards them as a shepherd his flock.
℞. The Lord will guard us,
  like a shepherd guarding his flock.
The Lord shall ransom Jacob,

he shall redeem him from the hand of his conqueror.

Shouting, they shall mount the heights of Zion, they shall come streaming to the Lord's blessings.

R̷. The Lord will guard us, like a shepherd guarding his flock.

Then the virgins shall make merry and dance, and young men and old as well.

I will turn their mourning into joy, I will console and gladden them after their sorrows.

R̷. The Lord will guard us, like a shepherd guarding his flock.

Years I and II

GOSPEL   Mt 13, 18-23
Alleluia

See no. 509.

✠ A reading from the holy gospel according to Matthew

He who hears the word of God and understands it, yields much fruit.

Jesus said to his disciples, "Mark well the parable of the sower. The seed along the path is the man who hears the message about God's reign without understanding it. The evil one approaches him to steal away what was sown in his mind. The seed that fell on patches of rock is the man who hears the message and at first receives it with joy. But he has no roots, so he lasts only for a time. When some setback or persecution involving the message occurs, he soon falters. What was sown among briers is the man who hears the message, but then worldly anxiety and the lure of money choke it off. Such a one produces no yield. But what was sown on good soil is the man who hears the message and takes it in. He it is who bears a yield of a hundred – or sixty– or thirty-fold."

   This is the gospel of the Lord.

---

400   SATURDAY OF THE SIXTEENTH WEEK OF THE YEAR

Year I

READING I   Ex 24, 3-8

A reading from the book of Exodus

This is the blood of the covenant which the Lord God has made with you.

When Moses came to the people and related all the words and ordinances of the Lord, they all answered with one voice, "We will do everything that the Lord has told us." Moses then wrote down all the words of the Lord and, rising early the next day, he erected at the foot of the mountain an altar and twelve pillars for the twelve tribes of Israel. Then, having sent certain young men of the Israelites to offer holocausts and sacrifice young bulls as peace offerings to the Lord, Moses took half of the blood and put it in large bowls; the other half he splashed on the altar. Taking the book of the covenant, he read it aloud to the people, who answered, "All that the Lord has said, we will heed and do." Then he took the blood and sprinkled it on the people, saying, "This is the blood of the covenant which the Lord has made with you in accordance with all these words of his."

   This is the Word of the Lord.

Responsorial Psalm   Ps 50, 1-2. 5-6. 14-15

R̷. (14) Offer to God a sacrifice of praise.

God the Lord has spoken and summoned the earth,
   from the rising of the sun to its setting.
From Zion, perfect in beauty,
   God shines forth.

R̷. Offer to God a sacrifice of praise.

"Gather my faithful ones before me,
   those who have made a covenant with me
   by sacrifice."
And the heavens proclaim his justice;
   for God himself is the judge.

R̷. Offer to God a sacrifice of praise.

"Offer to God praise as your sacrifice
   and fulfill your vows to the Most High;

Then call upon me in time of distress;
  I will rescue you, and you shall glorify me."
℟. Offer to God a sacrifice of praise.

Year II

READING I   Jer 7, 1-11
**A reading from the book of the prophet
Jeremiah**
Do you take this temple that bears my name for a robbers
den?

The following message came to Jeremiah from
the Lord: Stand at the gate of the house of the
Lord, and there proclaim this message: Hear
the word of the Lord, all you of Judah who
enter these gates to worship the Lord! Thus
says the Lord of hosts, the God of Israel: Reform your ways and your deeds, so that I may
remain with you in this place. Put not your
trust in the deceitful words: "This is the temple
of the Lord! The temple of the Lord! The temple
of the Lord!" Only if you thoroughly reform
your ways and your deeds; if each of you deals
justly with his neighbor; if you no longer oppress the resident alien, the orphan, and the
widow; if you no longer shed innocent blood in
this place, or follow strange gods to your own
harm, will I remain with you in this place, in
the land which I gave your fathers long ago
and forever.
   But here you are, putting your trust in deceitful words to your own loss! Are you to steal
and murder, commit adultery and perjury,
burn incense to Baal, go after strange gods that
you know not, and yet come to stand before me
in this house which bears my name, and say:
"We are safe; we can commit all these abominations again"? Has this house which bears my
name become in your eyes a den of thieves? I
too see what is being done, says the Lord.
           This is the Word of the Lord.

Responsorial Psalm   Ps 84, 3. 4. 5-6. 8. 11

℟. (2) How lovely is your dwelling-place,
   Lord, mighty God!
My soul yearns and pines
   for the courts of the Lord.

My heart and my flesh
   cry out for the living God.
℟. How lovely is your dwelling-place,
   Lord, mighty God!
Even the sparrow finds a home,
   and the swallow a nest
   in which she puts her young—
Your altars, O Lord of hosts,
   my king and my God!
℟. How lovely is your dwelling-place,
   Lord, mighty God!
Happy they who dwell in your house!
   continually they praise you.
Happy the men whose strength you are!
   they go from strength to strength.
℟. How lovely is your dwelling-place,
   Lord, mighty God!
I had rather one day in your courts
   than a thousand elsewhere;
I had rather lie at the threshold of the house of
   my God
   than dwell in the tents of the wicked.
℟. How lovely is your dwelling-place,
   Lord, mighty God!

Years I and II

GOSPEL   Mt 13, 24-30
Alleluia
See no. 509.

✠ **A reading from the holy gospel according
to Matthew**
Let them both grow until the harvest time.

Jesus proposed to the crowds another parable:
"The reign of God may be likened to a man
who sowed good seed in his field. While everyone was asleep, his enemy came and sowed
weeds through his wheat, and then made off.
When the crop began to mature and yield
grain, the weeds made their appearance as
well. The owner's slaves came to him and said,
'Sir, did you not sow good seed in your field?
Where are the weeds coming from?' He answered, 'I see an enemy's hand in this.' His
slaves said to him, 'Do you want us to go out
and pull them up?' 'No,' he replied, 'pull up the
weeds and you might take the wheat along

with them. Let them grow together until harvest; then at harvest time I will order the harvesters, first collect the weeds and bundle them up to burn, then gather the wheat into my barn.' "

This is the gospel of the Lord.

**401   MONDAY OF THE
SEVENTEENTH WEEK OF THE YEAR**

Year I

READING I   Ex 32, 15-24. 30-34

A reading from the book of Exodus

*This people has committed a grave sin, making themselves
gods of gold.*

Moses turned and came down the mountain with the two tablets of the commandments in his hands, tablets that were written on both sides, front and back; tablets that were made by God, having inscriptions on them that were engraved by God himself. Now, when Joshua heard the noise of the people shouting, he said to Moses, "That sounds like a battle in the camp." But Moses answered, "It does not sound like cries of victory, nor does it sound like cries of defeat; the sounds that I hear are cries of revelry." As he drew near the camp, he saw the calf and the dancing. With that, Moses' wrath flared up, so that he threw the tablets down and broke them on the base of the mountain. Taking the calf they had made, he fused it in the fire and then ground it down to powder, which he scattered on the water and made the Israelites drink.

Moses asked Aaron, "What did this people ever do to you that you should lead them into so grave a sin?" Aaron replied, "Let not my lord be angry. You know well enough how prone the people are to evil. They said to me, 'Make us a god to be our leader; as for the man Moses who brought us out of the land of Egypt, we do not know what has happened to him.' So I told them, 'Let anyone who has gold jewelry take it off.' They gave it to me, and I threw it into the fire, and this calf came out."

On the next day Moses said to the people, "You have committed a grave sin. I will go up to the Lord, then; perhaps I may be able to make atonement for your sin." So Moses went back to the Lord and said, "Ah, this people has indeed committed a grave sin in making a god of gold for themselves! If you would only forgive their sin! If you will not, then strike me out of the book that you have written." The Lord answered, "Him only who has sinned against me will I strike out of my book. Now, go and lead the people whither I have told you. My angel will go before you. When it is time for me to punish, I will punish them for their sin."

This is the Word of the Lord.

Responsorial Psalm   Ps 106, 19-20. 21-22. 23

℟. (1) Give thanks to the Lord for he is good.
They made a calf in Horeb
   and adored a molten image;
They exchanged their glory
   for the image of a grass-eating bullock.
℟. Give thanks to the Lord for he is good.
They forgot the God who had saved them,
   who had done great deeds in Egypt,
Wondrous deeds in the land of Ham,
   terrible things at the Red Sea.
℟. Give thanks to the Lord for he is good.
Then he spoke of exterminating them,
   but Moses, his chosen one,
Withstood him in the breach
   to turn back his destructive wrath.
℟. Give thanks to the Lord for he is good.
℟. Or: Alleluia.

Year II

READING I   Jer 13, 1-11

A reading from the book of the prophet Jeremiah

*Let this people become like loincloth, spoiled and good
for nothing.*

The Lord said to me: Go buy yourself a linen loincloth; wear it on your loins, but do not put it in water. I bought the loincloth, as the Lord commanded, and put it on. A second time the word of the Lord came to me thus: Take the loincloth which you bought and are wearing, and go now to the Parath; there hide it in a cleft of the rock. Obedient to the Lord's command, I went to the Parath and buried the loincloth. After a long interval, he said to me: Go now to the Parath and fetch the loincloth which I told you to hide there. Again I went to the Parath, sought out and took the loincloth from the place where I had hid it. But it was rotted, good for nothing! Then the message came to me from the Lord: Thus says the Lord: So also I will allow the pride of Judah to rot, the great pride of Jerusalem. This wicked people who refuse to obey my words, who walk in the stubbornness of their hearts, and follow strange gods to serve and adore them shall be like this loincloth which is good for nothing. For, as close as the loincloth clings to a man's loins, so had I made the whole house of Israel and the whole house of Judah cling to me, says the Lord; to be my people, my renown, my praise, my beauty. But they did not listen.

This is the Word of the Lord.

Responsorial Psalm   Dt 32, 18-19. 20. 21

℞. (18) You have forgotten God who gave you birth.

You were unmindful of the Rock that begot you.
   You forgot the God who gave you birth.
When the Lord saw this, he was filled with loathing
   and anger toward his sons and daughters.

℞. You have forgotten God who gave you birth.

"I will hide my face from them," he said.
   "and see what will then become of them.
What a fickle race they are,
   sons with no loyalty in them!

℞. You have forgotten God who gave you birth.

Since they have provoked me with their 'no-god'
   and angered me with their vain idols,
I will provoke them with a 'no-people';
   with a foolish nation I will anger them."

℞. You have forgotten God who gave you birth.

GOSPEL   **Years I and II**
Alleluia   Mt 13, 31-35

See no. 509.

✠ **A reading from the holy gospel according to Matthew**

When the seed grows it is the biggest shrub of all and the birds of the air come and nest in its branches.

Jesus proposed to the crowds another parable: "The reign of God is like a mustard seed which someone took and sowed in his field. It is the smallest seed of all, yet when full-grown it is the largest of plants. It becomes so big a shrub that the birds of the sky come and build their nests in its branches."

He offered them still another image: "The reign of God is like yeast which a woman took and kneaded into three measures of flour. Eventually the whole mass of dough began to rise." All these lessons Jesus taught the crowds in the form of parables. He spoke to them in parables only, to fulfill what had been said through the prophet:
   "I will open my mouth in parables,
      I will announce what has lain hidden since the creation of the world."
   This is the gospel of the Lord.

---

402   **TUESDAY OF THE SEVENTEENTH WEEK OF THE YEAR**

Year I

READING I   Ex 33, 7-11; 34, 5-9. 28

A reading from the book of Exodus

The Lord God spoke to Moses face to face.

The tent, which was called the meeting tent, Moses used to pitch at some distance away, outside the camp. Anyone who wished to consult the Lord would go to this meeting tent outside the camp. Whenever Moses went out to the tent, the people would all rise and stand at the entrance of their own tents, watching Moses until he entered the tent. As Moses entered the tent, the column of cloud would come down and stand at its entrance while the Lord spoke with Moses. On seeing the column of cloud stand at the entrance of the tent, all the people would rise and worship at the entrance of their own tents. The Lord used to speak to Moses face to face, as one man speaks to another. Moses would then return to the camp, but his young assistant, Joshua, son of Nun, would not move out of the tent.

Moses invoked the name of the Lord who stood with him there and proclaimed his name, "Lord." Thus the Lord passed before him and cried out, "The Lord, the Lord, a merciful and gracious God, slow to anger and rich in kindness and fidelity, continuing his kindness for a thousand generations, and forgiving wickedness and crime and sin; yet not declaring the guilty guiltless, but punishing children and grandchildren to the third and fourth generation for their fathers' wickedness!" Moses at once bowed down to the ground in worship. Then he said, "If I find favor with you, O Lord, do come along in our company. This is indeed a stiff-necked people; yet pardon our wickedness and sins, and receive us as your own."

So Moses stayed there with the Lord for forty days and forty nights, without eating any food or drinking any water, and he wrote on the tablets the words of the covenant, the ten commandments.

This is the Word of the Lord.

Responsorial Psalm Ps 103, 6-7. 8-9. 10-11. 12-13

℟. (8) The Lord is kind and merciful.

The Lord secures justice
  and the rights of all the oppressed.
He has made known his ways to Moses,
  and his deeds to the children of Israel.

℟. The Lord is kind and merciful.

Merciful and gracious is the Lord,
  slow to anger and abounding in kindness.
He will not always chide,
  nor does he keep his wrath forever.

℟. The Lord is kind and merciful.

Not according to our sins does he deal with us,
  nor does he requite us according to our
    crimes.
For as the heavens are high above the earth,
  so surpassing is his kindness toward those
    who fear him.

℟. The Lord is kind and merciful.

As far as the east is from the west,
  so far has he put our transgressions from us.
As a father has compassion on his children,
  so the Lord has compassion on those who
    fear him.

℟. The Lord is kind and merciful.

Year II

READING I   Jer 14, 17-22

**A reading from the book of the prophet
Jeremiah**

Remember, Lord, do not break your covenant with us.

Let my eyes stream with tears
  day and night, without rest,
Over the great destruction which overwhelms
  the virgin daughter of my people,
  over her incurable wound.
If I walk out into the field,
  look! those slain by the sword;
If I enter the city,
  look! those consumed by hunger.
Even the prophet and the priest
  forage in a land they know not.

Have you cast Judah off completely?
  Is Zion loathsome to you?
Why have you struck us a blow
  that cannot be healed?
We wait for peace, to no avail;
  for a time of healing, but terror comes instead.
We recognize, O Lord, our wickedness,
  the guilt of our fathers;
  that we have sinned against you.
For your name's sake spurn us not,
  disgrace not the throne of your glory;
  remember your covenant with us, and break
    it not.
Among the nations' idols is there any that
  gives rain?
  Or can the mere heavens send showers?
Is it not you alone, O Lord,
  our God, to whom we look?
  You alone have done all these things.

This is the Word of the Lord.

Responsorial Psalm   Ps 79, 8. 9. 11. 13

℞. (9) For the glory of your name,
  O Lord, deliver us.

Remember not against us the iniquities of the
    past;
  may your compassion quickly come to us,
  for we are brought very low.

℞. For the glory of your name,
  O Lord, deliver us.

Help us, O God our savior,
  because of the glory of your name;
Deliver us and pardon our sins
  for your name's sake.

℞. For the glory of your name,
  O Lord, deliver us.

Let the prisoners' sighing come before you;
  with your great power free those doomed to
  death.

Then we, your people and the sheep of your
    pasture,
  will give thanks to you forever;
  through all generations we will declare your
    praise.

℞. For the glory of your name,
  O Lord, deliver us.

GOSPEL   **Years I and II**
Alleluia   Mt 13, 35-43

See no. 509.

✠ A reading from the holy gospel according
    to Matthew

*Just as the weeds are gathered up and burnt in the fire, so
it will be at the end of time.*

Jesus dismissed the crowds and went home.
His disciples came to him with the request,
"Explain to us the parable of the weeds in the
field." He said in answer: "The farmer sowing
good seed is the Son of Man; the field is the
world, the good seed the citizens of the kingdom. The weeds are the followers of the evil
one and the enemy who sowed them is the
devil. The harvest is the end of the world, while
the harvesters are the angels. Just as weeds
are collected and burned, so it will be at the
end of the world. The Son of Man will dispatch
his angels to collect from his kingdom all who
draw others to apostasy, and all evildoers. The

angels will hurl them into the fiery furnace
where they will wail and grind their teeth.
Then the saints will shine like the sun in their
Father's kingdom. Let everyone heed what he
hears!"

This is the gospel of the Lord.

---

403   **WEDNESDAY OF THE**
SEVENTEENTH WEEK OF THE YEAR

Year I

READING I   Ex 34, 29-35

A reading from the book of Exodus

Seeing Moses' face, they would not approach him.

As Moses came down from Mount Sinai with
the two tablets of the commandments in his
hands, he did not know that the skin of his
face had become radiant while he conversed
with the Lord. When Aaron, then, and the
other Israelites saw Moses and noticed how
radiant the skin of his face had become, they
were afraid to come near him. Only after
Moses called to them did Aaron and all the
rulers of the community come back to him.
Moses then spoke to them. Later on, all the
Israelites came up to him, and he enjoined on
them all that the Lord had told him on Mount
Sinai. When he finished speaking with them,
he put a veil over his face. Whenever Moses
entered the presence of the Lord to converse
with him, he removed the veil until he came out
again. On coming out, he would tell the Israelites all that had been commanded. Then the
Israelites would see that the skin of Moses'
face was radiant; so he would again put the
veil over his face until he went in to converse
with the Lord.

This is the Word of the Lord.

Responsorial Psalm   Ps 99, 5. 6. 7. 9

℞. (9) Holy is the Lord our God.

Extol the Lord, our God,
  and worship at his footstool;
  holy is he!

℞. Holy is the Lord our God.

Moses and Aaron were among his priests,

and Samuel, among those who called upon
  his name;
they called upon the Lord, and he answered
  them.
℞. Holy is the Lord our God.
From the pillar of cloud he spoke to them;
  they heard his decrees and the law he gave
  them.
℞. Holy is the Lord our God.
Extol the Lord, our God,
  and worship at his holy mountain;
  for holy is the Lord, our God.
℞. Holy is the Lord our God.

READING I **Year II**

Jer 15, 10. 16-21

**A reading from the book of the prophet
Jeremiah**

Why is my suffering continued, Lord? If you come back, I
will take you into my service.

Woe to me, mother, that you gave me birth!
  a man of strife and contention to all the land!
I neither borrow nor lend,
  yet all curse me.

When I found your words, I devoured them;
  they became my joy and the happiness of my
  heart,
Because I bore your name,
  O Lord, God of hosts.
I did not sit celebrating
  in the circle of merrymakers;
Under the weight of your hand I sat alone
  because you filled me with indignation.
Why is my pain continuous,
  my wound incurable, refusing to be healed?
You have indeed become for me a treacherous
  brook,
  whose waters do not abide!
    Thus the Lord answered me:
If you repent, so that I restore you,
  in my presence you shall stand;
If you bring forth the precious without the vile,
  you shall be my mouthpiece.
Then it shall be they who turn to you,
  and you shall not turn to them;
And I will make you toward this people
  a solid wall of brass.

Though they fight against you,
  they shall not prevail,
For I am with you,
  to deliver and rescue you, says the Lord.
I will free you from the hand of the wicked,
  and rescue you from the grasp of the violent.
    This is the Word of the Lord.

Responsorial Psalm   Ps 59, 2-3. 4. 10-11. 17. 18

℞. (17) God is my refuge on the day of distress.
Rescue me from my enemies, O my God;
  from my adversaries defend me.
Rescue me from evildoers;
  from bloodthirsty men save me.
℞. God is my refuge on the day of distress.
For behold, they lie in wait for my life;
  mighty men come together against me,
Not for any offense or sin of mine, O Lord.
℞. God is my refuge on the day of distress.
  O my strength! for you I watch;
    for you, O God, are my stronghold,
    my gracious God!
May God come to my aid.
℞. God is my refuge on the day of distress.
But I will sing of your strength
  and revel at dawn in your kindness;
You have been my stronghold,
  my refuge in the day of distress.
℞. God is my refuge on the day of distress.
  O my strength! your praise will I sing;
    for you, O God, are my stronghold,
    my gracious God!
℞. God is my refuge on the day of distress.

GOSPEL **Years I and II**
Alleluia   Mt 13, 44-46
See no. 509.

✠ **A reading from the holy gospel according
to Matthew**

He sold everything he had and went and bought the field.

Jesus said to the crowds: "The reign of God is
like a buried treasure which a man found in a
field. He hid it again, and rejoicing at his find
went and sold all he had and bought that field.
Or again, the kingdom of heaven is like a
merchant's search for fine pearls. When he

found one really valuable pearl, he went back and put up for sale all that he had and bought it."

This is the gospel of the Lord.

---

404   **THURSDAY OF THE SEVENTEENTH WEEK OF THE YEAR**

Year I

READING I   Ex 40, 16-21. 34-38

A reading from the book of Exodus

The cloud covered the tent of meeting and the glory of the Lord God filled the tabernacle.

Moses did all that the Lord had commanded him. On the first day of the first month of the second year the Dwelling was erected. It was Moses who erected the Dwelling. He placed its pedestals, set up its boards, put in its bars, and set up its columns. He spread the tent over the Dwelling and put the covering on top of the tent, as the Lord had commanded him. He took the commandments and put them in the ark; he placed poles alongside the ark and set the propitiatory upon it. He brought the ark into the Dwelling and hung the curtain veil, thus screening off the ark of the commandments, as the Lord had commanded him.

Then the cloud covered the meeting tent, and the glory of the Lord filled the Dwelling. Moses could not enter the meeting tent, because the cloud settled down upon it and the glory of the Lord filled the Dwelling. Whenever the cloud rose from the Dwelling, the Israelites would set out on their journey. But if the cloud did not lift, they would not go forward; only when it lifted did they go forward. In the daytime the cloud of the Lord was seen over the Dwelling; whereas at night, fire was seen in the cloud by the whole house of Israel in all the stages of their journey.

This is the Word of the Lord.

Responsorial Psalm   Ps 84, 3. 4. 5-6. 8. 11

℟. (2) How lovely is your dwelling-place,
    Lord, mighty God!
My soul yearns and pines
    for the courts of the Lord.
My heart and my flesh
    cry out for the living God.
℟. How lovely is your dwelling-place,
    Lord, mighty God!
Even the sparrow finds a home,
    and the swallow a nest
    in which she puts her young—
Your altars, O Lord of hosts,
    my king and my God!
℟. How lovely is your dwelling-place,
    Lord, mighty God!
Happy they who dwell in your house!
    continually they praise you.
Happy the men whose strength you are!
They go from strength to strength;
℟. How lovely is your dwelling-place,
    Lord, mighty God!
I had rather one day in your courts
    than a thousand elsewhere;
I had rather lie at the threshold of the house
    of my God
    than dwell in the tents of the wicked.
℟. How lovely is your dwelling-place,
    Lord, mighty God!

Year II

READING I   Jer 18, 1-6

A reading from the book of the prophet Jeremiah

As the clay in the potter's hand, so you are in mine, house of Israel.

This word came to Jeremiah from the Lord: Rise up, be off to the potter's house; there I will give you my message. I went down to the potter's house and there he was, working at the wheel. Whenever the object of clay which he was making turned out badly in his hand, he tried again, making of the clay another object of whatever sort he pleased. Then the word of the Lord came to me: Can I not do to you, house of Israel, as this potter has done? says the Lord. Indeed, like clay in the hand of the potter, so are you in my hand, house of Israel.

This is the Word of the Lord.

Responsorial Psalm   Ps 146, 1-2. 2-4. 5-6

℟. (5) Blest are they whose help is the God of Jacob.

Praise the Lord, O my soul;
I will praise the Lord all my life;
  I will sing praise to my God while I live.
R̠. Blest are they whose help is the God of
  Jacob.
Put not your trust in princes,
  in man, in whom there is no salvation.
When his spirit departs he returns to his earth;
  on that day his plans perish.
R̠. Blest are they whose help is the God of
  Jacob.
Happy he whose help is the God of Jacob,
  whose hope is in the Lord, his God.
Who made heaven and earth,
  the sea and all that is in them.
R̠. Blest are they whose help is the God of
  Jacob.
R̠. Or: Alleluia.

Years I and II

GOSPEL   Mt 13, 47-53
Alleluia
See no. 509.

✠ A reading from the holy gospel according
  to Matthew
They gather the good ones in a basket, the bad are thrown
away.

Jesus said to the crowds: "The reign of God is
also like a dragnet thrown into the lake, which
collected all sorts of things. When it was full
they hauled it ashore and sat down to put what
was worthwhile into containers. What was
useless they threw away. That is how it will be
at the end of the world. Angels will go out and
separate the wicked from the just and hurl the
wicked into the fiery furnace, where they will
wail and grind their teeth.
  "Have you understood all this?" "Yes," they
answered; to which he replied, "Every scribe
who is learned in the reign of God is like the
head of a household who can bring from his
storeroom both the new and the old." When
Jesus had finished this parable he moved on
from that district.
  This is the gospel of the Lord.

**405   FRIDAY OF THE
SEVENTEENTH WEEK OF THE YEAR**

Year I

READING I   Lv 23, 1. 4-11. 15-16. 27. 34-37
A reading from the book of Leviticus
The solemn feasts of the Lord God are sacred assemblies.

The Lord said to Moses, "These are the festivals of the Lord which you shall celebrate at
their proper time with a sacred assembly. The
Passover of the Lord falls on the fourteenth
day of the first month, at the evening twilight.
The fifteenth day of this month is the Lord's
feast of Unleavened Bread. For seven days you
shall eat unleavened bread. On the first of these
days you shall hold a sacred assembly and do
no sort of work. On each of the seven days you
shall offer an oblation to the Lord. Then on
the seventh day you shall again hold a sacred
assembly and do no sort of work."
  The Lord said to Moses, "Speak to the Israelites and tell them: When you come into the
land which I am giving you, and reap your
harvest, you shall bring a sheaf of the first
fruits of your harvest to the priest, who shall
wave the sheaf before the Lord that it may be
acceptable for you.
  "Beginning with the day after the sabbath,
the day on which you bring the wave-offering
sheaf, you shall count seven full weeks, and
then on the day after the seventh week, the
fiftieth day, you shall present the new cereal
offering to the Lord. The tenth of this seventh
month is the Day of Atonement, when you
shall hold a sacred assembly and mortify yourselves and offer an oblation to the Lord. The
fifteenth day of this seventh month is the
Lord's feast of Booths, which shall continue for
seven days. On the first day there shall be a
sacred assembly, and you shall do no sort of
work. For seven days you shall offer an oblation to the Lord, and on the eighth day you
shall again hold a sacred assembly and offer an
oblation to the Lord. On that solemn closing
you shall do no sort of work.
  "These, therefore, are the festivals of the
Lord on which you shall proclaim a sacred
assembly, and offer as an oblation to the Lord

holocausts and cereal offerings, sacrifices and libations, as prescribed for each day."
This is the Word of the Lord.

Responsorial Psalm   Ps 81, 3-4. 5-6. 10-11

℟. (2) Sing with joy to God our help.
Take up a melody, and sound the timbrel,
the pleasant harp and the lyre.
Blow the trumpet at the new moon,
at the full moon, on our solemn feast;
℟. Sing with joy to God our help.
For it is a statute in Israel,
an ordinance of the God of Jacob,
Who made it a decree for Joseph
when he came forth from the land of Egypt.
℟. Sing with joy to God our help.
There shall be no strange god among you
nor shall you worship any alien god.
I, the Lord, am your God
who led you forth from the land of Egypt.
℟. Sing with joy to God our help.

Year II

READING I   Jer 26, 1-9
A reading from the book of the prophet Jeremiah

All the people gathered to worship the Lord.

In the beginning of the reign of Jehoiakim, son of Josiah, king of Judah, this message came from the Lord: Thus says the Lord: Stand in the court of the house of the Lord and speak to the people of all the cities of Judah who come to worship in the house of the Lord; whatever I command you, tell them, and omit nothing. Perhaps they will listen and turn back, each from his evil way, so that I may repent of the evil I have planned to inflict upon them for their evil deeds. Say to them: Thus says the Lord: If you disobey me, not living according to the law I placed before you and not listening to the words of my servants the prophets, whom I send you constantly though you do not obey them, I will treat this house like Shiloh, and make this the city which all the nations of the earth shall refer to when cursing another.
Now the priests, the prophets, and all the people heard Jeremiah speak these words in the house of the Lord. When Jeremiah finished speaking all that the Lord bade him speak to all the people, the priests and prophets laid hold of him, crying, "You must be put to death! Why do you prophesy in the name of the Lord: 'This house shall be like Shiloh,' and 'This city shall be desolate and deserted'?" And all the people gathered about Jeremiah in the house of the Lord.
This is the Word of the Lord.

Responsorial Psalm   Ps 69, 5. 8-10. 14

℟. (14) Lord, in your great love, answer me.
Those outnumber the hairs of my head
who hate me without cause.
Too many for my strength
are they who wrongfully are my enemies.
Must I restore what I did not steal?
℟. Lord, in your great love, answer me.
Since for your sake I bear insult,
and shame covers my face.
I have become an outcast to my brothers,
a stranger to my mother's sons,
Because zeal for your house consumes me,
and the insults of those who blaspheme you
fall upon me.
℟. Lord, in your great love, answer me.
But I pray to you, O Lord,
for the time of your favor, O God!
In your great kindness answer me
with your constant help.
℟. Lord, in your great love, answer me.

Years I and II

GOSPEL   Mt 13, 54-58
Alleluia

See no. 509.

✠ **A reading from the holy gospel according to Matthew**

Is this not the son of the carpenter? Where did he get all his wisdom?

Jesus went to his native place and spent his time teaching the people in their synagogue. They were filled with amazement, and said to one another, "Where did this man get such wisdom and miraculous powers? Isn't this the carpenter's son? Isn't Mary known to be his mother and James, Joseph, Simon, and Judas his brothers? Aren't his sisters our neighbors? Where did he get all this?" They found him altogether too much for them. Jesus said to them, "No prophet is without honor except in his native place, indeed in his own house." And he did not work many miracles there because of their lack of faith.

This is the gospel of the Lord.

---

406   SATURDAY OF THE SEVENTEENTH WEEK OF THE YEAR

Year I

READING I   Lv 25, 1. 8-17

A reading from the book of Leviticus

In the jubilee year you will reap all you possess.

The Lord said to Moses on Mount Sinai, "Seven weeks of years shall you count—seven times seven years—so that the seven cycles amount to forty-nine years. Then, on the tenth day of the seventh month let the trumpet resound; on this, the Day of Atonement, the trumpet blast shall re-echo throughout your land. This fiftieth year you shall make sacred by proclaiming liberty in the land for all its inhabitants. It shall be a jubilee for you, when every one of you shall return to his own property, every one to his own family estate. In this fiftieth year, your year of jubilee, you shall not sow, nor shall you reap the aftergrowth or pick the grapes from the untrimmed vines. Since this is the jubilee, which shall be sacred for you, you may not eat of its produce, except as taken directly from the field.

"In this year of jubilee, then, every one of you shall return to his own property. Therefore, when you sell any land to your neighbor or buy any from him, do not deal unfairly. On the basis of the number of years since the last jubilee shall you purchase the land from him; and so also, on the basis of the number of years for crops, shall he sell it to you. When the years are many, the price shall be so much the more; when the years are few, the price shall be so much the less. For it is really the number of crops that he sells you. Do not deal unfairly, then; but stand in fear of your God. I, the Lord, am your God."

This is the Word of the Lord.

Responsorial Psalm   Ps 67, 2-3. 5. 7-8

℟. (4) O God, let all the nations praise you!
May God have pity on us and bless us;
    may he let his face shine upon us.
So may your way be known upon earth;
    among all nations, your salvation.
℟. O God, let all the nations praise you!
May the nations be glad and exult
    because you rule the peoples in equity;
    the nations on the earth you guide.
℟. O God, let all the nations praise you!
The earth has yielded its fruits;
    God, our God, has blessed us.
May God bless us,
    and may all the ends of the earth fear him!
℟. O God, let all the nations praise you!

Year II

READING I   Jer 26, 11-16. 24

A reading from the book of the prophet Jeremiah

The Lord God himself sent me to say all the things you have heard.

The priests and prophets said to the princes and to all the people, "This man deserves death; he has prophesied against this city, as you have heard with your own ears." Jeremiah gave this answer to the princes and all the people: "It was the Lord who sent me to prophesy against this house and city all that you have heard. Now, therefore, reform your ways and your deeds; listen to the voice of the Lord your God, so that the Lord will repent of the evil with which he threatens you. As for me, I am in your hands; do with me what you think good and right. But mark well: if you put me to death, it is innocent blood you bring on yourselves, on this city and its citizens. For in truth it was the Lord who sent me to you, to speak all these things for you to hear."

Thereupon the princes and all the people said to the priests and the prophets, "This man does not deserve death; it is in the name of the Lord, our God, that he speaks to us." But Ahikam, son of Shaphan, protected Jeremiah, so that he was not handed over to the people to be put to death.

This is the Word of the Lord.

Responsorial Psalm   Ps 69, 15-16. 30-31. 33-34

℞. (14) Lord, in your great love, answer me.

Rescue me out of the mire; may I not sink!
   may I be rescued from my foes,
   and from the watery depths.
Let not the flood-waters overwhelm me,
   nor the abyss swallow me up,
   nor the pit close its mouth over me.

℞. Lord, in your great love, answer me.

But I am afflicted and in pain;
   let your saving help, O God, protect me.
I will praise the name of God in song,
   and I will glorify him with thanksgiving.

℞. Lord, in your great love, answer me.

"See, you lowly ones, and be glad;
   you who seek God, may your hearts be
      merry!
For the Lord hears the poor,
   and his own who are in bonds he spurns not.

℞. Lord, in your great love, answer me.

GOSPEL   Years I and II
Alleluia   Mt 14, 1-12

See no. 509.

✠ A reading from the holy gospel according
   to Matthew
Herod had John beheaded; the disciples went and told
Jesus.

On one occasion Herod the tetrarch, having heard of Jesus' reputation, exclaimed to his courtiers, "This man is John the Baptizer—it is he in person, raised from the dead; that is why such miraculous powers are at work in him!" Recall that Herod had had John arrested, put in chains, and imprisoned on account of Herodias, the wife of his brother Philip. That was because John had told him, "It is not right for you to live with her." Herod wanted to kill John but was afraid of the people, who re-

garded him as a prophet. Then on Herod's birthday Herodias' daughter performed a dance before the court which delighted Herod so much that he swore he would grant her anything she asked for. Prompted by her mother she said, "Bring me the head of John the Baptizer on a platter." The king immediately had his misgivings, but because of his oath and the guests who were present he gave orders that the request be granted. He sent the order to have John beheaded in prison. John's head was brought in on a platter and given to the girl, who took it to her mother. Later his disciples presented themselves to carry his body away and bury it. Afterward, they came and informed Jesus.

This is the gospel of the Lord.

407   **MONDAY OF THE**
      EIGHTEENTH WEEK OF THE YEAR

                              Year I

READING I   Nm 11, 4-15

   A reading from the book of Numbers
   I am not able to carry this nation by myself alone.

The Israelites lamented, "Would that we had meat for food! We remember the fish we used to eat without cost in Egypt, and the cucumbers, the melons, the leeks, the onions, and the garlic. But now we are famished; we see nothing before us but this manna."

Manna was like coriander seed and had the appearance of bdellium. When they had gone about and gathered it up, the people would grind it between millstones or pound it in a mortar, then cook it in a pot and make it into loaves, which tasted like cakes made with oil. At night, when the dew fell upon the camp, the manna also fell.

When Moses heard the people, family after family, crying at the entrance of their tents, so that the Lord became very angry, he was grieved. "Why do you treat your servant so badly?" Moses asked the Lord. "Why are you so displeased with me that you burden me with all this people? Was it I who conceived all this people? or was it I who gave them birth, that you tell me to carry them at my bosom, like a foster father carrying an infant, to the land you have promised under oath to their fathers? Where can I get meat to give to all this people? For they are crying to me, 'Give us meat for our food.' I cannot carry all this people by myself, for they are too heavy for me. If this is the way you will deal with me, then please do me the favor of killing me at once, so that I need no longer face this distress."

    This is the Word of the Lord.

Responsorial Psalm   Ps 81, 12-13. 14-15. 16-17

℞. (2) Sing with joy to God our help.
My people heard not my voice,
    and Israel obeyed me not;
So I gave them up to the hardness of their
    hearts;
    they walked according to their own coun-
    sels.
℞. Sing with joy to God our help.
If only my people would hear me,
    and Israel walk in my ways,
Quickly would I humble their enemies;
    against their foes I would turn my hand.
℞. Sing with joy to God our help.
Those who hated the Lord would seek to flatter
    me,
    but their fate would endure forever,
While Israel I would feed with the best of
    wheat,
    and with honey from the rock I would fill
    them.
℞. Sing with joy to God our help.

Year II

READING I   Jer 28, 1-17
    **A reading from the book of the prophet
                    Jeremiah**
Hananiah, the Lord God has not sent you; you have confided
            to the people what is false.
In [the beginning of] the reign of Zedekiah, king of Judah, in the fifth month of the fourth year, the prophet Hananiah, son of Azzur, from Gibeon, said to me in the house of the Lord in the presence of the priests and all the people:

"Thus says the Lord of hosts, the God of Israel: 'I will break the yoke of the king of Babylon. Within two years I will restore to this place all the vessels of the temple of the Lord which Nebuchadnezzar, king of Babylon, took away from this place to Babylon. And I will bring back to this place Jeconiah, son of Jehoiakim, king of Judah, and all the exiles of Judah who went to Babylon,' says the Lord, 'for I will break the yoke of the king of Babylon.' "

    The prophet Jeremiah answered the prophet Hananiah in the presence of the priests and all the people assembled in the house of the Lord, and said: Amen! thus may the Lord do! May he fulfill the things you have prophesied by bringing the vessels of the house of the Lord and all the exiles back from Babylon to this place! But now, listen to what I am about to state in your hearing and the hearing of all the people. From of old, the prophets who were before you and me prophesied war, woe, and pestilence against many lands and mighty kingdoms. But the prophet who prophesies peace is recognized as truly sent by the Lord only when his prophetic prediction is fulfilled.

    Thereupon the prophet Hananiah took the yoke from the neck of the prophet Jeremiah, broke it, and said in the presence of all the people: "Thus says the Lord: 'Even so, within two years I will break the yoke of Nebuchadnezzar, king of Babylon, from off the neck of all the nations.' " At that, the prophet Jeremiah went away.

    Some time after the prophet Hananiah had broken the yoke from off the neck of the prophet Jeremiah, the word of the Lord came to Jeremiah: Go tell Hananiah this: Thus says the Lord: By breaking a wooden yoke, you forge an iron yoke! For thus says the Lord of hosts, the God of Israel: A yoke of iron I will place on the necks of all these nations serving Nebuchadnezzar, king of Babylon, and they shall serve him; even the beasts of the field I give him.

    To the prophet Hananiah the prophet Jeremiah said: Hear this, Hananiah! The Lord has not sent you, and you have raised false confidence in this people. For this, says the Lord, I will dispatch you from the face of the earth; this very year you shall die, because you have preached rebellion against the Lord. That same year, in the seventh month, Hananiah the prophet died.

This is the Word of the Lord.

Responsorial Psalm   Ps 119, 29, 43. 79. 80. 95. 102

R̸. (68) Teach me your laws, O Lord.
Remove from me the way of falsehood,
 and favor me with your law.
R̸. Teach me your laws, O Lord.
Take not the word of truth from my mouth,
 for in your ordinances is my hope.
R̸. Teach me your laws, O Lord.
Let those turn to me who fear you
 and acknowledge your decrees.
R̸. Teach me your laws, O Lord.
Let my heart be perfect in your statutes,
 that I be not put to shame.
R̸. Teach me your laws, O Lord.
Sinners wait to destroy me,
 but I pay heed to your decrees.
R̸. Teach me your laws, O Lord.
From your ordinances I turn not away,
 for you have instructed me.
R̸. Teach me your laws, O Lord.

GOSPEL   `Years I and II`
Alleluia   Mt 14, 13-21
See no. 509.

✠ A reading from the holy gospel according to Matthew

Raising his eyes to heaven he said the blessing and gave the bread to his disciples who in turn gave it to the crowds.

When Jesus heard of the death of John the Baptizer, he withdrew by boat from there to a deserted place by himself. The crowds heard of it and followed him on foot from the towns. When he disembarked and saw the vast throng, his heart was moved with pity, and he cured their sick. As evening drew on, his disciples came to him with the suggestion: "This is a deserted place and it is already late. Dismiss the crowds so that they may go to the villages and buy some food for themselves." Jesus said to them: "There is no need for them

to disperse. Give them something to eat yourselves." "We have nothing here," they replied, "but five loaves and a couple of fish." "Bring them here," he said. Then he ordered the crowds to sit down on the grass. He took the five loaves and two fish, looked up to heaven, blessed and broke them and gave the loaves to the disciples, who in turn gave them to the people. All those present ate their fill. The fragments which remained, when gathered up, filled twelve baskets. Those who ate were about five thousand, not counting women and children.

This is the gospel of the Lord.

In year A, when the above gospel is read on the preceding Sunday, Mt 14, 22-36 is read on Monday (as below, no. 408).

**408   TUESDAY OF THE
EIGHTEENTH WEEK OF THE YEAR**

`Year I`

READING I   Nm 12, 1-13

A reading from the book of Numbers

Moses is at home in my house. How have you dared to speak against him?

Miriam and Aaron spoke against Moses on the pretext of the marriage he had contracted with a Cushite woman. They complained, "Is it through Moses alone that the Lord speaks? Does he not speak through us also?" And the Lord heard this. Now, Moses himself was by far the meekest man on the face of the earth. So at once the Lord said to Moses and Aaron and Miriam, "Come out, you three, to the meeting tent." And the three of them went. Then the Lord came down in the column of cloud, and standing at the entrance of the tent, called Aaron and Miriam. When both came forward, he said, "Now listen to the words of the Lord:

 Should there be a prophet among you,
  in visions will I reveal myself to him,
  in dreams will I speak to him;
 Not so with my servant Moses!
 Throughout my house he bears my trust:
  face to face I speak to him,
  plainly and not in riddles.

The presence of the Lord he beholds.
Why, then, did you not fear to speak against
my servant Moses?"

So angry was the Lord against them that
when he departed, and the cloud withdrew
from the tent, there was Miriam, a snow-white
leper! When Aaron turned and saw her a leper,
"Ah, my lord!" he said to Moses, "please do not
charge us with the sin that we have foolishly
committed! Let her not thus be like the still-
born babe that comes forth from its mother's
womb with its flesh half consumed." Then
Moses cried to the Lord, "Please, not this! Pray,
heal her!"

This is the Word of the Lord.

Responsorial Psalm   Ps 51, 3-4. 5-6. 6-7. 12-13

℞. (3) Be merciful, O Lord, for we have sinned.
Have mercy on me, O God, in your goodness;
   in the greatness of your compassion wipe
   out my offense.
Thoroughly wash me from my guilt
   and of my sin cleanse me.
℞. Be merciful, O Lord, for we have sinned.
For I acknowledge my offense,
   and my sin is before me always:
"Against you only have I sinned
   and done what is evil in your sight"—
℞. Be merciful, O Lord, for we have sinned.
That you may be justified in your sentence,
   vindicated when you condemn.
Indeed, in guilt was I born,
   and in sin my mother conceived me,
℞. Be merciful, O Lord, for we have sinned.
A clean heart create for me, O God,
   and a steadfast spirit renew within me.
Cast me not out from your presence,
   and your holy spirit take not from me.
℞. Be merciful, O Lord, for we have sinned.

Year II

READING I   Jer 30, 1-2. 12-15. 18-22

A reading from the book of the prophet
Jeremiah

Your sins are so great that I have done all this to you. Now
I will restore the tents of Jacob.

The following message came to Jeremiah from
the Lord: Thus says the Lord, the God of Israel:

Write all the words I have spoken to you in a
book.

Thus says the Lord:
Incurable is your wound,
   grievous your bruise;
There is none to plead your cause,
   no remedy for your running sore,
   no healing for you.
All your lovers have forgotten you,
   they do not seek you.
I struck you as an enemy would strike,
   punished you cruelly;
Why cry out over your wound?
   your pain is without relief.
Because of your great guilt,
   your numerous sins,
I have done this to you.

Thus says the Lord:
See! I will restore the tents of Jacob,
   his dwellings I will pity;
City shall be rebuilt upon hill,
   and palace restored as it was.
From them will resound songs of praise,
   the laughter of happy men.
I will make them not few, but many;
   they will not be tiny, for I will glorify them.
His sons shall be as of old,
   his assembly before me shall stand firm;
   I will punish all his oppressors.
His leader shall be one of his own,
   and his rulers shall come from his kin.
When I summon him, he shall approach me;
   how else should one take the deadly risk
   of approaching me? says the Lord.
You shall be my people,
   and I will be your God.
   This is the Word of the Lord.

Responsorial Psalm   Ps 102, 16-18. 19-21. 29. 22-23

℞. (17) The Lord will build up Zion again,
   and appear in all his glory.
The nations shall revere your name, O Lord,
   and all the kings of the earth your glory,
When the Lord has rebuilt Zion
   and appeared in his glory;
When he has regarded the prayer of the destitute,
   and not despised their prayer.

℞. The Lord will build up Zion again,
   and appear in all his glory.

Let this be written for the generation to come,
   and let his future creatures praise the Lord:
"The Lord looked down from his holy height,
   from heaven he beheld the earth,
To hear the groaning of the prisoners,
   to release those doomed to die."

℞. The Lord will build up Zion again,
   and appear in all his glory.

The children of your servants shall abide,
   and their posterity shall continue in your
   presence.
That the name of the Lord may be declared
   in Zion;
   and his praise, in Jerusalem,
When the peoples gather together,
   and the kingdoms, to serve the Lord.

℞. The Lord will build up Zion again,
   and appear in all his glory.

Years I and II

GOSPEL   Mt 14, 22-36
Alleluia

See no. 509.

✠ **A reading from the holy gospel according**
to Matthew

Order me to come to you across the water.

After the crowds had eaten their fill Jesus
insisted that his disciples get into a boat and
precede him to the other side. When he had
sent them away, he went up on the mountain
by himself to pray, remaining there alone as
evening drew on. Meanwhile the boat, already
several hundred yards out from shore, was
being tossed about in the waves raised by
strong head winds. At about three in the morn-
ing, he came walking toward them on the lake.
When the disciples saw him walking on the
water, they were terrified. "It is a ghost!" they
said, and in their fear they began to cry out.
Jesus hastened to reassure them: "Get hold of
yourselves! It is I. Do not be afraid!" Peter
spoke up and said, "Lord, if it is really you, tell
me to come to you across the water." "Come!"
he said. So Peter got out of the boat and began

to walk on the water, moving toward Jesus.
But when he perceived how strong the wind
was, becoming frightened, he began to sink
and cried out, "Lord, save me!" Jesus at once
stretched out his hand and caught him. "How
little faith you have!" he exclaimed. "Why did
you falter?" Once they had climbed into the
boat, the wind died down. Those who were in
the boat showed him reverence, declaring,
"Undoubtedly you are the Son of God!"

After making the crossing they reached the
shore at Gennesaret; and when the men of that
place recognized him they spread the word
throughout the region. People brought him all
the afflicted, with the plea that he let them do
no more than touch the tassel of his cloak. As
many as touched it were fully restored to
health.

      This is the gospel of the Lord.

OR

The following text may be substituted especially in year A
when the above gospel is read on Monday.

Any plant my heavenly Father has not planted will be pulled
up by the roots.

The scribes from Jerusalem approached Jesus
with the question: "Why do your disciples act
contrary to the tradition of our ancestors?
They do not wash their hands, for example,
before eating a meal."

   Jesus summoned the crowd and said to
them: "Give ear and try to understand. It is
not what goes into a man's mouth that makes
him impure; it is what comes out of his
mouth." His disciples approached him and
said, "Do you realize the Pharisees were scan-
dalized when they heard your pronounce-
ment?" "Every planting not put down by my
heavenly Father will be uprooted," he replied.
"Let them go their way; they are blind leaders
of the blind. If one blind man leads another,
both will end in a pit."

      This is the gospel of the Lord.

409   WEDNESDAY OF THE EIGHTEENTH WEEK OF THE YEAR

Year I

READING I   Nm 13, 1-2. 25–14, 1. 26-29. 34-35

A reading from the book of Numbers
They will have nothing of the land they desired.

The Lord said to Moses in the desert of Pharan, "Send men to reconnoiter the land of Canaan, which I am giving the Israelites." After reconnoitering the land for forty days they returned, met Moses and Aaron and the whole community of the Israelites in the desert of Paran at Kadesh, made a report to them all, and showed them the fruit of the country. They told Moses: "We went into the land to which you sent us. It does indeed flow with milk and honey, and here is its fruit. However, the people who are living in the land are fierce, and the towns are fortified and very strong. Besides, we saw descendants of the Anakim there. Amalekites live in the region of the Negeb; Hittites, Jebusites and Amorites dwell in the highlands, and Canaanites along the seacoast and the banks of the Jordan."

Caleb, however, to quiet the people toward Moses, said, "We ought to go up and seize the land, for we can certainly do so." But the men who had gone up with him said, "We cannot attack these people; they are too strong for us." So they spread discouraging reports among the Israelites about the land they had scouted, saying, "The land that we explored is a country that consumes its inhabitants. And all the people we saw there are huge men, veritable giants [the Anakim were a race of giants]; we felt like mere grasshoppers, and so we must have seemed to them."

At this, the whole community broke out with loud cries, and even in the night the people wailed.

The Lord said to Moses and Aaron: "How long will this wicked community grumble against me? I have heard the grumblings of the Israelites against me. Tell them: By my life, says the Lord, I will do to you just what I have heard you say. Here in the desert shall your dead bodies fall. Forty days you spent in scouting the land; forty years shall you suffer for your crimes: one year for each day. Thus you will realize what it means to oppose me. I, the Lord, have sworn to do this to all this wicked community that conspired against me: here in the desert they shall die to the last man."

This is the Word of the Lord.

Responsorial Psalm   Ps 106, 6-7. 13-14. 21-22. 23

℟. (4) Lord, remember us,
    for the love you bear your people.
We have sinned, we and our fathers;
    we have committed crimes; we have done
      wrong.
Our fathers in Egypt
    considered not your wonders.
℟. Lord, remember us,
    for the love you bear your people.
But soon they forgot his works;
    they waited not for his counsel.
They gave way to craving in the desert
    and tempted God in the wilderness.
℟. Lord, remember us,
    for the love you bear your people.
They forgot the God who had saved them,
    who had done great deeds in Egypt,
Wondrous deeds in the land of Ham,
    terrible things at the Red Sea.
℟. Lord, remember us,
    for the love you bear your people.
Then he spoke of exterminating them,
    but Moses, his chosen one,
Withstood him in the breach
    to turn back his destructive wrath.
℟. Lord, remember us,
    for the love you bear your people.
℟. Or: Alleluia.

Year II

READING I   Jer 31, 1-7

A reading from the book of the prophet Jeremiah
I have loved you with an everlasting love.

At that time, says the Lord,
I will be the God of all the tribes of Israel,
    and they shall be my people.

Thus says the Lord:
The people that escaped the sword
    have found favor in the desert.
As Israel comes forward to be given his rest,
    the Lord appears to him from afar:
With age-old love I have loved you;
    So I have kept my mercy toward you.
Again I will restore you, and you shall be
    rebuilt,
    O virgin Israel;
Carrying your festive tambourines,
    you shall go forth dancing with the merry-
    makers.
Again you shall plant vineyards
    on the mountains of Samaria;
    those who plant them shall enjoy the fruits.
Yes, a day will come when the watchmen
    will call out on Mount Ephraim:
"Rise up, let us go to Zion,
    to the Lord, our God."

For thus says the Lord:
Shout with joy for Jacob,
    exult at the head of the nations;
    proclaim your praise and say:
The Lord has delivered his people,
    the remnant of Israel.
                    This is the Word of the Lord.

Responsorial Psalm   Jer 31, 10. 11-12. 13

Ry. (10) The Lord will guard us,
    like a shepherd guarding his flock.
Hear the word of the Lord, O nations,
    proclaim it on distant coasts, and say:
He who scattered Israel, now gathers them to-
    gether,
    he guards them as a shepherd his flock.
Ry. The Lord will guard us,
    like a shepherd guarding his flock.
The Lord shall ransom Jacob,
    he shall redeem him from the hand of his
    conqueror.
Shouting, they shall mount the heights of Zion,
    they shall come streaming to the Lord's
    blessings.
Ry. The Lord will guard us,
    like a shepherd guarding his flock.
Then the virgins shall make merry and dance,

and young men and old as well.
I will turn their mourning into joy,
    I will console and gladden them after their
    sorrows.
Ry. The Lord will guard us,
    like a shepherd guarding his flock.

Years I and II

GOSPEL   Mt 15, 21-28
Alleluia
See no. 509.

✠ A reading from the holy gospel according
                    to Matthew
        Woman, you have great faith.
Jesus withdrew to the district of Tyre and
Sidon. It happened that a Canaanite woman
living in that locality presented herself, crying out to him, "Lord, Son of David, have
pity on me! My daughter is terribly troubled
by a demon." He gave her no word of response.
His disciples came up and began to entreat
him, "Get rid of her. She keeps shouting after
us." "My mission is only to the lost sheep of the
house of Israel," Jesus replied. She came forward then and did him homage with the plea,
"Help me, Lord!" But he answered, "It is not
right to take the food of sons and daughters
and throw it to the dogs." "Please, Lord," she
insisted, "even the dogs eat the leavings that
fall from their masters' tables." Jesus then
said in reply, "Woman, you have great faith!
Your wish will come to pass." That very moment her daughter got better.
                    This is the gospel of the Lord.

410   **THURSDAY OF THE**
        EIGHTEENTH WEEK OF THE YEAR

Year I

READING I   Nm 20, 1-13
        A reading from the book of Numbers
        He showed them his treasure, the font of living water.
The whole Israelite community arrived in the
desert of Zin in the first month, and the people
settled at Kadesh. It was here that Miriam
died, and here that she was buried.

As the community had no water, they held a council against Moses and Aaron. The people contended with Moses, exclaiming, "Would that we too had perished with our kinsmen in the Lord's presence! Why have you brought the Lord's community into this desert where we and our livestock are dying? Why did you lead us out of Egypt, only to bring us to this wretched place which has neither grain nor figs nor vines nor pomegranates? Here there is not even water to drink!" But Moses and Aaron went away from the assembly to the entrance of the meeting tent, where they fell prostrate.

Then the glory of the Lord appeared to them, and the Lord said to Moses, "Take the staff and assemble the community, you and your brother Aaron, and in their presence order the rock to yield its waters. From the rock you shall bring forth water for the community and their live-stock to drink." So Moses took the staff from its place before the Lord, as he was ordered. He and Aaron assembled the community in front of the rock, where he said to them, "Listen to me, you rebels! Are we to bring water for you out of this rock?" Then, raising his hand, Moses struck the rock twice with his staff, and water gushed out in abundance for the community and their livestock to drink. But the Lord said to Moses and Aaron, "Because you were not faithful to me in showing forth my sanctity be-fore the Israelites, you shall not lead this com-munity into the land I will give them."

These are the waters of Meribah, where the Israelites contended against the Lord, and where he revealed his sanctity among them. This is the Word of the Lord.

Responsorial Psalm   Ps 95, 1-2. 6-7. 8-9

R̂. (8) If today you hear his voice,
harden not your hearts.
Come, let us sing joyfully to the Lord;
let us acclaim the Rock of our salvation.
Let us greet him with thanksgiving;
let us joyfully sing psalms to him.
R̂. If today you hear his voice,
harden not your hearts.

Come, let us bow down in worship;
let us kneel before the Lord who made us.
For he is our God,
and we are the people he shepherds, the
flock he guides.
R̂. If today you hear his voice,
harden not your hearts.
Oh, that today you would hear his voice:
"Harden not your hearts as at Meribah,
as in the day of Massah in the desert,
Where your fathers tempted me;
they tested me though they had seen my
works."
R̂. If today you hear his voice,
harden not your hearts.

Year II

READING I   Jer 31, 31-34

A reading from the book of the prophet Jeremiah

I will make a new covenant with the house of Israel and never call their sin to mind.

The days are coming, says the Lord, when I will make a new covenant with the house of Israel and the house of Judah. It will not be like the covenant I made with their fathers the day I took them by the hand to lead them forth from the land of Egypt; for they broke my covenant, and I had to show myself their master, says the Lord. But this is the covenant which I will make with the house of Israel after those days, says the Lord. I will place my law within them, and write it upon their hearts; I will be their God, and they shall be my people. No longer will they have need to teach their friends and kinsmen how to know the Lord. All, from least to greatest, shall know me, says the Lord, for I will forgive their evildoing and remember their sin no more. This is the Word of the Lord.

Responsorial Psalm   Ps 51, 12-13. 14-15. 18-19

R̂. (12) Create a clean heart in me, O God.
A clean heart create for me, O God,
and a steadfast spirit renew within me.
Cast me not out from your presence,
and your holy spirit take not from me.

℟. Create a clean heart in me, O God.
**Give me back the joy of your salvation,
and a willing spirit sustain in me.
I will teach transgressors your ways,
and sinners shall return to you.**
℟. Create a clean heart in me, O God.
**For you are not pleased with sacrifices;
should I offer a holocaust, you would not accept it.
My sacrifice, O God, is a contrite spirit;
a heart contrite and humbled, O God, you will not spurn.**
℟. Create a clean heart in me, O God.

GOSPEL
Alleluia

| Years I and II |
| Mt 16, 13-23 |

See no. 509.

✠ A reading from the holy gospel according to Matthew
You are Peter, to you I will give the keys of the kingdom of heaven.

When Jesus came to the neighborhood of Caesarea Philippi, he asked his disciples this question: "Who do people say that the Son of Man is?" They replied, "Some say John the Baptizer, others Elijah, still others Jeremiah or one of the prophets." "And you," he said to them, "who do you say that I am?" "You are the Messiah," Simon Peter answered, "the Son of the living God!" Jesus replied, "Blest are you, Simon son of John! No mere man has revealed this to you, but my heavenly Father. I for my part declare to you, you are 'Rock,' and on this rock I will build my church, and the jaws of death shall not prevail against it. I will entrust to you the keys of the kingdom of heaven. Whatever you declare bound on earth shall be bound in heaven; whatever you declare loosed on earth shall be loosed in heaven." Then he strictly ordered his disciples not to tell anyone that he was the Messiah.

From then on Jesus [the Messiah] started to indicate to his disciples that he must go to Jerusalem to suffer greatly there at the hands of the elders, the chief priests, and the scribes, and to be put to death, and raised up on the third day. At this, Peter took him aside and began to remonstrate with him. "May you be spared, Master! God forbid that any such thing ever happen to you!" Jesus turned on Peter and said, "Get out of my sight, you satan! You are trying to make me trip and fall. You are not judging by God's standards but by man's."

This is the gospel of the Lord.

411 **FRIDAY OF THE
EIGHTEENTH WEEK OF THE YEAR**

| Year I |

READING I
Dt 4, 32-40

A reading from the book of Deuteronomy
The Lord God loved your fathers and chose their descendants after them.

Moses said to the people: "Ask now of the days of old, before your time, ever since God created man upon the earth; ask from one end of the sky to the other: Did anything so great ever happen before? Was it ever heard of? Did a people ever hear the voice of God speaking from the midst of fire, as you did, and live? Or did any God venture to go and take a nation for himself from the midst of another nation, by testings, by signs and wonders, by war, with his strong hand and outstretched arm, and by great terrors, all of which the Lord, your God, did for you in Egypt before your very eyes? All this you were allowed to see that you might know the Lord is God and there is no other. Out of the heavens he let you hear his voice to discipline you; on earth he let you see his great fire, and you heard him speaking out of the fire. For love of your fathers he chose their descendants and personally led you out of Egypt by his great power, driving out of your way nations greater and mightier than you, so as to bring you in and to make their land your heritage, as it is today. This is why you must now know, and fix in your heart, that the Lord is God in the heavens above and on earth below, and that there is no other. You must keep his statutes and commandments which I enjoin

on you today, that you and your children after you may prosper, and that you may have long life on the land which the Lord, your God, is giving you forever."
This is the Word of the Lord.

Responsorial Psalm   Ps 77, 12-13. 14-15. 16. 21

℞. (12) I remember the deeds of the Lord.
I remember the deeds of the Lord;
    yes, I remember your wonders of old.
And I meditate on your works;
    your exploits I ponder.
℞. I remember the deeds of the Lord.
O God, your way is holy;
    what great god is there like our God?
You are the God who works wonders;
    among the peoples you have made known
    your power.
℞. I remember the deeds of the Lord.
With your strong arm you redeemed your
    people,
    the sons of Jacob and Joseph.
You led your people like a flock
    under the care of Moses and Aaron.
℞. I remember the deeds of the Lord.

Year II

READING I   Na 2, 1. 3; 3, 1-3. 6-7
A reading from the book of the prophet Nahum
Woe to the city soaked in blood.
See, upon the mountains there advances
    the bearer of good news, announcing peace!
Celebrate your feast, O Judah,
    fulfill your vows!
For nevermore shall you be invaded
    by the scoundrel; he is completely destroyed.
The Lord will restore the vine of Jacob,
    the pride of Israel,
Though ravagers have ravaged them
    and ruined the tendrils.

Woe to the bloody city, all lies,
    full of plunder, whose looting never stops!
The crack of the whip, the rumbling sound of
    wheels;
    horses a-gallop, chariots bounding,
Cavalry charging,

The flame of the sword, the flash of the spear,
    the many slain, the heaping corpses,
    the endless bodies to stumble upon!
I will cast filth upon you,
    disgrace you and put you to shame;
Till everyone who sees you runs from you,
    saying,
    "Nineveh is destroyed; who can pity her?
Where can one find any to console her?"
This is the Word of the Lord.

Responsorial Psalm   Dt 32, 35-36. 39. 41

℞. (39) It is I who deal death and give life.
Close at hand is the day of their disaster,
    and their doom is rushing upon them!
Surely, the Lord shall do justice for his people;
    on his servants he shall have pity.
℞. It is I who deal death and give life.
"Learn then that I, I alone, am God,
    and there is no god besides me.
It is I who bring both death and life,
    I who inflict wounds and heal them.
℞. It is I who deal death and give life.
I will sharpen my flashing sword,
    and my hand shall lay hold of my quiver.
With vengeance I will repay my foes
    and requite those who hate me."
℞. It is I who deal death and give life.

GOSPEL   **Years I and II**
Alleluia   Mt 16, 24-28
See no. 509.

✠ **A reading from the holy gospel according
                to Matthew**
What can a man give in exchange for his life?
Jesus said to his disciples: "If a man wishes to come after me, he must deny his very self, take up his cross, and begin to follow in my footsteps. Whoever would save his life will lose it, but whoever loses his life for my sake will find it. What profit would a man show if he were to gain the whole world and ruin himself in the process? What can a man offer in exchange for his very self? The Son of Man will come with his Father's glory accompanied by his angels. When he does, he will repay each

man according to his conduct. I assure you, among those standing here there are some who will not experience death before they see the Son of Man come in his kingship."

This is the gospel of the Lord.

---

412 SATURDAY OF THE EIGHTEENTH WEEK OF THE YEAR

Year I

READING I   Dt 6, 4-13

A reading from the book of Deuteronomy

You shall love the Lord your God with your whole heart.

Moses said to the people: "Hear, O Israel! The Lord is our God, the Lord alone! Therefore, you shall love the Lord, your God, with all your heart, and with all your soul, and with all your strength. Take to heart these words which I enjoin on you today. Drill them into your children. Speak of them at home and abroad, whether you are busy or at rest. Bind them at your wrist as a sign and let them be as a pendant on your forehead. Write them on the doorposts of your houses and on your gates.

"When the Lord, your God, brings you into the land which he swore to your fathers, Abraham, Isaac and Jacob, that he would give you, a land with fine, large cities that you did not build, with houses full of goods of all sorts that you did not garner, with cisterns that you did not dig, with vineyards and olive groves that you did not plant; and when, therefore, you eat your fill, take care not to forget the Lord, who brought you out of the land of Egypt, that place of slavery. The Lord, your God, shall you fear; him shall you serve, and by his name shall you swear."

This is the Word of the Lord.

Responsorial Psalm   Ps 18, 2-3. 3-4. 47. 51

℞. (2) I love you, Lord, my strength.

I love you, O Lord, my strength,
    O Lord, my rock, my fortress, my deliverer.

℞. I love you, Lord, my strength.

My God, my rock of refuge,
    my shield, the horn of my salvation, my stronghold!
Praised be the Lord, I exclaim,
    and I am safe from my enemies.

℞. I love you, Lord, my strength.

The Lord live! And blessed be my rock!
    Extolled be God my savior.
You who gave great victories to your king
    and showed kindness to your anointed,
    to David and his posterity forever.

℞. I love you, Lord, my strength.

Year II

READING I   Hb 1, 12–2, 4

A reading from the book of the prophet Habakkuk

The upright man will live by his faithfulness.

Are you not from eternity, O Lord,
    my holy God, immortal?
O Lord, you have marked him for judgment,
    O Rock, you have readied him for punishment!
Too pure are your eyes to look upon evil,
    and the sight of misery you cannot endure.
Why, then, do you gaze on the faithless in silence
    while the wicked man devours
    one more just than himself?
You have made man like the fish of the sea,
    like creeping things without a ruler.
He brings them all up with his hook,
    he hauls them away with his net,
He gathers them in his seine;
    and so he rejoices and exults.
Therefore he sacrifices to his net,
    and burns incense to his seine;
For thanks to them his portion is generous,
    and his repast sumptuous.
Shall he, then, keep on brandishing his sword
    to slay peoples without mercy?
I will stand at my guard post,
    and station myself upon the rampart,
And keep watch to see what he will say to me,
    and what answer he will give to my complaint.

Then the Lord answered me and said:
  Write down the vision
Clearly upon the tablets,
  so that one can read it readily.
For the vision still has its time,
  presses on to fulfillment, and will not dis-
    appoint;
If it delays, wait for it,
  it will surely come, it will not be late.
The rash man has no integrity;
  but the just man, because of his faith, shall
    live.
              This is the Word of the Lord.

Responsorial Psalm   Ps 9, 8-9. 10-11. 12-13

℟. (11) You will never abandon those who
  seek you, Lord.
The Lord sits enthroned forever;
  he has set up his throne for judgment.
He judges the world with justice;
  he governs the peoples with equity.
℟. You will never abandon those who seek
  you, Lord.
The Lord is a stronghold for the oppressed,
  a stronghold in times of distress.
They trust in you who cherish your name,
  for you forsake not those who seek you, O
    Lord.
℟. You will never abandon those who seek
  you, Lord.
Sing praise to the Lord enthroned in Zion;
  proclaim among the nations his deeds;
For the avenger of blood has remembered;
  he has not forgotten the cry of the afflicted.
℟. You will never abandon those who seek
  you, Lord.

Years I and II

GOSPEL   Mt 17, 14-20
Alleluia
See no. 509.

✠ A reading from the holy gospel according
              to Matthew
If you have faith, nothing is impossible for you.
A man came up to Jesus and knelt before him.
"Lord," he said, "take pity on my son, who is

demented and in a serious condition. For example, he often falls into the fire and frequently into the water. I have brought him to
your disciples but they could not cure him."
In reply Jesus said: "What an unbelieving and
perverse lot you are! How long must I remain
with you? How long can I endure you? Bring
him here to me!" Then Jesus reprimanded him,
and the demon came out of him. That very
moment the boy was cured.
    The disciples approached Jesus at that point
and asked him privately, "Why could we not
expel it?" "Because you have so little trust,"
he told them. "I assure you, if you had faith
the size of a mustard seed, you would be able to
say to this mountain, 'Move from here to
there,' and it would move. Nothing would be
impossible for you."
              This is the gospel of the Lord.

---

413   **MONDAY OF THE**
          NINETEENTH WEEK OF THE YEAR

Year I

READING I   Dt 10, 12-22
    A reading from the book of Deuteronomy
Circumcise your hearts. Love the strangers, for you your-
    selves were strangers in the land of Egypt.
Moses said to the people: "And now, Israel,
what does the Lord, your God, ask of you but
to fear the Lord, your God, and follow his
ways exactly, to love and serve the Lord, your
God, with all your heart and all your soul, to
keep the commandments and statutes of the
Lord which I enjoin on you today for your own
good? Think! The heavens, even the highest
heavens, belong to the Lord, your God, as well
as the earth and everything on it. Yet in his
love for your fathers the Lord was so attached
to them as to choose you, their descendants,
in preference to all other peoples, as indeed
he has now done. Circumcise your hearts,
therefore, and be no longer stiff-necked. For
the Lord, your God, is the God of gods, the Lord
of lords, the great God, mighty and awesome,
who has no favorites, accepts no bribes; who
executes justice for the orphan and the widow,

and befriends the alien, feeding and clothing him. So you too must befriend the alien, for you were once aliens yourselves in the land of Egypt. The Lord, your God, shall you fear, and him shall you serve; hold fast to him and swear by his name. He is your glory, he, your God, who has done for you those great and terrible things which your own eyes have seen. Your ancestors went down to Egypt seventy strong, and now the Lord, your God, has made you as numerous as the stars of the sky."
This is the Word of the Lord.

Responsorial Psalm   Ps 147, 12-13. 14-15. 19-20

℟. (12) Praise the Lord, Jerusalem.
Glorify the Lord, O Jerusalem;
praise your God, O Zion.
For he has strengthened the bars of your gates;
he has blessed your children within you.
℟. Praise the Lord, Jerusalem.
He has granted peace in your borders;
with the best of wheat he fills you.
He sends forth his command to the earth;
swiftly runs his word!
℟. Praise the Lord, Jerusalem.
He has proclaimed his word to Jacob,
his statutes and his ordinances to Israel.
He has not done thus for any other nation;
his ordinances he has not made known to
them. Alleluia.
℟. Praise the Lord, Jerusalem.
℟. Or: Alleluia.

Year II

READING I   Ez 1, 2-5. 24-28
A reading from the book of the prophet
Ezekiel
It was something that looked like the Lord God.
In the fifth month of the fifth year, that is, of King Jehoiachin's exile, the word of the Lord came to the priest Ezekiel, the son of Buzi, in the land of the Chaldeans by the river Chebar.—There the hand of the Lord came upon me.
As I looked, a stormwind came from the North, a huge cloud with flashing fire [enveloped in brightness], from the midst of which

[the midst of the fire] something gleamed like electrum. Within it were figures resembling four living creatures that looked like this: their form was human. Then I heard the sound of their wings, like the roaring of mighty waters, like the voice of the Almighty. When they moved, the sound of the tumult was like the din of an army. [And when they stood still, they lowered their wings.]
Above the firmament over their heads, something like a throne could be seen, looking like sapphire. Upon it was seated, up above, one who had the appearance of a man. Upward from what resembled his waist I saw what gleamed like electrum; downward from what resembled his waist I saw what looked like fire; he was surrounded with splendor. Like the bow which appears in the clouds on a rainy day was the splendor that surrounded him. Such was the vision of the likeness of the glory of the Lord.
This is the Word of the Lord.

Responsorial Psalm   Ps 148, 1-2. 11-12. 12-14. 14

℟. Heaven and earth are filled with your glory.
Praise the Lord from the heavens,
praise him in the heights;
Praise him, all you his angels,
praise him, all you his hosts.
℟. Heaven and earth are filled with your glory.
Let the kings of the earth and all peoples,
the princes and all the judges of the earth,
Young men too, and maidens,
old men and boys,
℟. Heaven and earth are filled with your glory.
Praise the name of the Lord,
for his name alone is exalted;
His majesty is above earth and heaven,
℟. Heaven and earth are filled with your glory.
And he has lifted up the horn of his people.
Be this his praise from all his faithful ones,
from the children of Israel, the people close
to him. Alleluia.
℟. Heaven and earth are filled with your glory.
℟. Or: Alleluia.

GOSPEL

Years I and II

Alleluia   Mt 17, 22-27

See no. 509.

✠ **A reading from the holy gospel according
to Matthew**

They put him to death and he rose. The sons are freed
from tribute.

When Jesus and the disciples met in Galilee,
he said to them, "The Son of Man is going
to be delivered into the hands of men who will
put him to death, and he will be raised up on
the third day." At these words they were overwhelmed with grief.

When they entered Capernaum, the collectors of the temple tax approached Peter and
said, "Does your master not pay the temple
tax?" "Of course he does," Peter replied. Then
Jesus on entering the house asked, without
giving him time to speak: "What is your opinion, Simon? Do the kings of the world take
tax or toll from their sons, or from foreigners?"
When he replied, "From foreigners," Jesus observed: "Then their sons are exempt. But for
fear of disedifying them go to the lake, throw
in a line, and take out the first fish you catch.
Open its mouth and you will discover there
a coin worth twice the temple tax. Take it and
give it to them for you and me."

This is the gospel of the Lord.

---

414   TUESDAY OF THE
NINETEENTH WEEK OF THE YEAR

Year I

READING I   Dt 31, 1-8

A reading from the book of Deuteronomy

Be strong, Joshua, stand firm, you will lead this people
into the land of promise.

When Moses finished speaking to all Israel, he
said to them, "I am now one hundred and
twenty years old and am no longer able to
move about freely; besides, the Lord has told
me that I shall not cross this Jordan. It is the
Lord, your God, who will cross before you; he
will destroy these nations before you, that

you may supplant them. [It is Joshua who will
cross before you, as the Lord promised.] The
Lord will deal with them just as he dealt
with Sihon and Og, the kings of the Amorites
whom he destroyed, and with their country.
When, therefore, the Lord delivers them up to
you, you must deal with them exactly as I
have ordered you. Be brave and steadfast; have
no fear or dread of them, for it is the Lord,
your God, who marches with you; he will
never fail you or forsake you."

Then Moses summoned Joshua and in the
presence of all Israel said to him, "Be brave
and steadfast, for you must bring this people
into the land which the Lord swore to their
fathers he would give them; you must put them
in possession of their heritage. It is the Lord
who marches before you; he will be with you
and will never fail you or forsake you. So do
not fear or be dismayed."

This is the Word of the Lord.

Responsorial Psalm   Dt 32, 3-4. 7. 8. 9. 12

℟. (9) The portion of the Lord is his people.
For I will sing the Lord's renown.
    Oh, proclaim the greatness of our God!
The Rock—how faultless are his deeds,
    how right all his ways!

℟. The portion of the Lord is his people.
Think back on the days of old,
    reflect on the years of age upon age.
Ask your father and he will inform you,
    ask your elders and they will tell you.

℟. The portion of the Lord is his people.
When the Most High assigned the nations their
    heritage,
    when he parceled out the descendants of
    Adam,
He set up the boundaries of the peoples
    after the number of the sons of God.

℟. The portion of the Lord is his people.
While the Lord's own portion was Jacob,
    his hereditary share was Israel.
The Lord alone was their leader,
    no strange god was with him.

℟. The portion of the Lord is his people.

READING I   Ez 2, 8–3, 4

A reading from the book of the prophet Ezekiel

He gave me the scroll to eat and it tasted as sweet as honey.

The Lord said, "As for you, son of man, obey me when I speak to you: be not rebellious like this house of rebellion, but open your mouth and eat what I shall give you.

It was then I saw a hand stretched out to me, in which was a written scroll which he unrolled before me. It was covered with writing front and back, and written on it was: Lamentation and wailing and woe!

He said to me: Son of man, eat what is before you; eat this scroll, then go, speak to the house of Israel. So I opened my mouth and he gave me the scroll to eat. Son of man, he then said to me, feed your belly and fill your stomach with this scroll I am giving you. I ate it, and it was as sweet as honey in my mouth. He said: Son of man, go now to the house of Israel, and speak my words to them. This is the Word of the Lord.

Responsorial Psalm   Ps 119, 14. 24. 72. 103. 111. 131

℟. (103) How sweet to my taste is your promise!

In the way of your decrees I rejoice,
   as much as in all riches.

℟. How sweet to my taste is your promise!

Yes, your decrees are my delight;
   they are my counselors.

℟. How sweet to my taste is your promise!

The law of your mouth is to me more precious
   than thousands of gold and silver pieces.

℟. How sweet to my taste is your promise!

How sweet to my palate are your promises,
   sweeter than honey to my mouth!

℟. How sweet to my taste is your promise!

Your decrees are my inheritance forever;
   the joy of my heart they are.

℟. How sweet to my taste is your promise!

I gasp with open mouth
   in my yearning for your commands.

℟. How sweet to my taste is your promise!

GOSPEL   Mt 18, 1-5. 10. 12-14
Alleluia

See no. 509.

✠ **A reading from the holy gospel according to Matthew**

Be careful never to despise one of these little ones.

The disciples came up to Jesus with the question, "Who is of greatest importance in the kingdom of God?" He called a little child over and stood him in their midst and said: "I assure you, unless you change and become like little children, you will not enter the kingdom of God. Whoever makes himself lowly, becoming like this child, is of greatest importance in that heavenly reign.

"Whoever welcomes one such child for my sake welcomes me. See that you never despise one of these little ones. I assure you their angels in heaven constantly behold my heavenly Father's face.

"What is your thought on this: A man owns a hundred sheep and one of them wanders away; will he not leave the ninety-nine out on the hills and go in search of the stray? If he succeeds in finding it, believe me he is happier about this one than about the ninety-nine that did not wander away. Just so, it is no part of your heavenly Father's plan that a single one of these little ones shall ever come to grief." This is the gospel of the Lord.

---

415   **WEDNESDAY OF THE NINETEENTH WEEK OF THE YEAR**

READING I   Dt 34, 1-12

A reading from the book of Deuteronomy

Moses died here praising the Lord; since then there has not been raised such a prophet in Israel.

Moses went up from the plains of Moab to Mount Nebo, the headland of Pisgah which faces Jericho, and the Lord showed him all the land—Gilead, and as far as Dan, all Naphtali, the land of Ephraim and Manasseh, all the land of Judah as far as the Western Sea, the

Negeb, the circuit of the Jordan with the low-lands at Jericho, city of palms, and as far as Zoar. The Lord then said to him, "This is the land which I swore to Abraham, Isaac and Jacob that I would give to their descendants. I have let you feast your eyes upon it, but you shall not cross over." So there, in the land of Moab, Moses, the servant of the Lord, died as the Lord had said; and he was buried in the ravine opposite Beth-peor in the land of Moab, but to this day no one knows the place of his burial. Moses was one hundred and twenty years old when he died, yet his eyes were un-dimmed and his vigor unabated. For thirty days the Israelites wept for Moses in the plains of Moab, till they had completed the period of grief and mourning for Moses.

Now Joshua, son of Nun, was filled with the spirit of wisdom, since Moses had laid his hands upon him; and so the Israelites gave him their obedience, thus carrying out the Lord's command to Moses.

Since then no prophet has arisen in Israel like Moses, whom the Lord knew face to face. He had no equal in all the signs and wonders the Lord sent him to perform in the land of Egypt against Pharaoh and all his servants and against all his land, and for the might and the terrifying power that Moses exhibited in the sight of all Israel.

This is the Word of the Lord.

Responsorial Psalm   Ps 66, 1-3. 5. 8. 16-17

℟. (20. 9) Blessed be God who filled my soul with fire!
Shout joyfully to God, all you on earth,
  sing praise to the glory of his name;
  proclaim his glorious praise.
Say to God, "How tremendous are your deeds!"
℟. Blessed be God who filled my soul with fire!
Come and see the works of God,
  his tremendous deeds among men.
Bless our God, you peoples,
  loudly sound his praise.
℟. Blessed be God who filled my soul with fire!
Hear now, all you who fear God, while I de-clare
  what he has done for me.

When I appealed to him in words,
  praise was on the tip of my tongue.
℟. Blessed be God who filled my soul with fire!

Year II

READING I   Ez 9, 1-7; 10, 18-22

A reading from the book of the prophet Ezekiel

Mark a cross on the foreheads of all who deplore the filth practiced in Jerusalem.

The Lord cried loud for me to hear: Come, you scourges of the city! With that I saw six men coming from the direction of the upper gate which faces the north, each with a destroying weapon in his hand. In their midst was a man dressed in linen, with a writer's case at his waist. They entered and stood beside the bronze altar. Then he called to the man dressed in linen with the writer's case at his waist, saying to him: Pass through the city [through Jerusalem] and mark an X on the foreheads of those who moan and groan over all the abominations that are practiced within it. To the others I heard him say: Pass through the city after him and strike! Do not look on them with pity nor show any mercy! Old men, youths and maidens, women and children—wipe them out! But do not touch any marked with the X; begin at my sanctuary. So they began with the men [the elders] who were in front of the temple. Defile the temple, he said to them, and fill the courts with the slain; then go out and strike in the city.

Then the glory of the Lord left the threshold of the temple and rested upon the cherubim. These lifted their wings, and I saw them rise from the earth, the wheels rising along with them. They stood at the entrance of the eastern gate of the Lord's house, and the glory of the God of Israel was up above them. These were the living creatures I had seen beneath the God of Israel by the river Chebar, whom I now recognized to be cherubim. Each had four faces and four wings; something like human hands were under their wings. Their faces looked just like those I had seen by the river Chebar; each one went straight forward.

This is the Word of the Lord.

Responsorial Psalm   Ps 113, 1-2. 3-4. 5-6

℞. (4) The glory of the Lord is higher than the
    skies.

Praise, you servants of the Lord,
    praise the name of the Lord.
Blessed be the name of the Lord
    both now and forever.

℞. The glory of the Lord is higher than the
    skies.

From the rising to the setting of the sun
    is the name of the Lord to be praised.
High above all nations is the Lord;
    above the heavens is his glory.

℞. The glory of the Lord is higher than the
    skies.

Who is like the Lord, our God, who is en-
    throned on high
    and looks upon the heavens and the earth
    below?

℞. The glory of the Lord is higher than the
    skies.

℞. Or: Alleluia.

Years I and II

GOSPEL   Mt 18, 15-20
Alleluia

See no. 509.

✠ A reading from the holy gospel according
     to Matthew

If your brother listens to you, you will have won him back.

Jesus said to his disciples: "If your brother
should commit some wrong against you, go
and point out his fault, but keep it between the
two of you. If he listens to you, you have won
your brother over. If he does not listen, however, summon another, so that every case may
stand on the word of two or three witnesses.
If he ignores them refer it to the church.
If he ignores even the church, then treat him
as you would a Gentile or a tax collector.
I assure you, whatever you declare bound on
earth shall be held bound in heaven, and whatever you declare loosed on earth shall be held
loosed in heaven.

    "Again I tell you, if two of you join your
voices on earth to pray for anything whatever,
it shall be granted you by my Father in heaven.

Where two or three are gathered in my name,
there am I in their midst."
     This is the gospel of the Lord.

---

416   **THURSDAY OF THE
NINETEENTH WEEK OF THE YEAR**

Year I

READING I   Jos 3, 7-10. 11. 13-17
    A reading from the book of Joshua

The ark of the Lord God will precede you across the Jordan.

The Lord said to Joshua, "Today I will begin
to exalt you in the sight of all Israel, that
they may know I am with you, as I was with
Moses. Now command the priests carrying the
ark of the covenant to come to a halt in the
Jordan when they reach the edge of the
waters."

    So Joshua said to the Israelites, "Come here
and listen to the words of the Lord, your God."
He continued: "This is how you will know that
there is a living God in your midst, who at your
approach will dispossess the Canaanites. The
ark of the covenant of the Lord of the whole
earth will precede you into the Jordan. When
the soles of the feet of the priests carrying the
ark of the Lord, the Lord of the whole earth,
touch the water of the Jordan, it will cease to
flow; for the water flowing down from up-
stream will halt in a solid bank."

    The people struck their tents to cross the
Jordan, with the priests carrying the ark of the
covenant ahead of them. No sooner had these
priestly bearers of the ark waded into the
waters at the edge of the Jordan, which overflows all its banks during the entire season of
the harvest, than the waters flowing from up-
stream halted, backing up in a solid mass
for a very great distance indeed, from Adam,
a city in the direction of Zarethan; while those
flowing downstream toward the Salt Sea of the
Arabah disappeared entirely. Thus the people
crossed over opposite Jericho. While all Israel
crossed over on dry ground, the priests carrying the ark of the covenant of the Lord remained motionless on dry ground in the bed of

the Jordan until the whole nation had completed the passage.
This is the Word of the Lord.

Responsorial Psalm   Ps 114, 1-2. 3-4. 5-6

R̸. Alleluia.
When Israel came forth from Egypt,
    the house of Jacob from a people of alien
        tongue,
Judah became his sanctuary,
    Israel his domain.
R̸. Alleluia.
The sea beheld and fled;
    Jordan turned back.
The mountains skipped like rams,
    the hills like the lambs of the flock.
R̸. Alleluia.
Why is it, O sea, that you flee?
    O Jordan, that you turn back?
You mountains, that you skip like rams?
    You hills, like the lambs of the flock?
R̸. Alleluia.

READING I   **Year II**
Ez 12, 1-2
**A reading from the book of the prophet
Ezekiel**
You will leave in the daylight for them to see.
The word of the Lord came to me: Son of
man, you live in the midst of a rebellious house;
they have eyes to see but do not see, and ears
to hear but do not hear, for they are a rebellious house.
    This is the Word of the Lord.

Responsorial Psalm   Ps 78, 56-57. 58-59. 61-62

R̸. (7) Do not forget the works of the Lord!
They tempted and rebelled against God the
        Most High,
    and kept not his decrees.
They turned back and were faithless like their
        fathers;
    they recoiled like a treacherous bow.
R̸. Do not forget the works of the Lord!
They angered him with their high places
    and with their idols roused his jealousy.

God heard and was enraged
    and utterly rejected Israel.
R̸. Do not forget the works of the Lord!
And he surrendered his strength into captivity,
    his glory into the hands of the foe.
He abandoned his people to the sword
    and was enraged against his inheritance.
R̸. Do not forget the works of the Lord!

GOSPEL   **Years I and II**
Mt 18, 21—19, 1
Alleluia
See no. 509.

✠ **A reading from the holy gospel according
to Matthew**
I did not say to you to forgive seven times, but seventy
times seven.
Peter came up to Jesus and asked him, "Lord,
when my brother wrongs me, how often must I
forgive him? Seven times?" "No," Jesus replied, "not seven times; I say, seventy times
seven times. That is why the reign of God
may be said to be like a king who decided
to settle accounts with his officials. When he
began his auditing, one was brought in who
owed him a huge amount. As he had no way
of paying it, his master ordered him to be
sold, along with his wife, his children, and all
his property, in payment of the debt. At that
the official prostrated himself in homage and
said, 'My lord, be patient with me and I will
pay you back in full.' Moved with pity, the
master let the official go and wrote off the debt.
But when that same official went out he met a
fellow servant who owed him a mere fraction
of what he himself owed. He seized him and
throttled him. 'Pay back what you owe,' he
demanded. His fellow servant dropped to his
knees and began to plead with him, 'Just give
me time and I will pay you back in full.' But
he would hear none of it. Instead, he had him
put in jail until he paid back what he owed.
When his fellow servants saw what had happened they were badly shaken, and went to
their master to report the whole incident. His
master sent for him and said, 'You worthless
wretch! I canceled your entire debt when you
pleaded with me. Should you not have dealt

mercifully with your fellow servant, as I dealt with you?' Then in anger the master handed him over to the torturers until he paid back all that he owed. My heavenly Father will treat you in exactly the same way unless each of you forgives his brother from his heart."

When Jesus had finished this discourse, he left Galilee and came to the district of Judea across the Jordan.

This is the gospel of the Lord.

---

417   **FRIDAY OF THE**

NINETEENTH WEEK OF THE YEAR

Year I

READING I   Jos 24, 1-13

A reading from the book of Joshua

I brought your father from Mesopotamia, out of the land of Egypt and took you to your own land.

Joshua gathered together all the tribes of Israel at Shechem, summoning their elders, their leaders, their judges and their officers. When they stood in ranks before God, Joshua addressed all the people: "Thus says the Lord, the God of Israel: In times past your fathers, down to Terah, father of Abraham and Nahor, dwelt beyond the River and served other gods. But I brought your father Abraham from the region beyond the River and led him through the entire land of Canaan. I made his descendants numerous, and gave him Isaac. To Isaac I gave Jacob and Esau. To Esau I assigned the mountain region of Seir in which to settle, while Jacob and his children went down to Egypt.

"Then I sent Moses and Aaron, and smote Egypt with the prodigies which I wrought in her midst. Afterward I led you out of Egypt, and when you reached the sea, the Egyptians pursued your fathers to the Red Sea with chariots and horsemen. Because they cried out to the Lord, he put darkness between your people and the Egyptians, upon whom he brought the sea so that it engulfed them. After you witnessed what I did to Egypt, and dwelt a long time in the desert, I brought you into the land of the Amorites who lived east of the Jordan. They fought against you, but I delivered them into your power. You took possession of their land, and I destroyed them [the two kings of the Amorites] before you. Then Balak, son of Zippor, king of Moab, prepared to war against Israel. He summoned Balaam, son of Beor, to curse you; but I would not listen to Balaam. On the contrary, he had to bless you, and I saved you from him. Once you crossed the Jordan and came to Jericho, the men of Jericho fought against you, but I delivered them also into your power. And I sent the hornets ahead of you which drove them [the Amorites, Perizzites, Canaanites, Hittites, Girgashites, Hivites and Jebusites] out of your way; it was not your sword or your bow.

"I gave you a land which you had not tilled and cities which you had not built, to dwell in; you have eaten of vineyards and olive groves which you did not plant."

This is the Word of the Lord.

Responsorial Psalm   Ps 136, 1-3. 16-18. 21-22. 24

R̸. His love is everlasting.

Give thanks to the Lord, for he is good,
    for his mercy endures forever;
Give thanks to the God of gods,
    for his mercy endures forever;
Give thanks to the Lord of lords,
    for his mercy endures forever.

R̸. His love is everlasting.

Who led his people through the wilderness,
    for his mercy endures forever;
Who smote great kings,
    for his mercy endures forever;
And slew powerful kings,
    for his mercy endures forever.

R̸. His love is everlasting.

And made their land a heritage,
    for his mercy endures forever;
The heritage of Israel his servant,
    for his mercy endures forever;
And freed us from our foes,
    for his mercy endures forever.

R̸. His love is everlasting.
R̸. Or: Alleluia.

Year II

READING I   Ez 16, 1-15. 60. 63

A reading from the book of the prophet Ezekiel

I clothed you with my own splendor; you became a prostitute.

The word of the Lord came to me: Son of man, make known to Jerusalem her abominations. Thus says the Lord God to Jerusalem: By origin and birth you are of the land of Canaan; your father was an Amorite and your mother a Hittite. As for your birth, the day you were born your navel cord was not cut; you were neither washed with water nor anointed, nor were you rubbed with salt, nor swathed in swaddling clothes. No one looked on you with pity or compassion to do any of these things for you. Rather, you were thrown out on the ground as something loathsome, the day you were born.

Then I passed by and saw you weltering in your blood. I said to you: Live in your blood and grow like a plant in the field. You grew and developed, you came to the age of puberty; your breasts were formed, your hair had grown, but you were still stark naked. Again I passed by you and saw that you were now old enough for love. So I spread the corner of my cloak over you to cover your nakedness; I swore an oath to you and entered into a covenant with you; you became mine, says the Lord God. Then I bathed you with water, washed away your blood, and anointed you with oil. I clothed you with an embroidered gown, put sandals of fine leather on your feet; I gave you a fine linen sash and silk robes to wear. I adorned you with jewelry: I put bracelets on your arms, a necklace about your neck, a ring in your nose, pendants in your ears, and a glorious diadem upon your head. Thus you were adorned with gold and silver; your garments were of fine linen, silk, and embroidered cloth. Fine flour, honey, and oil were your food. You were exceedingly beautiful, with the dignity of a queen. You were renowned among the nations for your beauty, perfect as it was, because of my splen-dor which I had bestowed on you, says the Lord God.

But you were captivated by your own beauty, you used your renown to make yourself a harlot, and you lavished your harlotry on every passer-by, whose own you became. Yet I will remember the covenant I made with you when you were a girl, and I will set up an everlasting covenant with you, that you may remember and be covered with confusion, and that you may be utterly silenced for shame when I pardon you for all you have done, says the Lord God.

This is the Word of the Lord.

OR

READING I   Ez 16, 59-63

A reading from the book of the prophet Ezekiel

I will keep my covenant and you will be ashamed.

Thus speaks the Lord God: I will deal with you according to what you have done, you who despised your oath, breaking a covenant. Yet I will remember the covenant I made with you when you were a girl, and I will set up an everlasting covenant with you. Then you shall remember your conduct and be ashamed when I take your sisters, those older and younger than you, and give them to you as daughters, even though I am not bound by my covenant with you. For I will re-establish my covenant with you, that you may know that I am the Lord, that you may remember and be covered with confusion, and that you may be utterly silenced for shame when I pardon you for all you have done, says the Lord God.

This is the Word of the Lord.

Responsorial Psalm   Is 12, 2-3. 4. 5-6

R̸. You have turned from your anger to comfort me.

God indeed is my savior;
   I am confident and unafraid.
My strength and my courage is the Lord,
   and he has been my savior.
With joy you will draw water.

℟. You have turned from your anger to comfort me.

Give thanks to the Lord, acclaim his name;
   among the nations make known his deeds,
   proclaim how exalted is his name.

℟. You have turned from your anger to comfort me.

Sing praise to the Lord for his glorious achievement;
   let this be known throughout all the earth.

Shout with exultation, O city of Zion,
   for great in your midst
   is the Holy One of Israel!

℟. You have turned from your anger to comfort me.

Years I and II

GOSPEL   Mt 19, 3-12
Alleluia

See no. 509.

✠ **A reading from the holy gospel according to Matthew**

Because of the hardness of your hearts Moses permitted you to divorce your wives, but it was not like this from the beginning.

Some Pharisees came up to Jesus and said, to test him, "May a man divorce his wife for any reason whatever?" He replied, "Have you not read that at the beginning the Creator made them male and female and declared, 'For this reason a man shall leave his father and mother and cling to his wife, and the two shall become as one'? Thus they are no longer two but one flesh. Therefore, let no man separate what God has joined." They said to him, "Then why did Moses command divorce and the promulgation of a divorce decree?" "Because of your stubbornness Moses let you divorce your wives," he replied; "but at the beginning it was not that way. I now say to you whoever divorces his wife (lewd conduct is a separate case) and marries another commits adultery, and the man who marries a divorced woman commits adultery."

His disciples said to him, "If that is the case between man and wife, it is better not to marry." He said, "Not everyone can accept this teaching, only those to whom it is given

to do so. Some men are incapable of sexual activity from birth; some have been deliberately made so; and some there are who have freely renounced sex for the sake of God's reign. Let him accept this teaching who can."

This is the gospel of the Lord.

---

418   **SATURDAY OF THE NINETEENTH WEEK OF THE YEAR**

Year I

READING I   Jos 24, 14-29

A reading from the book of Joshua

Choose today whom you wish to serve.

Joshua said to the people, "Fear the Lord and serve him completely and sincerely. Cast out the gods your fathers served beyond the River and in Egypt, and serve the Lord. If it does not please you to serve the Lord, decide today whom you will serve, the gods your fathers served beyond the River or the gods of the Amorites in whose country you are dwelling. As for me and my household, we will serve the Lord."

But the people answered, "Far be it from us to forsake the Lord for the service of other gods. For it was the Lord, our God, who brought us and our fathers up out of the land of Egypt, out of a state of slavery. He performed those great miracles before our very eyes and protected us along our entire journey and among all the peoples through whom we passed. At our approach the Lord drove out [all the peoples, including] the Amorites who dwelt in the land. Therefore we also will serve the Lord, for he is our God."

Joshua in turn said to the people, "You may not be able to serve the Lord, for he is a holy God; he is a jealous God who will not forgive your transgressions or your sins. If, after the good he has done for you, you forsake the Lord and serve strange gods, he will do evil to you and destroy you."

But the people answered Joshua, "We will still serve the Lord." Joshua therefore said to the people, "You are your own witnesses that you have chosen to serve the Lord." They replied, "We are, indeed!" [Joshua continued:] "Now, therefore, put away the strange gods that are among you and turn your hearts to the Lord, the God of Israel." Then the people promised Joshua, "We will serve the Lord, our God, and obey his voice."

So Joshua made a covenant with the people that day and made statutes and ordinances for them at Shechem, which he recorded in the book of the law of God. Then he took a large stone and set it up there under the oak that was in the sanctuary of the Lord. And Joshua said to all the people, "This stone shall be our witness, for it has heard all the words which the Lord spoke to us. It shall be a witness against you, should you wish to deny your God." Then Joshua dismissed the people, each to his own heritage.

After these events, Joshua, son of Nun, servant of the Lord, died at the age of a hundred and ten.

> **This is the Word of the Lord.**

Responsorial Psalm   Ps 16, 1-2. 5. 7-8. 11

℟. You are my inheritance, O Lord.

Keep me, O God, for in you I take refuge;
    I say to the Lord, "My Lord are you.
    Apart from you I have no good."
O Lord, my allotted portion and my cup,
    you it is who hold fast my lot.

℟. You are my inheritance, O Lord.

I bless the Lord who counsels me;
    even in the night my heart exhorts me.
I set the Lord ever before me;
    with him at my right hand I shall not be
    disturbed.

℟. You are my inheritance, O Lord.

You will show me the path to life,
    fullness of joys in your presence,
    the delights at your right hand forever.

℟. You are my inheritance, O Lord.

READING I   Ez 18, 1-10. 13. 30-32

A reading from the book of the prophet Ezekiel

I will judge everyone according to his ways.

The word of the Lord came to me: Son of man, what is the meaning of this proverb that you recite in the land of Israel:

"Fathers have eaten green grapes,
    thus their children's teeth are on edge"?

As I live, says the Lord God: I swear that there shall no longer be anyone among you who will repeat this proverb in Israel. For all lives are mine; the life of the father is like the life of the son, both are mine; only the one who sins shall die.

If a man is virtuous—if he does what is right and just, if he does not eat on the mountains, nor raise his eyes to the idols of the house of Israel; if he does not defile his neighbor's wife, nor have relations with a woman in her menstrual period; if he oppresses no one, gives back the pledge received for a debt, commits no robbery; if he gives food to the hungry and clothes the naked; if he does not lend at interest nor exact usury; if he holds off from evildoing, judges fairly between a a man and his opponent; if he lives by my statutes and is careful to observe my ordinances, that man is virtuous—he shall surely live, says the Lord God.

But if he begets a son who is a thief, a murderer, or lends at interest and exacts usury —this son certainly shall not live. Because he practiced all these abominations, he shall surely die; his death shall be his own fault.

Therefore I will judge you, house of Israel, each one according to his ways, says the Lord God. Turn and be converted from all your crimes, that they may be no cause of guilt for you. Cast away from you all the crimes you have committed, and make for yourselves a new heart and a new spirit. Why should you die, O house of Israel? For I have no pleasure in the death of anyone who dies, says the Lord God. Return and live!

> **This is the Word of the Lord.**

Responsorial Psalm   Ps 51, 12-13. 14-15. 18-19

℟. (12) Create a clean heart in me, O God.

A clean heart create for me, O God,
    and a steadfast spirit renew within me.
Cast me not out from your presence,
    and your holy spirit take not from me.
℟. Create a clean heart in me, O God.

Give me back the joy of your salvation,
    and a willing spirit sustain in me.
I will teach transgressors your ways,
    and sinners shall return to you.
℟. Create a clean heart in me, O God.

For you are not pleased with sacrifices;
    should I offer a holocaust, you would not
    accept it.
My sacrifice, O God, is a contrite spirit;
    a heart contrite and humbled, O God, you
    will not spurn.
℟. Create a clean heart in me, O God.

GOSPEL   `Years I and II`

Alleluia   Mt 19, 13-15

See no. 509.

✠ **A reading from the holy gospel according
       to Matthew**

Do not prevent the little children from coming to me: to
them belongs the kingdom of heaven.

Children were brought to Jesus so that he
could place his hands on them in prayer. The
disciples began to scold them, but Jesus said,
"Let the children come to me. Do not hinder
them. The kingdom of God belongs to such as
these." And he laid his hands on their heads
before he left that place.
      This is the gospel of the Lord.

---

419   **MONDAY OF THE
    TWENTIETH WEEK OF THE YEAR**

`Year I`

READING I   Jgs 2, 11-19

A reading from the book of Judges

The Lord God appointed judges for them, but they would
not listen to them.

**The Israelites offended the Lord by serving the
Baals. Abandoning the Lord, the God of their**
fathers, who had led them out of the land of
Egypt, they followed the other gods of the
various nations around them, and by their worship of these gods provoked the Lord.
      Because they had thus abandoned him and
served Baal and the Ashtaroth, the anger of
the Lord flared up against Israel, and he delivered them over to plunderers who despoiled
them. He allowed them to fall into the power
of their enemies round about whom they were
no longer able to withstand. Whatever they
undertook, the Lord turned into disaster for
them, as in his warning he had sworn he would
do, till they were in great distress. Even when
the Lord raised up judges to deliver them from
the power of their despoilers, they did not
listen to their judges, but adandoned themselves to the worship of other gods. They
were quick to stray from the way their fathers
had taken, and did not follow their example
of obedience to the commandments of the
Lord. Whenever the Lord raised up judges
for them, he would be with the judge and save
them from the power of their enemies as long
as the judge lived; it was thus the Lord took
pity on their distressful cries of affliction under
their oppressors. But when the judge died,
they would relapse and do worse than their
fathers, following other gods in service and
worship, relinquishing none of their evil practices or stubborn conduct.
      This is the Word of the Lord.

Responsorial Psalm   Ps 106, 34-35. 36-37. 39-40. 43. 44

℟. (4) Lord, remember us,
    for the love you bear your people.
They did not exterminate the peoples,
    as the Lord had commanded them,
But mingled with the nations
    and learned their works.
℟. Lord, remember us,
    for the love you bear your people.

They served their idols,
    which became a snare for them.
They sacrificed their sons
    and their daughters to demons.
℟. Lord, remember us,
    for the love you bear your people.

They became defiled by their works,
 and wanton in their crimes.
And the Lord grew angry with his people,
 and abhorred his inheritance.
℟. Lord, remember us,
 for the love you bear your people.
Many times did he rescue them,
 but they embittered him with their counsels.
Yet he had regard for their affliction
 when he heard their cry.
℟. Lord, remember us,
 for the love you bear your people.

Year II

READING I   Ez 24, 15-24

A reading from the book of the prophet Ezekiel

Thus shall Ezekiel be to you a sign; all that he has done, you will do.

The word of the Lord came to me: Son of man, by a sudden blow I am taking away from you the delight of your eyes, but do not mourn or weep or shed any tears. Groan in silence, make no lament for the dead, bind on your turban, put your sandals on your feet, do not cover your beard, and do not eat the customary bread. That evening my wife died, and the next morning I did as I had been commanded. Then the people asked me, "Will you not tell us what all these things that you are doing mean for us?" I therefore spoke to the people that morning, saying to them: Thus the word of the Lord came to me: Say to the house of Israel: Thus says the Lord God: I will now desecrate my sanctuary, the stronghold of your pride, the delight of your eyes, the desire of your soul. The sons and daughters you left behind shall fall by the sword. Ezekiel shall be a sign for you: all that he did you shall do when it happens. Thus you shall know that I am the Lord. You shall do as I have done, not covering your beards nor eating the customary bread. Your turbans shall remain on your heads, your sandals on your feet. You shall not mourn or weep, but you shall rot away because of your sins and groan one to another.
This is the Word of the Lord.

Responsorial Psalm   Dt 32, 18-19. 20. 21

℟. (18) You have forgotten God who gave you birth.
You were unmindful of the Rock that begot you,
 You forgot the God who gave you birth.
When the Lord saw this, he was filled with loathing
 and anger toward his sons and daughters.
℟. You have forgotten God who gave you birth.
"I will hide my face from them," he said,
 "and see what will then become of them.
What a fickle race they are,
 sons with no loyalty in them!
℟. You have forgotten God who gave you birth.
Since they have provoked me with their 'no-god'
 and angered me with their vain idols,
I will provoke them with a 'no-people';
 with a foolish nation I will anger them."
℟. You have forgotten God who gave you birth.

Years I and II

GOSPEL   Mt 19, 16-22
Alleluia

See no. 509.

✠ **A reading from the holy gospel according to Matthew**

If you wish to be perfect, sell what you own, and your treasure will be in heaven.

A man came up to Jesus and said, "Teacher, what good must I do to possess everlasting life?" He answered, "Why do you question me about what is good? There is One who is good. If you wish to enter into life, keep the commandments." "Which ones?" he asked. Jesus replied, " 'You shall not kill'; 'You shall not commit adultery'; 'You shall not steal'; 'You shall not bear false witness'; 'Honor your father and your mother'; and 'Love your neighbor as yourself.' " The young man said to him, "I have kept all these; what do I need to do further?" Jesus told him, "If you seek perfection, go, sell your possessions, and give to the poor. You will then have treasure in

heaven. After that, come back and follow me."
Hearing these words, the young man went
away sad, for his possessions were many.
This is the gospel of the Lord.

---

420   **TUESDAY OF THE
TWENTIETH WEEK OF THE YEAR**

Year I

READING I   Jgs 6, 11-24

A reading from the book of Judges

Gideon, you will free Israel. Do I not send you?

The angel of the Lord came and sat under the
terebinth in Ophrah that belonged to Joash the
Abiezrite. While his son Gideon was beating
out wheat in the wine press to save it from
the Midianites, the angel of the Lord appeared
to him and said, "The Lord is with you, O
champion!" "My lord," Gideon said to him, "if
the Lord is with us, why has all this happened to us? Where are his wondrous deeds
of which our fathers told us when they said,
'Did not the Lord bring us up from Egypt?'
For now the Lord has abandoned us and has
delivered us into the power of Midian." The
Lord turned to him and said, "Go with the
strength you have and save Israel from the
power of Midian. It is I who send you." But he
answered him, "Please, my lord, how can I
save Israel? My family is the meanest in
Manasseh, and I am the most insignificant in
my father's house." "I shall be with you,"
the Lord said to him, "and you will cut down
Midian to the last man." He answered him, "If
I find favor with you, give me a sign that
you are speaking with me. Do not depart from
here, I pray you, until I come back to you and
bring out my offering and set it before you."
He answered, "I will await your return."

So Gideon went off and prepared a kid and
an ephah of flour in the form of unleavened
cakes. Putting the meat in a basket and the
broth in a pot, he brought them out to him
under the terebinth and presented them. The
angel of God said to him, "Take the meat and
unleavened cakes and lay them on this rock;
then pour out the broth." When he had done so,
the angel of the Lord stretched out the tip of
the staff he held, and touched the meat and
unleavened cakes. Thereupon a fire came up
from the rock which consumed the meat and
unleavened cakes, and the angel of the Lord
disappeared from sight. Gideon, now aware
that it had been the angel of the Lord, said,
"Alas, Lord God, that I have seen the angel
of the Lord face to face!" The Lord answered
him, "Be calm, do not fear. You shall not
die." So Gideon built there an altar to the
Lord and called it Yahweh-shalom.
This is the Word of the Lord.

Responsorial Psalm   Ps 85, 9. 11-12. 13-14

℟. (9) The Lord speaks of peace to his people.
I will hear what God proclaims;
  the Lord—for he proclaims peace
To his people, and to his faithful ones,
  and to those who put in him their hope.
℟. The Lord speaks of peace to his people.
Kindness and truth shall meet;
  justice and peace shall kiss.
Truth shall spring out of the earth,
  and justice shall look down from heaven.
℟. The Lord speaks of peace to his people.
The Lord himself will give his benefits;
  our land shall yield its increase.
Justice shall walk before him,
  and salvation, along the way of his steps.
℟. The Lord speaks of peace to his people.

Year II

READING I   Ez 28, 1-10

**A reading from the book of the prophet
Ezekiel**

You are a man and not God, yet you consider yourself equal
to God.

The word of the Lord came to me: Son of man,
say to the prince of Tyre: Thus says the Lord
God:
Because you are haughty of heart,
  and say, "A god am I!
I occupy a godly throne
  in the heart of the sea!"—
And yet you are a man, and not a god,
  however you may think yourself like a god.

Oh yes, you are wiser than Daniel,
  there is no secret that is beyond you.
By your wisdom and your intelligence
  you have made riches for yourself;
You have put gold and silver
  into your treasuries.
By your great wisdom applied to your trading
  you have heaped up your riches;
  your heart has grown haughty from your
    riches—
  therefore thus says the Lord God:
Because you have thought yourself
  to have the mind of a god,
Therefore I will bring against you
  foreigners, the most barbarous of nations.
They shall draw their swords
  against your beauteous wisdom,
  they shall run them through your splendid
    apparel.
They shall thrust you down to the pit, there to
    die
  a bloodied corpse, in the heart of the sea.
Will you then say, "I am a god!"
  when you face your murderers?
No, you are a man, not a god,
  handed over to those who will slay you.
You shall die the death of the uncircumcised
  at the hands of foreigners,
  for I have spoken,
    says the Lord God.
      This is the Word of the Lord.

Responsorial Psalm   Dt 32, 26-27. 27-28. 30. 35-36

℟. (39) It is I who deal death and give life.
"I would have said, 'I will make an end of them
  and blot out their name from men's memo-
  ries,'
Had I not feared the insolence of their enemies,
  feared that these foes would mistakenly
  boast,
℟. It is I who deal death and give life.
'Our own hand won the victory;
  the Lord had nothing to do with it.' "
For they are a people devoid of reason,
  having no understanding.
℟. It is I who deal death and give life.

"How could one man rout a thousand,
  or two men put ten thousand to flight,
Unless it was because their Rock sold them
  and the Lord delivered them up?"
℟. It is I who deal death and give life.
Close at hand is the day of their disaster,
  and their doom is rushing upon them!
Surely, the Lord shall do justice for his people;
  on his servants he shall have pity.
℟. It is I who deal death and give life.

Years I and II

GOSPEL   Mt 19, 23-30
Alleluia
See no. 509.

✠ A reading from the holy gospel according
             to Matthew

It is easier for a camel to pass through the eye of a needle
   than for a rich man to enter the kingdom of heaven.

Jesus said to his disciples: "I assure you, only
with difficulty will a rich man enter into the
kingdom of God. I repeat what I said: it is
easier for a camel to pass through a needle's
eye than for a rich man to enter the kingdom
of God." When the disciples heard this they
were completely overwhelmed, and exclaimed,
"Then who can be saved?" Jesus looked at
them and said, "For man it is impossible; but
for God all things are possible." Then it was
Peter's turn to say to him: "Here we have put
everything aside to follow you. What can we
expect from it?" Jesus said to them: "I give you
my solemn word, in the new age when the Son
of Man takes his seat upon a throne befitting
his glory, you who have followed me shall
likewise take your places on twelve thrones to
judge the twelve tribes of Israel. Moreover,
everyone who has given up home, brothers or
sisters, father or mother, wife or children or
property for my sake will receive many times
as much and inherit everlasting life. Many who
are first shall come last, and the last shall come
first."
      This is the gospel of the Lord.

421   **WEDNESDAY OF THE
TWENTIETH WEEK OF THE YEAR**

Year I

READING I   Jgs 9, 6-15

A reading from the book of Judges
It is said, the king will reign over us, when the Lord God
reigns among you (1 Sm 12, 12).

All the citizens of Shechem and all Beth-millo
came together and proceeded to make Abime-
lech king by the terebinth at the memorial
pillar in Shechem.

When this was reported to him, Jotham
went to the top of Mount Gerizim, and standing there, cried out to them in a loud voice:
"Hear me, citizens of Shechem, that God may
then hear you! Once the trees went to anoint a
king over themselves. So they said to the olive
tree, 'Reign over us.' But the olive tree answered them, 'Must I give up my rich oil,
whereby men and gods are honored, and go to
wave over the trees?' Then the trees said to the
fig tree, 'Come; you reign over us!' But the fig
tree answered them, 'Must I give up my
sweetness and my good fruit, and go to wave
over the trees?' Then the trees said to the vine,
'Come you, and reign over us.' But the vine
answered them, 'Must I give up my wine that
cheers gods and men, and go to wave over the
trees?' Then all the trees said to the buckthorn,
'Come you reign over us!' But the buckthorn
replied to the trees, 'If you wish to anoint me
king over you in good faith, come and take
refuge in my shadow. Otherwise, let fire come
from the buckthorn and devour the cedars of
Lebanon.' "

This is the Word of the Lord.

Responsorial Psalm   Ps 21, 2-3. 4-5. 6-7

℟. (2) Lord, your strength gives joy to the
    king.
O Lord, in your strength the king is glad;
    in your victory how greatly he rejoices!
You have granted him his heart's desire;
    you refused not the wish of his lips.
℟. Lord, your strength gives joy to the king.

For you welcomed him with goodly blessings,
    you placed on his head a crown of pure gold.
He asked life of you: you gave him
    length of days forever and ever.
℟. Lord, your strength gives joy to the king.
Great is his glory in your victory;
    majesty and splendor you conferred upon
    him.
For you made him a blessing forever;
    you gladdened him with the joy of your
    presence.
℟. Lord, your strength gives joy to the king.

Year II

READING I   Ez 34, 1-11

A reading from the book of the prophet Ezekiel
I will free my sheep from their hands and they will not prey
on them any more.

The word of the Lord came to me: Son of man,
prophesy against the shepherds of Israel, in
these words prophesy to them [to the shep-
herds]: Thus says the Lord God: Woe to the
shepherds of Israel who have been pasturing
themselves! Should not shepherds, rather, pasture sheep? You have fed off their milk, worn
their wool, and slaughtered the fatlings, but
the sheep you have not pastured. You did not
strengthen the weak nor heal the sick nor bind
up the injured. You did not bring back the
strayed nor seek the lost, but you lorded it over
them harshly and brutally. So they were scattered for lack of a shepherd, and became food
for all the wild beasts. My sheep were scattered and wandered over all the mountains
and high hills; my sheep were scattered over
the whole earth, with no one to look after
them or to search for them.

Therefore, shepherds, hear the word of the
Lord: As I live, says the Lord God, because my
sheep have been given over to pillage, and
because my sheep have become food for every
wild beast, for lack of a shepherd; because my
shepherds did not look after my sheep, but pastured themselves and did not pasture my
sheep; because of this, shepherds, hear the
word of the Lord: Thus says the Lord God: I
swear I am coming against these shepherds. I
will claim my sheep from them and put a stop

to their shepherding my sheep so that they may no longer pasture themselves. I will save my sheep, that they may no longer be food for their mouths.

For thus says the Lord God: I myself will look after and tend my sheep.
This is the Word of the Lord.

Responsorial Psalm   Ps 23, 1-3. 3-4. 5. 6

℟. (1) The Lord is my shepherd;
    there is nothing I shall want.

The Lord is my shepherd; I shall not want.
    In verdant pastures he gives me repose;
Beside restful waters he leads me;
    he refreshes my soul.

℟. The Lord is my shepherd;
    there is nothing I shall want.

He guides me in right paths
    for his name's sake.
Even though I walk in the dark valley
    I fear no evil; for you are at my side
With your rod and your staff
    that give me courage.

℟. The Lord is my shepherd;
    there is nothing I shall want.

You spread the table before me
    in the sight of my foes;
You anoint my head with oil;
    my cup overflows.

℟. The Lord is my shepherd;
    there is nothing I shall want.

Only goodness and kindness follow me
    all the days of my life;
And I shall dwell in the house of the Lord
    for years to come.

℟. The Lord is my shepherd;
    there is nothing I shall want.

Years I and II

GOSPEL   Mt 20, 1-16
Alleluia

See no. 509.

✠ A reading from the holy gospel according
    to Matthew

Are you jealous because I am generous?

Jesus told his disciples this parable: "The reign of God is like the case of the owner of an estate who went out at dawn to hire workmen for his vineyard. After reaching an agreement with them for the usual daily wage, he sent them out to his vineyard. He came out about midmorning and saw other men standing around the marketplace without work, so he said to them, 'You too go along to my vineyard and I will pay you whatever is fair.' At that they went away. He came out again around noon and midafternoon and did the same. Finally, going out in late afternoon he found still others standing around. To these he said, 'Why have you been standing here idle all day?' 'No one has hired us,' they told him. He said, 'You go to the vineyard too.' When evening came the owner of the vineyard said to his foreman, 'Call the workmen and give them their pay, but begin with the last group and end with the first.' When those hired late in the afternoon came up they received a full day's pay, and when the first group appeared they supposed they would get more; yet they received the same daily wage. Thereupon they complained to the owner, 'This last group did only an hour's work, but you have put them on the same basis as us who have worked a full day in the scorching heat.' 'My friend,' he said to one in reply, 'I do you no injustice. You agreed on the usual wage, did you not? Take your pay and go home. I intend to give this man who was hired last the same pay as you. I am free to do as I please with my money, am I not? Or are you envious because I am generous?' Thus the last shall be first and the first shall be last."
This is the gospel of the Lord.

---

422   **THURSDAY OF THE
TWENTIETH WEEK OF THE YEAR**

Year I

READING I   Jgs 11, 29-39

A reading from the book of Judges

Whoever first comes from the door of my house I will offer up as a holocaust.

The spirit of the Lord came upon Jephthah. He passed through Gilead and Manasseh, and through Mizpah-Gilead as well, and from there he went on to the Ammonites. Jephthah made a vow to the Lord. "If you deliver the Ammonites into my power," he said, "whoever comes out of the doors of my house to meet me when I return in triumph from the Ammonites shall belong to the Lord. I shall offer him up as a holocaust."

Jephthah then went on to the Ammonites to fight against them, and the Lord delivered them into his power, so that he inflicted a severe defeat on them, from Aroer to the approach of Minnith (twenty cities in all) and as far as Abel-keramin. Thus were the Ammonites brought into subjection by the Israelites. When Jephthah returned to his house in Mizpah, it was his daughter who came forth, playing the tambourines and dancing. She was an only child: he had neither son nor daughter besides her. When he saw her, he rent his garments and said, "Alas, daughter, you have struck me down and brought calamity upon me. For I have made a vow to the Lord and I cannot retract." "Father," she replied, "you have made a vow to the Lord. Do with me as you have vowed, because the Lord has wrought vengeance for you on your enemies the Ammonites." Then she said to her father, "Let me have this favor. Spare me for two months, that I may go off down the mountains to mourn my virginity with my companions." "Go," he replied, and sent her away for two months. So she departed with her companions and mourned her virginity on the mountains. At the end of the two months she returned to her father, who did to her as he had vowed.
This is the Word of the Lord.

Responsorial Psalm   Ps 40, 5. 7-8. 8-9. 10

℟. (8. 9) Here am I, Lord;
    I come to do your will.
Happy the man who makes the Lord his trust;
    who turns not to idolatry
    or to those who stray after falsehood.
℟. Here am I, Lord;
    I come to do your will.
Sacrifice or oblation you wished not,
    but ears open to obedience you gave me.

Holocausts or sin-offerings you sought not;
    then said I, "Behold I come";
℟. Here am I, Lord;
    I come to do your will.
"In the written scroll it is prescribed for me
    to do your will, O my God, is my delight,
    and your law is within my heart!"
℟. Here am I, Lord;
    I come to do your will.
I announced your justice in the vast assembly;
    I did not restrain my lips, as you, O Lord,
    know.
℟. Here am I, Lord;
    I come to do your will.

Year II

READING I   Ez 36, 23-28
A reading from the book of the prophet Ezekiel
I will give you a new heart and put a new spirit in you.
The Lord said: I will prove the holiness of my great name, profaned among the nations, in whose midst you have profaned it. Thus the nations shall know that I am the Lord, says the Lord God, when in their sight I prove my holiness through you. For I will take you away from among the nations, gather you from all the foreign lands, and bring you back to your own land. I will sprinkle clean water upon you to cleanse you from all your impurities, and from all your idols I will cleanse you. I will give you a new heart and place a new spirit within you, taking from your bodies your stony hearts and giving you natural hearts. I will put my spirit within you and make you live by my statutes, careful to observe my decrees. You shall live in the land I gave your fathers; you shall be my people, and I will be your God.
This is the Word of the Lord.

Responsorial Psalm   Ps 51, 12-13. 14-15. 18-19

℟. (Ez 36, 25) I will pour clean water on you
    and wash away all your sins.
A clean heart create for me, O God,
    and a steadfast spirit renew within me.
Cast me not out from your presence,
    and your holy spirit take not from me.

℟. I will pour clean water on you
  and wash away all your sins.
Give me back the joy of your salvation,
  and a willing spirit sustain in me.
I will teach transgressors your ways,
  and sinners shall return to you.
℟. I will pour clean water on you
  and wash away all your sins.
For you are not pleased with sacrifices;
  should I offer a holocaust, you would not
  accept it.
My sacrifice, O God, is a contrite spirit;
  a heart contrite and humbled, O God, you
  will not spurn.
℟. I will pour clean water on you
  and wash away all your sins.

Years I and II

GOSPEL Mt 22, 1-14
Alleluia
See no. 509.

✠ **A reading from the holy gospel according**
  to Matthew
Go out and find whomever you can, and invite them to the
wedding.
Jesus began to address the chief priests and
elders of the people, once more using parables.
"The reign of God may be likened to a king
who gave a wedding banquet for his son. He
dispatched his servants to summon the invited
guests to the wedding, but they refused to
come. A second time he sent other servants,
saying: 'Tell those who are invited, See, I have
my dinner prepared! My bullocks and corn-
fed cattle are killed; everything is ready. Come
to the feast.' Some ignored the invitation and
went their way, one to his farm, another to his
business. The rest laid hold of his servants, insulted them, and killed them. At this the king
grew furious and sent his army to destroy
those murderers and burn their city. Then he
said to his servants: 'The banquet is ready, but
those who were invited were unfit to come.
That is why you must go out into the byroads
and invite to the wedding anyone you come
upon.' The servants then went out into the
byroads and rounded up everyone they met,
bad as well as good. This filled the wedding
hall with banqueters.
"When the king came in to meet the guests,
however, he caught sight of a man not properly
dressed for a wedding feast. 'My friend,' he
said, 'how is it you came in here not properly
dressed?' The man had nothing to say. The
king then said to the attendants, 'Bind him
hand and foot and throw him out into the
night to wail and grind his teeth.' The invited
are many, the elect are few."
  This is the gospel of the Lord.

---

423 FRIDAY OF THE TWENTIETH
WEEK OF THE YEAR

Year I

READING I Ru 1, 1. 3-6. 14-16. 22
The beginning of the book of Ruth
Naomi came with Ruth the Moabitess and returned to
Bethlehem.
Once in the time of the judges there was a
famine in the land; so a man from Bethlehem
of Judah departed with his wife and two sons
to reside on the plateau of Moab. Elimelech,
the husband of Naomi, died, and she was left
with her two sons, who married Moabite
women, one named Orpah, the other Ruth.
When they had lived there about ten years,
both Mahlon and Chilion died also, and the
woman was left with neither her two sons
nor her husband. She then made ready to go
back from the plateau of Moab because word
reached her there that the Lord had visited his
people and given them food.
  Orpah kissed her mother-in-law good-bye,
but Ruth stayed with her.
  "See now!" she said, "your sister-in-law has
gone back to her people and her god. Go back
after your sister-in-law!" But Ruth said, "Do
not ask me to abandon or forsake you! for
wherever you go I will go, wherever you lodge
I will lodge, your people shall be my people,
and your God my God."
  Thus it was that Naomi returned with the
Moabite daughter-in-law, Ruth, who accompanied her back from the plateau of Moab.

They arrived in Bethlehem at the beginning of the barley harvest.
This is the Word of the Lord.

Responsorial Psalm   Ps 146, 5-6. 7. 8-9. 9-10

℟. (2) Praise the Lord, my soul!
Happy he whose help is the God of Jacob,
whose hope is in the Lord, his God,
Who made heaven and earth,
the sea and all that is in them;
℟. Praise the Lord, my soul!
Who keeps faith forever,
secures justice for the oppressed,
gives food to the hungry.
The Lord sets captives free;
℟. Praise the Lord, my soul!
The Lord gives sight to the blind.
The Lord raises up those that were bowed
down;
the Lord loves the just.
The Lord protects strangers;
℟. Praise the Lord, my soul!
The fatherless and the widow he sustains,
but the way of the wicked he thwarts.
The Lord shall reign forever;
your God, O Zion, through all generations.
Alleluia.
℟. Praise the Lord, my soul!
℟. Or: Alleluia.

Year II

READING I   Ez 37, 1-14

A reading from the book of the prophet Ezekiel
Dry bones, hear the word of the Lord. I will lead you back
to the soil, O house of Israel.

The hand of the Lord came upon me, and he led me out in the spirit of the Lord and set me in the center of the plain, which was now filled with bones. He made me walk among them in every direction so that I saw how many they were on the surface of the plain. How dry they were! He asked me: Son of man, can these bones come to life? "Lord God," I answered, "you alone know that." Then he said to me: Prophesy over these bones, and say to them: Dry bones, hear the word of the Lord! Thus says the Lord God to these bones: See! I will bring spirit into you, that you may come to life.

I will put sinews upon you, make flesh grow over you, cover you with skin, and put spirit in you so that you may come to life and know that I am the Lord. I prophesied as I had been told, and even as I was prophesying I heard a noise; it was a rattling as the bones came together, bone joining bone. I saw the sinews and the flesh come upon them, and the skin cover them, but there was no spirit in them. Then he said to me: Prophesy to the spirit, prophesy, son of man, and say to the spirit: Thus says the Lord God: From the four winds come, O spirit, and breathe into these slain that they may come to life. I prophesied as he told me, and the spirit came into them; they came alive and stood upright, a vast army. Then he said to me: Son of man, these bones are the whole house of Israel. They have been saying, "Our bones are dried up, our hope is lost, and we are cut off." Therefore, prophesy and say to them: Thus says the Lord God: O my people, I will open your graves and have you rise from them, and bring you back to the land of Israel. Then you shall know that I am the Lord, when I open your graves and have you rise from them, O my people! I will put my spirit in you that you may live, and I will settle you upon your land; thus you shall know that I am the Lord. I have promised, and I will do it, says the the Lord.

This is the Word of the Lord.

Responsorial Psalm   Ps 107, 2-3. 4-5. 6-7. 8-9

℟. (1) Give thanks to the Lord,
his love is everlasting.
Let the redeemed of the Lord say,
those whom he has redeemed from the hand
of the foe
And gathered from the lands,
from the east and the west, from the north
and the south.
℟. Give thanks to the Lord,
his love is everlasting.
They went astray in the desert wilderness;
the way to an inhabited city they did not
find.
Hungry and thirsty,
their life was wasting away within them.

Ry. Give thanks to the Lord,
  his love is everlasting.
They cried to the Lord in their distress;
  from their straits he rescued them.
And he led them by a direct way
  to reach an inhabited city.
Ry. Give thanks to the Lord,
  his love is everlasting.
Let them give thanks to the Lord for his kind-
  ness
  and his wondrous deeds to the children of
  men,
Because he satisfied the longing soul
  and filled the hungry soul with good things.
Ry. Give thanks to the Lord,
  his love is everlasting.
Ry. Or: Alleluia.

Years I and II

GOSPEL   Mt 22, 34-40
Alleluia
See no. 509.

✠ **A reading from the holy gospel according**
  to Matthew
  Love the Lord your God, and your neighbor as yourself.

When the Pharisees heard that Jesus had si-
lenced the Sadducees, they assembled in a
body; and one of them, a lawyer, in an attempt
to trip him up, asked him, "Teacher, which
commandment of the law is the greatest?"
Jesus said to him:
  " 'You shall love the Lord your God
  with your whole heart,
  with your whole soul,
  and with all your mind.'
This is the greatest and first commandment.
The second is like it:
  'You shall love your neighbor as yourself.'
On these two commandments the whole law is
based, and the prophets as well."
  This is the gospel of the Lord.

424   SATURDAY OF THE TWENTIETH
      WEEK OF THE YEAR

Year I

READING I   Ru 2, 1-3. 8-11; 4, 13-17
A reading from the book of Ruth
The Lord has not left your family without a successor. This
        was the father of David's father.

Naomi had a prominent kinsman named Boaz,
of the clan of her husband Elimelech. Ruth the
Moabite said to Naomi, "Let me go and glean
ears of grain in the field of anyone who will
allow me that favor." Naomi said to her, "Go,
my daughter," and she went. The field she
entered to glean after the harvesters happened
to be the section belonging to Boaz of the clan
of Elimelech.
  Boaz said to Ruth, "Listen, my daughter!
Do not go to glean in anyone else's field; you
are not to leave here. Stay here with my
woman servants. Watch to see which field is
to be harvested, and follow them; I have com-
manded the young men to do you no harm.
When you are thirsty, you may go and drink
from the vessels the young men have filled."
Casting herself prostrate upon the ground, she
said to him, "Why should I, a foreigner, be
favored with your notice?" Boaz answered
her: "I have had a complete account of what
you have done for your mother-in-law after
your husband's death; you have left your fa-
ther and your mother and the land of your
birth, and have come to a people whom you
did not know previously."
  Boaz took Ruth. When they came together
as man and wife, the Lord enabled her to con-
ceive and she bore a son. Then the women said
to Naomi, "Blessed is the Lord who has not
failed to provide you today with an heir! May
he become famous in Israel! He will be your
comfort and the support of your old age, for his
mother is the daughter-in-law who loves you.
She is worth more to you than seven sons!"
Naomi took the child, placed him on her lap,
and became his nurse. And the neighbor
women gave him his name, at the news that a
grandson had been born to Naomi. They called

him Obed. He was the father of Jesse, the father of David.
> **This is the Word of the Lord.**

Responsorial Psalm   Ps 128, 1-2. 3. 4. 5

℟. (4) See how the Lord blesses those who fear him.

Happy are you who fear the Lord,
> **who walk in his ways!**

For you shall eat the fruit of your handiwork;
> **happy shall you be, and favored.**

℟. See how the Lord blesses those who fear him.

Your wife shall be like a fruitful vine
> **in the recesses of your home;**

Your children like olive plants
> **around your table.**

℟. See how the Lord blesses those who fear him.

Behold, thus is the man blessed
> **who fears the Lord.**

℟. See how the Lord blesses those who fear him.

The Lord bless you from Zion:
> **may you see the prosperity of Jerusalem all the days of your life.**

℟. See how the Lord blesses those who fear him.

READING I   Year II   Ez 43, 1-7

A reading from the book of the prophet Ezekiel
The glory of God filled the temple.

The angel led me to the gate which faces the east, and there I saw the glory of the God of Israel coming from the east. I heard a sound like the roaring of many waters, and the earth shone with his glory. The vision was like that which I had seen when he came to destroy the city, and like that which I had seen by the river Chebar. I fell prone as the glory of the Lord entered the temple by way of the gate which faces the east, but spirit lifted me up and brought me to the inner court. And I saw that the temple was filled with the glory of the Lord. Then I heard someone speaking to me from the temple, while the man stood beside

me. The voice said to me: Son of man, this is where my throne shall be, this is where I will set the soles of my feet; here I will dwell among the Israelites forever.
> **This is the Word of the Lord.**

Responsorial Psalm   Ps 85, 9-10. 11-12. 13-14

℟. (10) The glory of the Lord will dwell in our land.

I will hear what God proclaims;
> **the Lord—for he proclaims peace.**

Near indeed is his salvation to those who fear him,
> **glory dwelling in our land.**

℟. The glory of the Lord will dwell in our land.

Kindness and truth shall meet;
> **justice and peace shall kiss.**

Truth shall spring out of the earth,
> **and justice shall look down from heaven.**

℟. The glory of the Lord will dwell in our land.

The Lord himself will give his benefits;
> **our land shall yield its increase.**

Justice shall walk before him,
> **and salvation, along the way of his steps.**

℟. The glory of the Lord will dwell in our land.

GOSPEL   Years I and II   Mt 23, 1-12
Alleluia

See no. 509.

✠ **A reading from the holy gospel according to Matthew**
They speak, but do not practice what they preach.

Jesus told the crowds and his disciples: "The scribes and the Pharisees have succeeded Moses as teachers; therefore, do everything and observe everything they tell you. But do not follow their example. Their words are bold but their deeds are few. They bind up heavy loads, hard to carry, to lay on other men's shoulders, while they themselves will not lift a finger to budge them. All their works are performed to be seen. They widen their phylacteries and wear huge tassels. They are fond of places of honor at banquets and the front seats in synagogues, of marks of respect in public and of being called 'Rabbi.' As to you,

avoid the title 'Rabbi.' One among you is your teacher, the rest are learners. Do not call anyone on earth your father. Only one is your father, the One in heaven. Avoid being called teachers. Only one is your teacher, the Messiah. The greatest among you will be the one who serves the rest. Whoever exalts himself shall be humbled, but whoever humbles himself shall be exalted."

This is the gospel of the Lord.

---

425   MONDAY OF THE
          TWENTY-FIRST WEEK
          OF THE YEAR

Year I

READING I   1 Thes 1, 2-5. 8-10

A reading from the first letter of Paul to the Thessalonians

You converted to God from idolatry, expecting his Son whom he raised from the dead.

We constantly remember you in our prayers, for we are mindful before our God and Father of the way you are proving your faith, laboring in love, and showing constancy in hope in our Lord Jesus Christ. We know, too, brothers beloved of God, how you were chosen. Our preaching of the gospel proved not a mere matter of words for you but one of power; it was carried on in the Holy Spirit and out of complete conviction. You know as well as we do what we proved to be like when, while still among you, we acted on your behalf.

This is true not only in Macedonia and Achaia; throughout every region your faith in God is celebrated, which makes it needless for us to say anything more. The people of those parts are reporting what kind of reception we had from you and how you turned to God from idols, to serve him who is the living and true God and to await from heaven the Son he raised from the dead—Jesus, who delivers us from the wrath to come.

This is the Word of the Lord.

Responsorial Psalm   Ps 149, 1-2. 3-4. 5-6. 9

℟. (4) The Lord takes delight in his people.
Sing to the Lord a new song
   of praise in the assembly of the faithful.
Let Israel be glad in their maker,
   let the children of Zion rejoice in their king.
℟. The Lord takes delight in his people.
Let them praise his name in the festive dance,
   let them sing praise to him with timbrel
      and harp.
For the Lord loves his people,
   and he adorns the lowly with victory.
℟. The Lord takes delight in his people.
Let the faithful exult in glory;
   let them sing for joy upon their couches;
   let the high praises of God be in their throats.
   This is the glory of all his faithful. Alleluia.
℟. The Lord takes delight in his people.
℟. Or: Alleluia.

Year II

READING I   2 Thes 1, 1-5. 11-12

The beginning of the second letter of Paul to the Thessalonians

The name of our Lord Jesus Christ will be glorified in you and you in him.

Paul, Silvanus and Timothy, to the church of the Thessalonians, who belong to God our Father and the Lord Jesus Christ. Grace and peace be yours from God the Father and the Lord Jesus Christ. It is no more than right that we thank God unceasingly for you, brothers, because your faith grows apace and your mutual love increases; so much so that in God's communities we can boast of your constancy and your faith in persecution and trial. You endure these as an expression of God's just judgment, in order to be found worthy of his reign—it is for his kingdom you suffer.

We pray for you always that our God may make you worthy of his call, and fulfill by his power every honest intention and work of faith. In this way the name of our Lord Jesus may be glorified in you and you in him, in accord with the gracious gift of our God and of the Lord Jesus Christ.

This is the Word of the Lord.

Responsorial Psalm   Ps 96, 1-2. 2-3. 4-5

℟. (3) Proclaim his marvelous deeds to all the
  nations.

Sing to the Lord a new song;
  sing to the Lord, all you lands;
  sing to the Lord; bless his name.

℟. Proclaim his marvelous deeds to all the
  nations.

Announce his salvation, day after day.
  Tell his glory among the nations;
  among all peoples, his wondrous deeds.

℟. Proclaim his marvelous deeds to all the
  nations.

For great is the Lord and highly to be praised;
  awesome is he, beyond all gods.

For all the gods of the nations are things of
  nought,
  but the Lord made the heavens.

℟. Proclaim his marvelous deeds to all the
  nations.

Years I and II

GOSPEL   Mt 23, 13-22

Alleluia

See no. 509.

✠ A reading from the holy gospel according
  to Matthew

Woe to you, blind leaders.

Jesus said, "Woe to you scribes and Pharisees,
you frauds! You shut the doors of the kingdom
of God in men's faces, neither entering yourselves nor admitting those who are trying to
enter. Woe to you scribes and Pharisees, you
frauds! You travel over sea and land to make a
single convert, but once he is converted you
make a devil of him twice as wicked as yourselves. It is an evil day for you, blind guides!
You declare, 'If a man swears by the temple it
means nothing, but if he swears by the gold
of the temple he is obligated.' Blind fools!
Which is more important, the gold or the temple which makes it sacred? Again you declare,
'If a man swears by the altar it means nothing,
but if he swears by the gift on the altar he is
obligated.' How blind you are! Which is more
important, the offering or the altar which
makes the offering sacred? The man who

swears by the altar is swearing by it and by
everything on it. The man who swears by the
temple is swearing by it and by him who
dwells there. The man who swears by heaven
is swearing by God's throne and by him who
is seated on that throne."

This is the gospel of the Lord.

---

426   **TUESDAY OF THE**
          TWENTY-FIRST WEEK
          OF THE YEAR

Year I

READING I   1 Thes 2, 1-8

**A reading from the first letter of Paul to the
  Thessalonians**

We wish to hand over to you not only the Good News, but
our lives as well.

You know well enough, brothers, that our
coming among you was not without effect.
Fresh from the humiliation we had suffered at
Philippi—about which you know—we drew
courage from our God to preach his good tidings to you in the face of great opposition. The
exhortation we deliver does not spring from
deceit or impure motives or any sort of trickery; rather, having met the test imposed on us
by God, as men entrusted with the good tidings
we speak like those who strive to please God,
"the tester of our hearts," rather than men.

We were not guilty, as you well know, of
flattering words or greed under any pretext, as
God is our witness! Neither did we seek glory
from men, you or any others, even though we
could have insisted on our own importance as
apostles of Christ.

On the contrary, while we were among you
we were as gentle as any nursing mother
fondling her little ones. So well disposed were
we to you, in fact, that we wanted to share
with you not only God's tidings but our very
lives, so dear had you become to us.

This is the Word of the Lord.

Responsorial Psalm   Ps 139, 1-3. 4-6

℟. (1) You have searched me
  and you know me, Lord.

O Lord, you have probed me and you know me;
   you know when I sit and when I stand;
   you understand my thoughts from afar.
My journeys and my rest you scrutinize,
   with all my ways you are familiar.
℞. You have searched me
   and you know me, Lord.
Even before a word is on my tongue,
   behold, O Lord, you know the whole of it.
Behind me and before, you hem me in
   and rest your hand upon me.
Such knowledge is too wonderful for me;
   too lofty for me to attain.
℞. You have searched me
   and you know me, Lord.

Year II

READING I   2 Thes 2, 1-3. 14-16

A reading from the second letter of Paul to the Thessalonians

Stand firm to the traditions that you have learned.

On the question of the coming of our Lord
Jesus Christ and our being gathered to him, we
beg you, brothers, not to be so easily agitated
or terrified, whether by an oracular utterance,
or rumor, or a letter alleged to be ours, into
believing that the day of the Lord is here.
   Let no one seduce you, no matter how.
   God called you through our preaching of the
good news so that you might achieve the glory
of our Lord Jesus Christ. Therefore, brothers,
stand firm. Hold fast to the traditions you received from us, either by our word or by letter.
May our Lord Jesus Christ himself, may God
our Father who loved us and in his mercy gave
us eternal consolation and hope, console your
hearts and strengthen them for every good
work and word.
         This is the Word of the Lord.

Responsorial Psalm   Ps 96, 10. 11-12. 13

℞. (13) The Lord comes to judge the earth.
Say among the nations: The Lord is king.
He has made the world firm, not to be moved;
   he governs the peoples with equity.
℞. The Lord comes to judge the earth.

Let the heavens be glad and the earth rejoice;
   let the sea and what fills it resound;
   let the plains be joyful and all that is in them!
Then shall all the trees of the forest exult
℞. The Lord comes to judge the earth.
Before the Lord, for he comes;
   for he comes to rule the earth.
He shall rule the world with justice
   and the peoples with his constancy.
℞. The Lord comes to judge the earth.

Years I and II

GOSPEL   Mt 23, 23-26
Alleluia

See no. 509.

✠ **A reading from the holy gospel according to Matthew**

You should have practiced these without neglecting other things.

Jesus said: "Woe to you scribes and Pharisees,
you frauds! You pay tithes on mint and herbs
and seeds while neglecting the weightier matters of the law, justice and mercy and good
faith. It is these you should have practiced,
without neglecting the others.
   "Blind guides! You strain out the gnat and
swallow the camel! Woe to you scribes and
Pharisees, you frauds! You cleanse the outside
of cup and dish, and leave the inside filled with
loot and lust! Blind Pharisee! First cleanse the
inside of the cup so that its outside may be
clean."
         This is the gospel of the Lord.

---

427   **WEDNESDAY OF THE**
           TWENTY-FIRST WEEK
           OF THE YEAR

Year I

READING I   1 Thes 2, 9-13

A reading from the first letter of Paul to the Thessalonians

Night and day we have worked among you preaching the Good News.

You must recall, brothers, our efforts and our
toil: how we worked day and night all the time

we preached God's good tidings to you in order not to impose on you in any way. You are witnesses, as is God himself, of how upright, just, and irreproachable our conduct was toward you who are believers. You likewise know how we exhorted every one of you, as a father does his children—how we encouraged and pleaded with you to make your lives worthy of the God who calls you to his kingship and glory. That is why we thank God constantly that in receiving his message from us you took it, not as the word of men, but as it truly is, the word of God at work within you who believe.

    This is the Word of the Lord.

Responsorial Psalm   Ps 139, 7-8. 9-10. 11-12

℟. (1) You have searched me
    and you know me, Lord.

Where can I go from your spirit?
    from your presence where can I flee?
If I go up to the heavens, you are there;
    if I sink to the nether world, you are present
      there.
℟. You have searched me
    and you know me, Lord.
If I take the wings of the dawn,
    if I settle at the farthest limits of the sea,
Even there your hand shall guide me,
    and your right hand hold me fast.
℟. You have searched me
    and you know me, Lord.
If I say, "Surely the darkness shall hide me,
    and night shall be my light"—
For you darkness itself is not dark,
    and night shines as the day.
℟. You have searched me
    and you know me, Lord.

Year II

READING I   2 Thes 3, 6-10. 16-18
A reading from the second letter of Paul to the Thessalonians
If anyone does not wish to work, he cannot eat.
We command you, brothers, in the name of the Lord Jesus Christ, to avoid any brother who wanders from the straight path and does not

follow the tradition you received from us. You know how you ought to imitate us. We did not live lives of disorder when we were among you, nor depend on anyone for food. Rather, we worked day and night, laboring to the point of exhaustion so as not to impose on any of you. Not that we had no claim on you, but that we might present ourselves as an example for you to imitate. Indeed, when we were with you we used to lay down the rule that anyone who would not work should not eat.

    May he who is the Lord of peace give you continued peace in every possible way. The Lord be with you all.

    This greeting is in my own hand—Paul's. I append this signature to every letter I write.

    May the grace of our Lord Jesus Christ be with you all.

    This is the Word of the Lord.

Responsorial Psalm   Ps 128, 1-2. 4-5.

℟. (1) Happy are those who fear the Lord.
Happy are you who fear the Lord,
    who walk in his ways!
For you shall eat the fruit of your handiwork;
    happy shall you be, and favored.
℟. Happy are those who fear the Lord.
Behold, thus is the man blessed
    who fears the Lord.
The Lord bless you from Zion:
    may you see the prosperity of Jerusalem
    all the days of your life.
℟. Happy are those who fear the Lord.

Years I and II

GOSPEL   Mt 23, 27-32
Alleluia
See no. 509.

✠ **A reading from the holy gospel according to Matthew**
You are the sons of those who murdered the prophets.
Jesus said: "Woe to you scribes and Pharisees, you frauds! You are like whitewashed tombs, beautiful to look at on the outside but inside full of filth and dead men's bones. Thus you present to view a holy exterior while hypocrisy and evil fill you within. Woe to you scribes

and Pharisees, you frauds! You erect tombs for the prophets and decorate the monuments of the saints. You say, 'Had we lived in our forefathers' time we would not have joined them in shedding the prophets' blood.' Thus you show that you are the sons of the prophets' murderers. Now it is your turn: fill up the vessel measured off by your forefathers."

This is the gospel of the Lord.

---

428   **THURSDAY OF THE TWENTY-FIRST WEEK OF THE YEAR**

Year I

READING I   1 Thes 3, 7-13

A reading from the first letter of Paul to the Thessalonians

May the Lord be generous in increasing your love for one another and for the whole human race.

We have been much consoled by your faith throughout our distress and trial—so much so that we shall continue to flourish only if you stand firm in the Lord!

What thanks can we give to God for all the joy we feel in his presence because of you, as we ask him fervently night and day that we may see you face to face and remedy any shortcomings in your faith? May God himself, who is our Father, and our Lord Jesus make our path to you a straight one! And may the Lord increase you and make you overflow with love for one another and for all, even as our love does for you. May he strengthen your hearts, making them blameless and holy before our God and Father at the coming of our Lord Jesus with all his holy ones.

This is the Word of the Lord.

Responsorial Psalm   Ps 90, 3-4. 12-13. 14. 17

℞. (14) Fill us with your love, O Lord,
and we will sing for joy!
You turn man back to dust,
saying, "Return, O children of men."
For a thousand years in your sight

are as yesterday, now that it is past,
or as a watch of the night.
℞. Fill us with your love, O Lord,
and we will sing for joy!
Teach us to number our days aright,
that we may gain wisdom of heart.
Return, O Lord! How long?
Have pity on your servants!
℞. Fill us with your love, O Lord,
and we will sing for joy!
Fill us at daybreak with your kindness,
that we may shout for joy and gladness all
our days.
And may the gracious care of the Lord our God
be ours;
prosper the work of our hands for us!
[Prosper the work of our hands!]
℞. Fill us with your love, O Lord,
and we will sing for joy!

Year II

READING I   1 Cor 1, 1-9

The beginning of the first letter of Paul to the Corinthians

You have been enriched in so many ways by Christ.

Paul, called by God's will to be an apostle of Christ Jesus, and Sosthenes our brother, send greetings to the church of God which is in Corinth; to you who have been consecrated in Christ Jesus and called to be a holy people, as to all those who, wherever they may be, call on the name of our Lord Jesus Christ, their Lord and ours. Grace and peace from God our Father and the Lord Jesus Christ.

I continually thank my God for you because of the favor he has bestowed on you in Christ Jesus, in whom you have been richly endowed with every gift of speech and knowledge. Likewise, the witness I bore to Christ has been so confirmed among you that you lack no spiritual gift as you wait for the revelation of our Lord Jesus Christ. He will strengthen you to the end, so that you will be blameless on the day of our Lord Jesus [Christ]. God is faithful, and it was he who called you to fellowship with his Son, Jesus Christ our Lord.

This is the Word of the Lord.

Responsorial Psalm   Ps 145, 2-3. 4-5. 6-7

℟. (1) I will praise your name for ever, Lord.
Every day will I bless you,
   and I will praise your name forever and ever.
Great is the Lord and highly to be praised;
   his greatness is unsearchable.

℟. I will praise your name for ever, Lord.
Generation after generation praises your
   works
   and proclaims your might.
They speak of the splendor of your glorious
   majesty
   and tell of your wondrous works.

℟. I will praise your name for ever, Lord.
They discourse of the power of your terrible
   deeds
   and declare your greatness.
They publish the fame of your abundant good-
   ness
   and joyfully sing of your justice.

℟. I will praise your name for ever, Lord.

Years I and II

GOSPEL   Mt 24, 42-51
Alleluia

See no. 509.

✠ **A reading from the holy gospel according**
   to Matthew

Stay awake and be ready.

Jesus said to his disciples: "Stay awake, therefore! You cannot know the day your Lord is
coming.

"Be sure of this: if the owner of the house
knew when the thief was coming he would
keep a watchful eye and not allow his house
to be broken into. You must be prepared in the
same way. The Son of Man is coming at the
time you least expect. Who is the faithful, farsighted servant whom the master has put in
charge of his household to dispense food at
need? Happy that servant whom his master
discovers at work on his return! I assure you,
he will put him in charge of all his property.
But if the servant is worthless and tells himself, 'My master is a long time in coming,'
and begins to beat his fellow servants, to eat
and drink with drunkards, that man's master

will return when he is not ready and least
expects him. He will punish him severely and
settle with him as is done with hypocrites.
There will be wailing then and grinding of
teeth."

        This is the gospel of the Lord.

---

429   **FRIDAY OF THE**
           TWENTY-FIRST WEEK
           OF THE YEAR

Year I

READING I   1 Thes 4, 1-8

A reading from the first letter of Paul to the
           Thessalonians

This is the will of God, your holiness.

Now, my brothers, we beg and exhort you in
the Lord Jesus that, even as you learned from
us how to conduct yourselves in a way pleasing to God—which you are indeed doing—so
you must learn to make still greater progress. You know the instructions we gave you
in the Lord Jesus. It is God's will that you
grow in holiness: that you abstain from immorality, each of you guarding his member in
sanctity and honor, not in passionate desire as
do the Gentiles who know not God; and that
each refrain from overreaching or cheating his
brother in the matter at hand; for the Lord is
an avenger of all such things, as we once indicated to you by our testimony. God has not
called us to immorality but to holiness; hence,
whoever rejects these instructions rejects, not
man, but God "who sends his holy Spirit upon
"

        This is the Word of the Lord.

Responsorial Psalm   Ps 97, 1. 2. 5-6. 10. 11-12

℟. (12) Let good men rejoice in the Lord.
The Lord is king; let the earth rejoice;
   let the many isles be glad.
Justice and judgment are the foundation of his
   throne.

℟. Let good men rejoice in the Lord.
The mountains melt like wax before the Lord,
   before the Lord of all the earth.

The heavens proclaim his justice,
and all peoples see his glory.
℟. Let good men rejoice in the Lord.
The Lord loves those that hate evil;
he guards the lives of his faithful ones;
from the hand of the wicked he delivers
them.
℟. Let good men rejoice in the Lord.
Light dawns for the just;
and gladness, for the upright of heart.
Be glad in the Lord, you just,
and give thanks to his holy name.
℟. Let good men rejoice in the Lord.

Year II

READING I   1 Cor 1, 17-25

A reading from the first letter of Paul to the
Corinthians

We are preaching a crucified Christ, to men a scandal but
to those who have been called, the wisdom of God.

Christ did not send me to baptize but to preach
the gospel—not with wordy "wisdom," however, lest the cross of Christ be rendered void
of its meaning!

The message of the cross is complete absurdity to those who are headed for ruin, but to
us who are experiencing salvation it is the
power of God. Scripture says,

"I will destroy the wisdom of the wise,
and thwart the cleverness of the
clever."

Where is the wise man to be found? Where the
scribe? Where is the master of worldly argument? Has not God turned the wisdom of this
world into folly? Since in God's wisdom the
world did not come to know him through its
"wisdom," it pleased God to save those who
believe through the absurdity of the preaching
of the gospel. Yes, Jews demand "signs" and
Greeks look for "wisdom," but we preach
Christ crucified, a stumbling block to Jews, and
an absurdity to gentiles; but to those who
are called, Jews and Greeks alike, Christ the
power of God and the wisdom of God. For God's
folly is wiser than men, and his weakness more
powerful than men.

This is the Word of the Lord.

Responsorial Psalm   Ps 33, 1-2. 4-5. 10. 11

℟. (5) The earth is full of the goodness of the
Lord.
Exult, you just, in the Lord;
praise from the upright is fitting.
Give thanks to the Lord on the harp;
with the ten-stringed lyre chant his praises.
℟. The earth is full of the goodness of the Lord.
For upright is the word of the Lord,
and all his works are trustworthy.
He loves justice and right;
of the kindness of the Lord the earth is full.
℟. The earth is full of the goodness of the Lord.
The Lord brings to nought the plans of nations;
he foils the designs of peoples.
But the plan of the Lord stands forever;
the design of his heart, through all genera-
tions.
℟. The earth is full of the goodness of the Lord.

Years I and II

GOSPEL   Mt 25, 1-13

Alleluia

See no. 509.

✠ A reading from the holy gospel according
to Matthew

The bridegroom is here, go out and meet him.

Jesus told this parable to his disciples: "The
reign of God can be likened to ten bridesmaids
who took their torches and went out to welcome the groom. Five of them were foolish,
while the other five were sensible. The foolish
ones, in taking their torches, brought no oil
along, but the sensible ones took flasks of oil
as well as their torches. The groom delayed his
coming, so they all began to nod, then to fall
asleep. At midnight someone shouted, 'The
groom is here! Come out and greet him!' At the
outcry all the virgins woke up and got their
torches ready. The foolish ones said to the
sensible, 'Give us some of your oil. Our torches
are going out.' But the sensible ones replied,
'No, there may not be enough for you and us.
You had better go to the dealers and buy yourselves some.' While they went off to buy it the
groom arrived, and the ones who were ready
went in to the wedding with him. Then the

door was barred. Later the other bridesmaids came back. 'Master, master!' they cried. 'Open the door for us.' But he answered, 'I tell you, I do not know you.' The moral is: keep your eyes open, for you know not the day or the hour."
   This is the gospel of the Lord.

---

430 **SATURDAY OF THE**
   TWENTY-FIRST WEEK
   OF THE YEAR

Year I

READING I   1 Thes 4, 9-12

A reading from the first letter of Paul to the Thessalonians
You have learned from God himself to love one another.

As regards brotherly love, there is no need for me to write you. God himself has taught you to love one another, and this you are doing with respect to all the brothers throughout Macedonia. Yet we exhort you to even greater progress, brothers. Make it a point of honor to remain at peace and attend to your own affairs. Work with your hands as we directed you to do, so that you will give good example to outsiders and want for nothing.
   This is the Word of the Lord.

Responsorial Psalm   Ps 98, 1. 7-8. 9

℟. (9) The Lord comes to rule the earth with justice.
Sing to the Lord a new song,
 for he has done wondrous deeds;
His right hand has won victory for him,
 his holy arm.
℟. The Lord comes to rule the earth with justice.
Let the sea and what fills it resound,
 the world and those who dwell in it;
Let the rivers clap their hands,
 the mountains shout with them for joy.
℟. The Lord comes to rule the earth with justice.
Before the Lord, for he comes,
 for he comes to rule the earth;

He will rule the world with justice
 and the peoples with equity.
℟. The Lord comes to rule the earth with justice.

Year II

READING I   1 Cor 1, 26-31

A reading from the first letter of Paul to the Corinthians
God has chosen the weak.

Brothers, you are among those called. Consider your own situation. Not many of you are wise, as men account wisdom; not many are influential; and surely not many are wellborn. God chose those whom the world considers absurd to shame the wise; he singled out the weak of this world to shame the strong. He chose the world's lowborn and despised, those who count for nothing, to reduce to nothing those who were something; so that mankind can do no boasting before God. God it is who has given you life in Christ Jesus. He has made him our wisdom and also our justice, our sanctification, and our redemption. This is just as you find it written, "Let him who would boast, boast in the Lord."
   This is the Word of the Lord.

Responsorial Psalm Ps 33, 12-13. 18-19. 20-21

℟. (12) Happy the people the Lord has chosen to be his own.
Happy the nation whose God is the Lord,
 the people he has chosen for his own inheritance.
From heaven the Lord looks down;
 he sees all mankind.
℟. Happy the people the Lord has chosen to be his own.
But see, the eyes of the Lord are upon those who fear him,
 upon those who hope for his kindness,
To deliver them from death
 and preserve them in spite of famine.
℟. Happy the people the Lord has chosen to be his own.
Our soul waits for the Lord,
 who is our help and our shield,

For in him our hearts rejoice;
in his holy name we trust.
R⁄. Happy the people the Lord has chosen to be
his own.

Years I and II

GOSPEL   Mt 25, 14-30
Alleluia

See no. 509.

✠ A reading from the holy gospel according
to Matthew

*You have been faithful in small things, enter into the joy
of your Master.*

Jesus told this parable to his disciples: "A
certain man was going on a journey. He called
in his servants and handed his funds over to
them according to each man's abilities. To one
he disbursed five thousand silver pieces, to a
second two thousand, and to a third a thousand.
Then he went away. Immediately the man who
received the five thousand went to invest it and
made another five. In the same way, the man
who received the two thousand doubled his figure. The man who received the thousand went
off instead and dug a hole in the ground, where
he buried his master's money. After a long absence, the master of those servants came home
and settled accounts with them. The man who
had received the five thousand came forward
bringing the additional five. 'My lord,' he said,
'you let me have five thousand. See, I have made
five thousand more.' His master said to him,
'Well done! You are an industrious and reliable
servant. Since you were dependable in a small
matter I will put you in charge of larger affairs.
Come, share your master's joy!' The man who
had received the two thousand then stepped
forward. 'My lord,' he said, 'you entrusted me
with two thousand and I have made two thousand more.' His master said to him, 'Cleverly
done! You too are an industrious and reliable
servant. Since you were dependable in a small
matter I will put you in charge of larger affairs.
Come, share your master's joy!'
"Finally the man who had received the thousand stepped forward. 'My lord,' he said, 'I
knew you were a hard man. You reap where

you did not sow and gather where you did not
scatter, so out of fear I went off and buried
your thousand silver pieces in the ground. Here
is your money back.' His master exclaimed:
'You worthless, lazy lout! You know I reap
where I did not sow and gather where I did not
scatter. All the more reason to deposit my
money with the bankers, so that on my return
I could have had it back with interest. You,
there! Take the thousand away from him and
give it to the man with the ten thousand. Those
who have, will get more until they grow rich,
while those who have not, will lose even the
little they have. Throw this worthless servant
into the darkness outside, where he can wail
and grind his teeth.' "
This is the gospel of the Lord.

---

431   **MONDAY OF THE
TWENTY-SECOND WEEK
OF THE YEAR**

Year I

READING I   1 Thes 4, 13-18
A reading from the first letter of Paul to the
Thessalonians

*The Lord himself will lead all who are asleep in Jesus
with him.*

We would have you be clear about those who
sleep in death, brothers; otherwise you might
yield to grief, like those who have no hope. For
if we believe that Jesus died and rose, God
will bring forth with him from the dead those
also who have fallen asleep believing in him.
We say to you, as if the Lord himself had said
it, that we who live, who survive until his coming, will in no way have an advantage over
those who have fallen asleep. No, the Lord himself will come down from heaven at the word
of command, at the sound of the archangel's
voice and God's trumpet; and those who have
died in Christ will rise first. Then we, the living, the survivors, will be caught up with
them in the clouds to meet the Lord in the air.
Thenceforth we shall be with the Lord unceasingly. Console one another with this message.
This is the Word of the Lord.

Responsorial Psalm   Ps 96, 1. 3. 4-5. 11-12. 13

℟. (13) The Lord comes to judge the earth.
Sing to the Lord a new song;
   sing to the Lord, all you lands.
Tell his glory among the nations;
   among all peoples, his wondrous deeds.
℟. The Lord comes to judge the earth.
For great is the Lord and highly to be praised;
   awesome is he, beyond all gods.
For all the gods of the nations are things of
   nought,
   but the Lord made the heavens.
℟. The Lord comes to judge the earth.
Let the heavens be glad and the earth rejoice;
   let the sea and what fills it resound;
   let the plains be joyful and all that is in them!
Then shall all the trees of the forest exult.
   The Lord comes to judge the earth.
Before the Lord, for he comes;
   for he comes to rule the earth.
He shall rule the world with justice
   and the peoples with his constancy.
℟. The Lord comes to judge the earth.

Year II

READING I   1 Cor 2, 1-5

A reading from the first letter of Paul to the Corinthians

I have announced to you the knowledge of Christ crucified.

As for myself, brothers, when I came to you I did not come proclaiming God's testimony with any particular eloquence or "wisdom." No, I determined that while I was with you I would speak of nothing but Jesus Christ and him crucified. When I came among you it was in weakness and fear, and with much trepidation. My message and my preaching had none of the persuasive force of "wise" argumentation, but the convincing power of the Spirit. As a consequence, your faith rests not on the wisdom of men but on the power of God.
    This is the Word of the Lord.

Responsorial Psalm   Ps 119, 97. 98. 99. 100. 101. 102

℟. (97) Lord, I love your commands.
How I love your law, O Lord!
   It is my meditation all the day.

℟. Lord, I love your commands.
Your command has made me wiser than my
   enemies,
   for it is ever with me.
℟. Lord, I love your commands.
I have more understanding than all my teach-
   ers
   when your decrees are my meditation.
℟. Lord, I love your commands.
I have more discernment than the elders,
   because I observe your precepts.
℟. Lord, I love your commands.
From every evil way I withhold my feet,
   that I may keep your words.
℟. Lord, I love your commands.
From your ordinances I turn not away,
   for you have instructed me.
℟. Lord, I love your commands.

Years I and II

GOSPEL   Lk 4, 16-30
Alleluia
See no. 509.

✠ **A reading from the holy gospel according to Luke**

He has sent me to bring the Good News to the poor. No prophet is ever accepted in his own country.

Jesus came to Nazareth where he had been reared, and entering the synagogue on the sabbath as he was in the habit of doing, he stood up to do the reading. When the book of the prophet Isaiah was handed him, he unrolled the scroll and found the passage where it was written:
    "The spirit of the Lord is upon me;
      therefore he has anointed me.
    He has sent me to bring glad tidings to the
      poor,
      to proclaim liberty to captives,
    Recovery of sight to the blind
      and release to prisoners,
    To announce a year of favor from the
      Lord."
Rolling up the scroll, he gave it back to the assistant and sat down. All in the synagogue had their eyes fixed on him. Then he began by saying to them, "Today this Scripture passage is fulfilled in your hearing." All who were

present spoke favorably of him; they marveled at the appealing discourse which came from his lips. They also asked, "Is not this Joseph's son?"

He said to them, "You will doubtless quote me the proverb, 'Physician, heal yourself,' and say, 'Do here in your own country the things we have heard you have done in Capernaum.' But in fact," he went on, "no prophet gains acceptance in his native place. Indeed, let me remind you, there were many widows in Israel in the days of Elijah when the heavens remained closed for three and a half years and a great famine spread over the land. It was to none of these that Elijah was sent, but to a widow of Zarephath near Sidon. Recall, too, the many lepers in Israel in the time of Elisha the prophet; yet not one was cured except Naaman the Syrian."

At these words the whole audience in the synagogue was filled with indignation. They rose up and expelled him from the town, leading him to the brow of the hill on which it was built and intending to hurl him over the edge. But he went straight through their midst and walked away.

This is the gospel of the Lord.

---

432   **TUESDAY OF THE**
TWENTY-SECOND WEEK
OF THE YEAR

Year I

READING I   1 Thes 5, 1-6. 9-11
A reading from the first letter of Paul to the Thessalonians

Christ has died for us, that we might live.

As regards specific times and moments, brothers, we do not need to write you; you know very well that the day of the Lord is coming like a thief in the night. Just when people are saying, "Peace and security," ruin will fall on them with the suddenness of pains overtaking a woman in labor, and there will be no escape. You are not in the dark, brothers, so that the day might catch you off guard, like a thief. No,

all of you are children of light and of the day. We belong neither to darkness nor to night; therefore let us not be asleep like the rest, but awake and sober!

God has not destined us for wrath but for acquiring salvation through our Lord Jesus Christ. He died for us that all of us, whether awake or asleep, together might live with him. Therefore, comfort and upbuild one another, as indeed you are doing.

This is the Word of the Lord.

Responsorial Psalm   Ps 27, 1. 4. 13-14

℟. (13) I believe that I shall see the good things of the Lord in the land of the living.

The Lord is my light and my salvation;
  whom should I fear?
The Lord is my life's refuge;
  of whom should I be afraid?

℟. I believe that I shall see the good things of the Lord in the land of the living.

One thing I ask of the Lord;
  this I seek:
To dwell in the house of the Lord
  all the days of my life,
That I may gaze on the loveliness of the Lord
  and contemplate his temple.

℟. I believe that I shall see the good things of the Lord in the land of the living.

I believe that I shall see the bounty of the Lord
  in the land of the living.
Wait for the Lord with courage;
  be stouthearted, and wait for the Lord.

℟. I believe that I shall see the good things of the Lord in the land of the living.

Year II

READING I   1 Cor 2, 10-16
A reading from the first letter of Paul to the Corinthians

The unspiritual man does not receive the gifts of God; the spiritual man judges all things.

The Spirit scrutinizes all matters, even the deep things of God. Who, for example, knows a man's innermost self but the man's own spirit within him? Similarly, no one knows what lies at the depths of God but the Spirit of God. The Spirit we have received is not the world's spirit but God's Spirit, helping us to recognize the gifts he has given us. We speak of these gifts, not in words of human wisdom but in words taught by the Spirit, thus interpreting spiritual things in spiritual terms. The natural man does not accept what is taught by the Spirit of God. For him, that is absurdity. He cannot come to know such teaching because it must be appraised in a spiritual way. The spiritual man, on the other hand, can appraise everything, though he himself can be appraised by no one. For "Who has known the mind of the Lord so as to instruct him?" But we have the mind of Christ.

This is the Word of the Lord.

Responsorial Psalm   Ps 145, 8-9. 10-11. 12-13. 13-14

℟. (17) The Lord is just in all his ways.
The Lord is gracious and merciful,
    slow to anger and of great kindness.
The Lord is good to all
    and compassionate toward all his works.
℟. The Lord is just in all his ways.
Let all your works give you thanks, O Lord,
    and let your faithful ones bless you.
Let them discourse of the glory of your kingdom
    and speak of your might,
℟. The Lord is just in all his ways.
Making known to men your might
    and the glorious splendor of your kingdom.
Your kingdom is a kingdom for all ages,
    and your dominion endures through all generations.
℟. The Lord is just in all his ways.
The Lord is faithful in all his words
    and holy in all his works.
The Lord lifts up all who are falling
    and raises up all who are bowed down.
℟. The Lord is just in all his ways.

Years I and II

GOSPEL   Lk 4, 31-37
Alleluia

See no. 509.

✠ **A reading from the holy gospel according to Luke**
I know who you are, the Holy One of God.

Jesus went down to Capernaum, a town of Galilee, where he began instructing the people on the sabbath day. They were spellbound by his teaching, for his words had authority.

In the synagogue there was a man with an unclean spirit, who shrieked in a loud voice: "Leave us alone! What do you want of us, Jesus of Nazareth? Have you come to destroy us? I know who you are: the Holy One of God." Jesus said to him sharply, "Be quiet! Come out of him." At that, the demon threw him to the ground before everyone's eyes and came out of him without doing him any harm. All were struck with astonishment, and they began saying to one another: "What is there about his speech? He commands the unclean spirits with authority and power, and they leave." His renown kept spreading through the surrounding country.

This is the gospel of the Lord.

---

433   **WEDNESDAY OF THE TWENTY-SECOND WEEK OF THE YEAR**

Year I

READING I   Col 1, 1-8

The beginning of the letter of Paul to the Colossians
The Good News which has reached you is spreading all over the world.

Paul, an apostle of Christ Jesus by the will of God, and Timothy our brother, to the holy ones at Colossae, faithful brothers in Christ. May God our Father give you grace and peace.

We always give thanks to God, the Father of our Lord Jesus Christ, in our prayers for you because we have heard of your faith in Christ Jesus and the love you bear toward all the saints—moved as you are by the hope held in store for you in heaven. You heard of this hope through the message of truth, the gospel, which has come to you, has borne fruit, and has continued to grow in your midst as it has everywhere in the world. This has been the case from the day you first heard it and comprehended God's gracious intention through the instructions of Epaphras, our dear fellow slave, who represents us as a faithful minister of Christ. He it was who told us of your love in the Spirit.

This is the Word of the Lord.

Responsorial Psalm   Ps 52, 10. 11

R̸. (10) I trust in the kindness of God for ever.
I, like a green olive tree
in the house of God,
Trust in the kindness of God
forever and ever.

R̸. I trust in the kindness of God for ever.
I will thank you always for what you have
done,
and proclaim the goodness of your name
before your faithful ones.

R̸. I trust in the kindness of God for ever.

Year II

READING I   1 Cor 3, 1-9

A reading from the first letter of Paul to the Corinthians

We are fellow workers with God; you are God's farm, God's building.

Brothers, I could not talk to you as spiritual men but only as men of flesh, as infants in Christ. I fed you with milk, and did not give you solid food because you were not ready for it. You are not ready for it even now, being still very much in a natural condition. For as long as there are jealousy and quarrels among you, are you not of the flesh? And is not your behavior that of ordinary men? When someone says, "I belong to Paul," and another, "I belong to Apollos," is it not clear that you are still at the human level?

After all, who is Apollos? And who is Paul? Simply ministers through whom you became believers, each of them doing only what the Lord assigned him. I planted the seed and Apollos watered it, but God made it grow. This means that neither he who plants nor he who

waters is of any special account, only God, who gives the growth. He who plants and he who waters work to the same end. Each will receive his wages in proportion to his toil. We are God's co-workers, while you are his cultivation, his building.

This is the Word of the Lord.

Responsorial Psalm   Ps 33, 12-13. 14-15. 20-21

R̸. (12) Happy the people the Lord has chosen to be his own.
Happy the nation whose God is the Lord,
the people he has chosen for his own inheritance.
From heaven the Lord looks down;
he sees all mankind.

R̸. Happy the people the Lord has chosen to be his own.
From his fixed throne he beholds
all who dwell on the earth,
He who fashioned the heart of each,
he who knows all their works.

R̸. Happy the people the Lord has chosen to be his own.
Our soul waits for the Lord,
who is our help and our shield,
For in him our hearts rejoice;
in his holy name we trust.

R̸. Happy the people the Lord has chosen to be his own.

Years I and II

GOSPEL   Lk 4, 38-44
Alleluia

See no. 509.

✠ **A reading from the holy gospel according to Luke**

I must preach the Good News to other towns as well, because that is what I was sent to do.

On leaving the synagogue, Jesus entered the house of Simon. Simon's mother-in-law was in the grip of a severe fever, and they interceded with him for her. He stood over her and addressed himself to the fever, and it left her. She got up immediately and waited on them.

At sunset, all who had people sick with a variety of diseases took them to him, and he laid hands on each of them and cured them. Demons departed from many, crying out as they did so, "You are the son of God!" He rebuked them and did not allow them to speak because they knew that he was the Messiah.

The next morning he left the town and set out into the open country. The crowds went in search of him, and when they found him they tried to keep him from leaving them. But he said to them, "To other towns I must announce the good news of the reign of God, because that is why I was sent." And he continued to preach in the synagogues of Judea. This is the gospel of the Lord.

---

434   THURSDAY OF THE TWENTY-SECOND WEEK OF THE YEAR

Year I

READING I   Col 1, 9-14

A reading from the letter of Paul to the Colossians

He has taken us out of the power of darkness and created a place for us in the kingdom of his Son.

Ever since we heard this we have been praying for you unceasingly and asking that you may attain full knowledge of his will through perfect wisdom and spiritual insight. Then you will lead a life worthy of the Lord and pleasing to him in every way. You will multiply good works of every sort and grow in the knowledge of God. By the might of his glory you will be endowed with the strength needed to stand fast, even to endure joyfully whatever may come, giving thanks to the Father for having made you worthy to share the lot of the saints in light. He rescued us from the power of darkness and brought us into the kingdom of his beloved Son. Through him we have redemption, the forgiveness of our sins. This is the Word of the Lord.

Responsorial Psalm   Ps 98, 2-3. 3-4. 5-6

℟. (2) The Lord has made known his salvation.

The Lord has made his salvation known:
in the sight of the nations he has revealed his justice.
He has remembered his kindness and his faithfulness
toward the house of Israel.
℟. The Lord has made known his salvation.
All the ends of the earth have seen
the salvation by our God.
Sing joyfully to the Lord, all you lands;
break into song; sing praise.
℟. The Lord has made known his salvation.
Sing praise to the Lord with the harp,
with the harp and melodious song.
With trumpets and the sound of the horn
sing joyfully before the King, the Lord.
℟. The Lord has made known his salvation.

Year II

READING I   1 Cor 3, 18-23

A reading from the first letter of Paul to the Corinthians

All things are yours, but you belong to Christ and Christ belongs to God.

Let no one delude himself. If any one of you thinks he is wise in a worldly way, he had better become a fool. In that way he will really be wise, for the wisdom of this world is absurdity with God. Scripture says, "He catches the wise in their craftiness"; and again, "The Lord knows how empty are the thoughts of the wise." Let there be no boasting about men. All things are yours, whether it be Paul, or Apollos, or Cephas, or the world, or life, or death, or the present, or the future: all these are yours, and you are Christ's and Christ is God's.

This is the Word of the Lord.

Responsorial Psalm   Ps 24, 1-2. 3-4. 5-6

℟. (1) To the Lord belongs the earth
and all that fills it.
The Lord's are the earth and its fullness;
the world and those who dwell in it.
For he founded it upon the seas
and established it upon the rivers.
℟. To the Lord belongs the earth
and all that fills it.

Who can ascend the mountain of the Lord?
or who may stand in his holy place?
He whose hands are sinless, whose heart is
clean,
who desires not what is vain.
℟. To the Lord belongs the earth
and all that fills it.
He shall receive a blessing from the Lord,
a reward from God his savior.
Such is the race that seeks for him,
that seeks the face of the God of Jacob.
℟. To the Lord belongs the earth
and all that fills it.

Years I and II

GOSPEL   Lk 5, 1-11
Alleluia

See no. 509.

✠ **A reading from the holy gospel according
to Luke**

They left everything and followed him.

As the crowd pressed in on Jesus to hear the
word of God, he saw two boats moored by the
side of the lake; the fishermen had disembarked and were washing their nets. He got
into one of the boats, the one belonging to
Simon, and asked him to pull out a short distance from the shore; then, remaining seated,
he continued to teach the crowds from the
boat. When he had finished speaking he said
to Simon, "Put out into deep water and lower
your nets for a catch." Simon answered,
"Master, we have been hard at it all night
long and have caught nothing; but if you say
so, I will lower the nets." Upon doing this they
caught such a great number of fish that their
nets were at the breaking point. They signaled
to their mates in the other boat to come and
help them. These came, and together they filled
the two boats until they nearly sank.

At the sight of this, Simon Peter fell at the
knees of Jesus saying, "Leave me, Lord. I am
a sinful man." For indeed, amazement at the
catch they had made seized him and all his
shipmates, as well as James and John, Zebedee's sons, who were partners with Simon.
Jesus said to Simon, "Do not be afraid. From
now on you will be catching men." With that

they brought their boats to land, left everything, and became his followers.
This is the gospel of the Lord.

435   **FRIDAY OF THE
TWENTY-SECOND WEEK
OF THE YEAR**

Year I

READING I   Col 1, 15-20

**A reading from the letter of Paul to the
Colossians**

All things were created through him and for him.

Christ is the image of the invisible God, the
first-born of all creatures. In him everything
in heaven and on earth was created, things
visible and invisible, whether thrones or dominations, principalities or powers; all were
created through him and for him. He is before
all else that is. In him everything continues in
being. It is he who is head of the body, the
church; he who is the beginning, the first-born
of the dead, so that primacy may be his in
everything. It pleased God to make absolute
fullness reside in him and, by means of him,
to reconcile everything in his person, everything, I say, both on earth and in the heavens,
making peace through the blood of his cross.
This is the Word of the Lord.

Responsorial Psalm   Ps 100, 1. 2. 3. 4. 5.
℟. (2) Come with joy into the presence of the
Lord.
Sing joyfully to the Lord, all you lands;
serve the Lord with gladness;
come before him with joyful song.
℟. Come with joy into the presence of the
Lord.
Know that the Lord is God;
he made us, his we are;
his people, the flock he tends.
℟. Come with joy into the presence of the Lord.
Enter his gates with thanksgiving,
his courts with praise;
Give thanks to him; bless his name.
℟. Come with joy into the presence of the Lord.

The Lord is good,
the Lord, whose kindness endures forever,
and his faithfulness, to all generations.
℞. Come with joy into the presence of the Lord.

Year II

READING I
1 Cor 4, 1-5

A reading from the first letter of Paul to the Corinthians

The Lord will reveal the intentions of men's hearts.

Men should regard us as servants of Christ and administrators of the mysteries of God. The first requirement of an administrator is that he prove trustworthy. It matters little to me whether you or any human court pass judgment on me. I do not even pass judgment on myself. Mind you, I have nothing on my conscience. But that does not mean that I am declaring myself innocent. The Lord is the one to judge me, so stop passing judgment before the time of his return. He will bring to light what is hidden in darkness and manifest the intentions of hearts. At that time, everyone will receive his praise from God.
This is the Word of the Lord.

Responsorial Psalm   Ps 37, 3-4. 5-6. 27-28. 39-40

℞. (39) The salvation of the just comes from the Lord.

Trust in the Lord and do good,
that you may dwell in the land and enjoy security.
Take delight in the Lord,
and he will grant you your heart's requests.
℞. The salvation of the just comes from the Lord.

Commit to the Lord your way;
trust in him, and he will act.
He will make justice dawn for you like the light;
bright as the noonday shall be your vindication.
℞. The salvation of the just comes from the Lord.

Turn from evil and do good,
that you may abide forever;

For the Lord loves what is right,
and forsakes not his faithful ones.
Criminals are destroyed
and the posterity of the wicked is cut off.
℞. The salvation of the just comes from the Lord.

The salvation of the just is from the Lord;
he is their refuge in time of distress.
And the Lord helps them and delivers them;
he delivers them from the wicked and saves them,
because they take refuge in him.
℞. The salvation of the just comes from the Lord.

GOSPEL
Lk 5, 33-39

Alleluia

See no. 509.

✠ **A reading from the holy gospel according to Luke**

When the bridegroom is taken from them, then they will fast.

The scribes and Pharisees said to Jesus: "John's disciples fast frequently and offer prayers; the disciples of the Pharisees do the same. Yours, on the contrary, eat and drink freely." Jesus replied: "Can you make guests of the groom fast while the groom is still with them? But when the days come that the groom is removed from their midst, they will surely fast in those days."

He then proposed to them this figure: "No one tears a piece from a new coat to patch an old one. If he does he will only tear the new coat, and the piece taken from it will not match the old. Moreover, no one pours new wine into old wineskins. Should he do so, the new wine will burst the old skins, the wine will spill out, and the skins will be lost. New wine should be poured into fresh skins. No one, after drinking old wine, wants new. He says, 'I find the old wine better.' "
This is the gospel of the Lord.

436   **SATURDAY OF THE
TWENTY-SECOND WEEK
OF THE YEAR**

Year I

READING I   Col 1, 21-23

A reading from the letter of Paul to the Colossians

He has reconciled you that you can appear holy and pure.

You yourselves were once alienated from him; you nourished hostility in your hearts because of your evil deeds. But now Christ has achieved reconciliation for you in his mortal body by dying, so as to present you to God holy, free of reproach and blame. But you must hold fast to faith, be firmly grounded and steadfast in it, unshaken in the hope promised you by the gospel you have heard. It is the gospel which has been announced to every creature under heaven, and I, Paul, am its servant.

This is the Word of the Lord.

Responsorial Psalm   Ps 54, 3-4. 6. 8

℟. (6) God himself is my help.

O God, by your name save me,
  and by your might defend my cause.
O God, hear my prayer;
  hearken to the words of my mouth.

℟. God himself is my help.

Behold, God is my helper;
  the Lord sustains my life.
Freely will I offer you sacrifice;
  I will praise your name, O Lord, for its
  goodness.

℟. God himself is my help.

Year II

READING I   1 Cor 4, 9-15

A reading from the first letter of Paul to the Corinthians

We hunger and thirst and are naked.

God has put us apostles at the end of the line, like men doomed to die in the arena. We have become a spectacle to the universe, to angels and men alike. We are fools on Christ's account. Ah, but in Christ you are wise! We are

the weak ones, you the strong! They honor you, while they sneer at us! Up to this very hour we go hungry and thirsty, poorly clad, roughly treated, wandering about homeless. We work hard at manual labor. When we are insulted we respond with a blessing. Persecution comes our way; we bear it patiently. We are slandered, and we try conciliation. We have become the world's refuse, the scum of all; that is the present state of affairs.

I am writing you in this way not to shame you but to admonish you as my beloved children. Granted you have ten thousand guardians in Christ, you have only one father. It was I who begot you in Christ Jesus through my preaching of the gospel.

This is the Word of the Lord.

Responsorial Psalm   Ps 145, 17-18. 19-20. 21

℟. (18) The Lord is near to all who call him.

The Lord is just in all his ways
  and holy in all his works.
The Lord is near to all who call upon him,
  to all who call upon him in truth.

℟. The Lord is near to all who call him.

He fulfills the desire of those who fear him,
  he hears their cry and saves them.
The Lord keeps all who love him,
  but all the wicked he will destroy.

℟. The Lord is near to all who call him.

May my mouth speak the praise of the Lord,
  and may all flesh bless his holy name forever
  and ever.

℟. The Lord is near to all who call him.

Years I and II

GOSPEL   Lk 6, 1-5

Alleluia

See no. 509.

✠ **A reading from the holy gospel according
to Luke**

*Why are you doing something that is forbidden on the
sabbath?*

Once on a sabbath Jesus was walking through the standing grain. His disciples were pulling off grain-heads, shelling them with their hands, and eating them. Some of the Pharisees asked,

"Why are you doing what is prohibited on the sabbath?" Jesus said to them: "Have you not read what David did when he and his men were hungry—how he entered God's house and took and ate the holy bread and gave it to his men, even though only priests are allowed to eat it?" Then he said to them, "The Son of Man is Lord even of the sabbath."

This is the gospel of the Lord.

---

437   MONDAY OF THE TWENTY-THIRD WEEK OF THE YEAR

Year I

READING I   Col 1, 24–2, 3

A reading from the letter of Paul to the Colossians

I am the servant of the Church to make known the word of God, a mystery hidden for generations.

Even now I find my joy in the suffering I endure for you. In my own flesh I fill up what is lacking in the sufferings of Christ for the sake of his body, the church. I became a minister of this church through the commission God gave me to preach among you his word in its fullness, that mystery hidden from ages and generations past but now revealed to his holy ones. God has willed to make known to them the glory beyond price which this mystery brings to the Gentiles—the mystery of Christ in you, your hope of glory. This is the Christ we proclaim while we admonish all men and teach them in the full measure of wisdom, hoping to make every man complete in Christ. For this I work and struggle, impelled by that energy of his which is so powerful a force within me.

I want you to know how hard I am struggling for you and for the Laodiceans and the many others who have never seen me in the flesh. I wish their hearts to be strengthened and themselves to be closely united in love, enriched with full assurance by their knowledge of the mystery of God—namely Christ—in whom every treasure of wisdom and knowledge is hidden.

This is the Word of the Lord.

Responsorial Psalm   Ps 62, 6-7. 9

℟. (8) In God is my safety and my glory.
Only in God be at rest, my soul,
    for from him comes my hope.
He only is my rock and my salvation,
    my stronghold; I shall not be disturbed.
℟. In God is my safety and my glory.
Trust in him at all times, O my people!
    Pour out your hearts before him;
    God is our refuge!
℟. In God is my safety and my glory.

Year II

READING I   1 Cor 5, 1-8

A reading from the first letter of Paul to the Corinthians

Get rid of the old yeast; Christ our passover has been sacrificed.

It is actually reported that there is lewd conduct among you, of a kind not even found among the pagans—a man living with his own father's wife. Still you continue to be self-satisfied, instead of grieving and getting rid of the offender! As for me, though absent in body I am present in spirit, and have already passed sentence in the name of our Lord Jesus Christ on the man who did this deed. United in spirit with you and empowered by our Lord Jesus, I hand him over to Satan for the destruction of his flesh, so that his spirit may be saved on the day of the Lord.

This boasting of yours is an ugly thing. Do you not know that a little yeast has its effect all through the dough? Get rid of the old yeast to make of yourselves fresh dough, unleavened loaves, as it were; Christ our Passover has been sacrificed. Let us celebrate the feast not with the old yeast, that of corruption and wickedness, but with the unleavened bread of sincerity and truth.

This is the Word of the Lord.

Responsorial Psalm   Ps 5, 5-6. 7. 12

℟. (9) Lead me in your justice, Lord.
For you, O God, delight not in wickedness;
    no evil man remains with you;

the arrogant may not stand in your sight.
You hate all evildoers;
R̂. Lead me in your justice, Lord.
You destroy all who speak falsehood;
   the bloodthirsty and the deceitful
   the Lord abhors.
R̂. Lead me in your justice, Lord.
But let all who take refuge in you
   be glad and exult forever.
Protect them, that you may be the joy
   of those who love your name.
R̂. Lead me in your justice, Lord.

Years I and II

GOSPEL   Lk 6, 6-11
Alleluia

See no. 509.

✠ A reading from the holy gospel according
            to Luke
They watched him to see if he would cure a man on the
sabbath.

On a sabbath Jesus came to teach in a synagogue where there was a man whose right
hand was withered. The scribes and Pharisees
were on the watch to see if he would perform
a cure on the sabbath so that they could find
a charge against him. He knew their thoughts,
however, and said to the man whose hand was
withered, "Get up and stand here in front."
The man rose and remained standing. Jesus
said to them, "I ask you, is it lawful to do good
on the sabbath—or evil? To preserve life—
or destroy it?" He looked around at them all
and said to the man, "Stretch out your hand."
The man did so and his hand was perfectly
restored.
   At this they became frenzied and began
asking one another what could be done to
Jesus.
            This is the gospel of the Lord.

438   **TUESDAY OF THE**
            TWENTY-THIRD WEEK
            OF THE YEAR

Year I

READING I   Col 2, 6-15
   A reading from the letter of Paul to the
                  Colossians
You must live your life in Christ, who has given you all
forgiveness.

Continue to live in Christ Jesus the Lord, in the
spirit in which you received him. Be rooted in
him and built up in him, growing ever stronger
in faith as you were taught, and overflowing
with gratitude. See to it that no one deceives
you through any empty, seductive philosophy
that follows mere human traditions, a philosophy based on cosmic powers rather than on
Christ.
   In Christ the fullness of deity resides in
bodily form. Yours is a share of this fullness,
in him who is the head of every principality
and power. You were also circumcised in him,
not with the circumcision administered by
hand but with Christ's circumcision, which
strips off the carnal body completely. In baptism you were not only buried with him but
also raised to life with him because you believed in the power of God who raised him
from the dead. Even when you were dead in
sin and your flesh was uncircumcised, God
gave you new life in company with Christ.
He pardoned all our sins. He canceled the
bond that stood against us with all its claims,
snatching it up and nailing it to the cross.
Thus did God disarm the principalities and
powers. He made a public show of them and,
leading them off captive, he triumphed in the
person of Christ.
            This is the Word of the Lord.

Responsorial Psalm   Ps 145, 1-2. 8-9. 10-11

R̂. (9) The Lord is compassionate to all his
      creatures.
I will extol you, O my God and King,
   and I will bless your name forever and ever.
Every day will I bless you,
   and I will praise your name forever and ever.

℞. The Lord is compassionate to all his creatures.

The Lord is gracious and merciful,
slow to anger and of great kindness.
The Lord is good to all
and compassionate toward all his works.
℞. The Lord is compassionate to all his creatures.

Let all your works give you thanks, O Lord,
and let your faithful ones bless you.
Let them discourse of the glory of your kingdom
and speak of your might.
℞. The Lord is compassionate to all his creatures.

Year II

READING I   1 Cor 6, 1-11
A reading from the first letter of Paul to the Corinthians
One brother contests another in front of unbelievers.

How can anyone with a case against another dare bring it for judgment to the wicked and not to God's holy people? Do you not know that the believers will judge the world? If the judgment of the world is to be yours, are you to be thought unworthy of judging in minor matters? Do you not know that we are to judge angels? Surely, then, we are up to deciding everyday affairs. If you have such matters to decide, do you accept as judges those who have no standing in the church? I say this in an attempt to shame you. Can it be that there is no one among you wise enough to settle a case between one member of the church and another? Must brother drag brother into court, and before unbelievers at that? Why, the very fact that you have lawsuits against one another is disastrous for you. Why not put up with injustice, and let yourselves be cheated? Instead, you yourselves injure and cheat your very own brothers. Can you not realize that the unholy will not fall heir to the kingdom of God? Do not deceive yourselves: no fornicators, idolators, or adulterers, no sodomites, thieves, misers, or drunkards, no slanderers or robbers will inherit God's kingdom. And such

were some of you; but you have been washed, consecrated, justified in the name of our Lord Jesus Christ and in the Spirit of our God.

This is the Word of the Lord.

Responsorial Psalm   Ps 149, 1-2. 3-4. 5-6. 9
℞. (4) The Lord takes delight in his people.
Sing to the Lord a new song
of praise in the assembly of the faithful.
Let Israel be glad in their maker,
let the children of Zion rejoice in their king.
℞. The Lord takes delight in his people.

Let them praise his name in the festive dance,
let them sing praise to him with timbrel and harp.
For the Lord loves his people,
and he adorns the lowly with victory.
℞. The Lord takes delight in his people.

Let the faithful exult in glory;
let them sing for joy upon their couches;
let the high praises of God be in their throats.
This is the glory of all his faithful. Alleluia.
℞. The Lord takes delight in his people.
℞. Or: Alleluia.

Years I and II

GOSPEL   Lk 6, 12-19
Alleluia

See no. 509.

✠ **A reading from the holy gospel according to Luke**
He spent the night in prayer. He chose twelve from his disciples and called them Apostles.

Jesus went out to the mountain to pray, spending the night in communion with God. At daybreak he called his disciples and selected twelve of them to be his apostles: Simon, to whom he gave the name Peter, and Andrew his brother, James and John, Philip and Bartholomew, Matthew and Thomas, James son of Alphaeus, and Simon called the Zealot, Judas son of James, and Judas Iscariot, who turned traitor.

    Coming down the mountain with them, he stopped at a level stretch where there were many of his disciples; a large crowd of people was with them from all Judea and Jerusalem

and the coast of Tyre and Sidon, people who came to hear him and be healed of their diseases. Those who were troubled with unclean spirits were cured; indeed, the whole crowd was trying to touch him because power went out from him which cured all.

This is the gospel of the Lord.

---

439   **WEDNESDAY OF THE TWENTY-THIRD WEEK OF THE YEAR**

Year I

READING I   Col 3, 1-11

A reading from the letter of Paul to the Colossians

You must die with Christ; put to death everything in you that belongs to earthly life.

Since you have been raised up in company with Christ, set your heart on what pertains to higher realms where Christ is seated at God's right hand. Be intent on things above rather than on things of earth. After all, you have died! Your life is hidden now with Christ in God. When Christ our life appears, then you shall appear with him in glory.

Put to death whatever in your nature is rooted in earth: fornication, uncleanness, passion, evil desires, and that lust which is idolatry. These are the sins which provoke God's wrath. Your own conduct was once of this sort, when these sins were your very life. You must put that aside now: all the anger and quick temper, the malice, the insults, the foul language. Stop lying to one another. What you have done is put aside your old self with its past deeds and put on a new man, cne who grows in knowledge as he is formed anew in the image of his Creator. There is no Greek or Jew here, circumcised or uncircumcised, foreigner, Scythian, slave, or freeman. Rather Christ is everything in all of you.

This is the Word of the Lord.

Responsorial Psalm   Ps 145, 2-3. 10-11. 12-13

℟. (9) The Lord is compassionate to all his creatures.

Every day will I bless you,
    and I will praise your name forever and ever.
Great is the Lord and highly to be praised;
    his greatness is unsearchable.
℟. The Lord is compassionate to all his creatures.

Let all your works give you thanks, O Lord,
    and let your faithful ones bless you.
Let them discourse of the glory of your kingdom
    and speak of your might.
℟. The Lord is compassionate to all his creatures.

Making known to men your might
    and the glorious splendor of your kingdom.
Your kingdom is a kingdom for all ages,
    and your dominion endures through all generations.
℟. The Lord is compassionate to all his creatures.

Year II

READING I   1 Cor 7, 25-31

A reading from the first letter of Paul to the Corinthians

Are you bound to a wife? Do not seek to be free. Are you free from a wife? Do not seek marriage.

I have not received any commandment from the Lord with respect to virgins, but I give my opinion as one who is trustworthy, thanks to the Lord's mercy. It is this: In the present time of stress it seems good to me for a person to continue as he is. Are you bound to a wife? Then do not seek your freedom. Are you free of a wife? If so, do not go in search of one. Should you marry, however, you will not be committing sin. Neither does a virgin commit a sin if she marries. Such people, however, will have trials in this life, and these I should like to spare you.

I tell you, brothers, the time is short. From now on those with wives should live as though they had none; those who weep should live as though they were not weeping, and those who rejoice as though they were not rejoicing; buyers should conduct themselves as though they owned nothing, and those who make use

of the world as though they were not using it, for the world as we know it is passing away.
This is the Word of the Lord.

Responsorial Psalm   Ps 45, 11-12. 14-15. 16-17

R̸. (11) Listen to me, daughter;
see and bend your ear.

Hear, O daughter, and see; turn your ear,
forget your people and your father's house.
So shall the king desire your beauty;
for he is your lord, and you must worship
him.

R̸. Listen to me, daughter;
see and bend your ear.

All glorious is the king's daughter as she
enters;
her raiment is threaded with spun gold.
In embroidered apparel she is borne in to the
king;
behind her the virgins of her train are
brought to you.

R̸. Listen to me, daughter;
see and bend your ear.

They are borne in with gladness and joy;
they enter the palace of the king.
The place of your fathers your sons shall have;
you shall make them princes through all the
land.

R̸. Listen to me, daughter;
see and bend your ear.

Years I and II

GOSPEL   Lk 6, 20-26
Alleluia

See no. 509.

✠ A reading from the holy gospel according
to Luke

Happy are the poor. Woe to you who are rich.

Jesus raised his eyes to his disciples and said:
"Blest are you poor; the reign of God is
yours.
Blest are you who hunger; you shall be filled.
Blest are you who are weeping; you shall
laugh.
Blest shall you be when men hate you,
when they ostracize you and insult you and
proscribe your name as evil because of the

Son of Man. On the day they do so, rejoice
and exult, for your reward shall be great in
heaven. Thus it was that their fathers treated
the prophets.
"But woe to you rich, for your consolation
is now.
Woe to you who are full; you shall go
hungry.
Woe to you who laugh now; you shall weep
in your grief.
Woe to you when all speak well of you.
Their fathers treated the false prophets in just
this way."
This is the gospel of the Lord.

---

440   **THURSDAY OF THE**
TWENTY-THIRD WEEK
OF THE YEAR

Year I

READING I   Col 3, 12-17

**A reading from the letter of Paul to the
Colossians**

Have charity, which is the bond of perfection.

Because you are God's chosen ones, holy
and beloved, clothe yourselves with heartfelt
mercy, with kindness, humility, meekness, and
patience. Bear with one another; forgive whatever grievances you have against one another.
Forgive as the Lord has forgiven you. Over all
these virtues put on love, which binds the rest
together and makes them perfect. Christ's
peace must reign in your hearts, since as members of the one body you have been called to
that peace. Dedicate yourselves to thankfulness. Let the word of Christ, rich as it is,
dwell in you. In wisdom made perfect, instruct
and admonish one another. Sing gratefully to
God from your hearts in psalms, hymns, and
inspired songs. Whatever you do, whether in
speech or in action, do it in the name of the
Lord Jesus. Give thanks to God the Father
through him.
This is the Word of the Lord.

Responsorial Psalm   Ps 150, 1-2. 3-4. 5-6

℞. (6) Let everything that breathes praise the
Lord!

Praise the Lord in his sanctuary,
    praise him in the firmament of his strength.
Praise him for his mighty deeds,
    praise him for his sovereign majesty.

℞. Let everything that breathes praise the
Lord!

Praise him with the blast of the trumpet,
    praise him with lyre and harp,
Praise him with timbrel and dance,
    praise him with strings and pipe.

℞. Let everything that breathes praise the
Lord!

Praise him with sounding cymbals,
    praise him with clanging cymbals.
Let everything that has breath
    praise the Lord! Alleluia.

℞. Let everything that breathes praise the
Lord!

℞. Or: Alleluia.

Year II

READING I   1 Cor 8, 1-7. 11-13

**A reading from the first letter of Paul to the
Corinthians**

By sinning against your weaker brothers, you have sinned
against Christ.

"Knowledge" inflates, but love upbuilds. If
a man thinks he knows something, that means
he has never really known it as he ought.
But if anyone loves God, that man is known
by him. So then, about this matter of eating
meats that have been offered to idols; we know
that an idol is really nothing, and that there is
no God but one. Even though there are so-
called gods in the heavens and on the earth—
there are, to be sure, many such "gods" and
"lords"—for us there is one God, the Father,
from whom all things come and for whom we
live; and one Lord Jesus Christ, through whom
everything was made and through whom we
live.

Not all, of course, possess this "knowledge."
Because some were so recently devoted to
idols, they eat meat, fully aware that it has
been sacrificed, and because their conscience is

weak, it is defiled by the eating. Because of
your "knowledge" the weak one perishes—
that brother for whom Christ died. When you
sin thus against your brothers and wound their
weak consciences, you are sinning against
Christ. Therefore, if food causes my brother
to sin I will never eat meat again, so that I
may not be an occasion of sin to him.
    This is the Word of the Lord.

Responsorial Psalm   Ps 139, 1-3. 13-14. 23-24

℞. (24) Guide me, Lord, along the everlasting way.

O Lord, you have probed me and you know me;
    you know when I sit and when I stand;
    you understand my thoughts from afar.
My journeys and my rest you scrutinize,
    with all my ways you are familiar.

℞. Guide me, Lord, along the everlasting way.

Truly you have formed my inmost being;
    you knit me in my mother's womb.
I give you thanks that I am fearfully, wonder-
        fully made;
    wonderful are your works.

℞. Guide me, Lord, along the everlasting way.

Probe me, O God, and know my heart;
    try me, and know my thoughts;
See if my way is crooked,
    and lead me in the way of old.

℞. Guide me, Lord, along the everlasting way.

Years I and II

GOSPEL   Lk 6, 27-38
Alleluia

See no. 509.

✠ **A reading from the holy gospel according
to Luke**

Be merciful, as your Father is merciful.

Jesus said to his disciples: "To you who hear
me, I say: Love your enemies, do good to
those who hate you; bless those who curse you
and pray for those who maltreat you. When
someone slaps you on one cheek, turn and
give him the other; when someone takes your
coat, let him have your shirt as well. Give to
all who beg from you. When a man takes what
is yours, do not demand it back. Do to others

what you would have them do to you. If you love those who love you, what credit is that to you? Even sinners love those who love them. If you do good to those who do good to you, how can you claim any credit? Sinners do as much. If you lend to those from whom you expect repayment, what merit is there in it for you? Even sinners lend to sinners, expecting to be repaid in full.

"Love your enemy and do good; lend without expecting repayment. Then will your recompense be great. You will rightly be called sons of the Most High, since he himself is good to the ungrateful and the wicked.

"Be compassionate, as your Father is compassionate. Do not judge, and you will not be judged. Do not condemn, and you will not be condemned. Pardon, and you shall be pardoned. Give, and it shall be given to you. Good measure pressed down, shaken together, running over, will they pour into the fold of your garment. For the measure you measure with will be measured back to you."

This is the gospel of the Lord.

---

441   **FRIDAY OF THE
TWENTY-THIRD WEEK
OF THE YEAR**

Year I

READING I   1 Tm 1, 1-2. 12-14

The beginning of the first letter of Paul to Timothy

I used to be a blasphemer, but the mercy of God was shown me.

Paul, an apostle of Christ Jesus by command of God our savior and Christ Jesus our hope, to Timothy, my own true child in faith. May grace, mercy and peace be yours from God the Father and Christ Jesus our Lord.

I thank Christ Jesus our Lord, who has strengthened me, that he has made me his servant and judged me faithful. I was once a blasphemer, a persecutor, a man filled with arrogance but because I did not know what I was doing in my unbelief, I have been treated mercifully, and the grace of our Lord has been

granted me in overflowing measure, along with the faith and love which are in Christ Jesus.

This is the Word of the Lord.

Responsorial Psalm   Ps 16, 1-2. 5. 7-8. 11

℟. (5) You are my inheritance, O Lord.
**Keep me, O God, for in you I take refuge;
I say to the Lord, "My Lord are you."
O Lord, my allotted portion and my cup,
you it is who hold fast my lot.**
℟. You are my inheritance, O Lord.
**I bless the Lord who counsels me;
even in the night my heart exhorts me.
I set the Lord ever before me;
with him at my right hand I shall not be
disturbed.**
℟. You are my inheritance, O Lord.
**You will show me the path to life,
fullness of joys in your presence,
the delights at your right hand forever.**
℟. You are my inheritance, O Lord.

Year II

READING I   1 Cor 9, 16-19. 22-27

A reading from the first letter of Paul to the Corinthians

I made myself all things to all men, to save some at any cost.

Preaching the gospel is not the subject of a boast; I am under compulsion and have no choice. I am ruined if I do not preach it! If I do it willingly, I have my recompense; if unwillingly, I am nonetheless entrusted with a charge. And this recompense of mine? It is simply this, that when preaching I offer the gospel free of charge and do not make full use of the authority the gospel gives me.

Although I am not bound to anyone, I made myself the slave of all so as to win over as many as possible. To the weak I became a weak person with a view to winning the weak. I have made myself all things to all men in order to save at least some of them. In fact, I do all that I do for the sake of the gospel in the hope of having a share in its blessings.

You know that while all the runners in the

stadium take part in the race, the award goes to one man. In that case, run so as to win! Athletes deny themselves all sorts of things. They do this to win a crown of leaves that withers, but we, a crown that is imperishable.

I do not run like a man who loses sight of the finish line. I do not fight as if I were shadowboxing. What I do is discipline my own body and master it, for fear that after having preached to others I myself should be rejected. **This is the Word of the Lord.**

Responsorial Psalm   Ps 84, 3. 4. 5-6. 8. 12

℟. (2) How lovely is your dwelling-place,
   Lord, mighty God!
My soul yearns and pines
   for the courts of the Lord.
My heart and my flesh
   cry out for the living God.
℟. How lovely is your dwelling-place,
   Lord, mighty God!

Even the sparrow finds a home,
   and the swallow a nest
   in which she puts her young—
Your altars, O Lord of hosts,
   my king and my God!
℟. How lovely is your dwelling-place,
   Lord, mighty God!

Happy they who dwell in your house!
   continually they praise you.
Happy the men whose strength you are!
They go from strength to strength.
℟. How lovely is your dwelling-place,
   Lord, mighty God!

For a sun and a shield is the Lord God;
   grace and glory he bestows;
The Lord withholds no good thing
   from those who walk in sincerity.
℟. How lovely is your dwelling-place,
   Lord, mighty God!

Years I and II

GOSPEL   Lk 6, 39-42
Alleluia

See no. 509.

✠ **A reading from the holy gospel according to Luke**

Can a blind man lead the blind?

Jesus used images in speaking to his disciples: "Can a blind man act as guide to a blind man? Will they not both fall into a ditch? A student is not above his teacher; but every student when he has finished his studies will be on a par with his teacher.

"Why look at the speck in your brother's eye when you miss the plank in your own? How can you say to your brother, 'Brother, let me remove the speck from your eye,' yet fail yourself to see the plank lodged in your own? Hypocrite, remove the plank from your own eye first; then you will see clearly enough to remove the speck from your brother's eye." **This is the gospel of the Lord.**

---

442   **SATURDAY OF THE**
           TWENTY-THIRD WEEK
           OF THE YEAR

Year I

READING I   1 Tm 1, 15-17

A reading from the first letter of Paul to Timothy

He came into the world to save sinners.

You can depend on this as worthy of full acceptance: that Christ Jesus came into the world to save sinners. Of these I myself am the worst. But on that very account I was dealt with more mercifully, so that in me, as an extreme case, Jesus Christ might display all his patience, and that I might become an example to those who would later have faith in him and gain everlasting life. To the King of ages, the immortal, the invisible, the only God, be honor and glory forever and ever! Amen.

This is the Word of the Lord.

Responsorial Psalm   Ps 113, 1-2. 3-4. 5. 6-7

℟. (2) Blessed be the name of the Lord for ever.

Praise, you servants of the Lord,
  praise the name of the Lord.
Blessed be the name of the Lord
  both now and forever.
R̷. Blessed be the name of the Lord for ever.
From the rising to the setting of the sun
  is the name of the Lord to be praised.
High above all nations is the Lord;
  above the heavens is his glory.
R̷. Blessed be the name of the Lord for ever.
Who is like the Lord, our God, who is en-
  throned on high
  and looks upon the heavens and the earth
  below?
He raises up the lowly from the dust;
  from the dunghill he lifts up the poor.
R̷. Blessed be the name of the Lord for ever.
R̷. Or: Alleluia.

Year II

READING I   1 Cor 10, 14-22
**A reading from the first letter of Paul to the
  Corinthians**
Though there are many of us, we are one body, because we
share in this one bread.
I am telling you, whom I love, to shun the
worship of idols, and I address you as one
addresses sensible people. You may judge for
yourselves what I am saying. Is not the cup of
blessing we bless a sharing in the blood of
Christ? And is not the bread we break a sharing
in the body of Christ? Because the loaf of bread
is one, we, many though we are, are one body,
for we all partake of the one loaf. Look at Israel
according to the flesh and see if those who eat
the sacrifices do not share in the altar!
  What am I saying—that meat offered to an
idol is really offered to that idol, or that an
idol is a reality? No, I mean that the Gentiles
sacrifice to demons and not to God, and I do
not want you to become sharers with demons.
You cannot drink the cup of the Lord and also
the cup of demons. You cannot partake of the
table of the Lord and likewise the table of
demons. Do we mean to provoke the Lord to
jealous anger? Surely we are not stronger than
he!
  This is the Word of the Lord.

Responsorial Psalm   Ps 116, 12-13. 17-18
R̷. (17) To you, Lord, I will offer a sacrifice
  of praise.
How shall I make a return to the Lord
  for all the good he has done for me?
The cup of salvation I will take up,
  and I will call upon the name of the Lord.
R̷. To you, Lord, I will offer a sacrifice of
  praise.
To you will I offer sacrifice of thanksgiving,
  and I will call upon the name of the Lord.
My vows to the Lord I will pay
  in the presence of all his people.
R̷. To you, Lord, I will offer a sacrifice of
  praise.

Years I and II

GOSPEL   Lk 6, 43-49
Alleluia
See no. 509.

✠ **A reading from the holy gospel according
  to Luke**
Why do you call me Lord, Lord, and not do what I say?
Jesus said to his disciples: "A good tree does
not produce decayed fruit any more than a decayed tree produces good fruit. Each tree is
known by its yield. Figs are not taken from
thornbushes, nor grapes picked from brambles.
A good man produces goodness from the good
in his heart; an evil man produces evil out of
his store of evil. Each man speaks from his
heart's abundance. Why do you call me 'Lord,
Lord,' and not put into practice what I teach
you? Any man who desires to come to me will
hear my words and put them into practice. I
will show you with whom he is to be compared. He may be likened to the man who, in
building a house, dug deeply and laid the foundation on a rock. When the floods came the
torrent rushed in on that house, but failed
to shake it because of its solid foundation. On
the other hand, anyone who has heard my
words but not put them into practice is like the
man who built his house on the ground without
any foundation. When the torrent rushed upon
it, it immediately fell in and was completely
destroyed."
  This is the gospel of the Lord.

443 **MONDAY OF THE**
TWENTY-FOURTH WEEK
OF THE YEAR

Year I

READING I   1 Tm 2, 1-8

**A reading from the first letter of Paul to
Timothy**

There should be prayers offered to God for everyone; he
wants everyone to be saved.

First of all, I urge that petitions, prayers, intercessions, and thanksgivings be offered for all
men, especially for kings and those in authority, that we may be able to lead undisturbed and tranquil lives in perfect piety and
dignity. Prayer of this kind is good, and God
our savior is pleased with it, for he wants all
men to be saved and come to know the truth.
And the truth is this:
  "God is one.
One also is the mediator between God and
    men,
  the man Christ Jesus,
    who gave himself as a ransom for all."
This truth was attested at the fitting time. I
have been made its herald and apostle (believe
me, I am not lying but speak the truth), the
teacher of the nations in the true faith.
    It is my wish, then, that in every place the
men shall offer prayers with blameless hands
held aloft, and be free from anger and dissension.
            This is the Word of the Lord.

Responsorial Psalm   Ps 28, 2. 7. 8-9

℟. (6) Blest be the Lord for he has heard my
    prayer.
**Hear the sound of my pleading, when I cry to
    you,**
  lifting up my hands toward your holy shrine.
℟. Blest be the Lord for he has heard my
    prayer.
The Lord is my strength and my shield.
  In him my heart trusts, and I find help;
**Then my heart exults, and with my song I give
    him thanks.**

℟. Blest be the Lord for he has heard my
    prayer.
The Lord is the strength of his people,
  the saving refuge of his anointed.
Save your people, and bless your inheritance;
  feed them, and carry them forever!
℟. Blest be the Lord for he has heard my
    prayer.

Year II

READING I   1 Cor 11, 17-26. 33

**A reading from the first letter of Paul to the
Corinthians**

If there are factions among you, it is not the Lord's supper
that you eat.

What I now have to say is not said in praise,
because your meetings are not profitable but
harmful. First of all, I hear that when you
gather for a meeting there are divisions among
you, and I am inclined to believe it. There may
even have to be factions among you for the
tried and true to stand out clearly. When you
assemble it is not to eat the Lord's Supper, for
everyone is in haste to eat his own supper.
One person goes hungry while another gets
drunk. Do you not have homes where you can
eat and drink? Would you show contempt for
the church of God, and embarrass those who
have nothing? What can I say to you? Shall I
praise you? Certainly not in this matter!
    I received from the Lord what I handed on to
you, namely, that the Lord Jesus on the night
in which he was betrayed took bread, and after
he had given thanks, broke it and said, "This
is my body, which is for you. Do this in remembrance of me." In the same way, after the supper, he took the cup, saying, "This cup is the
new covenant in my blood. Do this, whenever
you drink it, in remembrance of me." Every
time, then, you eat this bread and drink this
cup, you proclaim the death of the Lord until
he comes! Therefore, my brothers, when you
assemble for the meal, wait for one another.
            This is the Word of the Lord.

Responsorial Psalm   Ps 40, 7-8. 8-9. 10. 17

℟. (1 Cor 11, 26) Proclaim the death of the
Lord until he comes again.

Sacrifice or oblation you wished not,
but ears open to obedience you gave me.
Holocausts or sin-offerings you sought not;
then said I, "Behold I come."

℟. Proclaim the death of the Lord until he
comes again.

"In the written scroll it is prescribed for me,
to do your will, O my God, is my delight,
and your law is within my heart!"

℟. Proclaim the death of the Lord until he
comes again.

I announced your justice in the vast assembly;
I did not restrain my lips, as you, O Lord,
know.

℟. Proclaim the death of the Lord until he
comes again.

But may all who seek you,
exult and be glad in you.
And may those who love your salvation
say ever, "The Lord be glorified."

℟. Proclaim the death of the Lord until he
comes again.

Years I and II

GOSPEL   Lk 7, 1-10

Alleluia

See no. 509.

✠ A reading from the holy gospel according
to Luke

Not even in Israel have I found such faith.

When Jesus had finished his discourse in the
hearing of the people, he entered Capernaum.
A centurion had a servant he held in high
regard, who was at that moment sick to the
point of death. When he heard about Jesus he
sent some Jewish elders to him, asking him to
come and save the life of his servant. Upon
approaching Jesus they petitioned him earnestly. "He deserves this favor from you," they
said, "because he loves our people, and even
built our synagogue for us." Jesus set out with
them. When he was only a short distance from
the house, the centurion sent friends to tell
him: "Sir, do not trouble yourself, for I am not
worthy to have you enter my house. That is
why I did not presume to come to you myself.
Just give the order and my servant will be
cured. I too am a man who knows the meaning
of an order, having soldiers under my command. I say to one, 'On your way,' and off he
goes; to another, 'Come here,' and he comes;
to my slave, 'Do this,' and he does it." Jesus
showed amazement on hearing this, and turned
to the crowd which was following him to say,
"I tell you, I have never found so much faith
among the Israelites." When the deputation
returned to the house, they found the servant
in perfect health.

This is the gospel of the Lord.

---

444   TUESDAY OF THE
TWENTY-FOURTH WEEK
OF THE YEAR

Year I

READING I   1 Tm 3, 1-13

A reading from the first letter of Paul to
Timothy

The bishop must be blameless; deacons also must be
conscientious believers in the mystery of the faith.

You can depend on this: whoever wants to be
a bishop aspires to a noble task. A bishop must
be irreproachable, married only once, of even
temper, self-controlled, modest, and hospitable. He should be a good teacher. He must not
be addicted to drink. He ought not to be con-
tentious but, rather, gentle, a man of peace.
Nor can he be someone who loves money. He
must be a good manager of his own household,
keeping his children under control without
sacrificing his dignity; for if a man does not
know how to manage his own house, how can
he take care of the church of God? He should
not be a new convert, lest he become conceited and thus incur the punishment once
meted out to the devil. He must also be well
thought of by those outside the church, to
ensure that he not fall into disgrace and the devil's trap. In the same way, deacons must be
serious, straightforward, and truthful. They

may not overindulge in drink, or give in to greed. They must hold fast to the divinely revealed faith with a clear conscience. They should be put on probation first; then, if there is nothing against them, they may serve as deacons. The women, similarly, should be serious, not slanderous gossips. They should be temperate and entirely trustworthy. Deacons may be married but once and must be good managers of their children and their households. Those who serve well as deacons gain a worthy place for themselves and much assurance in their faith in Christ Jesus.

This is the Word of the Lord.

Responsorial Psalm   Ps 101, 1-2. 2-3. 5. 6

℟. (2) I will walk with blameless heart.
Of kindness and judgment I will sing;
   to you, O Lord, I will sing praise.
I will persevere in the way of integrity;
   when will you come to me?
℟. I will walk with blameless heart.
I will walk in the integrity of my heart,
   within my house;
I will not set before my eyes
   any base thing.
℟. I will walk with blameless heart.
Whoever slanders his neighbor in secret,
   him will I destroy.
The man of haughty eyes and puffed-up heart
   I will not endure.
℟. I will walk with blameless heart.
My eyes are upon the faithful of the land,
   that they may dwell with me.
He who walks in the way of integrity
   shall be in my service.
℟. I will walk with blameless heart.

Year II

READING I   1 Cor 12, 12-14. 27-31

A reading from the first letter of Paul to the Corinthians

Now you together are Christ's body, but each of you is a different part of it.

The body is one and has many members, but all the members, many though they are, are one body; and so it is with Christ. It was in one

Spirit that all of us, whether Jew or Greek, slave or free, were baptized into one body. All of us have been given to drink of the one Spirit. Now the body is not one member, it is many.

You, then, are the body of Christ. Every one of you is a member of it. Furthermore, God has set up in the church first apostles, second prophets, third teachers, then miracle workers, healers, assistants, administrators, and those who speak in tongues. Are all apostles? Are all prophets? Are all teachers? Do all work miracles or have the gift of healing? Do all speak in tongues, all have the gift of interpretation of tongues? Set your hearts on the greater gifts.

This is the Word of the Lord.

Responsorial Psalm   Ps 100, 1-2. 3. 4. 5

℟. (3) We are his people:
   the sheep of his flock.
Sing joyfully to the Lord, all you lands;
   serve the Lord with gladness;
   come before him with joyful song.
Know that the Lord is God;
   he made us, his we are;
   his people, the flock he tends.
℟. We are his people:
   the sheep of his flock.
Enter his gates with thanksgiving,
   his courts with praise;
Give thanks to him; bless his name.
℟. We are his people:
   the sheep of his flock.
Give thanks to him; bless his name, for he is good:
   the Lord, whose kindness endures forever,
   and his faithfulness, to all generations.
℟. We are his people:
   the sheep of his flock.

Years I and II

GOSPEL   Lk 7, 11-17
Alleluia

See no. 509.

✠ **A reading from the holy gospel according to Luke**

Young man, I tell you, arise.

Jesus went to a town called Naim, and his disciples and a large crowd accompanied him.

As he approached the gate of the town a dead man was being carried out, the only son of a widowed mother. A considerable crowd of townsfolk were with her. The Lord was moved with pity upon seeing her and said to her, "Do not cry." Then he stepped forward and touched the litter; at this, the bearers halted. He said, "Young man, I bid you get up." The dead man sat up and began to speak. Then Jesus gave him back to his mother. Fear seized them all and they began to praise God. "A great prophet has risen among us," they said; and, "God has visited his people." This was the report that spread about him throughout Judea and the surrounding country.

This is the gospel of the Lord.

445   WEDNESDAY OF THE TWENTY-FOURTH WEEK OF THE YEAR

Year I

READING I   1 Tm 3, 14-16

A reading from the first letter of Paul to Timothy

The mystery of our religion is very deep.

Although I hope to visit you soon, I am writing you about these matters so that if I should be delayed you will know what kind of conduct befits a member of God's household, the church of the living God, the pillar and bulwark of truth. Wonderful, indeed, is the mystery of our faith, as we say in professing it:

"He was manifested in the flesh,
    vindicated in the Spirit;
Seen by the angels;
    preached among the Gentiles,
Believed in throughout the world,
    taken up into glory."

This is the Word of the Lord.

Responsorial Psalm   Ps 111, 1-2. 3-4. 5-6

℟. (2) How great are the works of the Lord!
I will give thanks to the Lord with all my heart
    in the company and assembly of the just.

Great are the works of the Lord,
    exquisite in all their delights.
℟. How great are the works of the Lord!
Majesty and glory are his work,
    and his justice endures forever.
He has won renown for his wondrous deeds;
    gracious and merciful is the Lord.
℟. How great are the works of the Lord!
He has given food to those who fear him;
    he will forever be mindful of his covenant.
He has made known to his people the power of
    his works,
    giving them the inheritance of the nations.
℟. How great are the works of the Lord!
℟. Or: Alleluia.

Year II

READING I   1 Cor 12, 31—13, 13

A reading from the first letter of Paul to the Corinthians

There are three things that last: faith, hope, and love, and the greatest of these is love.

Set your hearts on the greater gifts.
I will show you the way that surpasses all the others. If I speak with human tongues and angelic as well, but do not have love, I am a noisy gong, a clanging cymbal. If I have the gift of prophecy and, with full knowledge, comprehend all mysteries, if I have faith great enough to move mountains, but have not love, I am nothing. If I give everything I have to feed the poor and hand over my body to be burned, but have not love, I gain nothing.

Love is patient; love is kind. Love is not jealous, it does not put on airs, it is not snobbish. Love is never rude, it is not self-seeking, it is not prone to anger; neither does it brood over injuries. Love does not rejoice in what is wrong but rejoices with the truth. There is no limit to love's forbearance, to its trust, its hope, its power to endure.

Love never fails. Prophecies will cease, tongues will be silent, knowledge will pass away. Our knowledge is imperfect and our prophesying is imperfect. When the perfect comes, the imperfect will pass away. When I was a child I used to talk like a child, think like a child, reason like a child. When I became a man I put childish ways aside. Now we see indistinctly, as in a mirror; then we shall see face to face. My knowledge is imperfect now; then I shall know even as I am known. There are in the end three things that last: faith, hope, and love, and the greatest of these is love.

This is the Word of the Lord.

Responsorial Psalm   Ps 33, 2-3. 4-5. 12. 22

℞. (12) Happy the people the Lord has chosen to be his own.

Give thanks to the Lord on the harp;
　with the ten-stringed lyre chant his praises.
Sing to him a new song;
　pluck the strings skillfully, with shouts of
　gladness.

℞. Happy the people the Lord has chosen to be his own.

For upright is the word of the Lord,
　and all his works are trustworthy.
He loves justice and right;
　of the kindness of the Lord the earth is full.

℞. Happy the people the Lord has chosen to be his own.

Happy the nation whose God is the Lord,
　the people he has chosen for his own inheritance.
May your kindness, O Lord, be upon us
　who have put our hope in you.

℞. Happy the people the Lord has chosen to be his own.

GOSPEL

Years I and II

Alleluia   Lk 7, 31-35

See no. 509.

✠ A reading from the holy gospel according to Luke

We played the pipes for you, and you wouldn't dance; we sang dirges, and you wouldn't cry.

Jesus said: "What comparison can I use for the men of today? What are they like? They are like children squatting in the city squares and calling to their playmates,

　'We piped you a tune but you did not dance,
　We sang you a dirge but you did not wail.'

I mean that John the Baptizer came neither eating bread nor drinking wine, and you say, 'He is mad!' The Son of Man came and he both ate and drank, and you say, 'Here is a glutton and a drunkard, a friend of tax collectors and sinners!' God's wisdom is vindicated by all who accept it."

This is the gospel of the Lord.

446　**THURSDAY OF THE TWENTY-FOURTH WEEK OF THE YEAR**

Year I

READING I   1 Tm 4, 12-16

A reading from the first letter of Paul to Timothy

Take care about what you do and teach; in this way you will save both yourself and those who listen to you.

Let no one look down on you because of your youth, but be a continuing example of love, faith and purity to believers. Until I arrive, devote yourself to the reading of Scripture, to preaching and teaching. Do not neglect the gift you received when, as a result of prophecy, the presbyters laid their hands on you. Attend to your duties; let them absorb you, so that everyone may see your progress. Watch yourself and watch your teaching. Persevere at both tasks. By doing so you will bring to salvation yourself and all who hear you.

This is the Word of the Lord.

Responsorial Psalm   Ps 111, 7-8. 9. 10

℞. (2) How great are the works of the Lord!
The works of his hands are faithful and just;
　sure are all his precepts,
Reliable forever and ever,
　wrought in truth and equity.

℞. How great are the works of the Lord!
He has sent deliverance to his people;
　he has ratified his covenant forever;
　holy and awesome is his name.

℞. How great are the works of the Lord!
The fear of the Lord is the beginning of wisdom;

prudent are all who live by it.
His praise endures forever.
℟. How great are the works of the Lord!
℟. Or: Alleluia.

READING I   1 Cor 15, 1-11

A reading from the first letter of Paul to the Corinthians

We preached and this is what you believed.

Brothers, I want to remind you of the gospel I preached to you, which you received and in which you stand firm. You are being saved by it at this very moment if you retain it as I preached it to you. Otherwise you have believed in vain. I handed on to you first of all what I myself received, that Christ died for our sins in accord with the Scriptures; that he was buried and, in accord with the Scriptures, rose on the third day; that he was seen by Cephas, then by the Twelve. After that he was seen by five hundred brothers at once, most of whom are still alive, although some have fallen asleep. Next he was seen by James; then by all the apostles. Last of all he was seen by me, as one born out of the normal course. I am the least of the apostles; in fact, because I persecuted the church of God, I do not even deserve the name. But by God's favor I am what I am. This favor of his to me has not proved fruitless. Indeed, I have worked harder than all the others, not on my own but through the favor of God. In any case, whether it be I or they, this is what we preach and this is what you believed.

          This is the Word of the Lord.

Responsorial Psalm   Ps 118, 1-2. 16-17. 28

℟. (1) Give thanks to the Lord, for he is good.
Give thanks to the Lord, for he is good,
    for his mercy endures forever.
Let the house of Israel say,
    "His mercy endures forever."
℟. Give thanks to the Lord, for he is good.
"The right hand of the Lord is exalted;
    the right hand of the Lord has struck with
    power."

I shall not die, but live,
    and declare the works of the Lord.
℟. Give thanks to the Lord, for he is good.
You are my God, and I give thanks to you;
    O my God, I extol you.
I give thanks to you because you heard me,
    and you have been my savior.
℟. Give thanks to the Lord, for he is good.
℟. Or: Alleluia.

GOSPEL   Lk 7, 36-50
Alleluia

See no. 509.

✠ **A reading from the holy gospel according to Luke**

Her many sins must have been forgiven her, because she loved much.

There was a certain Pharisee who invited Jesus to dine with him. Jesus went to the Pharisee's home and reclined to eat. A woman known in the town to be a sinner learned that he was dining in the Pharisee's home. She brought in a vase of perfumed oil and stood behind him at his feet, weeping so that her tears fell upon his feet. Then she wiped them with her hair, kissing them and perfuming them with the oil. When his host, the Pharisee, saw this, he said to himself, "If this man were a prophet, he would know who and what sort of woman this is that touches him—that she is a sinner." In answer to his thoughts, Jesus said to him, "Simon, I have something to propose to you." "Teacher," he said, "speak."

"Two men owed money to a certain money-lender; one owed a total of five hundred coins, the other fifty. Since neither was able to repay, he wrote off both debts. Which of them was more grateful to him?" Simon answered, "He, I presume, to whom he remitted the larger sum." Jesus said to him, "You are right."

Turning then to the woman, he said to Simon: "You see this woman? I came to your home and you provided me with no water for my feet. She has washed my feet with her tears and wiped them with her hair. You gave me no kiss, but she has not ceased kissing my feet since I entered. You did not anoint my head with oil, but she has anointed my feet with perfume. I tell you, that is why her many sins are forgiven—because of her great love. Little is forgiven the one whose love is small."

He said to her then, "Your sins are forgiven," at which his fellow guests began to ask among themselves, "Who is this that he even forgives sin?" Meanwhile he said to the woman, "Your faith has been your salvation. Now go in peace."

This is the gospel of the Lord.

---

447   **FRIDAY OF THE TWENTY-FOURTH WEEK OF THE YEAR**

Year I

READING I   1 Tm 6, 2-12

A reading from the first letter of Paul to Timothy

As a man dedicated to God, you must be just.

These are the things you must teach and preach. Whoever teaches in any other way, not holding to the sound doctrines of our Lord Jesus Christ and the teaching proper to true religion, should be recognized as both conceited and ignorant, a sick man in his passion for polemics and controversy. From these come envy, dissension, slander, evil suspicions—in a word, the bickering of men with twisted minds who have lost all sense of truth. Such men value religion only as a means of personal gain. There is, of course, great gain in religion—provided one is content with a sufficiency. We brought nothing into this world, nor have we the power to take anything out. If we have food and clothing we have all that we need. Those who want to be rich are falling into temptation, and a trap. They are letting themselves be captured by foolish and harmful desires which draw men down to ruin and destruction. The love of money is the root of all evil. Some men in their passion for it have strayed from the faith and have come to grief amid great pain.

Man of God that you are, flee from all this Instead, seek after integrity, piety, faith, love, steadfastness, and a gentle spirit. Fight the good fight of faith. Take firm hold on the everlasting life to which you were called when, in the presence of many witnesses, you made your profession of faith.

This is the Word of the Lord.

Responsorial Psalm   Ps 49, 6-7. 8-10. 17-18. 19-20

℞. (Mt 5, 3) Happy the poor in spirit;
the kingdom of heaven is theirs!

Why should I fear in evil days
when my wicked ensnarers ring me round?
They trust in their wealth;
the abundance of their riches is their boast.

℞. Happy the poor in spirit;
the kingdom of heaven is theirs!

Yet in no way can a man redeem himself,
or pay his own ransom to God;
Too high is the price to redeem one's life; he
would never have enough
to remain alive always and not see destruction.

℞. Happy the poor in spirit;
the kingdom of heaven is theirs!

Fear not when a man grows rich,
when the wealth of his house becomes great,
For when he dies, he shall take none of it;
his wealth shall not follow him down.

℞. Happy the poor in spirit;
the kingdom of heaven is theirs!

Though in his lifetime he counted himself
blessed,
"They will praise you for doing well for
yourself,"
He shall join the circle of his forebears
who shall never more see light.

℞. Happy the poor in spirit;
the kingdom of heaven is theirs!

Year II

READING I   1 Cor 15, 12-20

A reading from the first letter of Paul to the Corinthians

If Christ has not risen, your faith is in vain.

If Christ is preached as raised from the dead, how is it that some of you say there is no resurrection of the dead? If there is no resurrection of the dead, Christ himself has not been raised. And if Christ has not been raised, our preaching is void of content and your faith is empty too. Indeed, we should then be exposed as false witnesses of God, for we have borne witness before him that he raised up Christ; but he certainly did not raise him up if the dead are not raised. Why? Because if the dead are not raised, then Christ was not raised; and if Christ was not raised, your faith is worthless. You are still in your sins, and those who have fallen asleep in Christ are the deadest of the dead. If our hopes in Christ are limited to this life only, we are the most pitiable of men.

But as it is, Christ has been raised from the dead, the first fruits of those who have fallen asleep.

This is the Word of the Lord.

Responsorial Psalm   Ps 17, 1. 6-7. 8. 15

℟. (15) Lord, when your glory appears,
    my joy will be full.
Hear, O Lord, a just suit;
    attend to my outcry;
    hearken to my prayer from lips without
    deceit.
℟. Lord, when your glory appears,
    my joy will be full.
I call upon you, for you will answer me, O God;
    incline your ear to me; hear my word.
Show your wondrous kindness,
    O savior of those who hope in you.
℟. Lord, when your glory appears,
    my joy will be full.
Hide me in the shadow of your wings
    but I in justice shall behold your face;
    on waking, I shall be content in your presence.
℟. Lord, when your glory appears,
    my joy will be full.

Years I and II

GOSPEL   Lk 8, 1-3
Alleluia

See no. 509.

✠ **A reading from the holy gospel according to Luke**

There were women with them who provided for them out of their own resources.

Jesus journeyed through towns and villages preaching and proclaiming the good news of the kingdom of God. The Twelve accompanied him, and also some women who had been cured of evil spirits and maladies: Mary called the Magdalene, from whom seven devils had gone out, Joanna, the wife of Herod's steward Chuza, Susanna, and many others who were assisting them out of their means.

This is the gospel of the Lord.

---

448   **SATURDAY OF THE
            TWENTY-FOURTH WEEK
            OF THE YEAR**

Year I

READING I   1 Tm 6, 13-16
A reading from the first letter of Paul to Timothy

Do all that you have been told until the appearance of our Lord Jesus Christ.

Before God, who gives life to all, and before Christ Jesus, who in bearing witness made his noble profession before Pontius Pilate, I charge you to keep God's command without blame or reproach until our Lord Jesus Christ shall appear. This appearance God will bring to pass at his chosen time. He is the blessed and only ruler, the King of kings and Lord of lords who alone has immortality and who dwells in inapproachable light, whom no human being has ever seen or can see. To him be honor and everlasting rule! Amen.

This is the Word of the Lord.

Responsorial Psalm   Ps 100, 2. 3. 4. 5

℟. (2) Come with joy into the presence of the Lord.
Serve the Lord with gladness;
    come before him with joyful song.
℟. Come with joy into the presence of the Lord.

Know that the Lord is God;
   he made us, his we are;
   his people, the flock he tends.
℟. Come with joy into the presence of the
   Lord.
Enter his gates with thanksgiving,
   his courts with praise;
Give thanks to him; bless his name.
℟. Come with joy into the presence of the
   Lord.
For he is good:
   the Lord, whose kindness endures forever,
   and his faithfulness, to all generations.
℟. Come with joy into the presence of the
   Lord.

Year II

READING I   1 Cor 15, 35-37. 42-49
**A reading from the first letter of Paul to the
                Corinthians**
What is sown is perishable, but what is raised is imperishable.

Perhaps someone will say, "How are the dead
to be raised up? What kind of body will they
have?" A nonsensical question! The seed you
sow does not germinate unless it dies. When
you sow, you do not sow the full-blown plant,
but a kernel of wheat or some other grain. So
is it with the resurrection of the dead. What is
sown in the earth is subject to decay, what
rises is incorruptible. What is sown is ignoble,
what rises is glorious. Weakness is sown,
strength rises up. A natural body is put down
and a spiritual body comes up.
   If there is a natural body, be sure there is
also a spiritual body. Scripture has it that
Adam, the first man, became a living soul; the
last Adam has become a life-giving spirit. Take
note the spiritual was not first; first came
the natural and after that the spiritual. The
first man was of earth formed from dust, the
second is from heaven. Earthly men are like
the man of earth, heavenly men are like the
man of heaven. Just as we resemble the man
from earth, so shall we bear the likeness of
the man from heaven.
                    This is the Word of the Lord.

Responsorial Psalm   Ps 56, 10-12. 13-14
℟. (14) I will walk in the presence of God,
   with the light of the living.
Now I know that God is with me.
   In God, in whose promise I glory,
In God I trust without fear;
   what can flesh do against me?
℟. I will walk in the presence of God,
   with the light of the living.
I am bound, O God, by vows to you;
   your thank offerings I will fulfill.
For you have rescued me from death,
   my feet, too, from stumbling;
   that I may walk before God in the light of the
      living.
℟. I will walk in the presence of God,
   with the light of the living.

Years I and II

GOSPEL   Lk 8, 4-15
Alleluia
See no. 509.

✠ **A reading from the holy gospel according
                to Luke**
As for the seed in good ground, this is the people who have
heard the word and take it to themselves and yield a
harvest through their perseverance.

A large crowd was gathering, with people
resorting to Jesus from one town after another.
He spoke to them in a parable: "A farmer went
out to sow some seed. In the sowing, some fell
on the footpath where it was walked on and
the birds of the air ate it up. Some fell on rocky
ground, sprouted up, then withered through
lack of moisture. Some fell among briers, and
the thorns growing up with it stifled it. But
some fell on good soil, grew up, and yielded
grain a hundred-fold."
   As he said this he exclaimed: "Let everyone
who has ears attend to what he has heard."
His disciples began asking him what the meaning of this parable might be. He replied, "To
you the mysteries of the reign of God have
been confided, but to the rest in parables that,
   'Seeing they may not perceive,
      and hearing they may not understand.'
This is the meaning of the parable. The seed
is the word of God. Those on the footpath are

people who hear, but the devil comes and takes the word out of their hearts lest they believe and be saved. Those on the rocky ground are the ones who, when they hear the word, receive it with joy. They have no root; they believe for a while, but fall away in time of temptation. The seed fallen among briers are those who hear, but their progress is stifled by the cares and riches and pleasures of life and they do not mature. The seed on good ground are those who hear the word in a spirit of openness, retain it, and bear fruit through perseverance.''

This is the gospel of the Lord.

---

449 **MONDAY OF THE TWENTY-FIFTH WEEK OF THE YEAR**

Year I

READING I Ezr 1, 1-6

The beginning of the book of Ezra

These are the people of the Lord who went to Jerusalem to build the temple of the Lord God.

In the first year of Cyrus, king of Persia, in order to fulfill the word of the Lord spoken by Jeremiah, the Lord inspired King Cyrus of Persia to issue this proclamation throughout his kingdom, both by word of mouth and in writing: "Thus says Cyrus, king of Persia: 'All the kingdoms of the earth the Lord, the God of heaven, has given to me, and he has also charged me to build him a house in Jerusalem, which is in Judah. Whoever, therefore, among you belongs to any part of his people, let him go up, and may his God be with him! Let everyone who has survived, in whatever place he may have dwelt, be assisted by the people of that place with silver, gold, goods, and cattle, together with free-will offerings for the house of God in Jerusalem.' "

Then the family heads of Judah and Benjamin and the priests and Levites—everyone, that is, whom God had inspired to do so—prepared to go up to build the house of the Lord in Jerusalem. All their neighbors gave them help in every way, with silver, gold, goods, and cattle, and with many precious gifts besides all their free-will offerings.

This is the Word of the Lord.

Responsorial Psalm Ps 126, 1-2. 2-3. 4-5. 6

℟. (3) The Lord has done marvels for us.

When the Lord brought back the captives of Zion,
  we were like men dreaming.
Then our mouth was filled with laughter,
  and our tongue with rejoicing.

℟. The Lord has done marvels for us.

Then they said among the nations,
  "The Lord has done great things for them."
The Lord has done great things for us;
  we are glad indeed.

℟. The Lord has done marvels for us.

Restore our fortunes, O Lord,
  like the torrents in the southern desert.
Those that sow in tears
  shall reap rejoicing.

℟. The Lord has done marvels for us.

Although they go forth weeping,
  carrying the seed to be sown,
They shall come back rejoicing,
  carrying their sheaves.

℟. The Lord has done marvels for us.

Year II

READING I Prv 3, 27-34

A reading from the book of Proverbs

The Lord God's curse lies on the house of the wicked.

Refuse no one the good on which he has a claim
  when it is in your power to do it for him.
Say not to your neighbor, "Go, and come again,
  tomorrow I will give," when you can give at once.

Plot no evil against your neighbor,
  against him who lives at peace with you.
Quarrel not with a man without cause,
  with one who has done you no harm.

Envy not the lawless man
  and choose none of his ways:
To the Lord the perverse man is an abomination,
  but with the upright is his friendship.

The curse of the Lord is on the house of the
wicked,
but the dwelling of the just he blesses;
When he is dealing with the arrogant, he is
stern,
but to the humble he shows kindness.
This is the Word of the Lord.

Responsorial Psalm Ps 15, 2-3. 3-4. 5

℟. (1) He who does justice shall live on the
Lord's holy mountain.

He who walks blamelessly and does justice;
who thinks the truth in his heart
and slanders not with his tongue;

℟. He who does justice shall live on the Lord's
holy mountain.

Who harms not his fellow man,
nor takes up a reproach against his neighbor;
By whom the reprobate is despised,
while he honors those who fear the Lord;

℟. He who does justice shall live on the Lord's
holy mountain.

Who lends not his money at usury
and accepts no bribe against the innocent.
He who does these things
shall never be disturbed.

℟. He who does justice shall live on the Lord's
holy mountain.

Years I and II

GOSPEL Lk 8, 16-18

Alleluia

See no. 509.

✠ A reading from the holy gospel according
to Luke

Place your light on a stand so that the people may see it
when they enter.

Jesus said to the crowds: "No one lights a lamp
and puts it under a bushel basket or under a
bed; he puts it on a lampstand so that whoever
comes in can see it. There is nothing hidden
that will not be exposed, nothing concealed
that will not be known and brought to light.
Take heed, therefore, how you hear: to the man
who has, more will be given; and he who has
not, will lose even the little he thinks he has."
This is the gospel of the Lord.

450 **TUESDAY OF THE
TWENTY-FIFTH WEEK
OF THE YEAR**

Year I

READING I Ezr 6, 7-8. 12. 14-20

A reading from the book of Ezra

They completed the temple of God, and ate the passover.

King Darius issued an order to the officials of
West-of-Euphrates: "Let the governor and the
elders of the Jews continue the work on that
house of God; they are to rebuild it on its
former site. I also issue this decree concerning
your dealing with these elders of the Jews in
the rebuilding of that house of God: From the
royal revenue, the taxes of West-of-Euphrates,
let these men be repaid for their expenses, in
full and without delay. I, Darius, have issued
this decree; let it be carefully executed."

The elders of the Jews continued to make
progress in the building, supported by the message of the prophets, Haggai and Zechariah,
son of Iddo. They finished the building according to the command of the God of Israel
and the decrees of Cyrus and Darius [and of
Artaxerxes, king of Persia]. They completed
this house on the third day of the month Adar,
in the sixth year of the reign of King Darius.
The Israelites—priests, Levites, and the other
returned exiles—celebrated the dedication of
this house of God with joy. For the dedication
of this house of God, they offered one hundred
bulls, two hundred rams, and four hundred
lambs, together with twelve he-goats as a sin-
offering for all Israel, in keeping with the
number of the tribes of Israel. Finally, they set
up the priests in their classes and the Levites
in their divisions for the service of God in Jerusalem, as is prescribed in the book of Moses.

The exiles kept the Passover on the fourteenth day of the first month. The Levites,
every one of whom had purified himself for the
occasion, sacrificed the Passover for the rest
of the exiles, for their brethren the priests, and
for themselves.
This is the Word of the Lord.

Responsorial Psalm   Ps 122, 1-2. 3-4. 4-5

℟. (1) I rejoiced when I heard them say:
  let us go to the house of the Lord.

I rejoiced because they said to me,
  "We will go up to the house of the Lord."
And now we have set foot
  within your gates, O Jerusalem—

℟. I rejoiced when I heard them say:
  let us go to the house of the Lord.

Jerusalem, built as a city
  with compact unity.
To it the tribes go up,
  the tribes of the Lord,

℟. I rejoiced when I heard them say:
  let us go to the house of the Lord.

According to the decree for Israel,
  to give thanks to the name of the Lord.
In it are set up judgment seats,
  seats for the house of David.

℟. I rejoiced when I heard them say:
  let us go to the house of the Lord.

Year II

READING I   Prv 21, 1-6. 10-13

A reading from the book of Proverbs
The Lord looks to the heart.

Like a stream is the king's heart in the hand of
  the Lord;
  wherever it pleases him, he directs it.

All the ways of a man may be right in his own
  eyes,
  but it is the Lord who proves hearts.

To do what is right and just
  is more acceptable to the Lord than sacrifice.

Haughty eyes and a proud heart—
  the tillage of the wicked is sin.

The plans of the diligent are sure of profit,
  but all rash haste leads certainly to poverty.

He who makes a fortune by a lying tongue
  is chasing a bubble over deadly snares.

The soul of the wicked man desires evil;
  his neighbor finds no pity in his eyes.

When the arrogant man is punished, the simple
  are the wiser;
  when the wise man is instructed, he gains
  knowledge.

The just man appraises the house of the
  wicked:
  there is one who brings down the wicked to
  ruin.

He who shuts his ear to the cry of the poor
  will himself also call and not be heard.
  This is the Word of the Lord.

Responsorial Psalm   Ps 119, 1. 27. 30. 34. 35. 44

℟. (35) Guide me, Lord, in the way of your
  commands.

Happy are they whose way is blameless,
  who walk in the law of the Lord.

℟. Guide me, Lord, in the way of your commands.

Make me understand the way of your precepts,
  and I will meditate on your wondrous deeds.

℟. Guide me, Lord, in the way of your commands.

The way of truth I have chosen;
  I have set your ordinances before me.

℟. Guide me, Lord, in the way of your commands.

Give me discernment, that I may observe your
  law
  and keep it with all my heart.

℟. Guide me, Lord, in the way of your commands.

Lead me in the path of your commands,
  for in it I delight.

℟. Guide me, Lord, in the way of your commands.

And I will keep your law continually,
  forever and ever.

℟. Guide me, Lord, in the way of your commands.

Years I and II

GOSPEL   Lk 8, 19-21
Alleluia

See no. 509.

✠ **A reading from the holy gospel according to Luke**

My mother and my brothers are those who hear the word of God and put it into practice.

The mother and brothers of Jesus came to be with him, but they could not reach him because of the crowd. He was informed, "Your mother and your brothers are standing outside and wish to see you." He told them in reply, "My mother and my brothers are those who hear the word of God and act upon it."

This is the gospel of the Lord.

---

451 WEDNESDAY OF THE TWENTY-FIFTH WEEK OF THE YEAR

Year I

READING I Ezr 9, 5-9

A reading from the book of Ezra

Our God has not forgotten us in our slavery.

At the time of the evening sacrifice, I Ezra rose in my wretchedness, and with cloak and mantle torn I fell on my knees, stretching out my hands to the Lord my God.

I said: "My God, I am too ashamed and confounded to raise my face to you, O my God, for our wicked deeds are heaped up above our heads and our guilt reaches up to heaven. From the time of our fathers even to this day great has been our guilt, and for our wicked deeds we have been delivered over, we and our kings and our priests, to the will of the kings of foreign lands, to the sword, to captivity, to pillage, and to disgrace, as is the case today.

"And now, but a short time ago, mercy came to us from the Lord our God, who left us a remnant and gave us a stake in his holy place; thus our God has brightened our eyes and given us relief in our servitude. For slaves we are, but in our servitude our God has not abandoned us; rather, he has turned the good will of the kings of Persia toward us. Thus he has given us new life to raise again the house of our God and restore its ruins, and has granted us a fence in Judah and Jerusalem."

This is the Word of the Lord.

Responsorial Psalm Tb 13, 2. 3-4. 6. 7-8. 6

℟. (1) Blessed be God, who lives for ever.

He scourges and then has mercy;
   he casts down to the depths of the nether world,
   and he brings up from the great abyss.
No one can escape his hand.

℟. Blessed be God, who lives for ever.

For though he has scattered you among the Gentiles,
   he has shown you his greatness even there.
Exalt him before every living being,
   because he is the Lord our God,
   our Father and God forever.

℟. Blessed be God, who lives for ever.

So now consider what he has done for you,
   and praise him with full voice.
Bless the Lord of righteousness,
   and exalt the King of ages.

℟. Blessed be God, who lives for ever.

As for me, I exalt my God,
   and my spirit rejoices in the King of heaven.
Let all men speak of his majesty,
   and sing his praises in Jerusalem.

℟. Blessed be God, who lives for ever.

Turn back, you sinners! do the right before him:
   perhaps he may look with favor upon you
   and show you mercy."

℟. Blessed be God, who lives for ever.

Year II

READING I Prv 30, 5-9

A reading from the book of Proverbs

Give me neither poverty nor riches, but only the food which is necessary.

Every word of God is tested;
   he is a shield to those who take refuge in him.
Add nothing to his words,
   lest he reprove you, and you be exposed as a deceiver.

Two things I ask of you,
   deny them not to me before I die:
Put falsehood and lying far from me,
   give me neither poverty nor riches;
[provide me only with the food I need;]

Lest, being full, I deny you,
  saying, "Who is the Lord?"
Or, being in want, I steal,
  and profane the name of my God.
        This is the Word of the Lord.

Responsorial Psalm   Ps 119, 29. 72. 89. 101. 104. 163

℟. (105) Your word, O Lord, is a lamp for my
  feet.
**Remove from me the way of falsehood,
  and favor me with your law.**
℟. Your word, O Lord, is a lamp for my feet.
**The law of your mouth is to me more precious
  than thousands of gold and silver pieces.**
℟. Your word, O Lord, is a lamp for my feet.
**Your word, O Lord, endures forever;
  it is firm as the heavens.**
℟. Your word, O Lord, is a lamp for my feet.
**From every evil way I withhold my feet,
  that I may keep your words.**
℟. Your word, O Lord, is a lamp for my feet.
**Through your precepts I gain discernment;
  therefore I hate every false way.**
℟. Your word, O Lord, is a lamp for my feet.
**Falsehood I hate and abhor;
  your law I love.**
℟. Your word, O Lord, is a lamp for my feet.

Years I and II

GOSPEL   Lk 9, 1-6
Alleluia

See no. 509.

✠ **A reading from the holy gospel according
        to Luke**
He sent them to proclaim the kingdom of God and to heal
                the sick.

**Jesus called the Twelve together and gave
them power and authority to overcome all
demons and to cure diseases. He sent them
forth to proclaim the reign of God and heal the
afflicted. Jesus advised them: "Take nothing
for the journey, neither walking staff nor traveling bag; no bread, no money. No one is to
have two coats. Stay at whatever house you
enter and proceed from there. When people
will not receive you, leave that town and shake
its dust from your feet as a testimony against**

**them." So they set out and went from village
to village, spreading the good news everywhere and curing diseases.**
        This is the gospel of the Lord.

---

452   **THURSDAY OF THE
              TWENTY-FIFTH WEEK
              OF THE YEAR**

Year I

READING I   Hg 1, 1-8
**The beginning of the book of the prophet
                Haggai**
Build the temple and you will be acceptable to me.

**In the second year of King Darius, the word of
the Lord came through the prophet Haggai
to the governor of Judah, Zerubbabel, son of
Shealtiel, and to the high priest Joshua, son of
Jehozadak:**
  **Thus says the Lord of hosts: This people
says: "Not now has the time come to rebuild
the house of the Lord." (Then this word of the
Lord came through Haggai, the prophet:) Is it
time for you to dwell in your own paneled
houses, while this house lies in ruins?**
Now thus says the Lord of hosts:
  Consider your ways!
**You have sown much, but have brought in
    little;**
  you have eaten, but have not been satisfied;
**You have drunk, but have not been exhila-
    rated;**
  **have clothed yourselves, but not been
    warmed;**
**And he who earned wages
  earned them for a bag with holes in it.**

  **Thus says the Lord of hosts:
Consider your ways!
  Go up into the hill country;
  bring timber, and build the house
That I may take pleasure in it
  and receive my glory, says the Lord.**
        This is the Word of the Lord.

Responsorial Psalm   Ps 149, 1-2. 3-4. 5-6. 9

℟. (4) The Lord takes delight in his people.
Sing to the Lord a new song
  of praise in the assembly of the faithful.
Let Israel be glad in their maker,
  let the children of Zion rejoice in their king.
℟. The Lord takes delight in his people.
Let them praise his name in the festive dance,
  let them sing praise to him with timbrel and
  harp.
For the Lord loves his people,
  and he adorns the lowly with victory.
℟. The Lord takes delight in his people.
Let the faithful exult in glory;
  let them sing for joy upon their couches;
  let the high praises of God be in their throats.
This is the glory of all his faithful. Alleluia.
℟. The Lord takes delight in his people.

Year II

READING I   Eccl 1, 2-11

A reading from the book of Ecclesiastes

There is nothing new under the sun.

Vanity of vanities, says Qoheleth,
  vanity of vanities! All things are vanity!
What profit has man from all the labor
  which he toils at under the sun?
One generation passes and another comes,
  but the world forever stays.
The sun rises and the sun goes down;
  then it presses on to the place where it rises.
Blowing now toward the south, then toward
  the north,
  the wind turns again and again, resuming
  its rounds.
All rivers go to the sea,
  yet never does the sea become full.
To the place where they go,
  the rivers keep on going.
All speech is labored;
  there is nothing man can say.
The eye is not satisfied with seeing
  nor is the ear filled with hearing.
What has been, that will be; what has been
done, that will be done. Nothing is new under
the sun. Even the thing of which we say, "See,
this is new!" has already existed in the ages

that preceded us. There is no remembrance of
the men of old; nor of those to come will there
be any remembrance among those who come
after them.

This is the Word of the Lord.

Responsorial Psalm   Ps 90, 3-4. 5-6. 12-13. 14. 17

℟. (1) In every age, O Lord, you have been our
  refuge.
You turn man back to dust,
  saying, "Return, O children of men."
For a thousand years in your sight
  are as yesterday, now that it is past,
  or as a watch of the night.
℟. In every age, O Lord, you have been our
  refuge.
You make an end of them in their sleep;
  the next morning they are like the changing
  grass,
Which at dawn springs up anew,
  but by evening wilts and fades.
℟. In every age, O Lord, you have been our
  refuge.
Teach us to number our days aright,
  that we may gain wisdom of heart.
Return, O Lord! How long?
  Have pity on your servants!
℟. In every age, O Lord, you have been our
  refuge.
Fill us at daybreak with your kindness,
  that we may shout for joy and gladness all
  our days.
And may the gracious care of the Lord our God
  be ours;
  prosper the work of our hands for us!
  [Prosper the work of our hands!]
℟. In every age, O Lord, you have been our
  refuge.

Years I and II

GOSPEL   Lk 9, 7-9
Alleluia
See no. 509.

✠ A reading from the holy gospel according
  to Luke

I beheaded John, so who is this I hear so much about?

Herod the tetrarch heard of all that Jesus was
doing and he was perplexed, for some were

saying, "John has been raised from the dead"; others, "Elijah has appeared"; and still others, "One of the prophets of old has risen." But Herod said, "John I beheaded. Who is this man about whom I hear all these reports?" He was very curious to see him.

This is the gospel of the Lord.

---

453   FRIDAY OF THE
TWENTY-FIFTH WEEK
OF THE YEAR

Year I

READING I   Hg 1, 15—2, 9

A reading from the book of the prophet Haggai
A little while and I shall fill the temple with glory.

In the second year of King Darius, on the twenty-first day of the seventh month, the word of the Lord came through the prophet Haggai: Tell this to the governor of Judah, Zerubbabel, son of Shealtiel, and to the high priest Joshua, son of Jehozadak, and to the remnant of the people:
Who is left among you
    that saw this house in its former glory?
And how do you see it now?
    Does it not seem like nothing in your eyes?
But now take courage, Zerubbabel, says the Lord,
    and take courage, Joshua, high priest, son of Jehozadak,
And take courage, all you people of the land, says the Lord, and work!
    For I am with you, says the Lord of hosts.
This is the pact that I made with you
    when you came out of Egypt,
And my spirit continues in your midst;
    do not fear!

For thus says the Lord of hosts:
One moment yet, a little while,
    and I will shake the heavens and the earth,
    the sea and the dry land.
I will shake all the nations,
    and the treasures of all the nations will
    come in,

And I will fill this house with glory,
    says the Lord of hosts.
Mine is the silver and mine the gold
    says the Lord of hosts.
Greater will be the future glory of this house
    than the former, says the Lord of hosts;
And in this place I will give peace,
    says the Lord of hosts!

This is the Word of the Lord.

Responsorial Psalm   Ps 43, 1. 2. 3. 4

℟. (5) Hope in God; I will praise him,
    my savior and my God.
**Do me justice, O God, and fight my fight
    against a faithless people;**
from the deceitful and impious man rescue
    me.
℟. Hope in God; I will praise him,
    my savior and my God.
**For you, O God, are my strength.
    Why do you keep me so far away?**
Why must I go about in mourning,
    with the enemy oppressing me?
℟. Hope in God; I will praise him,
    my savior and my God.
**Send forth your light and your fidelity;
    they shall lead me on**
And bring me to your holy mountain,
    to your dwelling-place.
℟. Hope in God; I will praise him,
    my savior and my God.
**Then will I go in to the altar of God,
    the God of my gladness and joy;**
Then will I give you thanks upon the harp,
    O God, my God!
℟. Hope in God; I will praise him,
    my savior and my God.

Year II

READING I   Eccl 3, 1-11

A reading from the book of Ecclesiastes
There is a time for everything under heaven.

There is an appointed time for everything,
    and a time for every affair under the heav-
    ens.
A time to be born, and a time to die;
    a time to plant, and a time to uproot the
    plant.

A time to kill, and a time to heal;
a time to tear down, and a time to build.
A time to weep, and a time to laugh;
a time to mourn, and a time to dance.
A time to scatter stones, and a time to gather them;
a time to embrace, and a time to be far from embraces.
A time to seek, and a time to lose;
a time to keep, and a time to cast away.
A time to rend, and a time to sew;
a time to be silent, and a time to speak.
A time to love, and a time to hate;
a time of war, and a time of peace.
What advantage has the worker from his toil? I have considered the task which God has appointed for men to be busied about. He has made everything appropriate to its time, and has put the timeless into their hearts, without men's ever discovering, from beginning to end, the work which God has done.

This is the Word of the Lord.

Responsorial Psalm   Ps 144, 1-2. 3-4

℟. (1) Blessed be the Lord, my Rock!
Blessed be the Lord, my rock,
    my refuge and my fortress,
My stronghold, my deliverer,
    my shield, in whom I trust.
℟. Blessed be the Lord, my Rock!
Lord, what is man, that you notice him;
    the son of man, that you take thought of him?
Man is like a breath;
    his days, like a passing shadow.
℟. Blessed be the Lord, my Rock!

Years I and II

GOSPEL   Lk 9, 18-22
Alleluia

See no. 509.

✠ A reading from the holy gospel according to Luke

You are the Christ of God. The Son of Man must suffer much.

One day when Jesus was praying in seclusion and his disciples were with him, he put the question to them, "Who do the crowds say that I am?" "John the Baptizer," they replied, "and some say Elijah, while others claim that one of the prophets of old has returned from the dead." "But you—who do you say that I am?" he asked them. Peter said in reply, "The Messiah of God." He strictly forbade them to tell this to anyone. "The Son of Man," he said, "must first endure many sufferings, be rejected by the elders, the high priests and the scribes, and be put to death, and then be raised up on the third day."

This is the gospel of the Lord.

---

454   **SATURDAY OF THE
TWENTY-FIFTH WEEK
OF THE YEAR**

Year I

READING I   Zec 2, 5-9. 14-15

A reading from the book of the prophet Zechariah

I am coming, and I will live in your midst.

Again I raised my eyes and looked: there was a man with a measuring line in his hand. "Where are you going?" I asked. "To measure Jerusalem," he answered; "to see how great is its width and how great its length."

Then the angel who spoke with me advanced, and another angel came out to meet him and said to him, "Run, tell this to that young man: People will live in Jerusalem as though in open country, because of the multitude of men and beasts in her midst. But I will be for her an encircling wall of fire, says the Lord, and I will be the glory in her midst."

Sing and rejoice, O daughter Zion! See, I am coming to dwell among you, says the Lord. Many nations shall join themselves to the Lord on that day.

This is the Word of the Lord.

Responsorial Psalm   Jer 31, 10. 11-12. 13

℟. (10) The Lord will guard us,
    like a shepherd guarding his flock.

Hear the word of the Lord, O nations,
  proclaim it on distant coasts, and say:
He who scattered Israel, now gathers them together,
  he guards them as a shepherd his flock.
℟. The Lord will guard us,
  like a shepherd guarding his flock.
The Lord shall ransom Jacob,
  he shall redeem him from the hand of his
  conqueror.
Shouting, they shall mount the heights of Zion,
  they shall come streaming to the Lord's
  blessings.
℟. The Lord will guard us,
  like a shepherd guarding his flock.
Then the virgins shall make merry and dance,
  and young men and old as well.
I will turn their mourning into joy,
  I will console and gladden them after their
  sorrows.
℟. The Lord will guard us,
  like a shepherd guarding his flock.

Year II

READING I   Eccl 11, 9—12, 8

A reading from the book of Ecclesiastes

Remember your creator in the days of your youth before
the dust returns to the earth and the spirit to God.

Rejoice, O young man, while you are young
  and let your heart be glad in the days of your
  youth.
Follow the ways of your heart,
  the vision of your eyes;
Yet understand that as regards all this
  God will bring you to judgment.
Ward off grief from your heart
  and put away trouble from your presence,
  though the dawn of youth is fleeting.

Remember your Creator in the days of your
  youth,
  before the evil days come
And the years approach of which you will say,
  I have no pleasure in them;
Before the sun is darkened,
  and the light, and the moon, and the stars,
  while the clouds return after the rain;
When the guardians of the house tremble,
  and the strong men are bent,

And the grinders are idle because they are few,
  and they who look through the windows
  grow blind;
When the doors to the street are shut,
  and the sound of the mill is low;
When one waits for the chirp of a bird,
  but all the daughters of song are suppressed;
And one fears heights,
  and perils in the street;
When the almond tree blooms,
  and the locust grows sluggish
  and the caper berry is without effect,
Because man goes to his lasting home,
  and mourners go about the streets;
Before the silver cord is snapped
  and the golden bowl is broken,
And the pitcher is shattered at the spring,
  and the broken pulley falls into the well,
And the dust returns to the earth as it once
  was,
  and the life breath returns to God who gave
  it.

Vanity of vanities, says Qoheleth,
  all things are vanity!
    This is the Word of the Lord.

Responsorial Psalm   Ps 90, 3-4. 5-6. 12-13. 14. 17

℟. (1) In every age, O Lord, you have been our
  refuge.
You turn man back to dust,
  saying, "Return, O children of men."
For a thousand years in your sight
  are as yesterday, now that it is past,
  or as a watch of the night.
℟. In every age, O Lord, you have been our
  refuge.
You make an end of them in their sleep;
  the next morning they are like the changing
  grass,
Which at dawn springs up anew,
  but by evening wilts and fades.
℟. In every age, O Lord, you have been our
  refuge.
Teach us to number our days aright,
  that we may gain wisdom of heart.
Return, O Lord! How long?
  Have pity on your servants!

℟. In every age, O Lord, you have been our refuge.
Fill us at daybreak with your kindness,
    that we may shout for joy and gladness all
    our days.
And may the gracious care of the Lord our God
be ours;
    prosper the work of our hands for us!
    [Prosper the work of our hands!]
℟. In every age, O Lord, you have been our refuge.

Years I and II

GOSPEL   Lk 9, 43-45
Alleluia

See no. 509.

✠ **A reading from the holy gospel according**
             to Luke

The Son of Man is going to be handed over to men. They
were afraid to ask him what he had said.

In the midst of the disciples' amazement at all
that Jesus was doing, he said to his disciples:
"Pay close attention to what I tell you: The Son
of Man must be delivered into the hands of
men." They failed, however, to understand this
warning; its meaning was so concealed from
them they did not grasp it at all, and they were
afraid to question him about the matter.
             This is the gospel of the Lord.

---

455   **MONDAY OF THE**

          TWENTY-SIXTH WEEK

          OF THE YEAR

Year I

READING I   Zec 8, 1-8

A reading from the book of the prophet
             Zechariah

I will save my people from the east and the west.

This word of the Lord of hosts came: Thus says
the Lord of hosts:
I am intensely jealous for Zion,
    stirred to jealous wrath for her.
Thus says the Lord:
I will return to Zion,
    and I will dwell within Jerusalem;

Jerusalem shall be called the faithful city,
    and the mountain of the Lord of hosts,
    the holy mountain.
Thus says the Lord of hosts: Old men and old
women, each with staff in hand because of old
age, shall again sit in the streets of Jerusalem.
The city shall be filled with boys and girls play-
ing in her streets. Thus says the Lord of hosts:
Even if this should seem impossible in the eyes
of the remnant of this people, shall it in those
days be impossible in my eyes also, says the
Lord of hosts. Thus says the Lord of hosts: Lo,
I will rescue my people from the land of the
rising sun, and from the land of the setting sun.
I will bring them back to dwell within Jerusa-
lem. They shall be my people, and I will be their
God, with faithfulness and justice.
             This is the Word of the Lord.

Responsorial Psalm   Ps 102, 16-18. 19-21. 29. 22-23

℟. (17) The Lord will build up Zion again,
    and appear in all his glory.
And the nations shall revere your name, O
    Lord,
    and all the kings of the earth your glory,
When the Lord has rebuilt Zion
    and appeared in his glory;
When he has regarded the prayer of the desti-
    tute,
    and not despised their prayer.
℟. The Lord will build up Zion again,
    and appear in all his glory.
Let this be written for the generation to come,
    and let his future creatures praise the Lord:
"The Lord looked down from his holy height,
    from heaven he beheld the earth,
To hear the groaning of the prisoners,
    to release those doomed to die."
℟. The Lord will build up Zion again,
    and appear in all his glory.
The children of your servants shall abide,
    and their posterity shall continue in your
    presence.
That the name of the Lord may be declared in
    Zion;
    and his praise, in Jerusalem,

When the peoples gather together,
and the kingdoms, to serve the Lord.
℟. The Lord will build up Zion again,
and appear in all his glory.

READING I   Jb 1, 6-22

A reading from the book of Job

The Lord gave, the Lord has taken away, blessed be the name of the Lord.

One day, when the sons of God came to present themselves before the Lord, Satan also came among them. And the Lord said to Satan, "Whence do you come?" Then Satan answered the Lord and said, "From roaming the earth and patrolling it." And the Lord said to Satan, "Have you noticed my servant Job, and that there is no one on earth like him, blameless and upright, fearing God and avoiding evil?" But Satan answered the Lord and said, "Is it for nothing that Job is God-fearing? Have you not surrounded him and his family and all that he has with your protection? You have blessed the work of his hands, and his livestock are spread over the land. But now put forth your hand and touch anything that he has, and surely he will blaspheme you to your face." And the Lord said to Satan, "Behold, all that he has is in your power; only do not lay a hand upon his person." So Satan went forth from the presence of the Lord.

And so one day, while his sons and his daughters were eating and drinking wine in the house of their eldest brother, a messenger came to Job and said, "The oxen were ploughing and the asses grazing beside them, and the Sabeans carried them off in a raid. They put the herdsmen to the sword, and I alone have escaped to tell you." While he was yet speaking, another came and said, "Lightning has fallen from heaven and struck the sheep and their shepherds and consumed them; and I alone have escaped to tell you." While he was yet speaking, another came and said, "The Chaldeans formed three columns, seized the camels, carried them off, and put those tending them to the sword, and I alone have escaped to tell you." While he was yet speaking, another came and said, "Your sons and daughters were eating and drinking wine in the house of their eldest brother, when suddenly a great wind came across the desert and smote the four corners of the house. It fell upon the young people and they are dead; and I alone have escaped to tell you." Then Job began to tear his cloak and cut off his hair. He cast himself prostrate upon the ground, and said,

"Naked I came forth from my mother's womb,
and naked shall I go back again.
The Lord gave and the Lord has taken away;
blessed be the name of the Lord!"

In all this Job did not sin, nor did he say anything disrespectful of God.

This is the Word of the Lord.

Responsorial Psalm   Ps 17, 1. 2-3. 6-7

℟. (6) Lord, bend your ear and hear my prayer.
Hear, O Lord, a just suit;
attend to my outcry;
hearken to my prayer from lips without deceit.
℟. Lord, bend your ear and hear my prayer.
From you let my judgment come;
your eyes behold what is right.
Though you test my heart, searching it in the night,
though you try me with fire, you shall find no malice in me.
℟. Lord, bend your ear and hear my prayer.
I call upon you, for you will answer me, O God;
incline your ear to me; hear my word.
Show your wondrous kindness,
O savior of those who flee
from their foes to refuge at your right hand.
℟. Lord, bend your ear and hear my prayer.

GOSPEL   Lk 9, 46-50
Alleluia

See no. 509.

✠ A reading from the holy gospel according
to Luke

The least among you all is the one who is great.

A discussion arose among the disciples as to which of them was the greatest. Jesus, who knew their thoughts, took a little child and placed it beside him, after which he said to them, "Whoever welcomes this little child on my account welcomes me, and whoever welcomes me welcomes him who sent me; for the least one among you is the greatest."

It was John who said, "Master, we saw a man using your name to expel demons, and we tried to stop him because he is not of our company." Jesus told him in reply, "Do not stop him, for any man who is not against you is on your side."

This is the gospel of the Lord.

---

456 TUESDAY OF THE TWENTY-SIXTH WEEK OF THE YEAR

Year I

READING I
Zec 8, 20-23

A reading from the book of the prophet Zechariah

Many peoples will come to seek the Lord God in Jerusalem.

Thus says the Lord of hosts: There shall yet come peoples, the inhabitants of many cities; and the inhabitants of one city shall approach those of another, and say, "Come! let us go to implore the favor of the Lord"; and, "I too will go to seek the Lord." Many peoples and strong nations shall come to seek the Lord of hosts in Jerusalem and to implore the favor of the Lord. Thus says the Lord of hosts: In those days ten men of every nationality, speaking different tongues, shall take hold, yes, take hold of every Jew by the edge of his garment and say, "Let us go with you, for we have heard that God is with you."

This is the Word of the Lord.

Responsorial Psalm Ps 87, 1-3. 4-5. 6-7

℟. (Zec 8, 23) God is with us.
His foundation upon the holy mountains
   the Lord loves:
The gates of Zion,
   more than any dwelling of Jacob.
Glorious things are said of you,
   O city of God!

℟. God is with us.
I tell of Egypt and Babylon
   among those that know the Lord;
Of Philistia, Tyre, Ethiopia:
   "This man was born there."
And of Zion they shall say:
   "One and all were born in her;
And he who has established her
   is the Most High Lord."
℟. God is with us.
They shall note, when the peoples are enrolled:
   "This man was born there."
And all shall sing, in their festive dance:
   "My home is within you."
℟. God is with us.

Year II

READING I
Jb 3, 1-3. 11-17. 20-23

A reading from the book of Job

Why give light to a man of grief?

Job opened his mouth and cursed his day. Job spoke out and said:
Perish the day on which I was born,
   the night when they said, "The child is a boy!"

Why did I not perish at birth,
   come forth from the womb and expire?
Or why was I not buried away like an untimely birth,
   like babes that have never seen light?
Wherefore did the knees receive me?
   or why did I suck at the breasts?

For then I should have lain down and been tranquil;
   had I slept, I should then have been at rest
With kings and counselors of the earth
   who built where now there are ruins,
Or with princes who had gold
   and filled their houses with silver.
There the wicked cease from troubling,
   there the weary are at rest.

Why is light given to the toilers,
   and life to the bitter in spirit?
They wait for death and it comes not;
   they search for it rather than for hidden treasures,

Rejoice in it exultingly,
    and are glad when they reach the grave:
Men whose path is hidden from them,
    and whom God has hemmed in!
        This is the Word of the Lord.

Responsorial Psalm   Ps 88, 2-3. 4-5. 6. 7-8

℟. (3) Let my prayer come before you, Lord.
O Lord, my God, by day I cry out;
    at night I clamor in your presence.
Let my prayer come before you;
    incline your ear to my call for help.
℟. Let my prayer come before you, Lord.
For my soul is surfeited with troubles
    and my life draws near to the nether world.
I am numbered with those who go down into
        the pit;
    I am a man without strength.
℟. Let my prayer come before you, Lord.
My couch is among the dead,
    like the slain who lie in the grave,
Whom you remember no longer
    and who are cut off from your care.
℟. Let my prayer come before you, Lord.
You have plunged me into the bottom of the
        pit,
    into the dark abyss.
Upon me your wrath lies heavy,
    and with all your billows you overwhelm
        me.
℟. Let my prayer come before you, Lord.

Years I and II

GOSPEL   Lk 9, 51-56
Alleluia
See no. 509.

✠ A reading from the holy gospel according
                to Luke
He resolutely took the road to Jerusalem.

As the time approached when Jesus was to be
taken from this world, he firmly resolved to
proceed toward Jerusalem, and sent messengers on ahead of him. These entered a Samaritan town to prepare for his passing through,
but the Samaritans would not welcome him because he was on his way to Jerusalem. When
his disciples James and John saw this, they

said, "Lord, would you not have us call down
fire from heaven to destroy them?" He turned
toward them only to reprimand them. Then
they set off for another town.
        This is the gospel of the Lord.

457   **WEDNESDAY OF THE
             TWENTY-SIXTH WEEK
             OF THE YEAR**

                                        Year I
READING I   Neh 2, 1-8
        A reading from the book of Nehemiah
If it pleases the king, send me to the city of my ancestors
                and I will rebuild it.

In the month Nisan of the twentieth year of
King Artaxerxes, when the wine was in my
charge, I Nehemiah took some and offered it to
the king. As I had never before been sad in his
presence, the king asked me, "Why do you look
sad? If you are not sick, you must be sad at
heart." Though I was seized with great fear, I
answered the king: "May the king live forever!
How could I not look sad when the city where
my ancestors are buried lies in ruins, and its
gates have been eaten out by fire?" The king
asked me, "What is it, then, that you wish?" I
prayed to the God of heaven and then answered the king: "If it please the king, and if
your servant is deserving of your favor, send
me to Judah, to the city of my ancestors'
graves, to rebuild it." Then the king, and the
queen seated beside him, asked me how long
my journey would take and when I would return. I set a date that was acceptable to him,
and the king agreed that I might go.
    I asked the king further: "If it please the
king, let letters be given to me for the governors of West-of-Euphrates, that they may afford me safe-conduct till I arrive in Judah; also
a letter for Asaph, the keeper of the royal park,
that he may give me wood for timbering the
gates of the temple-citadel and for the city
wall and the house that I shall occupy." The
king granted my requests, for the favoring
hand of my God was upon me.
        This is the Word of the Lord.

Responsorial Psalm   Ps 137, 1-2. 3. 4-5. 6

℟. (6) Let my tongue be silenced, if I ever
    forget you!
**By the streams of Babylon
    we sat and wept
    when we remembered Zion.
On the aspens of that land
    we hung up our harps.**

℟. Let my tongue be silenced, if I ever forget
    you!

**Though there our captors asked of us
    the lyrics of our songs,
And our despoilers urged us to be joyous:
    "Sing for us the songs of Zion!"**

℟. Let my tongue be silenced, if I ever forget
    you!

**How could we sing a song of the Lord
    in a foreign land?
If I forget you, Jerusalem,
    may my right hand be forgotten!**

℟. Let my tongue be silenced, if I ever forget
    you!

**May my tongue cleave to my palate
    if I remember you not,
If I place not Jerusalem
    ahead of my joy.**

℟. Let my tongue be silenced, if I ever forget
    you!

Year II

READING I   Jb 9, 1-12. 14-16

A reading from the book of Job
Man's justice cannot be compared to God's.

**Job answered his friends and said:
I know well that it is so;
    but how can a man be justified before God?
Should one wish to contend with him,
    he could not answer him once in a thousand
    times.
God is wise in heart and mighty in strength;
    who has withstood him and remained un-
    scathed?**

**He removes the mountains before they know
    it;
    he overturns them in his anger.
He shakes the earth out of its place,
    and the pillars beneath it tremble.**

**He commands the sun, and it rises not;
    he seals up the stars.**
**He alone stretches out the heavens
    and treads upon the crests of the sea.**
**He made the Bear and Orion,
    the Pleiades and the constellations of the
    south;**
**He does great things past finding out,
    marvelous things beyond reckoning.
Should he come near me, I see him not;
    should he pass by, I am not aware of him;
Should he seize me forcibly, who can say him
    nay?**
**Who can say to him, "What are you doing?"
How much less shall I give him any answer,
    or choose out arguments against him!
Even though I were right, I could not answer
    him,
    but should rather beg for what was due me.**

**If I appealed to him and he answered my call,
    I could not believe that he would hearken to
    my words.**
        This is the Word of the Lord.

Responsorial Psalm   Ps 88, 10-11. 12-13. 14-15

℟. (3) Let my prayer come before you, Lord.
**Daily I call upon you, O Lord;
    to you I stretch out my hands.
Will you work wonders for the dead?
    Will the shades arise to give you thanks?**

℟. Let my prayer come before you, Lord.
**Do they declare your kindness in the grave,
    your faithfulness among those who have
    perished?
Are your wonders made known in the dark-
    ness,
    or your justice in the land of oblivion?**

℟. Let my prayer come before you, Lord.
**But I, O Lord, cry out to you;
    with my morning prayer I wait upon you.
Why, O Lord, do you reject me;
    why hide from me your face?**

℟. Let my prayer come before you, Lord.

Years I and II

GOSPEL   Lk 9, 57-62
Alleluia
See no. 509.

✠ A reading from the holy gospel according
to Luke

I will follow you wherever you go.

As Jesus and his disciples were making their
way along, someone said to Jesus, "I will be
your follower wherever you go." Jesus said to
him, "The foxes have lairs, the birds of the sky
have nests, but the Son of Man has nowhere to
lay his head." To another he said, "Come after
me." The man replied, "Let me bury my father
first." Jesus said to him, "Let the dead bury
their dead; come away and proclaim the kingdom of God." Yet another said to him, "I will
be your follower, Lord, but first let me take
leave of my people at home." Jesus answered
him, "Whoever puts his hand to the plow but
keeps looking back is unfit for the reign of
God."

This is the gospel of the Lord.

---

458   THURSDAY OF THE

TWENTY-SIXTH WEEK

OF THE YEAR

Year I

READING I   Neh 8, 1-4. 5-6. 7-12

A reading from the book of Nehemiah

Ezra opened the book of the law, blessed the people, and
they responded, Amen! Amen!

The whole people gathered as one man in the
open space before the Water Gate, and they
called upon Ezra the scribe to bring forth the
book of the law of Moses which the Lord prescribed for Israel. On the first day of the
seventh month, therefore, Ezra the priest
brought the law before the assembly, which
consisted of men, women, and those children
old enough to understand. Standing at one end
of the open place that was before the Water
Gate, he read out of the book from daybreak
until midday, in the presence of the men, the
women, and those children old enough to understand; and all the people listened attentively to the book of the law. Ezra the scribe
stood on a wooden platform that had been
made for the occasion.

25-22

Ezra opened the scroll so that all the people
might see it (for he was standing higher up
than any of the people); and, as he opened it,
all the people rose. Ezra blessed the Lord, the
great God, and all the people, their hands
raised high, answered, "Amen, amen!" Then
they bowed down and prostrated themselves
before the Lord, their faces to the ground. As
the people remained in their places Ezra read
plainly from the book of the law of God, interpreting it so that all could understand what
was read. Then [Nehemiah, that is, His Excellency, and] Ezra the priest-scribe [and the
Levites who were instructing the people] said
to all the people: "Today is holy to the Lord
your God. Do not be sad, and do not weep"—
for all the people were weeping as they heard
the words of the law. He said further: "Go, eat
rich foods and drink sweet drinks, and allot
portions to those who had nothing prepared;
for today is holy to our Lord. Do not be saddened this day, for rejoicing in the Lord must
be your strength!" [And the Levites quieted all
the people, saying, "Hush, for today is holy,
and you must not be saddened."] Then all the
people went to eat and drink, to distribute
portions, and to celebrate with great joy, for
they understood the words that had been ex-
pounded to them.

This is the Word of the Lord.

Responsorial Psalm   Ps 19, 8. 9. 10. 11

℟. (9) The precepts of the Lord give joy to the
heart.

The law of the Lord is perfect,
refreshing the soul;
The decree of the Lord is trustworthy,
giving wisdom to the simple.

℟. The precepts of the Lord give joy to the
heart.

The precepts of the Lord are right,
rejoicing the heart;
The command of the Lord is clear,
enlightening the eye;

℟. The precepts of the Lord give joy to the
heart.

The fear of the Lord is pure,
enduring forever;

The ordinances of the Lord are true,
all of them just.
℞. The precepts of the Lord give joy to the
heart.
They are more precious than gold,
than a heap of purest gold;
Sweeter also than syrup
or honey from the comb.
℞. The precepts of the Lord give joy to the
heart.

Year II

READING I   Jb 19, 21-27

A reading from the book of Job
I know that my Redeemer lives.

Job said:
Pity me, pity me, O you my friends,
for the hand of God has struck me!
Why do you hound me as though you were
divine,
and insatiably prey upon me?

Oh, would that my words were written down!
Would that they were inscribed in a record:
That with an iron chisel and with lead
they were cut in the rock forever!
But as for me, I know that my Vindicator lives,
and that he will at last stand forth upon the
dust;
Whom I myself shall see:
my own eyes, not another's, shall behold
him.
And from my flesh I shall see God;
my inmost being is consumed with longing.
This is the Word of the Lord.

Responsorial Psalm   Ps 27, 7-8. 8-9. 13-14

℞. (13) I believe that I shall see the good things
of the Lord in the land of the living.
Hear, O Lord, the sound of my call;
have pity on me, and answer me.
Of you my heart speaks; you my glance seeks;
℞. I believe that I shall see the good things of
the Lord in the land of the living.
Your presence, O Lord, I seek.
Hide not your face from me;
do not in anger repel your servant.
You are my helper: cast me not off.

℞. I believe that I shall see the good things of
the Lord in the land of the living.
I believe that I shall see the bounty of the Lord
in the land of the living.
Wait for the Lord with courage;
be stouthearted, and wait for the Lord.
℞. I believe that I shall see the good things of
the Lord in the land of the living.

Years I and II

GOSPEL   Lk 10, 1-12
Alleluia
See no. 509.

✠ **A reading from the holy gospel according
to Luke**
Your peace will rest on them.

Jesus appointed a further seventy-two and
sent them in pairs before him to every town
and place he intended to visit. He said to them:
"The harvest is rich but the workers are few;
therefore ask the harvest-master to send
workers to his harvest. Be on your way, and
remember: I am sending you as lambs in the
midst of wolves. Do not carry a walking staff
or traveling bag; wear no sandals and greet
no one along the way. On entering any house,
first say, 'Peace to this house.' If there is a
peaceable man there, your peace will rest on
him; if not, it will come back to you. Stay in
the one house eating and drinking what they
have, for the laborer is worth his wage. Do not
move from house to house.

"Into whatever city you go, after they welcome you, eat what they set before you, and
cure the sick there. Say to them, 'The reign of
God is at hand.' If the people of any town you
enter do not welcome you, go into its streets
and say, 'We shake the dust of this town from
our feet as testimony against you. But know
that the reign of God is near.' I assure you,
on that day the fate of Sodom will be less
severe than that of such a town."
This is the gospel of the Lord.

459   **FRIDAY OF THE**
TWENTY-SIXTH WEEK
OF THE YEAR

Year I

READING I   Bar 1, 15-22
A reading from the book of the prophet Baruch
We have sinned in the sight of the Lord and have not
believed.

Justice is with the Lord, our God; and we today are flushed with shame, we men of Judah
and citizens of Jerusalem, that we, with our
kings and rulers and priests and prophets, and
with our fathers, have sinned in the Lord's
sight and disobeyed him. We have neither
heeded the voice of the Lord, our God, nor
followed the precepts which the Lord set before us. From the time the Lord led our fathers
out of the land of Egypt until the present day,
we have been disobedient to the Lord, our God,
and only too ready to disregard his voice. And
the evils and the curse which the Lord enjoined
upon Moses, his servant, at the time he led
our fathers forth from the land of Egypt to give
us the land flowing with milk and honey, cling
to us even today. For we did not heed the voice
of the Lord, our God, in all the words of the
prophets whom he sent us, but each one of us
went off after the devices of his own wicked
heart, served other gods, and did evil in the
sight of the Lord, our God.
                    This is the Word of the Lord.

Responsorial Psalm   Ps 79, 1-2. 3-5. 8. 9
℟. (9) For the glory of your name,
    O Lord, deliver us.
O God, the nations have come into your in-
    heritance;
    they have defiled your holy temple,
    they have laid Jerusalem in ruins.
They have given the corpses of your servants
    as food to the birds of heaven,
    the flesh of your faithful ones to the beasts
    of the earth.
℟. For the glory of your name,
    O Lord, deliver us.

They have poured out their blood like water
    round about Jerusalem,
    and there is no one to bury them.
We have become the reproach of our neigh-
    bors,
    the scorn and derision of those around us.
O Lord, how long? Will you be angry forever?
    Will your jealousy burn like fire?
℟. For the glory of your name,
    O Lord, deliver us.
Remember not against us the iniquities of the
    past;
    may your compassion quickly come to us,
    for we are brought very low.
℟. For the glory of your name,
    O Lord, deliver us.
Help us, O God our savior,
    because of the glory of your name;
Deliver us and pardon our sins
    for your name's sake.
℟. For the glory of your name,
    O Lord, deliver us.

Year II

READING I   Jb 38, 1. 12-21; 40, 3-5
A reading from the book of Job
Have you ever given orders to the morning, or journeyed to
the depths of the sea?
The Lord addressed Job out of the storm and
said:

Have you ever in your lifetime commanded the
    morning
    and shown the dawn its place
For taking hold of the ends of the earth,
    till the wicked are shaken from its surface?
The earth is changed as is clay by the seal,
    and dyed as though it were a garment;
But from the wicked the light is withheld,
    and the arm of pride is shattered.

Have you entered into the sources of the sea,
    or walked about in the depths of the abyss?
Have the gates of death been shown to you,
    or have you seen the gates of darkness?
Have you comprehended the breadth of the
    earth?

Tell me, if you know all:
Which is the way to the dwelling place of light,

and where is the abode of darkness,
That you may take them to their boundaries
  and set them on their homeward paths?
You know, because you were born before
  them,
  and the number of your years is great!

Then Job answered the Lord and said:

Behold, I am of little account; what can I
  answer you?
I put my hand over my mouth.
Though I have spoken once, I will not do so
  again;
  though twice, I will do so no more.
      This is the Word of the Lord.

Responsorial Psalm   Ps 139, 1-3. 7-8. 9-10. 13-14

℟. (24) Guide me, Lord, along the everlasting
  way.

O Lord, you have probed me and you know me;
  you know when I sit and when I stand;
  you understand my thoughts from afar.
My journeys and my rest you scrutinize,
  with all my ways you are familiar.
℟. Guide me, Lord, along the everlasting way.
Where can I go from your spirit?
  from your presence where can I flee?
If I go up to the heavens, you are there;
  if I sink to the nether world, you are present there.
℟. Guide me, Lord, along the everlasting way.
If I take the wings of the dawn,
  if I settle at the farthest limits of the sea,
Even there your hand shall guide me,
  and your right hand hold me fast.
℟. Guide me, Lord, along the everlasting way.
Truly you have formed my inmost being;
  you knit me in my mother's womb.
I give you thanks that I am fearfully, wonder-
  fully made;
  wonderful are your works.
℟. Guide me, Lord, along the everlasting way.

Years I and II

GOSPEL   Lk 10, 13-16
Alleluia

See no. 509.

✠ **A reading from the holy gospel according
  to Luke**
He who rejects me, rejects him who sent me.

Jesus said: "It will go ill with you, Chorazin!
And just as ill with you, Bethsaida! If the
miracles worked in your midst had occurred in
Tyre and Sidon, they would long ago have
reformed in sackcloth and ashes. It will go
easier on the day of judgment for Tyre and
Sidon than for you. And as for you, Capernaum, 'Are you to be exalted to the skies? You
shall be hurled down to the realm of death!'
  "He who hears you, hears me. He who rejects you, rejects me. And he who rejects me,
rejects him who sent me."
      This is the gospel of the Lord.

460   **SATURDAY OF THE
           TWENTY-SIXTH WEEK
           OF THE YEAR**

                                              Year I

READING I   Bar 4, 5-12. 27-29
A reading from the book of the prophet Baruch
He who delivered you to your enemies, will rescue you and
              give you eternal joy.

Fear not, my people!
  Remember, Israel,
You were sold to the nations
  not for your destruction;
It was because you angered God
  that you were handed over to your foes.
For you provoked your Maker
  with sacrifices to demons, to no-gods;
You forsook the Eternal God who nourished
  you,
  and you grieved Jerusalem who fostered
  you.
She indeed saw coming upon you
  the anger of God; and she said:

"Hear, you neighbors of Zion!
  God has brought great mourning upon me,
For I have seen the captivity
  that the Eternal God has brought
  upon my sons and daughters.
With joy I fostered them;
  but with mourning and lament I let them go.

Let no one gloat over me, a widow,
   bereft of many:
For the sins of my children I am left desolate,
   because they turned from the law of God.

Fear not, my children; call out to God!
   He who brought this upon you will remember you.
As your hearts have been disposed to stray from God,
   turn now ten times the more to seek him;
For he who has brought disaster upon you
   will, in saving you, bring you back enduring joy."
      This is the Word of the Lord.

Responsorial Psalm   Ps 69, 33-35. 36-37

℟. (34) The Lord listens to the poor.
"See, you lowly ones, and be glad;
   you who seek God, may your hearts be merry!
For the Lord hears the poor,
   and his own who are in bonds he spurns not.
Let the heavens and the earth praise him,
   the seas and whatever moves in them!"
℟. The Lord listens to the poor.
For God will save Zion
   and rebuild the cities of Judah.
They shall dwell in the land and own it,
   and the descendants of his servants shall inherit it,
   and those who love his name shall inhabit it.
℟. The Lord listens to the poor.

Year II

READING I   Jb 42, 1-3. 5-6. 12-16
    A reading from the book of Job
I have seen you with my own eyes, and I repent all I
have said.

Then Job answered the Lord and said:

I know that you can do all things,
   and that no purpose of yours can be hindered.
I have dealt with great things that I do not understand;
   things too wonderful for me, which I cannot know.

I had heard of you by word of mouth,
   but now my eye has seen you.
Therefore I disown what I have said,
   and repent in dust and ashes.
Thus the Lord blessed the latter days of Job more than his earlier ones. For he had fourteen thousand sheep, six thousand camels, a thousand yoke of oxen, and a thousand she-asses. And he had seven sons and three daughters, of whom he called the first Jemimah, the second Keziah, and the third Keren-happuch. In all the land no other women were as beautiful as the daughters of Job; and their father gave them an inheritance among their brethren. After this, Job lived a hundred and forty years; and he saw his children, his grandchildren, and even his great-grandchildren.
      This is the Word of the Lord.

Responsorial Psalm   Ps 119, 66. 71. 75. 91. 125. 130

℟. (135) Lord, let your face shine on me.
Teach me wisdom and knowledge,
   for in your commands I trust.
℟. Lord, let your face shine on me.
It is good for me that I have been afflicted,
   that I may learn your statutes.
   Lord, let your face shine on me.
I know, O Lord, that your ordinances are just,
   and in your faithfulness you have afflicted me.
℟. Lord, let your face shine on me.
According to your ordinances they still stand firm:
   all things serve you.
℟. Lord, let your face shine on me.
I am your servant; give me discernment
   that I may know your decrees.
℟. Lord, let your face shine on me.
The revelation of your words sheds light,
   giving understanding to the simple.
℟. Lord, let your face shine on me.

Years I and II

GOSPEL   Lk 10, 17-24
Alleluia

See no. 509.

✠ A reading from the holy gospel according
to Luke

Rejoice because your names are written in heaven.

The seventy-two disciples returned in jubilation, saying, "Master, even the demons are subject to us in your name." He said in reply:
"I watched Satan fall from the sky like lightning. See what I have done; I have given you
power to tread on snakes and scorpions and all
the forces of the enemy, and nothing shall ever
injure you. Nevertheless, do not rejoice so
much in the fact that the devils are subject to
you as that your names are inscribed in
heaven."

At that moment Jesus rejoiced in the Holy
Spirit and said: "I offer you grateful praise,
O Father, Lord of heaven and earth, because
what you have hidden from the learned and the
clever you have revealed to the merest children.

"Yes, Father, you have graciously willed it
so. Everything has been given over to me by
my Father. No one knows the Son except the
Father and no one knows the Father except
the Son—and anyone to whom the Son wishes
to reveal him."

Turning to his disciples he said to them
privately: "Blest are the eyes that see what you
see. I tell you, many prophets and kings wished
to see what you see but did not see it, and to
hear what you hear but did not hear it."

This is the gospel of the Lord.

---

461   MONDAY OF THE
        TWENTY-SEVENTH WEEK
            OF THE YEAR

Year I

READING I   Jon 1, 1—2, 1. 11
The beginning of the book of the prophet Jonah

Jonah rose up and fled from the face of the Lord.

This is the word of the Lord that came to
Jonah, son of Amittai: "Set out for the great
city of Nineveh, and preach against it; their
wickedness has come up before me." But
Jonah made ready to flee to Tarshish away
from the Lord. He went down to Joppa, found
a ship going to Tarshish, paid the fare, and
went aboard to journey with them to Tarshish,
away from the Lord.

The Lord, however, hurled a violent wind
upon the sea, and in the furious tempest that
arose the ship was on the point of breaking
up. Then the mariners became frightened and
each one cried to his god. To lighten the ship
for themselves, they threw its cargo into the
sea. Meanwhile, Jonah had gone down into the
hold of the ship, and lay there fast asleep. The
captain came to him and said, "What are you
doing asleep? Rise up, call upon your God!
Perhaps God will be mindful of us so that
we may not perish."

Then they said to one another, "Come, let us
cast lots to find out on whose account we
have met with this misfortune." So they cast
lots, and thus singled out Jonah. "Tell us,"
they said, "what is your business? Where do
you come from? What is your country, and to
what people do you belong?" "I am a Hebrew,"
Jonah answered them; "I worship the Lord, the
God of heaven, who made the sea and the dry
land."

Now the men were seized with great fear
and said to him, "How could you do such a
thing!"—They knew that he was fleeing from
the Lord, because he had told them.—"What
shall we do with you," they asked, "that the
sea may quiet down for us?" For the sea was
growing more and more turbulent. Jonah said
to them, "Pick me up and throw me into the
sea, that it may quiet down for you; since I
know it is because of me that this violent storm
has come upon you."

Still the men rowed hard to regain the land,
but they could not, for the sea grew ever more
turbulent. Then they cried to the Lord: "We
beseech you, O Lord, let us not perish for
taking this man's life; do not charge us with
shedding innocent blood, for you, Lord, have
done as you saw fit." Then they took Jonah
and threw him into the sea, and the sea's
raging abated. Struck with great fear of the
Lord, the men offered sacrifice and made vows
to him.

But the Lord sent a large fish, that swallowed Jonah; and he remained in the belly of the fish three days and three nights. Then the Lord commanded the fish to spew Jonah upon the shore.

    This is the Word of the Lord.

Responsorial Psalm   Jon 2, 2. 3. 4. 5. 8

℟. (7) You will rescue my life from the pit, O Lord.

From the belly of the fish Jonah said this prayer to the Lord, his God:

℟. You will rescue my life from the pit, O Lord.

Out of my distress I called to the Lord,
  and he answered me;
From the midst of the nether world I cried for help,
  and you heard my voice.

℟. You will rescue my life from the pit, O Lord.

For you cast me into the deep, into the heart of the sea,
  and the flood enveloped me;
All your breakers and your billows
  passed over me.

℟. You will rescue my life from the pit, O Lord.

Then I said, "I am banished from your sight!
  yet would I again look upon your holy temple."

℟. You will rescue my life from the pit, O Lord.

When my soul fainted within me,
  I remembered the Lord;
My prayer reached you
  in your holy temple.

℟. You will rescue my life from the pit, O Lord.

READING I   `Year II`   Gal 1, 6-12

A reading from the letter of Paul to the Galatians

The Good News I preached is not from men, nor have I learned it from a revelation of men, but from Christ.

I am amazed that you are so soon deserting him who called you in accord with his gracious design in Christ, and are going over to another gospel. But there is no other. Some who wish to alter the gospel of Christ must have confused you. For if even we or an angel from heaven should preach to you a gospel not in accord with the one we delivered to you, let a curse be upon him! I repeat what I have just said: if anyone preaches a gospel to you other than the one you received, let a curse be upon him!

    Whom would you say I am trying to please at this point—men or God? Is this how I seek to ingratiate myself? If I were trying to win man's approval, I would surely not be serving Christ!

    I assure you, brothers, the gospel I proclaimed to you is no mere human invention. I did not receive it from any man, nor was I schooled in it. It came by revelation from Jesus Christ.

    This is the Word of the Lord.

Responsorial Psalm   Ps 111, 1-2. 7-8. 9. 10

℟. (5) The Lord will remember his covenant for ever.

I will give thanks to the Lord with all my heart
  in the company and assembly of the just.
Great are the works of the Lord,
  exquisite in all their delights.

℟. The Lord will remember his covenant for ever.

The works of his hands are faithful and just;
  sure are all his precepts,
Reliable forever and ever,
  wrought in truth and equity.

℟. The Lord will remember his covenant for ever.

He has sent deliverance to his people;
  he has ratified his covenant forever;
Holy and awesome is his name.
  His praise endures forever.

℟. The Lord will remember his covenant for ever.

℟. Or: Alleluia.

GOSPEL   Years I and II

Alleluia   Lk 10, 25-37

See no. 509.

✠ A reading from the holy gospel according
to Luke

Who is my neighbor?

On one occasion a lawyer stood up to pose
to Jesus this problem: "Teacher, what must I do
to inherit everlasting life?" Jesus answered
him: "What is written in the law? How do you
read it?" He replied:

"You shall love the Lord your God
with all your heart,
with all your soul,
with all your strength,
and with all your mind;
and your neighbor as yourself."

Jesus said, "You have answered correctly. Do
this and you shall live." But because he wished
to justify himself he said to Jesus, "And who is
my neighbor?" Jesus replied: "There was a
man going down from Jerusalem to Jericho
who fell in with robbers. They stripped him,
beat him, and then went off leaving him half-
dead. A priest happened to be going down the
same road; he saw him but continued on. Likewise there was a Levite who came the same
way; he saw him and went on. But a Samaritan
who was journeying along came on him and
was moved to pity at the sight. He approached
him and dressed his wounds, pouring in oil and
wine. He then hoisted him on his own beast
and brought him to an inn, where he cared for
him. The next day he took out two silver pieces
and gave them to the innkeeper with the request: 'Look after him, and if there is any
further expense I will repay you on my way
back.'

"Which of these three, in your opinion, was
neighbor to the man who fell in with the
robbers?" The answer came, "The one who
treated him with compassion." Jesus said to
him, "Then go and do the same."

This is the gospel of the Lord.

---

462   TUESDAY OF THE
TWENTY-SEVENTH WEEK
OF THE YEAR

                                              Year I

READING I   Jon 3, 1-10

A reading from the book of the prophet Jonah

Nineveh was converted from its evil ways and was spared
by the Lord.

The word of the Lord came to Jonah a second
time: "Set out for the great city of Nineveh,
and announce to it the message that I will tell
you." So Jonah made ready and went to Nineveh, according to the Lord's bidding. Now
Nineveh was an enormously large city; it took
three days to go through it. Jonah began his
journey through the city, and had gone but
a single day's walk, announcing, "Forty days
more and Nineveh shall be destroyed," when
the people of Nineveh believed God; they proclaimed a fast and all of them, great and small,
put on sackcloth.

When the news reached the king of Nineveh,
he rose from his throne, laid aside his robe,
covered himself with sackcloth, and sat in the
ashes. Then he had this proclaimed throughout
Nineveh, by decree of the king and his nobles:
"Neither man nor beast, neither cattle nor
sheep, shall taste anything; they shall not eat,
nor shall they drink water. Man and beast
shall be covered with sackcloth and call loudly
to God; every man shall turn from his evil
way and from the violence he has in hand.
Who knows, God may relent and forgive, and
withhold his blazing wrath, so that we shall
not perish." When God saw by their actions
how they turned from their evil way, he repented of the evil that he had threatened to do
to them; he did not carry it out.

This is the Word of the Lord.

Responsorial Psalm   Ps 130, 1-2. 3-4. 7-8

℟. (3) If you, O Lord, laid bare our guilt,
who could endure it?

Out of the depths I cry to you, O Lord;
Lord, hear my voice!
Let your ears be attentive
to my voice in supplication.

Ry. If you, O Lord, laid bare our guilt,
    who could endure it?
If you, O Lord, mark iniquities,
    Lord, who can stand?
But with you is forgiveness,
    that you may be revered.
Ry. If you, O Lord, laid bare our guilt,
    who could endure it?
Let Israel wait for the Lord,
For with the Lord is kindness
    and with him is plenteous redemption;
And he will redeem Israel
    from all their iniquities.
Ry. If you, O Lord, laid bare our guilt,
    who could endure it?

Year II

READING I   Gal 1, 13-24

A reading from the letter of Paul to the Galatians

He revealed his Son in me, that I might preach the Good News about him to the gentiles.

You have heard, I know, the story of my former way of life in Judaism. You know that I went to extremes in persecuting the church of God and tried to destroy it; I made progress in Jewish observance far beyond most of my contemporaries, in my excess of zeal to live out all the traditions of my ancestors.

But the time came when he who had set me apart before I was born and called me by his favor chose to reveal his Son to me, that I might spread among the Gentiles the good tidings concerning him. Immediately, without seeking human advisers or even going to Jerusalem to see those who were apostles before me, I went off to Arabia; later I returned to Damascus. Three years after that I went up to Jerusalem to get to know Cephas, with whom I stayed fifteen days. I did not meet any other apostles except James, the brother of the Lord. I declare before God that what I have just written is true.

Thereafter I entered the regions of Syria and Cilicia. The communities of Christ in Judea had no idea what I looked like; they had only heard that "he who was formerly persecuting us is now preaching the faith he tried to destroy," and they gave glory to God on my account.

This is the Word of the Lord.

Responsorial Psalm   Ps 139, 1-3. 13-14. 14-15

Ry. (24) Guide me, Lord, along the everlasting way.

O Lord, you have probed me and you know me;
    you know when I sit and when I stand;
    you understand my thoughts from afar.
My journeys and my rest you scrutinize,
    with all my ways you are familiar.
Ry. Guide me, Lord, along the everlasting way.
Truly you have formed my inmost being;
    you knit me in my mother's womb.
I give you thanks that I am fearfully, wonderfully made;
    wonderful are your works.
Ry. Guide me, Lord, along the everlasting way.
My soul also you knew full well;
    nor was my frame unknown to you
When I was made in secret,
    when I was fashioned in the depths of the earth.
Ry. Guide me, Lord, along the everlasting way.

Years I and II

GOSPEL   Lk 10, 38-42
Alleluia

See no. 509.

✠ **A reading from the holy gospel according to Luke**

Martha took up the duties in the house. Mary chose the better part.

Jesus entered a village where a woman named Martha welcomed him to her home. She had a sister named Mary, who seated herself at the Lord's feet and listened to his words. Martha, who was busy with all the details of hospitality, came to him and said, "Lord, are you not concerned that my sister has left me all alone to do the household tasks? Tell her to help me."

The Lord in reply said to her: "Martha, Martha, you are anxious and upset about many things; one thing only is required. Mary has

chosen the better portion and she shall not be deprived of it."

This is the gospel of the Lord.

---

463   **WEDNESDAY OF THE
TWENTY-SEVENTH WEEK
OF THE YEAR**

Year I

READING I   Jon 4, 1-11

A reading from the book of the prophet Jonah

Jonah, you worry over a plant. Am I not to feel sorry for the great city Nineveh?

Jonah was greatly displeased and became angry that God did not carry out the evil he threatened [against Nineveh]. "I beseech you, Lord," he prayed, "is not this what I said while I was still in my own country? This is why I fled at first to Tarshish. I knew that you are a gracious and merciful God, slow to anger, rich in clemency, loathe to punish. And now, Lord, please take my life from me; for it is better for me to die than to live." But the Lord asked, "Have you reason to be angry?"

Jonah then left the city for a place to the east of it, where he built himself a hut and waited under it in the shade, to see what would happen to the city. And when the Lord God provided a gourd plant, that grew up over Jonah's head, giving shade that relieved him of any discomfort, Jonah was very happy over the plant. But the next morning at dawn God sent a worm which attacked the plant, so that it withered. And when the sun arose, God sent a burning east wind; and the sun beat upon Jonah's head til he became faint. Then he asked for death, saying, "I would be better off dead than alive."

But God said to Jonah, "Have you reason to be angry over the plant?" "I have reason to be angry," Jonah answered, "angry enough to die." Then the Lord said, "You are concerned over the plant which cost you no labor and which you did not raise; it came up in one night and in one night it perished. And should

I not be concerned over Nineveh, the great city, in which there are more than a hundred and twenty thousand persons who cannot distinguish their right hand from their left, not to mention the many cattle?"

This is the Word of the Lord.

Responsorial Psalm   Ps 86, 3-4. 5-6. 9-10

℟. (15) Lord, you are tender and full of love.

**You are my God; have pity on me, O Lord,
for to you I call all the day.
Gladden the soul of your servant,
for to you, O Lord, I lift up my soul.**

℟. Lord, you are tender and full of love.

**For you, O Lord, are good and forgiving,
abounding in kindness to all who call upon you.
Hearken, O Lord, to my prayer
and attend to the sound of my pleading.**

℟. Lord, you are tender and full of love.

**All the nations you have made shall come
and worship you, O Lord,
and glorify your name.
For you are great, and you do wondrous deeds;
you alone are God.**

℟. Lord, you are tender and full of love.

Year II

READING I   Gal 2, 1-2. 7-14

**A reading from the letter of Paul to the
Galatians**

They recognized the grace that had been given to me.

After fourteen years, I went up to Jerusalem again with Barnabas, this time taking Titus with me. I went prompted by a revelation, and I laid out for their scrutiny the gospel as I present it to the Gentiles—all this in private conference with the leaders, to make sure the course I was pursuing, or had pursued, was not useless.

On the contrary, recognizing that I had been entrusted with the gospel for the uncircumcised, just as Peter was for the circumcised (for he who worked through Peter as his apostle among the Jews had been at work in me for the Gentiles), and recognizing, too, the favor bestowed on me, those who were the acknowledged pillars, James, Cephas, and John, gave Barnabas and me the handclasp of fellowship, signifying that we should go to the Gentiles as they to the Jews. The only stipulation was that we should be mindful of the poor—the one thing that I was making every effort to do.

When Cephas came to Antioch I directly withstood him, because he was clearly in the wrong. He had been taking his meals with the Gentiles before others came who were from James. But when they arrived he drew himself apart to avoid trouble with those who were circumcised. The rest of the Jews joined in his dissembling, till even Barnabas was swept away by their pretense. As soon as I observed that they were not being straightforward about the truth of the gospel, I had this to say to Cephas in the presence of all: "If you who are a Jew are living according to Gentile ways rather than Jewish, by what logic do you force the Gentiles to adopt Jewish ways?"
This is the Word of the Lord.

Responsorial Psalm   Ps 117, 1. 2

℟. (Mk 16, 15) Go out to all the world,
  and tell the Good News.
Praise the Lord, all you nations,
  glorify him, all you peoples!
℟. Go out to all the world,
  and tell the Good News.
For steadfast is his kindness toward us,
  and the fidelity of the Lord endures forever.
℟. Go out to all the world,
  and tell the Good News.
℟. Or: Alleluia.

Years I and II

GOSPEL   Lk 11, 1-4
Alleluia

See no. 509.

✠ A reading from the holy gospel according to Luke
Lord, teach us to pray.

One day Jesus was praying in a certain place. When he had finished, one of his disciples asked him, "Lord, teach us to pray as John

taught his disciples." He said to them, "When you pray, say:
  " 'Father,
  hallowed be your name,
  your kingdom come.
  Give us each day our daily bread.
  Forgive us our sins,
  for we too forgive all who do us wrong;
  and subject us not to the trial.' "
This is the gospel of the Lord.

---

464   ## THURSDAY OF THE TWENTY-SEVENTH WEEK OF THE YEAR

Year I

READING I   Mal 3, 13-20
A reading from the book of the prophet Malachi
The day is coming now like a burning furnace.

You have defied me in word, says the Lord,
  yet you ask, "What have we spoken against you?"
You have said, "It is vain to serve God,
  and what do we profit by keeping his command,
And going about in penitential dress
  in awe of the Lord of hosts?
Rather must we call the proud blessed;
  for indeed evildoers prosper,
  and even tempt God with impunity."
Then they who fear the Lord spoke with one another,
  and the Lord listened attentively;
And a record book was written before him
  of those who fear the Lord and trust in his name.
And they shall be mine, says the Lord of hosts,
  my own special possession, on the day I take action.
And I will have compassion on them,
  as a man has compassion on his son who serves him.
Then you will again see the distinction
  between the just and the wicked;
Between him who serves God,
  and him who does not serve him.

For lo, the day is coming, blazing like an oven,
    when all the proud and all evildoers will be
      stubble,
And the day that is coming will set them on
    fire,
    leaving them neither root nor branch,
says the Lord of hosts.
But for you who fear my name, there will arise
    the sun of justice with its healing rays.
      This is the Word of the Lord.

Responsorial Psalm   Ps 1, 1-2. 3. 4. 6

℞. (Ps 40, 5) Happy are they who hope in the
    Lord.
Happy the man who follows not
    the counsel of the wicked
Nor walks in the way of sinners,
    nor sits in the company of the insolent,
But delights in the law of the Lord
    and meditates on his law day and night.
℞. Happy are they who hope in the Lord.
He is like a tree
    planted near running water,
That yields its fruit in due season,
    and whose leaves never fade.
[Whatever he does, prospers.]
℞. Happy are they who hope in the Lord.
Not so the wicked, not so;
    they are like chaff which the wind drives
      away.
For the Lord watches over the way of the just,
    but the way of the wicked vanishes.
℞. Happy are they who hope in the Lord.

Year II

READING I   Gal 3, 1-5

**A reading from the letter of Paul to the
Galatians**

Was it because you practiced the law that you received the
spirit or because you believed what you heard?

My good people of Galatia, have you gone out
of your minds? Who has cast a spell over you—
you before whose eyes Jesus Christ was displayed to view upon his cross? I want to know
only one thing from you: how did you receive
the Spirit? Was it through observance of the
law or through faith in what you heard? How
could you be so stupid? After beginning in the

spirit, are you now to end in the flesh? Have
you had such remarkable experiences all to no
purpose—if indeed they were to no purpose? Is
it because you observe the law or because you
have faith in what you heard that God lavishes
the Spirit on you and works wonders in your
midst?
    This is the Word of the Lord.

Responsorial Psalm   Lk 1, 69-70. 71-72. 73-75

℞. (68) Blessed be the Lord God of Israel,
    for he has visited his people.
He has raised a horn of saving strength for us
    in the house of David his servant,
As he promised through the mouths of his holy
    ones,
    the prophets of ancient times.
℞. Blessed be the Lord God of Israel,
    for he has visited his people.
Salvation from our enemies
    and from the hands of all our foes.
He has dealt mercifully with our fathers
    and remembered the holy covenant he made.
℞. Blessed be the Lord God of Israel,
    for he has visited his people.
The oath he swore to Abraham our father he
    would grant us:
    that, rid of fear and delivered from the
      enemy,
We should serve him devoutly and through all
    our days,
    be holy in his sight.
℞. Blessed be the Lord God of Israel,
    for he has visited his people.

Years I and II

GOSPEL   Lk 11, 5-13
Alleluia

See no. 509.

✠ **A reading from the holy gospel according
to Luke**

Seek and it will be given to you.

Jesus said to his disciples: "If one of you
knows someone who comes to him in the
middle of the night and says to him, 'Friend,
lend me three loaves, for a friend of mine has
come in from a journey and I have nothing to
offer him'; and he from inside should reply,

'Leave me alone. The door is shut now and my children and I are in bed. I can't get up to look after your needs'—I tell you, even though he does not get up and take care of the man because of friendship, he will find himself doing so because of his persistence and give him as much as he needs.

"So I say to you, 'Ask and you shall receive; see and you shall find; knock and it shall be opened to you.'

"For whoever asks, receives; whoever seeks, finds; whoever knocks, is admitted. What father among you will give his son a snake if he asks for a fish, or hand him a scorpion if he asks for an egg? If you, with all your sins, know how to give your children good things, how much more will the heavenly Father give the Holy Spirit to those who ask him."

This is the gospel of the Lord.

---

465   **FRIDAY OF THE TWENTY-SEVENTH WEEK OF THE YEAR**

Year I

READING I   Jl 1, 13-15; 2, 1-2

A reading from the book of the prophet Joel

The day of the Lord God is coming, a day of darkness and gloom.

Gird yourselves and weep, O priests!
    wail, O ministers of the altar!
Come, spend the night in sackcloth,
    O ministers of my God!
The house of your God is deprived
    of offering and libation.
Proclaim a fast,
    call an assembly;
Gather the elders,
    all who dwell in the land,
Into the house of the Lord, your God,
    and cry to the Lord!

Alas, the day!
    for near is the day of the Lord,
    and it comes as ruin from the Almighty.

Blow the trumpet in Zion,
    sound the alarm on my holy mountain!

Let all who dwell in the land tremble,
    for the day of the Lord is coming;
Yes, it is near, a day of darkness and of gloom,
    a day of clouds and somberness!
Like dawn spreading over the mountains,
    a people numerous and mighty!
Their like has not been from of old,
    nor will it be after them,
    even to the years of distant generations.

This is the Word of the Lord.

Responsorial Psalm   Ps 9, 2-3. 6. 16. 8-9

℟. (9) The Lord will judge the world with justice.
I will give thanks to you, O Lord, with all my heart;
    I will declare all your wondrous deeds.
I will be glad and exult in you;
    I will sing praise to your name, Most High.
℟. The Lord will judge the world with justice.
You rebuked the nations and destroyed the wicked;
    their names you blotted out forever and ever.
The nations are sunk in the pit they have made;
    in the snare they set, their foot is caught.
℟. The Lord will judge the world with justice.
But the Lord sits enthroned forever;
    he has set up his throne for judgment.
He judges the world with justice;
    he governs the peoples with equity.
℟. The Lord will judge the world with justice.

Year II

READING I   Gal 3, 7-14

A reading from the letter of Paul to the Galatians

Those who rely on faith are blessed with the faith of Abraham.

Those who believe are sons of Abraham. Because Scripture saw in advance that God's way of justifying the Gentiles would be through faith, it foretold this good news to Abraham: "All nations shall be blessed in you." Thus it is that all who believe are blessed along with Abraham, the man of faith.

All who depend on observance of the law, on the other hand, are under a curse. It is written,

"Cursed is he who does not abide by everything written in the book of the law and carry it out." It should be obvious that no one is justified in God's sight by the law, for "the just man shall live by faith." But the law does not depend on faith. Its terms are: "Whoever does these things shall live by them." Christ has delivered us back from the power of the law's curse by becoming himself a curse for us, as it is written: "Accursed is anyone who is hanged on a tree." This has happened so that through Christ Jesus the blessing bestowed on Abraham might descend on the Gentiles in Christ Jesus, thereby making it possible for us to receive the promised Spirit through faith.

This is the Word of the Lord.

Responsorial Psalm   Ps 111, 1-2. 3-4. 5-6

℟. (5) The Lord will remember his covenant for ever.
I will give thanks to the Lord with all my heart
    in the company and assembly of the just.
Great are the works of the Lord,
    exquisite in all their delights.
℟. The Lord will remember his covenant for ever.
Majesty and glory are his work,
    and his justice endures forever.
He has won renown for his wondrous deeds;
    gracious and merciful is the Lord.
℟. The Lord will remember his covenant for ever.
He has given food to those who fear him;
    he will forever be mindful of his covenant.
He has made known to his people the power of his works,
    giving them the inheritance of the nations.
℟. The Lord will remember his covenant for ever.
℟. Or: Alleluia.

GOSPEL   Lk 11, 15-26
Alleluia
See no. 509.

✠ A reading from the holy gospel according to Luke
If by the finger of God I cast out devils, the kingdom of God has overtaken you.

As Jesus was casting out a devil, some of the crowd said, "It is by Beelzebul, the prince of devils, that he casts out devils." Others, to test him, were demanding of him a sign from heaven.

Because he knew their thoughts, he said to them: "Every kingdom divided against itself is laid waste. Any house torn by dissension falls. If Satan is divided against himself, how can his kingdom last?—since you say it is by Beelzebul that I cast out devils. If I cast out devils by Beelzebul, by whom do your people cast them out? In such a case, let them act as your judges. But if it is by the finger of God that I cast out devils, then the reign of God is upon you.

"When a strong man fully armed guards his courtyard, his possessions go undisturbed. But when someone stronger than he comes and overpowers him, such a one carries off the arms on which he was relying and divides the spoils. The man who is not with me is against me, and the man who does not gather with me scatters.

"When an unclean spirit has gone out of a man, it wanders through arid wastes, searching for a resting place; failing to find one, it says, 'I will go back where I came from.' It then returns, to find the house swept and tidied. Next it goes out and returns with seven other spirits far worse than itself, who enter in and dwell there. The result is that the last state of the man is worse than the first."

This is the gospel of the Lord.

466   SATURDAY OF THE TWENTY-SEVENTH WEEK OF THE YEAR

Year I

READING I   Jl 4, 12-21

A reading from the book of the prophet Joel

Put the sickle in because the harvest is ripe.

The Lord said:
Let the nations bestir themselves and come up
   to the Valley of Jehoshaphat;
For there will I sit in judgment
   upon all the neighboring nations.

Apply the sickle,
   for the harvest is ripe;
Come and tread,
   for the wine press is full;
The vats overflow,
   for great is their malice.
Crowd upon crowd
   in the valley of decision;
For near is the day of the Lord
   in the valley of decision.
Sun and moon are darkened,
   and the stars withhold their brightness.
The Lord roars from Zion,
   and from Jerusalem raises his voice;
The heavens and the earth quake,
   but the Lord is a refuge to his people,
   a stronghold to the men of Israel.

Then shall you know that I, the Lord, am your
   God,
   dwelling on Zion, my holy mountain;
Jerusalem shall be holy,
   and strangers shall pass through her no
   more.
And then, on that day,
   the mountains shall drip new wine,
   and the hills shall flow with milk;
And the channels of Judah
   shall flow with water:
A fountain shall issue from the house of the
   Lord,
   to water the Valley of Shittim.
Egypt shall be a waste,
   and Edom a desert waste,

Because of violence done to the people of
   Judah,
   because they shed innocent blood in their
   land.
But Judah shall abide forever,
   and Jerusalem for all generations.
I will avenge their blood,
   and not leave it unpunished.
The Lord dwells in Zion.
      This is the Word of the Lord.

Responsorial Psalm   Ps 97, 1-2. 5-6. 11-12

℟. (12) Let good men rejoice in the Lord.
The Lord is king; let the earth rejoice;
   let the many isles be glad.
Clouds and darkness are round about him,
   justice and judgment are the foundation of
   his throne.
℟. Let good men rejoice in the Lord.
The mountains melt like wax before the Lord,
   before the Lord of all the earth.
The heavens proclaim his justice,
   and all peoples see his glory.
℟. Let good men rejoice in the Lord.
Light dawns for the just;
   and gladness, for the upright of heart.
Be glad in the Lord, you just,
   and give thanks to his holy name.
℟. Let good men rejoice in the Lord.

Year II

READING I   Gal 3, 22-29

A reading from the letter of Paul to the Galatians

All of you are sons of God through faith.

Scripture has locked all things in under the constraint of sin. Why? So that the promise might be fulfilled, in those who believe, in consequence of faith in Jesus Christ.

Before faith came we were under the constraint of the law, locked in until the faith that was coming should be revealed. In other words, the law was our monitor until Christ came to bring about our justification through faith. But now that faith is here, we are no longer in the monitor's charge. Each one of you

is a son of God because of your faith in Christ Jesus. All of you who have been baptized into Christ have clothed yourselves with him. There does not exist among you Jew or Greek, slave or freeman, male or female. All are one in Christ Jesus. Furthermore, if you belong to Christ you are the descendants of Abraham, which means you inherit all that was promised.
This is the Word of the Lord.

Responsorial Psalm   Ps 105, 2-3. 4-5. 6-7

℟. (8) The Lord remembers his covenant for ever.
Sing to him, sing his praise,
    proclaim all his wondrous deeds.
Glory in his holy name;
    rejoice, O hearts that seek the Lord!
℟. The Lord remembers his covenant for ever.
Look to the Lord in his strength;
    seek to serve him constantly.
Recall the wondrous deeds that he has
        wrought,
    his portents, and the judgments he has ut-
        tered.
℟. The Lord remembers his covenant for ever.
You descendants of Abraham, his servants,
    sons of Jacob, his chosen ones!
He, the Lord, is our God;
    throughout the earth his judgments prevail.
℟. The Lord remembers his covenant for ever.
℟. Or: Alleluia.

Years I and II

GOSPEL   Lk 11, 27-28
Alleluia

See no. 509.

✠ A reading from the holy gospel according
            to Luke
Happy the womb that bore you! Happier still are those who
            hear the word of God.

While Jesus was speaking, a woman from the crowd called out, "Blest is the womb that bore you and the breasts that nursed you!" "Rather," he replied, "blest are they who hear the word of God and keep it."
This is the gospel of the Lord.

467   **MONDAY OF THE**
          TWENTY-EIGHTH WEEK
          OF THE YEAR

Year I

READING I   Rom 1, 1-7
    The beginning of the letter of Paul to the
                    Romans
Through Christ we received grace and our apostolic mission
    to preach the obedience of faith to the gentiles.

Greetings from Paul, a servant of Christ Jesus, called to be an apostle and set apart to proclaim the gospel of God which he promised long ago through his prophets, as the Holy Scriptures record—the gospel concerning his Son, who was descended from David according to the flesh but was made Son of God in power, according to the spirit of holiness, by his resurrection from the dead: Jesus Christ our Lord. Through him we have been favored with apostleship, that we may spread his name and bring to obedient faith all the Gentiles, among whom are you who have been called to belong to Jesus Christ.

To all in Rome, beloved of God and called to holiness, grace and peace from God our Father and the Lord Jesus Christ.
            This is the Word of the Lord.

Responsorial Psalm   Ps 98, 1. 2-3. 3-4

℟. (2) The Lord has made known his salvation.
Sing to the Lord a new song,
    for he has done wondrous deeds;
His right hand has won victory for him,
    his holy arm.
℟. The Lord has made known his salvation.
The Lord has made his salvation known:
    in the sight of the nations he has revealed his
        justice.
He has remembered his kindness and his faith-
        fulness
    toward the house of Israel.
℟. The Lord has made known his salvation.
All the ends of the earth have seen
    the salvation by our God.
Sing joyfully to the Lord, all you lands;
    break into song; sing praise.
℟. The Lord has made known his salvation.

Year II

READING I   Gal 4, 22-24. 26-27. 31—5, 1

A reading from the letter of Paul to the Galatians

We are the children, not of the slave girl, but of the free-born wife.

It is written that Abraham had two sons, one by the slave girl, the other by his freeborn wife. The son of the slave girl had been begotten in the course of nature, but the son of the free woman was the fruit of the promise. All this is clearly an allegory: the two women stand for the two covenants. One is from Mount Sinai and she brought forth children to slavery: this is Hagar. But the Jerusalem on high is freeborn, and it is she who is our mother. That is why Scripture says:

"Rejoice, you barren one who bear no children;
    break into song, you stranger to the pains of childbirth!
For many are the children of the wife deserted—
    far more than of her who has a husband!"

Therefore, my brothers, we are not children of a slave girl but of a mother who is free.

It was for liberty that Christ freed us. So stand firm, and do not take on yourselves the yoke of slavery a second time!

This is the Word of the Lord.

Responsorial Psalm   Ps 113, 1-2. 3-4. 5. 6-7

℟. (2) Blessed be the name of the Lord for ever.
Praise, you servants of the Lord,
    praise the name of the Lord.
Blessed be the name of the Lord
    both now and forever.
℟. Blessed be the name of the Lord for ever.
From the rising to the setting of the sun
    is the name of the Lord to be praised.
High above all nations is the Lord;
    above the heavens is his glory.
℟. Blessed be the name of the Lord for ever.
Who is like the Lord, our God,
    who looks upon the heavens and the earth below?

He raises up the lowly from the dust;
    from the dunghill he lifts up the poor.
℟. Blessed be the name of the Lord for ever.
℟. Or: Alleluia.

Years I and II

GOSPEL   Lk 11, 29-32

Alleluia

See no. 509.

✠ **A reading from the holy gospel according to Luke**

No sign will be given to this generation except the sign of Jonah the prophet.

While the crowds pressed around him Jesus began to speak to them in these words: "This is an evil age. It seeks a sign. But no sign will be given it except the sign of Jonah. Just as Jonah was a sign for the Ninevites, so will the Son of Man be a sign for the present age. The queen of the south will rise at the judgment along with the men of this generation, and she will condemn them. She came from the farthest corner of the world to listen to the wisdom of Solomon, but you have a greater than Solomon here. At the judgment, the citizens of Nineveh will rise along with the present generation, and they will condemn it. For at the preaching of Jonah they reformed, but you have a greater than Jonah here.

This is the gospel of the Lord.

468   **TUESDAY OF THE TWENTY-EIGHTH WEEK OF THE YEAR**

Year I

READING I   Rom 1, 16-25

A reading from the letter of Paul to the Romans

Men have known God, yet they refused to honor him.

I am not ashamed of the gospel. It is the power of God leading everyone who believes in it to salvation, the Jew first, then the Greek. For in the gospel is revealed the justice of God which begins and ends with faith; as Scripture says, "The just man shall live by faith."

The wrath of God is being revealed from heaven against the irreligious and perverse spirit of men who, in this perversity of theirs, hinder the truth. In fact, whatever can be known about God is clear to them; he himself made it so. Since the creation of the world, invisible realities, God's eternal power and divinity, have become visible, recognized through the things he has made. Therefore these men are inexcusable. They certainly had knowledge of God, yet they did not glorify him as God or give him thanks; they stultified themselves through speculating to no purpose, and their senseless hearts were darkened. They claimed to be wise, but turned into fools instead; they exchanged the glory of the immortal God for images representing mortal man, birds, beasts and snakes. In consequence, God delivered them up in their lusts to unclean practices; they engaged in the mutual degradation of their bodies, these men who exchanged the truth of God for a lie and worshiped and served the creature rather than the Creator—blessed be he forever, amen!

This is the Word of the Lord.

Responsorial Psalm   Ps 19, 2-3. 4-5

R̶∕. (2) The heavens proclaim the glory of God.
The heavens declare the glory of God,
   and the firmament proclaims his handiwork.
Day pours out the word to day,
   and night to night imparts knowledge.
R̶∕. The heavens proclaim the glory of God.
Not a word nor a discourse
   whose voice is not heard;
Through all the earth their voice resounds,
   and to the ends of the world, their message.
R̶∕. The heavens proclaim the glory of God.

Year II

READING I   Gal 5, 1-6
A reading from the letter of Paul to the Galatians

Whether you are circumcised or not is not important; what does matter is faith which expresses itself through love.

Christ freed us for liberty. So stand firm, and do not take on yourselves the yoke of slavery a second time! Pay close attention to me, Paul,

when I tell you that if you have yourselves circumcised, Christ will be of no use to you! I point out once more to all who receive circumcision that they are bound to the law in its entirety. Any of you who seek your justification in the law have severed yourselves from Christ and fallen from God's favor! It is in the spirit that we eagerly await the justification we hope for, and only faith can yield it. In Christ Jesus neither circumcision nor the lack of it counts for anything; only faith, which expresses itself through love.

This is the Word of the Lord.

Responsorial Psalm   Ps 119, 41. 43. 44. 45. 47. 48

R̶∕. (41) Let your loving kindness come to me, O Lord.
Let your kindness come to me, O Lord,
   your salvation according to your promise.
R̶∕. Let your loving kindness come to me, O Lord.
Take not the word of truth from my mouth,
   for in your ordinances is my hope.
R̶∕. Let your loving kindness come to me, O Lord.
And I will keep your law continually,
   forever and ever.
R̶∕. Let your loving kindness come to me, O Lord.
And I will walk at liberty,
   because I seek your precepts.
R̶∕. Let your loving kindness come to me, O Lord.
And I will delight in your commands,
   which I love.
R̶∕. Let your loving kindness come to me, O Lord.
And I will lift up my hands to your commands
   and meditate on your statutes.
R̶∕. Let your loving kindness come to me, O Lord.

Years I and II

GOSPEL   Lk 11, 37-41
Alleluia

See no. 509.

✠ A reading from the holy gospel according to Luke

Give alms and everything will be made clean for you.

As Jesus was speaking, a Pharisee invited him to dine at his house. He entered and reclined at table. Seeing this, the Pharisee was surprised that he had not first performed the ablutions prescribed before eating. The Lord said to him: "You Pharisees! You cleanse the outside of cup and dish, but within you are filled with rapaciousness. Fools! Did not he who made the outside make the inside too? But if you give what you have as alms, all will be wiped clean for you."

This is the gospel of the Lord.

---

469   **WEDNESDAY OF THE TWENTY-EIGHTH WEEK OF THE YEAR**

Year I

READING I   Rom 2, 1-11

A reading from the letter of Paul to the Romans

He will repay each one according to his works, Jews first, but Greeks as well.

Every one of you who judges another is inexcusable. By your judgment you convict yourself, since you do the very same things. "We know that God's judgment on men who do such things is just." Do you suppose, then, that you will escape his judgment, you who condemn these things in others yet do them yourself? Or do you presume on his kindness and forbearance? Do you not know that God's kindness is an invitation to you to repent? In spite of this, your hard and impenitent heart is storing up retribution for that day of wrath when the just judgment of God will be revealed, when he will repay every man for what he has done: eternal life to those who strive for glory, honor, and immortality by patiently doing right; wrath and fury to those who selfishly disobey the truth and obey wickedness. Yes, affliction and anguish will come upon every man who has done evil, the Jew first, then the Greek. But there will be glory, honor, and peace for everyone who has done

good, likewise the Jew first, then the Greek. With God there is no favoritism.

This is the Word of the Lord.

Responsorial Psalm   Ps 62, 2-3. 6-7. 9

℟. (13) Lord, you give back to every man according to his works.

Only in God is my soul at rest;
    from him comes my salvation.
He only is my rock and my salvation,
    my stronghold; I shall not be disturbed at all.
℟.Lord, you give back to every man
    according to his works.

Only in God be at rest, my soul,
    for from him comes my hope.
He only is my rock and my salvation,
    my stronghold; I shall not be disturbed.
℟.Lord, you give back to every man
    according to his works.

Trust in him at all times, O my people!
    Pour out your hearts before him;
    God is our refuge!
℟.Lord, you give back to every man
    according to his works.

Year II

READING I   Gal 5, 18-25

A reading from the letter of Paul to the Galatians

You cannot belong to Christ unless you crucify the flesh with its passions.

If you are guided by the spirit, you are not under the law. It is obvious what proceeds from the flesh: lewd conduct, impurity, licentiousness, idolatry, sorcery, hostilities, bickering, jealousy, outbursts of rage, selfish rivalries, dissensions, factions, envy, drunkenness, orgies, and the like. I warn you, as I have warned you before: those who do such things will not inherit the kingdom of God!

In contrast, the fruit of the spirit is love, joy, peace, patient endurance, kindness, generosity, faith, mildness, and chastity. Against such there is no law! Those who belong to Christ Jesus have crucified their flesh with its passions and desires. Since we live by the spirit, let us follow the spirit's lead.

This is the Word of the Lord.

Responsorial Psalm   Ps 1, 1-2. 3. 4. 6

℟. (Jn 8, 12) Those who follow you, Lord, will
   have the light of life.

Happy the man who follows not
   the counsel of the wicked
Nor walks in the way of sinners,
   nor sits in the company of the insolent,
But delights in the law of the Lord
   and meditates on his law day and night.

℟. Those who follow you, Lord, will have the
   light of life.

He is like a tree
   planted near running water,
That yields its fruit in due season,
   and whose leaves never fade.
   [Whatever he does, prospers.]

℟. Those who follow you, Lord, will have the
   light of life.

Not so the wicked, not so;
   they are like chaff which the wind drives
   away.
For the Lord watches over the way of the just,
   but the way of the wicked vanishes.

℟. Those who follow you, Lord, will have the
   light of life.

Years I and II

GOSPEL   Lk 11, 42-46
Alleluia

See no. 509.

✠ A reading from the holy gospel according
   to Luke
Alas for you pharisees—and you lawyers, woe to you!

The Lord said: "Woe to you Pharisees! You pay
tithes on mint and rue and all the garden
plants, while neglecting justice and the love of
God. These are the things you should practice,
without omitting the others. Woe to you Pharisees! You love the front seats in synagogues
and marks of respect in public. Woe to you!
You are like hidden tombs over which men
walk unawares."

   In reply one of the lawyers said to him,
"Teacher, in speaking this way you insult us
too." Jesus answered: "Woe to you lawyers
also! You lay impossible burdens on men but
will not lift a finger to lighten them."

   This is the gospel of the Lord.

**470   THURSDAY OF THE
           TWENTY-EIGHTH WEEK
           OF THE YEAR**

Year I

READING I   Rom 3, 21-29
A reading from the letter of Paul to the Romans
A man is justified by faith apart from the law.

The justice of God has been manifested apart
from the law, even though both law and prophets bear witness to it—that justice of God
which works through faith in Jesus Christ for
all who believe. All men have sinned and hence
are deprived of the glory of God. All men are
now undeservedly justified by the gift of God,
through the redemption wrought in Christ
Jesus. Through his blood, God made him the
means of expiation for all who believe. He did
so to manifest his own justice, for the sake of
remitting sins committed in the past—to manifest his justice in the present, by way of forbearance, so that he might be just and might
justify those who believe in Jesus.

   What occasion is there then for boasting?
It is ruled out. By what law, the law of works?
Not at all! By the law of faith. For we hold that
a man is justified by faith apart from obser-
vance of the law. Does God belong to the Jews
alone? Is he not also the God of the Gentiles?
Yes, of the Gentiles too. It is the same God.
   This is the Word of the Lord.

Responsorial Psalm   Ps 130, 1-2. 3-4. 5-6

℟. (7) With the Lord there is mercy,
   and fullness of redemption.

Out of the depths I cry to you, O Lord;
   Lord, hear my voice!
Let your ears be attentive
   to my voice in supplication.

℟. With the Lord there is mercy,
   and fullness of redemption.

If you, O Lord, mark iniquities,
   Lord, who can stand?
But with you is forgiveness,
   that you may be revered.

℟. With the Lord there is mercy,
   and fullness of redemption.

I trust in the Lord;
   my soul trusts in his word.
My soul waits for the Lord
   more than sentinels wait for the dawn.
℟. With the Lord there is mercy,
   and fullness of redemption.

Year II

READING I   Eph 1, 3-10
The beginning of the letter of Paul to the
Ephesians
Before the world was made, he chose us.

Paul, the apostle of Jesus Christ: Praised be
the God and Father of our Lord Jesus Christ:
God, who has bestowed on us in Christ every
spiritual blessing in the heavens! God chose
us in him before the world began, to be holy
and blameless in his sight, to be full of love;
he likewise predestined us through Christ
Jesus to be his adopted sons—such was his will
and pleasure—that all might praise the divine
favor he has bestowed on us in his beloved.

It is in Christ and through his blood that
we have been redeemed and our sins forgiven,
so immeasurably generous is God's favor to
us. God has given us the wisdom to understand
fully the mystery, the plan he was pleased to
decree in Christ, to be carried out in the fullness of time: namely, to bring all things in the
heavens and on earth into one under Christ's
headship.
                This is the Word of the Lord.

Responsorial Psalm   Ps 98, 1. 2-3. 3-4. 5-6

℟. (2) The Lord has made known his salvation.
Sing to the Lord a new song,
   for he has done wondrous deeds;
His right hand has won victory for him,
   his holy arm.
℟. The Lord has made known his salvation.
The Lord has made his salvation known:
   in the sight of the nations he has revealed
      his justice.
He has remembered his kindness and his faith-
      fulness
   toward the house of Israel.
℟. The Lord has made known his salvation.

All the ends of the earth have seen,
   the salvation by our God.
Sing joyfully to the Lord, all you lands;
   break into song; sing praise.
℟. The Lord has made known his salvation.
Sing praise to the Lord with the harp,
   with the harp and melodious song.
With trumpets and the sound of the horn
   sing joyfully before the King, the Lord.
℟. The Lord has made known his salvation.

Years I and II

GOSPEL   Lk 11, 47-54
Alleluia
See no. 509.

✠ A reading from the holy gospel according
                  to Luke
The blood of the prophets is required, from the blood of
Abel to the blood of Zechariah.

The Lord said: "Woe to you! You build the
tombs of the prophets, but it was your fathers
who murdered them. You show that you stand
behind the deeds of your fathers: they did the
murders and you erect the tombs. That is why
the wisdom of God has said, 'I will send them
prophets and apostles, and some of these they
will persecute and kill'; so that this generation
will have to account for the blood of all the
prophets shed since the foundation of the
world. Their guilt stretches from the blood of
Abel to the blood of Zechariah, who met his
death between the altar and the sanctuary!
Yes, I tell you, this generation will have to
account for it. Woe to you lawyers. You have
taken away the key of knowledge. You yourselves have not gained access, yet you have
stopped those who wish to enter!" After he
had left this gathering, the scribes and Pharisees began to manifest fierce hostility to him
and to make him speak on a multitude of
questions, setting traps to catch him in his
speech.
            This is the gospel of the Lord.

471   FRIDAY OF THE TWENTY-EIGHTH WEEK OF THE YEAR

Year I

READING I   Rom 4, 1-8

A reading from the letter of Paul to the Romans
Abraham believed in God, and his faith justified him.

What shall we say of Abraham our ancestor according to the flesh? Certainly if Abraham was justified by his deeds he has grounds for boasting, but not in God's view, for what does Scripture say? "Abraham believed God, and it was credited to him as justice." Now, when a man works, his wages are not regarded as a favor but as his due. But when a man does nothing, yet believes in him who justifies the sinful, his faith is credited as justice. Thus David congratulates the man to whom God credits justice without requiring deeds:
"Blest are they whose iniquities are forgiven, whose sins are covered over.
Blest is the man to whom the Lord imputes no guilt."
    This is the Word of the Lord.

Responsorial Psalm   Ps 32, 1-2. 5. 11

℟. (7) I turn to you, Lord, in time of trouble, and you fill me with the joy of salvation.
Happy is he whose fault is taken away, whose sin is covered.
Happy the man to whom the Lord imputes not guilt, in whose spirit there is no guile.
℟. I turn to you, Lord, in time of trouble, and you fill me with the joy of salvation.
Then I acknowledged my sin to you, my guilt I covered not.
I said, "I confess my faults to the Lord," and you took away the guilt of my sin.
℟. I turn to you, Lord, in time of trouble, and you fill me with the joy of salvation.
Be glad in the Lord and rejoice, you just; exult, all you upright of heart.
℟. I turn to you, Lord, in time of trouble, and you fill me with the joy of salvation.

Year II

READING I   Eph 1, 11-14

A reading from the letter of Paul to the Ephesians
We hoped in Christ before he came and we were sealed with the Holy Spirit.

In Christ we were chosen; for in the decree of God, who administers everything according to his will and counsel, we were predestined to praise his glory by being the first to hope in Christ. In him you too were chosen; when you heard the glad tidings of salvation, the word of truth, and believed in it, you were sealed with the Holy Spirit who had been promised. He is the pledge of our inheritance, the first payment against the full redemption of a people God has made his own to praise his glory.
    This is the Word of the Lord.

Responsorial Psalm   Ps 33, 1-2. 4-5. 12-13

℟. (12) Happy the people the Lord has chosen to be his own.
Exult, you just, in the Lord; praise from the upright is fitting.
Give thanks to the Lord on the harp; with the ten-stringed lyre chant his praises.
℟. Happy the people the Lord has chosen to be his own.
For upright is the word of the Lord, and all his works are trustworthy.
He loves justice and right; of the kindness of the Lord the earth is full.
℟. Happy the people the Lord has chosen to be his own.
Happy the nation whose God is the Lord, the people he has chosen for his own inheritance.
From heaven the Lord looks down; he sees all mankind.
℟. Happy the people the Lord has chosen to be his own.

Years I and II

GOSPEL   Lk 12, 1-7
Alleluia

See no. 509.

✠ A reading from the holy gospel according
to Luke

Every hair on your head has been numbered.

A crowd of thousands had gathered, so dense
that they were treading on one another. Jesus
began to speak first to his disciples: "Be on
guard against the yeast of the Pharisees, which
is hypocrisy. There is nothing concealed that
will not be revealed, nothing hidden that will
not be made known. Everything you have said
in the dark will be heard in the daylight; what
you have whispered in locked rooms will be
proclaimed from the rooftops.

"I say to you who are my friends: Do not be
afraid of those who kill the body and can do
no more. I will show you whom you ought to
fear. Fear him who has power to cast into
Gehenna after he has killed. Yes, I tell you,
fear him. Are not five sparrows sold for a few
pennies? Yet not one of them is neglected by
God. In very truth, even the hairs of your head
are counted! Fear nothing, then. You are worth
more than a flock of sparrows."

This is the gospel of the Lord.

---

472   **SATURDAY OF THE
TWENTY-EIGHTH WEEK
OF THE YEAR**

Year I

READING I   Rom 4, 13. 16-18

A reading from the letter of Paul to the Romans

In hope he believed against hope.

The promise made to Abraham and his descendants that they would inherit the world did not
depend on the law; it was made in view of the
justice that comes from faith. Hence all depends on faith, everything is a grace. Thus the
promise holds true for all Abraham's descendants, not only for those who have the law but
for all who have his faith. He is the father of us
all, which is why Scripture says, "I have made
you father of many nations." Yes, he is our
father in the sight of God in whom he believed,
the God who restores the dead to life and calls
into being those things which had not been.
Hoping against hope, Abraham believed and so

became the father of many nations, just as it
was once told him, "Numerous as this shall
your descendants be."

This is the Word of the Lord.

Responsorial Psalm   Ps 105, 6-7. 8-9. 42-43

℞. (8) The Lord remembers his covenant for
ever.

You descendants of Abraham, his servants,
sons of Jacob, his chosen ones!
He, the Lord, is our God;
throughout the earth his judgments prevail.

℞. The Lord remembers his covenant for ever.

He remembers forever his covenant
which he made binding for a thousand generations—
Which he entered into with Abraham
and by his oath to Isaac.

℞. The Lord remembers his covenant for ever.

For he remembered his holy word
to his servant Abraham.
And he led forth his people with joy;
with shouts of joy, his chosen ones.

℞. The Lord remembers his covenant for ever.
℞. Or: Alleluia.

Year II

READING I   Eph 1, 15-23

**A reading from the letter of Paul to the
Ephesians**

He made him the head of the Church, which is his body.

From the time I first heard of your faith in the
Lord Jesus and your love for all the members of
the church, I have never stopped thanking God
for you and recommending you in my prayers.
May the God of our Lord Jesus Christ, the Father of glory, grant you a spirit of wisdom and
insight to know him clearly. May he enlighten
your innermost vision that you may know the
great hope to which he has called you, the
wealth of glorious heritage to be distributed
among the members of the church, and the immeasurable scope of his power in us who believe. It is like the strength he showed in raising
Christ from the dead and seating him at his
right hand in heaven, high above every principality, power, virtue, and domination, and every

name that can be given in this age or in the age to come.

He has put all things under Christ's feet and made him head of the church, which is his body: the fullness of him, who fills the universe in all its parts.

       This is the Word of the Lord.

Responsorial Psalm   Ps 8, 2-3. 4-5. 6-7

℟. (7) You gave your Son authority over all your creation.

O Lord, our Lord,
  how glorious is your name over all the earth!
  You have exalted your majesty above the heavens.
Out of the mouths of babes and sucklings
  you have fashioned praise because of your foes.

℟. You gave your Son authority over all your creation.

When I behold your heavens, the work of your fingers,
  the moon and the stars which you set in place—
What is man that you should be mindful of him,
  or the son of man that you should care for him?

℟. You gave your Son authority over all your creation.

You have made him little less than the angels,
  and crowned him with glory and honor.
You have given him rule over the works of your hands,
  putting all things under his feet.

℟. You gave your Son authority over all your creation.

GOSPEL   **Years I and II**
Alleluia   Lk 12, 8-12
See no. 509.

✠ **A reading from the holy gospel according to Luke**

When the time comes the Holy Spirit will teach you what you must say.

Jesus said to his disciples: "I tell you, whoever acknowledges me before men—the Son of Man will acknowledge him before the angels of God. But the man who has disowned me in the presence of men will be disowned in the presence of the angels of God. Anyone who speaks against the Son of Man will be forgiven, but whoever blasphemes the Holy Spirit will never be forgiven. When they bring you before synagogues, rulers and authorities, do not worry about how to defend yourselves or what to say. The Holy Spirit will teach you at that moment all that should be said."

       This is the gospel of the Lord.

---

473   **MONDAY OF THE TWENTY-NINTH WEEK OF THE YEAR**   **Year I**

READING I   Rom 4, 20-25
A reading from the letter of Paul to the Romans
It was written for us when it says that our faith in him will be counted.

Abraham never questioned or doubted God's promise; rather, he was strengthened in faith and gave glory to God, fully persuaded that God could do whatever he had promised. Thus his faith was credited to him as justice.

    The words, "It was credited to him," were not written with him alone in view; they were intended for us too. For our faith will be credited to us also if we believe in him who raised Jesus our Lord from the dead, the Jesus who was handed over to death for our sins and raised up for our justification.

       This is the Word of the Lord.

Responsorial Psalm   Lk 1, 69-70. 71-72. 73-75

℟. (68) Blessed be the Lord God of Israel, for he has visited his people.

He has raised a horn of saving strength for us in the house of David his servant,
As he promised through the mouths of his holy ones,
  the prophets of ancient times.

℟. Blessed be the Lord God of Israel, for he has visited his people.

Salvation from our enemies
  and from the hands of all our foes.
He has dealt mercifully with our fathers
  and remembered the holy covenant he made.

℟. Blessed be the Lord God of Israel,
    for he has visited his people.
**The oath he swore to Abraham our father he
    would grant us:**
    **that, rid of fear and delivered from the en-
    emy,**
**We should serve him devoutly and through all
    our days**
    be holy in his sight.
℟. Blessed be the Lord God of Israel,
    for he has visited his people.

Year II

READING I   Eph 2, 1-10
A reading from the letter of Paul to the
Ephesians
He has raised us up with Christ and has given us a place
with him in heaven.

**You were dead because of your sins and
offenses, as you gave allegiance to the present
age and to the prince of the air, that spirit who
is even now at work among the rebellious. All
of us were once of their company; we lived at
the level of the flesh, following every whim
and fancy, and so by nature deserved God's
wrath like the rest. But God is rich in mercy;
because of his great love for us he brought us
to life with Christ when we were dead in sin.
By this favor you were saved. Both with and in
Christ Jesus he raised us up and gave us a place
in the heavens, that in the ages to come he
might display the great wealth of his favor,
manifested by his kindness to us in Christ
Jesus. I repeat, it is owing to his favor that
salvation is yours through faith. This is not
your own doing, it is God's gift; neither is
it a reward for anything you have accomplished, so let no one pride himself on it. We
are truly his handiwork, created in Christ
Jesus to lead the life of good deeds which God
prepared for us in advance.**
        This is the Word of the Lord.

Responsorial Psalm   Ps 100, 2. 3. 4. 5

℟. (3) The Lord made us, we belong to him.
Serve the Lord with gladness;
    come before him with joyful song.

℟. The Lord made us, we belong to him.
Know that the Lord is God;
    he made us, his we are;
    his people, the flock he tends.
℟. The Lord made us, we belong to him.
Enter his gates with thanksgiving,
    his courts with praise.
℟. The Lord made us, we belong to him.
**Give thanks to him; bless his name, for he is
    good:**
    the Lord, whose kindness endures forever,
    and his faithfulness, to all generations.
℟. The Lord made us, we belong to him.

Years I and II

GOSPEL   Lk 12, 13-21
Alleluia
See no. 509.

✠ **A reading from the holy gospel according
to Luke**
What good are your possessions?
**Someone in the crowd said to Jesus, "Teacher,
tell my brother to give me my share of our inheritance." He replied, "Friend, who has set me
up as your judge or arbiter?" Then he said to
the crowd, "Avoid greed in all its forms. A
man may be wealthy, but his possessions do
not guarantee him life."**

**He told them a parable in these words:
"There was a rich man who had a good harvest. 'What shall I do?' he asked himself. 'I
have no place to store my harvest. I know!' he
said. 'I will pull down my grain bins and build
larger ones. All my grain and my goods will go
there. Then I will say to myself: You have
blessings in reserve for years to come. Relax!
Eat heartily, drink well. Enjoy yourself.'**

**But God said to him, 'You fool! This very
night your life shall be required of you. To
whom will all this piled-up wealth of yours go?'
That is the way it works with the man who
grows rich for himself instead of growing rich
in the sight of God."**
        This is the gospel of the Lord.

474   TUESDAY OF THE
TWENTY-NINTH WEEK
OF THE YEAR

Year I

READING I   Rom 5, 12. 15. 17-19. 20-21

A reading from the letter of Paul to the Romans

If death reigns from one man's sin, how much more will those who receive the gift of grace reign.

Just as through one man sin entered the world and with sin death, so death came to all men inasmuch as all sinned. For if by the offense of the one man, all died, much more did the grace of God and the gracious gift of the one man, Jesus Christ, abound for all. If death began its reign through one man because of his offense, much more shall those who receive the overflowing grace and gift of justice live and reign through the one man, Jesus Christ.

To sum up, then: just as a single offense brought condemnation to all men, a single righteous act brought all men acquittal and life. Just as through one man's disobedience all became sinners, so through one man's obedience all shall become just.

Despite the increase of sin, grace has far surpassed it, so that, as sin reigned through death, grace may reign by way of justice leading to eternal life, through Jesus Christ our Lord.
      This is the Word of the Lord.

Responsorial Psalm   Ps 40, 7-8. 8-9. 10. 17

℟. (8. 9)Here am I, Lord;
  I come to do your will.
Sacrifice or oblation you wished not,
  but ears open to obedience you gave me.
Holocausts or sin-offerings you sought not;
  then said I, "Behold I come."
℟.Here am I, Lord;
  I come to do your will.
"In the written scroll it is prescribed for me,
To do your will, O my God, is my delight,
  and your law is within my heart!"
℟.Here am I, Lord;
  I come to do your will.
I announced your justice in the vast assembly;
  I did not restrain my lips, as you, O Lord, know.

℟.Here am I, Lord;
  I come to do your will.
But may all who seek you
  exult and be glad in you,
And may those who love your salvation
  say ever, "The Lord be glorified."
℟.Here am I, Lord;
  I come to do your will.

Year II

READING I   Eph 2, 12-22

A reading from the letter of Paul to the Ephesians

He is our peace; he has made the two into one.

In former times, you had no part in Christ and were excluded from the community of Israel. You were strangers to the covenant and its promise; you were without hope and without God in the world. But now in Christ Jesus you who once were far off have been brought near through the blood of Christ. It is he who is our peace, and who made the two of us one by breaking down the barrier of hostility that kept us apart. In his own flesh he abolished the law with its commands and precepts, to create in himself one new man from us who had been two, and to make peace reconciling both of us to God in one body through his cross which put that enmity to death. He came and "announced the good news of peace to you who were far off, and to those who were near"; through him we both have access in one Spirit to the Father.

This means that you are strangers and aliens no longer. No, you are fellow citizens of the saints and members of the household of God. You form a building which rises on the foundation of the apostles and prophets, with Christ Jesus himself as the capstone. Through him the whole structure is fitted together and takes shape as a holy temple in the Lord; in him you are being built into this temple, to become a dwelling place for God in the Spirit.
      This is the Word of the Lord.

Responsorial Psalm　　Ps 85, 9-10. 11-12. 13-14

℟. (9) The Lord speaks of peace to his people.
I will hear what God proclaims;
　　the Lord—for he proclaims peace.
Near indeed is his salvation to those who fear
　　him,
　　glory dwelling in our land.
℟. The Lord speaks of peace to his people.
Kindness and truth shall meet;
　　justice and peace shall kiss.
Truth shall spring out of the earth,
　　and justice shall look down from heaven.
℟. The Lord speaks of peace to his people.
The Lord himself will give his benefits;
　　our land shall yield its increase.
Justice shall walk before him,
　　and salvation, along the way of his steps.
℟. The Lord speaks of peace to his people.

Years I and II

GOSPEL　　Lk 12, 35-38
Alleluia

See no. 509.

✠ A reading from the holy gospel according
　　to Luke
Happy those servants whom the master finds awake when
he comes.
Jesus said to his disciples: "Let your belts be
fastened around your waists and your lamps
be burning ready. Be like men awaiting their
master's return from a wedding, so that when
he arrives and knocks, you will open for him
without delay. It will go well with those servants whom the master finds wide-awake on
his return. I tell you, he will put on an apron,
seat them at table, and proceed to wait on
them. Should he happen to come at midnight
or before sunrise and find them prepared, it
will go well with them."
　　This is the gospel of the Lord.

475　　**WEDNESDAY OF THE
TWENTY-NINTH WEEK
OF THE YEAR**

Year I

READING I　　Rom 6, 12-18
A reading from the letter of Paul to the Romans
Offer yourselves to God as dead men brought back to life.
Do not, therefore, let sin rule your mortal body
and make you obey its lusts; no more shall you
offer the members of your body to sin as
weapons for evil. Rather, offer yourselves to
God as men who have come back from the dead
to life, and your bodies to God as weapons for
justice. Sin will no longer have power over
you; you are now under grace, not under the
law.
　　What does all this lead to? Just because we
are not under the law but under grace, are we
free to sin? By no means! You must realize
that, when you offer yourselves to someone as
obedient slaves, you are the slave of the one
you obey, whether yours is the slavery of sin,
which leads to death, or of obedience, which
leads to justice. Thanks be to God, though once
you were slaves of sin, you sincerely obeyed
that rule of teaching which was imparted to
you; freed from your sin, you became slaves of
justice.
　　This is the Word of the Lord.

Responsorial Psalm　　Ps 124, 1-3. 4-6. 7-8

℟. (8)　Our help is in the name of the Lord.
Had not the Lord been with us,
　　let Israel say,
　　had not the Lord been with us—
When men rose up against us,
　　then would they have swallowed us alive.
When their fury was inflamed against us.
℟. Our help is in the name of the Lord.
Then would the waters have overwhelmed us;
The torrent would have swept over us;
　　over us then would have swept
　　the raging waters.
Blessed be the Lord, who did not leave us
　　a prey to their teeth.
℟. Our help is in the name of the Lord.

We were rescued like a bird
  from the fowlers' snare;
Broken was the snare,
  and we were freed.
Our help is in the name of the Lord,
  who made heaven and earth.
R̰. Our help is in the name of the Lord.

Year II

READING I   Eph 3, 2-12

A reading from the letter of Paul to the Ephesians

The mystery of Christ now revealed to us, was unknown to men in past generations.

I am sure you have heard of the ministry which God in his goodness gave me in your regard. That is why to me, Paul, a prisoner for Christ Jesus on behalf of you Gentiles, God's secret plan as I have briefly described it was revealed. When you read what I have said, you will realize that I know what I am talking about in speaking of the mystery of Christ, unknown to men in former ages but now revealed by the Spirit to the holy apostles and prophets. It is no less than this: in Christ Jesus the Gentiles are now co-heirs with the Jews, members of the same body and sharers of the promise through the preaching of the gospel.

Through the gift God in his goodness bestowed on me by the exercise of his power, I became a minister of the gospel. To me, the least of all believers, was given the grace to preach to the Gentiles the unfathomable riches of Christ and to enlighten all men on the mysterious design which for ages was hidden in God, the Creator of all. Now, therefore, through the church, God's manifold wisdom is made known to the principalities and powers of heaven, in accord with his age-old purpose, carried out in Christ Jesus our Lord. In Christ and through faith in him we can speak freely to God, drawing near him with confidence.
  This is the Word of the Lord.

Responsorial Psalm   Is 12, 2-3. 4. 5-6

R̰. (3) You will draw water joyfully from the springs of salvation.

God indeed is my savior;
  I am confident and unafraid.
My strength and my courage is the Lord,
  and he has been my savior.
With joy you will draw water
  at the fountain of salvation.
R̰. You will draw water joyfully from the springs of salvation.
Give thanks to the Lord, acclaim his name;
  among the nations make known his deeds,
  proclaim how exalted is his name.
R̰. You will draw water joyfully from the springs of salvation.
Sing praise to the Lord for his glorious achievement;
  let this be known throughout all the earth.
Shout with exultation, O city of Zion,
  for great in your midst
  is the Holy One of Israel!
R̰. You will draw water joyfully from the springs of salvation.

Years I and II

GOSPEL   Lk 12, 39-48
Alleluia

See no. 509.

✠ **A reading from the holy gospel according to Luke**

From the man who has received much, much will be demanded.

Jesus said to his disciples: "You know as well as I that if the head of the house knew when the thief was coming he would not let him break into his house. Be on guard, therefore. The Son of Man will come when you least expect him."

Peter said, "Do you intend this parable for us, Lord, or do you mean it for the whole world?" The Lord said, "Who in your opinion is that faithful, farsighted steward whom the master will set over his servants to dispense their ration of grain in season? That servant is fortunate whom his master finds busy when he returns. Assuredly, his master will put him in charge of all his property. But if the servant says to himself, 'My master is taking his time about coming,' and begins to abuse the housemen and servant girls, to eat and drink and get drunk, that servant's master will come back on a day when he does not expect him, at a time he does not know. He will punish him severely and rank him among those undeserving of trust. The slave who knew his master's wishes but did not prepare to fulfill them will get a severe beating, whereas the one who did not know them and who nonetheless deserved to be flogged will get off with fewer stripes. When much has been given a man, much will be required of him. More will be asked of a man to whom more has been entrusted."

This is the gospel of the Lord.

---

476 **THURSDAY OF THE TWENTY-NINTH WEEK OF THE YEAR**

Year I

READING I Rom 6, 19-23

A reading from the letter of Paul to the Romans
Now that you have been freed from sin, you have been made slaves of God.

I use the following example from human affairs because of your weak human nature. Just as formerly you enslaved your bodies to impurity and licentiousness for their degradation, make them now the servants of justice for their sanctification. When you were slaves of sin, you had freedom from justice. What benefit did you then enjoy? Things you are now ashamed of, all of them tending toward death. But now that you are freed from sin and have become slaves of God, your benefit is sanctification as you tend toward eternal life. The wages of sin is death, but the gift of God is eternal life in Christ Jesus our Lord.

This is the Word of the Lord.

Responsorial Psalm Ps 1, 1-2. 3. 4. 6

℟. (Ps 40, 5) Happy are they who hope in the Lord.

Happy the man who follows not
    the counsel of the wicked
Nor walks in the way of sinners,
    nor sits in the company of the insolent,

But delights in the law of the Lord
    and meditates on his law day and night.
℟. Happy are they who hope in the Lord.
He is like a tree
    planted near running water,
That yields its fruit in due season,
    and whose leaves never fade.
    [Whatever he does, prospers.]
℟. Happy are they who hope in the Lord.
Not so the wicked, not so;
    they are like chaff which the wind drives
    away.
For the Lord watches over the way of the just,
    but the way of the wicked vanishes.
℟. Happy are they who hope in the Lord.

Year II

READING I Eph 3, 14-21

A reading from the letter of Paul to the Ephesians
Planted in love and built on love, you will grasp the fullness of God.

That is why I kneel before the Father from whom every family in heaven and on earth takes its name; and I pray that he will bestow on you gifts in keeping with the riches of his glory. May he strengthen you inwardly through the workings of his Spirit. May Christ dwell in your hearts through faith, and may charity be the root and foundation of your life. Thus you will be able to grasp fully, with all the holy ones, the breadth and length and height and depth of Christ's love, and experience this love which surpasses all knowledge, so that you may attain to the fullness of God himself.

To him whose power now at work in us can do immeasurably more than we ask or imagine —to him be glory in the church and in Christ Jesus through all generations, world without end. Amen.

This is the Word of the Lord.

Responsorial Psalm Ps 33, 1-2. 4-5. 11-12. 18-19

℟. (5) The earth is full of the goodness of the Lord.

Exult, you just, in the Lord;
    praise from the upright is fitting.

Give thanks to the Lord on the harp;
  with the ten-stringed lyre chant his praises.
℟. The earth is full of the goodness of the Lord.
For upright is the word of the Lord,
  and all his works are trustworthy.
He loves justice and right;
  of the kindness of the Lord the earth is full.
℟. The earth is full of the goodness of the Lord.
But the plan of the Lord stands forever;
  the design of his heart, through all generations.
℟. The earth is full of the goodness of the Lord.
Happy the nation whose God is the Lord,
  the people he has chosen for his own inheritance.
℟. The earth is full of the goodness of the Lord.
But see, the eyes of the Lord are upon those
    who fear him,
  upon those who hope for his kindness,
To deliver them from death
  and preserve them in spite of famine.
℟. The earth is full of the goodness of the Lord.

Years I and II

GOSPEL   Lk 12, 49-53
Alleluia
See no. 509.

✠ A reading from the holy gospel according
            to Luke
I have not come to bring peace, but separation.
Jesus said to his disciples: "I have come to light
a fire on the earth. How I wish the blaze were
ignited! I have a baptism to receive. What
anguish I feel till it is over! Do you think I have
come to establish peace on the earth? I assure
you, the contrary is true; I have come for division. From now on, a household of five will be
divided three against two and two against
three; father will be split against son and
son against father, mother against daughter
and daughter against mother, mother-in-
law against daughter-in-law, daughter-in-law
against mother-in-law."
    This is the gospel of the Lord.

----

477   **FRIDAY OF THE**
        TWENTY-NINTH WEEK
        OF THE YEAR

Year I

READING I   Rom 7, 18-25
A reading from the letter of Paul to the
                Romans
Who will rescue me from this body of death?
I know that no good dwells in me, that is, in my
flesh; the desire to do right is there but not the
power. What happens is that I do, not the good
I will to do, but the evil I do not intend. But if
I do what is against my will, it is not I who do
it, but sin which dwells in me. This means that
even though I want to do what is right, a law
that leads to wrongdoing is always ready to
hand. My inner self agrees with the law of God,
but I see in my body's members another law at
war with the law of my mind; this makes me
the prisoner of the law of sin in my members.
What a wretched man I am! Who can free me
from this body under the power of death? All
praise to God, through Jesus Christ our Lord.
    This is the Word of the Lord.

Responsorial Psalm   Ps 119, 66. 68. 76. 77. 93. 94
℟. (68) Teach me your laws, O Lord.
Teach me wisdom and knowledge,
    for in your commands I trust.
℟. Teach me your laws, O Lord.
You are good and bountiful;
    teach me your statutes.
℟. Teach me your laws, O Lord.
Let your kindness comfort me
    according to your promise to your servants.
℟. Teach me your laws, O Lord.
Let your compassion come to me that I may
      live,
    for your law is my delight.
℟. Teach me your laws, O Lord.
Never will I forget your precepts,
    for through them you give me life.
℟. Teach me your laws, O Lord.
I am yours; save me,
    for I have sought your precepts.
℟. Teach me your laws, O Lord.

Year II

READING I
Eph 4, 1-6

A reading from the letter of Paul to the Ephesians

There is one body, one Lord, one faith, one baptism.

I plead with you as a prisoner for the Lord, to live a life worthy of the calling you have received, with perfect humility, meekness, and patience, bearing with one another lovingly. Make every effort to preserve the unity which has the Spirit as its origin and peace as its binding force. There is but one body and one Spirit, just as there is but one hope given all of you by your call. There is one Lord, one faith, one baptism; one God and Father of all, who is over all, and works through all, and is in all.
This is the Word of the Lord.

Responsorial Psalm
Ps 24, 1-2. 3-4. 5-6

℟. (6) Lord, this is the people that longs to see your face.

The Lord's are the earth and its fullness;
  the world and those who dwell in it.
For he founded it upon the seas
  and established it upon the rivers.

℟. Lord, this is the people that longs to see your face.

Who can ascend the mountain of the Lord?
  or who may stand in his holy place?
He whose hands are sinless, whose heart is clean,
  who desires not what is vain.

℟. Lord, this is the people that longs to see your face.

He shall receive a blessing from the Lord,
  a reward from God his savior.
Such is the race that seeks for him,
  that seeks the face of the God of Jacob.

℟. Lord, this is the people that longs to see your face.

Years I and II

GOSPEL
Lk 12, 54-59

Alleluia

See no. 509.

✠ A reading from the holy gospel according to Luke

You know how to interpret the face of the earth and the sky. How is it you do not know how to interpret these times?

Jesus said to the crowds: "When you see a cloud rising in the west, you say immediately that rain is coming—and so it does. When the wind blows from the south, you say it is going to be hot—and so it is. You hypocrites! If you can interpret the portents of earth and sky, why can you not interpret the present time? Tell me, why do you not judge for yourselves what is just? When you are going with your opponent to appear before a magistrate, try to settle with him on the way lest he turn you over to the judge, and the judge deliver you up to the jailer, and the jailer throw you into prison. I warn you, you will not be released from there until you have paid the last penny."
This is the gospel of the Lord.

478   **SATURDAY OF THE TWENTY-NINTH WEEK OF THE YEAR**

Year I

READING I
Rom 8, 1-11

A reading from the letter of Paul to the Romans

The Spirit of him who raised Jesus from the dead lives in you.

There is no condemnation now for those who are in Christ Jesus. The law of the spirit, the spirit of life in Christ Jesus, has freed you from the law of sin and death. The law was powerless because of its weakening by the flesh. Then God sent his Son in the likeness of sinful flesh as a sin offering, thereby condemning sin in the flesh, so that the just demands of the law might be fulfilled in us who live, not according to the flesh, but according to the spirit. Those who live according to the flesh are intent on the things of the flesh, those who live according to the spirit, on those of the spirit. The tendency of the flesh is toward death but that of the spirit toward life and peace. The flesh in its tendency is at enmity with God; it is not subject to God's law. Indeed, it cannot be; those who are in the flesh cannot please God. But you are not in the flesh; you are in the spirit, since the Spirit of God dwells in you. If anyone does not have the Spirit of Christ, he does not belong to Christ. If Christ is in you, the body is indeed dead because of sin, while the spirit lives because of justice. If the Spirit of him who raised Jesus from the dead dwells in you, then he who raised Christ from the dead will bring your mortal bodies to life also through his Spirit dwelling in you.

This is the Word of the Lord.

Responsorial Psalm   Ps 24, 1-2. 3-4. 5-6

℟. (6) Lord, this is the people that longs to see your face.

The Lord's are the earth and its fullness;
  the world and those who dwell in it.
For he founded it upon the seas
  and established it upon the rivers.

℟. Lord, this is the people that longs to see your face.

Who can ascend the mountain of the Lord?
  or who may stand in his holy place?
He whose hands are sinless, whose heart is clean,
  who desires not what is vain.

℟. Lord, this is the people that longs to see your face.

He shall receive a blessing from the Lord,
  a reward from God his savior.
Such is the race that seeks for him,
  that seeks the face of the God of Jacob.

℟. Lord, this is the people that longs to see your face.

Year II

READING I   Eph 4, 7-16

A reading from the letter of Paul to the Ephesians
Christ is the head by whom the whole body is fitted and joined together.

Each of us has received God's favor in the measure in which Christ bestows it. Thus you find Scripture saying:

"When he ascended on high, he took a host of captives
  and gave gifts to men."
"He ascended"—what does this mean but that he had first descended into the lower regions of the earth? He who descended is the very one who ascended high above the heavens, that he might fill all men with his gifts.

It is he who gave apostles, prophets, evangelists, pastors and teachers in roles of service for the faithful to build up the body of Christ, till we become one in faith and in the knowledge of God's Son, and form that perfect man who is Christ come to full stature.

Let us, then, be children no longer, tossed here and there, carried about by every wind of doctrine that originates in human trickery and skill in proposing error. Rather, let us profess to the truth in love and grow to the full maturity of Christ the head. Through him the whole body grows, and with the proper functioning of the members joined firmly together by each supporting ligament, builds itself up in love.

This is the Word of the Lord.

Responsorial Psalm   Ps 122, 1-2. 3-4. 4-5

℟. (1) I rejoiced when I heard them say:
  let us go to the house of the Lord.

I rejoiced because they said to me,
  "We will go up to the house of the Lord."
And now we have set foot
  within your gates, O Jerusalem—

℟. I rejoiced when I heard them say:
  let us go to the house of the Lord.

Jerusalem, built as a city
  with compact unity.
To it the tribes go up,
  the tribes of the Lord.

℟. I rejoiced when I heard them say:
  let us go to the house of the Lord.

According to the decree for Israel,
  to give thanks to the name of the Lord.
In it are set up judgment seats,
  seats for the house of David.

℟. I rejoiced when I heard them say:
  let us go to the house of the Lord.

Years I and II

GOSPEL   Lk 13, 1-9
Alleluia

See no. 509.

✠ A reading from the holy gospel according
to Luke

Unless you repent, you will all perish as they did.

Persons were present who told Jesus about the
Galileans whose blood Pilate had mixed with
their sacrifices. He said in reply: "Do you think
that these Galileans were the greatest sinners
in Galilee just because they suffered this? By
no means! But I tell you, you will all come to
the same end unless you reform. Or take those
eighteen who were killed by a falling tower in
Siloam. Do you think they were more guilty
than anyone else who lived in Jerusalem? Certainly not! But I tell you, you will all come to
the same end unless you reform."

Jesus spoke this parable: "A man had a fig
tree growing in his vineyard, and he came out
looking for fruit on it but did not find any. He
said to the vinedresser, 'Look here! For three
years now I have come in search of fruit on this
fig tree and found none. Cut it down. Why
should it clutter up the ground?' In answer, the
man said, 'Sir, leave it another year, while I hoe
around it and manure it; then perhaps it will
bear fruit. If not, it shall be cut down.' "
This is the gospel of the Lord.

---

479   **MONDAY OF THE
THIRTIETH WEEK
OF THE YEAR**

Year I

READING I   Rom 8, 12-17

A reading from the letter of Paul to the
Romans

The Spirit you received is the spirit of sons and it makes us
cry out: Abba, Father.

We are debtors, then, my brothers—but not to
the flesh, so that we should live according to
the flesh. If you live according to the flesh, you
will die; but if by the spirit you put to death the
evil deeds of the body, you will live.

All who are led by the Spirit of God are sons
of God. You did not receive a spirit of slavery
leading you back into fear, but a spirit of adoption through which we cry out, "Abba!" (that
is, "Father"). The Spirit himself gives witness
with our spirit that we are children of God. But
if we are children, we are heirs as well: heirs of
God, heirs with Christ, if only we suffer with
him so as to be glorified with him.
This is the Word of the Lord.

Responsorial Psalm   Ps 68, 2. 4. 6-7. 20-21

℟. (21) Our God is the God of salvation.
God arises; his enemies are scattered,
   and those who hate him flee before him.
But the just rejoice and exult before God;
   they are glad and rejoice.
℟. Our God is the God of salvation.
The father of orphans and the defender of
   widows
   is God in his holy dwelling.
God gives a home to the forsaken;
   he leads forth prisoners to prosperity.
℟. Our God is the God of salvation.
Blessed day by day be the Lord,
   who bears our burdens; God, who is our salvation.
God is a saving God for us;
   the Lord, my Lord, controls the passageways
   of death.
℟. Our God is the God of salvation.

Year II

READING I   Eph 4, 32—5, 8

A reading from the letter of Paul to the
Ephesians

Walk in love as Christ loved us.

Be kind to one another, compassionate, and
mutually forgiving, just as God has forgiven
you in Christ.

Be imitators of God as his dear children.
Follow the way of love, even as Christ loved
you. He gave himself for us as an offering to
God, a gift of pleasing fragrance.

As for lewd conduct or promiscuousness or
lust of any sort, let them not even be mentioned
among you; your holiness forbids this. Nor

should there be any obscene, silly, or suggestive talk; all that is out of place. Instead, give thanks. Make no mistake about this: no fornicator, no unclean or lustful person—in effect an idolator—has any inheritance in the kingdom of Christ and of God. Let no one deceive you with worthless arguments. These are sins that bring God's wrath down on the disobedient; therefore have nothing to do with them. There was a time when you were darkness, but now you are light in the Lord.
    This is the Word of the Lord.

Responsorial Psalm   Ps 1, 1-2. 3. 4. 6

R̷. (Eph 5, 1) Behave like God as his very dear children.
Happy the man who follows not
    the counsel of the wicked,
Nor walks in the way of sinners,
    nor sits in the company of the insolent,
But delights in the law of the Lord
    and meditates on his law day and night.
R̷. Behave like God as his very dear children.
He is like a tree
    planted near running water,
That yields its fruit in due season,
    and whose leaves never fade.
    [Whatever he does, prospers.]
R̷. Behave like God as his very dear children.
Not so the wicked, not so;
    they are like chaff which the wind drives
        away.
For the Lord watches over the way of the just,
    but the way of the wicked vanishes.
R̷. Behave like God as his very dear children.

Years I and II

GOSPEL   Lk 13, 10-17

Alleluia

See no. 509.

✠ A reading from the holy gospel according
        to Luke

*This daughter of Abraham, was it not right to untie her on
    the sabbath day?*

On a sabbath day Jesus was teaching in one of the synagogues. There was a woman there who for eighteen years had been possessed by a spirit which drained her strength. She was badly stooped—quite incapable of standing erect. When Jesus saw her, he called her to him and said, "Woman, you are free of your infirmity." He laid his hand on her, and immediately she stood up straight and began thanking God.
    The chief of the synagogue, indignant that Jesus should have healed on the sabbath, said to the congregation, "There are six days for working. Come on those days to be cured, not on the sabbath." The Lord said in reply, "O you hypocrites! Which of you does not let his ox or ass out of the stall on the sabbath to water it? Should not this daughter of Abraham here who has been in the bondage of Satan for eighteen years have been released from her shackles on the sabbath?" At these words, his opponents were covered with confusion; meanwhile, everyone else rejoiced at the marvels Jesus was accomplishing.
    This is the gospel of the Lord.

---

480   **TUESDAY OF THE
              THIRTIETH WEEK
              OF THE YEAR**

Year I

READING I   Rom 8, 18-25

**A reading from the letter of Paul to the
        Romans**

*The whole creation is eagerly waiting for God to reveal
    his sons.*

I consider the sufferings of the present to be as nothing compared with the glory to be revealed in us. Indeed, the whole created world eagerly awaits the revelation of the sons of God. Creation was made subject to futility, not of its own accord but by him who once subjected it; yet not without hope, because the world itself will be freed from its slavery to corruption and share in the glorious freedom of the children of God. Yes, we know that all creation groans and is in agony even until now. Not only that, but we ourselves, although we have the Spirit as first fruits, groan inwardly while we await the redemption of our bodies. In hope we were saved. But hope is not hope if its object is seen; how is it possible for one to hope for what he sees? And hoping for what we cannot see means awaiting it with patient endurance.

This is the Word of the Lord.

Responsorial Psalm   Ps 126, 1-2. 2-3. 4-5. 6

℟. (3) The Lord has done marvels for us.

When the Lord brought back the captives of Zion,
   we were like men dreaming.
Then our mouth was filled with laughter,
   and our tongue with rejoicing.

℟. The Lord has done marvels for us.

Then they said among the nations,
   "The Lord has done great things for them."
The Lord has done great things for us;
   we are glad indeed.

℟. The Lord has done marvels for us.

Restore our fortunes, O Lord,
   like the torrents in the southern desert.
Those that sow in tears
   shall reap rejoicing.

℟. The Lord has done marvels for us.

Although they go forth weeping,
   carrying the seed to be sown,
They shall come back rejoicing,
   carrying their sheaves.

℟. The Lord has done marvels for us.

Year II

READING I   Eph 5, 21-33
A reading from the letter of Paul to the Ephesians

This is a great mystery and it refers to Christ and the Church.

Defer to one another out of reverence for Christ. Wives should be submissive to their husbands as if to the Lord because the husband is head of his wife just as Christ is head of his body, the church, as well as its savior. As the church submits to Christ, so wives should submit to their husbands in everything.

Husbands, love your wives, as Christ loved the church. He gave himself up for her to make her holy, purifying her in the bath of water by the power of the word, to present to himself a glorious church, holy and immaculate, without stain or wrinkle or anything of that sort. Husbands should love their wives as they do their own bodies. He who loves his wife loves himself. Observe that no one ever hates his own flesh; no, he nourishes it and takes care of it as Christ cares for the church— for we are members of his body.

"For this reason a man shall leave his father
   and mother,
   and shall cling to his wife,
   and the two shall be made into one."

This is a great foreshadowing; I mean that it refers to Christ and the church. In any case, each one should love his wife as he loves himself, the wife for her part showing respect for her husband.

This is the Word of the Lord.

Responsorial Psalm   Ps 128, 1-2. 3. 4-5

℟. (1) Happy are those who fear the Lord.

Happy are you who fear the Lord,
   who walk in his ways!
For you shall eat the fruit of your handiwork;
   happy shall you be, and favored.

℟. Happy are those who fear the Lord.

Your wife shall be like a fruitful vine
   in the recesses of your home;
Your children like olive plants
   around your table.

℟. Happy are those who fear the Lord.

Behold, thus is the man blessed
   who fears the Lord.
The Lord bless you from Zion:
   may you see the prosperity of Jerusalem
   all the days of your life.

℟. Happy are those who fear the Lord.

Years I and II

GOSPEL   Lk 13, 18-21
Alleluia

See no. 509.

✠ **A reading from the holy gospel according to Luke**

The seed grew and became a mighty tree.

Jesus said: "What does the reign of God resemble? To what shall I liken it? It is like mustard seed which a man took and planted in his

garden. It grew and became a large shrub and the birds of the air nested in its branches."

He went on: "To what shall I compare the reign of God? It is like yeast which a woman took to knead into three measures of flour until the whole mass of dough began to rise."

This is the gospel of the Lord.

---

481   **WEDNESDAY OF THE THIRTIETH WEEK OF THE YEAR**

Year I

READING I   Rom 8, 26-30

A reading from the letter of Paul to the Romans
All things work to the good for those who love God.

The Spirit too helps us in our weakness, for we do not know how to pray as we ought; but the Spirit himself makes intercessions for us with groanings which cannot be expressed in speech. He who searches hearts knows what the Spirit means, for the Spirit intercedes for the saints as God himself wills.

We know that God makes all things work together for the good of those who have been called according to his decree. Those whom he foreknew he predestined to share the image of his Son, that the Son might be the first-born of many brothers. Those he predestined he likewise called; those he called he also justified; and those he justified he in turn glorified.

This is the Word of the Lord.

Responsorial Psalm   Ps 13, 4-5. 6

℞. (6) All my hope, O Lord,
    is in your loving kindness.
Look, answer me, O Lord, my God!
    Give light to my eyes that I may not sleep in
        death
Lest my enemy say, "I have overcome him";
    lest my foes rejoice at my downfall.
℞. All my hope, O Lord,
    is in your loving kindness.
Though I trusted in your kindness,

let my heart rejoice in your salvation;
    let me sing of the Lord, "He has been good to
        me."
℞. All my hope, O Lord,
    is in your loving kindness.

Year II

READING I   Eph 6, 1-9

A reading from the letter of Paul to the
Ephesians
Be obedient, not as servants of men but as servants of God.

Children, obey your parents in the Lord, for that is what is expected of you. "Honor your father and mother" is the first commandment to carry a promise with it—"that it may go well with you, and that you may have long life on earth."

Fathers, do not anger your children. Bring them up with the training and instruction befitting the Lord.

Slaves, obey your human masters with the reverence, the awe, and the sincerity you owe to Christ. Do not render service for appearance only and to please men, but do God's will with your whole heart as slaves of Christ. Give your service willingly, doing it for the Lord rather than men. You know that each one, whether slave or free, will be repaid by the Lord for whatever good he does.

Masters, act in a similar way toward your slaves. Stop threatening them. Remember that you and they have a Master in heaven who plays no favorites.

This is the Word of the Lord.

Responsorial Psalm   Ps 145, 10-11. 12-13. 13-14

℞. (13) The Lord is faithful in all his words.
**Let all your works give you thanks, O Lord,
    and let your faithful ones bless you.
Let them discourse of the glory of your king-
        dom
    and speak of your might.**
℞. The Lord is faithful in all his words.
**Making known to men your might
    and the glorious splendor of your kingdom.
Your kingdom is a kingdom for all ages,**

and your dominion endures through all gen-
erations.
℟. The Lord is faithful in all his words.
The Lord is faithful in all his words
and holy in all his works.
The Lord lifts up all who are falling
and raises up all who are bowed down.
℟. The Lord is faithful in all his words.

GOSPEL   Years I and II

Alleluia   Lk 13, 22-30

See no. 509.

✠ **A reading from the holy gospel according**
to Luke

Men from east and west will take their places at the feast
in the kingdom of God.

Jesus went through cities and towns teaching
—all the while making his way toward Jerusalem. Someone asked him, "Lord, are they few
in number who are to be saved?" He replied:
"Try to come in through the narrow door.
Many, I tell you, will try to enter and be unable.
When once the master of the house has risen to
lock the door and you stand outside knocking
and saying, 'Sir, open for us,' he will say in
reply, 'I do not know where you come from.'
Then you will begin to say, 'We ate and drank
in your company. You taught in our streets.'
But he will answer, 'I tell you, I do not know
where you come from. Away from me, you
evildoers!'

"There will be wailing and grinding of teeth
when you see Abraham, Isaac, Jacob, and all
the prophets safe in the kingdom of God, and
you yourselves rejected. People will come from
the east and the west, from the north and the
south, and will take their place at the feast in
the kingdom of God. Some who are last will be
first and some who are first will be last."
This is the gospel of the Lord.

482   **THURSDAY OF THE**
THIRTIETH WEEK
OF THE YEAR

Year I

READING I   Rom 8, 31-39

A reading from the letter of Paul to the Romans

Nothing can come between us and the love of God made
visible in Christ Jesus our Lord.

If God is for us, who can be against us? Is it
possible that he who did not spare his own Son
but handed him over for the sake of us all will
not grant us all things besides? Who shall bring
a charge against God's chosen ones? God, who
justifies? Who shall condemn them? Christ
Jesus, who died or rather was raised up, who is
at the right hand of God and who intercedes for
us?

Who will separate us from the love of
Christ? Trial, or distress, or persecution, or
hunger, or nakedness, or danger, or the sword?
As Scripture says: "For your sake we are being
slain all the day long; we are looked upon as
sheep all to be slaughtered." Yet in all this we are
more than conquerors because of him who has
loved us. For I am certain that neither death
nor life, neither angels nor principalities, nor
powers, neither the present nor the future,
neither height nor depth, nor any other creature, will be able to separate us from the love of
God that comes to us in Christ Jesus, our Lord.
This is the Word of the Lord.

Responsorial Psalm   Ps 109, 21-22. 26-27. 30-31

℟. (26) Save me, O Lord,
in your kindness.
Do you, O God, my Lord, deal kindly with me
for your name's sake;
in your generous kindness rescue me;
For I am wretched and poor,
and my heart is pierced within me.
℟. Save me, O Lord,
in your kindness.
Help me, O Lord, my God;
save me, in your kindness,
And let them know that this is your hand;
that you, O Lord, have done this.

℟. Save me, O Lord,
    in your kindness.
I will speak my thanks earnestly to the Lord,
    and in the midst of the throng I will praise
    him,
For he stood at the right hand of the poor man,
    to save him from those who would condemn
    him.
℟. Save me, O Lord,
    in your kindness.

Year II

READING I   Eph 6, 10-20

**A reading from the letter of Paul to the
Ephesians**

Put God's armor on so that you will be able to stand firm.

Draw your strength from the Lord and his
mighty power. Put on the armor of God so that
you may be able to stand firm against the tactics of the devil. Our battle ultimately is not
against human forces but against the principalities and powers, the rulers of this world of
darkness, the evil spirits in regions above. You
must put on the armor of God if you are to
resist on the evil day; do all that your duty requires, and hold your ground. Stand fast, with
the truth as the belt around your waist, justice
as your breastplate, and zeal to propagate the
the gospel of peace as your footgear. In all circumstances hold faith up before you as your
shield; it will help you extinguish the fiery
darts of the evil one. Take the helmet of salvation and the sword of the spirit, the word of
God.
    At every opportunity pray in the Spirit, us-
ing prayers and petitions of every sort. Pray
constantly and attentively for all in the holy
company. Pray for me that God may put his
word on my lips, that I may courageously
make known the mystery of the gospel—that
mystery for which I am an ambassador in
chains. Pray that I may have courage to proclaim it as I ought.
    This is the Word of the Lord.

Responsorial Psalm   Ps 144, 1. 2. 9-10

℟. (1) Blessed be the Lord, my Rock!

Blessed be the Lord, my rock,
    who trains my hands for battle, my fingers
    for war.
℟. Blessed be the Lord, my Rock!
My refuge and my fortress,
    my stronghold, my deliverer,
My shield, in whom I trust,
    who subdues peoples under me.
℟. Blessed be the Lord, my Rock!
O God, I will sing a new song to you;
    with a ten-stringed lyre I will chant your
    praise,
You who give victory to kings,
    and deliver David, your servant.
℟. Blessed be the Lord, my Rock!

Years I and II

GOSPEL   Lk 13, 31-35
Alleluia

See no. 509.

✠ **A reading from the holy gospel according
to Luke**

It is not right for the prophet to die outside Jerusalem.

Certain Pharisees came to Jesus. "Go on your
way!" they said. "Leave this place! Herod is
trying to kill you." His answer was: "Go tell
that fox, 'Today and tomorrow I cast out devils
and perform cures, and on the third day my
purpose is accomplished. For all that, I must
proceed on course today, tomorrow, and the
day after, since no prophet can be allowed to
die anywhere except in Jerusalem.'
    "O Jerusalem, Jerusalem, you slay the
prophets and stone those who are sent to you!
How often have I wanted to gather your children together as a mother bird collects her
young under her wings, and you refused me!
Your temple will be abandoned. I say to you,
you shall not see me until the time comes when
you say, 'Blessed is he who comes in the name
of the Lord.'"
    This is the gospel of the Lord.

483   FRIDAY OF THE
THIRTIETH WEEK OF THE YEAR

READING I   Rom 9, 1-5

A reading from the letter of Paul to the Romans
I would willingly be condemned if I could help my brothers.

**I speak the truth in Christ: I do not lie. My con-
science bears me witness in the Holy Spirit
that there is great grief and constant pain in
my heart. Indeed, I could even wish to be separated from Christ for the sake of my brothers,
my kinsmen the Israelites. Theirs were the
adoption, the glory, the covenants, the lawgiving, the worship, and the promises; theirs
were the patriarchs, and from them came the
Messiah (I speak of his human origins).
Blessed forever be God who is over all! Amen.**
        This is the Word of the Lord.

Responsorial Psalm   Ps 147, 12-13. 14-15. 19-20

℟. (12) Praise the Lord, Jerusalem.
Glorify the Lord, O Jerusalem;
    praise your God, O Zion.
For he has strengthened the bars of your gates;
    he has blessed your children within you.
℟. Praise the Lord, Jerusalem.
He has granted peace in your borders;
    with the best of wheat he fills you.
He sends forth his command to the earth;
    swiftly runs his word!
℟. Praise the Lord, Jerusalem.
He has proclaimed his word to Jacob,
    his statutes and his ordinances to Israel.
He has not done thus for any other nation;
    his ordinances he has not made known to
        them. Alleluia.
℟. Praise the Lord, Jerusalem.

READING I   Phil 1, 1-11

**The beginning of the letter of Paul to the
Philippians**
He who began this good work in you will see that it is
perfected in you when the day of Christ comes.

**Paul and Timothy, servants of Christ Jesus, to
all the holy ones at Philippi, with their bishops**
and deacons in Christ Jesus. Grace and peace
be yours from God our Father and from the
Lord Jesus Christ!
    **I give thanks to my God every time I think of
you—which is constantly, in every prayer I
utter—rejoicing, as I plead on your behalf, at
the way you have all continually helped promote the gospel from the very first day.**
    **I am sure of this much: that he who has be-
gun the good work in you will carry it through
to completion, right up to the day of Christ
Jesus. It is only right that I should entertain
such expectations in your regard since I hold
all of you dear—you who, to a man, are sharers
of my gracious lot when I lie in prison or am
summoned to defend the solid grounds on
which the gospel rests. God himself can testify
how much I long for each of you with the affection of Christ Jesus! My prayer is that your
love may more and more abound, both in understanding and wealth of experience, so that
with a clear conscience and blameless conduct
you may learn to value the things that really
matter, up to the very day of Christ. It is my
wish that you may be found rich in the harvest
of justice which Jesus Christ has ripened in
you, to the glory and praise of God.**
        This is the Word of the Lord.

Responsorial Psalm   Ps 111, 1-2. 3-4. 5-6

℟. (2) How great are the works of the Lord!
I will give thanks to the Lord with all my heart
    in the company and assembly of the just.
Great are the works of the Lord,
    exquisite in all their delights.
℟. How great are the works of the Lord!
Majesty and glory are his work,
    and his justice endures forever.
He has won renown for his wondrous deeds;
    gracious and merciful is the Lord.
℟. How great are the works of the Lord!
He has given food to those who fear him;
    he will forever be mindful of his covenant.
He has made known to his people the power of
    his works,
    giving them the inheritance of the nations.
℟. How great are the works of the Lord!
℟. Or: Alleluia.

GOSPEL   **Years I and II**   Lk 14, 1-6

Alleluia

See no. 509.

✠ A reading from the holy gospel according
to Luke

*Which of you here, if his ass or ox falls into a well, will
not pull him out on the sabbath day?*

When Jesus came on a sabbath to eat a meal
in the house of one of the leading Pharisees,
they observed him closely. Directly in front of
him was a man who suffered from dropsy.
Jesus asked the lawyers and the Pharisees, "Is
it lawful to cure on the sabbath or not?" At this
they kept silent. He took the man, healed him,
and sent him on his way. Then he addressed
himself to them: "If one of you has a son or an
ox and he falls into a pit, will he not immediately rescue him on the sabbath day?" This
they could not answer.

This is the gospel of the Lord.

---

484   **SATURDAY OF THE
THIRTIETH WEEK
OF THE YEAR**

Year I

READING I   Rom 11, 1-2. 11-12. 25-29

A reading from the letter of Paul to the Romans

*If the loss of the Jews brings reconciliation to the world,
what can we assume but that life comes from death?*

I ask, then, has God rejected his people? Of
course not! I myself am an Israelite, descended
from Abraham, of the tribe of Benjamin. No,
God has not rejected his people whom he foreknew.

I further ask, does their stumbling mean that
they are forever fallen? Not at all! Rather, by
their transgressions salvation has come to the
Gentiles to stir Israel to envy. But if their trans-
gression and their diminishing have meant
riches for the Gentile world, how much more
their full number!

Brothers, I do not want you to be ignorant
of this mystery lest you be conceited: blindness
has come upon part of Israel until the full number of Gentiles enter in, and then all Israel will

be saved. As Scripture says: "Out of Zion will
come the deliverer who shall remove all im-
piety from Jacob; and this is the covenant I will
make with them when I take away their sins."
In respect to the gospel, the Jews are enemies
of God for your sake; in respect to the election,
they are beloved by him because of the patriarchs. God's gifts and his call are irrevocable.

This is the Word of the Lord.

Responsorial Psalm   Ps 94, 12-13. 14-15. 17-18

℟. (14) The Lord will not abandon his people.
Happy the man whom you instruct, O Lord,
    whom by your law you teach,
Giving him rest from evil days.
℟. The Lord will not abandon his people.
For the Lord will not cast off his people,
    nor abandon his inheritance;
But judgment shall again be with justice,
    and all the upright of heart shall follow it.
℟. The Lord will not abandon his people.
Were not the Lord my help,
    I would soon dwell in the silent grave.
When I say, "My foot is slipping,"
    your kindness, O Lord, sustains me.
℟. The Lord will not abandon his people.

Year II

READING I   Phil 1, 18-26

A reading from the letter of Paul to the
Philippians

For me to live is Christ, and to die is gain.

All that matters is that in any and every way,
whether from specious motives or genuine
ones, Christ is being proclaimed! That is what
brings me joy. Indeed, I shall continue to rejoice in the conviction that "this will turn out
to my salvation," thanks to your prayers and
the support I receive from the Spirit of Jesus
Christ. I firmly trust and anticipate that I shall
never be put to shame for my hopes; I have full
confidence that now as always Christ will be
exalted through me, whether I live or die. For,
to me, "life" means Christ; hence dying is so
much gain. If, on the other hand, I am to go on
living in the flesh, that means productive toil
for me—and I do not know which to prefer. I

am strongly attracted by both: I long to be freed from this life and to be with Christ, for that is the far better thing; yet it is more urgent that I remain alive for your sakes. This fills me with confidence that I will stay with you, and persevere with you all, for your joy and your progress in the faith. My being with you once again should make you even prouder of me in Christ.

This is the Word of the Lord.

Responsorial Psalm   Ps 42, 2. 3. 5

℟. (3) My soul is thirsting for the living God.
As the hind longs for the running waters,
    so my soul longs for you, O God.
℟.My soul is thirsting for the living God.·
Athirst is my soul for God, the living God.
    When shall I go and behold the face of God?
℟.My soul is thirsting for the living God.
I went with the throng
    and led them in procession to the house of
    God.
Amid loud cries of joy and thanksgiving,
    with the multitude keeping festival.
℟.My soul is thirsting for the living God.

Years I and II

GOSPEL   Lk 14, 1. 7-11
Alleluia
See no. 509.

✠ A reading from the holy gospel according
    to Luke

*Everyone who exalts himself will be humbled, and the man
who humbles himself will be exalted.*

When Jesus came on a sabbath to eat a meal in the house of one of the leading Pharisees, they observed him closely. He went on to address a parable to the guests, noticing how they were trying to get the places of honor at the table: "When you are invited by someone to a wedding party, do not sit in the place of honor in case some greater dignitary has been invited. Then the host might come and say to you, 'Make room for this man,' and you would have to proceed shamefacedly to the lowest place. What you should do when you have been invited is go and sit in the lowest place, so that

when your host approaches you he will say, 'My friend, come up higher.' This will win you the esteem of your fellow guests. For everyone who exalts himself shall be humbled, and he who humbles himself shall be exalted."

This is the gospel of the Lord.

---

485   **MONDAY OF THE
THIRTY-FIRST WEEK
OF THE YEAR**

Year I

READING I   Rom 11, 29-36
A reading from the letter of Paul to the Romans
*God has consigned all men to disobedience only to show
mercy to them.*

God's gifts and his call are irrevocable. Just as you were once disobedient to God and now have received mercy through their disobedience, so they have become disobedient—since God wished to show you mercy—that they too may receive mercy. God has imprisoned all in disobedience that he might have mercy on all.

How deep are the riches and the wisdom and the knowledge of God! How inscrutable his judgments, how unsearchable his ways! For "who has known the mind of the Lord? Or who has ever been his counselor? Who has given him anything so as to deserve return?" For from him and through him and for him all things are: To him be glory forever. Amen.

This is the Word of the Lord.

Responsorial Psalm   Ps 69, 30-31. 33-34. 36-37

℟. (14) Lord, in your great love, answer me.
But I am afflicted and in pain;
    let your saving help, O God, protect me.
I will praise the name of God in song,
    and I will glorify him with thanksgiving.
    Lord, in your great love, answer me.
"See, you lowly ones, and be glad;
    you who seek God, may your hearts be
    merry!
For the Lord hears the poor,
    and his own who are in bonds he spurns
    not."

℟. Lord, in your great love, answer me.
For God will save Zion
  and rebuild the cities of Judah.
They shall dwell in the land and own it,
  and the descendants of his servants shall
    inherit it,
  and those who love his name shall inhabit it.
℟. Lord, in your great love, answer me.

Year II

READING I   Phil 2, 1-4

A reading from the letter of Paul to the Philippians

Be of one mind and make me happy.

In the name of the encouragement you owe me in Christ, in the name of the solace that love can give, of fellowship in spirit, compassion, and pity, I beg you: make my joy complete by your unanimity, possessing the one love, united in spirit and ideals. Never act out of rivalry or conceit; rather, let all parties think humbly of others as superior to themselves, each of you looking to others' interests rather than his own.
      This is the Word of the Lord.

Responsorial Psalm   Ps 131, 1. 2. 3

℟. In you, Lord, I have found my peace.
O Lord, my heart is not proud,
  nor are my eyes haughty;
I busy not myself with great things,
  nor with things too sublime for me.
℟. In you, Lord, I have found my peace.
Nay rather, I have stilled and quieted
  my soul like a weaned child.
Like a weaned child on its mother's lap,
  [so is my soul within me.]
℟. In you, Lord, I have found my peace.
O Israel, hope in the Lord,
  both now and forever.
℟. In you, Lord, I have found my peace.

Years I and II

GOSPEL   Lk 14, 12-14
Alleluia

See no. 509.

✠ **A reading from the holy gospel according to Luke**

Do not invite just your friends, but the poor and the crippled.

Jesus said to the chief of the Pharisees who had invited him to dinner: "Whenever you give a lunch or dinner, do not invite your friends or brothers or relatives or wealthy neighbors. They might invite you in return and thus repay you. No, when you have a reception, invite beggars and the crippled, the lame and the blind. You should be pleased that they cannot repay you, for you will be repaid in the resurrection of the just."
      This is the gospel of the Lord.

---

486   **TUESDAY OF THE**
             THIRTY-FIRST WEEK
             OF THE YEAR

Year I

READING I   Rom 12, 5-16

A reading from the letter of Paul to the Romans
We form one body and as parts of it we belong to each other.

We, though many, are one body in Christ and individually members one of another. We have gifts that differ according to the favor bestowed on each of us. One's gift may be prophecy; its use should be in proportion to his faith. It may be the gift of ministry; it should be used for service. One who is a teacher should use his gift for teaching; one with the power of exhortation should exhort. He who gives alms should do so generously; he who rules should exercise his authority with care; he who performs works of mercy should do so cheerfully.

   Your love must be sincere. Detest what is evil, cling to what is good. Love one another with the affection of brothers. Anticipate each other in showing respect. Do not grow slack but be fervent in spirit; he whom you serve is the Lord. Rejoice in hope, be patient under trial, persevere in prayer. Look on the needs of the saints as your own; be generous in offering hospitality. Bless your persecutors; bless and

do not curse them. Rejoice with those who rejoice, weep with those who weep. Have the same attitude toward all.

　　This is the Word of the Lord.

Responsorial Psalm　　Ps 131, 1. 2. 3

℞. In you, Lord, I have found my peace.

O Lord, my heart is not proud,
**　　nor are my eyes haughty;**
I busy not myself with great things,
**　　nor with things too sublime for me.**

℞. In you, Lord, I have found my peace.

Nay rather, I have stilled and quieted
**　　my soul like a weaned child.**
Like a weaned child on its mother's lap,
**　　[so is my soul within me.]**

℞. In you, Lord, I have found my peace.

O Israel, hope in the Lord,
**　　both now and forever.**

℞. In you, Lord, I have found my peace.

READING I　　　　　　Phil 2, 5-11
Year II

　　A reading from the letter of Paul to the Philippians

Because of his humility, God raised him on high.

Your attitude must be Christ's:
Though he was in the form of God,
**　　he did not deem equality with God**
**　　something to be grasped at.**
Rather, he emptied himself
**　　and took the form of a slave,**
**　　being born in the likeness of men.**

He was known to be of human estate
**　　and it was thus that he humbled himself,**
**　　obediently accepting even death,**
**　　death on a cross!**

Because of this,
**　　God highly exalted him**
**　　and bestowed on him the name**
**　　above every other name,**

So that at Jesus' name
**　　every knee must bend**
**　　in the heavens, on the earth,**
**　　and under the earth,**

and every tongue proclaim
to the glory of God the Father:
JESUS CHRIST IS LORD!

　　This is the Word of the Lord.

Responsorial Psalm　　Ps 22, 26-27. 28-30. 31-32

℞. (26) I will praise you, Lord, in the assembly of your people.

I will fulfill my vows before those who fear
**　　him.**
The lowly shall eat their fill;
**　　they who seek the Lord shall praise him:**
**　　"May your hearts be ever merry!"**

℞. I will praise you, Lord, in the assembly of your people.

All the ends of the earth
**　　shall remember and turn to the Lord;**
All the families of the nations
**　　shall bow down before him.**
For dominion is the Lord's,
**　　and he rules the nations.**
To him alone shall bow down
**　　all who sleep in the earth.**

℞. I will praise you, Lord, in the assembly of your people.

To him my soul shall live;
**　　my descendants shall serve him.**
Let the coming generation be told of the Lord
**　　that they may proclaim to a people yet to be**
**　　born**
**　　the justice he has shown.**

℞. I will praise you, Lord, in the assembly of your people.

GOSPEL　　　　　　Lk 14, 15-24
Years I and II

Alleluia

See no. 509.

✠ **A reading from the holy gospel according to Luke**

Go to the highway and force people to come that my house will be filled.

One of the guests at a party said to Jesus, "Happy is he who eats bread in the kingdom of God." Jesus responded: "A man was giving a large dinner and he invited many. At dinner time he sent his servant to say to those invited,

'Come along, everything is ready now.' But they began to excuse themselves, one and all. The first one said to the servant, 'I have bought some land and must go out and inspect it. Please excuse me.' Another said, 'I have bought five yoke of oxen and I am going out to test them. Please excuse me.' A third said, 'I am newly married and so I cannot come.' The servant, returning, reported all this to his master. The master of the house grew angry at the account. He said to his servant, 'Go out quickly into the streets and alleys of the town and bring in the poor and crippled, the blind and the lame.' The servant reported, after some time, 'Your orders have been carried out, my lord, and there is still room.' The master then said to the servant, 'Go out into the highways and along the hedgerows and force them to come in. I want my house to be full, but I tell you that not one of those invited shall taste a morsel of my dinner.' "

This is the gospel of the Lord.

---

487   WEDNESDAY OF THE THIRTY-FIRST WEEK OF THE YEAR

Year I

READING I   Rom 13, 8-10

A reading from the letter of Paul to the Romans

You fulfill the law if you love your neighbor.

Owe no debt to anyone except the debt that binds us to love another. He who loves his neighbor has fulfilled the law. The commandments, "You shall not commit adultery; you shall not murder; you shall not steal; you shall not covet," and any other commandment there may be are all summed up in this, "You shall love your neighbor as yourself." Love never does any wrong to the neighbor, hence love is the fulfillment of the law.

This is the Word of the Lord.

Responsorial Psalm   Ps 112, 1-2. 4-5. 9

℞. (5) Happy the man who is merciful and lends to those in need.

Happy the man who fears the Lord, who greatly delights in his commands. His posterity shall be mighty upon the earth; the upright generation shall be blessed.

℞. Happy the man who is merciful and lends to those in need.

He dawns through the darkness, a light for the upright; he is gracious and merciful and just. Well for the man who is gracious and lends, who conducts his affairs with justice.

℞. Happy the man who is merciful and lends to those in need.

Lavishly he gives to the poor; his generosity shall endure forever; his horn shall be exalted in glory.

℞. Happy the man who is merciful and lends to those in need.

℞. Or: Alleluia.

Year II

READING I   Phil 2, 12-18

A reading from the letter of Paul to the Philippians

Work out your salvation; God will put both the will and the action into you.

My dearly beloved, obedient as always to my urging, work with anxious concern to achieve your salvation, not only when I happen to be with you but all the more now that I am absent. It is God who, in his good will toward you, begets in you any measure of desire or achievement. In everything you do, act without grumbling or arguing; prove yourselves innocent and straightforward, children of God beyond reproach in the midst of a twisted and depraved generation—among whom you shine like the stars in the sky while holding fast to the word of life. As I look to the day of Christ, you give me cause to boast that I did not run the race in vain or work to no purpose. Even if my life is to be poured out as a libation over the sacrificial service of your faith, I am glad of it and rejoice with all of you. May you be glad on the same score, and rejoice with me!

This is the Word of the Lord.

Responsorial Psalm   Ps 27, 1. 4. 13-14

℞. (1) The Lord is my light and my salvation.
The Lord is my light and my salvation;
    whom should I fear?
The Lord is my life's refuge;
    of whom should I be afraid?
℞. The Lord is my light and my salvation.
One thing I ask of the Lord;
    this I seek:
To dwell in the house of the Lord
    all the days of my life,
That I may gaze on the loveliness of the Lord
    and contemplate his temple.
℞. The Lord is my light and my salvation.
I believe that I shall see the bounty of the Lord
    in the land of the living.
Wait for the Lord with courage;
    be stouthearted, and wait for the Lord.
℞. The Lord is my light and my salvation.

Years I and II

GOSPEL   Lk 14, 25-33
Alleluia

See no. 509.

✠ A reading from the holy gospel according
         to Luke

He who does not give up all his possessions cannot be my
disciple.

On one occasion when a great crowd was with
Jesus, he turned to them and said, "If anyone
comes to me without turning his back on his
father and mother, his wife and his children,
his brothers and sisters, indeed his very self, he
cannot be my follower. Anyone who does not
take up his cross and follow me cannot be my
disciple. If one of you decides to build a tower,
will he not first sit down and calculate the outlay to see if he has enough money to complete
the project? He will do that for fear of laying
the foundation and then not being able to complete the work; at which all who saw it would
then jeer at him, saying, 'That man began to
build what he could not finish.'

    "Or if a king is about to march on another
king to do battle with him, will he not sit down
first and consider whether, with ten thousand
men, he can withstand an enemy coming

against him with twenty thousand? If he cannot, he will send a delegation while the enemy
is still at a distance, asking for terms of peace.
In the same way, none of you can be my disciple if he does not renounce all his possessions."
      This is the gospel of the Lord.

---

488   **THURSDAY OF THE**
           THIRTY-FIRST WEEK
           OF THE YEAR

Year I

READING I   Rom 14, 7-12
A reading from the letter of Paul to the Romans

If we live, we live for the Lord; if we die, we die for the Lord.

None of us lives as his own master and none of
us dies as his own master. While we live we are
responsible to the Lord, and when we die we
die as his servants. Both in life and in death we
are the Lord's. That is why Christ died and
came to life again, that he might be Lord of
both the dead and the living. But you, how can
you sit in judgment on your brother? Or you,
how can you look down on your brother?
We shall all have to appear before the judgment seat of God. It is written, "As surely as I
live, says the Lord, every knee shall bend before me and every tongue shall give praise to
God."
    Every one of us will have to give an account
of himself before God.
      This is the Word of the Lord.

Responsorial Psalm   Ps 27, 1. 4. 13-14

℞. (13) I believe that I shall see the good things
      of the Lord in the land of the living.
The Lord is my light and my salvation;
    whom should I fear?
The Lord is my life's refuge;
    of whom should I be afraid?
℞. I believe that I shall see the good things of
      the Lord in the land of the living.
One thing I ask of the Lord;
    this I seek:
To dwell in the house of the Lord
    all the days of my life,

That I may gaze on the loveliness of the Lord
  and contemplate his temple.
℟. I believe that I shall see the good things of
  the Lord in the land of the living.
I believe that I shall see the bounty of the Lord
  in the land of the living.
Wait for the Lord with courage;
  be stouthearted, and wait for the Lord.
℟. I believe that I shall see the good things of
  the Lord in the land of the living.

| Year II |

READING I
Phil 3, 3-8

A reading from the letter of Paul to the Philippians

I count everything else as loss, if only I can gain Christ.

It is we who are the circumcision, who worship
in the spirit of God and glory in Christ Jesus
rather than putting our trust in the flesh—
though I can be confident even there. If anyone
thinks he has a right to put his trust in external
evidence, all the more can I! I was circumcised
on the eighth day, being of the stock of Israel
and the tribe of Benjamin, a Hebrew of Hebrew
origins; in legal observance I was a Pharisee,
and so zealous that I persecuted the church. I
was above reproach when it came to justice
based on the law.

But those things I used to consider gain I
have now reappraised as loss in the light of
Christ. I have come to rate all as loss in the
light of the surpassing knowledge of my Lord
Jesus Christ.

This is the Word of the Lord.

Responsorial Psalm
Ps 105, 2-3. 4-5. 6-7

℟. (3) Let hearts rejoice who search for the
  Lord.
Sing to him, sing his praise,
  proclaim all his wondrous deeds.
Glory in his holy name;
  rejoice, O hearts that seek the Lord!
℟. Let hearts rejoice who search for the Lord.
Look to the Lord in his strength;
  seek to serve him constantly.
Recall the wondrous deeds that he has
  wrought,

his portents, and the judgments he has ut-
  tered.
℟. Let hearts rejoice who search for the Lord.
You descendants of Abraham, his servants,
  sons of Jacob, his chosen ones!
He, the Lord, is our God;
  throughout the earth his judgments prevail.
℟. Let hearts rejoice who search for the Lord.
℟. Or: Alleluia.

| Years I and II |

GOSPEL
Lk 15, 1-10

Alleluia
See no. 509.

✠ A reading from the holy gospel according
  to Luke

There will be great rejoicing in heaven over one repentant sinner.

The tax collectors and sinners were all gathering around to hear Jesus, at which the Pharisees and the scribes murmured, "This man
welcomes sinners and eats with them." Then
he addressed this parable to them: "Who
among you, if he has a hundred sheep and loses
one of them, does not leave the ninety-nine in
the wasteland and follow the lost one until he
finds it? And when he finds it, he puts it on his
shoulders in jubilation. Once arrived home, he
invites friends and neighbors in and says to
them, 'Rejoice with me because I have found
my lost sheep.' I tell you, there will likewise
be more joy in heaven over one repentant
sinner than over ninety-nine righteous people
who have no need to repent.

"What woman, if she has ten silver pieces
and loses one, does not light a lamp and sweep
the house in a diligent search until she has retrieved what she lost? And when she finds it,
she calls in her friends and neighbors to say,
'Rejoice with me! I have found the silver piece
I lost.' I tell you, there will be the same kind of
joy before the angels of God over one repentant
sinner."

This is the gospel of the Lord.

489   **FRIDAY OF THE**
THIRTY-FIRST WEEK
OF THE YEAR

Year I

READING I   Rom 15, 14-21
A reading from the letter of Paul to the Romans
He has appointed me as a minister of Jesus Christ to make
the gentiles acceptable as an offering.

I am convinced, my brothers, that you are filled with goodness, that you have complete knowledge, and that you are able to give advice to one another. Yet I have written to you rather boldly in parts of this letter by way of reminder. I take this liberty because God has given me the grace to be a minister of Christ Jesus among the Gentiles, with the priestly duty of preaching the gospel of God so that the Gentiles may be offered up as a pleasing sacrifice, consecrated by the Holy Spirit. This means I can take glory in Christ Jesus for the work I have done for God. I will not dare to speak of anything except what Christ has done through me to win the Gentiles to obedience by word and deed, with mighty signs and marvels, by the power of God's Spirit. As a result, I have completed preaching the gospel of Christ from Jerusalem all the way around to Illyria. It has been a point of honor with me never to preach in places where Christ's name was already known, for I did not want to build on a foundation laid by another but rather to fulfill the words of Scripture, "They who received no word of him will see him, and they who have never heard will understand."
    This is the Word of the Lord.

Responsorial Psalm   Ps 98, 1. 2-3. 3-4
℞. (2) The Lord has revealed to the nations his
    saving power.
Sing to the Lord a new song,
    for he has done wondrous deeds;
His right hand has won victory for him,
    his holy arm.
℞. The Lord has revealed to the nations his
    saving power.

The Lord has made his salvation known:
    in the sight of the nations he has revealed his
    justice.
He has remembered his kindness and his faith-
    fulness
    toward the house of Israel.
℞. The Lord has revealed to the nations his
    saving power.
All the ends of the earth have seen
    the salvation by our God.
Sing joyfully to the Lord, all you lands;
    break into song; sing praise.
℞. The Lord has revealed to the nations his
    saving power.

Year II

READING I   Phil 3, 17—4, 1
**A reading from the letter of Paul to the
Philippians**
The Savior we await will transfigure these wretched bodies
to be like his own.

Be imitators of me, my brothers. Take as your guide those who follow the example that we set. Unfortunately, many go about in a way which shows them to be enemies of the cross of Christ. I have often said this to you before; this time I say it with tears. Such as these will end in disaster! Their only god is their belly, and their glory is in their shame. I am talking about those who are set upon the things of this world. As you well know, we have our citizenship in heaven; it is from there that we eagerly await the coming of our savior, the Lord Jesus Christ. He will give a new form to this lowly body of ours and remake it according to the pattern of his glorified body, by his power to subject everything to himself.
    For these reasons, my brothers, you whom I so love and long for, you who are my joy and my crown, continue, my dear ones, to stand firm in the Lord.
    This is the Word of the Lord.

Responsorial Psalm   Ps 122, 1-2. 3-4. 4-5
℞. (1) I rejoiced when I heard them say:
    let us go to the house of the Lord.
I rejoiced because they said to me,
    "We will go up to the house of the Lord."

And now we have set foot
within your gates, O Jerusalem.
R̸. I rejoiced when I heard them say:
let us go to the house of the Lord.

Jerusalem, built as a city
with compact unity.
To it the tribes go up,
the tribes of the Lord.
R̸. I rejoiced when I heard them say:
let us go to the house of the Lord.

According to the decree for Israel,
to give thanks to the name of the Lord.
In it are set up judgment seats,
seats for the house of David.
R̸. I rejoiced when I heard them say:
let us go to the house of the Lord.

Years I and II

GOSPEL   Lk 16, 1-8

Alleluia

See no. 509.

✠ A reading from the holy gospel according
to Luke

The children of this world are wiser in dealing with their
own kind than are the children of light.

Another time Jesus said to his disciples: "A
rich man had a manager who was reported to
him for dissipating his property. He summoned
him and said, 'What is this I hear about you?
Give me an account of your service, for it is
about to come to an end.' The manager thought
to himself, 'What shall I do next? My employer
is sure to dismiss me. I cannot dig ditches. I
am ashamed to go begging. I have it! Here is
a way to make sure that people will take me
into their homes when I am let go.'

"So he called in each of his master's debtors,
and said to the first, 'How much do you owe
my master?' The man replied, 'A hundred jars
of oil.' The manager said, 'Take your invoice,
sit down quickly, and make it fifty.' Then he
said to a second, 'How much do you owe?' The
answer came, 'A hundred measures of wheat,'
and the manager said, 'Take your invoice and
make it eighty.'

"The owner then gave his devious employee
credit for being enterprising! Why? Because

the worldly take more initiative than the other-
worldly when it comes to dealing with their
own kind."
This is the gospel of the Lord.

490   **SATURDAY OF THE**
THIRTY-FIRST WEEK
OF THE YEAR

Year I

READING I   Rom 16, 3-9. 16. 22-27

A reading from the letter of Paul to the Romans
Greet each other with a holy kiss.

Give my greetings to Prisca and Aquila; they
were my fellow workers in the service of
Christ Jesus and even risked their lives for the
sake of mine. Not only I but all the churches
of the Gentiles are grateful to them. Remember
me also to the congregation that meets in their
house. Greetings to my beloved Epaenetus; he
is the first offering that Asia made to Christ.
My greetings to Mary, who has worked hard
for you, and to Andronicus and Junias, my
kinsmen and fellow prisoners; they are out-
standing apostles, and they were in Christ even
before I was. Greetings to Ampliatus, who is
dear to me in the Lord; to Urbanus, our fellow
worker in the service of Christ; and to my beloved Stachys. Greet one another with a holy
kiss. All the churches of Christ send you
greetings.

I, Tertius, who have written this letter, send
you my greetings in the Lord. Greetings also
from Gaius, who is host to me and to the
whole church. Erastus, the city treasurer, and
our brother Quartus wish to be remembered to
you.

Now to him who is able to strengthen you in
the gospel which I proclaim when I preach
Jesus Christ, the gospel which reveals the
mystery hidden for many ages but now manifested through the writings of the prophets,
and, at the command of the eternal God, made
known to all the Gentiles that they may believe and obey—to him, the God who alone is

wise, may glory be given through Jesus Christ
unto endless ages. Amen.

This is the Word of the Lord.

Responsorial Psalm　　　　Ps 145, 2-3. 4-5. 10-11

℟. (1) I will praise your name for ever, Lord.
Every day will I bless you,
　　and I will praise your name forever and ever.
Great is the Lord and highly to be praised;
　　his greatness is unsearchable.

℟. I will praise your name for ever, Lord.
Generation after generation praises your
　　works
　　and proclaims your might.
They speak of the splendor of your glorious
　　majesty
　　and tell of your wondrous works.

℟. I will praise your name for ever, Lord.
Let all your works give you thanks, O Lord,
　　and let your faithful ones bless you.
Let them discourse of the glory of your king-
　　dom
　　and speak of your might.

℟. I will praise your name for ever, Lord.

Year II

READING I　　　　　　　　Phil 4, 10-19

**A reading from the letter of Paul to the
Philippians**

I possess all things with the help of him who gives me
strength.

It gave me great joy in the Lord that your concern for me bore fruit once more. You had been
concerned all along, of course, but lacked the
opportunity to show it. I do not say this because I am in want, for whatever the situation
I find myself in I have learned to be self-
sufficient. I am experienced in being brought
low, yet I know what it is to have an abundance. I have learned how to cope with every
circumstance—how to eat well or go hungry,
to be well provided for or do without. In him
who is the source of my strength I have
strength for everything.

　　Nonetheless, it was kind of you to want to
share in my hardships. You yourselves know,
my dear Philippians, that at the start of my

evangelizing, when I left Macedonia, not a
single congregation except yourselves shared
with me by giving me something for what it
had received. Even when I was at Thessalonica
you sent something for my needs, not once but
twice. It is not that I am eager for the gift;
rather, my concern is for the ever-growing
balance in your account. Herewith is my receipt which says that I have been fully paid,
and more. I am well supplied because of what
I received from you through Epaphroditus, a
fragrant offering, a sacrifice acceptable and
pleasing to God.

　　My God in turn will supply your needs fully,
in a way worthy of his magnificent riches in
Christ Jesus.

This is the Word of the Lord.

Responsorial Psalm　　　Ps 112, 1-2. 5-6. 8. 9

℟. (1) Happy the man who fears the Lord.
Happy the man who fears the Lord,
　　who greatly delights in his commands.
His posterity shall be mighty upon the earth;
　　the upright generation shall be blessed.

℟. Happy the man who fears the Lord.
Well for the man who is gracious and lends,
　　who conducts his affairs with justice;
He shall never be moved;
　　the just man shall be in everlasting remem-
　　brance.

℟. Happy the man who fears the Lord.
His heart is steadfast; he shall not fear.
Lavishly he gives to the poor;
　　his generosity shall endure forever;
　　his horn shall be exalted in glory.

℟. Happy the man who fears the Lord.
℟. Or: Alleluia.

Years I and II

GOSPEL　　　　　　　　　　Lk 16, 9-15

Alleluia

See no. 509.

✠ **A reading from the holy gospel according
to Luke**

If you cannot be trusted with money, who will trust you with
the true riches?

[Jesus said to his disciples:] "Make friends for
yourselves through your use of this world's

goods, so that when they fail you, a lasting reception will be yours. If you can trust a man in little things, you can also trust him in greater; while anyone unjust in a slight matter is also unjust in greater. If you cannot be trusted with elusive wealth, who will trust you with lasting? And if you have not been trustworthy with someone else's money, who will give you what is your own?

"No servant can serve two masters. Either he will hate the one and love the other or be attentive to the one and despise the other. You cannot give yourself to God and money." The Pharisees, who were avaricious men, heard all this and began to deride him. He said to them: "You justify yourselves in the eyes of men, but God reads your hearts. What man thinks important, God holds in contempt."

This is the gospel of the Lord.

---

491   **MONDAY OF THE**
        THIRTY-SECOND WEEK
        OF THE YEAR

Year I

READING I   Wis 1, 1-7

The beginning of the book of Wisdom
Wisdom is a spirit, a friend of man; the Spirit of the Lord fills the whole world.

Love justice, you who judge the earth;
  think of the Lord in goodness,
  and seek him in integrity of heart;
Because he is found by those who test him not,
  and he manifests himself to those who do not disbelieve him.
For perverse counsels separate a man from God,
  and his power, put to the proof, rebukes the foolhardy;
Because into a soul that plots evil wisdom enters not,
  nor dwells she in a body under debt of sin.
For the holy spirit of discipline flees deceit
  and withdraws from senseless counsels;
  and when injustice occurs it is rebuked.
For wisdom is a kindly spirit,
  yet she acquits not the blasphemer of his guilty lips;

Because God is the witness of his inmost self
  and the sure observer of his heart
  and the listener to his tongue.
For the spirit of the Lord fills the world,
  is all-embracing, and knows what man says.
    This is the Word of the Lord.

Responsorial Psalm   Ps 139, 1-3. 4-6. 7-8. 9-10

℟. (24) Guide me, Lord, along the everlasting way.

O Lord, you have probed me and you know me;
  you know when I sit and when I stand;
  you understand my thoughts from afar.
My journeys and my rest you scrutinize,
  with all my ways you are familiar.
℟. Guide me, Lord, along the everlasting way.
Even before a word is on my tongue,
  behold, O Lord, you know the whole of it.
Behind me and before, you hem me in
  and rest your hand upon me.
Such knowledge is too wonderful for me;
  too lofty for me to attain.
℟. Guide me, Lord, along the everlasting way.
Where can I go from your spirit?
  from your presence where can I flee?
If I go up to the heavens, you are there;
  if I sink to the nether world, you are present there.
℟. Guide me, Lord, along the everlasting way.
If I take the wings of the dawn,
  if I settle at the farthest limits of the sea,
Even there your hand shall guide me,
  and your right hand hold me fast.
℟. Guide me, Lord, along the everlasting way.

Year II

READING I   Ti 1, 1-9

The beginning of the letter of Paul to Titus
Appoint elders as I directed you.

Paul, a servant of God, sent as an apostle of Jesus Christ for the sake of the faith of those whom God has chosen, and to promote their knowledge of the truth as our religion embodies it, in the hope of that eternal life which God, who cannot lie, promised in endless ages past. This he has now manifested in his own good time as his word, in the preaching entrusted to me by the command of God our Savior. Paul to Titus, my own true child in our common faith: May grace and peace from God our Father, and Christ Jesus our Savior, be with you.

My purpose in leaving you in Crete was that you might accomplish what had been left undone, especially the appointment of presbyters in every town. As I instructed you, a presbyter must be irreproachable, married only once, the father of children who are believers and are known not to be wild and insubordinate. The bishop as God's steward must be blameless. He may not be self-willed or arrogant, a drunkard, a violent or greedy man. He should, on the contrary, be hospitable and a lover of goodness; steady, just, holy, and self-controlled. In his teaching he must hold fast to the authentic message, so that he will be able both to encourage men to follow sound doctrine and to refute those who contradict it. **This is the Word of the Lord.**

Responsorial Psalm   Ps 24, 1-2. 3-4. 5-6

R̥. (6) Lord, this is the people that longs to see your face.

The Lord's are the earth and its fullness;
 the world and those who dwell in it.
For he founded it upon the seas
 and established it upon the rivers.

R̥. Lord, this is the people that longs to see your face.

Who can ascend the mountain of the Lord?
 or who may stand in his holy place?
He whose hands are sinless, whose heart is clean,
 who desires not what is vain.

R̥. Lord, this is the people that longs to see your face.

He shall receive a blessing from the Lord,
 a reward from God his savior.
Such is the race that seeks for him,
 that seeks the face of the God of Jacob.

R̥. Lord, this is the people that longs to see your face.

GOSPEL
Alleluia   Lk 17, 1-6

See no. 509.

✠ **A reading from the holy gospel according to Luke**

If your brother returns to you seven times a day and says, I am sorry, you must forgive him.

Jesus said to his disciples: "Scandals will inevitably arise, but woe to him through whom they come. He would be better off thrown into the sea with a millstone around his neck than giving scandal to one of these little ones.

"Be on your guard. If your brother does wrong, correct him; if he repents, forgive him. If he sins against you seven times a day, and seven times a day turns back to you saying, 'I am sorry,' forgive him."

The apostles said to the Lord, "Increase our faith," and he answered: "If you had faith the size of a mustard seed, you could say to this sycamore, 'Be uprooted and transplanted into the sea,' and it would obey you."

This is the gospel of the Lord.

---

492   **TUESDAY OF THE THIRTY-SECOND WEEK OF THE YEAR**

Year I

READING I   Wis 2, 23—3, 9

A reading from the book of Wisdom

In the eyes of fools they were dead, but they are at peace.

For God formed man to be imperishable;
 the image of his own nature he made him.
But by the envy of the devil, death entered the world,
 and they who are in his possession experience it.

But the souls of the just are in the hands of God,
 and no torment shall touch them.
They seemed, in the view of the foolish, to be dead;

and their passing away was thought an affliction
and their going forth from us, utter destruction.
But they are in peace.
For if before men, indeed, they be punished,
  yet is their hope full of immortality;
Chastised a little, they shall be greatly blessed,
  because God tried them
  and found them worthy of himself.
As gold in the furnace, he proved them,
  and as sacrificial offerings he took them to
  himself.
In the time of their visitation they shall shine,
  and shall dart about as sparks through
  stubble;
They shall judge nations and rule over peoples,
  and the Lord shall be their king forever.
Those who trust in him shall understand truth,
  and the faithful shall abide with him in love:
Because grace and mercy are with his holy
  ones,
  and his care is with his elect.
    This is the Word of the Lord.

Responsorial Psalm   Ps 34, 2-3. 16-17. 18-19

℟. (2) I will bless the Lord at all times.
I will bless the Lord at all times;
  his praise shall be ever in my mouth.
Let my soul glory in the Lord;
  the lowly will hear me and be glad.
℟. I will bless the Lord at all times.
The Lord has eyes for the just,
  and ears for their cry.
The Lord confronts the evildoers,
  to destroy remembrance of them from the
  earth.
℟. I will bless the Lord at all times.
When the just cry out, the Lord hears them,
  and from all their distress he rescues them.
The Lord is close to the brokenhearted;
  and those who are crushed in spirit he saves.
℟. I will bless the Lord at all times.

Year II

READING I   Ti 2, 1-8. 11-14
A reading from the letter of Paul to Titus
We must live good lives while we wait in hope for the
  appearance of our Lord and God, Jesus Christ.

As for yourself, let your speech be consistent
with sound doctrine. Tell the older men that
they must be temperate, serious-minded, and
self-controlled; likewise sound in the faith,
loving, and steadfast. Similarly, the older
women must behave in ways that befit those
who belong to God. They must not be slanderous gossips or slaves to drink. By their good
example they must teach the younger women
to love their husbands and children, to be
sensible, chaste, busy at home, kindly, submissive to their husbands. Thus the word of
God will not fall into disrepute. Tell the young
men to keep themselves completely under control—nor may you yourself fail to set them
good example. Your teaching must have the
integrity of serious, sound words to which no
one can take exception. If it does, no opponent
will be able to find anything bad to say about
us, and hostility will yield to shame.
  The grace of God has appeared, offering
salvation to all men. It trains us to reject
godless ways and worldly desires, and live
temperately, justly, and devoutly in this age as
we await our blessed hope, the appearing of
the glory of the great God and of our Savior
Christ Jesus. It was he who sacrificed himself
for us, to redeem us from all unrighteousness
and to cleanse for himself a people of his own,
eager to do what is right.
    This is the Word of the Lord.

Responsorial Psalm   Ps 37, 3-4. 18. 23. 27. 29

℟. (39) The salvation of the just comes from
  the Lord.
Trust in the Lord and do good,
  that you may dwell in the land and enjoy
  security.
Take delight in the Lord,
  and he will grant you your heart's requests.
℟. The salvation of the just comes from the
  Lord.

The Lord watches over the lives of the whole-
hearted;
 their inheritance lasts forever.
By the Lord are the steps of a man made firm,
 and he approves his way.
℟. The salvation of the just comes from the
 Lord.
Turn from evil and do good,
 that you may abide forever;
The just shall possess the land
 and dwell in it forever.
℟. The salvation of the just comes from the
 Lord.

Years I and II

GOSPEL   Lk 17, 7-10
Alleluia

See no. 509.

✠ A reading from the holy gospel according
 to Luke

We are only servants: we have done our duty.

The Lord said: "If one of you had a servant
plowing or herding sheep and he came in from
the fields, would you say to him, 'Come and sit
down at table'? Would you not rather say,
'Prepare my supper. Put on your apron and
wait on me while I eat and drink. You can eat
and drink afterward'? Would he be grateful
to the servant who was only carrying out his
orders? It is quite the same with you who hear
me. When you have done all you have been
commanded to do, say, 'We are useless servants. We have done no more than our duty.' "
 This is the gospel of the Lord.

---

493   **WEDNESDAY OF THE**

        THIRTY-SECOND WEEK

        OF THE YEAR   **Year I**

READING I   Wis 6, 2-11

A reading from the book of Wisdom

Listen, kings, that you may learn wisdom.

Hear, therefore, kings, and understand;
 learn, you magistrates of the earth's ex-
 panse!
Hearken, you who are in power over the
 multitude

and lord it over throngs of peoples!
Because authority was given you by the Lord
 and sovereignty by the Most High,
 who shall probe your works and scrutinize
 your counsels!
Because, though you were ministers of his
 kingdom, you judged not rightly,
 and did not keep the law,
 nor walk according to the will of God,
Terribly and swiftly shall he come against you,
 because judgment is stern for the exalted—
For the lowly may be pardoned out of mercy
 but the mighty shall be mightily put to the
 test.
For the Lord of all shows no partiality,
 nor does he fear greatness,
Because he himself made the great as well as
 the small,
 and he provides for all alike;
 but for those in power a rigorous scrutiny
 impends.
To you, therefore, O princes, are my words
 addressed
 that you may learn wisdom and that you
 may not sin.
For those who keep the holy precepts hallowed
 shall be found holy,
 and those learned in them will have ready a
 response.
Desire therefore my words;
 long for them and you shall be instructed.
 This is the Word of the Lord.

Responsorial Psalm   Ps 82, 3-4. 6-7

℟. (8) Rise up, O God, bring judgment to the
 earth.
Defend the lowly and the fatherless;
 render justice to the afflicted and the destitute.
Rescue the lowly and the poor;
 from the hand of the wicked deliver them.
℟. Rise up, O God, bring judgment to the earth.
"I said: You are gods,
 all of you sons of the Most High;
Yet like men you shall die,
 and fall like any prince."
℟. Rise up, O God, bring judgment to the earth.

READING I
Year II

READING I   Ti 3, 1-7

A reading from the letter of Paul to Titus

There was a time when we were ignorant, but his compassion saved us.

Remind people to be loyally subject to the government and its officials, to obey the laws, to be ready to take on any honest employment. Tell them not to speak evil of anyone or be quarrelsome. They must be forbearing and display a perfect courtesy toward all men. We ourselves were once foolish, disobedient, and far from true faith; we were the slaves of our passions and of pleasures of various kinds. We went our way in malice and envy, hateful ourselves and hating one another. But when the kindness and love of God our Savior appeared, he saved us, not because of any righteous deeds we had done, but because of his mercy. He saved us through the baptism of new birth and renewal by the Holy Spirit. This Spirit he lavished on us through Jesus Christ our Savior, that we might be justified by his grace and become heirs, in hope, of eternal life.

　　　　This is the Word of the Lord.

Responsorial Psalm   Ps 23, 1-3. 3-4. 5. 6

℟. (1) The Lord is my shepherd;
　there is nothing I shall want.

The Lord is my shepherd; I shall not want.
　In verdant pastures he gives me repose;
Beside restful waters he leads me;
　he refreshes my soul.

℟. The Lord is my shepherd;
　there is nothing I shall want.

He guides me in right paths
　for his name's sake.
Even though I walk in the dark valley
　I fear no evil; for you are at my side
With your rod and your staff
　that give me courage.

℟. The Lord is my shepherd;
　there is nothing I shall want.

You spread the table before me
　in the sight of my foes;
You anoint my head with oil;
　my cup overflows.

℟. The Lord is my shepherd;
　there is nothing I shall want.

Only goodness and kindness follow me
　all the days of my life;
And I shall dwell in the house of the Lord
　for years to come.

℟. The Lord is my shepherd;
　there is nothing I shall want.

Years I and II

GOSPEL   Lk 17, 11-19
Alleluia

See no. 509.

✠ **A reading from the holy gospel according to Luke**

It seems that no one has come back to God to give praise, except this foreigner.

On his journey to Jerusalem Jesus passed along the borders of Samaria and Galilee. As he was entering a village, ten lepers met him. Keeping their distance, they raised their voices and said, "Jesus, Master, have pity on us!" When he saw them, he responded, "Go and show yourselves to the priests." On their way there they were cured. One of them, realizing that he had been cured, came back praising God in a loud voice. He threw himself on his face at the feet of Jesus and spoke his praises. This man was a Samaritan.

　　Jesus took the occasion to say, "Were not all ten made whole? Where are the other nine? Was there no one to return and give thanks to God except this foreigner?" He said to the man, "Stand up and go your way; your faith has been your salvation."

　　　　This is the gospel of the Lord.

---

494   **THURSDAY OF THE THIRTY-SECOND WEEK OF THE YEAR**

Year I

READING I   Wis 7, 22—8, 1

A reading from the book of Wisdom

Wisdom is a reflection of eternal light, a spotless mirror of the majesty of God.

In Wisdom is a spirit
　intelligent, holy, unique,

Manifold, subtle, agile,
  clear, unstrained, certain,
Not baneful, loving the good, keen,
  unhampered, beneficent, kindly,
Firm, secure, tranquil,
  all-powerful, all-seeing,
And pervading all spirits,
  though they be intelligent, pure, and very
  subtle.
For Wisdom is mobile beyond all motion,
  and she penetrates and pervades all things
  by reason of her purity.
For she is an aura of the might of God
  and a pure effusion of the glory of the
  Almighty;
  therefore nought that is sullied enters into
  her.
For she is the refulgence of eternal light,
  the spotless mirror of the power of God,
  the image of his goodness.
And she, who is one, can do all things,
  and renews everything while herself per-
  during;
And passing into holy souls from age to age,
  she produces friends of God and prophets.
For there is nought God loves, be it not one
  who dwells with Wisdom.
For she is fairer than the sun
  and surpasses every constellation of the
  stars.
Compared to light, she takes precedence;
  for that, indeed, night supplants,
  but wickedness prevails not over Wisdom.
Indeed, she reaches from end to end mightily
  and governs all things well.
         This is the Word of the Lord.

Responsorial Psalm   Ps 119, 89. 90. 91. 130. 135. 175

R̸. (89) Your word is for ever, O Lord.
Your word, O Lord, endures forever;
  it is firm as the heavens.
R̸. Your word is for ever, O Lord.
Through all generations your truth endures;
  you have established the earth, and it stands
    firm.
R̸. Your word is for ever, O Lord.

According to your ordinances they still stand
  firm:
  all things serve you.
R̸. Your word is for ever, O Lord.
The revelation of your words sheds light,
  giving understanding to the simple.
R̸. Your word is for ever, O Lord.
Let your countenance shine upon your servant,
  and teach me your statutes.
R̸. Your word is for ever, O Lord.
Let my soul live to praise you,
  and may your ordinances help me.
R̸. Your word is for ever, O Lord.

Year II

READING I   Phlm 7-20

A reading from the letter of Paul to
Philemon

Receive him, not as a slave any more, but a dear brother.
**I find great joy and comfort in your love,
because through you the hearts of God's people
have been refreshed.**

    **Therefore, although I feel that I have every
right to command you to do what ought to be
done, I prefer to appeal in the name of love.
Yes, I, Paul, ambassador of Christ and now a
prisoner for him, appeal to you for my child
whom I have begotten during my imprisonment. He has become in truth Onesimus [Use-
ful], for he who was formerly useless to you is
now useful indeed both to you and to me. It
is he I am sending you—and that means I am
sending my heart!**

    **I had wanted to keep him with me, that he
might serve me in your place while I am in
prison for the gospel; but I did not want to do
anything without your consent, that kindness
might not be forced on you but might be freely
bestowed. Perhaps he was separated from
you for a while for this reason: that you might
possess him forever, no longer as a slave
but as more than a slave, a beloved brother,
especially dear to me; and how much more
than a brother to you, since now you will know
him both as a man and in the Lord.**

    **If then you regard me as a partner, welcome
him as you would me. If he has done you an**

injury or owes you anything, charge it to me. I, Paul, write this in my own hand: I agree to pay —not to mention that you owe me your very self! You see, brother, I want to make you "useful" to me in the Lord. Refresh this heart of mine in Christ.

This is the Word of the Lord.

Responsorial Psalm   Ps 146, 7. 8-9. 9-10

℞. (5) Blest are they whose help is the God of Jacob.

Happy is he who
   secures justice for the oppressed,
   gives food to the hungry.
The Lord sets captives free.

℞. Blest are they whose help is the God of Jacob.

The Lord gives sight to the blind.
The Lord raises up those that were bowed down;
   the Lord loves the just.
The Lord protects strangers.

℞. Blest are they whose help is the God of Jacob.

The fatherless and the widow he sustains,
   but the way of the wicked he thwarts.
The Lord shall reign forever;
   your God, O Zion, through all generations.
   Alleluia.

℞. Blest are they whose help is the God of Jacob.

℞. Or: Alleluia.

Years I and II

GOSPEL   Lk 17, 20-25
Alleluia

See no. 509.

✠ A reading from the holy gospel according to Luke

The kingdom of God is among you.

Jesus, on being asked by the Pharisees when the reign of God would come, replied: "You cannot tell by careful watching when the reign of God will come. Neither is it a matter of reporting that it is 'here' or 'there.' The reign of God is already in your midst."

He said to the disciples: "A time will come when you will long to see one day of the Son of Man but will not see it. They will tell you he is to be found in this place or that. Do not go running about excitedly. The Son of Man in his day will be like the lightning that flashes from one end of the sky to the other. First, however, he must suffer much and be rejected by the present age."

This is the gospel of the Lord.

---

495   **FRIDAY OF THE THIRTY-SECOND WEEK OF THE YEAR**

Year I

READING I   Wis 13, 1-9
A reading from the book of Wisdom

If they are able to investigate the world, how have they been so slow to find its master?

For all men were by nature foolish who were in ignorance of God,
   and who from the good things seen did not succeed in knowing him who is,
   and from studying the works did not discern the artisan:
But either fire, or wind, or the swift air,
   or the circuit of the stars, or the mighty water,
   or the luminaries of heaven, the governors of the world, they considered gods.
Now if out of joy in their beauty they thought them gods,
   let them know how far more excellent is the Lord than these;
   for the original source of beauty fashioned them.
Or if they were struck by their might and energy,
   let them from these things realize how much more powerful is he who made them.
For from the greatness and the beauty of created things
   their original author, by analogy, is seen.
But yet, for these the blame is less;
For they indeed have gone astray perhaps,
   though they seek God and wish to find him.

For they search busily among his works,
   but are distracted by what they see, because
      the things seen are fair.
But again, not even these are pardonable.
For if they so far succeeded in knowledge
   that they could speculate about the world,
   how did they not more quickly find its Lord?
      This is the Word of the Lord.

Responsorial Psalm   Ps 19, 2-3. 4-5

℟. (2) The heavens proclaim the glory of God.
The heavens declare the glory of God,
   and the firmament proclaims his handiwork.
Day pours out the word to day,
   and night to night imparts knowledge.
℟. The heavens proclaim the glory of God.
Not a word nor a discourse
   whose voice is not heard;
Through all the earth their voice resounds,
   and to the ends of the world, their message.
℟. The heavens proclaim the glory of God.

Year II

READING I   2 Jn 4-9

A reading from the second letter of John
He who stands by that doctrine has the Father and the Son.

It has given me great joy to find some of your
children walking in the path of truth, just as
we were commanded by the Father. But now,
my Lady, I would make this request of you
(not as if I were writing you some new commandment; rather, it is a commandment we
have had from the start): let us love one another. This love involves our walking according to the commandments, and as you have
heard from the beginning, the commandment
is the way in which you should walk.

Many deceitful men have gone out into the
world, men who do not acknowledge Jesus
Christ as coming in the flesh. Such is the deceitful one! This is the antichrist! Look out that
you yourselves do not lose what you have
worked for; you must receive your reward in
full. Anyone who is so "progressive" that he
does not remain rooted in the teaching of
Christ does not possess God while anyone who

remains rooted in the teaching possesses both
the Father and the Son.
   This is the Word of the Lord.

Responsorial Psalm   Ps 119, 1. 2. 10. 11. 17. 18

℟. (1) Happy are they who follow the law
   of the Lord!
Happy are they whose way is blameless,
   who walk in the law of the Lord.
℟. Happy are they who follow the law of the
   Lord!
Happy are they who observe his decrees,
   who seek him with all their heart.
℟. Happy are they who follow the law of the
   Lord!
With all my heart I seek you;
   let me not stray from your commands.
℟. Happy are they who follow the law of the
   Lord!
Within my heart I treasure your promise,
   that I may not sin against you.
℟. Happy are they who follow the law of the
   Lord!
Be good to your servant, that I may live
   and keep your words.
℟. Happy are they who follow the law of the
   Lord!
Open my eyes, that I may consider
   the wonders of your law.
℟. Happy are they who follow the law of the
   Lord!

Years I and II
GOSPEL   Lk 17, 26-37
Alleluia
See no. 509.

✠ **A reading from the holy gospel according**
   to Luke
It will be the same when the day comes the Son of Man
is revealed.

Jesus said to his disciples: As it was in the
days of Noah, so will it be in the days of
the Son of Man. They ate and drank, they took
husbands and wives, right up to the day Noah
entered the ark—and when the flood came, it
destroyed them all. It was much the same in
the days of Lot: they ate and drank, they

bought and sold, they built and planted. But on the day Lot left Sodom, fire and brimstone rained down from heaven and destroyed them all.

"It will be like that on the day the Son of Man is revealed. On that day, if a man is on the rooftop and his belongings are in the house, he should not go down to get them; neither should the man in the field return home. Remember Lot's wife. Whoever tries to spare his life will lose it; whoever seems to forfeit it will keep it. I tell you, on that night there will be two men in one bed; one will be taken and the other left. Two women will be grinding grain together; one will be taken and the other left." "Where, Lord?" they asked him, and he answered, "Wherever the carcass is, there will the vultures gather."

This is the gospel of the Lord.

---

496   **SATURDAY OF THE THIRTY-SECOND WEEK OF THE YEAR**

Year I

READING I   Wis 18, 14-16; 19, 6-9

A reading from the book of Wisdom

It appeared over the Red Sea, the way was opened and they rejoiced like lambs.

For when peaceful stillness compassed everything
  and the night in its swift course was half spent,
Your all-powerful word from heaven's royal throne
  bounded, a fierce warrior, into the doomed land,
  bearing the sharp sword of your inexorable decree.
And as he alighted, he filled every place with death;
  he still reached to heaven, while he stood upon the earth.

For all creation, in its several kinds, was being made over anew,
  serving its natural laws,

that your children might be preserved unharmed.
The cloud overshadowed their camp;
  and out of what had before been water, dry land was seen emerging:
Out of the Red Sea an unimpeded road,
  and a grassy plain out of the mighty flood.
Over this crossed the whole nation sheltered by your hand,
  after they beheld stupendous wonders.
For they ranged about like horses,
  and bounded about like lambs,
  praising you, O Lord! their deliverer.
      This is the Word of the Lord.

Responsorial Psalm   Ps 105, 2-3. 36-37. 42-43

℟. (5) Remember the marvels the Lord has done.
Sing to him, sing his praise,
  proclaim all his wondrous deeds.
Glory in his holy name;
  rejoice, O hearts that seek the Lord!
℟. Remember the marvels the Lord has done.
Then he struck every first-born throughout their land,
  the firstfruits of all their manhood.
And he led them forth laden with silver and gold,
  with not a weakling among their tribes.
℟. Remember the marvels the Lord has done.
For he remembered his holy word
  to his servant Abraham.
And he led forth his people with joy;
  with shouts of joy, his chosen ones.
℟. Remember the marvels the Lord has done.
℟. Or: Alleluia.

Year II

READING I   3 Jn 5-8

A reading from the third letter of John

We must welcome our brothers and cooperate in their work of truth.

Beloved, you demonstrate fidelity by all that you do for the brothers even though they are strangers; indeed, they have testified to your love before the church. And you will do a good thing if, in a way that pleases God, you help them to continue their journey. It was for the sake of the Name that they set out, and they are accepting nothing from the pagans. Therefore, we owe it to such men to support them and thus to have our share in the work of truth.

This is the Word of the Lord.

Responsorial Psalm   Ps 112, 1-2. 3-4. 5-6

℟. (1) Happy the man who fears the Lord.
Happy the man who fears the Lord,
   who greatly delights in his commands.
His posterity shall be mighty upon the earth;
   the upright generation shall be blessed.
℟. Happy the man who fears the Lord.
Wealth and riches shall be in his house;
   his generosity shall endure forever.
He dawns through the darkness, a light for the
      upright;
   he is gracious and merciful and just.
℟. Happy the man who fears the Lord.
Well for the man who is gracious and lends,
   who conducts his affairs with justice;
He shall never be moved;
   the just man shall be in everlasting remem-
      brance.
℟. Happy the man who fears the Lord.
℟. Or: Alleluia.

Years I and II

GOSPEL   Lk 18, 1-8
Alleluia

See no. 509.

✠ A reading from the holy gospel according
         to Luke

God will see justice done to his chosen who cry to him.

Jesus told his disciples a parable on the necessity of praying always and not losing heart: "Once there was a judge in a certain city who respected neither God nor man. A widow in that city kept coming to him saying, 'Give me my rights against my opponent.' For a time he refused, but finally he thought, 'I care little for God or man, but this widow is wearing me out. I am going to settle in her favor or she will end by doing me violence.'" The Lord said, "Listen to what the corrupt judge has to say. Will not God then do justice to his chosen who call out to him day and night? Will he delay long over them, do you suppose? I tell you, he will give them swift justice. But when the Son of Man comes, will he find any faith on the earth?"

This is the gospel of the Lord.

497   **MONDAY OF THE**
THIRTY-THIRD WEEK
OF THE YEAR

Year I

READING I   1 Mc 1, 10-15. 41-43. 54-57. 62-63

A reading from the first book of Maccabees
A dreadful wrath visited Israel.

There sprang a sinful offshoot, Antiochus Epiphanes, son of King Antiochus, once a hostage at Rome. He became king in the year one hundred and thirty-seven of the kingdom of the Greeks.

In those days there appeared in Israel men who were breakers of the law, and they seduced many people, saying: "Let us go and make an alliance with the Gentiles all around us; since we separated from them, many evils have come upon us." The proposal was agreeable; some from among the people promptly went to the king, and he authorized them to introduce the way of living of the Gentiles. Thereupon they built a gymnasium in Jerusalem according to the Gentile custom. They covered over the mark of their circumcision and abandoned the holy covenant; they allied themselves with the Gentiles and sold themselves to wrongdoing.

Then the king wrote to his whole kingdom that all should be one people, each abandoning his particular customs. All the Gentiles conformed to the command of the king, and many Israelites were in favor of his religion; they sacrificed to idols and profaned the sabbath.

On the fifteenth day of the month Chislev, in the year one hundred and forty-five, the king erected the horrible abomination upon the altar of holocausts, and in the surrounding cities of Judah they built pagan altars. They also burnt incense at the doors of houses and in the streets. Any scrolls of the law which they found they tore up and burnt. Whoever was found with a scroll of the covenant, and whoever observed the law, was condemned to death by royal decree. But many in Israel were determined and resolved in their hearts not to eat anything unclean; they preferred to die rather than to be defiled with unclean food or to profane the holy covenant; and they did die. Terrible affliction was upon Israel.

This is the Word of the Lord.

Responsorial Psalm   Ps 119, 53. 61. 134. 150. 155. 158

℟. (88) Give me life, O Lord,
and I will do your commands.

Indignation seizes me because of the wicked
who forsake your law.
℟. Give me life, O Lord,
and I will do your commands.

Though the snares of the wicked are twined
about me,
your law I have not forgotten.
℟. Give me life, O Lord,
and I will do your commands.

Redeem me from the oppression of men,
that I may keep your precepts.
℟. Give me life, O Lord,
and I will do your commands.

I am attacked by malicious persecutors
who are far from your law.
℟. Give me life, O Lord,
and I will do your commands.

Far from sinners is salvation,
because they seek not your statutes.
℟. Give me life, O Lord,
and I will do your commands.

I beheld the apostates with loathing,
because they kept not to your promise.
℟. Give me life, O Lord,
and I will do your commands.

Year II

READING I   Rv 1, 1-4; 2, 1-5

The beginning of the book of Revelation

Remember how far you have fallen, and repent.

This is the revelation God gave to Jesus Christ, that he might show his servants what must happen very soon. He made it known by sending his angel to his servant John, who in reporting all he saw bears witness to the word of God and the testimony of Jesus Christ. Happy is the man who reads this prophetic message, and happy are those who hear it and heed what is written in it, for the appointed time is near!

To the seven churches in the province of Asia: John wishes you grace and peace—from him who is and who was and who is to come, and from the seven spirits before his throne.

I heard the Lord saying to me:

"To the presiding spirit of the church in Ephesus, write this:

" 'The One who holds the seven stars in his right hand and walks among the seven lampstands of gold has this to say: I know your deeds, your labors, and your patient endurance. I know you cannot tolerate wicked men; you have tested those self-styled apostles, who are nothing of the sort, and discovered that they are impostors. You are patient and endure hardship for my cause. Moreover, you do not become discouraged. I hold this against you, though: you have turned aside from your early love. Keep firmly in mind the heights from which you have fallen. Repent, and return to your former deeds.' "

This is the Word of the Lord.

Responsorial Psalm   Ps 1, 1-2. 3. 4. 6

℟. (Rv 2, 7) Those who are victorious I will
feed from the tree of life.

Happy the man who follows not
the counsel of the wicked
Nor walks in the way of sinners,
nor sits in the company of the insolent,
But delights in the law of the Lord
and meditates on his law day and night.

℟. Those who are victorious I will feed from
the tree of life.

He is like a tree
planted near running water,
That yields its fruit in due season,
and whose leaves never fade.
[Whatever he does, prospers.]

℟. Those who are victorious I will feed from
the tree of life.

Not so the wicked, not so;
they are like chaff which the wind drives
away.
For the Lord watches over the way of the just,
but the way of the wicked vanishes.

℟. Those who are victorious I will feed from
the tree of life.

Years I and II

GOSPEL

Lk 18, 35-43

Alleluia

See no. 509.

✠ A reading from the holy gospel according
to Luke

What do you want me to do? Lord, that I may see.

As Jesus drew near Jericho a blind man sat at
the side of the road begging. Hearing a crowd
go by the man asked, "What is that?" The
answer came that Jesus of Nazareth was passing by. He shouted out, "Jesus, Son of David,
have pity on me!" Those in the lead sternly
ordered him to be quiet, but he cried out all
the more, "Son of David, have pity on me!"
Jesus halted and ordered him to be brought
to him. When he had come close, Jesus asked
him, "What do you want me to do for you?"
"Lord," he answered, "I want to see." Jesus
said to him, "Receive your sight. Your faith
has healed you." At that very moment he was
given his sight and began to follow him, giving God the glory. All the people witnessed it
and they too gave praise to God.
This is the gospel of the Lord.

---

498   **TUESDAY OF THE**
THIRTY-THIRD WEEK
OF THE YEAR

Year I

READING I

2 Mc 6, 18-31

A reading from the second book of Maccabees

I have left the young an example of how to die a good
death for the venerable and holy laws.

Eleazar, one of the foremost scribes, a man of
advanced age and noble appearance, was being
forced to open his mouth to eat pork. But
preferring a glorious death to a life of de-
filement, he spat out the meat, and went for-
ward of his own accord to the instrument of
torture, as men ought to do who have the
courage to reject the food which it is unlaw-
ful to taste even for love of life. Those in charge
of that unlawful ritual meal took the man
aside privately, because of their long acquaint-
ance with him, and urged him to bring meat
of his own providing, such as he could legiti-
mately eat, and to pretend to be eating some of
the meat of the sacrifice prescribed by the
king; in this way he would escape the death
penalty, and be treated kindly because of their
old friendship with him. But he made up his
mind in a noble manner, worthy of his years,
the dignity of his advanced age, the merited
distinction of his gray hair, and of the ad-
mirable life he had lived from childhood; and
so he declared that above all he would be loyal
to the holy laws given by God.

He told them to send him at once to the
abode of the dead, explaining: "At our age
it would be unbecoming to make such a pretense; many young men would think the
ninety-year-old Eleazar had gone over to an
alien religion. Should I thus dissimulate for
the sake of a brief moment of life, they would
be led astray by me, while I would bring
shame and dishonor on my old age. Even if, for
the time being, I avoid the punishment of men,
I shall never, whether alive or dead, escape the
hands of the Almighty. Therefore, by manfully
giving up my life now, I will prove myself
worthy of my old age, and I will leave to the
young a noble example of how to die willingly

and generously for the revered and holy laws."

He spoke thus, and went immediately to the instrument of torture. Those who shortly before had been kindly disposed, now became hostile toward him because what he had said seemed to them utter madness. When he was about to die under the blows, he groaned and said: "The Lord in his holy knowledge knows full well that, although I could have escaped death, I am not only enduring terrible pain in my body from this scourging, but also suffering it with joy in my soul because of my devotion to him." This is how he died, leaving in his death a model of courage and an unforgettable example of virtue not only for the young but for the whole nation.

This is the Word of the Lord.

Responsorial Psalm   Ps 3, 2-3. 4-5. 6-8

Ry. (6) **The Lord upholds me.**

O Lord, how many are my adversaries!
    Many rise up against me!
Many are saying of me,
    "There is no salvation for him in God."
Ry. The Lord upholds me.

But you, O Lord, are my shield;
    my glory, you lift up my head!
When I call out to the Lord,
    he answers me from his holy mountain.
Ry. The Lord upholds me.

When I lie down in sleep,
    I wake again, for the Lord sustains me.
I fear not the myriads of people
    arrayed against me on every side.
Rise up, O Lord!
    Save me, my God!
Ry. The Lord upholds me.

Year II

READING I   Rv 3, 1-6. 14-22

A reading from the book of Revelation

If one of you hears me calling and opens the door, I will come and share his meal.

I, John, heard the Lord say to me: "To the presiding spirit of the church in Sardis, write this:

" 'The One who holds the seven spirits of God, the seven stars, has this to say: I know your conduct; I know the reputation you have of being alive, when in fact you are dead! Wake up, and strengthen what remains before it dies. I find that the sum of your deeds is less than complete in the sight of my God. Call to mind how you accepted what you heard; keep to it, and repent. If you do not rouse yourselves, I will come upon you like a thief, at a time you cannot know. I realize that you have in Sardis a few persons who have not soiled their garments; these shall walk with me in white because they are worthy.

" 'The victor shall go clothed in white. I will never erase his name from the book of the living, but will acknowledge him in the presence of my Father and his angels.

" 'Let him who has ears to hear heed the Spirit's word to the churches!

" 'To the presiding spirit of the church in Laodicea, write this:

" 'The Amen, the Witness faithful and true, the Source of God's creation, has this to say: I know your deeds; I know you are neither cold nor hot. How I wish you were one or the other—hot or cold! But because you are lukewarm, neither hot nor cold, I will spew you out of my mouth! You keep saying, "I am so rich and secure that I want for nothing." Little do you realize how wretched you are, how pitiable and poor, how blind and naked! Take my advice. Buy from me gold refined by fire if you would be truly rich. Buy white garments in which to be clothed, if the shame of your nakedness is to be covered. Buy ointment to smear on your eyes, if you would see once more. Whoever is dear to me I reprove and chastise. Be earnest about it, therefore. Repent!

" 'Here I stand, knocking at the door. If anyone hears me calling and opens the door, I will enter his house and have supper with him, and he with me. I will give the victor the right to sit with me on my throne, as I myself won the victory and took my seat beside my Father on his throne.

" 'Let him who has ears to hear heed the Spirit's word to the churches.' "

This is the Word of the Lord.

Responsorial Psalm   Ps 15, 2-3. 3-4. 5

℟. (Rv 3, 21) Him who is victorious I will sit
    beside me on my throne.

He who walks blamelessly and does justice;
    who thinks the truth in his heart
    and slanders not with his tongue;

℟. Him who is victorious I will sit beside me
    on my throne.

Who harms not his fellow man,
    nor takes up a reproach against his neighbor;
By whom the reprobate is despised,
    while he honors those who fear the Lord;

℟. Him who is victorious I will sit beside me
    on my throne.

Who lends not his money at usury
    and accepts no bribe against the innocent.
He who does these things
    shall never be disturbed.

℟. Him who is victorious I will sit beside me
    on my throne.

Years I and II

GOSPEL   Lk 19, 1-10
Alleluia

See no. 509.

✠ A reading from the holy gospel according
    to Luke

The Son of Man has come to seek out and save what was
lost.

On entering Jericho, Jesus passed through the
city. There was a man there named Zacchaeus,
the chief tax collector and a wealthy man. He
was trying to see what Jesus was like, but
being small of stature, was unable to do so because of the crowd. He first ran on in front,
then climbed a sycamore tree which was along
Jesus' route, in order to see him. When Jesus
came to the spot he looked up and said,
"Zacchaeus, hurry down. I mean to stay at
your house today." He quickly descended, and
welcomed him with delight. When this was
observed, everyone began to murmur, "He has
gone to a sinner's house as a guest." Zacchaeus
stood his ground and said to the Lord: "I
give half my belongings, Lord, to the poor.
If I have defrauded anyone in the least, I pay
him back fourfold." Jesus said to him: "Today

salvation has come to this house, for this is
what it means to be a son of Abraham. The Son
of Man has come to search out and save what
was lost."

    This is the gospel of the Lord.

---

499   **WEDNESDAY OF THE**
          THIRTY-THIRD WEEK
             OF THE YEAR

Year I

READING I   2 Mc 7, 1. 20-31
A reading from the second book of Maccabees
The creator of the world will give you breath and life.

Seven brothers with their mother were arrested and tortured with whips and scourges
by the king, to force them to eat pork in
violation of God's law.

    Most admirable and worthy of everlasting
remembrance was the mother, who saw her
seven sons perish in a single day, yet bore it
courageously because of her hope in the Lord.
Filled with a noble spirit that stirred her
womanly heart with manly courage, she exhorted each of them in the language of their
forefathers with these words: "I do not know
how you came into existence in my womb; it
was not I who gave you the breath of life,
nor was it I who set in order the elements
of which each of you is composed. Therefore,
since it is the Creator of the universe who
shapes each man's beginning, as he brings
about the origin of everything, he, in his mercy,
will give you back both breath and life, because you now disregard yourselves for the
sake of his law."

    Antiochus, suspecting insult in her words,
thought he was being ridiculed. As the youngest brother was still alive, the king appealed
to him, not with mere words, but with
promises on oath, to make him rich and happy
if he would abandon his ancestral customs:
he would make him his Friend and entrust
him with high office. When the youth paid
no attention to him at all, the king appealed
to the mother, urging her to advise her boy

to save his life. After he had urged her for a long time, she went through the motions of persuading her son. In derision of the cruel tyrant, she leaned over close to her son and said in their native language: "Son, have pity on me, who carried you in my womb for nine months, nursed you for three years, brought you up, educated and supported you to your present age. I beg you, child, to look at the heavens and the earth and see all that is in them; then you will know that God did not make them out of existing things; and in the same way the human race came into existence. Do not be afraid of this executioner, but be worthy of your brothers and accept death, so that in the time of mercy I may receive you again with them."

She had scarcely finished speaking when the youth said: "What are you waiting for? I will not obey the king's command. I obey the command of the law given to our forefathers through Moses. But you, who have contrived every kind of affliction for the Hebrews, will not escape the hands of God."

This is the Word of the Lord.

Responsorial Psalm   Ps 17, 1. 5-6. 8. 15

℟. (15) Lord, when your glory appears,
   my joy will be full.

Hear, O Lord, a just suit;
   attend to my outcry;
   hearken to my prayer from lips without deceit.

℟. Lord, when your glory appears,
   my joy will be full.

My steps have been steadfast in your paths,
   my feet have not faltered.
I call upon you, for you will answer me, O God;
   incline your ear to me; hear my word.

℟. Lord, when your glory appears,
   my joy will be full.

Hide me in the shadow of your wings.
But I in justice shall behold your face;
   on waking, I shall be content in your presence.

℟. Lord, when your glory appears,
   my joy will be full.

READING I   Rv 4, 1-11

A reading from the book of Revelation
Holy Lord God, the Almighty, who was and is to come.

After this I, John, had another vision: above me there was an open door to heaven, and I heard the trumpetlike voice which had spoken to me before. It said, "Come up here and I will show you what must take place in time to come." At once I was caught up in ecstasy. A throne was standing there in heaven, and on the throne was seated One whose appearance had a gemlike sparkle as of jasper and carnelian. Around the throne was a rainbow as brilliant as emerald. Surrounding this throne were twenty-four other thrones upon which were seated twenty-four elders; they were clothed in white garments and had crowns of gold on their heads. From the throne came flashes of lightning and peals of thunder; before it burned seven flaming torches, the seven spirits of God. The floor around the throne was like a sea of glass that was crystal-clear.

At the very center, around the throne itself, stood four living creatures covered with eyes front and back. The first creature resembled a lion, the second an ox; the third had the face of a man, while the fourth looked like an eagle in flight. Each of the four living creatures had six wings and eyes all over, inside and out.

Day and night, without pause, they sing:
"Holy, holy, holy, is the Lord God Almighty,
   He who was, and who is, and who is to come!"
Whenever these creatures give glory and honor and praise to the One seated on the throne, who lives forever and ever, the twenty-four elders fall down before the One seated on the throne, and worship him who lives forever and ever. They throw down their crowns before the throne and sing:
"O Lord our God, you are worthy
   to receive glory and honor and power!
For you have created all things;
   by your will they came to be and were made!"

This is the Word of the Lord.

Responsorial Psalm   Ps 150, 1-2. 3-4. 5-6

℞. (Rv 4, 8) Holy, holy, holy Lord, mighty
God!

Praise the Lord in his sanctuary,
     praise him in the firmament of his strength.
Praise him for his mighty deeds,
     praise him for his sovereign majesty.

℞. Holy, holy, holy Lord, mighty God!

Praise him with the blast of the trumpet,
     praise him with lyre and harp,
Praise him with timbrel and dance,
     praise him with strings and pipe.

℞. Holy, holy, holy Lord, mighty God!

Praise him with sounding cymbals,
     praise him with clanging cymbals.
Let everything that has breath
     praise the Lord! Alleluia.

℞. Holy, holy, holy Lord, mighty God!
℞. Or: Alleluia.

Years I and II

GOSPEL   Lk 19, 11-28
Alleluia

See no. 509.

✠ A reading from the holy gospel according
                   to Luke

Why did you not put my money in the bank?

While the disciples were listening Jesus went
on to tell a parable, because he was near
Jerusalem where they thought that the reign
of God was about to appear. He said: "A man
of noble birth went to a faraway country to
become its king, and then return. He summoned ten of his servants and gave them sums
of ten units each, saying to them, 'Invest this
until I get back.' But his fellow citizens despised him, and they immediately sent a
deputation after him with instructions to say,
'We will not have this man rule over us.' He
returned, however, crowned as king. Then he
sent for the servants to whom he had given the
money, to learn what profit each had made.
The first presented himself and said, 'Lord,
the sum you gave me has earned you another
ten.' 'Good man!' he replied. 'You showed yourself capable in a small matter. For that you can
take over ten villages.' The second came and

said, 'Your investment, my lord, has netted you
five.' His word to him was, 'Take over five
villages.' The third came in and said: 'Here is
your money, my lord, which I hid for safekeep-
ing. You see, I was afraid of you because you
are a hard man. You withdraw what you never
deposited. You reap what you never sowed.'
To him the king said: 'You worthless lout!
I intend to judge you on your own evidence.
You knew I was a hard man, withdrawing
what I never deposited, reaping what I never
sowed! Why, then, did you not put my money
out on loan, so that on my return I could
get it back with interest?' He said to those
standing around, 'Take from him what he has,
and give it to the man with the ten.' 'Yes,
but he already has ten,' they said. He responded with, 'The moral is: whoever has will
be given more, but the one who has not will
lose the little he has. Now about those enemies
of mine who did not want me to be king,
bring them in and slay them in my presence.' "
     Having spoken thus he went ahead with his
ascent to Jerusalem.
     This is the gospel of the Lord.

---

500   **THURSDAY OF THE**
             THIRTY-THIRD WEEK
             OF THE YEAR

Year I

READING I   1 Mc 2, 15-29

A reading from the first book of Maccabees

We will still follow the law of our ancestors.

The officers of the king in charge of enforcing
the apostasy came to the city of Modein to
organize the sacrifices. Many of Israel joined
them, but Mattathias and his sons gathered in
a group apart. Then the officers of the king
addressed Mattathias: "You are a leader, an
honorable and great man in this city, supported
by sons and kinsmen. Come now, be the first
to obey the king's command, as all the Gentiles
and the men of Judah and those who are left
in Jerusalem have done. Then you and your
sons shall be numbered among the King's
Friends, and shall be enriched with silver and

gold and many gifts." But Mattathias answered in a loud voice: "Although all the Gentiles in the king's realm obey him, so that each forsakes the religion of his fathers and consents to the king's orders, yet I and my sons and my kinsmen will keep to the covenant of our fathers. God forbid that we should forsake the law and the commandments. We will not obey the words of the king nor depart from our religion in the slightest degree."

As he finished saying these words, a certain Jew came forward in the sight of all to offer sacrifice on the altar in Modein according to the king's order. When Mattathias saw him, he was filled with zeal; his heart was moved and his just fury was aroused; he sprang forward and killed him upon the altar. At the same time, he also killed the messenger of the king who was forcing them to sacrifice, and he tore down the altar. Thus he showed his zeal for the law, just as Phinehas did with Zimri, son of Salu.

Then Mattathias went through the city shouting, "Let everyone who is zealous for the law and who stands by the covenant follow after me!" Thereupon he fled to the mountains with his sons, leaving behind in the city all their possessions. Many who sought to live according to righteousness and religious custom went out into the desert to settle there. **This is the Word of the Lord.**

Responsorial Psalm   Ps 50, 1-2. 5-6. 14-15

℟. (23) To the upright I will show the saving power of God.
God the Lord has spoken and summoned the earth,
    from the rising of the sun to its setting.
From Zion, perfect in beauty,
    God shines forth.
℟. To the upright I will show the saving power of God.

"Gather my faithful ones before me,
    those who have made a covenant with me by sacrifice."
And the heavens proclaim his justice;
    for God himself is the judge.

℟. To the upright I will show the saving power of God.

"Offer to God praise as your sacrifice
    and fulfill your vows to the Most High;
Then call upon me in time of distress;
    I will rescue you, and you shall glorify me."
℟. To the upright I will show the saving power of God.

Year II

READING I   Rv 5, 1-10

A reading from the book of Revelation
The lamb that was slain redeemed us from every nation by his blood.

I, John, saw in the right hand of the One who sat on the throne a scroll. It had writing on both sides and was sealed with seven seals. Then I saw a mighty angel who proclaimed in a loud voice: "Who is worthy to open the scroll and break its seals?" But no one in heaven or on earth or under the earth could be found to open the scroll or examine its contents. I wept bitterly because no one could be found worthy to open or examine the scroll. One of the elders said to me: "Do not weep. The Lion of the tribe of Judah, the Root of David, has won the right by his victory to open the scroll with the seven seals."

Then, between the throne with the four living creatures and the elders, I saw a Lamb standing, a Lamb that had been slain. He had seven horns and seven eyes; these eyes are the seven spirits of God, sent to all parts of the world. The Lamb came and received the scroll from the right hand of the One who sat on the throne. When he had taken the scroll, the four living creatures and the twenty-four elders fell down before the Lamb. Along with their harps, the elders were holding vessels of gold filled with aromatic spices, which were the prayers of God's holy people. This is the new hymn they sang:
"Worthy are you to receive the scroll
    and break open its seals,
    for you were slain.
With your blood you purchased for God
    men of every race and tongue,
    of every people and nation.

You made of them a kingdom,
    and priests to serve our God,
    and they shall reign on the earth."
        This is the Word of the Lord.

Responsorial Psalm   Ps 149, 1-2. 3-4. 5-6. 9

℟. (Rv 5, 10) The Lamb has made us a kingdom
    of priests to serve our God.

Sing to the Lord a new song
    of praise in the assembly of the faithful.
Let Israel be glad in their maker,
    let the children of Zion rejoice in their king.
℟. The Lamb has made us a kingdom of priests
    to serve our God.

Let them praise his name in the festive dance,
    let them sing praise to him with timbrel
    and harp.
For the Lord loves his people,
    and he adorns the lowly with victory.
℟. The Lamb has made us a kingdom of priests
    to serve our God.

Let the faithful exult in glory;
    let them sing for joy upon their couches;
    let the high praises of God be in their throats.
    This is the glory of all his faithful. Alleluia.
℟. The Lamb has made us a kingdom of priests
    to serve our God.

℟. Or: Alleluia.

GOSPEL   Lk 19, 41-44
Alleluia

See no. 509.

✠ **A reading from the holy gospel according**
        to Luke

If only you knew on what your peace depends.

Coming within sight of the city of Jerusalem,
Jesus wept over it and said: "If only you
had known the path to peace this day; but you
have completely lost it from view! Days will
come upon you when your enemies encircle
you with a rampart, hem you in, and press you
hard from every side. They will wipe you
out, you and your children within you. walls,
and leave not a stone on a stone within you,
because you failed to recognize the time of
your visitation."
        This is the gospel of the Lord.

501   **FRIDAY OF THE**
             THIRTY-THIRD WEEK
             OF THE YEAR

Year I

READING I   1 Mc 4, 36-37. 52-59

A reading from the first book of Maccabees

They offered with joy a sacrifice on the new altar which
they had dedicated.

Judas and his brothers said, "Now that our
enemies have been crushed, let us go up to
purify the sanctuary and rededicate it." So
the whole army assembled, and went up to
Mount Zion.

Early in the morning on the twenty-fifth day
of the ninth month, that is, the month of Chislev, in the year one hundred and forty-eight,
they arose and offered sacrifice according to
the law on the new altar of holocausts that
they had made. On the anniversary of the
day on which the Gentiles had defiled it, on
that very day it was reconsecrated with songs,
harps, flutes, and cymbals. All the people prostrated themselves and adored and praised
Heaven, who had given them success.

For eight days they celebrated the dedication of the altar and joyfully offered holocausts
and sacrifices of deliverance and praise. They
ornamented the facade of the temple with gold
crowns and shields; they repaired the gates
and the priests' chambers and furnished them
with doors. There was great joy among the
people now that the disgrace of the Gentiles
was removed. Then Judas and his brothers and
the entire congregation of Israel decreed that
the days of the dedication of the altar should
be observed with joy and gladness on the
anniversary every year for eight days, from
the twenty-fifth day of the month Chislev.
        This is the Word of the Lord.

Responsorial Psalm   1 Chr 29, 10. 11. 11-12. 12

℟. (13) We praise your glorious name, O
    mighty God.

Blessed may you be, O Lord,
  God of Israel our father,
  from eternity to eternity.
℟. We praise your glorious name, O mighty
  God.
Yours, O Lord, are grandeur and power,
  majesty, splendor, and glory.
For all in heaven and on earth is yours;
℟. We praise your glorious name, O mighty
  God.
Yours, O Lord, is the sovereignty;
  you are exalted as head over all.
Riches and honor are from you.
℟. We praise your glorious name, O mighty
  God.
And you have dominion over all,
  in your hand are power and might;
  it is yours to give grandeur and strength to
  all.
℟. We praise your glorious name, O mighty
  God.

Year II

READING I   Rv 10, 8-11

A reading from the book of Revelation
I took the book and swallowed it.

The voice which I, John, heard from heaven
spoke to me again and said, "Go, take the
open scroll from the hand of the angel standing
on the sea and on the land." I went up to the angel
and said to him, "Give me the little scroll."
He said to me, "Here, take it and eat it! It will
be sour in your stomach, but in your mouth it
will taste as sweet as honey." I took the little
scroll from the angel's hand and ate it. In my
mouth it tasted as sweet as honey, but when
I swallowed it my stomach turned sour. Then
someone said to me, "You must prophesy again
for many peoples, nations, languages and
kings."
    This is the Word of the Lord.

Responsorial Psalm   Ps 119, 14. 24. 72. 103. 111. 131

℟. (103) How sweet to my taste is your
  promise!
In the way of your decrees I rejoice,
  as much as in all riches.

℟. How sweet to my taste is your promise!
Yes, your decrees are my delight;
  they are my counselors.
℟. How sweet to my taste is your promise!
The law of your mouth is to me more precious
  than thousands of gold and silver pieces.
℟. How sweet to my taste is your promise!
How sweet to my palate are your promises,
  sweeter than honey to my mouth!
℟. How sweet to my taste is your promise!
Your decrees are my inheritance forever;
  the joy of my heart they are.
℟. How sweet to my taste is your promise!
I gasp with open mouth
  in my yearning for your commands.
℟. How sweet to my taste is your promise!

Years I and II

GOSPEL   Lk 19, 45-48
Alleluia

See no. 509.

✠ **A reading from the holy gospel according
          to Luke**
You have turned the house of the Lord into a robber's den.

Jesus entered the temple and began ejecting the
traders saying:"Scripture has it,
  'My house is meant for a house of prayer'
but you have made it 'a den of thieves.' "
    He was teaching in the temple area from day
to day. The chief priests and scribes meanwhile
were looking for a way to destroy him, as were
the leaders of the people, but they had no idea
how to achieve it, for indeed, the entire populace was listening to him and hanging on his
words.
    This is the gospel of the Lord.

502   **SATURDAY OF THE THIRTY-THIRD WEEK OF THE YEAR**

Year I

READING I   1 Mc 6, 1-13

A reading from the first book of Maccabees
On account of the evil I did in Jerusalem, I have suffered great misfortunes.

As King Antiochus was traversing the inland provinces, he heard that in Persia there was a city called Elymias, famous for its wealth in silver and gold, and that its temple was very rich, containing gold helmets, breastplates, and weapons left there by Alexander, son of Philip, king of Macedon, the first king of the Greeks. He went therefore and tried to capture and pillage the city. But he could not do so, because his plan became known to the people of the city who rose up in battle against him. So he retreated and in great dismay withdrew from there to return to Babylon.

While he was in Persia, a messenger brought him news that the armies sent into the land of Judah had been put to flight; that Lysias had gone at first with a strong army and been driven back by the Israelites; that they had grown strong by reason of the arms, men, and abundant possessions taken from the armies they had destroyed; that they had pulled down the Abomination which he had built upon the altar in Jerusalem; and that they had surrounded with high walls both the sanctuary, as it has been before, and his city of Beth-zur.

When the king heard this news, he was struck with fear and very much shaken. Sick with grief because his designs had failed, he took to his bed. There he remained many days, overwhelmed with sorrow, for he knew he was going to die.

So he called in all his Friends and said to them: "Sleep has departed from my eyes, for my heart is sinking with anxiety. I said to myself: 'Into what tribulation have I come, and in what floods of sorrow am I now! Yet I was kindly and beloved in my rule.' But I now recall the evils I did in Jerusalem, when I carried away all the vessels of gold and silver that were in it, and for no cause gave orders that the inhabitants of Judah be destroyed. I know that this is why these evils have overtaken me; and now I am dying, in bitter grief, in a foreign land."

This is the Word of the Lord.

Responsorial Psalm   Ps 9, 2-3. 4. 6. 16. 19

℟. (16) I will rejoice in your salvation, O Lord.
I will give thanks to you, O Lord, with all my heart;
    I will declare all your wondrous deeds.
I will be glad and exult in you;
    I will sing praise to your name, Most High.
℟. I will rejoice in your salvation, O Lord.
Because my enemies are turned back,
    overthrown and destroyed before you.
You rebuked the nations and destroyed the wicked;
    their name you blotted out forever and ever.
℟. I will rejoice in your salvation, O Lord.
In the snare they set, their foot is caught;
    for the needy shall not always be forgotten,
    nor shall the hope of the afflicted forever perish.
℟. I will rejoice in your salvation, O Lord.

Year II

READING I   Rv 11, 4-12

A reading from the book of Revelation
These two prophets have been a plague to the people of the earth.

To me, John, it was said: See my two witnesses; these are the two olive trees and the two lampstands which stand in the presence of the Lord of the earth. If anyone tries to harm them, fire will come out of the mouths of these witnesses to devour their enemies. Anyone attempting to harm them will surely be slain in this way. These witnesses have power to close up the sky so that no rain will fall during the time of their mission. They also have power to turn water into blood and to afflict the earth at will with any kind of plague.

When they have finished giving their testimony, the wild beast that comes up from the abyss will wage war against them and conquer and kill them. Their corpses will lie in the streets of the great city, which has the symbolic name "Sodom" or "Egypt," where also their Lord was crucified. Men from every people and race, language and nation, stare at their corpses for three and a half days but refuse to bury them. The earth's inhabitants gloat over them and in their merriment exchange gifts, because these two prophets harassed everyone on earth. But after the three and a half days, the breath of life which comes from God returned to them. When they stood on their feet sheer terror gripped those who saw them. The two prophets heard a loud voice from heaven say to them, "Come up here!" So they went up to heaven in a cloud as their enemies looked on.

This is the Word of the Lord.

Responsorial Psalm   Ps 144, 1. 2. 9-10

℟. (1) Blessed be the Lord, my Rock!

Blessed be the Lord, my rock,
   who trains my hands for battle, my fingers
      for war.
℟. Blessed be the Lord, my Rock!

My refuge and my fortress,
   my stronghold, my deliverer,
My shield, in whom I trust,
   who subdues peoples under me.
℟. Blessed be the Lord, my Rock!

O God, I will sing a new song to you;
   with a ten-stringed lyre I will chant your
      praise,
You who give victory to kings,
   and deliver David, your servant.
℟. Blessed be the Lord, my Rock!

Years I and II

GOSPEL   Lk 20, 27-40
Alleluia

See no. 509.

✠ A reading from the holy gospel according
to Luke

He is God not of the dead, but of the living.

Some Sadducees came forward (the ones who claim there is no resurrection) to pose this problem to Jesus: "Master, Moses prescribed

that if a man's brother dies leaving a wife and no child, the brother should marry the widow and raise posterity to his brother. Now there were seven brothers. The first one married and died childless. Next, the second brother married the widow, then the third, and so on. All seven died without leaving her any children. Finally the widow herself died. At the resurrection, whose wife will she be? Remember, seven married her."

Jesus said to them: "The children of this age marry and are given in marriage, but those judged worthy of a place in the age to come and of resurrection from the dead do not. They become like angels and are no longer liable to death. Sons of the resurrection, they are sons of God. Moses in the passage about the bush showed that the dead rise again when he called the Lord the God of Abraham, and the God of Isaac, and the God of Jacob. God is not the God of the dead but of the living. All are alive for him."

Some of the scribes responded, "Well said, Teacher." They did not dare ask him anything else.

This is the gospel of the Lord.

---

503   **MONDAY OF THE
THIRTY-FOURTH, OR LAST,
WEEK OF THE YEAR**

Year I

READING I   Dn 1, 1-6. 8-20

**The beginning of the book of the prophet
Daniel**

They have not found the equal of Daniel, Hananiah, Mishael,
and Azariah.

In the third year of the reign of Jehoiakim, king of Judah, King Nebuchadnezzar of Babylon came and laid siege to Jerusalem. The Lord handed over to him Jehoiakim, king of Judah, and some of the vessels of the temple of God, which he carried off to the land of Shinar, and placed in the temple treasury of his god.

The king told Ashpenaz, his chief chamberlain, to bring in some of the Israelites of royal blood and of the nobility, young men without any defect, handsome, intelligent and wise, quick to learn, and prudent in judgment, such as could take their place in the king's palace; they were to be taught the language and literature of the Chaldeans; after three years' training they were to enter the king's service. The king allotted them a daily portion of food and wine from the royal table. Among these were men of Judah: Daniel, Hananiah, Mishael, and Azariah.

But Daniel was resolved not to defile himself with the king's food or wine; so he begged the chief chamberlain to spare him this defilement. Though God had given Daniel the favor and sympathy of the chief chamberlain, he nevertheless said to Daniel, "I am afraid of my lord the king; it is he who allotted your food and drink. If he sees that you look wretched by comparison with the other young men of your age, you will endanger my life with the king." Then Daniel said to the steward whom the chief chamberlain had put in charge of Daniel, Hananiah, Mishael, and Azariah, "Please test your servants for ten days. Give us vegetables to eat and water to drink. Then see how we look in comparison with the other young men who eat from the royal table, and treat your servants according to what you see." He acceded to this request, and tested them for ten days; after ten days they looked healthier and better fed than any of the young men who ate from the royal table. So the steward continued to take away the food and wine they were to receive, and gave them vegetables.

To these four young men God gave knowledge and proficiency in all literature and science, and to Daniel the understanding of all visions and dreams. At the end of the time the king had specified for their preparation, the chief chamberlain brought them before Nebuchadnezzar. When the king had spoken with all of them, none was found equal to Daniel, Hananiah, Mishael, and Azariah; and so they entered the king's service. In any question of wisdom or prudence which the king put to them, he found them ten times better than all

the magicians and enchanters in his kingdom.
This is the Word of the Lord.

Responsorial Psalm   Dn 3, 52. 53. 54. 55. 56

℟. (52) Glory and praise for ever!
Blessed are you, O Lord, the God of our fathers,
  praiseworthy and exalted above all forever;
And blessed is your holy and glorious name,
  praiseworthy and exalted above all for all ages.
℟. Glory and praise for ever!
Blessed are you in the temple of your holy glory,
  praiseworthy and glorious above all forever.
℟. Glory and praise for ever!
Blessed are you on the throne of your kingdom,
  praiseworthy and exalted above all forever.
℟. Glory and praise for ever!
Blessed are you who look into the depths
  from your throne upon the cherubim,
  praiseworthy and exalted above all forever.
℟. Glory and praise for ever!
Blessed are you in the firmament of heaven,
  praiseworthy and glorious forever.
℟. Glory and praise for ever!

Year II

READING I   Rv 14, 1-3. 4-5
A reading from the book of Revelation
They had the names of Christ and his Father written on their foreheads.

I, John, saw the Lamb appear in my vision. He was standing on Mount Zion, and with him were the hundred and forty-four thousand who had his name and the name of his Father written on their foreheads. I heard a sound from heaven which resembled the roaring of the deep, or loud peals of thunder; the sound I heard was like the melody of harpists playing on their harps. They were singing a new hymn before the throne in the presence of the four living creatures and the elders. This hymn no one could learn except the hundred and forty-four thousand who had been ransomed from the world. They are pure and follow the Lamb wherever he goes. They have been ransomed as the first fruits of mankind for God and the Lamb. On their lips no deceit has been found; they are indeed without flaw.

This is the Word of the Lord.

Responsorial Psalm   Ps 24, 1-2. 3-4. 5-6

℟. (6) Lord, this is the people that longs to see
     your face.
The Lord's are the earth and its fullness;
     the world and those who dwell in it.
For he founded it upon the seas
     and established it upon the rivers.

℟. Lord, this is the people that longs to see
     your face.
Who can ascend the mountain of the Lord?
     or who may stand in his holy place?
He whose hands are sinless, whose heart is
     clean,
     who desires not what is vain.

℟. Lord, this is the people that longs to see
     your face.
He shall receive a blessing from the Lord,
     a reward from God his savior.
Such is the race that seeks for him,
     that seeks the face of the God of Jacob.

℟. Lord, this is the people that longs to see
     your face.

Years I and II

GOSPEL   Lk 21, 1-4
Alleluia

See no. 509, at the end.

✠ **A reading from the holy gospel according
to Luke**

He saw the poor widow give two small coins.

Jesus glanced up and saw the rich putting their offerings into the treasury, and also a poor widow putting in two copper coins. At that he said: "I assure you, this poor widow has put in more than all the rest. They make contributions out of their surplus, but she from her want has given what she could not afford— every penny she had to live on."

This is the gospel of the Lord.

---

504   **TUESDAY OF THE
THIRTY-FOURTH, OR LAST,
WEEK OF THE YEAR**

Year I

READING I   Dn 2, 31-45

A reading from the book of the prophet Daniel

The God of heaven will set up a kingdom which will never be destroyed, and it will absorb all the kingdoms of the world.

Daniel said to Nebuchadnezzar: "In your vision, O king, you saw a statue, very large and exceedingly bright, terrifying in appearance as it stood before you. The head of the statue was pure gold, its chest and arms were silver, its belly and thighs bronze, the legs iron, its feet partly iron and partly tile. While you looked at the statue, a stone which was hewn from a mountain without a hand being put to it, struck its iron and tile feet, breaking them in pieces. The iron, tile, bronze, silver, and gold all crumbled at once, fine as the chaff on the threshing floor in summer, and the wind blew them away without leaving a trace. But the stone that struck the statue became a great mountain and filled the whole earth.

"This was the dream; the interpretation we shall also give in the king's presence. You, O king, are the king of kings; to you the God of heaven has given dominion and strength, power and glory; men, wild beasts, and birds of the air, wherever they may dwell, he has handed over to you, making you ruler over them all; you are the head of gold. Another kingdom shall take your place, inferior to yours, then a third kingdom, of bronze, which shall rule over the whole earth. There shall be a fourth kingdom, strong as iron; it shall break in pieces and subdue all these others, just as iron breaks in pieces and crushes everything else. The feet and toes you saw, partly of potter's tile and partly of iron, mean that it shall be a divided kingdom, but yet have some of the hardness of iron. As you saw the iron mixed with clay tile, and the toes partly iron and partly tile, the kingdom shall be partly strong and partly fragile. The iron mixed with clay tile means that they shall seal their alliances by intermarriage, but they shall not stay united, any more than iron mixes with clay. In the lifetime of those kings the God of heaven will set up a kingdom that shall never be destroyed or delivered up to another people; rather, it shall break in pieces all these kingdoms and put an end to them, and it shall stand forever. That is the meaning of the stone you saw hewn from the mountain without a hand being put to it, which broke in pieces the tile, iron, bronze, silver, and gold. The great God has revealed to the king what shall be in the future; this is exactly what you dreamed, and its meaning is sure."

This is the Word of the Lord.

Responsorial Psalm   Dn 3, 57. 58. 59. 60. 61

℟. (59) Give glory and eternal praise to him.
Bless the Lord, all you works of the Lord,
    praise and exalt him above all forever.
℟. Give glory and eternal praise to him.
Angels of the Lord, bless the Lord,
    praise and exalt him above all forever.
℟. Give glory and eternal praise to him.
You heavens, bless the Lord,
    praise and exalt him above all forever.
℟. Give glory and eternal praise to him.
All you waters above the heavens, bless the Lord,
    praise and exalt him above all forever.
℟. Give glory and eternal praise to him.
All you hosts of the Lord, bless the Lord;
    praise and exalt him above all forever.
℟. Give glory and eternal praise to him.

Year II

READING I   Rv 14, 14-19
A reading from the book of Revelation.
Harvest time has come, and the harvest of the earth is ripe.

As I, John, watched, a white cloud appeared, and on the cloud sat One like a Son of Man wearing a gold crown on his head and holding a sharp sickle in his hand. Another angel came out of the temple and in a loud voice cried out to him who sat on the cloud, "Use your sickle and cut down the harvest, for now is the time

to reap; the earth's harvest is fully ripe." So the one sitting on the cloud wielded his sickle over all the earth and reaped the earth's harvest.

Then out of the temple in heaven came another angel, who likewise held a sharp sickle. A second angel, who was in charge of the fire at the altar of incense, cried out in a loud voice to the one who held the sharp sickle, "Use your sharp sickle and gather the grapes from the vines of the earth, for the clusters are ripe." So the angel wielded his sickle over the earth and gathered the grapes of the earth. He threw them into the huge winepress of God's wrath.

This is the Word of the Lord.

Responsorial Psalm   Ps 96, 10. 11-12. 13

℟. (13) The Lord comes to judge the earth.
Say among the nations: The Lord is king.
He has made the world firm, not to be moved;
    he governs the peoples with equity.
℟. The Lord comes to judge the earth.
Let the heavens be glad and the earth rejoice;
    let the sea and what fills it resound;
    let the plains be joyful and all that is in them!
Then shall all the trees of the forest exalt,
℟. The Lord comes to judge the earth.
Before the Lord, for he comes;
    for he comes to rule the earth.
He shall rule the world with justice
    and the peoples with his constancy.
℟. The Lord comes to judge the earth.

Years I and II

GOSPEL   Lk 21, 5-11
Alleluia
See no. 509, at the end.

✠ **A reading from the holy gospel according to Luke**
Not a single stone will be left on the other.

People were speaking of how the temple was adorned with precious stones and votive offerings. Jesus said, "These things you are contemplating—the day will come when not one stone will be left on another, but it will all be torn down." They asked him, "When will this occur, Teacher? And what will be the sign it is going to happen?" He said, "Take care not to be misled. Many will come in my name saying, 'I am he' and 'The time is at hand.' Do not follow them. Neither must you be perturbed when you hear of wars and insurrections. These things are bound to happen first, but the end does not follow immediately."

He said to them further: "Nation will rise against nation and kingdom against kingdom. There will be great earthquakes, plagues and famines in various places, and in the sky fearful omens and great signs."

This is the gospel of the Lord.

---

505   **WEDNESDAY OF THE THIRTY-FOURTH, OR LAST, WEEK OF THE YEAR**

Year I

READING I   Dn 5, 1-6. 13-14. 16-17. 23-28

A reading from the book of the prophet **Daniel**

The fingers of a human hand appeared and began to write on the wall.

King Belshazzar gave a great banquet for a thousand of his lords, with whom he drank. Under the influence of the wine, he ordered the gold and silver vessels which Nebuchadnezzar, his father, had taken from the temple in Jerusalem, to be brought in so that the king, his lords, his wives and his entertainers might drink from them. When the gold and silver vessels taken from the house of God in Jerusalem had been brought in, and while the king, his lords, his wives and his entertainers were drinking wine from them, they praised their gods of gold and silver, bronze and iron, wood and stone.

Suddenly, opposite the lampstand, the fingers of a human hand appeared, writing on the plaster of the wall in the king's palace. When the king saw the wrist and hand that wrote, his face blanched; his thoughts terrified him, his hip joints shook, and his knees knocked.

Then Daniel was brought into the presence of the king. The king asked him, "Are you the Daniel, the Jewish exile, whom my father, the king, brought from Judah? I have heard that the spirit of God is in you, that you possess brilliant knowledge and extraordinary wisdom. But I have heard that you can interpret dreams and solve difficulties; if you are able to read the writing and tell me what it means, you shall be clothed in purple, wear a gold collar about your neck, and be third in the government of the kingdom."

Daniel answered the king: "You may keep your gifts, or give your presents to someone else; but the writing I will read for you, O king, and tell you what it means. You have rebelled against the Lord of heaven. You had the vessels of his temple brought before you, so that you and your nobles, your wives and your entertainers, might drink wine from them; and you praised the gods of silver and gold, bronze and iron, wood and stone, that neither see nor hear nor have intelligence. But the God in whose hand is your life breath and the whole course of your life, you did not glorify. By him were the wrist and hand sent, and the writing set down.

"This is the writing that was inscribed: MENE, TEKEL, and PERES. These words mean: MENE, God has numbered your kingdom and put an end to it; TEKEL, you have been weighed on the scales and found wanting; PERES, your kingdom has been divided and given to the Medes and Persians."

This is the Word of the Lord.

Responsorial Psalm   Dn 3, 62. 63. 64. 65. 66. 67

℟. (59) Give glory and eternal praise to him.
Sun and moon, bless the Lord;
    praise and exalt him above all forever.
℟. Give glory and eternal praise to him.
Stars of heaven, bless the Lord;
    praise and exalt him above all forever.
℟. Give glory and eternal praise to him.
Every shower and dew, bless the Lord;
    praise and exalt him above all forever.
℟. Give glory and eternal praise to him.
All you winds, bless the Lord;
    praise and exalt him above all forever.
℟. Give glory and eternal praise to him.

Fire and heat, bless the Lord;
  praise and exalt him above all forever.
℞. Give glory and eternal praise to him.
[Cold and chill, bless the Lord;
  praise and exalt him above all forever.]
℞. Give glory and eternal praise to him.

READING I Year II Rv 15, 1-4

A reading from the book of Revelation

They sang the canticle of Moses and the canticle of the lamb.

I, John, saw in heaven another sign, great and awe-inspiring: seven angels holding the seven final plagues which would bring God's wrath to a climax.

I then saw something like a sea of glass mingled with fire. On the sea of glass were standing those who had won the victory over the beast and its image, and the number that signified its name. They were holding the harps used in worshiping God, and they sang the song of Moses, the servant of God, and the song of the Lamb:

"Mighty and wonderful are your works,
  Lord God Almighty!
Righteous and true are your ways,
  O King of the nations!
Who would dare refuse you honor,
  or the glory due your name, O Lord?
Since you alone are holy,
  all nations shall come
  and worship in your presence.
Your mighty deeds are clearly seen."
  This is the Word of the Lord.

Responsorial Psalm   Ps 98, 1. 2-3. 7-8. 9

℞. (Rv 15, 3) Great and wonderful are all your works,
  Lord, mighty God!
Sing to the Lord a new song,
  for he has done wondrous deeds;
His right hand has won victory for him,
  his holy arm.
℞. Great and wonderful are all your works,
  Lord, mighty God!

The Lord has made his salvation known:
  in the sight of the nations he has revealed his justice.
He has remembered his kindness and his faithfulness
  toward the house of Israel.
℞. Great and wonderful are all your works,
  Lord, mighty God!
Let the sea and what fills it resound,
  the world and those who dwell in it;
Let the rivers clap their hands,
  the mountains shout with them for joy
℞. Great and wonderful are all your works,
  Lord, mighty God!
Before the Lord, for he comes,
  for he comes to rule the earth;
He will rule the world with justice
  and the peoples with equity.
℞. Great and wonderful are all your works,
  Lord, mighty God!

GOSPEL Years I and II Lk 21, 12-19
Alleluia

See no. 509, at the end.

✠ **A reading from the holy gospel according to Luke**

You will be hated by all men because of my name, but not a hair of your head will be lost.

Jesus said to his disciples: "People will manhandle and persecute you, summoning you to synagogues and prisons, bringing you to trial before kings and governors, all because of my name. You will be brought to give witness on account of it. I bid you resolve not to worry about your defense beforehand, for I will give you words and a wisdom which none of your adversaries can take exception to or contradict. You will be delivered up even by your parents, brothers, relatives and friends, and some of you will be put to death. All will hate you because of me, yet not a hair of your head will be harmed. By patient endurance you will save your lives."
  This is the gospel of the Lord.

506   THURSDAY OF THE THIRTY-FOURTH, OR LAST, WEEK OF THE YEAR

Year I

READING I   Dn 6, 12-28

A reading from the book of the prophet Daniel

God sent his angels to seal the lions' jaws.

Men rushed into the upper chamber of Daniel's home and found him praying and pleading before his God. Then they went to remind the king about the prohibition: "Did you not decree, O king, that no one is to address a petition to god or man for thirty days, except to you, O king; otherwise he shall be cast into a den of lions?" The king answered them, "The decree is absolute, irrevocable under the Mede and Persian law." To this they replied, "Daniel, the Jewish exile, has paid no attention to you, O king, or to the decree you issued; three times a day he offers his prayer." The king was deeply grieved at this news and he made up his mind to save Daniel; he worked till sunset to rescue him. But these men insisted. "Keep in mind, O king," they said, "that under the Mede and Persian law every royal prohibition or decree is irrevocable." So the king ordered Daniel to be brought and cast into the lions' den. To Daniel he said, "May your God, whom you serve so constantly, save you." To forestall any tampering, the king sealed with his own ring and the rings of the lords the stone that had been brought to block the opening of the den.

Then the king returned to his palace for the night; he refused to eat and he dismissed the entertainers. Since sleep was impossible for him, the king rose very early the next morning and hastened to the lions' den. As he drew near, he cried out to Daniel sorrowfully, "O Daniel, servant of the living God, has the God whom you serve so constantly been able to save you from the lions?" Daniel answered the king: "O king, live forever! My God has sent his angel and closed the lions' mouths so that they have not hurt me. For I have been found innocent before him; neither to you have

I done any harm, O king!" This gave the king great joy. At his order Daniel was removed from the den, unhurt because he trusted in his God. The king then ordered the men who had accused Daniel, along with their children and their wives, to be cast into the lions' den. Before they reached the bottom of the den, the lions overpowered them and crushed all their bones.

Then King Darius wrote to the nations and peoples of every language, wherever they dwell on the earth: "All peace to you! I decree that throughout my royal domain the God of Daniel is to be reverenced and feared:

"For he is the living God, enduring forever;
  his kingdom shall not be destroyed,
  and his dominion shall be without end.
He is a deliverer and savior,
  working signs and wonders in heaven and
    on earth,
  and he delivered Daniel from the lions'
    power."

  This is the Word of the Lord.

Responsorial Psalm   Dn 3, 68. 69. 70. 71. 72. 73. 74

℟. (59) Give glory and eternal praise to him.
Dew and rain, bless the Lord;
  praise and exalt him above all forever.
℟. Give glory and eternal praise to him.
Frost and chill, bless the Lord;
  praise and exalt him above all forever.
℟. Give glory and eternal praise to him.
Ice and snow, bless the Lord;
  praise and exalt him above all forever.
℟. Give glory and eternal praise to him.
Nights and days, bless the Lord;
  praise and exalt him above all forever.
℟. Give glory and eternal praise to him.
Light and darkness, bless the Lord;
  praise and exalt him above all forever.
℟. Give glory and eternal praise to him.
Lightnings and clouds, bless the Lord;
  praise and exalt him above all forever.
℟. Give glory and eternal praise to him.
Let the earth bless the Lord,
  praise and exalt him above all forever.
℟. Give glory and eternal praise to him.

READING I   Rv 18, 1-2. 21-23; 19, 1-3. 9

A reading from the book of Revelation

Babylon the Great has fallen.

I, John, saw another angel coming down from heaven. His authority was so great that all the earth was lighted up by his glory. He cried out in a strong voice:

"Fallen, fallen is Babylon the great!
　She has become a dwelling place for demons.
She is a cage for every unclean spirit,
　a cage for every filthy and disgusting bird."

A powerful angel picked up a stone like a huge millstone and hurled it into the sea, and said:

"Babylon the great city
　shall be cast down like this with violence,
　and never more be found!
No tunes of harpists and minstrels,
　of flutists and trumpeters,
　shall ever again be heard in you!
No craftsmen in any trade
　shall ever again be found in you!
No sound of the millstone
　shall ever again be heard in you!
No light from a burning lamp
　shall ever again shine out in you!
No voices of bride and groom
　shall ever again be heard in you!
Because your merchants were the world's nobility,
　you led all nations astray by your sorcery."

After this I heard what sounded like the loud song of a great assembly in heaven. They were singing:

"Alleluia!
Salvation, glory, and might belong to our God,
　for his judgments are true and just!
He has condemned the great harlot
　who corrupted the earth with her harlotry.
He has avenged the blood of his servants
　which was shed by her hand."

Once more they sang, "Alleluia!" The angel then said to me: "Write this down: Happy are they who have been invited to the wedding feast of the Lamb."

This is the Word of the Lord.

Responsorial Psalm   Ps 100, 2. 3. 4. 5

℟. (Rv 19, 9) Blessed are they who are called to the wedding feast of the Lamb.

Sing joyfully to the Lord, all you lands;
　serve the Lord with gladness;
　come before him with joyful song.

℟. Blessed are they who are called to the wedding feast of the Lamb.

Know that the Lord is God;
　he made us, his we are;
　his people, the flock he tends.

℟. Blessed are they who are called to the wedding feast of the Lamb.

Enter his gates with thanksgiving,
　his courts with praise.
Give thanks to him; bless his name;

℟. Blessed are they who are called to the wedding feast of the Lamb.

For the Lord is good:
　the Lord, whose kindness endures forever,
　and his faithfulness, to all generations.

℟. Blessed are they who are called to the wedding feast of the Lamb.

GOSPEL   Lk 21, 20-28
Alleluia

See no. 509, at the end.

✠ **A reading from the holy gospel according to Luke**

Jerusalem will be desolate and the people will be led captive to every nation.

Jesus said to his disciples: "When you see Jerusalem encircled by soldiers, know that its devastation is near. Those in Judea at the time must flee to the mountains; those in the heart of the city must escape it; those in the country must not return. These indeed will be days of retribution, when all that is written must be fulfilled.

"The women who are pregnant or nursing at the breast will fare badly in those days! The distress in the land and the wrath against this people will be great. The people will fall before the sword; they will be led captive in the midst of the Gentiles. Jerusalem will be trampled by the Gentiles, until the times of the Gentiles are fulfilled.

"There will be signs in the sun, the moon and the stars. On the earth, nations will be in anguish, distraught at the roaring of the sea and the waves. Men will die of fright in anticipation of what is coming upon the earth. The powers in the heavens will be shaken. After that, men will see the Son of Man coming on a cloud with great power and glory. When these things begin to happen, stand up straight and raise your heads, for your ransom is near at hand."

> This is the gospel of the Lord.

---

507   FRIDAY OF THE THIRTY-FOURTH, OR LAST, WEEK OF THE YEAR

Year I

READING I   Dn 7, 2-14

A reading from the book of the prophet Daniel

I saw, coming out of the clouds, one like a son of man.

In the vision I saw during the night, suddenly the four winds of heaven stirred up the great sea, from which emerged four immense beasts, each different from the others. The first was like a lion, but with eagle's wings. While I watched, the wings were plucked; it was raised from the ground to stand on two feet like a man, and given a human mind. The second was like a bear; it was raised up on one side, and among the teeth in its mouth were three tusks. It was given the order, "Up, devour much flesh." After this I looked and saw another beast, like a leopard; on its back were four wings like those of a bird, and it had four heads. To this beast dominion was given. After this, in the visions of the night I saw the fourth beast, different from all the others, terrifying, horrible, and of extraordinary strength; it had great iron teeth with which it devoured and crushed, and what was left it trampled with its feet. I was considering the ten horns it had, when suddenly another, a little horn, sprang out of their midst, and three of the previous horns were torn away to make room for it.

This horn had eyes like a man, and a mouth that spoke arrogantly. As I watched,
Thrones were set up
    and the Ancient One took his throne.
His clothing was snow bright,
    and the hair on his head as white as wool;
His throne was flames of fire,
    with wheels of burning fire.
A surging stream of fire
    flowed out from where he sat;
Thousands upon thousands were ministering to him,
    and myriads upon myriads attended him.
    The court was convened, and the books were opened. I watched, then, from the first of the arrogant words which the horn spoke, until the beast was slain and its body thrown into the fire to be burnt up. The other beasts, which also lost their dominion, were granted a prolongation of life for a time and a season. As the visions during the night continued, I saw
One like a son of man coming,
    on the clouds of heaven;
When he reached the Ancient One
    and was presented before him,
He received dominion, glory, and kingship;
    nations and peoples of every language serve him.
His dominion is an everlasting dominion
    that shall not be taken away,
    his kingship shall not be destroyed.

> This is the Word of the Lord.

Responsorial Psalm   Dn 3, 75. 76. 77. 78. 79. 80. 81

℟. (59) Give glory and eternal praise to him.
Mountains and hills, bless the Lord;
    praise and exalt him above all forever.
℟. Give glory and eternal praise to him.
Everything growing from the earth, bless the Lord;
    praise and exalt him above all forever.
℟. Give glory and eternal praise to him.
You springs, bless the Lord;
    praise and exalt him above all forever.
℟. Give glory and eternal praise to him.
Seas and rivers, bless the Lord;
    praise and exalt him above all forever.
℟. Give glory and eternal praise to him.

You dolphins and all water creatures, bless
the Lord;
    praise and exalt him above all forever.
℟. Give glory and eternal praise to him.
All you birds of the air, bless the Lord;
    praise and exalt him above all forever.
℟. Give glory and eternal praise to him.
All you beasts, wild and tame, bless the Lord;
    praise and exalt him above all forever.
℟. Give glory and eternal praise to him.

Year II

READING I   Rv 20, 1-4. 11-21, 2

A reading from the book of Revelation

The dead were judged according to what they had done in
their lives. I saw the new Jerusalem coming down from
heaven.

I, John, saw an angel come down from heaven,
holding the key to the abyss and a huge chain
in his hand. He seized the dragon, the ancient
serpent, who is the devil or Satan, and chained
him up for a thousand years. The angel
hurled him into the abyss, which he closed and
sealed over him. He did this so that the dragon
might not lead the nations astray until the
thousand years are over. After this, the dragon
is to be released for a short time.

Then I saw some thrones. Those who were
sitting on them were empowered to pass judgment. I also saw the spirits of those who had
been beheaded for their witness to Jesus and
the word of God, those who had never worshiped the beast or its image nor accepted its
mark on their foreheads or their hands. They
came to life again and reigned with Christ for
a thousand years.

Next I saw a large white throne and the One
who sat on it. The earth and the sky fled from
his presence until they could no longer be
seen. I saw the dead, the great and the lowly,
standing before the throne. Lastly, among the
scrolls, the book of the living was opened.
The dead were judged according to their conduct as recorded on the scrolls. The sea gave
up its dead; then death and the nether world
gave up their dead. Each person was judged
according to his conduct. Then death and the
nether world were hurled into the pool of fire,
which is the second death; anyone whose name
was not found inscribed in the book of the
living was hurled into this pool of fire.

Then I saw new heavens and a new earth.
The former heavens and the former earth had
passed away, and the sea was no longer. I also
saw a new Jerusalem, the holy city, coming
down out of heaven from God, beautiful as a
bride prepared to meet her husband.
    This is the Word of the Lord.

Responsorial Psalm   Ps 84, 3. 4. 5-6. 8

℟. (Rv 21, 3) Here God lives among his people.
My soul yearns and pines
    for the courts of the Lord.
My heart and my flesh
    cry out for the living God.
℟. Here God lives among his people.
Even the sparrow finds a home,
    and the swallow a nest
    in which she puts her young—
Your altars, O Lord of hosts,
    my king and my God!
℟. Here God lives among his people.
Happy they who dwell in your house!
    continually they praise you.
Happy the men whose strength you are!
    They go from strength to strength.
℟. Here God lives among his people.

GOSPEL   **Years I and II**
Alleluia   Lk 21, 29-33

See no. 509, at the end.

✠ A reading from the holy gospel according
to Luke

When you see these things happen, know that the kingdom
of God is near.

Jesus told his disciples a parable: "Notice the
fig tree, or any other tree. You observe them
when they are budding and know for yourselves that summer is near. Likewise when you
see all the things happening of which I speak,
know that the reign of God is near. Let me
tell you this: the present generation will not
pass away until all this takes place. The heavens and the earth will pass away, but my
words will not pass."
    This is the gospel of the Lord.

508   **SATURDAY OF THE
THIRTY-FOURTH, OR LAST,
WEEK OF THE YEAR**

`Year I`

READING I   Dn 7, 15-27

**A reading from the book of the prophet
Daniel**

Kingdoms and power will be given to the people of the
Most High.

I, Daniel, found my spirit anguished within its
sheath of flesh, and I was terrified by the visions of my mind. I approached one of those
present and asked him what all this meant in
truth; in answer, he made known to me the
meaning of the things: "These four great beasts
stand for four kingdoms which shall arise on
the earth. But the holy ones of the Most High
shall receive the kingship, to possess it forever and ever."

But I wished to make certain about the
fourth beast, so very terrible and different
from the others, devouring and crushing with
its iron teeth and bronze claws, and trampling
with its feet what was left; about the ten horns
on its head, and the other one that sprang up,
before which three horns fell; about the horn
with the eyes and the mouth that spoke arrogantly, which appeared greater than its fellows. For, as I watched, that horn made war
against the holy ones and was victorious until
the Ancient One arrived; judgment was pronounced in favor of the holy ones of the Most
High, and the time came when the holy ones
possessed the kingdom. He answered me thus:
"The fourth beast shall be a fourth kingdom
on earth,
   different from all the others;
It shall devour the whole earth,
   beat it down, and crush it.
The ten horns shall be ten kings
   rising out of that kingdom;
   another shall rise up after them,
Different from those before him,
   who shall lay low three kings.
He shall speak against the Most High
   and oppress the holy ones of the Most High,

thinking to change the feast days and the
   law.
They shall be handed over to him
   for a year, two years, and a half-year.
But when the court is convened,
   and his power is taken away
   by final and absolute destruction,
Then the kingship and dominion and majesty
   of all the kingdoms under the heavens
   shall be given to the holy people of the
      Most High,
Whose kingdom shall be everlasting:
   all dominions shall serve and obey him."
      This is the Word of the Lord.

Responsorial Psalm   Dn 3, 82. 83. 84. 85. 86. 87

℟. (59) Give glory and eternal praise to him.
You sons of men, bless the Lord;
   praise and exalt him above all forever.
℟. Give glory and eternal praise to him.
O Israel, bless the Lord;
   praise and exalt him above all forever.
℟. Give glory and eternal praise to him.
Priests of the Lord, bless the Lord;
   praise and exalt him above all forever.
℟. Give glory and eternal praise to him.
Servants of the Lord, bless the Lord;
   praise and exalt him above all forever.
℟. Give glory and eternal praise to him.
Spirits and souls of the just, bless the Lord;
   praise and exalt him above all forever.
℟. Give glory and eternal praise to him.
Holy men of humble heart, bless the Lord;
   praise and exalt him above all forever.
℟. Give glory and eternal praise to him.

`Year II`

READING I   Rv 22, 1-7

A reading from the book of Revelation

It will never be night again, because the Lord God will
shine on them.

The angel then showed me, John, the river of
life-giving water, clear as crystal, which issued
from the throne of God and of the Lamb and
flowed down the middle of the streets. On
either side of the river grew the trees of life
which produce fruit twelve times a year, once
each month; their leaves serve as medicine for

the nations. Nothing deserving a curse shall be found there. The throne of God and of the Lamb shall be there, and his servants shall serve him faithfully. They shall see him face to face and bear his name on their foreheads. The night shall be no more. They will need no light from lamps or the sun, for the Lord God shall give them light, and they shall reign forever.

The angel said to me: "These words are trustworthy and true; the Lord, the God of prophetic spirits, has sent his angel to show his servants what must happen very soon.

"Remember, I am coming soon! Happy the man who heeds the prophetic message of this book!"

     This is the Word of the Lord.

Responsorial Psalm   Ps 95, 1-2. 3-5. 6-7

℞. (1 Cor 16, 22; Rv 21, 20) Marana tha! Come, Lord Jesus!
Come, let us sing joyfully to the Lord;
   let us acclaim the Rock of our salvation.
Let us greet him with thanksgiving;
   let us joyfully sing psalms to him.
℞. Marana tha! Come, Lord Jesus!
For the Lord is a great God,
   and a great king above all gods;
In his hands are the depths of the earth,
   and the tops of the mountains are his.

His is the sea, for he has made it,
   and the dry land, which his hands have formed.
℞. Marana tha! Come, Lord Jesus!
Come, let us bow down in worship;
   let us kneel before the Lord who made us.
For he is our God,
   and we are the people he shepherds, the flock he guides.
℞. Marana tha! Come, Lord Jesus!

Years I and II

GOSPEL   Lk 21, 34-36
Alleluia

See no. 509.

✠ A reading from the holy gospel according to Luke

Stay awake, that you might have the strength to survive all that is going to happen.

Jesus said to his disciples: "Be on guard lest your spirits become bloated with indulgence and drunkenness and worldly cares. The great day will suddenly close in on you like a trap. The day I speak of will come upon all who dwell on the face of the earth. So be on the watch. Pray constantly for the strength to escape whatever is in prospect, and to stand secure before the Son of Man."

     This is the gospel of the Lord.

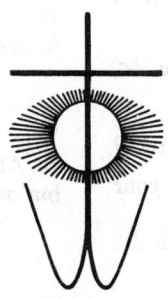

509 **ALLELUIA**

FOR WEEKDAYS OF THE YEAR

1 1 Sm 3, 9; Jn 6, 69

℟. Alleluia. **Speak, O Lord, your servant is listening;**
you have the words of everlasting life. ℟. Alleluia.

2 Ps 19, 9

℟. Alleluia. **Your words, O Lord, give joy to my heart,**
your teaching is light to my eyes. ℟. Alleluia.

3 Ps 25, 4. 5

℟. Alleluia. **Teach me your paths, my God, and lead me in your truth.** ℟. Alleluia.

4 Ps 27, 11

℟. Alleluia. **Teach me your way, O Lord, and lead me on a straight road.** ℟. Alleluia.

5 Ps 95, 8

℟. Alleluia. **If today you hear his voice, harden not your hearts.** ℟. Alleluia.

6 Ps 111, 8

℟. Alleluia. **Your laws are all made firm, O Lord,**
established for ever more. ℟. Alleluia.

7 Ps 119, 18

℟. Alleluia. **Unveil my eyes, O Lord, and I will see the marvels of your law.** ℟. Alleluia.

8 Ps 119, 27

℟. Alleluia. **Instruct me in the way of your rules, and I will reflect on all your wonders.** ℟. Alleluia.

9 Ps 119, 34

℟. Alleluia. **Teach me the meaning of your law, O Lord, and I will guard it with all my heart.** ℟. Alleluia.

10 Ps 119, 35. 29

℟. Alleluia. **Turn my heart to do your will; teach me your law, O God.** ℟. Alleluia.

11 Ps 119, 88

℟. Alleluia. **Give me life, O Lord, and I will do your commands.** ℟. Alleluia.

12 Ps 119, 105

℟. Alleluia. **Your word is a lamp for my feet, and a light on my path.** ℟. Alleluia.

13 Ps 119, 135

℟. Alleluia. **Let your face shine on your servant, and teach me your laws.** ℟. Alleluia.

14 Ps 130, 5

℟. Alleluia. **I hope in the Lord, I trust in his word.** ℟. Alleluia.

15 Ps 145, 13

℟. Alleluia. **The Lord is faithful in all his words and holy in his deeds.** ℟. Alleluia.

16 Ps 147, 2. 15

℟. Alleluia. **O praise the Lord, Jerusalem; he sends out his word to the earth.** ℟. Alleluia.

17 Mt 4, 4

℟. Alleluia. **Man does not live on bread alone, but on every word that comes from the mouth of God.** ℟. Alleluia.

18 Mt 11, 25

℟. Alleluia. **Blessed are you, Father, Lord of heaven and earth;**
you have revealed to little ones the mysteries of the kingdom. ℟. Alleluia.

19   See Lk 8, 15

℟. Alleluia. **Happy are they who have kept the word with a generous heart,**
and yield a harvest through perseverance. ℟. Alleluia.

20   Jn 6, 64. 69

℟. Alleluia. **Your words, Lord, are spirit and life,**
you have the words of everlasting life. ℟. Alleluia.

21   Jn 8, 12

℟. Alleluia. **I am the light of the world, says the Lord;**
the man who follows me will have the light of life. ℟. Alleluia.

22   Jn 10, 27

℟. Alleluia. **My sheep listen to my voice, says the Lord;**
I know them, and they follow me. ℟. Alleluia.

23   Jn 14, 5

℟. Alleluia. **I am the way, the truth, and the life, says the Lord;**
no one comes to the Father, except through me. ℟. Alleluia.

24   Jn 14, 23

℟. Alleluia. **If anyone loves me, he will hold to my words,**
and my Father will love him, and we will come to him. ℟. Alleluia.

25   Jn 15, 15

℟. Alleluia. **I call you my friends, says the Lord,**
for I have made known to you all that the Father has told me. ℟. Alleluia.

26   Jn 17, 17

℟. Alleluia. **Your word, O Lord, is truth;**
make us holy in the truth. ℟. Alleluia.

27   See Acts 16, 14

℟. Alleluia. **Open our hearts, O Lord,**
to listen to the words of your Son. ℟. Alleluia.

28   2 Cor 5, 19

℟. Alleluia. **God was in Christ, to reconcile the world to himself;**
and the Good News of reconciliation he has entrusted to us. ℟. Alleluia.

29   See Eph 1, 17-18

℟. Alleluia. **May the Father of our Lord Jesus Christ**
enlighten the eyes of our heart
that we might see how great is the hope
to which we are called. ℟. Alleluia.

30   Phil 2, 15-16

℟. Alleluia. **Shine on the world like bright stars;**
you are offering it the word of life. ℟. Alleluia.

31   Col 3, 16. 17

℟. Alleluia. **Give thanks to God our Father through Jesus Christ our Lord,**
and may the fullness of his message live within you. ℟. Alleluia.

32   1 Thes 2, 13

℟. Alleluia. **Receive this message not as the words of man,**
but as truly the word of God. ℟. Alleluia.

33   2 Thes 2, 14

℟. Alleluia. **God has called us with the gospel;**
the people won for him by Jesus Christ our Lord. ℟. Alleluia.

34   2 Tm 1, 10

℟. Alleluia. **Our Savior Jesus Christ has done away with death,**
and brought us life through his gospel. ℟. Alleluia.

35   Heb 4, 12

℟. Alleluia. **The word of God is living and active;**
it probes the thoughts and motives of our heart. ℟. Alleluia.

36 Jas 1, 18

℟. Alleluia. **The Father gave us birth by his message of truth,**
that we might be as the first fruits of his creation. ℟. Alleluia.

37 Jas 1, 21

℟. Alleluia. **Receive and submit to the word planted in you;**
it can save your souls. ℟. Alleluia.

38 1 Pt 1, 25

℟. Alleluia. **The word of the Lord stands for ever;**
it is the word given to you, the Good News. ℟. Alleluia.

39 1 Jn 2, 5

℟. Alleluia. **He who keeps the word of Christ, grows perfect in the love of God.** ℟. Alleluia.

FOR THE LAST WEEK

1 Mt 24, 42. 44

℟. Alleluia. **Be watchful and ready: you know not when the Son of Man is coming.** ℟. Alleluia.

2 Lk 21, 28

℟. Alleluia. **Lift up your heads and see; your redemption is near at hand.** ℟. Alleluia.

3 Lk 21, 36

℟. Alleluia. **Be watchful, pray constantly, that you may be worthy to stand before the Son of Man.** ℟. Alleluia.

4 Rv 2, 10

℟. Alleluia. **Be faithful until death, says the Lord,**
and I will give you the crown of life. ℟. Alleluia.

See also No. 164.

COMMON TEXTS FOR SUNG RESPONSORIAL PSALMS

See above nos. 174-175.

PROPER OF THE SAINTS

On celebrations in honor of the saints, in addition to the
texts referred to in individual cases, the readings given in
the common of saints may always be selected for pastoral
reasons.

JANUARY

January 1

OCTAVE OF CHRISTMAS
SOLEMNITY OF MARY,
MOTHER OF GOD

See the proper of seasons, no. 18.

January 2

510   **BASIL THE GREAT and
GREGORY NAZIANZEN,
bishops and doctors**

Memorial

Common of pastors or doctors, p. 846 or 858.

January 7

511   **RAYMOND OF PENYAFORT,
priest**

Common of pastors, p. 846, especially 2 Cor 5, 14-20
(Reading II, no. 722, § 7), p. 853.

January 13

512   **HILARY, bishop and doctor**

Common of pastors or doctors, p. 846 or 858.

OR

READING II   1 Jn 2, 18-25

A reading from the first letter of John

Whoever acknowledges the Son possesses the Father also.

Children, it is the final hour;
  just as you heard that the Antichrist was
    coming,
so now many such antichrists have appeared.

This makes us certain that it is the final
  hour.
It was from our ranks that they took their
  leave—
not that they really belonged to us;
for if they had really belonged to us,
they would have stayed with us.
It only served to show that none of them
  was ours.

But you have the anointing that comes from
  the Holy One,
so that all knowledge is yours.
My reason for having written you
is not that you do not know the truth
but that you do,
and that no lie has anything in common with
  the truth.
Who is the liar?
He who denies that Jesus is the Christ.
He is the antichrist,
denying the Father and the Son.
Anyone who denies the Son
has no claim on the Father,
but he who acknowledges the Son
can claim the Father as well.

As for you,
let what you heard from the beginning
remain in your hearts.
If what you heard from the beginning
does remain in your hearts,
then you in turn will remain in the Son and
  in the Father.
He himself made us a promise
and the promise is no less than this:
eternal life.
      This is the Word of the Lord.

January 17

513   **ANTHONY, abbot**

Common of saints [for religious], p. 867.

Memorial

OR

GOSPEL   Mt 19, 16-26

✠ A reading from the holy gospel according
to Matthew

If you wish to be perfect, go and sell what you have.

A man came up to Jesus and said, "Teacher,
what good must I do to possess everlasting
life?" He answered, "Why do you question me
about what is good? There is One who is good.
If you wish to enter into life, keep the commandments." "Which ones?" he asked. Jesus
replied, " 'You shall not kill'; 'You shall not
commit adultery'; 'You shall not steal'; 'You
shall not bear false witness'; 'Honor your father and your mother'; and 'Love your neighbor as yourself.' " The young man said to him,
"I have kept all these; what do I need to do
further?" Jesus told him, "If you seek perfection, go, sell your possessions, and give to the
poor. You will then have treasure in heaven.
Afterward, come back and follow me." Hearing
these words, the young man went away sad,
for his possessions were many.

Jesus said to his disciples: "I assure you,
only with difficulty will a rich man enter into
the kingdom of God. I repeat what I said:
it is easier for a camel to pass through a
needle's eye than for a rich man to enter the
kingdom of God." When the disciples heard
this they were completely overwhelmed, and
exclaimed, "Then who can be saved?" Jesus
looked at them and said, "For man it is impossible; but for God all things are possible."
This is the gospel of the Lord.

January 20

514   **FABIAN, pope and martyr**

Common of martyrs or pastors [for a pope], p. 837 or 846.

515   **SEBASTIAN, martyr**

Common of martyrs, p. 837.

January 21

516   **AGNES, virgin and martyr**

Memorial

Common of martyrs or virgins, p. 837 or 864.

January 22

517   **VINCENT, deacon and martyr**

Common of martyrs, p. 837.

January 24

518   **FRANCIS DE SALES,
bishop and doctor**

Memorial

Common of pastors or doctors, p. 846 or 858.

January 25

519   **CONVERSION OF PAUL,
apostle**

Feast

READING I   Acts 22, 3-16

A reading from the Acts of the Apostles

Rise and be baptized and wash away your sins, calling on
the name of Jesus.

Paul told the people: "I am a Jew, born in
Tarsus in Cilicia, but I was brought up in this
city. Here I sat at the feet of Gamaliel and was
educated strictly in the law of our fathers. I
was a staunch defender of God, just as all of
you are today. Furthermore I persecuted this
new way to the point of death. I arrested and
imprisoned both men and women.

"On this point the high priest and the whole
council of elders can bear me witness, for it
was from them that I received letters to our
brother Jews in Damascus. I set out with the
intention of bringing the prisoners I would
arrest back to Jerusalem for punishment. As I
was traveling along, approaching Damascus
around noon, a great light from the sky suddenly flashed all about me. I fell to the ground
and heard a voice say to me, 'Saul, Saul, why
do you persecute me?' I answered, 'Who are

you, sir?' He said to me, 'I am Jesus the Nazo-rean whom you are persecuting.' My com-panions saw the light but did not hear the voice speaking to me. 'What is it I must do, sir?' I asked, and the Lord replied, 'Get up and go into Damascus. There you will be told about everything you are destined to do.' But since I could not see because of the brilliance of the light, I had to be taken by the hand and led into Damascus by my companions.

"A certain Ananias, a devout observer of the law and well spoken of by all the Jews who lived there, came and stood by me. 'Saul, my brother,' he said, 'recover your sight.' In that instant I regained my sight and looked at him. The next thing he said was, 'The God of our fathers long ago designated you to know his will, to look upon the Just One, and to hear the sound of his voice; before all men you are to be his witness to what you have seen and heard. Why delay, then? Be baptized at once and wash away your sins as you call upon his name.' "

This is the Word of the Lord.

OR

READING I   Acts 9, 1-22

A reading from the Acts of the Apostles
Lord, what do you want me to do?

Saul, still breathing murderous threats against the Lord's disciples, went to the high priest and asked him for letters to the synagogues in Damascus which would empower him to ar-rest and bring to Jerusalem anyone he might find, man or woman, living according to the new way. As he traveled along and was ap-proaching Damascus, a light from the sky sud-denly flashed about him. He fell to the ground and at the same time heard a voice saying, "Saul, Saul, why do you persecute me?" "Who are you, sir?" he asked. The voice answered, "I am Jesus, the one you are persecuting. Get up and go into the city, where you will be told what to do." The men who were traveling with him stood there speechless. They had heard the voice but could see no one. Saul got up

from the ground unable to see, even though his eyes were open. They had to take him by the hand and lead him into Damascus. For three days he continued blind, during which time he neither ate nor drank.

There was a disciple in Damascus named Ananias to whom the Lord had appeared in a vision. "Ananias!" he said. "Here I am, Lord," came the answer. The Lord said to him, "Go at once to Straight Street, and at the house of Judas ask for a certain Saul of Tarsus. He is there praying." (Saul saw in a vision a man named Ananias coming to him and placing his hands on him so that he might recover his sight.) But Ananias protested: "Lord, I have heard from many sources about this man and all the harm he has done to your holy people in Jerusalem. He is here now with authoriza-tion from the chief priests to arrest any who invoke your name." The Lord said to him: "You must go! This man is the instrument I have chosen to bring my name to the Gentiles and their kings and to the people of Israel. I myself shall indicate to him how much he will have to suffer for my name." With that Ananias left. When he entered the house he laid his hands on Saul and said, "Saul, my brother, I have been sent by the Lord Jesus who appeared to you on the way here, to help you recover your sight and be filled with the Holy Spirit." Im-mediately something like scales fell from his eyes and he regained his sight. He got up and was baptized, and his strength returned to him after he had taken food.

Saul stayed some time with the disciples in Damascus, and soon began to proclaim in the synagogues that Jesus was the Son of God. Any who heard it were greatly taken aback. They kept saying: "Isn't this the man who worked such havoc in Jerusalem among those who invoke this name? Did he not come here purposely to apprehend such people and bring them before the chief priests?"

Saul for his part grew steadily more power-ful, and reduced the Jewish community of Damascus to silence with his proofs that this Jesus was the Messiah.

This is the Word of the Lord.

Responsorial Psalm   Ps 117, 1. 2

℟. (Mk 16, 15) Go out to all the world,
    and tell the Good News.

Praise the Lord, all you nations;
    glorify him, all you peoples!

℟. Go out to all the world,
    and tell the Good News.

For steadfast is his kindness toward us,
    and the fidelity of the Lord endures forever.

℟. Go out to all the world,
    and tell the Good News.

℟. Or: Alleluia.

GOSPEL   Mk 16, 15-18

Alleluia   Jn 15, 16

℟. Alleluia. I have chosen you from the world,
    says the Lord,
to go and bear fruit that will last. ℟. Alleluia.

✠ A reading from the holy gospel according
    to Mark

Go out to the whole world and make known the Good News.

Jesus appeared to the Eleven and said to them:
"Go into the whole world and proclaim the
good news to all creation. The man who believes in it and accepts baptism will be saved;
the man who refuses to believe in it will be
condemned. Signs like these will accompany
those who have professed their faith: they will
use my name to expel demons, they will speak
entirely new languages, they will be able to
handle serpents, they will be able to drink
deadly poison without harm, and the sick upon
whom they lay their hands will recover."
    This is the gospel of the Lord.

In votive Masses of St. Paul the readings are as above.

January 26

520   **TIMOTHY and TITUS,**

                    bishops

                                    Memorial

Common of pastors, p. 846, except:

READING I   2 Tm 1, 1-8

The beginning of the second letter of Paul to
                    Timothy

I have in mind your faith which is openly sincere.

**Paul, by the will of God an apostle of Christ
Jesus sent to proclaim the promise of life in
him, to Timothy, my child whom I love. May
grace, mercy, and peace from God the Father and from Christ Jesus our Lord be with
you.**

I thank God, the God of my forefathers
whom I worship with a clear conscience,
whenever I remember you in my prayers—as
indeed I do constantly, night and day. Recalling
your tears when we parted, I yearn to see you
again. That would make my happiness complete. I find myself thinking of your sincere
faith—faith which first belonged to your
grandmother Lois and to your mother Eunice,
and which (I am confident) you also have.

For this reason, I remind you to stir into
flame the gift of God bestowed when my hands
were laid on you. The Spirit God has given us
is no cowardly spirit, but rather one that
makes us strong, loving, and wise. Therefore,
never be ashamed of your testimony to our
Lord, nor of me, a prisoner for his sake, but
with the strength which comes from God bear
your share of the hardship which the gospel
entails.

        This is the Word of the Lord.

OR

READING I   Ti 1, 1-5

The beginning of the letter of Paul to Titus

To Titus, my beloved son in a common faith.

**Paul, a servant of God, sent as an apostle of
Jesus Christ for the sake of the faith of those
whom God has chosen, and to promote their
knowledge of the truth as our religion embodies it, in the hope of that eternal life which
God, who cannot lie, promised in endless ages
past. This he has now manifested in his own
good time as his word, in the preaching entrusted to me by the command of God our
Savior. Paul to Titus, my own true child in our
common faith: May grace and peace from God
our Father, and Christ Jesus our Savior, be
with you.**

My purpose in leaving you in Crete was
that you might accomplish what had been left

undone, especially the appointment of presbyters in every town, as I instructed you.
This is the Word of the Lord.

January 27
521   **ANGELA MERICI, virgin**

Common of virgins or saints [for teachers], p. 864 or 867.

January 28
522   **THOMAS AQUINAS,**

priest and doctor   Memorial

Common of doctors or pastors, p. 846 or 858.

January 31
523   **JOHN BOSCO, priest**   Memorial

Common of pastors or saints [for teachers], p. 846 or 867.

FEBRUARY

February 2
524   **PRESENTATION OF THE LORD**

Feast

READING I   Mal 3, 1-4

A reading from the book of the prophet Malachi

The Lord whom you seek will come to his temple.

The Lord God said:
Lo, I am sending my messenger
    to prepare the way before me;
And suddenly there will come to the temple
    the Lord whom you seek,
And the messenger of the covenant whom you
    desire.
Yes, he is coming, says the Lord of hosts.
But who will endure the day of his coming?
    And who can stand when he appears?
For he is like the refiner's fire,
    or like the fuller's lye.
He will sit refining and purifying [silver],
    and he will purify the sons of Levi,

Refining them like gold or like silver
    that they may offer due sacrifice to the Lord.
Then the sacrifice of Judah and Jerusalem
    will please the Lord,
    as in the days of old, as in years gone by.
This is the Word of the Lord.

Responsorial Psalm   Ps 24, 7. 8. 9. 10

℟. (8) Who is this king of glory?
    It is the Lord!
Lift up, O gates, your lintels;
    reach up, you ancient portals,
    that the king of glory may come in!
℟. Who is this king of glory?
    It is the Lord!
Who is this king of glory?
    The Lord, strong and mighty,
    the Lord, mighty in battle.
℟. Who is this king of glory?
    It is the Lord!
Lift up, O gates, your lintels;
    reach up, you ancient portals,
    that the king of glory may come in!
℟. Who is this king of glory?
    It is the Lord!
Who is this king of glory?
    The Lord of hosts; he is the king of glory.
℟. Who is this king of glory?
    It is the Lord!

READING II   Heb 2, 14-18

A reading from the letter to the Hebrews

He had to be made like his fellow men in all things.

Now, since the children are men of blood and flesh, Jesus likewise had a full share in these, that by his death he might rob the devil, the prince of death, of his power, and free those who through fear of death had been slaves their whole life long. Surely he did not come to help angels, but rather the children of Abraham; therefore he had to become like his brothers in every way, that he might be a merciful and faithful high priest before God on their behalf, to expiate the sins of the people. Since he was himself tested through what he suffered, he is able to help those who are tempted.
This is the Word of the Lord.

GOSPEL Lk 2, 22-40 or 1, 22-32

Alleluia Lk 2, 32

℞. Alleluia. This is the light of revelation to the nations,
and the glory of your people, Israel. ℞. Alleluia.

✠ A reading from the holy gospel according to Luke

My eyes have seen your saving power.

(Long Form)

When the day came to purify them according to the law of Moses, the couple brought Jesus up to Jerusalem so that he could be presented to the Lord, for it is written in the law of the Lord, "Every first-born male shall be consecrated to the Lord." They came to offer in sacrifice "a pair of turtledoves or two young pigeons," in accord with the dictate in the law of the Lord.

There lived in Jerusalem at the time a certain man named Simeon. He was just and pious, and awaited the consolation of Israel, and the Holy Spirit was upon him. It was revealed to him by the Holy Spirit that he would not experience death until he had seen the Anointed of the Lord. He came to the temple now, inspired by the Spirit; and when the parents brought in the child Jesus to perform for him the customary ritual of the law, he took him in his arms and blessed God in these words:
"Now, Master, you can dismiss your servant in peace;
    you have fulfilled your word.
For my eyes have witnessed your saving deed
    displayed for all the peoples to see:
A revealing light to the Gentiles,
    the glory of your people Israel."
The child's father and mother were marveling at what was being said about him. Simeon blessed them and said to Mary his mother: "This child is destined to be the downfall and the rise of many in Israel, a sign that will be opposed—and you yourself shall be pierced with a sword—so that the thoughts of many hearts may be laid bare."

There was also a certain prophetess, Anna by name, daughter of Phanuel of the tribe of Asher. She had seen many days, having lived seven years with her husband after her marriage and then as a widow until she was eighty-four. She was constantly in the temple, worshiping day and night in fasting and prayer. Coming on the scene at this moment, she gave thanks to God and talked about the child to all who looked forward to the deliverance of Jerusalem.

When the pair had fulfilled all the prescriptions of the law of the Lord, they returned to Galilee and their own town of Nazareth. The child grew in size and strength, filled with wisdom, and the grace of God was upon him.

This is the gospel of the Lord.

OR

(Short Form)

When the day came to purify them according to the law of Moses, the couple brought Jesus up to Jerusalem so that he could be presented to the Lord, for it is written in the law of the Lord, "Every first-born male shall be consecrated to the Lord." They came to offer in sacrifice "a pair of turtledoves or two young pigeons," in accord with the dictate in the law of the Lord.

There lived in Jerusalem at the time a certain man named Simeon. He was just and pious, and awaited the consolation of Israel, and the Holy Spirit was upon him. It was revealed to him by the Holy Spirit that he would not experience death until he had seen the Anointed of the Lord. He came to the temple now, inspired by the Spirit; and when the parents brought in the child Jesus to perform for him the customary ritual of the law, he took him in his arms and blessed God in these words:
"Now, Master, you can dismiss your servant in peace;
    you have fulfilled your word.
For my eyes have witnessed your saving deed
    displayed for all the peoples to see:

A revealing light to the Gentiles,
    the glory of your people Israel."
  This is the gospel of the Lord.

February 3

525   BLASE, bishop and martyr

Common of martyrs or pastors, p. 837 or 846.

---

526   ANSGAR, bishop

Common of pastors [for missionaries], p. 846.

February 5

527   AGATHA, virgin and martyr

Memorial

Common of martyrs or virgins, p. 837 or 864.

February 6

528   PAUL MIKI and COMPANIONS,

martyrs

Memorial

Common of martyrs, p. 837.

OR

READING I   Gal 2, 19-20

A reading from the letter of Paul to the
                Galatians

I live now, not I, but Christ lives in me.

It was through the law that I died to the law, to
live for God. I have been crucified with Christ,
and the life I live now is not my own; Christ
is living in me. I still live my human life,
but it is a life of faith in the Son of God, who
loved me and gave himself for me.
  This is the Word of the Lord.

GOSPEL   Mt 28, 16-20

✠ A reading from the holy gospel according
                to Matthew

Go out to the whole world; proclaim the Good News to
    all creation.

The eleven disciples made their way to Galilee,
to the mountain to which Jesus had summoned

them. At the sight of him, those who had enter-
tained doubts fell down in homage. Jesus came
forward and addressed them in these words:
    "Full authority has been given to me
    both in heaven and on earth;
    go, therefore, and make disciples of all the
        nations.
  Baptize them in the name
    'of the Father
    and of the Son,
    and of the Holy Spirit.'
  Teach them to carry out everything I have
    commanded you.
  And know that I am with you always,
    until the end of the world!"
  This is the gospel of the Lord.

February 8

529   JEROME EMILIANI

Comon of saints [for teachers], p. 867.

February 10

530   SCHOLASTICA, virgin

Memorial

Common of virgins or saints [for religious], p. 864 or 867.

February 11

531   OUR LADY OF LOURDES

Common of the Blessed Virgin Mary, p. 826.

OR

READING I   Is 66, 10-14

A reading from the book of the prophet
                Isaiah

Now toward her I send flowing peace, like a river.

Rejoice with Jerusalem and be glad because of
    her,
  all you who love her;
Exult, exult with her,
  all you who were mourning over her!
Oh, that you may suck fully
  of the milk of her comfort,
That you may nurse with delight
  at her abundant breasts!

For thus says the Lord:
Lo, I will spread prosperity over her like a
river,
and the wealth of the nations like an overflowing torrent.
As nurslings, you shall be carried in her arms,
and fondled in her lap;
As a mother comforts her son,
so will I comfort you;
in Jerusalem you shall find your comfort.

When you see this, your heart shall rejoice,
and your bodies flourish like the grass;
The Lord's power shall be known to his servants.
        This is the Word of the Lord.

February 14
532   CYRIL, monk, and METHODIUS,

     bishop   Memorial

Common of pastors [for missionaries] or saints, p. 846 or
867.

February 17
533   SEVEN FOUNDERS OF THE

     ORDER OF SERVITES

Common of saints [for religious], p. 867.

FEBRUARY 21
534   PETER DAMIAN, bishop

     and doctor

Common of doctors or pastors or saints [for religious], p.
858 or 846 or 867.

February 22
535   CHAIR OF PETER, apostle

                                  Feast

READING I   1 Pt 5, 1-4

A reading from the first letter of Peter
I myself am one of your leaders and a witness to the sufferings of Christ.

To the elders among you I, a fellow elder, a
witness of Christ's sufferings and sharer in the

glory that is to be revealed, make this appeal.
God's flock is in your midst; give it a shepherd's care. Watch over it willingly as God
would have you do, not under coercion; and
not for shameful profit either, but generously.
Be examples to the flock, not lording it over
those assigned to you, so that when the chief
shepherd appears you will win for yourselves
the unfading crown of glory.
        This is the Word of the Lord.

Responsorial Psalm   Ps 23, 1-3. 3-4. 5. 6

℟. (1) The Lord is my shepherd;
   there is nothing I shall want.
The Lord is my shepherd; I shall not want.
   In verdant pastures he gives me repose;
Beside restful waters he leads me;
   he refreshes my soul.
℟. The Lord is my shepherd;
   there is nothing I shall want.
He guides me in right paths
   for his name's sake.
Even though I walk in the dark valley
   I fear no evil; for you are at my side
With your rod and your staff
   that give me courage.
℟. The Lord is my shepherd;
   there is nothing I shall want.
You spread the table before me
   in the sight of my foes;
You anoint my head with oil;
   my cup overflows.
℟. The Lord is my shepherd;
   there is nothing I shall want.
Only goodness and kindness follow me
   all the days of my life;
And I shall dwell in the house of the Lord
   for years to come.
℟. The Lord is my shepherd;
   there is nothing I shall want.

GOSPEL   Mt 16, 13-19
Alleluia   Mt 16, 18

℟. Alleluia. **You are Peter, the rock on which I
will build my Church;**
the gates of hell will not hold out against
it. ℟. Alleluia.

✠ **A reading from the holy gospel according to Matthew**

You are Peter; and to you I will give the keys of the kingdom of heaven.

When Jesus came to the neighborhood of Caesarea Philippi, he asked his disciples this question: "Who do people say that the Son of Man is?" They replied, "Some say John the Baptizer, others Elijah, still others Jeremiah or one of the prophets." "And you," he said to them, "who do you say that I am?" "You are the Messiah," Simon Peter answered, "the Son of the living God!" Jesus replied, "Blest are you, Simon son of John! No mere man has revealed this to you, but my heavenly Father. I for my part declare to you, you are 'Rock,' and on this rock I will build my church, and the jaws of death shall not prevail against it. I will entrust to you the keys of the kingdom of heaven. Whatever you declare bound on earth shall be bound in heaven; whatever you declare loosed on earth shall be loosed in heaven."

This is the gospel of the Lord.

In votive Masses of St. Peter the readings are as above.

February 23

536   POLYCARP, bishop and martyr

Memorial

Common of martyrs or pastors, p. 837 or 846.

OR

READING II   Rv 2, 8-11

A reading from the book of Revelation

I know your affliction and your poverty.

To the presiding spirit of the church in Smyrna, write this:

"The First and the Last who once died but now lives has this to say: I know of your tribulation and your poverty, even though you are rich. I know the slander you endure from self-styled Jews who are nothing other than members of Satan's assembly. Have no fear of the sufferings to come. The devil will indeed cast some of you into prison to put you to the test;

you will be tried over a period of ten days. Remain faithful until death and I will give you the crown of life.

"Let him who has ears to hear heed the Spirit's word to the churches! The victor shall never be harmed by the second death."

This is the Word of the Lord.

MARCH

March 4

537   CASIMIR

Common of saints, p. 867.

March 7

538   PERPETUA and FELICITY,

martyrs   Memorial

Common of martyrs, p. 837.

March 8

539   JOHN OF GOD, religious

Common of saints [for religious; for those who work for the disadvantaged], p. 867, especially Mt 25, 31-46 (Gospel, no. 742, § 10), p. 884.

March 9

540   FRANCES OF ROME, religious

Common of saints, p. 867.

March 17

541   PATRICK, bishop

Common of pastors [for missionaries], p. 846.

March 18

542   CYRIL OF JERUSALEM,

bishop and doctor

Common of pastors or doctors, p. 846 or 858.

March 19

543   JOSEPH, HUSBAND OF MARY

Solemnity

READING I   2 Sm 7, 4-5. 12-14. 16

A reading from the second book of Samuel

The Lord will give to him the throne of his father, David.

The Lord spoke to Nathan and said: "Go, tell my servant David, 'When your time comes and you rest with your ancestors, I will raise up your heir after you, sprung from your loins, and I will make his kingdom firm. It is he who shall build a house for my name. And I will make his royal throne firm forever. I will be a father to him, and he shall be a son to me. Your house and your kingdom shall endure forever before me; your throne shall stand firm forever.' "

This is the Word of the Lord.

Responsorial Psalm   Ps 89, 2-3. 4-5. 27. 29

℞. (37) The son of David will live for ever.

The favors of the Lord I will sing forever;
   through all generations my mouth shall proclaim your faithfulness.

For you have said, "My kindness is established
   forever";
   in heaven you have confirmed your faithfulness.

℞. The son of David will live for ever.

"I have made a covenant with my chosen one,
   I have sworn to David my servant:

Forever will I confirm your posterity
   and establish your throne for all generations."

℞. The son of David will live for ever.

"He shall say of me, 'You are my father,
   my God, the Rock, my savior.'

Forever I will maintain my kindness toward
   him,
   and my covenant with him stands firm."

℞. The son of David will live for ever.

READING II   Rom 4, 13. 16-18. 22

A reading from the letter of Paul to the Romans

Against all hope he believed in hope.

Certainly the promise made to Abraham and his descendants that they would inherit the world did not depend on the law; it was made in view of the justice that comes from faith. Hence, all depends on faith, everything is a grace. Thus the promise holds true for all Abraham's descendants, not only for those who have the law but for all who have his faith. He is father of us all, which is why Scripture says, "I have made you father of many nations." Yes, he is our father in the sight of God in whom he believed, the God who restores the dead to life and calls into being those things which had not been. Hoping against hope, Abraham believed and so became the father of many nations, just as it was once told him, "Numerous as this shall your descendants be." Thus his faith was credited to him as justice.

This is the Word of the Lord.

GOSPEL   Mt 1, 16. 18-21. 24

Verse before the Gospel or Alleluia   Ps 84, 1

How happy they who dwell in your house, O
   Lord;
continually they sing your praise!

✠ A reading from the holy gospel according
                   to Matthew

Joseph did as the angel of the Lord commanded him.

Jacob was the father of Joseph the husband of Mary. It was of her that Jesus who is called the Messiah was born. Now this is how the birth of Jesus Christ came about. When his mother Mary was engaged to Joseph, but before they lived together, she was found with child through the power of the Holy Spirit. Joseph her husband, an upright man unwilling to expose her to the law, decided to divorce her quietly. Such was his intention when suddenly the angel of the Lord appeared in a dream and said to him: "Joseph, son of David, have no fear about taking Mary as your wife. It is by the Holy Spirit that she has conceived this child. She is to have a son and you are to name him Jesus because he will save his people from their sins." When Joseph awoke he did as the angel of the Lord had directed him.

This is the gospel of the Lord.

OR

GOSPEL   Lk 2, 41-51
Verse before the Gospel or Alleluia   Ps 84, 1

How happy they who dwell in your house, O
    Lord;
continually they sing your praise!

✠ A reading from the holy gospel according
                to Luke
See how your father and I have been in sorrow seeking you.

The parents of Jesus used to go every year to
Jerusalem for the feast of the Passover, and
when he was twelve they went up for the
celebration as was their custom. As they were
returning at the end of the feast, the child
Jesus remained behind unknown to his parents. Thinking he was in the party, they continued their journey for a day, looking for him
among their relatives and acquaintances.

Not finding him, they returned to Jerusalem
in search of him. On the third day they came
upon him in the temple sitting in the midst of
the teachers, listening to them and asking them
questions. All who heard him were amazed at
his intelligence and his answers.

When his parents saw him they were astonished, and his mother said to him: "Son, why
have you done this to us? You see that your
father and I have been searching for you in
sorrow." He said to them: "Why did you
search for me? Did you not know I had to be
in my Father's house?" But they did not grasp
what he said to them.

He went down with them then and came to
Nazareth, and was obedient to them.

This is the gospel of the Lord.

March 23
544   TURIBIUS DE MONGROVEJO,
                    bishop
Common of pastors, p. 846.

March 25
545   THE ANNUNCIATION
        OF OUR LORD
                                        Solemnity
READING I   Is 7, 10-14
A reading from the book of the prophet Isaiah
The virgin will conceive.

The Lord spoke to Ahaz: Ask for a sign from
the Lord, your God; let it be deep as the
nether world, or high as the sky! But Ahaz
answered, "I will not ask! I will not tempt the
Lord!" Then he said: Listen, O house of David!
Is it not enough for you to weary men, must
you also weary my God? Therefore the Lord
himself will give you this sign: the virgin shall
be with child, and bear a son, and shall name
him Immanuel.

    This is the Word of the Lord.

Responsorial Psalm   Ps 40, 7-8. 8-9. 10. 11

℟. (8. 9) Here am I, Lord;
    I come to do your will.
Sacrifice or oblation you wished not,
    but ears open to obedience you gave me.
Holocausts or sin-offerings you sought not;
    then said I, "Behold I come;
℟. Here am I, Lord;
    I come to do your will.
In the written scroll it is prescribed for me,
To do your will, O my God, is my delight,
    and your law is within my heart!"
℟. Here am I, Lord;
    I come to do your will.
I announced your justice in the vast assembly;
    I did not restrain my lips, as you, O Lord,
    know.
℟. Here am I, Lord;
    I come to do your will.
Your justice I kept not hid within my heart;
    your faithfulness and your salvation I have
        spoken of;
I have made no secret of your kindness and
        your truth
    in the vast assembly.
℟. Here am I Lord;
    I come to do your will.

READING II   Heb 10, 4-10

A reading from the letter to the Hebrews

In the scroll of the book it was written of me that I should obey your will, O God.

It is impossible for the blood of bulls and goats to take sins away. Wherefore, on coming into the world, Jesus said:

"Sacrifice and offering you did not desire,
    but a body you have prepared for me;
Holocausts and sin offerings you took no
    delight in.
Then I said, 'As is written of me in the
    book,
I have come to do your will, O God.' "

First he says,

"Sacrifices and offerings, holocausts and
    sin offerings
you neither desired nor delighted in."

(These are offered according to the prescriptions of the law.) Then he says,

"I have come to do your will."

In other words, he takes away the first covenant to establish the second.

By this "will," we have been sanctified through the offering of the body of Jesus Christ once for all.

This is the Word of the Lord.

GOSPEL   Lk 1, 26-38

Verse before the Gospel or Alleluia   Jn 1, 14

The Word of God became man and lived among
    us;
and we saw his glory.

✠ **A reading from the holy gospel according
    to Luke**

You are to conceive and bear a son.

The angel Gabriel was sent from God to a town of Galilee named Nazareth, to a virgin betrothed to a man named Joseph, of the house of David. The virgin's name was Mary. Upon arriving, the angel said to her: "Rejoice, O highly favored daughter! The Lord is with you. Blessed are you among women." She was deeply troubled by his words, and wondered what his greeting meant. The angel went on to say to her: "Do not fear, Mary. You have found favor with God. You shall conceive and bear a son and give him the name Jesus. Great will be his dignity and he will be called Son of the Most High. The Lord God will give him the throne of David his father. He will rule over the house of Jacob forever and his reign will be without end."

Mary said to the angel, "How can this be since I do not know man?" The angel answered her: "The Holy Spirit will come upon you and the power of the Most High will overshadow you; hence, the holy offspring to be born will be called Son of God. Know that Elizabeth your kinswoman has conceived a son in her old age; she who was thought to be sterile is now in her sixth month, for nothing is impossible with God."

Mary said: "I am the maidservant of the Lord. Let it be done to me as you say." With that the angel left her.

This is the gospel of the Lord.

APRIL

April 2

546   **FRANCIS OF PAOLA, hermit**

Common of saints [for religious], p. 868.

April 4

547   **ISIDORE, bishop and doctor**

Common of pastors or doctors, p. 846 or 858.

April 5

548   **VINCENT FERRER, priest**

Common of pastors [for missionaries], p. 846.

April 7

549   **JOHN BAPTIST DE LA SALLE,**

                 priest   Memorial

Common of pastors or saints [for teachers], p. 846 or 867.

April 11

550

STANISLAUS, bishop
and martyr

Common of martyrs or pastors, p. 837 or 846.

April 13

551

MARTIN I, pope and martyr

Common of martyrs or pastors [for a pope], p. 837 or 846.

April 21

552

ANSELM, bishop and doctor

Common of pastors or doctors, p. 846 or 858.

April 23

553

GEORGE, martyr

Common of martyrs, p. 837.

April 24

554

FIDELIS OF SIGMARINGEN,

priest and martyr

Common of martyrs or pastors, p. 837 or 846.

April 25

555

MARK, evangelist

READING I　　　　　　　　　　1 Pt 5, 5-14

A reading from the first letter of Peter

My son, Mark, sends you greetings.

In your relations with one another, clothe yourselves with humility, because God "is stern with the arrogant but to the humble he shows kindness." Bow humbly under God's mighty hand, so that in due time he may lift you high. Cast all your cares on him because he cares for you. Stay sober and alert. Your opponent the devil is prowling like a roaring lion looking for someone to devour. Resist him, solid in your faith, realizing that the brotherhood of believers is undergoing the same suf-

ferings throughout the world. The God of all grace, who called you to his everlasting glory in Christ, will himself restore, confirm, strengthen and establish those who have suffered a little while. Dominion be his throughout the ages! Amen.

I am writing briefly through Silvanus, whom I take to be a faithful brother to you. Herewith are expressed my encouragement and my testimony that this is the true grace of God. Be steadfast in it. The church in Babylon sends you greeting, as does Mark my son. Greet one another with the embrace of true love. To all of you who are in Christ, peace.

This is the Word of the Lord.

Responsorial Psalm　　　Ps 89, 2-3. 6-7. 16-17

℟. (2) For ever I will sing the goodness of the Lord.

The favors of the Lord I will sing forever;
　through all generations my mouth shall proclaim your faithfulness.
For you have said, "My kindness is established forever";
　in heaven you have confirmed your faithfulness.

℟. For ever I will sing the goodness of the Lord.

The heavens proclaim your wonders, O Lord,
　and your faithfulness, in the assembly of the holy ones.
For who in the skies can rank with the Lord?
Who is like the Lord among the sons of God?

℟. For ever I will sing the goodness of the Lord.

Happy the people who know the joyful shout;
　in the light of your countenance, O Lord, they walk.
At your name they rejoice all the day,
　and through your justice they are exalted.

℟. For ever I will sing the goodness of the Lord.

℟. Or: Alleluia.

GOSPEL   Mk 16, 15-20

Alleluia   1 Cor 1, 23-24

℟. Alleluia. **We preach a Christ who was crucified;**

he is the power and the wisdom of God. ℟. Alleluia.

✠ **A reading from the holy gospel according to Mark**

Make known the Good News to every creature.

Jesus appeared to the Eleven and told them: "Go into the world and proclaim the good news to all creation. The man who believes in it and accepts baptism will be saved; the man who refuses to believe in it will be condemned. Signs like these will accompany those who have professed their faith: they will use my name to expel demons, they will speak entirely new languages, they will be able to handle serpents, they will be able to drink deadly poison without harm, and the sick upon whom they lay their hands will recover." Then, after speaking to them, the Lord Jesus was taken up into heaven and took his seat at God's right hand. The Eleven went forth and preached everywhere. The Lord continued to work with them throughout and confirm the message through the signs which accompanied them. **This is the gospel of the Lord.**

April 28

556   **PETER CHANEL, priest**

and martyr

Common of martyrs or pastors [for missionaries], p. 837 or 846.

April 29

557   **CATHERINE OF SIENA,**

virgin

Common of virgins, p. 864.

Memorial

OR

READING I   1 Jn 1, 5—2, 2

A reading from the first letter of John

The blood of Christ cleanses us of all sin.

Here, then, is the message
we have heard from him
and announce to you:
that God is light;
in him there is no darkness.
If we say, "We have fellowship with him,"
while continuing to walk in darkness,
we are liars and do not act in truth.
But if we walk in light,
as he is in the light,
we have fellowship with one another,
and the blood of his Son Jesus cleanses us
    from all sin.
If we say, "We are free of the guilt of sin,"
we deceive ourselves; the truth is not to be
    found in us.
But if we acknowledge our sins,
he who is just can be trusted
to forgive our sins
and cleanse us from every wrong.
If we say, "We have never sinned,"
we make him a liar
and his word finds no place in us.

My little ones,
I am writing this to keep you from sin.
But if anyone should sin,
we have in the presence of the Father,
Jesus Christ, an intercessor who is just.
He is an offering for our sins,
and not for our sins only,
but for those of the whole world.
    This is the Word of the Lord.

April 30

558   **PIUS V, pope**

Common of pastors [for a pope], p. 837.

MAY

May 1

559   JOSEPH THE WORKER

READING I   Gn 1, 26—2, 3

A reading from the book of Genesis
Fill the earth and subdue it.

God said: "Let us make man in our image, after our likeness. Let them have dominion over the fish of the sea, the birds of the air, and the cattle, and over all the wild animals and all the creatures that crawl on the ground."

God created man in his image;
  in the divine image he created him;
  male and female he created them.

God blessed them, saying: "Be fertile and multiply; fill the earth and subdue it. Have dominion over the fish of the sea, the birds of the air, and all the living things that move on the earth." God also said: "See, I give you every seed-bearing plant all over the earth and every tree that has seed-bearing fruit on it to be your food; and to all the animals of the land, all the birds of the air, and all the living creatures that crawl on the ground, I give all the green plants for food." And so it happened. God looked at everything he had made, and he found it very good. Evening came, and morning followed—the sixth day.

Thus the heavens and the earth and all their array were completed. Since on the seventh day God was finished with the work he had been doing, he rested on the seventh day from all the work he had undertaken. So God blessed the seventh day and made it holy, because on it he rested from all the work he had done in creation.

    This is the Word of the Lord.

OR

READING I   Col 3, 14-15. 17. 23-24

A reading from the letter of Paul to the Colossians
Whatever the task, work heartily, as serving the Lord and not men.

Over all the virtues put on love, which binds the rest together and makes them perfect.

Christ's peace must reign in your hearts, since as members of the one body you have been called to that peace. Dedicate yourselves to thankfulness. Whatever you do, whether in speech or in action, do it in the name of the Lord Jesus. Give thanks to God the Father through him.

Whatever you do, work at it with your whole being. Do it for the Lord rather than for men, since you know full well you will receive an inheritance from him as your reward. Be slaves of Christ the Lord.

    This is the Word of the Lord.

Responsorial Psalm   Ps 90, 2. 3-4. 12-13. 14. 16

℟. (17) Lord, give success to the work of our hands.

Before the mountains were begotten
  and the earth and the world were brought forth,
  from everlasting to everlasting you are God.
℟. Lord, give success to the work of our hands.

You turn man back to dust,
  saying, "Return, O children of men."
For a thousand years in your sight
  are as yesterday, now that it is past,
  or as a watch of the night.
℟. Lord, give success to the work of our hands.

Teach us to number our days aright,
  that we may gain wisdom of heart.
Return, O Lord! How long?
  Have pity on your servants!
℟. Lord, give success to the work of our hands.

Fill us at daybreak with your kindness,
  that we may shout for joy and gladness all our days.
Let your work be seen by your servants
  and your glory by their children.
℟. Lord, give success to the work of our hands.
℟. Or: Alleluia.

GOSPEL   Mt 13, 54-58
Alleluia   Ps 67, 20

℟. Alleluia. Blessed be the Lord day after day,
the God who saves us and bears our burdens.
    ℟. Alleluia.

✠ A reading from the holy gospel according
            to Matthew
         Is not this the carpenter's son?

Jesus went to his native place and spent his
time teaching the people in their synagogue.
They were filled with amazement, and said
to one another, "Where did this man get such
wisdom and miraculous powers? Isn't this the
carpenter's son? Isn't Mary known to be his
mother and James, Joseph, Simon, and Judas
his brothers? Aren't his sisters our neighbors?
Where did he get all this?" They found him
altogether too much for them. Jesus said to
them, "No prophet is without honor except in
his native place, indeed in his own house."
And he did not work many miracles there because of their lack of faith.
        This is the gospel of the Lord.

May 2

560   **ATHANASIUS, bishop
            and doctor**
                                            Memorial
Common of pastors or doctors, p. 846 or 858.

OR

READING I   1 Jn 5, 1-5

A reading from the first letter of John
Our faith, this is the victory which overcomes the evils in
the world.

Everyone who believes that Jesus is the
        Christ
has been begotten of God.
Now, everyone who loves the father
loves the child he has begotten.
We can be sure that we love God's children
when we love God
and do what he has commanded.
The love of God consists in this:
that we keep his commandments—

and his commandments are not burdensome.
Everyone begotten of God conquers the
        world,
and the power that has conquered the world
is this faith of ours.
Who, then, is conqueror of the world?
The one who believes that Jesus is the Son
        of God.
        This is the Word of the Lord.

OR

GOSPEL   Mt 10, 22-25

✠ A reading from the holy gospel according
            to Matthew
If they persecute you in one city, take refuge in the next.

Jesus said to his disciples: "You will be hated
by all on account of me. But whoever holds
out till the end will escape death. When they
persecute you in one town, flee to the next.
I solemnly assure you, you will not have covered the towns of Israel before the Son of Man
comes.
    "No pupil outranks his teacher, no slave his
master. The pupil should be glad to become like
his teacher, the slave like his master."
        This is the gospel of the Lord.

May 3

561   **PHILIP and JAMES, apostles**
                                                Feast
READING I   1 Cor 15, 1-8

**A reading from the first letter of Paul to the
            Corinthians**
The Lord appeared to James, then to all the Apostles.

Brothers, I want to remind you of the gospel
I preached to you, which you received and in
which you stand firm. You are being saved by
it at this very moment if you retain it as I
preached it to you. Otherwise you have believed in vain. I handed on to you first of
all what I myself received, that Christ died
for our sins in accord with the Scriptures;
that he was buried and, in accord with the
Scriptures, rose on the third day; that he was
seen by Cephas, then by the Twelve. After
that he was seen by five hundred brothers at

once, most of whom are still alive, although some have fallen asleep. Next he was seen by James; then by all the apostles. Last of all he was seen by me, as one born out of the normal course.

This is the Word of the Lord.

Responsorial Psalm   Ps 19, 2-3. 4-5

℞. (5) Their message goes out through all the earth.

The heavens declare the glory of God,
   and the firmament proclaims his handiwork.
Day pours out the word to day,
   and night to night imparts knowledge.

℞. Their message goes out through all the earth.

Not a word nor a discourse
   whose voice is not heard;
Through all the earth their voice resounds,
   and to the ends of the world, their message.

℞. Their message goes out through all the earth.

℞. Or: Alleluia.

GOSPEL   Jn 14, 6-14
Alleluia   Jn 14, 6. 9

℞. Alleluia. I am the way, the truth, and the life, says the Lord;
Philip, whoever sees me sees the Father. ℞. Alleluia.

✠ A reading from the holy gospel according to John

Have I been with you so long and yet you do not know me?

Jesus told Thomas:
   "I am the way, and the truth, and the life;
no one comes to the Father but through me.
If you really knew me, you would know my Father also.
From this point on you know him; you have seen him."
   "Lord," Philip said to him, "show us the Father and that will be enough for us."
   "Philip," Jesus replied, "after I have been with you all this time, you still do not know me?
   "Whoever has seen me has seen the Father. How can you say, 'Show us the Father'?

Do you not believe that I am in the Father and the Father is in me?
The words I speak are not spoken of myself;
it is the Father who lives in me accomplishing his works.
Believe me that I am in the Father
   and the Father is in me,
or else, believe because of the works I do.
I solemnly assure you,
   the man who has faith in me
will do the works I do,
   and greater far than these.
Why? Because I go to the Father,
   and whatever you ask in my name
I will do,
so as to glorify the Father in the Son.
Anything you ask me in my name
I will do."

This is the gospel of the Lord.

May 12

562   **NEREUS and ACHILLEUS,**
                    martyrs

Common of martyrs, p. 837.

---

563   **PANCRAS, martyr**

Common of martyrs, p. 837.

May 14

564   **MATTHIAS, apostle**
                            Feast

READING I   Acts 1, 15-17. 20-26

A reading from the Acts of the Apostles
The lot fell to Matthias and he was numbered with the eleven Apostles.

In those days, Peter stood up in the center of the brothers; there must have been a hundred and twenty gathered together. "Brothers," he said, "the saying in Scripture uttered long ago by the Holy Spirit through the mouth of David was destined to be fulfilled in Judas, the one that guided those who arrested Jesus. He was one of our number and he had been given a

share in this ministry of ours.
"It is written in the Book of Psalms,
'Let his encampment be desolate.
May no one dwell on it.'
And again,
'May another take his office.'
It is entirely fitting, therefore, that one of those
who was of our company while the Lord Jesus
moved among us, from the baptism of John until the day he was taken up from us, should be
named as witness with us to his resurrection."
At that they nominated two, Joseph (called
Barsabbas, also known as Justus) and Matthias. Then they prayed: "O Lord, you read the
hearts of men. Make known to us which of these
two you choose for this apostolic ministry, replacing Judas, who deserted the cause and went
the way he was destined to go." They then
drew lots between the two men. The choice fell
to Matthias, who was added to the eleven apostles.

This is the Word of the Lord.

Responsorial Psalm   Ps 113, 1-2. 3-4. 5-6. 7-8

℞. (8) The Lord will give him a seat with the
leaders of his people.
Praise, you servants of the Lord,
praise the name of the Lord.
Blessed be the name of the Lord
both now and forever.
℞. The Lord will give him a seat with the
leaders of his people.
From the rising to the setting of the sun
is the name of the Lord to be praised.
High above all nations is the Lord;
above the heavens is his glory.
℞. The Lord will give him a seat with the
leaders of his people.
Who is like the Lord, our God, who is enthroned on high
and looks upon the heavens and the earth
below?
℞. The Lord will give him a seat with the
leaders of his people.
He raises up the lowly from the dust;
from the dunghill he lifts up the poor

To seat them with princes,
with the princes of his own people.
℞. The Lord will give him a seat with the
leaders of his people.
℞. Or: Alleluia.

GOSPEL   Jn 15, 9-17

Alleluia   Jn 15, 16

℞. Alleluia. I have chosen you from the world,
says the Lord,
to go out and bear fruit that will last. ℞.
Alleluia.

✠ **A reading from the holy gospel according
to John**
I shall no longer call you servants; I call you my friends.
Jesus said to his disciples:
"As the Father has loved me,
so I have loved you.
Live on in my love.
You will live in my love
if you keep my commandments,
even as I have kept my Father's commandments
and live in his love.
All this I tell you
that my joy may be yours
and your joy may be complete.
This is my commandment:
love one another
as I have loved you.
There is no greater love than this:
to lay down one's life for one's friends.
You are my friends
if you do what I command you.
I no longer speak of you as slaves,
for a slave does not know what his master
is about.
Instead, I call you friends,
since I have made known to you all that I
heard from my Father.
It was not you who chose me,
it was I who chose you
to go forth and bear fruit.
Your fruit must endure,
so that all you ask the Father in my name
he will give you.

The command I give you is this,
that you love one another."
This is the gospel of the Lord.

May 18

565   JOHN I, pope and martyr

Common of martyrs or pastors [for a pope], p. 837 or 846.

May 20

566   BERNARDINE OF SIENA, priest

Common of pastors [for missionaries], p. 846.

OR

READING I   Acts 4, 8-12

A reading from the Acts of the Apostles
There is no salvation in any other.

Peter, filled with the Holy Spirit, spoke up:
"Leaders of the people! Elders! If we must
answer today for a good deed done to a cripple
and explain how he was restored to health,
then you and all the people of Israel must
realize that it was done in the name of Jesus
Christ the Nazorean whom you crucified and
whom God raised from the dead. In the power
of that name this man stands before you perfectly sound. This Jesus is 'the stone rejected
by you the builders which has become the
cornerstone.' There is no salvation in anyone
else, for there is no other name in the whole
world given to men by which we are to be
saved."
This is the Word of the Lord.

May 25

567   VENERABLE BEDE, priest
and doctor

Common of pastors or doctors, p. 846 or 858.

---

568   GREGORY VII, pope

Common of pastors [for a pope], p. 846.

---

569   MARY MAGDALENE DE PAZZI,
virgin

Common of virgins or saints [for religious], p. 864 or 867.

May 26

570   PHILIP NERI, priest

Memorial

Common of pastors or saints [for religious], p. 846 or 867.

May 27

571   AUGUSTINE OF CANTERBURY,
bishop

Common of pastors [for missionaries], p. 846.

May 31

572   VISITATION

Feast

READING I   Zep 3, 14-18

A reading from the book of the prophet
Zephaniah
The King of Israel, the Lord, is in your midst.

Shout for joy, O daughter Zion!
    sing joyfully, O Israel!
Be glad and exult with all your heart,
    O daughter Jerusalem!
The Lord has removed the judgment against
    you,
    he has turned away your enemies;
The King of Israel, the Lord, is in your midst,
    you have no further misfortune to fear.
On that day, it shall be said to Jerusalem:
    Fear not, O Zion, be not discouraged!
The Lord, your God, is in your midst,
    a mighty savior;
He will rejoice over you with gladness,
    and renew you in his love.
He will sing joyfully because of you,
    as one sings at festivals.
This is the Word of the Lord.

OR

READING I
Rom 12, 9-16

A reading from the letter of Paul to the Romans

Contribute to the needs of God's people, and practice hospitality.

Your love must be sincere. Detest what is evil, cling to what is good. Love one another with the affection of brothers. Anticipate each other in showing respect. Do not grow slack but be fervent in spirit; he whom you serve is the Lord. Rejoice in hope, be patient under trial, persevere in prayer. Look on the needs of the saints as your own; be generous in offering hospitality. Bless your persecutors; bless and do not curse them. Rejoice with those who rejoice, weep with those who weep. Have the same attitude toward all. Put away ambitious thoughts and associate with those who are lowly.

This is the Word of the Lord.

Responsorial Psalm
Is 12, 2-3. 4. 5-6

℟. (6) Among you is the great and Holy One of Israel.

God indeed is my savior;
   I am confident and unafraid.
My strength and my courage is the Lord,
   and he has been my savior.
With joy you will draw water
   at the fountain of salvation.

℟. Among you is the great and Holy One of Israel.

Give thanks to the Lord, acclaim his name;
   among the nations make known his deeds,
   proclaim how exalted is his name.

℟. Among you is the great and Holy One of Israel.

Sing praise to the Lord for his glorious achievement;
   let this be known throughout all the earth.
Shout with exultation, O city of Zion,
   for great in your midst
   is the Holy One of Israel!

℟. Among you is the great and Holy One of Israel.

GOSPEL
Lk 1, 39-56

Alleluia   Lk 1, 45

℟. Alleluia. **Blessed are you, O Virgin Mary, for your firm believing, that the promises of the Lord would be fulfilled.** ℟. Alleluia.

✠ **A reading from the holy gospel according to Luke**

Why should I be honored with a visit from the mother of my Lord?

Mary set out, proceeding in haste into the hill country to a town of Judah, where she entered Zechariah's house and greeted Elizabeth. When Elizabeth heard Mary's greeting, the baby stirred in her womb. Elizabeth was filled with the Holy Spirit and cried out in a loud voice: "Blessed are you among women and blessed is the fruit of your womb. But who am I that the mother of my Lord should come to me? The moment your greeting sounded in my ears, the baby stirred in my womb for joy. Blessed is she who trusted that the Lord's words to her would be fulfilled."
Then Mary said:
"My being proclaims the greatness of the Lord,
   my spirit finds joy in God my savior,
For he has looked upon his servant in her lowliness;
   all ages to come shall call me blessed.
God who is mighty has done great things for me,
   holy is his name;
His mercy is from age to age
   on those who fear him.

"He has shown might with his arm;
   he has confused the proud in their inmost thoughts.
He has deposed the mighty from their thrones
   and raised the lowly to high places.
The hungry he has given every good thing,
   while the rich he has sent empty away.
He has upheld Israel his servant,
   ever mindful of his mercy;
Even as he promised our fathers,

promised Abraham and his descendants forever."

Mary remained with Elizabeth about three months and then returned home.

This is the gospel of the Lord.

Saturday following the Second Sunday after Pentecost

573 IMMACULATE HEART OF MARY

Common of the Blessed Virgin Mary, p. 826, except:

GOSPEL   Lk 2, 41-51

✠ **A reading from the holy gospel according to Luke**

She stored all these things in her heart.

The parents of Jesus used to go every year to Jerusalem for the feast of the Passover, and when he was twelve they went up for the celebration as was their custom. As they were returning at the end of the feast, the child Jesus remained behind unknown to his parents. Thinking he was in the party, they continued their journey for a day, looking for him among their relatives and acquaintances.

Not finding him, they returned to Jerusalem in search of him. On the third day they came upon him in the temple sitting in the midst of the teachers, listening to them and asking them questions. All who heard him were amazed at his intelligence and his answers.

When his parents saw him they were astonished, and his mother said to him: "Son, why have you done this to us? You see that your father and I have been searching for you in sorrow." He said to them: "Why did you search for me? Did you not know I had to be in my Father's house?" But they did not grasp what he said to them.

He went down with them then, and came to Nazareth, and was obedient to them. His mother meanwhile kept all these things in memory.

This is the gospel of the Lord.

JUNE

June 1

574 JUSTIN, martyr

Memorial

Common of martyrs, p. 837.

OR

READING I   1 Cor 1, 18-25

A reading from the first letter of Paul to the Corinthians

It was because God wanted to save those who have faith through the foolishness of the message that we preach.

The message of the cross is complete absurdity to those who are headed for ruin, but to us who are experiencing salvation it is the power of God. Scripture says,

"I will destroy the wisdom of the wise,

and thwart the cleverness of the clever."

Where is the wise man to be found? Where is the scribe? Where is the master of worldly argument? Has not God turned the wisdom of this world into folly? Since in God's wisdom the world did not come to know him through wisdom, it pleased God to save those who believe through the absurdity of the preaching of the gospel. Yes, Jews demand "signs" and Greeks look for "wisdom," but we preach Christ crucified, a stumbling block to Jews and an absurdity to Gentiles, but to those who are called, Jews and Greeks alike, Christ the power of God and the wisdom of God. For God's folly is wiser than men, and his weakness more powerful than men.

This is the Word of the Lord.

June 2

575 MARCELLINUS and PETER, martyrs

Common of martyrs, p. 837.

June 3

576   **CHARLES LWANGA and COMPANIONS, martyrs**

Common of martyrs, p. 837.   Memorial

June 5

577   **BONIFACE, bishop and martyr**
                                              Memorial
Common of martyrs or pastors [for missionaries], p. 837 or 846.

June 6

578   **NORBERT, bishop**

Common of pastors or saints [for religious], p. 846 or 867.

June 9

579   **EPHREM, deacon and doctor**

Common of doctors, p. 858.

June 11

580   **BARNABAS, apostle**
                                              Memorial

READING I   Acts 11, 21-26; 13, 1-3

A reading from the Acts of the Apostles

He was a good man, filled with the Holy Spirit and with faith.

A great number believed and were converted to the Lord. News of this eventually reached the ears of the church in Jerusalem, resulting in Barnabas' being sent to Antioch. On his arrival he rejoiced to see the evidence of God's favor. He encouraged them all to remain firm in their commitment to the Lord, since he himself was a good man filled with the Holy Spirit and faith. Thereby large numbers were added to the Lord. Then Barnabas went off to Tarsus to look for Saul; once he had found him, he brought him back to Antioch. For a whole year they met with the church and instructed great numbers. It was in Antioch that the disciples were called Christians for the first time.

There were in the church at Antioch certain prophets and teachers: Barnabas, Symeon known as Niger, Lucius of Cyrene, Manaen (who had been brought up with Herod the tetrarch), and Saul. On one occasion, while they were engaged in the liturgy of the Lord and were fasting, the Holy Spirit spoke to them: "Set apart Barnabas and Saul for me to do the work for which I have called them." Then, after they had fasted and prayed, they imposed hands on them and sent them off.

This is the Word of the Lord.

Responsorial Psalm   Ps 98, 1. 2-3. 3-4. 5-6

℟. (2) The Lord has revealed to the nations his saving power.

Sing to the Lord a new song,
  for he has done wondrous deeds;
His right hand has won victory for him,
  his holy arm.

℟. The Lord has revealed to the nations his saving power.

The Lord has made his salvation known:
  in the sight of the nations he has revealed his justice.
He has remembered his kindness and his faithfulness
  toward the house of Israel.

℟. The Lord has revealed to the nations his saving power.

All the ends of the earth have seen
  the salvation by our God.
Sing joyfully to the Lord, all you lands;
  break into song; sing praise.

℟. The Lord has revealed to the nations his saving power.

Sing praise to the Lord with the harp,
  with the harp and melodious song.
With trumpets and the sound of the horn
  sing joyfully before the King, the Lord.

℟. The Lord has revealed to the nations his saving power.

GOSPEL   Mt 10, 7-13

Alleluia

℟. Alleluia. We praise you, God; we acknowledge you as Lord;

your glorious band of apostles extols you. ℟. Alleluia.

✠ A reading from the holy gospel according to Matthew

You received without charge, give without charge.

Jesus said to his disciples: "As you go, make this announcement: 'The reign of God is at hand!' Cure the sick, raise the dead, heal the leprous, expel demons. The gift you have received, give as a gift. Provide yourselves with neither gold nor silver nor copper in your belts; no traveling bag, no change of shirt, no sandals, no walking staff. The workman, after all, is worth his keep.

"Look for a worthy citizen in every town or village you come to and stay with him until you leave. As you enter his home bless it. If the home is deserving, your blessing will descend on it. If it is not, your blessing will return to you."

This is the gospel of the Lord.

June 13

581　ANTHONY OF PADUA, priest and doctor

Memorial

Common of pastors or doctors or saints [for religious], p. 846 or 858 or 867.

June 19

582　ROMUALD, abbot

Common of saints [for religious], p. 867.

June 21

583　ALOYSIUS GONZAGA, religious

Memorial

Common of saints [for religious], p. 867.

June 22

584　PAULINUS OF NOLA, bishop

Common of pastors, p. 846.

OR

READING I　　　　　　2 Cor 8, 9-15

A reading from the second letter of Paul to the Corinthians

He was rich but he became poor for your sake: to make you rich out of his poverty.

You are well acquainted with the favor shown you by our Lord Jesus Christ: how for your sake he made himself poor though he was rich, so that you might become rich by his poverty. I am about to give you some advice on this matter of rich and poor. It will help you who began this good work last year, not only to carry it through but to do so willingly. Carry it through now to a successful completion, so that your ready resolve may be matched by giving according to your means. The willingness to give should accord with one's means, but not go beyond them. The relief of others ought not to impoverish you; there should be a certain equality. Your plenty at the present time should supply their need so that their surplus may one day supply your need, with equality as the result. It is written, "He who gathered much had no excess and he who gathered little had no lack."

This is the Word of the Lord.

585　JOHN FISHER, bishop and martyr and THOMAS MORE, martyr

Common of martyrs, p. 837.

June 24

586 **BIRTH OF JOHN THE BAPTIST**

Vigil

Solemnity

READING I
Jer 1, 4-10

A reading from the book of the prophet Jeremiah

Before I formed you in the womb, I knew you.

The word of the Lord came to me thus:

Before I formed you in the womb I knew you,
before you were born I dedicated you,
a prophet to the nations I appointed you.
"Ah, Lord God!" I said,
"I know not how to speak; I am too young."

But the Lord answered me,
Say not, "I am too young."
To whomever I send you, you shall go;
whatever I command you, you shall speak.
Have no fear before them,
because I am with you to deliver you, says
the Lord.

Then the Lord extended his hand and touched
my mouth, saying,
See, I place my words in your mouth!
This day I set you
over nations and over kingdoms,
To root up and to tear down,
to destroy and to demolish,
to build and to plant.
This is the Word of the Lord.

Responsorial Psalm   Ps 71, 1-2. 3-4. 5-6. 15. 17

℟. (6) Since my mother's womb, you have
been my strength.

In you, O Lord, I take refuge;
let me never be put to shame.
In your justice rescue me, and deliver me;
incline your ear to me, and save me.

℟. Since my mother's womb, you have been
my strength.

Be my rock of refuge,
a stronghold to give me safety,
for you are my rock and my fortress.
O my God, rescue me from the hand of the
wicked.

℟. Since my mother's womb, you have been
my strength.

For you are my hope, O Lord;
my trust, O God, from my youth.
On you I depend from birth;
from my mother's womb you are my
strength.

℟. Since my mother's womb, you have been
my strength.

My mouth shall declare your justice,
day by day your salvation.
O God, you have taught me from my youth,
and till the present I proclaim your won-
drous deeds.

℟. Since my mother's womb, you have been
my strength.

READING II
1 Pt 1, 8-12

A reading from the first letter of Peter

The prophets searched and inquired for this salvation.

It is true you have never seen Jesus Christ,
but in the present age you believe in him
without seeing him, and rejoice with inexpress-
ible joy touched with glory because you are
achieving faith's goal, your salvation. This is
the salvation which the prophets carefully
searched out and examined. They prophesied
a divine favor that was destined to be yours.
They investigated the times and the circum-
stances which the Spirit of Christ within them
was pointing to, for he predicted the suffer-
ings destined for Christ and the glories that
would follow. They knew by revelation that
they were providing, not for themselves but for
you, what has now been proclaimed to you by
those who preach the gospel to you in the
power of the Holy Spirit sent from heaven. Into
these matters angels long to search.
This is the Word of the Lord.

GOSPEL
Lk 1, 5-17

Alleluia Jn 1, 7; Lk 1, 17

℟. Alleluia. He came to bear witness to the
light,

to prepare an upright people for the Lord.
℟. Alleluia.

✠ A reading from the holy gospel according to Luke

A son is born to you and you will name him John.

In the days of Herod, king of Judea, there was a priest named Zechariah of the priestly class of Abijah; his wife was a descendant of Aaron named Elizabeth. Both were just in the eyes of God, blamelessly following all the commandments and ordinances of the Lord. They were childless, for Elizabeth was sterile; moreover, both were advanced in years.

Once, when it was the turn of Zechariah's class and he was fulfilling his functions as a priest before God, it fell to him by lot according to priestly usage to enter the sanctuary of the Lord and offer incense. While the full assembly of people was praying outside at the incense hour, an angel of the Lord appeared to him, standing at the right of the altar of incense. Zechariah was deeply disturbed upon seeing him, and overcome by fear.

The angel said to him: "Do not be frightened, Zechariah; your prayer has been heard. Your wife Elizabeth shall bear a son whom you shall name John. Joy and gladness will be yours, and many will rejoice at his birth; for he will be great in the eyes of the Lord. He will never drink wine or strong drink, and he will be filled with the Holy Spirit from his mother's womb. Many of the sons of Israel will he bring back to the Lord their God. God himself will go before him, in the spirit and power of Elijah, to turn the hearts of fathers to their children and the rebellious to the wisdom of the just, and to prepare for the Lord a people well-disposed."

This is the gospel of the Lord.

---

587   Mass during the Day

READING I   Is 49, 1-6

A reading from the book of the prophet Isaiah

Behold I will make you a light to the nations.

Hear me, O coastlands,
  listen, O distant peoples.
The Lord called me from birth,

from my mother's womb he gave me my
  name.
He made of me a sharp-edged sword
  and concealed me in the shadow of his arm.
He made me a polished arrow,
  in his quiver he hid me.
You are my servant, he said to me,
  Israel, through whom I show my glory.

Though I thought I had toiled in vain,
  and for nothing, uselessly, spent my
  strength,
Yet my reward is with the Lord,
  my recompense is with my God.
For now the Lord has spoken
  who formed me as his servant from the
  womb,
That Jacob may be brought back to him
  and Israel gathered to him;
And I am made glorious in the sight of the
  Lord,
  and my God is now my strength!
It is too little, he says, for you to be my
  servant,
  to raise up the tribes of Jacob,
  and restore the survivors of Israel;
I will make you a light to the nations,
  that my salvation may reach to the ends of
  the earth.

This is the Word of the Lord.

Responsorial Psalm   Ps 139, 1-3. 13-14. 14-15

℟. (14)I praise you for I am wonderfully made.
O Lord, you have probed me and you know me;
  you know when I sit and when I stand;
  you understand my thoughts from afar.
My journeys and my rest you scrutinize,
  with all my ways you are familiar.
℟. I praise you for I am wonderfully made.
Truly you have formed my inmost being;
  you knit me in my mother's womb.
I give you thanks that I am fearfully, wonderfully made;
  wonderful are your works.
℟. I praise you for I am wonderfully made.
My soul also you knew full well;
  nor was my frame unknown to you

When I was made in secret,
   when I was fashioned in the depths of the
   earth.
℟. I praise you for I am wonderfully made.

READING II   Acts 13, 22-26

A reading from the Acts of the Apostles

*Christ's coming was announced beforehand by the
preaching of John.*

Paul said: "God raised up David as their king;
on his behalf God testified, 'I have found David
son of Jesse to be a man after my own heart
who will fulfill my every wish.'

"According to his promise, God has brought
forth from this man's descendants Jesus, a
savior for Israel. John heralded the coming of
Jesus by proclaiming a baptism of repentance
to all the people of Israel. As John's career was
coming to an end, he would say, 'What you
suppose me to be I am not. Rather, look for the
one who comes after me. I am not worthy
to unfasten the sandals on his feet.' My
brothers, children of the family of Abraham
and you others who reverence our God, it was
to us that this message of salvation was sent
forth."

   This is the Word of the Lord.

GOSPEL   Lk 1, 57-66. 80

Alleluia   Lk 1, 76

℟. Alleluia. You, child, will be called the
   prophet of the Most High;
you will go before the Lord to prepare his
   ways.℟. Alleluia.

✠ A reading from the holy gospel according
   to Luke

John is his name.

When Elizabeth's time for delivery arrived, she
gave birth to a son. Her neighbors and relatives, upon hearing that the Lord had extended
his mercy to her, rejoiced with her. When they
assembled for the circumcision of the child on
the eighth day, they intended to name him after
his father Zechariah. At this his mother intervened, saying, "No, he is to be called John."

   They pointed out to her, "None of your
relatives has this name." Then, using signs,

they asked the father what he wished him to
be called.

   He signaled for a writing tablet and wrote
the words, "His name is John." This astonished them all. At that moment his mouth was
opened and his tongue loosed, and he began to
speak in praise of God.

   Fear descended on all in the neighborhood;
throughout the hill country of Judea these
happenings began to be recounted to the last
detail. All who heard stored these things up in
their hearts, saying, "What will this child be?"
and, "Was not the hand of the Lord upon
him?"

   The child grew up and matured in spirit. He
lived in the desert until the day when he made
his public appearance in Israel.

   This is the gospel of the Lord.

June 27
**588   CYRIL OF ALEXANDRIA,
   bishop and doctor**

Common of pastors or doctors, p. 846 or 858.

June 28
589   IRENAEUS, bishop and martyr

                                                    Memorial
Common of martyrs or doctors, p. 837 or 858.

OR

READING I   2 Tm 2, 22-26

A reading from the second letter of Paul to
   Timothy

*The Lord's servant must be kind to everyone, correcting
with gentleness.*

Pursue integrity, faith, love, and peace, along
with those who call on the Lord in purity of
heart. Have nothing to do with senseless, ignorant disputations. As you well know, they
only breed quarrels, and the servant of the
Lord must not be quarrelsome but must be
kindly toward all. He must be an apt teacher,
patiently and gently correcting those who contradict him, in the hope always that God will
enable them to repent and know the truth.

Thus, taken captive by God to do his will, they shall escape the devil's trap.
This is the Word of the Lord.

June 29
590   PETER AND PAUL, apostles

Vigil

Solemnity

READING I   Acts 3, 1-10

A reading from the Acts of the Apostles

What I have, I give to you; in the name of Jesus stand up and walk.

Once, when Peter and John were going up to the temple for prayer at the three o'clock hour, a man crippled from birth was being carried in. They would bring him every day and put him at the temple gate called "the Beautiful" to beg from the people as they entered. When he saw Peter and John on their way in, he begged them for an alms. Peter fixed his gaze on the man; so did John. "Look at us!" Peter said. The cripple gave them his whole attention, hoping to get something. Then Peter said: "I have neither silver nor gold, but what I have I give you! In the name of Jesus Christ the Nazorean, walk!" Then Peter took him by the right hand and pulled him up. Immediately the beggar's feet and ankles became strong; he jumped up, stood for a moment, then began to walk around. He went into the temple with them—walking, jumping about, and praising God. When the people saw him moving and giving praise to God, they recognized him as that beggar who used to sit at the Beautiful Gate of the temple. They were struck with astonishment—utterly stupefied at what had happened to him.
This is the Word of the Lord.

Responsorial Psalm   Ps 19, 2-3. 4-5

℟. (5) Their message goes out through all the earth.
The heavens declare the glory of God,
  and the firmament proclaims his handiwork.

Day pours out the word to day,
  and night to night imparts knowledge.
℟. Their message goes out through all the earth.
Not a word nor a discourse
  whose voice is not heard;
Through all the earth their voice resounds,
  and to the ends of the world, their message.
℟. Their message goes out through all the earth.

READING II   Gal 1, 11-20

A reading from the letter of Paul to the Galatians

God chose me while I was still in my mother's womb.

I assure you, brothers, the gospel I proclaimed to you is no mere human invention. I did not receive it from any man, nor was I schooled in it. It came by revelation from Jesus Christ. You have heard, I know, the story of my former way of life in Judaism. You know that I went to extremes in persecuting the church of God and tried to destroy it; I made progress in Jewish observance far beyond most of my contemporaries, in my excess of zeal to live out all the traditions of my ancestors.

But the time came when he who had set me apart before I was born and called me by his favor chose to reveal his Son to me, that I might spread among the Gentiles the good tidings concerning him. Immediately, without seeking human advisers or even going to Jerusalem to see those who were apostles before me, I went off to Arabia; later I returned to Damascus. Three years after that I went up to Jerusalem to get to know Cephas, with whom I stayed fifteen days. I did not meet any other apostles except James, the brother of the Lord. I declare before God that what I have just written is true.
This is the Word of the Lord.

GOSPEL   Jn 21, 15-19

Alleluia   Jn 21, 17

℟. Alleluia. **Lord, you know all things: you know that I love you.** ℟. Alleluia.

✠ A reading from the holy gospel according
to John

Feed my lambs, feed my sheep.

When Jesus had appeared to his disciples and
had eaten with them, he said to Simon Peter,
"Simon, son of John, do you love me more than
these?" "Yes, Lord," Peter said, "you know
that I love you." At which Jesus said, "Feed
my lambs."

A second time he put his question, "Simon,
son of John, do you love me?" "Yes, Lord,"
Peter said, "you know that I love you." Jesus
replied, "Tend my sheep."

A third time Jesus asked him, "Simon, son
of John, do you love me?" Peter was hurt
because he had asked a third time, "Do you
love me?" So he said to him: "Lord, you know
everything. You know well that I love you."
Jesus told him, "Feed my sheep.

"I tell you solemnly:
as a young man
you fastened your belt
and went about as you pleased;
but when you are older
you will stretch out your hands,
and another will tie you fast
and carry you off against your will."

(What he said indicated the sort of death by
which Peter was to glorify God.) When Jesus
had finished speaking he said to him, "Follow
me."

This is the gospel of the Lord.

---

591   Mass during the Day

READING I   Acts 12, 1-11

A reading from the Acts of the Apostles

Now I know it is indeed true: the Lord has saved me from
the power of Herod.

King Herod started to harass some of the
members of the church. He beheaded James the
brother of John, and when he saw that this
pleased certain of the Jews, he took Peter into
custody too. During the feast of Unleavened
Bread he had him arrested and thrown into
prison, with four squads of soldiers to guard
him. Herod intended to bring him before the
people after the Passover. Peter was thus de-
tained in prison, while the church prayed fervently to God on his behalf. During the night
before Herod was to bring him to trial, Peter
was sleeping between two soldiers, fastened
with double chains, while guards kept watch
at the door. Suddenly an angel of the Lord
stood nearby and light shone in the cell. He
tapped Peter on the side and woke him.
"Hurry, get up!" he said. With that, the chains
dropped from Peter's wrists. The angel said,
"Put on your belt and your sandals!" This he
did. Then the angel told him, "Now put on
your cloak and follow me."

Peter followed him out, but with no clear
realization that this was taking place through
the angel's help. The whole thing seemed to
him a mirage. They passed the first guard, then
the second, and finally came to the iron gate
leading out to the city, which opened for them
of itself. They emerged and made their way
down a narrow alley, when suddenly the angel
left him. Peter had recovered his senses by this
time, and said, "Now I know for certain that
the Lord has sent his angel to rescue me from
Herod's clutches and from all that the Jews
hoped for."

This is the Word of the Lord.

Responsorial Psalm   Ps 34, 2-3. 4-5. 6-7. 8-9

℟. (8) The angel of the Lord will rescue those
who fear him.

I will bless the Lord at all times;
his praise shall be ever in my mouth.
Let my soul glory in the Lord;
the lowly will hear me and be glad.

℟. The angel of the Lord will rescue those who
fear him.

Glorify the Lord with me,
let us together extol his name.
I sought the Lord, and he answered me
and delivered me from all my fears.

℟. The angel of the Lord will rescue those who
fear him.

Look to him that you may be radiant with joy,
and your faces may not blush with shame.

When the afflicted man called out, the Lord heard,
  and from all his distress he saved him.
℟. The angel of the Lord will rescue those who fear him.
The angel of the Lord encamps
  around those who fear him, and delivers them.
Taste and see how good the Lord is;
  happy the man who takes refuge in him.
℟. The angel of the Lord will rescue those who fear him.

READING II   2 Tm 4, 6-8. 17-18
A reading from the second letter of Paul to Timothy
All that remains now is the crown of righteousness.

I am already being poured out like a libation. The time of my dissolution is near. I have fought the good fight, I have finished the race, I have kept the faith. From now on a merited crown awaits me; on that Day the Lord, just judge that he is, will award it to me—and not only to me but to all who have looked for his appearing with eager longing. But the Lord stood by my side and gave me strength, so that through me the preaching task might be completed and all the nations might hear the gospel. That is how I was saved from the lion's jaws. The Lord will continue to rescue me from all attempts to do me harm and will bring me safe to his heavenly kingdom. To him be glory forever and ever. Amen.
    This is the Word of the Lord.

GOSPEL   Mt 16, 13-19
Alleluia Mt 16, 18
℟. Alleluia. You are Peter, the rock on which I will build my Church;
the gates of hell will not hold out against it.
℟. Alleluia.

✠ **A reading from the holy gospel according to Matthew**
You are Peter; and I will give you the keys of the Kingdom of heaven.

When Jesus came to the neighborhood of Caesarea Philippi, he asked his disciples this question: "Who do people say that the Son of Man is?" They replied, "Some say John the Baptizer, others Elijah, still others Jeremiah or one of the prophets." "And you," he said to them, "who do you say that I am?" "You are the Messiah," Simon Peter answered, "the Son of the living God!" Jesus replied, "Blest are you, Simon son of John! No mere man has revealed this to you, but my heavenly Father. I for my part declare to you, you are 'Rock,' and on this rock I will build my church, and the jaws of death shall not prevail against it. I will entrust to you the keys of the kingdom of heaven. Whatever you declare bound on earth shall be bound in heaven; whatever you declare loosed on earth shall be loosed in heaven."
    This is the gospel of the Lord.

For a votive Mass of St. Peter the readings are from no. 535, above.

For a votive Mass of St. Paul the readings are from no. 519, above.

June 30
592 **FIRST MARTYRS OF THE CHURCH OF ROME**
Common of martyrs, p. 837, especially Rom 8, 31-39 (no. 716, § 2), p. 842.

OR

GOSPEL   Mt 24, 4-13
✠ **A reading from the holy gospel according to Matthew**
You will be hated by all nations for my name's sake.

Jesus said to his disciples: "Be on guard! Let no one mislead you. Many will come attempting to impersonate me. 'I am the Messiah!' they will claim, and they will deceive many. You will hear of wars and rumors of wars. Do not be alarmed. Such things are bound to happen, but that is not yet the end. Nation will rise against nation, one kingdom against another. There will be famine and pestilence and earthquakes in many places. These are the early stages of the birth pangs. They will hand you over to torture and kill you. Indeed, you will be hated by all nations on my account. Many will falter then, betraying and hating one another.

False prophets will rise in great numbers to mislead many. Because of the increase of evil, the love of most will grow cold. The man who holds out to the end, however, is the one who will see salvation."

This is the gospel of the Lord.

JULY

July 3

593   **THOMAS, apostle**

Feast

READING I   Eph 2, 19-22

A reading from the letter of Paul to the Ephesians

You are part of the building built on the foundation of the apostles.

You are strangers and aliens no longer. No, you are fellow citizens of the saints and members of the household of God. You form a building which rises on the foundation of the apostles and prophets, with Christ Jesus himself as the capstone. Through him the whole structure is fitted together and takes shape as a holy temple in the Lord; in him you are being built into this temple, to become a dwelling place for God in the Spirit.

This is the Word of the Lord.

Responsorial Psalm   Ps 117, 1. 2

℟. (Mk 16, 15) Go out to all the world, and tell the Good News.

Praise the Lord, all you nations;
  glorify him, all you peoples!
℟. Go out to all the world,
  and tell the Good News.

For steadfast is his kindness toward us,
  and the fidelity of the Lord endures forever.
℟. Go out to all the world,
  and tell the Good News.

GOSPEL   Jn 20, 24-29

Alleluia   Jn 20, 29

℟. Alleluia. You believed in me, Thomas, because you have seen me;
happy those who have not seen me, but still believe! ℟. Alleluia.

✠ **A reading from the holy gospel according to John**

My Lord and my God.

Thomas (the name means "Twin"), one of the Twelve, was absent when Jesus came into the room. The other disciples kept telling him: "We have seen the Lord!" His answer was, "I'll never believe it without probing the nailprints in his hands, without putting my finger in the nailmarks and my hand into his side."

A week later, the disciples were once more in the room, and this time Thomas was with them. Despite the locked doors, Jesus came and stood before them. "Peace be with you," he said; then, to Thomas: "Take your finger and examine my hands. Put your hand into my side. Do not persist in your unbelief, but believe!" Thomas said in response, "My Lord and my God!" Jesus then said to him:

"You became a believer because you saw me.
Blest are they who have not seen and have believed."

This is the gospel of the Lord.

July 4

594   **ELIZABETH OF PORTUGAL**

Common of the saints [for those who work for the disadvantaged], p. 867.

July 5

595   **ANTHONY ZACCARIA, priest**

Common of pastors or saints [for teachers and for religious], p. 846 or 867.

July 6

596 **MARIA GORETTI, virgin and martyr**

Common of martyrs or virgins, p. 837 or 864.

OR

READING I   1 Cor 6, 13-15. 17-20

A reading from the first letter of Paul to the Corinthians

Your bodies are members of Christ.

The body is not for immorality; it is for the Lord, and the Lord is for the body. God, who rasied up the Lord, will raise us also by his power.

Do you not see that your bodies are members of Christ? But whoever is joined to the Lord becomes one spirit with him. Shun lewd conduct. Every other sin a man commits is outside his body, but the fornicator sins against his own body. You must know that your body is a temple of the Holy Spirit, who is within— the Spirit you have received from God. You are not your own. You have been purchased, and at what a price! So glorify God in your body.

This is the Word of the Lord.

July 11

597 **BENEDICT, abbot**

Memorial

Common of saints [for religious], p. 867.

OR

READING I   Prv 2, 1-9

A reading from the book of Proverbs

Apply your heart to learn wisdom.

My son, if you receive my words
and treasure my commands,
Turning your ear to wisdom,
inclining your heart to understanding;
Yes, if you call to intelligence,
and to understanding raise your voice;
If you seek her like silver,
and like hidden treasures search her out:

Then will you understand the fear of the Lord;
the knowledge of God you will find;
For the Lord gives wisdom,
from his mouth come knowledge and understanding;
He has counsel in store for the upright,
he is the shield of those who walk honestly,
Guarding the paths of justice,
protecting the way of his pious ones.
Then you will understand rectitude and justice,
honesty, every good path.

This is the Word of the Lord.

July 13

598 **HENRY**

Common of saints, p. 867.

July 14

599 **CAMILLUS DE LELLIS, priest**

Common of saints [for those who work for the disadvantaged], p. 867.

July 15

600 **BONAVENTURE, bishop and doctor**

Memorial

Common of pastors or doctors, p. 846 or 858.

July 16

601 **OUR LADY OF MT. CARMEL**

Common of the Blessed Virgin Mary, p. 826.

July 21

602 **LAWRENCE OF BRINDISI, priest and doctor**

Common of pastors or doctors, p. 846 or 858.

July 22

MARY MAGDALENE

Memorial

READING I   Sg 3, 1-4

A reading from the Song of Solomon

I have found him whom my heart loves.

On my bed at night I sought him
    whom my heart loves—
    I sought him but I did not find him.
I will rise then and go about the city;
    in the streets and crossings I will seek
Him whom my heart loves.
    I sought him but I did not find him.
The watchmen came upon me
    as they made their rounds of the city:
Have you seen him whom my heart loves?
I had hardly left them
    when I found him whom my heart loves.
            This is the Word of the Lord.

OR

READING I   2 Cor 5, 14-17

A reading from the second letter of Paul to the Corinthians

Even if we did once know Christ in the flesh, that is not how we know him now.

The love of Christ impels us who have reached
the conviction that since one died for all, all
died. He died for all so that those who live
might live no longer for themselves, but for
him who for their sakes died and was raised
up.
    Because of this we no longer look on anyone
in terms of mere human judgment. If at one
time we so regarded Christ, we no longer know
him by this standard. This means that if anyone is in Christ, he is a new creation. The old
order has passed away; now all is new!
            This is the Word of the Lord.

Responsorial Psalm   Ps 63, 2. 3-4. 5-6. 8-9

℟. (2) My soul is thirsting for you, O Lord my
    God.

O my God, you are my God whom I seek;
    for you my flesh pines and my soul thirsts
    like the earth, parched, lifeless and without
    water.

℟. My soul is thirsting for you, O Lord my
    God.

Thus have I gazed toward you in the sanctuary
    to see your power and your glory,
For your kindness is a greater good than life;
    my lips shall glorify you.

℟. My soul is thirsting for you, O Lord my
    God.

Thus will I bless you while I live;
    lifting up my hands, I will call upon your
    name.
As with the riches of a banquet shall my soul
    be satisfied,
    and with exultant lips my mouth shall praise
    you.

℟. My soul is thirsting for you, O Lord my
    God.

That you are my help,
    and in the shadow of your wings I shout
    for joy.
My soul clings fast to you;
    your right hand upholds me.

℟. My soul is thirsting for you, O Lord my
    God.

GOSPEL   Jn 20, 1-2. 11-18

Alleluia

℟. Alleluia. Tell us, Mary, what did you see on
    the way?
I saw the glory of the risen Christ, I saw his
    empty tomb. ℟. Alleluia.

✠ A reading from the holy gospel according
        to John

Woman, why are you weeping? For whom are you seeking?

Early in the morning on the first day of the
week, while it was still dark, Mary Magdalene
came to the tomb. She saw that the stone had
been moved away, so she ran off to Simon
Peter and the other disciple (the one Jesus
loved) and told them, "The Lord has been
taken from the tomb! We do not know where
they have put him!"
    Mary stood weeping beside the tomb. Even
as she wept, she stooped to peer inside, and
there she saw two angels in dazzling robes.
One was seated at the head and the other at
the foot of the place where Jesus' body had

lain. "Woman," they asked her, "why are you weeping?" She answered them, "Because the Lord has been taken away, and I do not know where they have put him." She had no sooner said this than she turned around and caught sight of Jesus standing there. But she did not know him. "Woman," he asked her, "why are you weeping? Who is it you are looking for?" She supposed he was the gardener, so she said, "Sir, if you are the one who carried him off, tell me where you have laid him and I will take him away." Jesus said to her, "Mary!" She turned to him and said [in Hebrew], "Rabboni!" (meaning "Teacher"). Jesus then said: "Do not cling to me, for I have not yet ascended to the Father. Rather, go to my brothers and tell them, 'I am ascending to my Father and your Father, to my God and your God!' " Mary Magdalene went to the disciples. "I have seen the Lord!" she announced. Then she reported what he had said to her.

   This is the gospel of the Lord.

July 23

604   **BRIDGET, religious**

Common of saints [for religious], p. 867.

July 25

605   **JAMES, apostle**

READING I   2 Cor 4, 7-15

A reading from the second letter of Paul to the Corinthians

We carry always in our bodies the death of Jesus.

We possess a treasure in earthen vessels to make it clear that its surpassing power comes from God and not from us. We are afflicted in every way possible, but we are not crushed; full of doubts, we never despair. We are persecuted but never abandoned; we are struck down but never destroyed. Continually we carry about in our bodies the dying of Jesus, so that in our bodies the life of Jesus may also be revealed. While we live we are constantly being delivered to death for Jesus' sake,

so that the life of Jesus may be revealed in our mortal flesh. Death is at work in us, but life in you. We have that spirit of faith of which the Scripture says, "Because I believed, I spoke out." We believe and so we speak, knowing that he who raised up the Lord Jesus will raise us up along with Jesus and place both us and you in his presence. Indeed, everything is ordered to your benefit, so that the grace bestowed in abundance may bring greater glory to God because they who give thanks are many.

   This is the Word of the Lord.

Responsorial Psalm Ps 126, 1-2. 2-3. 4-5. 6

R⁄. (5) Those who sow in tears, shall reap with shouts of joy.

When the Lord brought back the captives of Zion,
 we were like men dreaming.
Then our mouth was filled with laughter,
 and our tongue with rejoicing.

R⁄. Those who sow in tears, shall reap with shouts of joy.

Then they said among the nations,
 "The Lord has done great things for them."
The Lord has done great things for us;
 we are glad indeed.

R⁄. Those who sow in tears, shall reap with shouts of joy.

Restore our fortunes, O Lord,
 like the torrents in the southern desert.
Those that sow in tears
 shall reap rejoicing.

R⁄. Those who sow in tears, shall reap with shouts of joy.

Although they go forth weeping,
 carrying the seed to be sown,
They shall come back rejoicing,
 carrying their sheaves.

R⁄. Those who sow in tears, shall reap with shouts of joy.

GOSPEL   Mt 20, 20-28

Alleluia Jn 15, 16

R⁄. Alleluia. **I have chosen you from the world, says the Lord,**
to go and bear fruit that will last. R⁄. Alleluia.

✠ A reading from the holy gospel according
to Matthew

You shall indeed drink my cup.

The mother of Zebedee's sons came up to
Jesus accompanied by her sons, to do him
homage and ask of him a favor. "What is it you
want?" he said. She answered, "Promise me
that these sons of mine will sit, one at your
right hand and the other at your left, in your
kingdom." In reply Jesus said, "You do not
know what you are asking. Can you drink of
the cup I am to drink of?" "We can," they said.
He told them, "From the cup I drink of you
shall drink. Sitting at my right hand or my
left is not mine to give. That is for those for
whom it has been reserved by my Father."
The other ten, on hearing this, became indignant at the two brothers. Jesus then called
them together and said: "You know how those
who exercise authority among the Gentiles
lord it over them; their great ones make their
importance felt. It cannot be like that with
you. Anyone among you who aspires to greatness must serve the rest, and whoever wants
to rank first among you must serve the needs
of all. Such is the case with the Son of Man
who has come, not to be served by others but
to serve, to give his own life as a ransom for
the many."

This is the gospel of the Lord.

July 26

**606 JOACHIM and ANN, parents
of Mary**

Memorial

READING I Sir 44, 1. 10-15

A reading from the book of Sirach

Their name lives on for all generations.

Now will I praise those godly men,
our ancestors, each in his own time:
These were godly men
whose virtues have not been forgotten;
Their wealth remains in their families,
their heritage with their descendants;
Through God's covenant with them their family endures,
their posterity, for their sake.

And for all time their progeny will endure,
their glory will never be blotted out;
Their bodies are peacefully laid away,
but their name lives on and on.
At gatherings their wisdom is retold,
and the assembly proclaims their praise.
This is the Word of the Lord.

Responsorial Psalm Ps 132, 11. 13-14. 17-18

℟. (Lk 1, 32) God will give him the throne of
David, his father.

The Lord swore to David
a firm promise from which he will not withdraw:
"Your own offspring
I will set upon your throne."
℟. God will give him the throne of David, his
father.

For the Lord has chosen Zion;
he prefers her for his dwelling.
"Zion is my resting place forever;
in her will I dwell, for I prefer her."
℟. God will give him the throne of David, his
father.

"In her will I make a horn to sprout forth for
David;
I will place a lamp for my anointed.
His enemies I will clothe with shame,
but upon him my crown shall shine."
℟. God will give him the throne of David, his
father.

GOSPEL Mt 13, 16-17

Alleluia Lk 2, 25

℟. Alleluia. They yearned for the comforting
of Israel,
and the Holy Spirit dwelt in them. ℟. Alleluia.

✠ A reading from the holy gospel according
to Matthew

*Many prophets and just men have longed to see what
you see.*

Jesus said to his disciples: "Blest are your
eyes because they see and blest are your ears
because they hear. I assure you, many a
prophet and many a saint longed to see what
you see but did not see it, to hear what you
hear but did not hear it."

This is the gospel of the Lord.

July 29

607

MARTHA

Memorial

Common of saints, p. 867, except:

GOSPEL　Jn 11, 19-27

✠ A reading from the holy gospel according to John

I have believed that you are the Christ, the Son of the living God.

Many Jewish people had come out to console Martha and Mary over their brother. When Martha heard that Jesus was coming she went to meet him, while Mary sat at home. Martha said to Jesus, "Lord, if you had been here, my brother would never have died. Even now, I am sure that God will give you whatever you ask of him." "Your brother will rise again," Jesus assured her. "I know he will rise again," Martha replied, "in the resurrection on the last day." Jesus told her:

"I am the resurrection and the life:
whoever believes in me,
though he should die, will come to life;
and whoever is alive and believes in me
will never die.

Do you believe this?" "Yes, Lord," she replied. "I have come to believe that you are the Messiah, the Son of God: he who is to come into the world."

This is the gospel of the Lord.

OR

GOSPEL　Lk 10, 38-42

✠ A reading from the holy gospel according to Luke

Martha, Martha, you worry and fret about so many things.

Jesus entered a village where a woman named Martha welcomed him to her home. She had a sister named Mary, who seated herself at the Lord's feet and listened to his words. Martha, who was busy with all the details of hospitality, came to him and said, "Lord, are you not concerned that my sister has left me all alone to do the household tasks? Tell her to help me."

The Lord in reply said to her: "Martha, Martha, you are anxious and upset about many things; one thing only is required. Mary has chosen the better portion and she shall not be deprived of it."

This is the gospel of the Lord.

July 30

608

PETER CHRYSOLOGUS, bishop and doctor

Common of pastors or doctors, p. 846 or 858.

July 31

609

IGNATIUS OF LOYOLA, priest

Memorial

Common of pastors or saints [for religious], p. 846 or 867.

OR

READING I　1 Cor 10, 31-11, 1

A reading from the first letter of Paul to the Corinthians

Do all things for the glory of God.

Whether you eat or drink—whatever you do—you should do all for the glory of God. Give no offense to Jew or Greek or to the church of God, just as I try to please all in any way I can by seeking, not my own advantage, but that of the many, that they may be saved. Imitate me as I imitate Christ.

This is the Word of the Lord.

AUGUST

August 1

610

ALPHONSUS LIGUORI, bishop and doctor

Memorial

Common of pastors or doctors, p. 846 or 858.

OR

READING I　Rom 8, 1-4

A reading from the letter of Paul to the Romans

The law of the spirit of life in Christ Jesus has set me free from the law of sin and death.

There is no condemnation now for those who are in Christ Jesus. The law of the spirit, the spirit of life in Christ Jesus, has freed you from the law of sin and death. The law was powerless because of its weakening by the flesh. Then God sent his Son in the likeness of sinful flesh as a sin offering, thereby condemning sin in the flesh, so that the just demands of the law might be fulfilled in us who live, not according to the flesh, but according to the spirit.

This is the Word of the Lord.

August 2

611 **EUSEBIUS OF VERCELLI, bishop**

Common of pastors, p. 846.

August 4

612 **JOHN VIANNEY, priest**

Memorial

Common of pastors, p. 846, especially Ez 3, 17-21 (no. 719, § 8), p. 848.

OR

GOSPEL Mt 9, 35—10, 1

✠ A reading from the holy gospel according to Matthew

When he saw the crowds, he had compassion for them.

Jesus continued his tour of all the towns and villages. He taught in their synagogues, he proclaimed the good news of God's reign, and he cured every sickness and disease. At the sight of the crowds, his heart was moved with pity. They were lying prostrate from exhaustion, like sheep without a shepherd. He said to his disciples: "The harvest is good but laborers are scarce. Beg the harvest master to send out laborers to gather his harvest."

Then he summoned his twelve disciples and gave them authority to expel unclean spirits and to cure sickness and disease of every kind.

This is the gospel of the Lord.

August 5

613 **DEDICATION OF SAINT MARY MAJOR**

Common of the Blessed Virgin Mary, p. 826.

August 6

614 **TRANSFIGURATION**

Feast

READING I Dn 7, 9-10. 13-14

A reading from the book of the prophet Daniel

His raiment was as white as snow.

As Daniel watched:
Thrones were set up
  and the Ancient One took his throne.
His clothing was snow bright,
  and the hair on his head as white as wool;
His throne was flames of fire,
  with wheels of burning fire.
A surging stream of fire
  flowed out from where he sat;
Thousands upon thousands were ministering to him,
  and myriads upon myriads attended him.
The court was convened and the books were opened. As the visions during the night continued, I saw
One like a son of man coming,
  on the clouds of heaven;
When he reached the Ancient One
  and was presented before him,
He received dominion, glory, and kingship;
  nations and peoples of every language serve him.
His dominion is an everlasting dominion
  that shall not be taken away,
  his kingship shall not be destroyed.
    This is the Word of the Lord.

Responsorial Psalm Ps 97, 1-2. 5-6. 9

℟. (1. 9) The Lord is king, the most high over all the earth.

The Lord is king; let the earth rejoice;
  let the many isles be glad.
Clouds and darkness are round about him,
  justice and judgment are the foundation of his throne.

℟. The Lord is king, the most high over all the
  earth.
The mountains melt like wax before the Lord,
  before the Lord of all the earth.
The heavens proclaim his justice,
  and all peoples see his glory.
℟. The Lord is king, the most high over all the
  earth.
Because you, O Lord, are the Most High over
  all the earth,
  exalted far above all gods.
℟. The Lord is king, the most high over all the
  the earth.

READING II   2 Pt 1, 16-19
A reading from the second letter of Peter
We heard this voice from out of heaven.

It was not by way of cleverly concocted myths
that we taught you about the coming in power
of our Lord Jesus Christ, for we were eye-
witnesses of his sovereign majesty. He received glory and praise from God the Father
when that unique declaration came to him out
of the majestic splendor: "This is my beloved
Son on whom my favor rests." We ourselves
heard this said from heaven while we were in
his company on the holy mountain. Besides, we
possess the prophetic message as something
altogether reliable. Keep your attention closely
fixed on it, as you would on a lamp shining in a
dark place until the first streaks of dawn appear and the morning star rises in your hearts.
This is the Word of the Lord.

A

GOSPEL   Mt 17, 1-9
Alleluia Mt 17, 5

℟. Alleluia. **This is my Son, my beloved, in**
  whom is all my delight:
listen to him. ℟. Alleluia.

✠ **A reading from the holy gospel according**
  to Matthew
His face was shining like the sun.

Jesus took Peter, James, and his brother John
and led them up on a high mountain by themselves. He was transfigured before their eyes.
His face became as dazzling as the sun, his
clothes as radiant as light. Suddenly Moses and

Elijah appeared to them conversing with him.
Upon this, Peter said to Jesus, "Lord, how good
it is for us to be here! With your permission I
will erect three booths here, one for you, one
for Moses, and one for Elijah." He was still
speaking when suddenly a bright cloud overshadowed them. Out of the cloud came a voice
which said, "This is my beloved Son on whom
my favor rests. Listen to him." When they
heard this the disciples fell forward on the
ground, overcome with fear. Jesus came toward them and, laying his hand on them, said,
"Get up! Do not be afraid." When they looked
up they did not see anyone but Jesus.
  As they were coming down the mountainside Jesus commanded them, "Do not tell anyone of the vision until the Son of Man rises
from the dead."
  This is the gospel of the Lord.

B

GOSPEL   Mk 9, 2-10
✠ **A reading from the holy gospel according**
  to Mark
This is my Son, my beloved.

Jesus took Peter, James, and John off by themselves with him and led them up a high mountain. He was transfigured before their eyes and
his clothes became dazzlingly white—whiter
than the work of any bleacher could make
them. Elijah appeared to them along with
Moses; the two were in conversation with
Jesus. Then Peter spoke to Jesus: "Rabbi, how
good it is for us to be here. Let us erect three
booths on this site, one for you, one for Moses,
and one for Elijah." He hardly knew what to
say, for they were all overcome with awe. A
cloud came, overshadowing them, and out of
the cloud a voice: "This is my Son, my beloved. Listen to him." Suddenly looking around
they no longer saw anyone with them—only
Jesus.
  As they were coming down the mountain, he
strictly enjoined them not to tell anyone what
they had seen, before the Son of Man had risen
from the dead. They kept this word of his to

themselves, though they continued to discuss what "to rise from the dead" meant.

This is the gospel of the Lord.

GOSPEL   Lk 9, 28-36

✠ A reading from the holy gospel according to Luke

As he was praying his face was transformed.

Jesus took Peter, John and James, and went up onto a mountain to pray. While he was praying, his face changed in appearance and his clothes became dazzlingly white. Suddenly two men were talking with him—Moses and Elijah. They appeared in glory and spoke of his passage, which he was about to fulfill in Jerusalem. Peter and those with him had fallen into a deep sleep; but awakening, they saw his glory and likewise saw the two men who were standing with him. When these were leaving, Peter said to Jesus, "Master, how good it is for us to be here. Let us set up three booths, one for you, one for Moses, and one for Elijah." (He did not really know what he was saying.) While he was speaking, a cloud came and overshadowed them, and the disciples grew fearful as the others entered it. Then from the cloud came a voice which said, "This is my Son, my Chosen One. Listen to him." When the voice fell silent, Jesus was there alone. The disciples kept quiet, telling nothing of what they had seen at that time to anyone.

This is the gospel of the Lord.

August 7

615   SIXTUS II, pope and martyr, and companions, martyrs

Common of martyrs, p. 837.

616   CAJETAN, priest

Common of pastors or saints [for religious], p. 846 or 867.

August 8

617   DOMINIC, priest

Memorial

Common of pastors [for missionaries] or saints [for religious], p. 846 or 867.

August 10

618   LAWRENCE, deacon and martyr

Feast

READING I   2 Cor 9, 6-10

A reading from the second letter of Paul to the Corinthians

God loves a cheerful giver.

He who sows sparingly will reap sparingly, and he who sows bountifully will reap bountifully. Everyone must give according to what he has inwardly decided; not sadly, not grudgingly, for God loves a cheerful giver. God can multiply his favors among you so that you may always have enough of everything and even a surplus for good works, as it is written:

"He scattered abroad and gave to the poor,
    his justice endures forever."

He who supplies seed for the sower and bread for the eater will provide in abundance; he will multiply the seed you sow and increase your generous yield.

This is the Word of the Lord.

Responsorial Psalm   Ps 112, 1-2. 5-6. 7-8. 9

℞. (5) Happy the man who is merciful
    and lends to those in need.

Happy the man who fears the Lord,
    who greatly delights in his commands.
His posterity shall be mighty upon the earth;
    the upright generation shall be blessed.

℞. Happy the man who is merciful
    and lends to those in need.

Well for the man who is gracious and lends,
    who conducts his affairs with justice;
He shall never be moved;
    the just man shall be in everlasting remembrance.

℞. Happy the man who is merciful
    and lends to those in need.

An evil report he shall not fear;
    his heart is firm, trusting in the Lord.

His heart is steadfast; he shall not fear
  till he looks down upon his foes.
℟. Happy the man who is merciful
  and lends to those in need.
Lavishly he gives to the poor;
  his generosity shall endure forever;
  his horn shall be exalted in glory.
℟. Happy the man who is merciful
  and lends to those in need.

GOSPEL   Jn 12, 24-26
Alleluia   Jn 8, 12
℟. Alleluia. **I am the light of the world, says
  the Lord;**
the man who follows me will have the light of
  life. ℟. Alleluia.

✠ **A reading from the holy gospel according
  to John**
If anyone serves me the Father will honor him.

Jesus said to his disciples:
  "I solemnly assure you,
  unless the grain of wheat falls to the earth
    and dies,
  it remains just a grain of wheat.
  But if it dies,
  it produces much fruit.
  The man who loves his life
  loses it,
  while the man who hates his life in this
    world
  preserves it to life eternal.
  If anyone would serve me,
  let him follow me;
  where I am,
  there will my servant be.
  Anyone who serves me,
  the Father will honor."
    This is the gospel of the Lord.

AUGUST 11
619   **CLARE, virgin**
                              Memorial
Common of saints [for religious], p. 867.

620

August 13

**PONTIAN, pope and martyr,
  and HIPPOLYTUS, priest
  and martyr**

Common of martyrs or pastors, p. 837 or 846.

August 15
621   **ASSUMPTION**

Vigil

                              Solemnity
READING I   1 Chr 15, 3-4. 15. 16; 16, 1-2

A reading from the first book of Chronicles
They brought in the ark of God and set it inside the tent
  which David had pitched for it.

**David assembled all Israel in Jerusalem to
  bring the ark of the Lord to the place which he
  had prepared for it. David also called together
  the sons of Aaron and the Levites.**

The Levites bore the ark of God on their
  shoulders with poles, as Moses had ordained
  according to the word of the Lord.

David commanded the chiefs of the Levites
  to appoint their brethren as chanters, to play
  on musical instruments, harps, lyres, and cymbals, to make a loud sound of rejoicing.

They brought in the ark of God and set it
  within the tent which David had pitched for it.
  Then they offered up holocausts and peace
  offerings to God. When David had finished offering up the holocausts and peace offerings,
  he blessed the people in the name of the Lord.
    This is the Word of the Lord.

Responsorial Psalm   Ps 132, 6-7. 9-10. 13-14

℟. (8) Lord, go up to the place of your rest,
  you and the ark of your holiness.
**Behold, we heard of it in Ephrathah;
  we found it in the fields of Jaar.
Let us enter into his dwelling,
  let us worship at his footstool.**
℟. Lord, go up to the place of your rest,
  you and the ark of your holiness.

May your priests be clothed with justice;
  let your faithful ones shout merrily for joy.
For the sake of David your servant,
  reject not the plea of your anointed.
℟. Lord, go up to the place of your rest,
  you and the ark of your holiness.
For the Lord has chosen Zion;
  he prefers her for his dwelling.
"Zion is my resting place forever;
  in her will I dwell, for I prefer her."
℟. Lord, go up to the place of your rest,
  you and the ark of your holiness.

READING II   1 Cor 15, 54-57

A reading from the first letter of Paul to the Corinthians
He gives us victory through Jesus Christ.

When the corruptible frame takes on incorruptibility and the mortal immortality, then will the saying of Scripture be fulfilled: "Death is swallowed up in victory." "O death, where is your victory? O death, where is your sting?" The sting of death is sin, and sin gets its power from the law. But thanks be to God who has given us the victory through our Lord Jesus Christ.
          This is the Word of the Lord.

GOSPEL   Lk 11, 27-28

Alleluia   Lk 11, 28

℟. Alleluia. Blessed are they who hear the word of God
and keep it.℟. Alleluia.

✠ **A reading from the holy gospel according to Luke**
Blessed is the womb that bore you.

While Jesus was speaking to the crowd, a woman called out, "Blest is the womb that bore you and the breasts that nursed you!" "Rather," he replied, "blest are they who hear the word of God and keep it."
          This is the gospel of the Lord.

622   **Mass during the Day**
READING I   Rv 11, 19; 12, 1-6. 10

A reading from the book of Revelation
I saw a woman clothed with the sun and with the moon beneath her feet.

God's temple in heaven opened and in the temple could be seen the ark of his covenant.

A great sign appeared in the sky, a woman clothed with the sun, with the moon under her feet, and on her head a crown of twelve stars. Because she was with child, she wailed aloud in pain as she labored to give birth. Then another sign appeared in the sky: it was a huge dragon, flaming red, with seven heads and ten horns; on his head were seven diadems. His tail swept a third of the stars from the sky and hurled them down to the earth. Then the dragon stood before the woman about to give birth, ready to devour her child when it should be born. She gave birth to a son—a boy who is destined to shepherd all the nations with an iron rod. Her child was snatched up to God and to his throne. The woman herself fled into the desert, where a special place had been prepared for her by God.

Then I heard a loud voice in heaven say:
  "Now have salvation and power come,
    the reign of our God and the authority of
      his Anointed One."
          This is the Word of the Lord

Responsorial Psalm   Ps 45, 10. 11. 12. 16

℟. (10) The queen stands at your right hand,
  arrayed in gold.
The queen takes her place at your right hand
  in gold of Ophir.
℟. The queen stands at your right hand, arrayed in gold.
Hear, O daughter, and see; turn your ear,
  forget your people and your father's house.
℟. The queen stands at your right hand, arrayed in gold.
So shall the king desire your beauty;
  for he is your lord.
℟. The queen stands at your right hand, arrayed in gold.

They are borne in with gladness and joy;
they enter the palace of the king.
℞. The queen stands at your right hand, arrayed in gold.

READING II   1 Cor 15, 20-26
**A reading from the first letter of Paul to the
Corinthians**
As members of Christ all men will be raised, Christ first,
and after him all who belong to him.

Christ has been raised from the dead, the first
fruits of those who have fallen asleep. Death
came through a man; hence the resurrection of
the dead comes through a man also. Just as in
Adam all die, so in Christ all will come to life
again, but each one in proper order: Christ the
first fruits and then, at his coming, all those
who belong to him. After that will come the end,
when, after having destroyed every sovereignty, authority, and power, he will hand over the
kingdom to God the Father. Christ must reign
until God has put all enemies under his feet.
This is the Word of the Lord.

GOSPEL   Lk 1, 39-56
Alleluia

℞. Alleluia. **Mary is taken up to heaven,**
and the angels of God shout for joy. ℞. Alleluia.

✠ **A reading from the holy gospel according
to Luke**
He who is mighty has done great things for me; he has
exalted the humble.

Mary set out, proceeding in haste into the
hill country to a town of Judah, where she
entered Zechariah's house and greeted Elizabeth. When Elizabeth heard Mary's greeting,
the baby stirred in her womb. Elizabeth was
filled with the Holy Spirit and cried out in a
loud voice: "Blessed are you among women
and blessed is the fruit of your womb. But who
am I that the mother of my Lord should come
to me? The moment your greeting sounded in
my ears, the baby stirred in my womb for joy.
Blessed is she who trusted that the Lord's
words to her would be fulfilled."

Then Mary said:
"My being proclaims the greatness of the
Lord,
my spirit finds joy in God my savior,
For he has looked upon his servant in her
lowliness;
all ages to come shall call me blessed.
God who is mighty has done great things
for me,
holy is his name;
His mercy is from age to age
on those who fear him.
"He has shown might with his arm;
he has confused the proud in their inmost thoughts.
He has deposed the mighty from their
thrones
and raised the lowly to high places.
The hungry he has given every good thing,
while the rich he has sent empty away.
He has upheld Israel his servant,
ever mindful of his mercy;
Even as he promised our fathers,
promised Abraham and his descendants
forever."
Mary remained with Elizabeth about three
months and then returned home.
This is the gospel of the Lord.

August 16

623   **STEPHEN OF HUNGARY**

Common of saints, p. 867.

August 19

624   **JOHN EUDES, priest**

Common of pastors or saints, p. 846 or 867, especially Eph
3, 14-19 (no. 740, § 7), p. 877.

August 20

625   **BERNARD, abbot and doctor**
                                                    Memorial
Common of doctors or saints [for religious], p. 858 or 867.

August 21
626   **PIUS X, pope**

Memorial

Common of pastors [for a pope], p. 846, especially 1 Thes 2, 2-8 (no. 722, § 10), p. 854.

August 22
627   **QUEENSHIP OF MARY**

Memorial

Common of the Blessed Virgin Mary, p. 826, especially Is 9, 1-6 (no. 707, § 8), p. 828, and Lk 1, 39-47 (no. 712, § 4), p. 835.

August 23
628   **ROSE OF LIMA, virgin**

Common of virgins or saints [for religious], p. 864 or 867.

August 24
629   **BARTHOLOMEW, apostle**

Feast

READING I   Rv 21, 9-14

A reading from the book of Revelation
On the foundations are the names of the twelve Apostles of the Lamb.

An angel said to me, "Come, I will show you the woman who is the bride of the Lamb." He carried me away in spirit to the top of a very high mountain and showed me the holy city Jerusalem coming down out of heaven from God. It gleamed with the splendor of God. The city had the radiance of a precious jewel that sparkled like a diamond. Its wall, massive and high, had twelve gates at which twelve angels were stationed. Twelve names were written on the gates, the names of the twelve tribes of Israel. There were three gates facing east, three north, three south, and three west. The wall of the city had twelve courses of stones as its foundation, on which were written the names of the twelve apostles of the Lamb.

This is the Word of the Lord.

Responsorial Psalm   Ps 145, 10-11. 12-13. 17-18

℞. (12) Your friends tell the glory of your kingship, Lord.

Let all your works give you thanks, O Lord, and let your faithful ones bless you.
Let them discourse of the glory of your kingdom
and speak of your might.

℞. Your friends tell the glory of your kingship, Lord.

Making known to men your might
and the glorious splendor of your kingdom.
Your kingdom is a kingdom for all ages,
and your dominion endures through all generations.

℞. Your friends tell the glory of your kingship, Lord.

The Lord is just in all his ways
and holy in all his works.
The Lord is near to all who call upon him,
to all who call upon him in truth.

℞. Your friends tell the glory of your kingship, Lord.

GOSPEL   Jn 1, 45-51

Alleluia   Jn 1, 49

℞. Alleluia. **Master, you are the Son of God, you are the king of Israel.** ℞. Alleluia.

✠ A reading from the holy gospel according to John
There is a true Israelist, in whom there is no deceit.

Philip sought out Nathanael and told him, "We have found the one Moses spoke of in the law—the prophets too—Jesus, son of Joseph, from Nazareth." Nathanael's response to that was, "Can anything good come from Nazareth?" and Philip replied, "Come, see for yourself." When Jesus saw Nathanael coming toward him, he remarked: "This man is a real Israelite. There is no guile in him." "How do you know me?" Nathanael asked him. "Before Philip called you," Jesus answered, "I saw

you under the fig tree." "Rabbi," said Nathanael, "you are the Son of God; you are the
king of Israel." Jesus responded: "Do you believe just because I told you I saw you under
the fig tree? You will see much greater things
than that."

He went on to tell them, "I solemnly assure
you, you shall see the sky opened and the
angels of God ascending and descending on
the Son of Man."

This is the gospel of the Lord.

August 25
630   **LOUIS**

Common of saints, p. 867.

---

631   **JOSEPH CALASANZ, priest**

Common of pastors or saints [for teachers], p. 846 or 867.

August 27
632   **MONICA**

Memorial

Common of saints, p. 867, especially Sir 26, 1-4. 13-16 (no.
737, § 14), p. 871.

OR

GOSPEL   Lk 7, 11-17

✠ A reading from the holy gospel according
to Luke

She bore me in the arms of her prayer that you might say
to the son of the widow: Young man, I command you—
rise up.

Jesus went to a town called Naim, and his
disciples and a large crowd accompanied him.
As he approached the gate of the town a dead
man was being carried out, the only son of a
widowed mother. A considerable crowd of
townsfolk were with her. The Lord was moved
with pity upon seeing her and said to her, "Do
not cry." Then he stepped forward and touched
the litter; at this, the bearers halted. He said,
"Young man, I bid you get up." The dead man
sat up and began to speak. Then Jesus gave
hi... back to his mother. Fear seized them all
and they began to praise God. "A great prophet

has risen among us," they said; and, "God has
visited his people." This was the report that
spread about him throughout Judea and the
surrounding country.

This is the gospel of the Lord.

August 28
633   **AUGUSTINE, bishop and doctor**

Memorial

READING I   1 Jn 4, 7-16

A reading from the first letter of John

If we love one another, God will live in us.

Beloved,
let us love one another
because love is of God;
everyone who loves is begotten of God
and has knowledge of God.
The man without love has known nothing of
    God,
for God is love.
God's love was revealed in our midst in this
    way:
he sent his only Son to the world
that we might have life through him.
Love, then, consists in this:
not that we have loved God,
but that he has loved us
and has sent his Son as an offering for our
    sins.
Beloved,
if God has loved us so,
we must have the same love for one another.
God has never yet been seen.
Yet if we love one another
God dwells in us,
and his love is brought to perfection in us.
The way we know we remain in him
and he in us
is that he has given us of his Spirit.
We have seen for ourselves, and can testify,
that the Father has sent the Son as savior of
    the world.
When anyone acknowledges that Jesus is
    the Son of God,
God dwells in him
and he in God.

We have come to know and enter fully into the love God has for us.
God is love,
and he who lives in love
lives in God
and God in him.
This is the Word of the Lord.

GOSPEL   Mt 23, 8-12

✠ A reading from the holy gospel according to Matthew

You must not allow yourselves to be called teachers, for you have only one teacher, the Christ.

Jesus said to his disciples: "Avoid the title 'Rabbi.' One among you is your teacher, the rest are learners. Do not call anyone on earth your father. Only one is your father, the One in heaven. Avoid being called teachers. Only one is your teacher, the Messiah. The greatest among you will be the one who serves the rest. Whoever exalts himself shall be humbled, but whoever humbles himself shall be exalted."
This is the gospel of the Lord.

OR

Common of pastors or doctors, p. 846 or 858.

August 29

634   BEHEADING OF JOHN THE BAPTIST, martyr

Memorial

READING I   Jer 1, 17-19

A reading from the book of the prophet Jeremiah

Say to them everything that I tell you; do not be afraid of their presence.

The word of the Lord said to me:
Do you gird your loins;
   stand up and tell them
   all that I command you.
Be not crushed on their account,
   as though I would leave you crushed before them;
For it is I this day
   who have made you a fortified city,
A pillar of iron, a wall of brass,
   against the whole land:

Against Judah's kings and princes,
   against its priests and people.
They will fight against you, but not prevail over you,
   for I am with you to deliver you, says the Lord.
This is the Word of the Lord.

Responsorial Psalm   Ps 71, 1-2. 3-4. 5-6. 15. 17

℟. (15) I will sing of your salvation.
In you, O Lord, I take refuge;
   let me never be put to shame.
In your justice rescue me, and deliver me;
   incline your ear to me, and save me.
℟. I will sing of your salvation,
Be my rock of refuge,
   a stronghold to give me safety,
   for you are my rock and my fortress.
O my God, rescue me from the hand of the wicked.
℟. I will sing of your salvation.
For you are my hope, O Lord:
   my trust, O God, from my youth.
On you I depend from birth;
   from my mother's womb you are my strength.
℟. I will sing of your salvation.
My mouth shall declare your justice,
   day by day your salvation.
O God, you have taught me from my youth,
   and till the present I proclaim your wondrous deeds.
℟. I will sing of your salvation.

GOSPEL   Mk 6, 17-29

Alleluia   Mt 5, 10

℟. Alleluia. Happy are they who suffer persecution for justice' sake;
the kingdom of heaven is theirs. ℟. Alleluia.

✠ A reading from the holy gospel according to Mark

I want you to give me the head of John the Baptist on a dish.

Herod was the one who had ordered John arrested, chained, and imprisoned on account of Herodias, the wife of his brother Philip, whom he had married. That was because John had told Herod, "It is not right for you to live with your brother's wife." Herodias harbored a grudge against him for this and wanted to kill him but was unable to do so. Herod feared John, knowing him to be an upright and holy man, and kept him in custody. When he heard him speak he was very much disturbed; yet he felt the attraction of his words. Herodias had her chance one day when Herod held a birthday dinner for his court circle, military officers, and the leading men of Galilee. Herodias' own daughter came in at one point and performed a dance which delighted Herod and his guests. The king told the girl, "Ask for anything you want and I will give it to you." He went so far as to swear to her: "I will grant you whatever you ask, even to half my kingdom!" She went out and said to her mother, "What shall I ask for?" The mother answered, "The head of John the Baptizer." At that the girl hurried back to the king's presence and made her request: "I want you to give me, at once, the head of John the Baptizer on a platter." The king bitterly regretted the request; yet because of his oath and the presence of the guests, he did not want to refuse her. He promptly dispatched an executioner, ordering him to bring back the Baptizer's head. The man went and beheaded John in the prison. He brought in the head on a platter and gave it to the girl, and the girl gave it to her mother. Later, when his disciples heard about this, they came and carried his body away and laid it in a tomb.

This is the gospel of the Lord.

SEPTEMBER

September 3

635 **GREGORY THE GREAT, pope and doctor**

Memorial

Common of pastors [for the pope] or doctors, p. 846 or 858.

September 8

636 **BIRTH OF MARY**

Feast

READING I   Mi 5, 1-4

A reading from the book of the prophet Micah

This is the time when she who is in labor is to give birth.

You, Bethlehem-Ephrathah,
    too small to be among the clans of Judah,
From you shall come forth for me
    one who is to be ruler in Israel;
Whose origin is from of old,
    from ancient times.
(Therefore the Lord will give them up, until the time
    when she who is to give birth has borne,
And the rest of his brethren shall return
    to the children of Israel.)
He shall stand firm and shepherd his flock
    by the strength of the Lord,
    in the majestic name of the Lord, his God;
And they shall remain, for now his greatness
    shall reach to the ends of the earth;
    he shall be peace.

This is the Word of the Lord.

OR

READING I   Rom 8, 28-30

A reading from the letter of Paul to the Romans

Those whom God knew beforehand and predestined.

We know that God makes all things work together for the good of those who have been called according to his decree. Those whom he foreknew he predestined to share the image of his Son, that the Son might be the first-born of many brothers. Those he predestined he likewise called; those he called he also justified; and those he justified he in turn glorified.

This is the Word of the Lord.

Responsorial Psalm   Ps 13, 6. 6

℟. (Is 61, 9) With delight I rejoice in the Lord.
Though I trusted in your kindness,
    let my heart rejoice in your salvation.
℟. With delight I rejoice in the Lord.
Let me sing of the Lord, "He has been good to me."
℟. With delight I rejoice in the Lord.

GOSPEL   Mt 1, 1-16. 18-23 or 1, 18-23
Alleluia

℟. Alleluia. **Happy are you, holy Virgin Mary,
deserving of all praise;
from you arose the sun of justice, Christ the
Lord.** ℟. Alleluia.

✠ **The beginning of the holy gospel according
to Matthew**

She has conceived what is in her by the Holy Spirit.

**A family record of Jesus Christ, son of David,
son of Abraham. Abraham was the father of
Isaac, Isaac the father of Jacob, Jacob the
father of Judah and his brothers.**

> **Judah was the father of Perez and Zerah,
> whose mother was Tamar.
> Perez was the father of Hezron,
> Hezron the father of Ram.
> Ram was the father of Amminadab,
> Amminadab the father of Nahshon,
> Nahshon the father of Salmon.
> Salmon was the father of Boaz, whose
> mother was Rahab,
> Boaz was the father of Obed, whose
> mother was Ruth.
> Obed was the father of Jesse,
> Jesse the father of King David.**

> **David was the father of Solomon, whose
> mother had been the wife of Uriah.
> Solomon was the father of Rehoboam,
> Rehoboam the father of Abijah,
> Abijah the father of Asa.
> Asa was the father of Jehoshaphat,
> Jehoshaphat the father of Joram,
> Joram the father of Uzziah.
> Uzziah was the father of Jotham,
> Jotham the father of Ahaz,
> Ahaz the father of Hezekiah.
> Hezekiah was the father of Manasseh,
> Manasseh the father of Amos,
> Amos the father of Josiah.
> Josiah became the father of Jechoniah and
> his brothers at the time of the Baby-
> lonian exile.**

> **After the Babylonian exile
> Jechoniah was the father of Shealtiel,
> Shealtiel the father of Zerubbabel.
> Zerubbabel was the father of Abiud,**

> **Abiud the father of Eliakim,
> Eliakim the father of Azor.
> Azor was the father of Zadok,
> Zadok the father of Achim,
> Achim the father of Eliud.
> Eliud was the father of Eleazar,
> Eleazar the father of Matthan,
> Matthan the father of Jacob.
> Jacob was the father of Joseph the hus-
> band of Mary.**

> **It was of her that Jesus who is called the
> Messiah was born.**

**Now this is how the birth of Jesus Christ
came about. When his mother Mary was engaged to Joseph, but before they lived together,
she was found with child through the power
of the Holy Spirit. Joseph her husband, an upright man unwilling to expose her to the law,
decided to divorce her quietly. Such was his
intention when suddenly the angel of the Lord
appeared in a dream and said to him: "Joseph,
son of David, have no fear about taking Mary
as your wife. It is by the Holy Spirit that she
has conceived this child. She is to have a son
and you are to name him Jesus because he will
save his people from their sins." All this happened to fulfill what the Lord had said through
the prophet:**

> **"The virgin shall be with child
> and give birth to a son,
> and they shall call him Emmanuel,"**

a name which means "God is with us."

This is the gospel of the Lord.

OR (Short Form)

**Now this is how the birth of Jesus Christ came
about. When his mother Mary was engaged to
Joseph, but before they lived together, she was
found with child through the power of the
Holy Spirit. Joseph her husband, an upright
man unwilling to expose her to the law, decided to divorce her quietly. Such was his intention when suddenly the angel of the Lord
appeared in a dream and said to him: "Joseph,
son of David, have no fear about taking Mary
as your wife. It is by the Holy Spirit that she
has conceived this child. She is to have a son
and you are to name him Jesus because he will**

save his people from their sins." All this happened to fulfill what the Lord had said through the prophet:

"The virgin shall be with child
and give birth to a son,
and they shall call him Emmanuel,"

a name which means "God is with us."

This is the gospel of the Lord

September 13

637   ## JOHN CHRYSOSTOM, bishop
and doctor

Memorial

Common of pastors or doctors, p. 846 or 858.

September 14

638   ## TRIUMPH OF THE CROSS

Feast

READING I   Nm 21, 4-9

A reading from the book of Numbers

When those that were afflicted looked upon it, they were healed.

With their patience worn out by the journey, the people complained against God and Moses, "Why have you brought us up from Egypt to die in this desert, where there is no food or water? We are disgusted with this wretched food!"

In punishment the Lord sent among the people saraph serpents, which bit the people so that many of them died. Then the people came to Moses and said, "We have sinned in complaining against the Lord and you. Pray the Lord to take the serpents from us." So Moses prayed for the people, and the Lord said to Moses, "Make a saraph and mount it on a pole, and if anyone who has been bitten looks at it, he will recover." Moses accordingly made a bronze serpent and mounted it on a pole, and whenever anyone who had been bitten by a serpent looked at the bronze serpent, he recovered.

This is the Word of the Lord.

Responsorial Psalm   Ps 78, 1-2. 34-35. 36-37. 38

℞. (7) Do not forget the works of the Lord!

Hearken, my people, to my teaching;
    incline your ears to the words of my mouth.
I will open my mouth in a parable,
    I will utter mysteries from of old.

℞. Do not forget the works of the Lord!

While he slew them they sought him
    and inquired after God again,
Remembering that God was their rock
    and the Most High God, their redeemer.

℞. Do not forget the works of the Lord!

But they flattered him with their mouths
    and lied to him with their tongues,
Though their hearts were not steadfast toward him,
    nor were they faithful to his covenant.

℞. Do not forget the works of the Lord!

Yet he, being merciful, forgave their sin
    and destroyed them not;
Often he turned back his anger
    and let none of his wrath be roused.

℞. Do not forget the works of the Lord!

READING II   Phil 2, 6-11

A reading from the letter of Paul to the Philippians

He humbled himself, therefore God has exalted him.

Christ Jesus, though he was in the form of God,
    did not deem equality with God
    something to be grasped at.

Rather, he emptied himself
    and took the form of a slave,
    being born in the likeness of men.

He was known to be of human estate
    and it was thus that he humbled himself,
    obediently accepting even death,
    death on a cross!

Because of this,
    God highly exalted him
    and bestowed on him the name
    above every other name,

So that at Jesus' name
   every knee must bend
   in the heavens, on the earth,
   and under the earth,
   and every tongue proclaim
   to the glory of God the Father:
   JESUS CHRIST IS LORD!
       This is the Word of the Lord.

GOSPEL   Jn 3, 13-17
Alleluia

℟. Alleluia. **We adore you, O Christ, and we
praise you,
because by your cross you have redeemed the
world.** ℟. Alleluia.

✠ **A reading from the holy gospel according
to John**

The Son of Man must be lifted up.

Jesus said to Nicodemus:
"No one has gone up to heaven
except the One who came down from
   there—
the Son of Man [who is in heaven].
Just as Moses lifted up the serpent in the
   desert,
so must the Son of Man be lifted up,
that all who believe
may have eternal life in him.
Yes, God so loved the world
that he gave his only Son,
that whoever believes in him may not die
but may have eternal life.
God did not send the Son into the world
to condemn the world,
but that the world might be saved through
   him."
       This is the gospel of the Lord.

September 15

639   OUR LADY OF SORROWS

Memorial

READING I   Heb 5, 7-9

A reading from the letter to the Hebrews

He learned obedience and became the source of eternal
salvation.

**In the days when Christ was in the flesh, he
offered prayers and supplications with loud**
cries and tears to God, who was able to save
him from death, and he was heard because of
his reverence. Son though he was, he learned
obedience from what he suffered; and when
perfected, he became the source of eternal salvation for all who obey him.
       This is the Word of the Lord.

Responsorial Psalm   Ps 31, 2-3. 3-4. 5-6. 15-16. 20

℟. (17) **Save me, O Lord, in your steadfast
   love.**
In you, O Lord, I take refuge;
   let me never be put to shame.
In your justice rescue me,
   incline your ear to me,
   make haste to deliver me!
℟. **Save me, O Lord, in your steadfast love.**
Be my rock of refuge,
   a stronghold to give me safety.
You are my rock and my fortress;
   for your name's sake you will lead and guide
   me.
℟. **Save me, O Lord, in your steadfast love.**
You will free me from the snare they set for
   me,
   for you are my refuge.
Into your hands I commend my spirit;
   you will redeem me, O Lord, O faithful God.
℟. **Save me, O Lord, in your steadfast love.**
But my trust is in you, O Lord;
   I say, "You are my God."
In your hands is my destiny; rescue me
   from the clutches of my enemies and my
   persecutors.
℟. **Save me, O Lord, in your steadfast love.**
How great is the goodness, O Lord,
   which you have in store for those who fear
   you,
And which, toward those who take refuge in
   you,
   you show in the sight of men.
℟. **Save me, O Lord, in your steadfast love.**

SEQUENCE (OPTIONAL) (Prose Text)

**The sorrowful mother was standing in tears
beside the cross on which her Son was hanging. Her soul was full of grief and anguish and
sorrow, for the sword of prophecy pierced it.**

How sad now and how unhappy at the fate of her only Son was that mother, once called blessed; how the faithful mother grieved and lamented as she saw her glorious Son so shamefully treated.

Who is there who would not weep, were he to see Christ's mother in such great suffering? Or who could help feeling sympathy with the mother, were he to think of her sorrowing with her Son?

Yet she actually saw Jesus in agony and broken by the scourging—and this because of the sins of her own people. She saw her dear Son all the time he was dying and abandoned until he yielded up his soul.

Come then, mother, from whom all love springs, make me understand the meaning of your sorrow that I may mourn with you. Make my heart burn with love of Christ, my God, that he may look on me with favor.

Holy mother, do this for me. Pierce my heart once and forever with the wounds of your crucified Son. Let me share with you the pain of your Son's wounds, for he thought it right to bear such sufferings for me.

Grant that my tears of love may mingle with yours and that, as long as I live, I may feel the pains of my crucified Lord. To stand with you beside the cross and be your companion in grief is my own wish.

Virgin without equal among virgins, do not now turn down my request; grant that I may mourn with you. Grant that I carry about the dying state of Christ; grant that I be a sharer of his passion; grant that I relive his wounds.

Grant that I be wounded with his wounds; grant that I drink to my soul's content of the chalice of his cross and blood. Be a defense to me, virgin Mary, on the judgment day, and I will not burn and be consumed in the fires of hell.

When it is time, Lord Christ, for me to leave this world, give me through your mother's prayers the palm of victory. When my body is dead, grant that my soul be given the glory of paradise. Amen. (Alleluia)

OR (Poetic Text)

At the cross her station keeping,
Stood the mournful Mother weeping,
   Close to Jesus to the last.

Through her heart, his sorrow sharing,
All his bitter anguish bearing,
   Now at length the sword had passed.

Oh, how sad and sore distressed
Was that Mother highly blessed
   Of the sole begotten One!

Christ above in torment hangs,
She beneath beholds the pangs
   Of her dying, glorious Son.

Is there one who would not weep,
'Whelmed in miseries so deep,
   Christ's dear Mother to behold?

Can the human heart refrain
From partaking in her pain,
   In that mother's pain untold?

Bruised, derided, cursed, defiled,
She beheld her tender Child,
   All with bloody scourges rent.

For the sins of his own nation
Saw him hang in desolation
   Till his spirit forth he sent.

O sweet Mother! font of love,
Touch my spirit from above,
   Make my heart with yours accord.

Make me feel as you have felt;
Make my soul to glow and melt
   With the love of Christ, my Lord.

Holy Mother, pierce me through,
In my heart each wound renew
   Of my Savior crucified.

Let me share with you his pain,
Who for all our sins was slain,
   Who for me in torments died.

Let me mingle tears with you,
Mourning him who mourned for me,
   All the days that I may live.

By the cross with you to stay,
There with you to weep and pray,
   Is all I ask of you to give.

Virgin of all virgins blest!
Listen to my fond request:
  Let me share your grief divine.

Let me to my latest breath,
In my body bear the death
  Of that dying Son of yours.

Wounded with his every wound,
Steep my soul till it has swooned
  In his very blood away.

Be to me, O Virgin, nigh,
Lest in flames I burn and die,
  In his awful judgment day.

Christ, when you shall call me hence,
Be your Mother my defense,
  Be your cross my victory.

While my body here decays,
May my soul your goodness praise,
  Safe in heaven eternally.
Amen. (Alleluia.)

GOSPEL   Jn 19, 25-27
Alleluia

℟. Alleluia. **Happy are you, O Blessed Virgin
Mary;
without dying you won the martyr's crown
beside the cross of the Lord.** ℟. Alleluia.

✠ **A reading from the holy gospel according
to John**

How that loving mother was pierced with grief and anguish
when she saw the sufferings of her son.

**Near the cross of Jesus there stood his mother,
his mother's sister, Mary the wife of Clopas,
and Mary Magdalene. Seeing his mother there
with the disciple whom he loved, Jesus said to
his mother, "Woman, there is your son." In
turn he said to the disciple, "There is your
mother." From that hour onward, the disciple
took her into his care.**
        This is the gospel of the Lord.

                        OR
GOSPEL   Lk 2, 33-35
Alleluia

℟. Alleluia. **Happy are you, O Blessed Virgin
Mary;**

without dying you won the martyr's crown
  beside the cross of the Lord. ℟. Alleluia.

✠ **A reading from the holy gospel according
to Luke**

A sword will pierce your very soul.

**Mary and Joseph were marveling at what was
being said about Jesus. Simeon blessed them
and said to Mary his mother: "This child is
destined to be the downfall and the rise of
many in Israel, a sign that will be opposed—
and you yourself shall be pierced with a sword
—so that the thoughts of many hearts may be
laid bare."**
        This is the gospel of the Lord.

September 16
640   **CORNELIUS, pope and martyr,
and CYPRIAN, bishop and
martyr**

Memorial

Common of martyrs or pastors, p. 837 or 846.

September 17
641   **ROBERT BELLARMINE, bishop
and doctor**

Common of pastors or doctors, p. 846 or 858.

September 19
642   **JANUARIUS, bishop and martyr**

Common of martyrs or pastors, p. 837 or 846.

September 21
643   **MATTHEW, apostle and
evangelist**

Feast

READING I   Eph 4, 1-7. 11-13
**A reading from the letter of Paul to the
Ephesians**

It was his gift that some should be apostles, others
evangelists.

**I plead with you, as a prisoner for the Lord,
to live a life worthy of the calling you**

have received, with perfect humility, meekness, and patience, bearing with one another lovingly. Make every effort to preserve the unity which has the Spirit as its origin and peace as its binding force. There is but one body and one Spirit, just as there is but one hope given all of you by your call. There is one Lord, one faith, one baptism; one God and Father of all, who is over all, and works through all, and is in all.

Each of us has received God's favor in the measure in which Christ bestows it.

It is he who gave apostles, prophets, evangelists, pastors, and teachers in roles of service for the faithful to build up the body of Christ, till we become one in faith and in the knowledge of God's Son, and form that perfect man who is Christ come to full stature.

This is the Word of the Lord.

Responsorial Psalm   Ps 19, 2-3. 4-5

℟. (5) Their message goes out through all the earth.

The heavens declare the glory of God,
    and the firmament proclaims his handiwork.
Day pours out the word to day,
    and night to night imparts knowledge.

℟. Their message goes out through all the earth.

Not a word nor a discourse
    whose voice is not heard;
Through all the earth their voice resounds,
    and to the ends of the world, their message.

℟. Their message goes out through all the earth.

GOSPEL   Mt 9, 9-13
Alleluia

℟. Alleluia. We praise you, God; we acknowledge you as Lord;
your glorious band of apostles extols you. ℟. Alleluia.

✠ A reading from the holy gospel according to Matthew

Follow me. And standing up, he followed him.

As Jesus moved on, he saw a man named Matthew at his post where taxes were collected. He said to him, "Follow me." Matthew

got up and followed him. Now it happened that, while Jesus was at table in Matthew's house, many tax collectors and those known as sinners came to join Jesus and his disciples at dinner. The Pharisees saw this and complained to his disciples, "What reason can the Teacher have for eating with tax collectors and those who disregard the law?" Overhearing the remark, he said: "People who are in good health do not need a doctor; sick people do. Go and learn the meaning of the words, 'It is mercy I desire and not sacrifice.' I have come to call, not the self-righteous, but sinners."

This is the gospel of the Lord.

September 26
644   **COSMAS and DAMIAN,**
martyrs
Common of martyrs, p. 837.

September 27
645   **VINCENT DE PAUL, priest**
Memorial
Common of pastors [for missionaries] or saints [for those who work for the disadvantaged], p. 846 or 867, especially 1 Cor 1, 26-31 (no. 740, § 2), p. 875.

September 28
646   **WENCESLAUS, martyr**
Common of martyrs, p. 837.

September 29
647   **MICHAEL, GABRIEL, and**
RAPHAEL, archangels
Feast
READING I   Dn 7, 9-10. 13-14
A reading from the book of the prophet Daniel
Countless thousands ministered to him.

As Daniel watched:
Thrones were set up
    and the Ancient One took his throne.

His clothing was snow bright,
and the hair on his head as white as wool;
His throne was flames of fire,
with wheels of burning fire.
A surging stream of fire
flowed out from where he sat;
Thousands upon thousands were ministering
to him,
and myriads upon myriads attended him.
The court was convened, and the books were
opened. As the visions during the night continued, I saw
One like a son of man coming,
on the clouds of heaven;
When he reached the Ancient One
and was presented before him,
He received dominion, glory, and kingship;
nations and peoples of every language serve
him.
His dominion is an everlasting dominion
that shall not be taken away,
his kingship shall not be destroyed.
This is the Word of the Lord.

OR

READING I   Rv 12, 7-12

A reading from the book of Revelation
Michael and his angels battled with the dragon.

Then war broke out in heaven; Michael and his
angels battled against the dragon. Although
the dragon and his angels fought back, they
were overpowered and lost their place in
heaven. The huge dragon, the ancient serpent
known as the devil or Satan, the seducer of
the whole world, was driven out; he was
hurled down to earth and his minions with
him.
Then I heard a loud voice in heaven say:
"Now have salvation and power come,
the reign of our God and the authority of
his Anointed One.
For the accuser of our brothers is cast out,
who night and day accused them before our
God.
They defeated him by the blood of the Lamb
and by the word of their testimony;
love for life did not deter them from death.
So rejoice, you heavens,

and you that dwell therein!"
This is the Word of the Lord.

Responsorial Psalm   Ps 138, 1-2. 2-3. 4-5

℟. (1) In the sight of the angels
I will sing your praises, Lord.
**I will give thanks to you, O Lord, with all my
heart,**
[for you have heard the words of my mouth;]
in the presence of the angels I will sing your
praise;
**I will worship at your holy temple
and give thanks to your name,**
℟. In the sight of the angels
I will sing your praises, Lord.
Because of your kindness and your truth;
for you have made great above all things
your name and your promise.
When I called, you answered me;
you built up strength within me.
℟. In the sight of the angels
I will sing your praises, Lord.
**All the kings of the earth shall give thanks to
you, O Lord,**
when they hear the words of your mouth;
And they shall sing of the ways of the Lord:
"Great is the glory of the Lord."
℟. In the sight of the angels
I will sing your praises, Lord.

GOSPEL   Jn 1, 47-51
Alleluia   Ps 103, 21

℟. Alleluia. **Bless the Lord, all you his angels,
his ministers who do his will.** ℟. Alleluia.

✠ **A reading from the holy gospel according
to John**
Above the Son of Man you will see the angels of God
ascending and descending.

When Jesus saw Nathanael coming toward
him, he remarked: "This man is a real Israelite. There is no guile in him." "How do you
know me?" Nathanael asked him. "Before
Philip called you," Jesus answered, "I saw
you under the fig tree." "Rabbi," said Nathanael, "you are the Son of God; you are the

king of Israel." Jesus responded: "Do you believe just because I told you I saw you under the fig tree? You will see much greater things than that."

He went on to tell them, "I solemnly assure you, you shall see the sky opened and the angels of God ascending and descending on the Son of Man."

This is the gospel of the Lord.

September 30
648   JEROME, priest and doctor

Memorial
Common of doctors or pastors, p. 858 or 846.

OR

READING I   2 Tm 3, 14-17
A reading from the second letter of Paul to Timothy

All scripture is inspired by God and can profitably be used for teaching.

You, for your part, must remain faithful to what you have learned and believed because you know who your teachers were. Likewise, from your infancy you have known the sacred Scriptures, the source of the wisdom which through faith in Jesus Christ leads to salvation. All Scripture is inspired of God and is useful for teaching—for reproof, correction, and training in holiness so that the man of God may be fully competent and equipped for every kind of good work.

This is the Word of the Lord.

OCTOBER

October 1
649   THERESA OF THE CHILD JESUS, virgin

Memorial
Common of virgins or saints [for religious], p. 864 or 867.

OR

READING I   Is 66, 10-14
A reading from the book of the prophet Isaiah

Now toward her I send flowering peace, like a river.

Rejoice with Jerusalem and be glad because of her,
    all you who love her;
Exult, exult with her,
    all you who were mourning over her!
Oh, that you may suck fully
    of the milk of her comfort,
That you may nurse with delight
    at her abundant breasts!
    For thus says the Lord:
Lo, I will spread prosperity over her like a river,
    and the wealth of the nations like an overflowing torrent.
As nurslings, you shall be carried in her arms,
    and fondled in her lap;
As a mother comforts her son,
    so will I comfort you;
    in Jerusalem you shall find your comfort.

When you see this, your heart shall rejoice,
    and your bodies flourish like the grass;
The Lord's power shall be known to his servants.
    This is the Word of the Lord.

GOSPEL   Mt 18, 1-4
✠ A reading from the holy gospel according to Matthew

Unless you have the genuineness of little children, you will not enter into the kingdom of God.

The disciples came up to Jesus with the question, "Who is of greatest importance in the kingdom of God?" He called a little child over and stood him in their midst and said: "I assure you, unless you change and become like little children, you will not enter the kingdom of God. Whoever makes himself lowly, becoming like this child, is of greatest importance in that heavenly reign."

This is the gospel of the Lord.

October 2

650   GUARDIAN ANGELS

Memorial

READING I   Ex 23, 20-23

A reading from the book of Exodus

My angel will go before you.

The Lord said: "See, I am sending an angel before you, to guard you on the way and bring you to the place I have prepared. Be attentive to him and heed his voice. Do not rebel against him, for he will not forgive your sin. My authority resides in him. If you heed his voice and carry out all I tell you, I will be an enemy to your enemies and a foe to your foes.

"My angel will go before you and bring you to the Amorites, Hittites, Perizzites, Canaanites, Hivites and Jebusites; and I will wipe them out."

This is the Word of the Lord.

Responsorial Psalm   Ps 91, 1-2. 3-4. 5-6. 10-11

℟. (11) He has put his angels in charge of you,
    to guard you in all your ways.

You who dwell in the shelter of the Most High,
    who abide in the shadow of the Almighty,
Say to the Lord, "My refuge and my fortress,
    my God, in whom I trust."

℟. He has put his angels in charge of you,
    to guard you in all your ways.

For he will rescue you from the snare of the
        fowler,
    from the destroying pestilence.
With his pinions he will cover you,
    and under his wings you shall take refuge.

℟. He has put his angels in charge of you,
    to guard you in all your ways.

His faithfulness is a buckler and a shield.
    You shall not fear the terror of the night
    nor the arrow that flies by day;

Not the pestilence that roams in darkness
    nor the devastating plague at noon.

℟. He has put his angels in charge of you,
    to guard you in all your ways.

No evil shall befall you,
    nor shall affliction come near your tent,
For to his angels he has given command about
        you,
    that they guard you in all your ways.

℟. He has put his angels in charge of you,
    to guard you in all your ways.

GOSPEL   Mt 18, 1-5. 10

Alleluia   Ps 103, 21

℟. Alleluia. Bless the Lord, all you his angels, his ministers who do his will. ℟. Alleluia.

✠ **A reading from the holy gospel according to Matthew**

Their angels in heaven are always in the presence of my Father, who is in heaven.

The disciples came up to Jesus with the question, "Who is of greatest importance in the kingdom of God?" He called a little child over and stood him in their midst and said: "I assure you, unless you change and become like little children, you will not enter the kingdom of God. Whoever makes himself lowly, becoming like this child, is of greatest importance in that heavenly reign. Whoever welcomes one such child for my sake welcomes me.

"See that you never despise one of these little ones. I assure you, their angels in heaven constantly behold my heavenly Father's face."

This is the gospel of the Lord.

October 4

651   FRANCIS OF ASSISI

Memorial

READING I   Gal 6, 14-18

A reading from the letter of Paul to the Galatians

Through him the world is crucified to me and I to the world.

May I never boast of anything but the cross of our Lord Jesus Christ! Through it, the world

has been crucified to me and I to the world. It means nothing whether one is circumcised or not. All that matters is that one is created anew. Peace and mercy on all who follow this rule of life, and on the Israel of God.

Henceforth, let no man trouble me, for I bear the brand marks of Jesus in my body.

Brothers, may the favor of our Lord Jesus Christ be with your spirit. Amen.

This is the Word of the Lord.

OR

Common of saints [for religious], p. 867.

October 6
652 **BRUNO, priest**
Common of pastors or saints [for religious], p. 846 or 867.

October 7
653 **OUR LADY OF THE ROSARY**
Memorial
Common of the Blessed Virgin Mary, p. 826, especially Lk 1, 26-38 (no. 712, § 3), p. 834.

October 9
654 **DENIS, bishop and martyr, and COMPANIONS, martyrs**
Common of martyrs, p. 837.

---

655 **JOHN LEONARDI, priest**
Common of pastors or saints [for those who work for the disadvantaged], p. 846 or 867.

OCTOBER 14
656 **Callistus I, pope and martyr**
Common of martyrs or pastors [for a pope], p. 837 or 846.

October 15
657 **THERESA OF AVILA, virgin** **Memorial**
Common of virgins or saints [for religious], p. 864 or 867.

OR

READING I Rom 8, 22-27

A reading from the letter of Paul to the Romans
The Spirit himself intercedes for us with longings too deep for words.

We know that all creation groans and is in agony even until now. Not only that, but we ourselves, although we have the Spirit as first fruits, groan inwardly while we await the redemption of our bodies. In hope we were saved. But hope is not hope if its object is seen; how is it possible for one to hope for what he sees? And hoping for what we cannot see means awaiting it with patient endurance.

The Spirit too helps us in our weakness, for we do not know how to pray as we ought; but the Spirit himself makes intercession for us with groanings which cannot be expressed in speech. He who searches hearts knows what the Spirit means, for the Spirit intercedes for the saints as God himself wills.

This is the Word of the Lord.

October 16
658 **HEDWIG, religious**
Common of saints [for religious], p. 867.

---

659 **MARGARET MARY ALACOQUE, virgin**
Common of virgins or saints [for religious], p. 864 or 867, especially Eph 3, 14-19 (no. 740, § 7), p. 877.

October 17
660 **IGNATIUS OF ANTIOCH, bishop and martyr** **Memorial**

READING I Phil 3, 17—4, 1

A reading from the letter of Paul to the Philippians
Our homeland is in heaven.

Be imitators of me, my brothers. Take as your guide those who follow the example that we

set. Unfortunately, many go about in a way
which shows them to be enemies of the cross
of Christ. I have often said this to you before;
this time I say it with tears in my eyes.
Such as these will end in disaster! Their only
god is their belly and their glory is in their
shame. I am talking about those who are set
upon the things of this world. As you well
know, we have our citizenship in heaven; it is
from there that we eagerly await the coming
of our savior, the Lord Jesus Christ. He will
give a new form to this lowly body of ours
and remake it according to the pattern of his
glorified body, by his power to subject everything to himself.

For these reasons, my brothers, you whom I
so love and long for, you who are my joy and
my crown, continue, my dear ones, to stand
firm in the Lord.

This is the Word of the Lord.

GOSPEL   Jn 12, 24-26

✠ **A reading from the holy gospel according
to John**

If the grain of wheat in the ground dies, it yields a rich
harvest.

Jesus said to his disciples:
"I solemnly assure you,
 unless the grain of wheat falls to the earth
  and dies,
 it remains just a grain of wheat.
 But if it dies,
 it produces much fruit.
 The man who loves his life
 loses it,
 while the man who hates his life in this
  world
 preserves it to life eternal.
 If anyone would serve me,
 let him follow me;
 where I am,
 there will my servant be.
 Anyone who serves me,
 the Father will honor."

This is the gospel of the Lord.

OR

Common of martyrs or pastors, p. 837 or 846.

October 18
661   **LUKE, evangelist**
                                          Feast

READING I   2 Tm 4, 9-17

**A reading from the second letter of Paul to
Timothy**

Luke alone is with me.

Do your best to join me soon, for Demas, en-
amored of the present world, has left me and
gone to Thessalonica. Crescens has gone to
Galatia and Titus to Dalmatia. I have no one
with me but Luke. Get Mark and bring him
with you, for he can be of great service to me.
Tychicus I have sent to Ephesus. When you
come, bring the cloak I left in Troas with
Carpus, and the books, especially the parch-
ments.

Alexander the coppersmith did me a great
deal of harm; the Lord will repay him according to his deeds. Meanwhile, you too had better
be on guard, for he has strongly resisted our
preaching. At the first hearing of my case in
court, no one took my part. In fact everyone
abandoned me. May it not be held against
them! But the Lord stood by my side and gave
me strength, so that through me the preaching
task might be completed and all the nations
might hear the gospel.

This is the Word of the Lord.

Responsorial Psalm   Ps 145, 10-11. 12-13. 17-18

℟. (12) Your friends tell the glory of your kingship, Lord.

Let all your works give you thanks, O Lord,
 and let your faithful ones bless you.
Let them discourse of the glory of your kingdom
 and speak of your might.

℟. Your friends tell the glory of your kingship, Lord.

Making known to me your might
 and the glorious splendor of your kingdom.
Your kingdom is a kingdom for all ages,
 and your dominion endures through all generations.

℟. Your friends tell the glory of your kingship,
Lord.

The Lord is just in all his ways
and holy in all his works.
The Lord is near to all who call upon him,
to all who call upon him in truth.
R̝. Your friends tell the glory of your kingship,
Lord.

GOSPEL　　　　　　　　　　　　　Lk 10, 1-9

Alleluia　Jn 15, 16

R̝. Alleluia. I have chosen you from the world
says the Lord,
to go and bear fruit that will last. R̝. Alleluia.

✠ A reading from the holy gospel according
to Luke

The harvest is plentiful but the laborers are few.

The Lord appointed a further seventy-two and
sent them in pairs before him to every town
and place he intended to visit. He said to
them: "The harvest is rich but the workers are
few; therefore ask the harvest-master to send
workers to his harvest. Be on your way, and
remember: I am sending you as lambs in the
midst of wolves. Do not carry a walking staff
or traveling bag; wear no sandals and greet no
one along the way. On entering any house,
first say, 'Peace to this house.' If there is a
peaceable man there, your peace will rest on
him; if not, it will come back to you. Stay in
the one house eating and drinking what they
have, for the laborer is worth his wage. Do
not move from house to house.

"Into whatever city you go, after they welcome you, eat what they set before you, and
cure the sick there. Say to them, 'The reign
of God is at hand.' "

This is the gospel of the Lord.

October 19

662　　**ISAAC JOGUES, priest and
martyr, and COMPANIONS,
martyrs**

Common of martyrs or pastors [for missionaries], p. 837 or
846.

663　　**PAUL OF THE CROSS, priest**

Common of pastors, p. 846, especially I Cor 1, 18-25 (no.
722, § 2), p. 852.

OR

Common of saints [for religious], p. 867.

October 23

664　　**JOHN OF CAPISTRANO, priest**

Common of pastors [for missionaries], p. 846.

October 24

665　　**ANTHONY CLARET, bishop**

Common of pastors [for missionaries], p. 846.

October 28

666　　**SIMON and JUDE, apostles**

Feast

READING I　　　　　　　　　　Eph 2, 19-22

**A reading from the letter of Paul to the
Ephesians**

*You are part of the building built on the foundation of
the apostles.*

You are strangers and aliens no longer. No,
you are fellow citizens of the saints and members of the household of God. You form a
building which rises on the foundation of the
apostles and prophets, with Christ Jesus himself as the capstone. Through him the whole
structure is fitted together and takes shape
as a holy temple in the Lord; in him you are
being built into this temple, to become a dwelling place for God in the Spirit.

This is the Word of the Lord.

Responsorial Psalm　　　　　　Ps 19, 2-3. 4-5

R̝. (5) Their message goes out through all the
earth.

The heavens declare the glory of God,
and the firmament proclaims his handiwork.
Day pours out the word to day,
and night to night imparts knowledge.

℟. Their message goes out through all the
earth.
Not a word nor a discourse
    whose voice is not heard;
Through all the earth their voice resounds,
    and to the end of the world, their message.
℟. Their message goes out through all the
earth.

GOSPEL   Lk 6, 12-16
Alleluia

℟. Alleluia. **We praise you, God; we acknowl-**
    edge you as Lord;
Your glorious band of apostles extols you.
    ℟. Alleluia.

✠ **A reading from the holy gospel according**
    to Luke
He chose twelve from among them whom he named
Apostles.

Jesus went out to the mountain to pray, spend-
ing the night in communion with God. At day-
break he called his disciples and selected
twelve of them to be his apostles: Simon, to
whom he gave the name Peter, and Andrew
his brother, James and John, Philip and Bar-
tholomew, Matthew and Thomas, James son of
Alphaeus, and Simon called the Zealot, Judas
son of James, and Judas Iscariot, who turned
traitor.
        This is the gospel of the Lord.

**In votive Masses of the apostles, or of a single apostle, the
above readings are said.**

NOVEMBER

November 1

667

ALL SAINTS

Solemnity

READING I   Rv 7, 2-4. 9-14

A reading from the book of Revelation

I saw an immense crowd, beyond hope of counting, of
people from every nation, race, tribe and language.

I, John, saw another angel come up from the
east holding the seal of the living God. He
cried out at the top of his voice to the four
angels who were given power to ravage the
land and the sea, "Do no harm to the land or
the sea or the trees until we imprint this seal
on the foreheads of the servants of our God."
I heard the number of those who were so
marked—one hundred and forty-four thousand
from every tribe of Israel.

After this I saw before me a huge crowd
which no one could count from every nation,
race, people, and tongue. They stood before
the throne and the Lamb, dressed in long white
robes and holding palm branches in their
hands. They cried out in a loud voice, "Salvation is from our God, who is seated on the
throne, and from the Lamb!" All the angels
who were standing around the throne and the
elders and the four living creatures fell down
before the throne to worship God. They said:
"Amen! Praise and glory, wisdom, thanksgiving, and honor, power and might to our God
forever and ever. Amen!"

Then one of the elders asked me, "Who do
you think these are, all dressed in white? And
where have they come from?" I said to him,
"Sir, you should know better than I." He then
told me, "These are the ones who have survived the great period of trial; they have
washed their robes and made them white in the
blood of the Lamb.
        This is the Word of the Lord.

Responsorial Psalm   Ps 24, 1-2. 3-4. 5-6

℟. (6) Lord, this is the people that longs to see
    your face.
The Lord's are the earth and its fullness;
    the world and those who dwell in it.
For he founded it upon the seas
    and established it upon the rivers.
℟. Lord, this is the people that longs to see
    your face.
Who can ascend the mountain of the Lord?
    or who may stand in his holy place?
He whose hands are sinless, whose heart is
    clean,
    who desires not what is vain.
℟. Lord, this is the people that longs to see
    your face.

He shall receive a blessing from the Lord,
a reward from God his savior.
Such is the race that seeks for him,
that seeks the face of the God of Jacob.
℟. Lord, this is the people that longs to see
your face.

READING II   1 Jn 3, 1-3
A reading from the first letter of John
We shall see God as he really is.

See what love the Father has bestowed on us
in letting us be called children of God!
Yet that in fact is what we are.
The reason the world does not recognize us
is that it never recognized the Son.
Dearly beloved,
we are God's children now;
what we shall later be has not yet come to
light.
We know that when it comes to light
we shall be like him,
for we shall see him as he is.
Everyone who has this hope based on him
keeps himself pure, as he is pure.
This is the Word of the Lord.

GOSPEL   Mt 5, 1-12
Alleluia   Mt 11, 28

℟. Alleluia. Come to me, all you that labor and
are burdened,
and I will give you rest, says the Lord. ℟.
Alleluia.

✠ A reading from the holy gospel according
to Matthew
Rejoice and be glad for your reward will be great in heaven.

When Jesus saw the crowds he went up on the
mountainside. After he had sat down his disciples gathered around him, and he began to
teach them:
"How blest are the poor in spirit: the reign
of God is theirs.
Blest too are the sorrowing; they shall
be consoled.
[Blest are the lowly; they shall inherit the
land.]

Blest are they who hunger and thirst for
holiness;
they shall have their fill.
Blest are they who show mercy; mercy
shall be theirs.
Blest are the single-hearted, for they shall
see God.
Blest too the peacemakers; they shall be
called sons of God.
Blest are those persecuted for holiness'
sake; the reign of God is theirs.
Blest are you when they insult you and
persecute you and utter every kind of
slander against you because of me.
Be glad and rejoice, for your reward in
heaven is great."
This is the gospel of the Lord.

November 2
668   ALL SOULS
See the readings in the Masses for the dead, below, nos.
789-793.

November 3
669   MARTIN DE PORRES, religious
Common of saints [for religious], p. 867.

November 4
670   CHARLES BORROMEO, bishop
                                          Memorial
Common of pastors, p. 846.

November 9
**671   DEDICATION OF ST. JOHN
LATERAN**
                                          Feast
Common of the dedication of a church, p. 820.

November 10

672   **LEO THE GREAT, pope and doctor**

Memorial

Common of pastors [for a pope] or doctors, p. 846 or 858.

November 11

673   **MARTIN OF TOURS, bishop**

Memorial

Common of pastors or saints [for religious], p. 846 or 867.

OR

GOSPEL   Mt 25, 31-40

✠ A reading from the holy gospel according
to Matthew

*Whatever you have done to the very least of my brothers
you have done to me.*

Jesus said to his disciples: "When the Son of
Man comes in his glory, escorted by all the angels of heaven, he will sit upon his royal throne,
and all the nations will be assembled before him.
Then he will separate them into two groups, as
a shepherd separates sheep from goats. The
sheep he will place on his right hand, the goats
on his left. The king will say to those on his
right: 'Come, you have my Father's blessing!
Inherit the kingdom prepared for you from the
creation of the world. For I was hungry and you
gave me food, I was thirsty and you gave me
drink, I was a stranger and you welcomed me,
naked and you clothed me. I was ill and you
comforted me, in prison and you came to visit
me.' Then the just will ask him: 'Lord, when did
we see you hungry and feed you or see you
thirsty and give you drink? When did we welcome you away from home or clothe you in your
nakedness? When did we visit you when you
were ill or in prison?' The king will answer
them: 'I assure you, as often as you did it for
one of my least brothers, you did it for me.' "
This is the gospel of the Lord.

November 12

674   **JOSAPHAT, bishop and martyr**

Memorial

Common of martyrs or pastors, p. 837 or 846.

November 15

675   **ALBERT THE GREAT, bishop
and doctor**

Common of pastors or doctors, p. 846 or 858.

November 16

676   **MARGARET OF SCOTLAND**

Common of saints [for those who work for the disadvan-
taged], p. 867.

677   **GERTRUDE, virgin**

Common of virgins or saints [for religious], p. 864 or 867,
especially Eph 3, 14-19 (no. 740, § 7), p. 877.

November 17

678   **ELIZABETH OF HUNGARY,
religious**

Memorial

Common of saints [for those who work for the disadvan-
taged, or for religious], p. 867.

November 18

679   **DEDICATION OF THE CHURCHES
OF PETER AND PAUL, apostles**

READING I   Acts 28, 11-16. 30-31

A reading from the Acts of the Apostles

So we came to Rome.

After three months in Malta we set sail in a
ship which had passed the winter at the island.
It was an Alexandrian vessel with the "Heavenly Twins" as its figurehead. We put in at
Syracuse and spent three days there. Then we
sailed around the toe and arrived at Rhegium.
A day later a south wind began to blow which
enabled us to reach Puteoli in two days. Here
we found some of the brothers, who urged us
to stay on with them for a week.

This is how we finally came to Rome. Certain brothers from Rome who heard about us
came out as far as the Forum of Appius and the
Three Taverns to meet us. When Paul saw
them, he thanked God and took courage afresh.

Upon our entry into Rome Paul was allowed to take a lodging of his own, although a soldier was assigned to keep guard over him.

For two full years Paul stayed on in his rented lodgings, welcoming all who came to him. With full assurance, and without any hindrance whatever, he preached the reign of God and taught about the Lord Jesus Christ. **This is the Word of the Lord.**

Responsorial Psalm   Ps 98, 1. 2-3. 3-4. 5-6

R̷. (2) The Lord has revealed to the nations his
    saving power.
Sing to the Lord a new song,
    for he has done wondrous deeds;
His right hand has won victory for him,
    his holy arm.
R̷. The Lord has revealed to the nations his
    saving power.
The Lord has made his salvation known:
    in the sight of the nations he has revealed
    his justice.
He has remembered his kindness and his faith-
    fulness
    toward the house of Israel.
R̷. The Lord has revealed to the nations his
    saving power.
All the ends of the earth have seen
    the salvation by our God.
Sing joyfully to the Lord, all you lands;
    break into song; sing praise.
R̷. The Lord has revealed to the nations his
    saving power.
Sing praise to the Lord with the harp,
    with the harp and melodious song.
With trumpets and the sound of the horn
    sing joyfully before the King, the Lord.
R̷. The Lord has revealed to the nations his
    saving power.

GOSPEL   Mt 14, 22-33
Alleluia

R̷. Alleluia. We praise you, God; we acknowl-
    edge you as Lord;
your glorious band of apostles extols you. R̷.
    Alleluia.

✠ **A reading from the holy gospel according
to Matthew**
Tell me to come to you over the water.

While dismissing the crowds, Jesus insisted that his disciples get into the boat and precede him to the other side. When he had sent them away, he went up on the mountain by himself to pray, remaining there alone as evening drew on. Meanwhile the boat, already several hundred yards out from shore, was being tossed about in the waves raised by strong head winds. At about three in the morning, he came walking toward them on the lake. When the disciples saw him walking on the water, they were terrified. "It is a ghost!" they said, and in their fear they began to cry out. Jesus hastened to reassure them: "Get hold of yourselves! It is I. Do not be afraid!" Peter spoke up and said, "Lord, if it is really you, tell me to come to you across the water." "Come!" he said. So Peter got out of the boat and began to walk on the water, moving toward Jesus. But when he perceived how strong the wind was, becoming frightened he began to sink, and cried out, "Lord, save me!" Jesus at once stretched out his hand and caught him. "How little faith you have!" he exclaimed. "Why did you falter?" Once they had climbed into the boat, the wind died down. Those who were in the boat showed him reverence, declaring, "Beyond doubt you are the Son of God!"
This is the gospel of the Lord.

November 21

680   PRESENTATION OF MARY
                                      Memorial
Common of the Blessed Virgin Mary, p. 826.

November 22

681   CECILIA, virgin and martyr
                                      Memorial
Common of martyrs or virgins, p. 837 or 864.

November 23

682   **CLEMENT I, pope and martyr**

Common of martyrs or pastors [for a pope], p. 837 or 846.

---

683   **COLUMBAN, abbot**

Common of pastors [for missionaries] or saints [for religious], p. 846 or 867.

November 30

684   **ANDREW, apostle**

Feast

READING I   Rom 10, 9-18

A reading from the letter of Paul to the Romans

Faith comes from what is heard and what is heard comes from the preaching of Christ.

If you confess with your lips that Jesus is Lord, and believe in your heart that God raised him from the dead, you will be saved. Faith in the heart leads to justification, confession on the lips to salvation. Scripture says, "No one who believes in him will be put to shame." Here there is no difference between Jew and Greek; all have the same Lord, rich in mercy toward all who call upon him. "Everyone who calls on the name of the Lord will be saved."

But how shall they call on him in whom they have not believed? And how can they believe unless they have heard of him? And how can they hear unless there is someone to preach? And how can men preach unless they are sent? Scripture says, "How beautiful are the feet of those who announce good news!" But not all have believed the gospel. Isaiah asks, "Lord, who has believed what he has heard from us?" Faith, then, comes through hearing, and what is heard is the word of Christ. I ask you, have they not heard? Certainly they have, for "their voice has sounded over the whole earth, and their words to the limits of the world."

This is the Word of the Lord.

Responsorial Psalm   Ps 19, 2-3. 4-5

℟. (5) Their message goes out through all the earth.

The heavens declare the glory of God,
and the firmament proclaims his handiwork.
Day pours out the word to day,
and night to night imparts knowledge.

℟. Their message goes out through all the earth.

Not a word nor a discourse
whose voice is not heard;
Through all the earth their voice resounds,
and to the end of the world, their message.

℟. Their message goes out through all the earth.

GOSPEL   Mt 4, 18-22

Alleluia   Mt 4, 19

℟. Alleluia. Come follow me, says the Lord, and I will make you fishers of men. ℟. Alleluia.

✠ **A reading from the holy gospel according to Matthew**

Immediately they left their nets and followed him.

As Jesus was walking along the Sea of Galilee he watched two brothers, Simon now known as Peter, and his brother Andrew, casting a net into the sea. They were fishermen. He said to them, "Come after me and I will make you fishers of men." They immediately abandoned their nets and became his followers. He walked along farther and caught sight of two other brothers, James, Zebedee's son, and his brother John. They too were in their boat, getting their nets in order with their father, Zebedee. He called them, and immediately they abandoned boat and father to follow him.

This is the gospel of the Lord.

DECEMBER

December 3

685   **FRANCIS XAVIER, priest**

Memorial

Common of pastors [for missionaries], p. 846, especially 1 Cor 9, 16-19. 22-23 (no. 722, § 4), p. 852, and Mk 16, 15-20 (no. 724, § 5), p. 856.

December 4

686   **JOHN DAMASCENE, priest and doctor**

Common of pastors or doctors, p. 846 or 858, especially 2 Tm 1, 13-14; 2, 1-3 (no. 728, § 6), p. 862.

December 6

687   **NICHOLAS, bishop**

Common of pastors, p. 846.

December 7

688   **AMBROSE, bishop and doctor**

Common of pastors or doctors, p. 846 or 858.   **Memorial**

December 8

689   **IMMACULATE CONCEPTION**

                   Solemnity

READING I   Gn 3, 9-15. 20

A reading from the book of Genesis

I will place enmity between your seed and the seed of the woman.

After Adam had eaten of the tree the Lord God called to the man and asked him, "Where are you?" He answered, "I heard you in the garden; but I was afraid, because I was naked, so I hid myself." Then he asked, "Who told you that you were naked? You have eaten, then, from the tree of which I had forbidden you to eat!" The man replied, "The woman whom you put here with me—she gave me fruit from the tree, and so I ate it." The Lord God then asked the woman, "Why did you do such a thing?" The woman answered, "The serpent tricked me into it, so I ate it."

Then the Lord God said to the serpent:
"Because you have done this, you shall be banned
    from all the animals
    and from all the wild creatures;
On your belly shall you crawl,
    and dirt shall you eat
    all the days of your life.

I will put enmity between you and the woman,
    and between your offspring and hers;
He will strike at your head,
    while you strike at his heel."

The man called his wife Eve, because she became the mother of all the living.

          This is the Word of the Lord.

Responsorial Psalm   Ps 98, 1. 2-3. 3-4

℞. (1) Sing to the Lord a new song,
    for he has done marvelous deeds.

Sing to the Lord a new song,
    for he has done wondrous deeds;
His right hand has won victory for him,
    his holy arm.

℞. Sing to the Lord a new song,
    for he has done marvelous deeds.

The Lord has made his salvation known:
    in the sight of the nations he has revealed
    his justice.
He has remembered his kindness and his faithfulness
    toward the house of Israel.

℞. Sing to the Lord a new song,
    for he has done marvelous deeds.

All the ends of the earth have seen
    the salvation by our God.
Sing joyfully to the Lord, all you lands;
    break into song; sing praise.

℞. Sing to the Lord a new song,
    for he has done marvelous deeds.

READING II   Eph 1, 3-6. 11-12

A reading from the letter of Paul to the Ephesians

God chose us in Christ before the foundation of the world.

Praised be the God and Father of our Lord Jesus Christ, who has bestowed on us in Christ every spiritual blessing in the heavens! God chose us in him before the world began, to be holy and blameless in his sight, to be full of love; likewise he predestined us through Christ Jesus to be his adopted sons—such was his will and pleasure—that all might praise the divine favor he has bestowed on us in his beloved.

In him we were chosen; for in the decree of God, who administers everything according to his will and counsel, we were predestined to praise his glory by being the first to hope in Christ.

This is the Word of the Lord.

GOSPEL   Lk 1, 26-38
Alleluia   Lk 1, 28

℟. Alleluia. Hail, Mary, full of grace, the Lord is with you; blessed are you among women. ℟. Alleluia.

✠ A reading from the holy gospel according to Luke

Rejoice, favored one, the Lord is with you.

The angel Gabriel was sent from God to a town of Galilee named Nazareth, to a virgin betrothed to a man named Joseph, of the house of David. The virgin's name was Mary. Upon arriving, the angel said to her: "Rejoice, O highly favored daughter! The Lord is with you. Blessed are you among women." She was deeply troubled by his words, and wondered what his greeting meant. The angel went on to say to her: "Do not fear, Mary. You have found favor with God. You shall conceive and bear a son and give him the name Jesus. Great will be his dignity and he will be called Son of the Most High. The Lord God will give him the throne of David his father. He will rule over the house of Jacob forever and his reign will be without end."

Mary said to the angel, "How can this be since I do not know man?" The angel answered her: "The Holy Spirit will come upon you and the power of the Most High will overshadow you; hence, the holy offspring to be born will be called Son of God. Know that Elizabeth your kinswoman has conceived a son in her old age; she who was thought to be sterile is now in her sixth month, for nothing is impossible with God."

Mary said: "I am the maidservant of the Lord. Let it be done to me as you say." With that the angel left her.

This is the gospel of the Lord.

December 11

690   DAMASUS I, pope

Common of pastors [for a pope], p. 846.

December 12

691   JANE FRANCES DE CHANTAL, religious

Common of saints [for religious], p. 867.

December 13

692   LUCY, virgin and martyr

Common of martyrs or virgins, p. 837 or 864.   Memorial

December 14

693   JOHN OF THE CROSS, priest and doctor   Memorial

Common of pastors or doctors, p. 846 or 858, especially 1 Cor 2, 1-10 (no. 728, § 2), p. 861.

December 21

694   PETER CANISIUS, priest and doctor

Common of pastors or doctors, p. 846 or 858.

December 23

695   JOHN OF KANTY, priest

Common of pastors [for those who work for the disadvantaged], p. 846.

December 26

696   STEPHEN, first martyr

READING I   Acts 6, 8-10; 7, 54-59

A reading from the Acts of the Apostles

I can see heaven thrown open.

Stephen was a man filled with grace and power, who worked great wonders and signs among the people. Certain members of the so-called "Synagogue of Roman Freedmen" (that is, the Jews from Cyrene, Alexandria, Cilicia and Asia) would undertake to engage Stephen in debate, but they proved no match for the wisdom and spirit with which he spoke.

Those who listened to his words were stung to the heart; they ground their teeth in anger at him. Stephen meanwhile, filled with the Holy Spirit, looked to the sky above and saw the glory of God, and Jesus standing at God's right hand. "Look!" he exclaimed, "I see an opening in the sky, and the Son of Man standing at God's right hand." The onlookers were shouting aloud, holding their hands over their ears as they did so. Then they rushed at him as one man, dragged him out of the city, and began to stone him. The witnesses meanwhile were piling their cloaks at the feet of a young man named Saul. As Stephen was being stoned he could be heard praying, "Lord Jesus, receive my spirit."

This is the Word of the Lord.

Responsorial Psalm   Ps 31, 3-4. 6. 7. 8. 17. 21

℟. (6) Into your hands, O Lord,
   I entrust my spirit.

Be my rock of refuge,
   a stronghold to give me safety.
You are my rock and my fortress;
   for your name's sake you will lead and guide
   me.

℟. Into your hands, O Lord,
   I entrust my spirit.

Into your hands I commend my spirit;
   you will redeem me, O Lord, O faithful God.
But my trust is in the Lord.
   I will rejoice and be glad of your kindness.

℟. Into your hands, O Lord,
   I entrust my spirit.

Let your face shine upon your servant;
   save me in your kindness.
You hide them in the shelter of your presence
   from the plottings of men.

℟. Into your hands, O Lord,
   I entrust my spirit.

GOSPEL   Mt 10, 17-22

Alleluia   Ps 118, 26. 27

℟. Alleluia. **Blessed is he who comes in the name of the Lord;**
the Lord God shines upon us. ℟. Alleluia.

✠ **A reading from the holy gospel according to Matthew**

It is not you who will be speaking but the Spirit of your Father.

Jesus said to his apostles: "Be on your guard with respect to others. They will hale you into court, they will flog you in their synagogues. You will be brought to trial before rulers and kings, to give witness before them and before the Gentiles on my account. When they hand you over, do not worry about what you will say or how you will say it. When the hour comes, you will be given what you are to say. You yourselves will not be the speakers; the Spirit of your Father will be speaking in you.

"Brother will hand over brother to death, and the father his child; children will turn against parents and have them put to death. You will be hated by all on account of me. But whoever holds out till the end will escape death."

This is the gospel of the Lord.

December 27

697   **JOHN, apostle and evangelist**

READING I   1 Jn 1, 1-4

The beginning of the first letter of John

What we have seen and heard we are making known to you.

This is what we proclaim to you:
what was from the beginning,
what we have heard,
what we have seen with our eyes,
what we have looked upon
and our hands have touched—
we speak of the word of life.
(This life became visible;
we have seen and bear witness to it,
and we proclaim to you the eternal life
that was present to the Father

and became visible to us.)
What we have seen and heard
we proclaim in turn to you
so that you may share life with us.
This fellowship of ours is with the Father
and with his Son, Jesus Christ.
Indeed, our purpose in writing you this
is that our joy may be complete.
This is the Word of the Lord.

Responsorial Psalm   Ps 97, 1-2. 5-6. 11-12

℟. (12) Let good men rejoice in the Lord.
The Lord is king; let the earth rejoice;
    let the many isles be glad.
Clouds and darkness are round about him,
    justice and judgment are the foundation of
    his throne.
℟. Let good men rejoice in the Lord.
The mountains melt like wax before the Lord,
    before the Lord of all the earth.
The heavens proclaim his justice,
    and all peoples see his glory.
℟. Let good men rejoice in the Lord.
Light dawns for the just;
    and gladness, for the upright of heart.
Be glad in the Lord, you just,
    and give thanks to his holy name.
℟. Let good men rejoice in the Lord.

GOSPEL   Jn 20, 2-8
Alleluia

℟. Alleluia. We praise you, God; we acknowledge you as Lord;
your glorious band of apostles extols you. ℟.
Alleluia.

✠ **A reading from the holy gospel according
to John**
The other disciple outran Peter and came first to the tomb.

On the first day of the week Mary Magdalene
ran off to Simon Peter and the other disciple
(the one Jesus loved) and told them, "The Lord
has been taken from the tomb! We do not know
where they have put him!"
    At that, Peter and the other disciple started
out on their way toward the tomb. They were
running side by side, but then the other disciple outran Peter and reached the tomb first.
He did not enter but bent down to peer in,
and saw the wrappings lying on the ground.
Presently, Simon Peter came along behind him
and entered the tomb. He observed the wrappings on the ground and saw the piece of cloth
which had covered the head not lying with the
wrappings, but rolled up in a place by itself.
Then the disciple who had arrived first at the
tomb went in. He saw and believed.
    This is the gospel of the Lord.

December 28
698   HOLY INNOCENTS, martyrs
READING I   1 Jn 1, 5—2, 2

A reading from the first letter of John
The blood of Jesus Christ cleanses us of all sin.

Here, then, is the message
we have heard from Jesus Christ
and announce to you:
that God is light;
in him there is no darkness.

If we say, "We have fellowship with him,"
while continuing to walk in darkness,
we are liars and do not act in truth.
But if we walk in light,
as he is in the light,
we have fellowship with one another,
and the blood of his Son Jesus cleanses us
    from all sin.
If we say, "We are free of the guilt of sin,"
we deceive ourselves; the truth is not to be
    found in us.
But if we acknowledge our sins,
he who is just can be trusted
to forgive our sins
and cleanse us from every wrong.
If we say, "We have never sinned,"
we make him a liar
and his word finds no place in us.

My little ones,
I am writing this to keep you from sin.
But if anyone should sin,
we have in the presence of the Father,
Jesus Christ, an intercessor who is just.

He is an offering for our sins,
and not for our sins only,
but for those of the whole world.
This is the Word of the Lord.

Responsorial Psalm   Ps 124, 2-3. 4-5. 7-8

℟. (7) Our soul has escaped like a bird from
the hunter's net.
Had not the Lord been with us—
when men rose up against us,
Then would they have swallowed us alive.
When their fury was inflamed against us.
℟. Our soul has escaped like a bird from the
hunter's net.
Then would the waters have overwhelmed us;
the torrent would have swept over us;
Over us then would have swept
the raging waters.
℟. Our soul has escaped like a bird from the
hunter's net.
Broken was the snare,
and we were freed.
Our help is in the name of the Lord,
who made heaven and earth.
℟. Our soul has escaped like a bird from the
hunter's net.

GOSPEL   Mt 2, 13-18
Alleluia

℟. Alleluia. We praise you, God; we acknowledge you as Lord;
the radiant army of martyrs acclaims you.
℟. Alleluia.

✠ **A reading from the holy gospel according**
to Matthew
Herod killed all the male children who were in Bethlehem.
After the Magi had left, the angel of the Lord
suddenly appeared in a dream to Joseph with
the command: "Get up, take the child and his

mother, and flee to Egypt. Stay there until I
tell you otherwise. Herod is searching for the
child to destroy him." Joseph got up and took
the child and his mother and left that night for
Egypt. He stayed there until the death of
Herod, to fulfill what the Lord had said
through the prophet:
"Out of Egypt I have called my son."
Once Herod realized that he had been deceived
by the astrologers, he became furious. He ordered the massacre of all the boys two years
old and under in Bethlehem and its environs,
making his calculations on the basis of the
date he had learned from the astrologers. What
was said through Jeremiah the prophet was
then fulfilled:
"A cry was heard at Ramah,
sobbing and loud lamentation:
Rachel bewailing her children;
no comfort for her, since they are no
more."
This is the gospel of the Lord.

December 29

699   **THOMAS BECKET, bishop and**
martyr
Common of martyrs or pastors, p. 837 or 846.

December 31

700   **SYLVESTER I, pope**
Common of pastors [for a pope], p. 846.

COMMONS

On celebrations in honor of the saints, in addition to the texts referred to in individual cases, the readings given in the common of saints may always be selected for pastoral reasons.

DEDICATION OF A CHURCH

701 **READING I**

OUTSIDE EASTER SEASON

1 Gn 28, 11-18

A reading from the book of Genesis

The house of God and the gate of heaven.

When Jacob came upon a certain shrine, as the sun had already set, he stopped there for the night. Taking one of the stones at the shrine, he put it under his head and lay down to sleep at that spot. Then he had a dream: a stairway rested on the ground, with its top reaching to the heavens; and God's messengers were going up and down on it. And there was the Lord standing beside him and saying:

"I, the Lord, am the God of your forefather Abraham and the God of Isaac; the land on which you are lying I will give to you and your descendants. These shall be as plentiful as the dust of the earth, and through them you shall spread out east and west, north and south. In you and your descendants all the nations of the earth shall find blessing. Know that I am with you; I will protect you wherever you go, and bring you back to this land. I will never leave you until I have done what I promised you."

When Jacob awoke from his sleep, he exclaimed, "Truly, the Lord is in this spot, although I did not know it!" In solemn wonder he cried out: "How awesome is this shrine! This is nothing else but an abode of God, and that is the gateway to heaven!" Early the next morning Jacob took the stone that he had put under his head, set it up as a memorial stone, and poured oil on top of it.

This is the Word of the Lord.

---

2 1 Kgs 8, 22-23. 27-30

A reading from the first book of Kings

Let your eyes watch over this house.

Solomon stood before the altar of the Lord in the presence of the whole community of Israel, and stretching forth his hands toward heaven, he said, "Lord, God of Israel, there is no God like you in heaven above or on earth below; you keep your covenant of kindness with your servants who are faithful to you with their whole heart.

"Can it indeed be that God dwells among men on earth? If the heavens and the highest heavens cannot contain you, how much less this temple which I have built! Look kindly on the prayer and petition of your servant, O Lord, my God, and listen to the cry of supplication which I, your servant, utter before you this day. May your eyes watch night and day over this temple, the place where you have decreed you shall be honored; may you heed the prayer which I, your servant, offer in this place. Listen to the petitions of your servant and of your people Israel which they offer in this place. Listen from your heavenly dwelling and grant pardon."

This is the Word of the Lord.

---

3 2 Chr 5, 6-10. 13—6, 2

A reading from the second book of Chronicles

I have built a dwelling-place for you to live in for ever.

King Solomon and the entire community of Israel gathered about him before the ark were sacrificing sheep and oxen so numerous that they could not be counted or numbered. The priests brought the ark of the covenant of the Lord to its place beneath the wings of the cherubim in the sanctuary, the holy of holies of the temple. The cherubim had their wings spread out over the place of the ark, sheltering the ark and its poles from above. The poles were long enough so that their ends could be seen from that part of the holy place nearest the sanctuary; however, they could not be seen beyond. The ark has remained there to this day. There was nothing in it but the two tablets which Moses put there on Horeb, the tablets of the covenant which the Lord made with the Israelites at their departure from Egypt.

When the trumpeters and singers were heard as a single voice praising and giving thanks to the Lord, and when they raised the sound of the trumpets, cymbals and other musical instruments to "give thanks to the Lord, for he is good, for his mercy endures forever," the building of the Lord's temple was filled with a cloud. The priests could not continue to minister because of the cloud, since the Lord's glory filled the house of God.

Then Solomon said: "The Lord intends to dwell in the dark cloud. I have truly built you a princely house and dwelling, where you may abide forever."

This is the Word of the Lord.

---

4   1 Mc 4, 52-59

[For the consecration of an altar]

A reading from the first book of Maccabees

They dedicated the altar and the people celebrated with great joy.

Early in the morning on the twenty-fifth day of the ninth month, that is, the month of Chislev, in the year one hundred and forty-eight, they arose and offered sacrifice according to the law on the new altar of holocausts that they had made. On the anniversary of the day on which the Gentiles had defiled it, on that very day it was reconsecrated with songs, harps, flutes, and cymbals. All the people prostrated themselves and adored and praised Heaven, who had given them success.

For eight days they celebrated the dedication of the altar and joyfully offered holocausts and sacrifices of deliverance and praise. They ornamented the façade of the temple with gold crowns and shields; they repaired the gates and the priests' chambers and furnished them with doors. There was great joy among the people now that the disgrace of the Gentiles

was removed. Then Judas and his brothers and the entire congregation of Israel decreed that the days of the dedication of the altar should be observed with joy and gladness on the anniversary every year for eight days from the twenty-fifth day of the month Chislev.

This is the Word of the Lord.

---

5   Is 56, 1. 6-7

A reading from the book of the prophet Isaiah

My house will be called a house of prayer for all the peoples.

Thus says the Lord:
Observe what is right, do what is just;
    for my salvation is about to come,
    my justice, about to be revealed.

And the foreigners who join themselves to the Lord,
    ministering to him,
Loving the name of the Lord,
    and becoming his servants—
All who keep the sabbath free from profanation
    and hold to my covenant,
Them I will bring to my holy mountain
    and make joyful in my house of prayer;
Their holocausts and sacrifices
    will be acceptable on my altar,
For my house shall be called
    a house of prayer for all peoples.

This is the Word of the Lord.

---

6   Ez 43, 1-2. 4-7

A reading from the book of the prophet Ezekiel

The glory of the Lord God filled the temple.

The angel led me to the gate which faces the east, and there I saw the glory of the God of Israel coming from the east. I heard a sound like the roaring of many waters, and the earth shone with his glory. I fell prone as the glory of the Lord entered the temple by way of the gate which faces the east, but spirit lifted me up and brought me to the inner court. And I saw that the temple was filled with the glory of the Lord. Then I heard someone speaking to me from the temple, while the man stood beside me. The voice said to me: Son of man, this is where my throne shall be, this is where I will set the soles of my feet; here I will dwell among the Israelites forever.

This is the Word of the Lord.

---

702   **READING I**

DURING EASTER SEASON

1   Acts 7, 44-50

A reading from the Acts of the Apostles
God does not live in man-made houses.

[Stephen spoke to the people, the elders and the scribes:] "Our fathers in the desert had the meeting tent as God prescribed it when he spoke to Moses, ordering him to make it according to the pattern he had seen. The next generation of our fathers inherited it. Under Joshua, they brought it into the land during the conquest of those peoples whom God drove out to make room for our fathers. So it was until the time of David, who found favor with God and begged that he might 'find a dwelling place for' the house of 'Jacob.' It was Solomon who ultimately constructed the building for that house. Yet the Most High does not dwell in buildings made by human hands, for as the prophet says:

'The heavens are my throne,
    the earth is my footstool;
What kind of house can you build me?
asks the Lord.
    What is my resting-place to be like?
Did not my hand make all these things?' "

This is the Word of the Lord.

---

2   Rv 8, 3-4

[For the consecration of an altar]

A reading from the book of Revelation
The angel stood before the altar.

I, John, saw another angel come in holding a censer of gold. He took his place at the altar of incense and was given large amounts of incense to deposit on the altar of gold in front of the throne, together with the prayers of all

God's holy ones. From the angel's hand the smoke of the incense went up before God, and with it the prayers of God's people.

This is the Word of the Lord.

---

3   Rv 21, 1-5

A reading from the book of Revelation
Behold, the home of God is among men.

I, John, saw new heavens and a new earth. The former heavens and the former earth had passed away, and the sea was no longer. I also saw a new Jerusalem, the holy city, coming down out of heaven from God, beautiful as a bride prepared to meet her husband. I heard a loud voice from the throne cry out: "This is God's dwelling among men. He shall dwell with them and they shall be his people, and he shall be their God who is always with them. He shall wipe every tear from their eyes, and there shall be no more death or mourning, crying out or pain, for the former world has passed away."

The One who sat on the throne said to me, "See, I make all things new!"

This is the Word of the Lord.

---

4   Rv 21, 9-14

A reading from the book of Revelation
I will show you the bride the Lamb has married.

The angel said to me, "Come, I will show you the woman who is the bride of the Lamb." He carried me away in spirit to the top of a very high mountain and showed me the holy city Jerusalem coming down out of heaven from God. It gleamed with the splendor of God. The city had the radiance of a precious jewel that sparkled like a diamond. Its wall, massive and high, had twelve gates at which twelve angels were stationed. Twelve names were written on the gates, the names of the twelve tribes of Israel. There were three gates facing east, three north, three south, and three west. The wall of the city had twelve courses of stones as its foundation, on which were written the names of the twelve apostles of the Lamb.

This is the Word of the Lord.

703   RESPONSORIAL PSALM

1   1 Chr 29, 10. 11. 11-12. 12

℟. (13) We praise your glorious name, O
mighty God.

Blessed may you be, O Lord,
God of Israel our father,
from eternity to eternity.

℟. We praise your glorious name, O mighty
God.

Yours, O Lord, are grandeur and power,
majesty, splendor, and glory.
For all in heaven and on earth is yours.

℟. We praise your glorious name, O mighty
God.

Yours, O Lord, is the sovereignty;
you are exalted as head over all.
Riches and honor are from you.

℟. We praise your glorious name, O mighty
God.

You have dominion over all.
in your hand are power and might;
it is yours to give grandeur and strength to
all.

℟. We praise your glorious name, O mighty
God.

----

2   Ps 84, 3. 4. 5-6. 8. 11

℟. (2) How lovely is your dwelling-place,
Lord, mighty God!

My soul yearns and pines
for the courts of the Lord.
My heart and my flesh
cry out for the living God.

℟. How lovely is your dwelling-place,
Lord, mighty God!

Even the sparrow finds a home,
and the swallow a nest
in which she puts her young—
Your altars, O Lord of hosts,
my king and my God!

℟. How lovely is your dwelling-place,
Lord, mighty God!

Happy they who dwell in your house!
continually they praise you.

Happy the men whose strength you are!
They go from strength to strength.

℟. How lovely is your dwelling-place,
Lord, mighty God!

I had rather one day in your courts
than a thousand elsewhere;
I had rather lie at the threshold of the house
of my God
than dwell in the tents of the wicked.

℟. How lovely is your dwelling-place,
Lord, mighty God!

℟. Or: (Rv 21, 3) Here God lives among his
people.

----

3   Ps 95, 1-2. 3-5. 6-7

℟. (2) Let us come before the Lord and praise
him.

Come, let us sing joyfully to the Lord;
let us acclaim the Rock of our salvation.
Let us greet him with thanksgiving;
let us joyfully sing psalms to him.

℟. Let us come before the Lord and praise
him.

For the Lord is a great God,
and a great king above all gods;
In his hands are the depths of the earth,
and the tops of the mountains are his.
His is the sea, for he has made it,
and the dry land, which his hands have
formed.

℟. Let us come before the Lord and praise
him.

Come, let us bow down in worship;
let us kneel before the Lord who made us.
For he is our God,
and we are the people he shepherds, the
flock he guides.

℟. Let us come before the Lord and praise
him.

----

4   Ps 122, 1-2. 3-4. 4-5. 8-9

℟. (1) I rejoiced when I heard them say:
let us go to the house of the Lord.

I rejoiced because they said to me,
"We will go up to the house of the Lord."
And now we have set foot
within your gates, O Jerusalem—

℟. I rejoiced when I heard them say:
let us go to the house of the Lord.

Jerusalem, built as a city
　with compact unity.
To it the tribes go up,
　the tribes of the Lord.
℟. I rejoiced when I heard them say:
　let us go to the house of the Lord.
According to the decree for Israel,
　to give thanks to the name of the Lord.
In it are set up judgment seats,
　seats for the house of David.
℟. I rejoiced when I heard them say:
　let us go to the house of the Lord.
Because of my relatives and friends
　I will say, "Peace be within you!"
Because of the house of the Lord, our God,
　I will pray for your good.
℟. I rejoiced when I heard them say:
　let us go to the house of the Lord.
℟. Or: Let us go rejoicing to the house of the
　Lord.

704　　　　**READING II**

1　　　　　　　　　　　　1 Cor 3, 9-13. 16-17

**A reading from the first letter of Paul to the
Corinthians**

You are the temple of God.

You are God's building. Thanks to the favor
God showed me I laid a foundation as a wise
master-builder might do, and now someone
else is building upon it. Everyone, however,
must be careful how he builds. No one can lay
a foundation other than the one that has been
laid, namely Jesus Christ. If different ones
build on this foundation with gold, silver, precious stones, wood, hay or straw, the work
of each will be made clear. The Day will disclose it. That day will make its appearance
with fire, and fire will test the quality of each
man's work.

　Are you not aware that you are the temple
of God, and that the Spirit of God dwells in
you? If anyone destroys God's temple, God will
destroy him. For the temple of God is holy,
and you are that temple.

This is the Word of the Lord.

2　　　　　　　　　　　　　　Eph 2, 19-22

**A reading from the letter of Paul to the
Ephesians**

Through the Lord, the whole building is bound together as
one holy temple.

You are strangers and aliens no longer. No,
you are fellow citizens of the saints and members of the household of God. You form a building which rises on the foundation of the apostles and prophets, with Christ Jesus himself as
the capstone. Through him the whole structure
is fitted together and takes shape as a holy temple in the Lord; in him you are being built into
this temple, to become a dwelling place for God
in the Spirit.

This is the Word of the Lord.

3　　　　　　　　　　　　Heb 12, 18-19. 22-24

A reading from the letter to the Hebrews

You have come to Mount Zion and to the city of the living
God.

You have not drawn near to an untouchable
mountain and a blazing fire, and gloomy darkness and storm and trumpet blast, and a voice
speaking words such that those who heard
begged that they be not addressed to them.
No, you have drawn near to Mount Zion and
the city of the living God, the heavenly Jerusalem, to myriads of angels in festal gathering,
to the assembly of the first-born enrolled in
heaven, to God the judge of all, to the spirits
of just men made perfect, to Jesus, the mediator of a new covenant, and to the sprinkled
blood which speaks more eloquently than that
of Abel.

This is the Word of the Lord.

4　　　　　　　　　　　　　　1 Pt 2, 4-9

A reading from the first letter of Peter

As living stones, you will be built into a spiritual temple.

Come to the Lord, a living stone, rejected by
men but approved, nonetheless, and precious
in God's eyes. You too are living stones, built
as an edifice of spirit, into a holy priesthood,
offering spiritual sacrifices acceptable to God
through Jesus Christ. For Scripture has it:

"See, I am laying a cornerstone in Zion,
    an approved stone, and precious.
He who puts his faith in it shall not be
    shaken."
The stone is of value for you who have faith.
For those without faith, it is rather
    "A stone which the builders rejected,
    that became a cornerstone."
It is likewise "an obstacle and a stumbling
stone." Those who stumble and fall are the dis-
believers in God's word; it belongs to their
destiny to do so.

You, however, are "a chosen race, a royal
priesthood, a consecrated nation, a people he
claims for his own to proclaim the glorious
works" of the One who called you from darkness into his marvelous light.

     This is the Word of the Lord.

---

705   **ALLELUIA VERSE AND
        VERSE BEFORE THE GOSPEL**

1   2 Chr 7, 16

I have chosen and sanctified this house, says
    the Lord,
that my name may remain in it for all time.

2   Is 66, 1

Heaven is my throne and earth is my footstool,
    says the Lord;
what is the house that you would build for me?

3   Ez 37, 27

My dwelling-place shall be with them, says the
    Lord,
and I will be their God and they will be my
    people.

4   See Mt 7, 8

In my house, says the Lord, everyone who asks
    will receive;
whoever seeks shall find; and to him who
    knocks it shall be opened.

---

706   **GOSPEL**

1   Mt 5, 23-24

✠ **A reading from the holy gospel according
        to Matthew**

Go and make peace with your brother first, then come and
offer your gift.

Jesus said to his disciples: "If you bring your
gift to the altar and there recall that your
brother has anything against you, leave your
gift at the altar, go first to be reconciled with
your brother, and then come and offer your
gift."

     This is the gospel of the Lord.

2   Lk 19, 1-10

✠ **A reading from the holy gospel according
        to Luke**

Today salvation has come to this house.

Entering Jericho, Jesus passed through the
city. There was a man there named Zacchaeus,
the chief tax collector and a wealthy man.
He was trying to see what Jesus was like,
but being small of stature, was unable to do so
because of the crowd. He first ran on in front,
then climbed a sycamore tree which was along
Jesus' route, in order to see him. When Jesus
came to the spot he looked up and said,
"Zacchaeus, hurry down. I mean to stay at
your house today." He quickly descended, and
welcomed him with delight. When this was
observed, everyone began to murmur, "He has
gone to a sinner's house as a guest." Zacchaeus
stood his ground and said to the Lord: "I give
half my belongings, Lord, to the poor. If I have
defrauded anyone in the least, I pay him back
fourfold." Jesus said to him: "Today salvation
has come to this house, for this is what it
means to be a son of Abraham. The Son of Man
has come to search out and save what was
lost."

     This is the gospel of the Lord.

3   Jn 2, 13-22

✠ A reading from the holy gospel according
to John

He spoke about the temple of his own body.

As the Jewish Passover was near, Jesus went
up to Jerusalem. In the temple precincts he
came upon people engaged in selling oxen,
sheep and doves, and others seated changing
coins. He made a [kind of] whip of cords and
drove them all out of the temple area, sheep
and oxen alike, and knocked over the money-
changers' tables, spilling their coins. He told
those who were selling doves: "Get them out of
here! Stop turning my Father's house into a
marketplace!" His disciples recalled the words
of Scripture: "Zeal for your house consumes
me."

At this the Jews responded, "What sign can
you show us authorizing you to do these
things?" "Destroy this temple," was Jesus'
answer, "and in three days I will raise it up."
They retorted, "This temple took forty-six
years to build, and you are going to 'raise it
up in three days'!" Actually he was talking
about the temple of his body. Only after Jesus
had been raised from the dead did his disciples recall that he had said this, and come to
believe the Scripture and the word he had
spoken.

This is the gospel of the Lord.

4   Jn 4, 19-24

✠ A reading from the holy gospel according
to John

True worshipers will worship the Father in spirit and in
truth.

The [Samaritan] woman said to Jesus: "Sir,
I can see you are a prophet. Our ancestors
worshiped on this mountain, but you people
claim that Jerusalem is the place where men
ought to worship God." Jesus told her:

"Believe me, woman,
an hour is coming
when you will worship the Father
neither on this mountain
nor in Jerusalem.
You people worship what you do not understand,

while we understand what we worship;
after all, salvation is from the Jews.
Yet an hour is coming, and is already here,
when authentic worshipers
will worship the Father in Spirit and truth.
Indeed, it is just such worshipers
the Father seeks.
God is Spirit,
and those who worship him
must worship in Spirit and truth."

This is the gospel of the Lord.

COMMON OF THE
BLESSED VIRGIN MARY

707   **READING I**

OUTSIDE EASTER SEASON

1   Gn 3, 9-15. 20

A reading from the book of Genesis

I will put enmity between your offspring and her offspring.

[After Adam had eaten of the fruit of the tree,]
the Lord God then called to the man and asked
him, "Where are you?" He answered, "I heard
you in the garden; but I was afraid, because
I was naked, so I hid myself." Then he asked,
"Who told you that you were naked? You have
eaten, then, from the tree of which I had
forbidden you to eat!" The man replied, "The
woman whom you put here with me—she gave
me fruit from the tree, and so I ate it." The
Lord God then asked the woman, "Why did
you do such a thing?" The woman answered,
"The serpent tricked me into it, so I ate it."

Then the Lord God said to the serpent:
"Because you have done this, you shall be
banned
from all the animals
and from all the wild creatures;
On your belly shall you crawl,
and dirt shall you eat
all the days of your life.
I will put enmity between you and the woman,
and between your offspring and hers;
He will strike at your head,
while you strike at his heel."

The man called his wife Eve, because she became the mother of all the living.
This is the Word of the Lord.

---

2   Gn 12, 1-7

A reading from the book of Genesis
He spoke to our fathers, to Abraham and his seed for ever.

**The Lord said to Abram: "Go forth from the land of your kinsfolk and from your father's house to a land that I will show you.
"I will make of you a great nation,
   and I will bless you;
I will make your name great,
   so that you will be a blessing.

"I will bless those who bless you
   and curse those who curse you.
All the communities of the earth
   shall find blessing in you."
Abram went as the Lord directed him, and Lot went with him. Abram was seventy-five years old when he left Haran. Abram took his wife Sarai, his brother's son Lot, all the possessions that they had accumulated, and the persons they had acquired in Haran, and they set out for the land of Canaan. When they came to the land of Canaan, Abram passed through the land as far as the sacred place at Shechem, by the terebinth of Moreh. (The Canaanites were then in the land.)
The Lord appeared to Abram and said, "To your descendants I will give this land." So Abram built an altar there to the Lord who had appeared to him.**
This is the Word of the Lord.

---

3   2 Sm 7, 1-5. 8-11. 16

A reading from the second book of Samuel
God will give him the seat of David, his father.

When King David was settled in his palace, and the Lord had given him rest from his enemies on every side, he said to Nathan the prophet, "Here I am living in a house of cedar, while the ark of God dwells in a tent!" Nathan answered the king, "Go, do whatever you have in mind, for the Lord is with you." But that night the Lord spoke to Nathan and said: "Go,

tell my servant David, 'Thus says the Lord: Should you build me a house to dwell in? It was I who took you from the pasture and from the care of the flock to be commander of my people Israel. I have been with you wherever you went, and I have destroyed all your enemies before you. And I will make you famous like the great ones of the earth. I will fix a place for my people Israel; I will plant them so that they may dwell in their place without further disturbance. Neither shall the wicked continue to afflict them as they did of old, since the time I first appointed judges over my people Israel. I will give you rest from all your enemies. The Lord also reveals to you that he will establish a house for you. Your house and your kingdom shall endure forever before me; your throne shall stand firm forever.' "**
This is the Word of the Lord.

---

4   1 Chr 15, 3-4. 15-16; 16, 1-2

A reading from the first book of Chronicles
They brought the ark of God in and put it inside the tent that David had pitched for it.

**David assembled all Israel in Jerusalem to bring the ark of the Lord to the place which he had prepared for it. David also called together the sons of Aaron and the Levites. The Levites bore the ark of God on their shoulders with poles, as Moses had ordained according to the word of the Lord.
David commanded the chiefs of the Levites to appoint their brethren as chanters, to play on musical instruments, harps, lyres, and cymbals to make a loud sound of rejoicing.
They brought in the ark of God and set it within the tent which David had pitched for it. Then they offered up holocausts and peace offerings to God. When David had finished offering up the holocausts and peace offerings, he blessed the people in the name of the Lord.**
This is the Word of the Lord.

---

5   Prv 8, 22-31

A reading from the book of Proverbs
Mary, seat of wisdom.

[Thus speaks the Wisdom of God:]
"The Lord begot me, the firstborn of his ways,
  the forerunner of his prodigies of long ago;
From of old I was poured forth,
  at the first, before the earth.
When there were no depths I was brought
    forth,
  when there were no fountains or springs of
    water;
Before the mountains were settled into place,
  before the hills, I was brought forth;
While as yet the earth and the fields were not
    made,
  nor the first clods of the world.
"When he established the heavens I was there,
  when he marked out the vault over the face
    of the deep;
When he made firm the skies above,
  when he fixed fast the foundations of the
    earth;
When he set for the sea its limit,
  so that the waters should not transgress his
    command;
Then was I beside him as his craftsman,
  and I was his delight day by day,
Playing before him all the while,
  playing on the surface of his earth;
[and I found delight in the sons of men.]"
      This is the Word of the Lord.

---

6   Sir 24, 1. 3-4. 8-12. 19-21

A reading from the book of Sirach
Mary, seat of wisdom.

Wisdom sings her own praises,
  before her own people she proclaims her
    glory.
"From the mouth of the Most High I came
    forth,
  and mistlike covered the earth.
In the highest heavens did I dwell,
  my throne on a pillar of cloud.
"Then the Creator of all gave me his command,

and he who formed me chose the spot for my
    tent,
Saying, 'In Jacob make your dwelling,
  in Israel your inheritance.'
Before all ages, in the beginning, he created me,
  and through all ages I shall not cease to be.
In the holy tent I ministered before him,
  and in Zion I fixed my abode.
Thus in the chosen city he has given me rest,
  in Jerusalem is my domain.
I have struck root among the glorious people,
  in the portion of the Lord, his heritage.
"You will remember me as sweeter than honey,
  better to have than the honey comb.
He who eats of me will hunger still,
  he who drinks of me will thirst for more;
He who obeys me will not be put to shame,
  he who serves me will never fail."
      This is the Word of the Lord.

---

7   Is 7, 10-14

A reading from the book of the prophet Isaiah
Behold, the virgin shall conceive.

The Lord spoke to Ahaz: Ask for a sign from
the Lord, your God; let it be deep as the
nether world, or high as the sky! But Ahaz
answered, "I will not ask! I will not tempt
the Lord!" Then he said: Listen, O house of
David! Is it not enough for you to weary
men, must you also weary my God? Therefore the Lord himself will give you this sign:
the virgin shall be with child, and bear a son,
and shall name him Immanuel.

      This is the Word of the Lord.

---

8   Is 9, 1-6

A reading from the book of the prophet Isaiah
A Son is born to us.

The people who walked in darkness
  have seen a great light;
Upon those who dwelt in the land of gloom
  a light has shone.
You have brought them abundant joy
  and great rejoicing,

As they rejoice before you as at the harvest,
    as men make merry when dividing spoils.
For the yoke that burdened them,
    the pole on their shoulder,
And the rod of their taskmaster
    you have smashed, as on the day of Midian.
For every boot that tramped in battle,
    every cloak rolled in blood,
    will be burned as fuel for flames.

For a child is born to us, a son is given us;
    upon his shoulder dominion rests.
They name him Wonder-Counselor, God-Hero,
    Father-Forever, Prince of Peace.
His dominion is vast
    and forever peaceful,
From David's throne, and over his kingdom,
    which he confirms and sustains
By judgment and justice,
    both now and forever.
The zeal of the Lord of hosts will do this!
    This is the Word of the Lord.

---

9   Is 61, 9-11

A reading from the book of the prophet Isaiah

I will rejoice in my God.

The descendants of my people shall be re-
    nowned among the nations,
    and their offspring among the peoples;
All who see them shall acknowledge them
    as a race the Lord has blessed.

I rejoice heartily in the Lord,
    in my God is the joy of my soul;
For he has clothed me with a robe of salvation,
    and wrapped me in a mantle of justice,
Like a bridegroom adorned with a diadem,
    like a bride bedecked with her jewels.
As the earth brings forth its plants,
    and a garden makes its growth spring up,
So will the Lord God make justice and praise
    spring up before all the nations.
    This is the Word of the Lord.

---

10   Mi 5, 1-4

A reading from the book of the prophet Micah

The remnant will return when she who is pregnant gives
birth.

You, Bethlehem-Ephrathah,
    too small to be among the clans of Judah,
From you shall come forth for me
    one who is to be ruler in Israel;
Whose origin is from of old,
    from ancient times.
(Therefore the Lord will give them up, until the
    time
    when she who is to give birth has borne,
And the rest of his brethren shall return
    to the children of Israel.)
He shall stand firm and shepherd his flock
    by the strength of the Lord,
    in the majestic name of the Lord, his God;
And they shall remain, for now his greatness
    shall reach to the ends of the earth;
    he shall be peace.
    This is the Word of the Lord.

---

11   Zec 2, 14-17

**A reading from the book of the prophet
Zechariah**

Rejoice, daughter of Zion, for I am coming.

Sing and rejoice, O daughter Zion! See, I am
coming to dwell among you, says the Lord.
Many nations shall join themselves to the Lord
on that day, and they shall be his people, and
he will dwell among you, and you shall know
that the Lord of hosts has sent me to you. The
Lord will possess Judah as his portion in the
holy land, and he will again choose Jerusalem.
Silence, all mankind, in the presence of the
Lord! for he stirs forth from his holy dwelling.
    This is the Word of the Lord.

---

708   **READING I**

DURING EASTER SEASON

1   Acts 1, 12-14

A reading from the Acts of the Apostles

They all joined in continuous prayer together with Jesus' mother, Mary.

[After Jesus had ascended to heaven,] the apostles returned to Jerusalem from the mount called Olivet near Jerusalem—a mere sabbath's journey away. Entering the city, they went to the upstairs room where they were staying: Peter and John and James and Andrew; Philip and Thomas, Bartholomew and Matthew; James son of Alpheus; Simon, the Zealot party member, and Judas son of James. Together they devoted themselves to constant prayer. There were some women in their company, and Mary the mother of Jesus, and his brothers.

This is the Word of the Lord.

2   Rv 11, 19; 12, 1-6. 10

A reading from the book of Revelation

A great sign appeared in the heavens.

God's temple in heaven opened and in the temple could be seen the ark of his covenant.

A great sign appeared in the sky, a woman clothed with the sun, with the moon under her feet, and on her head a crown of twelve stars. Because she was with child, she wailed aloud in pain as she labored to give birth. Then another sign appeared in the sky: it was a huge dragon, flaming red, with seven heads and ten horns; on his heads were seven diadems. His tail swept a third of the stars from the sky and hurled them down to the earth. Then the dragon stood before the woman about to give birth, ready to devour her child when it should be born. She gave birth to a son—a boy destined to shepherd all the nations with an iron rod. Her child was snatched up to God and to his throne. The woman herself fled into the desert, where a special place had been prepared for her by God.

Then I heard a loud voice in heaven say: "Now have salvation and power come,

the reign of our God and the authority of his Anointed One."

This is the Word of the Lord.

3   Rv 21, 1-5

A reading from the book of Revelation

I saw the new Jerusalem, as beautiful as a bride all dressed for her husband.

I, John, saw new heavens and a new earth. The former heavens and the former earth had passed away, and the sea was no longer. I also saw a new Jerusalem, the holy city, coming down out of heaven from God, beautiful as a bride prepared to meet her husband. I heard a loud voice from the throne cry out: "This is God's dwelling among men. He shall dwell with them and they shall be his people, and he shall be their God who is always with them. He shall wipe every tear from their eyes, and there shall be no more death or mourning, crying out or pain, for the former world has passed away."

The One who sat on the throne said to me, "See, I make all things new!"

This is the Word of the Lord.

709   **RESPONSORIAL PSALM**

1   1 Sm 2, 1. 4-5. 6-7. 8

℟. (1) My heart rejoices in the Lord, my Savior.

As Hannah worshiped the Lord, she said:
"My heart exults in the Lord,
 my horn is exalted in my God.
I have swallowed up my enemies;
 I rejoice in my victory.

℟. My heart rejoices in the Lord, my Savior.

The bows of the mighty are broken,
 while the tottering gird on strength.
The well-fed hire themselves out for bread,
 while the hungry batten on spoil.
The barren wife bears seven sons,
 while the mother of many languishes.

℟. My heart rejoices in the Lord, my Savior.

The Lord puts to death and gives life;
 he casts down to the nether world;
 he raises up again.

The Lord makes poor and makes rich,
  he humbles, he also exalts.
℟. My heart rejoices in the Lord, my Savior.
He raises the needy from the dust;
  from the ash heap he lifts up the poor,
To seat them with nobles
  and make a glorious throne their heritage."
℟. My heart rejoices in the Lord, my Savior.

---

2   Jdt 13, 18. 19. 20

℟. (9) You are the highest honor of our race.
Blessed are you, daughter, by the Most High
God, above all the women on earth; and
blessed be the Lord God, the creator of heaven
and earth.
℟. You are the highest honor of our race.
Your deed of hope will never be forgotten by
those who tell of the might of God.
℟. You are the highest honor of our race.
May God make this redound to your everlast-
ing honor, rewarding you with blessings, be-
cause you risked your life when your people
were being oppressed, and you averted our
disaster, walking uprightly before our God.
And all the people answered, "Amen! Amen!"
℟. You are the highest honor of our race.

---

3   Ps 45, 11-12. 14-15. 16-17

℟. (11) Listen to me, daughter;
  see and bend your ear.
Hear, O daughter, and see; turn your ear,
  forget your people and your father's house.
So shall the king desire your beauty;
  for he is your lord, and you must worship
  him.
℟. Listen to me, daughter;
  see and bend your ear.
All glorious is the king's daughter as she
  enters;
  her raiment is threaded with spun gold.
In embroidered apparel she is borne in to the
  king;
  behind her the virgins of her train are
  brought to you.
℟. Listen to me, daughter;
  see and bend your ear.

They are borne in with gladness and joy;
  they enter the palace of the king.
The place of your fathers your sons shall have;
  you shall make them princes through all
  the land.
℟. Listen to me, daughter;
  see and bend your ear.

---

4   Ps 113, 1-2. 3-4. 5-6. 7-8

℟. (2) Blessed be the name of the Lord for ever.
Praise, you servants of the Lord,
  praise the name of the Lord.
Blessed be the name of the Lord
  both now and forever.
℟. Blessed be the name of the Lord for ever.
From the rising to the setting of the sun
  is the name of the Lord to be praised.
High above all nations is the Lord;
  above the heavens is his glory.
℟. Blessed be the name of the Lord for ever.
Who is like the Lord, our God, who is en-
  throned on high
  and looks upon the heavens and the earth
  below?
℟. Blessed be the name of the Lord for ever.
He raises up the lowly from the dust;
  from the dunghill he lifts up the poor
To seat them with princes,
  with the princes of his own people.
℟. Blessed be the name of the Lord for ever.
℟. Or: Alleluia.

---

5   Lk 1, 46-47. 48-49. 50-51. 52-53. 54-55

℟. (49) The Almighty has done great things
  for me and holy is his name.
Mary said:
"My being proclaims the greatness of the Lord,
  my spirit finds joy in God my savior.
℟. The Almighty has done great things for me
  and holy is his name.
For he has looked upon his servant in her
  lowliness;
  all ages to come shall call me blessed.
God who is mighty has done great things for
  me,
  holy is his name.

℞. The Almighty has done great things for me
and holy is his name.
**His mercy is from age to age
on those who fear him.
He has shown might with his arm;**
he has confused the proud in their inmost
thoughts.
℞. The Almighty has done great things for me
and holy is his name.
**He has deposed the mighty from their thrones
and raised the lowly to high places.
The hungry he has given every good thing,
while the rich he has sent empty away.**
℞. The Almighty has done great things for me
and holy is his name.
**He has upheld Israel his servant,
ever mindful of his mercy;
Even as he promised our fathers,**
promised Abraham and his descendants forever."
℞. The Almighty has done great things for me
and holy is his name.
℞. Or: O Blessed Virgin Mary, you carried the
Son of the eternal Father.

---

710   **READING II**

1   Rom 5, 12. 17-19

A reading from the letter of Paul to the Romans
However great the number of sins committed, grace was
even greater.

**Just as through one man sin entered the world
and with sin death, so death came to all men
inasmuch as all sinned. If death began its reign
through one man because of his offense, much
more shall those who receive the overflowing
grace and gift of justice live and reign through
the one man, Jesus Christ.**
   **To sum up, then: just as a single offense
brought condemnation to all men, a single
righteous act brought all men acquittal and
life. Just as through one man's disobedience all
became sinners, so through one man's obedience all shall become just.**
      This is the Word of the Lord.

---

2   Rom 8, 28-30

A reading from the letter of Paul to the Romans
God knew them and called them to justification.

**We know that God makes all things work
together for the good of those who have been
called according to his decree. Those whom he
foreknew he predestined to share the image of
his Son, that the Son might be the first-born of
many brothers. Those he predestined he likewise called; those he called he also justified;
and those he justified he in turn glorified.**
      This is the Word of the Lord.

---

3   Gal 4, 4-7

**A reading from the letter of Paul to the
Galatians**
God sent his Son, born of a woman.

**When the designated time had come, God sent
forth his Son born of a woman, born under the
law, to deliver from the law those who were
subjected to it, so that we might receive our
status as adopted sons. The proof that you are
sons is the fact that God has sent forth into
our hearts the spirit of his Son which cries out
"Abba!" ("Father!") You are no longer a slave
but a son! And the fact that you are a son
makes you an heir, by God's design.**
      This is the Word of the Lord.

---

4   Eph 1, 3-6. 11-12

**A reading from the letter of Paul to the
Ephesians**
Before the world was made, God chose us in Christ.

**Praised be the God and Father of our Lord
Jesus Christ, who has bestowed on us in Christ
every spiritual blessing in the heavens! God
chose us in him before the world began, to be
holy and blameless in his sight, to be full of
love; he likewise predestined us through Christ
Jesus to be his adopted sons—such was his will
and pleasure—that all might praise the divine
favor he has bestowed on us in his beloved.**
   **In him we were chosen; for in the decree of
God, who administers everything according
to his will and counsel, we were predestined**

to praise his glory by being the first to hope in Christ.

This is the Word of the Lord.

---

711   **ALLELUIA VERSE AND VERSE BEFORE THE GOSPEL**

1   Lk 1, 28

Hail, Mary, full of grace, the Lord is with you; blessed are you among women.

2   Lk 1, 45

Blessed are you, O Virgin Mary, for your firm believing,
that the promises of the Lord would be fulfilled.

3   See Lk 2, 19

Blessed is the Virgin Mary who kept the word of God,
and pondered it in her heart.

4

Happy are you, holy Virgin Mary, deserving of all praise;
from you rose the sun of justice, Christ the Lord.

---

712   **GOSPEL**

1   Mt 1, 1-16. 18-23 or 1, 18-23

(Long Form)

✠ **The beginning of the holy gospel according to Matthew**

She has conceived and what is in her is by the Holy Spirit.

A family record of Jesus Christ, son of David, son of Abraham. Abraham was the father of Isaac, Isaac the father of Jacob, Jacob the father of Judah and his brothers.
Judah was the father of Perez and Zerah, whose mother was Tamar.
Perez was the father of Hezron,
Hezron the father of Ram.
Ram was the father of Amminadab,
Amminadab the father of Nahshon,
Nahshon the father of Salmon.
Salmon was the father of Boaz, whose mother was Rahab,
Boaz was the father of Obed, whose mother was Ruth.
Obed was the father of Jesse,
Jesse the father of King David.
David was the father of Solomon, whose mother had been the wife of Uriah.
Solomon was the father of Rehoboam,
Rehoboam the father of Abijah,
Abijah the father of Asa.
Asa was the father of Jehoshaphat,
Jehoshaphat the father of Joram,
Joram the father of Uzziah.
Uzziah was the father of Jotham,
Jotham the father of Ahaz,
Ahaz the father of Hezekiah.
Hezekiah was the father of Manasseh,
Manasseh the father of Amos,
Amos the father of Josiah.
Josiah became the father of Jechoniah and his brothers at the time of the Babylonian exile.
After the Babylonian exile
Jechoniah was the father of Shealtiel,
Shealtiel the father of Zerubbabel.
Zerubbabel was the father of Abiud,
Abiud the father of Eliakim,
Eliakim the father of Azor.
Azor was the father of Zadok,
Zadok the father of Achim,
Achim the father of Eliud.
Eliud was the father of Eleazar,
Eleazar the father of Matthan,
Matthan the father of Jacob.
Jacob was the father of Joseph the husband of Mary.
It was of her that Jesus who is called the Messiah was born.

Now this is how the birth of Jesus Christ came about. When his mother Mary was engaged to Joseph, but before they lived together, she was found with child through the power of the Holy Spirit. Joseph her husband, an upright man unwilling to expose her to the law, decided to divorce her quietly. Such was his intention when suddenly the angel of the Lord appeared in a dream and said to him: "Joseph, son of David, have no fear about taking Mary as your wife. It is by the Holy Spirit that she has conceived this child. She is to have a son and you are to name him Jesus because he will save his people from their sins." All this happened to fulfill what the Lord had said through the prophet:

"The virgin shall be with child
and give birth to a son,
and they shall call him Emmanuel,"

a name which means "God is with us."

This is the gospel of the Lord.

OR
(Short Form)

✠ A reading from the holy gospel according to Matthew

She has conceived and what is in her is by the Holy Spirit.

Now this is how the birth of Jesus Christ came about. When his mother Mary was engaged to Joseph, but before they lived together, she was found with child through the power of the Holy Spirit. Joseph her husband, an upright man unwilling to expose her to the law, decided to divorce her quietly. Such was his intention when suddenly the angel of the Lord appeared in a dream and said to him: "Joseph, son of David, have no fear about taking Mary as your wife. It is by the Holy Spirit that she has conceived this child. She is to have a son and you are to name him Jesus because he will save his people from their sins." All this happened to fulfill what the Lord had said through the prophet:

"The virgin shall be with child
and give birth to a son,
and they shall call him Emmanuel,"

a name which means "God is with us."

This is the gospel of the Lord.

---

2   Mt 2, 13-15. 19-23

✠ A reading from the holy gospel according to Matthew

Take the child and his mother and flee into Egypt.

After the astrologers had departed from Bethlehem, the angel of the Lord suddenly appeared in a dream to Joseph with the command: "Get up, take the child and his mother, and flee to Egypt. Stay there until I tell you otherwise. Herod is searching for the child to destroy him." Joseph got up and took the child and his mother and left that night for Egypt. He stayed there until the death of Herod, to fulfill what the Lord had said through the prophet:

"Out of Egypt I have called my son."

But after Herod's death, the angel of the Lord appeared in a dream to Joseph in Egypt with the command: "Get up, take the child and his mother, and set out for the land of Israel. Those who had designs on the life of the child are dead." He got up, took the child and his mother, and returned to the land of Israel. He heard, however, that Archelaus had succeeded his father Herod as king of Judea, and he was afraid to go back there. Instead, because of a warning received in a dream, Joseph went to the region of Galilee. There he settled in a town called Nazareth. In this way what was said through the prophets was fulfilled:

"He shall be called a Nazorean."

This is the gospel of the Lord.

---

3   Lk 1, 26-38

✠ A reading from the holy gospel according to Luke

You will conceive and bear a son.

The angel Gabriel was sent from God to a town of Galilee named Nazareth, to a virgin betrothed to a man named Joseph, of the house of David. The virgin's name was Mary. Upon arriving, the angel said to her: "Rejoice, O highly favored daughter! The Lord is with you. Blessed are you among women." She was deeply troubled by his words, and wondered what his greeting meant. The angel went on to say to her: "Do not fear, Mary. You have found favor with God. You shall conceive and bear a son and give him the name Jesus. Great will be his dignity and he will be called Son of the Most High. The Lord God will give him the throne of David his father. He will rule over the house of Jacob forever and his reign will be without end."

Mary said to the angel, "How can this be

since I do not know man?" The angel answered her: "The Holy Spirit will come upon you and the power of the Most High will overshadow you; hence, the holy offspring to be born will be called Son of God. Know that Elizabeth your kinswoman has conceived a son in her old age; she who was thought to be sterile is now in her sixth month, for nothing is impossible with God."

Mary said: "I am the maidservant of the Lord. Let it be done to me as you say." With that the angel left her.

This is the gospel of the Lord.

---

4   Lk 1, 39-47

✠ A reading from the holy gospel according to Luke

Blessed is she who believed.

Mary set out, proceeding in haste into the hill country to a town of Judah, where she entered Zechariah's house and greeted Elizabeth. When Elizabeth heard Mary's greeting, the baby stirred in her womb. Elizabeth was filled with the Holy Spirit and cried out in a loud voice: "Blessed are you among women and blessed is the fruit of your womb. But who am I that the mother of my Lord should come to me? The moment your greeting sounded in my ears, the baby stirred in my womb for joy. Blessed is she who trusted that the Lord's words to her would be fulfilled."

Then Mary said:

"My being proclaims the greatness of the Lord,

my spirit finds joy in God my savior."

This is the gospel of the Lord.

---

5   Lk 2, 1-14

✠ A reading from the holy gospel according to Luke

She gave birth to a son, her firstborn.

In those days Caesar Augustus published a decree ordering a census of the whole world. This first census took place while Quirinius was governor of Syria. Everyone went to register, each to his own town. And so Joseph went from the town of Nazareth in Galilee to Judea, to David's town of Bethlehem—because he was of the house and lineage of David—to register with Mary, his espoused wife, who was with child.

While they were there the days of her confinement were completed. She gave birth to her first-born son and wrapped him in swaddling clothes and laid him in a manger, because there was no room for them in the place where travelers lodged.

There were shepherds in the locality, living in the fields and keeping night watch by turns over their flocks. The angel of the Lord appeared to them as the glory of the Lord shone around them, and they were very much afraid. The angel said to them: "You have nothing to fear! I come to proclaim good news to you—tidings of great joy to be shared by the whole people. This day in David's city a savior has been born to you, the Messiah and Lord. Let this be a sign to you: in a manger you will find an infant wrapped in swaddling clothes." Suddenly, there was with the angel a multitude of the heavenly host, praising God and saying,

"Glory to God in high heaven,

peace on earth to those on whom his favor rests."

This is the gospel of the Lord.

---

6   Lk, 2, 15-19

✠ A reading from the holy gospel according to Luke

Mary treasured all these things and pondered them in her heart.

The shepherds said to one another: "Let us go over to Bethlehem and see this event which the Lord has made known to us." They went in haste and found Mary and Joseph, and the baby lying in the manger; once they saw, they understood what had been told them concerning this child. All who heard of it were astonished at the report given them by the shepherds.

Mary treasured all these things and reflected on them in her heart.

This is the gospel of the Lord.

7   Lk 2, 27-35

✠ A reading from the holy gospel according
to Luke

A sword will pierce your own soul.

Simeon came to the temple, inspired by the
Spirit; and when the parents brought in the
child Jesus to perform for him the customary
ritual of the law, he took him in his arms and
blessed God in these words:

"Now, Master, you can dismiss your servant in peace;
you have fulfilled your word.
For my eyes have witnessed your saving
deed
displayed for all the peoples to see:
A revealing light to the Gentiles,
the glory of your people Israel."

The child's father and mother were marveling at what was being said about him. Simeon
blessed them and said to Mary his mother:
"This child is destined to be the downfall and
the rise of many in Israel, a sign that will be
opposed—and you yourself shall be pierced
with a sword—so that the thoughts of many
hearts may be laid bare."

This is the gospel of the Lord.

---

8   Lk 2, 41-52

✠ A reading from the holy gospel according
to Luke

Your father and I have been looking for you.

The parents of Jesus used to go every year to
Jerusalem for the feast of the Passover, and
when he was twelve they went up for the
celebration as was their custom. As they were
returning at the end of the feast, the child
Jesus remained behind unknown to his parents. Thinking he was in the party, they continued their journey for a day, looking for him
among their relatives and acquaintances.

Not finding him, they returned to Jerusalem in search of him. On the third day they
came upon him in the temple sitting in the
midst of the teachers, listening to them and
asking them questions. All who heard him
were amazed at his intelligence and his answers.

When his parents saw him they were astonished, and his mother said to him: "Son,
why have you done this to us? You see that
your father and I have been searching for you
in sorrow." He said to them: "Why did you
search for me? Did you not know I had to be in
my Father's house?" But they did not grasp
what he said to them.

He went down with them then, and came to
Nazareth, and was obedient to them. His
mother meanwhile kept all these things in
memory. Jesus, for his part, progressed steadily in wisdom and age and grace before God
and men.

This is the gospel of the Lord.

---

9   Lk 11, 27-28

✠ A reading from the holy gospel according
to Luke

Happy the womb that bore you!

While Jesus was speaking to the crowd a
woman called out, "Blest is the womb that
bore you and the breasts that nursed you!"
"Rather," he replied, "blest are they who hear
the word of God and keep it."

This is the gospel of the Lord.

---

10   Jn 2, 1-11

✠ A reading from the holy gospel according
to John

The mother of Jesus was at the wedding feast with him.

There was a wedding at Cana in Galilee, and
the mother of Jesus was there. Jesus and his
disciples had likewise been invited to the celebration. At a certain point the wine ran out,
and Jesus' mother told him, "They have no
more wine." Jesus replied, "Woman, how does
this concern of yours involve me? My hour
has not yet come." His mother instructed those
waiting on table, "Do whatever he tells you."
As prescribed for Jewish ceremonial washings,
there were at hand six stone water jars, each
one holding fifteen to twenty-five gallons. "Fill
those jars with water," Jesus ordered, at which
they filled them to the brim. "Now," he said,
"draw some out and take it to the waiter in

charge." They did as he instructed them. The waiter in charge tasted the water made wine, without knowing where it had come from; only the waiters knew, since they had drawn the water. Then the waiter in charge called the groom over and remarked to him: "People usually serve the choice wine first; then when the guests have been drinking a while, a lesser vintage. What you have done is keep the choice wine until now." Jesus performed this first of his signs at Cana in Galilee. Thus did he reveal his glory, and his disciples believed in him.

This is the gospel of the Lord.

11　　　　　　　　　　　　　　　　Jn 19, 25-27

✠ A reading from the holy gospel according to John

Woman, this is your son. This is your mother.

Near the cross of Jesus there stood his mother, his mother's sister, Mary the wife of Clopas, and Mary Magdalene. Seeing his mother there with the disciple whom he loved, Jesus said to his mother, "Woman, there is your son." In turn he said to the disciple, "There is your mother." From that hour onward, the disciple took her into his care.

This is the gospel of the Lord.

COMMON OF MARTYRS

713　　　　　　**READING I**
OUTSIDE EASTER SEASON

1　　　　　　　　　　　　　　　　2 Chr 24, 18-22

A reading from the second book of Chronicles

Zechariah, whom you murdered between the sanctuary and the altar.

The princes of Judah forsook the temple of the Lord, the God of their fathers, and began to serve the sacred poles and the idols; and because of this crime of theirs, wrath came upon Judah and Jerusalem. Although prophets were sent to them to convert them to the Lord, the people would not listen to their warnings. Then the spirit of God possessed Zechariah, son of Jehoiada the priest. He took his stand above

the people and said to them: "God says, 'Why are you transgressing the Lord's commands, so that you cannot prosper? Because you have abandoned the Lord, he has abandoned you.' " But they conspired against him, and at the king's order they stoned him to death in the court of the Lord's temple. Thus King Joash was unmindful of the devotion shown him by Jehoiada, Zechariah's father, and slew his son. And as he was dying, he said, "May the Lord see and avenge."

This is the Word of the Lord.

2　　　　　　　　　　　　　　　2 Mc 6, 18. 21. 24-31

A reading from the second book of Maccabees

Because of the awe the Lord inspires in me, I will suffer gladly.

Eleazar, one of the foremost scribes, a man of advanced age and noble appearance, was being forced to open his mouth to eat pork. Those in charge of that unlawful ritual meal took the man aside privately, because of their long acquaintance with him, and urged him to bring meat of his own providing, such as he could legitimately eat, and to pretend to be eating some of the meat of the sacrifice prescribed by the king. He told them: "At our age it would be unbecoming to make such a pretense; many young men would think the ninety-year old Eleazar had gone over to an alien religion. Should I thus dissimulate for the sake of a brief moment of life, they would be led astray by me, while I would bring shame and dishonor on my old age. Even if, for the time being, I avoid the punishment of men, I shall never, whether alive or dead, escape the hands of the Almighty. Therefore, by manfully giving up my life now, I will prove myself worthy of my old age, and I will leave to the young a noble example of how to die willingly and generously for the revered and holy laws."

He spoke thus, and went immediately to the instrument of torture. Those who shortly before had been kindly disposed, now became hostile toward him because what he had said seemed to them utter madness. When he was about to die under the blows, he groaned and said: "The Lord in his holy knowledge knows full well that, although I could have escaped death, I am not only enduring terrible pain in my body from this scourging, but also suffering it with joy in my soul because of my devotion to him." This is how he died, leaving in his death a model of courage and an unforgettable example of virtue not only for the young but for the whole nation.

This is the Word of the Lord.

---

3   2 Mc 7, 1-2. 9-14

A reading from the second book of Maccabees
We are prepared to die rather than to break the laws of our ancestors.

It happened that seven brothers with their mother were arrested and tortured with whips and scourges by the king, to force them to eat pork in violation of God's law. One of the brothers, speaking for the others, said: "What do you expect to achieve by questioning us? We are ready to die rather than transgress the laws of our ancestors."

[The second brother] at the point of death said: "You accursed fiend, you are depriving us of this present life, but the King of the world will raise us up to live again forever. It is for his laws that we are dying."

After him the third suffered their cruel sport. He put out his tongue at once when told to do so, and bravely held out his hands, as he spoke these noble words: "It was from Heaven that I received these; for the sake of his laws I disdain them; from him I hope to receive them again." Even the king and his attendants marveled at the young man's courage, because he regarded his sufferings as nothing.

After he had died, they tortured and maltreated the fourth brother in the same way. When he was near death, he said, "It is my choice to die at the hands of men with the God-given hope of being restored to life by him; but for you, there will be no resurrection to life."

This is the Word of the Lord.

---

4   2 Mc 7, 1. 20-23. 27-29

A reading from the second book of Maccabees
Because of her hopes in the Lord, this admirable mother bore their deaths with honor.

It happened that seven brothers with their mother were arrested and tortured with whips and scourges by the king, to force them to eat pork in violation of God's law.

Most admirable and worthy of everlasting remembrance was the mother, who saw her seven sons perish in a single day, yet bore it courageously because of her hope in the Lord. Filled with a noble spirit that stirred her womanly heart with manly courage, she exhorted each of them in the language of their forefathers with these words: "I do not know how you came into existence in my womb; it was not I who gave you the breath of life, nor was it I who set in order the elements of which each of you is composed. Therefore, since it is the Creator of the universe who shapes each man's beginning, as he brings about the origin of everything, he, in his mercy, will give you back both breath and life, because you now disregard yourselves for the sake of his law.

"Son, have pity on me, who carried you in my womb for nine months, nursed you for three years, brought you up, educated and supported you to your present age. I beg you, child, to look at the heavens and the earth and see all that is in them; then you will know that God did not make them out of existing things; and in the same way the human race came into existence. Do not be afraid of this executioner, but be worthy of your brothers and accept death, so that in the time of mercy I may receive you again with them."

This is the Word of the Lord.

---

5   Wis 3, 1-9

A reading from the book of Wisdom
He accepted them as a holocaust.

The souls of the just are in the hand of God,
    and no torment shall touch them.
They seemed, in the view of the foolish, to be
    dead;

and their passing away was thought an affliction
and their going forth from us, utter destruction.
But they are in peace.
For if before men, indeed, they be punished,
yet is their hope full of immortality;
Chastised a little, they shall be greatly blessed,
because God tried them
and found them worthy of himself.
As gold in the furnace, he proved them,
and as sacrificial offerings he took them to himself.
In the time of their visitation they shall shine,
and shall dart about as sparks through stubble;
They shall judge nations and rule over peoples,
and the Lord shall be their King forever.
Those who trust in him shall understand truth,
and the faithful shall abide with him in love:
Because grace and mercy are with his holy ones,
and his care is with his elect.
This is the Word of the Lord.

---

6   Sir 51, 1-8

A reading from the book of Sirach

You redeemed me, true to the greatness of your mercy
and of your name.

I give you thanks, O God of my father;
I praise you, O God my savior!
I will make known your name, refuge of my life;
you have been my helper against my adversaries.
You have saved me from death,
and kept back my body from the pit.
From the clutches of the nether world you have snatched my feet;
you have delivered me, in your great mercy
From the scourge of a slanderous tongue,
and from lips that went over to falsehood;
From the snare of those who watched for my downfall,
and from the power of those who sought my life;
From many a danger you have saved me,
from flames that hemmed me in on every side;

From the midst of unremitting fire,
from the deep belly of the nether world;
From deceiving lips and painters of lies,
from the arrows of dishonest tongues.
I was at the point of death,
my soul was nearing the depths of the nether world;
I turned every way, but there was no one to help me,
I looked for one to sustain me, but could find no one.
But then I remembered the mercies of the Lord,
his kindness through ages past;
For he saves those who take refuge in him,
and rescues them from every evil.
This is the Word of the Lord.

---

714   **READING I**

DURING EASTER SEASON

1   Acts 7, 55-60

A reading from the Acts of the Apostles

Lord Jesus, receive my spirit.

Stephen, filled with the Holy Spirit, looked to the sky above and saw the glory of God, and Jesus standing at God's right hand. "Look!" he exclaimed, "I see an opening in the sky, and the Son of Man standing at God's right hand." The onlookers were shouting aloud, holding their hands over their ears as they did so. Then they rushed at him as one man, dragged him out of the city, and began to stone him. The witnesses meanwhile were piling their cloaks at the feet of a young man named Saul. As Stephen was being stoned he could be heard praying, "Lord Jesus, receive my spirit." He fell to his knees and cried out in a loud voice, "Lord, do not hold this sin against them." And with that he died.
This is the Word of the Lord.

---

2   Rv 7, 9-17

A reading from the book of Revelation

These are the people who have been through the great persecution.

I, John, saw before me a huge crowd which no one could count from every nation and race, people and tongue. They stood before the throne and the Lamb, dressed in long white robes and holding palm branches in their hands. They cried out in a loud voice, "Salvation is from our God, who is seated on the throne, and from the Lamb!" All the angels who were standing around the throne and the elders and the four living creatures fell down before the throne to worship God. They said: "Amen! Praise and glory, wisdom, thanksgiving, and honor, power and might to our God forever and ever. Amen!"

Then one of the elders asked me, "Who are these, all dressed in white? And where have they come from?" I said to him, "Sir, you should know better that I." He then told me, "These are the ones who have survived the great period of trial; they have washed their robes and made them white in the blood of the Lamb.

"It was this that brought them before God's throne:
day and night they minister to him in his temple;
he who sits on the throne will give them shelter.
Never again shall they know hunger or thirst, nor shall the sun or its heat beat down on them,
for the Lamb on the throne will shepherd them.
He will lead them to springs of life-giving water,
and God will wipe every tear from their eyes."

    This is the Word of the Lord.

---

3   Rv 12, 10-12

A reading from the book of Revelation

Even in the face of death these martyrs would not cling to life.

I, John, heard a loud voice in heaven say:
"Now have salvation and power come,
the reign of our God and the authority of his Anointed One.
For the accuser of our brothers is cast out, who night and day accused them before our God.

They defeated him by the blood of the Lamb and by the word of their testimony;
love for life did not deter them from death.
So rejoice, you heavens,
and you that dwell therein!"

    This is the Word of the Lord.

---

4   Rv 21, 5-7

A reading from the book of Revelation

He who conquers shall have this heritage.

The One who sat on the throne said to me, "See, I make all things new!" Then he said, "Write these matters down, for the words are trustworthy and true!" He went on to say: "These words are already fulfilled! I am the Alpha and the Omega, the Beginning and the End. To anyone who thirsts I will give to drink without cost from the spring of life-giving water. He who wins the victory shall inherit these gifts; I will be his God and he shall be my son."

    This is the Word of the Lord.

---

715   **RESPONSORIAL PSALM**

1   Ps 31, 3-4. 6. 7. 8. 17. 21

℟. (6) Into your hands, O Lord,
    I entrust my spirit.
Be my rock of refuge,
    a stronghold to give me safety.
You are my rock and my fortress;
    for your name's sake you will lead and guide me.
℟. Into your hands, O Lord,
    I entrust my spirit.
Into your hands I commend my spirit;
    you will redeem me, O Lord, O faithful God.
My trust is in the Lord.
    I will rejoice and be glad of your kindness.
℟. Into your hands, O Lord,
    I entrust my spirit.
Let your face shine upon your servant;
    save me in your kindness.
You hide them in the shelter of your presence
    from the plottings of men.
℟. Into your hands, O Lord,
    I entrust my spirit.

2   Ps 34, 2-3. 4-5. 6-7. 8-9

℟. (5) The Lord set me free from all my fears.

I will bless the Lord at all times;
  his praise shall be ever in my mouth.
Let my soul glory in the Lord;
  the lowly will hear me and be glad.

℟. The Lord set me free from all my fears.

Glorify the Lord with me,
  let us together extol his name.
I sought the Lord, and he answered me
  and delivered me from all my fears.

℟. The Lord set me free from all my fears.

Look to him that you may be radiant with joy,
  and your faces may not blush with shame.
When the afflicted man called out, the Lord
    heard,
  and from all his distress he saved him.

℟. The Lord set me free from all my fears.

The angel of the Lord encamps
    around those who fear him, and delivers
    them.
Taste and see how good the Lord is;
  happy the man who takes refuge in him.

℟. The Lord set me free from all my fears.

---

3   Ps 124, 2-3. 4-5. 7-8

℟. (3) Our soul has escaped like a bird from
    the hunter's net.

Had not the Lord been with us—
  when men rose up against us,
Then would they have swallowed us alive,
  when their fury was inflamed against us.

℟. Our soul has escaped like a bird from the
    hunter's net.

Then would the waters have overwhelmed us;
  the torrent would have swept over us;
Over us then would have swept
  the raging waters.

℟. Our soul has escaped like a bird from the
    hunter's net.

Broken was the snare,
  and we were freed.
Our help is in the name of the Lord,
  who made heaven and earth.

℟. Our soul has escaped like a bird from the
    hunter's net.

---

4   Ps 126, 1-2. 2-3. 4-5. 6

℟. (5) Those who sow in tears, shall reap with
    shouts of joy.

When the Lord brought back the captives of
    Zion,
  we were like men dreaming.
Then our mouth was filled with laughter,
  and our tongue with rejoicing.

℟. Those who sow in tears, shall reap with
    shouts of joy.

Then they said among the nations,
  "The Lord has done great things for them."
The Lord has done great things for us;
  we are glad indeed.

℟. Those who sow in tears, shall reap with
    shouts of joy.

Restore our fortunes, O Lord,
  like the torrents in the southern desert.
Those that sow in tears
  shall reap rejoicing.

℟. Those who sow in tears, shall reap with
    shouts of joy.

Although they go forth weeping,
  carrying the seed to be sown,
They shall come back rejoicing,
  carrying their sheaves.

℟. Those who sow in tears, shall reap with
    shouts of joy.

---

716   **READING II**

1   Rom 5, 1-5

A reading from the letter of Paul to the Romans
We boast about our sufferings.

Now that we have been justified by faith, we
are at peace with God through our Lord Jesus
Christ. Through him we have gained access
by faith to the grace in which we now stand,
and we boast of our hope for the glory of God.
But not only that—we even boast of our afflictions! We know that affliction makes for
endurance, and endurance for tested virtue,
and tested virtue for hope. And this hope will
not leave us disappointed, because the love of
God has been poured out in our hearts through
the Holy Spirit who has been given to us.
  This is the Word of the Lord.

2 Rom 8, 31-39

A reading from the letter of Paul to the Romans

Neither death nor life can ever come between us and the love of God.

If God is for us, who can be against us? Is it possible that he who did not spare his own Son but handed him over for the sake of us all will not grant us all things besides? Who shall bring a charge against God's chosen ones? God, who justifies? Who shall condemn them? Christ Jesus, who died or rather was raised up, who is at the right hand of God and who intercedes for us?

Who will separate us from the love of Christ? Trial, or distress, or persecution, or hunger, or nakedness, or danger, or the sword? As Scripture says: "For your sake we are being slain all the day long; we are looked upon as sheep to be slaughtered." Yet in all this we are more than conquerors because of him who has loved us. For I am certain that neither death nor life, neither angels nor principalities, neither the present nor the future, nor powers, neither height nor depth nor any other creature, will be able to separate us from the love of God that comes to us in Christ Jesus, our Lord.

This is the Word of the Lord.

---

3 2 Cor 4, 7-15

A reading from the second letter of Paul to the Corinthians

We carry in our bodies the death and life of Jesus.

We possess our treasure in earthen vessels to make it clear that its surpassing power comes from God and not from us. We are afflicted in every way possible, but we are not crushed; full of doubts, we never despair. We are persecuted but never abandoned; we are struck down but never destroyed. Continually we carry about in our bodies the dying of Jesus, so that in our bodies the life of Jesus may also be revealed. While we live we are constantly being delivered to death for Jesus' sake, so that the life of Jesus may be revealed in our mortal flesh. Death is at work in us, but life in you.

We have that spirit of faith of which the Scripture says, "Because I believed, I spoke out." We believed and so we speak, knowing that he who raised up the Lord Jesus will raise us up along with Jesus and place both us and you in his presence. Indeed, everything is ordered to your benefit, so that the grace bestowed in abundance may bring greater glory to God because they who give thanks are many.

This is the Word of the Lord.

---

4 2 Cor 6, 4-10

A reading from the second letter of Paul to the Corinthians

We are said to be dying and yet here we are alive.

In all that we do we strive to present ourselves as ministers of God, acting with patient endurance amid trials, difficulties, distresses, beatings, imprisonments, and riots; as men familiar with hard work, sleepless nights, and fastings; conducting ourselves with innocence, knowledge, and patience, in the Holy Spirit, in sincere love; as men with the message of truth and the power of God; wielding the weapons of righteousness with right hand and left, whether honored or dishonored, spoken of well or ill. We are called imposters, yet we are truthful; nobodies who in fact are well known; dead, yet here we are, alive; punished, but not put to death; sorrowful, though we are always rejoicing; poor, yet we enrich many. We seem to have nothing, yet everything is ours!

This is the Word of the Lord.

---

5 2 Tm 2, 8-13; 3, 10-12

A reading from the second letter of Paul to Timothy

You must be aware that anybody who tries to live in devotion to Christ is certain to suffer persecution.

Remember that the Lord Jesus Christ, a descendant of David, was raised from the dead. This is the gospel I preach; in preaching it I suffer as a criminal, even to the point of being thrown into chains—but there is no chaining the word of God! Therefore I bear with all of this for the sake of those whom God has chosen, in order that they may obtain the salvation to be found in Christ Jesus and with it eternal glory.

You can depend on this:
If we have died with him
we shall also live with him;
If we hold out to the end
we shall reign with him.
But if we deny him he will deny us. If we are unfaithful he will still remain faithful for he cannot deny himself.

You have followed closely my teaching and my conduct. You have observed my resolution, fidelity, patience, love, and endurance, through persecutions and sufferings in Antioch. Iconium, and Lystra. You know what persecutions I have had to bear, and you know how the Lord saved me from them all. Anyone who wants to live a godly life in Christ Jesus can expect to be persecuted.

This is the Word of the Lord.

---

6   Heb 10, 32-36

A reading from the letter to the Hebrews
You have suffered greatly.

Recall the days gone by when, after you had been enlightened, you endured a great contest of suffering. At times you were publicly exposed to insult and trial; at other times you associated yourselves with those who were being so dealt with. You even joined in the sufferings of those who were in prison and joyfully assented to the confiscation of your goods, knowing that you had better and more permanent possessions. Do not, then, surrender your confidence; it will have great reward. You need patience to do God's will and receive what he has promised.

This is the Word of the Lord.

---

7   Jas 1, 2-4. 12

A reading from the letter of James
Happy the man who stands firm when trials come.

My brothers, count it pure joy when you are involved in every sort of trial. Realize that when your faith is tested this makes for endurance. Let endurance come to its perfection so that you may be fully mature and lacking in nothing.

Happy the man who holds out to the end through trial! Once he has been proved, he will receive the crown of life the Lord has promised to those who love him.

This is the Word of the Lord.

---

8   1 Pt 3, 14-17

A reading from the first letter of Peter
There is no need to be afraid or to worry about them.

Even if you should have to suffer for justice' sake, happy will you be. "Fear not and do not stand in awe of what this people fears. Venerate the Lord," that is, Christ, in your hearts. Should anyone ask you the reason for this hope of yours, be ever ready to reply, but speak gently and respectfully. Keep your conscience clear so that, whenever you are defamed, those who libel your way of life in Christ may be disappointed. If it should be God's will that you suffer, it is better to do so for good deeds than for evil ones.

This is the Word of the Lord.

---

9   1 Pt 4, 12-19

A reading from the first letter of Peter
Be glad when you are sharing in the suffering of Christ.

Do not be surprised, beloved, that a trial by fire is occurring in your midst. It is a test for you, but it should not catch you off guard. Rejoice, instead, insofar as you share Christ's sufferings. When his glory is revealed, you will rejoice exultantly. Happy are you when you are insulted for the sake of Christ, for then God's Spirit in its glory has come to rest on you. See to it that none of you suffers for being a murderer, a thief, a malefactor, or a destroyer of another's rights. If anyone suffers for being a Christian, however, he ought not to be ashamed. He should rather glorify God in virtue of that name. The season of judgment has begun, and begun with God's own household. If it begins this way with us, what must be the end for those who refuse obedience to the gospel of God? And if "the just man is saved only with difficulty, what is to become of the godless and the sinner?" Accordingly, let those who suffer as God's will requires continue in good deeds and entrust their lives to a faithful Creator.

This is the Word of the Lord.

---

10 .... 1 Jn 5, 1-5

A reading from the first letter of John

Our faith, this is the victory which overcomes the evils in the world.

Everyone who believes that Jesus is the Christ
has been begotten by God.
Now, everyone who loves the father
loves the child he has begotten.
We can be sure that we love God's children
when we love God
and do what he has commanded.
The love of God consists in this:
that we keep his commandments—
and his commandments are not burdensome.
Everyone begotten of God conquers the world,
and the power that has conquered the world
is this faith of ours.
Who, then, is conqueror of the world?
The one who believes that Jesus is the Son of God.

This is the Word of the Lord.

---

717   ALLELUIA VERSE AND VERSE BEFORE THE GOSPEL

1 Mt 5, 10

Happy are they who suffer persecution for justice' sake;
the kingdom of heaven is theirs.

2 2 Cor 1, 3-4

Blessed be the Father of mercies and the God of all comfort,
who consoles us in all our afflictions.

3 Jas 1, 12

Happy the man who stands firm when trials come;
he has proved himself, and will win the crown of life.

4 1 Pt 4, 14

If you are insulted for the name of Christ, blessed are you,
for the Spirit of God rests upon you.

5

We praise you, God; we acknowledge you as Lord;
the radiant army of martyrs acclaims you.

---

718   GOSPEL

1 Mt 10, 17-22

✠ **A reading from the holy gospel according to Matthew**

You will be dragged before governors and kings on account of me, to bear witness before them and all the people.

Jesus said to his apostles: "Be on your guard with respect to others. They will hale you into court, they will flog you in their synagogues. You will be brought to trial before rulers and kings, to give witness before them and before the Gentiles on my account. When they hand you over, do not worry about what you will say or how you will say it. When the hour comes, you will be given what you are to say. You yourselves will not be the speakers; the Spirit of your Father will be speaking in you.

"Brother will hand over brother to death, and the father his child; children will turn against parents and have them put to death. You will be hated by all on account of me. But whoever holds out till the end will escape death."

This is the gospel of the Lord.

2 Mt 10, 28-33

✠ A reading from the holy gospel according
to Matthew

Do not fear those who kill the body.

Jesus said to his disciples: "Do not fear those
who deprive the body of life but cannot destroy the soul. Rather, fear him who can destroy both body and soul in Gehenna. Are not
two sparrows sold for next to nothing? Yet not
a single sparrow falls to the ground without
your Father's consent. As for you, every hair of
your head has been counted; so do not be
afraid of anything. You are worth more than
an entire flock of sparrows. Whoever acknowledges me before men I will acknowledge before
my Father in heaven. Whoever disowns me before men I will disown before my Father in
heaven."
    This is the gospel of the Lord.

3 Mt 10, 34-39

✠ A reading from the holy gospel according
to Matthew

It is not peace I have come to bring, but a sword.

Jesus said to his disciples: "Do not suppose
that my mission on earth is to spread peace.
My mission is to spread, not peace, but division. I have come to set a man at odds with
his father, a daughter with her mother, a
daughter-in-law with her mother-in-law: in
short, to make a man's enemies those of his
own household. Whoever loves father or
mother, son or daughter more than me is not
worthy of me. He who will not take up his
cross and come after me is not worthy of me.
He who seeks only himself brings himself to
ruin, whereas he who brings himself to nought
for me discovers who he is."
    This is the gospel of the Lord.

4 Lk 9, 23-26

✠ A reading from the holy gospel according
to Luke

Anyone who loses his life for my sake, that man will save
his life.

Jesus said to all: "Whoever wishes to be my
follower must deny his very self, take up his

cross each day, and follow in my steps. Whoever would save his life will lose it, and whoever loses his life for my sake will save it.
What profit does he show who gains the whole
world and destroys himself in the process? If
a man is ashamed of me and my doctrine, the
Son of Man will be ashamed of him when he
comes in his glory and that of his Father and
his holy angels."
    This is the gospel of the Lord.

5 Jn 12, 24-26

✠ A reading from the holy gospel according
to John

If the grain of wheat in the ground dies, it yields a rich
harvest.

Jesus said to his disciples:
    "I solemnly assure you,
    unless the grain of wheat falls to the earth
        and dies,
    it remains just a grain of wheat.
    But if it dies,
    it produces much fruit.
    The man who loves his life
    loses it,
    while the man who hates his life in this
        world
    preserves it to life eternal.
    If anyone would serve me,
    let him follow me;
    where I am,
    there will my servant be.
    Anyone who serves me,
    the Father will honor."
        This is the gospel of the Lord.

6 Jn 15, 18-21

✠ A reading from the holy gospel according
to John

If they have persecuted me, they will persecute you too.

Jesus said to his disciples:
    "If you find that the world hates you,
    know it has hated me before you.
    If you belonged to the world,
    it would love you as its own;
    the reason it hates you
    is that you do not belong to the world.

But I chose you out of the world.
Remember what I told you:
no slave is greater than his master.
They will harry you
as they harried me.
They will respect your words
as much as they respected mine.
All this they will do to you because of my
    name,
for they know nothing of him who sent
    me."
    This is the gospel of the Lord.

---

7   **Jn 17, 11-19**

✠ A reading from the holy gospel according
    to John
    The world hates them.

Jesus looked up to heaven and prayed:
    "O Father most holy,
protect them with your name which you
    have given me,
[that they may be one, even as we are
    one.]
As long as I was with them,
I guarded them with your name which
    you gave me.
I kept careful watch,
and not one of them was lost,
none but him who was destined to be
    lost—
in fulfillment of Scripture.
Now, however, I come to you;
I say all this while I am still in the world
that they may share my joy completely.
I gave them your word,
and the world has hated them for it;
they do not belong to the world,
[any more than I belong to the world].
I do not ask you to take them out of the
    world,
but to guard them from the evil one.
They are not of the world,
any more than I am of the world.
Consecrate them by means of truth—
'Your word is truth.'
As you have sent me into the world,
so I have sent them into the world;

I consecrate myself for their sakes now,
that they may be consecrated in truth."
    This is the gospel of the Lord.

COMMON OF PASTORS

719   **READING I**

OUTSIDE EASTER SEASON

1   Ex 32, 7-14

A reading from the book of Exodus
He thought of destroying them but Moses, his chosen one,
    interceded in hopes of turning away his anger.

The Lord said to Moses, "Go down at once
to your people, whom you brought out of the
land of Egypt, for they have become depraved.
They have soon turned aside from the way I
pointed out to them, making for themselves a
molten calf and worshiping it, sacrificing to it
and crying out, 'This is your God, O Israel,
who brought you out of the land of Egypt!'
I see how stiff-necked this people is," continued
the Lord to Moses. "Let me alone, then, that
my wrath may blaze up against them to consume them. Then I will make of you a great
nation."

But Moses implored the Lord, his God, saying, "Why, O Lord, should your wrath blaze
up against your own people, whom you
brought out of the land of Egypt with such
great power and with so strong a hand? Why
should the Egyptians say, 'With evil intent
he brought them out, that he might kill them
in the mountains and exterminate them from
the face of the earth'? Let your blazing wrath
die down; relent in punishing your people.
Remember your servants Abraham, Isaac and
Israel, and how you swore to them by your
own self, saying, 'I will make your descendants as numerous as the stars in the sky; and
all this land that I promised, I will give your
descendants as their perpetual heritage.'" So
the Lord relented in the punishment he had
threatened to inflict on his people.
    This is the Word of the Lord.

---

2   Dt 10, 8-9

A reading from the book of Deuteronomy

The Lord God is the inheritance of those who serve him.

Moses said to the people: "At that time the Lord set apart the tribe of Levi to carry the ark of the covenant of the Lord, to be in attendance before the Lord and minister to him, and to give blessings in his name, as they have done to this day. For this reason, Levi has no share in the heritage with his brothers; the Lord himself is his heritage, as the Lord, your God, has told him."

This is the Word of the Lord.

---

3   1 Sm 16, 1. 6-13

A reading from the first book of Samuel

Come, anoint the young shepherd; he is the one who will be king.

The Lord said to Samuel: "Fill your horn with oil, and be on your way. I am sending you to Jesse of Bethlehem, for I have chosen my king from among his sons." As Jesse and his sons came, he looked at Eliab and thought, "Surely the Lord's anointed is here before him." But the Lord said to Samuel: "Do not judge from his appearance or from his lofty stature, because I have rejected him. Not as man sees does God see, because man sees the appearance but the Lord looks into the heart." Then Jesse called Abinadab and presented him before Samuel, who said, "The Lord has not chosen him." Next Jesse presented Shammah, but Samuel said, "The Lord has not chosen this one either." In the same way Jesse presented seven sons before Samuel, but Samuel said to Jesse, "The Lord has not chosen any one of these." Then Samuel asked Jesse, "Are these all the sons you have?" Jesse replied, "There is still the youngest, who is tending the sheep." Samuel said to Jesse, "Send for him; we will not begin the sacrificial banquet until he arrives here." Jesse sent and had the young man brought to them. He was ruddy, a youth handsome to behold and making a splendid appearance. The Lord said, "There—anoint him, for this is he!" Then Samuel, with the horn of oil in hand, anointed him in the midst of his brothers; and from that day on, the spirit of the Lord rushed upon David.

This is the Word of the Lord.

---

4   Is 6, 1-8

A reading from the book of the prophet Isaiah

Whom shall I send? Who will be our messenger?

In the year King Uzziah died, I saw the Lord seated on a high and lofty throne, with the train of his garment filling the temple. Seraphim were stationed above; each of them had six wings: with two they veiled their faces, with two they veiled their feet, and with two they hovered aloft.

"Holy, holy, holy is the Lord of hosts!" they cried one to the other. "All the earth is filled with his glory!" At the sound of that cry, the frame of the door shook and the house was filled with smoke.

Then I said, "Woe is me, I am doomed! For I am a man of unclean lips, living among a people of unclean lips; yet my eyes have seen the King, the Lord of hosts!" Then one of the seraphim flew to me, holding an ember which he had taken with tongs from the altar.

He touched my mouth with it. "See," he said, "now that this has touched your lips, your wickedness is removed, your sin purged."

Then I heard the voice of the Lord saying, "Whom shall I send? Who will go for us?" "Here I am," I said; "send me!"

This is the Word of the Lord.

---

5   Is 52, 7-10

[For missionaries]

A reading from the book of the prophet Isaiah

All the ends of the earth shall see the salvation of our God.

How beautiful upon the mountains
   are the feet of him who brings glad tidings,
Announcing peace, bearing good news,
   announcing salvation, and saying to Zion,
   "Your God is King!"
Hark! Your watchmen raise a cry,
   together they shout for joy,
For they see directly, before their eyes,
   the Lord restoring Zion.

Break out together in song,
  O ruins of Jerusalem!
For the Lord comforts his people,
  he redeems Jerusalem.
The Lord has bared his holy arm
  in the sight of all the nations;
All the ends of the earth will behold
  the salvation of our God.
    This is the Word of the Lord.

---

6   **Is 61, 1-3**

A reading from the book of the prophet Isaiah
The Lord God anointed me and sent me to bring Good News
to the poor.
The spirit of the Lord God is upon me,
  because the Lord has anointed me;
He has sent me to bring glad tidings to the
    lowly,
  to heal the brokenhearted,
To proclaim liberty to the captives
  and release to the prisoners,
To announce a year of favor from the Lord
  and a day of vindication by our God,
  to comfort all who mourn;
To place on those who mourn in Zion
  a diadem instead of ashes,
To give them oil of gladness in place of mourn-
    ing,
  a glorious mantle instead of a listless spirit.
    This is the Word of the Lord.

---

7   **Jer 1, 4-9**

**A reading from the book of the prophet
Jeremiah**
Go to those to whom I send you.
The word of the Lord came to me thus:
Before I formed you in the womb I knew you,
  before you were born I dedicated you,
  a prophet to the nations I appointed you.
    "Ah, Lord God!" I said,
    "I know not how to speak; I am too
        young."
But the Lord answered me,
  Say not, "I am too young."
    To whomever I send you, you shall go;
whatever I command you, you shall speak.

Have no fear before them,
  because I am with you to deliver you, says
    the Lord.
Then the Lord extended his hand and touched
    my mouth, saying,
  See, I place my words in your mouth!
    This is the Word of the Lord.

---

8   **Ez 3, 17-21**

A reading from the book of the prophet Ezekiel
I have appointed you as sentry to the house of Israel.
The word of the Lord came to me: Son of
man, I have appointed you a watchman for
the house of Israel. When you hear a word
from my mouth, you shall warn them for me.
If I say to the wicked man, You shall surely
die; and you do not warn him or speak out to
dissuade him from his wicked conduct so that
he may live: that wicked man shall die for his
sin, but I will hold you responsible for his
death. If, on the other hand, you have warned
the wicked man, yet he has not turned away
from his evil nor from his wicked conduct,
then he shall die for his sin, but you shall save
your life.
  If a virtuous man turns away from virtue
and does wrong when I place a stumbling
block before him, he shall die. He shall die for
his sin, and his virtuous deeds shall not be
remembered; but I will hold you responsible
for his death if you did not warn him. When,
on the other hand, you have warned a virtuous
man not to sin, and he has in fact not sinned,
he shall surely live because of the warning, and
you shall save your own life.
    This is the Word of the Lord.

---

9   **Ez 34, 11-16**

A reading from the book of the prophet Ezekiel
As a shepherd keeps all his flock in view, so shall I keep my
sheep in view.
Thus says the Lord God: I myself will look after
and tend my sheep. As a shepherd tends his
flock when he finds himself among his scattered
sheep, so will I tend my sheep. I will rescue
them from every place where they were scattered when it was cloudy and dark. I will lead

them out from among the peoples and gather them from the foreign lands; I will bring them back to their own country and pasture them upon the mountains of Israel [in the land's ravines and all its inhabited places]. In good pastures will I pasture them, and on the mountain heights of Israel shall be their grazing ground. There they shall lie down on good grazing ground, and in rich pastures shall they be pastured on the mountains of Israel. I myself will pasture my sheep; I myself will give them rest, says the Lord God. The lost I will seek out, the strayed I will bring back, the injured I will bind up, the sick I will heal [but the sleek and the strong I will destroy], shepherding them rightly.

This is the Word of the Lord.

720　　　　　　**READING I**
　　　　　DURING EASTER SEASON

1　　　　　　　　　　　　　　　Acts 13, 46-49

[For missionaries]

A reading from the Acts of the Apostles
We must turn to the gentiles.

Paul and Barnabas said to the Jews: "The word of God has to be declared to you first of all; but since you reject it and thus convict yourselves as unworthy of everlasting life, we now turn to the Gentiles. For thus were we instructed by the Lord: 'I have made you a light to the nations, a means of salvation to the ends of the earth.'" The Gentiles were delighted when they heard this and responded to the word of the Lord with praise. All who were destined for life everlasting believed in it. Thus the word of the Lord was carried throughout that area.

This is the Word of the Lord.

2　　　　　　　　　　　　Acts 20, 17-18. 28-32. 36

A reading from the Acts of the Apostles
Be on guard for yourselves and for all whom the Holy Spirit has made you the overseers.

Paul sent word from Miletus to Ephesus, summoning the elders of that church. When they came to him he delivered this address: "Keep watch over yourselves, and over the whole flock the Holy Spirit has given you to guard. Shepherd the church of God, which he has acquired at the price of his own blood. I know that when I am gone, savage wolves will come among you who will not spare the flock. From your own number, men will present themselves distorting the truth and leading astray any who follow them. Be on guard, therefore. Do not forget that for three years, night and day, I never ceased warning you individually even to the point of tears. I commend you now to the Lord, and to that gracious word of his which can enlarge you, and give you a share among all who are consecrated to him."

After this discourse, Paul knelt down with them all and prayed.

This is the Word of the Lord.

3　　　　　　　　　　　　　　　Acts 26, 19-23

[For missionaries]

A reading from the Acts of the Apostles
The Christ is he who proclaimed that light now shines for the whole world.

Paul said: "King Agrippa, I could not disobey that heavenly vision. I preached a message of reform and of conversion to God, first to the people of Damascus, then to the people of Jerusalem and all the country of Judea; yes, even to the Gentiles. I urged them to act in conformity with their change of heart. That is why the Jews seized me in the temple court and tried to murder me. But I have had God's help to this very day, and so I stand here to testify to great and small alike. Nothing that I say differs from what the prophets and Moses foretold: namely, that the Messiah must suffer, and that, as the first to rise from the dead, he will proclaim light to our people and to the Gentiles."

This is the Word of the Lord.

721   **RESPONSORIAL PSALM**

1   Ps 16, 1-2. 5. 7-8. 11

℟. (5) You are my inheritance, O Lord.

Keep me, O God, for in you I take refuge;
  I say to the Lord, "My Lord are you."
O Lord, my allotted portion and my cup,
  you it is who hold fast my lot.

℟. You are my inheritance, O Lord.

I bless the Lord who counsels me;
  even in the night my heart exhorts me.
I set the Lord ever before me;
  with him at my right hand I shall not be
  disturbed.

℟. You are my inheritance, O Lord.

You will show me the path to life,
  fullness of joys in your presence,
  the delights at your right hand forever.

℟. You are my inheritance, O Lord.

---

2   Ps 23, 1-3. 3-4. 5. 6

℟. (1) The Lord is my shepherd;
  there is nothing I shall want.

The Lord is my shepherd; I shall not want.
  In verdant pastures he gives me repose;
Beside restful waters he leads me;
  he refreshes my soul.

℟. The Lord is my shepherd;
  there is nothing I shall want.

He guides me in right paths
  for his name's sake.
Even though I walk in the dark valley
  I fear no evil; for you are at my side
With your rod and your staff
  that give me courage.

℟. The Lord is my shepherd;
  there is nothing I shall want.

You spread the table before me
  in the sight of my foes;
You anoint my head with oil;
  my cup overflows.

℟. The Lord is my shepherd;
  there is nothing I shall want.

Only goodness and kindness follow me
  all the days of my life;
And I shall dwell in the house of the Lord
  for years to come.

℟. The Lord is my shepherd;
  there is nothing I shall want.

---

3   Ps 89, 2-3. 4-5. 21-22. 25. 27

℟. (2) For ever I will sing the goodness of the
  Lord.

The favors of the Lord I will sing forever;
  through all generations my mouth shall pro-
  claim your faithfulness.
For you have said, "My kindness is established
  forever";
  in heaven you have confirmed your faith-
  fulness.

℟. For ever I will sing the goodness of the
  Lord.

"I have made a covenant with my chosen one,
  I have sworn to David my servant:
Forever will I confirm your posterity
  and establish your throne for all generations."

℟. For ever I will sing the goodness of the
  Lord.

I have found David, my servant;
  with my holy oil I have anointed him,
That my hand may be always with him,
  and that my arm may make him strong.

℟. For ever I will sing the goodness of the
  Lord.

My faithfulness and my kindness shall be with
  him,
  and through my name shall his horn be
  exalted.
He shall say of me, "You are my father,
  my God, the Rock, my savior."

℟. For ever I will sing the goodness of the
  Lord.

---

4   Ps 96, 1-2. 2-3. 7-8. 10

℟. (3) Proclaim his marvelous deeds to all the
  nations.

Sing to the Lord a new song;
  sing to the Lord, all you lands.
Sing to the Lord; bless his name.

℟. Proclaim his marvelous deeds to all the
  nations.

Announce his salvation, day after day.
  Tell his glory among the nations;
Among all peoples, his wondrous deeds.

℟. Proclaim his marvelous deeds to all the nations.

Give to the Lord, you families of nations,
give to the Lord glory and praise;
give to the Lord the glory due his name!
℟. Proclaim his marvelous deeds to all the nations.

Say among the nations: The Lord is king.
He has made the world firm, not to be moved;
He governs the peoples with equity.
℟. Proclaim his marvelous deeds to all the nations.

---

5   Ps 110, 1. 2. 3. 4

℟. (4) You are a priest for ever,
in the line of Melchizedek.

The Lord said to my Lord: "Sit at my right hand
till I make your enemies your footstool."
℟. You are a priest for ever,
in the line of Melchizedek.

The scepter of your power the Lord will stretch forth from Zion:
"Rule in the midst of your enemies.
℟. You are a priest for ever,
in the line of Melchizedek.

Yours is princely power in the day of your birth, in holy splendor;
before the daystar, like the dew, I have begotten you."
℟. You are a priest for ever,
in the line of Melchizedek.

The Lord has sworn, and he will not repent:
"You are a priest forever, according to the order of Melchizedek."
℟. You are a priest for ever,
in the line of Melchizedek.

---

6   Ps 117, 1. 2

℟. (Mk 16, 15) Go out to all the world,
and tell the Good News.

Praise the Lord, all you nations;
glorify him, all you peoples!
℟. Go out to all the world,
and tell the Good News.

For steadfast is his kindness toward us,
and the fidelity of the Lord endures forever.
℟. Go out to all the world,
and tell the Good News.
℟. Or: Alleluia.

---

722   **READING II**

1   Rom 12, 3-13

A reading from the letter of Paul to the Romans
Our gifts differ according to the grace given to us.

In virtue of the favor given to me, I warn each of you not to think more highly of himself than he ought. Let him estimate himself soberly, in keeping with the measure of faith that God has apportioned him. Just as each of us has one body with many members, and not all the members have the same function, so too we, though many, are one body in Christ and individually members of one another. We have gifts that differ according to the favor bestowed on each of us. One's gift may be prophecy; its use should be in proportion to his faith. It may be the gift of ministry; it should be used for service. One who is a teacher should use his gift for teaching; one with the power of exhortation should exhort. He who gives alms should do so generously; he who rules should exercise his authority with care; he who performs works of mercy should do so cheerfully.

Your love must be sincere. Detest what is evil, cling to what is good. Love one another with the affection of brothers. Anticipate each other in showing respect. Do not grow slack but be fervent in spirit; he whom you serve is the Lord. Rejoice in hope, be patient under trial, persevere in prayer. Look on the needs of the saints as your own; be generous in offering hospitality.

This is the Word of the Lord.

2   1 Cor 1, 18-25

[For missionaries]

A reading from the first letter of Paul to the Corinthians

It was because God wanted to save those who have faith through the foolishness of the message that we preach.

The message of the cross is complete absurdity to those who are headed for ruin, but to us who are experiencing salvation it is the power of God. Scripture says,

"I will destroy the wisdom of the wise, and thwart the cleverness of the clever."

Where is the wise man to be found? Where the scribe? Where the master of worldly argument? Has not God turned the wisdom of this world into folly? Since in God's wisdom the world did not come to know him through its wisdom, it pleased God to save those who believe through the absurdity of the preaching of the gospel. Yes, Jews demand "signs" and Greeks look for "wisdom," but we preach Christ crucified, a stumbling block to Jews and an absurdity to Gentiles, but to those who are called, Jews and Greeks alike, Christ the power of God and the wisdom of God. For God's folly is wiser than men, and his weakness more powerful than men.

This is the Word of the Lord.

---

3   1 Cor 4, 1-5

A reading from the first letter of Paul to the Corinthians

We are to be as Christ's servants, stewards entrusted with the mysteries of God.

Men should regard us as servants of Christ and administrators of the mysteries of God. The first requirement of an administrator is that he prove trustworthy. It matters little to me whether you or any human court pass judgment on me. I do not even pass judgment on myself. Mind you, I have nothing on my conscience. But that does not mean that I am declaring myself innocent. The Lord is the one to judge me, so stop passing judgment before the time of his return. He will bring to light what is hidden in darkness and manifest the

intentions of hearts. At that time, everyone will receive his praise from God.

This is the Word of the Lord.

---

4   1 Cor 9, 16-19. 22-23

A reading from the first letter of Paul to the Corinthians

Unless I preach the gospel, I shall be punished.

Preaching the gospel is not the subject of a boast; I am under compulsion and have no choice. I am ruined if I do not preach it! If I do it willingly, I have my recompense; if unwillingly, I am nonetheless entrusted with a charge. And this recompense of mine? It is simply this, that when preaching I offer the gospel free of charge and do not make full use of the authority the gospel gives me.

Although I am not bound to anyone, I made myself the slave of all so as to win over as many as possible. To the weak I became a weak person with a view to winning the weak. I have made myself all things to all men in order to save at least some of them. In fact, I do all that I do for the sake of the gospel in the hope of having a share in its blessings.

This is the Word of the Lord.

---

5   2 Cor 3, 1-6

A reading from the second letter of Paul to the Corinthians

God has given us the qualifications to be ministers of the new covenant.

Am I beginning to speak well of myself again? Or do I need letters of recommendation to you or from you as others might? You are my letter, known and read by all men, written on your hearts. Clearly you are a letter of Christ which I have delivered, a letter written not with ink but by the Spirit of the living God, not on tablets of stone but on tablets of flesh in the heart.

This great confidence in God is ours, through Christ. It is not that we are entitled of ourselves to take credit for anything. Our sole credit is from God, who has made us qualified

ministers of a new covenant, a covenant not of a written law but of spirit.
This is the Word of the Lord.

---

6   2 Cor 4, 1-2. 5-7

A reading from the second letter of Paul to the Corinthians

We preach Jesus Christ as Lord, with ourselves as your servants for Jesus' sake.

Because we possess the ministry through God's mercy, we do not give in to discouragement. Rather, we repudiate shameful, underhanded practices. We do not resort to trickery or falsify the word of God. We proclaim the truth openly and commend ourselves to every man's conscience before God. It is not ourselves we preach but Christ Jesus as Lord, and ourselves as your servants for Jesus' sake. For God, who said, "Let light shine out of darkness," has shone in our hearts, that we in turn might make known the glory of God shining on the face of Christ. This treasure we possess in earthen vessels to make it clear that its surpassing power comes from God and not from us.
This is the Word of the Lord.

---

7   2 Cor 5, 14-20

A reading from the second letter of Paul to the Corinthians

God gave us the work of reconciliation.

The love of Christ impels us who have reached the conviction that since one died for all, all died. He died for all so that those who live might live no longer for themselves, but for him who for their sakes died and was raised up.

Because of this we no longer look on anyone in terms of mere human judgment. If at one time we so regarded Christ, we no longer know him by this standard. This means that if anyone is in Christ, he is a new creation. The old order has passed away; now all is new! All this has been done by God, who has reconciled us to himself through Christ and has given us the ministry of reconciliation. I mean that God, in Christ, was reconciling the world to himself,

not counting men's transgressions against them, and that he has entrusted the message of reconciliation to us. This makes us ambassadors for Christ, God as it were appealing through us. We implore you, in Christ's name: be reconciled to God!
This is the Word of the Lord.

---

8   Eph 4, 1-7. 11-13

A reading from the letter of Paul to the Ephesians

In the work of service we help in building up the body of Christ.

I plead with you as a prisoner for the Lord, to live a life worthy of the calling you have received, with perfect humility, meekness, and patience, bearing with one another lovingly. Make every effort to preserve the unity which has the Spirit as its origin and peace as its binding force. There is but one body and one Spirit, just as there is but one hope given all of you by your call. There is one Lord, one faith, one baptism; one God and Father of all, who is over all, and works through all, and is in all.

Each of us has received God's favor in the measure in which Christ bestows it.

It is he who gave apostles, prophets, evangelists, pastors and teachers in roles of service for the faithful to build up the body of Christ, till we become one in faith and in the knowledge of God's Son, and form that perfect man who is Christ come to full stature.
This is the Word of the Lord.

---

9   Col 1, 24-29

A reading from the letter of Paul to the Colossians

I became the servant of the Church when God made me responsible for delivering his message to you.

Even now I find my joy in the suffering I endure for you. In my own flesh I fill up what is lacking in the sufferings of Christ for the sake of his body, the church. I became a minister of this church through the commission God gave me to preach among you his word in its fullness, that mystery hidden from ages and generations past but now revealed to his holy ones. God has willed to make known to them the glory beyond price which this mystery brings to the Gentiles—the mystery of Christ in you, your hope of glory. This is the Christ we proclaim while we admonish all men and teach them in the full measure of wisdom, hoping to make every man complete in Christ. For this I work and struggle, impelled by that energy of his which is so powerful a force within me.

This is the Word of the Lord.

10   1 Thes 2, 2-8

A reading from the first letter of Paul to the Thessalonians

We were eager to hand over to you not only the Good News but our whole lives as well.

We drew courage from our God to preach his good tidings to you in the face of great opposition. The exhortation we deliver does not spring from deceit or impure motives or any sort of trickery; rather, having met the test imposed on us by God, as men entrusted with the good tidings, we speak like those who strive to please God, "the tester of our hearts," rather than men.

We were not guilty, as you well know, of flattering words or greed under any pretext, as God is our witness! Neither did we seek glory from men, you or any others, even though we could have insisted on our own importance as apostles of Christ.

On the contrary, while we were among you we were as gentle as any nursing mother fondling her little ones. So well disposed were we to you, in fact, that we wanted to share with you not only God's tidings but our very lives so dear, had you become to us.

This is the Word of the Lord.

11   2 Tm 1, 13-14; 2, 1-3

A reading from the second letter of Paul to Timothy

You have been entrusted to look after something precious; guard it with the help of the Holy Spirit who lives in us.

Take as a model of sound teaching what you have heard me say, in faith and love in Christ

Jesus. Guard the rich deposit of faith with the help of the Holy Spirit who dwells within us.

So you, my son, must be strong in the grace which is ours in Christ Jesus. The things which you have heard from me through many witnesses you must hand on to trustworthy men who will be able to teach others. Bear hardship along with me as a good soldier of Christ Jesus.

This is the Word of the Lord.

12   2 Tm 4, 1-5

A reading from the second letter to Paul to Timothy

Preach the Good News; fulfill your ministry.

In the presence of God and of Christ Jesus, who is coming to judge the living and the dead, and by his appearing and his kingly power, I charge you to preach the word, to stay with this task, whether convenient or inconvenient—correcting, reproving, appealing—constantly teaching and never losing patience. For the time will come when people will not tolerate sound doctrine, but, following their own desires, will surround themselves with teachers who tickle their ears. They will stop listening to the truth and will wander off to fables. As for you, be steady and self-possessed; put up with hardship, perform your work as an evangelist, fulfill your ministry.

This is the Word of the Lord.

13   1 Pt 5, 1-4

A reading from the first letter of Peter

Be the shepherds of the flock of God that is entrusted to you.

To the elders among you I, a fellow elder, a witness of Christ's sufferings and sharer in the glory that is to be revealed, make this appeal. God's flock is in your midst; give it a shepherd's care. Watch over it willingly as God would have you do, not under coercion; and not for shameful profit either, but generously. Be examples to the flock, not lording it over those assigned to you, so that when the chief Shepherd appears you will win for yourselves the unfading crown of glory.

This is the Word of the Lord.

723   **ALLELUIA VERSE AND**
VERSE BEFORE THE GOSPEL

1   Mt 28, 19-20

Go and teach all people my gospel.
I am with you always, until the end of the
   world.

2   Mk 1, 17

Come, follow me, says the Lord,
and I will make you fishers of men.

3   Lk 4, 18-19

The Lord sent me to bring Good News to the
   poor,
and freedom to prisoners.

4   Jn 10, 14

I am the good shepherd, says the Lord;
I know my sheep, and mine know me.

5   Jn 15, 15

I call you my friends, says the Lord,
for I have made known to you all that the
   Father has told me.

6   2 Cor 5, 19

God was in Christ, to reconcile the world to
   himself;
and the Good News of reconciliation he has
   entrusted to us.

---

724   **GOSPEL**

1   Mt 16, 13-19

[For a pope]

✠ A reading from the holy gospel according
       to Matthew
You are Peter and on this rock I will build my Church.

When Jesus came to the neighborhood of Caesarea Philippi, he asked his disciples this question: "Who do people say that the Son of Man
is?" They replied, "Some say John the Baptizer,
others Elijah, still others Jeremiah or one of
the prophets." "And you," he said to them,
"who do you say that I am?" "You are the
Messiah," Simon Peter answered, "the Son of

the living God!" Jesus replied, "Blest are you,
Simon son of John! No mere man has revealed
this to you, but my heavenly Father. I for my
part declare to you, you are 'Rock,' and on this
rock I will build my church, and the jaws of
death shall not prevail against it. I will entrust
to you the keys of the kingdom of heaven.
Whatever you declare bound on earth shall be
bound in heaven; whatever you declare loosed
on earth shall be loosed in heaven."
   This is the gospel of the Lord.

---

2   Mt 23, 8-12

✠ A reading from the holy gospel according
       to Matthew
The greatest among you must be your servant.

Jesus said to his disciples: "Avoid the title
'Rabbi.' One among you is your teacher, the
rest are learners. Do not call anyone on earth
your father. Only one is your father, the One in
heaven. Avoid being called teachers. Only one
is your teacher, the Messiah. The greatest
among you will be the one who serves the rest.
Whoever exalts himself shall be humbled, but
whoever humbles himself shall be exalted."
   This is the gospel of the Lord.

---

3   Mt 28, 16-20

[For missionaries]

✠ A reading from the holy gospel according
       to Matthew
Go and make disciples of all the nations.

The eleven disciples made their way to Galilee,
to the mountain to which Jesus had summoned
them. At the sight of him, those who had
entertained doubts fell down in homage. Jesus
came forward and addressed them in these
words:
    "Full authority has been given to me
    both in heaven and on earth;
    go, therefore, and make disciples of all the
      nations.
    Baptize them in the name
     'of the Father
     and of the Son,
     and of the Holy Spirit.'

Teach them to carry out everything I have
commanded you.
And know that I am with you always,
until the end of the world!"
This is the gospel of the Lord.

4   Mk 1, 14-20

✠ A reading from the holy gospel according
to Mark
I will make you into fishers of men.

After John's arrest, Jesus appeared in Galilee
proclaiming God's good news: "This is the
time of fulfillment. The reign of God is at hand!
Reform your lives and believe in the good
news!"

As he made his way along the Sea of Galilee,
he observed Simon and his brother Andrew
casting their nets into the sea; they were fishermen. Jesus said to them, "Come after me;
I will make you fishers of men." They immediately abandoned their nets and became
his followers. Proceeding a little farther along,
he caught sight of James, Zebedee's son, and
his brother John. They too were in their boat
putting their nets in order. He summoned them
on the spot. They abandoned their father Zebedee, who was in the boat with the hired men,
and went off in his company.
This is the gospel of the Lord.

5   Mk 16, 15-20

[For missionaries]

✠ A reading from the holy gospel according
to Mark
Go out to the whole world; proclaim the Good News to all
creation.

Jesus appeared to the Eleven and said to
them: "Go into the whole world and proclaim
the good news to all creation. The man who
believes in it and accepts baptism will be
saved; the man who refuses to believe in it
will be condemned. Signs like these will accompany those who have professed their
faith: they will use my name to expel demons,
they will speak entirely new languages, they
will be able to handle serpents, they will be

able to drink deadly poison without harm,
and the sick upon whom they lay their hands
will recover." Then, after speaking to them,
the Lord Jesus was taken up into heaven and
took his seat at God's right hand. The Eleven
went forth and preached everywhere. The Lord
continued to work with them throughout and
confirm the message through the signs which
accompanied them.
This is the gospel of the Lord.

6   Lk 5, 1-11

[For missionaries]

✠ A reading from the holy gospel according
to Luke
I will place my trust in your words.

As Jesus stood by the Lake of Gennesaret, and
the crowd pressed in on him to hear the word
of God, he saw two boats moored by the side
of the lake; the fishermen had disembarked and
were washing their nets. He got into one of the
boats, the one belonging to Simon, and asked
him to pull out a short distance from the shore;
then, remaining seated, he continued to teach
the crowds from the boat. When he had finished speaking he said to Simon, "Put out into
deep water and lower your nets for a catch."
Simon answered, "Master, we have been hard
at it all night long and have caught nothing;
but if you say so, I will lower the nets." Upon
doing this they caught such a great number of
fish that their nets were at the breaking point.
They signaled to their mates in the other boat
to come and help them. These came, and together they filled the two boats until they
nearly sank.

At the sight of this, Simon Peter fell at the
knees of Jesus saying, "Leave me, Lord. I am
a sinful man." For indeed, amazement at the
catch they had made seized him and all his
shipmates, as well as James and John, Zebedee's sons, who were partners with Simon.
Jesus said to Simon, "Do not be afraid. From
now on you will be catching men." With that
they brought their boats to land, left everything, and became his followers.
This is the gospel of the Lord.

7   Lk 10, 1-9

✠ A reading from the holy gospel according
to Luke

The harvest is rich but the laborers are few.

The Lord appointed a further seventy-two and
sent them in pairs before him to every town
and place he intended to visit. He said to them:
"The harvest is rich but the workers are few;
therefore ask the harvest-master to send
workers to his harvest. Be on your way, and
remember: I am sending you as lambs in the
midst of wolves. Do not carry a walking staff
or traveling bag; wear no sandals and greet no
one along the way. On entering any house, first
say, 'Peace to this house.' If there is a peaceable
man there, your peace will rest on him; if
not, it will come back to you. Stay in the one
house eating and drinking what they have,
for the laborer is worth his wage. Do not move
from house to house.

"Into whatever city you go, after they welcome you, eat what they set before you, and
cure the sick there. Say to them, 'The reign of
God is at hand.' "

This is the gospel of the Lord.

---

8   Lk 22, 24-30

✠ A reading from the holy gospel according
to Luke

*I confer a kingdom on you, just as my Father conferred
one on me.*

A dispute arose among the apostles about who
should be regarded as the greatest. Jesus said:
"Earthly kings lord it over their people. Those
who exercise authority over them are called
their benefactors. Yet it cannot be that way
with you. Let the greater among you be as the
junior, the leader as the servant. Who, in fact,
is the greater—he who reclines at table or he
who serves the meal? Is it not the one who
reclines at table? Yet I am in your midst as the
one who serves you. You are the ones who
have stood loyally by me in my temptations.
I for my part assign to you the dominion my
Father has assigned to me. In my kingdom you
will eat and drink at my table, and you will

sit on thrones judging the twelve tribes of
Israel."

This is the gospel of the Lord.

---

9   Jn 10, 11-16

✠ A reading from the holy gospel according
to John

*The good shepherd is one who lays down his life for his
sheep.*

Jesus said:
"I am the good shepherd;
the good shepherd lays down his life for
the sheep.
The hired hand who is no shepherd,
nor owner of the sheep—
catches sight of the wolf coming
and runs away, leaving the sheep
to be snatched and scattered by the wolf.
That is because he works for pay;
he has no concern for the sheep.

"I am the good shepherd.
I know my sheep
and my sheep know me
in the same way that the Father knows me
and I know the Father;
for these sheep I will give my life.
I have other sheep
that do not belong to this fold.
I must lead them, too,
and they shall hear my voice.
There shall be one flock then, one
shepherd."

This is the gospel of the Lord.

---

10   Jn 15, 9-17

✠ A reading from the holy gospel according
to John

I shall not call you servants anymore; I call you friends.

Jesus said to his disciples:
"As the Father has loved me,
so I have loved you.
Live on in my love.
You will live in my love
if you keep my commandments,
even as I have kept my Father's commandments,
and live in his love.

All this I tell you
that my joy may be yours
and your joy may be complete.
This is my commandment:
love one another
as I have loved you.
There is no greater love than this:
to lay down one's life for one's friends.
You are my friends
if you do what I command you.
I no longer speak of you as slaves,
for a slave does not know what his master
   is about.
Instead, I call you friends,
since I have made known to you all that I
   heard from my Father.
It was not you who chose me,
it was I who chose you
to go forth and bear fruit.
Your fruit must endure,
so that all you ask the Father in my name
he will give you.
The command I give you is this:
that you love one another."
   This is the gospel of the Lord.

_____

11   Jn 21, 15-17

[For a pope]

✠ A reading from the holy gospel according
                to John

Take care of my lambs and my sheep.

Jesus appeared to his disciples again and when
they had eaten their meal, he said to Simon
Peter, "Simon, son of John, do you love me
more than these?" "Yes, Lord," Peter said,
"you know that I love you." At which Jesus
said, "Feed my lambs."

A second time he put his question, "Simon,
son of John, do you love me?" "Yes, Lord,"
Peter said, "you know that I love you." Jesus
replied, "Tend my sheep."

A third time Jesus asked him, "Simon, son of
John, do you love me?" Peter was hurt because he had asked a third time, 'Do you love
me?" So he said to him: "Lord, you know
everything. You know well that I love you."
Jesus told him, "Feed my sheep."
   This is the gospel of the Lord.

COMMON OF DOCTORS
OF THE CHURCH

725   **READING I**

OUTSIDE EASTER SEASON

1   1 Kgs 3, 11-14

A reading from the first book of Kings

I give you a heart wise and shrewd.

The Lord said to Solomon: "Because you have
asked—not for a long life for yourself, nor
for riches, nor for the life of your enemies,
but for understanding so that you may know
what is right—I do as you requested. I give
you a heart so wise and understanding that
there has never been anyone like you up to
now, and after you there will come no one to
equal you. In addition, I give you what you
have not asked for, such riches and glory that
among kings there is not your like. And if you
follow me by keeping my statutes and commandments, as your father David did, I will
give you a long life."
   This is the Word of the Lord.

_____

2   Wis 7, 7-10. 15-16

A reading from the book of Wisdom

I have loved wisdom more than health and beauty.

I prayed, and prudence was given me;
   I pleaded, and the spirit of Wisdom came to
   me.
I preferred her to scepter and throne,
And deemed riches nothing in comparison with
   her,
   nor did I liken any priceless gem to her;
Because all gold, in view of her, is a little sand,
   and before her, silver is to be accounted
   mire.
Beyond health and comeliness I loved her,
And I chose to have her rather than the light,
   because the splendor of her never yields to
   sleep.

Now God grant I speak suitably
   and value these endowments at their worth:
For he is the guide of Wisdom
   and the director of the wise.

For both we and our words are in his hand,
as well as all prudence and knowledge of
crafts.
>   This is the Word of the Lord.

---

3   Sir 15, 1-6

A reading from the book of Sirach

He filled him with the spirit of wisdom and understanding.

He who fears the Lord will do this;
   he who is practiced in the law will come to
     wisdom.
Motherlike she will meet him,
   like a young bride she will embrace him,
Nourish him with the bread of understanding,
   and give him the water of learning to drink.
He will lean upon her and not fall,
   he will trust in her and not be put to shame.
She will exalt him above his fellows;
   in the assembly she will make him eloquent.
Joy and gladness he will find,
   an everlasting name inherit.
>   This is the Word of the Lord.

---

4   Sir 39, 6-11

A reading from the book of Sirach

Understanding will fill him up.

If it pleases the Lord Almighty,
   he will be filled with the spirit of under-
     standing;
He will pour forth his words of wisdom
   and in prayer give thanks to the Lord,
Who will direct his knowledge and his counsel,
   as he meditates upon his mysteries.
He will show the wisdom of what he has
     learned
   and glory in the law of the Lord's covenant.
Many will praise his understanding;
   his fame can never be effaced;
Unfading will be his memory,
   through all generations his name will live;
Peoples will speak of his wisdom,
   and in assembly sing his praises.
While he lives he is one out of a thousand,
   and when he dies his renown will not cease.
>   This is the Word of the Lord.

---

726   **READING I**
DURING EASTER SEASON

1   Acts, 2, 14. 22-24. 32-36

A reading from the Acts of the Apostles

God has made him both Lord and Christ.

[On the day of Pentecost] Peter stood up with
the Eleven, raised his voice, and addressed
them: "Men of Israel, listen to me! Jesus the
Nazorean was a man whom God sent to you
with miracles, wonders and signs as his credentials. These God worked through him in
your midst, as you well know. He was delivered up by the set purpose and plan of God;
you even made use of pagans to crucify and
kill him. God freed him from death's bitter
pangs, however, and raised him up again, for
it was impossible that death should keep its
hold on him.

"This is the Jesus God has raised up, and
we are his witnesses. Exalted at God's right
hand, he first received the promised Holy Spirit
from the Father, then poured this Spirit out on
us. This is what you now see and hear. David
did not go up to heaven, yet David says,
   'The Lord said to my Lord,
     Sit at my right hand
       until I make your enemies your foot-
         stool.'
Therefore let the whole house of Israel know
beyond any doubt that God has made both
Lord and Messiah this Jesus whom you crucified."
>   This is the Word of the Lord.

---

2   Acts 13, 26-33

A reading from the Acts of the Apostles

God fulfilled the promise by raising Jesus from the dead.

When Paul came to Antioch in Pisidia, he
spoke in the synagogue and said: "My brothers, children of the family of Abraham and
you others who reverence our God, it was
to us that this message of salvation was sent
forth. The inhabitants of Jerusalem and their
rulers failed to recognize him, and in condemning him they fulfilled the words of the prophets
which we read sabbath after sabbath. Even
though they found no charge against him

which deserved death, they begged Pilate to have him executed. Once they had thus brought about all that had been written of him, they took him down from the tree and laid him in a tomb. Yet God raised him from the dead, and for many days thereafter Jesus appeared to those who had come up with him from Galilee to Jerusalem. These are his witnesses now before the people.

"We ourselves announce to you the good news that what God promised our fathers he has fulfilled for us, their children, in raising up Jesus, according to what is written in the second psalm, 'You are my son; this day I have begotten you.' "
This is the Word of the Lord.

---

727   RESPONSORIAL PSALM

1   Ps 19, 8. 9. 10. 11

℞. (10) The judgments of the Lord are true, and all of them are just.

The law of the Lord is perfect, refreshing the soul;
The decree of the Lord is trustworthy, giving wisdom to the simple.

℞. The judgments of the Lord are true, and all of them are just.

The precepts of the Lord are right, rejoicing the heart;
The command of the Lord is clear, enlightening the eye.

℞. The judgments of the Lord are true, and all of them are just.

The fear of the Lord is pure, enduring forever;
The ordinances of the Lord are true, all of them just.

℞. The judgments of the Lord are true, and all of them are just.

They are more precious than gold, than a heap of purest gold;
Sweeter also than syrup or honey from the comb.

℞. The judgments of the Lord are true, and all of them are just.
℞. Or: Your words, Lord, are spirit and life.

---

2   Ps 37, 3-4. 5-6. 30-31

℞. (30) The mouth of the just man murmurs wisdom.

Trust in the Lord and do good, that you may dwell in the land and enjoy security.
Take delight in the Lord, and he will grant you your heart's requests.

℞. The mouth of the just man murmurs wisdom.

Commit to the Lord your way; trust in him, and he will act.
He will make justice dawn for you like the light;
bright as the noonday shall be your vindication.

℞. The mouth of the just man murmurs wisdom.

The mouth of the just man tells of wisdom and his tongue utters what is right.
The law of his God is in his heart, and his steps do not falter.

℞. The mouth of the just man murmurs wisdom.

---

3   Ps 119, 9. 10. 11. 12. 13. 14

℞. (12) Lord, teach me your decrees.

How shall a young man be faultless in his way?
By keeping to your words.

℞. Lord, teach me your decrees.

With all my heart I seek you;
let me not stray from your commands.

℞. Lord, teach me your decrees.

Within my heart I treasure your promise, that I may not sin against you.

℞. Lord, teach me your decrees.

Blessed are you, O Lord;
teach me your statutes.

℞. Lord, teach me your decrees.

With my lips I declare all the ordinances of your mouth.

℞. Lord, teach me your decrees.

In the way of your decrees I rejoice, as much as in all riches.

℞. Lord, teach me your decrees.

728　　　**READING II**

1　　　　　　　　　　　　　　　　　　1 Cor 1, 18-25

A reading from the first letter of Paul to the Corinthians

It has pleased God to save those who have faith through the foolishness of the message that we preach.

The message of the cross is complete absurdity to those who are headed for ruin, but to us who are experiencing salvation it is the power of God. Scripture says,

"I will destroy the wisdom of the wise,

and thwart the cleverness of the clever."

Where is the wise man to be found? Where the scribe? Where the master of worldly argument? Has not God turned the wisdom of this world into folly. Since in God's wisdom the world did not come to know him through wisdom, it pleased God to save those who believe through the absurdity of the preaching of the gospel. Yes, Jews demand "signs" and Greeks look for "wisdom," but we preach Christ crucified, a stumbling block to Jews and an absurdity to Gentiles, but to those who are called, Jews and Greeks alike, Christ the power of God and the wisdom of God. For God's folly is wiser than men, and his weakness more powerful than men.

　　　　　　This is the Word of the Lord.

————————

2　　　　　　　　　　　　　　　　　　1 Cor 2, 1-10

A reading from the first letter of Paul to the Corinthians

We teach the wisdom of God in mystery.

Brothers, when I came to you I did not come proclaiming God's testimony with any particular eloquence or "wisdom." No, I determined that while I was with you I would speak of nothing but Jesus Christ and him crucified. When I came among you it was in weakness and fear, and with much trepidation. My message and my preaching had none of the persuasive force of "wise" argumentation, but the convincing power of the Spirit. As a consequence, your faith rests not on the wisdom of men but on the power of God.

There is, to be sure, a certain wisdom which we express among the spiritually mature. It is not a wisdom of this age, however, nor of the rulers of this age, who are men headed for destruction. No, what we utter is God's wisdom: a mysterious, a hidden wisdom. God planned it before all ages for our glory. None of the rulers of this age knew the mystery; if they had known it, they would never have crucified the Lord of glory. Of this wisdom it is written:

"Eye has not seen, ear has not heard,

nor has it so much as dawned on man

what God has prepared for those who love him."

Yet God has revealed this wisdom to us through the Spirit.

　　　　　　This is the Word of the Lord.

————————

3　　　　　　　　　　　　　　　　　　1 Cor 2, 10-16

A reading from the first letter of Paul to the Corinthians

We are those who have the mind of Christ.

The spirit scrutinizes all matters, even the deep things of God. Who, for example, knows a man's innermost self but the man's own spirit within him? Similarly, no one knows what lies at the depths of God but the Spirit of God. The Spirit we have received is not the world's spirit but God's Spirit, helping us to recognize the gifts he has given us. We speak of these, not in words of human wisdom but in words taught by the Spirit, thus interpreting spiritual things in spiritual terms. The natural man does not accept what is taught by the Spirit of God. For him, that is absurdity. He cannot come to know such teaching because it must be appraised in a spiritual way. The spiritual man, on the other hand, can appraise everything, though he himself can be appraised by no one. For, "Who has known the mind of the Lord so as to instruct him?" But we have the mind of Christ.

　　　　　　This is the Word of the Lord.

————————

4   Eph 3, 8-12

A reading from the letter of Paul to the Ephesians

The mission is to proclaim to all peoples the infinite treasure of Christ.

To me, the least of all believers, was given the grace to preach to the Gentiles the unfathomable riches of Christ and to enlighten all men on the mysterious design which for ages was hidden in God, the Creator of all. Now, therefore, through the church, God's manifold wisdom is made known to the principalities and powers of heaven, in accord with his age-old purpose, carried out in Christ Jesus our Lord. In Christ and through faith in him we can speak freely to God, drawing near him with confidence.

This is the Word of the Lord.

---

5   Eph 4, 1-7. 11-13

A reading from the letter of Paul to the Ephesians

Our mission is to build up the body of Christ.

I plead with you as a prisoner for the Lord, to live a life worthy of the calling you have received, with perfect humility, meekness, and patience, bearing with one another lovingly. Make every effort to preserve the unity which has the Spirit as its origin and peace as its binding force. There is but one body and one Spirit, just as there is but one hope given all of you by your call. There is one Lord, one faith, one baptism; one God and Father of all, who is over all, and works through all, and is in all.

Each of us has received God's favor in the measure in which Christ bestows it. It is he who gave apostles, prophets, evangelists, pastors, and teachers in roles of service for the faithful to build up the body of Christ, till we become one in faith and in the knowledge of God's Son, and form that perfect man who is Christ come to full stature.

This is the Word of the Lord.

---

6   2 Tm 1, 13-14; 2, 1-3

A reading from the second letter of Paul to Timothy

You have been trusted to look after something precious; guard it with the help of the Holy Spirit who lives in us.

Take as a model of sound teaching what you have heard me say, in faith and love in Christ Jesus. Guard the rich deposit of faith with the help of the Holy Spirit who dwells within us.

So you, my son, must be strong in the grace which is ours in Christ Jesus. The things which you have heard from me through many witnesses you must hand on to trustworthy men who will be able to teach others. Bear hardship along with me as a good soldier of Christ Jesus.

This is the Word of the Lord.

---

7   2 Tm 4, 1-5

A reading from the second letter of Paul to Timothy

Preach the Good News; fulfill your ministry.

In the presence of God and of Christ Jesus, who is coming to judge the living and the dead, and by his appearing and his kingly power, I charge you to preach the word, to stay with this task whether convenient or inconvenient— correcting, reproving, appealing—constantly teaching and never losing patience. For the time will come when people will not tolerate sound doctrine, but, following their own desires, will surround themselves with teachers who tickle their ears. They will stop listening to the truth and will wander off to fables. As for you, be steady and self-possessed; put up with hardship, perform your work as an evangelist, fulfill your ministry.

This is the Word of the Lord.

---

729   ALLELUIA VERSE AND
           VERSE BEFORE THE GOSPEL

1   Mt 5, 16

Let your light shine before men,
that they may see your good works and glorify
    your Father.

2   1 Cor 1, 18

The message of the cross is folly to those who
    turn away,
but to those who are saved it is the power
    of God.

3   1 Cor 2, 7

We teach a secret and hidden wisdom of God,
which he decreed for our glory before time
began.

4

The seed is the word of God, Christ is the
    sower;
all who come to him will live for ever.

---

730   **GOSPEL**

1   Mt 5, 13-16

✠ A reading from the holy gospel according
              to Matthew

You are the light of the world.

Jesus said to his disciples: "You are the salt
of the earth. But what if salt goes flat? How can
you restore its flavor? Then it is good for
nothing but to be thrown out and trampled
underfoot.

"You are the light of the world. A city set
on a hill cannot be hidden. Men do not light
a lamp and then put it under a bushel basket.
They set it on a stand where it gives light to
all in the house. In the same way, your light
must shine before men so that they may see
goodness in your acts and give praise to your
heavenly Father."

This is the gospel of the Lord.

---

2   Mt 23, 8-12

✠ A reading from the holy gospel according
              to Matthew

You must not allow yourselves to be called teachers, for you
have only one teacher, the Christ.

Jesus said to his disciples: "Avoid the title
'Rabbi.' One among you is your teacher, the
rest are learners. Do not call anyone on earth
your father. Only one is your father, the One in
heaven. Avoid being called teachers. Only one
is your teacher, the Messiah. The greatest
among you will be the one who serves the
rest. Whoever exalts himself shall be humbled,
but whoever humbles himself shall be exalted."

This is the gospel of the Lord.

---

3   Mk 4, 1-10. 13-20 or 4, 1-9

✠ A reading from the holy gospel according
              to Mark

The sower went out to sow seed.

(Long Form)

Jesus began to teach beside the lake. Such a
huge crowd gathered around him that he went
and sat in a boat on the water, while the crowd
remained on the shore nearby. He began to instruct them at great length, by the use of
parables, and in the course of his teaching
said: "Listen carefully to this. A farmer went
out sowing. Some of what he sowed landed
on the footpath, where the birds came along
and ate it. Some of the seed landed on rocky
ground where it had little soil; it sprouted
immediately because the soil had no depth.
Then, when the sun rose and scorched it, it
began to wither for lack of roots. Again, some
landed among thorns, which grew up and
choked it off, and there was no yield of grain.
Some seed, finally, landed on good soil and
yielded grain that sprang up to produce at a
rate of thirty- and sixty- and a hundredfold."
Having spoken this parable, he added: "Let
him who has ears to hear me, hear!"

Now when he was away from the crowd,
those present with the Twelve questioned him
about the parables. He said to them: "You
do not understand this parable? How then are
you going to understand other figures like it?
What the sower is sowing is the word. Those
on the path are the ones to whom, as soon
as they hear the word, Satan comes to carry
off what was sown in them. Similarly, those
sown on rocky ground are people who on
listening to the word accept it joyfully at the
outset. Being rootless, they last only a while.
When some pressure or persecution overtakes
them, because of the word, they falter. Those

sown among thorns are another class. They have listened to the word, but anxieties over life's demands, and the desire for wealth, and cravings of other sorts come to choke it off; it bears no yield. But those sown on good soil are the ones who listen to the word, take it to heart, and yield at thirty- and sixty- and a hundred-fold."

This is the gospel of the Lord.

OR

(Short Form)

Jesus began to teach beside the lake. Such a huge crowd gathered around him that he went and sat in a boat on the water, while the crowd remained on the shore nearby. He began to instruct them at great length, by the use of parables, and in the course of his teaching said: "Listen carefully to this. A farmer went out sowing. Some of what he sowed landed on the footpath, where the birds came along and ate it. Some of the seed landed on rocky ground where it had little soil; it sprouted immediately because the soil had no depth. Then, when the sun rose and scorched it, it began to wither for lack of roots. Again, some landed among thorns, which grew up and choked it off, and there was no yield of grain. Some seed, finally, landed on good soil and yielded grain that sprang up to produce at a rate of thirty and sixty and hundredfold." Having spoken this parable, he added: "Let him who has ears to hear me, hear!"

This is the gospel of the Lord.

COMMON OF VIRGINS

731   **READING I**

OUTSIDE EASTER SEASON

1

Sg 8, 6-7

A reading from the Song of Solomon
Love is as strong as death.

Set me as a seal on your heart,
    as a seal on your arm;

For stern as death is love,
    relentless as the nether world is devotion;
    its flames are a blazing fire.
Deep waters cannot quench love,
    nor floods sweep it away.
Were one to offer all he owns to purchase love,
    he would be roundly mocked.

This is the Word of the Lord.

2

Hos 2, 16. 17. 21-22

A reading from the book of the prophet Hosea
I will betroth you to myself for ever.

I will lead her into the desert
    and speak to her heart.
She shall respond there as in the days of her
    youth,
    when she came up from the land of Egypt.

I will espouse you to me forever:
    I will espouse you in right and in justice,
    in love and in mercy;
I will espouse you in fidelity,
    and you shall know the Lord.

This is the Word of the Lord.

---

732   **READING I**

DURING EASTER SEASON

1

Rv 19, 1. 5-9

A reading from the book of Revelation
Happy are those who are invited to the wedding feast of
the Lamb.

I, John, heard what sounded like the loud song of a great assembly in heaven. They were singing:

"Alleluia!
Salvation, glory, and might belong to our
    God."
    A voice coming from the throne cried out:
    "Praise our God, all you his servants,
    the small and the great, who revere him!"
    Then I heard what sounded like the shouts of a great crowd, or the roaring of the deep, or mighty peals of thunder, as they cried:
    "Alleluia!

The Lord is king,
  our God, the Almighty!
Let us rejoice and be glad,
  and give him glory!
For this is the wedding day of the Lamb;
  his bride has prepared herself for the
  wedding.
She has been given a dress to wear
  made of finest linen, brilliant white."
(The linen dress is the virtuous deeds of God's
saints.)
    The angel then said to me: "Write this down:
Happy are they who have been invited to the
wedding feast of the Lamb."
      This is the Word of the Lord.

---

2   Rv 21, 1-5

A reading from the book of Revelation

I saw the new Jerusalem, as beautiful as a bride all dressed
for her husband.

I, John, saw new heavens and a new earth.
The former heavens and the former earth had
passed away, and the sea was no longer.
I also saw a new Jerusalem, the holy city,
coming down out of heaven from God, beautiful as a bride prepared to meet her husband.
I heard a loud voice from the throne cry out:
"This is God's dwelling among men. He shall
dwell with them and they shall be his people,
and he shall be their God who is always with
them. He shall wipe every tear from their eyes,
and there shall be no more death or mourning,
crying out or pain, for the former world has
passed away."
    The One who sat on the throne said to me,
"See, I make all things new!"
      This is the Word of the Lord.

---

733   **RESPONSORIAL PSALM**

1   Ps 45, 11-12. 14-15. 16-17

℟. (11) Listen to me, daughter;
  see and bend your ear.
Hear, O daughter, and see; turn your ear,
  forget your people and your father's house.

So shall the king desire your beauty;
  for he is your lord, and you must worship
  him.
℟. Listen to me, daughter;
  see and bend your ear.
All glorious is the king's daughter as she
  enters;
  her raiment is threaded with spun gold.
In embroidered apparel she is borne in to the
  king;
  behind her the virgins of her train are
  brought to you.
℟. Listen to me, daughter;
  see and bend your ear.
They are borne in with gladness and joy;
  they enter the palace of the king.
The place of your fathers your sons shall have;
  you shall make them princes through all the
  land.
℟. Listen to me, daughter;
  see and bend your ear.
℟. Or: (Mt 25, 6) The bridegroom is here;
  let us go out to meet Christ the Lord.

---

2   Ps 148, 1-2. 11-12. 13-14. 14

℟. Alleluia.
Praise the Lord from the heavens,
  praise him in the heights;
Praise him, all you his angels,
  praise him, all you his hosts.
℟. Alleluia.
Let the kings of the earth and all peoples,
  the princes and all the judges of the earth,
Young men too, and maidens,
  old men and boys.
℟. Alleluia.
Praise the name of the Lord,
  for his name alone is exalted;
His majesty is above earth and heaven.
℟. Alleluia.
He has lifted up the horn of his people.
  Be this his praise from all his faithful ones;
From the children of Israel, the people close
  to him. Alleluia.
℟. Alleluia.

734   READING II

1   1 Cor 7, 25-35

A reading from the first letter of Paul to the Corinthians

A virgin can devote herself to the work of the Lord.

With respect to virgins, I have not received any commandment from the Lord, but I give my opinion as one who is trustworthy, thanks to the Lord's mercy. It is this: In the present time of stress it seems good to me for a person to continue as he is. Are you bound to a wife? Then do not seek your freedom. Are you free of a wife? If so, do not go in search of one. Should you marry, however, you will not be committing sin. Neither does a virgin commit a sin if she marries. Such people, however, will have trials in this life, and these I should like to spare you.

I tell you, brothers, the time is short. From now on those with wives should live as though they had none; those who weep should live as though they were not weeping, and those who rejoice as though they were not rejoicing; buyers should conduct themselves as though they owned nothing, and those who make use of the world as though they were not using it, for the world as we know it is passing away.

I should like you to be free of all worries. The unmarried man is busy with the Lord's affairs, concerned with pleasing the Lord; but the married man is busy with this world's demands and occupied with pleasing his wife. This means he is divided. The virgin—indeed, any unmarried woman—is concerned with things of the Lord, in pursuit of holiness in body and spirit. The married woman, on the other hand, has the cares of this world to absorb her and is concerned with pleasing her husband. I am going into this with you for your own good. I have no desire to place restrictions on you, but I do want to promote what is good, what will help you to devote yourselves entirely to the Lord.

This is the Word of the Lord.

2   2 Cor 10, 17—11, 2

A reading from the second letter of Paul to the Corinthians

I have betrothed you to one man, as a chaste virgin for Christ.

"Let him who would boast, boast in the Lord." It is not the man who recommends himself who is approved but the man whom the Lord recommends.

You must endure a little of my folly. Put up with me, I beg you! I am jealous of you with the jealousy of God himself, since I have given you in marriage to one husband, presenting you as a chaste virgin to Christ.

This is the Word of the Lord.

735   ALLELUIA VERSE AND VERSE BEFORE THE GOSPEL

1

This is the wise bridesmaid, whom the Lord found waiting;
at his coming, she went in with him to the wedding feast.

2

Come, bride of Christ, and receive the crown, which the Lord has prepared for you for ever.

736   GOSPEL

1   Mt 19, 3-12

✠ A reading from the holy gospel according to Matthew

There are some who have chosen to remain single for the sake of the kingdom of God.

Some of the Pharisees came up to Jesus and said, to test him, "May a man divorce his wife for any reason whatever?" He replied, "Have you not read that at the beginning the Creator made them male and female and declared, 'For this reason a man shall leave his father and mother and cling to his wife, and the two shall become as one'? Thus they are no longer two but one flesh. Therefore, let no man separate what God has joined." They said to him, "Then why did Moses command divorce and the promulgation of a divorce decree?" "Because of your stubbornness Moses let you divorce your wives," he replied; "but at the beginning it was not that way. I now say to you, whoever divorces his wife (lewd conduct is a separate case) and marries another commits adultery, and the man who marries a divorced woman commits adultery."

His disciples said to him, "If that is the case between man and wife, it is better not to marry." He said, "Not everyone can accept this teaching, only those to whom it is given to do so. Some men are incapable of sexual activity from birth; some have been deliberately made so; and some there are who have freely renounced sex for the sake of God's reign. Let him accept this teaching who can."

This is the gospel of the Lord.

---

2   Mt 25, 1-13

✠ A reading of the holy gospel according to Matthew

The bridegroom is here; go out and meet him.

Jesus told this parable to his disciples: "The reign of God can be likened to ten bridesmaids who took their torches and went out to welcome the groom. Five of them were foolish, while the other five were sensible. The foolish ones, in taking their torches, brought no oil along, but the sensible ones took flasks of oil as well as their torches. The groom delayed his coming, so they all began to nod, then to fall asleep. At midnight someone shouted, 'The groom is here! Come out and greet him!' At the outcry all the virgins woke up and got their torches ready. The foolish ones said to the sensible, 'Give us some of your oil. Our torches are going out.' But the sensible ones replied, 'No, there may not be enough for you and us. You had better go to the dealers and buy yourselves some.' While they went off to buy it the groom arrived, and the ones who were ready went in to the wedding with him. Then the door was barred. Later the other bridesmaids came back. 'Master, master!' they cried. 'Open the door for us.' But he answered, 'I

tell you, I do not know you.' The moral is: keep your eyes open, for you know not the day or the hour."

This is the gospel of the Lord.

---

3   Lk 10, 38-42

✠ A reading of the holy gospel according to Luke

Jesus accepts the hospitality of Martha and praises the attentiveness of Mary.

Jesus entered a village where a woman named Martha welcomed him to her home. She had a sister named Mary, who seated herself at the Lord's feet and listened to his words. Martha, who was busy with all the details of hospitality, came to him and said, "Lord, are you not concerned that my sister has left me all alone to do the household tasks? Tell her to help me."

The Lord in reply said to her: "Martha, Martha, you are anxious and upset about many things; one thing only is required. Mary has chosen the better portion and she shall not be deprived of it."

This is the gospel of the Lord.

COMMON OF SAINTS

737   READING I
          OUTSIDE EASTER SEASON

1   Gn 12, 1-4

A reading from the book of Genesis

Leave your country, your family, and come.

The Lord said to Abram: "Go forth from the land of your kinsfolk and from your father's house to a land that I will show you.

"I will make of you a great nation,
    and I will bless you;
I will make your name great,
    so that you will be a blessing.
I will bless those who bless you
    and curse those who curse you.
All the communities of the earth
    shall find blessing in you."

Abram went as the Lord directed him.

This is the Word of the Lord.

2   Lv 19, 1-2. 17-18

A reading from the book of Leviticus

Love your neighbor as you love yourself.

The Lord said to Moses, "Speak to the whole Israelite community and tell them: Be holy, for I, the Lord, your God, am holy.

"You shall not bear hatred for your brother in your heart. Though you may have to reprove your fellow man, do not incur sin because of him. Take no revenge and cherish no grudge against your fellow countrymen. You shall love your neighbor as yourself. I am the Lord."

This is the Word of the Lord.

---

3   Dt 6, 3-9

A reading from the book of Deuteronomy

Love the Lord your God with your whole heart.

Moses said to the people: "Hear, Israel, and be careful to observe the commandments, that you may grow and prosper the more, in keeping with the promise of the Lord, the God of your fathers, to give you a land flowing with milk and honey.

"Hear, O Israel! The Lord is our God, the Lord alone! Therefore, you shall love the Lord, your God, with all your heart, and with all your soul, and with all your strength. Take to heart these words which I enjoin on you today. Drill them into your children. Speak of them at home and abroad, whether you are busy or at rest. Bind them at your wrist as a sign and let them be as a pendant on your forehead. Write them on the doorposts of your houses and on your gates."

This is the Word of the Lord.

---

4   Dt 10, 8-9

[For religious]

A reading from the book of Deuteronomy

The Lord God is your inheritance.

Moses said to the people: "At that time the Lord set apart the tribe of Levi to carry the ark of the covenant of the Lord, to be in attendance before the Lord and minister to him, and to give blessings in his name, as they have done to this day. For this reason, Levi

has no share in the heritage with his brothers; the Lord himself is his heritage, as the Lord, your God, has told him."

This is the Word of the Lord.

---

5   1 Kgs 19, 4-9. 11-15

[For religious]

A reading from the first book of Kings

Go out and stand on the mountaintop in the presence of your God.

Elijah went a day's journey into the desert, until he came to a broom tree and sat beneath it. He prayed for death: "This is enough, O Lord! Take my life, for I am no better than my fathers." He lay down and fell asleep under the broom tree, but then an angel touched him and ordered him to get up and eat. He looked and there at his head was a hearth cake and a jug of water. After he ate and drank, he lay down again, but the angel of the Lord came back a second time, touched him, and ordered, "Get up and eat, else the journey will be too long for you!" He got up, ate and drank; then, strengthened by that food, he walked forty days and forty nights to the mountain of God, Horeb.

There he came to a cave, where he took shelter. Then the Lord said, "Go outside and stand on the mountain before the Lord; the Lord will be passing by." A strong and heavy wind was rending the mountains and crushing rocks before the Lord—but the Lord was not in the wind. After the wind there was an earthquake—but the Lord was not in the earthquake. After the earthquake there was fire—but the Lord was not in the fire. After the fire there was a tiny whispering sound. When he heard this, Elijah hid his face in his cloak and went and stood at the entrance of the cave. A voice said to him, "Elijah, why are you here?" He replied, "I have been most zealous for the Lord, the God of hosts. But the Israelites have forsaken your covenant, torn down your altars, and put your prophets to the sword. I alone am left, and they seek to take my life." "Go, take the road back to the desert near Damascus," the Lord said to him.

This is the Word of the Lord.

6   1 Kgs 19, 16. 19-21

[For religious]

A reading from the first book of Kings

Elisha rose up and followed Elijah.

The Lord said to Elijah: "You shall anoint
Elisha, son of Shaphat of Abel-meholah, as
prophet to succeed you.

Elijah set out, and came upon Elisha, son of
Shaphat, as he was plowing with twelve yoke
of oxen; he was following the twelfth. Elijah
went over to him and threw his cloak over him.
Elisha left the oxen, ran after Elijah, and said,
"Please, let me kiss my father and mother
goodbye, and I will follow you." "Go back!"
Elijah answered. "Have I done anything to
you?" Elisha left him and, taking the yoke
of oxen, slaughtered them; he used the plowing
equipment for fuel to boil their flesh, and gave
it to his people to eat. Then he left and followed
Elijah as his attendant.

This is the Word of the Lord.

7   Tb 8, 5-7

A reading from the book of Tobit

You and I must pray that the Lord may have mercy on us.

On their wedding night Sarah got up, and she
and Tobiah started to pray and beg that deliverance might be theirs. He began with these
words:

"Blessed are you, O God of our fathers;
    praised be your name forever and ever.
Let the heavens and all your creation
    praise you forever.
You made Adam and you gave him his wife
        Eve
    to be his help and support;
    and from these two the human race de-
        scended.
You said, 'It is not good for the man to be
        alone;
    let us make him a partner like himself.'
Now, Lord, you know that I take this wife of
        mine
    not because of lust,
    but for a noble purpose.

Call down your mercy on me and on her,
    and allow us to live together to a happy
        old age."

This is the Word of the Lord.

8   Tb 12, 6-13

[For those who work for the disadvantaged]

A reading from the book of Tobit

It is good to pray while fasting and giving alms.

The angel said to Tobit and his son: "Thank
God! Give him the praise and the glory. Before all the living, acknowledge the many good
things he has done for you, by blessing and
extolling his name in song. Before all men,
honor and proclaim God's deeds, and do not be
slack in praising him. A king's secret it is
prudent to keep, but the works of God are to
be declared and made known. Praise them with
due honor. Do good, and evil will not find
its way to you. Prayer and fasting are good,
but better than either is almsgiving accompanied by righteousness. A little with righteousness is better than abundance with wickedness. It is better to give alms than to store
up gold; for almsgiving saves one from death
and expiates every sin. Those who regularly
give alms shall enjoy a full life; but those
habitually guilty of sin are their own worst
enemies.

"I will now tell you the whole truth; I will
conceal nothing at all from you. I have already
said to you, 'A king's secret it is prudent to
keep, but the works of God are to be made
known with due honor.' I can now tell you that
when you, Tobit, and Sarah prayed, it was I
who presented and read the record of your
prayer before the Glory of the Lord; and I did
the same thing when you used to bury the
dead. When you did not hesitate to get up and
leave your dinner in order to go and bury the
dead, I was sent to put you to the test."

This is the Word of the Lord.

9   Jdt 8, 2-8

[For widows]

A reading from the book of Judith

She feared the Lord greatly.

Judith's husband, Manasseh, of her own tribe and clan, had died at the time of the barley harvest. While he was in the field supervising those who bound the sheaves, he suffered sunstroke; and he died of this illness in Bethulia, his native city. He was buried with his forefathers in the field between Dothan and Balamon. The widowed Judith remained three years and four months at home, where she set up a tent for herself on the roof of her house. She put sackcloth about her loins and wore widow's weeds. She fasted all the days of her widowhood, except sabbath eves and sabbaths, new moon eves and new moons, feastdays and holidays of the house of Israel. She was beautifully formed and lovely to behold. Her husband, Manasseh, had left her gold and silver, servants and maids, livestock and fields, which she was maintaining. No one had a bad word to say about her, for she was a very God-fearing woman.

This is the Word of the Lord.

---

10   Est C, 1-7. 10

A reading from the book of Esther

I was fearful that I might confer on man the honor due to God.

Mordecai recalled all that the Lord had done and he prayed to him and said: "O Lord God, almighty King, all things are in your power, and there is no one to oppose you in your will to save Israel. You made heaven and earth and every wonderful thing under the heavens. You are Lord of all, and there is no one who can resist you, Lord. You know all things. You know, O Lord, that it was not out of insolence or pride or desire for fame that I acted thus in not bowing down to the proud Haman. Gladly would I have kissed the soles of his feet for the salvation of Israel. But I acted as I did so as not to place the honor of man above that of God. I will not bow down to anyone but you, my Lord. It is not out of pride that I am

acting thus. Hear my prayer; have pity on your inheritance and turn our sorrow into joy: thus we shall live to sing praise to your name, O Lord. Do not silence those who praise you."

This is the Word of the Lord.

---

11   Prv 31, 10-13. 19-20. 30-31

A reading from the book of Proverbs

It is the wise woman whom the Lord will praise.

When one finds a worthy wife,
   her value is far beyond pearls.
Her husband, entrusting his heart to her,
   has an unfailing prize.
She brings him good, and not evil,
   all the days of her life.
She obtains wool and flax
   and makes cloth with skillful hands.
She puts her hands to the distaff,
   and her fingers ply the spindle.
She reaches out her hands to the poor,
   and extends her arms to the needy.
Charm is deceptive and beauty fleeting;
   the woman who fears the Lord is to be
   praised.
Give her a reward of her labors,
   and let her works praise her at the city gates.

This is the Word of the Lord.

---

12   Sir 2, 7-11

A reading from the book of Sirach

You who fear the Lord, believe him, hope in him, love him.

You who fear the Lord, wait for his mercy,
   turn not away lest you fall.
You who fear the Lord, trust him,
   and your reward will not be lost.
You who fear the Lord, hope for good things,
   for lasting joy and mercy.
Study the generations long past and understand;
   has anyone hoped in the Lord and been
   disappointed?
Has anyone persevered in his fear and been
   forsaken?
   has anyone called upon him and been rebuffed?
Compassionate and merciful is the Lord;
   he forgives sins, he saves in time of trouble.

This is the Word of the Lord.

---

13   Sir 3, 17-24

A reading from the book of Sirach

Humble yourselves and you will find grace in the eyes of
God.

My son, conduct your affairs with humility,
    and you will be loved more than a giver of
        gifts.
Humble yourself the more, the greater you are,
    and you will find favor with God.
For great is the power of God;
    by the humble he is glorified.
What is too sublime for you, seek not,
    into things beyond your strength search not.
What is committed to you, attend to;
    for what is hidden is not your concern.
With what is too much for you meddle not,
    when shown things beyond human under-
        standing.
Their own opinion has misled many,
    and false reasoning unbalanced their judg-
        ment.
Where the pupil of the eye is missing, there
    is no light,
    and where there is no knowledge, there is no
        wisdom.
            This is the Word of the Lord.

---

14   Sir 26, 1-4. 13-16

A reading from the book of Sirach

The beauty of a good wife in a well-kept house is like the
beauty of the rising sun.

Happy the husband of a good wife,
    twice-lengthened are his days;
A worthy wife brings joy to her husband,
    peaceful and full is his life.
A good wife is a generous gift
    bestowed upon him who fears the Lord;
Be he rich or poor, his heart is content,
    and a smile is ever on his face.

A gracious wife delights her husband,
    her thoughtfulness puts flesh on his bones;
A gift from the Lord is her governed speech,
    and her firm virtue is of surpassing worth.
Choicest of blessings is a modest wife,
    priceless her chaste person.
Like the sun rising in the Lord's heavens,

the beauty of a virtuous wife is the radiance
    of her home.
            This is the Word of the Lord.

---

15   Is 58, 6-11

[For those who work for the disadvantaged]

A reading from the book of the prophet Isaiah

Share your bread with the hungry.

Thus says the Lord:
This is the fasting that I wish:
    releasing those bound unjustly,
    untying the thongs of the yoke;
Setting free the oppressed,
    breaking every yoke;
Sharing your bread with the hungry,
    sheltering the oppressed and the homeless;
Clothing the naked when you see them,
    and not turning your back on your own.

Then your light shall break forth like the dawn,
    and your wound shall quickly be healed;
Your vindication shall go before you,
    and the glory of the Lord shall be your rear
        guard.
Then you shall call, and the Lord will answer,
    you shall cry for help, and he will say: Here
        I am!
If you remove from your midst oppression,
    false accusation and malicious speech;
If you bestow your bread on the hungry
    and satisfy the afflicted;
Then light shall rise for you in darkness,
    and the gloom shall become for you like
        midday;
Then the Lord will guide you always
    and give you plenty even on the parched
        land.
He will renew your strength,
    and you shall be like a watered garden,
    like a spring whose water never fails.
            This is the Word of the Lord.

16   Jer 20, 7-9

**A reading from the book of the prophet
Jeremiah**

The desire to speak the word of the Lord seemed to be like
a fire burning in my heart.

You duped me, O Lord, and I let myself be
    duped;

you were too strong for me, and you tri-
    umphed.
All the day I am an object of laughter;
    everyone mocks me.
Whenever I speak, I must cry out,
    violence and outrage is my message;
The word of the Lord has brought me
    derision and reproach all the day.
I say to myself, I will not mention him,
    I will speak in his name no more.
But then it becomes like fire burning in my
    heart,
    imprisoned in my bones;
I grow weary holding it in,
    I cannot endure it.
          This is the Word of the Lord.

17   Mi 6, 6-8

A reading from the book of the prophet Micah

What is good has been explained to you, man; this is what
the Lord God asks of you.

With what shall I come before the Lord,
    and bow before God most high?
Shall I come before him with holocausts,
    with calves a year old?
Will the Lord be pleased with thousands of
    rams,
    with myriad streams of oil?
Shall I give my first-born for my crime,
    the fruit of my body for the sin of my soul?
You have been told, O man, what is good,
    and what the Lord requires of you:
Only to do the right and to love goodness,
    and to walk humbly with your God.
          This is the Word of the Lord.

18   Zep 2, 3; 3, 12-13

**A reading from the book of the prophet
Zephaniah**

Without the Lord, I shall be left destitute in the midst of the
world.

Seek the Lord, all you humble of the earth,
    who have observed his law;
Seek justice, seek humility;
    perhaps you may be sheltered
    on the day of the Lord's anger.

But I will leave as a remnant in your midst
    a people humble and lowly,
Who shall take refuge in the name of the Lord:
    the remnant of Israel.
They shall do no wrong
    and speak no lies;
Nor shall there be found in their mouths
    a deceitful tongue;
They shall pasture and couch their flocks
    with none to disturb them.
          This is the Word of the Lord.

---

738   **READING I**
        DURING EASTER SEASON

1   Acts 4, 32-35

[For religious]

A reading from the Acts of the Apostles

The whole group of believers was united, heart and soul.

**The community of believers were of one heart
and one mind. None of them ever claimed anything as his own; rather, everything was held
in common. With power the apostles bore
witness to the resurrection of the Lord Jesus,
and great respect was paid to them all; nor was
there anyone needy among them, for all who
owned property or houses sold them and donated the proceeds. They used to lay them at
the feet of the apostles to be distributed to
everyone according to his need.**
        This is the Word of the Lord.

---

2   Rv 3, 14. 20-22

A reading from the book of Revelation

I will come in to share his meal, side by side with him.

**The Amen, the faithful Witness and true, the
Source of God's creation, has this to say: "Here
I stand, knocking at the door. If anyone hears
me calling and opens the door, I will enter his
house and have supper with him, and he with
me. I will give the victor the right to sit with
me on my throne, as I myself won the victory
and took my seat beside my Father on his
throne.
"Let him who has ears to hear heed the Spirit's word to the churches."**
        This is the Word of the Lord.

3   Rv 19, 1. 5-9

A reading from the book of Revelation

Happy are those who are invited to the wedding feast of the Lamb.

I, John, heard what sounded like the loud song of a great assembly in heaven. They were singing:
"Alleluia!
Salvation, glory, and might belong to our God."
A voice coming from the throne cried out:
"Praise our God, all you his servants,
the small and the great, who revere him!"
Then I heard what sounded like the shouts of a great crowd, or the roaring of the deep, or mighty peals of thunder, as they cried:
"Alleluia!
The Lord is king,
our God, the Almighty!
Let us rejoice and be glad,
and give him glory!
For this is the wedding day of the Lamb,
his bride has prepared herself for the wedding.
She has been given a dress to wear
made of finest linen, brilliant white."
(The linen dress is the virtuous deeds of God's saints.)
The angel then said to me: "Write this down: Happy are they who have been invited to the wedding feast of the Lamb."
This is the Word of the Lord.

---

4   Rv 21, 5-7

A reading from the book of Revelation

The Lord said: I will give water from the well of life to anybody who is thirsty.

The One who sat on the throne said to me, "See, I make all things new!" Then he said, "Write these matters down, for the words are trustworthy and true!" He went on to say: "These words are already fulfilled! I am the Alpha and the Omega, the Beginning and the End. To anyone who thirsts I will give drink without cost from the spring of life-giving water. He who wins the victory shall inherit these gifts; I will be his God and he shall be my son."
This is the Word of the Lord.

---

739   **RESPONSORIAL PSALM**

1   Ps 1, 1-2. 3. 4. 6

℟. (Ps 40, 5) Happy are they who hope in the Lord.
Happy the man who follows not
the counsel of the wicked
Nor walks in the way of sinners,
nor sits in the company of the insolent,
But delights in the law of the Lord
and meditates on his law day and night.
℟. Happy are they who hope in the Lord.
He is like a tree
planted near running water,
That yields its fruit in due season,
and whose leaves never fade.
[Whatever he does, prospers.]
℟. Happy are they who hope in the Lord.
Not so the wicked, not so;
they are like chaff which the wind drives
away.
For the Lord watches over the way of the just,
but the way of the wicked vanishes.
℟. Happy are they who hope in the Lord.
℟. Or: (Ps 92, 13-14) The just man will flourish
like a palm tree
in the garden of the Lord.

---

2   Ps 15, 2-3. 3-4. 5

℟. (1) He who does justice shall live on the Lord's holy mountain.
He who walks blamelessly and does justice;
who thinks the truth in his heart
and slanders not with his tongue;
℟. He who does justice shall live on the Lord's holy mountain.
Who harms not his fellow man,
nor takes up a reproach against his neighbor;
By whom the reprobate is despised,
while he honors those who fear the Lord.
℟. He who does justice shall live on the Lord's holy mountain.

Who lends not his money at usury
  and accepts no bribe against the innocent.
He who does these things
  shall never be disturbed.
℟. He who does justice shall live on the Lord's
  holy mountain.

---

3   Ps 16, 1-2. 5. 7-8. 11

℟. (5) You are my inheritance, O Lord.
Keep me, O God, for in you I take refuge;
  I say to the Lord, "My Lord are you."
O Lord, my allotted portion and my cup,
  you it is who hold fast my lot.
℟. You are my inheritance, O Lord.
I bless the Lord who counsels me;
  even in the night my heart exhorts me.
I set the Lord ever before me;
  with him at my right hand I shall not be
  disturbed.
℟. You are my inheritance, O Lord.
You will show me the path to life,
  fullness of joys in your presence,
  the delights at your right hand forever.
℟. You are my inheritance, O Lord.

---

4   Ps 34, 2-3. 4-5. 6-7. 8-9. 10-11

℟. (2) I will bless the Lord at all times.
I will bless the Lord at all times;
  his praise shall be ever in my mouth.
Let my soul glory in the Lord;
  the lowly will hear me and be glad.
℟. I will bless the Lord at all times.
Glorify the Lord with me,
  let us together extol his name.
I sought the Lord, and he answered me
  and delivered me from all my fears.
℟. I will bless the Lord at all times.
Look to him that you may be radiant with joy,
  and your faces may not blush with shame.
When the afflicted man called out, the Lord
  heard,
  and from all his distress he saved him.
℟. I will bless the Lord at all times.
The angel of the Lord encamps
  around those who fear him, and delivers
  them.

Taste and see how good the Lord is;
  happy the man who takes refuge in him.
℟. I will bless the Lord at all times.
Fear the Lord, you his holy ones,
  for nought is lacking to those who fear him.
The great grow poor and hungry;
  but those who seek the Lord want for no
  good thing.
℟. I will bless the Lord at all times.
℟. Or: (9) Taste and see the goodness of the
  Lord.

---

5   Ps 103, 1-2. 3-4. 8-9. 13-14. 17-18

℟. (1) Oh, bless the Lord, my soul.
Bless the Lord, O my soul;
  and all my being, bless his holy name.
Bless the Lord, O my soul,
  and forget not all his benefits.
℟. Oh, bless the Lord, my soul.
He pardons all your iniquities,
  he heals all your ills.
He redeems your life from destruction,
  he crowns you with kindness and compas-
  sion.
℟. Oh, bless the Lord, my soul.
Merciful and gracious is the Lord,
  slow to anger and abounding in kindness.
He will not always chide,
  nor does he keep his wrath forever.
℟. Oh, bless the Lord, my soul.
As a father has compassion on his children,
  so the Lord has compassion on those who
  fear him,
For he knows how we are formed;
  he remembers that we are dust.
℟. Oh, bless the Lord, my soul.
But the kindness of the Lord is from eternity
  to eternity toward those who fear him,
And his justice toward children's children
  among those who keep his covenant.
℟. Oh, bless the Lord, my soul.

---

6   Ps 112, 1-2. 3-4. 5-6. 7-8. 9

℟. (1) Happy the man who fears the Lord.
Happy the man who fears the Lord,
  who greatly delights in his commands.

His posterity shall be mighty upon the earth;
  the upright generation shall be blessed.
℞. Happy the man who fears the Lord.
Wealth and riches shall be in his house;
  his generosity shall endure forever.
He dawns through the darkness, a light for the
  upright;
  he is gracious and merciful and just.
℞. Happy the man who fears the Lord.
Well for the man who is gracious and lends,
  who conducts his affairs with justice;
He shall never be moved;
  the just man shall be in everlasting remem-
  brance.
℞. Happy the man who fears the Lord.
An evil report he shall not fear;
  his heart is firm, trusting in the Lord.
His heart is steadfast; he shall not fear
  Till he looks down upon his foes.
℞. Happy the man who fears the Lord.
Lavishly he gives to the poor;
  his generosity shall endure forever;
  his horn shall be exalted in glory.
℞. Happy the man who fears the Lord.
℞. Or: Alleluia.

---

7   Ps 128, 1-2. 3. 4-5

℞. (1) Happy are those who fear the Lord.
Happy are you who fear the Lord,
  who walk in his ways!
For you shall eat the fruit of your handiwork;
  happy shall you be, and favored.
℞. Happy are those who fear the Lord.
Your wife shall be like a fruitful vine
  in the recesses of your home;
Your children like olive plants
  around your table.
℞. Happy are those who fear the Lord.
Behold, thus is the man blessed
  who fears the Lord.
The Lord bless you from Zion:
  may you see the prosperity of Jerusalem
  all the days of your life.
℞. Happy are those who fear the Lord.

---

8   Ps 131, 1. 2. 3

℞. In you, Lord, I have found my peace.
O Lord, my heart is not proud,
  nor are my eyes haughty;
I busy not myself with great things,
  nor with things too sublime for me.
℞. In you, Lord, I have found my peace.
Nay rather, I have stilled and quieted
  my soul like a weaned child.
Like a weaned child on its mother's lap,
  [so is my soul within me.]
℞. In you, Lord, I have found my peace.
O Israel, hope in the Lord,
  both now and forever.
℞. In you, Lord, I have found my peace.

---

740   **READING II**

1   Rom 8, 26-30

A reading from the letter of Paul to the Romans
With those he justified, he shared his glory.

The Spirit too helps us in our weakness, for
we do not know how to pray as we ought;
but the Spirit himself makes intercession for
us with groanings which cannot be expressed
in speech. He who searches hearts knows what
the Spirit means, for the Spirit intercedes for
the saints as God himself wills.

We know that God makes all things work
together for the good of those who have been
called according to his decree. Those whom he
foreknew he predestined to share the image of
his Son, that the Son might be the first-born of
many brothers. Those he predestined he likewise called; those he called he also justified;
and those he justified he in turn glorified.

This is the Word of the Lord.

---

2   1 Cor 1, 26-31

**A reading from the first letter of Paul to the
Corinthians**
God has chosen those who are nothing at all.

Brothers, you are among those called. Consider your own situation. Not many of you are
wise, as men account wisdom; not many are
influential; and surely not many are well-born.

God chose those whom the world considers absurd to shame the wise; he singled out the weak of this world to shame the strong. He chose the world's low-born and despised, those who count for nothing, to reduce to nothing those who were something; so that mankind can do no boasting before God. God it is who has given you life in Christ Jesus. He has made him our wisdom and also our justice, our sanctification, and our redemption. This is just as you find it written, "Let him who would boast, boast in the Lord."

> **This is the Word of the Lord.**

---

3   1 Cor 12, 31—13, 13 or 13, 4-13

A reading from the first letter of Paul to the Corinthians

Love never ends.

(Long Form)

Set your hearts on the greater gifts.

Now I will show you the way which surpasses all the others. If I speak with human tongues and angelic as well, but do not have love, I am a noisy gong, a clanging cymbal. If I have the gift of prophecy and, with full knowledge, comprehend all mysteries, if I have faith great enough to move mountains, but have not love, I am nothing. If I give everything I have to feed the poor and hand over my body to be burned, but have not love, I gain nothing.

Love is patient; love is kind. Love is not jealous, it does not put on airs, it is not snobbish. Love is never rude, it is not self-seeking, it is not prone to anger; neither does it brood over injuries. Love does not rejoice in what is wrong but rejoices with the truth. There is no limit to love's forbearance, to its trust, its hope, its power to endure.

Love never fails. Prophecies will cease, tongues will be silent, knowledge will pass away. Our knowledge is imperfect and our prophesying is imperfect. When the perfect comes, the imperfect will pass away. When I was a child I used to talk like a child, think like a child, reason like a child. When I became a man I put childish ways aside. Now we

see indistinctly, as in a mirror; then we shall see face to face. My knowledge is imperfect now; then I shall know even as I am known. There are in the end three things that last: faith, hope, and love, and the greatest of these is love.

> **This is the Word of the Lord.**

OR
(Short Form)

Love is patient; love is kind. Love is not jealous, it does not put on airs, it is not snobbish. Love is never rude, it is not self-seeking, it is not prone to anger; neither does it brood over injuries. Love does not rejoice in what is wrong but rejoices with the truth. There is no limit to love's forbearance, to its trust, its hope, its power to endure.

Love never fails. Prophecies will cease, tongues will be silent, knowledge will pass away. Our knowledge is imperfect and our prophesying is imperfect. When the perfect comes, the imperfect will pass away. When I was a child I used to talk like a child, think like a child, reason like a child. When I became a man I put childish ways aside. Now we see indistinctly, as in a mirror; then we shall see face to face. My knowledge is imperfect now; then I shall know even as I am known. There are in the end three things that last: faith, hope, and love, and the greatest of these is love.

> **This is the Word of the Lord.**

---

4   2 Cor 10, 17—11, 2

A reading from the second letter of Paul to the Corinthians

I arranged for you to marry Christ so that I might give you away as a chaste virgin to this one husband.

"Let him who would boast, boast in the Lord." It is not the man who recommends himself who is approved but the man whom the Lord recommends.

You must endure a little of my folly. Put up with me, I beg you! I am jealous of you with the jealousy of God himself, since I have given you in marriage to one husband, presenting you as a chaste virgin to Christ.

> **This is the Word of the Lord.**

5   Gal 2, 19-20

A reading from the letter of Paul to the Galatians

I live now, not I but Christ lives in me.

It was through the law that I died to the law, to live for God. I have been crucified with Christ, and the life I live now is not my own; Christ is living in me. I still live my human life, but it is a life of faith in the Son of God, who loved me and gave himself for me.

This is the Word of the Lord.

---

6   Gal 6, 14-16

A reading from the letter of Paul to the Galatians

Through which the world is crucified to me, and I to the world.

May I never boast of anything but the cross of our Lord Jesus Christ! Through it, the world has been crucified to me and I to the world. It means nothing whether one is circumcised or not. All that matters is that one is created anew. Peace and mercy on all who follow this rule of life, and on the Israel of God.

This is the Word of the Lord.

---

7   Eph 3, 14-19

A reading from the letter of Paul to the Ephesians

To know the love of Christ, which is beyond all knowledge.

I kneel before the Father from whom every family in heaven and on earth takes its name; and I pray that he will bestow on you gifts in keeping with the riches of his glory. May he strengthen you inwardly through the working of his Spirit. May Christ dwell in your hearts through faith, and may charity be the root and foundation of your life. Thus you will be able to grasp fully, with all the holy ones, the breadth and length and height and depth of Christ's love, and experience this love which surpasses all knowledge, so that you may attain to the fullness of God himself.

This is the Word of the Lord.

---

8   Eph 6, 10-13, 18

A reading from the letter of Paul to the Ephesians

Put on God's armor.

Draw your strength from the Lord and his mighty power. Put on the armor of God so that you may be able to stand firm against the tactics of the devil. Our battle ultimately is not against human forces but against the principalities and powers, the rulers of this world of darkness, the evil spirits in regions above. You must put on the armor of God if you are to resist on the evil day; do all that your duty requires, and hold your ground.

At every opportunity pray in the Spirit, using prayers and petitions of every sort. Pray constantly and attentively for all in the holy company.

This is the Word of the Lord.

---

9   Phil 3, 8-14

A reading from the letter of Paul to the Philippians

I am racing for the finish, for the prize to which God calls us upwards to receive in Christ Jesus.

I have come to rate all as loss in the light of the surpassing knowledge of my Lord Jesus Christ. For his sake I have forfeited everything; I have accounted all else rubbish so that Christ may be my wealth and I may be in him, not having any justice of my own based on observance of the law. The justice I possess is that which comes through faith in Christ. It has its origin in God and is based on faith. I wish to know Christ and the power flowing from his resurrection; likewise to know how to share in his sufferings by being formed into the pattern of his death. Thus do I hope that I may arrive at resurrection from the dead.

It is not that I have reached it yet, or have already finished my course; but I am racing to grasp the prize if possible, since I have been grasped by Christ [Jesus]. Brothers, I do not think of myself as having reached the finish line. I give no thought to what lies behind but push on to what is ahead. My entire attention is on the finish line as I run toward the prize to which God calls me—life on high in Christ Jesus.

This is the Word of the Lord.

---

10   Phil 4, 4-9

A reading from the letter of Paul to the Philippians

Fill your minds with everything that is holy.

Rejoice in the Lord always! I say it again. Rejoice! Everyone should see how unselfish you are. The Lord himself is near. Dismiss all anxiety from your minds. Present your needs to God in every form of prayer and in petitions full of gratitude. Then God's own peace, which is beyond all understanding, will stand guard over your hearts and minds, in Christ Jesus.

Finally, my brothers, your thoughts should be wholly directed to all that is true, all that deserves respect, all that is honest, pure, admirable, decent, virtuous, or worthy of praise. Live according to what you have learned and accepted, what you have heard me say and seen me do. Then will the God of peace be with you.

This is the Word of the Lord.

---

11   1 Tm 5, 3-10

[For widows]

A reading from the first letter of Paul to Timothy

A woman who is a widow and left without anybody can give herself up to God.

Honor the claims of widows who are real widows—that is, who are alone and bereft. If a widow has any children or grandchildren, let these learn that piety begins at home and that they should fittingly support their parents and grandparents; this is the way God wants it to be. The real widow, left destitute, is one who has set her hope on God and continues night and day in supplications and prayers. A widow who gives herself up to selfish indulgence, however, leads a life of living death.

Make the following rules about widows, so that no one may incur blame. If anyone does not provide for his own relatives and especially for members of his immediate family, he has denied the faith; he is worse than an unbeliever. To be on the church's roll of widows, a widow should be not less than sixty years of age. She must have been married only once. Her good character will be attested to by her good deeds. Has she brought up children? Has she been hospitable to strangers? Has she washed the feet of Christian visitors? Has she given help to those in distress? In a word, has she been eager to do every possible good work?

This is the Word of the Lord.

---

12   Jas 2, 14-17

A reading from the letter of James

If good works do not go with faith then it is quite dead.

My brothers, what good is it to profess faith without practicing it? Such faith has no power to save one, has it? If a brother or sister has nothing to wear and no food for the day, and you say to them, "Good-bye and good luck! Keep warm and well fed," but do not meet their bodily needs, what good is that? So it is with the faith that does nothing in practice. It is thoroughly lifeless.

This is the Word of the Lord.

---

13   1 Pt 3, 1-9

A reading from the first letter of Peter

Holy women hoped in God.

You married women must obey your husbands, so that any of them who do not believe in the word of the gospel may be won over apart from preaching, through their wives' conduct. They have only to observe the reverent purity of your way of life. The affectation of an elaborate hairdress, the wearing of golden jewelry, or the donning of rich robes is not for you. Your adornment is rather the hidden character of the heart, expressed in the unfading beauty of a calm and gentle disposition. This is precious in God's eyes. The holy women of past ages used to adorn themselves in this way, reliant on God and obedient to their husbands—for example, Sarah, who was subject to Abraham and called him her master. You

are her children when you do what is right and
let no fears alarm you.

You husbands, too, must show consideration
for those who share your lives. Treat women
with respect as the weaker sex, heirs just as
much as you to the gracious gift of life. If you
do so, nothing will keep your prayers from
being answered.

In summary, then, all of you should be likeminded, sympathetic, loving toward one another, kindly disposed, and humble. Do not
return evil for evil or insult for insult. Return a
blessing instead. This you have been called to
do, that you may receive a blessing as your
inheritance.

This is the Word of the Lord.

---

14   **1 Pt 4, 7-11**

A reading from the first letter of Peter
Each one of you has received a special gift; put yourselves
at the service of others.

Remain calm so that you will be able to pray.
Above all, let your love for one another be
constant, for love covers a multitude of sins.
Be mutually hospitable without complaining.
As generous distributors of God's manifold
grace, put your gifts at the service of one another, each in the measure he has received. The
one who speaks is to deliver God's message.
The one who serves is to do it with the strength
provided by God. Thus, in all of you God is
to be glorified through Jesus Christ: to him be
glory and dominion throughout the ages.
Amen.

This is the Word of the Lord.

---

15   **1 Jn 3, 14-18**

[For those who work for the disadvantaged]

A reading from the first letter of John
We should lay down our lives for our brothers.

That we have passed from death to life we
    know
because we love the brothers.
The man who does not love is among the
    living dead.

Anyone who hates his brother is a murderer,
and you know that eternal life
abides in no murderer's heart.
The way we came to understand love
was that he laid down his life for us;
we too must lay down our lives for our
    brothers.
I ask you, how can God's love survive in a
    man
who has enough of this world's goods
yet closes his heart to his brother
when he sees him in need?
Little children,
let us love in deed
and not merely talk about it.

This is the Word of the Lord.

---

16   **1 Jn 4, 7-16**

A reading from the first letter of John
If we love one another, God will live in us.

Beloved,
let us love one another
because love is of God;
everyone who loves is begotten of God
and has knowledge of God.
The man without love has known nothing of
    God,
for God is love.
God's love was revealed in our midst in this
    way:
he sent his only Son to the world
that we might have life through him.
Love, then, consists in this:
not that we have loved God
but that he has loved us
and has sent his Son as an offering for our
    sins.
Beloved,
if God has loved us so,
we must have the same love for one another.
No one has ever seen God.
Yet if we love one another
God dwells in us,
and his love is brought to perfection in us.
The way we know we remain in him
and he in us
is that he has given us of his Spirit.

We have seen for ourselves, and can testify,
that the Father has sent the Son as savior
of the world.
When anyone acknowledges that Jesus is
the Son of God,
God dwells in him
and he in God.
We have come to know and to believe in
the love God has for us.
God is love,
and he who abides in love
abides in God,
and God in him.
        This is the Word of the Lord.

___

17   1 Jn 5, 1-5

A reading from the first letter of John
This is the victory over the world—our faith.

Everyone who believes that Jesus is the
Christ
has been begotten of God.
Now, everyone who loves the father
loves the child he has begotten.
We can be sure that we love God's children
when we love God
and do what he has commanded.
The love of God consists in this:
that we keep his commandments—
and his commandments are not burdensome.
Everyone begotten of God conquers the
world,
and the power that has conquered the world
is this faith of ours.
Who, then, is conqueror of the world?
The one who believes that Jesus is the Son of
God.
        This is the Word of the Lord.

___

741   **ALLELUIA VERSE AND**
         VERSE BEFORE THE GOSPEL

1   Mt 5, 3

Happy the poor in spirit;
the kingdom of heaven is theirs!

2   Mt 5, 6

Happy those who hunger and thirst for what
is right;
they shall be satisfied.

3   Mt 5, 8

Happy are the pure of heart, for they shall see
God.

4   Mt 11, 25

Blessed are you, Father, Lord of heaven and
earth;
you have revealed to little ones the mysteries
of the kingdom.

5   Mt 11, 28

Come to me, all you that labor and are burdened,
and I will give you rest, says the Lord.

6   Jn 8, 12

I am the light of the world, says the Lord;
the man who follows me will have the light of
life.

7   Jn 8, 31-32

If you stay in my word, you will indeed be my
disciples,
and you will know the truth, says the Lord.

8   Jn 13, 34

I give you a new commandment:
love one another as I have loved you.

9   Jn 14, 23

If anyone loves me, he will hold to my words,
and my Father will love him, and we will come
to him.

10   Jn 15, 4-5

Live in me and let me live in you, says the Lord;
my branches bear much fruit.

___

GOSPEL

1
                                   Mt 5, 1-12

✠ **A reading from the holy gospel according to Matthew**

Rejoice and be glad, for your reward will be great in heaven.

When Jesus saw the crowds he went up on the mountainside. After he had sat down his disciples gathered around him, and he began to teach them:

"**How blest are the poor in spirit: the reign of God is theirs.**

Blest too are the sorrowing; they shall be consoled.

[Blest are the lowly; they shall inherit the land.]

Blest are they who hunger and thirst for holiness;

they shall have their fill.

Blest are they who show mercy; mercy shall be theirs.

Blest are the single-hearted for they shall see God.

Blest too the peacemakers; they shall be called sons of God.

Blest are those persecuted for holiness' sake; the reign of God is theirs.

Blest are you when they insult you and persecute you

and utter every kind of slander against you because of me.

Be glad and rejoice, for your reward in heaven is great."

This is the gospel of the Lord.

2
                                  Mt 5, 13-16

✠ **A reading from the holy gospel according to Matthew**

You are the light of the world.

Jesus said to his disciples: "You are the salt of the earth. But what if salt goes flat? How can you restore its flavor? Then it is good for nothing but to be thrown out and trampled underfoot.

"**You are the light of the world. A city set on a hill cannot be hidden. Men do not light a lamp and then put it under a bushel basket. They set it on a stand where it gives light to all in the**

house. In the same way, your light must shine before men so that they may see goodness in your acts and give praise to your heavenly Father.**"

This is the gospel of the Lord.

3
                                 Mt 11, 25-30

✠ **A reading from the holy gospel according to Matthew**

You have hidden these things from the learned and the clever and revealed them to children.

On one occasion Jesus said: "Father, Lord of heaven and earth, to you I offer praise; for what you have hidden from the learned and the clever you have revealed to the merest children. Father, it is true. You have graciously willed it so. Everything has been given over to me by my Father. No one knows the Son but the Father, and no one knows the Father but the Son—and anyone to whom the Son wishes to reveal him.

"**Come to me, all you who are weary and find life burdensome, and I will refresh you. Take my yoke upon your shoulders and learn from me, for I am gentle and humble of heart. Your souls will find rest, for my yoke is easy and my burden light.**"

This is the gospel of the Lord.

4
                                 Mt 13, 44-46

✠ **A reading from the holy gospel according to Matthew**

He sold all that he had and bought the field.

Jesus said to the crowds: "The reign of God is like buried treasure which a man found in a field. He hid it again, and rejoicing at his find went and sold all he had and bought that field. Or again, the kingdom of heaven is like a merchant's search for fine pearls. When he found one really valuable pearl, he went back and put up for sale all that he had and bought it."

This is the gospel of the Lord.

5   Mt 16, 24-27

✠ A reading from the holy gospel according
to Matthew

The man who loses his life on account of me will really
save his life.

Jesus said to his disciples: "If a man wishes to
come after me, he must deny his very self, take
up his cross, and begin to follow in my footsteps.
Whoever would save his life will lose it, but
whoever loses his life for my sake will find it.
What profit would a man show if he were to
gain the whole world and ruin himself in the
process? What can a man offer in exchange
for his very self? The Son of Man will come
with his Father's glory accompanied by his
angels. When he does, he will repay each man
according to his conduct."
                This is the gospel of the Lord.

---

6   Mt 18, 1-4

✠ A reading from the holy gospel according
to Matthew

Unless you have the genuineness of little children, you will
not enter into the kingdom of God.

The disciples came up to Jesus with the question, "Who is of greatest importance in the
kingdom of God?" He called a little child over
and stood him in their midst and said: "I assure
you, unless you change and become like little
children, you will not enter the kingdom of
God. Whoever makes himself lowly, becoming
like this child, is of greatest importance in that
heavenly reign."
                This is the gospel of the Lord.

7   Mt 19, 3-12

[For religious]

✠ A reading from the holy gospel according
to Matthew

Some persons have chosen to remain single for the sake
of the kingdom of heaven.

Some Pharisees came up to Jesus and said, to
test him, "May a man divorce his wife for any
reason whatever?" He replied, "Have you not
read that at the beginning the Creator made
them male and female and declared, 'For this
reason a man shall leave his father and mother
and cling to his wife, and the two shall become

as one?' Thus they are no longer two but one
flesh. Therefore, let no man separate what
God has joined." They said to him, "Then why
did Moses command divorce and the promulgation of a divorce decree?" "Because of
your stubbornness Moses let you divorce your
wives," he replied; "but at the beginning it was
not that way. I now say to you, whoever
divorces his wife (lewd conduct is a separate
case) and marries another commits adultery,
and the man who marries a divorced woman
commits adultery."

His disciples said to him, "If that is the case
between man and wife, it is better not to
marry." He said, "Not everyone can accept this
teaching, only those to whom it is given to do
so. Some men are incapable of sexual activity
from birth; some have been deliberately made
so; and some there are who have freely renounced sex for the sake of God's reign. Let
him accept this teaching who can."
                This is the gospel of the Lord.

---

8   Mt 25, 1-13.

✠ A reading from the holy gospel according
to Matthew

The groom is coming; go and meet him.

Jesus told this parable to his disciples: "The
reign of God can be likened to ten bridesmaids
who took their torches and went out to welcome the groom. Five of them were foolish,
while the other five were sensible. The foolish
ones, in taking their torches, brought no oil
along, but the sensible ones took flasks of oil
as well as their torches. The groom delayed his
coming, so they all began to nod, then to fall
asleep. At midnight someone shouted, 'The
groom is here! Come out and greet him!' At the
outcry all the virgins woke up and got their
torches ready. The foolish ones said to the
sensible, 'Give us some of your oil. Our torches
are going out.' But the sensible ones replied,
'No, there may not be enough for you and us.
You had better go to the dealers and buy yourselves some.' While they went off to buy it the
groom arrived, and the ones who were ready
went in to the wedding with him. Then the
door was barred. Later the other bridesmaids

came back. 'Master, master!' they cried. 'Open the door for us.' But he answered, 'I tell you, I do not know you.' The moral is: keep your eyes open, for you know not the day or the hour."

This is the gospel of the Lord.

---

9   Mt 25, 14-30 or 25, 14-23

✠ **A reading from the holy gospel according to Matthew**

Because you have been faithful in a few things, enter into the joy of your Lord.

(Long Form)

Jesus told his disciples this parable: "It is the case of a man who was going on a journey. He called in his servants and handed his funds over to them according to each man's abilities. To one he disbursed five thousand silver pieces, to a second two thousand, and to a third a thousand. Then he went away. Immediately the man who received the five thousand went to invest it and made another five. In the same way, the man who received the two thousand doubled his figure. The man who received the thousand went off instead and dug a hole in the ground, where he buried his master's money. After a long absence, the master of those servants came home and settled accounts with them. The man who had received the five thousand came forward bringing the additional five. 'My lord,' he said, 'you let me have five thousand. See, I have made five thousand more.' His master said to him, 'Well done! You are an industrious and reliable servant. Since you were dependable in a small matter I will put you in charge of larger affairs. Come, share your master's joy!' The man who had received the two thousand then stepped forward. 'My lord,' he said, 'you entrusted me with two thousand and I have made two thousand more.' His master said to him, 'Cleverly done! You too are an industrious and reliable servant. Since you were dependable in a small matter I will put you in charge of larger affairs. Come, share your master's joy!'

"Finally the man who had received the thousand stepped forward. 'My lord,' he said, 'I knew you were a hard man. You reap where you did not sow and gather where you did not scatter, so out of fear I went off and buried your thousand silver pieces in the ground. Here is your money back.' His master exclaimed: 'You worthless, lazy lout! You know I reap where I did not sow and gather where I did not scatter. All the more reason to deposit my money with the bankers, so that on my return I could have had it back with interest. You, there! Take the thousand away from him and give it to the man with the ten thousand. Those who have, will get more until they grow rich, while those who have not, will lose even the little they have. Throw this worthless servant into the darkness outside, where he can wail and grind his teeth.' "

This is the gospel of the Lord.

OR
(Short Form)

Jesus told his disciples this parable: "It is the case of a man who was going on a journey. He called in his servants and handed his funds over to them according to each man's abilities. To one he disbursed five thousand silver pieces, to a second two thousand, and to a third a thousand. Then he went away. Immediately the man who received the five thousand went to invest it and made another five. In the same way, the man who received the two thousand doubled his figure. The man who received the thousand went off instead and dug a hole in the ground, where he buried his master's money. After a long absence, the master of those servants came home and settled accounts with them. The man who had received the five thousand came forward bringing the additional five. 'My lord,' he said, 'you let me have five thousand. See, I have made five thousand more.' His master said to him, 'Well done! You are an industrious and reliable servant. Since you were dependable in a small matter I will put you in charge of larger affairs. Come, share your master's joy!' The man who had received the two thousand then stepped forward. 'My lord,' he said, 'you entrusted me with two thousand and I have made two thousand more.' His master said to him, 'Cleverly done! You too are an industrious and reliable servant. Since you were dependable in a small matter I will put you in charge of larger affairs. Come, share your master's joy!' "

This is the gospel of the Lord.

---

10   Mt 25, 31-46 or 25, 31-40

[For those who work for the disadvantaged]

✠ A reading from the holy gospel according to Matthew

Whatever you have done to the very least of my brothers you have done to me.

(Long Form)

Jesus said to his disciples: "When the Son of Man comes in his glory, escorted by all the angels of heaven, he will sit upon his royal throne, and all the nations will be assembled before him. Then he will separate them into two groups, as a shepherd separates sheep from goats. The sheep he will place on his right hand, the goats on his left. The king will say to those on his right: 'Come. You have my Father's blessing! Inherit the kingdom prepared for you from the creation of the world. For I was hungry and you gave me food, I was thirsty and you gave me drink. I was a stranger and you welcomed me, naked and you clothed me. I was ill and you comforted me, in prison and you came to visit me.' Then the just will ask him: 'Lord, when did we see you hungry and feed you or see you thirsty and give you drink? When did we welcome you away from home or clothe you in your nakedness? When did we visit you when you were ill or in prison?' The king will answer them: 'I assure you, as often as you did it for one of my least brothers, you did it for me.'

"Then he will say to those on his left: 'Out of my sight, you condemned, into that everlasting fire prepared for the devil and his angels! I was hungry and you gave me no food, I was thirsty and you gave me no drink. I was away from home and you gave me no welcome, naked and you gave me no clothing. I was ill and in prison and you did not come to comfort me.' Then they in turn will ask: 'Lord, when did we see you hungry or thirsty or away

from home or naked or ill or in prison and not attend you in your needs?' He will answer them: 'I assure you, as often as you neglected to do it to one of these least ones, you neglected to do it to me.' These will go off to eternal punishment and the just to eternal life."

This is the gospel of the Lord.

OR

(Short Form)

Jesus said to his disciples: "When the Son of Man comes in his glory, escorted by all the angels of heaven, he will sit upon his royal throne, and all the nations will be assembled before him. Then he will separate them into two groups, as a shepherd separates sheep from goats. The sheep he will place on his right hand, the goats on his left. The king will say to those on his right: 'Come. You have my Father's blessing! Inherit the kingdom prepared for you from the creation of the world. For I was hungry and you gave me food, I was thirsty and you gave me drink. I was a stranger and you welcomed me, naked and you clothed me. I was ill and you comforted me, in prison and you came to visit me.' Then the just will ask him: 'Lord, when did we see you hungry and feed you or see you thirsty and give you drink? When did we welcome you away from home or clothe you in your nakedness? When did we visit you when you were ill or in prison?' The king will answer them: 'I assure you, as often as you did it for one of my least brothers, you did it for me.' "

This is the gospel of the Lord.

---

11   Mk 3, 31-35

✠ A reading from the holy gospel according to Mark

He who has done the will of God is my brother, my sister, and my mother.

The mother of Jesus and his brothers arrived, and as they stood outside [the house] they sent word to Jesus to come out. The crowd seated around him told him, "Your mother and your brothers and sisters are outside asking for you." He said in reply, "Who are my mother and my brothers?" And gazing around him at those seated in the circle he continued, "These are my mother and my brothers. Whoever does the will of God is brother and sister and mother to me."

This is the gospel of the Lord.

---

12   Mk 9, 34-37

[For teachers]

✠ A reading from the holy gospel according to Mark

Whenever you have accepted graciously a small child, you have accepted me.

The disciples of Jesus had been arguing along the way about who was the most important. So he sat down and called the Twelve around him and said, "If anyone wishes to rank first, he must remain the last one of all and the servant of all." Then he took a little child, stood him in their midst, and putting his arms around him, said to them, "Whoever welcomes a child such as this for my sake welcomes me. And whoever welcomes me welcomes, not me, but him who sent me."

This is the gospel of the Lord.

[For teachers]

13   Mk 10, 13-16

✠ A reading from the holy gospel according to Mark

Do not keep the children from me.

People were bringing their little children to Jesus to have him touch them, but the disciples were scolding them for this. Jesus became indignant when he noticed it and said to them: "Let the children come to me and do not hinder them. It is to just such as these that the kingdom of God belongs. I assure you that whoever does not accept the kingdom of God like a little child shall not enter into it." Then he embraced them and blessed them, placing his hands on them.

This is the gospel of the Lord.

---

14   Mk 10, 17-30 or 10, 17-27

[For religious]

✠ A reading from the holy gospel according to Mark

Sell whatever you have, and come, follow me.

(Long Form)

As Jesus was setting out on a journey a man came running up, knelt down before him and asked, "Good Teacher, what must I do to share in everlasting life?" Jesus answered, "Why do you call me good? No one is good but God alone. You know the commandments:

    'You shall not kill;

    You shall not commit adultery;

    You shall not steal;

    You shall not bear false witness;

    You shall not defraud;

    Honor your father and your mother.' "

He replied, "Teacher, I have kept all these since my childhood." Then Jesus looked at him with love and told him, "There is one thing more you must do. Go and sell what you have and give to the poor; you will then have treasure in heaven. After that come and follow me." At these words the man's face fell. He went away sad, for he had many possessions. Jesus looked around and said to his disciples, "How hard it is for the rich to enter the kingdom of God!" The disciples could only marvel at his words. So Jesus repeated what he had said: "My sons, how hard it is to enter the kingdom of God! It is easier for a camel to pass through a needle's eye than for a rich man to enter the kingdom of God."

They were completely overwhelmed at this, and exclaimed to one another, "Then who can be saved?" Jesus fixed his gaze on them and said, "For man it is impossible but not for God. With God all things are possible."

Peter was moved to say to him: "We have put aside everything to follow you!" Jesus answered: "I give you my word, there is no one who has given up home, brothers or sisters, mother or father, children or property, for me and for the gospel who will not receive in this present age a hundred times as many homes, brothers and sisters, mothers, children and property—and persecution besides—and in the age to come, everlasting life."

This is the gospel of the Lord.

OR

(Short Form)

As Jesus was setting out on a journey a man came running up, knelt down before him and asked, "Good Teacher, what must I do to share in everlasting life?" Jesus answered, "Why do you call me good? No one is good but God alone. You know the commandments:

'You shall not kill;
You shall not commit adultery;
You shall not steal;
You shall not bear false witness;
You shall not defraud;
Honor your father and your mother.' "

He replied, "Teacher, I have kept all these since my childhood." Then Jesus looked at him with love and told him, "There is one thing more you must do. Go and sell what you have and give to the poor; you will then have treasure in heaven. After that come and follow me." At these words the man's face fell. He went away sad, for he had many possessions. Jesus looked around and said to his disciples, "How hard it is for the rich to enter the kingdom of God!" The disciples could only marvel at his words. So Jesus repeated what he had said: "My sons, how hard it is to enter the kingdom of God! It is easier for a camel to pass through a needle's eye than for a rich man to enter the kingdom of God."

They were completely overwhelmed at this, and exclaimed to one another, "Then who can be saved?" Jesus fixed his gaze on them and said, "For man it is impossible but not for God. With God all things are possible."

This is the gospel of the Lord.

---

15   Lk 9, 57-62

[For religious]

✠ A reading from the holy gospel according to Luke

I will follow you, wherever you go.

As Jesus and his disciples were making their way along, someone said to him, "I will be your follower wherever you go." Jesus said to him, "The foxes have lairs, the birds of the sky have nests, but the Son of Man has nowhere to lay his head." To another he said, "Come after me." The man replied, "Let me bury my father first." Jesus said to him, "Let the dead bury their dead; come away and proclaim the kingdom of God." Yet another said to him, "I will be your follower, Lord, but first let me take leave of my people at home." Jesus answered him, "Whoever puts his hand to the plow but keeps looking back is unfit for the reign of God."

This is the gospel of the Lord.

---

16   Lk 10, 38-42

✠ A reading from the holy gospel according to Luke

Jesus accepts the hospitality of Martha and praises the attentiveness of Mary.

Jesus entered a village where a woman named Martha welcomed him to her home. She had a sister named Mary, who seated herself at the Lord's feet and listened to his words. Martha, who was busy with all the details of hospitality, came to him and said, "Lord, are you not concerned that my sister has left me all alone to do the household tasks? Tell her to help me."

The Lord in reply said to her: "Martha, Martha, you are anxious and upset about many things; one thing only is required. Mary has chosen the better portion and she shall not be deprived of it."

This is the gospel of the Lord.

---

17   Lk 12, 32-34

[For religious]

✠ A reading from the holy gospel according to Luke

It has pleased the Father to give you the kingdom.

Jesus said to his disciples: "Do not live in fear, little flock. It has pleased your Father to give you the kingdom. Sell what you have and give alms. Get purses for yourselves that do not wear out, a never-failing treasure with the Lord which no thief comes near nor any moth destroys. Wherever your treasure lies, there your heart will be."

This is the gospel of the Lord.

---

18   Lk 12, 35-40

✠ A reading from the holy gospel according to Luke

Be prepared.

Jesus said to his disciples: "Let your belts be fastened around your waists and your lamps be burning ready. Be like men awaiting their master's return from a wedding, so that when he arrives and knocks, you will open for him without delay. It will go well with those servants whom the master finds wide-awake on his return. I tell you, he will put on an apron, seat them at table, and proceed to wait on them. Should he happen to come at midnight or before sunrise and find them prepared, it will go well with them. You know as well as I that if the head of the house knew when the thief was coming he would not let him break into his house. Be on guard, therefore. The Son of Man will come when you least expect him."

This is the gospel of the Lord.

---

19   Lk 14, 25-33

[For religious]

✠ A reading from the holy gospel according to Luke

Unless you are ready to give up all that you possess, you cannot be my disciple.

On one occasion when a great crowd was with Jesus, he turned to them and said, "If anyone comes to me without turning his back on his father and mother, his wife and his children, his brothers and sisters, indeed his very self, he cannot be my follower. Anyone who does not take up his cross and follow me cannot be my disciple. If one of you decides to build a tower, will he not first sit down and calculate the outlay to see if he has enough money to complete the project? He will do that for fear of laying the foundation and then not being able to complete the work; at which all who saw it

would then jeer at him, saying, 'That man began to build what he could not finish.'

"Or if a king is about to march on another king to do battle with him, will he not sit down first and consider whether, with ten thousand men, he can withstand an enemy coming against him with twenty thousand? If he cannot, he will send a delegation while the enemy is still at a distance, asking for terms of peace. In the same way, none of you can be my disciple if he does not renounce all his possessions."

This is the gospel of the Lord.

---

20   Jn 15, 1-8

✠ A reading from the holy gospel according to John

Whoever stays with me, with me in him, bears fruit in abundance.

Jesus said to his disciples:
    "I am the true vine
    and my Father is the vinegrower.
    He prunes away
    every barren branch,
    but the fruitful ones
    he trims clean
    to increase their yield.
    You are clean already,
    thanks to the word I have spoken to you.
    Live on in me, as I do in you.
    No more than a branch can bear fruit of
        itself
    apart from the vine,
    can you bear fruit
    apart from me.
    I am the vine, you are the branches.
    He who lives in me and I in him,
    will produce abundantly,
    for apart from me you can do nothing.
    A man who does not live in me
    is like a withered, rejected branch,
    picked up to be thrown in the fire and
        burnt.
    If you live in me,
    and my words stay part of you,
    you may ask what you will—
    it will be done for you.
    My Father has been glorified

in your bearing much fruit
and becoming my disciples.''
This is the gospel of the Lord.

---

21   Jn 15, 9-17

✠ **A reading from the holy gospel according
to John**

You are my friends if you do what I command you.

Jesus said to his disciples:
  ''As the Father has loved me,
  so I have loved you.
  Live on in my love.
  You will live in my love
  if you keep my commandments,
  even as I have kept my Father's command-
    ments,
  and live in his love.
  All this I tell you
  that my joy may be yours
  and your joy may be complete.
  This is my commandment:
  love one another
  as I have loved you.
  There is no greater love than this:
  to lay down one's life for one's friends.
  You are my friends
  if you do what I command you.
  I no longer speak of you as slaves,
  for a slave does not know what his master
    is about.
  Instead, I call you friends,
  since I have made known to you all that I
    heard from my Father.
  It was not you who chose me,
  it was I who chose you
  to go forth and to bear fruit.
  Your fruit must endure
  so that all you ask the Father in my name
  he will give you.
  The command I give you is this,
  that you love one another.''
      This is the gospel of the Lord.

---

22   Jn 17, 20-26

✠ **A reading from the holy gospel according
to John**

I want those you have given me to be with me where I am.

Jesus looked up to heaven and prayed:
  ''Holy Father,
  I do not pray for my disciples alone.
  I pray also for those who will believe in
    me through their word,
  that all may be one
  as you, Father, are in me, and I in you;
  I pray that they may be [one] in us,
  that the world may believe that you sent
    me.
  I have given them the glory you gave me
  that they may be one, as we are one—
  I living in them, you living in me—
  that their unity may be complete.
  So shall the world know that you sent me,
  and that you loved them as you loved me.

  ''Father,
  all those you gave me
  I would have in my company
  where I am,
  to see this glory of mine
  which is your gift to me,
  because of the love you bore me before
    the world began.
  Just Father,
  the world has not known you,
  but I have known you;
  and these men have known that you sent
    me.
  To them I have revealed your name,
  and I will continue to reveal it
  so that your love for me may live in them,
  and I may live in them.''
      This is the gospel of the Lord.

RITUAL MASSES

743   **THE PREPARATION AND BAPTISM OF ADULTS**

Beginning of the Catechumenate

READING I   Gn 12, 1-4

A reading from the book of Genesis

Leave your country, and come into the land I will show you.

The Lord said to Abram: "Go forth from the land of your kinsfolk and from your father's house to a land that I will show you.

"I will make of you a great nation,
and I will bless you;
I will make your name great,
so that you will be a blessing.
I will bless those who bless you
and curse those who curse you.
All the communities of the earth
shall find blessing in you."

Abram went as the Lord directed him, and Lot went with him.

This is the Word of the Lord.

Responsorial Psalm   Ps 33, 4-5. 12-13. 18-19. 20. 22

℟. (12) Happy the people the Lord has chosen to be his own.

For upright is the word of the Lord,
and all his works are trustworthy.
He loves justice and right;
of the kindness of the Lord the earth is full.

℟. Happy the people the Lord has chosen to be his own.

Happy the nation whose God is the Lord,
the people he has chosen for his own inheritance.
From heaven the Lord looks down;
he sees all mankind.

℟. Happy the people the Lord has chosen to be his own.

But see, the eyes of the Lord are upon those who fear him,
upon those who hope for his kindness,
To deliver them from death
and preserve them in spite of famine.

℟. Happy the people the Lord has chosen to be his own.

Our soul waits for the Lord,
who is our help and our shield.
May your kindness, O Lord, be upon us
who have put our hope in you.

℟. Happy the people the Lord has chosen to be his own.

℟. Or: Lord, let your mercy be on us,
as we place our trust in you.

GOSPEL   Jn 1, 35-42

Verse before the Gospel   Jn 1, 41. 17

We have found the Messiah:
Jesus Christ, who brings us truth and grace.

✠ **A reading from the holy gospel according to John**

Look, there is the Lamb of God. We have found the Messiah.

John was [at Bethany, beyond the Jordan] again with two of his disciples. As he watched Jesus walk by he said, "Look! There is the Lamb of God!" The two disciples heard what he said, and followed Jesus. When Jesus turned around and noticed them following him, he asked them, "What are you looking for?" They said to him, "Rabbi (which means Teacher), where do you stay?" "Come and see," he answered. So they went to see where he was lodged, and stayed with him that day. (It was about four in the afternoon).

One of the two who had followed him after hearing John was Simon Peter's brother Andrew. The first thing he did was seek out his brother Simon and tell him, "We have found the Messiah" (which means the Anointed)! He brought him to Jesus, who looked at him and said, "You are Simon, son of John; your name shall be Cephas (which is rendered Peter)."

This is the gospel of the Lord.

Other appropriate texts may also be used.

---

744   **Election**

If this is done on the first Sunday of Lent, the readings of any series for this Sunday may be used.

If this is done on a weekday and the readings of the day are not appropriate, readings from those assigned to the First Sunday of Lent (nos. 22-24), or other suitable readings, should be selected.

---

745   First Scrutiny

The readings are always taken from the Third Sunday of Lent, series A, with their own chants (above, no. 28).

---

746   Second Scrutiny

The readings are always taken from the Fourth Sunday of Lent, series A, with their own chants (above, no. 31).

---

747   Third Scrutiny

The readings are always taken from the Fifth Sunday of Lent, series A, with their own chants (above, no. 34).

---

748   Presentation of the Creed

READING I   Dt 6, 1-7

A reading from the book of Deuteronomy

Listen, Israel: You shall love the Lord your God with all your heart.

Moses said to the people: "These then are the commandments, the statutes and decrees which the Lord, your God, has ordered that you be taught to observe in the land into which you are crossing for conquest, so that you and your son and your grandson may fear the Lord, your God, and keep, throughout the days of your lives, all his statutes and commandments which I enjoin on you, and thus have long life. Hear then, Israel, and be careful to observe them, that you may grow and prosper the more, in keeping with the promise of the Lord, the God of your fathers, to give you a land flowing with milk and honey.

"Hear, O Israel! The Lord is our God, the Lord alone! Therefore, you shall love the Lord, your God, with all your heart, and with all your soul, and with all your strength. Take to heart these words which I enjoin on you today. Drill them into your children. Speak of them at home and abroad, whether you are busy or at rest."

This is the Word of the Lord.

Responsorial Psalm   Ps 19, 8. 9. 10. 11

℞. (Jn 6, 69) Lord, you have the words of ever-lasting life.

The law of the Lord is perfect,
    refreshing the soul;
The decree of the Lord is trustworthy,
    giving wisdom to the simple.
℞. Lord, you have the words of everlasting life.
The precepts of the Lord are right,
    rejoicing the heart;
The command of the Lord is clear,
    enlightening the eye.
℞. Lord, you have the words of everlasting life.
The fear of the Lord is pure,
    enduring forever;
The ordinances of the Lord are true,
    all of them just.
℞. Lord, you have the words of everlasting life.
They are more precious than gold,
    than a heap of purest gold;
Sweeter also than syrup
    or honey from the comb.
℞. Lord, you have the words of everlasting life.

READING II   Rom 10, 8-13

A reading from the letter of Paul to the Romans

By confessing your faith in God you are saved.

What does the Scripture say? "The word is near you, on your lips and in your heart (that is, the word of faith which we preach)." For if you confess with your lips that Jesus is Lord, and believe in your heart that God raised him from the dead, you will be saved. Faith in the heart leads to justification, confession on the lips to salvation. Scripture says, "No one who believes in him will be put to shame." Here there is no difference between Jew and Greek; all have the same Lord, rich in mercy toward all who call upon him. "Everyone who calls on the name of the Lord will be saved."

This is the Word of the Lord.

OR

READING II   1 Cor 15, 1-8 or 15, 1-4

A reading from the first letter of Paul to the
Corinthians

The gospel will save you only if you keep believing what
I preached to you.

(Long Form)

Brothers, I want to remind you of the gospel I
preached to you, which you received and in
which you stand firm. You are being saved by
it at this very moment if you retain it as I
preached it to you. Otherwise you have believed in vain. I handed on to you first of all
what I myself received, that Christ died for our
sins in accord with the Scriptures; that he was
buried and, in accord with the Scriptures, rose
on the third day; that he was seen by Cephas,
then by the Twelve. After that he was seen by
five hundred brothers at once, most of whom
are still alive, although some have fallen
asleep. Next he was seen by James; then by all
the apostles. Last of all he was seen by me.

This is the Word of the Lord.

OR
(Short Form)

Brothers, I want to remind you of the gospel
I preached to you, which you received and in
which you stand firm. You are being saved by
it at this very moment if you retain it as I
preached it to you. Otherwise you have believed in vain. I handed on to you first of all
what I myself received, that Christ died for
our sins in accord with the Scriptures; that he
was buried and, in accord with the Scriptures,
rose on the third day.

This is the Word of the Lord.

GOSPEL   Mt 16, 13-18

Verse before the Gospel   Jn 3, 16

God loved the world so much, he gave us his
    only Son,
that all who believe in him might have eternal
    life.

✠ A reading from the holy gospel according
            to Matthew

On this rock I will build my Church.

When Jesus came to the neighborhood of Caesarea Philippi, he asked his disciples this question: "Who do people say that the Son of Man
is?" They replied, "Some say John the Baptizer,
others Elijah, still others Jeremiah or one of the
prophets." "And you," he said to them, "who
do you say that I am?" "You are the Messiah,"
Simon Peter answered, "the Son of the living
God!" Jesus replied, "Blest are you, Simon son
of John! No mere man has revealed this to
you, but my heavenly Father. I for my part declare to you, you are 'Rock,' and on this rock I
will build my church, and the jaws of death
shall not prevail against it."

This is the gospel of the Lord.

OR

GOSPEL   Jn 12, 44-50

Verse before the Gospel   Jn 3, 16

God loved the world so much, he gave us his
    only Son,
that all who believe in him might have eternal
    life.

✠ A reading from the holy gospel according
            to John

I, the light, have come into the world, so that whoever
believes in me need not remain in the dark any more.

Jesus proclaimed aloud:
    "Whoever puts faith in me
    believes not so much in me
    as in him who sent me;
    and whoever looks on me
    is seeing him who sent me.
I have come to the world as its light,
    to keep anyone who believes in me
    from remaining in the dark.
If anyone hears my words and does not
    keep them,
I am not the one to condemn him,
for I did not come to condemn the world
    but to save it.
Whoever rejects me and does not accept my
    words
    already has his judge,
    namely, the word I have spoken—
    it is that which will condemn him on the
    last day.

For I have not spoken on my own;
no, the Father who sent me
has commanded me
what to say and how to speak.
Since I know that his commandment means
    eternal life,
whatever I say
is spoken just as he instructed me."
    This is the gospel of the Lord.

---

749   Presentation of the Lord's Prayer

READING I   Hos 11, 1. 3-4. 8-9

A reading from the book of the prophet Hosea
    I have led you with cords of love.

The Lord said:
When Israel was a child I loved him,
    Out of Egypt I called my son.
Yet it was I who taught Ephraim to walk,
    who took them in my arms;
I drew them with human cords,
    with bands of love;
I fostered them like one
    who raises an infant to his cheeks;
Yet, though I stooped to feed my child,
    they did not know that I was their healer.
My heart is overwhelmed,
    my pity is stirred.
I will not give vent to my blazing anger,
    I will not destroy Ephraim again;
For I am God and not man,
    the Holy One present among you;
I will not let the flames consume you.
    This is the Word of the Lord.

Responsorial Psalm   Ps 23, 1-3. 3-4. 5. 6

℟. (1) The Lord is my shepherd;
    there is nothing I shall want.
The Lord is my shepherd; I shall not want.
    In verdant pastures he gives me repose;
Beside restful waters he leads me;
    he refreshes my soul.
℟. The Lord is my shepherd;
    there is nothing I shall want.
He guides me in right paths
    for his name's sake.
Even though I walk in the dark valley
    I fear no evil; for you are at my side

With your rod and your staff
    that give me courage.
℟. The Lord is my shepherd;
    there is nothing I shall want.
You spread the table before me
    in the sight of my foes;
You anoint my head with oil;
    my cup overflows.
℟. The Lord is my shepherd;
    there is nothing I shall want.
Only goodness and kindness follow me
    all the days of my life;
And I shall dwell in the house of the Lord
    for years to come.
℟. The Lord is my shepherd;
    there is nothing I shall want.

OR

Responsorial Psalm   Ps 103, 1-2. 8. 10. 11-12. 13. 18

℟. (13) As a father is kind to his children,
    so kind is the Lord to those who fear him.
Bless the Lord, O my soul;
    and all my being, bless his holy name.
Bless the Lord, O my soul,
    and forget not all his benefits.
℟. As a father is kind to his children,
    so kind is the Lord to those who fear him.
Merciful and gracious is the Lord,
    slow to anger and abounding in kindness.
Not according to our sins does he deal with us,
    nor does he requite us according to our
    crimes.
℟. As a father is kind to his children,
    so kind is the Lord to those who fear him.
For as the heavens are high above the earth
    so surpassing is his kindness toward those
    who fear him.
As far as the east is from the west,
    so far has he put our transgressions from us.
℟. As a father is kind to his children,
    so kind is the Lord to those who fear him.
As a father has compassion on his children,
    so the Lord has compassion on those who
    fear him,
    on those who keep his covenant
    and remember to fulfill his precepts.
℟. As a father is kind to his children,
    so kind is the Lord to those who fear him.

READING II   Rom 8, 14-17. 26-27

A reading from the letter of Paul to the Romans

You have received the Spirit of sonship and it makes us cry
out, "Abba, Father!"

All who are led by the Spirit of God are sons of
God. You did not receive a spirit of slavery
leading you back into fear, but a spirit of adoption through which we cry out, "Abba!" (that
is, "Father"). The Spirit himself gives witness
with our spirit that we are children of God. But
if we are children, we are heirs as well: heirs
of God, heirs with Christ, if only we suffer
with him so as to be glorified with him.

The Spirit too helps us in our weakness, for
we do not know how to pray as we ought; but
the Spirit himself makes intercession for us
with groanings which cannot be expressed in
speech. He who searches hearts knows what
the Spirit means, for the Spirit intercedes for
the saints as God himself wills.

This is the Word of the Lord.

OR

READING II   Gal 4, 4-7

**A reading from the letter of Paul to the
Galatians**

God has sent the Spirit of his Son into our hearts: the Spirit
that cries, "Abba, Father!"

When the designated time had come, God sent
forth his Son born of a woman, born under the
law, to deliver from the law those who were
subjected to it, so that we might receive our
status as adopted sons. The proof that you are
sons is the fact that God has sent forth into our
hearts the spirit of his Son which cries out
"Abba!" ("Father!"). You are no longer a slave
but a son! And the fact that you are a son makes
you an heir, by God's design.

This is the Word of the Lord.

GOSPEL   Lk 11, 1-2; Mt 6, 9-13

Verse before the Gospel   Rom 8, 15
You have received the Spirit which makes us
    God's children,
and in that Spirit we call God our Father.

✠ **A reading from the holy gospel according
to Luke and Matthew**

Lord, teach us to pray.

One day Jesus was praying in a certain place.
When he had finished, one of his disciples
asked him, "Lord, teach us to pray as John
taught his disciples." He said to them, "When
you pray, say:
    'Our Father in heaven,
    hallowed be your name,
    your kingdom come,
    your will be done
    on earth as it is in heaven.
    Give us today our daily bread,
    and forgive us the wrong we have done
    as we forgive those who wrong us.
    Subject us not to the trial
    but deliver us from the evil one.' "
    This is the gospel of the Lord.

750   Rites of Immediate Preparation

GOSPEL   Mk 7, 31-37

✠ **A reading from the holy gospel according
to Mark**

Ephphetha, that is, be opened.

Jesus left Tyrian territory and returned by way
of Sidon to the Sea of Galilee, into the district
of the Ten Cities. Some people brought him a
deaf man who had a speech impediment and
begged him to lay his hand on him. Jesus took
him off by himself away from the crowd. He
put his fingers into the man's ears and, spitting, touched his tongue; then he looked up to
heaven and emitted a groan. He said to him,
"Ephphatha!" (that is, "Be opened!"). At once
the man's ears were opened; he was freed from
the impediment, and began to speak plainly.
Then he enjoined them strictly not to tell anyone; but the more he ordered them not to, the
more they proclaimed it. Their amazement
went beyond all bounds: "He has done everything well! He makes the deaf hear and the
mute speak!"
    This is the gospel of the Lord.

751   Baptism during the Easter Vigil

The readings are taken from those assigned to the Easter Vigil (above, no. 42); Isaiah 55 (reading V) and Ezekiel 36 (reading VII) may be chosen in addition to Exodus (reading III).

---

752   Christian Initiation apart from the Easter Vigil

OLD TESTAMENT READING

1   Gn 15, 1-6. 18

A reading from the book of Genesis

So shall your descendants be. To your descendants I give this land.

The word of the Lord came to Abram in a vision:

"Fear not, Abram!
I am your shield;
I will make your reward very great."

But Abram said, "O Lord God, what good will your gifts be, if I keep on being childless and have as my heir the steward of my house, Eliezer?" Abram continued, "See, you have given me no offspring, and so one of my servants will be my heir." Then the word of the Lord came to him: "No, that one shall not be your heir; your own issue shall be your heir." He took him outside and said: "Look up at the sky and count the stars, if you can. Just so," he added, "shall your descendants be." Abram put his faith in the Lord, who credited it to him as an act of righteousness.

It was on that occasion that the Lord made a covenant with Abram.

This is the Word of the Lord.

---

2   Gn 17, 1-8

A reading from the book of Genesis

I will establish my covenant between myself and you, and your descendants after you, generation after generation, a covenant in perpetuity.

When Abram was ninety-nine years old, the Lord appeared to him and said: "I am God the Almighty. Walk in my presence and be blameless. Between you and me I will establish my covenant, and I will multiply you exceedingly."

When Abram prostrated himself, God continued to speak to him: "My covenant with you is this: you are to become the father of a host of nations. No longer shall you be called Abram; your name shall be Abraham, for I am making you the father of a host of nations. I will render you exceedingly fertile; I will make nations of you; kings shall stem from you. I will maintain my covenant with you and your descendants after you throughout the ages as an everlasting pact, to be your God and the God of your descendants after you. I will give to you and to your descendants after you the land in which you are now staying, the whole land of Canaan, as a permanent possession; and I will be their God."

This is the Word of the Lord.

---

3   Gn 35, 1-4. 6-7

A reading from the book of Genesis

Get rid of the foreign gods you have with you.

God said to Jacob: "Go up now to Bethel. Settle there and build an altar there to the God who appeared to you while you were fleeing from your brother Esau." So Jacob told his family and all the others who were with him: "Get rid of the foreign gods that you have among you; then purify yourselves and put on fresh clothes. We are now to go up to Bethel, and I will build an altar there to the God who answered me in my hour of distress and who has been with me wherever I have gone." They therefore handed over to Jacob all the foreign gods in their possession and also the rings they had in their ears.

Thus Jacob and all the people who were with him arrived in Luz [that is, Bethel] in the land of Canaan. There he built an altar and named the place Bethel.

This is the Word of the Lord.

---

4   Dt 30, 15-20

A reading from the book of Deuteronomy

Choose life, then, so that you and your descendants may live.

Moses said to the people: "Here, then, I have today set before you life and prosperity, death

and doom. If you obey the commandments of the Lord, your God, which I enjoin on you today, loving him, and walking in his ways, and keeping his commandments, statutes and decrees, you will live and grow numerous, and the Lord, your God, will bless you in the land you are entering to occupy. If, however, you turn away your hearts and will not listen, but are led astray and adore and serve other gods, I tell you now that you will certainly perish; you will not have a long life on the land which you are crossing the Jordan to enter and occupy. I call heaven and earth today to witness against you: I have set before you life and death, the blessing and the curse. Choose life, then, that you and your descendants may live, by loving the Lord, your God, heeding his voice, and holding fast to him. For that will mean life for you, a long life for you to live on the land which the Lord swore he would give to your fathers Abraham, Isaac and Jacob."
This is the Word of the Lord.

5 Jos 24, 1-2. 15-17. 18-25

A reading from the book of Joshua
We will serve the Lord because he is our God.

Joshua gathered together all the tribes of Israel at Shechem, summoning their elders, their leaders, their judges and their officers. When they stood in ranks before God, Joshua addressed all the people: "If it does not please you to serve the Lord, decide today whom you will serve, the gods your fathers served beyond the River or the gods of the Amorites in whose country you are dwelling. As for me and my household, we will serve the Lord." But the people answered, "Far be it from us to forsake the Lord for the service of other gods. For it was the Lord, our God, who brought us and our fathers up out of the land of Egypt, out of a state of slavery. He performed those great miracles before our very eyes and protected us along our entire journey and among all the peoples through whom we passed. Therefore we also will serve the Lord, for he is our God."
Joshua in turn said to the people, "You may not be able to serve the Lord, for he is a holy

God; he is a jealous God who will not forgive your transgressions or your sins. If, after the good he has done for you, you forsake the Lord and serve strange gods, he will do evil to you and destroy you."
But the people answered Joshua, "We will still serve the Lord." Joshua therefore said to the people, "You are your own witnesses that you have chosen to serve the Lord." They replied, "We are, indeed!" Joshua said, "Now, therefore, put away the strange gods that are among you and turn your hearts to the Lord, the God of Israel." Then the people promised Joshua, "We will serve the Lord, our God, and obey his voice."
So Joshua made a covenant with the people that day.
This is the Word of the Lord.

6 2 Kgs 5, 9-15

A reading from the second book of Kings
Naaman went down and washed himself seven times in the river Jordan and became clean.

Naaman [the mighty army commander of the king of Aram] came with his horses and chariots and stopped at the door of Elisha's house. The prophet sent him the message: "Go and wash seven times in the Jordan, and your flesh will heal, and you will be clean." But Naaman went away angry, saying, "I thought that he would surely come out and stand there to invoke the Lord his God, and would move his hand over the spot, and thus cure the leprosy. Are not the rivers of Damascus, the Abana and Pharpar, better than all the waters of Israel? Could I not wash in them and be cleansed?" With this, he turned about in anger and left.
But his servants came up and reasoned with him. "My father," they said, "if the prophet had told you to do something extraordinary, would you not have done it? All the more now, since he said to you, 'Wash and be clean,' should you do as he said." So Naaman went down and plunged into the Jordan seven times at the word of the man of God. His flesh became again like the flesh of a little child, and he was clean.

He returned with his whole retinue to the man of God.
This is the Word of the Lord.

---

7   Is 44, 1-3

A reading from the book of the prophet Isaiah
I will pour my spirit upon your descendants.

Hear, O Jacob, my servant,
  Israel, whom I have chosen.
Thus says the Lord who made you,
  your help, who formed you from the womb:
Fear not, O Jacob, my servant,
  the darling whom I have chosen.
I will pour out water upon the thirsty ground,
  and streams upon the dry land;
I will pour out my spirit upon your offspring,
  and my blessing upon your descendants.
This is the Word of the Lord.

---

8   Jer 31, 31-34

A reading from the book of the prophet Jeremiah
In their heart I will write my law.

The days are coming, says the Lord, when I will make a new covenant with the house of Israel and the house of Judah. It will not be like the covenant I made with their fathers the day I took them by the hand to lead them forth from the land of Egypt; for they broke my covenant, and I had to show myself their master, says the Lord. But this is the covenant which I will make with the house of Israel after those days, says the Lord. I will place my law within them, and write it upon their hearts; I will be their God, and they shall be my people. No longer will they have need to teach their friends and kinsmen how to know the Lord. All, from least to greatest, shall know me, says the Lord, for I will forgive their evil-doing and remember their sin no more.
This is the Word of the Lord.

---

9   Ez 36, 24-28

A reading from the book of the prophet Ezekiel
I shall pour clean water over you and you shall be cleansed of all your sins.

Thus says the Lord God: I will take you away from among the nations, gather you from all the foreign lands, and bring you back to your own land. I will sprinkle clean water upon you to cleanse you from all your impurities, and from all your idols I will cleanse you. I will give you a new heart and place a new spirit within you, taking from your bodies your stony hearts and giving you natural hearts. I will put my spirit within you and make you live by my statutes, careful to observe my decrees. You shall live in the land I gave your fathers; you shall be my people, and I will be your God.
This is the Word of the Lord.

Or the Old Testament readings for the Easter Vigil.

---

753   NEW TESTAMENT READING

1   Acts 2, 14. 36-40. 41-42

A reading from the Acts of the Apostles
Everyone of you must be baptized in the name of Jesus Christ.

In the days of Pentecost, Peter stood up with the Eleven, raised his voice, and addressed them: "Let the whole house of Israel know beyond any doubt that God has made both Lord and Messiah this Jesus whom you crucified."

When they heard this, they were deeply shaken. They asked Peter and the other apostles, "What are we to do, brothers?" Peter answered: "You must reform and be baptized, each one of you, in the name of Jesus Christ, that your sins may be forgiven; then you will receive the gift of the Holy Spirit. It was to you and your children that the promise was made, and to all those still far off whom the Lord our God calls."

In support of his testimony he used many other arguments. Those who accepted his message were baptized; some three thousand were added that day.

They devoted themselves to the apostles' instruction and the communal life, to the breaking of bread and the prayers.
This is the Word of the Lord.

---

2   Acts 8, 26-38

A reading from the Acts of the Apostles

If you believe with your whole heart, you should be baptized.

An angel of the Lord then addressed himself to Philip: "Head south toward the road which goes from Jerusalem to Gaza, the desert route." Philip began the journey. It happened that an Ethiopian eunuch, a court official in charge of the entire treasury of Candace (a name meaning queen) of the Ethiopians, had come on a pilgrimage to Jerusalem and was returning home. He was sitting in his carriage reading the prophet Isaiah. The Spirit said to Philip, "Go and catch up with that carriage." Philip ran ahead and heard the man reading the prophet Isaiah. He said to him, "Do you really grasp what you are reading?" "How can I," the man replied, "unless someone explains it to me?" With that, he invited Philip to get in and sit down beside him. This was the passage of Scripture he was reading:

"Like a sheep he was led to the slaughter,
 like a lamb before its shearer he was silent
 and opened not his mouth.
In his humiliation he was deprived of justice.
 Who will ever speak of his posterity,
 for he is deprived of his life on earth?"

The eunuch said to Philip, "Tell me, if you will, of whom the prophet says this—himself or someone else?" Philip launched out with this Scripture passage as his starting point, telling him the good news of Jesus. As they moved along the road they came to some water, and the eunuch said, "Look, there is some water right there. What is to keep me from being baptized?" He ordered the carriage stopped, and Philip went down into the water with the eunuch and baptized him.
This is the Word of the Lord.

---

3   Rom 6, 3-11 or 6, 3-4. 8-11

A reading of the letter of Paul to the Romans

When we were baptized we joined Jesus in death so that we might walk in the newness of his life.

(Long Form)

Are you not aware that we who were baptized into Christ Jesus were baptized into his death? Through baptism into his death we were buried with him, so that, just as Christ was raised from the dead by the glory of the Father, we too might live a new life. If we have been united with him through likeness to his death, so shall we be through a like resurrection. This we know: our old self was crucified with him so that the sinful body might be destroyed and we might be slaves to sin no longer. A man who is dead has been freed from sin. If we have died with Christ, we believe that we are also to live with him. We know that Christ, once raised from the dead, will never die again; death has no more power over him. His death was death to sin, once for all; his life is life for God. In the same way, you must consider yourselves dead to sin but alive for God in Christ Jesus.
This is the Word of the Lord.

OR
(Short Form)

Are you not aware that we who were baptized into Christ Jesus were baptized into his death? Through baptism into his death we were buried with him, so that, just as Christ was raised from the dead by the glory of the Father, we too might live a new life.

If we have died with Christ, we believe that we are also to live with him. We know that Christ, once raised from the dead, will never die again; death has no more power over him. His death was death to sin, once for all; his life is life for God. In the same way, you must consider yourselves dead to sin but alive for God in Christ Jesus.
This is the Word of the Lord.

4   Rom 8, 28-32. 35. 37-39

A reading from the letter of Paul to the Romans
Who can ever come between us and the love of Christ.

We know that God makes all things work together for the good of those who have been called according to his decree. Those whom he foreknew he predestined to share the image of his Son, that the Son might be the first-born of many brothers. Those he predestined he likewise called; those he called he also justified; and those he justified he in turn glorified. What shall we say after that? If God is for us, who can be against us? Is it possible that he who did not spare his own Son but handed him over for the sake of us all will not grant us all things besides?

Who will separate us from the love of Christ? Trial, or distress, or persecution, or hunger, or nakedness, or danger, or the sword?

Yet in all this we are more than conquerors because of him who has loved us. For I am certain that neither death nor life, neither angels nor principalities, neither the present nor the future, nor powers, neither height nor depth nor any other creature, will be able to separate us from the love of God that comes to us in Christ Jesus, our Lord.
        This is the Word of the Lord.

---

5   1 Cor 12, 12-13

A reading from the first letter of Paul to the Corinthians
In the one Spirit we were all baptized into one body.

The body is one and has many members, but all the members, many though they are, are one body; and so it is with Christ. It was in one Spirit that all of us, whether Jew or Greek, slave or free, were baptized into one body. All of us have been given to drink of the one Spirit.
        This is the Word of the Lord.

---

6   Gal 3, 26-28

A reading from the letter of Paul to the Galatians
All baptized in Christ, have put on Christ.

Each one of you is a son of God because of your faith in Christ Jesus. All of you who have been baptized into Christ have clothed yourselves with him. There does not exist among you Jew or Greek, slave or freeman, male or female. All are one in Christ Jesus.
        This is the Word of the Lord.

---

7   Eph 1, 3-10. 13-14

A reading from the letter of Paul to the Ephesians
The Father chose us to be his adopted sons through Jesus Christ.

Praised be the God and Father of our Lord Jesus Christ, who has bestowed on us in Christ every spiritual blessing in the heavens! God chose us in him before the world began, to be holy and blameless in his sight, to be full of love; he likewise predestined us through Christ Jesus to be his adopted sons—such was his will and pleasure—that all might praise the divine favor he has bestowed on us in his beloved.

It is in Christ and through his blood that we have been redeemed and our sins forgiven, so immeasurably generous is God's favor to us. God has given us the wisdom to understand fully the mystery, the plan he was pleased to decree in Christ, to be carried out in the fullness of time: namely, to bring all things in the heavens and on earth into one under Christ's headship.

In him you too were chosen; when you heard the glad tidings of salvation, the word of truth, and believed in it, you were sealed with the Holy Spirit who had been promised. He is the pledge of our inheritance, the first payment against the full redemption of a people God has made his own, to praise his glory.
        This is the Word of the Lord.

---

8   Eph 4, 1-6

A reading from the letter of Paul to the Ephesians
There is one Lord, one faith, one baptism.

I plead with you as a prisoner for the Lord, to live a life worthy of the calling you have received, with perfect humility, meekness, and patience, bearing with one another lovingly. Make every effort to preserve the unity which has the Spirit as its origin and peace as its binding force. There is but one body and one Spirit, just as there is but one hope given all of you by your call. There is one Lord, one faith, one baptism; one God and Father of all, who is over all, and works through all, and is in all.

This is the Word of the Lord.

---

9   Col 3, 9-17

A reading from the letter of Paul to the Colossians

As the chosen ones of God, you have put on the new man.

What you have done is put aside your old self with its past deeds and put on a new man, one who grows in knowledge as he is formed anew in the image of his Creator. There is no Greek or Jew here, circumcised or uncircumcised, foreigner, Scythian, slave, or freeman. Rather, Christ is everything in all of you.

Because you are God's chosen ones, holy and beloved, clothe yourselves with heartfelt mercy, with kindness, humility, meekness, and patience. Bear with one another; forgive whatever grievances you have against one another. Forgive as the Lord has forgiven you. Over all these virtues put on love, which binds the rest together and makes them perfect. Christ's peace must reign in your hearts, since as members of the one body you have been called to that peace. Dedicate yourselves to thankfulness. Let the word of Christ, rich as it is, dwell in you. In wisdom made perfect, instruct and admonish one another. Sing gratefully to God from your hearts in psalms, hymns, and inspired songs. Whatever you do, whether in speech or in action, do it in the name of the Lord Jesus. Give thanks to God the Father through him.

This is the Word of the Lord.

---

10   Ti 3, 4-7

A reading from the letter of Paul to Titus

We are saved by the cleansing water of rebirth and by being renewed with the Holy Spirit.

When the kindness and love of God our Savior appeared, he saved us, not because of any righteous deeds we had done, but because of his mercy. He saved us through the baptism of new birth and renewal by the Holy Spirit. This Spirit he lavished on us through Jesus Christ our Savior, that we might be justified by his grace and become heirs, in hope, of eternal life.

This is the Word of the Lord.

---

11   Heb 10, 22-25

A reading from the letter to the Hebrews

Free our hearts from any trace of bad conscience and wash our bodies with pure water.

Let us draw near in utter sincerity and absolute confidence, our hearts sprinkled clean from the evil which lay on our conscience and our bodies washed in pure water. Let us hold unswervingly to our profession which gives us hope, for he who made the promise deserves our trust. We must consider how to rouse each other to love and good deeds. We should not absent ourselves from the assembly, as some do, but encourage one another; and this all the more because you see that the Day draws near.

This is the Word of the Lord.

---

12   1 Pt 2, 4-5. 9-10

A reading from the first letter of Peter

You are a chosen race, a royal priesthood.

Come to Christ, a living stone, rejected by men but approved, nonetheless, and precious in God's eyes. You too are living stones, built as an edifice of spirit, into a holy priesthood, offering spiritual sacrifices acceptable to God through Jesus Christ.

You, however, are "a chosen race, a royal priesthood, a consecrated nation, a people he claims for his own to proclaim the glorious works" of the One who called you from darkness into his marvelous light. Once you were "no people," but now you are God's people; once there was "no mercy for you," but now you have found mercy.

This is the Word of the Lord.

---

13   Rv 19, 1. 5-9

A reading from the book of Revelation

Happy are those who are invited to the wedding feast of the Lamb.

I, John, heard what sounded like the loud song of a great assembly in heaven. They were singing:

"Alleluia!

Salvation, glory, and might belong to our God."

A voice coming from the throne cried out: "Praise our God, all you his servants, the small and the great, who revere him!"

Then I heard what sounded like the shouts of a great crowd, or the roaring of the deep, or mighty peals of thunder, as they cried:

"Alleluia!

The Lord is king,
    our God, the Almighty!
Let us rejoice and be glad,
    and give him glory!
For this is the wedding day of the Lamb;
    his bride has prepared herself for the wedding.
She has been given a dress to wear
    made of finest linen, brilliant white."

(The linen dress is the virtuous deeds of God's saints.)

The angel then said to me: "Write this down: Happy are they who have been invited to the wedding feast of the Lamb."

This is the Word of the Lord.

RESPONSORIAL PSALM

1   Ps 8, 4-5. 6-7. 8-9

℟. (2) O Lord, our God,
    how wonderful your name in all the earth!
When I behold your heavens, the work of your fingers,
    the moon and the stars which you set in place—
What is man that you should be mindful of him,
    or the son of man that you should care for him?
℟. O Lord, our God,
    how wonderful your name in all the earth!

You have made him little less than the angels,
    and crowned him with glory and honor.
You have given him rule over the works of your hands,
    putting all things under his feet.
℟. O Lord, our God,
    how wonderful your name in all the earth!
All sheep and oxen,
    yes, and the beasts of the field,
The birds of the air, the fishes of the sea,
    and whatever swims the paths of the seas.
℟. O Lord, our God,
    how wonderful your name in all the earth!
℟. Or: (Eph 5, 14) Wake up and rise from death:
    Christ will shine upon you!

---

2   Ps 23, 1-3. 3-4. 5. 6

℟. (1) The Lord is my shepherd;
    there is nothing I shall want.
The Lord is my shepherd; I shall not want.
    In verdant pastures he gives me repose;
Beside restful waters he leads me;
    he refreshes my soul.
℟. The Lord is my shepherd;
    there is nothing I shall want.
He guides me in right paths
    for his name's sake.
Even though I walk in the dark valley
    I fear no evil; for you are at my side
With your rod and your staff
    that give me courage.
℟. The Lord is my shepherd;
    there is nothing I shall want.
You spread the table before me
    in the sight of my foes;
You anoint my head with oil;
    my cup overflows.
℟. The Lord is my shepherd;
    there is nothing I shall want.
Only goodness and kindness follow me
    all the days of my life;
And I shall dwell in the house of the Lord
    for years to come.
℟. The Lord is my shepherd;
    there is nothing I shall want.

℟. Or: (1 Pt 2, 25) You were all like lost sheep:
but now you have returned to the shepherd
of your souls.

---

3   Ps 27, 1. 4. 8-9. 13-14

℟. (1) The Lord is my light and my salvation.
The Lord is my light and my salvation;
  whom should I fear?
The Lord is my life's refuge;
  of whom should I be afraid?
℟. The Lord is my light and my salvation.
One thing I ask of the Lord;
  this I seek:
To dwell in the house of the Lord
  all the days of my life,
That I may gaze on the loveliness of the Lord
  and contemplate his temple.
℟. The Lord is my light and my salvation.
Your presence, O Lord, I seek.
  Hide not your face from me;
  do not in anger repel your servant.
You are my helper: cast me not off;
  forsake me not, O God my savior.
℟. The Lord is my light and my salvation.
I believe that I shall see the bounty of the Lord
  in the land of the living.
Wait for the Lord with courage;
  be stouthearted, and wait for the Lord.
℟. The Lord is my light and my salvation.
℟. Or: (Eph 5, 14) Wake up and rise from
death:
  Christ will shine upon you!

---

4   Ps 32, 1-2. 5. 11

℟. (1) Happy are those whose sins are forgiven.
Happy is he whose fault is taken away,
  whose sin is covered.
Happy the man to whom the Lord imputes not
  guilt,
  in whose spirit there is no guile.
℟. Happy are those whose sins are forgiven.
Then I acknowledged my sin to you,
  my guilt I covered not.
I said, "I confess my faults to the Lord,"
  and you took away the guilt of my sin.

℟. Happy are those whose sins are forgiven.
Be glad in the Lord, and rejoice, you just;
  exult, all you upright of heart.
℟. Happy are those whose sins are forgiven.
℟. Or: (11) Let the just exult and rejoice in the
Lord.

---

5   Ps 34, 2-3. 6-7. 8-9. 14-15. 16-17. 18-19

℟. (6) Come to him and receive his light!
I will bless the Lord at all times;
  his praise shall be ever in my mouth.
Let my soul glory in the Lord;
  the lowly will hear me and be glad.
℟. Come to him and receive his light!
Look to him that you may be radiant with joy,
  and your faces may not blush with shame.
When the afflicted man called out, the Lord
  heard,
  and from all his distress he saved him.
℟. Come to him and receive his light!
The angel of the Lord encamps
  around those who fear him, and delivers
  them.
Taste and see how good the Lord is;
  happy the man who takes refuge in him.
℟. Come to him and receive his light!
Keep your tongue from evil
  and your lips from speaking guile;
Turn from evil, and do good;
  seek peace, and follow after it.
℟. Come to him and receive his light!
The Lord has eyes for the just,
  and ears for their cry.
The Lord confronts the evildoers,
  to destroy remembrance of them from the
  earth.
℟. Come to him and receive his light!
When the just cry out, the Lord hears them,
  and from all their distress he rescues them.
The Lord is close to the brokenhearted;
  and those who are crushed in spirit he saves.
℟. Come to him and receive his light!

6   Ps 42, 2-3; 43, 3. 4

℟. (Ps 42, 3) My soul is thirsting for the living God.

As the hind longs for the running waters,
  so my soul longs for you, O God.
Athirst is my soul for God, the living God.
  When shall I go and behold the face of God?
℟. My soul is thirsting for the living God.
Send forth your light and your fidelity;
  they shall lead me on
And bring me to your holy mountain,
  to your dwelling-place.
℟. My soul is thirsting for the living God.
Then will I go in to the altar of God,
  the God of my gladness and joy;
Then will I give you thanks upon the harp,
O God, my God!
℟. My soul is thirsting for the living God.

---

7   Ps 51, 3-4. 8-9. 12-13. 14. 17

℟. (12) Create a clean heart in me, O God.

Have mercy on me, O God, in your goodness;
  in the greatness of your compassion wipe
  out my offense.
Thoroughly wash me from my guilt
  and of my sin cleanse me.
℟. Create a clean heart in me, O God.
Behold, you are pleased with sincerity of heart,
  and in my inmost being you teach me wisdom.
Cleanse me of sin with hyssop, that I may be
  purified;
  wash me, and I shall be whiter than snow.
℟. Create a clean heart in me, O God.
A clean heart create for me, O God,
  and a steadfast spirit renew within me.
Cast me not out from your presence,
  and your holy spirit take not from me.
℟. Create a clean heart in me, O God.
Give me back the joy of your salvation,
  and a willing spirit sustain in me.
O Lord, open my lips,
  and my mouth shall proclaim your praise.
℟. Create a clean heart in me, O God.
℟. Or: (Ez 36, 26) I will give you a new heart, a
  new spirit within you.

8

℟. (2) My soul is thirsting for you, O Lord my God.

O God, you are my God whom I seek;
  for you my flesh pines and my soul thirsts
  like the earth, parched, lifeless and without
  water.
℟. My soul is thirsting for you, O Lord my God.
Thus have I gazed toward you in the sanctuary
  to see your power and your glory,
For your kindness is a greater good than life;
  my lips shall glorify you.
℟. My soul is thirsting for you O Lord my God.
Thus will I bless you while I live;
  lifting up my hands, I will call upon your
  name.
As with the riches of a banquet shall my soul
  be satisfied,
  and with exultant lips my mouth shall praise
  you.
℟. My soul is thirsting for you, O Lord my God.
That you are my help,
  and in the shadow of your wings I shout for
  joy.
My soul clings fast to you.
℟. My soul is thirsting for you, O Lord my God.

---

9   Ps 66, 1-3. 5-6. 8-9. 16-17

℟. (1) Let all the earth cry out to God with joy.

Shout joyfully to God, all you on earth,
  sing praise to the glory of his name;
  proclaim his glorious praise.
Say to God, "How tremendous are your deeds!"
℟. Let all the earth cry out to God with joy.
Come and see the works of God,
  his tremendous deeds among men.
He has changed the sea into dry land;
  through the river they passed on foot;
  therefore let us rejoice in him.
℟. Let all the earth cry out to God with joy.
Bless our God, you peoples,
  loudly sound his praise;
He has given life to our souls,
  and has not let our feet slip.

℞. Let all the earth cry out to God with joy.
Hear now, all you who fear God, while I declare
what he has done for me.
When I appealed to him in words,
praise was on the tip of my tongue.
℞. Let all the earth cry out to God with joy.

---

10   Ps 89, 3-4. 16-17. 21-22. 25. 27

℞. (2) For ever I will sing the goodness of the Lord.
You have said, "My kindness is established forever";
in heaven you have confirmed your faithfulness:
"I have made a covenant with my chosen one,
I have sworn to David my servant."
℞. For ever I will sing the goodness of the Lord.
Happy the people who know the joyful shout;
in the light of your countenance, O Lord, they walk.
At your name they rejoice all the day,
and through your justice they are exalted.
℞. For ever I will sing the goodness of the Lord.
I have found David, my servant;
with my holy oil I have anointed him,
That my hand may be always with him,
and that my arm may make him strong.
℞. For ever I will sing the goodness of the Lord.
My faithfulness and my kindness shall be with him,
and through my name shall his horn be exalted.
"He shall say of me, 'You are my father,
my God, the Rock, my savior.' "
℞. For ever I will sing the goodness of the Lord.

---

11   Ps 126, 1-2. 2-3. 4-5. 6

℞. (3) The Lord has done great things for us; we are filled with joy.
When the Lord brought back the captives of Zion,
we were like men dreaming.

Then our mouth was filled with laughter,
and our tongue with rejoicing.
℞. The Lord has done great things for us; we are filled with joy.
Then they said among the nations,
"The Lord has done great things for them."
The Lord has done great things for us;
we are glad indeed.
℞. The Lord has done great things for us; we are filled with joy.
Restore our fortunes, O Lord,
like the torrents in the southern desert.
Those that sow in tears
shall reap rejoicing.
℞. The Lord has done great things for us; we are filled with joy.
Although they go forth weeping,
carrying the seed to be sown,
They shall come back rejoicing,
carrying their sheaves.
℞. The Lord has done great things for us; we are filled with joy.

---

755   **ALLELUIA VERSE AND**
                VERSE BEFORE THE GOSPEL

1   Jn 3, 16
God so loved the world that he gave us his only Son,
that all who believe in him might have eternal life.

2   Jn 8, 12
I am the light of the world, says the Lord;
the man who follows me will have the light of life.

3   Jn 14, 5
I am the way, the truth, and the life, says the Lord;
no one comes to the Father, except through me.

4   Eph 4, 5-6
One Lord, one faith, one baptism.
One God, the Father of all.

5　　　　　　　　　　　　　　　　　Col 2, 19

In baptism we have died with Christ,
and we have risen to new life in him.

6　　　　　　　　　　　　　　　　　Col 3, 1

If then you have been raised with Christ, seek
　the things that are above,
where Christ is seated at the right hand of God.

7　　　　　　　　　　　　　　　　　2 Tm 1, 10

Our Savior Jesus Christ has done away with
　death,
and brought us life through his gospel.

8　　　　　　　　　　　　　　　　　1 Pt 2, 9

You are a chosen race, a royal priesthood, a
　holy people.
Praise God who called you out of darkness and
　into his marvelous light.

756　　　　　　**GOSPEL**

1　　　　　　　　　　　　　　　　　Mt 16, 24-27

✠ A reading from the holy gospel according
　　　　　　to Matthew
If anyone wishes to follow me, let him deny himself.

Jesus said to his disciples: "If a man wishes to
come after me, he must deny his very self, take
up his cross, and begin to follow in my footsteps. Whoever would save his life will lose it,
but whoever loses his life for my sake will find
it. What profit would a man show if he were
to gain the whole world and ruin himself in the
process? What can a man offer in exchange for
his very self? The Son of Man will come with
his Father's glory accompanied by his angels.
When he does, he will repay each man according to his conduct."
　　　This is the gospel of the Lord.

2　　　　　　　　　　　　　　　　　Mt 28, 18-20

✠ A reading from the holy gospel according
　　　　　　to Matthew
Go and teach all the nations, baptizing them in the name of
　the Father, and of the Son, and of the Holy Spirit.

Jesus came forward and addressed the eleven
disciples in these words:

"Full authority has been given to me
both in heaven and on earth;
go, therefore, and make disciples of all the
　nations.
Baptize them in the name
　'of the Father
　and of the Son,
　and of the Holy Spirit.'
Teach them to carry out everything I have
　commanded you.
And know that I am with you always,
　until the end of the world!"
　　　This is the gospel of the Lord.

3　　　　　　　　　　　　　　　　　Mk 1, 9-11

✠ A reading from the holy gospel according
　　　　　　to Mark
Jesus was baptized by John in the Jordan.

Jesus came from Nazareth in Galilee and was
baptized in the Jordan by John. Immediately
on coming up out of the water he saw the sky
rent in two and the Spirit descending on him
like a dove. Then a voice came from the
heavens: "You are my beloved Son. On you my
favor rests."
　　　This is the gospel of the Lord.

4　　　　　　　　　　　　　　　　　Mk 10, 13-16

✠ A reading from the holy gospel according
　　　　　　to Mark
Anyone who does not welcome the kingdom of God like a
　little child will never enter it.

People were bringing their little children to
Jesus to have him touch them, but the disciples
were scolding them for this. Jesus became indignant when he noticed it and said to them:
"Let the children come to me and do not hinder
them. It is to just such as these that the kingdom of God belongs. I assure you that whoever
does not accept the kingdom of God like a little
child shall not enter into it." Then he embraced
them and blessed them, placing his hands on
them.
　　　This is the gospel of the Lord.

---

5   Mk 16, 15-16. 19-20

✠ A reading from the holy gospel according
to Mark

He who believes and is baptized will be saved.

Jesus appeared to the Eleven and said to them:
"Go into the whole world and proclaim the
good news to all creation. The man who believes in it and accepts baptism will be saved;
the man who refuses to believe in it will be condemned."

Then, after speaking to them, the Lord Jesus
was taken up into heaven and took his seat
at God's right hand. The Eleven went forth and
preached everywhere. The Lord continued to
work with them throughout and confirm the
message through the signs which accompanied
them.

This is the gospel of the Lord.

6   Lk 24, 44-53

✠ A reading from the holy gospel according
to Luke

In the name of Jesus, repentance for the forgiveness of sins
should be preached to all the nations.

Jesus said to his disciples: "Recall those words
I spoke to you when I was still with you:
everything written about me in the law of
Moses and the prophets and psalms had to be
fulfilled." Then he opened their minds to the
understanding of the Scriptures.

He said to them: "Thus it is written that the
Messiah must suffer and rise from the dead on
the third day. In his name, penance for the remission of sins is to be preached to all the
nations, beginning at Jerusalem. You are witnesses of this. See, I send down upon you the
promise of my Father. Remain here in the city
until you are clothed with power from on
high."

He then led them out near Bethany, and with
hands upraised, blessed them. As he blessed,
he left them, and was taken up to heaven.
They fell down to do him reverence, then
returned to Jerusalem filled with joy. There
they were to be found in the temple constantly
speaking the praises of God.

This is the gospel of the Lord.

7   Jn 1, 1-5. 9-14. 16-18

✠ A reading from the holy gospel according
to John

He gave power to become children of God to all who believe
in his name.

In the beginning was the Word;
the Word was in God's presence,
and the Word was God.
He was present to God in the beginning.
Through him all things came into being,
and apart from him nothing came to be.
Whatever came to be in him, found life,
life for the light of men.
The light shines on in darkness,
a darkness that did not overcome it.
The real light which gives light to every man
was coming into the world.
He was in the world,
and through him the world was made,
yet the world did not know who he was.
To his own he came,
yet his own did not accept him.
Any who did accept him
he empowered to become children of God.
These are they who believe in his name—who
were begotten not by blood, nor by carnal
desire, nor by man's willing it, but by God.
The Word became flesh
and made his dwelling among us,
and we have seen his glory:
the glory of an only Son coming from the
Father,
filled with enduring love.

Of his fullness
we have all had a share—
love following upon love.
For while the law was a gift through Moses,
this enduring love came through Jesus Christ.
No one has ever seen God. It is God the only
Son, ever at the Father's side, who has revealed
him.

This is the gospel of the Lord.

8   Jn 1, 29-34

✠ A reading from the holy gospel according
to John

Look, there is the Lamb of God that takes away the sins of
the world.

The next day, when John caught sight of Jesus
coming toward him, he exclaimed:
"Look there! The Lamb of God
who takes away the sin of the world!
It is he of whom I said:
'After me is to come a man
who ranks ahead of me,
because he was before me.'
I confess I did not recognize him, though the
very reason I came baptizing with water was
that he might be revealed to Israel."
John gave this testimony also:
"I saw the Spirit descend
like a dove from the sky,
and it came to rest on him.
But I did not recognize him. The one who sent
me to baptize with water told me, 'When you
see the Spirit descend and rest on someone, it
is he who is to baptize with the Holy Spirit.'
Now I have seen for myself and have testified,
'This is God's chosen One.' "
This is the gospel of the Lord.

---

9   Jn 3, 1-6

✠ A reading from the holy gospel according
to John

Unless a man is born from above, he cannot see the
kingdom of God.

A certain Pharisee named Nicodemus, a member of the Jewish Sanhedrin, came to Jesus at
night. "Rabbi," he said, "we know you are a
teacher come from God, for no man can perform signs and wonders such as you perform
unless God is with him." Jesus gave him this
answer:
"I solemnly assure you,
no one can see the rule of God
unless he is begotten from above."
"How can a man be born again once he is old?"
retorted Nicodemus. "Can he return to his
mother's womb and be born over again?" Jesus
replied:

"I solemnly assure you,
no one can enter into God's kingdom
without being begotten of water and
Spirit.
Flesh begets flesh,
Spirit begets spirit."
This is the gospel of the Lord.

---

10   Jn 3, 16-21

✠ A reading from the holy gospel according
to John

Everyone who believes in him will have everlasting life.

Jesus said to Nicodemus:
"God so loved the world
that he gave his only Son,
that whoever believes in him may not die
but may have eternal life.
God did not send the Son into the world
to condemn the world,
but that the world might be saved through
him.
Whoever believes in him avoids condemnation,
but whoever does not believe is already
condemned
for not believing in the name of God's
only Son.
The judgment in question is this:
the light came into the world,
but men loved darkness rather than light
because their deeds were wicked.
Everyone who practices evil
hates the light;
he does not come near it
for fear his deeds will be exposed.
But he who acts in truth
comes into the light,
to make clear
that his deeds are done in God."
This is the gospel of the Lord.

11   Jn 12, 44-50

✠ **A reading from the holy gospel according
to John**

I, the light, have come into the world.

Jesus proclaimed aloud:
"Whoever puts faith in me
believes not so much in me
as in him who sent me;
and whoever looks on me
is seeing him who sent me.
I have come to the world as its light,
to keep anyone who believes in me
from remaining in the dark.
If anyone hears my words and does not
keep them,
I am not the one to condemn him,
for I did not come to condemn the world
but to save it.
Whoever rejects me and does not accept
my words
already has his judge,
namely, the word I have spoken—
it is that which will condemn him on the
last day.
For I have not spoken on my own;
no, the Father who sent me
has commanded me
what to say and how to speak.
Since I know that his commandment
means eternal life,
whatever I say
is spoken just as he instructed me."
This is the gospel of the Lord.

12   Jn 15, 1-11

✠ **A reading from the holy gospel according
to John**

Whoever remains in me, and I in him, bears fruit in plenty.

Jesus said to his disciples:
"I am the true vine
and my Father is the vinegrower.
He prunes away
every barren branch,
but the fruitful ones
he trims clean
to increase their yield.
You are clean already,

thanks to the word I have spoken to you.
Live on in me, as I do in you.
No more than a branch can bear fruit of
itself
apart from the vine,
can you bear fruit
apart from me.
I am the vine, you are the branches.
He who lives in me and I in him,
will produce abundantly,
for apart from me you can do nothing.
A man who does not live in me
is like a withered, rejected branch,
picked up to be thrown in the fire and
burnt.
If you live in me,
and my words stay part of you,
you may ask what you will—
it will be done for you.
My Father has been glorified
in your bearing much fruit
and becoming my disciples.

"As the Father has loved me,
so I have loved you.
Live on in my love.
You will live in my love
if you keep my commandments,
even as I have kept my Father's commandments,
and live in his love.
All this I tell you
that my joy may be yours
and your joy may be complete."
This is the gospel of the Lord.

BAPTISM OF CHILDREN

OLD TESTAMENT READING

1   Ex 17, 3-7

A reading from the book of Exodus
Give to us water, that we may drink.

In their thirst for water the people grumbled against Moses, saying, "Why did you ever make us leave Egypt? Was it just to have us die here of thirst with our children and our livestock?" So Moses cried out to the Lord, "What shall I do with this people? A little more and they will stone me!" The Lord answered Moses, "Go over there in front of the people, along with some of the elders of Israel, holding in your hand as you go, the staff with which you struck the river. I will be standing there in front of you on the rock in Horeb. Strike the rock, and the water will flow from it for the people to drink."

This Moses did, in the presence of the elders of Israel. The place was called Massah and Meribah, because the Israelites quarreled there and tested the Lord, saying, "Is the Lord in our midst or not?"

This is the Word of the Lord.

2   Ez 36, 24-28

A reading from the book of the prophet Ezekiel
I will pour out on you clean water and you will be cleansed from all your sins.

Thus says the Lord God: I will take you away from among the nations, gather you from all the foreign lands, and bring you back to your own land. I will sprinkle clean water upon you to cleanse you from all your impurities, and from all your idols I will cleanse you. I will give you a new heart and place a new spirit within you, taking from your bodies your stony hearts and giving you natural hearts. I will put my spirit within you and make you live by my statutes, careful to observe my decrees. You shall live in the land I gave your fathers; you shall be my people, and I will be your God.

This is the Word of the Lord.

3   Ez 47, 1-9. 12

A reading from the book of the prophet Ezekiel
I see the water flowing from the temple and all who were touched by it were saved.

Then the angel brought me back to the entrance of the temple of the Lord, and I saw water flowing out from beneath the threshold of the temple toward the east, for the facade of the temple was toward the east; the water flowed down from the southern side of the temple, south of the altar. He led me outside by the north gate, and around to the outer gate facing the east, where I saw water trickling from the southern side. Then when he had walked off to the east with a measuring cord in his hand, he measured off a thousand cubits and had me wade through the water, which was ankle-deep. He measured off another thousand and once more had me wade through the water, which was now knee-deep. Again he measured off a thousand and had me wade; the water was up to my waist. Once more he measured off a thousand, but there was now a river through which I could not wade; for the water had risen so high it had become a river that could not be crossed except by swimming. He asked me, "Have you seen this, son of man?" Then he brought me to the bank of the river, where he had me sit. Along the bank of the river I saw very many trees on both sides. He said to me, "This water flows into the eastern district down upon the Arabah, and empties into the sea, the salt waters, which it makes fresh. Wherever the river flows, every sort of living creature that can multiply shall live, and there shall be abundant fish, for wherever this water comes the sea shall be made fresh. Along both banks of the river, fruit trees of every kind shall grow; their leaves shall not fade, nor their fruit fail. Every month they shall bear fresh fruit, for they shall be watered by the flow from the sanctuary. Their fruit shall serve for food, and their leaves for medicine."

This is the Word of the Lord.

758   NEW TESTAMENT READING

1   Rom 6, 3-5

A reading from the letter of Paul to the Romans
When we were baptized we joined Jesus in death so that we
might walk in the newness of his life.

Are you not aware that we who were baptized into Christ Jesus were baptized into his
death? Through baptism into his death we
were buried with him, so that, just as Christ
was raised from the dead by the glory of the
Father, we too might live a new life. If we have
been united with him through likeness to his
death, so shall we be through a like resurrection.

This is the Word of the Lord.

2   Rom 8, 28-32

A reading from the letter of Paul to the Romans
We have become more like God's own Son.

We know that God makes all things work together for the good of those who have been
called according to his decree. Those whom he
foreknew he predestined to share the image of
his Son, that the Son might be the first-born of
many brothers. Those he predestined he likewise called; those he called he also justified;
and those he justified he in turn glorified. What
shall we say after that? If God is for us, who
can be against us? Is it possible that he who did
not spare his own Son but handed him over for
the sake of us all will not grant us all things
besides?

This is the Word of the Lord.

3   1 Cor 12, 12-13

**A reading from the first letter of Paul to the
Corinthians**
In the one Spirit we were all baptized into one body.

The body is one and has many members, but all
the members, many though they are, are one
body; and so it is with Christ. It was in one
Spirit that all of us, whether Jew or Greek,
slave or free, were baptized into one body. All
of us have been given to drink of the one
Spirit.

This is the Word of the Lord.

4   Gal 3, 26-28

**A reading from the letter of Paul to the
Galatians**
All baptized in Christ have put on Christ.

Each one of you is a son of God because of
your faith in Christ Jesus. All of you who have
been baptized into Christ have clothed yourselves with him. There does not exist among
you Jew or Greek, slave or freeman, male or
female. All are one in Christ Jesus.

This is the Word of the Lord.

5   Eph 4, 1-6

**A reading from the letter of Paul to the
Ephesians**
One Lord, one faith, one baptism.

I plead with you as a prisoner for the Lord, to
live a life worthy of the calling you have received, with perfect humility, meekness, and
patience, bearing with one another lovingly.
Make every effort to preserve the unity which
has the Spirit as its origin and peace as its binding force. There is but one body and one Spirit,
just as there is but one hope given all of you
by your call. There is one Lord, one faith, one
baptism; one God and Father of all, who is over
all, and works through all, and is in all.

This is the Word of the Lord.

6   1 Pt 2, 4-5. 9-10

A reading from the first letter of Peter
You are a chosen race, a royal priesthood.

Come to Christ, a living stone, rejected by men
but approved, nonetheless, and precious in
God's eyes. You too are living stones, built
as an edifice of spirit, into a holy priesthood,
offering spiritual sacrifices acceptable to God
through Jesus Christ.

You, however, are "a chosen race, a royal
priesthood, a consecrated nation, a people he
claims for his own to proclaim the glorious
works" of the One who called you from darkness into his marvelous light. Once you were
"no people," but now you are God's people;

once there was "no mercy for you," but now you have found mercy.
    This is the Word of the Lord.

---

759   RESPONSORIAL PSALM

1   Ps 23, 1-3. 3-4. 5. 6

℟. (1) The Lord is my shepherd;
    there is nothing I shall want.
The Lord is my shepherd; I shall not want.
    In verdant pastures he gives me repose;
Beside restful waters he leads me;
    he refreshes my soul.
℟. The Lord is my shepherd;
    there is nothing I shall want.
He guides me in right paths
    for his name's sake.
Even though I walk in the dark valley
    I fear no evil; for you are at my side
With your rod and your staff
    that give me courage.
℟. The Lord is my shepherd;
    there is nothing I shall want.
You spread the table before me
    in the sight of my foes;
You anoint my head with oil;
    my cup overflows.
℟. The Lord is my shepherd;
    there is nothing I shall want.
Only goodness and kindness follow me
    all the days of my life;
And I shall dwell in the house of the Lord
    for years to come.
℟. The Lord is my shepherd;
    there is nothing I shall want.

---

2   Ps 27, 1. 4. 8-9. 13-14

℟. (1) The Lord is my light and my salvation.
The Lord is my light and my salvation;
    whom should I fear?
The Lord is my life's refuge;
    of whom should I be afraid?
℟. The Lord is my light and my salvation.
One thing I ask of the Lord;
    this I seek:
To dwell in the house of the Lord
    all the days of my life,

That I may gaze on the loveliness of the Lord
    and contemplate his temple.
℟. The Lord is my light and my salvation.
Your presence, O Lord, I seek.
Hide not your face from me;
    do not in anger repel your servant.
You are my helper: cast me not off.
℟. The Lord is my light and my salvation.
I believe that I shall see the bounty of the Lord
    in the land of the living.
Wait for the Lord with courage;
    be stouthearted, and wait for the Lord.
℟. The Lord is my light and my salvation.
℟. Or: (Eph 5, 14) Wake up and rise from
    death:
    Christ will shine upon you!

---

3   Ps 34, 2-3. 6-7. 8-9. 14-15. 16-17. 18-19

℟. (6) Come to him and receive his light!
I will bless the Lord at all times;
    his praise shall be ever in my mouth.
Let my soul glory in the Lord;
    the lowly will hear me and be glad.
℟. Come to him and receive his light!
Look to him that you may be radiant with joy,
    and your faces may not blush with shame.
When the afflicted man called out, the Lord
    heard,
    and from all his distress he saved him.
℟. Come to him and receive his light!
The angel of the Lord encamps
    around those who fear him, and delivers
    them.
Taste and see how good the Lord is;
    happy the man who takes refuge in him.
℟. Come to him and receive his light!
Keep your tongue from evil
    and your lips from speaking guile;
Turn from evil, and do good;
    seek peace, and follow after it.
℟. Come to him and receive his light!
The Lord has eyes for the just,
    and ears for their cry.
The Lord confronts the evildoers,
    to destroy remembrance of them from the
    earth.
℟. Come to him and receive his light!

When the just cry out, the Lord hears them,
  and from all their distress he rescues them.
The Lord is close to the brokenhearted;
  and those who are crushed in spirit he saves.
℞. Come to him and receive his light!
℞. Or: (9) Taste and see the goodness of the
  Lord.

**760   ALLELUIA VERSE AND
VERSE BEFORE THE GOSPEL**

1   Jn 3, 16

God loved the world so much, he gave us his
  only Son,
that all who believe in him might have eternal
  life.

2   Jn 8, 12

I am the light of the world, says the Lord;
the man who follows me will have the light of
  life.

3   Jn 14, 6

I am the way, the truth, and the life, says the
  Lord;
no one comes to the Father, except through me.

4   Eph 4, 5-6

One Lord, one faith, one baptism.
One God, the Father of all.

5   2 Tm 1, 10

Our Savior Jesus Christ has done away with
  death,
and brought us life through his gospel.

6   1 Pt 2, 9

You are a chosen race, a royal priesthood, a
  holy people.
Praise God who called you out of darkness and
  into his marvelous light.

---

761   GOSPEL

1   Mt 22, 35-40

✠ **A reading from the holy gospel according
to Matthew**

This is the first and most important commandment.

One of the Pharisees, a lawyer, in an attempt
to trip Jesus up, asked him, "Teacher, which
commandment of the law is the greatest?"
Jesus said to him:
    " 'You shall love the Lord your God
    with your whole heart,
    with your whole soul,
    and with all your mind.'
This is the greatest and first commandment.
The second is like it:
    'You shall love your neighbor as yourself.'
On these two commandments the whole law is
based, and the prophets as well."
        This is the gospel of the Lord.

---

2   Mt 28, 18-20

✠ **A reading from the holy gospel according
to Matthew**

Go and teach all the nations, baptizing them in the name
of the Father, and of the Son, and of the Holy Spirit.

Jesus came forward and addressed the eleven
disciples in these words:
        "Full authority has been given to me
        both in heaven and on earth;
        go, therefore, and make disciples of all the
            nations.
    Baptize them in the name
        'of the Father
        and of the Son,
        and of the Holy Spirit.'
    Teach them to carry out everything I have
            commanded you.
    And know that I am with you always,
            until the end of the world!"
        This is the gospel of the Lord.

3   Mk 1, 9-11

✠ **A reading from the holy gospel according to Mark**

Jesus was baptized by John in the Jordan.

Jesus came from Nazareth in Galilee and was baptized in the Jordan by John. Immediately on coming up out of the water he saw the sky rent in two and the Spirit descending on him like a dove. Then a voice came from the heavens: "You are my beloved Son. On you my favor rests."

This is the gospel of the Lord.

---

4   Mk 10, 13-16

✠ **A reading from the holy gospel according to Mark**

Let the children come to me.

People were bringing their little children to Jesus to have him touch them, but the disciples were scolding them for this. Jesus became indignant when he noticed it and said to them: "Let the children come to me and do not hinder them. It is to just such as these that the kingdom of God belongs. I assure you that whoever does not accept the kingdom of God like a little child shall not enter into it." Then he embraced them and blessed them, placing his hands on them.

This is the gospel of the Lord.

---

5   Mk 12, 28-34 or 12, 28-31

✠ **A reading from the holy gospel according to Mark**

Hear Israel, love the Lord God with your whole heart.

(Long Form)

One of the scribes decided to ask Jesus, "Which is the first of all the commandments?" Jesus replied: "This is the first:

'Hear, O Israel! The Lord our God is Lord alone!
Therefore you shall love the Lord your God
with all your heart,
with all your soul,
with all your mind,
and with all your strength.'

This is the second,
'You shall love your neighbor as yourself.' There is no other commandment greater than these." The scribe said to him: "Excellent, Teacher! You are right in saying, 'He is the One, there is no other than he.' Yes, 'to love him with all our heart, with all our thoughts and with all our strength, and to love our neighbor as ourselves' is worth more than any burnt offering or sacrifice." Jesus approved the insight of this answer and told him, "You are not far from the reign of God." And no one had the courage to ask him any more questions.

This is the gospel of the Lord.

OR
(Short Form)

One of the scribes decided to ask Jesus, "Which is the first of all the commandments?" Jesus replied: "This is the first:

'Hear, O Israel! The Lord our God is Lord alone!
Therefore you shall love the Lord your God
with all your heart,
with all your soul,
with all your mind,
and with all your strength.'

This is the second,
'You shall love your neighbor as yourself.' There is no other commandment greater than these."

This is the gospel of the Lord.

---

6   Jn 3, 1-6

✠ **A reading from the holy gospel according to John**

Unless a man is born from above, he cannot see the kingdom of God.

A certain Pharisee named Nicodemus, a member of the Jewish Sanhedrin, came to Jesus at night. "Rabbi," he said, "we know you are a teacher come from God, for no man can perform signs and wonders such as you perform unless God is with him." Jesus gave him this answer:

"I solemnly assure you,
no one can see the rule of God
unless he is begotten from above."

"How can a man be born again once he is old?" retorted Nicodemus. "Can he return to his mother's womb and be born over again?" Jesus replied:

"I solemnly assure you,
no one can enter into God's kingdom
without being begotten of water and Spirit.
Flesh begets flesh,
Spirit begets spirit."
This is the gospel of the Lord.

---

7   Jn 4, 5-14

✠ **A reading from the holy gospel according to John**

The water I give will become a fountain of living water springing up into life eternal.

The journey of Jesus brought him to a Samaritan town named Shechem near the plot of land which Jacob had given to his son Joseph. This was the site of Jacob's well. Jesus, tired from his journey, sat down at the well.

The hour was about noon. When a Samaritan woman came to draw water, Jesus said to her, "Give me a drink." (His disciples had gone off to the town to buy provisions.) The Samaritan woman said to him, "You are a Jew. How can you ask me, a Samaritan and a woman, for a drink?" (Recall that Jews have nothing to do with Samaritans.) Jesus replied:

"If only you recognized God's gift,
and who it is that is asking you for a drink,
you would have asked him instead,
and he would have given you living water."

"Sir," she challenged him, "you don't have a bucket and this well is deep. Where do you expect to get this flowing water? Surely you don't pretend to be greater than our ancestor Jacob, who gave us this well and drank from it with his sons and his flocks?" Jesus replied:

"Everyone who drinks this water
will be thirsty again.
But whoever drinks the water I give him
will never be thirsty;
no, the water I give

shall become a fountain within him,
leaping up to provide eternal life."
This is the gospel of the Lord.

---

8   Jn 6, 44-47

✠ **A reading from the holy gospel according to John**

He who believes has eternal life.

Jesus said to the crowd:

"No one can come to me
unless the Father who sent me draws him;
I will raise him up on the last day.
It is written in the prophets:
'They shall all be taught by God.'
Everyone who has heard the Father
and learned from him
comes to me.
Not that anyone has seen the Father—
only the one who is from God
has seen the Father.
Let me firmly assure you,
he who believes has eternal life."
This is the gospel of the Lord.

---

9   Jn 7, 37-39

✠ **A reading from the holy gospel according to John**

Streams of living water shall flow from his heart.

Jesus stood up and cried out:

"If anyone thirsts, let him come to me;
let him drink who believes in me.
Scripture has it:
'From within him rivers of living water shall flow.'" (Here he was referring to the Spirit, whom those that came to believe in him were to receive.)
This is the gospel of the Lord.

---

10   Jn 9, 1-7

✠ **A reading from the holy gospel according to John**

He leaves, and washes, and returns able to see.

As Jesus walked along, he saw a man who had been blind from birth. His disciples asked him,

"Rabbi, was it his sin or his parents' that caused him to be born blind?" "Neither," answered Jesus:

"It was no sin, either of this man
or of his parents.
Rather, it was to let God's works show
forth in him.
We must do the deeds of him who sent me
while it is day.
The night comes on
when no one can work.
While I am in the world
I am the light of the world."

With that Jesus spat on the ground, made mud with his saliva, and smeared the man's eyes with the mud. Then he told him, "Go, wash in the pool of Siloam." (This name means "One who has been sent.") So the man went off and washed, and came back able to see.

This is the gospel of the Lord.

---

11   Jn 15, 1-11

✠ A reading from the holy gospel according to John

Whoever remains in me, and I in him, bears fruit in plenty.

Jesus said to his disciples:
"I am the true vine
and my Father is the vinegrower.
He prunes away
every barren branch,
but the fruitful ones
he trims clean
to increase their yield.
You are clean already,
thanks to the word I have spoken to you.
Live on in me, as I do in you.
No more than a branch can bear fruit of
itself
apart from the vine,
can you bear fruit
apart from me.
I am the vine, you are the branches.
He who lives in me and I in him,
will produce abundantly,
for apart from me you can do nothing.
A man who does not live in me
is like a withered, rejected branch,

picked up to be thrown in the fire and
burnt.
If you live in me,
and my words stay part of you,
you may ask what you will—
it will be done for you.
My Father has been glorified
in your bearing much fruit
and becoming my disciples.

"As the Father has loved me,
so I have loved you.
Live on in my love.
You will live in my love
if you keep my commandments,
even as I have kept my Father's commandments,
and live in his love.
All this I tell you
that my joy may be yours
and your joy may be complete."

This is the gospel of the Lord.

---

12   Jn 19, 31-35

✠ A reading from the holy gospel according to John

He opened his side and out came blood and water.

Since it was the Preparation Day, the Jews did not want to have the bodies left on the cross during the sabbath, for that sabbath was a solemn feast day. They asked Pilate that the legs be broken and the bodies be taken away. Accordingly, the soldiers came and broke the legs of the men crucified with Jesus, first of the one, then of the other. When they came to Jesus and saw that he was already dead, they did not break his legs. One of the soldiers thrust a lance into his side, and immediately blood and water flowed out. (This testimony has been given by an eyewitness and his testimony is true. He tells what he knows is true, so that you may believe.)

This is the gospel of the Lord.

762   **RECEPTION OF THE BAPTIZED INTO THE FULL COMMUNION OF THE CHURCH**

Readings may be taken in whole or in part from the Mass of the day or from the Mass for the Unity of Christians (below, nos. 811-815), or from the Mass of Christian initiation (above, nos. 752-756).

CONFIRMATION

763   **OLD TESTAMENT READING**

1   Is 11, 1-4

A reading from the book of the prophet Isaiah
On him the Spirit of the Lord rests.

A shoot shall sprout from the stump of Jesse,
   and from his roots a bud shall blossom.
The spirit of the Lord shall rest upon him:
   a spirit of wisdom and of understanding,
A spirit of counsel and of strength,
   a spirit of knowledge and of fear of the Lord,
   and his delight shall be the fear of the Lord.
Not by appearance shall he judge,
   nor by hearsay shall he decide,
But he shall judge the poor with justice,
   and decide aright for the land's afflicted.
        This is the Word of the Lord.

2   Is 42, 1-3

A reading from the book of the prophet Isaiah
I have endowed my servant with my Spirit.

Here is my servant whom I uphold,
   my chosen one with whom I am pleased,
Upon whom I have put my spirit;
   he shall bring forth justice to the nations,
Not crying out, not shouting,
   not making his voice heard in the street.
A bruised reed he shall not break,
   and a smoldering wick he shall not quench.
        This is the Word of the Lord.

3   Is 61, 1-3. 6. 8-9

A reading from the book of the prophet Isaiah
The Lord God has anointed me and has sent me to bring Good News to the poor, to give them the oil of gladness.

The spirit of the Lord God is upon me,
   because the Lord has anointed me;
He has sent me to bring glad tidings to the lowly,
   to heal the brokenhearted,
To proclaim liberty to the captives
   and release to the prisoners,
To announce a year of favor from the Lord
   and a day of vindication by our God,
   to comfort all who mourn;
To place on those who mourn in Zion
   a diadem instead of ashes.
To give them oil of gladness in place of mourning,
   a glorious mantle instead of a listless spirit.
You yourselves shall be named priests of the Lord,
   ministers of our God you shall be called.
I will give them their recompense faithfully,
   a lasting covenant I will make with them.
Their descendants shall be renowned among the nations,
   and their offspring among the peoples;
All who see them shall acknowledge them
   as a race the Lord has blessed.
        This is the Word of the Lord.

4   Ez 36, 24-28

A reading from the book of the prophet Ezekiel
I will place a new Spirit in your midst.

The Lord God said: I will take you away from among the nations, gather you from all the foreign lands, and bring you back to your own land. I will sprinkle clean water upon you to cleanse you from all your impurities, and from all your idols I will cleanse you. I will give you a new heart and place a new spirit within you, taking from your bodies your stony hearts and giving you natural hearts. I will put my spirit within you and make you live by my statutes, careful to observe my decrees. You shall live in the land I gave your

fathers; you shall be my people, and I will be your God.

This is the Word of the Lord.

5   Jl 2, 23; 3, 1-3

A reading from the book of the prophet Joel

I will pour out my Spirit on all mankind.

Do you, O children of Zion, exult
  and rejoice in the Lord, your God!
You shall eat and be filled,
  and shall praise the name of the Lord, your
    God,
Because he has dealt wondrously with you;
  my people shall nevermore be put to shame.
And you shall know that I am in the midst of
    Israel;
  I am the Lord, your God, and there is no
    other;
my people shall nevermore be put to shame.
Then afterward I will pour out
  my spirit upon all mankind.
Your sons and daughters shall prophesy,
  your old men shall dream dreams,
  your young men shall see visions;
Even upon the servants and the handmaids,
  in those days, I will pour out my spirit.
And I will work wonders in the heavens and on
    the earth.

This is the Word of the Lord.

764   **NEW TESTAMENT READING**

1   Acts 1, 3-8

A reading from the Acts of the Apostles

You will receive the power of the Holy Spirit, and you will be my witnesses.

In the time after his suffering Jesus showed his apostles in many convincing ways that he was alive, appearing to them over the course of forty days and speaking to them about the reign of God. On one occasion when he met with them, he told them not to leave Jerusalem: "Wait, rather, for the fulfillment of my Father's promise, of which you have heard me speak. John baptized with water, but within a few days you will be baptized with the Holy Spirit."

While they were with him they asked, "Lord, are you going to restore the rule to Israel now?" His answer was: "The exact time

it is not yours to know. The Father has reserved that to himself. You will receive power when the Holy Spirit comes down on you; then you are to be my witnesses in Jerusalem, throughout Judea and Samaria, yes, even to the ends of the earth."

This is the Word of the Lord.

2   Acts 2, 1-6. 14. 22-23. 32-33

A reading from the Acts of the Apostles

They were all filled with the Holy Spirit, and began to speak.

When the day of Pentecost came it found the apostles gathered in one place. Suddenly from up in the sky there came a noise like a strong, driving wind which was heard all through the house where they were seated. Tongues as of fire appeared, which parted and came to rest on each of them. All were filled with the Holy Spirit. They began to express themselves in foreign tongues and make bold proclamation as the Spirit prompted them.

Staying in Jerusalem at the time were devout Jews of every nation under heaven. These heard the sound, and assembled in a large crowd. They were much confused because each one heard these men speaking his own language.

Peter stood up with the Eleven, raised his voice, and addressed them: "You who are Jews, indeed all of you staying in Jerusalem! Listen to what I have to say. Men of Israel, listen to me: Jesus the Nazorean was a man whom God sent to you with miracles, wonders and signs as his credentials. These God worked through him in your midst, as you well know. He was delivered up by the set purpose and plan of God; you even made use of pagans to crucify and kill him. This is the Jesus God has raised up, and we are his witnesses. Exalted at God's right hand, he first received the promised holy Spirit from the Father, then poured this Spirit out on us."

This is the Word of the Lord.

3   Acts 8, 1. 4. 14-17

A reading from the Acts of the Apostles

They laid hands on them, and they received the Holy Spirit.

A certain day saw the beginning of a great persecution of the church in Jerusalem. All except the apostles scattered throughout the countryside of Judea and Samaria.

The members of the church who had been dispersed went about preaching the word.

When the apostles in Jerusalem heard that Samaria had accepted the word of God, they sent Peter and John to them. The two went down to these people and prayed that they might receive the Holy Spirit. It had not as yet come down upon any of them since they had only been baptized in the name of the Lord Jesus. The pair upon arriving imposed hands on them and they received the Holy Spirit.

This is the Word of the Lord.

---

4 Acts 10, 1. 33-34. 37-44

A reading from the Acts of the Apostles

The Holy Spirit came down on all those listening to the word of God.

In Caesarea there was a centurion named Cornelius, of the Roman cohort Italica, who was religious and God-fearing. The same was true of his whole household.

Cornelius said to Peter: "I sent for you immediately, and you have been kind enough to come. All of us stand before God at this moment to hear whatever directives the Lord has given you."

Peter proceeded to address them in these words: "I take it you know what has been reported all over Judea about Jesus of Nazareth, beginning in Galilee with the baptism John preached; of the way God anointed him with the Holy Spirit and power. He went about doing good works and healing all who were in the grip of the devil, and God was with him. We are witnesses to all that he did in the land of the Jews and in Jerusalem. They killed him finally, 'hanging him on a tree,' only to have God raise him up on the third day and grant that he be seen, not by all, but only by such witnesses as had been chosen beforehand by God—by us who ate and drank with him after he rose from the dead. He commissioned us to preach to the people and to bear witness that he is the one set apart by God as judge of the living and the dead. To him all the prophets testify, saying that everyone who believes in him has forgiveness of sins through his name."

Peter had not finished these words when the Holy Spirit descended upon all who were listening to Peter's message.

This is the Word of the Lord.

---

5 Acts 19, 1-6

A reading from the Acts of the Apostles

Did you receive the Holy Spirit when you became believers?

Paul came to Ephesus. There he found some disciples to whom he put the question, "Did you receive the Holy Spirit when you became believers?" They answered, "We have not so much as heard that there is a Holy Spirit." "Well, how were you baptized?" he persisted. They replied, "With the baptism of John." Paul then explained, "John's baptism was a baptism of repentance. He used to tell the people about the one who would come after him in whom they were to believe—that is, Jesus." When they heard this, they were baptized in the name of the Lord Jesus. As Paul laid his hands on them, the Holy Spirit came down on them.

This is the Word of the Lord.

---

6 Rom 5, 1-2. 5-8

A reading from the letter of Paul to the Romans

The love of God has been poured into our hearts by the Holy Spirit which has been given to us.

Now that we have been justified by faith, we are at peace with God through our Lord Jesus Christ. Through him we have gained access by faith to the grace in which we now stand, and we boast of our hope for the glory of God. And this hope will not leave us disappointed, because the love of God has been poured out in our hearts through the Holy Spirit who has been given to us. At the appointed time, when we were still powerless, Christ died for us godless men. It is rare that anyone should lay down his life for a just man, though it is barely possible that for a good man someone may have the courage to die. It is precisely in this that God proves his love for us: that while we were still sinners, Christ died for us.

This is the Word of the Lord.

7   Rom 8, 14-17

A reading from the letter of Paul to the Romans

The Spirit himself and our spirit bear united witness that
we are children of God.

All who are led by the Spirit of God are sons of
God. You did not receive a spirit of slavery
leading you back into fear, but a spirit of
adoption through which we cry out, "Abba!"
(that is, "Father"). The Spirit himself gives
witness with our spirit that we are children
of God. But if we are children, we are heirs
as well: heirs of God, heirs with Christ, if
only we suffer with him so as to be glorified
with him.

This is the Word of the Lord.

---

8   Rom 8, 26-27

A reading from the letter of Paul to the Romans

The Spirit himself will express our plea in a way that could
never be put to words.

The Spirit helps us in our weakness, for we
do not know how to pray as we ought; but the
Spirit himself makes intercession for us with
groanings which cannot be expressed in
speech. He who searches hearts knows what
the Spirit means, for the Spirit intercedes for
the saints as God himself wills.

This is the Word of the Lord.

---

9   1 Cor 12, 4-13

**A reading from the first letter of Paul to the
Corinthians**

There is one and the same Spirit giving to each as he wills.

There are different gifts but the same Spirit;
there are different ministries but the same
Lord; there are different works but the same
God who accomplishes all of them in everyone. To each person the manifestation of the
Spirit is given for the common good. To one
the Spirit gives wisdom in discourse, to
another the power to express knowledge.
Through the Spirit one receives faith; by the
same Spirit another is given the gift of healing,
and still another miraculous powers. Prophecy
is given to one; to another power to distinguish
one spirit from another. One receives the gift

of tongues, another that of interpreting the
tongues. But it is one and the same Spirit who
produces all these gifts, distributing them to
each as he wills.

The body is one and has many members, but
all the members, many though they are, are one
body; and so it is with Christ. It was in one
Spirit that all of us, whether Jew or Greek,
slave or free, were baptized into one body. All
of us have been given to drink of the one Spirit.

This is the Word of the Lord.

---

10   Gal 5, 16-17. 22-23. 24-25

**A reading from the letter of Paul to the
Galatians**

If we live in the Spirit, let us be directed by the Spirit.

Live in accord with the spirit and you will not
yield to the cravings of the flesh. The flesh lusts
against the spirit and the spirit against the flesh;
the two are directly opposed. This is why you
do not do what your will intends.

In contrast, the fruit of the spirit is love, joy,
peace, patient endurance, kindness, generosity,
faith, mildness, and chastity. Those who belong to Christ Jesus have crucified their flesh
with its passions and desires. Since we live
by the spirit, let us follow the spirit's lead.

This is the Word of the Lord.

---

11   Eph 1, 3. 4. 13-19

**A reading from the letter of Paul to the
Ephesians**

You have been signed with the seal of the Holy Spirit of
the promise.

Praised be the God and Father of our Lord
Jesus Christ! God chose us in him before the
world began. In him you too were chosen;
when you heard the glad tidings of salvation,
the word of truth, and believed in it, you were
sealed with the Holy Spirit who had been
promised. He is the pledge of our inheritance,
the first payment against the full redemption
of a people God has made his own, to praise his
glory.

For my part, from the time I first heard of
your faith in the Lord Jesus and your love for

all the members of the church, I have never stopped thanking God for you and recommending you in my prayers. May the God of our Lord Jesus Christ, the Father of glory, grant you a spirit of wisdom and insight to know him clearly. May he enlighten your innermost vision that you may know the great hope to which he has called you, the wealth of his glorious heritage to be distributed among the members of the church, and the immeasurable scope of his power in us who believe.

This is the Word of the Lord.

---

12   **Eph 4, 1-6**

A reading from the letter of Paul to the Ephesians

There is one body, one Spirit, and one baptism.

I plead with you as a prisoner for the Lord, to live a life worthy of the calling you have received, with perfect humility, meekness, and patience, bearing with one another lovingly. Make every effort to preserve the unity which has the Spirit as its origin and peace as its binding force. There is but one body and one Spirit, just as there is but one hope given all of you by your call. There is one Lord, one faith, one baptism; one God and Father of all, who is over all, and works through all, and is in all.

This is the Word of the Lord.

---

765 **RESPONSORIAL PSALM**

1   **Ps 22, 23-24. 26-27. 28. 31-32**

℟. (23) I will proclaim your name to my brothers.

I will proclaim your name to my brethren; in the midst of the assembly I will praise you:

"You who fear the Lord, praise him; all you descendants of Jacob, give glory to him."

℟. I will proclaim your name to my brothers.

So by your gift will I utter praise in the vast assembly;

I will fulfill my vows before those who fear him.

The lowly shall eat their fill; they who seek the Lord shall praise him: "May your hearts be ever merry!"

℟. I will proclaim your name to my brothers.

All the ends of the earth shall remember and turn to the Lord;

All the families of the nations shall bow down before him.

And to him my soul shall live; my descendants shall serve him.

Let the coming generation be told of the Lord that they may proclaim to a people yet to be born the justice he has shown.

℟. I will proclaim your name to my brothers.

℟. Or: (Jn 15, 26-27) When the Holy Spirit comes to you, you will be my witness.

---

2   **Ps 23, 1-3. 3-4. 5-6**

℟. (1) The Lord is my shepherd; there is nothing I shall want.

The Lord is my shepherd; I shall not want. In verdant pastures he gives me repose;

Beside restful waters he leads me; he refreshes my soul.

℟. The Lord is my shepherd; there is nothing I shall want.

He guides me in right paths for his name's sake.

Even though I walk in the dark valley I fear no evil; for you are at my side

With your rod and your staff that give me courage.

℟. The Lord is my shepherd; there is nothing I shall want.

You spread the table before me in the sight of my foes;

You anoint my head with oil; my cup overflows.

Only goodness and kindness follow me all the days of my life;

And I shall dwell in the house of the Lord for years to come.

℟. The Lord is my shepherd; there is nothing I shall want.

3   Ps 96, 1-2. 2-3. 9-10. 11-12

℟. (3) Proclaim his marvelous deeds to all the
    nations.

Sing to the Lord a new song;
    sing to the Lord, all you lands.
Sing to the Lord; bless his name.
℟. Proclaim his marvelous deeds to all
    nations.
Announce his salvation, day after day.
    Tell his glory among the nations;
Among all peoples, his wondrous deeds.
℟. Proclaim his marvelous deeds to all the
    nations.
Worship the Lord in holy attire.
    Tremble before him, all the earth;
    say among the nations: the Lord is king.
℟. Proclaim his marvelous deeds to all the
    nations.
Let the heavens be glad and the earth rejoice;
    let the sea and what fills it resound;
    let the plains be joyful and all that is in
    them!
Then shall all the trees of the forest exult.
℟. Proclaim his marvelous deeds to all the
    nations.

_____

4   Ps 104, 1. 24. 27-28. 30-31. 33-34

℟. (30) Lord, send out your Spirit,
    and renew the face of the earth.
Bless the Lord, O my soul!
    O Lord, my God, you are great indeed!
How manifold are your works, O Lord!
    In wisdom you have wrought them all—
    the earth is full of your creatures.
℟. Lord, send out your Spirit,
    and renew the face of the earth.
They all look to you
    to give them food in due time.
When you give it to them, they gather it;
    when you open your hand, they are filled
    with good things.
℟. Lord, send out your Spirit,
    and renew the face of the earth.
When you send forth your spirit, they are
    created,
    and you renew the face of the earth.
May the glory of the Lord endure forever;
    may the Lord be glad in his works!

℟. Lord, send out your Spirit,
    and renew the face of the earth.
I will sing to the Lord all my life;
    I will sing praise to my God while I live.
Pleasing to him be my theme;
    I will be glad in the Lord.
℟. Lord, send out your Spirit,
    and renew the face of the earth.

_____

5   Ps 117, 1. 2

℟. (Acts 1, 8) You will be my witnesses to all
    the world.
    Alleluia.
Praise the Lord, all you nations;
    glorify him, all you peoples!
℟. You will be my witnesses to all the world.
For steadfast is his kindness toward us,
    and the fidelity of the Lord endures forever.
℟. You will be my witnesses to all the world.
℟. Or: Alleluia.

_____

6   Ps 145, 2-3. 4-5. 8-9. 10-11. 15-16. 21

℟. (1) I will praise your name for ever, Lord.
Every day will I bless you,
    and I will praise your name forever and
    ever.
Great is the Lord and highly to be praised;
    his greatness is unsearchable.
℟. I will praise your name for ever, Lord.
Generation after generation praises your
    works
    and proclaims your might.
They speak of the splendor of your glorious
    majesty
    and tell of your wondrous works.
℟. I will praise your name for ever, Lord.
The Lord is gracious and merciful,
    slow to anger and of great kindness.
The Lord is good to all
    and compassionate toward all his works.
℟. I will praise your name for ever, Lord.
Let all your works give you thanks, O Lord,
    and let your faithful ones bless you.
Let them discourse of the glory of your king-
    dom
    and speak of your might.

℟. I will praise your name for ever, Lord.
The eyes of all look hopefully to you,
 and you give them their food in due season;
You open your hand
 and satisfy the desire of every living thing.
℟. I will praise your name for ever, Lord.
May my mouth speak the praise of the Lord,
 and may all flesh bless his holy name
 forever and ever.
℟. I will praise your name for ever, Lord.

---

766   ALLELUIA VERSE AND
VERSE BEFORE THE GOSPEL

1   Jn 14, 16

The Father will send you the Holy Spirit, says
 the Lord,
to be with you for ever.

2   Jn 15, 26. 27

The Spirit of truth will bear witness to me, says
 the Lord,
and you also will be my witnesses.

3   Jn 16, 33; 14, 26

When the Spirit of truth comes, he will teach
 you all truth
and bring to your mind all I have told you.

4   Rv 1, 5. 6

Jesus Christ, you are the faithful witness, first-
 born from the dead;
you have made us a kingdom of priests to serve
 our God and Father.

5

Come, Holy Spirit, fill the hearts of your faith-
 ful;
and kindle in them the fire of your love.

6

Come, Holy Spirit;
shine on us the radiance of your light.

---

767   GOSPEL

1   Mt 5, 1-12

✠ **A reading from the holy gospel according**
 to Matthew

Theirs is the kingdom of heaven.

When Jesus saw the crowds he went up on the
mountainside. After he had sat down his dis-
ciples gathered around him, and he began to
teach them:
   "How blest are the poor in spirit: the reign
    of God is theirs.
   Blest too are the sorrowing; they shall be
    consoled.
   [Blest are the lowly; they shall inherit the
    land.]
   Blest are they who hunger and thirst for
    holiness;
   they shall have their fill.
   Blest are they who show mercy;
    mercy shall be theirs.
   Blest are the single-hearted for they shall
    see God.
   Blest too the peacemakers; they shall be
    called sons of God.
   Blest are those persecuted for holiness'
    sake; the reign of God is theirs.
   Blest are you when they insult you and
    persecute you and utter every kind of
    slander against you because of me.
   Be glad and rejoice, for your reward in
    heaven is great."
   This is the gospel of the Lord.

2   Mt 16, 24-27

✠ **A reading from the holy gospel according**
 to Matthew

If anyone wishes to follow me, let him deny himself.

Jesus said to his disciples: "If a man wishes
to come after me, he must deny his very self,
take up his cross and begin to follow in my
footsteps. Whoever would save his life will
lose it, but whoever loses his life for my sake
will find it. What profit would a man show if
he were to gain the whole world and ruin him-
self in the process? What can a man offer in

exchange for his very self? The Son of Man will come with his Father's glory accompanied by his angels. When he does, he will repay each man according to his conduct."

This is the gospel of the Lord.

---

3   Mt 25, 14-30

✠ A reading from the holy gospel according to Matthew

Because you have been faithful in small matters, come into the joy of your master.

Jesus told this parable to his disciples: "This is the case of a man who was going on a journey. He called in his servants and handed his funds over to them according to each man's abilities. To one he disbursed five thousand silver pieces, to a second two thousand, and to a third a thousand. Then he went away. Immediately the man who received the five thousand went to invest it and made another five. In the same way, the man who received the two thousand doubled his figure. The man who received the thousand went off instead and dug a hole in the ground, where he buried his master's money. After a long absence, the master of those servants came home and settled accounts with them. The man who had received the five thousand came forward bringing the additional five. 'My lord,' he said, 'you let me have five thousand. See, I have made five thousand more.' His master said to him, 'Well done! You are an industrious and reliable servant. Since you were dependable in a small matter I will put you in charge of larger affairs. Come, share your master's joy!' The man who had received the two thousand then stepped forward. 'My lord,' he said, 'you entrusted me with two thousand and I have made two thousand more.' His master said to him, 'Cleverly done! You too are an industrious and reliable servant. Since you were dependable in a small matter I will put you in charge of larger affairs. Come, share your master's joy!'

"Finally the man who had received the thousand stepped forward. 'My lord,' he said, 'I knew you were a hard man. You reap where you did not sow and gather where you did not scatter, so out of fear I went off and buried your thousand silver pieces in the ground. Here is your money back.' His master exclaimed: 'You worthless, lazy lout! You know I reap where I did not sow and gather where I did not scatter. All the more reason to deposit my money with the bankers, so that on my return I could have had it back with interest. You, there! Take the thousand away from him and give it to the man with the ten thousand. Those who have, will get more until they grow rich, while those who have not, will lose even the little they have. Throw this worthless servant into the darkness outside, where he can wail and grind his teeth.' "

This is the gospel of the Lord.

---

4   Mk 1, 9-11

✠ A reading from the holy gospel according to Mark

He saw the Spirit descending and remaining on him.

Jesus came from Nazareth in Galilee and was baptized in the Jordan by John. Immediately on coming up out of the water he saw the sky rent in two and the Spirit descending on him like a dove. Then a voice came from the heavens: "You are my beloved Son. On you my favor rests."

This is the gospel of the Lord.

---

5   Lk 4, 16-22

✠ A reading from the holy gospel according to Luke

The Spirit of the Lord is upon me.

Jesus came to Nazareth where he had been reared, and entering the synagogue on the sabbath as he was in the habit of doing, he stood up to do the reading. When the book of the prophet Isaiah was handed him, he unrolled the scroll and found the passage where it was written:

"The spirit of the Lord is upon me;
   therefore he has anointed me.
He has sent me to bring glad tidings to the
      poor,
   to proclaim liberty to captives,

Recovery of sight to the blind
and release to prisoners,
To announce a year of favor from the
    Lord."
Rolling up the scroll, he gave it back to the
assistant and sat down. All in the synagogue
had their eyes fixed on him. Then he began
by saying to them, "Today this Scripture passage is fulfilled in your hearing." All who were
present spoke favorably of him.
    This is the gospel of the Lord.

---

6   Lk 8, 4-10. 11-15

✠ A reading from the holy gospel according
                to Luke
Some seed fell into rich soil. These are the people who
    receive the word and bear fruit in patience.

A large crowd was gathering, with people resorting to Jesus from one town after another.
He spoke to them in a parable: "A farmer
went out to sow some seed. In the sowing,
some fell on the footpath where it was walked
on and the birds of the air ate it up. Some fell
on rocky ground, sprouted up, then withered
through lack of moisture. Some fell among
briers, and the thorns growing up with it
stifled it. But some fell on good soil, grew
up, and yielded grain a hundred-fold."
    As he said this he exclaimed: "Let everyone
who has ears attend to what he has heard."
His disciples began asking him what the meaning of this parable might be. He replied, "To
you the mysteries of the reign of God have
been confided. The seed is the word of God.
Those on the footpath are people who hear,
but the devil comes and takes the word out
of their hearts lest they believe and be saved.
Those on the rocky ground are the ones who,
when they hear the word, receive it with joy.
They have no root; they believe for a while,
but fall away in time of temptation. The seed
fallen among briers are those who hear, but
their progress is stifled by the cares and riches
and pleasures of life and they do not mature.
The seed on good ground are those who hear
the word in a spirit of openness, retain it, and

bear fruit through perseverance."
    This is the gospel of the Lord.

---

7   Lk 10, 21-24

✠ A reading from the holy gospel according
                to Luke
I bless you, Father, for revealing these things to children.

Jesus rejoiced in the Holy Spirit and said: "I
offer you praise, O Father, Lord of heaven and
earth, because what you have hidden from the
learned and the clever you have revealed to the
merest children.
    "Yes, Father, you have graciously willed
it so. Everything has been given over to me by
my Father. No one knows the Son except
the Father and no one knows the Father except
the Son—and anyone to whom the Son wishes
to reveal him."
    Turning to his disciples he said to them
privately: "Blest are the eyes that see what
you see. I tell you, many prophets and kings
wished to see what you see but did not see it,
and to hear what you hear but did not hear it."
    This is the gospel of the Lord.

---

8   Jn 7, 37-39

✠ A reading from the holy gospel according
                to John
From the heart of God shall flow fountains of living water.

Jesus stood up and cried out:
    "If anyone thirsts, let him come to me;
        let him drink who believes in me.
    Scripture has it:
'From within him rivers of living water shall
flow.' "
(Here he was referring to the Spirit, whom
those that came to believe in him were to
receive. There was, of course, no Spirit as
yet, since Jesus had not yet been glorified.)
    This is the gospel of the Lord.

---

9   Jn 14, 15-17

✠ A reading from the holy gospel according
to John

The Spirit of truth will be with you for ever.

Jesus said to his disciples:
"If you love me
and obey the commands I give you,
I will ask the Father
and he will give you another Paraclete—
to be with you always:
the Spirit of truth,
whom the world cannot accept,
since it neither sees him nor recognizes
him;
but you can recognize him
because he remains with you
and will be within you."
This is the gospel of the Lord.

---

10   Jn 14, 23-26

✠ A reading from the holy gospel according
to John

The Holy Spirit will teach you everything.

Jesus said to his disciples:
"Anyone who loves me
will be true to my word,
and my Father will love him;
we will come to him
and make our dwelling place with him.
He who does not love me does not keep
my words.
Yet the word you hear is not mine;
it comes from the Father who sent me.
This much have I told you while I was still
with you;
the Paraclete, the Holy Spirit
whom the Father will send in my name,
will instruct you in everything,
and remind you of all that I told you."
This is the gospel of the Lord.

---

11   Jn 15, 18-21. 26-27

✠ A reading from the holy gospel according
to John

*The Spirit of truth who issues from the Father, will be my
witness.*

Jesus said to his disciples:
"If you find that the world hates you,
know it has hated me before you.
If you belonged to the world,
it would love you as its own;
the reason it hates you
is that you do not belong to the world.
But I chose you out of the world.
Remember what I told you:
no slave is greater than his master.
They will harry you
as they harried me.
They will respect your words
as much as they respected mine.
All this they will do to you because of
my name,
for they know nothing of him who sent
me.
When the Paraclete comes,
the Spirit of truth who comes from the
Father—
and whom I myself will send from the
Father—
he will bear witness on my behalf.
You must bear witness as well,
for you have been with me from the beginning."
This is the gospel of the Lord.

---

12   Jn 16, 5-7. 12-13

✠ A reading from the holy gospel according
to John

The Spirit of truth will lead you to the complete truth.

Jesus said to his disciples:
"Now that I go back to him who sent me,
not one of you asks me, 'Where are you
going?'
Because I have had all this to say to you
you are overcome with grief.
Yet I tell you the sober truth:
it is much better for you that I go.
If I fail to go,

the Paraclete will never come to you,
whereas if I go,
I will send him to you.
I have much more to tell you,
but you cannot bear it now.
When he comes, however,
being the Spirit of truth
he will guide you to all truth."
This is the gospel of the Lord.

**768   FIRST COMMUNION
OF CHILDREN**

Readings may be taken either in whole or in part from the
Mass of the day, or from the Mass of Christian initiation
(above, nos. 752-756) or from the votive Mass of the Holy
Eucharist (below, nos. 904-909).

HOLY ORDERS

769   OLD TESTAMENT READING

1   Nm 3, 5-9

[For deacons]

A reading from the book of Numbers

Gather the tribe of Levi so that they can serve Aaron the
priest.

Now the Lord said to Moses: "Summon the
tribe of Levi and present them to Aaron the
priest, as his assistants. They shall discharge
his obligations and those of the whole community before the meeting tent by serving at
the Dwelling. They shall have custody of all the
furnishings of the meeting tent and discharge
the duties of the Israelites in the service of the
Dwelling. You shall give the Levites to Aaron
and his sons; they have been set aside from
among the Israelites as dedicated to me."
This is the Word of the Lord.

---

2   Nm 11, 11-12. 14-17. 24-25

[For priests]

A reading from the book of Numbers

I will give them your spirit so that they may share with you
the burden of this people.

Moses asked the Lord, "Why are you so displeased with me that you burden me with all

this people? Was it I who conceived all this
people? or was it I who gave them birth, that
you tell me to carry them at my bosom, like
a foster father carrying an infant, to the land
you have promised under oath to their fathers?
I cannot carry all this people by myself, for
they are too heavy for me. If this is the way
you will deal with me, then please do me the
favor of killing me at once, so that I need no
longer face this distress."
Then the Lord said to Moses, "Assemble for
me seventy of the elders of Israel, men you
know for true elders and authorities among
the people, and bring them to the meeting tent.
When they are in place beside you, I will come
down and speak with you there. I will also take
some of the spirit that is on you and will bestow it on them, that they may share the
burden of the people with you. You will then
not have to bear it by yourself."
So Moses went out and told the people what
the Lord had said. Gathering seventy elders of
the people, he had them stand around the tent.
The Lord then came down in the cloud and
spoke to him. Taking some of the spirit that
was on Moses, he bestowed it on the seventy
elders, and as the spirit came to rest on them
they prophesied.
This is the Word of the Lord.

---

3   Is 61, 1-3

[For bishops and priests]

A reading from the book of the prophet Isaiah

The Lord has anointed me and sent me to bring Good News
to the poor and to give them the oil of gladness.

The spirit of the Lord God is upon me,
  because the Lord has anointed me;
He has sent me to bring glad tidings to the
  lowly,
  to heal the brokenhearted,
To proclaim liberty to the captives
  and release to the prisoners,
To announce a year of favor from the Lord
  and a day of vindication by our God,
  to comfort all who mourn;
To place on those who mourn in Zion
  a diadem instead of ashes.
This is the Word of the Lord.

25-30

4 Jer 1, 4-9

A reading from the book of the prophet Jeremiah

You will go to all the places to which I will send you.

The word of the Lord came to me thus:
Before I formed you in the womb I knew you,
  before you were born I dedicated you,
  a prophet to the nations I appointed you.
"Ah, Lord God!" I said,
  "I know not how to speak; I am too young."

But the Lord answered me,
Say not, "I am too young."
  To whomever I send you, you shall go;
  whatever I command you, you shall speak.
Have no fear before them,
  because I am with you to deliver you, says
    the Lord.

Then the Lord extended his hand and touched
my mouth, saying,
See, I place my words in your mouth!
    This is the Word of the Lord.

---

770 **NEW TESTAMENT READING**
1 Acts 6, 1-7

[For deacons]

A reading from the Acts of the Apostles

They chose seven men filled with the Holy Spirit.

As the number of disciples grew, the ones who
spoke Greek complained that their widows
were being neglected in the daily distribution
of food, as compared with the widows of those
who spoke Hebrew. The Twelve assembled
the community of the disciples and said, "It
is not right for us to neglect the word of God
in order to wait on the tables. Look around
among your own number, brothers, for seven
men acknowledged to be deeply spiritual and
prudent, and we shall appoint them to this
task. This will permit us to concentrate on
prayer and the ministry of the word." The
proposal was unanimously accepted by the
community. Following this they selected
Stephen, a man filled with faith and the Holy
Spirit; Philip, Prochorus, Nicanor, Timon,
Parmenas and Nicolaus of Antioch, who had

been a convert to Judaism. They presented
these men to the apostles, who first prayed
over them and then imposed hands on them.
  The word of God continued to spread, while
at the same time the number of the disciples
in Jerusalem increased enormously.
    This is the Word of the Lord.

---

2 Acts 8, 26-40

[For deacons]

A reading from the Acts of the Apostles

Beginning with this text of scripture he explained the Good
News of Jesus to him.

An angel of the Lord addressed himself to
Philip: "Head south toward the road which
goes from Jerusalem to Gaza, the desert
route." Philip began the journey. It happened
that an Ethiopian eunuch, a court official in
charge of the entire treasury of Candace (a
name meaning queen) of the Ethiopians, had
come on a pilgrimage to Jerusalem and was
returning home. He was sitting in his carriage
reading the prophet Isaiah. The Spirit said to
Philip, "Go and catch up with that carriage."
Philip ran ahead and heard the man reading the
prophet Isaiah. He said to him, "Do you really
grasp what you are reading?" "How can I,"
the man replied, "unless someone explains it to
me?" With that, he invited Philip to get in and
sit down beside him. This was the passage of
Scripture he was reading:
"Like a sheep he was led to the slaughter,
  like a lamb before its shearer he was silent
  and opened not his mouth.
In his humiliation he was deprived of justice.
  Who will ever speak of his posterity,
  for he is deprived of his life on earth?"
The eunuch said to Philip, "Tell me, if you will,
of whom the prophet says this—himself or
someone else?" Philip launched out with this
Scripture passage as his starting point, telling
him the good news of Jesus. As they moved
along the road they came to some water, and
the eunuch said, "Look, there is some water
right there. What is to keep me from being
baptized?" He ordered the carriage stopped,
and Philip went down into the water with the
eunuch and baptized him. When they came out

of the water, the Spirit of the Lord snatched Philip away and the eunuch saw him no more. Nevertheless the man went on his way rejoicing. Philip found himself at Azotus next, and he went about announcing the good news in all the towns until he reached Caesarea.

This is the Word of the Lord.

---

3   Acts 10, 37-43

A reading from the Acts of the Apostles

We are witnesses to everything Jesus did in the countryside around Judea and in Jerusalem.

Peter addressed the crowd in these words: "I take it you know what has been reported all over Judea about Jesus of Nazareth, beginning in Galilee with the baptism John preached; of the way God anointed him with the Holy Spirit and power. He went about doing good works and healing all who were in the grip of the devil, and God was with him. We are witnesses to all that he did in the land of the Jews and in Jerusalem. They killed him finally, 'hanging him on a tree,' only to have God raise him up on the third day and grant that he be seen, not by all, but only by such witnesses as had been chosen beforehand by God—by us who ate and drank with him after he rose from the dead. He commissioned us to preach to the people and to bear witness that he is the one set apart by God as judge of the living and the dead. To him all the prophets testify, saying that everyone who believes in him has forgiveness of sins through his name."

This is the Word of the Lord.

---

4   Acts 20, 17-18. 28-32. 36

[For bishops and priests]

A reading from the Acts of the Apostles

Keep watch for yourselves and for all the flock of which the Holy Spirit has made you overseers to govern the Church of God.

Paul sent word from Miletus to Ephesus, summoning the elders of that church. When they came to him he delivered this address: "Keep watch over yourselves, and over the whole flock the Holy Spirit has given you to guard. Shepherd the Church of God, which he has acquired at the price of his own blood. I know that when I am gone, savage wolves will come among you who will not spare the flock. From your own number, men will present themselves distorting the truth and leading astray any who follow them. Be on guard, therefore. Do not forget that for three years, night and day, I never ceased warning you individually even to the point of tears. I commend you now to the Lord, and to that gracious word of his which can enlarge you, and give you a share among all who are consecrated to him."

After this discourse, Paul knelt down with them all and prayed.

This is the Word of the Lord.

---

5   Rom 12, 4-8

A reading from the letter of Paul to the Romans

Our gifts differ according to the grace given to each of us.

Just as each of us has one body with many members, and not all the members have the same function, so too we, though many, are one body in Christ and individually members one of another. We have gifts that differ according to the favor bestowed on each of us. One's gift may be prophecy; its use should be in proportion to his faith. It may be the gift of ministry; it should be used for service. One who is a teacher should use his gift for teaching; one with the power of exhortation should exhort. He who gives alms should do so generously; he who rules should exercise his authority with care; he who performs works of mercy should do so cheerfully.

This is the Word of the Lord.

---

6   2 Cor 4, 1-2. 5-7

A reading from the second letter of Paul to the Corinthians

We are teaching Jesus Christ, but we are your servants for Jesus' sake.

Because we possess the ministry through God's mercy, we do not give in to discouragement. Rather, we repudiate shameful, underhanded practices. We do not resort to trickery or falsify the word of God. We proclaim the truth openly and commend ourselves to every man's conscience before God. It is not ourselves we preach but Christ Jesus as Lord, and ourselves as your servants for Jesus' sake. For God, who said, "Let light shine out of darkness," has shone in our hearts, that we in turn might make known the glory of God shining on the face of Christ. This treasure we possess in earthen vessels to make it clear that its surpassing power comes from God and not from us.

This is the Word of the Lord.

7   2 Cor 5, 14-20

A reading from the second letter of Paul to the Corinthians

He gave us the ministry of reconciliation.

The love of Christ impels us who have reached the conviction that since one died for all, all died. He died for all so that those who live might live no longer for themselves, but for him who for their sakes died and was raised up.

Because of this we no longer look on anyone in terms of mere human judgment. If at one time we so regarded Christ, we no longer know him by this standard. This means that if anyone is in Christ, he is a new creation. The old order has passed away; now all is new! All this has been done by God, who has reconciled us to himself through Christ and has given us the ministry of reconciliation. I mean that God, in Christ, was reconciling the world to himself, not counting men's transgressions against them, and that he has entrusted the message of reconciliation to us. This makes us ambassadors for Christ, God as it were appealing through us. We implore you, in Christ's name: be reconciled to God!

This is the Word of the Lord.

8   Eph 4, 1-7. 11-13

A reading from the letter of Paul to the Ephesians

Unity in the work of service, building up the body of Christ.

I plead with you as a prisoner for the Lord, to live a life worthy of the calling you have received, with perfect humility, meekness, and patience, bearing with one another lovingly.

Make every effort to preserve the unity which has the Spirit as its origin and peace as its binding force. There is but one body and one Spirit, just as there is but one hope given all of you by your call. There is one Lord, one faith, one baptism; one God and Father of all, who is over all, and works through all, and is in all.

Each of us has received God's favor in the measure in which Christ bestows it.

It is he who gave apostles, prophets, evangelists, pastors, and teachers in roles of service for the faithful to build up the body of Christ, till we become one in faith and in the knowledge of God's Son, and form that perfect man who is Christ come to full stature.

This is the Word of the Lord.

9   1 Tm 3, 8-13

[For deacons]

A reading from the first letter of Paul to Timothy

They must be conscientious believers in the mystery of faith.

Deacons must be serious, straightforward, and truthful. They may not overindulge in drink, or give in to greed. They must hold fast to the divinely revealed faith with a clear conscience. They should be put on probation first; then, if there is nothing against them, they may serve as deacons. The women, similarly, should be serious, not slanderous gossips. They should be temperate and entirely trustworthy. Deacons may be married but once and must be good managers of their children and their households. Those who serve well as deacons gain a worthy place for themselves and much assurance in their faith in Christ Jesus.

This is the Word of the Lord.

10   1 Tm 4, 12-16

[For bishops]

A reading from the first letter of Paul to Timothy

Do not neglect the spiritual gift given you when the elders laid hands on you.

Let no one look down on you because of your youth, but be a continuing example of love, faith, and purity to believers. Until I arrive, devote yourself to the reading of Scripture, to preaching and teaching. Do not neglect the gift you received when, as a result of prophecy, the presbyters laid their hands on you. Attend to your duties; let them absorb you, so that everyone may see your progress. Watch yourself and watch your teaching. Persevere at both tasks. By doing so you will bring to salvation yourself and all who hear you.

This is the Word of the Lord.

OR

1 Tm 4, 12-16 beginning: Be a continuous example of love, faith and purity, etc. . . . .

---

11   2 Tm 1, 6-14

[For bishops]

A reading from the second letter of Paul to Timothy

Rekindle the gift that God gave you when I laid my hands on you.

I remind you to stir into flame the gift of God bestowed when my hands were laid on you. The Spirit God has given us is no cowardly spirit, but rather one that makes us strong, loving, and wise. Therefore, never be ashamed of your testimony to our Lord, nor of me, a prisoner for his sake, but with the strength which comes from God bear your share of the hardship which the gospel entails.

God has saved us and has called us to a holy life, not because of any merit of ours but according to his own design—the grace held out to us in Christ Jesus before the world began but now made manifest through the appearance of our Savior. He has robbed death of its power and has brought life and immortality into clear light through the gospel. In the service of this gospel I have been appointed preacher and apostle and teacher, and for its sake I undergo present hardships. But I am not ashamed, for I know him in whom I have believed, and I am confident that he is able to guard what has been entrusted to me until that Day. Take as a model of sound teaching what you have heard me say, in faith and love in Christ Jesus. Guard the rich deposit of faith

with the help of the Holy Spirit who dwells within us.

This is the Word of the Lord.

12   Heb 5, 1-10

A reading from the letter to the Hebrews

Christ was acclaimed by God a high priest of the order of Melchizedek.

Every high priest is taken from among men and made their representative before God, to offer gifts and sacrifices for sins. He is able to deal patiently with erring sinners, for he is himself beset by weakness and so must make sin offerings for himself as well as for the people. One does not take this honor on his own initiative, but only when called by God as Aaron was. Even Christ did not glorify himself with the office of high priest; he received it from the One who said to him,

"You are my son;
today I have begotten you";

just as he says in another place,

"You are a priest forever,
according to the order of Melchizedek."

In the days when he was in the flesh, he offered prayers and supplications with loud cries and tears to God, who was able to save him from death, and he was heard because of his reverence. Son though he was, he learned obedience from what he suffered; and when perfected, he became the source of eternal salvation for all who obey him, designated by God as high priest according to the order of Melchizedek.

This is the Word of the Lord.

---

13   1 Pt 4, 7-11

A reading from the first letter of Peter

As good stewards be responsible for the different graces of God.

Remain calm so you will be able to pray. Above all, let your love for one another be constant, for love covers a multitude of sins. Be mutually hospitable without complaining. As generous distributors of God's manifold grace, put your gifts at the service of one another, each in the

measure he has received. **The one who speaks is to deliver God's message. The one who serves is to do it with the strength provided by God. Thus, in all of you God is to be glorified through Jesus Christ: to him be glory and dominion throughout the ages. Amen.**
                This is the Word of the Lord.

---

14   1 Pt 5, 1-4
        A reading from the first letter of Peter
Be shepherds of the flock of God which is entrusted to you.
To the elders among you I, a fellow elder, a witness of Christ's sufferings and sharer in the glory that is to be revealed, make this appeal. God's flock is in your midst; give it a shepherd's care. Watch over it willingly as God would have you do, not under coercion; and not for shameful profit either, but generously. Be examples to the flock, not lording it over those assigned to you, so that when the chief Shepherd appears you will win for yourselves the unfading crown of glory.
                This is the Word of the Lord.

---

771   RESPONSORIAL PSALM
1   Ps 23, 1-3. 3-4. 5. 6
℟. (1) The Lord is my shepherd;
    there is nothing I shall want.
**The Lord is my shepherd; I shall not want.
    In verdant pastures he gives me repose;
Beside restful waters he leads me;
    he refreshes my soul.**
℟. The Lord is my shepherd;
    there is nothing I shall want.
**He guides me in right paths
    for his name's sake.
Even though I walk in the dark valley
    I fear no evil; for you are at my side
With your rod and your staff
    that give me courage.**
℟. The Lord is my shepherd;
    there is nothing I shall want.
**You spread the table before me
    in the sight of my foes;**

**You anoint my head with oil;
    my cup overflows.**
℟. The Lord is my shepherd;
    there is nothing I shall want.
**Only goodness and kindness follow me
    all the days of my life;
And I shall dwell in the house of the Lord
    for years to come.**
℟. The Lord is my shepherd;
    there is nothing I shall want.

---

2   Ps 84, 3-4. 5-6. 8. 11
℟. (5) How happy they who dwell in your
    house, O Lord.
**My soul yearns and pines
    for the courts of the Lord.
My heart and my flesh
    cry out for the living God.
Even the sparrow finds a home,
    and the swallow a nest
    in which she puts her young—
Your altars, O Lord of hosts,
    my king and my God!**
℟. How happy they who dwell in your house,
    O Lord.
**Happy they who dwell in your house!
    continually they praise you.
Happy the men whose strength you are!
    They go from strength to strength.**
℟. How happy they who dwell in your house,
    O Lord.
**I had rather one day in your courts
    than a thousand elsewhere;
I had rather lie at the threshold of the house
    of my God
    than dwell in the tents of the wicked.**
℟. How happy they who dwell in your house,
    O Lord.

---

3   Ps 89, 21-22. 25. 27
℟. (2) For ever I will sing the goodness of the
    Lord.
**I have found David, my servant;
    with my holy oil I have anointed him,
That my hand may be always with him,
    and that my arm may make him strong.**

R/. For ever I will sing the goodness of the Lord.
My faithfulness and my kindness shall be with him,
and through my name shall his horn be exalted.
He shall say of me, "You are my father, my God, the Rock, my savior."
R/. For ever I will sing the goodness of the Lord.

---

4 Ps 96, 1-2. 2-3. 10

R/. Go out to the world and teach all nations, alleluia.
Sing to the Lord a new song;
sing to the Lord, all you lands.
Sing to the Lord; bless his name.
R/. Go out to the world and teach all nations, alleluia.
Announce his salvation, day after day.
Tell his glory among the nations;
among all peoples, his wondrous deeds.
R/. Go out to the world and teach all nations, alleluia.
Say among the nations: The Lord is king.
He has made the world firm, not to be moved;
he governs the peoples with equity.
R/. Go out to the world and teach all nations, alleluia.

---

5 Ps 100, 2. 3. 4. 5

R/. (Jn 15, 14) You are my friends if you do what I command you,
says the Lord.
Sing joyfully to the Lord, all you lands;
serve the Lord with gladness;
come before him with joyful song.
R/. You are my friends if you do what I command you,
says the Lord.
Know that the Lord is God;
he made us, his we are;
his people, the flock he tends.
R/. You are my friends if you do what I command you,
says the Lord.

Enter his gates with thanksgiving,
his courts with praise.
Give thanks to him; bless his name.
R/. You are my friends if you do what I command you,
says the Lord.
The Lord is good:
the Lord, whose kindness endures forever,
and his faithfulness, to all generations.
R/. You are my friends if you do what I command you,
says the Lord.

---

6 Ps 110, 1. 2. 3. 4

R/. Priest for ever, like Melchizedek of old, the Lord Christ offered bread and wine.
The Lord said to my Lord: "Sit at my right hand
till I make your enemies your footstool."
R/. Priest for ever, like Melchizedek of old, the Lord Christ offered bread and wine.
The scepter of your power the Lord will stretch forth from Zion:
"Rule in the midst of your enemies."
R/. Priest for ever, like Melchizedek of old, the Lord Christ offered bread and wine.
"Yours is princely power in the day of your birth, in holy splendor;
before the daystar, like the dew, I have begotten you."
R/. Priest for ever, like Melchizedek of old, the Lord Christ offered bread and wine.
The Lord has sworn, and he will not repent:
"You are a priest forever, according to the order of Melchizedek."
R/. Priest for ever, like Melchizedek of old, the Lord Christ offered bread and wine.
R/. Or: You are a priest for ever, in the line of Melchizedek.

---

7 Ps 116, 12-13. 17-18

R/. (1 Cor 10, 16) Our blessing-cup is a communion with the blood of Christ.
How shall I make a return to the Lord for all the good he has done for me?
The cup of salvation I will take up,
and I will call upon the name of the Lord.

℟. Our blessing-cup is a communion with the blood of Christ.
**To you will I offer sacrifice of thanksgiving,
and I will call upon the name of the Lord.
My vows to the Lord I will pay
in the presence of all his people.**
℟. Our blessing-cup is a communion with the blood of Christ.
℟. Or: Alleluia.

8   Ps 117, 1.2

℟. (Mk 16, 15) Go out to all the world,
and tell the Good News.
Alleluia.
**Praise the Lord, all you nations;
glorify him, all you peoples!**
℟. Go out to all the world,
and tell the Good News.
**For steadfast is his kindness toward us,
and the fidelity of the Lord endures forever.**
℟. Go out to all the world,
and tell the Good News.
℟. Or: Alleluia.

**772   ALLELUIA VERSE AND
VERSE BEFORE THE GOSPEL**

1   Mt 28, 19-20

Go and teach all people my gospel.
I am with you always, until the end of the world.

2   Lk 4, 18-19

The Lord sent me to bring Good News to the poor,
and freedom to prisoners.

3   Jn 10, 14

I am the good shepherd, says the Lord;
I know my sheep, and mine know me.

4   Jn 15, 15

I call you my friends, says the Lord,
for I have made known to you all that the Father has told me.

773   **GOSPEL**

1   Mt 5, 13-16

✠ A reading from the holy gospel according to Matthew

You are the light of the world.

Jesus said to his disciples: "You are the salt of the earth. But what if salt goes flat? How can you restore its flavor? Then it is good for nothing but to be thrown out and trampled underfoot.

"You are the light of the world. A city set on a hill cannot be hidden. Men do not light a lamp and then put it under a bushel basket. They set it on a stand where it gives light to all in the house. In the same way, your light must shine before men so that they may see goodness in your acts and give praise to your heavenly Father."

This is the gospel of the Lord.

2   Mt 9, 35-38

✠ A reading from the holy gospel according to Matthew

Ask the Lord of the harvest to send laborers to the harvest.

Jesus toured all the towns and villages. He taught in their synagogues, he proclaimed the good news of God's reign, and he cured every sickness and disease. At the sight of the crowds, his heart was moved with pity. They were lying prostrate from exhaustion, like sheep without a shepherd. He said to his disciples: "The harvest is good but laborers are scarce. Beg the harvest master to send out laborers to gather his harvest."

This is the gospel of the Lord.

3   Mt 10, 1-5

✠ A reading from the holy gospel according to Matthew

Proclaim that the kingdom of God is at hand.

Jesus summoned his twelve disciples and gave them authority to expel unclean spirits and to cure sickness and disease of every kind.

The names of the twelve apostles are these: first Simon, now known as Peter, and his brother Andrew; James, Zebedee's son, and his brother John; Philip and Bartholomew, Thomas and Matthew the tax collector; James, son of Alphaeus, and Thaddeus; Simon the Zealot Party member, and Judas Iscariot, who betrayed him. Jesus sent these men on mission as the Twelve.

This is the gospel of the Lord.

---

4   Mt 20, 25-28

✠ A reading from the holy gospel according to Matthew

Jesus chose twelve apostles and sent them to preach.

Jesus called his disciples together and said: "You know how those who exercise authority among the Gentiles lord it over them; their great ones make their importance felt. It cannot be like that with you. Anyone among you who aspires to greatness must serve the rest, and whoever wants to rank first among you must serve the needs of all. Such is the case with the Son of Man who has come, not to be served by others but to serve, to give his own life as a ransom for the many."

This is the gospel of the Lord.

---

5   Lk 10, 1-9

✠ A reading from the holy gospel according to Luke

The harvest is rich but the laborers are few.

The Lord appointed a further seventy-two and sent them in pairs before him to every town and place he intended to visit. He said to them: "The harvest is rich but the workers are few; therefore ask the harvest-master to send workers to this harvest. Be on your way, and remember: I am sending you as lambs in the midst of wolves. Do not carry a walking staff or traveling bag; wear no sandals and greet no one along the way. On entering any house, first say, 'Peace to this house.' If there is a peaceable man there, your peace will rest on him; if not, it will come back to you. Stay in the one house eating and drinking what they have, for the laborer is worth his wage. Do not move from house to house.

"Into whatever city you go, after they welcome you, eat what they set before you, and cure the sick there. Say to them, 'The reign of God is at hand.' "

This is the gospel of the Lord.

---

6   Lk 12, 35-44

✠ A reading from the holy gospel according to Luke

Happy those servants whom the master finds awake when he comes.

Jesus said to his disciples: "Let your belts be fastened around your waists and your lamps be burning ready. Be like men awaiting their master's return from a wedding, so that when he arrives and knocks, you will open for him without delay. It will go well with those servants whom the master finds wide-awake on his return. I tell you, he will put on an apron, seat them at table, and proceed to wait on them. Should he happen to come at midnight or before sunrise and find them prepared, it will go well with them. You know as well as I that if the head of the house knew when the thief was coming he would not let him break into his house. Be on guard, therefore. The Son of Man will come when you least expect him."

Peter said, "Do you intend this parable for us, Lord, or do you mean it for the whole world?" The Lord said, "Who in your opinion is that faithful, farsighted steward whom the master will set over his servants to dispense their ration of grain in season? That servant is fortunate whom his master finds busy when he returns. Assuredly, his master will put him in charge of all his property."

This is the gospel of the Lord.

---

7   Lk 22, 14-20. 24-30

✠ A reading from the holy gospel according to Luke

Do this in memory of me. I come among you as one who serves.

When the hour arrived, Jesus took his place at table, and the apostles with him. He said to them: "I have greatly desired to eat this Passover with you before I suffer. I tell you, I will not eat again until it is fulfilled in the kingdom of God."

Then taking a cup he offered a blessing in thanks and said: "Take this and divide it among you; I tell you, from now on I will not drink of the fruit of the vine until the coming of the reign of God."

Then taking bread and giving thanks, he broke it and gave it to them, saying: "This is my body to be given for you. Do this as a remembrance of me." He did the same with the cup after eating, saying as he did so: "This cup is the new covenant in my blood, which will be shed for you."

A dispute arose among them about who should be regarded as the greatest. He said: "Earthly kings lord it over their people. Those who exercise authority over them are called their benefactors. Yet it cannot be that way with you. Let the greater among you be as the junior, the leader as the servant. Who, in fact, is the greater—he who reclines at table or he who serves the meal? Is it not the one who reclines at table? Yet I am in your midst as the one who serves you. You are the ones who have stood loyally by me in my temptations. I for my part assign to you the dominion my Father has assigned to me. In my kingdom you will eat and drink at my table, and you will sit on thrones judging the twelve tribes of Israel."

This is the gospel of the Lord.

---

8   Jn 10, 11-16

✠ A reading from the holy gospel according to John

The good shepherd lays down his life for his sheep.

Jesus said:

"I am the good shepherd;
the good shepherd lays down his life for the
    sheep.
The hired hand who is no shepherd
nor owner of the sheep
catches sight of the wolf coming
and runs away, leaving the sheep
to be snatched and scattered by the wolf.
That is because he works for pay;
he has no concern for the sheep.

"I am the good shepherd.
I know my sheep
and my sheep know me
in the same way that the Father knows me
and I know the Father;
for these sheep I will give my life.
I have other sheep
that do not belong to this fold.
I must lead them, too,
and they shall hear my voice.
There shall be one flock then, one shepherd."
    This is the gospel of the Lord.

---

9   Jn 12, 24-26

✠ A reading from the holy gospel according to John

If a man serves me, he must follow me.

Jesus answered Philip and Andrew:

"I solemnly assure you,
unless the grain of wheat falls to the earth
    and dies,
it remains just a grain of wheat.
But if it dies,
it produces much fruit.
The man who loves his life
loses it,
while the man who hates his life in this
    world
preserves it to life eternal.
If anyone would serve me,
let him follow me;
where I am,
there will my servant be.
Anyone who serves me,
the Father will honor."
    This is the gospel of the Lord.

---

10   Jn 15, 9-17

✠ A reading from the holy gospel according to John

I shall not call you servants; you are my friends.

Jesus said to his disciples:

"As the Father has loved me,
so I have loved you.
Live on in my love.
You will live in my love

if you keep my commandments,
even as I have kept my Father's command-
    ments,
and live in his love.
All this I tell you
that my joy may be yours
and your joy may be complete.
This is my commandment:
love one another
as I have loved you.
There is no greater love than this:
to lay down one's life for one's friends.
You are my friends
if you do what I command you.
I no longer speak of you as slaves,
for a slave does not know what his master is
    about.
Instead, I call you friends,
since I have made known to you all that I
    heard from my Father.
It was not you who chose me,
it was I who chose you
to go forth and bear fruit.
Your fruit must endure,
so that all you ask the Father in my name
he will give you.
The command I give you is this:
that you love one another."
    This is the gospel of the Lord.

---

11   Jn 17, 6. 14-19

✠ **A reading from the holy gospel according
to John**

For them I consecrate myself so that they too may be
consecrated in truth.

Jesus looked up to heaven and said:
    "I have made your name known
to those you gave me out of the world.
These men you gave me were yours;
they have kept your word.
I gave them your word,
and the world has hated them for it;
they do not belong to the world,
[any more than I belong to the world].
I do not ask you to take them out of the
    world,
but to guard them from the evil one.
They are not of the world,

any more than I am of the world.
Consecrate them by means of truth—
    Your word is truth.'
As you have sent me into the world,
so I have sent them into the world;
I consecrate myself for their sakes now,
that they may be consecrated in truth."
    This is the gospel of the Lord.

---

12   Jn 20, 19-23

✠ **A reading from the holy gospel according
to John**

As the Father has sent me, I send you: Receive the Holy
Spirit.

On the evening of that first day of the week,
even though the disciples had locked the doors
of the place where they were for fear of the
Jews, Jesus came and stood before them.
"Peace be with you," he said. When he had said
this, he showed them his hands and his side. At
the sight of the Lord the disciples rejoiced.
"Peace be with you," he said again.
    "As the Father has sent me,
        so I send you."
Then he breathed on them and said:
    "Receive the Holy Spirit.
    If you forgive men's sins,
    they are forgiven them;
    if you hold them bound,
    they are held bound."
    This is the gospel of the Lord.

---

13   Jn 21, 15-17

✠ **A reading from the holy gospel according
to John**

Feed my lambs, feed my sheep.

Jesus appeared to his disciples again and when
they had eaten their meal, he said to Simon
Peter, "Simon, son of John, do you love me
more than these?" "Yes, Lord," Peter said, "you
know that I love you." At which Jesus said,
"Feed my lambs."
    A second time he put his question, "Simon,
son of John, do you love me?" "Yes, Lord,"
Peter said, "you know that I love you." Jesus
replied, "Tend my sheep."

A third time Jesus asked him, "Simon, son of John, do you love me?" Peter was hurt because he had asked a third time, "Do you love me?" So he said to him: "Lord, you know everything. You know well that I love you." Jesus told him, "Feed my sheep."

    This is the gospel of the Lord.

MARRIAGE

774   **OLD TESTAMENT READING**

1   Gn 1, 26-28. 31

A reading from the book of Genesis
Male and female he created them.

God said: "Let us make man in our image, after our likeness. Let them have dominion over the fish of the sea, the birds of the air, and the cattle, and over all the wild animals and all the creatures that crawl on the ground."

    God created man in his image;
        in the divine image he created him;
    male and female he created them.
God blessed them, saying: "Be fertile and multiply; fill the earth and subdue it. Have dominion over the fish of the sea, the birds of the air, and all the living things that move on the earth." God looked at everything he had made, and he found it very good.

    This is the Word of the Lord.

---

2   Gn 2, 18-24

A reading from the book of Genesis
And they will be two in one flesh.

The Lord God said: "It is not good for the man to be alone. I will make a suitable partner for him." So the Lord God formed out of the ground various wild animals and various birds of the air, and he brought them to the man to see what he would call them; whatever the man called each of them would be its name. The man gave names to all the cattle, all the birds of the air, and all the wild animals; but none proved to be the suitable partner for the man.

So the Lord God cast a deep sleep on the man, and while he was asleep, he took out one of his ribs and closed up its place with flesh. The Lord God then built up into a woman the rib that he had taken from the man. When he brought her to the man, the man said:

    "This one, at last, is bone of my bones
        and flesh of my flesh;
    This one shall be called 'woman,'
        for out of 'her man' this one has been
            taken."
That is why a man leaves his father and mother and clings to his wife, and the two of them become one body.

    This is the Word of the Lord.

---

3   Gn 24, 48-51. 58-67

A reading from the book of Genesis
Isaac loved Rebekah, and so he was consoled for the loss
of his mother.

The servant of Abraham said to Laban: "I bowed down in worship to the Lord, blessing the Lord, the God of my master Abraham, who had led me on the right road to obtain the daughter of my master's kinsman for his son. If, therefore, you have in mind to show true loyalty to my master, let me know; but if not, let me know that, too. I can then proceed accordingly."

    Laban and his household said in reply: "This thing comes from the Lord; we can say nothing to you either for or against it. Here is Rebekah, ready for you; take her with you, that she may become the wife of your master's son, as the Lord has said."

    So they called Rebekah and asked her, "Do you wish to go with this man?" She answered, "I do." At this they allowed their sister Rebekah and her nurse to take leave, along with Abraham's servant and his men. Invoking a blessing on Rebekah, they said:

    "Sister, may you grow
        into thousands of myriads;
    And may your descendants gain possession
        of the gates of their enemies!"
Then Rebekah and her maids started out; they mounted their camels and followed the man. So the servant took Rebekah and went on his way.

    Meanwhile Isaac had gone from Beer-lahairoi and was living in the region of the Negeb. One day toward evening he went out . . . in the field, and as he looked around, he noticed that camels were approaching. Rebekah, too, was looking about, and when she saw him, she alighted from her camel and asked the servant, "Who is the man out there, walking through the fields toward us?" "That is my master," replied the servant. Then she covered herself with her veil.

The servant recounted to Isaac all the things he had done. Then Isaac took Rebekah into his tent; he married her, and thus she became his wife. In his love for her Isaac found solace after the death of his mother Sarah.

This is the Word of the Lord.

---

4   Tb 7, 9-10. 11-15

A reading from the book of Tobit

May God join you together and fill you with his blessings.

Tobiah said to Raphael, "Brother Azariah, ask Raguel to let me marry my kinswoman Sarah." Raguel overheard the words; so he said to the boy: "Eat and drink and be merry tonight, for no man is more entitled to marry my daughter Sarah than you, brother. Besides, not even I have the right to give her to anyone but you, because you are my closest relative. But I will explain the situation to you very frankly. She is yours according to the decree of the Book of Moses. Your marriage to her has been decided in heaven! Take your kinswoman; from now on you are her love, and she is your beloved. She is yours today and ever after. And tonight, son, may the Lord of heaven prosper you both. May he grant you mercy and peace." Then Raguel called his daughter Sarah, and she came to him. He took her by the hand and gave her to Tobiah with the words: "Take her according to the law. According to the decree written in the Book of Moses she is your wife. Take her and bring her back safely to your father. And may the God of heaven grant both of you peace and prosperity." He then called her mother and told her to bring a scroll, so that he might draw up a marriage contract stating that he gave Sarah to Tobiah as his wife according to the decree of the Mosaic law. Her mother brought the scroll, and he drew up the contract, to which he affixed their seals. Afterward they began to eat and drink.

This is the Word of the Lord.

---

5   Tb 8, 5-7

A reading from the book of Tobit

May God bring us to old age together.

On the wedding night Sarah got up, and she and Tobiah started to pray and beg that deliverance might be theirs. He began with these words:

"Blessed are you, O God of our fathers;
  praised be your name forever and ever.
Let the heavens and all your creation
  praise you forever.
You made Adam and you gave him his wife Eve
  to be his help and support;
  and from these two the human race descended.
You said, 'It is not good for the man to be alone;
  let us make him a partner like himself.'
Now, Lord, you know that I take this wife of mine
  not because of lust,
  but for a noble purpose.
Call down your mercy on me and on her,
  and allow us to live together to a happy old age."

This is the Word of the Lord.

---

6   Sg 2, 8-10. 14. 16; 8, 6-7

A reading from the Song of Songs

For love is as strong as death.

Hark! my lover—here he comes
  springing across the mountains,
  leaping across the hills.
My lover is like a gazelle
  or a young stag.
Here he stands behind our wall,
  gazing through the windows,
  peering through the lattices.
My lover speaks; he says to me,
  "Arise, my beloved, my beautiful one,
  and come!

"O my dove in the clefts of the rock,
  in the secret recesses of the cliff,
Let me see you,
  let me hear your voice,
For your voice is sweet,
  and you are lovely."

My lover belongs to me and I to him.
  [He said to me:]
Set me as a seal on your heart,
  as a seal on your arm;
For stern as death is love,
  relentless as the nether world is devotion;
  its flames are a blazing fire.
Deep waters cannot quench love,
  nor floods sweep it away.
       This is the Word of the Lord.

---

7   Sir 26, 1-4. 13-16

A reading from the book of Sirach
Like the sun rising is the beauty of a good wife in a
    well-kept house.

Happy the husband of a good wife,
  twice-lengthened are his days;
A worthy wife brings joy to her husband,
  peaceful and full is his life.
A good wife is a generous gift
  bestowed upon him who fears the Lord;
Be he rich or poor, his heart is content,
  and a smile is ever on his face.
A gracious wife delights her husband,
  her thoughtfulness puts flesh on his bones;
A gift from the Lord is her governed speech,
  and her firm virtue is of surpassing worth.
Choicest of blessings is a modest wife,
  priceless her chaste person.
Like the sun rising in the Lord's heavens,
  the beauty of a virtuous wife is the radiance
    of her home.
       This is the Word of the Lord.

---

8   Jer 31, 31-32. 33-34

A reading from the book of the prophet
Jeremiah
I will make a new covenant with the house of Israel and
    Judah.

The days are coming, says the Lord, when I
will make a new covenant with the house of
Israel and the house of Judah. It will not be like
the covenant I made with their fathers the day
I took them by the hand to lead them forth
from the land of Egypt. But this is the covenant
which I will make with the house of Israel
after those days, says the Lord. I will place
my law within them, and write it upon their
hearts; I will be their God, and they shall be my
people. No longer will they have need to
teach their friends and kinsmen how to know
the Lord. All, from least to greatest, shall
know me, says the Lord.
       This is the Word of the Lord.

---

775   NEW TESTAMENT READING

1   Rom 8, 31-35. 37-39

A reading from the letter of Paul to the Romans
Who will separate us from the love of Christ?

If God is for us, who can be against us? Is it
possible that he who did not spare his own
Son but handed him over for the sake of us all
will not grant us all things besides? Who shall
bring a charge against God's chosen ones?
God, who justifies? Who shall condemn them?
Christ Jesus, who died or rather was raised up,
who is at the right hand of God and who
intercedes for us?

   Who will separate us from the love of
Christ? Trial, or distress, or persecution, or
hunger, or nakedness, or danger, or the sword?
Yet in all this we are more than conquerors
because of him who has loved us. For I am
certain that neither death nor life, neither angels nor principalities, neither the present nor
the future, nor powers, neither height nor
depth nor any other creature, will be able to
separate us from the love of God that comes to
us in Christ Jesus, our Lord.
       This is the Word of the Lord.

2   Rom 12, 1-2. 9-18 or 12, 1-2. 9-13

A reading from the letter of Paul to the Romans

Offer to God your bodies as a living and holy sacrifice, truly pleasing to him.

(Long Form)

Brothers, I beg you through the mercy of God to offer your bodies as a living sacrifice holy and acceptable to God, your spiritual worship. Do not conform yourselves to this age but be transformed by the renewal of your mind, so that you may judge what is God's will, what is good, pleasing and perfect.

Your love must be sincere. Detest what is evil, cling to what is good. Love one another with the affection of brothers. Anticipate each other in showing respect. Do not grow slack but be fervent in spirit; he whom you serve is the Lord. Rejoice in hope, be patient under trial, persevere in prayer. Look on the needs of the saints as your own; be generous in offering hospitality. Bless your persecutors; bless and do not curse them. Rejoice with those who rejoice, weep with those who weep. Have the same attitude toward all. Put away ambitious thoughts and associate with those who are lowly. Do not be wise in your own estimation. Never repay injury with injury. See that your conduct is honorable in the eyes of all. If possible, live peaceably with everyone.

This is the Word of the Lord.

OR
(Short Form)

Brothers, I beg you through the mercy of God to offer your bodies as a living sacrifice holy and acceptable to God, your spiritual worship. Do not conform yourselves to this age but be transformed by the renewal of your mind so that you may judge what is God's will, what is good, pleasing and perfect.

Your love must be sincere. Detest what is evil, cling to what is good. Love one another with the affection of brothers. Anticipate each other in showing respect. Do not grow slack but be fervent in spirit; he whom you serve is the Lord. Rejoice in hope, be patient under trial, persevere in prayer. Look on the needs

of the saints as your own; be generous in offering hospitality.

This is the Word of the Lord.

---

3   1 Cor 6, 13-15. 17-20

A reading from the first letter of Paul to the Corinthians

Your body is a temple of the Spirit.

The body is not for immorality; it is for the Lord, and the Lord is for the body. God, who raised up the Lord, will raise us also by his power. Do you not see that your bodies are members of Christ? But whoever is joined to the Lord becomes one spirit with him. Shun lewd conduct. Every other sin a man commits is outside his body, but the fornicator sins against his own body. You must know that your body is a temple of the Holy Spirit, who is within—the Spirit you have received from God. You are not your own. You have been purchased, and at what a price! So glorify God in your body.

This is the Word of the Lord.

---

4   1 Cor 12, 31—13, 8

A reading from the first letter of Paul to the Corinthians

If I am without love, it will do me no good whatever.

Set your hearts on the greater gifts. I will show you the way which surpasses all the others. If I speak with human tongues and angelic as well, but do not have love, I am a noisy gong, a clanging cymbal. If I have the gift of prophecy and, with full knowledge, comprehend all mysteries, if I have faith great enough to move mountains, but have not love, I am nothing. If I give everything I have to feed the poor and hand over my body to be burned, but have not love, I gain nothing.

Love is patient; love is kind. Love is not jealous, it does not put on airs, it is not snobbish. Love is never rude, it is not self-seeking, it is not prone to anger; neither does it brood over injuries. Love does not rejoice in what is wrong but rejoices with the truth. There is no limit to love's forbearance, to its trust, its hope, its power to endure.

> Love never fails.
> > **This is the Word of the Lord.**

---

5   Eph 5, 2. 21-33 or 5, 2. 25-32

A reading from the letter of Paul to the Ephesians

This mystery has many implications, and I am saying it applies to Christ and the Church.

(Long Form)

Follow the way of love, even as Christ loved you. He gave himself for us.

Defer to one another out of reverence for Christ.

Wives should be submissive to their husbands as if to the Lord because the husband is head of his wife just as Christ is head of his body the church, as well as its savior. As the church submits to Christ, so wives should submit to their husbands in everything.

Husbands, love your wives, as Christ loved the church. He gave himself up for her to make her holy, purifying her in the bath of water by the power of the word, to present to himself a glorious church, holy and immaculate, without stain or wrinkle or anything of that sort. Husbands should love their wives as they do their own bodies. He who loves his wife loves himself. Observe that no one ever hates his own flesh; no, he nourishes it and takes care of it as Christ cares for the church—for we are members of his body.

> "For this reason a man shall leave his father
> > and mother,
> > and shall cling to his wife,
> > and the two shall be made into one."

This is a great foreshadowing; I mean that it refers to Christ and the church. In any case, each one should love his wife as he loves himself, the wife for her part showing respect for her husband.

> > **This is the Word of the Lord.**

OR
(Short Form)

Follow the way of love, even as Christ loved you. He gave himself for us.

Husbands, love your wives, as Christ loved the church. He gave himself up for her to make her holy, purifying her in the bath of water by the power of the word, to present to himself a glorious church, holy and immaculate, without stain or wrinkle or anything of that sort. Husbands should love their wives as they do their own bodies. He who loves his wife loves himself. Observe that no one ever hates his own flesh; no, he nourishes it and takes care of it as Christ cares for the church—for we are members of his body.

> "For this reason a man shall leave his father
> > and mother,
> > and shall cling to his wife,
> > and the two shall be made into one."

This is a great foreshadowing; I mean that it refers to Christ and the church.

> > **This is the Word of the Lord.**

---

6   Col 3, 12-17

A reading from the letter of Paul to the Colossians

Above all have love, which is the bond of perfection.

Because you are God's chosen ones, holy and beloved, clothe yourselves with heartfelt mercy, with kindness, humility, meekness, and patience. Bear with one another; forgive whatever grievances you have against one another. Forgive as the Lord has forgiven you. Over all these virtues put on love, which binds the rest together and makes them perfect. Christ's peace must reign in your hearts, since as members of the one body you have been called to that peace. Dedicate yourselves to thankfulness. Let the word of Christ, rich as it is, dwell in you. In wisdom made perfect, instruct and admonish one another. Sing gratefully to God from your hearts in psalms, hymns, and inspired songs. Whatever you do, whether in speech or in action, do it in the name of the

Lord Jesus. Give thanks to God the Father through him.

This is the Word of the Lord.

---

7   1 Pt 3, 1-9

A reading from the first letter of Peter

You should agree with one another, be sympathetic and love the brothers.

You married women must obey your husbands, so that any of them who do not believe in the word of the gospel may be won over apart from preaching, through their wives' conduct. They have only to observe the reverent purity of your way of life. The affectation of an elaborate hairdress, the wearing of golden jewelry, or the donning of rich robes is not for you. Your adornment is rather the hidden character of the heart, expressed in the unfading beauty of a calm and gentle disposition. This is precious in God's eyes. The holy women of past ages used to adorn themselves in this way, reliant on God and obedient to their husbands —for example, Sarah, who was subject to Abraham and called him her master. You are her children when you do what is right and let no fears alarm you.

You husbands, too, must show consideration for those who share your lives. Treat women with respect as the weaker sex, heirs just as much as you to the gracious gift of life. If you do so, nothing will keep your prayers from being answered.

In summary, then, all of you should be likeminded, sympathetic, loving toward one another, kindly disposed, and humble. Do not return evil for evil or insult for insult. Return a blessing instead. This you have been called to do, that you may receive a blessing as your inheritance.

This is the Word of the Lord.

---

8   1 Jn 3, 18-24

A reading from the first letter of John

Our love is to be something real and active.

Little children,
let us love in deed and in truth,
and not merely talk about it.

This is our way of knowing we are committed to the truth
and are at peace before him
no matter what our consciences may charge us with;
for God is greater than our hearts
and all is known to him.
Beloved,
if our consciences have nothing to charge us with,
we can be sure that God is with us
and that we will receive at his hands
whatever we ask.
Why? Because we are keeping his commandments
and doing what is pleasing in his sight.
His commandment is this:
we are to believe in the name of his Son, Jesus Christ,
and are to love one another as he commanded us.
Those who keep his commandments remain in him
and he in them.
And this is how we know that he remains in us:
from the Spirit that he gave us.

This is the Word of the Lord.

---

9   1 Jn 4, 7-12

A reading from the first letter of John

God is love.

Beloved,
let us love one another
because love is of God;
everyone who loves is begotten of God
and has knowledge of God.
The man without love has known nothing of God,
for God is love.
God's love was revealed in our midst in this way:
he sent his only Son to the world
that we might have life through him.
Love, then, consists in this:
not that we have loved God,
but that he has loved us

and has sent his Son as an offering for our
sins.
Beloved,
if God has loved us so,
we must have the same love for one another.
No one has ever seen God.
Yet if we love one another
God dwells in us,
and his love is brought to perfection in us.
        This is the Word of the Lord.

---

10   Rv 19, 1. 5-9

A reading from the book of Revelation

Happy are those who are invited to the wedding feast of
the Lamb.

I, John, heard what sounded like the loud song
of a great assembly in heaven. They were singing:
    "Alleluia!
Salvation, glory, and might belong to our
God."
    A voice coming from the throne cried out:
"Praise our God, all you his servants, the small
and the great, who revere him!" Then I heard
what sounded like the shouts of a great crowd,
or the roaring of the deep, or mighty peals of
thunder, as they cried:
    "Alleluia!
The Lord is king,
    our God, the Almighty!
Let us rejoice and be glad,
    and gave him glory!
For this is the wedding day of the Lamb,
    his bride has prepared herself for the wed-
    ding.
She has been given a dress to wear
    made of finest linen, brilliant white."
(The linen dress is the virtuous deeds of God's
saints.)
    The angel then said to me: "Write this down:
Happy are they who have been invited to the
wedding feast of the Lamb."
        This is the Word of the Lord.

---

776   **RESPONSORIAL PSALM**

1   Ps 33, 12. 18. 20-21. 22

℟. (5) The earth is full of the goodness of the
    Lord.
Happy the nation whose God is the Lord,
    the people he has chosen for his own inheri-
    tance.
But see, the eyes of the Lord are upon those
    who fear him,
    upon those who hope for his kindness.
℟. The earth is full of the goodness of the Lord.
Our soul waits for the Lord,
    who is our help and our shield,
For in him our hearts rejoice;
    in his holy name we trust.
℟. The earth is full of the goodness of the Lord.
May your kindness, O Lord, be upon us
    who have put our hope in you.
℟. The earth is full of the goodness of the Lord.

---

2   Ps 34, 2-3. 4-5. 6-7. 8-9

℟. (2) I will bless the Lord at all times.
I will bless the Lord at all times;
    his praise shall be ever in my mouth.
Let my soul glory in the Lord;
    the lowly will hear me and be glad.
℟. I will bless the Lord at all times.
Glorify the Lord with me,
    let us together extol his name.
I sought the Lord, and he answered me
    and delivered me from all my fears.
℟. I will bless the Lord at all times.
Look to him that you may be radiant with joy,
    and your faces may not blush with shame.
When the afflicted man called out, the Lord
    heard,
    and from all his distress he saved him.
℟. I will bless the Lord at all times.
The angel of the Lord encamps
    around those who fear him, and delivers
    them.
Taste and see how good the Lord is;
    happy the man who takes refuge in him.
℟. I will bless the Lord at all times.
℟. Or: (9) Taste and see the goodness of the
    Lord.

3   Ps 103, 1-2. 8. 13. 17-18

℟. (8) The Lord is kind and merciful.
Bless the Lord, O my soul;
  and all my being, bless his holy name.
Bless the Lord, O my soul,
  and forget not all his benefits.
℟. The Lord is kind and merciful.
Merciful and gracious is the Lord,
  slow to anger and abounding in kindness.
As a father has compassion on his children,
  so the Lord has compassion on those who
  fear him.
℟. The Lord is kind and merciful.
But the kindness of the Lord is from eternity
  to eternity toward those who fear him,
And his justice toward children's children
  among those who keep his covenant.
℟. The Lord is kind and merciful.
℟. Or: (17) The Lord's kindness is everlasting
  to those who fear him.

---

4   Ps 112, 1-2. 3-4. 5-7. 7-8. 9

℟. (1) Happy are those who do what the
  Lord commands.
Happy the man who fears the Lord,
  who greatly delights in his commands.
His posterity shall be mighty upon the earth;
  the upright generation shall be blessed.
℟. Happy are those who do what the Lord
  commands.
Wealth and riches shall be in his house;
  his generosity shall endure forever.
He dawns through the darkness, a light for the
  upright;
  he is gracious and merciful and just.
℟. Happy are those who do what the Lord
  commands.
Well for the man who is gracious and lends,
  who conducts his affairs with justice;
He shall never be moved;
  the just man shall be in everlasting remem-
  brance.
℟. Happy are those who do what the Lord
  commands.
An evil report he shall not fear.
  His heart is firm, trusting in the Lord.
His heart is steadfast; he shall not fear
  till he looks down upon his foes.

℟. Happy are those who do what the Lord
  commands.
Lavishly he gives to the poor;
  his generosity shall endure forever;
  his horn shall be exalted in glory.
℟. Happy are those who do what the Lord
  commands.
℟. Or: Alleluia.

---

5   Ps 128, 1-2. 3. 4-5

℟. (1) Happy are those who fear the Lord.
Happy are you who fear the Lord,
  who walk in his ways!
For you shall eat the fruit of your handiwork;
  happy shall you be, and favored.
℟. Happy are those who fear the Lord.
Your wife shall be like a fruitful vine
  in the recesses of your home;
Your children like olive plants
  around your table.
℟. Happy are those who fear the Lord.
Behold, thus is the man blessed
  who fears the Lord.
The Lord bless you from Sion:
  may you see the prosperity of Jerusalem
  all the days of your life.
℟. Happy are those who fear the Lord.
℟. Or: (4) See how the Lord blesses those who
  fear him.

---

6   Ps 145, 8-9. 10. 15. 17-18

℟. (9) The Lord is compassionate to all his
  creatures.
The Lord is gracious and merciful,
  slow to anger and of great kindness.
The Lord is good to all
  and compassionate toward all his works.
℟. The Lord is compassionate to all his creatures.
Let all your works give you thanks, O Lord,
  and let your faithful ones bless you.
The eyes of all look hopefully to you,
  and you give them their food in due season.
℟. The Lord is compassionate to all his creatures.
The Lord is just in all his ways
  and holy in all his works.

The Lord is near to all who call upon him,
   to all who call upon him in truth.
℞. The Lord is compassionate to all his creatures.

_____

7   Ps 148, 1-2. 3-4. 9-10. 11-12. 12-14

℞. (12) Let all praise the name of the Lord.
Praise the Lord from the heavens,
   praise him in the heights;
Praise him, all you his angels,
   praise him, all you his hosts.
℞. Let all praise the name of the Lord.
Praise him, sun and moon;
   praise him, all you shining stars.
Praise him, you highest heavens,
   and you waters above the heavens.
℞. Let all praise the name of the Lord.
You mountains and all you hills,
   you fruit trees and all you cedars;
You wild beasts and all tame animals,
   you creeping things and you winged fowl.
℞. Let all praise the name of the Lord.
Let the kings of the earth and all peoples,
   the princes and all the judges of the earth,
Young men too, and maidens,
   old men and boys.
℞. Let all praise the name of the Lord.
Praise the name of the Lord,
   for his name alone is exalted;
His majesty is above earth and heaven,
   and he has lifted up the horn of his people.
℞. Let all praise the name of the Lord.
℞. Or: Alleluia.

_____

777   **ALLELUIA VERSE AND**
        VERSE BEFORE THE GOSPEL

1   1 Jn 4, 8. 11

God is love;
let us love one another as he has loved us.

2   1 Jn 4, 12

If we love one another,
God will live in us in perfect love.

3   1 Jn 4, 16

He who lives in love, lives in God,
and God in him.

4   1 Jn 4, 7

Everyone who loves is born of God and knows
him.

_____

778   **GOSPEL**

1   Mt 5, 1-12

✠ **A reading from the holy gospel according**
        to Matthew
Rejoice and be glad, for your reward will be great in heaven.

When Jesus saw the crowds he went up on
the mountainside. After he had sat down his
disciples gathered around him, and he began
to teach them:
    "How blest are the poor in spirit: the reign
       of God is theirs.
    Blest too are the sorrowing; they shall
       be consoled.
    [Blest are the lowly; they shall inherit the
       land.]
    Blest are they who hunger and thirst for
       holiness;
    they shall have their fill.
    Blest are they who show mercy;
    mercy shall be theirs.
    Blest are the single-hearted for they shall
       see God.
    Blest too the peacemakers; they shall be
       called sons of God.
    Blest are those persecuted for holiness'
       sake; the reign of God is theirs.
    Blest are you when they insult you and
       persecute you and utter every kind of
       slander against you because of me.
    Be glad and rejoice, for your reward in
       heaven is great."
       This is the gospel of the Lord.

_____

2   Mt 5, 13-16

✠ A reading from the holy gospel according
to Matthew

You are the light of the world.

Jesus said to his disciples: "You are the salt
of the earth. But what if salt goes flat? How
can you restore its flavor? Then it is good for
nothing but to be thrown out and trampled
underfoot.

"You are the light of the world. A city set on
a hill cannot be hidden. Men do not light a lamp
and then put it under a bushel basket. They
set it on a stand where it gives light to all
in the house. In the same way, your light must
shine before men so that they may see goodness in your acts and give praise to your
heavenly Father."

This is the gospel of the Lord.

---

3   Mt 7, 21. 24-29 or 7, 21. 24-25

✠ A reading from the holy gospel according
to Matthew

He built his house on rock.

(Long Form)

Jesus said to his disciples: "None of those who
cry out, 'Lord, Lord,' will enter the kingdom of
God but only the one who does the will of my
Father in heaven.

"Anyone who hears my words and puts
them into practice is like the wise man who
built his house on rock. When the rainy season
set in, the torrents came and the winds blew
and buffeted his house. It did not collapse; it
had been solidly set on rock. Anyone who
hears my words but does not put them into
practice is like the foolish man who built his
house on sandy ground. The rains fell, the torrents came, the winds blew and lashed against
his house. It collapsed under all this and was
completely ruined."

Jesus finished this discourse and left the
crowds spellbound at his teaching. The reason
was that he taught with authority and not like
the scribes.

This is the gospel of the Lord.

OR
(Short Form)

Jesus said to his disciples: "None of those who
cry out, 'Lord, Lord,' will enter the kingdom
of God but only the one who does the will of
my Father in heaven.

"Anyone who hears my words and puts
them into practice is like the wise man who
built his house on rock. When the rainy season
set in, the torrents came and the winds blew
and buffeted his house. It did not collapse;
it had been solidly set on rock."

This is the gospel of the Lord.

---

4   Mt 19, 3-6

✠ A reading from the holy gospel according
to Matthew

So then, what God has united, man must not divide.

Some Pharisees came up to Jesus and said, to
test him, "May a man divorce his wife for
any reason whatever?" He replied, "Have you
not read that at the beginning the Creator
made them male and female and declared,
'For this reason a man shall leave his father
and mother and cling to his wife, and the two
shall become as one'? Thus they are no longer
two but one flesh. Therefore, let no man separate what God has joined."

This is the gospel of the Lord.

---

5   Mt 22, 35-40

✠ A reading from the holy gospel according
to Matthew

*This is the greatest and the first commandment. The
second is similar to it.*

One of the Pharisees, a lawyer, in an attempt
to trip up Jesus, asked him, "Teacher, which
commandment of the law is the greatest?"
Jesus said to him:

"'You shall love the Lord your God
with your whole heart,
with your whole soul,
and with all your mind.'

This is the greatest and first commandment.
The second is like it:

'You shall love your neighbor as yourself.'

On these two commandments the whole law is based, and the prophets as well."
This is the gospel of the Lord.

---

6   Mk 10, 6-9

✠ A reading from the holy gospel according to Mark

They are no longer two, therefore, but one body.

Jesus said: "At the beginning of creation God made them male and female; for this reason a man shall leave his father and mother and the two shall become as one. They are no longer two but one flesh. Therefore let no man separate what God has joined."
This is the gospel of the Lord.

---

7   Jn 2, 1-11

✠ A reading from the holy gospel according to John

This was the first of the signs given by Jesus; it was given at Cana in Galilee.

There was a wedding at Cana in Galilee, and the mother of Jesus was there. Jesus and his disciples had likewise been invited to the celebration. At a certain point the wine ran out, and Jesus' mother told him, "They have no more wine." Jesus replied, "Woman, how does this concern of yours involve me? My hour has not yet come." His mother instructed those waiting on table, "Do whatever he tells you." As prescribed for Jewish ceremonial washings, there were at hand six stone water jars, each one holding fifteen to twenty-five gallons. "Fill those jars with water," Jesus ordered, at which they filled them to the brim. "Now," he said, "draw some out and take it to the waiter in charge." They did as he instructed them. The waiter in charge tasted the water made wine, without knowing where it had come from; only the waiters knew, since they had drawn the water. Then the waiter in charge called the groom over and remarked to him: "People usually serve the choice wine first; then when the guests have been drinking a while, a lesser vintage. What you have done is keep the choice wine until now." Jesus performed this first of

his signs at Cana in Galilee. Thus did he reveal his glory, and his disciples believed in him.
This is the gospel of the Lord.

---

8   Jn 15, 9-12

✠ A reading from the holy gospel according to John

Remain in my love.

Jesus said to his disciples:
"As the Father has loved me,
so I have loved you.
Live on in my love.
You will live in my love
if you keep my commandments,
even as I have kept my Father's commandments,
and live in his love.
All this I tell you
that my joy may be yours
and your joy may be complete.
This is my commandment:
love one another
as I have loved you."
This is the gospel of the Lord.

---

9   Jn 15, 12-16

✠ A reading from the holy gospel according to John

This is my commandment: love one another.

Jesus said to his disciples:
"This is my commandment:
love one another
as I have loved you.
There is no greater love than this:
to lay down one's life for one's friends.
You are my friends
if you do what I command you.
I no longer speak of you as slaves,
for a slave does not know what his master is about.
Instead, I call you friends,
since I have made known to you all that I heard from my Father.
It was not you who chose me,
it was I who chose you
to go forth and bear fruit.

Your fruit must endure,
so that all you ask the Father in my name
he will give you."
    This is the gospel of the Lord.

---

10   Jn 17, 20-26 or 17, 20-23

✠ A reading from the holy gospel according
        to John
        May they be completely one.

(Long Form)

Jesus looked up to heaven and prayed:
    "Holy Father,
    I do not pray for my disciples alone.
    I pray also for those who will believe in me
        through their word,
    that all may be one
    as you, Father, are in me, and I in you;
    I pray that they may be [one] in us,
    that the world may believe that you sent me.
    I have given them the glory you gave me
    that they may be one, as we are one—
    I living in them, you living in me—
    that their unity may be complete.
    So shall the world know that you sent me,
    and that you loved them as you loved me.
    Father,
    all those you gave me
    I would have in my company
    where I am,
    to see this glory of mine
    which is your gift to me,
    because of the love you bore me before the
        world began.
    Just Father,
    the world has not known you,
    but I have known you;
    and these men have known that you sent me.
    To them I have revealed your name,
    and I will continue to reveal it
    so that your love for me may live in them,
    and I may live in them."
        This is the gospel of the Lord.

OR
(Short Form)

Jesus looked up to heaven and prayed:
    "Holy Father,

I do not pray for my disciples alone.
I pray also for those who will believe in me
    through their word,
that all may be one
as you, Father, are in me, and I in you;
I pray that they may be [one] in us,
that the world may believe that you sent me.
I have given them the glory you gave me
that they may be one, as we are one—
I living in them, you living in me—
that their unity may be complete.
So shall the world know that you sent me,
and that you loved them as you loved me."
    This is the gospel of the Lord.

BLESSING OF ABBOTS
AND ABBESSES

779   **OLD TESTAMENT READING**
1   Prv 2, 1-9

A reading from the book of Proverbs
        Incline your heart to understanding.

My son, if you receive my words
    and treasure my commands,
Turning your ear to wisdom,
    inclining your heart to understanding;
Yes, if you call to intelligence,
    and to understanding raise your voice;
If you seek her like silver,
    and like hidden treasures search her out:

Then will you understand the fear of the Lord;
    the knowledge of God you will find;
For the Lord gives wisdom,
    from his mouth come knowledge and under-
        standing;
He has counsel in store for the upright,
    he is the shield of those who walk honestly,
Guarding the paths of justice,
    protecting the way of his pious ones.

Then you will understand rectitude and jus-
        tice,
    honesty, every good path.
        This is the Word of the Lord.

2   Prv 4, 7-13

A reading from the book of Proverbs
I will point out to you the way of wisdom.

"The beginning of wisdom is: get wisdom;
at the cost of all you have, get understanding.

Extol her, and she will exalt you;
she will bring you honors if you embrace her;

She will put on your head a graceful diadem;
a glorious crown will she bestow on you."

Hear, my son, and receive my words,
and the years of your life shall be many.

On the way of wisdom I direct you,
I lead you on straightforward paths.

When you walk, your step will not be impeded,
and should you run, you will not stumble.

Hold fast to instruction, never let her go;
keep her, for she is your life.

This is the Word of the Lord.

---

780   NEW TESTAMENT READING

1   Acts 2, 42-47

A reading from the Acts of the Apostles
All those who believed were equal and held everything in common.

The brethren devoted themselves to the apostles' instruction and the communal life, to the breaking of bread and the prayers. A reverent fear overtook them all, for many wonders and signs were performed by the apostles. They shared all things in common; they would sell their property and goods, dividing everything on the basis of each one's need. They went to the temple area together every day, while in their homes they broke bread. With exultant and sincere hearts they took their meals in common, praising God and winning the approval of all the people. Day by day the Lord added to their number those who were being saved.

This is the Word of the Lord.

---

2   Eph 4, 1-6

A reading from the letter of Paul to the Ephesians
Do all you can to preserve the unity of the Spirit in the bond of peace.

I plead with you as a prisoner for the Lord, to live a life worthy of the calling you have received, with perfect humility, meekness, and patience, bearing with one another lovingly. Make every effort to preserve the unity which has the Spirit as its origin and peace as its binding force. There is but one body and one Spirit, just as there is but one hope given all of you by your call. There is one Lord, one faith, one baptism; one God and Father of all, who is over all, and works through all, and is in all.

This is the Word of the Lord.

---

3   Col 3, 12-17

A reading from the letter of Paul to the Colossians
Love one another: that is the bond of perfection.

Because you are God's chosen ones, holy and beloved, clothe yourselves with heartfelt mercy, with kindness, humility, meekness, and patience. Bear with one another, forgive whatever grievances you have against one another. Forgive as the Lord has forgiven you. Over all these virtues put on love, which binds the rest together and makes them perfect. Christ's peace must reign in your hearts, since as members of the one body you have been called to that peace. Dedicate yourselves to thankfulness. Let the word of Christ, rich as it is, dwell in you. In wisdom made perfect, instruct and admonish one another. Sing gratefully to God from your hearts in psalms, hymns, and inspired songs. Whatever you do, whether in speech or in action, do it in the name of the Lord Jesus. Give thanks to God the Father through him.

This is the Word of the Lord.

---

4   Heb 13, 1-2. 7-8. 17-18

A reading from the letter to the Hebrews

Be obedient and behave honorably. Pray for us.

Love your fellow Christian always. Do not neglect to show hospitality, for by that means some have entertained angels without knowing it. Remember your leaders who spoke the word of God to you; consider how their lives ended, and imitate their faith. Jesus Christ is the same yesterday, today, and forever.

Obey your leaders and submit to them, for they keep watch over you as men who must render an account. So act that they may fulfill their task with joy, not with sorrow, for that would be harmful to you. Pray for us; we are confident that we have a good conscience, wishing, as we do, to act rightly in every respect.

This is the Word of the Lord.

---

5   1 Pt 5, 1-4

A reading from the first letter of Peter

Be the shepherds of those entrusted to you.

To the elders among you I, a fellow elder, a witness of Christ's sufferings and sharer in the glory that is to be revealed, make this appeal. God's flock is in your midst; give it a shepherd's care. Watch over it willingly as God would have you do, not under coercion; and not for shameful profit either, but generously. Be examples to the flock, not lording it over those assigned to you, so that when the chief shepherd appears you will win for yourselves the unfading crown of glory.

This is the Word of the Lord.

---

781   **RESPONSORIAL PSALM**

1   Ps 1, 1-2. 3. 4. 6

℟. (Ps 40, 5) Happy are they who hope in the Lord.

Happy the man who follows not
  the counsel of the wicked
Nor walks in the way of sinners,
  nor sits in the company of the insolent,

But delights in the law of the Lord
  and meditates on his law day and night.
℟. Happy are they who hope in the Lord.
He is like a tree
  planted near running water,
That yields its fruit in due season,
  and whose leaves never fade.
  [Whatever he does, prospers.]
℟. Happy are they who hope in the Lord.
Not so the wicked, not so;
  they are like chaff which the wind drives
  away.
For the Lord watches over the way of the just,
  but the way of the wicked vanishes.
℟. Happy are they who hope in the Lord.

---

2   Ps 34, 2-3. 4-5. 10-11. 12-13

℟. (12) Listen to me, my children:
  I will teach you to honor the Lord.
I will bless the Lord at all times;
  his praise shall be ever in my mouth.
Let my soul glory in the Lord;
  the lowly will hear me and be glad.
℟. Listen to me, my children:
  I will teach you to honor the Lord.
Glorify the Lord with me,
  let us together extol his name.
I sought the Lord, and he answered me
  and delivered me from all my fears.
℟. Listen to me, my children:
  I will teach you to honor the Lord.
Fear the Lord, you his holy ones,
  for naught is lacking to those who fear him.
The great grow poor and hungry;
  but those who seek the Lord want for no
  good thing.
℟. Listen to me, my children:
  I will teach you to honor the Lord.
Come, children, hear me;
  I will teach you the fear of the Lord.
Which of you desires life,
  and takes delight in prosperous days?
℟. Listen to me, my children:
  I will teach you to honor the Lord.

3   Ps 92, 2-3. 5-6. 13-14. 15-16

℟. (2) Lord, it is good to give thanks to you.

It is good to give thanks to the Lord,
  to sing praise to your name, Most High,
To proclaim your kindness at dawn
  and your faithfulness throughout the night.

℟. Lord, it is good to give thanks to you.

For you make me glad, O Lord, by your deeds;
  at the works of your hands I rejoice.
How great are your works, O Lord!
  How very deep are your thoughts!

℟. Lord, it is good to give thanks to you.

The just man shall flourish like the palm tree,
  like a cedar of Lebanon shall he grow.
They that are planted in the house of the Lord
  shall flourish in the courts of our God.

℟. Lord, it is good to give thanks to you.

They shall bear fruit even in old age;
  vigorous and sturdy shall they be,
Declaring how just is the Lord,
  my Rock, in whom there is no wrong.

℟. Lord, it is good to give thanks to you.

**782   ALLELUIA VERSE AND
        VERSE BEFORE THE GOSPEL**

1   Mt 23, 9. 10

You have one Father, your Father in heaven;
you have one teacher: the Lord Jesus Christ!

2   Col 3, 15

May the peace of Christ rule in your hearts,
that peace to which all of you are called as one
  body.

783   GOSPEL

1   Mt 23, 8-12

✠ A reading from the holy gospel according
            to Matthew

The greater among you must be your servant.

Jesus said to his disciples: "Avoid the title,
'Rabbi.' One among you is your teacher, the
rest are learners. Do not call anyone on earth
your father. Only one is your father, the One in
heaven. Avoid being called teachers. Only one
is your teacher, the Messiah. The greatest
among you will be the one who serves the rest.
Whoever exalts himself shall be humbled, but
whoever humbles himself shall be exalted."
            This is the gospel of the Lord.

2   Lk 12, 35-44

✠ A reading from the holy gospel according
            to Luke

The master will place him as the head of his household.

Jesus said to his disciples: "Let your belts be
fastened around your waists and your lamps
be burning ready. Be like men awaiting their
master's return from a wedding, so that when
he arrives and knocks, you will open for him
without delay. It will go well with those servants whom the master finds wide-awake on
his return. I tell you, he will put on an
apron, seat them at table, and proceed to wait
on them. Should he happen to come at midnight or before sunrise and find them prepared,
it will go well with them. You know as well as
I that if the head of the house knew when the
thief was coming he would not let him break
into his house. Be on guard, therefore. The
Son of Man will come when you least expect
him."

Peter said, "Do you intend this parable for
us, Lord, or do you mean it for the whole
world?" The Lord said, "Who in your opinion
is that faithful, farsighted steward whom the
master will set over his servants to dispense
their ration of grain in season? That servant is
fortunate whom his master finds busy when he
returns. Assuredly, his master will put him in
charge of all his property."
            This is the gospel of the Lord.

3   Lk 22, 24-27

✠ A reading from the holy gospel according
            to Luke

I am here among you as one who serves.

A dispute arose among the disciples about who
should be regarded as the greatest. Jesus said:
"Earthly kings lord it over their people. Those

who exercise authority over them are called their benefactors. Yet it cannot be that way with you. Let the greater among you be as the junior, the leader as the servant. Who, in fact, is the greater—he who reclines at table or he who serves the meal? Is it not the one who reclines at table? Yet I am in your midst as the one who serves you."

This is the gospel of the Lord.

CONSECRATION OF VIRGINS AND RELIGIOUS PROFESSION

784 OLD TESTAMENT READING

1 Gn 12, 1-4

A reading from the book of Genesis

Leave your country, your family, and come.

The Lord said to Abram: "Go forth from the land of your kinsfolk and from your father's house to a land that I will show you.

"I will make of you a great nation,
and I will bless you;
I will make your name great,
so that you will be a blessing.
I will bless those who bless you
and curse those who curse you.
All the communities of the earth
shall find blessing in you."

Abram went as the Lord directed him, and Lot went with him.

This is the Word of the Lord.

---

2 1 Sm 3, 1-10

A reading from the first book of Samuel

Speak, Lord, your servant is listening.

During the time young Samuel was minister to the Lord under Eli, a revelation of the Lord was uncommon and vision infrequent. One day Eli was asleep in his usual place. His eyes had lately grown so weak that he could not see. The lamp of God was not yet extinguished, and Samuel was sleeping in the temple of the Lord where the ark of God was. The Lord called to Samuel, who answered, "Here I am." He ran to Eli and said, "Here I am. You called me." "I did not call you," Eli said. "Go back to sleep." So he went back to sleep. Again the Lord called Samuel, who rose and went to Eli. "Here I am," he said. "You called me." But he answered, "I did not call you, my son. Go back to sleep." At that time Samuel was not familiar with the Lord, because the Lord had not revealed anything to him as yet. The Lord called Samuel again, for the third time. Getting up and going to Eli, he said, "Here I am. You called me." Then Eli understood that the Lord was calling the youth. So he said to Samuel, "Go to sleep, and if you are called, reply, 'Speak, Lord, for your servant is listening.'" When Samuel went to sleep in his place, the Lord came and revealed his presence, calling out as before, "Samuel, Samuel!" Samuel answered, "Speak, for your servant is listening."

This is the Word of the Lord.

---

3 1 Kgs 19, 4-9. 11-15

A reading from the first book of Kings

Go out and stand on the mountain before the Lord.

Elijah went a day's journey into the desert, until he came to a broom tree and sat beneath it. He prayed for death: "This is enough, O Lord! Take my life, for I am no better than my fathers." He lay down and fell asleep under the broom tree, but then an angel touched him and ordered him to get up and eat. He looked and there at his head was a hearth cake and a jug of water. After he ate and drank, he lay down again, but the angel of the Lord came back a second time, touched him, and ordered, "Get up and eat, else the journey will be too long for you!" He got up, ate and drank; then strengthened by that food, he walked forty days and forty nights to the mountain of God, Horeb.

There he came to a cave, where he took shelter. Then the Lord said, "Go outside and stand on the mountain before the Lord; the Lord will be passing by." A strong and heavy wind was rending the mountains and crushing rocks before the Lord—but the Lord was not in the wind. After the wind there was an earthquake—but the Lord was not in the earthquake. After the earthquake there was fire—but the Lord was not in the fire. After the fire there was a tiny whispering sound. When he heard this, Elijah hid his face in his cloak and went and stood at the entrance of the cave. A voice said to him, "Elijah, why are you here?" He replied, "I have been most zealous for the Lord, the God of hosts. But the Israelites have forsaken your covenant, torn down your altars, and put your prophets to the sword. I alone am left, and they seek to take my life." "Go, take the road back to the desert near Damascus," the Lord said to him.

This is the Word of the Lord.

---

4   1 Kgs 19, 16. 19-21

A reading from the first book of Kings
Elisha left and followed Elijah.

The Lord said to Elijah: "You shall anoint Elisha, son of Shaphat of Abel-meholah, as prophet to succeed you."

Elijah set out, and came upon Elisha, son of Shaphat, as he was plowing with twelve yoke of oxen; he was following the twelfth. Elijah went over to him and threw his cloak over him. Elisha left the oxen, ran after Elijah, and said, "Please, let me kiss my father and mother goodbye, and I will follow you." "Go back!" Elijah answered. "Have I done anything to you?" Elisha left him and, taking the yoke of oxen, slaughtered them; he used the plowing equipment for fuel to boil their flesh, and gave it to his people to eat. Then he left and followed Elijah as his attendant.

This is the Word of the Lord.

---

5   Sg 2, 8-14

A reading from the Song of Songs
Rise, my love, and come.

Hark! my lover—here he comes
    springing across the mountains,
    leaping across the hills.
My lover is like a gazelle
    or a young stag.

Here he stands behind our wall,
    gazing through the windows,
    peering through the lattices.
My lover speaks; he says to me,
    "Arise, my beloved, my beautiful one,
    and come!
For see, the winter is past,
    the rains are over and gone.
The flowers appear on the earth,
    the time of pruning the vines has come,
    and the song of the dove is heard in our land.
The fig tree puts forth its figs,
    and the vines, in bloom, give forth fragrance.
Arise, my beloved, my beautiful one,
    and come!
O my dove in the clefts of the rock,
    in the secret recesses of the cliff,
Let me see you,
    let me hear your voice,
For your voice is sweet,
    and you are lovely."

This is the Word of the Lord.

---

6   Sg 8, 6-7

A reading from the Song of Songs
Love is strong as death.

Set me as a seal on your heart,
    as a seal on your arm;
For stern as death is love,
    relentless as the nether world is devotion;
    its flames are a blazing fire.
Deep waters cannot quench love,
    nor floods sweep it away.
Were one to offer all he owns to purchase love,
    he would be roundly mocked.

This is the Word of the Lord.

---

7   Is 61, 9-11

A reading from the book of the prophet Isaiah
I exult for joy in the Lord.

The descendants of my people shall be renowned among the nations,
    and their offspring among the peoples;
All who see them shall acknowledge them
    as a race the Lord has blessed.
I rejoice heartily in the Lord,
    in my God is the joy of my soul;

For he has clothed me with a robe of salvation.
  and wrapped me in a mantle of justice,
Like a bridegroom adorned with a diadem,
  like a bride bedecked with her jewels.
As the earth brings forth its plants,
  and a garden makes its growth spring up,
So will the Lord God make justice and praise
  spring up before all the nations.
         This is the Word of the Lord.

8   Hos 2, 16. 21-22

A reading from the book of the prophet Hosea
         I will betroth you to myself for ever.

I will allure her;
  I will lead her into the desert
  and speak to her heart.
I will espouse you to me forever:
  I will espouse you in right and in justice,
  in love and in mercy;
I will espouse you in fidelity,
  and you shall know the Lord.
         This is the Word of the Lord.

---

785   NEW TESTAMENT READING

1   Acts 2, 42-47

A reading from the Acts of the Apostles
All those who believed were equal and held everything in
common.

The brethren devoted themselves to the apostles' instruction and the communal life, to the breaking of bread and the prayers. A reverent fear overtook them all, for many wonders and signs were performed by the apostles.

They shared all things in common; they would sell their property and goods, dividing everything on the basis of each one's need. They went to the temple area together every day, while in their homes they broke bread. With exultant and sincere hearts they took their meals in common, praising God and winning the approval of all the people. Day by day the Lord added to their number those who were being saved.
         This is the Word of the Lord.

---

2   Acts 4, 32-35

A reading from the Acts of the Apostles
         One heart and one soul.

The community of believers were of one heart and one mind. None of them ever claimed anything as his own; rather, everything was held in common. With power the apostles bore witness to the resurrection of the Lord Jesus, and great respect was paid to them all; nor was there anyone needy among them, for all who owned property or houses sold them and donated the proceeds. They used to lay them at the feet of the apostles to be distributed to everyone according to his need.
         This is the Word of the Lord.

---

3   Rom 6, 3-11

A reading from the letter of Paul to the Romans
         Let us walk in newness of life.

We who were baptized into Christ Jesus were baptized into his death. Through baptism into his death we were buried with him, so that, just as Christ was raised from the dead by the glory of the Father, we too might live a new life. If we have been united with him through likeness to his death, so shall we be through a like resurrection. This we know: our old self was crucified with him so that the sinful body might be destroyed and we might be slaves to sin no longer. A man who is dead has been freed from sin. If we have died with Christ, we believe that we are also to live with him. We know that Christ, once raised from the dead, will never die again; death has no more power over him. His death was death to sin, once for all; his life is life for God. In the same way, you must consider yourselves dead to sin but alive for God in Christ Jesus.
         This is the Word of the Lord.

---

4   Rom 12, 1-13

A reading from the letter of Paul to the Romans
Offer your bodies as a living, holy sacrifice, truly pleasing
to God.

Brothers, I beg you through the mercy of God to offer your bodies as a living sacrifice holy and acceptable to God, your spiritual worship. Do not conform yourselves to this age but be transformed by the renewal of your mind, so that you may judge what is God's will, what is good, pleasing and perfect.

Thus, in virtue of the favor given to me, I warn each of you not to think more highly of himself than he ought. Let him estimate himself soberly, in keeping with the measure of faith that God has apportioned him. Just as each of us has one body with many members, and not all the members have the same function, so too we, though many, are one body in Christ and individually members one of another. We have gifts that differ according to the favor bestowed on each of us. One's gift may be prophecy; its use should be in proportion to his faith. It may be the gift of ministry; it should be used for service. One who is a teacher should use his gift for teaching; one with the power of exhortation should exhort. He who gives alms should do so generously; he who rules should exercise his authority with care; he who performs works of mercy should do so cheerfully.

Your love must be sincere. Detest what is evil, cling to what is good. Love one another with the affection of brothers. Anticipate each other in showing respect. Do not grow slack but be fervent in spirit; he whom you serve is the Lord. Rejoice in hope, be patient under trial, persevere in prayer. Look on the needs of the saints as your own; be generous in offering hospitality.

This is the Word of the Lord.

---

5   1 Cor 1, 22-31

A reading from the first letter of Paul to the Corinthians

To many, preaching a crucified Christ is madness; to us, it is the power of God.

Jews demand "signs" and Greeks look for "wisdom," but we preach Christ crucified, a stumbling block to Jews and an absurdity to Gentiles, but to those who are called, Jews and Greeks alike, Christ the power of God and the wisdom of God. For God's folly is wiser than men, and his weakness more powerful than men.

Brothers, you are among those called. Consider your own situation. Not many of you are wise, as men account wisdom; not many are influential; and surely not many are wellborn. God chose those whom the world considers absurd to shame the wise; he singled out the weak of this world to shame the strong. He chose the world's lowborn and despised, those who count for nothing, to reduce to nothing those who were something; so that mankind can do no boasting before God. God it is who has given you life in Christ Jesus. He has made him our wisdom and also our justice, our sanctification, and our redemption. This is just as you find it written, "Let him who would boast, boast in the Lord."

This is the Word of the Lord.

---

6   1 Cor 7, 25-35

A reading from the first letter of Paul to the Corinthians

An unmarried woman can devote herself to the Lord's work.

With respect to virgins, I have not received any commandment from the Lord, but I give my opinion as one who is trustworthy, thanks to the Lord's mercy. It is this: In the present time of stress it seems good to me for a person to continue as he is. Are you bound to a wife? Then do not seek your freedom. Are you free of a wife? If so, do not go in search of one. Should you marry, however, you will not be committing sin. Neither does a virgin commit a sin if she marries. Such people, however, will have trials in this life, and these I should like to spare you.

I tell you, brothers, the time is short. From now on those with wives should live as though they had none; those who weep should live as though they were not weeping, and those who rejoice as though they were not rejoicing; buyers should conduct themselves as though they owned nothing, and those who make use of the world as though they were not using it, for the world as we know it is passing away.

I should like you to be free of all worries. The unmarried man is busy with the Lord's affairs, concerned with pleasing the Lord; but the married man is busy with this world's demands and occupied with pleasing his wife. This means he is divided. The virgin—indeed, any unmarried woman—is concerned with things of the Lord, in pursuit of holiness in body and spirit. The married woman, on the other hand, has the cares of this world to absorb her and is concerned with pleasing her husband. I am going into this with you for your own good. I have no desire to place restrictions on you, but I do want to promote what is good, what will help you to devote yourselves entirely to the Lord.

This is the Word of the Lord.

---

7   Eph 1, 3-14

A reading from the letter of Paul to the Ephesians

The Father chose us in Christ to be holy and spotless in love.

Praised be the God and Father of our Lord Jesus Christ who has bestowed on us in Christ every spiritual blessing in the heavens! God chose us in him before the world began, to be holy and blameless in his sight, to be full of love; he likewise predestined us through Christ Jesus to be his adopted sons—such was his will and pleasure—that all might praise the divine favor he has bestowed on us in his beloved.

It is in Christ and through his blood that we have been redeemed and our sins forgiven, so immeasurably generous is God's favor to us. God has given us the wisdom to understand fully the mystery, the plan he was pleased to decree in Christ, to be carried out in the fullness of time: namely, to bring all things in the heavens and on earth into one under Christ's headship.

In him we were chosen; for in the decree of God, who administers everything according to his will and counsel, we were predestined to praise his glory by being the first to hope in Christ. In him you too were chosen; when you heard the glad tidings of salvation, the word of truth, and believed in it, you were sealed with the Holy Spirit who had been promised. He is the pledge of our inheritance, the first payment against the full redemption of a people God has

made his own, to praise his glory.

This is the Word of the Lord.

---

8   Phil 2, 1-4

A reading from the letter of Paul to the Philippians

Be united in your convictions and in your love.

In the name of the encouragement you owe me in Christ, in the name of the solace that love can give, of fellowship in spirit, compassion, and pity, I beg you; make my joy complete by your unanimity, possessing the one love, united in spirit and ideals. Never act out of rivalry or conceit; rather, let all parties think humbly of others as superior to themselves, each of you looking to others' interests rather than his own.

This is the Word of the Lord.

---

9   Phil 3, 8-14

A reading from the letter of Paul to the Philippians

I look on everything as useless if only I can know Christ.

I have come to rate all as loss in the light of the surpassing knowledge of my Lord Jesus Christ. For his sake I have forfeited everything; I have accounted all else rubbish so that Christ may be my wealth and I may be in him, not having any justice of my own based on observance of the law. The justice I possess is that which comes through faith in Christ. It has its origin in God and is based on faith. I wish to know Christ and the power flowing from his resurrection; likewise to know how to share in his sufferings by being formed into the pattern of his death. Thus do I hope that I may arrive at resurrection from the dead.

It is not that I have reached it yet, or have already finished my course; but I am racing to grasp the prize if possible, since I have been grasped by Christ [Jesus]. Brothers, I do not think of myself as having reached the finish line. I give no thought to what lies behind but push on to what is ahead. My entire attention is on the finish line as I run toward the prize to which God calls me—life on high in Christ Jesus.

This is the Word of the Lord.

---

10   Col 3, 1-4

A reading from the letter of Paul to the Colossians

Let your thoughts be on heavenly things, not on the things that are on the earth.

Since you have been raised up in company with Christ, set your heart on what pertains to higher realms where Christ is seated at God's right hand. Be intent on things above rather than on things of earth. After all, you have died! Your life is hidden now with Christ in God. When Christ our life appears, then you shall appear with him in glory.

This is the Word of the Lord.

---

11   Col 3, 12-17

A reading from the letter of Paul to the Colossians

Above everything, have love for each other because that is the bond of perfection.

Because you are God's chosen ones, holy and beloved, clothe yourselves with heartfelt mercy, with kindness, humility, meekness, and patience. Bear with one another, forgive whatever grievances you have against one another. Forgive as the Lord has forgiven you. Over all these virtues put on love, which binds the rest together and makes them perfect. Christ's peace must reign in your hearts, since as members of the one body you have been called to that peace. Dedicate yourselves to thankfulness. Let the word of Christ, rich as it is, dwell in you. In wisdom made perfect, instruct and admonish one another. Sing gratefully to God from your hearts in psalms, hymns, and inspired songs. Whatever you do, whether in speech or in action, do it in the name of the Lord Jesus. Give thanks to God the Father through him.

This is the Word of the Lord.

---

12   1 Thes 4, 1-3. 7-12

A reading from the first letter of Paul to the Thessalonians

What God wants is for you to be holy.

My brothers, we beg and exhort you in the Lord Jesus that, even as you learned from us how to conduct yourselves in a way pleasing to God—which you are indeed doing—so you must learn to make still greater progress. You know the instructions we gave you in the Lord Jesus. It is God's will that you grow in holiness. God has not called us to immorality but to holiness; hence, whoever rejects these instructions rejects, not man, but God "who sends his holy Spirit upon us."

As regards brotherly love, there is no need for me to write you. God himself has taught you to love one another, and this you are doing with respect to all the brothers throughout Macedonia. Yet we exhort you to even greater progress, brothers. Make it a point of honor to remain at peace and attend to your own affairs. Work with your hands as we directed you to do, so that you will give good example to outsiders and want for nothing.

This is the Word of the Lord.

---

13   1 Pt 1, 3-9

A reading from the first letter of Peter

You have not seen the Christ, yet you love him.

Praised be the God and Father of our Lord Jesus Christ,
he who in his great mercy gave us new birth;
a birth unto hope which draws its life
from the resurrection of Jesus Christ from the dead;
a birth to an imperishable inheritance
incapable of fading or defilement,
which is kept in heaven for you
who are guarded with God's power through faith;
a birth to a salvation which stands ready to be revealed in the last days.

There is cause for rejoicing here. You may for a time have to suffer the distress of many trials; but this is so that your faith, which is more precious than the passing splendor of fire-tried gold, may by its genuineness lead to praise, glory and honor when Jesus Christ appears. Although you have never seen him, you love him, and without seeing him, you now believe in him and rejoice with inexpressible joy touched with glory because you are achieving faith's goal, your salvation.

This is the Word of the Lord.

---

14   1 Jn 4, 7-16

A reading from the first letter of John
As long as we love one another God will live in us.

Beloved,
let us love one another
because love is of God;
everyone who loves is begotten of God
and has knowledge of God.
The man without love has known nothing of
   God,
for God is love.
God's love was revealed in our midst in this
   way:
he sent his only Son to the world
that we might have life through him.
Love, then, consists in this:
not that we have loved God,
but that he has loved us
and has sent his Son as an offering for our
   sins.
Beloved,
if God has loved us so,
we must have the same love for one another.
No one has ever seen God.
Yet if we love one another
God dwells in us,
and his love is brought to perfection in us.
The way we know we remain in him
and he in us
is that he has given us of his Spirit.
We have seen for ourselves, and can testify,
that the Father has sent the Son as savior
   of the world.
When anyone acknowledges that Jesus is
   the Son of God,
God dwells in him
and he in God.

We have come to know and to believe in
the love God has for us.
This is the Word of the Lord.

---

15   Rv 3, 14. 20-22

A reading from the book of Revelation
I will share a meal side by side with him.

The Amen, the faithful Witness and true, the Source of God's creation, has this to say: "Here I stand, knocking at the door. If anyone hears me calling and opens the door, I will enter his house and have supper with him, and he with me. I will give the victor the right to sit with me on my throne, as I myself won the victory and took my seat beside my Father on his throne.

" 'Let him who has ears to hear heed the Spirit's word to the churches. "

This is the Word of the Lord.

---

16   Rv 22, 12-14. 16-17. 20

A reading from the book of Revelation
Come, Lord Jesus!

I, John, heard a voice saying to me: "Remember, I am coming soon! I bring with me the reward that will be given to each man as his conduct deserves. I am the Alpha and the Omega, the First and the Last, the Beginning and the End! Happy are they who wash their robes so as to have free access to the trees of life and enter the city through its gates!

"It is I, Jesus, who have sent my angel to give you this testimony about the churches. I am the Root and Offspring of David, the Morning Star shining bright."

The Spirit and the Bride say, "Come!" Let him who hears answer, "Come!" Let him who is thirsty come forward; let all who desire it accept the gift of life-giving water.

The One who gives this testimony says, "Yes, I am coming soon!" Amen! Come, Lord Jesus!

This is the Word of the Lord.

---

786   RESPONSORIAL PSALM

1   Ps 24, 1-2. 3-4. 5-6

℟. (6) Lord, this is the people that longs to see your face.

The Lord's are the earth and its fullness;
  the world and those who dwell in it.
For he founded it upon the seas
  and established it upon the rivers.

℟. Lord, this is the people that longs to see your face.

Who can ascend the mountain of the Lord?
  or who may stand in his holy place?
He whose hands are sinless, whose heart is clean,
  who desires not what is vain.

℟. Lord, this is the people that longs to see your face.

He shall receive a blessing from the Lord,
  a reward from God his savior.
Such is the race that seeks for him,
  that seeks the face of the God of Jacob.

℟. Lord, this is the people that longs to see your face.

2   Ps 27, 1. 4. 5. 8-9. 9. 11

℟. (8) I long to see your face, O Lord.

The Lord is my light and my salvation;
  whom should I fear?
The Lord is my life's refuge;
  of whom should I be afraid?

℟. I long to see your face, O Lord.

One thing I ask of the Lord;
  this I seek:
To dwell in the house of the Lord
  all the days of my life,
That I may gaze on the loveliness of the Lord
  and contemplate his temple.

℟. I long to see your face, O Lord.

For he will hide me in his abode
  in the day of trouble;
He will conceal me in the shelter of his tent,
  he will set me high upon a rock.

℟. I long to see your face, O Lord.

Your presence, O Lord, I seek.
  Hide not your face from me;
  do not in anger repel your servant.
You are my helper: cast me not off.

℟. I long to see your face, O Lord.
Forsake me not, O God my savior.
  Show me, O Lord, your way,
And lead me on a level path,
  because of my adversaries.

℟. I long to see your face, O Lord.

3   Ps 33, 2-3. 4-5. 11-12. 13-14. 18-19. 20-21

℟. (12) Happy the people the Lord has chosen to be his own.

Give thanks to the Lord on the harp;
  with the ten-stringed lyre chant his praises.
Sing to him a new song;
  pluck the strings skillfully, with shouts of gladness.

℟. Happy the people the Lord has chosen to be his own.

For upright is the word of the Lord,
  and all his works are trustworthy.
He loves justice and right;
  of the kindness of the Lord the earth is full.

℟. Happy the people the Lord has chosen to be his own.

But the plan of the Lord stands forever;
  the design of his heart, through all generations.
Happy the nation whose God is the Lord,
  the people he has chosen for his own inheritance.

℟. Happy the people the Lord has chosen to be his own.

From heaven the Lord looks down;
  he sees all mankind.
From his fixed throne he beholds
  all who dwell on the earth.

℟. Happy the people the Lord has chosen to be his own.

But see, the eyes of the Lord are upon those who fear him,
  upon those who hope for his kindness,
To deliver them from death
  and preserve them in spite of famine.

℟. Happy the people the Lord has chosen to be his own.

Our soul waits for the Lord,
  who is our help and our shield,
For in him our hearts rejoice;
  in his holy name we trust.

℟. Happy the people the Lord has chosen to be his own.

---

4   Ps 34, 2-3. 4-5. 6-7. 8-9

℟. (2) I will bless the Lord at all times.
I will bless the Lord at all times;
    his praise shall be ever in my mouth.
Let my soul glory in the Lord;
    the lowly will hear me and be glad.
℟. I will bless the Lord at all times.
Glorify the Lord with me,
    let us together extol his name.
I sought the Lord, and he answered me
    and delivered me from all my fears.
℟. I will bless the Lord at all times.
Look to him that you may be radiant with joy,
    and your faces may not blush with shame.
When the afflicted man called out, the Lord
    heard,
    and from all his distress he saved him.
℟. I will bless the Lord at all times.
The angel of the Lord encamps
    around those who fear him, and delivers
    them.
Taste and see how good the Lord is;
    happy the man who takes refuge in him.
℟. I will bless the Lord at all times.
℟. Or: (9) Taste and see the goodness of the Lord.

OR

                                         Ps 34, 10-11. 12-13. 14-15. 17. 19

℟. (2) I will bless the Lord at all times.
Fear the Lord, you his holy ones,
    for naught is lacking to those who fear him.
The great grow poor and hungry;
    but those who seek the Lord want for no
    good thing.
℟. I will bless the Lord at all times.
Come, children, hear me;
    I will teach you the fear of the Lord.
Which of you desires life,
    and takes delight in prosperous days?
℟. I will bless the Lord at all times.
Keep your tongue from evil
    and your lips from speaking guile;

Turn from evil, and do good;
    seek peace, and follow after it.
℟. I will bless the Lord at all times.
The Lord confronts the evildoers,
    to destroy remembrance of them from the
    earth.
The Lord is close to the brokenhearted;
    and those who are crushed in spirit he saves.
℟. I will bless the Lord at all times.
℟. Or: (9) Taste and see the goodness of the Lord.

---

5   Ps 40, 2. 4. 7-8. 8-9. 10. 12

℟. (8. 9) Here am I, Lord;
    I come to do your will.
I have waited, waited for the Lord,
    and he stooped toward me and heard my cry.
And he put a new song into my mouth,
    a hymn to our God.
℟. Here am I, Lord;
    I come to do your will.
Sacrifice or oblation you wished not,
    but ears open to obedience you gave me.
Holocausts or sin-offerings you sought not;
    then said I, "Behold I come."
℟. Here am I, Lord;
    I come to do your will.
"In the written scroll it is prescribed for me,
    To do your will, O my God, is my delight,
        and your law is within my heart!"
℟. Here am I, Lord;
    I come to do your will.
I announced your justice in the vast assembly;
    I did not restrain my lips, as you, O Lord,
    know.
℟. Here am I, Lord;
    I come to do your will.
Withhold not, O Lord, your compassion from
    me;
    may your kindness and your truth ever pre-
    serve me.
℟. Here am I, Lord;
    I come to do your will.

---

6   Ps 45, 11-12. 14-15. 16-17

℟. (Mt 25, 6) The bridegroom is here;
    let us go out to meet Christ the Lord.

Hear, O daughter, and see; turn your ear,
  forget your people and your father's house.
So shall the king desire your beauty;
  for he is your lord, and you must worship
  him.
℟. The bridegroom is here;
  let us go out to meet Christ the Lord.
All glorious is the king's daughter as she
  enters;
  her raiment is threaded with spun gold.
In embroidered apparel she is borne in to the
  king;
  behind her the virgins of her train are
  brought to you.
℟. The bridegroom is here;
  let us go out to meet Christ the Lord.
They are borne in with gladness and joy;
  they enter the palace of the king.
The place of your fathers your sons shall have;
  you shall make them princes through all the
  land.
℟. The bridegroom is here;
  let us go out to meet Christ the Lord.

7   Ps 63, 2. 3-4. 5-6. 8-9

℟. (2) My soul is thirsting for you, O Lord my
  God.
O God, you are my God whom I seek;
  for you my flesh pines and my soul thirsts
  like the earth, parched, lifeless and without
  water.
℟. My soul is thirsting for you, O Lord my
  God.
Thus have I gazed toward you in the sanctuary
  to see your power and your glory,
For your kindness is a greater good than life;
  my lips shall glorify you.
℟. My soul is thirsting for you, O Lord my
  God.
Thus will I bless you while I live;
  lifting up my hands, I will call upon your
  name.
As with the riches of a banquet shall my soul
  be satisfied,
  and with exultant lips my mouth shall praise
  you.
℟. My soul is thirsting for you, O Lord my
  God.

That you are my help,
  and in the shadow of your wings I shout for
  joy.
My soul clings fast to you;
  your right hand upholds me.
℟. My soul is thirsting for you, O Lord my
  God.

8   Ps 84, 3. 4. 5-6. 8. 11. 12

℟. (2) How lovely is your dwelling-place,
  Lord, mighty God!
My soul yearns and pines
  for the courts of the Lord.
My heart and my flesh
  cry out for the living God.
℟. How lovely is your dwelling-place,
  Lord, mighty God!
Even the sparrow finds a home,
  and the swallow a nest
  in which she puts her young—
Your altars, O Lord of hosts,
  my king and my God!
℟. How lovely is your dwelling-place,
  Lord, mighty God!
Happy they who dwell in your house!
  continually they praise you.
Happy the men whose strength you are!
  They go from strength to strength.
℟. How lovely is your dwelling-place,
  Lord, mighty God!
I had rather one day in your courts
  than a thousand elsewhere;
I had rather lie at the threshold of the house
  of my God
  than dwell in the tents of the wicked.
℟. How lovely is your dwelling-place,
  Lord, mighty God!
For a sun and a shield is the Lord God;
  grace and glory he bestows;
The Lord withholds no good thing
  from those who walk in sincerity.
℟. How lovely is your dwelling-place,
  Lord, mighty God!

9   Ps 100, 2. 3. 4. 5

℟. (2) Come with joy into the presence of the
    Lord.

Sing joyfully to the Lord, all you lands;
   serve the Lord with gladness;
   come before him with joyful song.

℟. Come with joy into the presence of the
    Lord.

Know that the Lord is God;
   he made us, his we are;
   his people, the flock he tends.

℟. Come with joy into the presence of the
    Lord.

Enter his gates with thanksgiving,
   his courts with praise.

Give thanks to him; bless his name.

℟. Come with joy into the presence of the
    Lord.

The Lord is good:
   the Lord, whose kindness endures forever,
   and his faithfulness, to all generations.

℟. Come with joy into the presence of the
    Lord.

---

787   **ALLELUIA VERSE AND**
            VERSE BEFORE THE GOSPEL

1   Ps 133, 1

See how good it is, how pleasant,
that brothers live in unity.

2   Mt 11, 25

Blessed are you, Father, Lord of heaven and
    earth;
you have revealed to little ones the mysteries
    of the kingdom.

3   Jn 13, 34

I give you a new commandment:
love one another as I have loved you.

4   Jn 15, 5

I am the vine and you are the branches, says
    the Lord:
he who lives in me, and I in him, will bear
    much fruit.

5   2 Cor 8, 9

Jesus Christ was rich but he became poor,
to make you rich out of his poverty.

6   Gal 6, 14

My only glory is the cross of our Lord Jesus
    Christ,
which crucifies the world to me and me to
    the world.

7   Phil 3, 8-9

I count all things worthless but this:
to gain Jesus Christ and to be found in him.

---

788   **GOSPEL**

1   Mt 11, 25-30

✠ **A reading from the holy gospel according**
            to Matthew

You have hidden these things from the learned and clever
and revealed them to children.

On one occasion Jesus said: "Father, Lord of
heaven and earth, to you I offer praise; for
what you have hidden from the learned and
the clever you have revealed to the merest
children. Father, it is true. You have graciously
willed it so. Everything has been given over to
me by my Father. No one knows the Son but
the Father, and no one knows the Father but
the Son—and anyone to whom the Son wishes
to reveal him.

"Come to me, all you who are weary and
find life burdensome, and I will refresh you.
Take my yoke upon your shoulders and learn
from me, for I am gentle and humble of heart.
Your souls will find rest, for my yoke is easy
and my burden light."

            This is the gospel of the Lord.

2   Mt 16, 24-27

✠ **A reading from the holy gospel according**
            to Matthew

Anyone who loses his life for my sake will find it.

Jesus said to his disciples: "If a man wishes
to come after me, he must deny his very self,
take up his cross, and begin to follow in my

footsteps. Whoever would save his life will lose it, but whoever loses his life for my sake will find it. What profit would a man show if he were to gain the whole world and ruin himself in the process? What can a man offer in exchange for his very self? The Son of Man will come with his Father's glory accompanied by his angels. When he does, he will repay each man according to his conduct."

This is the gospel of the Lord.

---

3   Mt 19, 3-12

✠ A reading from the holy gospel according to Matthew

There are some persons who choose to remain unmarried for the sake of the kingdom of heaven.

Some Pharisees came up to Jesus and said, to test him, "May a man divorce his wife for any reason whatever?" He replied, "Have you not read that at the beginning the Creator made them male and female and declared, 'For this reason a man shall leave his father and mother and cling to his wife, and the two shall become as one'? Thus they are no longer two but one flesh. Therefore, let no man separate what God has joined." They said to him, "Then why did Moses command divorce and the promulgation of a divorce decree?" "Because of your stubbornness Moses let you divorce your wives," he replied; "but at the beginning it was not that way. I now say to you, whoever divorces his wife (lewd conduct is a separate case) and marries another commits adultery, and the man who marries a divorced woman commits adultery."

His disciples said to him, "If that is the case between man and wife, it is better not to marry." He said, "Not everyone can accept this teaching, only those to whom it is given to do so. Some men are incapable of sexual activity from birth; some have been deliberately made so; and some there are who have freely renounced sex for the sake of God's reign. Let him accept this teaching who can."

This is the gospel of the Lord.

---

4   Mt 19, 16-26

✠ A reading from the holy gospel according to Matthew

If you wish to be perfect, go and sell everything you have and come follow me.

A man came up to Jesus and said, "Teacher, what good must I do to possess everlasting life?" He answered, "Why do you question me about what is good? There is One who is good. If you wish to enter into life, keep the commandments." "Which ones?" he asked. Jesus replied, " 'You shall not kill'; 'You shall not commit adultery'; 'You shall not steal'; 'You shall not bear false witness'; 'Honor your father and your mother'; and 'Love your neighbor as yourself.' " The young man said to him, "I have kept all these; what do I need to do further?" Jesus told him, "If you seek perfection, go, sell your possessions, and give to the poor. You will then have treasure in heaven. Afterward, come back and follow me." Hearing these words, the young man went away sad, for his possessions were many.

Jesus said to his disciples: "I assure you, only with difficulty will a rich man enter into the kingdom of God. I repeat what I said: it is easier for a camel to pass through a needle's eye than for a rich man to enter the kingdom of God." When the disciples heard this they were completely overwhelmed, and exclaimed, "Then who can be saved?" Jesus looked at them and said, "For man it is impossible; but for God all things are possible."

This is the gospel of the Lord.

---

5   Mt 25, 1-13

✠ A reading from the holy gospel according to Matthew

Look, the bridegroom is coming; go out and meet him.

Jesus told this parable to his disciples: "The reign of God can be likened to ten bridesmaids who took their torches and went out to welcome the groom. Five of them were foolish, while the other five were sensible. The foolish ones, in taking their torches, brought no oil along, but the sensible ones took flasks of oil as well as their torches. The groom delayed his coming, so they all began to nod, then to fall asleep. At midnight someone shouted, 'The groom is here! Come out and greet him!' At the outcry all the virgins woke up and got their torches ready. The foolish ones said to the sensible, 'Give us some of your oil. Our torches are going out.' But the sensible ones replied, 'No, there may not be enough for you and us. You had better go to the dealers and buy yourselves some.' While they went off to buy it the groom arrived, and the ones who were ready went in to the wedding with him. Then the door was barred. Later the other bridesmaids came back. 'Master, master!' they cried. 'Open the door for us.' But he answered, 'I tell you, I do not know you.' The moral is: keep your eyes open, for you know not the day or the hour."

This is the gospel of the Lord.

---

6   Mk 3, 31-35

✠ A reading from the holy gospel according to Mark

The man who does the will of God is my brother, my sister, and my mother.

Jesus' mother and his brothers arrived, and as they stood outside they sent word to him to come out. The crowd seated around him told him, "Your mother and your brothers and sisters are outside asking for you." He said in reply, "Who are my mother and my brothers?" And gazing around him at those seated in the circle he continued, "These are my mother and my brothers. Whoever does the will of God is brother and sister and mother to me."

This is the gospel of the Lord.

---

7   Mk 10, 24-30

✠ A reading from the holy gospel according to Mark

We have left everything and followed you.

Jesus said to his disciples: "My sons, how hard it is to enter the kingdom of God! It is easier for a camel to pass through a needle's eye than for a rich man to enter the kingdom of God."

They were completely overwhelmed at this, and exclaimed to one another, "Then who can be saved?" Jesus fixed his gaze on them and said, "For man it is impossible but not for God. With God all things are possible."

Peter was moved to say to him: "We have put aside everything to follow you!" Jesus answered: "I give you my word, there is no one who has given up home, brothers or sisters, mother or father, children or property, for me and for the gospel who will not receive in this present age a hundred times as many homes, brothers and sisters, mothers, children and property—and persecution besides—and in the age to come, everlasting life."

This is the gospel of the Lord.

---

8   Lk 9, 57-62

✠ A reading from the holy gospel according to Luke

Once the hand is laid on the plough, no one who looks back is fit for the kingdom of God.

As Jesus and his disciples were making their way along, someone said to him, "I will be your follower wherever you go." Jesus said to him, "The foxes have lairs, the birds of the sky have nests, but the Son of Man has nowhere to lay his head." To another he said, "Come after me." The man replied, "Let me bury my father first." Jesus said to him, "Let the dead bury their dead; come away and proclaim the kingdom of God." Yet another said to him, "I will be your follower, Lord, but first let me take leave of my people at home." Jesus answered him, "Whoever puts his hand to the plow but keeps looking back is unfit for the reign of God."

This is the gospel of the Lord.

---

9   Lk 10, 38-42

✠ A reading from the holy gospel according to Luke

Jesus accepts the hospitality of Martha and praises the attentiveness of Mary.

Jesus entered a village where a woman named Martha welcomed him to her home. She had a sister named Mary, who seated herself at the

Lord's feet and listened to his words. Martha, who was busy with all the details of hospitality, came to him and said, "Lord, are you not concerned that my sister has left me all alone to do the household tasks? Tell her to help me."

The Lord in reply said to her: "Martha, Martha, you are anxious and upset about many things; one thing only is required. Mary has chosen the better portion and she shall not be deprived of it."

This is the gospel of the Lord.

---

10   Lk 11, 27-28

✠ A reading from the holy gospel according to Luke

Happy are they who hear the word of God and keep it.

While Jesus was speaking to the crowd a woman from the crowd called out, "Blest is the womb that bore you and the breasts that nursed you!" "Rather," he replied, "blest are they who hear the word of God and keep it."

This is the gospel of the Lord.

---

11   Jn 12, 24-26

✠ A reading from the holy gospel according to John

If a grain of wheat falls on the ground and dies, it yields a rich harvest.

Jesus told his disciples:
"I solemnly assure you,
   unless the grain of wheat falls to the earth
      and dies,
   it remains just a grain of wheat.
But if it dies,
   it produces much fruit.
The man who loves his life
loses it,
while the man who hates his life in this
      world
preserves it to life eternal.
If anyone would serve me,
let him follow me;
where I am,
there will my servant be.
Anyone who serves me,

the Father will honor."
This is the gospel of the Lord.

---

12   Jn 15, 1-8

✠ A reading from the holy gospel according to John

Whoever remains in me, with me in him, bears fruit in plenty.

Jesus said to his disciples:
"I am the true vine
and my Father is the vinegrower.
He prunes away
every barren branch,
but the fruitful ones
he trims clean
to increase their yield.
You are clean already,
thanks to the word I have spoken to you.
Live on in me, as I do in you.
No more than a branch can bear fruit of
      itself
apart from the vine,
can you bear fruit
apart from me.
I am the vine, you are the branches.
He who lives in me and I in him,
will produce abundantly,
for apart from me you can do nothing.
A man who does not live in me
is like a withered, rejected branch,
picked up to be thrown in the fire and burnt.
If you live in me,
and my words stay part of you,
you may ask what you will—
it will be done for you.
My Father has been glorified
in your bearing much fruit
and becoming my disciples."
This is the gospel of the Lord.

---

13   Jn 15, 9-17

✠ A reading from the holy gospel according to John

You are my friends if you do what I command you.

Jesus said to his disciples:
"As the Father has loved me,

so I have loved you.
Live on in my love.
You will live in my love
if you keep my commandments,
even as I have kept my Father's commandments,
and live in his love.
All this I tell you
that my joy may be yours
and your joy may be complete.
This is my commandment:
love one another
as I have loved you.
There is no greater love than this:
to lay down one's life for one's friends.
You are my friends
if you do what I command you.
I no longer speak of you as slaves,
for a slave does not know what his master
   is about.
Instead, I call you friends,
since I have made known to you all that I
   heard from my Father.
It was not you who chose me,
it was I who chose you
to go forth and bear fruit.
Your fruit must endure,
so that all you ask the Father in my name
he will give you.
The command I give you is this:
that you love one another.''
    This is the gospel of the Lord.

---

14   Jn 17, 20-26

✠ **A reading from the holy gospel according
   to John**

I want those you have given me to be with me where I am.

Jesus looked up to heaven and prayed:
   "Holy Father,
   I do not pray for my disciples alone.
   I pray also for those who will believe in me
      through their word,
   that all may be one
   as you, Father, are in me, and I in you;
   I pray that they may be [one] in us,
   that the world may believe that you sent me.
   I have given them the glory you gave me

that they may be one, as we are one—
   I living in them, you living in me—
   that their unity may be complete.
So shall the world know that you sent me,
and that you loved them as you loved me.
Father,
   all those you gave me
   I would have in my company
   where I am,
   to see this glory of mine
   which is your gift to me,
   because of the love you bore me before the
      world began.
Just Father,
   the world has not known you,
   but I have known you;
   and these men have known that you sent me.
   To them I have revealed your name,
   and I will continue to reveal it
   so that your love for me may live in them,
   and I may live in them."
    This is the gospel of the Lord.

MASSES FOR THE DEAD

789   **OLD TESTAMENT READING**

1   Jb 19, 1. 23-27

A reading from the book of Job

I know that my redeemer lives.

Job answered and said:
Oh, would that my words were written down!
   Would that they were inscribed in a record:
That with an iron chisel and with lead
   they were cut in the rock forever!
But as for me, I know that my Vindicator lives,
   and that he will at last stand forth upon the
      dust;
Whom I myself shall see:
   my own eyes, not another's, shall behold
      him,
And from my flesh I shall see God;
   my inmost being is consumed with longing.
    This is the Word of the Lord.

---

2   Wis 3, 1-9 or 3, 1-6. 9

A reading from the book of Wisdom
He accepted them as a holocaust.

(Long Form)

The souls of the just are in the hand of God,
and no torment shall touch them.
They seemed, in the view of the foolish, to be
dead;
and their passing away was thought an affliction
and their going forth from us, utter destruction.
But they are in peace.
For if before men, indeed, they be punished,
yet is their hope full of immortality;
Chastised a little, they shall be greatly blessed,
because God tried them
and found them worthy of himself.
As gold in the furnace, he proved them,
and as sacrificial offerings he took them to
himself.
In the time of their visitation they shall shine,
and shall dart about as sparks through
stubble;
They shall judge nations and rule over peoples,
and the Lord shall be their King forever.
Those who trust in him shall understand truth,
and the faithful shall abide with him in love:
Because grace and mercy are with his holy
ones,
and his care is with his elect.
This is the Word of the Lord.

OR
(Short Form)

But the souls of the just are in the hand of God,
and no torment shall touch them.
They seemed, in the view of the foolish, to be
dead;
and their passing away was thought an affliction
and their going forth from us, utter destruction.
But they are in peace.
For if before men, indeed, they be punished,
yet is their hope full of immortality;

Chastised a little, they shall be greatly blessed,
because God tried them
and found them worthy of himself.
As gold in the furnace, he proved them,
and as sacrificial offerings he took them to
himself.
Those who trust in him shall understand truth,
and the faithful shall abide with him in love:
Because grace and mercy are with his holy
ones,
and his care is with his elect.
This is the Word of the Lord.

3   Wis 4, 7-14

A reading from the book of Wisdom
A blameless life is a ripe old age.

The just man, though he die early, shall be at
rest.
For the age that is honorable comes not with
the passing of time,
nor can it be measured in terms of years.
Rather, understanding is the hoary crown for
men,
and an unsullied life, the attainment of old
age.
He who pleased God was loved;
he who lived among sinners was trans-
ported—
Snatched away, lest wickedness pervert his
mind
or deceit beguile his soul;
For the witchery of paltry things obscures
what is right
and the whirl of desire transforms the innocent mind.
Having become perfect in a short while, he
reached the fullness of a long career;
for his soul was pleasing to the Lord,
therefore he sped him out of the midst of
wickedness.
But the people saw and did not understand,
nor did they take this into account.
This is the Word of the Lord.

4   Is 25, 6. 7-9

A reading from the book of the prophet Isaiah
The Lord God will destroy death forever.

On this mountain the Lord of hosts
  will provide for all peoples.
On this mountain he will destroy
  the veil that veils all peoples,
The web that is woven over all nations;
  he will destroy death forever.
The Lord God will wipe away
  the tears from all faces;
The reproach of his people he will remove
  from the whole earth; for the Lord has
  spoken.

On that day it will be said:
"Behold our God, to whom we looked to save
  us!
  This is the Lord for whom we looked;
  let us rejoice and be glad that he has saved
  us!"
              This is the Word of the Lord.

5   Lam 3, 17-26

A reading from the book of Lamentations
It is good to wait in silence for the Lord God to save.

My soul is deprived of peace,
  I have forgotten what happiness is;
I tell myself my future is lost,
  all that I hoped for from the Lord.
The thought of my homeless poverty
  is wormwood and gall;
Remembering it over and over
  leaves my soul downcast within me.
But I will call this to mind,
  as my reason to have hope:

The favors of the Lord are not exhausted,
  his mercies are not spent;
They are renewed each morning,
  so great is his faithfulness.
My portion is the Lord, says my soul;
  therefore will I hope in him.

Good is the Lord to one who waits for him,
  to the soul that seeks him;
It is good to hope in silence
  for the saving help of the Lord.
              This is the Word of the Lord.

6   Dn 12, 1-3

A reading from the book of the prophet Daniel
Of those who lie sleeping in the dust of the earth many will
awake.

[I, Daniel, mourned and I heard this word of
the Lord:]

"At that time there shall arise
  Michael, the great prince,
  guardian of your people;
It shall be a time unsurpassed in distress
  since nations began until that time.
At that time your people shall escape,
  everyone who is found written in the book.
Many of those who sleep
  in the dust of the earth shall awake;
Some shall live forever,
  others shall be an everlasting horror and
  disgrace.
But the wise shall shine brightly
  like the splendor of the firmament,
And those who lead the many to justice
  shall be like the stars forever."
              This is the Word of the Lord.

7   2 Mc 12, 43-46

A reading from the second book of Maccabees
It is good and holy to think of the dead rising again.

Judas [the ruler of Israel] then took up a
collection among all his soldiers, amounting to
two thousand silver drachmas, which he sent
to Jerusalem to provide for an expiatory sacrifice. In doing this he acted in a very excellent
and noble way, inasmuch as he had the resurrection of the dead in view; for if he were
not expecting the fallen to rise again, it would
have been useless and foolish to pray for them
in death. But if he did this with a view to the
splendid reward that awaits those who had
gone to rest in godliness, it was a holy and
pious thought. Thus he made atonement for the
dead that they might be freed from this sin.
              This is the Word of the Lord.

790   NEW TESTAMENT READING

1   Acts 10, 34-43 or 10, 34-36. 42-43

A reading from the Acts of the Apostles

God has appointed Jesus to judge everyone, alive and dead.

(Long Form)

Peter proceeded to address the people in these words: "I begin to see how true it is that God shows no partiality. Rather, the man of any nation who fears God and acts uprightly is acceptable to him. This is the message he has sent to the son of Israel, 'the good news of peace' proclaimed through Jesus Christ who is Lord of all. I take it you know what has been reported all over Judea about Jesus of Nazareth, beginning in Galilee with the baptism John preached; of the way God anointed him with the Holy Spirit and power. He went about doing good works and healing all who were in the grip of the devil, and God was with him. We are witnesses to all that he did in the land of the Jews and in Jerusalem. They killed him finally, 'hanging him on a tree,' only to have God raise him up on the third day and grant that he be seen, not by all, but only by such witnesses as had been chosen beforehand by God—by us who ate and drank with him after he rose from the dead. He commissioned us to preach to the people and to bear witness that he is the one set apart by God as judge of the living and the dead. To him all the prophets testify, saying that everyone who believes in him has forgiveness of sins through his name."

This is the Word of the Lord.

OR

(Short Form)

Peter proceeded to address the people in these words: "I begin to see how true it is that God shows no partiality. Rather, the man of any nation who fears God and acts uprightly is acceptable to him. This is the message he has sent to the sons of Israel, 'the good news of peace' proclaimed through Jesus Christ who is Lord of all. He commisioned us to preach to the people and to bear witness that he is the one set

apart by God as judge of the living and the dead. To him all the prophets testify, saying that eveyone who believes in him has forgiveness of sins through his name."

This is the Word of the Lord.

---

2   Rom 5, 5-11

A reading from the letter of Paul to the Romans

Having been justified by his blood, he will be saved from God's anger through him.

Hope will not leave us disappointed, because the love of God has been poured out in our hearts through the Holy Spirit who has been given to us. At the appointed time, when we were still powerless, Christ died for us godless men. It is rare that anyone should lay down his life for a just man, though it is barely possible that for a good man someone may have the courage to die. It is precisely in this that God proves his love for us: that while we were still sinners, Christ died for us. Now that we have been justified by his blood, it is all the more certain that we shall be saved by him from God's wrath. For if, when we were God's enemies, we were reconciled to him by the death of his Son, it is all the more certain that we who have been reconciled will be saved by his life. Not only that; we go so far as to make God our boast through our Lord Jesus Christ, through whom we have now received reconciliation.

This is the Word of the Lord.

---

3   Rom 5, 17-21

A reading from the letter of Paul to the Romans

However great the number of sins committed, grace was even greater.

If death began its reign through one man because of his offense, much more shall those who receive the overflowing grace and gift of justice live and reign through the one man, Jesus Christ.

To sum up, then: just as a single offense brought condemnation to all men, a single righteous act brought all men acquittal and life. Just as through one man's disobedience all became sinners, so through one man's obedience all shall become just.

The law came in order to increase offenses; but despite the increase of sin, grace has far surpassed it, so that, as sin reigned through death, grace may reign by way of justice leading to eternal life, through Jesus Christ our Lord.

This is the Word of the Lord.

---

4   Rom 6, 3-9 or 6, 3-4. 8-9

A reading from the letter of Paul to the Romans
Let us walk in the newness of life.

(Long Form)

Are you not aware that we who were baptized into Christ Jesus were baptized into his death? Through baptism into his death we were buried with him, so that, just as Christ was raised from the dead by the glory of the Father, we too might live a new life. If we have been united with him through likeness to his death, so shall we be through a like resurrection. This we know: our old self was crucified with him so that the sinful body might be destroyed and we might be slaves to sin no longer. A man who is dead has been freed from sin. If we have died with Christ, we believe that we are also to live with him. We know that Christ, once raised from the dead, will never die again; death has no more power over him.

This is the Word of the Lord.

OR

(Short Form)

Are you not aware that we who were baptized into Christ Jesus were baptized into his death? Through baptism into his death we were buried with him, so that, just as Christ was raised from the dead by the glory of the Father, we too might live a new life. If we have died with Christ, we believe that we are also to live with him. We know that Christ, once raised from the dead, will never die again; death has no more power over him.

This is the Word of the Lord.

---

5   Rom 8, 14-23

A reading from the letter of Paul to the Romans
We wait for our bodies to be set free.

All who are led by the Spirit of God are sons of God. You did not receive a spirit of slavery leading you back into fear, but a spirit of adoption through which we cry out, "Abba!" (that is, "Father"). The Spirit himself gives witness with our spirit that we are children of God. But if we are children, we are heirs as well: heirs of God, heirs with Christ, if only we suffer with him so as to be glorified with him.

I consider the sufferings of the present to be as nothing compared with the glory to be revealed in us. Indeed, the whole created world eagerly awaits the revelation of the sons of God. Creation was made subject to futility, not of its own accord but by him who once subjected it; yet not without hope, because the world itself will be freed from its slavery to corruption and share in the glorious freedom of the children of God. Yes, we know that all creation groans and is in agony even until now. Not only that, but we ourselves, although we have the Spirit as first fruits, groan inwardly while we await the redemption of our bodies.

This is the Word of the Lord.

---

6   Rom 8, 31-35. 37-39

A reading from the letter of Paul to the Romans
Nothing can really come between us and the love of Christ.

If God is for us, who can be against us? Is it possible that he who did not spare his own Son but handed him over for the sake of us all will not grant us all things besides? Who shall bring a charge against God's chosen ones? God, who justifies? Who shall condemn them? Christ Jesus, who died or rather was raised up, who is at the right hand of God and who intercedes for us?

Who will separate us from the love of Christ? Trial, or distress, or persecution, or hunger, or nakedness, or danger, or the sword? Yet in all this we are more than conquerors because of him who has loved us. For I am certain that neither death nor life, neither angels nor principalities, neither the present nor the future, nor powers, neither height nor depth nor any other creature, will be able to separate us from the love of God that comes to us in Christ Jesus, our Lord.

This is the Word of the Lord.

---

7   Rom 14, 7-9. 10-12

A reading from the letter of Paul to the Romans
Alive or dead, we belong to the Lord.

None of us lives as his own master and none of us dies as his own master. While we live we are responsible to the Lord, and when we die we die as his servants. Both in life and in death we are the Lord's. That is why Christ died and came to life again, that he might be Lord of both the dead and the living. We shall all have to appear before the judgment seat of God. It is written, "As surely as I live, says the Lord, every knee shall bend before me and every tongue shall give praise to God."

Every one of us will have to give an account of himself before God.

This is the Word of the Lord.

---

8   1 Cor 15, 20-24. 25-28

A reading from the first letter of Paul to the Corinthians
All men will be brought to life in Christ.

Christ has been raised from the dead, the first fruits of those who have fallen asleep. Death came through a man; hence the resurrection of the dead comes through a man also. Just as in Adam all die, so in Christ all will come to life again, but each one in proper order: Christ the first fruits and then, at his coming, all those who belong to him. After that will come the end, when, after having destroyed every sovereignty, authority, and power, he will hand over the kingdom to God the Father. Christ must reign until God has put all enemies under his feet, and the last enemy to be destroyed is death. Scripture reads that God "has placed all things under his feet." But when it says that everything has been made subject, it is clear that he who has made everything subject to Christ is excluded. When,

finally, all has been subjected to the Son, he will then subject himself to the One who made all things subject to him, so that God may be all in all.

This is the Word of the Lord.

---

9   1 Cor 15, 51-57

A reading from the first letter of Paul to the Corinthians
Death is swallowed up in victory.

I am going to tell you a mystery. Not all of us shall fall asleep, but all of us are to be changed —in an instant, in the twinkling of an eye, at the sound of the last trumpet. The trumpet will sound and the dead will be raised incorruptible, and we shall be changed. This corruptible body must be clothed with incorruptibility, this mortal body with immortality. When the corruptible frame takes on incorruptibility and the mortal immortality, then will the saying of Scripture be fulfilled: "Death is swallowed up in victory." "O death, where is your victory? O death, where is your sting?" The sting of death is sin, and sin gets its power from the law. But thanks be to God who has given us the victory through our Lord Jesus Christ.

This is the Word of the Lord.

---

10   2 Cor 5, 1. 6-10

A reading from the second letter of Paul to the Corinthians
We have an everlasting home in heaven.

We know that when the earthly tent in which we dwell is destroyed we have a dwelling provided for us by God, a dwelling in the heavens, not made by hands but to last forever.

Therefore we continue to be confident. We know that while we dwell in the body we are away from the Lord. We walk by faith, not by sight. I repeat, we are full of confidence and would much rather be away from the body and at home with the Lord. This being so, we make it our aim to please him whether we are with him or away from him. The lives of all of us are to be revealed before the tribunal of

Christ so that each one may receive his recompense, good or bad, according to his life in the body.

This is the Word of the Lord.

---

11   Phil 3, 20-21

A reading from the letter of Paul to the Philippians

Jesus will transfigure these wretched bodies of ours to be like his glorious body.

We have our citizenship in heaven; it is from there that we eagerly await the coming of our savior, the Lord Jesus Christ. He will give a new form to this lowly body of ours and remake it according to the pattern of his glorified body, by his power to subject everything to himself.

This is the Word of the Lord.

---

12   1 Thes 4, 13-18

A reading from the first letter of Paul to the Thessalonians

We shall stay with the Lord for ever.

We would have you be clear about those who sleep in death, brothers; otherwise you might yield to grief, like those who have no hope. For if we believe that Jesus died and rose, God will bring forth with him from the dead those also who have fallen asleep believing in him. We say to you, as if the Lord himself had said it, that we who live, who survive until his coming, will in no way have an advantage over those who have fallen asleep. No, the Lord himself will come down from heaven at the word of command, at the sound of the archangel's voice and God's trumpet; and those who have died in Christ will rise first. Then we, the living, the survivors, will be caught up with them in the clouds to meet the Lord in the air. Thenceforth we shall be with the Lord unceasingly. Console one another with this message.

This is the Word of the Lord.

---

13   2 Tm 2, 8-13

A reading from the second letter of Paul to Timothy

If we have died with him, then we shall live with him.

Remember that Jesus Christ, a descendant of David, was raised from the dead. This is the gospel I preach; in preaching it I suffer as a criminal, even to the point of being thrown into chains—but there is no chaining the word of God! Therefore I bear with all of this for the sake of those whom God has chosen, in order that they may obtain the salvation to be found in Christ Jesus and with it eternal glory.

You can depend on this:
If we have died with him
   we shall also live with him;
If we hold out to the end
   we shall also reign with him.
But if we deny him he will deny us. If we are unfaithful he will still remain faithful; for he cannot deny himself.

This is the Word of the Lord.

---

14   1 Jn 3, 1-2

A reading from the first letter of John

We shall see him as he really is.

See what love the Father has bestowed on us
in letting us be called children of God!
Yet that in fact is what we are.
The reason the world does not recognize us
is that it never recognized the Son.
Dearly beloved,
we are God's children now;
what we shall later be has not yet come to
   light.
We know that when it comes to light
we shall be like him,
for we shall see him as he is.

This is the Word of the Lord.

---

15   1 Jn 3, 14-16

A reading from the first letter of John

We have passed out of death and into life because we love the brothers.

That we have passed from death to life we know

because we love the brothers.
The man who does not love is among the living dead.
Anyone who hates his brother is a murderer, and you know that eternal life abides in no murderer's heart.
The way we came to understand love was that he laid down his life for us; we too must lay down our lives for our brothers.
This is the Word of the Lord.

---

16   Rv 14, 13

A reading from the book of Revelation

Happy are those who die in the Lord.

I, John, heard a voice from heaven say to me: "Write this down: Happy now are the dead who die in the Lord!" The Spirit added, "Yes, they shall find rest from their labors, for their good works accompany them."
This is the Word of the Lord.

---

17   Rv 20, 11—21, 1

A reading from the book of Revelation

The dead have been judged according to their works.

I, John, saw a large white throne and the One who sat on it. The earth and the sky fled from his presence until they could no longer be seen. I saw the dead, the great and the lowly, standing before the throne. Lastly, among the scrolls, the book of the living was opened. The dead were judged according to their conduct as recorded on the scrolls. The sea gave up its dead; then death and the nether world gave up their dead. Each person was judged according to his conduct. Then death and the nether world were hurled into the pool of fire which is the second death; anyone whose name was not found inscribed in the book of the living was hurled into this pool of fire.

Then I saw new heavens and a new earth. The former heavens and the former earth had passed away, and the sea was no longer there.
This is the Word of the Lord.

---

18   Rv 21, 1-5. 6-7

A reading from the book of Revelation

There will be no more death.

I, John, saw new heavens and a new earth. The former heavens and the former earth had passed away, and the sea was no longer. I also saw a new Jerusalem, the holy city, coming down out of heaven from God, beautiful as a bride prepared to meet her husband. I heard a loud voice from the throne cry out: "This is God's dwelling among men. He shall dwell with them and they shall be his people, and he shall be their God who is always with them. He shall wipe every tear from their eyes, and there shall be no more death or mourning, crying out or pain, for the former world has passed away."

The One who sat on the throne said to me, "See, I make all things new!" I am the Alpha and the Omega, the Beginning and the End. To anyone who thirsts I will give to drink without cost from the spring of life-giving water. He who wins the victory shall inherit these gifts; I will be his God and he shall be my son."
This is the Word of the Lord.

---

791   **RESPONSORIAL PSALM**

1   Ps 23, 1-3. 3-4. 5. 6.

℟. (1) The Lord is my shepherd; there is nothing I shall want.
The Lord is my shepherd; I shall not want.
    In verdant pastures he gives me repose;
Beside restful waters he leads me;
    he refreshes my soul.
℟. The Lord is my shepherd; there is nothing I shall want.
He guides me in right paths
    for his name's sake.
Even though I walk in the dark valley
    I fear no evil; for you are at my side
With your rod and your staff
    that give me courage.
℟. The Lord is my shepherd; there is nothing I shall want.
You spread the table before me
    in the sight of my foes;

You anoint my head with oil;
my cup overflows.
℞. The Lord is my shepherd;
there is nothing I shall want.
Only goodness and kindness follow me
all the days of my life;
And I shall dwell in the house of the Lord
for years to come.
℞. The Lord is my shepherd;
there is nothing I shall want.
℞. Or: (4) Though I walk in the valley of darkness,
I fear no evil, for you are with me.

---

2   Ps 25, 6-7. 17-18. 20-21
℞. (1) To you, O Lord, I lift my soul.
Remember that your compassion, O Lord,
and your kindness are from of old.
In your kindness remember me,
because of your goodness, O Lord.
℞. To you, O Lord, I lift my soul.
Relieve the troubles of my heart,
and bring me out of my distress.
Put an end to my affliction and my suffering,
and take away all my sins.
℞. To you, O Lord, I lift my soul.
Preserve my life, and rescue me;
let me not be put to shame, for I take refuge
in you.
Let integrity and uprightness preserve me,
because I wait for you, O Lord.
℞. To you, O Lord, I lift my soul.
℞. Or: (3) No one who waits for you, O Lord,
will ever be put to shame.

---

3   Ps 27, 1. 4. 7. 8. 9. 13-14
℞. (1) The Lord is my light and my salvation.
The Lord is my light and my salvation;
whom should I fear?
The Lord is my life's refuge;
of whom should I be afraid?
℞. The Lord is my light and my salvation.
One thing I ask of the Lord;
this I seek:

To dwell in the house of the Lord
all the days of my life,
That I may gaze on the loveliness of the Lord
and contemplate his temple.
℞. The Lord is my light and my salvation.
Hear, O Lord, the sound of my call;
have pity on me, and answer me.
Your presence, O Lord, I seek.
Hide not your face from me.
℞. The Lord is my light and my salvation.
I believe that I shall see the bounty of the Lord
in the land of the living.
Wait for the Lord with courage;
be stouthearted, and wait for the Lord.
℞. The Lord is my light and my salvation.
℞. Or: (13) I believe that I shall see the good
things of the Lord in the land of the living.

---

4   Pss 42, 2. 3. 5; 43, 3. 4. 5
℞. (Ps 42, 3) My soul is thirsting for the living
God:
when shall I see him face to face?
As the hind longs for the running waters,
so my soul longs for you, O God.
℞. My soul is thirsting for the living God:
when shall I see him face to face?
Athirst is my soul for God, the living God.
When shall I go and behold the face of God?
℞. My soul is thirsting for the living God:
when shall I see him face to face?
When I went with the throng
and led them in procession to the house of
God,
Amid loud cries of joy and thanksgiving,
with the multitude keeping festival.
℞. My soul is thirsting for the living God:
when shall I see him face to face?
Send forth your light and your fidelity;
they shall lead me on
And bring me to your holy mountain,
to your dwelling-place.
℞. My soul is thirsting for the living God:
when shall I see him face to face?
Then will I go in to the altar of God,
the God of my gladness and joy;
Then will I give you thanks upon the harp,
O God, my God!

℞. My soul is thirsting for the living God:
when shall I see him face to face?
Why are you so downcast, O my soul?
Why do you sigh within me?
Hope in God! For I shall again be thanking him,
in the presence of my savior and my God.
℞. My soul is thirsting for the living God:
when shall I see him face to face?

---

5   Ps 63, 2-3. 3-4. 5-6. 8-9

℞. (2) My soul is thirsting for you, O Lord my
God.
O God, you are my God whom I seek;
for you my flesh pines and my soul thirsts
like the earth, parched, lifeless and without
water.
℞. My soul is thirsting for you, O Lord my
God.
Thus have I gazed toward you in the sanctuary
to see your power and your glory.
For your kindness is a greater good than life;
my lips shall glorify you.
℞. My soul is thirsting for you, O Lord my
God.
Thus will I bless you while I live;
lifting up my hands, I will call upon your
name.
As with the riches of a banquet shall my soul
be satisfied,
and with exultant lips my mouth shall praise
you.
℞. My soul is thirsting for you, O Lord my
God.
You are my help,
and in the shadow of your wings I shout
for joy.
My soul clings fast to you;
your right hand upholds me.
℞. My soul is thirsting for you, O Lord my
God.

---

6   Ps 103, 8. 10. 13-14. 15-16. 17-18

℞. (8) The Lord is kind and merciful.
Merciful and gracious is the Lord,
slow to anger and abounding in kindness.
Not according to our sins does he deal with us,
nor does he requite us according to our
crimes.

℞. The Lord is kind and merciful.
As a father has compassion on his children,
so the Lord has compassion on those who
fear him,
For he knows how we are formed;
he remembers that we are dust.
℞. The Lord is kind and merciful.
Man's days are like those of grass;
like a flower of the field he blooms;
The wind sweeps over him and he is gone,
and his place knows him no more.
℞. The Lord is kind and merciful.
But the kindness of the Lord is from eternity
to eternity toward those who fear him,
And his justice toward children's children
among those who keep his covenant
and remember to fulfill his precepts.
℞. The Lord is kind and merciful.
℞. Or: (Ps 37, 39) The salvation of the just
comes from the Lord.

---

7   Pss 115, 5. 6; 116, 10-11. 15-16

℞. (Ps 115, 9) I will walk in the presence of
the Lord,
in the land of the living.
They have mouths but speak not;
they have eyes but see not;
They have ears but hear not;
they have noses but smell not.
℞. I will walk in the presence of the Lord,
in the land of the living.
I believed, even when I said,
"I am greatly afflicted";
I said in my alarm,
"No man is dependable."
℞. I will walk in the presence of the Lord,
in the land of the living.
Precious in the eyes of the Lord
is the death of his faithful ones.
O Lord, I am your servant;
you have loosed my bonds.
℞. I will walk in the presence of the Lord,
in the land of the living.
℞. Or: Alleluia.

---

8   Ps 122, 1-2. 3-4. 4-5. 6-7. 8-9

℞. (1) I rejoiced when I heard them say:
    let us go to the house of the Lord.
I rejoiced because they said to me,
    "We will go up to the house of the Lord."
And now we have set foot
    within your gates, O Jerusalem.
℞. I rejoiced when I heard them say:
    let us go to the house of the Lord.
Jerusalem, built as a city
    with compact unity.
To it the tribes go up,
    the tribes of the Lord.
℞. I rejoiced when I heard them say:
    let us go to the house of the Lord.
According to the decree for Israel,
    to give thanks to the name of the Lord.
In it are set up judgment seats,
    seats for the house of David.
℞. I rejoiced when I heard them say:
    let us go to the house of the Lord.
Pray for the peace of Jerusalem!
    May those who love you prosper!
May peace be within your walls,
    prosperity in your buildings.
℞. I rejoiced when I heard them say:
    let us go to the house of the Lord.
Because of my relatives and friends
    I will say, "Peace be within you!"
Because of the house of the Lord, our God,
    I will pray for your good.
℞. I rejoiced when I heard them say:
    let us go to the house of the Lord.
℞. Or: Let us go rejoicing to the house of the
    Lord.

---

9   Ps 130, 1-2. 3-4. 4-6. 7-8

℞. (1) Out of the depths, I cry to you, Lord.
Out of the depths I cry to you, O Lord;
    Lord, hear my voice!
Let your ears be attentive
    to my voice in supplication.
℞. Out of the depths, I cry to you, Lord.
If you, O Lord, mark iniquities,
    Lord, who can stand?
But with you is forgiveness,
    that you may be revered.

℞. Out of the depths, I cry to you, Lord.
I trust in the Lord;
    my soul trusts in his word.
My soul waits for the Lord
    more than sentinels wait for the dawn.
More than sentinels wait for the dawn,
    let Israel hope in the Lord.
℞. Out of the depths, I cry to you, Lord.
For with the Lord is kindness
    and with him is plenteous redemption;
And he will redeem Israel
    from all their iniquities.
℞. Out of the depths, I cry to you, Lord.
℞. Or: (5) I hope in the Lord,
    I trust in his word.

---

10   Ps 143, 1-2. 5-6. 7. 8. 10

℞. (1) O Lord, hear my prayer.
O Lord, hear my prayer;
    hearken to my pleading in your faithfulness;
    in your justice answer me.
And enter not into judgment with your ser-
    vant,
    for before you no living man is just.
℞. O Lord, hear my prayer.
I remember the days of old;
    I meditate on all your doings,
    the works of your hands I ponder.
I stretch out my hands to you;
    my soul thirsts for you like parched land.
℞. O Lord, hear my prayer.
Hasten to answer me, O Lord,
    for my spirit fails me.
At dawn let me hear of your kindness,
    for in you I trust.
℞. O Lord, hear my prayer.
Teach me to do your will,
    for you are my God.
May your good spirit guide me
    on level ground.
℞. O Lord, hear my prayer.

792 **ALLELUIA VERSE AND VERSE BEFORE THE GOSPEL**

1   Mt 11, 25

Blessed are you, Father, Lord of heaven and earth;
you have revealed to little ones the mysteries of the kingdom.

2   Mt 25, 34

Come, you whom my Father has blessed, says the Lord;
inherit the kingdom prepared for you since the foundation of the world.

3   Jn 3, 16

God loved the world so much, he gave us his only Son,
that all who believe in him might have eternal life.

4   Jn 6, 39

This is the will of my Father, says the Lord,
that I should lose nothing of all that he has given to me,
and that I should raise it up on the last day.

5   Jn 6, 40

This is the will of my Father, says the Lord,
all who believe in the Son will have eternal life
and I will raise them to life again on the last day.

6   Jn 11, 25. 26

I am the resurrection and the life, said the Lord:
he who believes in me will not die for ever.

7   Phil 3, 20

Our true home is in heaven,
and Jesus Christ whose return we long for will come from heaven to save us.

8   2 Tm 2, 11-12

If we die with Christ, we shall live with him,
and if we are faithful to the end, we shall reign with him.

9   Rv 1, 5-6

Jesus Christ is the firstborn of the dead;
glory and kingship be his for ever and ever. Amen.

10   Rv 14, 13

Happy are those who have died in the Lord;
let them rest from their labors for their good deeds go with them.

---

793   **GOSPEL**

1   Mt 5, 1-12

✠ A reading from the holy gospel according to Matthew

Rejoice and be glad, for your reward will be great in heaven.

When Jesus saw the crowds he went up on the mountainside. After he had sat down his disciples gathered around him, and he began to teach them:

"How blest are the poor in spirit: the reign of God is theirs.

Blest too are the sorrowing; they shall be consoled.

[Blest are the lowly; they shall inherit the land.]

Blest are they who hunger and thirst for holiness;
they shall have their fill.

Blest are they who show mercy; mercy shall be theirs.

Blest are the single-hearted,
for they shall see God.

Blest too the peacemakers; they shall be called sons of God.

Blest are those persecuted for holiness' sake; the reign of God is theirs.

Blest are you when they insult you and persecute you and utter every kind of slander against you because of me.

Be glad and rejoice, for your reward in heaven is great."

This is the gospel of the Lord.

---

2   Mt 11, 25-30

✠ A reading from the holy gospel according
to Matthew

*You have hidden these things from the learned and have
revealed them to children.*

On one occasion Jesus said: "Father, Lord
of heaven and earth, to you I offer praise; for
what you have hidden from the learned and
the clever you have revealed to the merest
children. Father, it is true. You have graciously
willed it so. Everything has been given over to
me by my Father. No one knows the Son but
the Father, and no one knows the Father but
the Son—and anyone to whom the Son wishes
to reveal him.

"Come to me, all you who are weary and find
life burdensome, and I will refresh you. Take
my yoke upon your shoulders and learn from
me, for I am gentle and humble of heart. Your
souls will find rest, for my yoke is easy and my
burden light."

This is the gospel of the Lord.

3   Mt 25, 1-13

✠ A reading from the holy gospel according
to Matthew

Look, the bridegroom is coming; go out and meet him.

Jesus told his disciples this parable: "The reign
of God can be likened to ten bridesmaids who
took their torches and went out to welcome
the groom. Five of them were foolish, while the
other five were sensible. The foolish ones, in
taking their torches, brought no oil along, but
the sensible ones took flasks of oil as well as
their torches. The groom delayed his coming,
so they all began to nod, then to fall asleep. At
midnight someone shouted, 'The groom is here!
Come out and greet him!' At the outcry all
the virgins woke up and got their torches
ready. The foolish ones said to the sensible,
'Give us some of your oil. Our torches are going
out.' But the sensible ones replied, 'No, there
may not be enough for you and us. You had
better go to the dealers and buy yourselves
some.' While they went off to buy it the groom
arrived, and the ones who were ready went in
to the wedding with him. Then the door was

barred. Later the other bridesmaids came back.
'Master, master!' they cried. 'Open the door
for us.' But he answered, 'I tell you, I do not
know you.' The moral is: keep your eyes open,
for you know not the day or the hour."

This is the gospel of the Lord.

4   Mt 25, 31-46

✠ A reading from the holy gospel according
to Matthew

Come, you whom my Father has blessed.

Jesus said to his disciples: "When the Son of
Man comes in his glory, escorted by all the angels of heaven, he will sit upon his royal throne,
and all the nations will be assembled before
him. Then he will separate them into two
groups, as a shepherd separates sheep from
goats. The sheep he will place on his right
hand, the goats on his left. The king will say to
those on his right: 'Come. You have my
Father's blessing! Inherit the kingdom prepared for you from the creation of the world.
For I was hungry and you gave me food, I
was thirsty and you gave me drink. I was a
stranger and you welcomed me, naked and
you clothed me. I was ill and you comforted
me, in prison and you came to visit me.' Then
the just will ask him: 'Lord, when did we see
you hungry and feed you or see you thirsty
and give you drink? When did we welcome you
away from home or clothe you in your nakedness? When did we visit you when you were
ill or in prison?' The king will answer them:
'I assure you, as often as you did it for one of
my least brothers, you did it for me.'

"Then he will say to those on his left: 'Out
of my sight, you condemned, into that everlasting fire prepared for the devil and his
angels! I was hungry and you gave me no food,
I was thirsty and you gave me no drink. I was
away from home and you gave me no welcome, naked and you gave me no clothing. I
was ill and in prison and you did not come to
comfort me.' Then they in turn will ask: 'Lord,
when did we see you hungry or thirsty or away
from home or naked or ill or in prison and not
attend you in your needs?' He will answer

them: 'I assure you, as often as you neglected to do it to one of these least ones, you neglected to do it to me.' These will go off to eternal punishment and the just to eternal life."
This is the gospel of the Lord.

---

5   Mk 15, 33-39; 16, 1-6 or 15, 33-39

✠ A reading from the holy gospel according to Mark
Jesus gave a loud cry and breathed his last.

(Long Form)

When noon came, darkness fell on the whole countryside and lasted until midafternoon. At that time Jesus cried in a loud voice, "Eloi, Eloi, lama sabachthani?" which means, "My God, my God, why have you forsaken me?" A few of the bystanders who heard it remarked, "Listen! He is calling on Elijah!" Someone ran off, and soaking a sponge in sour wine, stuck it on a reed to try to make him drink. The man said, "Now let's see whether Elijah comes to take him down."

Then Jesus, uttering a loud cry, breathed his last. At that moment the curtain in the sanctuary was torn in two from top to bottom. The centurion who stood guard over him, on seeing the manner of his death, declared, "Clearly this man was the Son of God!"

When the sabbath was over, Mary Magdalene, Mary the mother of James, and Salome brought perfumed oils with which they intended to go and anoint Jesus. Very early, just after sunrise on the first day of the week, they came to the tomb. They were saying to one another, "Who will roll back the stone for us from the entrance to the tomb?" When they looked, they found that the stone had been rolled back. (It was a huge one.) On entering the tomb they saw a young man sitting at the right, dressed in a white robe. This frightened them thoroughly, but he reassured them: "You need not be amazed! You are looking for Jesus of Nazareth, the one who was crucified. He has been raised up; he is not here. See the place where they laid him."
This is the gospel of the Lord.

OR
(Short Form)

When noon came, darkness fell on the whole countryside and lasted until midafternoon. At that time Jesus cried in a loud voice, "Eloi, Eloi, lama sabachthani?" which means, "My God, my God, why have you forsaken me?" A few of the bystanders who heard it remarked, "Listen! He is calling on Elijah!" Someone ran off, and soaking a sponge in sour wine, stuck it on a reed to try to make him drink. The man said, "Now let's see whether Elijah comes to take him down."

Then Jesus, uttering a loud cry, breathed his last. At that moment the curtain in the sanctuary was torn in two from top to bottom. The centurion who stood guard over him, on seeing the manner of his death, declared, "Clearly this man was the Son of God!"
This is the gospel of the Lord.

---

6   Lk 7, 11-17

✠ A reading from the holy gospel according to Luke
Young man, I say to you, get up.

Jesus went to a town called Naim, and his disciples and a large crowd accompanied him. As he approached the gate of the town, a dead man was being carried out, the only son of a widowed mother. A considerable crowd of townsfolk were with her. The Lord was moved with pity upon seeing her and said to her, "Do not cry." Then he stepped forward and touched the litter; at this, the bearers halted. He said, "Young man, I bid you get up." The dead man sat up and began to speak. Then Jesus gave him back to his mother. Fear seized them all and they began to praise God. "A great prophet has risen among us," they said; and, "God has visited his people." This was the report that spread about him throughout Judea and the surrounding country.
This is the gospel of the Lord.

---

7   Lk 12, 35-40

✠ **A reading from the holy gospel according to Luke**

Be like men waiting for the arrival of their master.

Jesus told his disciples: "Let your belts be fastened around your waists and your lamps be burning ready. Be like men awaiting their master's return from a wedding, so that when he arrives and knocks, you will open for him without delay. It will go well with those servants whom the master finds wide-awake on his return. I tell you, he will put on an apron, seat them at table, and proceed to wait on them. Should he happen to come at midnight or before sunrise and find them prepared, it will go well with them. You know as well as I that if the head of the house knew when the thief was coming he would not let him break into his house. Be on guard, therefore. The Son of Man will come when you least expect him." This is the gospel of the Lord.

---

8   Lk 23, 33. 39-43

✠ **A reading from the holy gospel according to Luke**

Today you will be with me in paradise.

When Jesus and the others came to Skull Place, as it was called, they crucified him there and the criminals as well, one on his right and the other on his left. One of the criminals hanging in crucifixion blasphemed him: "Aren't you the Messiah? Then save yourself and us." But the other one rebuked him: "Have you no fear of God, seeing you are under the same sentence? We deserve it, after all. We are only paying the price for what we've done, but this man has done nothing wrong." He then said, "Jesus, remember me when you enter upon your reign." And Jesus replied, "I assure you: this day you will be with me in paradise." This is the gospel of the Lord.

---

9   Lk 23, 44-49; 24, 1-6 or 23, 44-49

✠ **A reading from the holy gospel according to Luke**

Father, into your hands I commit my spirit.

(Long Form)

It was around midday, and darkness came over the whole land until midafternoon with an eclipse of the sun. The curtain in the sanctuary was torn in two. Jesus uttered a loud cry and said,
"Father, into your hands I commend my spirit."
After he had said this, he expired. The centurion, upon seeing what had happened, gave glory to God by saying, "Surely this was an innocent man." After the crowd assembled for this spectacle witnessed what had happened, they returned beating their breasts. All his friends and the women who had accompanied him from Galilee were standing at a distance watching everything.

On the first day of the week, at dawn, the women came to the tomb bringing the spices they had prepared. They found the stone rolled back from the tomb; but when they entered the tomb, they did not find the body of the Lord Jesus. While they were still at a loss over what to think of this, two men in dazzling garments stood beside them. Terrified, the women bowed to the ground. The men said to them: "Why do you search for the Living One among the dead? He is not here; he has been raised up."
This is the gospel of the Lord.

OR
(Short Form)

It was around midday, and darkness came over the whole land until midafternoon with an eclipse of the sun. The curtain in the sanctuary was torn in two. Jesus uttered a loud cry and said,
"Father, into your hands I commend my spirit."
After he had said this, he expired. The centurion, upon seeing what had happened, gave glory to God by saying, "Surely this was an innocent

man." After the crowd assembled for this spectacle witnessed what had happened, they returned beating their breasts. All his friends and the women who had accompanied him from Galilee were standing at a distance watching everything.

This is the gospel of the Lord.

---

10   Lk 24, 13-35 or 24, 13-16. 28-35

✠ A reading from the holy gospel according to Luke

Was it not necessary that the Christ should suffer and so enter into his glory?

(Long Form)

Two of the disciples of Jesus on that same day [the first day of the week] were making their way to a village named Emmaus seven miles distant from Jerusalem, discussing as they went all that had happened. In the course of their lively exchange, Jesus approached and began to walk along with them. However, they were restrained from recognizing him. He said to them, "What are you discussing as you go your way?" They halted in distress and one of them, Cleopas by name, asked him, "Are you the only resident of Jerusalem who does not know the things that went on there these past few days?" He said to them, "What things?" They said: "All those that had to do with Jesus of Nazareth, a prophet powerful in word and deed in the eyes of God and all the people; how our chief priests and leaders delivered him up to be condemned to death, and crucified him. We were hoping that he was the one who would set Israel free. Besides all this, today, the third day since these things happened, some women of our group have just brought us some astonishing news. They were at the tomb before dawn and failed to find his body, but returned with the tale that they had seen a vision of angels who declared he was alive. Some of our number went to the tomb and found it to be just as the women said; but him they did not see."

Then he said to them, "What little sense you have! How slow you are to believe all that the prophets have announced! Did not the Messiah have to undergo all this so as to enter into his glory?" Beginning, then, with Moses and all the prophets, he interpreted for them every passage of Scripture which referred to him. By now they were near the village to which they were going, and he acted as if he were going farther. But they pressed him: "Stay with us. It is nearly evening—the day is practically over." So he went in to stay with them.

When he had seated himself with them to eat, he took bread, pronounced the blessing, then broke the bread and began to distribute it to them. With that their eyes were opened and they recognized him; whereupon he vanished from their sight. They said to one another, "Were not our hearts burning inside us as he talked to us on the road and explained the Scriptures to us?" They got up immediately and returned to Jerusalem, where they found the Eleven and the rest of the company assembled. They were greeted with, "The Lord has been raised! It is true! He has appeared to Simon." Then they recounted what had happened on the road and how they had come to know him in the breaking of bread.

This is the gospel of the Lord.

OR
(Short Form)

Two of the disciples of Jesus on that same day [the first day of the week] were making their way to a village named Emmaus seven miles distant from Jerusalem, discussing as they went all that had happened. In the course of their lively exchange, Jesus approached and began to walk along with them. However, they were restrained from recognizing him.

By now they were near the village to which they were going, and he acted as if he were going farther. But they pressed him: "Stay with us. It is nearly evening—the day is practically over." So he went in to stay with them.

When he had seated himself with them to eat, he took bread, pronounced the blessing, then broke the bread and began to distribute it to them. With that their eyes were opened and they recognized him; whereupon he vanished from their sight. They said to one another,

"Were not our hearts burning inside us as he talked to us on the road and explained the Scriptures to us?" They got up immediately and returned to Jerusalem, where they found the Eleven and the rest of the company assembled. They were greeted with, "The Lord has been raised! It is true! He has appeared to Simon." Then they recounted what had happened on the road and how they had come to know him in the breaking of bread.
　　　This is the gospel of the Lord.

11　　　　　　　　　　　　　　　　　　　　　　Jn 6, 37-40

✠ A reading from the holy gospel according to John

Whoever believes in Jesus has eternal life and I will raise him up on the last day.

Jesus said to the crowd:
　"All that the Father gives me shall come to me;
　no one who comes will I ever reject,
　because it is not to do my own will
　that I have come down from heaven,
　but to do the will of him who sent me.
　It is the will of him who sent me
　that I should lose nothing of what he has given me;
　rather, that I should raise it up on the last day.
　Indeed, this is the will of my Father,
　that everyone who looks upon the Son
　and believes in him
　shall have eternal life.
　Him I will raise up on the last day."
　　　This is the gospel of the Lord.

12　　　　　　　　　　　　　　　　　　　　　　Jn 6, 51-58

✠ A reading from the holy gospel according to John

Anyone who eats this bread will live for ever; and I will raise him up on the last day.

Jesus told the crowd:
　"I myself am the living bread
　come down from heaven.
　If anyone eats this bread
　he shall live forever;
　the bread I will give
　is my flesh, for the life of the world."

At this the Jews quarreled among themselves, saying, "How can he give us his flesh to eat?" Thereupon Jesus said to them:
　"Let me solemnly assure you,
　if you do not eat the flesh of the Son of Man
　and drink his blood,
　you have no life in you.
　He who feeds on my flesh
　and drinks my blood
　has life eternal,
　and I will raise him up on the last day.
　For my flesh is real food
　and my blood real drink.
　The man who feeds on my flesh
　and drinks my blood
　remains in me, and I in him.
　Just as the Father who has life sent me
　and I have life because of the Father,
　so the man who feeds on me
　will have life because of me.
　This is the bread that came down from heaven.
　Unlike your ancestors who ate and died nonetheless,
　the man who feeds on this bread shall live forever."
　　　This is the gospel of the Lord.

13　　　　　　　　　　　　Jn 11, 17-27 or 11, 21-27

✠ A reading from the holy gospel according to John

I am the resurrection and the life.

(Long Form)

When Jesus arrived at Bethany, he found that Lazarus had already been in the tomb four days. The village was not far from Jerusalem— just under two miles—and many Jewish people had come out to console Martha and Mary over their brother. When Martha heard that Jesus was coming she went to meet him, while Mary sat at home. Martha said to Jesus, "Lord, if you had been here, my brother would never have died. Even now, I am sure that God will give you whatever you ask of him." "Your brother will rise again," Jesus assured her. "I know he will rise again," Martha replied, "in the resurrection on the last day." Jesus told her:

> "I am the resurrection and the life:
> whoever believes in me,
> though he should die, will come to life;
> and whoever is alive and believes in me
> will never die.

Do you believe this?" "Yes, Lord," she replied. "I have come to believe that you are the Messiah, the Son of God: he who is to come into the world."

> This is the gospel of the Lord.

OR
(Short Form)

Martha said to Jesus, "Lord, if you had been here, my brother would never have died. Even now, I am sure that God will give you whatever you ask of him." "Your brother will rise again," Jesus assured her. "I know he will rise again," Martha replied, "in the resurrection on the last day." Jesus told her:

> "I am the resurrection and the life:
> whoever believes in me,
> though he should die, will come to life;
> and whoever is alive and believes in me
> will never die.

Do you believe this?" "Yes, Lord," she replied. "I have come to believe that you are the Messiah, the Son of God: he who is to come into the world."

> This is the gospel of the Lord.

---

14   Jn 11, 32-45

✠ A reading from the holy gospel according to John

Lazarus, come out.

When Mary the sister of Lazarus came to the place where Jesus was, seeing him, she fell at his feet and said to him, "Lord, if you had been here my brother would never have died." When Jesus saw her weeping, and the Jewish folk who had accompanied her also weeping, he was troubled in spirit, moved by the deepest emotions. "Where have you laid him?" he asked. "Lord, come and see," they said. Jesus began to weep, which caused the Jews to remark, "See how much he loved him!" But

some said, "He opened the eyes of that blind man. Why could he not have done something to stop this man from dying?" Once again troubled in spirit, Jesus approached the tomb. It was a cave with a stone laid across it. "Take away the stone," Jesus directed. Martha, the dead man's sister, said to him, "Lord, it has been four days now; surely there will be a stench!" Jesus replied, "Did I not assure you that if you believed you would see the glory of God?" They then took away the stone and Jesus looked upward and said:

> "Father, I thank you for having heard me.
> I know that you always hear me
> but I have said this for the sake of the
>   crowd,
> that they may believe that you sent me."

Having said this, he called loudly, "Lazarus, come out!" The dead man came out, bound hand and foot with linen strips, his face wrapped in a cloth. "Untie him," Jesus told them, "and let him go free."

This caused many of the Jews who had come to visit Mary, and had seen what Jesus did, to put their faith in him.

> This is the gospel of the Lord.

---

15   Jn 12, 23-28 or 12, 23-26

✠ A reading from the holy gospel according to John

If a grain of wheat falls on the ground and dies, it yields a rich harvest.

(Long Form)

Jesus told his disciples:

> "The hour has come
> for the Son of Man to be glorified.
> I solemnly assure you,
> unless the grain of wheat falls to the earth
>   and dies,
> it remains just a grain of wheat.
> But if it dies,
> it produces much fruit.
> The man who loves his life
> loses it,
> while the man who hates his life in this
>   world
> preserves it to life eternal.

If anyone would serve me,
let him follow me;
where I am,
there will my servant be.
Anyone who serves me,
the Father will honor.
My soul is troubled now,
yet what should I say—
Father, save me from this hour?
But it was for this that I came to this hour.
Father, glorify your name!"

Then a voice came from the sky:
"I have glorified it,
and will glorify it again."
This is the gospel of the Lord.

OR
(Short Form)

Jesus told his disciples:
"The hour has come
for the Son of Man to be glorified.
I solemnly assure you,
unless the grain of wheat falls to the earth
and dies,
it remains just a grain of wheat.
But if it dies,
it produces much fruit.
The man who loves his life
loses it,
while the man who hates his life in this
world
preserves it to life eternal.
If anyone would serve me,
let him follow me;
where I am,
there will my servant be.
Anyone who serves me,
the Father will honor."
This is the gospel of the Lord.

16   Jn 14, 1-6

✠ A reading from the holy gospel according
to John

There are many rooms in my Father's house.

Jesus said to his disciples:
"Do not let your hearts be troubled.
Have faith in God
and faith in me.

In my Father's house there are many dwelling places;
otherwise, how could I have told you
that I was going to prepare a place for you?
I am indeed going to prepare a place for you,
and then I shall come back to take you with
me,
that where I am you also may be.
You know the way that leads where I go."
"Lord," said Thomas, "we do not know
where you are going. How can we know the
way?" Jesus told him:
"I am the way, and the truth, and the life;
no one comes to the Father but through me."
This is the gospel of the Lord.

17   Jn 17, 24-26

✠ A reading from the holy gospel according
to John

Father, I want those you have given me to be with me
where I am.

Raising his eyes to heaven, Jesus prayed and
said:
"Father,
all those you gave me
I would have in my company
where I am,
to see this glory of mine
which is your gift to me,
because of the love you bore me before the
world began.
Just Father,
the world has not known you,
but I have known you;
and these men have known that you sent me.
To them I have revealed your name,
and I will continue to reveal it
so that your love for me may live in them,
and I may live in them."
This is the gospel of the Lord.

BURIAL OF BAPTIZED CHILDREN

794 OLD TESTAMENT READING

1   Is 25, 6. 7-9

A reading from the book of the prophet Isaiah
The Lord God will destroy death for ever.

On this mountain the Lord of hosts
   will provide for all peoples
   a feast of rich foods.
On this mountain he will destroy
   the veil that veils all peoples,
The web that is woven over all nations;
   he will destroy death forever.
The Lord God will wipe away
   the tears from all faces;
The reproach of his people he will remove
   from the whole earth; for the Lord has
   spoken.

On that day it will be said:
"Behold our God, to whom we looked to save
   us!
   This is the Lord for whom we looked;
   let us rejoice and be glad that he has saved
   us!"
        This is the Word of the Lord.

---

2   Lam 3, 17-26

A reading from the book of Lamentations
It is good to wait in silence for the Lord God to save.

My soul is deprived of peace,
   I have forgotten what happiness is;
I tell myself my future is lost,
   all that I hoped for from the Lord.
The thought of my homeless poverty
   is wormwood and gall;
Remembering it over and over
   leaves my soul downcast within me.
But I will call this to mind,
   as my reason to have hope:

The favors of the Lord are not exhausted,
   his mercies are not spent;
They are renewed each morning,
   so great is his faithfulness.

My portion is the Lord, says my soul;
   therefore will I hope in him.

Good is the Lord to one who waits for him,
   to the soul that seeks him;
It is good to hope in silence
   for the saving help of the Lord.
        This is the Word of the Lord.

---

795 NEW TESTAMENT READING

1   Rom 6, 3-4. 8-9

A reading from the letter of Paul to the Romans
We believe that we shall return to life with Christ.

Are you not aware that we who were baptized
into Christ Jesus were baptized into his death?
Through baptism into his death we were buried
with him, so that, just as Christ was raised
from the dead by the glory of the Father, we
too might live a new life. If we have died with
Christ, we believe that we are also to live with
him. We know that Christ, once raised from
the dead, will never die again; death has no
more power over him.
        This is the Word of the Lord.

---

2   Rom 14, 7-9

A reading from the letter of Paul to the Romans
Alive or dead we belong to the Lord.

None of us lives as his own master and none of
us dies as his own master. While we live we are
responsible to the Lord, and when we die we
die as his servants. Both in life and in death we
are the Lord's. That is why Christ died and
came to life again, that he might be Lord of
both the dead and the living.
        This is the Word of the Lord.

---

3   1 Cor 15, 20-23

**A reading from the first letter of Paul to the
Corinthians**
All men will be brought to life in Christ.

Christ has been raised from the dead, the first
fruits of those who have fallen asleep. Death
came through a man; hence the resurrection of

the dead comes through a man also. Just as in Adam all die, so in Christ all will come to life again, but each one in proper order: Christ the first fruits and then, at his coming, all those who belong to him.
This is the Word of the Lord.

---

4   Eph 1, 3-5

A reading from the letter of Paul to the Ephesians

The Father chose us in Christ, before the creation of the world to be holy.

Praised be the God and Father of our Lord Jesus Christ, who has bestowed on us in Christ every spiritual blessing in the heavens! God chose us in him before the world began, to be holy and blameless in his sight, to be full of love; he likewise predestined us through Christ Jesus to be his adopted sons—such was his will and pleasure.
This is the Word of the Lord.

---

5   1 Thes 4, 13-14. 18

A reading from the first letter of Paul to the Thessalonians

We shall stay with the Lord for ever.

We would have you be clear about those who sleep in death, brothers; otherwise you might yield to grief, like those who have no hope. For if we believe that Jesus died and rose, God will bring forth with him from the dead those also who have fallen asleep believing in him. Console one another with this message.
This is the Word of the Lord.

---

6   Rv 7, 9-10. 15-17

A reading from the book of Revelation

God will wipe away all tears from their eyes.

I, John, saw before me a huge crowd which no one could count from every nation and race, people and tongue. They stood before the throne and the Lamb, dressed in long white robes and holding palm branches in their hands. They cried out in a loud voice, "Salvation is from our God, who is seated on the throne, and from the Lamb!"

"It was this that brought them before God's throne:
  day and night they minister to him in his temple;
he who sits on the throne will give them shelter.
Never again shall they know hunger or thirst,
  nor shall the sun or its heat beat down on them,
  for the Lamb on the throne will shepherd them.
He will lead them to springs of life-giving water,
  and God will wipe every tear from their eyes."
This is the Word of the Lord.

---

7   Rv 21, 1. 3-5

A reading from the book of Revelation

There will be no more death.

I, John, saw new heavens and a new earth. I heard a loud voice from the throne cry out: "This is God's dwelling among men. He shall dwell with them and they shall be his people, and he shall be their God who is always with them. He shall wipe every tear from their eyes, and there shall be no more death or mourning, crying out or pain, for the former world has passed away."
  The One who sat on the throne said to me, "See, I make all things new!"
This is the Word of the Lord.

---

796   **RESPONSORIAL PSALM**

1   Ps 23, 1-3. 3-4. 5. 6

℟. (1) The Lord is my shepherd;
  there is nothing I shall want.
The Lord is my shepherd; I shall not want.
  In verdant pastures he gives me repose;
Beside restful waters he leads me;
  he refreshes my soul.
℟. The Lord is my shepherd;
  there is nothing I shall want.
He guides me in right paths
  for his name's sake.

Even though I walk in the dark valley
  I fear no evil; for you are at my side
With your rod and your staff
  that give me courage.
℟. The Lord is my shepherd;
  there is nothing I shall want.
You spread the table before me
  in the sight of my foes;
You anoint my head with oil;
  my cup overflows.
℟. The Lord is my shepherd;
  there is nothing I shall want.
Only goodness and kindness follow me
  all the days of my life;
And I shall dwell in the house of the Lord
  for years to come.
℟. The Lord is my shepherd;
  there is nothing I shall want.

---

2   Ps 25, 4-5. 6. 7. 20-21
℟. (1) To you, O Lord, I lift my soul.
Your ways, O Lord, make known to me;
  teach me your paths.
Guide me in your truth and teach me,
  for you are God my savior.
℟. To you, O Lord, I lift my soul.
Remember that your compassion, O Lord,
  and your kindness are from of old.
In your kindness remember me,
  because of your goodness, O Lord.
℟. To you, O Lord, I lift my soul.
Preserve my life, and rescue me;
  let me not be put to shame, for I take refuge
  in you.
Let integrity and uprightness preserve me,
  because I wait for you, O Lord.
℟. To you, O Lord, I lift my soul.

---

3   Pss 42, 2. 3. 5; 43, 3. 4. 5
℟. (Ps 42, 3) My soul is thirsting for the liv-
  ing God:
  when shall I see him face to face?
As the hind longs for the running waters,
  so my soul longs for you, O God.
℟. My soul is thirsting for the living God:
  when shall I see him face to face?
Athirst is my soul for God, the living God.
  When shall I go and behold the face of God?

℟. My soul is thirsting for the living God:
  when shall I see him face to face?
I went with the throng
  and led them in procession to the house of
  God,
Amid loud cries of joy and thanksgiving,
  with the multitude keeping festival.
℟. My soul is thirsting for the living God:
  when shall I see him face to face?
Send forth your light and your fidelity;
  they shall lead me on
And bring me to your holy mountain,
  to your dwelling-place.
℟. My soul is thirsting for the living God:
  when shall I see him face to face?
Then will I go in to the altar of God,
  the God of my gladness and joy;
Then will I give you thanks upon the harp,
  O God, my God!
℟. My soul is thirsting for the living God:
  when shall I see him face to face?
Why are you so downcast, O my soul?
  Why do you sigh within me?
Hope in God! For I shall again be thanking him,
  in the presence of my savior and my God.
℟. My soul is thirsting for the living God:
  when shall I see him face to face?

---

4   Ps 148, 1-2. 11-12. 12-14. 14
℟. (12) Let all praise the name of the Lord.
Praise the Lord from the heavens,
  praise him in the heights;
Praise him, all you his angels,
  praise him, all you his hosts.
℟. Let all praise the name of the Lord.
Let the kings of the earth and all peoples,
  the princes and all the judges of the earth,
Young men too, and maidens,
  old men and boys,
℟. Let all praise the name of the Lord.
Praise the name of the Lord,
  for his name alone is exalted;
His majesty is above earth and heaven,
℟. Let all praise the name of the Lord.
He has lifted up the horn of his people.
  Be this his praise from all his faithful ones,
  from the children of Israel, the people close
  to him. Alleluia.

℞. Let all praise the name of the Lord.
℞. Or: Alleluia.

---

797 ALLELUIA VERSE AND VERSE BEFORE THE GOSPEL

1   Mt 11, 25

Blessed are you, Father, Lord of heaven and earth;
you have revealed to little ones the mysteries of the kingdom.

2   Jn 6, 39

This is the will of my Father, says the Lord,
that I should lose nothing of all that he has given to me,
and that I should raise it up on the last day.

3   2 Cor 1, 3-4

Blessed be the Father of mercies and the God of all comfort,
who consoles us in all our afflictions.

---

798 GOSPEL

1   Mt 11, 25-30

✠ A reading from the holy gospel according to Matthew

You have hidden these things from the learned and revealed them to children.

On one occasion Jesus spoke thus: "Father, Lord of heaven and earth, to you I offer praise; for what you have hidden from the learned and the clever you have revealed to the merest children. Father, it is true. You have graciously willed it so. Everything has been given over to me by my Father. No one knows the Son but the Father, and no one knows the Father but the Son—and anyone to whom the Son wishes to reveal him.

"Come to me, all you who are weary and find life burdensome, and I will refresh you. Take my yoke upon your shoulders and learn from me, for I am gentle and humble of heart. Your souls will find rest, for my yoke is easy and my burden light."

This is the gospel of the Lord.

---

2   Jn 6, 37-40

✠ A reading from the holy gospel according to John

This is the will of my Father, that I should lose nothing of all that he has given to me.

Jesus said to the crowd:
"All that the Father gives me shall come to me;
no one who comes will I ever reject,
because it is not to do my own will
that I have come down from heaven,
but to do the will of him who sent me.
It is the will of him who sent me
that I should lose nothing of what he has given me;
rather, that I should raise it up on the last day.
Indeed, this is the will of my Father,
that everyone who looks upon the Son
and believes in him
shall have eternal life.
Him I will raise up on the last day."
This is the gospel of the Lord.

---

3   Jn 6, 51-58

✠ A reading from the holy gospel according to John

Anyone who eats this bread will live for ever; and I will raise him up on the last day.

Jesus said to the crowd:
"I myself am the living bread
come down from heaven.
If anyone eats this bread
he shall live forever;
the bread I will give
is my flesh, for the life of the world."
At this the Jews quarreled among themselves, saying, "How can he give us his flesh to eat?" Thereupon Jesus said to them:
"Let me solemnly assure you,
if you do not eat the flesh of the Son of Man
and drink his blood,
you have no life in you.
He who feeds on my flesh
and drinks my blood
has life eternal,
and I will raise him up on the last day.

For my flesh is real food
and my blood real drink.
The man who feeds on my flesh
and drinks my blood
remains in me, and I in him.
Just as the Father who has life sent me
and I have life because of the Father,
so the man who feeds on me
will have life because of me.
This is the bread that came down from heaven.
Unlike your ancestors who ate and died nonetheless,
the man who feeds on this bread shall live forever."
    This is the gospel of the Lord.

---

4   Jn 11, 32-38. 40

✠ **A reading from the holy gospel according to John**
If you believe you will see the glory of God.

When Mary, the sister of Lazarus, came to the place where Jesus was, seeing him, she fell at his feet and said to him, "Lord, if you had been here my brother would never have died." When Jesus saw her weeping, and the Jewish folk who had accompanied her also weeping, he was troubled in spirit, moved by the deepest emotions. "Where have you laid him?" he asked. "Lord, come and see," they said. Jesus began to weep, which caused the Jews to remark, "See how much he loved him!" But some said, "He opened the eyes of that blind man. Why could he not have done something to stop this man from dying?" Once again troubled in spirit, Jesus approached the tomb. Jesus said: "Did I not assure you that if you believed you would see the glory of God?"
    This is the gospel of the Lord.

BURIAL OF NON-BAPTIZED CHILDREN

799   **READING I**
1   Is 25, 6. 7-8

A reading from the book of the prophet Isaiah
The Lord God will destroy death for ever.

On this mountain the Lord of hosts
    will provide for all peoples
    a feast of rich food.
On this mountain he will destroy
    the veil that veils all peoples,
The web that is woven over all nations;
    he will destroy death forever.
The Lord God will wipe away
    the tears from all faces.
        This is the Word of the Lord.

---

2   Lam 3, 17-26

A reading from the book of Lamentations
It is good to wait in silence for the Lord God to save.

My soul is deprived of peace,
    I have forgotten what happiness is;
I tell myself my future is lost,
    all that I hoped for from the Lord.
The thought of my homeless poverty
    is wormwood and gall;
Remembering it over and over
    leaves my soul downcast within me.
But I will call this to mind,
    as my reason to have hope:

The favors of the Lord are not exhausted,
    his mercies are not spent;
They are renewed each morning,
    so great is his faithfulness.
My portion is the Lord, says my soul;
    therefore will I hope in him.

Good is the Lord to one who waits for him,
    to the soul that seeks him;
It is good to hope in silence
    for the saving help of the Lord.
        This is the Word of the Lord.

Responsorial Psalm   Ps 25, 4-5. 6. 7. 17. 20

℟. (1) To you, O Lord, I lift my soul.
Your ways, O Lord, make known to me,
    teach me your paths.
Guide me in your truth and teach me,
    for you are God my savior.
℟. To you, O Lord, I lift my soul.
Remember that your compassion, O Lord,
    and your kindness are from of old.
In your kindness remember me,
    because of your goodness, O Lord.
℟. To you, O Lord, I lift my soul.
Relieve the troubles of my heart,
    and bring me out of my distress.
Preserve my life, and rescue me;
    let me not be put to shame, for I take refuge
    in you.
℟. To you, O Lord, I lift my soul.
℟. Or: (3) No one who waits for you, O Lord,
    will ever be put to shame.

GOSPEL   Mk 15, 33-46

✠ A reading from the holy gospel according
to Mark

Jesus gave a loud cry and breathed his last.

When noon came, darkness fell on the whole
countryside and lasted until midafternoon. At
that time Jesus cried in a loud voice, "Eloi,
Eloi, lama sabachthani?" which means, "My
God, my God, why have you forsaken me?"
A few of the bystanders who heard it remarked, "Listen! He is calling on Elijah!"
Someone ran off, and soaking a sponge in
sour wine, stuck it on a reed to try to make
him drink. The man said, "Now let's see
whether Elijah comes to take him down."

Then Jesus, uttering a loud cry, breathed his
last. At that moment the curtain in the sanctuary was torn in two from top to bottom. The
centurion who stood guard over him, on seeing
the manner of his death, declared, "Clearly
this man was the Son of God!" There were also
women present looking on from a distance.
Among them were Mary Magdalene, Mary the
mother of James the younger and Joses, and
Salome. These women had followed Jesus
when he was in Galilee and attended to his
needs. There were also many others who had
come up with him to Jerusalem.

As it grew dark (it was Preparation Day,
that is, the eve of the sabbath), Joseph from
Arimathea arrived—a distinguished member
of the Sanhedrin. He was another who looked
forward to the reign of God. He was bold
enough to seek an audience with Pilate and
urgently requested the body of Jesus. Pilate
was surprised that Jesus should have died so
soon. He summoned the centurion and inquired
whether Jesus was already dead. Learning
from him that he was dead, Pilate released
the corpse to Joseph. Then, having bought a
linen shroud, Joseph took him down, wrapped
him in the linen, and laid him in a tomb which
had been cut out of rock. Finally he rolled a
stone across the entrance of the tomb.

This is the gospel of the Lord.

MASSES FOR VARIOUS OCCASIONS

I. FOR THE CHURCH FOR THE ELECTION OF A POPE OR BISHOP

800   OLD TESTAMENT READING

Is 61, 1-3

A reading from the book of the prophet Isaiah

The Lord God has anointed me and has sent me to bring Good News to the poor.

The spirit of the Lord God is upon me,
because the Lord has anointed me;
He has sent me to bring glad tidings to the lowly,
to heal the brokenhearted,
To proclaim liberty to the captives
and release to the prisoners,
To announce a year of favor from the Lord
and a day of vindication by our God,
to comfort all who mourn;
To place on those who mourn in Zion
a diadem instead of ashes,
To give them oil of gladness in place of mourning,
a glorious mantle instead of a listless spirit.
This is the Word of the Lord.

---

801   NEW TESTAMENT READING

1   Eph 4, 11-16

A reading from the letter of Paul to the Ephesians

The body of Christ grows until it has built itself up in love.

It is Christ who gave apostles, prophets, evangelists, pastors and teachers in roles of service for the faithful to build up the body of Christ, till we become one in faith and in the knowledge of God's Son, and form that perfect man who is Christ come to full stature.

Let us, then, be children no longer, tossed here and there, carried about by every wind of doctrine that originates in human trickery and skill in proposing error. Rather, let us profess the truth in love and grow to the full maturity of Christ the head. Through him the whole body grows, and with the proper functioning of the members joined firmly together by each supporting ligament, builds itself up in love.

This is the Word of the Lord.

---

2   Heb 5, 1-10

A reading from the letter of Paul to the Hebrews

Jesus was acclaimed by God with the title of high priest of the order of Melchizedek.

Every high priest is taken from among men and made their representative before God, to offer gifts and sacrifices for sins. He is able to deal patiently with erring sinners, for he is himself beset by weakness and so must make sin offerings for himself as well as for the people. One does not take this honor on his own initiative, but only when called by God as Aaron was. Even Christ did not glorify himself with the office of high priest; he received it from the One who said to him,
"You are my son;
today I have begotten you";
just as he says in another place,
"You are a priest forever,
according to the order of Melchizedek."
In the days when he was in the flesh, he offered prayers and supplications with loud cries and tears to God, who was able to save him from death, and he was heard because of his reverence. Son though he was, he learned

obedience from what he suffered; and when perfected, he became the source of eternal salvation for all who obey him, designated by God as high priest according to the order of Melchizedek.

This is the Word of the Lord.

---

802   **RESPONSORIAL PSALM**

Ps 89, 4-5. 21-22. 25. 27

℞. (2) For ever I will sing the goodness of the Lord.

I have made a covenant with my chosen one;
  I have sworn to David my servant:
Forever will I confirm your posterity
  and establish your throne for all generations.

℞. For ever I will sing the goodness of the Lord.

I have found David, my servant;
  with my holy oil I have anointed him,
That my hand may be always with him,
  and that my arm may make him strong.

℞. For ever I will sing the goodness of the Lord.

My faithfulness and my kindness shall be with him,
  and through my name shall his horn be exalted.
He shall say of me, "You are my father,
  my God, the Rock, my savior."

℞. For ever I will sing the goodness of the Lord.

---

803   **ALLELUIA VERSE AND**
       VERSE BEFORE THE GOSPEL

Jn 10, 11

I am the good shepherd, says the Lord;
the good shepherd gives his life for his sheep.

---

804   **GOSPEL**

1   Jn 15, 9-17

✠ **A reading from the holy gospel according to John**

I chose you, and I commissioned you to go out and bear fruit.

Jesus said to his disciples:
  "As the Father has loved me,
  so I have loved you.
Live on in my love.
You will live in my love
  if you keep my commandments,
  even as I have kept my Father's commandments,
  and live in his love.
All this I tell you
  that my joy may be yours
  and your joy may be complete.
This is my commandment:
  love one another
  as I have loved you.
There is no greater love than this:
  to lay down one's life for one's friends.
You are my friends
  if you do what I command you.
I no longer speak of you as slaves,
  for a slave does not know what his master is about.
Instead, I call you friends,
  since I have made known to you all that I heard from my Father.
It was not you who chose me,
  it was I who chose you
  to go forth and bear fruit.
Your fruit must endure,
  so that all you ask the Father in my name he will give you.
The command I give you is this,
  that you love one another."

      This is the gospel of the Lord.

---

2   Jn 17, 11. 17-23

✠ **A reading from the holy gospel according to John**

As you sent me into the world, I have sent them into the world.

Jesus looked up to heaven and prayed:

"O Father most holy,
protect them with your name which you
   have given me,
[that they may be one, even as we are one.]
Consecrate them by means of truth—
'Your word is truth.'
As you have sent me into the world,
so I have sent them into the world;
I consecrate myself for their sakes now,
that they may be consecrated in truth.

"I do not pray for them alone.
I pray also for those who will believe in me
   through their word,
that all may be one
as you, Father, are in me, and I in you;
I pray that they may be [one] in us,
that the world may believe that you sent me.
I have given them the glory you gave me
that they may be one, as we are one—
I living in them, you living in me—
that their unity may be complete.
So shall the world know that you sent me,
and that you loved them as you loved me."
   This is the gospel of the Lord.

805   FOR POPE OR BISHOP
Including their anniversaries

Appropriate texts may be taken from those proposed in the
common of pastors, above, nos. 719-724.

FOR VOCATIONS OF
PRIESTS AND RELIGIOUS

806   OLD TESTAMENT READING
1   Gn 12, 1-4

A reading from the book of Genesis
Leave your country, your family, and come.

The Lord said to Abram: "Go forth from the
land of your kinsfolk and from your father's
house to a land that I will show you.
"I will make of you a great nation,
   and I will bless you;
I will make your name great,
   so that you will be a blessing.

I will bless those who bless you
   and curse those who curse you.
All the communities of the earth
   shall find blessing in you."
Abram went as the Lord directed him.
   This is the Word of the Lord.

2   Ex 3, 1-6. 9-12
A reading from the book of Exodus
I shall be with you.

Moses was tending the flock of his father-in-
law Jethro, the priest of Midian. Leading the
flock across the desert, he came to Horeb, the
mountain of God. There an angel of the Lord
appeared to him in fire flaming out of a bush.
As he looked on, he was surprised to see that
the bush, though on fire, was not consumed.
So Moses decided, "I must go over to look at
this remarkable sight, and see why the bush is
not burned."

   When the Lord saw him coming over to look
at it more closely, God called out to him from
the bush, "Moses! Moses!" He answered,
"Here I am." God said, "Come no nearer! Remove the sandals from your feet, for the place
where you stand is holy ground. I am the God
of your father," he continued, "the God of
Abraham, the God of Isaac, the God of Jacob."
Moses hid his face, for he was afraid to look
at God. So indeed the cry of the Israelites has
reached me, and I have truly noted that the
Egyptians are oppressing them. Come, now! I
will send you to Pharaoh to lead my people,
the Israelites, out of Egypt."

   But Moses said to God, "Who am I that I
should go to Pharaoh and lead the Israelites
out of Egypt?" He answered, "I will be with
you; and this shall be your proof that it is I who
have sent you: when you bring my people out
of Egypt, you will worship God on this very
mountain."
   This is the Word of the Lord.

3   1 Sm 3, 1-10

A reading from the first book of Samuel
Speak, O Lord, your servant is listening.

During the time young Samuel was minister to the Lord under Eli, a revelation of the Lord was uncommon and vision infrequent. One day Eli was asleep in his usual place. His eyes had lately grown so weak that he could not see. The lamp of God was not yet extinguished, and Samuel was sleeping in the temple of the Lord where the ark of God was. The Lord called to Samuel, who answered, "Here I am." He ran to Eli and said, "Here I am. You called me." "I did not call you," Eli said. "Go back to sleep." So he went back to sleep. Again the Lord called Samuel, who rose and went to Eli. "Here I am," he said. "You called me." But he answered, "I did not call you, my son. Go back to sleep." At that time Samuel was not familiar with the Lord, because the Lord had not revealed anything to him as yet. The Lord called Samuel again, for the third time. Getting up and going to Eli, he said, "Here I am. You called me." Then Eli understood that the Lord was calling the youth. So he said to Samuel, "Go to sleep, and if you are called, reply, 'Speak, Lord, for your servant is listening.'" When Samuel went to sleep in his place, the Lord came and revealed his presence, calling out as before, "Samuel, Samuel!" Samuel answered, "Speak, for your servant is listening."

This is the Word of the Lord.

---

4   1 Kgs 19, 16. 19-21

A reading from the first book of Kings
Elisha rose up and followed Elijah.

The Lord said to Elijah: "You shall anoint Elisha, son of Shaphat of Abel-meholah, as prophet to succeed you.

Elijah set out, and came upon Elisha, son of Shaphat, as he was plowing with twelve yoke of oxen; he was following the twelfth. Elijah went over to him and threw his cloak over him. Elisha left the oxen, ran after Elijah, and said, "Please, let me kiss my father and mother good-bye, and I will follow you." "Go back!" Elijah answered. "Have I done anything to you?" Elisha left him and, taking the yoke of oxen, slaughtered them; he used the plowing equipment for fuel to boil their flesh, and gave it to his people to eat. Then he left and followed Elijah as his attendant.

This is the Word of the Lord.

---

5   Is 6, 6-8

A reading from the book of the prophet Isaiah
Whom shall I send? Who will be our messenger?

In the year King Uzziah died, I saw the Lord seated on a high and lofty throne, with the train of his garment filling the temple. Seraphim were stationed above; each of them had six wings: with two they veiled their faces, with two they veiled their feet, and with two they hovered aloft.

"Holy, holy, holy is the Lord of hosts!" they cried one to the other. "All the earth is filled with his glory!" At the sound of that cry, the frame of the door shook and the house was filled with smoke.

Then I said, "Woe is me, I am doomed! For I am a man of unclean lips, living among a people of unclean lips; yet my eyes have seen the King, the Lord of hosts!" Then one of the seraphim flew to me, holding an ember which he had taken with tongs from the altar.

He touched my mouth with it. "See," he said, "now that this has touched your lips, your wickedness is removed, your sin purged."

Then I heard the voice of the Lord saying, "Whom shall I send? Who will go for us?" "Here I am," I said; "send me!"

This is the Word of the Lord.

---

6   Jer 1, 4-9

A reading from the book of the prophet Jeremiah
Go to those to whom I send you.

The word of the Lord came to me thus:
Before I formed you in the womb I knew you,
    before you were born I dedicated you,
a prophet to the nations I appointed you.
"Ah, Lord God!" I said,
    "I know not how to speak; I am too young."

But the Lord answered me,
Say not, "I am too young."
    To whomever I send you, you shall go;
    whatever I command you, you shall speak.
Have no fear before them,
    because I am with you to deliver you, says
    the Lord.

Then the Lord extended his hand and touched
my mouth, saying,
See, I place my words in your mouth!
            This is the Word of the Lord.

----

7   Jer 20, 7-9
    A reading from the book of the prophet
                    Jeremiah
        It seemed to be like a fire burning in my heart.
You duped me, O Lord, and I let myself be
    duped;
    you were too strong for me, and you
    triumphed.
All the day I am an object of laughter;
    everyone mocks me.
Whenever I speak, I must cry out,
    violence and outrage is my message;
The word of the Lord has brought me
    derision and reproach all the day.
I say to myself, I will not mention him,
    I will speak in his name no more.
But then it becomes like fire burning in my
    heart,
    imprisoned in my bones;
I grow weary holding it in,
    I cannot endure it.
            This is the Word of the Lord.

----

807   **NEW TESTAMENT READING**

1   2 Cor 5, 14-20
            [For priestly vocations]
A reading from the second letter of Paul to the
                    Corinthians
        Jesus has given us the ministry of reconciliation.
The love of Christ impels us who have reached
the conviction that since one died for all, all
died. He died for all so that those who live
might live no longer for themselves, but for

him who for their sakes died and was raised up.
    Because of this we no longer look on anyone
in terms of mere human judgment. If at one
time we so regarded Christ, we no longer know
him by this standard. This means that if anyone is in Christ, he is a new creation. The old
order has passed away; now all is new! All
this has been done by God, who has reconciled
us to himself through Christ and has given us
the ministry of reconciliation. I mean that God,
in Christ, was reconciling the world to himself,
not counting men's transgressions against
them, and that he has entrusted the message of
reconciliation to us. This makes us ambassadors for Christ, God as it were appealing
through us. We implore you, in Christ's name:
be reconciled to God!
            This is the Word of the Lord.

----

2   Phil 3, 8-14
    A reading from the letter of Paul to the
                    Philippians
    I look on everything as useless, if only I can know Christ.
I have come to rate all as loss in the light of
the surpassing knowledge of my Lord Jesus
Christ. For his sake I have forfeited everything; I have accounted all else rubbish so that
Christ may be my wealth and I may be in him,
not having any justice of my own based on
observance of the law. The justice I possess is
that which comes through faith in Christ. It
has its origin in God and is based on faith. I
wish to know Christ and the power flowing
from his resurrection; likewise to know how to
share in his sufferings by being formed into the
pattern of his death. Thus do I hope that I may
arrive at resurrection from the dead.
    It is not that I have reached it yet, or have
already finished my course; but I am racing
to grasp the prize if possible, since I have
been grasped by Christ [Jesus]. Brothers, I do
not think of myself as having reached the
finish line. I give no thought to what lies
behind but push on to what is ahead. My entire
attention is on the finish line as I run toward
the prize to which God calls me—life on high in
Christ Jesus.
            This is the Word of the Lord.

3   Heb 5, 1-10

[For priestly vocations]

A reading from the letter of Paul to the Hebrews

Jesus was acclaimed by God with the title of high priest of the order of Melchizedek.

Every high priest is taken from among men and made their representative before God, to offer gifts and sacrifices for sins. He is able to deal patiently with erring sinners, for he is himself beset by weakness and so must make sin offerings for himself as well as for the people. One does not take this honor on his own initiative, but only when called by God as Aaron was. Even Christ did not glorify himself with the office of high priest; he received it from the One who said to him,

> **"You are my son;**
>   **today I have begotten you";**
> **just as he says in another place,**
> **"You are a priest forever,**
>   **according to the order of Melchizedek."**

In the days when he was in the flesh, he offered prayers and supplications with loud cries and tears to God, who was able to save him from death, and he was heard because of his reverence. Son though he was, he learned obedience from what he suffered; and when perfected, he became the source of eternal salvation for all who obey him, designated by God as high priest according to the order of Melchizedek.

             This is the Word of the Lord.

---

808   **RESPONSORIAL PSALM**

1   Ps 16, 1-2. 5. 7-8. 11

℟. (5) You are my inheritance, O Lord.
Keep me, O God, for in you I take refuge;
    I say to the Lord, "My Lord are you."
O Lord, my allotted portion and my cup,
    you it is who hold fast my lot.
℟. You are my inheritance, O Lord.
I bless the Lord who counsels me;
    even in the night my heart exhorts me.
I set the Lord ever before me;
    with him at my right hand I shall not be disturbed.

℟. You are my inheritance, O Lord.
You will show me the path to life,
    fullness of joys in your presence,
    the delights at your right hand forever.
℟. You are my inheritance, O Lord.

---

2   Ps 27, 1. 4. 5. 8-9. 9. 11

℟. (8) I long to see your face, O Lord.
The Lord is my light and my salvation;
    whom should I fear?
The Lord is my life's refuge;
    of whom should I be afraid?
℟. I long to see your face, O Lord.
One thing I ask of the Lord;
    this I seek:
To dwell in the house of the Lord
    all the days of my life,
That I may gaze on the loveliness of the Lord
    and contemplate his temple.
℟. I long to see your face, O Lord.
For he will hide me in his abode
    in the day of trouble;
He will conceal me in the shelter of his tent,
    he will set me high upon a rock.
℟. I long to see your face, O Lord.
Your presence, O Lord, I seek.
    Hide not your face from me;
Do not in anger repel your servant.
    You are my helper: cast me not off.
℟. I long to see your face, O Lord.
Forsake me not, O God my savior.
    Show me, O Lord, your way,
And lead me on a level path,
    because of my adversaries.
℟. I long to see your face, O Lord.

---

3   Ps 40, 2. 4. 7-8. 8-9. 10. 12

℟. (8. 9) Here am I, Lord;
    I come to do your will.
I have waited, waited for the Lord,
    and he stooped toward me and heard my cry.
And he put a new song into my mouth,
    a hymn to our God.
℟. Here am I, Lord;
    I come to do your will.
Sacrifice or oblation you wished not,
    but ears open to obedience you gave me.

Holocausts or sin offerings you sought not;
  then said I, "Behold I come."
℟. Here am I, Lord;
  I come to do your will.

"In the written scroll it is prescribed for me,
  to do your will, O my God, is my delight,
And your law is within my heart!"
℟. Here am I, Lord;
  I come to do your will.

I announced your justice in the vast assembly;
  I did not restrain my lips, as you, O Lord,
  know.
℟. Here am I, Lord;
  I come to do your will.

Withhold not, O Lord, your compassion from
  me;
  may your kindness and your truth ever preserve me.
℟. Here am I, Lord;
  I come to do your will.

---

4   Ps 84, 3-4. 5-6. 8. 11

℟. (5) How happy they who dwell in your
house, O Lord.
My soul yearns and pines
  for the courts of the Lord.
My heart and my flesh
  cry out for the living God.
Even the sparrow finds a home,
  and the swallow a nest
  in which she puts her young—
Your altars, O Lord of hosts,
  my king and my God!
℟. How happy they who dwell in your house,
  O Lord.
Happy they who dwell in your house!
  continually they praise you.
Happy the men whose strength you are!
  They go from strength to strength.
℟. How happy they who dwell in your house,
  O Lord.
I had rather one day in your courts
  than a thousand elsewhere;
I had rather lie at the threshold of the house
  of my God
  than dwell in the tents of the wicked.
℟. How happy they who dwell in your house,
  O Lord.

---

809   **ALLELUIA VERSE AND**
VERSE BEFORE THE GOSPEL

1   Mt 4, 19

Come follow me, says the Lord,
and I will make you fishers of men.

2   Jn 15, 5

I am the vine and you are the branches, says
  the Lord:
he who lives in me, and I in him, will bear
  much fruit.

3   Jn 15, 16

I have chosen you from the world, says the
  Lord,
to go and bear fruit that will last.

4   Phil 3, 8-9

I count all things worthless but this:
to gain Jesus Christ and to be found in him.

---

810   **GOSPEL**

1   Mt 9, 35-38

✠ A reading from the holy gospel according
to Matthew
The harvest is rich but the laborers are few.
Jesus toured all the towns and villages. He
taught in their synagogues, he proclaimed the
good news of God's reign, and he cured every
sickness and disease. At the sight of the
crowds, his heart was moved with pity. They
were lying prostrate from exhaustion, like
sheep without a shepherd. He said to his disciples: "The harvest is good but laborers are
scarce. Beg the harvest master to send out
laborers to gather his harvest."
    This is the gospel of the Lord.

---

2   Mk 10, 17-27

✠ A reading from the holy gospel according
to Mark
Go and sell everything you own and follow me.
As Jesus was setting out on a journey a man
came running up, knelt down before him and

asked, "Good Teacher, what must I do to share in everlasting life?" Jesus answered, "Why do you call me good? No one is good but God alone. You know the commandments:

'You shall not kill;
You shall not commit adultery;
You shall not steal;
You shall not bear false witness;
You shall not defraud;
Honor your father and your mother.' "

He replied, "Teacher, I have kept all these since my childhood." Then Jesus looked at him with love and told him, "There is one thing more you must do. Go and sell what you have and give to the poor; you will then have treasure in heaven. After that come and follow me." At these words the man's face fell. He went away sad, for he had many possessions. Jesus looked around and said to his disciples, "How hard it is for the rich to enter the kingdom of God!" The disciples could only marvel at his words. So Jesus repeated what he had said: "My sons, how hard it is to enter the kingdom of God! It is easier for a camel to pass through a needle's eye than for a rich man to enter the kingdom of God."

They were completely overwhelmed at this, and exclaimed to one another, "Then who can be saved?" Jesus fixed his gaze on them and said, "For man it is impossible but not for God. With God all things are possible."

This is the gospel of the Lord.

---

3   Mk 10, 28-30

✠ A reading from the holy gospel according to Mark

You will be repaid a hundred times over—not without persecutions—now in this present time and in the world to come, eternal life.

Peter was moved to say to Jesus: "We have put aside everything to follow you!" Jesus answered: "I give you my word, there is no one who has given up home, brothers or sisters, mother or father, children or property, for me and for the gospel who will not receive in this present age a hundred times as many homes, brothers and sisters, mothers, children and

property—and persecution besides—and in the age to come, everlasting life."

This is the gospel of the Lord.

---

4   Lk 5, 1-11

[For priestly vocations]

✠ A reading from the holy gospel according to Luke

From this moment on, you will be fishers of men.

As the crowd pressed in on Jesus to hear the word of God, he saw two boats moored by the side of the lake; the fishermen had disembarked and were washing their nets. He got into one of the boats, the one belonging to Simon, and asked him to pull out a short distance from the shore; then, remaining seated, he continued to teach the crowds from the boat. When he had finished speaking he said to Simon, "Put out into deep water and lower your nets for a catch." Simon answered, "Master, we have been hard at it all night long and have caught nothing; but if you say so, I will lower the nets." Upon doing this they caught such a great number of fish that their nets were at the breaking point. They signaled to their mates in the other boat to come and help them. These came, and together they filled the two boats until they nearly sank.

At the sight of this, Simon Peter fell at the knees of Jesus saying, "Leave me, Lord. I am a sinful man." For indeed, amazement at the catch they had made seized him and all his shipmates, as well as James and John, Zebedee's sons, who were partners with Simon. Jesus said to Simon, "Do not be afraid. From now on you will be catching men." With that they brought their boats to land, left everything, and became his followers.

This is the gospel of the Lord.

---

5   Lk 9, 57-62

✠ A reading from the holy gospel according to Luke

Once the hand is laid on the plough, no one who looks back is fit for the kingdom of God.

As Jesus and his disciples were making their way along, someone said to him, "I will be your follower wherever you go." Jesus said to him, "The foxes have lairs, the birds of the sky have nests, but the Son of Man has nowhere to lay his head." To another he said, "Come after me." The man replied, "Let me bury my father first." Jesus said to him, "Let the dead bury their dead; come away and proclaim the kingdom of God." Yet another said to him, "I will be your follower, Lord, but first let me take leave of my people at home." Jesus answered him, "Whoever puts his hand to the plow but keeps looking back is unfit for the reign of God."

This is the gospel of the Lord.

---

6   Lk 14, 25-33

✠ A reading from the holy gospel according to Luke

Anyone who does not carry his cross and come after me cannot be my disciple.

On one occasion when a great crowd was with him, Jesus turned to them and said, "If anyone comes to me without turning his back on his father and mother, his wife and his children, his brothers and sisters, indeed his very self, he cannot be my follower. Anyone who does not take up his cross and follow me cannot be my disciple. If one of you decides to build a tower, will he not first sit down and calculate the outlay to see if he has enough money to complete the project? He will do that for fear of laying the foundation and then not being able to complete the work; at which all who saw it would then jeer at him, saying, 'That man began to build what he could not finish.'

"Or if a king is about to march on another king to do battle with him, will he not sit down first and consider whether, with ten thousand men, he can withstand an enemy coming against him with twenty thousand? If he cannot, he will send a delegation while the enemy is still at a distance, asking for terms of peace. In the same way, none of you can be my disciple if he does not renounce all his possessions."

This is the gospel of the Lord.

---

7   Jn 1, 35-51 or 1, 35-42

✠ A reading from the holy gospel according to John

Follow me.

(Long Form)

John was [at Bethany beyond the Jordan] again with two of his disciples. As he watched Jesus walk by he said: "Look! There is the Lamb of God!" The two disciples heard what he said, and followed Jesus. When Jesus turned around and noticed them following him, he asked them, "What are you looking for?" They said to him, "Rabbi (which means Teacher), where do you stay?" "Come and see," he answered. So they went to see where he was lodged, and stayed with him that day. (It was about four in the afternoon.)

One of the two who had followed him after hearing John was Simon Peter's brother Andrew. The first thing he did was seek out his brother Simon and tell him, "We have found the Messiah" (which means the Anointed)! He brought him to Jesus, who looked at him and said, "You are Simon, son of John; your name shall be Cephas (which is rendered Peter)."

The next day he wanted to set out for Galilee, but first he came upon Philip. "Follow me," Jesus said to him. Now Philip was from Bethsaida, the same town as Andrew and Peter. Philip sought out Nathanael and told him, "We have found the one Moses spoke of in the law—the prophets too—Jesus, son of Joseph, from Nazareth." Nathanael's response to that was, "Can anything good come from Nazareth?" and Philip replied, "Come, see for yourself." When Jesus saw Nathanael coming toward him, he remarked: "This man is a real Israelite. There is no guile in him." "How do you know me?" Nathanael asked him. "Before Philip called you," Jesus answered, "I saw you under the fig tree." "Rabbi," said Nathanael, "you are the Son of God; you are the king of Israel." Jesus responded: "Do you believe just because I told you I saw you under the fig tree? You will see much greater things than that."

He went on to tell them, "I solemnly assure

you, you shall see the sky opened and the angels of God ascending and descending on the Son of Man."

> This is the gospel of the Lord.

OR (Short Form)

John was [at Bethany beyond the Jordan] again with two of his disciples. As the watched Jesus walk by he said: "Look! There is the Lamb of God!" The two disciples heard what he said, and followed Jesus. When Jesus turned around and noticed them following him, he asked them, "What are you looking for?" They said to him, "Rabbi (which means Teacher), where do you stay?" "Come and see," he answered. So they went to see where he was lodged, and stayed with him that day. (It was about four in the afternoon.)

One of the two who had followed him after hearing John was Simon Peter's brother Andrew. The first thing he did was seek out his brother Simon and tell him, "We have found the Messiah" (which means the Anointed)! He brought him to Jesus, who looked at him and said, "You are Simon, son of John; your name shall be Cephas (which is rendered Peter)."

> This is the gospel of the Lord.

8
                                            Jn 15, 9-17

✠ A reading from the holy gospel according to John
You did not choose me; no, I chose you.

Jesus said to his disciples:
"As the Father has loved me,
so I have loved you.
Live on in my love.
You will live in my love
if you keep my commandments,
even as I have kept my Father's commandments,
and live in his love.
All this I tell you
that my joy may be yours
and your joy may be complete.
This is my commandment:
love one another
as I have loved you.

There is no greater love than this:
to lay down one's life for one's friends.
You are my friends
if you do what I command you.
I no longer speak of you as slaves,
for a slave does not know what his master is about.
Instead, I call you friends,
since I have made known to you all that I heard from my Father.
It was not you who chose me,
it was I who chose you
to go forth and bear fruit.
Your fruit must endure,
so that all you ask the Father in my name he will give you.
The command I give you is this,
that you love one another."

> This is the gospel of the Lord.

FOR UNITY OF CHRISTIANS

811   **OLD TESTAMENT READING**
1
                                            Dt 30, 1-4

A reading from the book of Deuteronomy
He will gather you once again out of all the peoples where he has scattered you.

Moses told the people: "When all these things which I have set before you, the blessings and the curses, are fulfilled in you, and from among whatever nations the Lord, your God, may have dispersed you, you ponder them in your heart: then, provided that you and your children return to the Lord, your God, and heed his voice with all your heart and all your soul, just as I now command you, the Lord, your God, will change your lot; and taking pity on you, he will again gather you from all the nations wherein he has scattered you. Though you may have been driven to the farthest corner of the world, even from there will the Lord, your God, gather you; even from there will he bring you back."

> This is the Word of the Lord.

---

2   Ez 36, 23-28

A reading from the book of the prophet Ezekiel

I will take you from among the nations, and I will give you a new heart.

Thus says the Lord God: I will prove the holiness of my great name, profaned among the nations, in whose midst you have profaned it. Thus the nations shall know that I am the Lord, says the Lord God, when in their sight I prove my holiness through you. For I will take you away from among the nations, gather you from all the foreign lands, and bring you back to your own land. I will sprinkle clean water upon you to cleanse you from all your impurities, and from all your idols I will cleanse you. I will give you a new heart and place a new spirit within you, taking from your bodies your stony hearts and giving you natural hearts. I will put my spirit within you and make you live by my statutes, careful to observe my decrees. You shall live in the land I gave your fathers; you shall be my people, and I will be your God.

This is the Word of the Lord.

---

3   Ez 37, 15-19. 21-22. 26-28

A reading from the book of the prophet Ezekiel

They will no longer be two nations.

Thus the word of the Lord came to me: Now, son of man, take a single stick, and write on it: Judah and those Israelites who are associated with him. Then take another stick and write on it: Joseph [the stick of Ephraim] and all the house of Israel associated with him. Then join the two sticks together, so that they form one stick in your hand. When your countrymen ask you, "Will you not tell us what you mean by all this?", answer them: Thus says the Lord God: [I will take the stick of Joseph, which is in the hand of Ephraim, and of the tribes of Israel associated with him, and I will join to it the stick of Judah, making them a single stick; they shall be one in my hand.] I will take the Israelites from among the nations to which they have come, and

gather them from all sides to bring them back to their land. I will make them one nation upon the land, in the mountains of Israel, and there shall be one prince for them all. Never again shall they be two nations, and never again shall they be divided into two kingdoms.

I will make with them a covenant of peace; it shall be an everlasting covenant with them, and I will multiply them, and put my sanctuary among them forever. My dwelling shall be with them; I will be their God, and they shall be my people. Thus the nations shall know that it is I, the Lord, who make Israel holy, when my sanctuary shall be set up among them forever.

This is the Word of the Lord.

---

4   Zep 3, 16-20

A reading from the book of the prophet Zephaniah

At the proper time, I will gather you together.

Fear not, O Zion, be not discouraged!
The Lord, your God, is in your midst,
   a mighty savior;
He will rejoice over you with gladness,
   and renew you in his love.
He will sing joyfully because of you,
   as one sings at festivals.

I will remove disaster from among you,
   so that none may recount your disgrace.
Yes, at that time I will deal
   with all who oppress you:
I will save the lame,
   and assemble the outcasts;
I will give them praise and renown
   in all the earth, when I bring about their
   restoration.
At that time I will bring you home,
   and at that time I will gather you;
For I will give you renown and praise,
   among all the peoples of the earth,
When I bring about your restoration
   before your very eyes, says the Lord.
This is the Word of the Lord.

812   NEW TESTAMENT READING

1   1 Cor 1, 10-13

A reading from the first letter of Paul to the Corinthians

There should not be serious differences between you. Has Christ been divided?

I beg you, brothers, in the name of our Lord Jesus Christ, to agree in what you say. Let there be no factions; rather, be united in mind and judgment. I have been informed, my brothers, by certain members of Chloe's household that you are quarreling among yourselves. This is what I mean: one of you, it seems, will say, "I belong to Paul," another, "I belong to Apollos," still another, "Cephas has my allegiance," and the fourth, "I belong to Christ." Has Christ, then, been divided into parts? Was it Paul who was crucified for you? Was it in Paul's name that you were baptized?

This is the Word of the Lord.

---

2   Eph 2, 19-22

A reading from the letter of Paul to the Ephesians

You are part of a building that has the apostles and prophets for its foundations, and Christ Jesus himself for its cornerstone.

You are strangers and aliens no longer. No, you are fellow citizens of the saints and members of the household of God. You form a building which rises on the foundation of the apostles and prophets, with Christ Jesus himself as the capstone. Through him the whole structure is fitted together and takes shape as a holy temple in the Lord; in him you are being built into this temple, to become a dwelling place for God in the Spirit.

This is the Word of the Lord.

---

3   Eph 4, 1-6

A reading from the letter of Paul to the Ephesians

Do all you can to preserve the unity of the Spirit in the bond of peace.

I plead with you, as a prisoner for the Lord, to live a life worthy of the calling you have received, with perfect humility, meekness, and patience, bearing with one another lovingly. Make every effort to preserve the unity which has the Spirit as its origin and peace as its binding force. There is but one body and one Spirit, just as there is but one hope given all of you by your call. There is one Lord, one faith, one baptism; one God and Father of all, who is over all, and works through all, and is in all.

This is the Word of the Lord.

---

4   Eph 4, 30—5, 2

A reading from the letter of Paul to the Ephesians

Forgive each other as readily as God forgave you in Christ.

Do nothing to sadden the Holy Spirit with whom you were sealed against the day of redemption. Get rid of all bitterness, all passion and anger, harsh words, slander, and malice of every kind. In place of these, be kind to one another, compassionate, and mutually forgiving, just as God has forgiven you in Christ.

Be imitators of God as his dear children. Follow the way of love, even as Christ loved you. He gave himself for us as an offering to God, a gift of pleasing fragrance.

This is the Word of the Lord.

---

5   Phil 2, 1-13

A reading from the letter of Paul to the Philippians

Be united in your convictions and united in your love.

In the name of the encouragement you owe me in Christ, in the name of the solace that love can give, of fellowship in spirit, compassion, and pity, I beg you: make my joy complete by your unanimity, possessing the one love, united in spirit and ideals. Never act out of rivalry or conceit; rather, let all parties think humbly of others as superior to themselves, each of you looking to others' interests rather than his own.

Your attitude must be Christ's:

Though he was in the form of God,
  he did not deem equality with God
  something to be grasped at.

Rather, he emptied himself
and took the form of a slave,
being born in the likeness of men.
He was known to be of human estate
and it was thus that he humbled himself,
obediently accepting even death,
death on a cross!
Because of this,
God highly exalted him
and bestowed on him the name
above every other name,
so that at Jesus' name
every knee must bend
in the heavens, on the earth,
and under the earth,
and every tongue proclaim
to the glory of God the Father:
JESUS CHRIST IS LORD!
So then, my dearly beloved, obedient as always to my urging, work with anxious concern to achieve your salvation, not only when I happen to be with you but all the more now that I am absent. It is God who, in his good will toward you, begets in you any measure of desire or achievement.

This is the Word of the Lord.

---

6   Col 3, 9-17

A reading from the letter of Paul to the Colossians

You have been called together into the unity of one body.

What you have done is put aside your old self with its past deeds and put on a new man, one who grows in knowledge as he is formed anew in the image of his Creator. There is no Greek or Jew here, circumcised or uncircumcised, foreigner, Scythian, slave, or freeman. Rather, Christ is everything in all of you.

Because you are God's chosen ones, holy and beloved, clothe yourselves with heartfelt mercy, with kindness, humility, meekness, and patience. Bear with one another; forgive whatever grievances you have against one another. Forgive as the Lord has forgiven you. Over all these virtues put on love, which binds the rest together and makes them perfect. Christ's

peace must reign in your hearts, since as members of the one body you have been called to that peace. Dedicate yourselves to thankfulness. Let the word of Christ, rich as it is, dwell in you. In wisdom made perfect, instruct and admonish one another. Sing gratefully to God from your hearts in psalms, hymns, and inspired songs. Whatever you do, whether in speech or in action, do it in the name of the Lord Jesus. Give thanks to God the Father through him.

This is the Word of the Lord.

---

7   1 Tm 2, 5-8

A reading from the first letter of Paul to Timothy

There is only one mediator between God and mankind, himself a man, Christ Jesus.

"God is one.
One also is the mediator between God and men,
the man Christ Jesus,
who gave himself as a ransom for all."
This truth was attested at the fitting time. I have been made its herald and apostle (believe me, I am not lying but speak the truth), the teacher of the nations in the true faith.

It is my wish, then, that in every place the men shall offer prayers with blameless hands held aloft, and be free from anger and dissension.

This is the Word of the Lord.

---

8   1 Jn 4, 9-15

A reading from the first letter of John

If God loved us so much, then we should love one another.

God's love was revealed in our midst in this way:
he sent his only Son to the world
that we might have life through him.
Love, then, consists in this:
not that we have loved God,
but that he has loved us
and has sent his Son as an offering for our sins.
Beloved,
if God has loved us so,

we must have the same love for one another.
No one has ever seen God.
Yet if we love one another
God dwells in us,
and his love is brought to perfection in us.
The way we know we remain in him
and he in us
is that he has given us of his Spirit.
We have seen for ourselves, and can testify,
that the Father has sent the Son as savior
of the world.
When anyone acknowledges that Jesus is
the Son of God,
God dwells in him
and he in God.
  This is the Word of the Lord.

---

813   RESPONSORIAL PSALM

1   Jer 31, 10. 11-12. 13-14

℟. (See 10) Lord, gather your scattered people,
  and guard them like a shepherd guarding his
  flock.
Hear the word of the Lord, O nations,
  proclaim it on distant coasts, and say:
He who scattered Israel, now gathers them
  together,
  he guards them as a shepherd his flock.
℟. Lord, gather your scattered people,
  and guard them like a shepherd guarding his
  flock.
The Lord shall ransom Jacob,
  he shall redeem him from the hand of his
  conqueror.
Shouting, they shall mount the heights of Zion,
  they shall come streaming to the Lord's
  blessings.
℟. Lord, gather your scattered people,
  and guard them like a shepherd guarding his
  flock.
Then the virgins shall make merry and dance,
  and young men and old as well.
I will turn their mourning into joy,
  I will console and gladden them after their
  sorrows.
I will lavish choice portions upon the priests,
  and my people shall be filled with my
  blessings,
  says the Lord.

℟. Lord, gather your scattered people,
  and guard them like a shepherd guarding his
  flock.

---

2   Ps 23, 1-3. 3-4. 5. 6

℟. (1) The Lord is my shepherd;
  there is nothing I shall want.
The Lord is my shepherd; I shall not want.
  In verdant pastures he gives me repose;
Beside restful waters he leads me;
  he refreshes my soul.
℟. The Lord is my shepherd;
  there is nothing I shall want.
He guides me in right paths
  for his name's sake.
Even though I walk in the dark valley
  I fear no evil; for you are at my side
With your rod and your staff
  that give me courage.
℟. The Lord is my shepherd;
  there is nothing I shall want.
You spread the table before me
  in the sight of my foes;
You anoint my head with oil;
  my cup overflows.
℟. The Lord is my shepherd;
  there is nothing I shall want.
Only goodness and kindness follow me
  all the days of my life;
And I shall dwell in the house of the Lord
  for years to come.
℟. The Lord is my shepherd;
  there is nothing I shall want.

---

3   Ps 100, 2. 3. 4. 5

℟. (3) We are his people:
  the sheep of his flock.
Sing joyfully to the Lord, all you lands;
  serve the Lord with gladness;
  come before him with joyful song.
℟. We are his people:
  the sheep of his flock.
Know that the Lord is God;
  he made us, his we are;
  his people, the flock he tends.
℟. We are his people:
  the sheep of his flock.

Enter his gates with thanksgiving,
  his courts with praise.
Give thanks to him;
  bless his name.
℟. We are his people:
  the sheep of his flock.
The Lord is good:
  the Lord, whose kindness endures forever,
  and his faithfulness, to all generations.
℟. We are his people:
  the sheep of his flock.
℟. Or: (2) Come with joy into the presence of
  the Lord.

---

4   Ps 118, 22-23. 25-26. 28

℟. (22) The stone rejected by the builders has
  become the cornerstone.
The stone which the builders rejected
  has become the cornerstone.
By the Lord has this been done;
  it is wonderful in our eyes.
℟. The stone rejected by the builders has be-
  come the cornerstone.
O Lord, grant salvation!
  O Lord, grant prosperity!
Blessed is he who comes in the name of the
  Lord;
  we bless you from the house of the Lord.
℟. The stone rejected by the builders has be-
  come the cornerstone.
You are my God, and I give thanks to you;
  O my God, I extol you.
I give thanks to you because you heard me;
  you have been my salvation.
℟. The stone rejected by the builders has be-
  come the cornerstone.
℟. Or: Alleluia.

---

5   Ps 122, 1-2. 3-4. 4-5. 6-7. 8-9

℟. (1) I rejoiced when I heard them say:
  let us go to the house of the Lord.
I rejoiced because they said to me,
  "We will go up to the house of the Lord."
And now we have set foot
  within your gates, O Jerusalem.
℟. I rejoiced when I heard them say:
  let us go to the house of the Lord.

Jerusalem, built as a city
  with compact unity.
To it the tribes go up,
  the tribes of the Lord.
℟. I rejoiced when I heard them say:
  let us go to the house of the Lord.
According to the decree for Israel,
  to give thanks to the name of the Lord.
In it are set up judgment seats,
  seats for the house of David.
℟. I rejoiced when I heard them say:
  let us go to the house of the Lord.
Pray for the peace of Jerusalem!
  May those who love you prosper!
May peace be within your walls,
  prosperity in your buildings.
℟. I rejoiced when I heard them say:
  let us go to the house of the Lord.
Because of my relatives and friends
  I will say, "Peace be within you!"
Because of the house of the Lord, our God,
  I will pray for your good.
℟. I rejoiced when I heard them say:
  let us go to the house of the Lord.
℟. Or: Let us go rejoicing to the house of the
  Lord.
℟. Or: (Is 66, 10) Rejoice with Jerusalem, and
  be glad,
  gather together, all you who love her.

---

814   ALLELUIA VERSE AND
               VERSE BEFORE THE GOSPEL

1   Jn 17, 21

May all be one as you are, Father, and I in you;
let the world believe that you sent me, says the
  Lord.

2   Eph 4, 5-6

One Lord, one faith, one baptism.
One God, the Father of all.

3   Col 3, 15

May the peace of Christ rule in your hearts,
that peace to which all of you are called as one
  body.

4

Lord, let your Church be gathered from the
ends of the earth into your kingdom,
for glory and power is yours through Jesus
Christ for ever.

5

The Church of the Lord is a single light;
it shines everywhere, yet the Church is not
divided.

---

815   **GOSPEL**

1   Mt 18, 19-22

✠ A reading from the holy gospel according
to Matthew

*Where two or there meet in my name, I shall be there with
them.*

Jesus said to his disciples: "If two of you join
your voices on earth to pray for anything
whatever, it shall be granted you by my Father
in heaven. Where two or three are gathered in
my name, there am I in their midst."

Then Peter came up and asked him, "Lord,
when my brother wrongs me, how often must
I forgive him? Seven times?" "No," Jesus replied, "not seven times; I say, seventy times
seven times."

This is the gospel of the Lord.

---

2   Lk 9, 49-55

✠ A reading from the holy gospel according
to Luke

Anyone who is not against you is for you.

John said to Jesus: "Master, we saw a man
using your name to expel demons, and we tried
to stop him because he is not of our company."
Jesus told him in reply, "Do not stop him, for
any man who is not against you is on your
side."

As the time approached when he was to be
taken from this world, he firmly resolved to
proceed toward Jerusalem, and sent messengers on ahead of him. These entered a Samaritan town to prepare for his passing through,
but the Samaritans would not welcome him

because he was on his way to Jerusalem. When
his disciples James and John saw this, they
said, "Lord, would you not have us call down
fire from heaven to destroy them?" He turned
toward them only to reprimand them. "You do
not know of what spirit you are," he said. "The
Son of Man has not come to destroy but to save
souls."

This is the gospel of the Lord.

---

3   Jn 10, 11-16

✠ A reading from the holy gospel according
to John

There will be only one flock, and one shepherd.

Jesus said:
"I am the good shepherd;
the good shepherd lays down his life for the
sheep.
The hired hand who is no shepherd,
nor owner of the sheep,
catches sight of the wolf coming
and runs away, leaving the sheep
to be snatched and scattered by the wolf.
That is because he works for pay;
he has no concern for the sheep.

"I am the good shepherd.
I know my sheep
and my sheep know me
in the same way that the Father knows me
and I know the Father;
for these sheep I will give my life.
I have other sheep
that do not belong to this fold.
I must lead them, too,
and they shall hear my voice.
There shall be one flock then, one shepherd."
This is the gospel of the Lord.

---

4   Jn 11, 45-52

✠ A reading from the holy gospel according
to John

*He will gather together in unity the scattered children of
God.*

Many of the Jews who had come to visit Mary
and Martha, [the sisters of Lazarus,] and had
seen what Jesus did, put their faith in him.

Some others, however, went to the Pharisees and reported what Jesus had done. The result was that the chief priests and the Pharisees called a meeting of the Sanhedrin. "What are we to do," they said, "with this man performing all sorts of signs? If we let him go on like this, the whole world will believe in him. Then the Romans will come in and sweep away our sanctuary and our nation." One of their number named Caiaphas, who was high priest that year, addressed them at this point: "You have no understanding whatever! Can you not see that it is better for you to have one man die [for the people] than to have the whole nation destroyed?" (He did not say this on his own. It was rather as high priest for that year that he prophesied that Jesus would die for the nation—and not for this nation only, but to gather into one all the dispersed children of God.)

> This is the gospel of the Lord.

---

5   Jn 13, 1-15

✠ A reading from the holy gospel according to John

I have given you an example so that you may copy what I have done to you.

Before the feast of Passover, Jesus realized that the hour had come for him to pass from this world to the Father. He had loved his own in this world, and would show his love for them to the end. The devil had already induced Judas, son of Simon Iscariot, to hand Jesus over; and so, during the supper, Jesus—fully aware that he had come from God and was going to God, the Father who had handed everything over to him—rose from the meal and took off his cloak. He picked up a towel and tied it around himself. Then he poured water into a basin and began to wash his disciples' feet and dry them with the towel he had around him. Thus he came to Simon Peter, who said to him, "Lord, are you going to wash my feet?" Jesus answered, "You may not realize now what I am doing, but later you will understand." Peter replied, "You shall never wash my feet!" "If I do not wash you," Jesus answered, "you will have no share in my

heritage." "Lord," Simon Peter said to him, "then not only my feet, but my hands and head as well." Jesus told him, "The man who has bathed has no need to wash [except for his feet]; he is entirely cleansed, just as you are; though not all." (The reason he said, "Not all are washed clean," was that he knew his betrayer.)

After he had washed their feet, he put his cloak back on and reclined at table once more. He said to them:

> "Do you understand what I just did for you?
> You address me as 'Teacher' and 'Lord,'
> and fittingly enough,
> for that is what I am.
> But if I washed your feet—
> I who am Teacher and Lord—
> then you must wash each other's feet.
> What I just did was to give you an example:
> as I have done, so you must do."
> This is the gospel of the Lord.

---

6   Jn 17, 1-11

✠ A reading from the holy gospel according to John

These disciples were yours and you gave them to me, and they have kept your word.

Jesus looked up to heaven and prayed:

> "Father, the hour has come!
> Give glory to your Son
> that your Son may give glory to you,
> inasmuch as you have given him authority over all mankind,
> that he may bestow eternal life on those you gave him.
> (Eternal life is this:
> to know you, the only true God,
> and him whom you have sent, Jesus Christ.)
> I have given you glory on earth
> by finishing the work you gave me to do.
> Do you now, Father, give me glory at your side,
> a glory I had with you before the world began.

I have made your name known
to those you gave me out of the world.
These men you gave me were yours;
they have kept your word.
Now they realize
that all that you gave me comes from you.
I entrusted to them
the message you entrusted to me,
and they received it.
They have known that in truth I came from
  you,
they have believed it was you who sent me.

"For these I pray—
not for the world
but for these you have given me,
for they are really yours.
(Just as all that belongs to me is yours,
so all that belongs to you is mine.)
It is in them that I have been glorified.
I am in the world no more,
but these are in the world
as I come to you."
  This is the gospel of the Lord.

---

7   Jn 17, 11-19

✠ A reading from the holy gospel according
              to John
      May these people be one as we are one!
Jesus looked up to heaven and prayed:
  "O Father most holy,
  protect them with your name which you
      have given me,
  [that they may be one, even as we are one.]
  As long as I was with them,
  I guarded them with your name which you
      gave me.
  I kept careful watch,
  and not one of them was lost,
  none but him who was destined to be lost—
  in fulfillment of Scripture.
  Now, however, I come to you;
  I say all this while I am still in the world
  that they may share my joy completely.
  I gave them your word,
  and the world has hated them for it;
  they do not belong to the world,
  [any more than I belong to the world].

I do not ask you to take them out of the
  world,
but to guard them from the evil one.
They are not of the world,
any more than I am of the world.
Consecrate them by means of truth—
'Your word is truth.'
As you have sent me into the world,
so I have sent them into the world;
I consecrate myself for their sakes now,
that they may be consecrated in truth."
  This is the gospel of the Lord.

---

8   Jn 17, 20-26

✠ A reading from the holy gospel according
              to John
      May these be completely one!
Jesus looked up to heaven and prayed:
  "Holy Father,
  I do not pray for my disciples alone.
  I pray also for those who will believe in me
      through their word,
  that all may be one
  as you, Father, are in me, and I in you;
  I pray that they may be [one] in us,
  that the world may believe that you sent me.
  I have given them the glory you gave me
  that they may be one, as we are one—
  I living in them, you living in me—
  that their unity may be complete.
  So shall the world know that you sent me,
  and that you loved them as you loved me.
  Father,
  all those you gave me
  I would have in my company
  where I am,
  to see this glory of mine
  which is your gift to me,
  because of the love you bore me before the
      world began.
  Just Father,
  the world has not known you,
  but I have known you;
  and these men have known that you sent me.
  To them I have revealed your name,
  and I will continue to reveal it
  so that your love for me may live in them,

and I may live in them."
This is the gospel of the Lord.

FOR THE SPREAD OF
THE GOSPEL

816   OLD TESTAMENT READING

1   Is 2, 1-5

A reading from the book of the prophet Isaiah
All the nations will stream to the mountain of the Lord God.

This is what Isaiah, son of Amoz, saw concerning Judah and Jerusalem.
   In days to come,
The mountain of the Lord's house
   shall be established as the highest mountain
   and raised above the hills.
All nations shall stream toward it;
   many peoples shall come and say:
"Come, let us climb the Lord's mountain,
   to the house of the God of Jacob,
That he may instruct us in his ways,
   and we may walk in his paths."
For from Zion shall go forth instruction,
   and the word of the Lord from Jerusalem.
He shall judge between the nations,
   and impose terms on many peoples.
They shall beat their swords into plowshares
   and their spears into pruning hooks;
One nation shall not raise the sword against
      another,
   nor shall they train for war again.

O house of Jacob, come,
   let us walk in the light of the Lord!
      This is the Word of the Lord.

---

2   Is 56, 1. 6-7

A reading from the book of the prophet Isaiah
My house will be called a house of prayer for all the peoples.

Thus says the Lord:
Observe what is right, do what is just;
   for my salvation is about to come,
   my justice, about to be revealed.

The foreigners who join themselves to the
      Lord,
   ministering to him,

Loving the name of the Lord,
   and becoming his servants—
All who keep the sabbath free from pro-
      fanation
   and hold to my covenant,
Them I will bring to my holy mountain
   and make joyful in my house of prayer;
Their holocausts and sacrifices
   will be acceptable on my altar,
For my house shall be called
   a house of prayer for all peoples.
      This is the Word of the Lord.

---

3   Is 60, 1-6

A reading from the book of the prophet Isaiah
All peoples will walk in your light.

Rise up in splendor, Jerusalem! Your light
      has come,
   the glory of the Lord shines upon you.
See, darkness covers the earth,
   and thick clouds cover the peoples;
But upon you the Lord shines,
   and over you appears his glory.
Nations shall walk by your light,
   and kings by your shining radiance.
Raise your eyes and look about;
   they all gather and come to you:
Your sons come from afar,
   and your daughters in the arms of their
      nurses.

Then you shall be radiant at what you see,
   your heart shall throb and overflow,
For the riches of the sea shall be emptied out
      before you,
   the wealth of nations shall be brought to
      you.
Caravans of camels shall fill you,
   dromedaries from Midian and Ephah;
All from Sheba shall come
   bearing gold and frankincense,
   and proclaiming the praises of the Lord.
      This is the Word of the Lord.

4   Jon 3, 10—4, 11

A reading from the book of the prophet Jonah
Shall I not show mercy to Nineveh?

When God saw by their actions how the Ninevites turned from their evil way, he repented of the evil that he had threatened to do to them; he did not carry it out.

But this was greatly displeasing to Jonah, and he became angry. "I beseech you, Lord," he prayed, "is not this what I said while I was still in my own country? This is why I fled at first to Tarshish. I knew that you are a gracious and merciful God, slow to anger, rich in clemency, loathe to punish. And now, Lord, please take my life from me; for it is better for me to die than to live." But the Lord asked, "Have you reason to be angry?"

Jonah then left the city for a place to the east of it, where he built himself a hut and waited under it in the shade, to see what would happen to the city. And when the Lord God provided a gourd plant, that grew up over Jonah's head, giving shade that relieved him of any discomfort, Jonah was very happy over the plant. But the next morning at dawn God sent a worm which attacked the plant, so that it withered. And when the sun arose, God sent a burning east wind; and the sun beat upon Jonah's head till he became faint. Then he asked for death, saying, "I would be better off dead than alive."

But God said to Jonah, "Have you reason to be angry over the plant?" "I have reason to be angry," Jonah answered, "angry enough to die." Then the Lord said, "You are concerned over the plant which cost you no labor and which you did not raise; it came up in one night and in one night it perished. And should I not be concerned over Nineveh, the great city, in which there are more than a hundred and twenty thousand persons who cannot distinguish their right hand from their left, not to mention the many cattle?"

This is the Word of the Lord.

---

5   Zec 8, 20-23

A reading from the book of the prophet Zechariah
Many great nations will come to seek the Lord God in Jerusalem.

Thus says the Lord of hosts: There shall yet come peoples, the inhabitants of many cities; and the inhabitants of one city shall approach those of another, and say, "Come! let us go to implore the favor of the Lord"; and, "I too will go to seek the Lord." Many peoples and strong nations shall come to seek the Lord of hosts in Jerusalem and to implore the favor of the Lord. Thus says the Lord of hosts: In those days ten men of every nationality, speaking different tongues, shall take hold, yes, take hold of every Jew by the edge of his garment and say, "Let us go with you, for we have heard that God is with you."

This is the Word of the Lord.

---

817   **NEW TESTAMENT READING**

1   Acts 1, 3-8

A reading from the Acts of the Apostles
You will be my witnesses to the ends of the earth.

In the time after his suffering Jesus showed his apostles in many convincing ways that he was alive, appearing to them over the course of forty days and speaking to them about the reign of God. On one occasion when he met with them, he told them not to leave Jerusalem: "Wait, rather, for the fulfillment of my Father's promise, of which you have heard me speak. John baptized with water, but within a few days you will be baptized with the Holy Spirit."

While they were with him they asked, "Lord, are you going to restore the rule to Israel now?" His answer was: "The exact time it is not yours to know. The Father has reserved that to himself. You will receive power when the Holy Spirit comes down on you; then you are to be my witnesses in Jerusalem, throughout Judea and Samaria, yes, even to the ends of the earth."

This is the Word of the Lord.

2   Acts 11, 19-26

A reading from the Acts of the Apostles

The disciples started preaching to the Greeks, proclaiming
the Good News of the Lord Jesus.

Those in the community who had been dispersed by the persecution that arose because of Stephen went as far as Phoenicia, Cyprus and Antioch, making the message known to none but Jews. However, some men of Cyprus and Cyrene among them who had come to Antioch began to talk even to the Greeks, announcing the good news of the Lord Jesus to them. The hand of the Lord was with them and a great number of them believed and were converted to the Lord. News of this eventually reached the ears of the church in Jerusalem, resulting in Barnabas' being sent to Antioch. On his arrival he rejoiced to see the evidence of God's favor. He encouraged them all to remain firm in their commitment to the Lord, since he himself was a good man filled with the Holy Spirit and faith. Thereby large numbers were added to the Lord. Then Barnabas went off to Tarsus to look for Saul; once he had found him, he brought him back to Antioch. For a whole year they met with the church and instructed great numbers. It was in Antioch that the disciples were called Christians for the first time.

This is the Word of the Lord.

---

3   Acts 13, 46-49

A reading from the Acts of the Apostles

We must turn to all nations.

Paul and Barnabas said to the Jews: "The word of God has to be declared to you first of all; but since you reject it and thus convict yourselves as unworthy of everlasting life, we now turn to the Gentiles. For thus were we instructed by the Lord: 'I have made you a light to the nations, a means of salvation to the ends of the earth.'" The Gentiles were delighted when they heard this and responded to the word of the Lord with praise. All who were destined for life everlasting believed in it. Thus the word of the Lord was carried throughout that area.

This is the Word of the Lord.

---

4   Rom 10, 9-18

A reading from the letter of Paul to the Romans

How will they hear without someone preaching? How will
they preach unless they are sent?

If you confess with your lips that Jesus is Lord, and believe in your heart that God raised him from the dead, you will be saved. Faith in the heart leads to justification, confession on the lips to salvation. Scripture says, "No one who believes in him will be put to shame." Here there is no difference between Jew and Greek; all have the same Lord, rich in mercy toward all who call upon him. "Everyone who calls on the name of the Lord will be saved."

But how shall they call on him in whom they have not believed? And how can they believe unless they have heard of him? And how can they hear unless there is somone to preach? And how can men preach unless they are sent? Scripture says, "How beautiful are the feet of those who announce good news!" But not all have believed the gospel. Isaiah asks, "Lord, who has believed what he has heard from us?" Faith, then, comes through hearing, and what is heard is the word of Christ. I ask you, have they not heard? Certainly they have, for "their voice has sounded over the whole earth, and their words to the limits of the world."

This is the Word of the Lord.

---

5   Eph 3, 2-12

A reading from the letter of Paul to the Ephesians

The mystery of Christ has now been revealed and all nations
are inheritors of the promise.

I am sure you have heard of the ministry which God in his goodness gave me in your regard. God's secret plan as I have briefly described it was revealed to me. When you read what I have said, you will realize that I know what I am talking about in speaking of the mystery of Christ, unknown to men in former ages but now revealed by the Spirit to the holy apostles and prophets. It is no less than this: in Christ Jesus the Gentiles are now co-heirs with the Jews, members of the same body and sharers of the promise through the preaching of the gospel.

Through the gift God in his goodness bestowed on me by the exercise of his power, I became a minister of the gospel. To me, the least of all believers, was given the grace to preach to the Gentiles the unfathomable riches of Christ and to enlighten all men on the mysterious design which for ages was hidden in God, the Creator of all. Now, therefore, through the church, God's manifold wisdom is made known to the principalities and powers of heaven, in accord with his age-old purpose, carried out in Christ Jesus our Lord. In Christ and through faith in him we can speak freely to God, drawing near him with confidence.

This is the Word of the Lord.

---

6   1 Tm 2, 1-8

A reading from the first letter of Paul to Timothy

God wills that all men be saved.

First of all, I urge that petitions, prayers, intercessions, and thanksgivings be offered for all men, especially for kings and those in authority, that we may be able to lead undisturbed and tranquil lives in perfect piety and dignity. Prayer of this kind is good, and God our savior is pleased with it, for he wants all men to be saved and come to know the truth. And the truth is this:

"God is one.

One also is the mediator between God and men,
    the man Christ Jesus,
who gave himself as a ransom for all."

This truth was attested at the fitting time. I have been made its herald and apostle (believe me, I am not lying but speak the truth), the teacher of the nations in the true faith.

It is my wish, then, that in every place the men shall offer prayers with blameless hands held aloft, and be free from anger and dissension.

This is the Word of the Lord.

---

818   **RESPONSORIAL PSALM**

1   Ps 19, 2-3. 4-5

℟. (5) Their message goes out through all the earth.
The heavens declare the glory of God,
    and the firmament proclaims his handiwork.
Day pours out the word to day,
    and night to night imparts knowledge.
℟. Their message goes out through all the earth.
Not a word nor a discourse
    whose voice is not heard;
Through all the earth their voice resounds,
    and to the ends of the world, their message.
℟. Their message goes out through all the earth.

---

2   Ps 67, 2-3. 5. 7-8

℟. (4) O God, let all the nations praise you!
May God have pity on us and bless us;
    may he let his face shine upon us.
So may your way be known upon earth;
    among all nations, your salvation.
℟. O God, let all the nations praise you!
May the nations be glad and exult
    because you rule the peoples in equity;
    the nations on the earth you guide.
℟. O God, let all the nations praise you!
The earth has yielded its fruits;
    God, our God, has blessed us.
May God bless us,
    and may all the ends of the earth fear him!
℟. O God, let all the nations praise you!
℟. Or: (3) Let all the nations know your saving power.

---

3   Ps 96, 1-2. 2-3. 7-8. 9-10

℟. (3) Proclaim his marvelous deeds to all the nations.
Sing to the Lord a new song;
    sing to the Lord, all you lands.
Sing to the Lord; bless his name.
℟. Proclaim his marvelous deeds to all the nations.
Announce his salvation, day after day.
    Tell his glory among the nations;

Among all peoples, his wondrous deeds.
℟. Proclaim his marvelous deeds to all the nations.
Give to the Lord, you families of nations,
give to the Lord glory and praise;
give to the Lord the glory due his name!
℟. Proclaim his marvelous deeds to all the nations.
Worship the Lord in holy attire.
Tremble before him, all the earth;
Say among the nations: The Lord is king.
℟. Proclaim his marvelous deeds to all the nations.
℟. Or: Go out to the world
and teach all nations, alleluia.

---

4   Ps 98, 1. 2-3. 3-4. 5-6

℟. (2) The Lord has revealed to the nations his saving power.
Sing to the Lord a new song,
for he has done wondrous deeds;
His right hand has won victory for him,
his holy arm.
℟. The Lord has revealed to the nations his saving power.
The Lord has made his salvation known:
in the sight of the nations he has revealed his justice.
He has remembered his kindness and his faithfulness
toward the house of Israel.
℟. The Lord has revealed to the nations his saving power.
All the ends of the earth have seen
the salvation by our God.
Sing joyfully to the Lord, all you lands;
break into song; sing praise.
℟. The Lord has revealed to the nations his saving power.
Sing praise to the Lord with the harp,
with the harp and melodious song.
With trumpets and the sound of the horn
sing joyfully before the King, the Lord.
℟. The Lord has revealed to the nations his saving power.
℟. Or: (3) All the ends of the earth have seen the saving power of God.

---

5   Ps 117, 1. 2

℟. (Mk 16, 15) Go out to all the world, and tell the Good News.
Praise the Lord, all you nations;
glorify him, all you peoples!
℟. Go out to all the world, and tell the Good News.
For steadfast is his kindness toward us,
and the fidelity of the Lord endures forever.
℟. Go out to all the world, and tell the Good News.

**819   ALLELUIA VERSE AND
VERSE BEFORE THE GOSPEL**

1   Mt 28, 19-20

Go and teach all people my gospel.
I am with you always, until the end of the world.

2   Mk 16, 15

Go out to all the world,
and tell the Good News.

3   Jn 3, 16

God loved the world so much, he gave us his only Son,
that all who believe in him might have eternal life.

---

820   GOSPEL

1   Mt 28, 16-20

✠ A reading from the holy gospel according
to Matthew
Go and teach all nations.

The eleven disciples made their way to Galilee, to the mountain to which Jesus had summoned them. At the sight of him, those who had entertained doubts fell down in homage. Jesus came forward and addressed them in these words:
"Full authority has been given to me
both in heaven and on earth;
go, therefore, and make disciples of all
the nations.

Baptize them in the name
   'of the Father
   and of the Son,
   and of the Holy Spirit.'
Teach them to carry out everything I have
   commanded you.
And know that I am with you always,
   until the end of the world!"
This is the gospel of the Lord.

---

2   Mk 16, 15-20

✠ A reading from the holy gospel according
   to Mark

Go into the whole world and preach the gospel.

Jesus appeared to the Eleven and said to them:
"Go into the whole world and proclaim the
good news to all creation. The man who believes in it and accepts baptism will be saved;
the man who refuses to believe in it will be
condemned. Signs like these will accompany
those who have professed ther faith: they
will use my name to expel demons, they will
speak entirely new languages, they will be
able to handle serpents, they will be able to
drink deadly poison without harm, and the
sick upon whom they lay their hands will recover." Then, after speaking to them, the Lord
Jesus was taken up into heaven and took his
seat at God's right hand. The Eleven went
forth and preached everywhere. The Lord continued to work with them throughout and confirm the message through the signs which accompanied them.
   This is the gospel of the Lord.

---

3   Lk 24, 44-53

✠ A reading from the holy gospel according
   to Luke

In the name of Jesus, repentance for the forgiveness of sins
should be preached to all the nations.

Jesus said to his disciples: "Recall those words
I spoke to you when I was still with you:
everything written about me in the law of
Moses and the prophets and psalms had to be
fulfilled." Then he opened their minds to the
understanding of the Scriptures.

He said to them: "Thus it is written that the
Messiah must suffer and rise from the dead on
the third day. In his name, penance for the remission of sins is to be preached to all the
nations, beginning at Jerusalem. You are witnesses of this. See, I send down upon you the
promise of my Father. Remain here in the city
until you are clothed with power from on
high."
   He then led them out near Bethany, and with
hands upraised, blessed them. As he blessed, he
left them, and was taken up to heaven. They
fell down to do him reverence, then returned to
Jerusalem filled with joy. There they were to
be found in the temple constantly, speaking the
praises of God.
   This is the gospel of the Lord.

---

4   Jn 11, 45-52

✠ A reading from the holy gospel according
   to John

Jesus died so that the scattered children of God might be
gathered together in unity.

Many of the Jews who had come to visit Mary
and Martha, [the sisters of Lazarus], and had
seen what Jesus did, put their faith in him.
Some others, however, went to the Pharisees
and reported what Jesus had done. The result
was that the chief priests and the Pharisees
called a meeting of the Sanhedrin. "What are
we to do," they said, "with this man performing all sorts of signs? If we let him go on like
this, the whole world will believe in him. Then
the Romans will come in and sweep away our
sanctuary and our nation." One of their number named Caiaphas, who was high priest that
year, addressed them at this point: "You have
no understanding whatever! Can you not see
that it is better for you to have one man die
[for the people] than to have the whole nation
destroyed?" (He did not say this on his own. It
was rather as high priest for that year that he
prophesied that Jesus would die for the nation—and not for this nation only, but to
gather into one all the dispersed children of
God.)
   This is the gospel of the Lord.

5　　　　　　　　　　　　　Jn 17, 11. 17-23

✠ A reading from the holy gospel according to John

As you sent me into the world, I have sent my followers into the world.

Jesus looked up to heaven and prayed:
"O Father most holy,
　protect them with your name which you
　　have given me,
　[that they may be one, even as we are one.]
Consecrate them by means of truth—
'Your word is truth.'
As you have sent me into the world,
so I have sent them into the world;
I consecrate myself for their sakes now,
that they may be consecrated in truth.

"I do not pray for them alone.
I pray also for those who will believe in me
　through their word,
that all may be one
as you, Father, are in me, and I in you;
I pray that they may be [one] in us,
that the world may believe that you sent
　me.
I have given them the glory you gave me
that they may be one, as we are one—
I living in them, you living in me—
that their unity may be complete.
So shall the world know that you sent me,
and that you loved them as you loved me."
　　This is the gospel of the Lord.

FOR PERSECUTED CHRISTIANS

821　　**OLD TESTAMENT READING**

1　　　　　　　　　　　　Est C, 1-4. 8-10

A reading from the book of Esther

Have mercy on your people; some men want to destroy your heritage.

Mordecai prayed to the Lord and said: "O Lord God, almighty King, all things are in your power, and there is no one to oppose you in your will to save Israel. You made heaven and earth and every wonderful thing under the heavens. You are Lord of all, and there is no

one who can resist you, Lord. And now, Lord God, King, God of Abraham, spare your people, for our enemies plan our ruin and are bent upon destroying the inheritance that was yours from the beginning. Do not spurn your portion, which you redeemed for yourself out of Egypt. Hear my prayer; have pity on your inheritance and turn our sorrow into joy: thus we shall live to sing praise to your name, O Lord. Do not silence those who praise you."
　　This is the Word of the Lord.

2　　　　　　　　　　1 Mc 2, 49-52. 57-64

A reading from the first book of Maccabees

All who hope in the Lord will not falter.

When the time came for Mattathias to die, he said to his sons: "Arrogance and scorn have now grown strong; it is a time of disaster and violent anger. Therefore, my sons, be zealous for the law and give your lives for the covenant of our fathers.
"Remember the deeds that our fathers did in
　　their times,
　and you shall win great glory and an ever-
　　lasting name.
Was not Abraham found faithful in trial,
　and it was reputed to him as uprightness?
David, for his piety,
　received as a heritage a throne of everlasting
　　royalty.
Elijah, for his burning zeal for the law,
　was taken up to heaven.
Hananiah, Azariah and Mishael, for their faith,
　were saved from the fire.
Daniel, for his innocence,
　was delivered from the jaws of lions.
And so, consider this from generation to gen-
　　eration,
　that none who hope in him shall fail in
　　strength.
Do not fear the words of a sinful man,
　for his glory ends in corruption and worms.
Today he is exalted, and tomorrow he is not to
　　be found,
　because he has returned to his dust,
　and his schemes have perished.

Children! be courageous and strong in keeping
the law,
for by it you shall be glorified."
This is the Word of the Lord.

---

3   Is 41, 8-10. 13-14

A reading from the book of the prophet Isaiah

You are my servant; I have chosen you, I have not rejected
you.

Thus said the Lord God:
But you, Israel, my servant,
Jacob, whom I have chosen,
offspring of Abraham my friend—
You whom I have taken from the ends of the
earth
and summoned from its far-off places,
You whom I have called my servant,
whom I have chosen and will not cast off—
Fear not, I am with you;
be not dismayed; I am your God.
I will strengthen you, and help you,
and uphold you with my right hand of justice.

For I am the Lord, your God,
who grasp your right hand;
It is I who say to you, "Fear not,
I will help you."
Fear not, O worm Jacob,
O maggot Israel;
I will help you, says the Lord;
your redeemer is the Holy One of Israel.
This is the Word of the Lord.

---

4   Dn 3, 25. 34-43

A reading from the book of the prophet Daniel

Do not abandon us for ever for the sake of your name.

In the fire Azariah stood up and prayed aloud:
For your name's sake, do not deliver us up
forever,
or make void your covenant.
Do not take away your mercy from us,
for the sake of Abraham, your beloved,
Isaac your servant, and Israel your holy one,
To whom you promised to multiply their offspring
like the stars of heaven,
or the sand on the shore of the sea.

For we are reduced, O Lord, beyond any other
nation,
brought low everywhere in the world this
day
because of our sins.
We have in our day no prince, prophet, or
leader,
no holocaust, sacrifice, oblation, or incense,
no place to offer first fruits, to find favor
with you.
But with contrite heart and humble spirit
let us be received;
As though it were holocausts of rams and
bullocks,
or thousands of fat lambs,
So let our sacrifice be in your presence today
as we follow you unreservedly;
for those who trust in you cannot be put to
shame.
And now we follow you with our whole heart,
we fear you and we pray to you.
Do not let us be put to shame,
but deal with us in your kindness and great
mercy.
Deliver us by your wonders,
and bring glory to your name, O Lord.
This is the Word of the Lord.

---

822   **NEW TESTAMENT READING**

1   Acts 4, 1-5. 18-21

A reading from the Acts of the Apostles

We cannot promise to stop proclaiming what we have seen
and heard.

While Peter and John were still addressing the
crowd, [after the crippled man was cured] the
priests, the captain of the temple guard, and
the Sadducees came up to them, angry because
they were teaching the people and proclaiming
the resurrection of the dead in the person of
Jesus. It was evening by now, so they arrested
them and put them in jail for the night. Despite
this, many of those who had heard the speech
believed; the number of the men came to about
five thousand.

The leaders, the elders, and the scribes assembled the next day in Jerusalem. So they

called back Peter and John and made it clear that under no circumstances were they to speak the name of Jesus or teach about him. Peter and John answered, "Judge for yourselves whether it is right in God's sight for us to obey you rather than God. Surely we cannot help speaking of what we have heard and seen." At that point they were dismissed with further warnings. The court could find no way to punish them because of the people, all of whom were praising God for what had happened.

This is the Word of the Lord.

---

2   Acts 4, 23-31

A reading from the Acts of the Apostles

Now Lord, take note of their threats.

After being released, Peter and John went back to their own people and told them what the priests and elders had said. All raised their voices in prayer to God on hearing the story: "Sovereign Lord, 'who made heaven and earth and sea and all that is in them,' you have said by the Holy Spirit through the lips of our father David your servant:
'Why did the Gentiles rage,
    the peoples conspire in folly?
The kings of the earth were aligned,
    the princes gathered together
    against the Lord and against his anointed.'
Indeed, they gathered in this very city against your holy Servant, Jesus, 'whom you anointed' —Herod and Pontius Pilate in league with 'the Gentiles' and 'the peoples' of Israel. They have brought about the very things which in your powerful providence you planned long ago. But now, O Lord, look at the threats they are leveling against us. Grant to your servants, even as they speak your words, complete assurance by stretching forth your hand in cures and signs and wonders to be worked in the name of Jesus, your holy Servant."

The place where they were gathered shook as they prayed. They were filled with the Holy Spirit and continued to speak of God's word with confidence.

This is the Word of the Lord.

---

3   Acts 5, 27-32. 40-42

A reading from the Acts of the Apostles

The apostles left, glad to have had the honor of suffering humiliation for the sake of Jesus' name.

The high priest began the interrogation of the apostles in this way: "We gave you strict orders not to teach about that name, yet you have filled Jerusalem with your teaching and are determined to make us responsible for that man's blood." To this, Peter and the apostles replied: "Better for us to obey God than men! The God of our fathers has raised up Jesus whom you put to death, 'hanging him on a tree.' He whom God has exalted at his right hand as ruler and savior is to bring repentance to Israel and forgiveness of sins. We testify to this. So too does the Holy Spirit, whom God has given to those that obey him."

This speech persuaded them. In spite of it, however, the Sanhedrin called in the apostles and had them whipped. They ordered them not to speak again about the name of Jesus, and afterward dismissed them. The apostles for their part left the Sanhedrin full of joy that they had been judged worthy of ill-treatment for the sake of the Name. Day after day, both in the temple and at home, they never stopped teaching and proclaiming the good news of Jesus the Messiah.

This is the Word of the Lord.

---

4   Phil 1, 27-30

A reading from the letter of Paul to the Philippians

He has given you the privilege not only of believing in Christ, but of suffering for him as well.

Conduct yourselves in a way worthy of the gospel of Christ. If you do, whether I come and see you myself or hear about your behavior from a distance, it will be clear that you are standing firm in unity of spirit and exerting yourselves with one accord for the faith of the gospel. Do not be intimidated by your opponents in any situation. Their opposition foreshadows downfall for them, but salvation for you. All this is as God intends, for it is your special privilege to take Christ's part—not only to believe in him but also to suffer for him. Yours is the same struggle as mine, the one in which you formerly saw me engaged and now hear that I am caught up.

This is the Word of the Lord.

---

5   Heb 12, 2-13

A reading from the letter of Paul to the Hebrews

What son is there whom his father does not discipline?

Let us keep our eyes fixed on Jesus, who inspires and perfects our faith. For the sake of the joy which lay before him he endured the cross, heedless of its shame. He has taken his seat at the right of the throne of God. Remember how he endured the opposition of sinners; hence do not grow despondent or abandon the struggle. In your fight against sin you have not yet resisted to the point of shedding blood. Moreover, you have forgotten the encouraging words addressed to you as sons:

"My sons, do not disdain the discipline of the Lord
    nor lose heart when he reproves you;
For, whom the Lord loves, he disciplines;
    he scourges every son he receives."

Endure your trials as the discipline of God, who deals with you as sons. For what son is there whom his father does not discipline? If you do not know the discipline of sons, you are not sons but bastards. If we respected our earthly fathers who corrected us, should we not all the more submit to the Father of spirits, and live? They disciplined us as seemed right to them, to prepare us for the short span of mortal life; but God does so for our true profit, that we may share his holiness. At the time it is administered, all discipline seems a cause for grief and not for joy, but later it brings forth the fruit of peace and justice to those who are trained in its school. So strengthen your drooping hands and your weak knees. Make straight the paths you walk on, that your halting limbs may not be dislocated but healed.

This is the Word of the Lord.

---

6   1 Pt 1, 3-9

A reading from the first letter of Peter

You will rejoice, though now for a little while you may have to suffer.

Praised be the God and Father of our Lord Jesus Christ,

he who in his great mercy gave us new birth;
a birth unto hope which draws its life
from the resurrection of Jesus Christ from the dead;
a birth to an imperishable inheritance
incapable of fading or defilement,
which is kept in heaven for you
who are guarded with God's power through faith;
a birth to a salvation which stands ready to be revealed in the last days.

There is cause for rejoicing here. You may for a time have to suffer the distress of many trials; but this is so that your faith, which is more precious than the passing splendor of fire-tried gold, may by its genuineness lead to praise, glory, and honor when Jesus Christ appears. Although you have never seen him, you love him, and without seeing you now believe in him, and rejoice with inexpressible joy touched with glory because you are achieving faith's goal, your salvation.

This is the Word of the Lord.

---

7   Rv 7, 9-10. 14-17

A reading from the book of Revelation

These are they who have come out of the great tribulation.

I, John, saw before me a huge crowd which no one could count from every nation, race, people, and tongue. They stood before the throne and the Lamb, dressed in long white robes and holding palm branches in their hands. They cried out in a loud voice, "Salvation is from our God, who is seated on the throne, and from the Lamb!"

"These are the ones who have survived the great period of trial; they have washed their robes and made them white in the blood of the Lamb."

"It was this that brought them before God's throne:

day and night they minster to him in his
temple;
he who sits on the throne will give them
shelter.
Never again shall they know hunger or thirst,
nor shall the sun or its heat beat down on
them,
for the Lamb on the throne will shepherd
them.
He will lead them to springs of life-giving
water,
and God will wipe every tear from their
eyes."
This is the Word of the Lord.

---

823   RESPONSORIAL PSALM

1   Ps 2, 1-3. 4-6. 10-11

℟. (13) Happy are all who put their trust in the
Lord.
Why do the nations rage
and the peoples utter folly?
The kings of the earth rise up,
and the princes conspire together
against the Lord and against his anointed:
"Let us break their fetters
and cast their bonds from us!"
℟. Happy are all who put their trust in the
Lord.
He who is throned in heaven laughs;
the Lord derides them.
Then in anger he speaks to them;
he terrifies them in his wrath:
"I myself have set up my king
on Zion, my holy mountain."
℟. Happy are all who put their trust in the
Lord.
And now, O kings, give heed;
take warning, you rulers of the earth.
Serve the Lord with fear, and rejoice before
him.
℟. Happy are all who put their trust in the
Lord.

---

2   Ps 27, 1. 2. 3. 5

℟. (9) Do not abandon me, O God my Savior.

The Lord is my light and my salvation;
whom should I fear?
The Lord is my life's refuge;
of whom should I be afraid?
℟. Do not abandon me, O God my Savior.
When evildoers come at me
to devour my flesh,
My foes and my enemies
themselves stumble and fall.
℟. Do not abandon me, O God my Savior.
Though an army encamp against me,
my heart will not fear;
Though war be waged upon me,
even then will I trust.
℟. Do not abandon me, O God my Savior.
For he will hide me in his abode
in the day of trouble;
He will conceal me in the shelter of his tent,
he will set me high upon a rock.
℟. Do not abandon me, O God my Savior.
℟. Or: (1) The Lord is my light and my salva-
tion.

---

3   Ps 123, 1-2. 2

℟. (3) Have mercy on us, Lord, have mercy.
To you I lift up my eyes
who are enthroned in heaven.
Behold, as the eyes of servants
are on the hands of their masters,
℟. Have mercy on us, Lord, have mercy.
As the eyes of a maid
are on the hands of her mistress,
So are our eyes on the Lord, our God,
till he have pity on us.
℟. Have mercy on us, Lord, have mercy.
℟. Or: (See 2) Our eyes are fixed on the Lord,
pleading for his mercy.

---

4   Ps 124, 2-3. 4-5. 7-8

℟. (7) Our soul has escaped like a bird from the
hunter's net.
Had not the Lord been with us—
when men rose up against us,
Then would they have swallowed us alive,
when their fury inflamed against us.
℟. Our soul has escaped like a bird from the
hunter's net.

Then would the waters have overwhelmed us;
  the torrent would have swept over us;
Over us then would have swept
  the raging waters.
℟. Our soul has escaped like a bird from the
  hunter's net.
Broken was the snare,
  and we were freed.
Our help is in the name of the Lord,
  who made heaven and earth.
℟. Our soul has escaped like a bird from the
  hunter's net.

---

824   ALLELUIA VERSE AND VERSE BEFORE THE GOSPEL

1   Mt 5, 10

Happy are they who suffer persecution for
  justice' sake;
the kingdom of heaven is theirs.

2   2 Cor 1, 3-4

Blessed be the Father of mercies and the God
  of all comfort,
who consoles us in all our afflictions.

3   Jas 1, 12

Happy the man who stands firm when trials
  come;
he has proved himself, and will win the crown
  of life.

4   1 Pt 4, 14

If you are insulted for the name of Christ,
  blessed are you,
for the Spirit of God rests upon you.

---

825   GOSPEL

1   Mt 5, 1-12

✠ A reading from the holy gospel according
                  to Matthew

Happy are you when people persecute you and speak all
kinds of calumny against you.

When Jesus saw the crowds he went up on the
mountainside. After he had sat down his disciples gathered around him, and he began to
teach them:

"How blest are the poor in spirit: the reign
  of God is theirs.
Blest too are the sorrowing; they shall be
  consoled.
[Blest are the lowly; they shall inherit the
  land.]
Blest are they who hunger and thirst for
  holiness;
they shall have their fill.
Blest are they who show mercy; mercy
  shall be theirs.
Blest are the single-hearted for they shall
  see God.
Blest too the peacemakers; they shall be
  called sons of God.
Blest are those persecuted for holiness'
  sake; the reign of God is theirs.
Blest are you when they insult you and
  persecute you and utter every kind of
  slander against you because of me.
Be glad and rejoice, for your reward in
  heaven is great."
    This is the gospel of the Lord.

---

2   Mt 10, 17-22

✠ A reading from the holy gospel according
                  to Matthew

You will be hated by all men on account of my name.

Jesus said to his apostles: "Be on your guard
with respect to others. They will hale you into
court, they will flog you in their synagogues.
You will be brought to trial before rulers and
kings to give witness before them and before
the Gentiles on my account. When they hand
you over, do not worry about what you will
say or how you will say it. When the hour
comes, you will be given what you are to say.
You yourselves will not be the speakers; the
Spirit of your Father will be speaking in you.
  "Brother will hand over brother to death,
and the father his child; children will turn
against parents and have them put to death.
You will be hated by all on account of me."
    This is the gospel of the Lord.

3   Mt 10, 26-33

✠ A reading from the holy gospel according
to Matthew

Do not fear those who can kill only the body.

Jesus said to his disciples: "Do not let them
intimidate you. Nothing is concealed that will
not be revealed, and nothing hidden that will
not become known. What I tell you in darkness, speak in the light. What you hear in
private, proclaim from housetops.

"Do not fear those who deprive the body of
life but cannot destroy the soul. Rather, fear
him who can destroy both body and soul in
Gehenna. Are not two sparrows sold for next
to nothing? Yet not a single sparrow falls to the
ground without your Father's consent. As for
you, every hair of your head has been counted;
so do not be afraid of anything. You are worth
more than an entire flock of sparrows. Whoever acknowledges me before men I will acknowledge before my Father in heaven. Whoever disowns me before men I will disown
before my Father in heaven."
This is the gospel of the Lord.

---

4   Jn 15, 18-21. 26—16, 4

✠ A reading from the holy gospel according
to John

If they have persecuted me, they will certainly persecute
you.

Jesus said to his disciples:
"If you find that the world hates you,
know it has hated me before you.
If you belonged to the world,
it would love you as its own;
the reason it hates you
is that you do not belong to the world.
But I chose you out of the world.
Remember what I told you:
no slave is greater than his master.
They will harry you
as they harried me.
They will respect your words
as much as they respected mine.
All this they will do to you because of my
name,
for they know nothing of him who sent
me.

When the Paraclete comes,
the Spirit of truth who comes from the
Father—
and whom I myself will send from the
Father—
he will bear witness on my behalf.
You must bear witness as well,
for you have been with me from the beginning.

"I have told you all this
to keep your faith from being shaken.
Not only will they expel you from synagogues;
a time will come
when anyone who puts you to death
will claim to be serving God!
All this they will do [to you]
because they knew neither the Father nor
me.

"But I have told you these things
that when their hour comes
you may remember my telling you of
them.
I did not speak of this with you from the
beginning
because I was with you."
This is the gospel of the Lord.

---

5   Jn 17, 11-19

✠ A reading from the holy gospel according
to John

The world has hated them.

Jesus looked up to heaven and prayed:
"O Father most holy,
protect them with your name which you
have given me,
[that they may be one, even as we are
one.]
As long as I was with them,
I guarded them with your name which
you gave me.
I kept careful watch,
and not one of them was lost,
none but him who was destined to be
lost—
in fulfillment of Scripture.
Now, however, I come to you;

I say all this while I am still in the world
that they may share my joy completely.
I gave them your word,
and the world has hated them for it;
they do not belong to the world,
[any more than I belong to the world].
I do not ask you to take them out of the
world,
but to guard them from the evil one.
They are not of the world,
any more than I am of the world.
Consecrate them by means of truth—
'Your word is truth.'
As you have sent me into the world,
so I have sent them into the world;
I consecrate myself for their sakes now,
that they may be consecrated in truth."
This is the gospel of the Lord.

PASTORAL OR SPIRITUAL
MEETINGS

826   **OLD TESTAMENT READING**

Dt 30, 10-14

A reading from the book of Deuteronomy

The word is very near to you for your observance.

Moses said to the people: "Heed the voice of
the Lord, your God, and keep his commandments and statutes that are written in this book
of the law, and return to the Lord, your God,
with all your heart and all your soul.

"For this command which I enjoin on you
today is not too mysterious and remote for
you. It is not up in the sky, that you should
say, 'Who will go up in the sky to get it for us
and tell us of it, that we may carry it out?'
Nor is it across the sea, that you should say,
'Who will cross the sea to get it for us and tell
us of it, that we may carry it out?' No, it is
something very near to you, already in your
mouths and in your hearts; you have only to
carry it out."
This is the Word of the Lord.

827   **NEW TESTAMENT READING**

Phil 2, 1-4

**A reading from the letter of Paul to the
Philippians**

Have the same convictions, the same love, the same
concern for unity.

In the name of the encouragement you owe
me in Christ, in the name of the solace that
love can give, of fellowship in spirit, compassion, and pity, I beg you: make my joy complete by your unanimity, possessing the one
love, united in spirit and ideals. Never act out
of rivalry or conceit; rather, let all parties
think humbly of others as superior to themselves, each of you looking to others' interests
rather than his own.
This is the Word of the Lord.

828   **RESPONSORIAL PSALM**

Ps 19, 8. 9. 10. 11

℞. (See Jn 6, 69) Lord, you have the words of
everlasting life.
The law of the Lord is perfect,
refreshing the soul;
The decree of the Lord is trustworthy,
giving wisdom to the simple.
℞. Lord, you have the words of everlasting
life.
The precepts of the Lord are right,
rejoicing the heart;
The command of the Lord is clear,
enlightening the eye.
℞. Lord, you have the words of everlasting
life.
The fear of the Lord is pure,
enduring forever;
The ordinances of the Lord are true,
all of them just.
℞. Lord, you have the words of everlasting
life.
They are more precious than gold,
than a heap of purest gold;
Sweeter also than syrup
or honey from the comb.
℞. Lord, you have the words of everlasting
life.

ALLELUIA VERSE AND
VERSE BEFORE THE GOSPEL

1   Ps 132, 1

See how good it is, how pleasant,
that brothers live in unity.

---

830   **GOSPEL**

1   Mt 18, 15-20

✠ A reading from the holy gospel according
to Matthew

Where two or three meet in my name, I shall be there with
them.

Jesus said to his disciples: "If your brother
should commit some wrong against you, go
go and point out his fault, but keep it between
the two of you. If he listens to you, you have
won your brother over. If he does not listen,
however, summon another, so that every case
may stand on the word of two or three witnesses. If he ignores them, refer it to the
church. If he ignores even the church, then
treat him as you would a Gentile or a tax collector. I assure you, whatever you declare
bound on earth shall be held bound in heaven,
and whatever you declare loosed on earth shall
be held loosed in heaven.

"Again I tell you, if two of you join your
voices on earth to pray for anything whatever,
it shall be granted you by my Father in heaven.
Where two or three are gathered in my name,
there am I in their midst."

This is the gospel of the Lord.

---

2   Mk 6, 30-34

✠ A reading from the holy gospel according
to Mark

You must come away to some lonely place all by yourselves
and rest for a while.

The apostles returned to Jesus and reported to
him all that they had done and what they had
taught. He said to them, "Come by yourselves
to an out-of-the-way place and rest a little."
People were coming and going in great numbers, making it impossible for them to so much
as eat. So Jesus and the apostles went off in the
boat by themselves to a deserted place. People
saw them leaving, and many got to know
about it. People from all the towns hastened
on foot to the place, arriving ahead of them.
Upon disembarking Jesus saw a vast crowd.
He pitied them for they were like sheep without a shepherd; and he began to teach them at
great length.

This is the gospel of the Lord.

---

3   Jn 14, 23-29

✠ A reading from the holy gospel according
to John

The Advocate, the Holy Spirit, will teach you everything.

Jesus said to his disciples:
   "Anyone who loves me
   will be true to my word,
   and my Father will love him;
   we will come to him
   and make our dwelling place with him.
   He who does not love me does not keep
      my words.
   Yet the word you hear is not mine;
   it comes from the Father who sent me.
   This much have I told you while I was still
      with you;
   the Paraclete, the Holy Spirit
   whom the Father will send in my name,
   will instruct you in everything,
   and remind you of all that I told you.
   'Peace' is my farewell to you,
   my peace is my gift to you;
   I do not give it to you as the world gives
      peace.
   Do not be distressed or fearful.
   You have heard me say,
   'I go away for a while, and I come back to
      you.'
   If you truly loved me
   you would rejoice to have me go to the Fa-
      ther,
   for the Father is greater than I.
   I tell you this now, before it takes place,
   so that when it takes place you may be-
      lieve."
   This is the gospel of the Lord.

II. FOR CIVIL NEEDS

FOR PEACE AND JUSTICE

831   OLD TESTAMENT READING

1   Is 9, 1-6

A reading from the book of the prophet Isaiah

Wide is the dominion of the Lord, in a peace that has no end.

The people who walked in darkness
  have seen a great light;
Upon those who dwelt in the land of gloom
  a light has shone.
You have brought them abundant joy
  and great rejoicing,
As they rejoice before you as at the harvest,
  as men make merry when dividing spoils.
For the yoke that burdened them,
  the pole on their shoulder,
And the rod of their taskmaster
  you have smashed, as on the day of Midian.
For every boot that tramped in battle,
  every cloak rolled in blood,
  will be burned as fuel for flames.

For a child is born to us, a son is given us;
  upon his shoulder dominion rests.
They named him Wonder-Counselor, God-
  Hero,
  Father-Forever, Prince of Peace.
His dominion is vast
  and forever peaceful,
From David's throne, and over his kingdom,
  which he confirms and sustains
By judgment and justice,
  both now and forever.
The zeal of the Lord of hosts will do this!
    This is the Word of the Lord.

---

2   Is 32, 15-20.

A reading from the book of the prophet Isaiah

The effect of justice will be peace.

The spirit from on high
  will be poured out on us.
Then will the desert become an orchard
  and the orchard be regarded as a forest.

Right will dwell in the desert
  and justice abide in the orchard.
Justice will bring about peace;
  right will produce calm and security.
My people will live in peaceful country,
  in secure dwellings and quiet resting places.
Happy are you who sow beside every stream,
  and let the ox and the ass go freely!
    This is the Word of the Lord.

---

3   Is 57, 15-19

A reading from the book of the prophet Isaiah

Peace to the far and near.

For thus says he who is high and exalted,
  living eternally, whose name is the Holy
    One:
On high I dwell, and in holiness,
  and with the crushed and dejected in spirit,
To revive the spirits of the dejected,
  to revive the hearts of the crushed.
I will not accuse forever,
  nor always be angry;
For their spirits would faint before me,
  the souls that I have made.
Because of their wicked avarice I was angry,
  and struck them, hiding myself in wrath,
  as they went their own rebellious way.
I saw their ways,
  but I will heal them and lead them;
I will give full comfort
  to them and to those who mourn for them,
  I, the Creator, who gave them life.

Peace, peace to the far and the near,
  says the Lord; and I will heal them.
    This is the Word of the Lord.

---

832   NEW TESTAMENT READING

1   Phil 4, 6-9

**A reading from the letter of Paul to the
    Philippians**

May the peace of God guard your hearts and your thoughts.

Dismiss all anxiety from your minds. Present
your needs to God in every form of prayer and
in petitions full of gratitude. Then God's own
peace, which is beyond all understanding, will

stand guard over your hearts and minds, in Christ Jesus.

Finally, my brothers, your thoughts should be wholly directed to all that is true, all that deserves respect, all that is honest, pure, admirable, decent, virtuous, or worthy of praise. Live according to what you have learned and accepted, what you have heard me say and seen me do. Then will the God of peace be with you.

This is the Word of the Lord.

---

2   Col 3, 12-15

A reading from the letter of Paul to the Colossians

May the peace of Christ reign in your hearts.

Because you are God's chosen ones, holy and beloved, clothe yourselves with heartfelt mercy, with kindness, humility, meekness, and patience. Bear with one another; forgive whatever grievances you have against one another. Forgive as the Lord has forgiven you. Over all these virtues put on love, which binds the rest together and makes them perfect. Christ's peace must reign in your hearts, since as members of the one body you have been called to that peace. Dedicate yourselves to thankfulness.

This is the Word of the Lord.

---

3   Jas 3, 13-18

A reading from the letter of James

The harvest of justice is sown in peace by those who make peace.

If one of you is wise and understanding, let him show this in practice through a humility filled with good sense. Should you instead nurse bitter jealousy and selfish ambition in your hearts, at least refrain from arrogant and false claims against the truth. Wisdom like this does not come from above. It is earthbound, a kind of animal, even devilish cunning. Where there are jealousy and strife, there also are inconstancy and all kinds of vile behavior. Wisdom from above, by contrast, is first of all inno-cent. It is also peaceable, lenient, docile, rich in

sympathy and the kindly deeds that are its fruits, impartial and sincere. The harvest of justice is sown in peace for those who cultivate peace.

This is the Word of the Lord.

---

833   **RESPONSORIAL PSALM**

1   Ps 72, 1-2. 3-4. 7-8. 12-13. 17

℟. (7) Justice shall flourish in his time,
and fullness of peace for ever.

**O God, with your judgment endow the king,
and with your justice the king's son;**
He shall govern your people with justice
and your afflicted ones with judgment.

℟. Justice shall flourish in his time,
and fullness of peace for ever.

**The mountains shall yield peace for the people,
and the hills justice.**
He shall defend the afflicted among the people,
save the children of the poor.

℟. Justice shall flourish in his time,
and fullness of peace for ever.

**Justice shall flower in his days,
and profound peace, till the moon be no more.**
May he rule from sea to sea,
and from the River to the ends of the earth.

℟. Justice shall flourish in his time,
and fullness of peace for ever.

**For he shall rescue the poor man when he cries out,
and the afflicted when he has no one to help him.**
He shall have pity for the lowly and the poor;
the lives of the poor he shall save.

℟. Justice shall flourish in his time,
and fullness of peace for ever.

**May his name be blessed forever;
as long as the sun his name shall remain.**
In him shall all the tribes of the earth be blessed;
all the nations shall proclaim his happiness.

℟. Justice shall flourish in his time,
and fullness of peace for ever.

2   Ps 85, 9-10. 11-12. 13-14

℟. (9) The Lord speaks of peace to his people.

I will hear what God proclaims;
    the Lord—for he proclaims peace
To his people, and to his faithful ones,
Near indeed is his salvation to those who fear
    him,
    glory dwelling in our land.

℟. The Lord speaks of peace to his people.

Kindness and truth shall meet;
    justice and peace shall kiss.
Truth shall spring out of the earth,
    and justice shall look down from heaven.

℟. The Lord speaks of peace to his people.

The Lord himself will give his benefits;
    our land shall yield its increase.
Justice shall walk before him,
    and salvation, along the way of his steps.

℟. The Lord speaks of peace to his people.

---

3   Ps 122, 1-2. 3-4. 4-5. 6-7. 8-9

℟. (Sir 36, 18) Give peace, O Lord, to those
    who wait for you.

I rejoiced because they said to me,
    "We will go up to the house of the Lord."
And now we have set foot
    within your gates, O Jerusalem.

℟. Give peace, O Lord, to those who wait for
    you.

Jerusalem, built as a city
    with compact unity.
To it the tribes go up,
    the tribes of the Lord.

℟. Give peace, O Lord, to those who wait for
    you.

According to the decree for Israel,
    to give thanks to the name of the Lord.
In it are set up judgment seats,
    seats for the house of David.

℟. Give peace, O Lord, to those who wait for
    you.

Pray for the peace of Jerusalem!
    May those who love you prosper!
May peace be within your walls,
    prosperity in your buildings.

℟. Give peace, O Lord, to those who wait for
    you.

Because of my relatives and friends
    I will say, "Peace be within you!"
Because of the house of the Lord, our God,
    I will pray for your good.

℟. Give peace, O Lord, to those who wait for
    you.

---

834   **ALLELUIA VERSE AND
          VERSE BEFORE THE GOSPEL**

1   Mt 5, 9

Happy the peacemakers;
they shall be called sons of God.

2   Jn 14, 27

Peace I leave with you, says the Lord,
my own peace I give you.

---

835   **GOSPEL**

1   Mt 5, 1-12

✠ A reading from the holy gospel according
         to Matthew

Happy the peacemakers; they shall be called sons of God.

When Jesus saw the crowds he went up on the
mountainside. After he had sat down his disciples gathered around him, and he began to
teach them:

    "How blest are the poor in spirit: the reign
       of God is theirs.
    Blest too are the sorrowing; they shall be
       consoled.
    [Blest are the lowly; they shall inherit the
       land.]
    Blest are they who hunger and thirst for
       holiness;
    they shall have their fill.
    Blest are they who show mercy; mercy
       shall be theirs.
    Blest are the single-hearted for they shall
       see God.
    Blest too the peacemakers; they shall be
       called sons of God.
    Blest are those persecuted for holiness'
       sake; the reign of God is theirs.

Blest are you when they insult you and persecute you and utter every kind of slander against you because of me.
Be glad and rejoice, for your reward in heaven is great."
This is the gospel of the Lord.

---

2   Mt 5, 38-48

✠ A reading from the holy gospel according to Matthew

I say this to you: offer the wicked man no resistance.

Jesus said to his disciples: "You have heard the commandment, 'An eye for an eye, a tooth for a tooth.' But what I say to you is: offer no resistance to injury. When a person strikes you on the right cheek, turn and offer him the other. If anyone wants to go to law over your shirt, hand him your coat as well. Should anyone press you into service for one mile, go with him two miles. Give to the man who begs from you. Do not turn your back on the borrower.

"You have heard the commandment, 'You shall love your countryman but hate your enemy.' My command to you is: love your enemies, pray for your persecutors. This will prove that you are sons of your heavenly Father, for his sun rises on the bad and the good, he rains on the just and the unjust. If you love those who love you, what merit is there in that? Do not tax collectors do as much? And if you greet your brothers only, what is so praiseworthy about that? Do not pagans do as much? In a word, you must be perfected as your heavenly Father is perfect."
This is the gospel of the Lord.

---

3   Jn 14, 23-29

✠ A reading from the holy gospel according to John

Peace is what I give to you.

Jesus said to his disciples:
"Anyone who loves me
will be true to my word,
and my Father will love him;
we will come to him
and make our dwelling place with him.

He who does not love me does not keep my words.
Yet the word you hear is not mine;
it comes from the Father who sent me.
This much have I told you while I was still with you;
the Paraclete, the Holy Spirit
whom the Father will send in my name,
will instruct you in everything,
and remind you of all that I told you.
'Peace' is my farewell to you,
my peace is my gift to you;
I do not give it to you as the world gives peace.
Do not be distressed or fearful.
You have heard me say,
'I go away for a while, and I come back to you.'
If you truly loved me
you would rejoice to have me go to the Father,
for the Father is greater than I.
I tell you this now, before it takes place,
so that when it takes place you may believe."
This is the gospel of the Lord.

---

4   Jn 20, 19-23

✠ A reading from the holy gospel according to John

Peace to you.

On the evening of the first day of the week, even though the disciples had locked the doors of the place where they were for fear of the Jews, Jesus came and stood before them. "Peace be with you," he said. When he had said this, he showed them his hands and his side. At the sight of the Lord the disciples rejoiced. "Peace be with you," he said again.
"As the Father has sent me,
so I send you."
Then he breathed on them and said:
"Receive the Holy Spirit.
If you forgive men's sins,
they are forgiven them;
if you hold them bound,
they are held bound."
This is the gospel of the Lord.

IN TIME OF WAR AND CIVIL DISTURBANCES

836   OLD TESTAMENT READING

1   Gn 4, 3-10

A reading from the book of Genesis

Cain attacked his brother, Abel, and killed him.

In the course of time Cain brought an offering to the Lord from the fruit of the soil, while Abel, for his part, brought one of the best firstlings of his flock. The Lord looked with favor on Abel and his offering, but on Cain and his offering he did not. Cain greatly resented this and was crestfallen. So the Lord said to Cain: "Why are you so resentful and crestfallen? If you do well, you can hold up your head; but if not, sin is a demon lurking at the door: his urge is toward you, yet you can be his master."

Cain said to his brother Abel, "Let us go out in the field." When they were in the field, Cain attacked his brother Abel and killed him. Then the Lord asked Cain, "Where is your brother Abel?" He answered, "I do not know. Am I my brother's keeper?" The Lord then said: "What have you done! Listen: your brother's blood cries out to me from the soil!"

This is the Word of the Lord.

---

2   Mi 4, 1-4

A reading from the book of the prophet Micah

There will be no more training for war.

In days to come
  the mount of the Lord's house
Shall be established higher than the mountains;
  it shall rise high above the hills,
And peoples shall stream to it:
  Many nations shall come, and say,
"Come, let us climb the mount of the Lord,
  to the house of the God of Jacob,
That he may instruct us in his ways,
  that we may walk in his paths."
For from Zion shall go forth instruction,
  and the word of the Lord from Jerusalem.
He shall judge between many peoples

and impose terms on strong and distant nations;
They shall beat their swords into plowshares,
  and their spears into pruning hooks;
One nation shall not raise the sword against another,
  nor shall they train for war again.
Every man shall sit under his own vine
  or under his own fig tree, undisturbed;
  for the mouth of the Lord of hosts has spoken.

This is the Word of the Lord.

---

3   Zec 9, 9-10

A reading from the book of the prophet Zechariah

The weapons of war will be banished.

Thus says the Lord:
Rejoice heartily, O daughter Zion,
  shout for joy, O daughter Jerusalem!
See, your king shall come to you;
  a just savior is he,
Meek, and riding on an ass,
  on a colt, the foal of an ass.
He shall banish the chariot from Ephraim,
  and the horse from Jerusalem;
The warrior's bow shall be banished,
  and he shall proclaim peace to the nations.
His dominion shall be from sea to sea,
  and from the River to the ends of the earth.

This is the Word of the Lord.

---

837   NEW TESTAMENT READING

1   Gal 5, 17-26

A reading from the letter of Paul to the Galatians

When self-indulgence is at work the results are obvious: feuds and wrangling, jealousy, bad temper and quarrels.

The flesh lusts against the spirit and the spirit against the flesh; the two are directly opposed. This is why you do not do what your will intends. If you are guided by the spirit, you are not under the law. It is obvious what proceeds from the flesh: lewd conduct, impurity, licentiousness, idolatry, sorcery, hostilities, bickering, jealousy, outbursts of rage, selfish rivalries, dissensions, factions, envy, drunkenness, orgies, and the like. I warn you, as I have warned you before: those who do such things will not inherit the kingdom of God!

In contrast, the fruit of the spirit is love, joy, peace, patient endurance, kindness, generosity, faith, mildness, and chastity. Against such there is no law! Those who belong to Christ Jesus have crucified their flesh with its passions and desires. Since we live by the spirit, let us follow the spirit's lead. Let us never be boastful, or challenging, or jealous toward one another.

This is the Word of the Lord.

---

2   Eph 4, 30—5, 2

A reading from the letter of Paul to the Ephesians

Let all bitterness, wrath, anger, and slander be put away from you.

Do nothing to sadden the Holy Spirit with whom you were sealed against the day of redemption. Get rid of all bitterness, all passion and anger, harsh words, slander, and malice of every kind. In place of these, be kind to one another, compassionate, and mutually forgiving, just as God has forgiven you in Christ.

Be imitators of God as his dear children. Follow the way of love, even as Christ loved you. He gave himself for us as an offering to God, a gift of pleasing fragrance.

This is the Word of the Lord.

---

3   Jas 4, 1-10

A reading from the letter of James

What causes war and fighting among you?

Where do the conflicts and disputes among you originate? Is it not your inner cravings that make war within your members? What you desire you do not obtain, and so you resort to murder. You envy and you cannot acquire, so you quarrel and fight. You do not obtain because you do not ask. You ask and you do not receive because you ask wrongly, with a view to squandering what you receive on your pleasures. O you unfaithful ones, are you not aware that love of the world is enmity to God? A man is marked out as God's enemy if he chooses to

be the world's friend. Do you suppose it is to no purpose that Scripture says, "The spirit he has implanted in us tends toward jealousy"? Yet he bestows a greater gift, for the sake of which it is written,

"God resists the proud
    but bestows his favor on the lowly."

Therefore submit to God; resist the devil and he will take flight. Draw close to God, and he will draw close to you. Cleanse your hands, you sinners; purify your hearts, you backsliders. Begin to lament, to mourn, and to weep; let your laughter be turned into mourning and your joy into sorrow. Be humbled in the sight of the Lord and he will raise you on high.

This is the Word of the Lord.

---

838   **RESPONSORIAL PSALM**

1   Ps 72, 2. 3-4. 7-8. 12-13. 17

℟. (7) Justice shall flourish in his time,
    and fullness of peace for ever.

**O God, with your judgment endow the king,
    and with your justice, the king's son;**
**He shall govern your people with justice
    and your afflicted ones with judgment.**

℟. Justice shall flourish in his time,
    and fullness of peace for ever.

**The mountains shall yield peace for the people,
    and the hills justice.**
**He shall defend the afflicted among the people,
    save the children of the poor.**

℟. Justice shall flourish in his time,
    and fullness of peace for ever.

**Justice shall flower in his days,
    and profound peace, till the moon be no
    more.**
**May he rule from sea to sea,
    and from the River to the ends of the earth.**

℟. Justice shall flourish in his time,
    and fullness of peace for ever.

**For he shall rescue the poor man when he cries
    out,
    and the afflicted when he has no one to help
    him.**
**He shall have pity for the lowly and the poor;
    the lives of the poor he shall save.**

℟. Justice shall flourish in his time,
  and fullness of peace for ever.
May his name be blessed forever;
  as long as the sun his name shall remain.
In him shall all the tribes of the earth be
  blessed;
  all the nations shall proclaim his happiness.
℟. Justice shall flourish in his time,
  and fullness of peace for ever.

---

2   Ps 85, 9-10. 11-12. 13-14

℟. (9) The Lord speaks of peace to his people.
I will hear what God proclaims;
  the Lord—for he proclaims peace.
Near indeed is his salvation to those who fear
  him,
  glory dwelling in our land.
℟. The Lord speaks of peace to his people.
Kindness and truth shall meet;
  justice and peace shall kiss.
Truth shall spring out of the earth,
  and justice shall look down from heaven.
℟. The Lord speaks of peace to his people.
The Lord himself will give his benefits;
  our land shall yield its increase.
Justice shall walk before him,
  and salvation, along the way of his steps.
℟. The Lord speaks of peace to his people.

---

839   **ALLELUIA VERSE AND**
        VERSE BEFORE THE GOSPEL

1   Mt 5, 9

Happy the peacemakers;
they shall be called sons of God.

2   2 Cor 1, 3-4

Blessed be the Father of mercies and the God
  of all comfort,
who consoles us in all our afflictions.

840   **GOSPEL**

1   Mt 5, 20-24

✠ **A reading from the holy gospel according**
        to Matthew
Anyone who is angry with his brother will answer for it
before the law.

Jesus said to his disciples: "I tell you, unless
your holiness surpasses that of the scribes and
Pharisees you shall not enter the kingdom of
God.

"You have heard the commandment im-
posed on your forefathers, 'You shall not com-
mit murder; every murderer shall be liable to
judgment.' What I say to you is: everyone who
grows angry with his brother shall be liable to
judgment; any man who uses abusive language
toward his brother shall be answerable to the
Sanhedrin, and if he holds him in contempt he
risks the fires of Gehenna. If you bring your
gift to the altar and there recall that your
brother has anything against you, leave your
gift at the altar, go first to be reconciled with
your brother, and then come and offer your
gift."
      This is the gospel of the Lord.

---

2   Jn 15, 9-12

✠ **A reading from the holy gospel according**
        to John
This is my commandment: love one another as I have loved
you.

Jesus said to his disciples:
  "As the Father has loved me,
  so I have loved you.
  Live on in my love.
  You will live in my love
  if you keep my commandments,
  even as I have kept my Father's command-
    ments,
  and live in his love.
  All this I tell you
  that my joy may be yours
  and your joy may be complete.
  This is my commandment:
  love one another
  as I have loved you.
      This is the gospel of the Lord.

Readings from the Mass for peace and justice may also be
used, above, nos. 831-835.

III. FOR VARIOUS PUBLIC NEEDS

BEGINNING OF THE NEW YEAR

841   OLD TESTAMENT READING

1   Gn 1, 14-18

A reading from the book of Genesis
Let there be lights to indicate festivals, days and years.

God said: "Let there be lights in the dome of the sky, to separate day from night. Let them mark the fixed times, the days and the years, and serve as luminaries in the dome of the sky, to shed light upon the earth." And so it happened: God made the two great lights, the greater one to govern the day, and the lesser one to govern the night; and he made the stars. God set them in the dome of the sky, to shed light upon the earth, to govern the day and the night, and to separate the light from the darkness. God saw how good it was.

This is the Word of the Lord.

---

2   Nm 6, 22-27

A reading from the book of Numbers
They will call my name down on the sons of Israel, and I will bless them.

The Lord said to Moses: "Speak to Aaron and his sons and tell them: This is how you shall bless the Israelites. Say to them:
The Lord bless you and keep you!
The Lord let his face shine upon you, and be gracious to you!
The Lord look upon you kindly and give you peace!
So shall they invoke my name upon the Israelites, and I will bless them."

This is the Word of the Lord.

---

842   NEW TESTAMENT READING

1   1 Cor 7, 29-31

A reading from the first letter of Paul to the Corinthians
The world as we know it is passing away.

I tell you, brothers, the time is short. From now on those with wives should live as though they had none; those who weep should live as though they were not weeping, and those who rejoice as though they were not rejoicing; buyers should conduct themselves as though they owned nothing, and those who make use of the world as though they were not using it, for the world as we know it is passing away.

This is the Word of the Lord.

---

2   Jas 4, 13-15

A reading from the letter of James
You never know what will happen tomorrow.

Come now, you who say, "Today or tomorrow we shall go to such and such a town, spend a year there, trade, and come off with a profit!" You have no idea what kind of life will be yours tomorrow. You are a vapor that appears briefly and vanishes. You should say, "If the Lord wills it, we shall live to do this or that."

This is the Word of the Lord.

---

843   RESPONSORIAL PSALM

1   Ps 8, 4-5. 6-7. 8-9

℟. (2) O Lord, our God,
how wonderful your name in all the earth!
When I behold your heavens, the work of your fingers,
the moon and the stars which you set in place—
What is man that you should be mindful of him,
or the son of man that you should care for him?
℟. O Lord, our God,
how wonderful your name in all the earth!
You have made him little less than the angels,
and crowned him with glory and honor.

You have given him rule over the works of
   your hands,
   putting all things under his feet:
R℣. O Lord, our God,
   how wonderful your name in all the earth!
All sheep and oxen,
   yes, and the beasts of the field,
The birds of the air, the fishes of the sea,
   and whatever swims the paths of the seas.
R℣. O Lord, our God,
   how wonderful your name in all the earth!

---

2   Ps 49, 2-3. 6-7. 8-10. 11. 17-18

R℣. (Mt 5, 3) Happy the poor in spirit;
   the kingdom of heaven is theirs!
Hear this, all you peoples;
   hearken, all who dwell in the world,
Of lowly birth or high degree,
   rich and poor alike.
R℣. Happy the poor in spirit;
   the kingdom of heaven is theirs!
Why should I fear in evil days
   when my wicked ensnarers ring me round?
They trust in their wealth;
   the abundance of their riches is their boast.
R℣. Happy the poor in spirit;
   the kingdom of heaven is theirs!
Yet in no way can a man redeem himself,
   or pay his own ransom to God;
Too high is the price to redeem one's life; he
   would never have enough
   to remain alive always and not see destruction.
R℣. Happy the poor in spirit;
   the kingdom of heaven is theirs!
For he can see that wise men die,
   and likewise the senseless and the stupid
   pass away,
   leaving to others their wealth.
R℣. Happy the poor in spirit;
   the kingdom of heaven is theirs!
Fear not when a man grows rich,
   when the wealth of his house becomes great,
For when he dies, he shall take none of it;
   his wealth shall not follow him down.
R℣. Happy the poor in spirit;
   the kingdom of heaven is theirs!

R℣. Or: (Mt 6, 33) Seek first the kingdom of
   God and his holiness.

---

3   Ps 90, 2. 3-4. 5-6. 12-13. 14-16

R℣. (17) Lord, give success to the work of our
   hands.
Before the mountains were begotten
   and the earth and the world were brought
   forth,
   from everlasting to everlasting you are God.
R℣. Lord, give success to the work of our hands.
You turn man back to dust,
   saying, "Return, O children of men."
For a thousand years in your sight
   are as yesterday, now that it is past,
   or as a watch of the night.
R℣. Lord, give success to the work of our hands.
You make an end of them in their sleep;
   the next morning they are like the changing
   grass,
Which at dawn springs up anew,
   but by evening wilts and fades.
R℣. Lord, give success to the work of our hands.
Teach us to number our days aright,
   that we may gain wisdom of heart.
Return, O Lord! How long?
   Have pity on your servants!
R℣. Lord, give success to the work of our hands.
Fill us at daybreak with your kindness,
   that we may shout for joy and gladness all
   our days.
Let your work be seen by your servants
   and your glory by their children.
R℣. Lord, give success to the work of our hands.

---

844   **ALLELUIA VERSE AND**
        VERSE BEFORE THE GOSPEL

1   1 Chr 29, 10. 11

Blessed are you, O Lord our God;
all things in heaven and earth are yours.

2

Day after day we bless you;
we praise your name without ceasing.

845   GOSPEL

1   Mt 6, 31-34

✠ **A reading from the holy gospel according to Matthew**

Do not worry about tomorrow.

Jesus said to his disciples: "Stop worrying over questions like, 'What are we to eat, or what are we to drink, or what are we to wear?' The unbelievers are always running after these things. Your heavenly Father knows all that you need. Seek first his kingship over you, his way of holiness, and all these things will be given you besides. Enough, then, of worrying about tomorrow. Let tomorrow take care of itself. Today has troubles enough of its own."

This is the gospel of the Lord.

----

2   Lk 12, 35-40

✠ **A reading from the holy gospel according to Luke**

See that you are prepared.

Jesus said to his disciples: "Let your belts be fastened around your waists and your lamps be burning ready. Be like men awaiting their master's return from a wedding, so that when he arrives and knocks, you will open for him without delay. It will go well with those servants whom the master finds wide-awake on his return. I tell you, he will put on an apron, seat them at table, and proceed to wait on them. Should he happen to come at midnight or before sunrise and find them prepared, it will go well with them. You know as well as I that if the head of the house knew when the thief was coming he would not let him break into his house. Be on guard, therefore. The Son of Man will come when you least expect him."

This is the gospel of the Lord.

BLESSING OF MAN'S LABOR

846   OLD TESTAMENT READING

1   Gn 1, 26—2. 3

A reading from the book of Genesis

Fill the earth and conquer it.

God said: "Let us make man in our image, after our likeness. Let them have dominion over the fish of the sea, the birds of the air, and the cattle, and over all the wild animals and all the creatures that crawl on the ground."

God created man in his image;
in the divine image he created him;
male and female he created them.

God blessed them, saying: "Be fertile and multiply; fill the earth and subdue it. Have dominion over the fish of the sea, the birds of the air, and all the living things that move on the earth." God also said: "See, I give you every seed-bearing plant over all the earth and every tree that has seed-bearing fruit on it to be your food; and to all the animals of the land, all the birds of the air, and all the living creatures that crawl on the ground, I give all the green plants for food." And so it happened. God looked at everything he had made, and he found it very good. Evening came, and morning followed—the sixth day.

Thus the heavens and the earth and all their array were completed. Since on the seventh day God was finished with the work he had been doing, he rested on the seventh day from all the work he had undertaken. So God blessed the seventh day and made it holy, because on it he rested from all the work he had done in creation.

This is the Word of the Lord.

----

2   Gn 2, 4-9. 15

A reading from the book of Genesis

God took Adam and settled him in the garden of Eden to cultivate and take care of it.

At the time when the Lord God made the earth and the heavens—while as yet there was no field shrub on earth and no grass of the field had sprouted, for the Lord God had sent no rain upon the earth and there was no man to till the soil, but a stream was welling up out of the earth and was watering all the surface of the ground—the Lord God formed man out of the clay of the ground and blew into his nostrils the breath of life, and so man became a living being.

Then the Lord God planted a garden in Eden, in the east, and he placed there the man whom he had formed. Out of the ground the Lord God made various trees grow that were delightful to look at and good for food, with the tree of life in the middle of the garden and the tree of the knowledge of good and bad.

The Lord God then took the man and settled him in the garden of Eden, to cultivate and care for it.

This is the Word of the Lord.

847   NEW TESTAMENT READING

2 Thes 3, 6-12. 16

A reading from the second letter of Paul to the Thessalonians

Do not let anyone have any food if he refuses to do any work.

We command you, brothers, in the name of the Lord Jesus Christ, to avoid any brother who wanders from the straight path and does not follow the tradition you received from us. You know how you ought to imitate us. We did not live lives of disorder when we were among you, nor depend on anyone for food. Rather, we worked day and night, laboring to the point of exhaustion so as not to impose on any of you. Not that we had no claim on you, but that we might present ourselves as an example for you to imitate. Indeed, when we were with you we used to lay down the rule that anyone who would not work should not eat.

We hear that some of you are unruly, not keeping busy but acting like busybodies. We enjoin all and we urge them strongly in the Lord Jesus Christ to earn the food they eat by working quietly.

May he who is the Lord of peace give you continued peace in every possible way. The Lord be with you all.

This is the Word of the Lord.

848   RESPONSORIAL PSALM

1   Ps 90, 2. 3-4. 12-13. 14. 16

℟. (17) Lord, give success to the work of our hands.

Before the mountains were begotten
    and the earth and the world were brought forth,
    from everlasting to everlasting you are God.
℟. Lord, give success to the work of our hands.
You turn man back to dust,
    saying, "Return, O children of men."
For a thousand years in your sight
    are as yesterday, now that it is past,
    or as a watch of the night.
℟. Lord, give success to the work of our hands.
Teach us to number our days aright,
    that we may gain wisdom of heart.
Return, O Lord! How long?
    Have pity on your servants!
℟. Lord, give success to the work of our hands.
Fill us at daybreak with your kindness,
    that we may shout for joy and gladness all our days.
Let your work be seen by your servants
    and your glory by their children.
℟. Lord, give success to the work of our hands.

2   Ps 127, 1. 2

℟. The Lord will build a house for us
    and guard our city.
Unless the Lord build the house,
    they labor in vain who build it.
Unless the Lord guard the city,
    in vain does the guard keep vigil.
℟. The Lord will build a house for us
    and guard our city.
It is vain for you to rise early,
    or put off your rest,
You that eat hard-earned bread,
    for he gives to his beloved in sleep.
℟. The Lord will build a house for us
    and guard our city.

849   **ALLELUIA VERSE AND
VERSE BEFORE THE GOSPEL**

1   Ps 68, 20

Blessed be the Lord day after day,
the God who saves us and bears our burdens.

2   Mt 11, 28

Come to me, all you that labor and are burdened,
and I will give you rest, says the Lord.

---

850   **GOSPEL**

1   Mt 6, 31-34

✠ A reading from the holy gospel according
to Matthew

Do not worry about tomorrow.

Jesus said to his disciples: "Stop worrying over
questions like, 'What are we to eat, or what are
we to drink, or what are we to wear?' The unbelievers are always running after these things.
Your heavenly Father knows all that you need.
Seek first his kingship over you, his way of holiness, and all these things will be given you
besides. Enough, then, of worrying about tomorrow. Let tomorrow take care of itself. Today has troubles enough of its own."
This is the gospel of the Lord.

---

2   Mt 25, 14-30

✠ A reading from the holy gospel according
to Matthew

You are faithful in small things; come and join in your
master's happiness.

Jesus told his disciples this parable: "A man
was going on a journey. He called in his servants and handed his funds over to them according to each man's abilities. To one he disbursed five thousand silver pieces, to a second
two thousand, and to a third a thousand. Then
he went away. Immediately the man who received the five thousand went to invest it and
made another five. In the same way, the man
who received the two thousand doubled his

figure. The man who received the thousand
went off instead and dug a hole in the ground,
where he buried his master's money. After a
long absence, the master of those servants
came home and settled accounts with them.
The man who had received the five thousand
came forward bringing the additional five. 'My
lord,' he said, 'you let me have five thousand.
See, I have made five thousand more.' His master said to him, 'Well done! You are an industrious and reliable servant. Since you were dependable in a small matter I will put you in
charge of larger affairs. Come, share your master's joy!' The man who had received the two
thousand then stepped forward. 'My lord,' he
said, 'you entrusted me with two thousand and
I have made two thousand more.' His master
said to him, 'Cleverly done! You too are an
industrious and reliable servant. Since you
were dependable in a small matter I will put
you in charge of larger affairs. Come, share
your master's joy!'
"Finally the man who had received the thousand stepped forward. 'My lord,' he said, 'I
knew you were a hard man. You reap where
you did not sow and gather where you did not
scatter, so out of fear I went off and buried
your thousand silver pieces in the ground. Here
is your money back.' His master exclaimed:
'You worthless, lazy lout! You know I reap
where I did not sow and gather where I did not
scatter. All the more reason to deposit my
money with the bankers, so that on my return
I could have had it back with interest. You,
there! Take the thousand away from him and
give it to the man with the ten thousand. Those
who have, will get more until they grow rich,
while those who have not, will lose even the little they have. Throw this worthless servant into
the darkness outside, where he can wail and
grind his teeth.' "
This is the gospel of the Lord.

FOR PRODUCTIVE LAND

851   OLD TESTAMENT READING

Gn 1, 11-12

A reading from the book of Genesis

Let the earth produce vegetation and seed-bearing plants.

God said, "Let the earth bring forth vegetation: every kind of plant that bears seed and every kind of fruit tree on earth that bears fruit with its seed in it." And so it happened: the earth brought forth every kind of plant that bears seed and every kind of fruit tree on earth that bears fruit with its seed in it. God saw how good it was.

This is the Word of the Lord.

852   NEW TESTAMENT READING

2 Cor 9, 8-11

A reading from the second letter of Paul to the Corinthians

God will provide bread for man to eat.

God can multiply his favors among you so that you may always have enough of everything and even a surplus for good works, as it is written:

"He scattered abroad and gave to the poor, his justice endures forever."

He who supplies seed for the sower and bread for the eater will provide in abundance; he will multiply the seed you sow and increase your generous yield. In every way your liberality is enriched; through us it results in thanks offered to God.

This is the Word of the Lord.

853   RESPONSORIAL PSALM

Ps 104, 1-2. 14-15. 24. 27-28

℟. (24) The earth is full of your riches, O Lord.
Bless the Lord, O my soul!
O Lord, my God, you are great indeed!
You are clothed with majesty and glory,
    robed in light as with a cloak.

℟. The earth is full of your riches, O Lord.

You raise grass for the cattle,
    and vegetation for men's use,
Producing bread from the earth,
    and wine to gladden men's hearts,
So that their faces gleam with oil,
    and bread fortifies the hearts of men.

℟. The earth is full of your riches, O Lord.
How manifold are your works, O Lord!
    In wisdom you have wrought them all—
    the earth is full of your creatures.

℟. The earth is full of your riches, O Lord.
They all look to you
    to give them food in due time.
When you give it to them, they gather it;
    when you open your hand, they are filled
    with good things.

℟. The earth is full of your riches, O Lord.

854   ALLELUIA VERSE AND
**   VERSE BEFORE THE GOSPEL**

Ps 126, 5

Those who sow in tears, shall reap with shouts
    of joy.

855   GOSPEL
1

Mt 13, 1-9

✠ **A reading from the holy gospel according**
to Matthew

The sower went out to sow seed.

On leaving the house, Jesus sat down by the lakeshore. Such great crowds gathered around him that he went and took his seat in a boat while the crowd stood along the shore. He addressed them at length in parables, speaking in this fashion:

"One day a farmer went out sowing. Part of what he sowed landed on a footpath, where birds came and ate it up. Part of it fell on rocky ground, where it had little soil. It sprouted at once since the soil had no depth, but when the sun rose and scorched it, it began to wither for lack of roots. Again, part of the seed fell among thorns, which grew up and choked it. Part of it, finally, landed on good soil and yielded grain one hundred- or sixty- or thirty-fold. Let everyone heed what he hears!'' This is the gospel of the Lord.

---

2   Mk 4, 26-29

✠ **A reading from the holy gospel according to Mark**

A man throws seed on the land. While he sleeps, the seed is sprouting and growing without him knowing it.

Jesus said to the crowds: "This is how it is with the reign of God. A man scatters seed on the ground. He goes to bed and gets up day after day. Through it all the seed sprouts and grows without his knowing how it happens. The soil produces of itself first the blade, then the ear, finally the ripe wheat in the ear. When the crop is ready he 'wields the sickle, for the time is ripe for harvest.' "

This is the gospel of the Lord.

Readings from the Mass for the blessing of man's labor may also be used, above, nos. 846-850.

AFTER THE HARVEST

856   **OLD TESTAMENT READING**

1   Dt 8, 7-18

A reading from the book of Deuteronomy

Be mindful of the Lord your God, how he elected you and showed you his favor.

Moses told the people: "The Lord, your God, is bringing you into a good country, a land with streams of water, with springs and fountains welling up in the hills and valleys, a land of wheat and barley, of vines and fig trees and pomegranates, of olive trees and of honey, a land where you can eat bread without stint and where you will lack nothing, a land whose stones contain iron and in whose hills you can mine copper. But when you have eaten your fill, you must bless the Lord, your God, for the good country he has given you. Be careful not to forget the Lord, your God, by neglecting his commandments and decrees and statutes which I enjoin on you today: lest, when you

have eaten your fill, and have built fine houses and lived in them, and have increased your herds and flocks, your silver and gold, and all your property, you then become haughty of heart and unmindful of the Lord, your God, who brought you out of the land of Egypt, that place of slavery; who guided you through the vast and terrible desert with its saraph serpents and scorpions, its parched and water-less ground; who brought forth water for you from the flinty rock and fed you in the desert with manna, a food unknown to your fathers, that he might afflict you and test you, but also make you prosperous in the end. Otherwise, you might say to yourselves, 'It is my own power and the strength of my own hand that has obtained for me this wealth.' Remember then, it is the Lord, your God, who gives you the power to acquire wealth, by fulfilling, as he has now done, the covenant which he swore to your fathers."

This is the Word of the Lord.

---

2   Jl 2, 21-24. 26-27

A reading from the book of the prophet Joel

He provided his elect with great abundance.

Fear not, O land!
    exult and rejoice!
    for the Lord has done great things.
Fear not, beasts of the field!
    for the pastures of the plain are green;
The tree bears its fruit,
    the fig tree and the vine give their yield.

And do you, O children of Zion, exult
    and rejoice in the Lord, your God!
He has given you the teacher of justice:
    he has made the rain come down for you,
    the early and the late rain as before.
The threshing floors shall be full of grain
    and the vats shall overflow with wine and
    oil.

You shall eat and be filled,
    and shall praise the name of the Lord, your
    God,
Because he has dealt wondrously with you;
    my people shall nevermore be put to shame.

And you shall know that I am in the midst of
  Israel;
I am the Lord, your God, and there is no
  other;
My people shall nevermore be put to shame.
  This is the Word of the Lord.

857   NEW TESTAMENT READING

1 Tm 6, 6-11. 17-19

A reading from the first letter of Paul to
Timothy

Warn the rich not to set their hopes on money.

There is, of course, this great gain in religion—
provided one is content with a sufficiency. We
brought nothing into this world, nor have we
the power to take anything out. If we have
food and clothing we have all that we need.
Those who want to be rich are falling into
temptation and a trap. They are letting themselves be captured by foolish and harmful desires which drag men down to ruin and
destruction. The love of money is the root
of all evil. Some men in their passion for it
have strayed from the faith and have come to
grief amid great pain.

Man of God that you are, flee from all this.
Instead, seek after integrity, piety, faith, love,
steadfastness, and a gentle spirit.

Tell those who are rich in this world's goods
not to be proud, and not to rely on so uncertain
a thing as wealth. Let them trust in the God
who provides us richly with all things for our
use. Charge them to do good, to be rich in good
works and generous, sharing what they have.
Thus will they build a secure foundation for the
future, for receiving that life which is life
indeed.

This is the Word of the Lord.

858   RESPONSORIAL PSALM

Ps 67, 2-3. 5. 7-8

℟. (17) The earth has yielded its fruit,
  the Lord our God has blessed us.
May God have pity on us and bless us;
  may he let his face shine upon us.

So may your way be known upon earth;
  among all nations, your salvation.
℟. The earth has yielded its fruit,
  the Lord our God has blessed us.
May the nations be glad and exult
  because you rule the peoples in equity;
  the nations on the earth you guide.
℟. The earth has yielded its fruit,
  the Lord our God has blessed us.
The earth has yielded its fruits;
  God, our God, has blessed us.
May God bless us,
  and may all the ends of the earth fear him!
℟. The earth has yielded its fruit,
  the Lord our God has blessed us.
℟. Or: (4) O God, let all the nations praise you!

**859   ALLELUIA VERSE AND
VERSE BEFORE THE GOSPEL**

Ps 126, 5

Those who sow in tears, shall reap with shouts
of joy.

860   GOSPEL

1   Lk 12, 15-21

✠ A reading from the holy gospel according
to Luke

A man's life is not made secure by what he owns, even
when he has more than he needs.

Jesus said to the crowd, "Avoid greed in all
its forms. A man may be wealthy, but his
possessions do not guarantee him life." He told
them a parable in these words: "There was a
rich man who had a good harvest. 'What shall
I do?' he asked himself. 'I have no place to
store my harvest. I know!' he said. 'I will pull
down my grain bins and build larger ones. All
my grain and my goods will go there. Then I
will say to myself: You have blessings in reserve for years to come. Relax! Eat heartily,
drink well. Enjoy yourself.' But God said to
him, 'You fool! This very night your life shall
be required of you. To whom will all this piled-
up wealth of yours go?' That is the way it

works with the man who grows rich for himself instead of growing rich in the sight of God."

This is the gospel of the Lord.

---

2 Lk 17, 11-19

✠ **A reading from the holy gospel according to Luke**

He threw himself at the feet of Jesus and thanked him.

On his journey to Jerusalem Jesus passed along the borders of Samaria and Galilee. As he was entering a village, ten lepers met him. Keeping their distance, they raised their voices and said, "Jesus, Master, have pity on us!" When he saw them, he responded, "Go and show yourselves to the priests." On their way there they were cured. One of them, realizing that he had been cured, came back praising God in a loud voice. He threw himself on his face at the feet of Jesus and spoke his praises. This man was a Samaritan.

Jesus took the occasion to say, "Were not all ten made whole? Where are the other nine? Was there no one to return and give thanks to God except this foreigner?" He said to the man: "Stand up and go your way; your faith has been your salvation."

This is the gospel of the Lord.

Readings from the Mass in thanksgiving may also be used, below, nos. 881–885.

FOR THOSE SUFFERING FROM FAMINE OR HUNGER

861 OLD TESTAMENT READING

1 Dt 24, 17-22

A reading from the book of Deuteronomy

Whatever you have left over from your work, leave for the stranger, the orphan, and the widow.

Moses told the people: "You shall not violate the rights of the alien or of the orphan, nor take the clothing of a widow as a pledge. For, remember, you were once slaves in Egypt, and the Lord, your God, ransomed you from

there; that is why I command you to observe this rule.

"When you reap the harvest in your field and overlook a sheaf there, you shall not go back to get it; let it be for the alien, the orphan or the widow, that the Lord, your God, may bless you in all your undertakings. When you knock down the fruit of your olive trees, you shall not go over the branches a second time; let what remains be for the alien, the orphan, and the widow. When you pick your grapes, you shall not go over the vineyard a second time; let what remains be for the alien, the orphan, and the widow. For remember that you were once slaves in Egypt; that is why I command you to observe this rule."

This is the Word of the Lord.

---

2 Jb 31, 16-20. 24-25. 31-32

A reading from the book of Job

If I have taken my share of bread alone and have not given a share of it to the orphan, then I have been insensitive.

If I have denied anything to the poor,
    or allowed the eyes of the widow to languish
While I ate my portion alone,
    with no share in it for the fatherless,
Though like a father God has reared me from
    my youth,
    guiding me even from my mother's womb—

If I have seen a wanderer without clothing,
    or a poor man without covering,
Whose limbs have not blessed me
    when warmed with the fleece of my sheep;

Had I put my trust in gold
    or called fine gold my security;
Or had I rejoiced that my wealth was great,
    or that my hand had acquired abundance—

Had not the men of my tent exclaimed,
    "Who has not been fed with his meat!"
Because no stranger lodged in the street,
    but I opened my door to wayfarers.

This is the Word of the Lord.

3   Is 58, 6-11

A reading from the book of the prophet Isaiah

Share your bread with the hungry.

Thus says the Lord:
This is the fasting that I wish:
    releasing those bound unjustly,
    untying the thongs of the yoke;
Setting free the oppressed,
    breaking every yoke;
Sharing your bread with the hungry,
    sheltering the oppressed and the homeless;
Clothing the naked when you see them,
    and not turning your back on your own.

Then your light shall break forth like the dawn,
    and your wound shall quickly be healed;
Your vindication shall go before you,
    and the glory of the Lord shall be your rear
    guard.
Then you shall call, and the Lord will answer,
    you shall cry for help, and he will say: Here
    I am!
If you remove from your midst oppression,
    false accusation and malicious speech;
If you bestow your bread on the hungry
    and satisfy the afflicted;
Then light shall rise for you in the darkness,
    and the gloom shall become for you like
    midday;
Then the Lord will guide you always
    and give you plenty even on the parched
    land.
He will renew your strength,
    and you shall be like a watered garden,
    like a spring whose water never fails.
        This is the Word of the Lord.

---

862   **NEW TESTAMENT READING**

1   Acts 11, 27-30

A reading from the Acts of the Apostles

The disciples decided to send relief during the famine, each
to contribute what he could afford, to the brothers living
in Judea.

Certain prophets came down from Jerusalem
to Antioch. One of them named Agabus was
inspired to stand up and proclaim that there
was going to be a severe famine all over the
world. (It did in fact occur while Claudius was
emperor.) This made the disciples determine
to set something aside, each according to his
means, and send it to the relief of the brothers
who lived in Judea. They did this, dispatching
it to the elders in the care of Barnabas and
Saul.
        This is the Word of the Lord.

---

2   2 Cor 8, 1-5. 9-15

**A reading from the second letter of Paul to the
Corinthians**

Your surplus now should supply the present need of others.

Brothers, I should like you to know of the grace
of God conferred on the churches of Macedonia. In the midst of severe trial their overflowing joy and deep poverty have produced
an abundant generosity. According to their
means—indeed I can testify even beyond their
means—and voluntarily, they begged us insistently for the favor of sharing in this service
to members of the church. Beyond our hopes
they first gave themselves to God and then to
us by the will of God.
    You are well acquainted with the favor
shown you by our Lord Jesus Christ: how for
your sake he made himself poor though he
was rich, so that you might become rich by his
poverty. I am about to give you some advice on
this matter of rich and poor. It will help you
who began this good work last year, not only
to carry it through but to do so willingly. Carry
it through now to a successful completion, so
that your ready resolve may be matched by
giving according to your means. The willingness to give should accord with one's means,
not go beyond them. The relief of others ought
not to impoverish you; there should be a certain equality. Your plenty at the present time
should supply their need so that their surplus
may one day supply your need, with equality
as the result. It is written, "He who gathered
much had no excess and he who gathered little
had no lack."
        This is the Word of the Lord.

---

3   2 Cor 9, 6-15

A reading from the second letter of Paul to the Corinthians

Each person should give to those in need what he has decided in his own mind, not grudgingly or because he is made to.

He who sows sparingly will reap sparingly, and he who sows bountifully will reap bountifully. Everyone must give according to what he has inwardly decided; not sadly, not grudgingly, for God loves a cheerful giver. God can multiply his favors among you so that you may always have enough of everything and even a surplus for good works, as it is written:

"He scattered abroad and gave to the poor, his justice endures forever."

He who supplies seed for the sower and bread for the eater will provide in abundance; he will multiply the seed you sow and increase your generous yield. In every way your liberality is enriched; through us it results in thanks offered to God. The administering of this public benefit not only supplies the needs of the members of the church but also overflows in much gratitude to God. Because of your praiseworthy service they are glorifying God for your obedient faith in the gospel of Christ, and for your generosity in sharing with them and with all. They pray for you longingly because of the surpassing grace God has given you. Thanks be to God for his indescribable gift! This is the Word of the Lord.

---

863   **RESPONSORIAL PSALM**

1   Ps 22, 23-24. 26-27. 28. 31-32

R̷. (27) **The poor shall eat and shall have their fill.**

I will proclaim your name to my brethren;
  in the midst of the assembly I will praise you:
"You who fear the Lord, praise him;
  all you descendants of Jacob, give glory to him."

R̷. The poor shall eat and shall have their fill.

So by your gift will I utter praise in the vast assembly;

I will fulfill my vows before those who fear him.
The lowly shall eat their fill;
  they who seek the Lord shall praise him:
  "May your hearts be ever merry!"

R̷. The poor shall eat and shall have their fill.

All the ends of the earth
  shall remember and turn to the Lord;
All the families of the nations
  shall bow down before him.
And to him my soul shall live;
  my descendants shall serve him.
Let the coming generation be told of the Lord
  that they may proclaim to a people yet to be born
  the justice he has shown.

R̷. The poor shall eat and shall have their fill.

---

2   Ps 107, 2-3. 4-5. 6-7. 8-9

R̷. (1) Give thanks to the Lord,
  his love is everlasting.
Thus let the redeemed of the Lord say,
  those whom he has redeemed from the hand of the foe
And gathered from the lands,
  from the east and the west, from the north and the south.

R̷. Give thanks to the Lord,
  his love is everlasting.
They went astray in the desert wilderness;
  the way to an inhabited city they did not find.
Hungry and thirsty,
  their life was wasting away within them.

R̷. Give thanks to the Lord,
  his love is everlasting.
They cried to the Lord in their distress;
  from their straits he rescued them.
And he led them by a direct way
  to reach an inhabited city.

R̷. Give thanks to the Lord,
  his love is everlasting.
Let them give thanks to the Lord for his kindness
  and his wondrous deeds to the children of men,
Because he satisfied the longing soul
  and filled the hungry soul with good things.

℞. Give thanks to the Lord,
his love is everlasting.
℞. Or: Alleluia.

---

3   Ps 112, 1-2. 3-4. 5-7. 7-8. 9

℞. (1. 9) Blessed is the man who gives to the poor.

Happy the man who fears the Lord,
  who greatly delights in his commands.
His posterity shall be mighty upon the earth
  the upright generation shall be blessed.
℞. Blessed is the man who gives to the poor.
Wealth and riches shall be in his house;
  his generosity shall endure forever.
He dawns through the darkness, a light for the
  upright;
  he is gracious and merciful and just.
℞. Blessed is the man who gives to the poor.
Well for the man who is gracious and lends,
  who conducts his affairs with justice;
He shall never be moved;
  the just man shall be in everlasting remembrance.
℞. Blessed is the man who gives to the poor.
An evil report he shall not fear;
  his heart is firm, trusting in the Lord.
His heart is steadfast; he shall not fear
  till he looks down upon his foes.
℞. Blessed is the man who gives to the poor.
Lavishly he gives to the poor;
  his generosity shall endure forever;
  his horn shall be exalted in glory.
℞. Blessed is the man who gives to the poor.
℞. Or: Alleluia.

---

864   **ALLELUIA VERSE AND**
              VERSE BEFORE THE GOSPEL

1   Mt 25, 34

Come, you whom my Father has blessed, says
  the Lord;
inherit the kingdom prepared for you since the
  foundation of the world.

2   2 Cor 8, 9

Jesus Christ was rich but he became poor,
to make you rich out of his poverty.

---

865   **GOSPEL**

1   Mt 25, 31-46

✠ A reading from the holy gospel according
       to Matthew

I was hungry and you gave me food.

Jesus said to his disciples: "When the Son of
Man comes in his glory, escorted by all the
angels of heaven, he will sit upon his royal
throne, and all the nations will be assembled
before him. Then he will separate them into
two groups, as a shepherd separates sheep
from goats. The sheep he will place on his right
hand, the goats on his left. The king will say to
those on his right: 'Come. You have my
Father's blessing! Inherit the kingdom prepared for you from the creation of the world.
For I was hungry and you gave me food, I was
thirsty and you gave me drink. I was a stranger
and you welcomed me, naked and you clothed
me. I was ill and you comforted me, in prison
and you came to visit me.' Then the just will
ask him: 'Lord, when did we see you hungry
and feed you or see you thirsty and give you
drink? When did we welcome you away from
home or clothe you in your nakedness? When
did we visit you when you were ill or in
prison?' The king will answer them: 'I assure
you, as often as you did it for one of my least
brothers, you did it for me.'

"Then he will say to those on his left: 'Out of
my sight, you condemned, into that everlasting
fire prepared for the devil and his angels! I was
hungry and you gave me no food, I was thirsty
and you gave me no drink. I was away from
home and you gave me no welcome, naked and
you gave me no clothing. I was ill and in
prison and you did not come to comfort me.'
Then they in turn will ask: 'Lord, when did we
see you hungry or thirsty or away from home
or naked or ill or in prison and not attend
you in your needs?' He will answer them: 'I
assure you, as often as you neglected to do it
to one of these least ones, you neglected to do
it to me.' These will go off to eternal punishment and the just to eternal life."

    This is the gospel of the Lord.

2   Mk 6, 34-44

✠ A reading from the holy gospel according
to Mark

Share with others what you have to eat.

Jesus saw a vast crowd. He pitied them, for
they were like sheep without a shepherd; and
he began to teach them at great length. It was
now getting late and his disciples came to him
with a suggestion: "This is a deserted place and
it is already late. Why do you not dismiss them
so that they can go to the crossroads and
villages around here and buy themselves something to eat?" "You give them something to
eat," Jesus replied. At that they said, "Are we
to go and spend two hundred days' wages for
bread to feed them?" "How many loaves have
you?" Jesus asked. "Go and see." When they
learned the number they answered, "Five, and
two fish." He told them to make the people
sit down on the green grass in groups or
parties. The people took their places in hundreds and fifties, neatly arranged like flower
beds. Then, taking the five loaves and the two
fish, Jesus raised his eyes to heaven, pronounced a blessing, broke the loaves, and gave
them to the disciples to distribute. He divided
the two fish among all of them and they ate
until they had their fill. They gathered up
enough leftovers to fill twelve baskets, besides
what remained of the fish. Those who had
eaten the loaves numbered five thousand men.
This is the gospel of the Lord.

----

3   Lk 14, 12-14

✠ A reading from the holy gospel according
to Luke

When you have a party, invite the poor.

Jesus said to the chief of the Pharisees who had
invited him: "Whenever you give a lunch or
dinner, do not invite your friends or brothers or
relatives or wealthy neighbors. They might
invite you in return and thus repay you. No,
when you have a reception, invite beggars and
the crippled, the lame and the blind. You
should be pleased that they cannot repay you,

for you will be repaid in the resurrection of the
just."
This is the gospel of the Lord.

----

4   Lk 16, 19-31

✠ A reading from the holy gospel according
to Luke

*Remember the blessings given to the poor man named
Lazarus.*

Jesus said to the Pharisees: "Once there was a
rich man who dressed in purple and linen and
feasted splendidly every day. At his gate lay
a beggar named Lazarus who was covered
with sores. Lazarus longed to eat the scraps
that fell from the rich man's table. The dogs
even came and licked his sores. Eventually the
beggar died. He was carried by angels to the
bosom of Abraham. The rich man likewise died
and was buried. From the abode of the dead
where he was in torment, he raised his eyes
and saw Abraham afar off, and Lazarus resting
in his bosom.

"He called out, 'Father Abraham, have pity
on me. Send Lazarus to dip the tip of his finger
in water to refresh my tongue, for I am tortured in these flames.' 'My child,' replied
Abraham, 'remember that you were well off in
your lifetime, while Lazarus was in misery.
Now he has found consolation here, but you
have found torment. And that is not all. Between you and us there is fixed a great abyss,
so that those who might wish to cross from
here to you cannot do so, nor can anyone cross
from your side to us.'

" 'Father, I ask you, then,' the rich man said,
'send him to my father's house where I have
five brothers. Let him be a warning to them so
that they may not end in this place of torment.'
Abraham answered, 'They have Moses and the
prophets. Let them hear them.' 'No, Father
Abraham,' replied the rich man. 'But if someone would only go to them from the dead, then
they would repent.' Abraham said to him, 'If
they do not listen to Moses and the prophets,
they will not be convinced even if one should
rise from the dead.' "
This is the gospel of the Lord.

FOR REFUGEES AND EXILES

866   OLD TESTAMENT READING

1   Dt 10, 17-19

A reading from the book of Deuteronomy
The Lord God loves the stranger and gives him food and
clothing.

Moses told the people: "The Lord, your God,
is the God of gods, the Lord of lords, the
great God, mighty and awesome, who has no
favorites, accepts no bribes; who executes justice for the orphan and the widow, and befriends the alien, feeding and clothing him. So
you too must befriend the alien, for you were
once aliens yourselves in the land of Egypt."
This is the Word of the Lord.

---

2   Dt 24, 17-22

A reading from the book of Deuteronomy
Whatever you have left over from your work, leave for the
stranger.

Moses told the people: "You shall not violate
the rights of the alien or of the orphan, nor take
the clothing of a widow as a pledge. For,
remember, you were once slaves in Egypt, and
the Lord, your God, ransomed you from there;
that is why I command you to observe this
rule.

"When you reap the harvest in your field
and overlook a sheaf there, you shall not go
back to get it; let it be for the alien, the orphan
or the widow, that the Lord, your God, may
bless you in all your undertakings. When you
knock down the fruit of your olive trees, you
shall not go over the branches a second time;
let what remains be for the alien, the orphan,
and the widow. When you pick your grapes,
you shall not go over the vineyard a second
time; let what remains be for the alien, the
orphan, and the widow. For remember that you
were once slaves in Egypt; that is why I command you to observe this rule."
This is the Word of the Lord.

---

867   NEW TESTAMENT READING

1   Rom 12, 9-16

A reading from the letter of Paul to the Romans
Take special care to be hospitable.

Your love must be sincere. Detest what is
evil, cling to what is good. Love one another
with the affection of brothers. Anticipate each
other in showing respect. Do not grow slack
but be fervent in spirit; he whom you serve is
the Lord. Rejoice in hope, be patient under
trial, persevere in prayer. Look on the needs of
the saints as your own; be generous in offering
hospitality. Bless your persecutors; bless and
do not curse them. Rejoice with those who rejoice, weep with those who weep. Have the
same attitude toward all. Put away ambitious
thoughts and associate with those who are
lowly.
This is the Word of the Lord.

---

2   Heb 11, 13-16

**A reading from the letter of Paul to the
Hebrews**
They indicate that they are in search of their real homeland.

All [the patriarchs] died in faith. They did not
obtain what had been promised but saw and
saluted it from afar. By acknowledging themselves to be strangers and foreigners on the
earth, they showed that they were seeking a
homeland. If they had been thinking back to
the place from which they had come, they
would have had the opportunity of returning
there. But they were searching for a better, a
heavenly home. Wherefore God is not ashamed
to be called their God, for he has prepared a
city for them.
This is the Word of the Lord.

---

3   Heb 13, 1-3. 14-16

**A reading from the letter of Paul to the
Hebrews**
Remember always to welcome strangers.

Love your fellow Christians always. Do not
neglect to show hospitality, for by that means
some have entertained angels without knowing it. Be as mindful of prisoners as if you were

sharing their imprisonment, and of the ill-treated as of yourselves, for you may yet suffer as they do.

For here we have no lasting city; we are seeking one which is to come. Through him let us continually offer God a sacrifice of praise, that is, the fruit of lips which acknowledge his name.

Do not neglect good deeds and generosity; God is pleased by sacrifices of that kind.

This is the Word of the Lord.

---

868   RESPONSORIAL PSALM

1   Tb 13, 1-2. 3-4. 6

℟. (1) Blessed be God, who lives for ever.

Blessed be God who lives forever
  because his kingdom lasts for all ages.
For he scourges and then has mercy;
  he casts down to the depths of the nether
    world,
  and he brings up from the great abyss.
No one can escape his hand.
℟. Blessed be God, who lives for ever.

Praise him, you Israelites, before the Gentiles,
  for though he has scattered you among them,
  he has shown you his greatness even there.
Exalt him before every living being,
  because he is the Lord our God,
  our Father and God forever.
℟. Blessed be God, who lives for ever.

So now consider what he has done for you,
  and praise him with full voice.
Bless the Lord of righteousness,
  and exalt the King of the ages.
℟. Blessed be God, who lives for ever.

In the land of my exile I praise him,
  and show his power and majesty to a sinful
    nation.
℟. Blessed be God, who lives for ever.

"Turn back, you sinners! do the right before
    him:
  perhaps he may look with favor upon you
  and show you mercy.
℟. Blessed be God, who lives for ever.

2   Ps 107, 33-34. 35-36. 41-42

℟. (2) Give thanks to the Lord,
  his love is everlasting.

He changed rivers into desert,
  water springs into thirsty ground,
Fruitful land into salt marsh,
  because of the wickedness of its inhabitants.
℟. Give thanks to the Lord,
  his love is everlasting.

He changed the desert into pools of water,
  waterless land into water springs.
And there he settled the hungry,
  and they built a city to dwell in.
℟. Give thanks to the Lord,
  his love is everlasting.

He lifted up the needy out of misery
  and made the families numerous like flocks.
The upright see this and rejoice,
  and all wickedness closes its mouth.
℟. Give thanks to the Lord,
  his love is everlasting.
℟. Or: Alleluia.

3   Ps 121, 1-2. 3-4. 5-6. 7-8

℟. (2) Our help is from the Lord
  who made heaven and earth.

I lift up my eyes toward the mountains;
  whence shall help come to me?
My help is from the Lord,
  who made heaven and earth.
℟. Our help is from the Lord
  who made heaven and earth.

May he not suffer your foot to slip;
  may he slumber not who guards you:
Indeed he neither slumbers nor sleeps,
  the guardian of Israel.
℟. Our help is from the Lord
  who made heaven and earth

The Lord is your guardian; the Lord is your
    shade;
  he is beside you at your right hand.
The sun shall not harm you by day,
  nor the moon by night.

℞. Our help is from the Lord
   who made heaven and earth.
The Lord will guard you from all evil;
   he will guard your life.
The Lord will guard your coming and your
   going,
   both now and forever.
℞. Our help is from the Lord
   who made heaven and earth.

---

869   ALLELUIA VERSE AND
        VERSE BEFORE THE GOSPEL

1   2 Cor 1, 3-4
Blessed be the Father of mercies and the God
   of all comfort,
who consoles us in all our afflictions.

2   Heb 13, 14
We do not have an eternal city in this life,
but we look for one in the life to come.

---

870   GOSPEL

1   Mt 2, 13-15. 19-23
✠ A reading from the holy gospel according
   to Matthew
Take the child and his mother and flee into Egypt.

After the astrologers had left, the angel of the
Lord suddenly appeared in a dream to Joseph
with the command: "Get up, take the child
and his mother, and flee to Egypt. Stay there
until I tell you otherwise. Herod is searching
for the child to destroy him." Joseph got up and
took the child and his mother and left that
night for Egypt. He stayed there until the death
of Herod, to fulfill what the Lord had said
through the prophet:
   "Out of Egypt I have called my son."
   But after Herod's death, the angel of the
Lord appeared in a dream to Joseph in Egypt
with the command: "Get up, take the child and
his mother, and set out for the land of Israel.
Those who had designs on the life of the child
are dead." He got up, took the child and his

mother, and returned to the land of Israel. He
heard, however, that Archelaus had succeeded
his father Herod as king of Judea, and he was
afraid to go back there. Instead, because of a
warning received in a dream, Joseph went to
the region of Galilee. There he settled in a town
called Nazareth. In this way what was said
through the prophets was fulfilled:
   "He shall be called a Nazorean."
   This is the gospel of the Lord.

---

2   Lk 10, 25-37
✠ A reading from the holy gospel according
   to Luke
Who is my neighbor?
On one occasion a lawyer stood up to pose
this problem to Jesus: "Teacher, what must I
do to inherit everlasting life?" Jesus answered
him: "What is written in the law? How do you
read it?" He replied:
   "You shall love the Lord your God
   with all your heart,
   with all your soul,
   with all your strength,
   and with all your mind;
   and your neighbor as yourself."
Jesus said, "You have answered correctly. Do
this and you shall live." But because he wished
to justify himself he said to Jesus, "And who is
my neighbor?" Jesus replied: "There was a
man going down from Jerusalem to Jericho
who fell in with robbers. They stripped him,
beat him, and then went off leaving him half-
dead. A priest happened to be going down the
same road; he saw him but continued on. Likewise there was a Levite who came the same
way; he saw him and went on. But a Samaritan
who was journeying along came on him and
was moved to pity at the sight. He approached
him and dressed his wounds, pouring in oil
and wine as a means to heal. He then hoisted
him on his own beast and brought him to an
inn, where he cared for him. The next day he
took out two silver pieces and gave them to the
innkeeper with the request: 'Look after him,
and if there is any further expense I will repay
you on my way back.'

"Which of these three, in your opinion, was neighbor to the man who fell in with the robbers?" The answer came, "The one who treated him with compassion." Jesus said to him, "Then go and do the same."

This is the gospel of the Lord.

FOR THE SICK

871   OLD TESTAMENT READING

1   2 Kgs 20, 1-6

A reading from the second book of Kings

I have seen your tears, and I have cured you.

In those days, when [King] Hezekiah was mortally ill, the prophet Isaiah, son of Amoz, came and said to him: "Thus says the Lord: 'Put your house in order, for you are about to die; you shall not recover.'" He turned his face to the wall and prayed to the Lord: "O Lord, remember how faithfully and wholeheartedly I conducted myself in your presence, doing what was pleasing to you!" And Hezekiah wept bitterly.

Before Isaiah had left the central courtyard, the word of the Lord came to him: "Go back and tell Hezekiah, the leader of my people: 'Thus says the Lord, the God of your forefather David: I have heard your prayer and seen your tears. I will heal you. In three days you shall go up to the Lord's temple; I will add fifteen years to your life. I will rescue you and this city from the hand of the king of Assyria; I will be a shield to this city for my own sake, and for the sake of my servant David.'"

This is the Word of the Lord.

---

2   Is 53, 1-5. 10-11

A reading from the book of the prophet Isaiah

He is the one who bore our sufferings.

Who would believe what we have heard?
  To whom has the arm of the Lord been revealed?
He grew up like a sapling before him,
  like a shoot from the parched earth;

There was in him no stately bearing to make us look at him,
  nor appearance that would attract us to him.
He was spurned and avoided by men,
  a man of suffering, accustomed to infirmity,
One of those from whom men hide their faces,
  spurned, and we held him in no esteem.

Yet it was our infirmities that he bore,
  our sufferings that he endured,
While we thought of him as stricken,
  as one smitten by God and afflicted.
But he was pierced for our offenses,
  crushed for our sins;
Upon him was the chastisement that makes us whole,
  by his stripes we were healed.

[But the Lord was pleased
  to crush him in infirmity.]

If he gives his life as an offering for sin,
  he shall see his descendants in a long life,
  and the will of the Lord shall be accomplished through him.

Because of his affliction
  he shall see the light in fullness of days;
Through his suffering, my servant shall justify many,
  and their guilt he shall bear.

This is the Word of the Lord.

---

872   NEW TESTAMENT READING

1   Acts 28, 7-10

A reading from the Acts of the Apostles

All the people on the island who had sicknesses came to the apostle Paul and were cured.

In the vicinity of [Miletus] the principal island, was the estate of Publius, the chief figure on the island. He took us in and gave us kind hospitality for three days. It happened that Publius' father was sick in bed, laid up with chronic fever and dysentery. Paul went in to see the man and, praying, laid his hands on him and cured him. After this happened, the rest of the sick on the island began to come to Paul and they too were healed. They paid us much

honor, and when we eventually set sail they brought us provisions for our needs.
This is the Word of the Lord.

---

2   2 Cor 4, 10-18

A reading from the second letter of Paul to the Corinthians
We are consigned to death for the sake of Jesus.

Continually we carry about in our bodies the dying of Jesus, so that in our bodies the life of Jesus may also be revealed. While we live we are constantly being delivered to death for Jesus' sake, so that the life of Jesus may be revealed in our mortal flesh. Death is at work in us, but life in you. We have that spirit of faith of which the Scripture says, "Because I believed, I spoke out." We believe and so we speak, knowing that he who raised up the Lord Jesus will raise us up along with Jesus and place both us and you in his presence. Indeed, everything is ordered to your benefit, so that the grace bestowed in abundance may bring greater glory to God because they who give thanks are many.

We do not lose heart because our inner being is renewed each day, even though our body is being destroyed at the same time. The present burden of our trial is light enough, and earns for us an eternal weight of glory beyond all comparison. We do not fix our gaze on what is seen but on what is unseen. What is seen is transitory; what is not seen lasts forever.
This is the Word of the Lord.

---

3   2 Cor 12, 7-10

A reading from the second letter of Paul to the Corinthians
My grace is enough for you: my power is at its best in weakness.

I was given a thorn in the flesh, an angel of Satan to beat me and keep me from getting proud. Three times I begged the Lord that this might leave me. He said to me, "My grace is enough for you, for in weakness power reaches perfection." And so I willingly boast of my weaknesses instead, that the power of Christ may rest upon me.

Therefore I am content with weakness, with mistreatment, with distress, with persecutions and difficulties for the sake of Christ; for when I am powerless, it is then that I am strong.
This is the Word of the Lord.

---

4   Jas 5, 13-16

A reading from the letter of James
The prayer of faith will save the infirm man.

If anyone among you is suffering hardship, he must pray. If a person is in good spirits, he should sing a hymn of praise. Is there anyone sick among you? He should ask for the elders of the church. They in turn are to pray over him, anointing him with oil in the Name of the Lord. This prayer uttered in faith will reclaim the one who is ill, and the Lord will restore him to health. If he has committed any sins, forgiveness will be his. Hence, declare your sins to one another, and pray for one another, that you may find healing.
This is the Word of the Lord.

---

873   **RESPONSORIAL PSALM**

1   Is 38, 10. 11. 12. 16

℟. (17) You saved my life, O Lord;
    I shall not die.
Once I said,
    "In the noontime of life I must depart!
To the gates of the nether world I shall be consigned
    for the rest of my years."
℟. You saved my life, O Lord;
    I shall not die.
I said, "I shall see the Lord no more
    in the land of the living.
No longer shall I behold my fellow men
    among those who dwell in the world."
℟. You saved my life, O Lord;
    I shall not die.
My dwelling, like a shepherd's tent,
    is struck down and borne away from me;
You have folded up my life, like a weaver
    who severs the last thread.
℟. You saved my life, O Lord;
    I shall not die.

Those live whom the Lord protects;
  yours alone is . . . the life of my spirit.
You have given me health and life.
℟. You saved my life, O Lord;
  I shall not die.

---

2   Ps 102, 2-3. 24-25. 19-21
℟. (2) O Lord, hear my prayer,
  and let my cry come to you.
O Lord, hear my prayer,
  and let my cry come to you.
Hide not your face from me
  in the day of my distress.
Incline your ear to me;
  in the day when I call, answer me speedily.
℟. O Lord, hear my prayer,
  and let my cry come to you.
He has broken down my strength in the way;
  he has cut short my days.
  I say: O my God,
Take me not hence in the midst of my days;
  through all generations your years endure.
℟. O Lord, hear my prayer,
  and let my cry come to you.
Let this be written for the generation to come,
  and let his future creatures praise the Lord:
"The Lord looked down from his holy height,
  from heaven he beheld the earth,
To hear the groaning of the prisoners,
  to release those doomed to die."
℟. O Lord, hear my prayer,
  and let my cry come to you.

---

874   ALLELUIA VERSE AND
        VERSE BEFORE THE GOSPEL
1   Mt 8, 17
He took our sicknesses away,
and carried our diseases for us.

2   2 Cor 1, 3-4
Blessed be the Father of mercies and the God of
  all comfort,
who consoles us in all our afflictions.

---

3   Col 1, 24
I will make up in my own body what is lacking
  in the suffering of Christ,
for the sake of his body, the Church.

---

875   GOSPEL
1   Mt 8, 14-17

✠ **A reading from the holy gospel according**
        to Matthew
  He took our infirmities on himself.

Jesus entered Peter's house and found Peter's
mother-in-law in bed with a fever. He took her
by the hand and the fever left her. She got up
at once and began to wait on him.
  As evening drew on, they brought him many
who were possessed. He expelled the spirits by
a simple command and cured all who were afflicted, thereby fulfilling what had been said
through Isaiah the prophet :
  "It was our infirmities he bore,
    our sufferings he endured."
    This is the gospel of the Lord.

---

2   Mk 16, 15-20

✠ **A reading from the holy gospel according**
        to Mark
  They will place their hands on the sick and they will recover.

Jesus appeared to the Eleven and said to
them: "Go into the whole world and proclaim
the good news to all creation. The man who
believes in it and accepts baptism will be
saved; the man who refuses to believe in it will
be condemned. Signs like these will accompany those who have professed their faith:
they will use my name to expel demons, they
will speak entirely new languages, they will
be able to handle serpents, they will be able
to drink deadly poison without harm, and the
sick upon whom they lay their hands will
recover." Then, after speaking to them, the
Lord Jesus was taken up into heaven and took
his seat at God's right hand. The Eleven went
forth and preached everywhere. The Lord continued to work with them throughout and
confirm the message through the signs which
accompanied them.
    This is the gospel of the Lord.

3   Lk 22, 39-43

✠ **A reading from the holy gospel according to Luke**

Father, let your will be done, not mine.

Jesus went out [from the Cenacle] and made his way, as was his custom, to the Mount of Olives; his disciples accompanied him. On reaching the place he said to them, "Pray that you may not be put to the test." He withdrew from them about a stone's throw, then went down on his knees and prayed in these words: "Father, if it is your will, take this cup from me; yet not my will but yours be done." An angel then appeared to him from heaven to strengthen him.

This is the gospel of the Lord.

---

4   Jn 15, 1-8

✠ **A reading from the holy gospel according to John**

The Father prunes every branch that bears fruit to make it bear even more.

Jesus said to his disciples:
"I am the true vine
and my Father is the vinegrower.
He prunes away
every barren branch,
but the fruitful ones
he trims clean
to increase their yield.
You are clean already,
thanks to the word I have spoken to you.
Live on in me, as I do in you.
No more than a branch can bear fruit of
    itself
apart from the vine,
can you bear fruit
apart from me.
I am the vine, you are the branches.
He who lives in me and I in him,
will produce abundantly,
for apart from me you can do nothing.
A man who does not live in me
is like a withered, rejected branch,
picked up to be thrown in the fire and
    burnt.
If you live in me,

and my words stay part of you,
you may ask what you will—
it will be done for you.
My Father has been glorified
in your bearing much fruit
and becoming my disciples."

This is the gospel of the Lord.

FOR ANY NEED

876   **OLD TESTAMENT READING**

1   Est C, 2-4. 8-10

A reading from the book of Esther

Change us into joyful people.

Mordecai prayed to the Lord and said: "O Lord God, almighty King, all things are in your power, and there is no one to oppose you in your will to save Israel. You made heaven and earth and every wonderful thing under the heavens. You are Lord of all, and there is no one who can resist you, Lord. And now, Lord God, King, God of Abraham, spare your people, for our enemies plan our ruin and are bent upon destroying the inheritance that was yours from the beginning. Do not spurn your portion, which you redeemed for yourself out of Egypt. Hear my prayer; have pity on your inheritance and turn our sorrow into joy: thus we shall live to sing praise to your name, O Lord. Do not silence those who praise you."

This is the Word of the Lord.

---

2   Lam 3, 17-26

A reading from the book of Lamentations

It is good to wait in silence for the Lord God to save.

My soul is deprived of peace,
    I have forgotten what happiness is;
I tell myself my future is lost,
    all that I hoped for from the Lord.
The thought of my homeless poverty
    is wormwood and gall;
Remembering it over and over
    leaves my soul downcast within me.
But I will call this to mind,
    as my reason to have hope:

The favors of the Lord are not exhausted,
 his mercies are not spent;
They are renewed each morning,
 so great is his faithfulness.
My portion is the Lord, says my soul;
 therefore will I hope in him.
Good is the Lord to one who waits for him,
 to the soul that seeks him;
It is good to hope in silence
 for the saving help of the Lord.
    This is the Word of the Lord.

---

3   Dn 3, 25. 34-43

A reading from the book of the prophet Daniel
Grant us deliverance worthy of your wonderful deeds.

In the fire Azariah stood up and prayed aloud:
"For your name's sake, do not deliver us up
 forever,
 or make void your covenant.
Do not take away your mercy from us,
 for the sake of Abraham, your beloved,
 Isaac your servant, and Israel your holy one,
To whom you promised to multiply their offspring
 like the stars of heaven,
 or the sand on the shore of the sea.
For we are reduced, O Lord, beyond any other
 nation,
 brought low everywhere in the world this
 day
 because of our sins.
We have in our day no prince, prophet, or
 leader,
 no holocaust, sacrifice, oblation, or incense,
 no place to offer first fruits, to find favor
 with you.
But with contrite heart and humble spirit
 let us be received;
As though it were holocausts of rams and bullocks,
 or thousands of fat lambs,
So let our sacrifice be in your presence today
 as we follow you unreservedly;
 for those who trust in you cannot be put to
 shame.
And now we follow you with our whole heart,
 we fear you and we pray to you.

Do not let us be put to shame,
 but deal with us in your kindness and great
 mercy.
Deliver us by your wonders,
 and bring glory to your name, O Lord."
    This is the Word of the Lord.

---

877   NEW TESTAMENT READING

1   Rom 8, 18-30

A reading from the letter of Paul to the Romans
We know that by turning everything to their good, God
cooperates with all those who love him.

I consider the sufferings of the present to be as
nothing compared with the glory to be revealed
in us. Indeed, the whole created world eagerly
awaits the revelation of the sons of God. Creation was made subject to futility, not of its own
accord but by him who once subjected it; yet
not without hope, because the world itself will
be freed from its slavery to corruption and
share in the glorious freedom of the children of
God. Yes, we know that all creation groans and
is in agony even until now. Not only that, but
we ourselves, although we have the Spirit as
first fruits, groan inwardly while we await the
redemption of our bodies. In hope we were
saved. But hope is not hope if its object is
seen; how is it possible for one to hope for
what he sees? And hoping for what we cannot
see means awaiting it with patient endurance.

The Spirit too helps us in our weakness, for
we do not know how to pray as we ought; but
the Spirit himself makes intercession for us
with groanings which cannot be expressed in
speech. He who searches hearts knows what
the Spirit means, for the Spirit intercedes
for the saints as God himself wills.

We know that God makes all things work
together for the good of those who have been
called according to his decree. Those whom he
foreknew he predestined to share the image of
his Son, that the Son might be the first-born of
many brothers. Those he predestined he likewise called; those he called he also justified;
and those he justified he in turn glorified.
    This is the Word of the Lord.

2 Rom 8, 31-39

A reading from the letter of Paul to the Romans

Neither death nor life can ever come between us and the love of God.

If God is for us, who can be against us? Is it possible that he who did not spare his own Son but handed him over for the sake of us all will not grant us all things besides? Who shall bring a charge against God's chosen ones? God, who justifies? Who shall condemn them? Christ Jesus, who died or rather was raised up, who is at the right hand of God and who intercedes for us?

Who will separate us from the love of Christ? Trial, or distress, or persecution, or hunger, or nakedness, or danger, or the sword? As Scripture says: "For your sake we are being slain all the day long; we are looked upon as sheep to be slaughtered." Yet in all this we are more than conquerors because of him who has loved us. For I am certain that neither death nor life, neither angels nor principalities, neither the present nor the future, nor powers, neither height nor depth nor any other creature, will be able to separate us from the love of God that comes to us in Christ Jesus, our Lord.

This is the Word of the Lord.

3 Jas 1, 2-4. 12

A reading from the letter of James

Happy the man who stands firm when trials come.

My brothers, count it pure joy when you are involved in every sort of trial. Realize that when your faith is tested this makes for endurance. Let endurance come to its perfection so that you may be fully mature and lacking in nothing.

Happy the man who holds out to the end through trial! Once he has been proved he will receive the crown of life the Lord has promised to those who love him.

This is the Word of the Lord.

4 Rv 21, 1-5. 6-7

A reading from the book of Revelation

There will be no more death, and no more mourning or sadness.

I, John, saw new heavens and a new earth. The former heavens and the former earth had passed away, and the sea was no longer. I also saw a new Jerusalem, the holy city, coming down out of heaven from God, beautiful as a bride prepared to meet her husband. I heard a loud voice from the throne cry out: "This is God's dwelling among men. He shall dwell with them and they shall be his people and he shall be their God who is always with them. He shall wipe every tear from their eyes, and there shall be no more death or mourning, crying out or pain, for the former world has passed away."

The One who sat on the throne said to me, "See, I make all things new! I am the Alpha and the Omega, the Beginning and the End. To anyone who thirsts I will give drink without cost from the spring of life-giving water.

"He who wins the victory shall inherit these gifts; I will be his God and he shall be my son."

This is the Word of the Lord.

---

878 **RESPONSORIAL PSALM**

1 Ps 80, 2. 3. 5-7

℞. (4) Let us see your face, Lord,
   and we shall be saved.
O shepherd of Israel, hearken!
   From your throne upon the cherubim, shine forth.
Rouse your power,
   and come to save us.
℞. Let us see your face, Lord,
   and we shall be saved.
O Lord of hosts, how long will you burn with anger
   while your people pray?
You have fed them with the bread of tears
   and given them tears to drink in ample measure.
You have left us to be fought over by our neighbors,

and our enemies mock us.
℟. Let us see your face, Lord,
and we shall be saved.

---

2 Ps 85, 2-4. 5-6. 7-8

℟. (8) Lord, let us see your kindness,
and grant us your salvation.
You have favored, O Lord, your land;
you have restored the well-being of Jacob.
You have forgiven the guilt of your people;
you have covered all their sins.
You have withdrawn all your wrath;
you have revoked your burning anger.
℟. Lord, let us see your kindness,
and grant us your salvation.
Restore us, O God our savior,
and abandon your displeasure against us.
Will you be ever angry with us,
prolonging your anger to all generations?
℟. Lord, let us see your kindness,
and grant us your salvation.
Will you not instead give us life;
and shall not your people rejoice in you?
Show us, O Lord, your kindness,
and grant us your salvation.
℟. Lord, let us see your kindness,
and grant us your salvation.

---

3 Ps 123, 1-2. 2

℟. (3) Have mercy on us, Lord, have mercy.
To you I lift up my eyes
who are enthroned in heaven.
Behold, as the eyes of servants
are on the hands of their masters,
℟. Have mercy on us, Lord, have mercy.
As the eyes of a maid
are on the hands of her mistress,
So are our eyes on the Lord, our God,
till he have pity on us.
℟. Have mercy on us, Lord, have mercy.
℟. Or: (2) Our eyes are fixed on the Lord,
pleading for his mercy.

---

879 **ALLELUIA VERSE AND**
VERSE BEFORE THE GOSPEL

1 Ps 33, 22

Lord, let your mercy be on us,
as we place our trust in you.

2 2 Cor 1, 3-4

Blessed be the Father of mercies and the God of
all comfort,
who consoles us in all our afflictions.

3 Jas 1, 12

Happy the man who stands firm when trials
come;
he has proved himself, and will win the crown
of life.

---

880 **GOSPEL**

1 Mt 7, 7-11

✠ A reading from the holy gospel according
to Matthew
Everyone who searches, finds.

Jesus said to his disciples: "Ask, and you will
receive. Seek, and you will find. Knock, and it
will be opened to you. For the one who asks,
receives. The one who seeks, finds. The one
who knocks, enters. Would one of you hand his
son a stone when he asks for a loaf, or a poison-
ous snake when he asks for a fish? If you,
with all your sins, know how to give your
children what is good, how much more will
your heavenly Father give good things to anyone who asks him!"
This is the gospel of the Lord.

---

2 Mk 4, 35-41

✠ A reading from the holy gospel according
to Mark
Who can this be? Even the wind and the sea obey him.

That day as evening drew on Jesus said to his
disciples, "Let us cross over to the farther
shore." Leaving the crowd, they took him away
in the boat in which he was sitting, while the
other boats accompanied him. It happened that

a bad squall blew up. The waves were breaking over the boat and it began to ship water badly. Jesus was in the stern through it all, sound asleep on a cushion. They finally woke him and said to him, "Teacher, doesn't it matter to you that we are going to drown?" He awoke and rebuked the wind and said to the sea: "Quiet! Be still!" The wind fell off and everything grew calm. Then he said to them, "Why are you so terrified? Why are you lacking in faith?" A great awe overcame them at this. They kept saying to one another, "Who can this be that the wind and the sea obey him?"

This is the gospel of the Lord.

---

3   Lk 18, 1-8

✠ A reading from the holy gospel according to Luke

God will see justice done to his chosen who cry to him.

Jesus told his disciples this parable on the necessity of praying always and not losing heart: "Once there was a judge in a certain city who respected neither God nor man. A widow in that city kept coming to him saying, 'Give me my rights against my opponent.' For a time he refused, but finally he thought, 'I care little for God or man, but this widow is wearing me out. I am going to settle in her favor or she will end by doing me violence.' " The Lord said, "Listen to what the corrupt judge has to say. Will not God then do justice to his chosen who call out to him day and night? Will he delay long over them, do you suppose? I tell you, he will give them swift justice. But when the Son of Man comes, will he find any faith on the earth?"

This is the gospel of the Lord.

IN THANKSGIVING

881   **OLD TESTAMENT READING**

1   1 Kgs 8, 55-61

A reading from the first book of Kings

Blessed be the Lord God who has granted rest to his people.

Solomon stood and blessed the whole community of Israel, saying in a loud voice:

"Blessed be the Lord who has given rest to his people Israel, just as he promised. Not a single word has gone unfulfilled of the entire generous promise he made through his servant Moses. May the Lord, our God, be with us as he was with our fathers and may he not forsake us nor cast us off. May he draw our hearts to himself, that we may follow him in everything and keep the commands, statutes, and ordinances which he enjoined on our fathers. May this prayer I have offered to the Lord, our God, be present to him day and night, that he may uphold the cause of his servant and of his people Israel as each day requires, that all the peoples of the earth may know the Lord is God and there is no other. You must be wholly devoted to the Lord, our God, observing his statutes and keeping his commandments, as on this day."

This is the Word of the Lord.

---

2   Sir 50, 22-24

A reading from the book of Sirach

God does great deeds everywhere.

And now, bless the God of all,
  who has done wondrous things on earth;
Who fosters men's growth from their mother's
  womb,
  and fashions them according to his will!
May he grant you joy of heart
  and may peace abide among you;
May his goodness toward us endure in Israel
  as long as the heavens are above.

This is the Word of the Lord.

---

3   Is 63, 7-9

A reading from the book of the prophet Isaiah

Let me sing the praises of the Lord's goodness, and of his marvelous deeds to the house of Israel.

The favors of the Lord I will recall,
  the glorious deeds of the Lord,
Because of all he has done for us;
  for he is good to the house of Israel,
He has favored us according to his mercy
  and his great kindness.

He said: They are indeed my people,
  children who are not disloyal;

So he became their savior
in their every affliction.
It was not a messenger or an angel,
but he himself who saved them.
Because of his love and pity
he redeemed them himself,
Lifting them and carrying them
all the days of old.

> This is the Word of the Lord.

---

4   Zep 3, 14-15

A reading from the book of the prophet Zephaniah

The king of Israel, the Lord God, is in your midst.

Shout for joy, O daughter Zion!
sing joyfully, O Israel!
Be glad and exult with all your heart,
O daughter Jerusalem!
The Lord has removed the judgment against
you,
he has turned away your enemies;
The King of Israel, the Lord, is in your midst,
you have no further misfortune to fear.

> This is the Word of the Lord.

---

882   NEW TESTAMENT READING

1   1 Cor 1, 3-9

A reading from the first letter of Paul to the Corinthians

I never stop thanking God for you.

Grace and peace from God our Father and the Lord Jesus Christ.

I continually thank my God for you because of the favor he has bestowed on you in Christ Jesus, in whom you have been richly endowed with every gift of speech and knowledge. Likewise, the witness I bore to Christ has been so confirmed among you that you lack no spiritual gift as you wait for the revelation of our Lord Jesus Christ. He will strengthen you to the end, so that you will be blameless on the day of our Lord Jesus [Christ]. God is faithful, and it was he who called you to fellowship with his Son, Jesus Christ our Lord.

> This is the Word of the Lord.

---

2   Eph 1, 3-14

A reading from the letter of Paul to the Ephesians

God made us his adopted sons to make us praise the glory of his gifts.

Praised be the God and Father of our Lord Jesus Christ, who has bestowed on us in Christ every spiritual blessing in the heavens! God chose us in him before the world began, to be holy and blameless in his sight, to be full of love; he likewise predestined us through Christ Jesus to be his adopted sons—such was his will and pleasure—that all might praise the divine favor he has bestowed on us in his beloved.

It is in Christ and through his blood that we have been redeemed and our sins forgiven, so immeasurably generous is God's favor to us. God has given us the wisdom to understand fully the mystery, the plan he was pleased to decree in Christ, to be carried out in the fullness of time: namely, to bring all things in the heavens and on earth into one under Christ's headship.

In him we were chosen; for in the decree of God, who administers everything according to his will and counsel, we were predestined to praise his glory by being the first to hope in Christ. In him you too were chosen; when you heard the glad tidings of salvation, the word of truth, and believed in it, you were sealed with the Holy Spirit who had been promised. He is the pledge of our inheritance, the first payment against the full redemption of a people God has made his own, to praise his glory.

> This is the Word of the Lord.

---

3   Col 3, 12-17

A reading from the letter of Paul to the Colossians

Give thanks to God the Father through Christ.

Because you are God's chosen ones, holy and beloved, clothe yourselves with heartfelt mercy, with kindness, humility, meekness, and patience. Bear with one another; forgive whatever grievances you have against one another. Forgive as the Lord has forgiven you. Over all these virtues put on love, which binds the rest together and makes them perfect. Christ's peace must reign in your hearts, since as members of the one body you have been called to that peace. Dedicate yourselves to thankfulness. Let the word of Christ, rich as it is, dwell in you. In wisdom made perfect, instruct and admonish one another. Sing gratefully to God from your hearts in psalms, hymns, and inspired songs. Whatever you do, whether in speech or in action, do it in the name of the Lord Jesus. Give thanks to God the Father through him.

This is the Word of the Lord.

---

883   **RESPONSORIAL PSALM**

1   1 Chr 29, 10. 11. 11-12. 12

℞. (13) We praise your glorious name, O mighty God.

Blessed may you be, O Lord,
  God of Israel our father,
  from eternity to eternity.

℞. We praise your glorious name, O mighty God.

Yours, O Lord, are grandeur and power,
  majesty, splendor, and glory.
For all in heaven and on earth is yours.

℞. We praise your glorious name, O mighty God.

Yours, O Lord, is the sovereignty;
  you are exalted as head over all.
Riches and honor are from you,

℞. We praise your glorious name, O mighty God.

And you have dominion over all.
  In your hand are power and might;
It is yours to give grandeur and strength to all.

℞. We praise your glorious name, O mighty God.

---

2   Ps 113, 1-2. 3-4. 5-6. 7-8

℞. (2) Blessed be the name of the Lord for ever.

Praise, you servants of the Lord,
  praise the name of the Lord.

Blessed be the name of the Lord
  both now and forever.

℞. Blessed be the name of the Lord for ever.

From the rising to the setting of the sun
  is the name of the Lord to be praised.
High above all nations is the Lord;
  above the heavens is his glory.

℞. Blessed be the name of the Lord for ever.

Who is like the Lord, our God, who is enthroned on high
  and looks upon the heavens and the earth below?

℞. Blessed be the name of the Lord for ever.

He raises up the lowly from the dust;
  from the dunghill he lifts up the poor
To seat them with princes,
  with the princes of his own people.

℞. Blessed be the name of the Lord for ever.
℞. Or: Alleluia.

---

3   Ps 138, 1-2. 2-3. 4-5

℞. (2) Lord, I thank you for your faithfulness and love.

I will give thanks to you, O Lord, with all my heart,
  [for you have heard the words of my mouth;]
  in the presence of the angels I will sing your praise;
I will worship at your holy temple
  and give thanks to your name.

℞. Lord, I thank you for your faithfulness and love.

Because of your kindness and your truth;
  for you have made great above all things your name and your promise.
When I called, you answered me;
  you built up strength within me.

℞. Lord, I thank you for your faithfulness and love.

All the kings of the earth shall give thanks to you, O Lord,
  when they hear the words of your mouth;
And they shall sing of the ways of the Lord:
  "Great is the glory of the Lord."

℞. Lord, I thank you for your faithfulness and love.

---

4   Ps 145, 2-3. 4-5. 6-7. 8-9. 10-11

℞. (1) I will praise your name for ever, Lord.
Every day will I bless you,
  and I will praise your name forever and ever.
Great is the Lord and highly to be praised;
  his greatness is unsearchable.
℞. I will praise your name for ever, Lord.
Generation after generation praises your
  works
  and proclaims your might.
They speak of the splendor of your glorious
  majesty
  and tell of your wondrous works.
℞. I will praise your name for ever, Lord.
They discourse of the power of your terrible
  deeds
  and declare your greatness.
They publish the fame of your abundant good-
  ness
  and joyfully sing of your justice.
℞. I will praise your name for ever, Lord.
The Lord is gracious and merciful,
  slow to anger and of great kindness.
The Lord is good to all
  and compassionate toward all his works.
℞. I will praise your name for ever, Lord.
Let all your works give you thanks, O Lord,
  and let your faithful ones bless you.
Let them discourse of the glory of your king-
  dom
  and speak of your might.
℞. I will praise your name for ever, Lord.

---

884   ALLELUIA VERSE AND
            VERSE BEFORE THE GOSPEL

1   Eph 1, 3
Blessed be God, the Father of our Lord Jesus
  Christ,
for he has blessed us with every spiritual gift
  in Christ.

2   1 Thes 5, 18
For all things give thanks to God,
  because this is what he expects of you in
  Christ Jesus.

3
We praise you, God; we acknowledge you as
  Lord;
your Church praises you around the world.

---

885   GOSPEL

1   Mk 5, 18-20

✠ A reading from the holy gospel according
            to Mark
              Tell what the Lord has done for you.

As Jesus was getting into the boat, the man
who had been possessed was pressing to ac-
company him. Jesus did not grant his request,
but told him instead: "Go home to your family
and make it clear to them how much the Lord
in his mercy has done for you." At that the man
went off and began to proclaim throughout the
Ten Cities what Jesus had done for him. They
were all amazed at what they heard.
        This is the gospel of the Lord.

---

2   Lk 17, 11-19

✠ A reading from the holy gospel according
            to Luke
          He threw himself at the feet of Jesus and thanked him.

On his journey to Jerusalem Jesus passed along
the borders of Samaria and Galilee. As he was
entering a village, ten lepers met him. Keeping
their distance, they raised their voices and
said, "Jesus, Master, have pity on us!" When
he saw them, he responded, "Go and show
yourselves to the priests." On their way there
they were cured. One of them, realizing that
he had been cured, came back praising God in a
loud voice. He threw himself on his face at the
feet of Jesus and spoke his praises. This man
was a Samaritan.
  Jesus took the occasion to say, "Were not all
ten made whole? Where are the other nine?
Was there no one to return and give thanks to
God except this foreigner?" He said to the
man, "Stand up and go your way; your faith
has been your salvation."
        This is the gospel of the Lord.

IV. FOR PARTICULAR NEEDS

FOR FORGIVENESS OF SINS

886 **OLD TESTAMENT READING**

1   Is 55, 6-9

A reading from the book of the prophet Isaiah

Turn back to the Lord God who is rich in forgiving.

Seek the Lord while he may be found,
  call him while he is near.
Let the scoundrel forsake his way,
  and the wicked man his thoughts;
Let him turn to the Lord for mercy;
  to our God, who is generous in forgiving.
For my thoughts are not your thoughts,
  nor are your ways my ways, says the Lord.
As high as the heavens are above the earth,
  so high are my ways above your ways
  and my thoughts above your thoughts.

This is the Word of the Lord.

---

2   Ez 18, 21-23. 30-32

A reading from the book of the prophet Ezekiel

Repent, renounce all your sin.

Thus says the Lord: If the wicked man turns away from all the sins he committed, if he keeps all my statutes and does what is right and just, he shall surely live, he shall not die. None of the crimes he committed shall be remembered against him; he shall live because of the virtue he has practiced. Do I indeed derive any pleasure from the death of the wicked? says the Lord God. Do I not rather rejoice when he turns from his evil way that he may live?

Therefore I will judge you, house of Israel, each one according to his ways, says the Lord God. Turn and be converted from all your crimes, that they may be no cause of guilt for you. Cast away from you all the crimes you have committed, and make for yourselves a new heart and a new spirit. Why should you die, O house of Israel? For I have no pleasure in the death of anyone who dies, says the Lord God. Return and live!

This is the Word of the Lord.

---

3   Jl 2, 12-18

A reading from the book of the prophet Joel

Let your hearts be broken, not your garments torn.

Even now, says the Lord,
  return to me with your whole heart,
  with fasting, and weeping, and mourning;
Rend your hearts, not your garments,
  and return to the Lord, your God.
For gracious and merciful is he,
  slow to anger, rich in kindness,
  and relenting in punishment.
Perhaps he will again relent
  and leave behind him a blessing,
Offerings and libations
  for the Lord, your God.
Blow the trumpet in Zion!
  proclaim a fast,
  call an assembly;
Gather the people,
  notify the congregation;
Assemble the elders,
  gather the children
  and the infants at the breast;
Let the bridegroom quit his room,
  and the bride her chamber.
Between the porch and the altar
  let the priests, the ministers of the Lord,
    weep,
And say, "Spare, O Lord, your people,
  and make not your heritage a reproach,
  with the nations ruling over them!
Why should they say among the peoples,
  'Where is their God?' "
Then the Lord was stirred to concern for his land and took pity on his people.

This is the Word of the Lord.

4   Jon 3, 1-10

A reading from the book of the prophet Jonah

The inhabitants of Nineveh have turned away from their evil ways.

The word of the Lord came to Jonah: "Set out for the great city of Nineveh, and announce to it the message that I will tell you." So Jonah made ready and went to Nineveh, according to the Lord's bidding. Now Nineveh was an enormously large city; it took three days to go through it. Jonah began his journey through the city, and had gone but a single day's walk announcing, "Forty days more and Nineveh shall be destroyed," when the people of Nineveh believed God; they proclaimed a fast and all of them, great and small, put on sackcloth.

When the news reached the king of Nineveh, he rose from his throne, laid aside his robe, covered himself with sackcloth, and sat in the ashes. Then he had this proclaimed throughout Nineveh, by decree of the king and his nobles: "Neither man nor beast, neither cattle nor sheep, shall taste anything; they shall not eat, nor shall they drink water. Man and beast shall be covered with sackcloth and call loudly to God; every man shall turn from his evil way and from the violence he has in hand. Who knows, God may relent and forgive, and withhold his blazing wrath, so that we shall not perish." When God saw by their actions how they turned from their evil way, he repented of the evil that he had threatened to do to them; he did not carry it out.

This is the Word of the Lord.

---

887   NEW TESTAMENT READING

1   Rom 6, 2-4. 12-14

A reading from the letter of Paul to the Romans
Consider yourselves dead to sin but alive to God.

How can we who died to sin go on living in it? Are you not aware that we who were baptized into Christ Jesus were baptized into his death? Through baptism into his death we were buried with him, so that, just as Christ was raised from the dead by the glory of the Father, we too might live a new life.

Do not, therefore, let sin rule your mortal body and make you obey its lusts; no more shall you offer the members of your body to sin as weapons for evil. Rather, offer yourselves to God as men who have come back from the dead to life, and your bodies to God as weapons for justice. Sin will no longer have power over you; you are now under grace, not under the law.

This is the Word of the Lord.

---

2   1 Jn 1, 5—2, 2

A reading from the first letter of John
The blood of Jesus purifies us from all sin.

Here, then, is the message
we have heard from Jesus Christ
and announce to you:
that God is light;
in him there is no darkness.
If we say, "We have fellowship with him,"
while continuing to walk in darkness,
we are liars and do not act in truth.
But if we walk in light,
as he is in the light,
we have fellowship with one another,
and the blood of his Son Jesus cleanses us
    from sin.
If we say, "We are free of the guilt of sin,"
we deceive ourselves; the truth is not to be
    found in us.
But if we acknowledge our sins,
he who is just can be trusted
to forgive our sins
and cleanse us from every wrong.
If we say, "We have never sinned,"
we make him a liar
and his word finds no place in us.

My little ones,
I am writing this to keep you from sin.
But if anyone should sin,
we have in the presence of the Father,
Jesus Christ, an intercessor who is just.
He is an offering for our sins,
and not for our sins only,
but for those of the whole world.

This is the Word of the Lord.

---

888   RESPONSORIAL PSALM

1   Ps 51, 3-4. 5-6. 12-13. 14. 17

℟. (3) Be merciful, O Lord, for we have sinned.
Have mercy on me, O God, in your goodness;
    in the greatness of your compassion wipe
        out my offense;
Thoroughly wash me from my guilt
    and of my sin cleanse me.
℟. Be merciful, O Lord, for we have sinned.

For I acknowledge my offense,
  and my sin is before me always:
"Against you only have I sinned,
  and done what is evil in your sight."
℞. Be merciful, O Lord, for we have sinned.
A clean heart create for me, O God,
  and a steadfast spirit renew within me.
Cast me not out from your presence,
  and your holy spirit take not from me.
℞. Be merciful, O Lord, for we have sinned.
Give me back the joy of your salvation,
  and a willing spirit sustain in me.
O Lord, open my lips,
  and my mouth shall proclaim your praise.
℞. Be merciful, O Lord, for we have sinned.

---

2   Ps 103, 1-2. 3-4. 8-9. 11-12

℞. (10) Lord, do not deal with us as our sins
  deserve,
  nor punish us for our faults.
Bless the Lord, O my soul;
  and all my being, bless his holy name.
Bless the Lord, O my soul,
  and forget not all his benefits.
℞. Lord, do not deal with us as our sins deserve,
  nor punish us for our faults.
He pardons all your iniquities,
  he heals all your ills.
He redeems your life from destruction,
  he crowns you with kindness and compassion.
℞. Lord, do not deal with us as our sins
  deserve,
  nor punish us for our faults.
Merciful and gracious is the Lord,
  slow to anger and abounding in kindness.
He will not always chide,
  nor does he keep his wrath forever.
℞. Lord, do not deal with us as our sins
  deserve,
  nor punish us for our faults.
For as the heavens are high above the earth,
  so surpassing is his kindness toward those
  who fear him.
As far as the east is from the west,
  so far has he put our transgressions from us.

℞. Lord, do not deal with us as our sins
  deserve,
  nor punish us for our faults.
℞. Or: (8) The Lord is kind and merciful.

---

3   Ps 130, 1-2. 3-4. 4-6. 7-8

℞. (3) If you, O Lord, laid bare our guilt,
  who could endure it?
Out of the depths I cry to you, O Lord;
  Lord, hear my voice!
Let your ears be attentive
  to my voice in supplication.
℞. If you, O Lord, laid bare our guilt,
  who could endure it?
If you, O Lord, mark iniquities,
  Lord, who can stand?
But with you is forgiveness,
  that you may be revered.
℞. If you, O Lord, laid bare our guilt,
  who could endure it?
My soul trusts in his word.
  My soul waits for the Lord
More than sentinels wait for the dawn.
  Let Israel wait for the Lord.
℞. If you, O Lord, laid bare our guilt,
  who could endure it?
For with the Lord is kindness
  and with him is plenteous redemption;
And he will redeem Israel
  from all their iniquities.
℞. If you, O Lord, laid bare our guilt,
  who could endure it?

---

889   **ALLELUIA VERSE AND
VERSE BEFORE THE GOSPEL**

1   Ez 33, 11
I do not wish the sinner to die, says the Lord,
but to turn to me and live.

2   Mk 1, 15
The kingdom of God is near:
repent and believe the Good News!

3   Rv 1, 5

Jesus Christ, you are the faithful witness,
    first-born from the dead;
you have loved us and washed away our sins
    in your blood.

---

890   **GOSPEL**

1   Mt 9, 1-8

✠ A reading from the holy gospel according
                to Matthew

They praised God for giving such power to men.

Jesus entered the boat, made the crossing, and
came back to his own town. There the people
at once brought to him a paralyzed man lying
on a mat. When Jesus saw their faith he said
to the paralytic, "Have courage, son, your sins
are forgiven." At that some of the scribes said
to themselves, "The man blasphemes." Jesus
was aware of what they were thinking and
said: "Why do you harbor evil thoughts?
Which is less trouble to say, 'Your sins are
forgiven' or 'Stand up and walk'? To help you
realize that the Son of Man has authority on
earth to forgive sins"—he then said to the
paralyzed man—"Stand up! Roll up your mat,
and go home." The man stood up and went
toward his home. At the sight, a feeling of awe
came over the crowd, and they praised God for
giving such authority to men.
          This is the gospel of the Lord.

---

2   Mk 1, 1-8. 14-15

✠ The beginning of the holy gospel according
                to Mark

Repent and believe the Good News.

Here begins the gospel of Jesus Christ, the
Son of God. In Isaiah the prophet it is written:
    "I send my messenger before you
        to prepare your way:
    a herald's voice in the desert, crying,
    'Make ready the way of the Lord,
        clear him a straight path.' "
    Thus it was that John the Baptizer appeared
in the desert proclaiming a baptism of repentance which led to the forgiveness of sins. All

the Judean countryside and the people of Jerusalem went out to him in great numbers.
They were being baptized by him in the Jordan
River as they confessed their sins. John was
clothed in camel's hair, and wore a leather
belt around his waist. His food was grasshoppers and wild honey. The theme of his
preaching was: "One more powerful than I is
to come after me. I am not fit to stoop and
untie his sandal straps. I have baptized you in
water; he will baptize you in the Holy Spirit."
    After John's arrest, Jesus appeared in Gali-
lee proclaiming God's good news: "This is the
time of fulfillment. The reign of God is at
hand! Reform your lives and believe in the
good news!"
          This is the gospel of the Lord.

---

3   Lk 7, 36-50

✠ A reading from the holy gospel according
                to Luke

Her many sins are forgiven because she has loved much.

A certain Pharisee invited Jesus to dine with
him. Jesus went to the Pharisee's home and
reclined to eat. A woman known in the town to
be a sinner learned that he was dining in the
Pharisee's home. She brought in a vase of
perfumed oil and stood behind him at his feet,
weeping so that her tears fell upon his feet.
Then she wiped them with her hair, kissing
them and perfuming them with the oil. When
his host, the Pharisee, saw this, he said to
himself, "If this man were a prophet, he would
know who and what sort of woman this is that
touches him—that she is a sinner." In answer to his thoughts, Jesus said to him,
"Simon, I have something to propose to you."
"Teacher," he said, "speak."
    "Two men owed money to a certain money-
lender; one owed a total of five hundred coins,
the other fifty. Since neither was able to repay,
he wrote off both debts. Which of them was
more grateful to him?" Simon answered, "He, I
presume, to whom he remitted the larger sum."
Jesus said to him, "You are right."
    Turning then to the woman, he said to Si-
mon: "You see this woman? I came to your

home and you provided me with no water for my feet. She has washed my feet with her tears and wiped them with her hair. You gave me no kiss, but she has not ceased kissing my feet since I entered. You did not anoint my head with oil, but she has anointed my feet with perfume. I tell you, that is why her many sins are forgiven—because of her great love. Little is forgiven the one whose love is small."

He said to her then, "Your sins are forgiven," at which his fellow guests began to ask among themselves, "Who is this that he even forgives sins?" Meanwhile he said to the woman, "Your faith has been your salvation. Now go in peace."

This is the gospel of the Lord.

---

4   Lk 15, 1-3. 11-32

✠ A reading from the holy gospel according to Luke

It was only right we should celebrate and rejoice because your brother here was dead and has come to life.

The tax collectors and sinners were all gathering around Jesus to hear him, at which the Pharisees murmured, "This man welcomes sinners and eats with them." Then he addressed this parable to them: "A man had two sons. The younger of them said to his father, 'Father, give me the share of the estate that is coming to me.' So the father divided up the property. Some days later this younger son collected all his belongings and went off to a distant land, where he squandered his money on dissolute living. After he had spent everything, a great famine broke out in that country and he was in dire need. So he attached himself to one of the propertied class of the place, who sent him to his farm to take care of the pigs. He longed to fill his belly with the husks that were fodder for the pigs, but no one made a move to give him anything. Coming to his senses at last, he said: 'How many hired hands at my father's place have more than enough to eat, while here I am starving! I will break away and return to my father, and say to him, "Father, I have sinned against God and against you; I no longer deserve to be called your son. Treat me like one of your hired hands." ' With that he

set off for his father's house. While he was still a long way off, his father caught sight of him and was deeply moved. He ran out to meet him, threw his arms around his neck, and kissed him. The son said to him, 'Father, I have sinned against God and against you; I no longer deserve to be called your son.' The father said to his servants: 'Quick! bring out the finest robe and put it on him; put a ring on his finger and shoes on his feet. Take the fatted calf and kill it. Let us eat and celebrate because this son of mine was dead and has come back to life. He was lost and is found.' Then the celebration began.

"Meanwhile the elder son was out on the land. As he neared the house on his way home, he heard the sound of music and dancing. He called one of the servants and asked him the reason for the dancing and the music. The servant answered, 'Your brother is home, and your father has killed the fatted calf because he has him back in good health.' The son grew angry at this and would not go in; but his father came out and began to plead with him.

"He said in reply to his father: 'For years now I have slaved for you. I never disobeyed one of your orders, yet you never gave me so much as a kid goat to celebrate with my friends. Then, when this son of yours returns after having gone through your property with loose women, you kill the fatted calf for him.'

" 'My son,' replied the father, 'you are with me always, and everything I have is yours. But we had to celebrate and rejoice! This brother of yours was dead, and has come back to life. He was lost, and is found.' "

This is the gospel of the Lord.

---

5   Lk 24, 46-48

✠ A reading from the holy gospel according to Luke

Jesus sent his apostles to preach repentance for the forgiveness of sins.

Jesus said to his disciples: "Thus it is written that the Messiah must suffer and rise from the dead on the third day. In his name, penance for the remission of sins is to be preached to all the nations, beginning at Jerusalem. You are witnesses of this."

This is the gospel of the Lord.

FOR A HAPPY DEATH

891   OLD TESTAMENT READING

Is 25, 6-10

A reading from the book of the prophet Isaiah

He will destroy death for ever.

On this mountain the Lord of hosts
    will provide for all peoples
A feast of rich food and choice wines,
    juicy, rich food and pure, choice wines.
On this mountain he will destroy
    the veil that veils all peoples,
The web that is woven over all nations;
    he will destroy death forever.
The Lord God will wipe away
    the tears from all faces;
The reproach of his people he will remove
    from the whole earth; for the Lord has
    spoken.
    On that day it will be said:
"Behold our God, to whom we looked to save
    us!
This is the Lord for whom we looked;
    let us rejoice and be glad that he has
    saved us!"
For the hand of the Lord will rest on this
    mountain.

This is the Word of the Lord.

---

892   NEW TESTAMENT READING

Rom 14, 7-9. 10-12

A reading from the letter of Paul to the Romans

Whether alive or dead, we belong to the Lord.

None of us lives as his own master and none of us dies as his own master. While we live we are responsible to the Lord, and when we die we die as his servants. Both in life and in death we are the Lord's. That is why Christ died and came to life again, that he might be Lord of both the dead and the living. We shall all have to appear before the judgment seat of God. It is written, "As surely as I live, says the Lord,

every knee shall bend before me and every tongue shall give praise to God."

Every one of us will have to give an account of himself before God.

This is the Word of the Lord.

---

893   RESPONSORIAL PSALM

Ps 31, 2. 6. 8-9. 15-16. 17. 25

℟. (Lk 23, 46) Father, I put my life in your hands.
In you, O Lord, I take refuge;
    let me never be put to shame.
    In your justice rescue me.
Into your hands I commend my spirit;
    you will redeem me, O Lord, O faithful God.
℟. Father, I put my life in your hands.
You have seen my affliction
    and watched over me in my distress,
Not shutting me up in the grip of the enemy
    but enabling me to move about at large.
℟. Father, I put my life in your hands.
My trust is in you, O Lord;
    I say, "You are my God."
In your hands is my destiny; rescue me
    from the clutches of my enemies and my
    persecutors.
℟. Father, I put my life in your hands.
Let your face shine upon your servant;
    save me in your kindness.
Take courage and be stouthearted,
    all you who hope in the Lord.
℟. Father, I put my life in your hands.

**894   ALLELUIA VERSE AND
VERSE BEFORE THE GOSPEL**

Jn 13, 1

When Jesus knew that his hour had come to
    depart out of this world to the Father,
having loved his own who were in the world,
    he loved them to the end.

895   **GOSPEL**

Lk 23, 39-46

✠ A reading from the holy gospel according
to Luke

Father, into your hands I commit my spirit.

One of the criminals hanging in crucifixion
blasphemed Jesus: "Aren't you the Messiah?
Then save yourself and us." But the other one
rebuked him: "Have you no fear of God, seeing you are under the same sentence? We
deserve it, after all. We are only paying the
price for what we've done, but this man has
done nothing wrong." He then said, "Jesus,
remember me when you enter upon your
reign." And Jesus replied, "I assure you: this
day you will be with me in paradise."

It was now around midday, and darkness
came over the whole land until midafternoon
with an eclipse of the sun. The curtain in the
sanctuary was torn in two. Jesus uttered a
loud cry and said,

"Father, into your hands I commend my
spirit."

This is the gospel of the Lord.

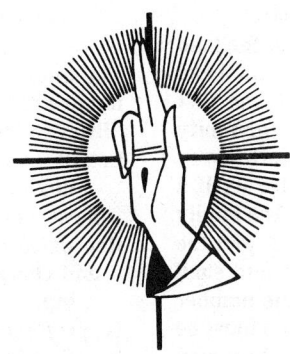

VOTIVE MASSES

Reading I is used in the Easter season where a votive Mass is celebrated in accord with no. 333 in the instruction in the Roman Missal.

HOLY TRINITY

896

See Trinity Sunday, nos. 165-167.

TRIUMPH OF THE HOLY CROSS

897   **READING I**

OUTSIDE EASTER SEASON

1   Ex 12, 1-8. 11-14

A reading from the book of Exodus
The law concerning the paschal supper.

The Lord said to Moses and Aaron in the land of Egypt, "This month shall stand at the head of your calendar; you shall reckon it the first month of the year. Tell the whole community of Israel: On the tenth of this month every one of your families must procure for itself a lamb, one apiece for each household. If a family is too small for a whole lamb, it shall join the nearest household in procuring one and shall share in the lamb in proportion to the number of persons who partake of it. The lamb must be a year-old male and without blemish. You may take it from either the sheep or the goats. You shall keep it until the fourteenth day of this month, and then, with the whole assembly of Israel present, it shall be slaughtered during the evening twilight. They shall take some of its blood and apply it to the two doorposts and the lintel of every house in which they partake of the lamb. That same night they shall eat its roasted flesh with unleavened bread and bitter herbs.

"This is how you are to eat it: with your loins girt, sandals on your feet and your staff in hand, you shall eat like those who are in flight. It is the Passover of the Lord. For on this same night I will go through Egypt, striking down every first-born of the land, both man and beast, and executing judgment on all the gods of Egypt—I, the Lord! But the blood will mark the houses where you are. Seeing the blood, I will pass over you; thus, when I strike the land of Egypt, no destructive blow will come upon you.

"This day shall be a memorial feast for you, which all your generations shall celebrate with pilgrimage to the Lord, as a perpetual institution."

This is the Word of the Lord.

---

2   Wis 2, 1. 12-22

A reading from the book of Wisdom
They condemned him to a violent death.

The impious said among themselves, thinking not aright:
"Brief and troublous is our lifetime;
Let us beset the just one, because he is obnoxious to us;
   he sets himself against our doings,
Reproaches us for transgressions of the law
   and charges us with violations of our training.
He professes to have knowledge of God
   and styles himself a child of the Lord.
To us he is the censure of our thoughts;
   merely to see him is a hardship for us,
Because his life is not like other men's,
   and different are his ways.
He judges us debased;
   he holds aloof from our paths as from things impure.
He calls blest the destiny of the just
   and boasts that God is his Father.
Let us see whether his words be true;
   let us find out what will happen to him.
For if the just one be the son of God, he will defend him
   and deliver him from the hand of his foes.

With revilement and torture let us put him
to the test
that we may have proof of his gentleness
and try his patience.
Let us condemn him to a shameful death;
for according to his own words, God will
take care of him."
These were their thoughts, but they erred;
for their wickedness blinded them,
And they knew not the hidden counsels of God;
neither did they count on the recompense of
holiness
nor discern the innocent souls' reward.
This is the Word of the Lord.

---

3   Is 50, 4-9

A reading from the book of the prophet Isaiah
I did not cover my face against insult.

The Lord God has given me
a well-trained tongue,
That I might know how to speak to the weary
a word that will rouse them.
Morning after morning
he opens my ear that I may hear;
And I have not rebelled,
have not turned back.
I gave my back to those who beat me,
my cheeks to those who plucked my beard;
My face I did not shield
from buffets and spitting.
The Lord God is my help,
therefore I am not disgraced;
I have set my face like flint,
knowing that I shall not be put to shame.
He is near who upholds my right;
if anyone wishes to oppose me,
let us appear together.
Who disputes my right?
Let him confront me.
See, the Lord God is my help;
who will prove me wrong?
This is the Word of the Lord.

---

4   Is 52, 13—53, 12

A reading from the book of the prophet Isaiah
He became vulnerable himself, bearing the faults of many.

See, my servant shall prosper,
he shall be raised high and greatly exalted.
Even as many were amazed at him—
so marred was his look beyond that of man,
and his appearance beyond that of mortals—
So shall he startle many nations,
because of him kings shall stand speechless;
For those who have not been told shall see,
those who have not heard shall ponder it.

Who would believe what we have heard?
To whom has the arm of the Lord been revealed?
He grew up like a sapling before him,
like a shoot from the parched earth;
There was in him no stately bearing to make
us look at him,
nor appearance that would attract us to him.
He was spurned and avoided by men,
a man of suffering, accustomed to infirmity,
One of those from whom men hide their faces,
spurned, and we held him in no esteem.

Yet it was our infirmities that he bore,
our sufferings that he endured,
While we thought of him as stricken,
as one smitten by God and afflicted.
But he was pierced for our offenses,
crushed for our sins;
Upon him was the chastisement that makes us
whole,
by his stripes we were healed.
We had all gone astray like sheep,
each following his own way;
But the Lord laid upon him
the guilt of us all.

Though he was harshly treated, he submitted
and opened not his mouth;
Like a lamb led to the slaughter
or a sheep before the shearers,
he was silent and opened not his mouth.
Oppressed and condemned, he was taken
away,
and who would have thought anymore of his
destiny?

When he was cut off from the land of the
living,
    and smitten for the sin of his people,
A grave was assigned him among the wicked
    and a burial place with evildoers,
Though he had done no wrong
    not spoken any falsehood.
[But the Lord was pleased
    to crush him in infirmity.]

If he gives his life as an offering for sin,
    he shall see his descendants in a long life,
    and the will of the Lord shall be accom-
    plished through him.
Because of his affliction
    he shall see the light in fullness of days;
Through his suffering, my servant shall justify
    many.
    and their guilt he shall bear.
Therefore I will give him his portion among the
    great,
    and he shall divide the spoils with the
    mighty,
Because he surrendered himself to death
    and was counted among the wicked;
And he shall take away the sins of many,
    and win pardon for their offenses.
        This is the Word of the Lord.

---

5   Zec 12, 10-11; 13, 6-7

**A reading from the book of the prophet
Zechariah**

They will look on the one they have pierced.

The Lord said: I will pour out on the house of
David and on the inhabitants of Jerusalem a
spirit of grace and petition; and they shall look
on him whom they have thrust through, and
they shall mourn for him as one mourns for an
only son, and they shall grieve over him as one
grieves over a first-born.

On that day the mourning in Jerusalem shall
be as great as the mourning of Hadadrimmon,
in the plain of Megiddo.

And if anyone asks the prophet, "What are
these wounds on your chest?" he shall answer, "With these I was wounded in the house
of my dear ones."

Awake, O sword, against my shepherd,

against the man who is my associate,
    says the Lord of hosts.
Strike the shepherd
    that the sheep may be dispersed,
    and I will turn my hand against the little
    ones.
        This is the Word of the Lord.

---

898   **READING I**

DURING EASTER SEASON

1   Act 10, 34-43

A reading from the Acts of the Apostles

The one they killed hung on the wood, then God raised him
on the third day.

Peter proceeded to address the people in these
words: "I begin to see how true it is that God
shows no partiality. Rather, the man of any
nation who fears God and acts uprightly is acceptable to him. This is the message he has
sent to the sons of Israel, 'the good news of
peace' proclaimed through Jesus Christ who is
Lord of all. I take it you know what has been
reported all over Judea about Jesus of Nazareth, beginning in Galilee with the baptism
John preached; of the way God anointed him
with the Holy Spirit and power. He went about
doing good works and healing all who were in
the grip of the devil, and God was with him.
We are witnesses to all that he did in the land
of the Jews and in Jerusalem. They killed him
finally, 'hanging him on a tree,' only to have
God raise him up on the third day and grant
that he be seen, not by all, but only by such witnesses as had been chosen beforehand by God
—by us who ate and drank with him after he
rose from the dead. He commissioned us to
preach to the people and to bear witness that
he is the one set apart by God as judge of the
living and the dead. To him all the prophets
testify, saying that everyone who believes in
him has forgiveness of sins through his name."
        This is the Word of the Lord.

---

2   Acts 13, 26-33

A reading from the Acts of the Apostles
By raising Jesus from the dead God has fulfilled his
promise.

[When Paul came to Antioch in Pisidia, he spoke in the synagogue:] "My brothers, children of the family of Abraham and you others who reverence our God, it was to us that this message of salvation was sent forth. The inhabitants of Jerusalem and their rulers failed to recognize him, and in condemning him they fulfilled the words of the prophets which we read sabbath after sabbath. Even though they found no charge against him which deserved death, they begged Pilate to have him executed. Once they had thus brought about all that had been written of him, they took him down from the tree and laid him in a tomb. Yet God raised him from the dead, and for many days thereafter Jesus appeared to those who had come up with him from Galilee to Jerusalem. These are his witnesses now before the people.

"We ourselves announce to you the good news that what God promised our fathers he has fulfilled for us, their children, in raising up Jesus, according to what is written in the second psalm, 'You are my son; this day I have begotten you.' "
This is the Word of the Lord.

---

3   Rv 1, 5-8

A reading from the book of Revelation
He was the firstborn of the dead, who loved us and washed
us clean of our sins in his own blood.

Grace and peace to you from Jesus Christ the faithful witness, the first-born from the dead and ruler of the kings of earth. To him who loves us and freed us from our sins by his own blood, who has made us a royal nation of priests in the service of his God and Father— to him be glory and power forever and ever! Amen.
See, he comes amid the clouds!
    Every eye shall see him,
    even of those who pierced him.
All the peoples of the earth
    shall lament him bitterly.

So it is to be! Amen!
The Lord God says, "I am the Alpha and the Omega, the One who is and who was and who is to come, the Almighty!"
This is the Word of the Lord.

---

4   Rv 5, 6-12

A reading from the book of Revelation
You redeemed men for God with your own blood.

Between the throne with the four living creatures and the elders, I, John, saw a Lamb standing, a Lamb that had been slain. He had seven horns and seven eyes; these eyes are the seven spirits of God, sent to all parts of the world. The Lamb came and received the scroll from the right hand of the One who sat on the throne. When he had taken the scroll, the four living creatures and the twenty-four elders fell down before the Lamb. Along with their harps, the elders were holding vessels of gold filled with aromatic spices, which were the prayers of God's holy people. This is the new hymn they sang:
"Worthy are you to receive the scroll
    and break open its seals,
    for you were slain.
With your blood you purchased for God
    men of every race and tongue,
    of every people and nation.
You made of them a kingdom,
    and priests to serve our God,
    and they shall reign on the earth."
    As my vision continued, I heard the voices of many angels who surrounded the throne and the living creatures and the elders. They were countless in number, thousands and tens of thousands, and they all cried out:
"Worthy is the Lamb that was slain
    to receive power and riches, wisdom and
        strength,
    honor and glory and praise!"
This is the Word of the Lord.

899   RESPONSORIAL PSALM

1   Ps 22, 8-9. 17-18. 19-20. 23-24

℟. (2) My God, my God, why have you abandoned me?

All who see me scoff at me;
    they mock me with parted lips, they wag
        their heads:
"He relied on the Lord; let him deliver him,
    let him rescue hin, if he loves him."

℟. My God, my God, why have you abandoned
me?

Indeed, many dogs surround me,
    a pack of evildoers closes in upon me;
They have pierced my hands and my feet;
    I can count all my bones.

℟. My God, my God, why have you abandoned
me?

They divide my garments among them,
    and for my vesture they cast lots.
But you, O Lord, be not far from me;
    O my help, hasten to aid me.

℟. My God, my God, why have you abandoned
me?

I will proclaim your name to my brethren;
    in the midst of the assembly I will praise
        you:
"You who fear the Lord, praise him;
    all you descendants of Jacob, give glory to
        him;
    revere him, all you descendants of Israel!"

℟. My God, my God, why have you abandoned
me?

℟. Or: (Mt 26, 42) My Father, your will be
done!

---

2   Ps 31, 2. 6. 12-13. 15-16. 17. 25

℟. (Lk 23, 46) Father, I put my life in your
hands.

In you, O Lord, I take refuge;
    let me never be put to shame.
    In your justice rescue me.
Into your hands I commend my spirit;
    you will redeem me, O Lord, O faithful God.

℟. Father, I put my life in your hands.

For all my foes I am an object of reproach,
    a laughingstock to my neighbors, and a
        dread to my friends;

they who see me abroad flee from me.
I am forgotten like the unremembered dead;
    I am like a dish that is broken.

℟. Father, I put my life in your hands.

But my trust is in you, O Lord;
    I say, "You are my God."
In your hands is my destiny; rescue me
    from the clutches of my enemies and my
        persecutors.

℟. Father, I put my life in your hands.

Let your face shine upon your servant;
    save me in your kindness.
Take courage and be stouthearted,
    all you who hope in the Lord.

℟. Father, I put my life in your hands.

---

3   Ps 55, 5-6. 13. 14-15. 17-18. 23

℟. (23) Throw your cares on the Lord,
and he will support you.

My heart quakes within me;
    the terror of death has fallen upon me.
Fear and trembling come upon me,
    and horror overwhelms me.

℟. Throw your cares on the Lord,
and he will support you.

If an enemy had reviled me,
    I could have borne it;
If he who hates me had vaunted himself
    against me,
    I might have hidden from him.

℟. Throw your cares on the Lord,
and he will support you.

But you, my other self,
    my companion and my bosom friend!
You, whose comradeship I enjoyed;
    at whose side I walked in procession in the
        the house of God!

℟. Throw your cares on the Lord,
and he will support you.

But I will call upon God,
    and the Lord will save me.
In the evening, and at dawn, and at noon,
    I will grieve and moan,
    and he will hear my voice.

℟. Throw your cares on the Lord,
and he will support you.

Cast your care upon the Lord,
    and he will support you;

never will he permit the just man to be disturbed.
℟. Throw your cares on the Lord,
and he will support you.

---

4   Ps 69, 8-10. 15-16. 17-19. 20-21. 22. 27. 31. 33-34
℟. (14) Lord, in your great love, answer me.
For your sake I bear insult,
and shame covers my face.
I have become an outcast to my brothers,
a stranger to my mother's sons,
Because zeal for your house consumes me,
and the insults of those who blaspheme you
fall upon me.
℟. Lord, in your great love, answer me.
Rescue me out of the mire; may I not sink!
may I be rescued from my foes,
and from the watery depths.
Let not the flood-waters overwhelm me,
nor the abyss swallow me up,
nor the pit close its mouth over me.
℟. Lord, in your great love, answer me.
Answer me, O Lord, for bounteous is your
kindness;
in your great mercy turn toward me.
Hide not your face from your servant;
in my distress, make haste to answer me.
Come and ransom my life;
as an answer for my enemies, redeem me.
℟. Lord, in your great love, answer me.
You know my reproach, my shame and my
ignominy;
before you are all my foes.
Insult has broken my heart, and I am weak;
I looked for sympathy, but there was none;
for comforters, and I found none.
℟. Lord, in your great love, answer me.
Rather they put gall in my food,
and in my thirst they gave me vinegar to
drink.
For they kept after him whom you smote,
and added to the pain of him you wounded.
℟. Lord, in your great love, answer me.
I will praise the name of God in song,
and I will glorify him with thanksgiving:
"See, you lowly ones, and be glad;
you who see God, may your hearts be merry!

For the Lord hears the poor,
and his own who are in bonds he spurns not."
℟. Lord, in your great love, answer me.
℟. Or: (21) I looked for sympathy, there was
none;
for consolers, not one could I find.

---

5   Ps 118, 5-7. 10-12. 13-15. 16-18. 19-21. 22-24
℟. (1) Give thanks to the Lord for he is good;
his love is everlasting.
In my straits I called upon the Lord;
the Lord answered me and set me free.
The Lord is with me; I fear not;
what can man do against me?
The Lord is with me to help me,
and I shall look down upon my foes.
℟. Give thanks to the Lord for he is good;
his love is everlasting.
All the nations encompassed me;
in the name of the Lord I crushed them.
They encompassed me on every side;
in the name of the Lord I crushed them.
They encompassed me like bees,
they flared up like fire among thorns;
in the name of the Lord I crushed them.
℟. Give thanks to the Lord for he is good;
his love is everlasting.
I was hard pressed and was falling,
but the Lord helped me.
My strength and my courage is the Lord,
and he has been my savior.
The joyful shout of victory
in the tents of the just:
"The right hand of the Lord has struck with
power.
℟. Give thanks to the Lord for he is good;
his love is everlasting.
The right hand of the Lord is exalted;
the right hand of the Lord has struck with
power."
I shall not die, but live,
and declare the works of the Lord.
Though the Lord has indeed chastised me,
yet he has not delivered me to death.
℟. Give thanks to the Lord for he is good;
his love is everlasting.
Open to me the gates of justice;
I will enter them and give thanks to the Lord.

This gate is the Lord's;
 the just shall enter it.
I will give thanks to you, for you have answered me
 and have been my savior.
Ry. Give thanks to the Lord for he is good;
 his love is everlasting.
The stone which the builders rejected
 has become the cornerstone.
By the Lord has this been done;
 it is wonderful in our eyes.
This is the day the Lord has made;
 let us be glad and rejoice in it.
Ry. Give thanks to the Lord for he is good;
 his love is everlasting.
Ry. Or: Alleluia.

---

900   **READING II**

1   1 Cor 1, 18-25

**A reading from the first letter of Paul to the
Corinthians**

We have preached to you Christ crucified.

The message of the cross is complete absurdity
to those who are headed for ruin, but to us who
are experiencing salvation it is the power of
God. Scripture says,
"I will destroy the wisdom of the wise,
 and thwart the cleverness of the clever."
Where is the wise man to be found? Where the
scribe? Where is the master of worldly argument? Has not God turned the wisdom of this
world into folly? Since in God's wisdom the
world did not come to know him through
wisdom, it pleased God to save those who
believe through the absurdity of the preaching
of the gospel. Yes, Jews demand "signs" and
Greeks look for "wisdom," but we preach
Christ crucified, a stumbling block to Jews
and an absurdity to Gentiles; but to those who
are called, Jews and Greeks alike, Christ the
power of God and the wisdom of God. For God's
folly is wiser than men, and his weakness more
powerful than men.
   This is the Word of the Lord.

---

2   Eph 2, 13-18

**A reading from the letter of Paul to the
Ephesians**

He is our peace, destroying the hostility in your body.

In Christ Jesus you who once were far off have
been brought near through the blood of Christ.
It is he who is our peace, and who made the
two of us one by breaking down the barrier of
hostility that kept us apart. In his own flesh
he abolished the law with its commands and
precepts, to create in himself one new man
from us who had been two and to make peace,
reconciling both of us to God in one body
through his cross, which put that enmity to
death. He came and "announced the good news
of peace to you who were far off, and to those
who were near"; through him we both have
access in one Spirit to the Father.
   This is the Word of the Lord.

---

3   Phil 2, 6-11

**A reading from the letter of Paul to the
Philippians**

He humiliated himself, but God raised him on high.

Christ Jesus, though he was in the form of God,
 did not deem equality with God
 something to be grasped at.
Rather, he emptied himself
 and took the form of a slave,
 being born in the likeness of men.

He was known to be of human estate
 and it was thus that he humbled himself,
 obediently accepting even death,
 death on a cross!

Because of this,
 God highly exalted him
 and bestowed on him the name
 above every other name.

So that at Jesus' name
 every knee must bend
 in the heavens, on the earth,
 and under the earth,
 and every tongue proclaim
 to the glory of God the Father:
JESUS CHRIST IS LORD!
   This is the Word of the Lord.

4   Phil 3, 8-14

A reading from the letter of Paul to the Philippians

All I want is to know Christ and the power of his resurrection and to share in his sufferings.

I have come to rate all as loss in the light of the surpassing knowledge of my Lord Jesus Christ. For his sake I have forfeited everything; I have accounted all else rubbish so that Christ may be my wealth and I may be in him, not having any justice of my own based on observance of the law. The justice I possess is that which comes through faith in Christ. It has its origin in God and is based on faith. I wish to know Christ and the power flowing from his resurrection; likewise to know how to share in his sufferings by being formed into the pattern of his death. Thus do I hope that I may arrive at resurrection from the dead.

It is not that I have reached it yet, or have already finished my course; but I am racing to grasp the prize if possible, since I have been grasped by Christ [Jesus]. Brothers, I do not think of myself as having reached the finish line. I give no thought to what lies behind but push on to what is ahead. My entire attention is on the finish line as I run toward the prize to which God calls me—life on high in Christ Jesus.

This is the Word of the Lord.

---

5   Heb 5, 7-9

A reading from the letter to the Hebrews

He learned obedience and became the source of eternal life.

In the days when Christ was in the flesh, he offered prayers and supplications with loud cries and tears to God, who was able to save him from death, and he was heard because of his reverence. Son though he was, he learned obedience from what he suffered; and when perfected, he became the source of eternal salvation for all who obey him.

This is the Word of the Lord.

---

901   **ALLELUIA VERSE AND VERSE BEFORE THE GOSPEL**

1   Phil 2, 8-9

Christ became obedient for us even to death, dying on the cross.
Therefore God raised him on high
and gave him a name above all other names.

2

We adore you, O Christ, and we praise you, because by your cross you have redeemed the world.

3

The tree of Adam made us slaves, the cross-tree set us free.
The evil fruit was snare, but the Son of God is ransom.

---

902   **GOSPEL**

1   Mk 8, 31-34

✠ A reading from the holy gospel according to Mark

The Son of Man was destined to suffer much.

Jesus began to teach his disciples that the Son of Man had to suffer much, be rejected by the elders, the chief priests, and the scribes, be put to death, and rise three days later. He said this quite openly. Peter then took him aside and began to remonstrate with him. At this he turned around and, eyeing the disciples, reprimanded Peter in turn: "Get out of my sight, you satan! You are not judging by God's standards but by man's!"

He summoned the crowd with his disciples and said to them: "If a man wishes to come after me, he must deny his very self, take up his cross, and follow in my steps."

This is the gospel of the Lord.

---

2   Mk 12, 1-12

✠ A reading from the holy gospel according
to Mark

They seized the beloved son and killed him and threw him
out of the vineyard.

Jesus began to tell the chief priests, scribes and
elders this parable: "A man planted a vineyard,
put a hedge around it, dug out a vat, and
erected a tower. Then he leased it to tenant
farmers and went on a journey. In due time he
dispatched a man in his service to the tenants
to obtain from them his share of produce from
the vineyard. But they seized him, beat him,
and sent him off empty-handed. The second
time he sent them another servant; him too
they beat over the head and treated shamefully. He sent yet another and they killed him.
So too with many others; some they beat; some
they killed. He still had one to send—the son
whom he loved. He sent him to them as a last
resort, thinking, 'They will have to respect my
son.' But those tenants said to one another,
'Here is the one who will inherit everything.
Come, let us kill him, and the inheritance will
be ours.' Then they seized and killed him and
dragged him outside the vineyard. What do
you suppose the owner of the vineyard will do?
He will come and destroy those tenants and
turn his vineyard over to others. Are you not
familiar with this passage of Scripture:

'The stone rejected by the builders
    has become the keystone of the struc-
    ture.
It was the Lord who did it
    and we find it marvelous to behold'?"

They wanted to arrest him at this, yet they
had reason to fear the crowd. (They knew well
enough that he meant the parable for them.)
Finally they left him and went off.

This is the gospel of the Lord.

---

3   Lk 24, 35-48

✠ A reading from the holy gospel according
to Luke

See my hands and my feet.

The disciples recounted what had happened on
the road and how they had come to know Jesus
in the breaking of bread.

While they were still speaking about all this,
he himself stood in their midst [and said to
them, "Peace to you."] In their panic and fright
they thought they were seeing a ghost. He said
to them, "Why are you disturbed? Why do such
ideas cross your mind? Look at my hands and
my feet; it is really I. Touch me, and see that
a ghost does not have flesh and bones as I do."
[As he said this he showed them his hands
and feet.] They were still incredulous for sheer
joy and wonder, so he said to them, "Have
you anything here to eat?" They gave him a
piece of cooked fish, which he took and ate in
their presence. Then he said to them, "Recall
those words I spoke to you when I was still
with you: everything written about me in the
law of Moses and the prophets and psalms had
to be fulfilled." Then he opened their minds to
the understanding of the Scriptures.

He said to them: "Thus it is written that
the Messiah must suffer and rise from the dead
on the third day. In his name, penance for the
remission of sins is to be preached to all the
nations, beginning at Jerusalem. You are witnesses of this."

This is the gospel of the Lord.

---

4   Jn 12, 31-36

✠ A reading from the holy gospel according
to John

When I am lifted up from the earth I will draw all men
to myself.

Jesus said to the crowd:

"Now has judgment come upon this world,
now will this world's prince be driven out,
and I—once I am lifted up from earth—
will draw all men to myself."

(This statement of his indicated the sort of
death he was going to die.) The crowd objected
to his words: "We have heard it said in the law
that the Messiah is to remain forever. How can
you claim that the Son of Man must be lifted
up? Just who is this 'Son of Man'?" Jesus
answered:

"The light is among you only a little longer.
Walk while you still have it
or darkness will come over you.
The man who walks in the dark

does not know where he is going.
While you have the light,
keep faith in the light;
Thus you will become sons of light."
This is the gospel of the Lord.

903 READING FROM THE ACCOUNT OF THE LORD'S PASSION

1   Mk 14, 32-41

✠ A reading from the holy gospel according
to Mark

My soul is sorrowful to the point of death.

Jesus and his disciples went to a place named
Gethsemani. "Sit down here while I pray," he
said to them; at the same time he took along
with him Peter, James, and John. Then he
began to be filled with fear and distress. He
said to them, "My heart is filled with sorrow to
the point of death. Remain here and stay
awake." He advanced a little and fell to the
ground, praying that if it were possible this
hour might pass him by. He kept saying, "Abba
(O Father), you have the power to do all things.
Take this cup away from me. But let it be as
you would have it, not as I." When he returned
he found them asleep. He said to Peter,
"Asleep, Simon? You could not stay awake for
even an hour? Be on guard and pray that you
may not be put to the test. The spirit is willing
but nature is weak." Going back again he
began to pray in the same words. Once again
he found them asleep on his return. They could
not keep their eyes open, nor did they know
what to say to him. He returned a third time
and said to them, "Still sleeping? Still taking
your ease? It will have to do. The hour is on us.
You will see that the Son of Man is to be
handed over into the clutches of evil men."
This is the gospel of the Lord.

2   Mt 26, 47-56

✠ A reading from the holy gospel according
to Matthew

*You have come with swords and clubs to capture me, as if
I were a thief.*

While Jesus was still speaking to his disciples,
Judas, one of the Twelve, arrived accompanied

by a great crowd with swords and clubs. They
had been sent by the chief priests and elders of
the people. His betrayer had arranged to give
them a signal, saying, "The man I shall embrace is the one; take hold of him." He immediately went over to Jesus, said to him,
"Peace, Rabbi," and embraced him. Jesus answered, "Do what you are here for, friend!"
At that moment they stepped forward to lay
hands on Jesus, and arrested him. Suddenly
one of those who accompanied Jesus put his
hand to his sword, drew it, and slashed at the
high priest's servant, cutting off his ear. Jesus
said to him: "Put back your sword where it
belongs. Those who use the sword are sooner
or later destroyed by it. Do you not suppose I
can call on my Father to provide at a moment's
notice more than twelve legions of angels? But
then how would the Scriptures be fulfilled
which say it must happen this way?"
At that very time Jesus said to the crowd:
"Am I a brigand, that you have come armed
with swords and clubs to arrest me? From day
to day I sat teaching in the temple precincts,
yet you never arrested me. Nonetheless, all this
has happened in fulfillment of the writings of
the prophets." Then all the disciples deserted
him and fled.
This is the gospel of the Lord.

3   Mk 14, 55-65

✠ A reading from the holy gospel according
to Mark

They all gave their verdict: he deserved to die.

The chief priests with the whole Sanhedrin
were busy soliciting testimony against Jesus
that would lead to his death, but they could not
find any. Many spoke against him falsely
under oath but their testimony did not agree.
Some, for instance, on taking the stand, testified falsely by alleging, "We heard him declare,
'I will destroy this temple made by human
hands,' and 'In three days I will construct
another not made by human hands.'" Even so,
their testimony did not agree.
The high priest rose to his feet before the
court and began to interrogate Jesus: "Have

you no answer to what these men testify against you?" But Jesus remained silent; he made no reply. Once again the high priest interrogated him: "Are you the Messiah, the Son of the Blessed One?" Then Jesus answered: "I am; and you will see the Son of Man seated at the right hand of the Power and coming with the clouds of heaven." At that the high priest tore his robes and said: "What further need do we have of witnesses? You have heard the blasphemy. What is your verdict?" They all concurred in the verdict "guilty," with its sentence of death. Some of them then began to spit on him. They blindfolded him and hit him, saying, "Play the prophet!" while the officers manhandled him.

This is the gospel of the Lord.

---

4   Mk 15, 1-15

✠ A reading from the holy gospel according to Mark

What am I to do with the man you call King of the Jews? Crucify him.

As soon as it was daybreak the chief priests, with the elders and scribes (that is, the whole Sanhedrin), reached a decision. They bound Jesus, led him away, and handed him over to Pilate. Pilate interrogated him: "Are you the king of the Jews?" "You are the one who is saying it," Jesus replied. The chief priests, meanwhile, brought many accusations against him. Pilate interrogated him again: "Surely you have some answer? See how many accusations they are leveling against you." But greatly to Pilate's surprise, Jesus made no further response.

Now on the occasion of a festival he would release for them one prisoner—any man they asked for. There was a prisoner named Barabbas jailed along with the rebels who had committed murder in the uprising. When the crowd came up to press their demand that he honor the custom, Pilate rejoined, "Do you want me to release the king of the Jews for you?" He was aware, of course, that it was out of jealousy that the chief priests had handed him over. Meanwhile, the chief priests incited the crowd to have him release Barabbas instead. Pilate again asked them, "What am I to do with the man you call the king of the Jews?" They shouted back, "Crucify him!" Pilate protested, "Why? What crime has he committed?" They only shouted the louder, "Crucify him!" So Pilate, who wished to satisfy the crowd, released Barabbas to them; and after he had had Jesus scourged, he handed him over to be crucified.

This is the gospel of the Lord.

---

5   Mk 15, 16-20

✠ A reading from the holy gospel according to Mark

They dressed him up in purple and put a crown of thorns on him.

The soldiers led Jesus away into the hall known as the praetorium; at the same time they assembled the whole cohort. They dressed him in royal purple, then wove a crown of thorns and put it on him, and began to salute him, "All hail! King of the Jews!" Continually striking Jesus on the head with a reed and spitting at him, they genuflected before him and pretended to pay him homage. When they had finished mocking him, they stripped him of the purple, dressed him in his own clothes, and led him out to crucify him.

This is the gospel of the Lord.

---

6   Mt 27, 33-50

✠ A reading from the holy gospel according to Matthew

Jesus cried out with a loud voice and gave up the spirit.

Upon arriving at a site called Golgotha (a name which means Skull Place), they gave Jesus a drink of wine flavored with gall, which he tasted but refused to drink.

When they had crucified him, they divided his clothes among them by casting lots; then they sat down there and kept watch over him. Above his head they had put the charge against him in writing:

"THIS IS JESUS, KING OF THE JEWS."

Two insurgents were crucified along with him, one at his right and one at his left. People going by kept insulting him, tossing their heads and saying: "So you are the one who was going to destroy the temple and rebuild it in three days! Save yourself, why don't you? Come down off that cross if you are God's Son!" The chief priests, the scribes and the elders also joined in the jeering: "He saved others but he cannot save himself! So he is the king of Israel! Let's see him come down from that cross and then we will believe in him. He relied on God; let God rescue him now if he wants to. After all, he claimed, 'I am God's Son.' " The insurgents who had been crucified with him kept taunting him in the same way.

From noon onward, there was darkness over the whole land until midafternoon. Then toward midafternoon, Jesus cried out in a loud tone, "Eli, Eli, lema sabachthani?", that is, "My God, my God, why have you forsaken me?" This made some of the bystanders who heard it remark, "He is invoking Elijah!" Immediately one of them ran off and got a sponge. He soaked it in cheap wine, and sticking it on a reed, tried to make him drink. Meanwhile the rest said, "Leave him alone. Let's see whether Elijah comes to his rescue." Once again Jesus cried out in a loud voice, and then gave up his spirit.

This is the gospel of the Lord.

7   Lk 23, 33-34. 39-46

✠ A reading from the holy gospel according to Luke

Father, into your hands I commit my spirit.

When they came to Skull Place, as it was called, they crucified Jesus there and the criminals as well, one on his right and the other on his left. [Jesus said, "Father, forgive them; they do not know what they are doing."] They divided his garments, rolling dice for them.

One of the criminals hanging in crucifixion blasphemed him: "Aren't you the Messiah? Then save yourself and us." But the other one rebuked him: "Have you no fear of God, seeing you are under the same sentence? We deserve it, after all. We are only paying the price for what we've done, but this man has done nothing wrong." He then said, "Jesus,

remember me when you enter upon your reign." And Jesus replied, "I assure you: this day you will be with me in paradise."

It was now around midday, and darkness came over the whole land until midafternoon with an eclipse of the sun. The curtain in the sanctuary was torn in two. Jesus uttered a loud cry and said,

"Father, into your hands I commend my spirit."

This is the gospel of the Lord.

8   Jn 19, 28-37

✠ A reading from the holy gospel according to John

He was pierced with a lance and blood and water flowed from his side.

Jesus, realizing that everything was now finished to bring the Scripture to fulfillment said, "I am thirsty." There was a jar there, full of common wine. They stuck a sponge soaked in this wine on some hyssop and raised it to his lips. When Jesus took the wine, he said, "Now it is finished." Then he bowed his head, and delivered over his spirit.

Since it was the Preparation Day the Jews did not want to have the bodies left on the cross during the sabbath, for that sabbath was a solemn feast day. They asked Pilate that the legs be broken and the bodies be taken away. Accordingly, the soldiers came and broke the legs of the men crucified with Jesus, first of the one, then of the other. When they came to Jesus and saw that he was already dead, they did not break his legs. One of the soldiers thrust a lance into his side, and immediately blood and water flowed out. (This testimony has been given by an eyewitness and his testimony is true. He tells what he knows is true, so that you may believe.) These events took place for the fulfillment of Scripture:

"Break none of his bones."

There is still another Scripture passage which says:

"They shall look on him whom they have pierced."

This is the gospel of the Lord.

9   Mk 15, 33-39; 16, 1-6

✠ **A reading from the holy gospel according to Mark**

My God, my God, why have you abandoned me? You are looking for Jesus of Nazareth whom they crucified; he has risen.

When noon came, darkness fell on the whole countryside and lasted until midafternoon. At that time Jesus cried in a loud voice, "Eloi, Eloi, lama sabachthani?" which means, "My God, my God, why have you forsaken me?" A few of the bystanders who heard it remarked, "Listen! He is calling Elijah!" Someone ran off, and soaking a sponge in sour wine, stuck it on a reed to try to make him drink. The man said, "Now let's see whether Elijah comes to take him down."

Then Jesus, uttering a loud cry, breathed his last. At that moment the curtain in the sanctuary was torn in two from top to bottom. The centurion who stood guard over him, on seeing the manner of his death, declared, "Clearly this man was the Son of God!"

When the Sabbath was over, Mary Magdalene, Mary the mother of James and Salome bought perfumed oils with which they intended to go and anoint Jesus. Very early, just after sunrise on the first day of the week, they came to the tomb. They were saying to one another, "Who will roll back the stone for us from the entrance to the tomb?" When they looked, they found that the stone had been rolled back. (It was a huge one.) On entering the tomb they saw a young man sitting at the right, dressed in a white robe. This frightened them thoroughly, but he reassured them: "You need not be amazed! You are looking for Jesus of Nazareth, the one who was crucified. He has been raised up; he is not here. See the place where they laid him."

This is the gospel of the Lord.

HOLY EUCHARIST

904   ## READING I
OUTSIDE EASTER SEASON

1   Gn 14, 18-20

A reading from the book of Genesis

Melchizedek offered bread and wine to God.

Melchizedek, king of Salem, brought out bread and wine, and being a priest of God Most High, he blessed Abram with these words:
"Blessed be Abram by God Most High,
   the creator of heaven and earth;
And blessed be God Most High,
   who delivered your foes into your hand."
Then Abram gave him a tenth of everything.
           This is the Word of the Lord.

---

2   Ex 16, 2-4. 12-15

A reading from the book of Exodus

The Lord will rain bread on us from heaven.

In the desert the whole Israelite community grumbled against Moses and Aaron. The Israelites said to them, "Would that we had died at the Lord's hand in the land of Egypt, as we sat by our fleshpots and ate our fill of bread! But you had to lead us into this desert to make the whole community die of famine!"

Then the Lord said to Moses, "I will now rain down bread from heaven for you. Each day the people are to go out and gather their daily portion; thus will I test them, to see whether they follow my instructions or not. I have heard the grumbling of the Israelites. Tell them: In the evening twilight you shall eat flesh, and in the morning you shall have your fill of bread, so that you may know that I, the Lord, am your God."

In the evening quail came up and covered the camp. In the morning a dew lay all about the camp, and when the dew evaporated, there on the surface of the desert were fine flakes like hoarfrost on the ground. On seeing it, the Israelites asked one another, "What is this?" for they did not know what it was. But Moses told them, "This is the bread which the Lord has given you to eat."

           This is the Word of the Lord.

3   Ex 24, 3-8

A reading from the book of Exodus

This is the blood marking the covenant the Lord has made with you.

When Moses came to the people and related all the words and ordinances of the Lord, they all answered with one voice, "We will do everything that the Lord has told us." Moses then wrote down all the words of the Lord and, rising early the next day, he erected at the foot of the mountain an altar and twelve pillars for the twelve tribes of Israel. Then, having sent certain young men of the Israelites to offer holocausts and sacrifice young bulls as peace offerings to the Lord, Moses took half of the blood and put it in large bowls; the other half he splashed on the altar. Taking the book of the covenant, he read it aloud to the people, who answered, "All that the Lord has said, we will heed and do." Then he took the blood and sprinkled it on the people, saying, "This is the blood of the covenant which the Lord has made with you in accordance with all these words of his."

This is the Word of the Lord.

---

4   Dt 8, 2-3. 14-16

A reading from the book of Deuteronomy

He gave you food finer than any you have ever known.

Moses said to the people: "Remember how for forty years now the Lord, your God, has directed all your journeying in the desert, so as to test you by affliction and find out whether or not it was your intention to keep his commandments. He therefore let you be afflicted with hunger, and then fed you with manna, a food unknown to you and your fathers, in order to show you that not by bread alone does man live, but by every word that comes forth from the mouth of the Lord.

"Remember the Lord, your God, who brought you out of the land of Egypt, that place of slavery; who guided you through the vast and terrible desert with its saraph serpents and scorpions, its parched and waterless ground; who brought forth water for you from the flinty rock and fed you in the desert with manna, a food unknown to your fathers."

This is the Word of the Lord.

---

5   1 Kgs 19, 4-8

A reading from the first book of Kings

In the strength of that food, Elijah walked to the mountain of God.

Elijah left his servant at Beer-sheba of Judah and went a day's journey into the desert, until he came to a broom tree and sat beneath it. He prayed for death: "This is enough, O Lord! Take my life, for I am no better than my fathers." He lay down and fell asleep under the broom tree, but then an angel touched him and ordered him to get up and eat. He looked and there at his head was a hearth cake and a jug of water. After he ate and drank, he lay down again, but the angel of the Lord came back a second time, touched him, and ordered, "Get up and eat, else the journey will be too long for you!" He got up, ate and drank; then, strengthened by that food, he walked forty days and forty nights to the mountain of God, Horeb.

This is the Word of the Lord.

---

6   Prv 9, 1-6

A reading from the book of Proverbs

Eat the bread and drink the wine which I have prepared for you.

Wisdom has built her house,
    she has set up her seven columns;
She has dressed her meat, mixed her wine,
    yes, she has spread her table.
She has sent out her maidens; she calls
    from the heights out over the city:
"Let whoever is simple turn in here;
    to him who lacks understanding, I say,
Come, eat of my food,
    and drink of the wine I have mixed!
Forsake foolishness that you may live;
    advance in the way of understanding."

This is the Word of the Lord.

905

READING I

DURING EASTER SEASON

1   Acts 2, 42-47

A reading from the Acts of the Apostles

They continued in fellowship with the apostles and in the breaking of bread.

The brethren devoted themselves to the apostles' instruction and the communal life, to the breaking of bread and the prayers. A reverent fear overtook them all, for many wonders and signs were performed by the apostles. Those who believed shared all things in common; they would sell their property and goods, dividing everything on the basis of each one's need. They went to the temple area together every day, while in their homes they broke bread. With exultant and sincere hearts they took their meals in common, praising God and winning the approval of all the people. Day by day the Lord added to their number those who were being saved.

This is the Word of the Lord.

2   Acts 10, 34. 37-43

A reading from the Acts of the Apostles

After he was raised from the dead, we ate and drank with him.

Peter proceeded to address the people in these words: "I take it you know what has been reported all over Judea about Jesus of Nazareth, beginning in Galilee with the baptism John preached; of the way God anointed him with the Holy Spirit and power. He went about doing good works and healing all who were in the grip of the devil, and God was with him. We are witnesses to all that he did in the land of the Jews and in Jerusalem. They killed him finally, 'hanging him on a tree,' only to have God raise him up on the third day and grant that he be seen, not by all, but only by such witnesses as had been chosen beforehand by God—by us who ate and drank with him after he rose from the dead. He commissioned us to preach to the people and to bear witness that he is the one set apart by God as judge of the living and the dead. To him all the prophets

testify, saying that everyone who believes in him has forgiveness of sins through his name." **This is the Word of the Lord.**

906

RESPONSORIAL PSALM

1   Ps 23, 1-3. 3-4. 5. 6

℟. (1) The Lord is my shepherd;
    there is nothing I shall want.
The Lord is my shepherd; I shall not want.
    In verdant pastures he gives me repose;
Beside restful waters he leads me;
    he refreshes my soul.
℟. The Lord is my shepherd;
    there is nothing I shall want.
He guides me in right paths
    for his name's sake.
Even though I walk in the dark valley
    I fear no evil; for you are at my side
With your rod and your staff
    that give me courage.
℟. The Lord is my shepherd;
    there is nothing I shall want.
You spread the table before me
    in the sight of my foes;
You anoint my head with oil;
    my cup overflows.
℟. The Lord is my shepherd;
    there is nothing I shall want.
Only goodness and kindness follow me
    all the days of my life;
And I shall dwell in the house of the Lord
    for years to come.
℟. The Lord is my shepherd;
    there is nothing I shall want.

2   Ps 34, 2-3. 4-5. 6-7. 8-9. 10-11

℟. (9) Taste and see the goodness of the Lord.
I will bless the Lord at all times;
    his praise shall be ever in my mouth.
Let my soul glory in the Lord;
    the lowly will hear me and be glad.
℟. Taste and see the goodness of the Lord.
Glorify the Lord with me,
    let us together extol his name.
I sought the Lord, and he answered me
    and delivered me from all my fears.

℟. Taste and see the goodness of the Lord.
Look to him that you may be radiant with joy,
   and your faces may not blush with shame.
When the afflicted man called out, the Lord
   heard,
   and from all his distress he saved him.
℟. Taste and see the goodness of the Lord.
The angel of the Lord encamps
   around those who fear him, and delivers
   them.
Taste and see how good the Lord is;
   happy the man who takes refuge in him.
℟. Taste and see the goodness of the Lord.
Fear the Lord, you his holy ones,
   for naught is lacking to those who fear him.
The great grow poor and hungry;
   but those who seek the Lord want for no
   good thing.
℟. Taste and see the goodness of the Lord.

---

3   Ps 78, 3.4. 23-24. 25. 54

℟. (24) The Lord gave them bread from heaven.
What we have heard and know,
   and what our fathers have declared to us,
The glorious deeds of the Lord and his strength
   and the wonders that he wrought.
℟. The Lord gave them bread from heaven.
He commanded the skies above
   and the doors of heaven he opened;
He rained manna upon them for food
   and gave them heavenly bread.
℟. The Lord gave them bread from heaven.
The bread of the mighty was eaten by men;
   even a surfeit of provisions he sent them.
And he brought them to his holy land,
   to the mountains his right hand had won.
℟. The Lord gave them bread from heaven.

---

4   Ps 110, 1. 2. 3. 4

℟. Priest for ever, like Melchizedek of old,
   the Lord Christ offered bread and wine.
The Lord said to my Lord: "Sit at my right
   hand
   till I make your enemies your footstool."
℟. Priest for ever, like Melchizedek of old,
   the Lord Christ offered bread and wine.
The scepter of your power the Lord will
   stretch forth from Sion:
   "Rule in the midst of your enemies."

℟. Priest for ever, like Melchizedek of old,
   the Lord Christ offered bread and wine.
"Yours is princely power in the day of your
   birth, in holy splendor;
   before the daystar, like the dew, I have be-
   gotten you."
℟. Priest for ever, like Melchizedek of old,
   the Lord Christ offered bread and wine.
The Lord has sworn, and he will not repent:
   "You are a priest forever, according to the
   order of Melchizedek."
℟. Priest for ever, like Melchizedek of old,
   the Lord Christ offered bread and wine.
℟. Or: (4) You are a priest for ever,
   in the line of Melchizedek.

---

5   Ps 116, 12-13. 15. 16. 17-18

℟. (1 Cor 10, 16) Our blessing-cup is a communion with the blood of Christ.
How shall I make a return to the Lord
   for all the good he has done for me?
The cup of salvation I will take up,
   and I will call upon the name of the Lord.
℟. Our blessing-cup is a communion with the
   blood of Christ.
Precious in the eyes of the Lord
   is the death of his faithful ones.
I am your servant, the son of your handmaid;
   you have loosed my bonds.
℟. Our blessing-cup is a communion with the
   blood of Christ.
To you will I offer sacrifice of thanksgiving,
   and I will call upon the name of the Lord.
My vows to the Lord I will pay
   in the presence of all his people.
℟. Our blessing-cup is a communion with the
   blood of Christ.
℟. Or: Alleluia.

---

6   Ps 145, 10-11. 15-16. 17-18

℟. (16) The hand of the Lord feeds us;
   he answers all our needs.
Let all your works give you thanks, O Lord,
   and let your faithful ones bless you.
Let them discourse of the glory of your king-
   dom
   and speak of your might.

℞. The hand of the Lord feeds us;
  he answers all our needs.
The eyes of all look hopefully to you,
  and you give them their food in due season;
You open your hand
  and satisfy the desire of every living thing.
℞. The hand of the Lord feeds us;
  he answers all our needs.
The Lord is just in all his ways
  and holy in all his works.
The Lord is near to all who call upon him,
  to all who call upon him in truth.
℞. The hand of the Lord feeds us;
  he answers all our needs.

---

7   Ps 147, 12-13. 14-15. 19-20
℞. (Jn 6, 59) Whoever eats this bread will live
  for ever.
Glorify the Lord, O Jerusalem;
  praise your God, O Zion.
For he has strengthened the bars of your gates,
  he has blessed your children within you.
℞. Whoever eats this bread will live for ever.
He has granted peace in your borders;
  with the best of wheat he fills you.
He sends forth his command to the earth;
  swiftly runs his word!
℞. Whoever eats this bread will live for ever.
He has proclaimed his word to Jacob,
  his statutes and his ordinances to Israel.
He has not done thus for any other nation;
  his ordinances he has not made known to
  them. Alleluia.
℞. Whoever eats this bread will live for ever.
℞. Or: Alleluia.

---

907   **READING II**
1   1 Cor 10, 16-17
A reading from the first letter of Paul to the
                      Corinthians
Though we are many, we are one bread and one body.

Is not the cup of blessing we bless a sharing in
the blood of Christ? And is not the bread we
break a sharing in the body of Christ? Because
the loaf of bread is one, we many though we

are, are one body, for we all partake of the one
loaf.
              This is the Word of the Lord.

---

2   1 Cor 11, 23-26
A reading from the first letter of Paul to the
                      Corinthians
Each time you eat this bread and drink this cup, you are
proclaiming the death of the Lord Jesus.

I received from the Lord what I handed on to
you, namely, that the Lord Jesus on the night
in which he was betrayed took bread, and after
he had given thanks, broke it and said, "This is
my body, which is for you. Do this in remembrance of me." In the same way, after the supper, he took the cup, saying, "This cup is the
new covenant in my blood. Do this, whenever
you drink it, in remembrance of me." Every
time, then, you eat this bread and drink this
cup, you proclaim the death of the Lord until
he comes!
              This is the Word of the Lord.

---

3   Heb 9, 11-15
A reading from the letter to the Hebrews
The blood of Christ purifies our hearts from sin.

When Christ came as high priest of the good
things which came to be, he entered once for
all into the sanctuary, passing through the
greater and more perfect tabernacle not made
by hands, that is, not belonging to this creation.
He entered, not with the blood of goats and
calves but with his own blood, and achieved
eternal redemption. For if the blood of goats
and bulls and the sprinkling of a heifer's ashes
can sanctify those who are defiled so that their
flesh is cleansed, how much more will the
blood of Christ, who through eternal spirit
offered himself up unblemished to God, cleanse
our consciences from dead works to worship
the living God!
    This is why he is mediator of a new cov-
enant: since his death has taken place for
deliverance from transgressions committed
under the first covenant, those who are called
may receive the promised eternal inheritance.
              This is the Word of the Lord.

908   **ALLELUIA VERSE AND**
VERSE BEFORE THE GOSPEL

1   Jn 6, 51-52

I am the living bread from heaven, says the
   Lord;
if anyone eats this bread he will live for ever.

2   Jn 6, 57

Whoever eats my flesh and drinks my blood
will live in me and I in him, says the Lord.

3   Jn 6, 58

As the living Father sent me, and I live because of the Father,
so he who eats me will live because of me.

---

909   **GOSPEL**

1   Mk 14, 12-16. 22-26

✠ A reading from the holy gospel according
                    to Mark
      This is my body. This is my blood.

On the first day of Unleavened Bread, when
it was customary to sacrifice the paschal lamb,
his disciples said to Jesus, "Where do you wish
us to go to prepare the Passover supper for
you?" He sent two of his disciples with these
instructions: "Go into the city and you will
come upon a man carrying a water jar. Follow
him. Whatever house he enters, say to the
owner, 'The Teacher asks, Where is my guest-
room where I may eat the Passover with my
disciples?' Then he will show you an upstairs
room, spacious, furnished, and all in order.
That is the place you are to get ready for us."
The disciples went off. When they reached the
city they found it just as he had told them, and
they prepared the Passover supper.

During the meal he took bread, blessed and
broke it, and gave it to them. "Take this,"
he said, "this is my body." He likewise took a
cup, gave thanks and passed it to them, and
they all drank from it. He said to them: "This
is my blood, the blood of the covenant, to be
poured out on behalf of many. I solemnly
assure you, I will never again drink of the
fruit of the vine until the day when I drink it
new in the reign of God."

After singing songs of praise, they walked
out to the Mount of Olives.
      This is the gospel of the Lord.

2   Lk 9, 11-17

✠ A reading from the holy gospel according
                    to Luke
     All the people ate and were satisfied.

Jesus spoke to the crowd of the reign of God,
and he healed all who were in need of healing.

As sunset approached the Twelve came and
said to him, "Dismiss the crowd so that they
can go into the villages and farms in the neighborhood and find themselves lodging and food,
for this is certainly an out-of-the-way place."
He answered them, "Why do you not give
them something to eat yourselves?" They replied, "We have nothing but five loaves and
two fishes. Or shall we ourselves go and buy
food for all these people?" (There were about
five thousand men.) Jesus said to his disciples,
"Have them sit down in groups of fifty or so."
They followed his instructions and got them all
seated. Then, taking the five loaves and the
two fishes, Jesus raised his eyes to heaven,
pronounced a blessing over them, broke them,
and gave them to his disciples for distribution
to the crowd. They all ate until they had
enough. What they had left, over and above,
filled twelve baskets.
      This is the gospel of the Lord.

---

3   Lk 24, 13-35

✠ A reading from the holy gospel according
                    to Luke
  They recognized the Lord when he broke the bread with
                     them.

Two of the disciples of Jesus that same day
[the first of the week] were making their way
to a village named Emmaus seven miles distant
from Jerusalem, discussing as they went all
that had happened. In the course of their lively
exchange, Jesus approached and began to walk
along with them. However they were restrained from recognizing him. He said to

them, "What are you discussing as you go your way?" They halted in distress and one of them, Cleopas by name, asked him, "Are you the only resident of Jerusalem who does not know the things that went on there these past few days?" He said to them, "What things?" They said: "All those that had to do with Jesus of Nazareth, a prophet powerful in word and deed in the eyes of God and all the people; how our chief priests and leaders delivered him up to be condemned to death, and crucified him. We were hoping that he was the one who would set Israel free. Besides all this, today, the third day since these things happened, some women of our group have just brought us some astonishing news. They were at the tomb before dawn and failed to find his body, but returned with the tale that they had seen a vision of angels who declared he was alive. Some of our number went to the tomb and found it to be just as the women said; but him they did not see."

Then he said to them, "What little sense you have! How slow you are to believe all that the prophets have announced! Did not the Messiah have to undergo all this so as to enter into his glory?" Beginning, then, with Moses and all the prophets, he interpreted for them every passage of Scripture which referred to him. By now they were near the village to which they were going, and he acted as if he were going farther. But they pressed him: "Stay with us. It is nearly evening—the day is practically over." So he went in to stay with them.

When he had seated himself with them to eat, he took bread, pronounced the blessing, then broke the bread and began to distribute it to them. With that their eyes were opened and they recognized him; whereupon he vanished from their sight. They said to one another, "Were not our hearts burning inside us as he talked to us on the road and explained the Scriptures to us?" They got up immediately and returned to Jerusalem, where they found the Eleven and the rest of the company assembled. They were greeted with, "The Lord has been raised! It is true! He has appeared to Simon." Then they recounted what had happened on the road and how they had come to know him in the breaking of bread.

This is the gospel of the Lord.

---

4   Jn 6, 1-15

✠ **A reading from the holy gospel according to John**

He gave the people all the food they wanted.

Jesus crossed the Sea of Galilee [to the shore] of Tiberias; a vast crowd kept following him because they saw the signs he was performing for the sick. Jesus then went up the mountain and sat down there with his disciples. The Jewish feast of Passover was near; when Jesus looked up and caught sight of a vast crowd coming toward him, he said to Philip, "Where shall we buy bread for these people to eat?" (He knew well what he intended to do but he asked this to test Philip's response.) Philip replied, "Not even with two hundred days' wages could we buy loaves enough to give each of them a mouthful!"

One of Jesus' disciples, Andrew, Simon Peter's brother, remarked to him, "There is a lad here who has five barley loaves and a couple of dried fish, but what good is that for so many?" Jesus said, "Get the people to recline." Even though the men numbered about five thousand, there was plenty of grass for them to find a place on the ground. Jesus then took the loaves of bread, gave thanks, and passed them around to those reclining there; he did the same with the dried fish, as much as they wanted. When they had had enough, he told his disciples, "Gather up the crusts that are left over so that nothing will go to waste." At this, they gathered twelve baskets full of pieces left over by those who had been fed with the five barley loaves.

When the people saw the sign he had performed they began to say, "This is undoubtedly the Prophet who is to come into the world." At that, Jesus realized that they would come and carry him off to make him king, so he fled back to the mountain alone.

This is the gospel of the Lord.

---

5   Jn 6, 24-35

✠ A reading from the holy gospel according
to John

*If you come to me, you will never be hungry. He who
believes in me will never know thirst.*

Once the crowd saw that neither Jesus nor his
disciples were there, they too embarked in the
boats and went to Capernaum looking for
Jesus.

When they found him on the other side of
the lake, they said to him, "Rabbi, when did
you come here?" Jesus answered them:
"I assure you,
you are not looking for me because you have
seen signs
but because you have eaten your fill of the
loaves.
You should not be working for perishable
food
but for food that remains unto life eternal,
food which the Son of Man will give you;
it is on him that God the Father has set
his seal."
At this they said to him, "What must we do
to perform the works of God?" Jesus replied:
"This is the work of God:
have faith in the One whom he sent."
"So that we can put faith in you," they asked
him, "what sign are you going to perform for
us to see? What is the 'work' you do? Our ancestors had manna to eat in the desert; according to Scripture, 'He gave them bread from the
heavens to eat.' " Jesus said to them:
"I solemnly assure you,
it was not Moses who gave you bread from
the heavens;
it is my Father who gives you the real heavenly bread.
God's bread comes down from heaven
and gives life to the world."
"Sir, give us this bread always," they besought
him.
Jesus explained to them:
"I myself am the bread of life.
No one who comes to me shall ever be
hungry,
no one who believes in me shall thirst again."
This is the gospel of the Lord.

6   Jn 6, 41-51

✠ A reading from the holy gospel according
to John

I am the living bread from heaven.

At this the Jews started to murmur in protest
against Jesus because he claimed, "I am the
bread that came down from heaven." They
kept saying: "Is this not Jesus, the son of
Joseph? Do we not know his father and
mother? How can he claim to have come down
from heaven?"
"Stop your murmuring," Jesus told them.

"No one can come to me
unless the Father who sent me draws him;
I will raise him up on the last day.
It is written in the prophets:
'They shall all be taught by God.'
Everyone who has heard the Father
and learned from him
comes to me.
Not that anyone has seen the Father—
only the one who is from God
has seen the Father.
Let me firmly assure you,
he who believes has eternal life.
I am the bread of life.
Your ancestors ate manna in the desert, but
they died.
This is the bread that comes down from
heaven,
for a man to eat and never die.

"I myself am the living bread
come down from heaven.
If anyone eats this bread
he shall live forever."
This is the gospel of the Lord.

_____

7   Jn 6, 51-58

✠ A reading from the holy gospel according
to John

My flesh and blood are true food and drink.

Jesus said to the crowd of the Jews:
"I myself am the living bread
come down from heaven.
If anyone eats this bread
he shall live forever;

the bread I will give
is my flesh for the life of the world."
At this the Jews quarreled among themselves, saying, "How can he give us his flesh
to eat?" Thereupon Jesus said to them:
"Let me solemnly assure you,
if you do not eat the flesh of the Son of Man
and drink his blood,
you have no life in you.
He who feeds on my flesh
and drinks my blood
has life eternal,
and I will raise him up on the last day.
For my flesh is real food
and my blood real drink.
The man who feeds on my flesh
and drinks my blood
remains in me, and I in him.
Just as the Father who has life sent me
and I have life because of the Father,
so the man who feeds on me
will have life because of me.
This is the bread that came down from
    heaven.
Unlike your ancestors who ate and died
    nonetheless,
the man who feeds on this bread shall live
    forever."
    This is the gospel of the Lord.

8   Jn 21, 1-14

✠ A reading from the holy gospel according
to John
Jesus gave the food to his apostles.

At the Sea of Tiberias, Jesus showed himself
to the disciples [once again]. This is how the
appearance took place. Assembled were Simon
Peter, Thomas ("the Twin"), Nathanael (from
Cana in Galilee), Zebedee's sons, and two other
disciples. Simon Peter said to them, "I am going
out to fish." "We will join you," they replied,
and went off to get into their boat. All through
the night they caught nothing. Just after daybreak Jesus was standing on the shore, though
none of the disciples knew it was Jesus. He said
to them, "Children, have you caught anything
to eat?" "Not a thing," they answered. "Cast

your net off to the starboard side," he suggested, "and you will find something." So they
made a cast, and took so many fish they could
not haul the net in. Then the disciple Jesus loved
cried out to Peter, "It is the Lord!" On hearing
it was the Lord, Simon Peter threw on some
clothes—he was stripped—and jumped into
the water.
    Meanwhile the other disciples came in the
boat, towing the net full of fish. Actually they
were not far from land—no more than a hundred yards.
    When they landed, they saw a charcoal fire
there with a fish laid on it and some bread.
"Bring some of the fish you just caught," Jesus
told them. Simon Peter went aboard and
hauled ashore the net loaded with sizable fish
—one hundred fifty-three of them! In spite of
the great number, the net was not torn.
    "Come and eat your meal," Jesus told them.
Not one of the disciples presumed to inquire
"Who are you?" for they knew it was the Lord.
Jesus came over, took the bread and gave it
to them, and did the same with the fish. This
marked the third time that Jesus appeared
to the disciples after being raised from the
dead.
    This is the gospel of the Lord.

──────────

SACRED HEART

910   READING I

OUTSIDE EASTER SEASON

1   Ex 34, 4-6. 8-9

A reading from the book of Exodus
Our God is merciful and compassionate.

Early in the morning Moses went up Mount
Sinai as the Lord had commanded him, taking
along the two stone tablets.
    Having come down in a cloud, the Lord
stood with him there and proclaimed his name,
"Lord." Thus the Lord passed before him and
cried out, "The Lord, the Lord, a merciful and
gracious God, slow to anger and rich in kindness and fidelity." Moses at once bowed down
to the ground in worship. Then he said, "If I

find favor with you, O Lord, do come along in our company. This is indeed a stiff-necked people; yet pardon our wickedness and sins, and receive us as your own."

This is the Word of the Lord.

2　　　　　　　　　　　　　　　　　　Dt 7, 6-11

A reading from the book of Deuteronomy
God has chosen you because he loves you.

Moses said to the people: "You are a people sacred to the Lord, your God; he has chosen you from all the nations on the face of the earth to be a people peculiarly his own. It was not because you are the largest of all nations that the Lord set his heart on you and chose you, for you are really the smallest of all nations. It was because the Lord loved you and because of his fidelity to the oath he had sworn to your fathers, that he brought you out with his strong hand from the place of slavery, and ransomed you from the hand of Pharaoh, king of Egypt. Understand, then, that the Lord, your God, is God indeed, the faithful God who keeps his merciful covenant down to the thousandth generation toward those who love him and keep his commandments, but who repays with destruction the person who hates him; he does not dally with such a one, but makes him personally pay for it. You shall therefore carefully observe the commandments, the statutes and the decrees which I enjoin on you today."

This is the Word of the Lord.

3　　　　　　　　　　　　　　　　　　Dt 10 12-22

A reading from the book of Deuteronomy
God loves his chosen ones and their children.

Moses said to the people: "And now, Israel, what does the Lord, your God, ask of you but to fear the Lord, your God, and follow his ways exactly, to love and serve the Lord, your God, with all your heart and all your soul, to keep the commandments and statutes of the Lord which I enjoin on you today for your own good? Think! The heavens, even the highest heavens, belong to the Lord, your God, as well as the earth and everything on it. Yet in his

love for your fathers the Lord was so attached to them as to choose you, their descendants, in preference to all other peoples, as indeed he has now done. Circumcise your hearts, therefore, and be no longer stiff-necked. For the Lord, your God, is the God of gods, the Lord of lords, the great God, mighty and awesome, who has no favorites, accepts no bribes; who executes justice for the orphan and the widow, and befriends the alien, feeding and clothing him. So you too must befriend the alien, for you were once aliens yourselves in the land of Egypt. The Lord, your God, shall you fear, and him shall you serve; hold fast to him and swear by his name. He is your glory, he, your God, who has done for you those great and terrible things which your own eyes have seen. Your ancestors went down to Egypt seventy strong, and now the Lord, your God, has made you as numerous as the stars of the sky."

This is the Word of the Lord.

4　　　　　　　　　　　　　　　　　　Is 49, 13-15

A reading from the book of the prophet Isaiah
Even if a mother forgets her child, I will never forget you.

Sing out, O heavens, and rejoice, O earth,
　break forth into song, you mountains.
For the Lord comforts his people
　and shows mercy to his afflicted.

But Sion said, "The Lord has forsaken me;
　my Lord has forgotten me."
Can a mother forget her infant,
　be without tenderness for the child of her
　　womb?
Even should she forget,
　I will never forget you.

This is the Word of the Lord.

5　　　　　　　　　　　　　　　　　　Jer 31, 1-4

A reading from the book of the prophet Jeremiah
I have loved you with a love that will never end.

At that time, says the Lord,
　I will be the God of all the tribes of Israel,
　and they shall be my people.

Thus says the Lord:
The people that escaped the sword
  have found favor in the desert.
As Israel comes forward to be given his rest,
  the Lord appears to him from afar:
With age-old love I have loved you;
  so I have kept my mercy toward you.
Again I will restore you, and you shall be
  rebuilt,
  O virgin Israel;
Carrying your festive tambourines,
  you shall go forth dancing with the merrymakers.
      This is the Word of the Lord.

6   Ez 34, 11-16

**A reading from the book of the prophet
Ezekiel**
I will take care of my flock.

Thus says the Lord God: I myself will look
after and tend my sheep. As a shepherd tends
his flock when he finds himself among his
scattered sheep, so will I tend my sheep. I
will rescue them from every place where they
were scattered when it was cloudy and dark.
I will lead them out from among the peoples
and gather them from the foreign lands; I
will bring them back to their own country and
pasture them upon the mountains of Israel
[in the land's ravines and all its inhabited
places]. In good pastures will I pasture them,
and on the mountain heights of Israel shall be
their grazing ground. There they shall lie down
on good grazing ground, and in rich pastures
shall they be pastured on the mountains of
Israel. I myself will pasture my sheep; I myself
will give them rest, says the Lord God. The lost
I will seek out, the strayed I will bring back,
the injured I will bind up, the sick I will heal
[but the sleek and the strong I will destroy],
shepherding them rightly.
      This is the Word of the Lord.

7   Hos 11, 1. 3-4. 8-9

A reading from the book of the prophet Hosea
My heart is saddened at the thought of parting.

The Lord said:
When Israel was a child I loved him,

out of Egypt I called my son.
Yet it was I who taught Ephraim to walk,
  who took them in my arms;
I drew them with human cords,
  with bands of love;
I fostered them like one
  who raises an infant to his cheeks;
Yet, though I stooped to feed my child,
  they did not know that I was their healer.

My heart is overwhelmed,
  my pity is stirred.
I will not give vent to my blazing anger,
  I will not destroy Ephraim again;
For I am God and not man,
  the Holy One present among you;
I will not let the flames consume you.
      This is the Word of the Lord.

911   **READING I
                    DURING EASTER SEASON**

1   Rv 3, 14. 20-22

A reading from the book of Revelation
I will come to eat with you.

The Amen, the faithful Witness and true, the
Source of God's creation, has this to say: "Here
I stand, knocking at the door. If anyone hears
me calling and opens the door, I will enter his
house and have supper with him, and he with
me. I will give the victor the right to sit with
me on my throne, as I myself won the victory
and took my seat beside my Father on his
throne.
  " Let him who has ears to hear heed the
Spirit's word to the churches. "
      This is the Word of the Lord.

2   Rv 5, 6-12

A reading from the book of Revelation
You brought us back to God by shedding your blood for us.

Between the throne with the four living creatures and the elders, I, John, saw a Lamb
standing, a Lamb that had been slain. He had
seven horns and seven eyes; these eyes are the
seven spirits of God, sent to all parts of the
world. The Lamb came and received the scroll

from the right hand of the One who sat on the throne. When he had taken the scroll, the four living creatures and the twenty-four elders fell down before the Lamb. Along with their harps, the elders were holding vessels of gold filled with aromatic spices, which were the prayers of God's holy people. This is the new hymn they sang:

"Worthy are you to receive the scroll
    and break open its seals,
    for you were slain.
With your blood you purchased for God
    men of every race and tongue,
    of every people and nation.
You made of them a kingdom,
    and priests to serve our God,
    and they shall reign on the earth."

As my vision continued, I heard the voices of many angels who surrounded the throne and the living creatures and the elders. They were countless in number, thousands and tens of thousands, and they all cried out:

"Worthy is the Lamb that was slain
    to receive power and riches, wisdom and
      strength,
    honor and glory and praise!"
    This is the Word of the Lord.

---

912   RESPONSORIAL PSALM

1   Is 12, 2-3. 4. 5-6

℞. (3) You will draw water joyfully
    from the springs of salvation.
God indeed is my savior;
    I am confident and unafraid.
My strength and my courage is the Lord,
    and he has been my savior.
With joy you will draw water
    at the fountain of salvation.
℞. You will draw water joyfully
    from the springs of salvation.
Give thanks to the Lord, acclaim his name;
    among the nations make known his deeds,
    proclaim how exalted is his name.
℞. You will draw water joyfully
    from the springs of salvation.
Sing praise to the Lord for his glorious achievement;

let this be known throughout all the earth.
Shout with exultation, O city of Zion,
    for great in your midst
    is the Holy One of Israel!
℞. You will draw water joyfully
    from the springs of salvation.

---

2   Ps 23, 1-3. 3-4. 5. 6

℞. (1) The Lord is my shepherd;
    there is nothing I shall want.
The Lord is my shepherd; I shall not want.
    In verdant pastures he gives me repose;
Beside restful waters he leads me;
    he refreshes my soul.
℞. The Lord is my shepherd;
    there is nothing I shall want.
He guides me in right paths
    for his name's sake.
Even though I walk in the dark valley
    I fear no evil; for you are at my side
With your rod and your staff
    that give me courage.
℞. The Lord is my shepherd;
    there is nothing I shall want.
You spread the table before me
    in the sight of my foes;
You anoint my head with oil;
    my cup overflows.
℞. The Lord is my shepherd;
    there is nothing I shall want.
Only goodness and kindness follow me
    all the days of my life;
And I shall dwell in the house of the Lord
    for years to come.
℞. The Lord is my shepherd;
    there is nothing I shall want.

---

3   Ps 25, 4-5. 6-7. 8-9. 10. 14

℞. (6) Remember your mercies, O Lord.
Your ways, O Lord, make known to me;
    teach me your paths,
Guide me in your truth and teach me,
    for you are God my savior.
℞. Remember your mercies, O Lord.
Remember that your compassion, O Lord,
    and your kindness are from of old.

In your kindness remember me
   because of your goodness, O Lord.
℟. Remember your mercies, O Lord.
Good and upright is the Lord;
   thus he shows sinners the way.
He guides the humble to justice,
   he teaches the humble his way.
℟. Remember your mercies, O Lord.
All the paths of the Lord are kindness and
   constancy
   toward those who keep his covenant and his
   decrees.
The friendship of the Lord is with those who
   fear him,
   and his covenant, for their instruction.
℟. Remember your mercies, O Lord.

---

4   Ps 33, 1-2. 4-5. 11-12. 18-19. 20-21
℟. (5) The earth is full of the goodness of the
   Lord.
Exult, you just, in the Lord;
   praise from the upright is fitting.
Give thanks to the Lord on the harp;
   with the ten-stringed lyre chant his praises.
℟. The earth is full of the goodness of the Lord.
For upright is the word of the Lord,
   and all his works are trustworthy.
He loves justice and right;
   of the kindness of the Lord the earth is full.
℟. The earth is full of the goodness of the Lord.
But the plan of the Lord stands forever;
   the design of his heart, through all gener-
   ations.
Happy the nation whose God is the Lord,
   the people he has chosen for his own inheritance.
℟. The earth is full of the goodness of the Lord.
But see, the eyes of the Lord are upon those
   who fear him,
   upon those who hope for his kindness,
To deliver them from death
   and preserve them in spite of famine.
℟. The earth is full of the goodness of the Lord.
Our soul waits for the Lord,
   who is our help and our shield,

For in him our hearts rejoice;
   in his holy name we trust.
℟. The earth is full of the goodness of the Lord.
℟. Or: (Mt 11, 29) Learn from me,
   for I am gentle and lowly in heart.

---

5   Ps 34, 2-3. 4-5. 6-7. 8-9. 17-18. 19. 23
℟. (9) Taste and see the goodness of the Lord.
I will bless the Lord at all times;
   his praise shall be ever in my mouth.
Let my soul glory in the Lord;
   the lowly will hear me and be glad.
℟. Taste and see the goodness of the Lord.
Glorify the Lord with me,
   let us together extol his name.
I sought the Lord, and he answered me
   and delivered me from all my fears.
℟. Taste and see the goodness of the Lord.
Look to him that you may be radiant with joy,
   and your faces may not blush with shame.
When the afflicted man called out, the Lord
   heard,
   and from all his distress he saved him.
℟. Taste and see the goodness of the Lord.
The angel of the Lord encamps
   around those who fear him, and delivers
   them.
Taste and see how good the Lord is;
   happy the man who takes refuge in him.
℟. Taste and see the goodness of the Lord.
The Lord confronts the evildoers,
   to destroy remembrance of them from the
   earth.
When the just cry out, the Lord hears them,
   and from all their distress he rescues them.
℟. Taste and see the goodness of the Lord.
The Lord is close to the brokenhearted;
   and those who are crushed in spirit he saves.
The Lord redeems the lives of his servants;
   no one incurs guilt who takes refuge in him.
℟. Taste and see the goodness of the Lord.

---

6   Ps 103, 1-2. 3-4. 6-7. 8. 10
℟. (17) The Lord's kindness is everlasting
   to those who fear him.
Bless the Lord, O my soul;
   and all my being, bless his holy name.

Bless the Lord, O my soul,
  and forget not all his benefits.
R̶⁄. The Lord's kindness is everlasting
  to those who fear him.
He pardons all your iniquities,
  he heals all your ills.
He redeems your life from destruction,
  he crowns you with kindness and compas-
    sion.
R̶⁄. The Lord's kindness is everlasting
  to those who fear him.
The Lord secures justice
  and the rights of all the oppressed.
He has made known his ways to Moses,
  and his deeds to the children of Israel.
R̶⁄. The Lord's kindness is everlasting
  to those who fear him.
Merciful and gracious is the Lord,
  slow to anger and abounding in kindness.
Not according to our sins does he deal with us,
  nor does he requite us according to our
    crimes.
R̶⁄. The Lord's kindness is everlasting
  to those who fear him.

---

913   **READING II**

1   Rom 5, 5-11

A reading from the letter of Paul to the Romans
God has poured out his love into our hearts.

Hope will not leave us disappointed, because
the love of God has been poured out in our
hearts through the Holy Spirit who has been
given to us. At the appointed time, when we
were still powerless, Christ died for us godless
men. It is rare that anyone should lay down his
life for a just man, though it is barely possible
that for a good man someone may have the
courage to die. It is precisely in this that God
proves his love for us: that while we were still
sinners, Christ died for us. Now that we have
been justified by his blood, it is all the more
certain that we shall be saved by him from
God's wrath. For if, when we were God's
enemies, we were reconciled to him by the
death of his Son, it is all the more certain that
we who have been reconciled will be saved by

his life. Not only that; we go so far as to make
God our boast through our Lord Jesus Christ,
through whom we have now received reconciliation.

  This is the Word of the Lord.

---

2   Eph 1, 3-10

**A reading from the letter of Paul to the
Ephesians**
He has lavished his rich graces upon us.

Praised be the God and Father of our Lord
Jesus Christ, who has bestowed on us in Christ
every spiritual blessing in the heavens! God
chose us in him before the world began, to be
holy and blameless in his sight, to be full of
love; likewise he predestined us through Christ
Jesus to be his adopted sons—such was his
will and pleasure—that all might praise the
divine favor he has bestowed on us in his
beloved.

  It is in Christ and through his blood that we
have been redeemed and our sins forgiven,
so immeasurably generous is God's favor to us.
God has given us the wisdom to understand
fully the mystery, the plan he was pleased to
decree in Christ, to be carried out in the fullness of time: namely, to bring all things in the
heavens and on earth into one under Christ's
headship.

  This is the Word of the Lord.

---

3   Eph 3, 8-12

**A reading from the letter of Paul to the
Ephesians**
God has given me the privilege of proclaiming the riches
of Christ to all the nations.

To me, the least of all believers, was given the
grace to preach to the Gentiles the unfathomable riches of Christ and to enlighten all men
on the mysterious design which for ages was
hidden in God, the Creator of all. Now, therefore, through the church, God's manifold wisdom is made known to the principalities and
powers of heaven, in accord with his age-old
purpose, carried out in Christ Jesus our Lord.
In Christ and through faith in him we can

speak freely to God, drawing near him with confidence.

This is the Word of the Lord.

---

4   Eph 3, 14-19

A reading from the letter of Paul to the Ephesians

I pray that you will grasp the unbounded love of Christ.

I kneel before the Father from whom every family in heaven and on earth takes its name; and I pray that he will bestow on you gifts in keeping with the riches of his glory. May he strengthen you inwardly through the working of his Spirit. May Christ dwell in your hearts through faith, and may charity be the root and foundation of your life. Thus you will be able to grasp fully, with all the holy ones, the breadth and length and height and depth of Christ's love, and experience this love which surpasses all knowledge, so that you may attain to the fullness of God himself.

This is the Word of the Lord.

---

5   Phil 1, 8-11

A reading from the letter of Paul to the Philippians

May your life be filled with the perfection which comes through Jesus Christ.

God himself can testify how much I long for each of you with the affection of Christ Jesus! My prayer is that your love may more and more abound, both in understanding and wealth of experience, so that with a clear conscience and blameless conduct you may learn to value the things that really matter, up to the very day of Christ. It is my wish that you may be found rich in the harvest of justice which Jesus Christ has ripened in you, to the glory and praise of God.

This is the Word of the Lord.

---

6   1 Jn 4, 7-16

A reading from the first letter of John

We love God because he has loved us first.

Beloved,
let us love one another
because love is of God;

everyone who loves is begotten of God
and has knowledge of God.
The man without love has known nothing of God,
for God is love.
God's love was revealed in our midst in this way:
he sent his only Son to the world
that we might have life through him.
Love, then, consists in this:
not that we have loved God,
but that he has loved us
and has sent his Son as an offering for our sins.
Beloved,
if God has loved us so,
we must have the same love for one another.
No one has ever seen God.
Yet if we love one another
God dwells in us,
and his love is brought to perfection in us.
The way we know we remain in him
and he in us
is that he has given us of his Spirit.
We have seen for ourselves, and can testify,
that the Father has sent the Son as savior of the world.
When anyone acknowledges that Jesus is the Son of God,
God dwells in him
and he in God.
We have come to know and to believe in the love God has for us.
God is love,
and he who abides in love
abides in God
and God in him.

This is the Word of the Lord.

---

914   **ALLELUIA VERSE AND VERSE BEFORE THE GOSPEL**

1   Mt 11, 25

Blessed are you, Father, Lord of heaven and earth;
you have revealed to little ones the mysteries of the kingdom.

2   Mt 11, 28

Come to me, all you that labor and are
  burdened,
and I will give you rest, says the Lord.

3   Mt 11, 29

Take my yoke upon you;
learn from me, for I am gentle and lowly in
  heart.

4   Jn 10, 14

I am the good shepherd, says the Lord;
I know my sheep, and mine know me.

5   Jn 15, 9

As the Father has loved me, so have I loved
  you;
remain in my love.

6   1 Jn 4, 10

God first loved us
and sent his Son to take away our sins.

---

915   **GOSPEL**

1   Mt 11, 25-30

✠ A reading from the holy gospel according
              to Matthew
I am meek and humble of heart.

Jesus said: ':Father, Lord of heaven and earth,
to you I offer praise; for what you have hidden from the learned and the clever you have
revealed to the merest children. Father, it is
true. You have graciously willed it so. Everything has been given over to me by my Father.
No one knows the Son but the Father, and no
one knows the Father but the Son—and anyone to whom the Son wishes to reveal him.
  "Come to me, all you who are weary and
find life burdensome, and I will refresh you.
Take my yoke upon your shoulders and learn
from me, for I am gentle and humble of heart.
Your souls will find rest, for my yoke is easy
and my burden light."
          This is the gospel of the Lord.

---

2   Lk 15, 1-10

✠ A reading from the holy gospel according
              to Luke
Heaven is filled with joy when one sinner turns back to God.

The tax collectors and sinners were all gathering around Jesus to hear him, at which the Pharisees murmured, "This man welcomes sinners
and eats with them." Then he addressed this
parable to them: "Who among you, if he has a
hundred sheep and loses one of them, does not
leave the ninety-nine in the wasteland and follow the lost one until he finds it? And when he
finds it, he puts it on his shoulders in jubilation.
Once arrived home, he invites friends and neighbors in and says to them, 'Rejoice with me because I have found my lost sheep.' I tell you,
there will likewise be more joy in heaven over
one repentant sinner than over ninety-nine
righteous people who have no need to repent.
  "What woman, if she has ten silver pieces
and loses one, does not light a lamp and sweep
the house in a diligent search until she has
retrieved what she lost? And when she finds it,
she calls in her friends and neighbors to say,
'Rejoice with me! I have found the silver piece
I lost.' I tell you, there will be the same kind
of joy before the angels of God over one repentant sinner."
          This is the gospel of the Lord.

---

3   Lk 15, 1-3. 11-32

✠ A reading from the holy gospel according
              to Luke
We are celebrating because your brother has come back
                    from death.

The tax collectors and sinners were all gathering around Jesus to hear him, at which the
Pharisees murmured, "This man welcomes sinners and eats with them." Then he addressed
this parable to them:
  "A man had two sons. The younger of them
said to his father, 'Father, give me the share of
the estate that is coming to me.' So the father
divided up the property. Some days later this
younger son collected all his belongings and

went off to a distant land, where he squandered his money on dissolute living. After he had spent everything, a great famine broke out in that country and he was in dire need. So he attached himself to one of the propertied class of the place, who sent him to his farm to take care of the pigs. He longed to fill his belly with the husks that were fodder for the pigs, but no one made a move to give him anything. Coming to his senses at last, he said: 'How many hired hands at my father's place have more than enough to eat, while here I am starving! I will break away and return to my father, and say to him, "Father, I have sinned against God and against you; I no longer deserve to be called your son. Treat me like one of your hired hands."' With that he set off for his father's house. While he was still a long way off, his father caught sight of him and was deeply moved. He ran out to meet him, threw his arms around his neck, and kissed him. The son said to him, 'Father, I have sinned against God and against you; I no longer deserve to be called your son.' The father said to his servants: 'Quick! bring out the finest robe and put it on him; put a ring on his finger and shoes on his feet. Take the fatted calf and kill it. Let us eat and celebrate because this son of mine was dead and has come back to life. He was lost and is found.' Then the celebration began.

"Meanwhile the elder son was out on the land. As he neared the house on his way home, he heard the sound of music and dancing. He called one of the servants and asked him the reason for the dancing and the music. The servant answered, 'Your brother is home, and your father has killed the fatted calf because he has him back in good health.' The son grew angry at this and would not go in; but his father came out and began to plead with him.

"He said in reply to his father: 'For years now I have slaved for you. I never disobeyed one of your orders, yet you never gave me so much as a kid goat to celebrate with my friends. Then, when this son of yours returns after having gone through your property with loose women, you kill the fatted calf for him.'

" 'My son,' replied the father, 'you are with me always, and everything I have is yours. But we had to celebrate and rejoice! This brother of yours was dead, and has come back to life. He was lost, and is found.' "
　　　This is the gospel of the Lord.

---

4   Jn 10, 11-18

✠ A reading from the holy gospel according to John

A good shepherd is ready to die for his flock.

Jesus said to his disciples:
　"I am the good shepherd;
　the good shepherd lays down his life for the sheep.
　The hired hand who is no shepherd,
　nor owner of the sheep,
　catches sight of the wolf coming
　and runs away, leaving the sheep
　to be snatched and scattered by the wolf.
　That is because he works for pay;
　he has no concern for the sheep.

　"I am the good shepherd.
　I know my sheep
　and my sheep know me
　in the same way that the Father knows me
　and I know the Father;
　for these sheep I will give my life.
　I have other sheep
　that do not belong to this fold.
　I must lead them, too,
　and they shall hear my voice.
　There shall be one flock then, one shepherd.
　The Father loves me for this:
　that I lay down my life
　to take it up again.
　No one takes it from me;
　I lay it down freely.
　I have power to lay it down,
　and I have power to take it up again.
　This command I received from my Father."
　　　This is the gospel of the Lord.

---

5   Jn 15, 1-8

✠ A reading from the holy gospel according
to John

Live in me as I live in you.

Jesus said to his disciples:
"I am the true vine
and my Father is the vinegrower.
He prunes away
every barren branch,
but the fruitful ones
he trims clean
to increase their yield.
You are clean already,
thanks to the word I have spoken to you.
Live on in me, as I do in you.
No more than a branch can bear fruit of
itself
apart from the vine,
can you bear fruit
apart from me.
I am the vine, you are the branches.
He who lives in me and I in him,
will produce abundantly,
for apart from me you can do nothing.
A man who does not live in me
is like a withered, rejected branch,
picked up to be thrown in the fire and burnt.
If you live in me,
and my words stay part of you,
you may ask what you will—
it will be done for you.
My Father has been glorified
in your bearing much fruit
and becoming my disciples."
    This is the gospel of the Lord.

6   Jn 15, 9-17

✠ A reading from the holy gospel according
to John

Love one another as much as I love you.

Jesus said to his disciples:
"As the Father has loved me,
so I have loved you.
Live on in my love.
You will live in my love
if you keep my commandments,
even as I have kept my Father's commandments,

and live in his love.
All this I tell you
that my joy may be yours
and your joy may be complete.
This is my commandment:
love one another
as I have loved you.
There is no greater love than this:
to lay down one's life for one's friends.
You are my friends
if you do what I command you.
I no longer speak of you as slaves,
for a slave does not know what his master
is about.
Instead, I call you friends,
since I have made known to you all that I
heard
from my Father.
It was not you who chose me,
it was I who chose you
to go forth and bear fruit.
Your fruit must endure,
so that all you ask the Father in my name
he will give you.
The command I give you is this,
that you love one another."
    This is the gospel of the Lord.

7   Jn 17, 20-26

✠ A reading from the holy gospel according
to John

Father, you loved them as you loved me.

Jesus looked up to heaven and prayed:
"Holy Father,
I do not pray for my disciples alone.
I pray also for those who will believe in me
through their word,
that all may be one
as you, Father, are in me, and I in you;
I pray that they may be [one] in us,
that the world may believe that you sent me.
I have given them the glory you gave me
that they may be one, as we are one—
I living in them, you living in me—
that their unity may be complete.
So shall the world know that you sent me,
and that you loved them as you loved me.

Father,
all those you gave me
I would have in my company
where I am,
to see this glory of mine
which is your gift to me,
because of the love you bore me before the
    world began.
Just Father,
the world has not known you,
but I have known you;
and these men have known that you sent me.
To them I have revealed your name,
and I will continue to reveal it
so that your love for me may live in them,
and I may live in them."
    This is the gospel of the Lord.

_____

8   Jn 19, 31-37

✠ **A reading from the holy gospel according
    to John**
When they pierced his side with a spear, blood and water
            flowed out.

Since it was the Preparation Day the Jews
did not want to have the bodies left on the
cross during the sabbath, for that sabbath was
a solemn feast day. They asked Pilate that
the legs be broken and the bodies be taken
away. Accordingly, the soldiers came and
broke the legs of the men crucified with Jesus,
first of the one, then of the other. When they
came to Jesus and saw that he was already
dead, they did not break his legs. One of the
soldiers thrust a lance into his side, and immediately blood and water flowed out. (This
testimony has been given by an eyewitness,
and his testimony is true. He tells what he
knows is true, so that you may believe.) These
events took place for the fulfillment of Scripture:
    "Break none of his bones."
There is still another Scripture passage which
says:
    "They shall look on him whom they have
        pierced."
    This is the gospel of the Lord.

_____

PRECIOUS BLOOD

916   **READING I**

OUTSIDE EASTER SEASON

1   Ex 12, 21-27

A reading from the book of Exodus
When the Lord sees the blood on the door, he will pass
            over your home.

Moses called all the elders of Israel and said
to them, "Go and procure lambs for your
families, and slaughter them as Passover vic-
tims. Then take a bunch of hyssop, and dipping
it in the blood that is in the basin, sprinkle
the lintel and the two doorposts with this
blood. But none of you shall go outdoors until
morning. For the Lord will go by, striking
down the Egyptians. Seeing the blood on the
lintel and the two doorposts, the Lord will
pass over that door and not let the destroyer
come into your houses to strike you down.
    "You shall observe this as a perpetual ordi-
nance for yourselves and your descendants.
Thus, you must also observe this rite when
you have entered the land which the Lord
will give you as he promised. When your
children ask you, 'What does this rite of yours
mean?' you shall reply, 'This is the Passover
sacrifice of the Lord, who passed over the
houses of the Israelites in Egypt; when he
struck down the Egyptians, he spared our
houses.' "
    This is the Word of the Lord.

_____

2   Ex 24, 3-8

A reading from the book of Exodus
This is the blood marking the covenant which the Lord
            has made with you.

When Moses came to the people and related
all the words and ordinances of the Lord,
they all answered with one voice, "We will
do everything that the Lord has told us." Moses
then wrote down all the words of the Lord
and, rising early the next day, he erected at
the foot of the mountain an altar and twelve
pillars for the twelve tribes of Israel. Then,
having sent certain young men of the Israelites
to offer holocausts and sacrifice young bulls

as peace offerings to the Lord, Moses took half of the blood and put it in large bowls; the other half he splashed on the altar. Taking the book of the covenant, he read it aloud to the people, who answered, "All that the Lord has said, we will heed and do." Then he took the blood and sprinkled it on the people, saying, "This is the blood of the covenant which the Lord has made with you in accordance with all these words of his."

This is the Word of the Lord.

---

917   **READING I**
          DURING EASTER SEASON

1   Rv 1, 5-8

A reading from the book of Revelation

Because he loves us, he has washed away our sins with his blood.

[Grace and peace] from Jesus Christ the faithful witness, the first-born from the dead and ruler of the kings of earth. To him who loves us and freed us from our sins by his own blood, who has made us a royal nation of priests in the service of his God and Father—to him be glory and power forever and ever! Amen.

See, he comes amid the clouds!
    Every eye shall see him,
    even of those who pierced him.
All the peoples of the earth
    shall lament him bitterly.
So it is to be! Amen!
The Lord God says, "I am the Alpha and the Omega, the One who is and who was and who is to come, the Almighty!"

This is the Word of the Lord.

---

2   Rv 7, 9-14

A reading from the book of Revelation

They have washed their robes in the blood of the Lamb.

I, John, saw before me a huge crowd which no one could count from every nation and race, people and tongue. They stood before the throne and the Lamb, dressed in long white robes and holding palm branches in their hands. They cried out in a loud voice, "Salvation is from our God, who is seated on the throne, and from the Lamb!" All the angels who were standing around the throne and the elders and the four living creatures fell down before the throne to worship God. They said: "Amen! Praise and glory, wisdom, thanksgiving, and honor, power and might to our God forever and ever. Amen!"

Then one of the elders asked me, "Who are these, all dressed in white? And where have they come from?" I said to him, "Sir, you should know better than I." He then told me, "These are the ones who have survived the great period of trial; they have washed their robes and made them white in the blood of the Lamb."

This is the Word of the Lord.

---

918   **RESPONSORIAL PSALM**

1   Ps 40, 2. 4. 7-8. 8-9. 10

℟. (8. 9) Here am I, Lord;
    I come to do your will.

I have waited, waited for the Lord,
    and he stooped toward me and heard my cry.
And he put a new song into my mouth,
    a hymn to our God.

℟. Here am I, Lord;
    I come to do your will.

Sacrifice or oblation you wished not,
    but ears open to obedience you gave me.
Holocausts or sin-offerings you sought not;
    then said I, "Behold I come."

℟. Here am I, Lord;
    I come to do your will.

In the written scroll it is prescribed for me,
To do your will, O my God, is my delight,
    and your law is within my heart!"

℟. Here am I, Lord;
    I come to do your will.

I announced your justice in the vast assembly;
    I did not restrain my lips, as you, O Lord, know.

℟. Here am I, Lord;
    I come to do your will.

2   Ps 116, 12-13. 15-16. 17-18

℞. (1 Cor 10, 16) Our blessing-cup is a communion with the blood of Christ.

How shall I make a return to the Lord
for all the good he has done for me?
The cup of salvation I will take up,
and I will call upon the name of the Lord.
℞. Our blessing-cup is a communion with the blood of Christ.
Precious in the eyes of the Lord
is the death of his faithful ones.
I am your servant, the son of your handmaid.
You have loosed my bonds.
℞. Our blessing-cup is a communion with the blood of Christ.
To you will I offer sacrifice of thanksgiving,
and I will call upon the name of the Lord.
My vows to the Lord I will pay
in the presence of all his people.
℞. Our blessing-cup is a communion with the blood of Christ.
℞. Or: Alleluia.

---

919   **READING II**

1   Heb 9, 11-15

A reading from the letter to the Hebrews
The Lord has entered the sanctuary by shedding his own blood.

When Christ came as high priest of the good things which came to be, he entered once for all into the sanctuary, passing through the greater and more perfect tabernacle not made by hands, that is, not belonging to this creation. He entered, not with the blood of goats and calves but with his own blood, and achieved eternal redemption. For if the blood of goats and bulls and the sprinkling of a heifer's ashes can sanctify those who are defiled so that their flesh is cleansed, how much more will the blood of Christ, who through eternal spirit offered himself up unblemished to God, cleanse our consciences from dead works to worship the living God! This is why he is mediator of a new covenant: since his death has taken place for

deliverance from transgressions committed under the first covenant, those who are called may receive the promised eternal inheritance.
This is the Word of the Lord.

---

2   Heb 12, 18-19. 22-24

A reading from the letter to the Hebrews
Jesus brings you to the Father by shedding his blood for you.

You have not drawn near to an untouchable mountain and a blazing fire, and gloomy darkness and storm and trumpet blast, and a voice speaking words such that those who heard begged that they be not addressed to them. No, you have drawn near to Mount Zion and the city of the living God, the heavenly Jerusalem, to myriads of angels in festal gathering, to the assembly of the first-born enrolled in heaven, to God the judge of all, to the spirits of just men made perfect, to Jesus, the mediator of a new covenant, and to the sprinkled blood which speaks more eloquently than that of Abel.
This is the Word of the Lord.

---

3   1 Pt 1, 17-21

A reading from the first letter of Peter
You have been redeemed by the precious blood of Jesus Christ.

In prayer you call upon a Father who judges each one justly on the basis of his actions. Since this is so, conduct yourselves reverently during your sojourn in a strange land. Realize that you were delivered from the futile way of life your fathers handed on to you, not by any diminishable sum of silver or gold, but by Christ's blood beyond all price: the blood of a spotless, unblemished lamb chosen before the world's foundation and revealed for your sake in these last days. It is through him that you are believers in God, the God who raised him from the dead and gave him glory. Your faith and hope, then, are centered in God.
This is the Word of the Lord.

---

4   1 Jn 5, 4-8

A reading from the first letter of John

The Spirit, the water, and the blood give witness.

Everyone begotten of God conquers the
world,
and the power that has conquered the world
is this faith of ours.
Who, then, is conqueror of the world?
The one who believes that Jesus is the Son
of God.
Jesus Christ it is who came through water
and blood—
not in water only,
but in water and in blood.
It is the Spirit who testifies to this,
and the Spirit is truth.
Thus there are three that testify,
the Spirit and the water and the blood—
and these three are of one accord.

This is the Word of the Lord.

---

920   **ALLELUIA VERSE AND
VERSE BEFORE THE GOSPEL**

1   Rv 1, 5

Jesus Christ, you are the faithful witness, first-
born from the dead;
you have loved us and washed away our sins
in your blood.

2   Rv 5, 9

You are worthy, O Lord, to receive the book
and open its seals,
for you were killed, and have redeemed us for
God in your blood.

---

921   **GOSPEL**

1   Mk 14, 12-16. 22-26

✠ **A reading from the holy gospel according
to Mark**

This is my body. This is my blood.

On the first day of Unleavened Bread, when it
was customary to sacrifice the paschal lamb,
his disciples said to Jesus, "Where do you wish
us to go to prepare the Passover supper for
you?" He sent two of his disciples with these
instructions: "Go into the city and you will

come upon a man carrying a water jar. Follow
him. Whatever house he enters, say to the
owner, 'The Teacher asks, Where is my guest-
room where I may eat the Passover with my
disciples?' Then he will show you an upstairs
room, spacious, furnished, and all in order.
That is the place you are to get ready for us."
The disciples went off. When they reached the
city they found it just as he had told them,
and they prepared the Passover supper.

During the meal he took bread, blessed and
broke it, and gave it to them. "Take this,"
he said, "this is my body." He likewise took
a cup, gave thanks and passed it to them, and
they all drank from it. He said to them: "This
is my blood, the blood of the covenant, to be
poured out on behalf of many. I solemnly
assure you, I will never again drink the fruit
of the vine until the day when I drink it new in
the reign of God."

After singing songs of praise, they walked
out to the Mount of Olives.

This is the gospel of the Lord.

---

2   Mk 15, 16-20

As in no. 903, § 5, p. 1074.

---

3   Lk 22, 39-44

✠ **A reading from the holy gospel according
to Luke**

While he prayed in agony, his sweat became like drops
of blood.

Jesus went out and made his way, as was his
custom, to the Mount of Olives; his disciples
accompanied him. On reaching the place he
said to them, "Pray that you may not be put
to the test." He withdrew from them about a
stone's throw, then went down on his knees
and prayed in these words: "Father, if it is your
will, take this cup from me; yet not my will
but yours be done." An angel then appeared to
him from heaven to strengthen him. In his
anguish he prayed with all the greater intensity, and his sweat became like drops of blood
falling to the ground.

This is the gospel of the Lord.

4   Jn 19, 31-37

As in no. 915, § 8, p. 1094.

HOLY NAME

922   READING I
OUTSIDE EASTER SEASON

1   Ex 3, 13-15

A reading from the book of Exodus

I am who am is my name forever.

Moses, hearing the voice of the Lord from the burning bush, said to him, "Who am I that I should go to Pharoah and lead the Israelites out of Egypt? When I go to the Israelites and say to them, 'The God of your fathers has sent me to you,' if they ask me, 'What is his name?' what am I to tell them?" God replied, "I am who am." Then he added, "This is what you shall tell the Israelites: I AM sent me to you."

God spoke further to Moses, "Thus shall you say to the Israelites: The Lord, the God of your fathers, the God of Abraham, the God of Isaac, the God of Jacob, has sent me to you. "This is my name forever;
    this is my title for all generations."
        This is the Word of the Lord.

2   Sir 51, 8-12

A reading from the book of Sirach

Lord, I will praise your name without ceasing.

I remembered the mercies of the Lord,
    his kindness through ages past;
For he saves those who take refuge in him,
    and rescues them from every evil.
So I raised my voice from the very earth,
    from the gates of the nether world, my cry.
I called out: O Lord, you are my father,
    you are my champion and my savior;
Do not abandon me in time of trouble,
    in the midst of storms and dangers.
I will ever praise your name
    and be constant in my prayers to you.
Thereupon the Lord heard my voice,
    he listened to my appeal;
He saved me from evil of every kind
    and preserved me in time of trouble.
For this reason I thank him and I praise him;
    I bless the name of the Lord.
        This is the Word of the Lord.

923   READING I
DURING EASTER SEASON

1   Acts 3, 1-10

As on June 29, no. 590, p. 779.

2   Acts 4, 8-12

As on May 20 (Reading I), no. 566, p. 771.

3   Acts 5, 27-32. 40-42

As in no. 822, § 3, p. 1016.

924   RESPONSORIAL PSALM

1   Is 12, 2-3. 4. 5-6

℟. (4) Praise the Lord and call upon his name.
God indeed is my savior;
    I am confident and unafraid.
My strength and my courage is the Lord,
    and he has been my savior.
With joy you will draw water
    at the fountain of salvation.
℟. Praise the Lord and call upon his name.
Give thanks to the Lord, acclaim his name;
    among the nations make known his deeds,
    proclaim how exalted is his name.
℟. Praise the Lord and call upon his name.
Sing praise to the Lord for his glorious achievement;
    let this be known throughout all the earth.
Shout with exultation, O city of Zion,
    for great in your midst
    is the Holy One of Israel!
℟. Praise the Lord and call upon his name.

2   Ps 113, 1-2. 3-4. 5-6

℟. (2) Blessed be the name of the Lord for ever.
Praise, you servants of the Lord,
    praise the name of the Lord.
Blessed be the name of the Lord
    both now and forever.
℟. Blessed be the name of the Lord for ever.
From the rising to the setting of the sun
    is the name of the Lord to be praised.
High above all nations is the Lord;
    above the heavens is his glory.

℟. Blessed be the name of the Lord for ever.
Who is like the Lord, our God, who is enthroned on high
  and looks upon the heavens and the earth below?
℟. Blessed be the name of the Lord for ever.
℟. Or: Alleluia.

925

1   READING II

                                        1 Cor 1, 1-3

The beginning of the first letter of Paul to the Corinthians

<small>We call on the name of the Lord Jesus.</small>

Paul, called by God's will to be an apostle of Christ Jesus, and Sosthenes our brother, send greetings to the church of God which is in Corinth; to you who have been consecrated in Christ Jesus and called to be a holy people, as to all those who, wherever they may be, call on the name of our Lord Jesus Christ, their Lord and ours. Grace and peace from God our Father and the Lord Jesus Christ.
  This is the Word of the Lord.

---

2   Phil 2, 6-11

<small>As in no. 900, § 3, p. 1070.</small>

---

3   Col 3, 12-17

<small>As in no. 882, § 3, p. 1054.</small>

---

926   ALLELUIA VERSE AND
            VERSE BEFORE THE GOSPEL

1   Ps 96, 2

Sing to the Lord and bless his name,
proclaim his salvation day after day.

2   Dn 3, 52

Praise to your holy and glorious name,
may you be praised for ever.

927   GOSPEL

1   Mt 1, 18-25

✠ **A reading from the holy gospel according to Matthew**

<small>You are to call him Jesus.</small>

This is how the birth of Jesus Christ came about. When his mother Mary was engaged to

Joseph, but before they lived together, she was found with child through the power of the Holy Spirit. Joseph her husband, an upright man unwilling to expose her to the law, decided to divorce her quietly. Such was his intention when suddenly the angel of the Lord appeared in a dream and said to him: "Joseph, son of David, have no fear about taking Mary as your wife. It is by the Holy Spirit that she has conceived this child. She is to have a son and you are to name him Jesus because he will save his people from their sins." All this happened to fulfill what the Lord had said through the prophet:
  "The virgin shall be with child
  and give birth to a son,
  and they shall call him Emmanuel,"
a name which means "God is with us." When Joseph awoke he did as the angel of the Lord had directed him and received her into his home as his wife. He had no relations with her at any time before she bore a son, whom he named Jesus.
  This is the gospel of the Lord.

---

2   Lk 2, 16-21

<small>As in no. 18, Gospel, p. 40.</small>

---

3   Jn 14, 6-14

<small>As on May 3, no. 561, Gospel, p. 769.</small>

HOLY SPIRIT

928

<small>The readings for Pentecost may be used, above nos. 63–64, or those for Confirmation, above nos. 763–767.</small>

ALL OR ONE
OF THE APOSTLES

929

<small>The readings for the feast of Simon and Jude are used, above no. 666.</small>

INDEX OF READINGS *

	Sunday			Weekday	
	A	B	C	I	II
GENESIS					
1, 1–2, 2*	42	42	42		
1-19				329	
20–2, 4				330	
2, 5-9, 15-17				331	
7-9; 3, 1-7	22				
18-25				332	
18-24		141			
3, 1-8				333	
9-24				334	
9-15		90			
4, 1-15. 25				335	
6, 5-8; 7, 1-5. 10				336	
8, 6-13. 20-22				337	
9, 1-13				338	
8-15		23			
11, 1-9	63	63	63	339	
12, 1-9				371	
1-4	25				
13, 2. 5-18				372	
14, 18-20			170		
15, 1-12. 17-18				373	
5-12. 17-18			27		
16, 1-12. 15-16*				374	
17, 1. 9-10. 15-22 ...				375	
3-9			255	255	
18, 1-15				376	
1-10			109		
20-32			112		
19, 15-29				378	
21, 5. 8-20				379	
22, 1-19				380	
1-18*	42	42	42		
1-2. 9. 10-13. 15-18		26			
23, 1-4. 19; 24, 1-8. 62-67				381	
27, 1-5. 15-29				382	
28, 10-22				383	
32, 23-33				384	
37, 3-4. 12-13. 17-28...			235	235	
41, 55-57; 42, 5-7. 17-24				385	
44, 18-21. 23-29; 45. 1-5				386	
46, 1-7. 28-30				387	
49, 2. 8-10			194	194	
29-33; 50, 15-24 ...				388	
EXODUS					
1, 8-14.22				389	
2, 1-15				390	
3, 1-8. 13-15			30		
1-6. 9-12				391	
11-20				392	
11, 10–12, 14				393	
12, 1-8.11-14	40	40	40		
37-42				394	
14, 5-18				395	
15–15, 1	42	42	42		
21–15, 1				396	
16, 1-5. 9-15				397	
2-4. 12-15		114			
17, 1-7			237	237	
3-7	28				
8-13			148		
19, 1-2. 9-11. 16-20				398	
2-6	92				
3-8. 16-20	63	63	63		
20, 1-17*				399	
22, 20-26	149				
24, 3-8		169			
32, 7-14				400	
7-11. 13-14			248	248	
15-24. 30-34				401	
33, 7-11; 34, 5-9. 28 ...				402	
34, 4-6. 8-9	165				
29-35				403	
40, 14-19. 32-36				404	
LEVITICUS					
13, 1-2. 44-46		78			
19, 1-2. 11-18			225	225	
1-2. 17-18	80				
23, 1. 4-11. 15-16. 27. 34-37				405	
25, 1. 8-17				406	
NUMBERS					
6, 22-27	18	18	18		
11, 4-15				407	
25-29		138			
12, 1-13				408	
13, 2-3. 26–14, 1. 26-29 34-35				409	
20, 1-13				410	
21, 4-9			253	253	
24, 2-7 15-17			188	188	
DEUTERONOMY					
4, 1-2. 6-8		126			
1. 5-9			240	240	
32-40				411	
32-34. 39-40		166			
5, 12-15		87			
6, 2-6		153			
4-13				412	
7, 6-11	171				
8, 2-3. 14-16	168				
10, 12-22				413	
11, 18. 26-28	86				
18, 15-20		72			
26, 4-10			24		
16-19			230	230	
30, 10-14			106		
15-20			221	221	
31, 1-8				414	
34, 1-12				415	
JOSHUA					
3, 7-10. 11. 13-17 ...				416	
5, 9. 10-12			33		
24, 1-13				417	
1-2. 15-17. 18		123			
14-29				418	
JUDGES					
2, 11-19				419	
6, 11-24				420	
9, 6-15				421	
11, 29-39				422	
13, 2-7. 24-25			196	196	
RUTH					
1, 1. 3-6. 14-16. 22..				423	
2, 1-3. 8-11; 4, 13-17				424	
1. SAMUEL (Vulg. 1Kings)					
1, 1-8					305
9-20					306
24-28			199	199	
3, 1-10. 19-20					307
3-10. 19		66			
4, 1-11					308
8, 4-7. 10-22					309
9, 1-4. 17-19; 10, 1 ...					310
15, 16-23					311
16, 1-13					312
1. 6-7. 10-13	31				
17, 32-33. 37. 40-51..					313
18, 6-9; 19, 1-7					314
24, 3-21					315
26, 2. 7-9. 12-13.					
22-23		82			

* The long and short readings of the same pericope are indicated by an asterisk. The numbers here indicated refer to sections, not to pages.

	Sunday			Weekday	
	A	**B**	**C**	**I**	**II**
DANIEL					
5, 1-6. 13-14. 16-17..					
23-28				505	
6, 12-28				506	
7, 2-14				507	
13-14		162			
15-27				508	
9, 4-10				231	231
12, 1-3		159			
13, 1-9. 15-17. 19-30.					
33-62*				252	252
HOSEA					
2, 16. 17. 21-22		84			383
6, 1-6				243	243
3-6	89				
8, 4-7. 11-13					384
10, 1-3. 7-8. 12					385
11, 1. 3-4. 8-9		172			386
14, 2-10				242	242
					387
JOEL					
1, 13-15; 2, 1-2				465	
2, 12-18				220	220
3, 1-5	63	63	63		
4, 12-21				466	
AMOS					
2, 6-10. 13-16					377
3, 1-8; 4, 11-12					378
5, 14-15. 21-24					379
6, 1. 4-7				139	
7, 10-17					380
12-15		105			
8, 4-6. 9-12					381
4-7				136	
9, 11-15					382
OBADIAH					
JONAH					
1, 1—2, 1.11				461	
3, 1-10				462	
				227	227
1-5. 10		69			
4, 1-11				463	
MICAH					
2, 1-5					394
5, 1-4				12	
6, 1-4. 6-8					395
7, 7-9				244	244
14-15. 18-20				236	236
					396.
NAHUM					
1, 15; 2, 1. 3; 3, 1-3.					
6-7					411
HABAKKUK					
1, 2-3; 2, 2-4				142	
12—2, 4					412
ZEPHANIAH					
2, 3; 3, 12-13	71				
3, 1-2. 9-13				189	189
14-18			9	198	198
HAGGAI					
1, 1-8				452	
1. 15—2, 9				453	
ZECHARIAH					
2, 5-9. 14-15				454	
8, 1-8				455	
20-23				456	
9, 9-10	101				
12, 10-11			97		
MALACHI					
1, 14—2, 2. 8-10	152				
3, 1-4. 23-24				200	200
13—4, 2				464	
19-20			160		

	Sunday			Weekday
	A	**B**	**C**	**I & II**
MATTHEW				
1, 1-25*	13	13	13	
1-17				194
18-24	10			195
2, 1-12	20	20	20	
13-15. 19-23	17			
3, 1-12	4			
13-17	21			
4, 1-11	22			
12-17. 23-25				213
12-23*	68			
5, 1-12	71			359
13-16	74			360
17-37*	77			
17-19*				240
				361
20-26				229
				362
27-32				363
33-37				364
38-48	80			
38-42				365
43-48				230
				366
6, 1-6. 16-18				220
				367
6, 7-15				226
				368
19-23				369
24-34	83			370
1-5				371
6. 12-14				372
7-12				228
15-20				373
21-29				374
21. 24-27				179
21-27	86			
8, 1-4				375
5-17				376
5-11				176
18-22				377
23-27				378
28-34				379
9, 1-8				380
9-13	89			381
14-17				382
14-15				222
18-26				383
27-31				180
32-38				384
35—10, 1. 6-8				181
36—10, 8	92			
10, 1-7				385
7-15				386
16-23				387
24-33				388
26-33	95			
34—11, 1				389
37-42	98			
11, 2-11	7			
11-15				185
16-19				186
20-24				390
25-30			101	
			171	
25-27				391
28-30				184
				392
12, 1-8				393
14-21				394
38-42				395
46-50				396

	Sunday			Weekday
	A	**B**	**C**	**I & II**
MATTHEW				
13, 1-23*	104			
1-9				397
10-17				398
18-23				399
24-43*	107			
24-30				400
31-35				401
36-43				402
44-52*	110			
44-46				403
47-53				404
54-58				405
14, 1-12	113			406
13-21				407
22-36	116			408
22-33				
15, 1-2. 10-14				408
21-28	119			409
29-37				178
16, 13-23	122			410
13-20				
21-27	125			
24-28				411
17, 1-9	25			
10-13				187
14-20				412
22-27				413
18, 1-5. 10. 12-14				414
12-14				183
15-20	128			415
21—19, 1				416
21-25				239
21-35	131			
19, 3-12				417
13-15				418
16-22				419
23-30				420
20, 1-16	134			421
17-28				233
21, 1-11	37			
23-27				188
28-32	137			189
33-43. 45-46				235
33-43	140			
22, 1-14*	143			422
15-21	146			
34-40	149			423
23, 1-12	152			232
				424
13-22				425
23-26				426
27-32				427
24, 37-44	1			
42-51				428
25, 1-13	155			429
14-30*	158			430
31-46	161			225
26, 14—27, 66*	38			
14-25				260
28, 1-10	42			
8-15				261
16-20	59	166		
MARK				
1, 1-8		5		
6-11		21		210
12-15		23		
14-20*		69		305
21-28		72		306
29-39		75		307
40-45		78		308

	Sunday			Weekday
	A	**B**	**C**	**I & II**
MARK				
2, 1-12		81		309
13-17				310
18-22		84		311
23—3, 6*		87		
23-28				312
3, 1-6				313
7-12				314
13-19				315
20-35		90		
20-21				316
22-30				317
31-35				318
4, 1-20				319
21-25				320
26-34		93		321
35-44		96		322
5, 1-20				323
21-43*		99		324
6, 1-6		102		325
7-13		105		326
14-29				327
30-34		108		328
34-44				214
45-52				215
53-56				329
7, 1-13				330
1-8. 14-15. 21-23		126		
14-23				331
24-30				332
31-37		129		333
8, 1-10				334
11-13				335
14-21				336
22-26				337
27-35		132		
27-33				338
8,34—9, 1				339
9, 2-13				340
2-10		26		
14-29				341
30-37		135		342
38. 43-45. 47-48		138		
38-40				343
41-50				344
10, 1-12				345
2-16*		141		
13-16				346
17-30*		144		
17-27				347
28-31				348
32-45				349
35-45*		147		
46-52		150		350
11, 1-10		37		
21-26				351
27-33				352
12, 1-12				353
13-17				354
18-27				355
28-34		153		242
				356
35-37				357
38-44*		156		358
13, 24-32		159		
33-37		2		
14, 1—15, 47*		38		
12-16. 22-26		169		
16, 1-8		42		
9-15				266
15-20		59		

1 CORINTHIANS

	Sunday			Weekday	
	A	B	C	I	II
6, 1-11					438
13-15. 17-20		66			
7, 25-31					439
29-31		69			
32-35		72			
8, 1-7. 11-13					440
9, 16-19. 22-27					441
16-19. 22-23		75			
10, 1-6. 10-12			30		
10-22					442
16-17	168				
31—11, 1		78			
11, 17-26. 33					443
23-26	40	40	40		
			170		
12, 3-7. 12-13	64	64	64		
4-11			67		
12-30*			70		
12-14. 27-31					444
31—13, 13*			73		445
15, 1-11*			76		446
12-20					447
12. 16-20			79		
20-26. 28	161				
35-37. 42-49					448
45-49			82		
54-58			85		

2 CORINTHIANS

	A	B	C	I	II
1, 1-7				355	
18-22		81		360	
3, 1-6		84			
4-11				361	
15—4, 1. 3-6				362	
4, 6-11		87			
7-15				363	
13—5, 1		90			
5, 6-10		93			
14-17		96			
14-21				364	
17-21			33		
20—6, 2				220	220
6, 1-10				365	
8, 1-9				366	
7. 9. 13-15		99			
9, 6-11				367	
11, 1-11				368	
18. 21-30				369	
12, 1-10				370	
7-10		102			
13, 11-13	165				

GALATIANS

	A	B	C	I	II
1, 1-2. 6-10			88		
6-12					461
11-19			91		
13-24					462
2, 1-2. 7-14					463
16. 19-21			94		
3, 1-5					464
7-14					465
22-29					466
26-29			97		
4, 4-7	18	18	18		
22-24. 26-27. 31—5, 1					
5, 1. 13-18			100		
1-6					467
18-25					468
6, 14-18			103		469

EPHESIANS

	A	B	C	I	II
1, 1. 3-10					470
3-14*		105			
3-6. 15-18	19	19	19		

EPHESIANS

	Sunday			Weekday	
	A	B	C	I	II
11-14					471
15-23					472
17-23	59	59	59		
2, 1-10					473
4-10		32			
12-22					474
13-18		108			
3, 2-12					475
2-3. 5-6	20	20	20		
8-12. 14-19		172			
14-21					476
4, 1-6			111		477
7-16					478
17. 20-24			114		
30—5, 2			117		
32—5, 8,					479
5, 8-14	31				
15-20			120		
21-33					480
21-32			123		
6, 1-9					481
10-20					482

PHILIPPIANS

	A	B	C	I	II
1, 1-11					483
4-6. 8-11			6		
18-26					484
20-24. 27	134				
2, 1-11*	137				
1-4					485
5-11					486
6-11	38	38	38		
12-18					487
3, 3-8					488
8-14			36		
17—4, 1*			27		489
4, 4-7			9		
6-9	140				
10-19					490
12-14. 19-20	143				

COLOSSIANS

	A	B	C	I	II
1, 1-8				433	
9-14				434	
12-20			163		
15-20			106	435	
21-23				436	
24—2, 3				437	
24-28			109		
2, 6-15				438	
12-14			112		
3, 1-11				439	
1-5. 9-11			115		
1-4	43	43	43		
12-21	17	17	17		
12-17				440	

1 THESSALONIANS

	A	B	C	I	II
1, 1-5	146				
2-5. 8-10				425	
5-10	149				
2, 1-8				426	
7-9. 13	152				
9-13				427	
3, 7-13				428	
12—4, 2			3		
4, 1-8				429	
9-12				430	
13-18*	155				431
5, 1-6. 9-11	158				432
1-6					
16-24		8			

2 THESSALONIANS

	A	B	C	I	II
1, 1-5. 11-19					425
11—2, 2			154		
2, 1-3. 14-17					426
16—3, 5			157		
3, 6-10. 16-18					427
7-12			160		

1 TIMOTHY

	A	B	C	I	II
1, 1-2. 12-14				441	
12-17			133		
15-17				442	
2, 1-8			136	443	
3, 1-13				444	
14-16				445	
4, 12-16				446	
6, 2-12				447	
11-16			139		
13-16				448	

2 TIMOTHY

	A	B	C	I	II
1, 1-3. 6-12					355
6-8. 13-14			142		
8-10	25				
2, 8-15					356
8-13			145		
3, 10-17					357
14—4, 2			148		
4, 1-8					358
6-8. 16-18			151		

TITUS

	A	B	C	I	II
1, 1-9					491
2, 1-8. 11-14					492
11-14	14	14	14		
3, 1-7					493
4-7	15	15	15		

PHILEMON

	A	B	C	I	II
7-20					494
9-10. 12-17			130		

HEBREWS

	A	B	C	I	II
1, 1-6	16	16	16	305	
2, 5-12				306	
9-11		141			
14-18				307	
3, 7-14				308	
4, 1-5. 11				309	
12-16				310	
12-13		144			
14-16		147			
14-16; 5, 7-9	41	41	41		
5, 1-10				311	
1-6		150			
7-9			35		
6, 10-20				312	
7, 1-3. 15-17				313	
23-28		153			
25—8, 6				314	
8, 6-13				315	
9, 2-3. 11-14				316	
11-15		169			
15. 24-28				317	
24-28		156			
10, 1-10				318	
5-10			12		
11-18				319	
11-14. 18		159			
19-25				320	
10, 32-39				321	
11, 1-7				340	
1-2. 8-19*			118	322	
32-40				323	
12, 1-4			121	324	
4-7. 11-15				325	

HEBREWS

	A	B	C	I	II
5-7. 11-13			124		
18-19. 21-24				326	
18-19. 22-24			127		
13, 1-8				327	
15-17. 20-21				328	

JAMES

	A	B	C	I	II
1, 1-11					335
12-18					336
17-18. 21-22. 27		126			
19-27					337
2, 1-9					338
1-5		129			
14-24. 26					339
14-18		132			
3; 1-10					340
13-18					341
16—4, 3		135			
4, 1-10					342
13-17					343
5, 1-6		138			344
7-10	7				
9-12					345
13-20					346

1 PETER

	A	B	C	I	II
1, 3-9	44				347
10-16					348
17-21	47				
18-25					349
2, 2-5. 9-12					350
4-9	53				
20-25	50				
3, 15-18	56				
18-22		23			
4, 7-13					351
13-16	60				

2 PETER

	A	B	C	I	II
1, 2-7					353
3, 8-14		5			
12-15. 17-18					354

1 JOHN

	A	B	C	I	II
2, 1-5		48			
3-11				203	203
12-17				204	204
18-21				205	205
22-28				206	206
29—3, 6				207	207
3, 1-2		51			
7-10				208	208
11-21				209	209
18-24		54			
22—4, 6				213	213
4, 7-16	171				
7-10		57		214	214
11-18				215	215
11-16		61			
19- 5, 4				216	216
5, 1-6		45			
5-13				210	210
				217	217
14-21				211	211
				218	218

2 JOHN

	A	B	C	I	II
4-9					495

3 JOHN

	A	B	C	I	II
5-8					496

JUDE

	A	B	C	I	II
17. 20-25					352

REVELATION

	A	B	C	I	II
1, 1-4; 2, 1-5					497
5-8	39	39	39		
		162			

	Sunday			Weekday	
	A	B	C	I	II
REVELATION					
9-11. 12-13. 17-19..			46		
3, 1-6. 14-22					498
4, 1-11					499
5, 1-10					500
11-14			49		
7, 9. 14-17			52		
10, 8-11					501
11, 4-12					502
14, 1-3. 4-5					503
14-19					504
15, 1-4					505
18, 1-2. 21-23; **19,** 1-3. 9					506
20, 1-4. 11–21, 2					507
21, 1-5			55		
10-14. 22-23			58		
22, 1-7					508
12-14. 16-17. 20...			62		

	Proper of Saints	Commons	Ritual Masses	Various Masses	Votive Masses
GENESIS					
1, 11-12 ·				851	
14-18				841	
26-28. 31			774		
26—2, 3	559				846
2, 4-9. 15					846
18-24			774		
3, 9-15. 20	689	707			
4, 3-10				836	
12, 1-4		737	743, 784	806	
1-7		707			
14, 18-20					904
15, 1-6. 18			752		
17, 1-8			752		
24, 48-51. 58-67..			774		
28, 11-18		701			
35, 1-4. 6-7			752		
EXODUS					
3, 1-6. 9-12			806		
13-15					922
12, 1-8. 11-14					897
21-27					916
16, 2-4. 12-15					904
17, 3-7			757		
23, 20-23	650				
24, 3-8					904, 916
32, 7-14		719			
34, 4-6. 8-9					910
LEVITICUS					
19, 1-2. 17-18 ...		737			
NUMBERS					
3, 5-10			769		
6, 22-27				841	
11, 11-12. 14-17.					
24-25			769		
21, 4-9	638				
DEUTERONOMY					
6, 1-7			748		
3-9		737			
7, 6-11					910
8, 2-3. 14-16 ...					904
7-18				856	
10, 8-9		719, 737			
12-22					910
17-19 ,.....				866	
24, 17-22				861, 866	
30, 1-4				811	
10-14				826	
15-20			752		
JOSHUA					
24, 1-2. 15-17.					
18-25 ...			752		
1 SAMUEL					
(Vulg. 1 Kings)					
3, 1-10			784	806	
16, 1 6-13...		719			
2 SAMUEL					
(Vulg. 2 Kings)					
7, 1-5. 8-11. 16		707			
4-5. 12-14. 16	543				
1 KINGS					
(Vulg. 3 Kings)					
3, 11-14		725			
8, 22-23. 27-30		70?			
55-61				881	

	Proper of Saints	Commons	Ritual Masses	Various Masses	Votive Masses
1 KINGS					
19, 4-8					904
4-9. 11-15 .		737	784		
16. 19-21 ..		737	784	806	
2 KINGS					
(Vulg. 4 Kings)					
5, 9-15......			752		
20, 1-6				871	
1 CHRONICLES					
(Vulg. 1 Para.)					
15, 3-4. 15-16					
16, 1-2		707			
2 CHRONICLES					
(Vulg. 2 Para)					
5, 6-10. 13—6, 2		701			
24, 18-22		713			
1 MACCABEES					
2, 49-52. 57-64				821	
4, 52-59 ,,,,,		701			
2 MACCABEES					
6, 18. 21. 24-31		713			
7, 1-2. 9-14 ...		713			
1. 20-23.					
27-29....		713			
12, 43-46			789		
TOBIT					
7, 9-10. 11-15 ..			774		
8, 5-7		737	774		
12, 6-13		737			
JUDITH					
8, 2-8		737			
13, 18. 19. 20 ..		709			
ESTHER					
C. 1-4. 8-10....				821	
2-4. 8-10....				876	
1-7. 10		737			
JOB					
19, 1. 23-27....			789		
31, 16-20. 24-25.					
31-32....				861	
PROVERBS					
2, 1-9	597		779		
4, 7-13			779		
8, 22-31		707			
9, 1-6					904
31, 10-13. 19-20.					
30-31 ...		737			
SONG OF SONGS					
2, 8-10. 14. 16;					
8, 6-7 ...			774		
8-14			784		
3, 1-4	603				
8, 6-7		731	784		
WISDOM					
2, 1. 12-22 ...					897
3, 1-9*		713	789		
4, 7-15			789		
7, 7-10. 15-16		725			
SIRACH					
(Vulg. Eccles)					
2, 7-13		737			
3, 17-24		737			
15, 1-6		725			
24, 1. 3-4. 8-12-					
19-21.......		707			
26, 1-4. 13-16 ..	632	737	774		
39, 6-11		725			
44, 1. 10-15 ...	606				
50, 24-26				881	
51, 1-8		713			
11-17					922

	Proper of Saints	Commons	Ritual Masses	Various Masses	Votive Masses
ISAIAH					
2, 1-5				816	
6, 1-8			719		
7, 10-14	545		707		
9, 1-6	627		707	831	
11, 1-4			763		
25, 6. 7-8			799		
6. 7-9			789, 794		
6-10				891	
32, 15-20				831	
41, 8-10. 13-14.				821	
42, 1-3			763		
44, 1-3			752		
49, 1-6	587				
13-15					910
50, 4-9					897
52, 7-10			719		
13—53, 12..					897
53, 1-5. 10-11 ..			871		
55, 6-9			886		
56, 1. 6-7		701	816		
57, 15-19			831		
58, 6-11		737	861		
60, 1-6			816		
61, 1-3		719	769	800	
1-3. 6. 8 -9			763		
6-8			806		
9-11		707	784		
63, 7-9			881		
66, 10-14	531, 649				
JEREMIAH					
1, 4-9		719	769	806	
4-10	586				
17-19	634				
20, 7-9		737	806		
31, 1-4					910
31-32. 33-34			774		
31-34			752		
LAMENTATIONS					
3, 17-26			789, 794	876	
			799		
EZEKIEL					
3, 17-21	612	719			
18, 21-23. 30-32				886	
34, 11-16		719			910
36, 23-28				811	
24-28			752, 757		
			763		
37, 15-19. 21-22					
26-28				811	
43, 1-2. 4-7 ...		701			
47, 1-9. 12 ...			757		
DANIEL					
3, 25. 34-43 ..				821, 876	
7, 9-10. 13-14 ..	615, 647				
12, 1-3			789		
HOSEA					
2, 16. 17. 21-22		731	784		
11, 1-4. 8-9 ..					910
JOEL					
2, 12-18				886	
21-24. 26-27				856	
23. 26-30 ..			763		
JONAH					
3, 1-10				886	
10—4, 11 ..				816	
MICAH					
4, 1-4				836,	
5, 1-4	636	707			
6, 6-8		737			

	Proper of Saints	Commons	Ritual Masses	Various Masses	Votive Masses
ZEPHANIAH					
2, 3; 3, 12-13		737			
3, 14-18	572				
14-15				881	
16-20				811	
ZECHARIAH					
2, 14-17		707			
8, 20-23				816	
9, 9-10				836	
12, 10-11; 13, 6-7 ...					897
MALACHI					
3, 1-4	524				
MATTHEW					
1, 1-16. 18-23*	636	712			
16. 18-21. 24	543				
18-25					927
2, 13-15. 19-23		712		870	
13-18	698				
4, 18-22	684				
5, 1-12	667	742	767, 778 793	825, 835	
13-16		730, 742	773, 778		
20-24				840	
23-24		706			
38-48				835	
6, 9-13			749		
31-34				845, 850	
7, 7-11				880	
21. 24-29*..			778		
8, 14-17				875	
9, 1-8				890	
9-13	643				
35-38			773	810	
35—10, 1..	612				
10. 1-5			773		
7-13	580				
17-22	696	718		825	
22-25	560				
26-33				825	
28-33		718			
34-39		718			
11, 25-30	651	742	788, 793 798		915
13, 1-9				855	
16-17	606				
44-46		742			
54-58	559				
14, 22-33	679				
16, 13-18				748	
13-19	535, 591	724			
24-27		742	756, 767 788		
17, 1-9	615				
18, 1-4	649	742			
1-5. 10	650				
15-20				830	
19-22				815	
19, 3-6			778		
3-12		736, 742	788		
16-26	513		788		
20, 20-28	605				
25-28			773		
22, 35-40			761, 778		
23, 8-12	633	724, 730	783		
24, 4-13	592				
25, 1-13		736, 742	788, 793		
14-30*		742	767	850	
31- 46*	539, 673	742	793	865	
26, 47-56					903
27, 33-50					903

	Proper of Saints	Commons	Ritual Masses	Various Masses	Votive Masses
MATTHEW					
28, 16-20	528	724		820	
18-20			756, 761		
MARK					
1, 1-8. 14-15..					890
9-11			756, 761		
			767		
14-20*		724			
3, 31-35		742	788		
4, 1-10. 13-20*		730			
26-29				855	
35-41				880	
5, 18-20				885	
6, 17-29	634				
30-34				830	
34-44				865	
7, 31-37				750	
8, 31-34					902
9, 2-10	615				
33-37		742			
10, 6-9			778		
13-16		742	756, 761		
17-30*		742		810	
24-30			788		
28-30				810	
12, 1-12					902
28-34*			761		
14, 12-16. 22-26					909, 921
32-41					903
55-65					903
15, 1-15					903
16-20					903, 921
33-46			799		
33-39; 16, 1-6*			793		903
16, 15-16. 19-20			756		
15-18	519			820, 875	
15-20	555, 685	724			
LUKE					
1, 5-17	586				
26-38	545	712			
	653, 689				
39-47	627	712			
39-56	572, 622				
57-66. 80 ..	587				
2, 1-14		712			
15-19		712			
16-21					927
22-40*	524				
27-35		712			
33-35	639				
41-51	543				
	573				
41-52		712			
4, 16-22			767		
5, 1-11		724		810	
6, 12-16	666				
7, 11-17	632		793		
36-50				890	
8, 4-10. 11-15 ..			767		
9 11-17					909
23-26		718			
28-36	615				
49-56				815	
57-62		742	788	810	

INDEX OF RESPONSORIAL PSALMS

APPENDIX

VOTIVE MASS FOR THANKSGIVING DAY

OLD TESTAMENT READING

Dt 8, 7-18

A reading from the book of Deuteronomy

Remember the Lord your God since it was he who gave you this strength.

Moses told the people: "The Lord, your God, is bringing you into a good country, a land with streams of water, with springs and fountains welling up in the hills and valleys, a land of wheat and barley, of vines and fig trees and pomegranates, of olive trees and of honey, a land where you can eat bread without stint and where you will lack nothing, a land whose stones contain iron and in whose hills you can mine copper. But when you have eaten your fill, you must bless the Lord, your God, for the good country he has given you. Be careful not to forget the Lord, your God, by neglecting his commandments and decrees and statutes which I enjoin on you today: lest, when you have eaten your fill, and have built fine houses and lived in them, and have increased your herds and flocks, your silver and gold, and all your property, you then become haughty of heart and unmindful of the Lord, your God, who brought you out of the land of Egypt, that place of slavery; who guided you through the vast and terrible desert with its saraph serpents and scorpions, its parched and waterless ground; who brought forth water for you from the flinty rock and fed you in the desert with manna, a food unknown to your fathers, that he might afflict you and test you, but also make you prosperous in the end. Otherwise, you might say to yourselves, 'It is my own power and the strength of my own hand that has obtained for me this wealth.' Remember then, it is the Lord, your God, who gives you the power to acquire wealth, by fulfilling, as he has now done, the covenant which he swore to your fathers."

This is the Word of the Lord.

2

1 Kgs 8, 55-61

A reading from the first book of Kings

Blessed be the Lord God who has granted rest to his people.

Solomon stood and blessed the whole community of Israel, saying in a loud voice: "Blessed be the Lord who has given rest to his people Israel, just as he promised. Not a single word has gone unfulfilled of the entire generous promise he made through his servant Moses. May the Lord, our God, be with us as he was with our fathers and may he not forsake us nor cast us off. May he draw our hearts to himself, that we may follow him in everything and keep the commands, statutes, and ordinances which he enjoined on our fathers. May this prayer I have offered to the Lord, our God, be present to him day and night, that he may uphold the cause of his servant and of his people Israel as each day requires, that all the peoples of the earth may know the Lord is God and there is no other. You must be wholly devoted to the Lord, our God, observing his statutes and keeping his commandments, as on this day."

This is the Word of the Lord.

3

Sir 50, 22-24

A reading from the book of Sirach

God does great deeds everywhere.

And now, bless the God of all,
    who has done wondrous things on earth;
Who fosters men's growth from their mother's
    womb,
    and fashions them according to his will!
May he grant you joy of heart
    and may peace abide among you;
May his goodness toward us endure in Israel
    as long as the heavens are above.
This is the Word of the Lord.

4

Is 63, 7-9

A reading from the book of the prophet Isaiah

I will sing the praises of the Lord for the multitude of gifts he has given to the house of Israel.

The favors of the Lord I will recall,
    the glorious deeds of the Lord,
Because of all he has done for us;
    for he is good to the house of Israel,

He has favored us according to his mercy
and his great kindness.
He said: They are indeed my people,
children who are not disloyal;
So he became their savior
in their every affliction.
It was not a messenger or an angel,
but he himself who saved them.
Because of his love and pity
he redeemed them himself,
Lifting them and carrying them
all the days of old.
This is the Word of the Lord.

---

5   Jl 2, 21-24. 26-27

A reading from the book of the prophet Joel
The threshing-floors will be filled with grain.

Fear not, O land!
exult and rejoice!
for the Lord has done great things.
Fear not, beasts of the field!
for the pastures of the plain are green;
The tree bears its fruit,
the fig tree and the vine give their yield.

And do you, O children of Zion, exult
and rejoice in the Lord, your God!
He has given you the teacher of justice:
he has made the rain come down for you,
the early and the late rain as before.
The threshing floors shall be full of grain
and the vats shall overflow with wine and oil.

You shall eat and be filled,
and shall praise the name of the Lord, your
God,
Because he has dealt wondrously with you;
my people shall nevermore be put to shame.
And you shall know that I am in the midst of
Israel;
I am the Lord, your God, and there is no
other;
My people shall nevermore be put to shame.
This is the Word of the Lord.

---

6   Zep 3, 14-15

**A reading from the book of the prophet
Zephaniah**
The Lord, the King of Israel, is in your midst.

Shout for joy, O daughter Zion!
sing joyfully, O Israel!
Be glad and exult with all your heart,
O daughter Jerusalem!
The Lord has removed the judgment against
you,
he has turned away your enemies;
The King of Israel, the Lord, is in your midst,
you have no further misfortune to fear.
This is the Word of the Lord.

NEW TESTAMENT READING

1   1 Cor 1, 3-9

**A reading from the first letter of Paul to the
Corinthians**
I give thanks always to my God for you.

Grace and peace from God our Father and the
Lord Jesus Christ.
I continually thank my God for you because
of the favor he has bestowed on you in Christ
Jesus, in whom you have been richly endowed
with every gift of speech and knowledge. Likewise, the witness I bore to Christ has been so
confirmed among you that you lack no spiritual gift as you wait for the revelation of our
Lord Jesus Christ. He will strengthen you to
the end, so that you will be blameless on the
day of our Lord Jesus [Christ]. God is faithful,
and it was he who called you to fellowship
with his Son, Jesus Christ our Lord.
This is the Word of the Lord.

---

2   Eph 1, 3-14

**A reading from the first letter of Paul to the
Ephesians**
In praise of the glory of his grace.

Praised be the God and Father of our Lord
Jesus Christ, who has bestowed on us in Christ
every spiritual blessing in the heavens! God
chose us in him before the world began, to be
holy and blameless in his sight, to be full of

love; he likewise predestined us through Christ Jesus to be his adopted sons—such was his will and pleasure—that all might praise the divine favor he has bestowed on us in his beloved.

It is in Christ and through his blood that we have been redeemed and our sins forgiven, so immeasurably generous is God's favor to us. God has given us the wisdom to understand fully the mystery, the plan he was pleased to decree in Christ, to be carried out in the fullness of time: namely, to bring all things in the heavens and on earth into one under Christ's headship.

In him we were chosen; for in the decree of God, who administers everything according to his will and counsel, we were predestined to praise his glory by being the first to hope in Christ. In him you too were chosen; when you heard the glad tidings of salvation, the word of truth, and believed in it, you were sealed with the Holy Spirit who had been promised. He is the pledge of our inheritance, the first payment against the full redemption of a people God has made his own, to praise his glory.

This is the Word of the Lord.

---

3 Col 3, 12-17

A reading from the letter of Paul to the Colossians

Giving thanks to God the Father through Christ.

Because you are God's chosen ones, holy and beloved, clothe yourselves with heartfelt mercy, with kindness, humility, meekness, and patience. Bear with one another; forgive whatever grievances you have against one another. Forgive as the Lord has forgiven you. Over all these virtues put on love, which binds the rest together and makes them perfect. Christ's peace must reign in your hearts, since as members of the one body you have been called to that peace. Dedicate yourselves to thankfulness. Let the word of Christ, rich as it is, dwell in you. In wisdom made perfect, instruct and admonish one another. Sing gratefully to God from your hearts in psalms, hymns, and inspired songs. Whatever you do, whether in speech or in action, do it in the name of the Lord Jesus. Give thanks to God the Father through him.

This is the Word of the Lord.

---

4 1 Tm 6, 6-11. 17-19

A reading from the first letter of Paul to Timothy

Warn the wealthy not to hope in the uncertainty of riches.

There is great gain in religion, provided one is content with a sufficiency. We brought nothing into this world, nor have we the power to take anything out. If we have food and clothing we have all that we need. Those who want to be rich are falling into temptation and a trap. They are letting themselves be captured by foolish and harmful desires which drag men down to ruin and destruction. The love of money is the root of all evil. Some men in their passion for it have strayed from the faith and have come to grief amid great pain.

Man of God that you are, flee from all this. Instead, seek after integrity, piety, faith, love, steadfastness and a gentle spirit.

Tell those who are rich in this world's goods not to be proud, and not to rely on so uncertain a thing as wealth. Let them trust in the God who provides us richly with all things for our use. Charge them to do good, to be rich in good works and generous, sharing what they have. Thus will they build a secure foundation for the future, for receiving that life which is life indeed.

This is the Word of the Lord.

RESPONSORIAL PSALM

1 Ps 67, 2-3. 5, 7-8

℟. (7) The earth has yielded its fruits;
God, our God, has blessed us.

May God have pity on us and bless us;
may he let his face shine upon us.

So may your way be known upon earth;
among all nations, your salvation.

℟. The earth has yielded its fruits;
God, our God, has blessed us.

May the nations be glad and exult
because you rule the peoples in equity;
the nations on the earth you guide.

℟. The earth has yielded its fruits;
  God, our God, has blessed us.
The earth has yielded its fruits;
  God, our God, has blessed us.
May God bless us,
  and may all the ends of the earth fear him!
℟. The earth has yielded its fruits;
  God, our God, has blessed us.
℟. Or: May the peoples praise you, O God;
  may all the peoples praise you!

---

2   1 Chr 29, 10-11. 11-12. 12
℟. (13) We praise the majesty of your name.
Blessed may you be, O Lord,
  God of Israel our father,
  from eternity to eternity.
℟. We praise the majesty of your name.
Yours, O Lord, are grandeur and power,
  majesty, splendor, and glory;
For all in heaven and on earth is yours.
℟. We praise the majesty of your name.
Yours, O Lord, is the sovereignty;
  you are exalted as head over all.
Riches and honor are from you.
℟. We praise the majesty of your name.
And you have dominion over all—
  In your hand are power and might;
It is yours to give grandeur and strength to all.
℟. We praise the majesty of your name.

---

3   Ps 113, 1-2. 3-4, 5-6. 7-8
℟. (2) Blessed be the name of the Lord
  both now and forever.
Praise, you servants of the Lord,
  praise the name of the Lord.
Blessed be the name of the Lord
  both now and forever.
℟. Blessed be the name of the Lord
  both now and forever.
From the rising to the setting of the sun
  is the name of the Lord to be praised.
High above all nations is the Lord;
  above the heavens is his glory.
℟. Blessed be the name of the Lord
  both now and forever.

Who is like the Lord, our God, who is enthroned
  on high
  and looks upon the heavens and the earth
  below?
℟. Blessed be the name of the Lord
  both now and forever.
He raises up the lowly from the dust;
  from the dunghill he lifts up the poor
To seat them with princes,
  with the princes of his own people.
℟. Blessed be the name of the Lord
  both now and forever.
℟. Or: Alleluia.

---

4   Ps 138, 1-2. 2-3. 4-5
℟. (2) I will give thanks to your name,
  because of your kindness and your truth.
I will give thanks to you, O Lord, with all my
  heart,
  [for you have heard the words of my mouth;]
  in the presence of the angels I will sing your
  praise;
I will worship at your holy temple.
℟. I will give thanks to your name,
  because of your kindness and your truth.
I will give thanks to your name,
  because of your kindness and your truth;
For you have made great above all things
  your name and your promise.
When I called, you answered me;
  you built up strength within me.
℟. I will give thanks to your name,
  because of your kindness and your truth.
All the kings of the earth shall give thanks to
  you, O Lord,
  when they hear the words of your mouth;
And they shall sing of the ways of the Lord:
  "Great is the glory of the Lord."
℟. I will give thanks to your name,
  because of your kindness and your truth.

---

5   Ps 145, 2-3. 4-5. 6-7. 8-9. 10-11
℟. (1) I will bless your name, O Lord, forever
  and ever.
Every day will I bless you,
  and I will praise your name forever and ever.

Great is the Lord and highly to be praised;
  his greatness is unsearchable.
℟. I will bless your name, O Lord, forever and
  ever.
Generation after generation praises your works
  and proclaims your might.
They speak of the splendor of your glorious
  majesty
and tell of your wondrous works.
℟. I will bless your name, O Lord, forever and
  ever.
They discourse of the power of your terrible
  deeds
  and declare your greatness.
They publish the fame of your abundant goodness
  and joyfully sing of your justice.
℟. I will bless your name, O Lord, forever and
  ever.
The Lord is gracious and merciful,
  slow to anger and of great kindness.
The Lord is good to all
  and compassionate toward all his works.
℟. I will bless your name, O Lord, forever and
  ever.
Let all your works give you thanks, O Lord,
  and let your faithful ones bless you.
Let them discourse of the glory of your kingdom
  and speak of your might.
℟. I will bless your name, O Lord, forever and
  ever.

ALLELUIA VERSE

1   Ps 126, 5
Those that sow in tears
  shall reap rejoicing

2   Eph 1, 3
May the God and Father of our Lord
  Jesus Christ be praised:
God, who has bestowed on us in Christ
  every spiritual blessing in the heavens!

3   1 Thess 5, 18
Rejoice always, never cease praying,
  render constant thanks;
such is God's will for you in Christ Jesus.

4   Ambrosian hymn
We praise you, O God, we acclaim you the
  Lord.
The holy Church throughout the world wor-
  ships you.

GOSPEL

1   Mk 5, 18-20
✠ A reading from the holy gospel according
        to Mark
Announce what great things the Lord has done for you.

As Jesus was getting into the boat, the man
who had been possessed was pressing to accompany him. Jesus did not grant his request,
but told him instead: "Go home to your family
and make it clear to them how much the Lord
in his mercy has done for you." At that the man
went off and began to proclaim throughout the
Ten Cities what Jesus had done for him. They
were all amazed at what they heard.
        This is the gospel of the Lord.

2   Lk 12, 15-21
✠ A reading from the holy gospel according
        to Luke
The security of a man's life does not come from this pos-
sessions even when he has them in abundance.

Jesus said to the crowd, "Avoid greed in all
its forms. A man may be wealthy, but his
possessions do not guarantee him life." He told
them a parable in these words: "There was a
rich man who had a good harvest. 'What shall
I do?' he asked himself. 'I have no place to
store my harvest. I know!' he said. 'I will pull
down my grain bins and build larger ones. All
my grain and my goods will go there. Then I
will say to myself: You have blessings in reserve for years to come. Relax! Eat heartily,

drink well. Enjoy yourself.' But God said to him, 'You fool! This very night your life shall be required of you. To whom will all this piled-up wealth of yours go?' That is the way it works with the man who grows rich for himself instead of growing rich in the sight of God."

This is the gospel of the Lord.

---

3   Lk 17, 11-19

✠ A reading from the holy gospel according to Luke

He threw himself on his face before Jesus and thanked him.

On his journey to Jerusalem Jesus passed along the borders of Samaria and Galilee. As he was entering a village, ten lepers met him. Keeping their distance, they raised their voices and said, "Jesus, Master, have pity on us!" When he saw them, he responded, "Go and show yourselves to the priests." On their way there they were cured. One of them, realizing that he had been cured, came back praising God in a loud voice. He threw himself on his face at the feet of Jesus and spoke his praises. This man was a Samaritan.

Jesus took the occasion to say, "Were not all ten made whole? Where are the other nine? Was there no one to return and give thanks to God except this foreigner" He said to the man, "Stand up and go your way; your faith has been your salvation."

This is the gospel of the Lord.